THE ROUGH GUIDE TO

South Africa
Lesotho & Swaziland

This eighth edition updated by

Hilary Heuler
Jeroen van M

ROUGH
GUIDES

roughguides.com

Contents

Introduction to
South Africa

South Africa is a large, diverse and incredibly beautiful country. The size of France and Spain combined, and roughly twice the size of Texas, it varies from the picturesque Garden Route towns of the Western Cape to the raw subtropical coast of northern KwaZulu-Natal, with the vast Karoo semi-desert across at its centre and one of Africa's premier safari destinations, Kruger National Park, in the northeast. In addition, its big cities attract immigrants from across Africa, making them great, bubbling cultural crucibles.

Many visitors are pleasantly surprised by South Africa's excellent **infrastructure**, which draws favourable comparison with countries such as Australia or the United States. Good air links and bus routes, excellent roads and plenty of first-class B&Bs and guesthouses make South Africa perfect for touring. If you're on a budget, the network of hostels and backpacker buses provide cost-efficient means of exploring.

Yet, despite all these facilities, South Africa is also something of an enigma; after two decades of democracy, the "**rainbow nation**" is still struggling to find its identity. Apartheid is dead, but its heritage still shapes South Africa in very physical ways. This is all too evident in the layout of the towns and cities, where the historically poorer African areas are usually tucked out of sight.

South Africa's **population** doesn't reduce simply to black and white. The majority are **Africans** (79 percent of the population); **whites** make up nine percent, as do **coloureds** – the descendants of white settlers, slaves and Africans, who speak English and Afrikaans and comprise the majority in the Western Cape. The rest are mostly **Indians** (2.5 percent), resident mainly in KwaZulu-Natal and descendants of indentured labourers, who came to South Africa at the beginning of the twentieth century.

But perhaps a better indication of South Africa's diversity is the plethora of official languages, most of which represent distinct cultures with rural roots in different corners of the country. Each region has its own particular style of architecture, craftwork, food and sometimes dress. Perhaps more exciting still are the cities, where

ABOVE KNYSNA, WESTERN CAPE **RIGHT** VINEYARDS, WESTERN CAPE

the whole country comes together in an alchemical blend of rural and urban, traditional and thoroughly modern.

Crime isn't the indiscriminate phenomenon that press reports suggest, but it is an issue. Really, it's a question of perspective – taking care, but not becoming paranoid. The odds of becoming a victim are highest in downtown Johannesburg, where violent crime is a daily reality; there is less risk in other cities.

Where to go

While you could circuit South Africa in a matter of weeks, it's more satisfying to focus on a specific region. Each of the nine provinces has compelling reasons to visit, although, depending on the time of year and your interests, you'd be wise to concentrate on either the **west** or the **east**.

The **west**, best visited in the warmer months (Nov–April), has the outstanding attraction of **Cape Town**, worth experiencing for its unbeatable location beneath Table Mountain. Half a day's drive from here can take you to any other destination in the **Western Cape**, a province that owes its character to the longest-established colonial heritage in the country. You'll find gabled Cape Dutch architecture, historic towns and vineyard-covered mountains in the **Winelands**; forested coast along the **Garden Route**; and a dry interior punctuated by Afrikaner *dorps* (towns) in the **Little Karoo**.

If the west sounds too pretty and you're after a more "African" experience, head for the **eastern** flank of the country, best visited in the cooler months (May–Oct).

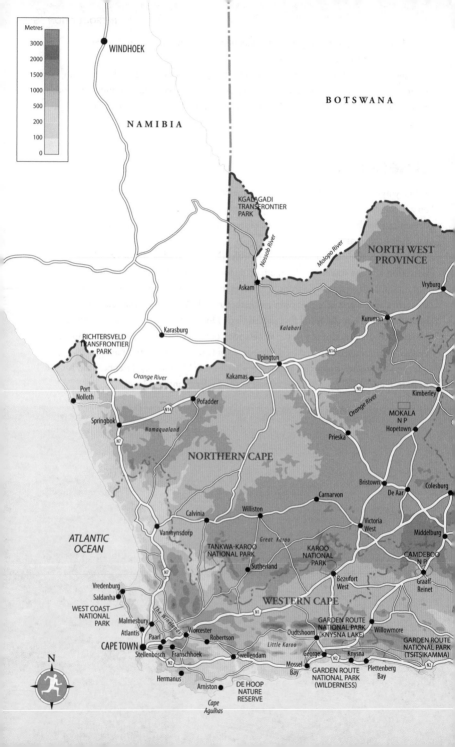

FACT FILE

• With a **population** of 51 million people, South Africa has eleven official **languages**: Zulu, Xhosa, Afrikaans, Pedi, English, Ndebele, Sotho, Setswana, siSwati, Venda and Tsonga.

• The country is a **multiparty democracy**, the head of state being President Jacob Zuma. Parliament sits in Cape Town, the **legislative capital**, while Pretoria is the **executive capital**, from where the president and his cabinet run the country. Each of the nine provinces has its own government.

• South African President **Jacob Zuma**'s three-spouse household is modest compared with the fourteen-wife ménage of Swazi King Mswati; King Letsie of Lesotho has been married just once.

• **Nelson Mandela**'s widow, Graca Machel, who was previously married to the late president of Mozambique, Samora Machel, is the only woman to have been first lady of two different countries.

• South Africa is the only country in the world to have manufactured **nuclear weapons** and then to have voluntarily dismantled them.

Johannesburg is likely to be your point of entry to this area: its frenetic street life, soaring office blocks and lively mix of people make it quite unlike anywhere else in the country. Half a day away by car lie **Limpopo** and **Mpumalanga** provinces, which share the mighty **Kruger National Park**. Of South Africa's roughly two dozen major parks, Kruger is unrivalled on the continent for its cross section of mammal species.

A visit to Kruger combines perfectly with KwaZulu-Natal to the south, and an excellent short cut between the two is through tiny, landlocked **Swaziland**, which has a distinct Swazi culture and a number of well-managed game parks. **KwaZulu-Natal** itself offers superb game and birdlife; **Hluhluwe-Imfolozi Park** is the best place in the world to see endangered rhinos, and there are several other outstanding small game reserves nearby, such as Ithala, Mkhuze and Ndumo. For hiking and nature, the high point of the province – literally – is the soaring **Drakensberg**, half a day's drive from Durban. **Durban** is one of the few South African cities worth visiting in its own right: a busy cultural melting pot with a bustling Indian district and lively beachfront. The long stretch of beaches north and south of Durban is the most developed in the country, but north towards the Mozambique border lies South Africa's wildest stretch of coast.

Long sandy **beaches**, developed only in pockets, are characteristic of much of the 2798km of shoreline that curves from the cool Atlantic along the Northern Cape round to the subtropical Indian Ocean that foams onto KwaZulu-Natal's shores. Much of the **Eastern Cape** coast is hugely appealing: for strolling, sunbathing or simply taking in backdrops of mountains and hulking sand dunes. **Scuba diving**, especially in KwaZulu-Natal, opens up a world of coral reefs rich with colourful fish, and south of the Western Cape winelands, along the **Whale Coast**, is one of South Africa's major wildlife attractions – some of the best shore-based **whale-watching** in the world.

With time in hand, you might want to drive through the sparse but exhilarating **interior**, with its open horizons, switchback mountain passes, rocks, scrubby vegetation and isolated *dorps*. The **Northern Cape** and **North West Province** can reveal surprises, such

FROM TOP WHITE RHINOS, EASTERN CAPE; BEACH VOLLEYBALL, CAMPS BAY, CAPE TOWN

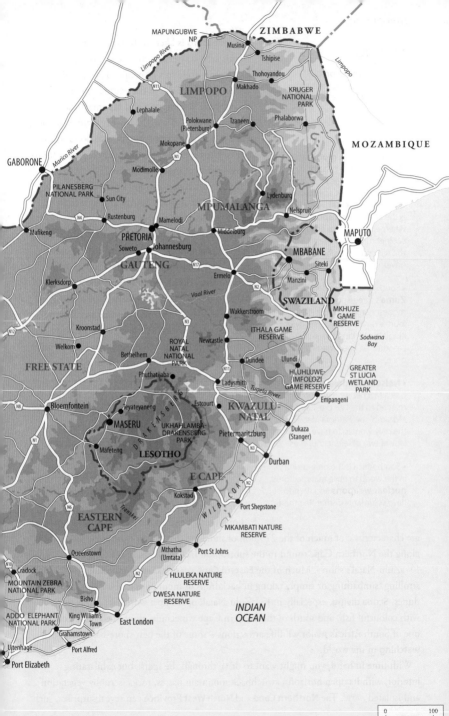

as the Martian landscapes of the Richtersveld and the lion country of the remote but thrilling Kgalagadi Transfrontier Park.

From the staunchly Afrikaner heartland of **Free State**, you're well poised to visit the undeveloped kingdom of **Lesotho**, set in the mountains between Free State and KwaZulu-Natal. Lesotho has few vestiges of royalty left, but does offer plenty of spectacular highland scenery, best explored on a sturdy, sure-footed Basotho pony.

When to go

South Africa is predominantly sunny, but when it does get cold you feel it, since everything is geared to fine weather. **Midwinter** in the southern hemisphere is in June and July, while **midsummer** is during December and January, when the country shuts down for its annual holiday.

South Africa has distinct climatic zones. In **Cape Town** and the **Garden Route** coastal belt, summers tend to be warm, mild and unpredictable; rain can fall at any time of the year and winter days can be cold and wet. Many Capetonians regard March to May as the perfect season, when the winds drop; it's beautifully mild and the tourists have gone. Subtropical **KwaZulu-Natal** has warm, sunny winters and tepid seas; in common with the **Lesotho** highlands, the province's Drakensberg range has misty days in summer and mountain snow in winter. **Johannesburg** and **Pretoria** lie on the highveld plateau and have a near-perfect climate; summer days are hot and frequently broken by dramatic thunder showers; winters are dry with chilly nights. East of Johannesburg, the **lowveld**, the low-lying wedge along the Mozambique border that includes the **Kruger National Park** and much of **Swaziland**, is subject to similar summer and winter rainfall patterns to the highveld, but experiences far greater extremes of temperature because of its considerably lower altitude.

HOUSE OF THE SPIRITS

For thousands of years, San Bushman shamans in South Africa decorated rock faces with powerful religious images. These finely realized paintings, found in mountainous areas across South Africa, include animals, people, and humans changing into animals. Archeologists now regard the images as metaphors for religious experiences, one of the most significant of which is the healing trance dance, still practised by the few surviving Bushman communities. Rockfaces can be seen as portals between the human and spiritual world: when we gaze at Bushman rock art, we are looking into the house of the spirits.

ABOVE LILAC-BREASTED ROLLER, KRUGER NATIONAL PARK

Author picks

Having returned to his home country after two decades, our author, Tony, is still constantly amazed by South Africa, where he's watched a whale breach over his morning coffee, trodden grapes with a high-court judge and run into a baboon during a morning jog. Chance encounters aside, here are some of the other things that make his home so special.

Oldest artistic tradition The haunting rock paintings of the Drakensberg hark back to a mythological time of shamans, animals and shape-shifters. **See p.388**

In the raw Taking an outdoor shower at one of the Kruger's private lodges is an unforgettable way to experience the African wild. **See p.549**

Soweto on spokes Bike tours of South Africa's largest township get you out of the bus and onto the street. **See p.468**

Walk with leviathans The five-day Whale Trail in De Hoop Nature Reserve is stunningly beautiful throughout the year – and sublime in season when there are whales around every corner. **See p.207**

Hottest rave Revel in a spectacular week of performance, music, madness and fire at the Afrika Burn festival in the Northern Cape's Tankwa Karoo desert. **See p.60**

Mother of all asteroids The Vredefort dome is part of the world's oldest, widest and deepest meteorite impact crater. **See p.442**

Go out on a limb Absorb the 360 degree vertiginous views of Cape Town and Table Mountain from the elegant timber and steel Boomslang (tree snake) Walkway as it slithers through the upper boughs of the forest canopy at Kirstenbosch Botanical Gardens. **See p.106**

Switched on switchbacks Few drives are more dramatic than taking the Swartberg Pass, which carves through mountains to reach the Karoo hamlet of Prince Albert. **See p.180**

Our author recommendations don't end here. We've flagged up our favourite places – a perfectly sited hotel, an atmospheric café, a special restaurant – throughout the guide, highlighted with the ★ symbol.

28

things not to miss

It's not possible to see everything that South Africa, Lesotho and Swaziland has to offer in one trip – and we don't suggest you try. What follows is a selective and subjective taste of the country's highlights, including outstanding national parks, spectacular wildlife, adventure sports and beautiful architecture. All entries have a page reference to take you straight into the guide, where you can find out more. Coloured numbers refer to chapters in the Guide section.

1

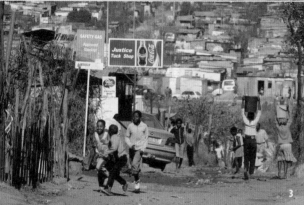

1 THE WILD COAST
This part of the Eastern Cape offers peace and seclusion along a remote and spectacular subtropical coastline.

2 HLUHLUWE-IMFOLOZI PARK
KwaZulu-Natal's finest game reserve provides an unsurpassed variety of wildlife-spotting activities, from night drives to self-guided walks and even donkey trails.

3 SOWETO
A tour around the vast, sprawling township – South Africa's largest – gives visitors a graphic insight into how the majority of black South Africans live.

4 INDIAN CULTURE
Durban, Africa's busiest port, boasts a large Indian population, brightly coloured Hindu temples, buzzing markets and zinging curries.

8

9

13

14

15

16

17 PONY TREKKING
Page 586
The perfect way to experience the ruggedly beautiful "mountain kingdom" of Lesotho.

18 KRUGER NATIONAL PARK
Page 539
Get spine-tinglingly close to hippos and other big game at Southern Africa's ultimate wildlife destination.

19 RAFTING
Page 631
Swaziland's Great Usutu River offers exhilarating whitewater rafting.

20 RICHTERSVELD TRANSFRONTIER
Page 290
Fierce, rugged and hot, the Richtersveld has some of the most dramatic mountainscape in the country, sparsely populated by science-fiction vegetation.

21 LIVE MUSIC
Page 479
Johannesburg offers the best nightlife in South Africa, attracting top musical performers from around the country and abroad.

22 TABLE MOUNTAIN CABLEWAY
Page 108
The most spectacular way to ascend Cape Town's famous landmark is also the easiest – the revolving cable car.

21

22

23 MADIKWE GAME RESERVE

Page 512

This massive game park sees remarkably few visitors, yet boasts excellent lodges and superb wildlife-spotting opportunities, from wild dogs to lions and elephants.

24 DE HOOP NATURE RESERVE

Page 207

Slide down mountainous dunes or watch whales from the high vantage point they provide.

25 THE BULUNGULA LODGE

Page 343

At a beautiful river mouth on the Wild Coast, this backpacker lodge offers an all-too-rare opportunity to experience rural African life.

26 ROBBEN ISLAND

Page 102

Just half an hour from Cape Town is the notorious offshore jail where political prisoners, including Nelson Mandela, were incarcerated.

27 WHALE-WATCHING

Page 201

Regularly visiting the southern Cape Coast, whales often approach surprisingly close to the shore.

28 GAMKASKLOOF

Page 191

Go to Hell (Die Hel) down one of the spectacular passes of the Little Karoo, where you'll find exciting drives and mountain biking.

26

27

28

Itineraries

The following itineraries take you from South Africa's southwestern corner to its northeastern extent, covering the classic attractions – such as Cape Town and Kruger National Park – as well as far less-visited sights. Stitched together, the three itineraries could constitute a two-month grand tour, sweeping across the country's major themes, from safaris, beaches and epic landscapes to ethnic art and culture, colonial architecture and urban life.

WESTERN CAPE CIRCUIT

South Africa's oldest urban centres are in the Western Cape, a province that packs a huge variety. You could cover its highlights in three weeks, but four would be better.

❶ Cape Town Southern Africa's oldest, most beautiful and most unmissable city has it all: an extraordinary natural setting, beautiful historic architecture and a buzzing urban life. **See p.80**

❷ The Winelands Limewashed Cape Dutch manors surrounded by vineyards beneath mauve mountains house some of the country's best restaurants and guesthouses. **See p.164**

❸ Whale Coast Monumental dunes and wild surf are reason enough to visit De Hoop Nature Reserve, but it's also one of the world's top spots for land-based whale-watching. **See p.193**

❹ Garden Route South Africa's quintessential route takes in pretty coastal towns, such as Knysna, as well as national parks with ancient forests and dramatic coastline. **See p.208**

❺ Little Karoo The R62 cuts through the semi-arid Little Karoo's mountain passes, taking in sculptural rock formations, hot springs and some lovely historic villages. **See p.179**

❻ Swartland The closest place to Cape Town to see the veld glowing with wild flowers in spring is Darling. **See p.238**

❼ Cederberg San rock-art sites and grotesque gargoyle-like rock formations give the Western Cape's mountain wilderness its otherworldly atmosphere. **See p.246**

THE EAST

The eastern flank of the country boasts game reserves, beaches and ethnic culture. You'll need three weeks for this tour.

❶ Johannesburg Africa's economic powerhouse buzzes with a thriving arts scene, well-established café culture and Soweto, the country's most populous township. **See p.448**

❷ Kruger National Park The size of a small country and brimming with wildlife, Kruger is up there with the continent's top game reserves. **See p.539**

❸ Swaziland One of the world's few remaining absolute monarchies retains its tribal traditions through a number of ceremonies. **See p.610**

❹ iSimangaliso Wetland UNESCO World Heritage Site that offers scuba diving in the subtropical waters of Sodwana Bay and where loggerhead and leatherback turtles come ashore to nest in summer. **See p.404**

❺ KwaZulu-Natal game reserves Hluhluwe-Imfolozi is the province's premier game reserve, roamed by big cats, rhinos and elephants;

ABOVE ROCK FORMATIONS, CEDERBERG MOUNTAINS; MSWATI III, KING OF SWAZILAND

a number of minor reserves such as Ithala, Mkhuze and Phinda also have a lot to offer. **See p.401, p.416, p.408 & p.409**

❻ Zulu heartland Geometrically patterned basketry and several festivals, including Shaka Day, keep alive the proud traditions of KwaZulu-Natal's dominant ethnic group. **See p.416**

❼ Ukhahlamba Drakensberg The dramatic landscapes make for breathtaking hikes and the chance to see the rock art of the San. **See p.388**

❽ Durban The subtropical vegetation, popular beachfront and cocktail of Zulu, Indian and English colonial cultures make Durban a compelling stay for a couple of days. **See p.355**

THE FRONTIER

Allow three weeks to explore the dry interior of the Great Karoo and the contrastingly verdant Wild Coast.

❶ Port Elizabeth Four thousand English settlers made landfall here in 1820 and today their descendants' families are drawn to its safe sandy beaches. **See p.300**

❷ Big Game Country Addo, the only Big Five national park in the southern half of the country, is also close to Shamwari and Kwande, two of the top private game reserves. **See p.307**

❸ Graaff-Reinet Totally surrounded by the mountainous Camdeboo National Park, whose highlight is the deep Valley of Desolation, this eighteenth-century Cape-Dutch Karoo outpost is perfect for exploring on foot. **See p.324**

❹ Cradock The atmospherically dusty frontier town sits on the west bank of the Great Fish River, the fractious nineteenth-century border between the English-governed Cape Colony and the traditional Xhosa chiefdoms. **See p.321**

❺ Grahamstown Edgy blend of cultured university town and rural backwater, this Settler City glories in extensive Georgian- and Victorian-colonial streetscapes. **See p.316**

❻ Hogsback A lush Afromontane highland resort elevated above baking valleys where herders graze their livestock. **See p.332**

❼ Madiba Country Boys still herd cattle, just as Nelson Mandela did, around Qunu, the village where he grew up; at nearby Mthatha, a museum tells the story of his life. **See p.344**

❽ Wild Coast Immerse yourself in Xhosa culture and life at Bulungula Lodge, in an unspoilt region of traditional villages, undulating hills, lush forests and hundreds of kilometres of undeveloped sandy beaches. **See p.336**

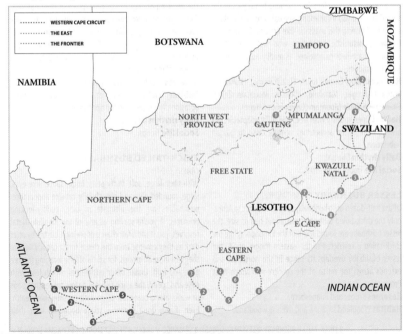

Wildlife

Apart from Kruger, Kgalagadi Transfrontier, Hluhluwe-Imfolozi, Addo Elephant, the Pilanesberg and a number of private parks, where you'll see the Big Five (lion, leopard, buffalo, elephant and rhino), more than a hundred other reserves offer numerous smaller predators and dozens of herbivores, including endangered species, in invariably beautiful settings.

This field guide provides a quick reference to help you identify some of the **mammals** most likely to be encountered in South Africa. It includes species found throughout the country as well a number whose range is more restricted. The photos show easily identified markings and features. The notes give pointers about the kind of habitat in which you are likely to see each mammal; its daily rhythm; the kind of social groups it usually forms; and some of the reserves you're most likely to find it in.

PRIMATES

Southern Africa has the lowest diversity of primates on the continent, a mere five species excluding Homo sapiens. They include two varieties of bushbaby, two monkeys and one species of baboon – the largest and most formidable of the lot. Great apes such as gorillas and chimpanzees aren't found in the wild in Southern Africa.

CHACMA BABOON *PAPIO (URSINUS) CYNOCEPHALUS*
Apart from humans, baboons are the primates most widely found in South Africa. Males can be intimidating and are bold enough to raid vehicles or accommodation in search of food, undeterred by the presence of people. Troops are led by a dominant male and are governed by complex social relations in which gender, precedence, physical strength and family ties determine status. Every adult male enjoys dominance over every female. Grooming forms part of the social glue and you'll commonly see baboons lolling about while performing this massage-like activity. Baboons are highly opportunistic omnivores who will tuck into a scorpion or a newborn antelope as readily as raid a citrus farm for oranges.
Reserves Addo, Garden Route (Tsitsikamma), Hluhluwe-Imfolozi, Kruger, Marakele, Mkhuze, Mountain Zebra, Pilanesberg, Table Mountain (Cape of Good Hope).
Habitat Open country with trees and cliffs; adaptable, but always near water; sometimes venture close to human habitation.
Daily rhythm Diurnal.
Social life Troops of 15–100.

LESSER BUSHBABY *GALAGO MOHOLI*
Of the half-dozen or so bushbaby species endemic to Africa, only the thick-tailed bushbaby and, about half its size, the lesser bushbaby are found south of the Limpopo. While the thick-tailed is restricted to the eastern fringes of SA, the lesser bushbaby overlaps its range in the northeast and extends across the north of the country into North West Province.
Reserves Kruger and Pilanesberg.
Habitat Woodland savanna and riverine woodland.

Daily rhythm Nocturnal.
Social life Small family groups.

SAMANGO (OR SYKES') MONKEY
CERCOPITHECUS MITIS
In striking contrast with the cheekier, upfront disposition of vervets, the rarer samango monkeys are shy and may only give themselves away through their loud explosive call or the breaking of branches as they go about their business. Samangos are larger than vervets and have long cheek hair. Like vervets, they're highly social and live in troops of females under the proprietorship of a dominant male, but unlike their relatives they are more inclined to fan out when looking for food.
Reserves Hluhluwe-Imfolozi, Isimangaliso and Ndumo.
Habitat Prefer higher reaches of gallery forest; occasionally venture into the open to forage.
Daily rhythm Diurnal.
Social life Troops.

THICK-TAILED BUSHBABY *OTOLEMUR CRASSICAUDATUS*
With their large, soft, fluffy pelts, huge, saucer-like eyes, large, rounded ears and superficially cat-like appearance, bushbabies are the ultimate in cute, cuddly-looking primates. If you're staying at any of the KwaZulu-Natal reserves, you stand a fair chance of seeing a bushbaby after dark as they emerge from the dense forest canopy, where they rest in small groups, for spells of lone foraging for tree gum and fruit. Unlike other bushbabies, which leap with ease and speed, the thick-tailed is a slow mover that hops or walks along branches, often with considerable stealth. Even if you don't see one, you're bound to hear their

1 THICK-TAILED BUSHBABY; **2** LESSER BUSHBABY; **3** SAMANGO MONKEY; **4** VERVET MONKEY; **5** CHACMA BABOON >

piercing scream cut through the sounds of the night. Bushbabies habituate easily to humans and will sometimes come into lodge dining rooms, scavenging for titbits.
Reserves Hluhluwe-Imfolozi, Isimangaliso, Kruger.
Habitat Dry and riverine woodland; arboreal.
Daily rhythm Nocturnal.
Social life Small groups of a mating pair or one or two females with young; males territorial with ranges that overlap several female ranges.

VERVET MONKEY *CERCOPITHECUS AETHIOPS*

A widespread primate you may see outside reserves, living around nearby farms and even on suburban fringes, where opportunities for scavenging are promising. Vervets are principally vegetarians but are not averse to eating invertebrates, small lizards, nestlings and eggs, as well as biscuits and sweets. Vervet society is made up of family groups of females and young, defended by associate males, and is highly caste-ridden. A mother's rank determines that of her daughter from infancy, and lower-ranking adult females risk being castigated if they fail to show due respect to these "upper-crust" youngsters.
Reserves Eastern half of SA: virtually every game reserve in KwaZulu-Natal, Limpopo, Mpumalanga and Northwest, as well as along the coast from Mossel Bay to northern KwaZulu-Natal.
Habitat Will forage in grasslands, but rarely far from woodland; particularly along river courses; arboreal and terrestrial.
Daily rhythm Diurnal.
Social life Troops.

DOG-RELATIVES AND ALLIED SPECIES

AARDWOLF *PROTELES CRISTATUS*

The hyena-like aardwolf is far smaller than the spotted hyena and far lighter, as well as being less shaggy, with vertical dark stripes along its tawny body. It is further distinguished from other hyenas by its insectivorous diet and its particular preference for harvester termites, which it laps up en masse (up to 200,000 in one night) with its broad sticky tongue. Far more widely distributed in South Africa than hyenas, but shy and not often seen.
Reserves Addo, Bontebok, Isimangaliso, Kruger and Pilanesberg.
Habitat Most habitats, except dense forest.
Daily rhythm Nocturnal; sometimes active in the cooler hours just before dusk or after dawn.
Social life Solitary.

BAT-EARED FOX *OTOCYON MEGALOTIS*

The bat-eared fox can easily be distinguished from the jackals by its outsized ears, its shorter, pointier muzzle and its considerably smaller-size. The bat-eared fox's black Zorro mask helps distinguish it from the similar-sized Cape fox, *Vulpes chama*, which inhabitats an overlapping range. Like other dogs, the bat-eared fox is an omnivore, but it favours termites and larvae, which is where its large radar-like ears come in handy. With these it can triangulate the precise position of dung-beetle larvae up to 30cm underground and dig them out.
Reserves Addo, Bontebok, Karoo, Kgalagadi, Kruger, Mountain Zebra and Pilanesberg.
Habitat Open countryside; short-scrubland; lightly forested areas.
Daily rhythm Nocturnal and diurnal.
Social life Family groups of 2–6.

BLACK-BACKED JACKAL *CANIS MESOMELAS*

The member of the dog family you're most likely to see is the black-backed jackal, found especially in the country's reserves. It bears a strong resemblance to a small, skinny German Shepherd, but with a muzzle more like that of a fox, and is distinguished from the grey, side-striped jackal (see below) by the white-flecked black saddle on its back, to which it owes its name. Jackals are omnivorous scavenger-hunters, who get most of their food from catching small creatures such as insects, lizards, snakes or birds, but will also tackle baby antelope and larger birds, and they are cheeky enough to steal pieces of prey from under the noses of lions or hyenas at a kill.
Reserves Addo, Hluhluwe-Imfolozi, Karoo, Kgalagadi, Kruger, Mkhuze, Mountain Zebra, Pilanesberg.
Habitat Broad range, from moist mountain regions to desert; avoid dense woodland.
Daily rhythm Normally nocturnal, but diurnal in safety of game reserves.
Social life Mostly monogamous pairs, but also seen singly and in small family groups.

SIDE-STRIPED JACKAL *CANIS ADJUSTUS*

Like its black-backed relative, the side-striped jackal is omnivorous, with a diet that takes in carrion, small animals, reptiles, birds and insects, as well as wild fruit and berries. The fact that the black-backed jackal seeks a drier habitat, in contrast to the side-striped's preference for well-watered woodland, is an identification pointer.
Reserves Isimangaliso, Kruger.
Habitat Well-watered woodland.
Daily rhythm Mainly nocturnal.
Social life Solitary or pairs.

SPOTTED HYENA *CROCUTA CROCUTA*

The largest carnivores after lions are hyenas, and apart from the lion, the spotted hyena is the meat-eater you will see most often. Although considered a scavenger *par excellence*, the spotted hyena is a formidable hunter, most often found where antelope and zebra are present. Exceptionally efficient consumers, with immensely strong teeth and jaws, spotted hyenas eat virtually every part of their prey, including bones and hide and, where used to humans, often steal shoes, unwashed pans and refuse from tents. They are most active at night, when they issue their unnerving whooping cries. Clans of twenty or so are dominated by females, who are larger than the males and compete with each other for rank.

Reserves Addo, Hluhluwe-Imfolozi, Kgalagadi and Kruger.

Habitat Wide variety of habitat apart from dense forest.

Daily rhythm Generally nocturnal from dusk, but diurnal in many parks.

Social life Highly social, usually living in extended family groups.

WILD DOG *LYCAON PICTUS*

Once the widely distributed hunters of the African plains, wild dogs have been brought to the edge of extinction. The world's second most threatened dog relative, the South African population consists of just five hundred individuals, of which two hundred are in the Kruger National Park. For many years they were shot on sight, having gained an unjustified reputation as cruel and wanton killers of cattle and sheep. More recent scientific evidence reveals them to be economical and efficient hunters – and more successful at it than any other African species. Capable of sustaining high speeds (up to 50km/h) over long distances, wild dogs lunge at their prey en masse, tearing it to pieces – a gruesome finish, but no more grisly than the suffocating muzzle-bite of a lion. The entire pack of ten to fifteen animals participates in looking after the pups, bringing back food and regurgitating it for them.

Reserves Kruger (best place) as well as Hluhluwe-Imfolozi, Madikwe, Marakele, Mkhuze, Pilanesberg and Tswalu.

Habitat Open savanna in the vicinity of grazing herds.

Daily rhythm Diurnal.

Social life Nomadic packs.

CATS

Apart from lions, which notably live in social groups, cats are solitary carnivores. With the exception of the cheetah, which is anatomically distinct from the other cats, the remaining members of the family are so similar, says mammal ecologist Richard Estes, that big cats are just "jumbo versions" of the domestic cat, "distinguished mainly by a modification of the larynx that enables them to roar".

CARACAL *CARACAL CARACAL*

Although classified as a small cat, the caracal is a fairly substantial animal. An unmistakeable and awesome hunter, with great climbing agility, it's able to take prey, such as adult impala and sheep, which far exceed its own weight of 8–18kg kilos. More commonly it will feed on birds, which it pounces on, sometimes while still in flight, as well as smaller mammals, including dassies (see p.40).

Reserves Addo, Karoo, Kgalagadi, Kruger, Mountain Zebra (one of the best places), Table Mountain (Cape of Good Hope).

Habitat Open bush and plains; occasionally arboreal.

Daily rhythm Mainly nocturnal.

Social life Solitary.

CHEETAH *ACINONYX JUBATUS*

In the flesh the cheetah is so different from the leopard that it's hard to see how there could ever be any confusion. Cheetahs are the greyhounds of the big-cat world, with small heads, long legs and an exterior decor of fine spots. Unlike leopards, cheetahs never climb trees, being designed rather for activity on the open plains. Hunting is normally a solitary activity, down to keen eyesight and an incredible burst of speed that can take the animal up to 100km/h for a few seconds. Because they're lighter than lions and less powerful than leopards, cheetahs can't rely on strength to bring down their prey. Instead they resort to tripping or knocking the victim off balance by striking its hindquarters, and then pouncing.

Reserves Addo, Hluhluwe-Imfolozi, Kgalagadi, Kruger, and Mountain Zebra.

Habitat Savanna in the vicinity of plains game.

Daily rhythm Diurnal.

Social life Solitary or temporary nuclear family groups.

LEOPARD *PANTHERA PARDUS*

The lion may be king, but most successful and arguably most beautiful of the large cats is the leopard, which survives from the southern coastal strip of Africa all the way to China. Highly adaptable, they can subsist in extremes of aridity or cold, as well as in proximity to human habitation, where they happily prey on domestic animals – which accounts for their absence in the sheep-farming regions of central South Africa, due to extermination by farmers. Powerfully built, they can bring down prey twice their weight and drag an impala (see p.34) their own weight up a tree. The chase is not part of the leopard's tactical repertoire; they hunt by stealth, getting to within 2m of their target before pouncing.

1 SERVAL; **2** LION; **3** CARACAL; **4** LEOPARD; **5** CHEETAH >

Reserves Kruger, Hluhluwe-Imfolozi, Kruger, Marakele and Pilanesberg; best places are the private reserves in Sabi Sands, abutting Kruger, which trade on their leopards being highly accustomed to humans; also present in rugged, mountainous southern W. Cape, but secretive and rarely seen.

Habitat Highly adaptable; frequently arboreal.

Daily rhythm Nocturnal; also cooler daylight hours.

Social life Solitary.

LION *PANTHERA LEO*

The most compelling and largest of the cats for most safari-goers are lions, the most massive predators in Africa. It's fortunate then that, despite having the most limited distribution of any cat in South Africa, lions are the ones you're most likely to see. Lazy, gregarious and sizeable, lions rarely attempt to hide, making them relatively easy to find, especially if someone else has already found them – a gathering of stationary vehicles frequently signals lions. Their fabled reputation as cold, efficient hunters is ill-founded, as lions are only successful around thirty percent of the time, and only if operating as a group. Males don't hunt at all if they can help it and will happily enjoy a free lunch courtesy of the females of the pride.

Reserves Healthy populations in Kgalagadi and Kruger; limited numbers in Addo, Hluhluwe-Imfolozi, Mapungubwe, Marakele and Pilanesberg.

Habitat Wherever there's water and shade except thick forest.

Daily rhythm Diurnal and nocturnal.

Social life Prides of three to forty, more usually around twelve.

SERVAL *FELIS SERVAL*

Long-legged and spotted, servals bear some resemblance to, but are far smaller than, cheetahs and are more rarely seen. Efficient hunters, servals use their large rounded ears to pinpoint prey (usually small rodents, birds or reptiles), which they pounce on with both front paws after performing impressive athletic leaps.

Reserves Hluhluwe-Imfolozi, Ithala, Kruger, Pilanesberg, Ukhahlamba Drakensberg.

Habitat Reed beds or tall grasslands near water.

Daily rhythm Normally nocturnal, but can be seen during daylight hours.

Social life Usually solitary.

SMALLER CARNIVORES

CIVET *CIVETTICTIS CIVETTA*

The civet (or African civet) is a stocky animal resembling a large, terrestrial genet. Civets were formerly kept in captivity for their musk (once an ingredient in perfume), which is secreted from glands near the tail. Civets aren't often seen, but they're predictable creatures, wending their way along the same path at the same time, night after night. Civets are omnivores that will scavenge for carrion and feed on small rodents, birds, reptiles and even fruit. Found in Northern SA, Mpumalanga and extreme north of KwaZulu-Natal.

Reserves Kruger and Pilanesberg.

Habitat Open, especially riverine, woodland.

Daily rhythm Nocturnal.

Social life Solitary.

HONEY BADGER *MELLIVORA CAPENSIS*

The unusual honey badger, related to the European badger, has a reputation for defending itself extremely fiercely. Primarily an omnivorous forager, it will tear open bees' nests (to which it is led by a small bird, the honey guide), its thick, loose hide rendering it impervious to stings.

Reserves Addo, Hluhluwe-Imfolozi , Karoo, Kgalagadi, Kruger and Pilanesberg.

Habitat Wide range except forest.

Daily rhythm Mainly nocturnal.

Social life Solitary, sometimes pairs.

SMALL-SPOTTED GENET *GENETTA GENETTA*

Small-spotted genets are reminiscent of slender elongated cats, and were once domesticated around the Mediterranean (but cats turned out to be better mouse hunters). In fact, they are viverrids, related to mongooses, and are frequently seen after dark around national-park lodges, where some live a semi-domesticated existence. They're difficult to distinguish from the less widely distributed, large-spotted genet, *Genetta tigrina*, which has bigger spots and a black (instead of white) tip to its tail.

Reserves Addo, Bontebok, Karoo, Kgalagadi, Kruger, Mountain Zebra, Pilanesberg, Table Mountain (Cape of Good Hope).

Habitat Wide range: light bush country, even arid areas; partly arboreal.

Daily rhythm Nocturnal. But becomes active at dusk.

Social life Solitary.

WATER MONGOOSE *ATILAX PALUDINOSUS*

Most species of mongoose, of which there are nearly a dozen in South Africa, are also tolerant of humans and, even when disturbed, can usually be observed for some time. If you keep your eyes peeled when driving on the open road, you'll often see mongooses darting across your path. Social arrangements differ from species to species, some being solitary while others live in packs. The water mongoose, one of the most widely distributed of the mongooses, resembles an otter, but is a lot smaller and

lighter. Foragers, they'll root for anything edible – mostly crabs and amphibians, but also invertebrates, eggs, lizards and small rodents. Water mongooses are found in a deep swathe across Southern Africa, sweeping down from Mpumalanga in the northeast to the Cape Peninsula in the southwest.

Reserves Bontebok, Hluhluwe-Imfolozi, Karoo, Kruger, Mkhuze, Table Mountain (Cape of Good Hope).

Habitat Well-watered areas, such as alongside streams, rivers and lakes.

Daily rhythm Mainly nocturnal, but also active at dusk and dawn.

Social life Solitary.

ANTELOPE

South Africa has roughly a third of all antelope species in Africa, and antelope are the most often seen family of animals in the country's game reserves. You'll even spot some on farmland along the extensive open stretches that separate interior towns. South African antelope are subdivided into a number of tribes, and like buffalo, giraffe and domestic cattle, they are ruminants – animals that have four stomachs and chew the cud.

BLACK WILDEBEEST *CONNOCHAETES GNOU*
Black wildebeest were brought to the edge of extinction in the nineteenth century and now number around three thousand in South Africa, though you will find them in a handful of parks in the country. You can tell them apart from their blue relatives by their darker colour (brown rather than the black suggested by their name) and long white tail. Black Wildebeest (1–1.2m high at the shoulder; 160–180kg) are also significantly shorter and lighter than their blue cousins (1.7m; 380kg). Black wildebeest appear to be under threat again, this time not from hunting, but hybridization, since black and blue wildebeest can interbreed and produce fertile offspring. Conservationists fear that the rarer black species will be bred out of existence. The problem is taken so seriously by KwaZulu-Natal wildlife authorities that no park in the province is stocked with both species.

Reserves Karoo, Mountain Zebra and Ukhahlamba Drakensberg.

Habitat Low scrub and open grassland.

Daily rhythm Diurnal.

Social life Cows and offspring wander freely through bull territories; during rut bulls try to keep females within their territory.

BLUE DUIKER *PHILANTOMBA MONTICOLA*
The smallest South African antelope, the blue duiker, weighs in at around 4kg, has an arched back and stands 35cm at the shoulder (roughly the height of a domestic cat). Pairs stick together and remain vigilant as a defence against predators, which can include leopards, baboons and even large birds of prey. Duiker are found in the forested areas of coastal strip from George in the Western Cape to northern KwaZulu-Natal, but are extremely shy and so seldom seen.

Reserves Garden Route (Knysna), Isimangaliso and Ndumo.

Habitat Forests and dense bushland.

Daily rhythm Mainly diurnal.

Social life Monogamous couples.

BLUE WILDEBEEST *CONNOCHAETES TAURINUS*
All hartebeest are sociable but the exemplar of this is the blue wildebeest (sometimes known as the brindled gnu), which, in East Africa, gather in hundreds of thousands for their annual migration. You won't see these numbers in South Africa, but you'll see smaller herds. Blue wildebeest are often seen in association with zebra.

Reserves Hluhluwe-Imfolozi, Ithala, Kgalagadi, Kruger, KwaZulu-Natal, Mapungubwe and Mkhuze.

Habitat Grasslands.

Daily rhythm Diurnal, occasionally nocturnal.

Social life Intensely gregarious in a wide variety of associations from small groups to sizeable herds.

BONTEBOK *DAMALISCUS DORCAS DORCAS*
Better-looking version of the tsessebe, from which it's distinguished by its chocolate-brown colouring and white facial and rump markings. Bontebok, which were historically limited to a small range in the southern Cape, teetered on the edge of extinction, but their survival is now secured on several reserves and farms. A subspecies, the blesbok, *Damaliscus dorcas phillipsi*, is found in the Free State and northern Eastern Cape.

Reserves Bontebok, De Hoop, Table Mountain (Cape of Good Hope), West Coast.

Habitat Coastal plain where Cape fynbos occurs.

Daily rhythm Diurnal.

Social life Rams hold territories; ewes and lamb herds numbering up to ten wander freely between territories.

BUSHBUCK *TRAGELAPHUS SCRIPTUS*
Despite a distinct family resemblance, you could never confuse a kudu with a bushbuck, which is considerably shorter and, in the males, has a single twist to its horns, in contrast to the kudu's two or three turns. They also differ in being the only solitary members of the tribe, one reason you're less likely to spot them. Often seen in thickets or heard crashing through them. Not to be confused with the larger nyala.

1 BUSHBUCK; **2** NYALA; **3** ELAND >

Reserves Addo, Garden Route (Wilderness and Knysna), Isimangaliso, Kruger, Mapungubwe, Pilanesberg; also most reserves (even minor ones) in KwaZulu-Natal.
Habitat Thick bush and woodland near water.
Daily rhythm Mainly nocturnal, but also active during the day when cool.
Social life Solitary, but casually sociable; sometimes graze in small groups.

COMMON (OR GREY) DUIKER *SYLVICAPRA GRIMMIA*

Of the duikers, the one you're most likely to see is the common duiker (sometimes called the grey duiker, reflecting its colouring), which occurs all over South Africa and is among the antelopes most tolerant of human habitation. When under threat it freezes in the undergrowth, but if chased will dart off in an erratic zigzagging run designed to throw pursuers off balance. The common duiker has a characteristic rounded back, is about 50cm high at the shoulder, and rams have short, straight horns.
Reserves Addo, Bontebok, Hluhluwe-Imfolozi, Ithala, Karoo, Kruger, Mkhuze, Mountain Zebra, Pilanesberg and Table Mountain (Cape of Good Hope)
Habitat Adaptable; prefers scrub and bush.
Daily rhythm Nocturnal and diurnal.
Social life Mostly solitary, but sometimes in pairs.

ELAND *TAUROTRAGUS ORYX*

Eland, the largest living antelope, is built like an ox and moves with the slow deliberation of one, though it's also a superb jumper. Once widely distributed, herds now survive only in pockets of northeast SA and protected areas of the Drakensberg in KwaZulu-Natal; also small introduced populations in numerous other reserves.
Reserves Addo, Ithala, Karoo, Kgalagadi, Kruger, Marakele, Mountain Zebra, Pilanesberg and Table Mountain (Cape of Good Hope).
Habitat Highly adaptable; semi-desert to mountains, but prefers scrubby plains.
Daily rhythm Nocturnal and diurnal.
Social life Non-territorial herds of up to sixty.

GEMSBOK (OR ORYX) *ORYX GAZELLA*

If you encounter a herd of these highly gregarious grazers, you should be left in no doubt as to what they are. Gemsbok are highly adapted for survival in the arid country they inhabit, able to go for long periods without water, relying instead on melons and vegetation for moisture. They tolerate temperatures above 40°C by raising their normal body temperature of 35°C above that of the surrounding air, losing heat by conduction and radiation; their brains are kept cool by a supply of blood from their noses.

Reserves Addo, Augrabies, Karoo, Kgalagadi, Mokala, Pilanesberg and Tankwa Karoo.
Habitat Open grasslands; waterless wastelands; tolerant of prolonged drought.
Daily rhythm Nocturnal and diurnal.
Social life Highly hierarchical mixed herds of up to fifteen, led by a dominant male.

IMPALA *AEPYCEROS MELAMPUS*

Larger and heavier than springbok, which they superficially resemble, impala are elegant and athletic. Prodigious jumpers, they have been recorded leaping distances of 11m and heights of 3m. Only the males carry the distinctive lyre-shaped pair of horns. They are so common in the reserves of the northeast and of KwaZulu-Natal that some jaded rangers look on them as the goats of the savanna – a perception that carries more than a germ of truth, as these flexible feeders are both browsers and grazers.
Reserves Hluhluwe-Imfolozi, Ithala, Kruger, Mapungubwe, Marakele, Mkhuze and Pilanesberg.
Habitat Open savanna, near light woodland cover.
Daily rhythm Diurnal.
Social life Large herds of females overlap with several male territories; during the rut (first five months of the year) dominant males will cut out harem herds of around twenty and expend considerable amounts of effort driving off the any potential rivals.

KLIPSPRINGER *OREOTRAGUS OREOTRAGUS*

Another dwarf antelope (about 60cm at the shoulder) you could well see is the stocky klipspringer, whose Afrikaans name (meaning "rock hopper") reflects its goat-like adaptation to living on *koppies* and cliffs – the only antelope to do so, making it unmistakeable. It's also the only one to walk on the tips of its hooves. They occur sporadically throughout SA where there are rocky outcrops.
Reserves Addo, Augrabies, Garden Route (Tsitsikamma), Karoo, Kruger, Mapungubwe, Mkhuze, Mountain Zebra, Pilanesberg and Table Mountain (Cape of Good Hope).
Habitat Rocky terrain.
Daily rhythm Diurnal; most active in morning and late afternoon.
Social life Monogamous pairs or small family groups.

KUDU *TRAGELAPHUS STREPSICEROS*

The magnificent kudu is more elegantly built than the eland, and males are adorned with sensational spiralled horns that can easily reach 1.5m in length. Known for their athleticism, kudu can vault over a 2m fence with no difficulty.
Reserves Northern Limpopo and North West provinces, and in Mpumalanga and northeastern KwaZulu-Natal; Addo, Ithala, Hluhluwe-Imfolozi, Karoo, Kgalagadi, Kruger, Marakele, Mountain Zebra and Pilanesberg.

1 BLUE WILDEBEEST; 2 TSESSEBE; 3 BLACK WILDEBEEST; 4 SABLE; 5 ROAN >

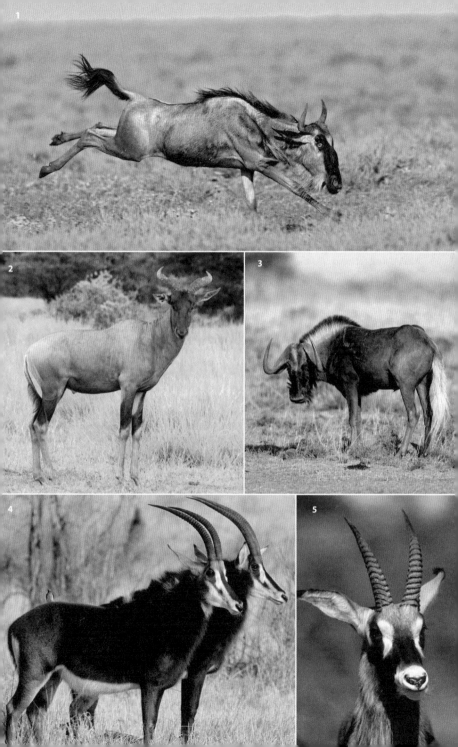

Habitat Semi-arid, hilly or undulating bush country; tolerant of drought.
Daily rhythm Diurnal when secure, otherwise nocturnal.
Social life Males usually solitary or in small transient groups; females in small groups with young.

NYALA *TRAGELAPHUS ANGASII*
Nyalas are midway in size between the kudu and bushbuck, with which they could be confused at first glance. Telling pointers are their size, the sharp vertical white stripes on the side of the nyala (up to fourteen on the male, eighteen on the female), orange legs, and, in the males, a short stiff mane from neck to shoulder. Females tend to group with their two last offspring and gather with other females in small herds, rarely exceeding ten. Males become more solitary the older they get.
Reserves Kruger and around three dozen reserves in KwaZulu-Natal, of which Hluhluwe-Imfolozi, Mkhuze, Ndumo and have the largest populations.
Habitat Dense woodland near water.
Daily rhythm Mainly nocturnal with some diurnal activity.
Social life Non-territorial; basic unit is female and two offspring.

ROAN *HIPPOTRAGUS EQUINUS*
The roan looks very similar to but is larger than a sable (it's Africa's second-largest antelope), with less impressive horns and lighter colouring. You're more likely to see them in open savanna than sables.
Reserves Kruger NP.
Habitat Tall grassland near water.
Daily rhythm Nocturnal and diurnal; peak afternoon feeding.
Social life Small herds led by dominant bull; herds of immature males; sometimes pairs in season.

SABLE *HIPPOTRAGUS NIGER*
The magnificent sable has a sleek, black upper body set in sharp counterpoint to its white underparts and facial markings, as well as its massive backwardly curving horns, making it the thoroughbred of the ruminants, particularly when galloping majestically across the savanna.
Reserves Kruger and Marakele reserves.
Habitat Open woodland with medium to tall grass near water.
Daily rhythm Nocturnal and diurnal.
Social life Highly hierarchical female herds of up to three dozen; territorial bulls divide into sub-territories, through which cows roam.

SPRINGBOK *ANTIDORCAS MARSUPIALIS*
Springboks are South Africa's only gazelle. Their characteristic horns and dark horizontal patch on their sides, separating their reddish tawny upper body from their white underparts, are definitive identifiers. Springbok are recorded as having reached nearly 90km/h and are noted for "pronking", a movement in which they arch their backs and straighten their legs as they leap into the air. Indigenous to the (often arid) northern reaches of South Africa, where they were once seen in their hundreds, they are now more widespread in reserves and on farms where they are raised for their venison and hides.
Reserves Addo, Augrabies, Chelmsford NR (biggest population in KZN), Golden Gate, Karoo, Kgalagadi, Mountain Zebra, Pilanesberg, Tankwa Karoo and West Coast.
Habitat Wide range of open country, from deserts to wetter savanna.
Daily rhythm Seasonally variable, but usually cooler times of day.
Social life Highly gregarious, sometimes in huge herds of hundreds or even thousands; various herding combinations of males, females and young.

TSESSEBE *DAMALISCUS LUNATUS*
Somewhat ungainly in appearance because, according to legend, it arrived late when the Creator was dishing out the goodies, the tsessebe turns out to be a thoroughbred when it comes to speed. One of the fastest antelope on the African plains, a fleeing tsessebe can reach 70km/h. Males often stand sentry on termite hills, marking territory against rivals (rather than defending it against predators). Tricky customers, tsessebe bulls will sometimes falsely give an alarm signal to deter females from wandering out of their territory.
Reserves Restricted to northern extremities of SA; best place is Kruger NP; also present in Ithala, Marakele and Pilanesberg.
Habitat Savanna woodland.
Daily rhythm Diurnal.
Social life Females and young form permanent herds usually of about half a dozen, but up to thirty individuals with a territorial bull.

WATERBUCK *KOBUS ELLIPSIPRYMNUS*
Waterbuck are largest of the near-aquatic Kob tribe, which live close to water. They are sturdy animals – 1.3m at the shoulder, and a distinctive white horseshoe marking on their rump. Only the males have horns. Unable to reach or sustain significant speed, they rely on cover to evade predators. It is also claimed that the oily, musky secretion and powerful odour waterbuck emit from their hair is distasteful to predators and acts as a deterrent. They are common and rather tame where they occur, predominantly in KwaZulu-Natal, Limpopo and Mpumalanga.

Reserves Hluhluwe-Imfolozi, Isimangaliso, Ithala, Kruger, Mapungubwe, Marakele and Mkhuze.
Habitat Open woodland and savanna, near permanent water.

Daily rhythm Nocturnal and diurnal.
Social life Sociable animals, they usually gather in small herds of up to ten, and occasionally up to thirty.

OTHER HOOFED RUMINANTS

Alongside cattle, sheep, goats and antelope, buffalo and giraffe are also hoofed ruminants. Bacteria in their digestive systems process plant matter into carbohydrates, while the dead bacteria are absorbed as protein – a highly efficient arrangement that makes them economical consumers, far more so than non-ruminants such as elephants, which pass vast quantities of what they eat as unutilized fibre. Species that concentrate on grasses are grazers; those eating leaves are browsers.

BUFFALO *SYNCERUS CAFFER*

You won't have to be in the Kruger or most of the other reserves in South Africa for long to see buffalo, a common safari animal that, as one of the Big Five, appears on every hunter's shopping list. Don't let their resemblance to domestic cattle or water buffalo (to which they are not at all closely related) or apparent docility lull you into complacency; lone bulls, in particular, are noted and feared even by hardened hunters as dangerous and relentless killers. Herds consist of clans and you'll be able to spot distinct units within the group: at rest, clan members often cuddle up close to each other. There are separate pecking orders among females and males, the latter being forced to leave the herd during adolescence (at about three years) or once they're over the hill, to form bachelor herds, which you can recognize by their small numbers. To distinguish males from females, look for their heavier horns bisected by a distinct boss, or furrow. Once found throughout South Africa, natural populations survive in the Eastern Cape, KwaZulu-Natal and Mpumalanga and have been widely reintroduced elsewhere.
Reserves Addo, Hluhluwe, Isimangaliso, Karoo, Kruger and Mountain Zebra.
Habitat Wide range of habitats, always near water.
Daily rhythm Nocturnal and diurnal, but inactive during heat of the day.

Social life Buffalo are non-territorial and gather in large herds of hundreds or even sometimes thousands. Herds under one or more dominant bulls consist of clans of a dozen or so related females under a leading cow.

GIRAFFE *GIRAFFA CAMELOPARDALIS*

Giraffe are among the easiest animals to spot because their long necks make them visible above the low scrub. The tallest mammals on earth, they spend their daylight hours browsing on the leaves of trees too high up for other species; combretum and acacias are favourites. Their highly flexible lips and prehensile tongues give them almost hand-like agility and enable them to select the most nutritious leaves while avoiding deadly-sharp acacia thorns. At night they lie down and spend the evening ruminating. If you encounter a bachelor herd, look out for young males testing their strength with neck wrestling. When the female comes into oestrus, which can happen at any time of year, the dominant male mates with her. She will give birth after a fourteen-month gestation. Over half of all young, however, fall prey to lions or hyenas in their early years.
Reserves Hluhluwe-Imfolozi, Ithala, Kgalagadi, Kruger, Mapungubwe, Mkhuze and Pilanesberg.
Habitat Wooded savanna and thorn country.
Daily rhythm Diurnal.
Social life Loose, non-territorial, leaderless herds.

NON-RUMINANTS

Non-ruminating mammals have more primitive digestive systems than animals that chew the cud. Although both have bacteria in their gut that convert vegetable matter into carbohydrates, the less efficient system of the non-ruminants means they have to consume more raw material and process it faster. The upside is they can handle food that's far more fibrous.

AFRICAN ELEPHANT *LOXODONTA AFRICANA*

Elephants were once found throughout South Africa. Now you'll only see them in a handful of reserves. When encountered in the flesh, elephants seem even bigger than you would imagine. You'll need little persuasion from those flapping warning ears to back off if you're too close, but they are at the same time amazingly graceful. In a matter

of moments a large herd can merge into the trees and disappear, silent on their padded, carefully placed feet, their presence betrayed only by the noisy cracking of branches as they strip trees and uproot saplings. Elephants are the most engaging of animals to watch, perhaps because their interactions, behaviour patterns and personality have so many human parallels. Like people,

they lead complex, interdependent social lives, growing from helpless infancy through self-conscious adolescence to adulthood. Babies are born with other cows in close attendance, after a 22-month gestation. Calves suckle for two to three years. Basic family units are composed of a group of related females, tightly protecting their young and led by a venerable matriarch. Bush mythology has it that elephants become ashamed after killing a human, covering the body with sticks and grass. They certainly pay much attention to the disposal of their own dead relatives, often dispersing the bones and spending time near the remains. Old animals die in their 70s or 80s, when their last set of teeth wears out so that they are no longer able to feed themselves.

Reserves Addo (the only population to survive naturally in the southern two-thirds of the country), Hluhluwe-Imfolozi, Ithala, Kruger, Mkhuze, Pilanesberg and Tembe.

Habitat Wide range of habitats, wherever there are trees or water.

Daily rhythm Nocturnal and diurnal; sleeps as little as four hours a day.

Social life Highly complex; cows and offspring in herds headed by matriarch; bulls solitary or in bachelor herds.

ROCK DASSIE (OR HYRAX) *PROCAVIA CAPENSIS*
Dassies look like they ought to be rodents but, amazingly, despite being fluffy and rabbit-sized, their closest relatives (admittedly from some way back) are elephants. Their name (pronounced like "dusty" without the "t") is the Afrikaans version of *dasje*, meaning "little badger", given to them by the first Dutch settlers. Like reptiles, hyraxes have poor body control systems and rely on shelter against both the cold and hot sunlight. They wake up sluggish and seek out rocks to catch the early morning sun – this is one of the best times to look out for them. One adult stands sentry against predators and issues a low-pitched warning cry in response to a threat. Dassies are found throughout South Africa (except the Northern Cape, and KwaZulu-Natal coastal belt) and are frequently sighted.

Reserves Bontebok, Garden Route (Tsitsikamma), Karoo, Kruger, Mountain Zebra, Pilanesberg, Table Mountain (Cape of Good Hope), Ukhahlamba Drakensberg.

Habitat Rocky areas, from mountains to isolated outcrops and coastal cliffs.

Daily rhythm Diurnal.

Social life Colonies of a dominant male and eight or more related females and their offspring.

RHINOS AND HIPPOS

"Hook-lipped" and "square-lipped" are technically more accurate terms for the two species of rhino. "Black" and "white" are based on a linguistic misunderstanding – somewhere along the line, the German "*weid*", which refers to the square-lipped's wide mouth, was misheard as "white". The term has stuck, despite both rhinos being a greyish muddy colour. The shape of their lips is highly significant as it indicates their respective diets and consequently their favoured habitat. Rhinos give birth to a single calf after a gestation period of fifteen to eighteen months, and the baby is not weaned until it is at a least a year old, sometimes two. Their population grows slowly compared with most animals, another factor contributing to their predicament.

BLACK RHINO *DICEROS BICORNIS*
The cantankerous, far rarer and smaller black rhino has the narrow prehensile lips of a browser, suited to picking leaves off trees and bushes. A solitary animal, it relies on the camouflage of dense thickets, which is why they are so much more difficult to see. South Africa's two thousand individuals make up forty percent of Africa's remaining black rhinos.

Reserves Addo, Augrabies, Hluhluwe-Imfolozi, Isimangaliso, Ithala, Karoo, Kruger, Marakele, Mkhuze and Pilanesberg.

Habitat Thick bush.

Daily rhythm Active day and night, resting between periods of activity.

Social life Solitary.

WHITE RHINO *CERATOTHERIUM SIMUM*
Twice as heavy as its black counterpart, the white rhino is also aggressive. Diet and habitat account for the greater sociability of the white rhino, which relies on

safety in numbers under the exposure of open grassland, while its wide, flatter mouth is well suited to chomping away at grasses like a lawnmower. By the end of the nineteenth century, the only place white rhinos survived was the Hluhluwe-Imfolozi reserve (where they still thrive), but they have since been introduced to a number of reserves.

Reserves Hluhluwe-Imfolozi, Ithala, Kruger, Marakele, Mkhuze, Ndumo, Pilanesberg and Tembe.

Habitat Savanna.

Daily rhythm Active day and night, resting between periods of activity.

Social life Mother/s and calves, or small same-sex herds of immature animals; old males solitary.

HIPPOPOTAMUS *HIPPOPOTAMUS AMPHIBIUS*
Hippos are highly adaptable animals that once inhabited South African waterways from the Limpopo in the north to the marshes of the Cape Peninsula in the south. Today

1

2

RHINOS: LAST CHANCE TO SEE?

Two species of **rhinoceros** are found in Africa: the hook-lipped or black rhino and the much heavier square-lipped or white rhino. Both have come close to extinction and have all but disappeared in the African wild. South Africa has the biggest populations in Africa by far, with more than 20,000 white and roughly 2000 black rhinos, making it the best place on earth to view these ancient mammals.

Sadly, **rhino poaching** in South Africa is escalating annually with over a thousand animals falling to poachers in 2013. The main market for rhino horn is in Asia, where it is used as an ingredient in traditional medicine. Here, a single 3kg horn can fetch up to US$300,000, making it more expensive per kilo than gold. So lucrative is the trade that sophisticated criminal syndicates have moved in, using helicopters and night-vision equipment to slaughter the mammals under cover of night.

Efforts are being made to protect the rhinos – 343 suspected poachers were arrested in 2013, and more than 50 were killed by anti-poaching units in shoot-outs – but this is insufficient to save the animals, who are now being killed faster than they can reproduce. Tactics such as removing the rhinos' horns have proved unsuccessful, because even the remaining stumps are still hugely valuable, and some conservationists argue that more resources need to be thrown at the problem. In 2014, two conservation companies announced a plan to move one hundred rhinos across South Africa's border into Botswana, whose vast and remote wildernesses, it is hoped, will prove inaccessible to poachers. Indeed, there is reason to be positive about this project – since its creation over two decades ago, not a single rhino has been poached in Botswana's Khama Rhino Sanctuary.

they're far more restricted. You'll see them elsewhere, in places where they've been reintroduced. Hippos need fresh water deep enough to submerge themselves, with a surrounding of suitable grazing grass. By day, they need to spend most of their time in water to protect their thin, hairless skin. After dark, hippos leave the water to spend the whole night grazing, often walking up to 10km in one session. Their grunting and jostling in the water may give the impression of loveable buffoons, but throughout Africa they are feared, and rightly so, as they are reckoned to be responsible for more human deaths on the continent than any other animal. When disturbed, lone bulls and cows with calves can become extremely aggressive. Their fearsomely long incisors can slash through a canoe with ease; on land they can charge at speeds up to 30km/h, with a tight turning circle.

Reserves Addo, Isimangaliso, Kruger and Pilanesberg.

Habitat Slow-flowing rivers, dams and lakes.

Daily rhythm Principally nocturnal, leaving the water to graze at night.

Social life Bulls solitary; others live in family groups known as pods, headed by a matriarch.

ZEBRAS

Zebras are closely related to horses and, together with them, donkeys and wild asses, form the equid family. Of the three species of zebra, two live in South Africa. Zebras congregate in family herds of a breeding stallion and two mares (or more) and their foals. Unattached males will often form bachelor herds. Among plains zebras, offspring leave the family group after between one and two years, while mountain zebras are far more tolerant in allowing adolescents to remain in the family.

BURCHELL'S ZEBRA *EQUUS QUAGGA*

A highly successful herbivore that can survive in a variety of grassland habitats, which accounts for its geographical range, the Burchell's or plains zebra has small ears and thick, black stripes, with lighter "shadows".

Reserves Addo, Hluhluwe-Imfolozi, Isimangaliso, Ithala, Kruger, Mapungubwe, Mkhuze, Pilanesberg.

Habitat Savanna, with or without trees.

Daily rhythm Active day and night, resting intermittently.

Social life Harems of several mares and foals, led by a dominant stallion, usually group together in large herds; harems highly stable and harem mares typically remain with the same male for life.

CAPE MOUNTAIN ZEBRA *EQUUS ZEBRA ZEBRA*

The Cape mountain zebra only narrowly escaped extinction, but now survives in healthy if limited numbers in several reserves in the southern half of SA, wherever there is suitably mountainous terrain. Characteristics that distinguish the two zebras are the dewlap on the mountain

zebra's lower neck, its absence of shadow stripes, its larger ears, and stripes that go all the way down to its hooves – the Burchell's stripes fade out as they progress down its legs.
Reserves Bontebok, Karoo, Mountain Zebra, Table Mountain (Cape of Good Hope) and Tankwa Karoo.

Habitat Mountainous areas and their immediate surrounds.
Daily rhythm Active by day.
Social life Harems of stallions with four or five mares and their foals.

OTHER MAMMALS

AARDVARK *ORYCTEROPUS AFER*
One of Africa's – indeed the world's – strangest animals, a solitary mammal weighing up to 70kg. Its name, Afrikaans for "earth pig", is an apt description, as it holes up during the day in large burrows that are excavated with remarkable speed and energy. It emerges at night to visit termite mounds within a radius of up to 5km, digging for its main diet. It's most likely to be common in bush country that's well scattered with termite mounds. Found throughout South Africa, but rarely seen.
Reserves Addo, Hluhluwe-Imfolozi, Karoo, Kgalagadi, Kruger, Mapungubwe and Mountain Zebra.
Habitat Open or wooded termite country; softer soil preferred.
Daily rhythm Nocturnal.
Social life Solitary.

PANGOLIN *MANIS TEMMINCKII*
Equally unusual – scale-covered mammals, resembling armadillos and feeding on ants and termites. Under attack they roll themselves into a ball. Pangolins occur widely in South Africa, north of the Orange River.
Reserves Kgalagadi and Kruger.
Habitat Wide range apart from desert and forest.
Daily rhythm Nocturnal.
Social life Solitary.

PORCUPINE *HYSTRIX AFRICAEAUSTRALIS*
The most singular and largest (up to 90cm) of the African rodents is the porcupine, which is quite unmistakeable with its coat of many quills. Porcupines are widespread and present in most reserves but, because they're nocturnal, you may only see shed quills. Rarely seen, but common away from croplands, where it is hunted as a pest.

Reserves Virtually all.
Habitat Adaptable to a wide range of habitats.
Daily rhythm Nocturnal; sometimes active at dusk.
Social life Family groups.

SPRINGHARES *PEDETES CAPENSIS*
If you go on a night drive in the Kruger or one of several other reserves in the north of the country, you'd be most unlucky not to see the glinting eyes of spring hares which, despite their resemblance to rabbit-sized kangaroos, are in fact true rodents.
Reserves Kgalagadi, Kruger, Mountain Zebra and Pilanesberg.
Habitat Savanna; softer soil areas preferred.
Daily rhythm Nocturnal.
Social life Burrows, usually with a pair and their young; often linked into a network, almost like a colony.

WARTHOG *PHACOCHOERUS AETHIOPICUS*
If you're visiting the Kruger, Pilanesberg or the KwaZulu-Natal parks, families of warthogs will become a familiar sight, trotting across the savanna with their tails erect like communications antennae. Boars join family groups only to mate; they're distinguished from sows by their prominent face warts, which are thought to be defensive pads protecting their heads during often violent fights.
Reserves Addo, Hluhluwe-Imfolozi, Isimangaliso. Ithala, Kruger, Mkhuze and Pilanesberg.
Habitat Savanna.
Daily rhythm Diurnal.
Social life Family groups usually consist of a mother and her litter of two to four piglets, or occasionally two or three females and their young.

TRAIN CROSSING THE KAAIMANS RIVER

Basics

Getting there

As sub-Saharan Africa's economic and tourism hub, South Africa is well served with flights from London and the rest of Europe. The majority of these touch down at Johannesburg's OR Tambo International, but there are also frequent flights into Cape Town. From North America there are a relatively small number of nonstop flights into Johannesburg.

Airfares depend on the **season**, with the highest prices and greatest demand in June, July, August, December and the first week of January. You get the best prices during the low season in October and November and from the last three weeks of January until March.

Flights from the UK and Ireland

From London there are nonstop flights with British Airways, South African Airways (SAA) and Virgin Atlantic to Johannesburg and Cape Town. Flying time from the UK is around eleven hours to Jo'burg, about an hour longer to Cape Town; nonstop fares from London start from £1600 in high season and £900 in low season. You can save up to £200 by flying via mainland Europe or the Middle East, and changing plane at least once.

From the Republic of Ireland, a number of European carriers fly out of Dublin to South Africa via their hub airports.

Flights from the US and Canada

From the US there are regular nonstop **flights** from New York (JFK) and Washington (IAD) operated by South African Airways in partnership with United Airlines. These take between fifteen and sixteen hours. Most other flights stop off in Europe, the Middle East or Asia and involve a change of plane. There are no direct flights **from Canada**; you'll have to change planes in the US, Europe or Asia, with journey times that can last up to thirty hours.

On direct flights from the US to Jo'burg, expect the high/low season fare to start from $2500/1400 from Washington DC and $2000/1700 from New York for a round trip; you might save from $200 to as much as $900 if you fly **via Europe**. Fares from Vancouver to Jo'burg start at Can$1900.

Flights from Australia and New Zealand

There are nonstop flights **from Sydney** (which take 14hr) and **Perth** (just under 11hr) to Johannesburg, with onward connections to Cape Town. Flights **from New Zealand** tend to be via Sydney. South African Airways and Qantas both fly nonstop to South Africa from Australia; several Asian, African and Middle Eastern airlines fly to South Africa via their hub cities, and tend to be less expensive, but their routings often entail long stopovers.

Direct flights from Sydney to Johannesburg start at Aus$3000 in high season and Aus$2000 in low; a flight to Europe with a stopover in South Africa, or even a round-the-world ticket, may provide better value than a straightforward return.

AIRLINES

British Airways Ⓦ ba.com.
Qantas Airways Ⓦ qantas.com.au.
South African Airways Ⓦ flysaa.com.
United Airlines Ⓦ united.com.
Virgin Atlantic Ⓦ virgin-atlantic.com.

AGENTS AND OPERATORS

Abercrombie & Kent Australia ☎ 1300 851 924,
Ⓦ abercrombiekent.com.au; UK ☎ 0845 485 1551,
Ⓦ abercrombiekent.co.uk; US ☎ 1 800 554 7016,
Ⓦ abercrombiekent.com. Classy operator whose packages feature Cape Town, Johannesburg, Kruger and luxury rail travel.
Absolute Africa UK ☎ 020 8742 0226, Ⓦ absoluteafrica.com. Adventure camping overland trips.
Acacia African Adventures Australia ☎ 02 8011 3686, UK ☎ 020 7706 4700, Ⓦ acacia-africa.com. Camping-based trips along classic South African routes.
Adventure Center US ☎ 1 800 228 8747, Ⓦ adventurecenter.com. Wide variety of affordable packages, including luxury rail journeys from Victoria Falls or Johannesburg to Cape Town.

A BETTER KIND OF TRAVEL

At Rough Guides we are passionately committed to travel. We believe it helps us understand the world we live in and the people we share it with – and of course tourism is vital to many developing economies. But the scale of modern tourism has also damaged some places irreparably, and climate change is accelerated by most forms of transport, especially flying. All Rough Guides' flights are carbon-offset, and every year we donate money to a variety of environmental charities.

Adventures Abroad US ☎ 1 800 665 3998, ⓦ adventures-abroad .com. Small-group and activity tours, including family-friendly trips.

Africa Travel Centre UK ☎ 020 7843 3500, ⓦ africatravel.co.uk. Experienced Africa specialists, who are agents for many South Africa-based overland operators.

Classic Safari Company Australia ☎ 1300 30 218, ⓦ classicsafaricompany.com.au. Luxury tailor-made safaris to southern Africa.

Cox & Kings UK ☎ 020 7873 5000, US ☎ 1 800 999 1758, ⓦ coxandkings.com. Packaged self-drive holidays in South Africa as well as pick-and-mix tailor-made tours.

Exodus UK ☎ 0845 287 3647, ⓦ exodus.co.uk. Small-group adventure tour operator with plenty of South Africa offerings, including activity packages.

Expert Africa UK ☎ 020 8232 9777, US ☎ 1 800 242 2434, ⓦ expertafrica.com. Small-group tours for independent travellers, as well as tailor-made trips. Strong on Cape Town and the Western Cape.

Explore Worldwide UK ☎ 0843 775 1343, ⓦ explore.co.uk; US ☎ 1 800 715 1746, ⓦ exploreworldwide.com. Good range of small-group tours, expeditions and safaris.

Goway Travel Experiences US ☎ 1 800 557 2841, ⓦ goway.com. Wide range of packages from three to fourteen days, including family trips taking in the highlights and game reserves.

Joe Walsh Tours Ireland ☎ 01 241 0800, ⓦ joewalshtours.ie. Budget airline fares as well as beach and safari packages.

Journeys International US ☎ 1 800 255 8735, ⓦ journeys.travel. Small-group trips with a range of safaris.

Journeys Worldwide Australia ☎ 07 3221 4788, ⓦ journeysworldwide.com.au. Escorted tours.

Kuoni Travel UK ☎ 0844 488 0581, ⓦ kuoni.co.uk. Flexible package holidays, including safaris, escorted tours and golfing packages. Good deals for families.

North South Travel UK ☎ 01245 608 291, ⓦ northsouthtravel .co.uk. Discounted airline fares worldwide. Profits are used to support projects in the developing world, especially the promotion of sustainable tourism.

Oasis Overland UK ☎ 01963 363 400, ⓦ oasisoverland.co.uk. One of the smaller overland companies, often running budget trips through Africa.

Okavango Tours and Safaris UK ☎ 020 8347 4030, ⓦ okavango.com. Top-notch outfit offering fully flexible and individual tours across South Africa.

Rainbow Tours UK ☎ 020 7666 1250, ⓦ rainbowtours.co.uk. Knowledgeable and sensitive South Africa specialists whose trips emphasize eco-friendly and community-based tourism.

Safari Consultants UK ☎ 01787 888 590, ⓦ safari-consultants .co.uk. Company offering individually tailored upmarket holidays across southern Africa, and specializing in activity-based trips, including walking safaris.

STA Travel Australia ☎ 134 782, New Zealand ☎ 0800 474 400, South Africa ☎ 0861 781 781, UK ☎ 0333 321 0099, US ☎ 1800 781 4040, ⓦ statravel.com. Worldwide specialists in independent travel offering good discounts for students and under-26s. Also sells student IDs, travel insurance, car rental, rail passes and more.

Trailfinders Ireland ☎ 02 1464 8800, UK ☎ 020 7368 1200, ⓦ trailfinders.com. One of the best-informed and most efficient agents for independent travellers.

Travel CUTS Canada ☎ 1 800 667 2887, ⓦ travelcuts.com. Canadian youth and student travel firm.

Tribes UK ☎ 01473 890 499, US ☎ 1 800 474 2056, ⓦ tribes.co.uk. Unusual and off-the-beaten-track Fairtrade safaris and cultural tours.

USIT Ireland ☎ 01 602 1906. Ireland's main student and youth travel specialists.

Wilderness Travel US ☎ 1 800 368 2794, ⓦ wildernesstravel .com. Hiking, cultural and wildlife adventures.

Getting around

Despite the large distances, travelling around most of South Africa is fairly straightforward, with a reasonably well-organized network of public transport, a good range of car rental companies, the best road system in Africa, and the continent's most comprehensive network of internal flights. The only weak point is public transport in urban areas, which is almost universally poor and often dangerous. Urban South Africans who can afford to do so tend to use private transport, and if you plan to spend much time in any one town, this is an option seriously worth considering. It's virtually impossible to get to the national parks and places off the beaten track by public transport; even if you do manage, you're likely to need a car once you're there.

Buses

South Africa's three established **intercity bus** companies are Greyhound (☎083 915 9000, ⓦgreyhound.co.za), Intercape (☎021 380 4400, ⓦintercape.co.za) and Translux (☎086 158 9282, ⓦtranslux.co.za); between them, they reach most towns in the country. Travel on these buses is safe, reasonable value and comfortable, and the vehicles are invariably equipped with air conditioning and toilets. Fares vary according to the time of year, with peak fares corresponding approximately to school holidays and costing around thirty percent more than in low season. As a rough indication, expect to pay the following fares from Cape Town: R270 to Paarl; R360 to Mossel Bay; R450 to Port Elizabeth; R400 to East London; R470 to Mthatha; R535 to Durban; and R575 to Johannesburg.

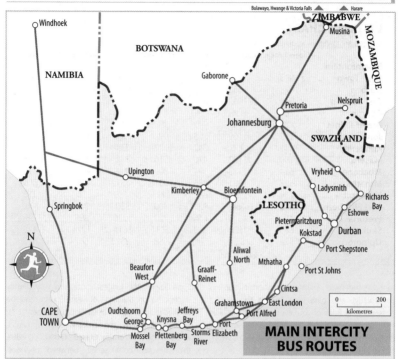

Bulawayo, Hwange & Victoria Falls ▲ ▲ Harare

ZIMBABWE
Musina
MOZAMBIQUE
BOTSWANA
NAMIBIA
Gaborone
Windhoek
Nelspruit
Pretoria
Johannesburg
SWAZILAND
Upington
Vryheid
Kimberley Bloemfontein Ladysmith
Richards Bay
Springbok
LESOTHO
Eshowe
Pietermaritzburg
Kokstad Durban
N
Aliwal North Mthatha Port Shepstone
Beaufort West Graaff-Reinet Port St Johns
Cintsa
Grahamstown East London
CAPE TOWN Oudtshoorn Jeffreys Bay Port Alfred
George Knysna
Mossel Bay Plettenberg Bay Storms River Port Elizabeth

0 — 200 kilometres

MAIN INTERCITY BUS ROUTES

Translux and Greyhound also operate the no-frills budget bus lines City to City (Ⓦcitytocity.co.za) and Citiliner (Ⓦcitiliner.co.za) respectively, which run along a range of routes around the country: check their websites for schedules and prices. You'll also find a host of small private companies running certain routes – your best bet is to enquire at the bus station the day before you travel.

Baz Bus (☎0861 229 287, Ⓦbazbus.com) operates an extremely useful hop-on/hop-off bus network aimed at backpackers and budget travellers, with intercity buses stopping off at backpacker accommodation en route. Its services run up and down the coast in both directions between Cape Town and Port Elizabeth (5 weekly), and between Port Elizabeth and Durban (4 weekly). Inland, it runs buses between Durban and Johannesburg (4 weekly). A number of independently run **shuttle services** connect with Baz services and go to Stellenbosch, Hermanus and Oudtshoorn in the Western Cape; to Hogsback, Coffee Bay, Mpande and Port St Johns in the Eastern Cape; to additional points in Durban, Southern Drakensberg and Southbroom in KwaZulu-Natal; and to Pretoria in Gauteng. Tickets can be bought through hostels,

online, at Baz offices in Cape Town and at Durban's central tourist offices.

Minibus taxis

Minibus taxis provide transport to two-thirds of South Africans, travelling everywhere in the country, covering relatively short hops from town to town, commuter trips from township to town and back, and routes within larger towns and cities. However, the problems associated with them – dangerous drivers and violent feuds between the different taxi associations competing for custom – mean that you should take local advice before using them. This is particularly true in cities, where minibus taxi ranks tend to be a magnet for petty criminals. The other problem with minibus taxis is that there is rarely much room to put **luggage**. Despite the drawbacks, minibus taxis are often the only option for getting around in **remote areas**, where you're unlikely to encounter trouble. You should, however, be prepared for some long waits, due to their infrequency.

Fares are low and comparable to what you might pay on the inexpensive intercity buses. Try

DISTANCE CHART
Figures are given in kilometres

	Bloemfontein	Cape Town	Durban	East London	George	Graaff-Reinet	Johannesburg
Bloemfontein	–	998	628	546	764	422	396
Cape Town	998	–	1660	1042	436	672	1405
Durban	628	1660	–	667	1240	945	598
East London	546	1042	667	–	630	388	992
George	764	436	1240	630	–	342	1168
Graaff-Reinet	422	672	945	388	342	–	826
Johannesburg	396	1405	598	992	1168	826	–
Kimberley	175	960	842	722	734	501	467
Maseru	150	1187	476	516	837	503	415
Mbabane	614	1483	394	802	1189	922	310
Mthatha	527	1181	436	231	851	509	866
Nelspruit	754	1779	689	1214	1509	1167	358
Port Elizabeth	676	756	927	300	330	251	1062
Pretoria	454	1324	656	322	1226	895	58
Skukuza	880	1888	809	1334	1616	1274	478
Upington	576	821	1243	958	857	667	875

to have the exact change (on shorter journeys particularly), and pass your fare to the row of passengers in front of you; eventually all the fares end up with the conductor, who dishes out any change. It's a good idea to check with locals which taxi routes are safe to use.

Trains

Travelling by **train** is just about the slowest way of getting around South Africa: the journey from Johannesburg to Cape Town, for example, takes 29 hours – compared with 19 hours by bus. **Overnighting** on the train, though, is more comfortable than the bus and does at least save you the cost of accommodation en route. Families with children get their own private compartment on the train, and under-5s travel free.

The **Passenger Rail Agency of South Africa (Prasa)** runs most of the intercity rail services. Its standard service, Shosholoza Meyl (☎086 000 8888, 🌐shosholoza-meyl.co.za), offers **Tourist Class** travel in two- or four-person compartments equipped with washbasins. The seats are comfortable and convert into **bunks**; you can rent sheets and blankets for the night (R40 per person), which are brought around by a bedding attendant who'll make up your bed. It's best to buy your bedding voucher when you book your train ticket. Services run between Johannesburg and Cape Town, Port Elizabeth, East London and Durban. Tourist class **fares** from Johannesburg range from R310 per person to Durban (the shortest route) to R630 to

Cape Town (the longest route) but vary slightly depending on the time of year. Tickets must be booked in advance at train stations or online.

Prasa also runs the twice-weekly, upmarket, air-conditioned **Premier Classe** (☎086 000 8888, 🌐premierclasse.co.za) service between Johannesburg and Cape Town. It also runs three times a week from Johannesburg to Port Elizabeth and Durban. The trains offer a choice of single, double, triple and four-person compartments, with gowns and toiletries provided, plus four-course lunches and five-course dinners served in a luxury dining car – all included in the fare. The Premier Classe **fare** from Johannesburg to Cape Town is R2650, to Durban R1050, and to Port Elizabeth R1950.

South Africa also offers a handful of **luxury trains**, with plush carriages and pricey fares. The celebrated **Blue Train** (🌐www.bluetrain.co.za) runs between Cape Town and Pretoria with fares starting at R13,795 per person sharing a double berth for the 29-hour journey; between Durban and Pretoria fares start at R7,810 per person for the 19-hour journey. The dress code is "smart casual" during the day, and formal wear for the evening meal. Bookings can be made online, or with Blue Train in Pretoria (☎012 334 8459) or Cape Town (☎021 449 2672).

Rovos Rail (Cape Town ☎021 421 4020; Pretoria ☎012 315 8242; 🌐rovos.com) also runs luxury rail trips between Pretoria and Cape Town (from R15,200), Durban (R15,200) and Victoria Falls in Zimbabwe (R19,900), at three levels of luxury, with prices to match.

Kimberley	Maseru	Mbabane	Mthatha	Nelspruit	Port Elizabeth	Pretoria	Skukuza	Upington
175	150	614	527	754	676	454	880	576
960	1187	1483	1181	1779	756	1324	1888	821
842	476	394	436	689	927	656	809	1243
722	516	802	231	1214	300	322	1334	958
734	837	1189	851	1509	330	1226	1616	857
501	503	922	509	1167	251	895	1274	667
467	415	310	866	358	1062	58	478	875
–	326	684	779	832	763	525	952	401
326	–	326	402	620	660	473	707	734
684	489	–	626	96	1001	300	257	1008
779	402	626	–	983	490	903	1099	1178
832	620	96	983	–	1373	328	120	1144
763	660	1001	490	1373	–	1119	1459	902
525	473	300	903	328	1119	–	436	813
952	707	257	1099	120	1459	436	–	1252
401	734	1008	1178	1144	2902	813	1252	–

A word of warning about **security** on trains: never leave valuables unattended in your compartment unless it is locked, and always close the window if leaving your carriage.

Domestic flights

Flying between destinations in South Africa compares favourably with the cost of covering long distances in a rental car, stopping over at places en route, and, with several competing **budget airlines**, you can sometimes pick up good deals.

The biggest airline offering **domestic flights** is **South African Airways** (SAA), with its subsidiaries **SA Airlink** and **SA Express** (reservations for all three go through SAA). SAA's main competitor is British Airways Comair, while the budget airlines Kulula and Mango have more limited networks, but generally offer better deals on the major routes. For the coastal towns of Margate and Plettenburg, Cemair runs a limited service.

On SAA and its associates, one-way tourist-class fares cost around R1400 from Cape Town to Johannesburg or Durban, while the budget airlines generally charge around R1000 on the Cape Town to Johannesburg route, provided you book well ahead.

SOUTH AFRICAN DOMESTIC AIRLINES

British Airways Comair ☎ 086 043 5922, ⓦ ba.com. Domestic flights serving Cape Town, Durban, Port Elizabeth, Johannesburg and Port Elizabeth with links to the rest of Africa, Harare, Livingstone, Mauritius and Windhoek.

Cemair ☎ 011 395 4473, ⓦ flycemair.co.za. The only airline that flies to the coastal resorts of Plettenberg Bay in the Western Cape and Margate in KwaZulu-Natal, with connections from Cape Town and Jo'burg.
Kulula ☎ 086 158 5852, ⓦ kulula.com. Budget flights from Cape Town, Durban, George, East London, Johannesburg and Nairobi.
Mango ☎ 086 116 2646, ⓦ flymango.com. SAA's budget airline provides cheap flights from Johannesburg to Cape Town, Durban, George, Port Elizabeth and Zanzibar; and from Cape Town to Bloemfontein, Durban, Jo'burg, Durban and Port Elizabeth.
South African Airways ☎ 086 135 9722, ⓦ flysaa.com. Together with SA Airlink and SA Express, SAA serves the major hubs of Johannesburg, Cape Town and Durban. Other destinations include Bloemfontein, East London, George, Hoedspruit, Kimberley, Margate, Mmabatho, Mthatha, Nelspruit (for Kruger National Park), Phalaborwa, Pietermaritzburg, Plettenberg Bay, Polokwane, Skukuza, Sun City, Ulundi and Upington.

Driving

Short of joining a tour, the only way to get to national parks and the more remote coastal areas is by **car**. Likewise, some of the most interesting places off the beaten track are only accessible in your own vehicle, as buses tend to ply just the major routes.

South Africa is ideal for driving, with a generally **well-maintained** network of highways and a high proportion of secondary and tertiary roads that are tarred and can be driven at speed. **Renting a vehicle** is not prohibitively expensive and, for a small group, it can work out to be a cheap option.

Filling stations are frequent on the major routes of the country, and usually open 24 hours. Off the beaten track, though, stations are less frequent, so fill up whenever you get the chance. Stations are rarely self-service; instead, poorly paid attendants fill up your car, check oil, water and tyre pressure if you ask them to, and often clean your windscreen even if you don't. A **tip** of R5–10 is always appreciated.

Parking is pretty straightforward, but due to the high levels of car break-ins, attendants, known as "**car guards**", are present virtually anywhere you'll find parking, for example at shopping malls. A tip of R2–5 during the day and R10 or more at night is generally appreciated.

Rules of the road and driving tips

Foreign driving licences are valid in South Africa for up to six months provided they are printed in English. If you don't have such a licence, you'll need to get an **International Driving Permit** (available from national motoring organizations) before arriving in South Africa. When driving, you are obliged by law to carry your driving **licence** and (unless you're a South African resident) your passport (or certified copies) at all times, although in reality, in the very rare event of your being stopped, the police will probably let you off with a warning if you're not carrying the required documents.

South Africans drive on the **left-hand side** of the road; speed limits range from 60km/h in built-up areas to 100km/h on rural roads and 120km/h on highways and major arteries. In addition to roundabouts, which follow the British rule of giving way to the right, there are four-way stops, where the rule is that the person who got there first leaves first. Note that traffic lights are called **robots** in South Africa.

The only real challenge you'll face on the roads is other drivers. South Africa has among the world's worst road **accident** statistics – the result of recklessness, drunken drivers (see p.72) and unroadworthy, overloaded vehicles. Keep your distance from cars in front, as domino-style pile-ups are common. Watch out also for overtaking traffic coming towards you: overtakers often assume that you will head for the **hard shoulder** to avoid an accident (it is legal to drive on the hard shoulder, but be careful as pedestrians frequently use it). If you do pull into the hard shoulder to let a car overtake, the other driver will probably thank you by flashing the hazard lights. If oncoming cars flash their headlights at you, it probably means there is a speed trap ahead.

Another potential **hazard** is animals on the road in rural areas, especially at night, so drive slowly then. Also, the large distances between major towns mean that falling asleep at the wheel, especially when travelling through long stretches of flat landscape in the Karoo or the Free State, is a real danger. Plan your car journeys to include breaks and stopovers. Finally, in urban areas, there's a small risk of being car-jacked; see p.71 for safety hints.

South Africa's motoring organization, the **Automobile Association** (AA; ☎083 843 22, ⓦ aa .co.za), provides useful information about road conditions as well as maps.

Car rental

Prebooking your **rental car** with a travel agent is the cheapest option, and will provide more favourable terms and conditions (such as unlimited mileage and lower insurance excesses). Don't rely on being able to just arrive at the airport and pick up a vehicle without reserving.

As a rough guideline, for a **one-week rental** expect to pay from R220 a day (with a R7500 insurance excess) including two hundred free kilometres a day. Most companies stipulate that drivers must be 23 or over and have been driving for at least two years. Note that to collect your vehicle, you will need to produce a credit (not debit) card.

Major rental companies usually allow you to return the car to a different city from where you hired it, though they will usually levy a charge for this. If you're planning to drive into **Lesotho** and **Swaziland**, check that the company allows it – some don't. **Insurance** often doesn't cover you if you drive on unsealed roads, so check for this too. Local firms are almost always cheaper than chains, but usually have restrictions on how far you can take the vehicle.

Camper vans and **4WD vehicles** equipped with rooftop tents can be a good idea for getting to remote places where accommodation is scarce.

ENGLISH/AFRIKAANS STREET NAMES

Many towns have **bilingual street names** with English and Afrikaans alternatives sometimes appearing along the same road. This applies particularly in Afrikaans areas away from the large cities, where direct translations are sometimes used. Often the Afrikaans name will bear little resemblance to the English one, something it's worth being aware of when trying to map read. Some terms you may encounter on Afrikaans signage are listed in Language (see p.667).

Expect to pay from R1000 a day for a vehicle that sleeps two. Some companies knock fifteen to twenty percent off the price if you book at short notice (one week or less in advance). Vans come fully equipped with crockery, cutlery and linen and usually a toilet and shower. The downside of camper vans and 4WDs is that they struggle up hills and guzzle a lot of fuel (15 litres per 100km in the smaller vans), which could partly offset any savings on accommodation.

RENTAL AGENCIES

Cheap Motorhome Rental ⓦ cheapmotorhomes.co.za. Booking agency that sources competitive motorhome rentals.
Drive Africa Cape Town ⓣ 021 447 1144, ⓦ driveafrica.co.za. Competitive motor-home deals and cheap car rental. If you're planning to be on the road for three months or longer, consider their rental-purchase agreement, where you buy a car and they guarantee to buy it back for an agreed price.
Kea Rentals ⓦ kea.co.za. Good-value motor-home rental.
Maui ⓦ maui.co.za. One of the biggest rental outlets for camper vans and 4WDs.
Tempest ⓣ 086 003 1666, ⓦ tempestcarhire.co.za. Offers very competitive car rental rates.

Cycling

It's easy to see why **cycling** is popular in South Africa: you can get to stunning destinations on good roads unclogged by traffic, many towns have decent cycle shops for spares and equipment, and an increasing number of backpacker hostels rent out mountain bikes for reasonable rates, so you don't have to transport your bike into the country. You'll need to be fit though, as South Africa is a hilly place, and many roads have punishing gradients. The **weather** can make life difficult, too: if it isn't raining, there is a good chance of it being very hot, so carry plenty of liquids. Cycling on the main intercity roads is not recommended.

Hitching

Hitching in most areas of South Africa is not recommended, particularly in large towns and cities. Even in rural areas it's **risky** and, while you might encounter wonderful hospitality and interesting companions, it's generally advisable not to hitch at all.

If you must hitchhike, avoid hitching alone and being dropped off in isolated areas between *dorps* (small towns). Ask drivers where they are going before you say where you want to go, and keep your **bags** with you: having them locked in the boot makes a hasty escape more difficult. Check the **notice boards** in backpacker lodges for people offering or looking to share lifts – that way, you can meet the driver in advance.

Accommodation

Accommodation in South Africa may seem expensive compared with other African countries, but standards are generally high and you get exceptional value for money. Even the most modest backpacker lodge will provide a minimum of fresh sheets and clean rooms. Other than in the very cheapest rooms, a private bath or shower is almost always provided, and you'll often have the use of a garden or swimming pool. South Africa also has some outstanding boutique hotels, luxury guesthouses, lodges and country retreats – invariably in beautiful settings – at fairly reasonable prices. The country's national parks and reserves feature a range of accommodation, from fairly basic restcamps to incredibly slick game lodges (see p.66), while you'll also find a backpacker hostel in most areas, plus no shortage of camping and self-catering options.

Advance booking is vital if you're travelling in high season or if you plan to stay in a national park or in popular areas such as Cape Town or the Garden Route. South Africa's **peak season** is during the midsummer Christmas school holiday period. The Easter school holiday is less intense, when South African families migrate to the coast and inland resorts. At Christmas and Easter, **prices** for budget and mid-priced accommodation (but not backpacker lodges or camping) can double,

> ### ACCOMMODATION PRICES
> Accommodation prices given in the Guide for **hotels, guest houses** and **B&Bs** are for the cheapest double room with breakfast in high season, unless otherwise stated. In the case of luxury **safari lodges**, such as those around the Kruger National Park, prices are per person sharing a double room and include meals and two safari activities (for example, game drives or guided walks) per day. **Camping prices** are per tent, unless otherwise stated.

and most places get booked up months ahead (see p.76).

Hotels

Most of South Africa's **budget hotels** are throwbacks to the 1950s and 1960s, and little more than watering holes that earn their keep from the bar.

Mid-range hotels usually charge from R1000 a room. Along the coastal holiday strips such as the Garden Route, southern KwaZulu-Natal and all the major seaside towns in between, these hotels are ubiquitous and frequently offer rooms on the **beachfront**. Many of the mid-priced hotels – especially those on main routes in the interior – are fully booked during the week by travelling salesmen, but over the weekend, when they're often empty, you can usually negotiate reasonable **discounts**.

A large number of mid-range and **upmarket establishments** belong to hotel **chains**, which offer reliable but sometimes soulless accommodation. Protea (W proteahotels.com) is the largest group in the country, with other big-players including Tsogo Sun (W tsogosunhotels.com), Holiday Inn (W ichotels.com) and Three Cities (W threecities.co.za).

Country lodges and boutique hotels

You can get incredible value and a really memorable stay in South Africa at small, characterful establishments – something the country excels at. You'll find hip **boutique hotels** in the cities and *dorps* and luxurious **country lodges** in exceptional natural surroundings, including eco-lodges in the middle of forests, places perched on the edges of cliffs, and magical hideaways in the middle of nowhere. At these places you can expect to be pampered and there will often be a spa on site. There are also numerous first-rate **safari camps** and **game lodges**, which fulfil all those Out-of-Africa fantasies (see p.66). You can pay from R1600 a room, though rates more usually start at R2000.

B&Bs and guesthouses

The most ubiquitous form of accommodation in South Africa is in **B&Bs** and **guesthouses**. The official difference between the two is that the owner lives on site at a B&B. The most basic B&Bs are just one or two rooms in a private home, with washing facilities shared with the owners. In reality, the distinction is a little hazy once you move up a notch to B&Bs and guesthouses that provide en-suite rooms (as is usually the case). **Rates** for en-suite rooms in both start at around R500, for which you can expect somewhere clean, comfortable and relaxed, but usually away from the beach or other action. Moving up a notch, you'll be paying from R800 for a room with a bit extra, and anything from R1200 upwards should offer the works: a great location, comfort and good service.

Since the late 1990s, **township tours** have become popular, with township dwellers offering **B&B** accommodation to tourists in their homes; expect to pay from R500 per room per night for an authentic South African experience.

Along many roads in the countryside you will see signs for "**Bed en Ontbyt**" (Afrikaans for "bed and breakfast"), signalling **farmstay** accommodation, with rooms in the main homestead or in a cottage in its garden. Some also offer hiking, horseriding and other **activities**. Tourist offices almost always have lists of farms in their area that rent out rooms or cottages.

Caravan parks, resorts and camping

Caravanning was once the favourite way to have a cheap family holiday in South Africa, and this accounts for the very large number of caravan parks dotted across the length and breadth of the country. However, their popularity has declined and with it the standard of many of the country's municipal caravan parks and campsites. Today, **municipal campsites** are generally pretty scruffy, though you may find the odd pleasant one in rural areas, or near small *dorps*. Staying in a municipal campsite adjoining a city or large town is often more grief than it's worth; not only will facilities be run-down, but theft is a big risk. Municipal sites cost around R100 per tent.

All in all, you're best off heading for the privately owned **resorts**, where for roughly the same price you get greater comfort. Although private resorts sometimes give off a holiday-camp vibe, they usually provide good washing and cooking **facilities**, self-catering chalets, shops selling basic goods, braai stands and swimming pools.

Virtually all **national parks** – and many provincial reserves – have campsites, and in some of the really remote places, such as parts of KwaZulu-Natal, camping may be your only option. Use of a **campsite** will cost R150–280 per site depending on the popularity of the park and the facilities. At

ONLINE ACCOMMODATION RESOURCES

B&BS, GUESTHOUSES AND SELF-CATERING

ⓦ **budgetgetaways.co.za** The best resource for affordable (under R400/person) self-catering accommodation in the Western Cape.

ⓦ **greenwoodguides.com/south-africa** Although properties pay to be listed, this site's handpicked selection is interesting and quirky.

ⓦ **portfoliocollection.com** While properties have to pay to be listed, they also have to meet fairly rigorous standards.

ⓦ **safarinow.com** One of the oldest and best South African online booking sites covers all types of accommodation – not just safaris – with user reviews and rankings.

BACKPACKERS

ⓦ **bazbus.co.za** Website of South Africa's biggest backpacker bus service also provides links to lodges with an online booking facility.

ⓦ **hihostels.com** Hostelling International acts as a booking agent for over a dozen of South Africa's backpacker lodges.

ⓦ **hostelbookers.com** International website with clear navigation and good coverage of South African hostels, including user reviews and ratings.

CAMPING AND CARAVAN PARKS

ⓦ **campsa.co.za** Comprehensive online directory of Southern African campsites and caravan parks.

national parks you can expect well-maintained washing facilities and there are often communal kitchen areas or, at the very least, a braai stand and running water, as well as a decent communal shower, toilet and washing facilities (known locally as "ablutions").

Camping rough is not recommended anywhere in the country.

Backpacker lodges

The cheapest beds in South Africa are in **dormitories** at backpacker lodges (or hostels), which cost from R150 per person. These are generally well-run operations with clean linen and helpful staff. In the cities and tourist resorts you'll have a number of places to choose from and almost all towns of any significance have at least one.

Apart from dorm beds, most also have **private rooms** (R450–550) – sometimes even with private bathrooms – and an increasing number have **family rooms** that work out at around R180 per person. They usually have communal kitchens, an on-site restaurant, TV, internet access and often other facilities such as bike rental. When choosing a hostel, it's worth checking out the **ambience** as some are party joints, while others have a quieter atmosphere.

The lodges are invariably good meeting points, with a constant stream of travellers passing through, and useful **notice boards** filled with advertisements for hostels and backpacker facilities throughout the country. Many lodges operate reasonably priced **excursions** into the surrounding areas, and will pick you up from train stations or bus stops (especially Baz Bus stops) if you phone in advance.

Self-catering cottages and apartments

Self-catering accommodation in cottages, apartments and small complexes can provide cheap accommodation in a variety of locations – on farms, near beaches, in forests and wilderness areas, as well as in practically every town and city.

There's a wide range of this type of accommodation with prices depending on facilities, location and level of luxury: expect to pay from R350 a night for something basic to R1000 or over for a luxurious beach stay. **Apartments** often sleep up to six, so this can be very economical if you're travelling as a family or in a group. You can save a lot of money by cooking for yourself, and you'll get a sense of **freedom** and **privacy** which is missing from even the nicest guesthouse or B&B. Standards are high: cottages or apartments generally come fully equipped with crockery and cutlery, and even microwaves and TVs in the more modern places. Linen and towels are often provided; check before you book in.

Eating and drinking

South Africa doesn't really have a coherent indigenous cuisine, although attempts have been made to elevate Cape Cuisine to this status. Meat is a big feature of South African meals, as is the vast array of available seafood, which includes a wide variety of fish, lobster (crayfish), oysters and mussels. Locally

grown fruit and vegetables are generally of a high standard.

There is no great tradition of street food and people on the move tend to pick up a pie or chicken and chips from one of the fast-food chains. Drinking is dominated by South Africa's often superb wines and by a handful of unmemorable lagers, though the recent upsurge of local microbreweries has dramatically improved the quality of beers on offer. In the cities, and to a far lesser extent beyond them, there are numerous excellent restaurants where you can taste a spectrum of international styles.

Breakfast, lunch and dinner

Most B&Bs, hotels and guesthouses serve a **breakfast** of eggs with bacon and usually some kind of sausage. Muesli, fruit, yoghurt, croissants and pastries are also becoming increasingly popular. **Lunch** is eaten around 1pm and **dinner** in the evening around 7pm or 8pm; the two can be pretty much interchangeable as far as the menu goes, usually along the lines of meat, chicken or fish and veg.

Styles of cooking

Traditional African food tends to focus around stiff grain **porridge** called *mielie pap* or *pap* (pronounced: "pup"), made of maize meal and accompanied by meat or vegetable-based sauces. Among white South Africans, Afrikaners have evolved a style of cooking known as **boerekos** (see opposite), which can be heavy-going if you're not used to it.

Some of the best-known South African **foods** are mentioned below, while there's a list of South African culinary terms, including other local foods, in the Language section (see p.672).

Braais

Braai (which rhymes with "dry") is an abbreviation of *braaivleis*, an Afrikaans word translated as "meat grill". More than simply the process of cooking over an outdoor fire, however, a braai is a cultural event that is central to the South African identity. A braai is an intensely social event, usually among family and friends and accompanied by gallons of **beer**. It's also probably the only occasion when you'll catch an unreconstructed South African man cooking.

You can braai anything, but a traditional barbecue meal consists of huge slabs of **steak**, **lamb cutlets** and **boerewors** ("farmer's sausage"), with ostrich and venison becoming increasingly popular. Potatoes, onions and butternut squash wrapped in aluminium foil and placed in the embers are the usual accompaniment.

Potjiekos and boerekos

A variant on the braai is **potjiekos** – pronounced "poy-key-kos" – (pot food), in which the food is cooked in a three-legged cast-iron cauldron (the *potjie*), preferably outdoors over an open fire. In a similar vein, but cooked indoors, **boerekos** (literally "farmer's food") is a style of cooking enjoyed mainly by Afrikaners. Much of it is similar to English food, but taken to cholesterol-rich extremes, with even the vegetables prepared with butter and sugar. *Boerekos* comes into its own in its variety of over-the-top **desserts**, including *koeksisters* (plaited doughnuts saturated with syrup) and *melktert* ("milk tart"), a solid, rich custard in a flan case.

Cape Cuisine

Styles of cooking brought to South Africa by **Asian** and **Madagascan** slaves have evolved into **Cape Cuisine** (sometimes known as Cape Malay food). Characterized by mild, semi-sweet **curries** with strong Indonesian influences, Cape Cuisine is worth sampling, especially in Cape Town, where it developed and is associated with the Muslim community. Dishes include *bredie* (stew), of which *waterblommetjiebredie*, made using water hyacinths, is a speciality; *bobotie*, a spicy minced dish served under a savoury custard; and *sosaties*, a local version of kebab using minced meat. For **dessert**, dates stuffed with almonds make a light and delicious end to a meal, while *malva* pudding is a rich combination of milk, sugar, cream and apricot jam.

Although Cape Cuisine can be delicious, there isn't that much **variety** and few restaurants specialize in it. Despite this, most of the dishes considered as Cape Cuisine have actually crept into the South African diet, many becoming part of the Afrikaner culinary vocabulary.

Other ethnic and regional influences

Although South Africa doesn't really have distinct **regional** cuisines, you will find local specialities in different parts of the country. KwaZulu-Natal, for instance, particularly around Durban and Pietermaritzburg, is especially good for **Indian** food. The South African contribution to this great multifaceted tradition is the humble **bunny chow**, a cheap takeaway consisting of a hollowed-out half-loaf of white bread originally filled with curried beans, but nowadays with anything from curried chicken to sardines.

VEGETARIAN FOOD

While not quite a **vegetarian** paradise, South Africa is nevertheless vegetarian-savvy and you'll find at least one vegetarian dish in most restaurants. Even steakhouses will have something palatable on the menu and generally offer good salad bars. If you're self-catering in the larger cities, delicious dips and breads can be found at delis and Woolworths and Pick 'n Pay supermarkets, as can the range of frozen vegetarian sausages and burgers made by Fry's (ⓦ frysvegetarian.co.za).

Portuguese food made early inroads into the country because of South Africa's proximity to Mozambique. The Portuguese influence is predominantly seen in the use of hot and spicy peri-peri seasoning, which goes extremely well with braais. The best-known example of this is delicious peri-peri chicken, which you will find all over the country.

Eating out

Restaurants in South Africa offer good value compared with Britain or North America. In every city you'll find places where you can eat a decent main course for under R150, while for R250 you can splurge on the best. All the cities and larger towns boast some restaurants with imaginative menus. As a rule, restaurants are **licensed**, though Muslim establishments serving Cape Cuisine don't allow alcohol at all.

An attractive phenomenon in the big cities, especially Cape Town, has been the rise of continental-style **cafés** – easy-going places where you can eat as well as in a regular restaurant, or just drink **coffee** all night without feeling obliged to order food. Service tends to be slick and friendly, and a reasonable meal in one of these cafés is unlikely to set you back more than R100.

Don't confuse these with traditional South African cafés, found in even the tiniest country town. The equivalent of **corner stores** elsewhere, they commonly sell a few magazines, soft drinks, sweets, crisps and an odd collection of tins and dry goods, though no sit-down meals.

If popularity is the yardstick, then South Africa's real national cuisine is to be found in its **franchise restaurants**, which you'll find in every town of any size. The usual international names like **KFC**, **McDonald's** and **Wimpy** are omnipresent, as are South Africa's own home-grown offerings, such as the American-style steakhouse chain, **Spur**, and the much-exported **Nando's** chain, which grills excellent Portuguese-style chicken, served under a variety of spicy sauces. Expect to pay around R60 for a burger and chips or chicken meal at any of these places, and twice that for a good-sized steak.

Drinking

White South Africans do a lot of their drinking **at home**, so pubs and bars are not quite the centres of social activity they are in the US or the UK, though in the African townships **shebeens** (informal bars) do occupy this role. A growing number of sports bars with huge screens draw in crowds when there's a big match on, but at other times they are relaxed places for a drink. You'll also find drinking spots in city centres and suburbs that conform more to European-style café-bars than British pubs, and which serve booze, coffee and light meals. The closest thing to British-style pubs is the themed restaurant-bar franchises, such the *Keg* chain or *O'Hagans Irish Pub and Grill*.

Beer, wines and spirits can by law be sold from Monday to Saturday between 9am and 6pm at **bottle stores** (the equivalent of the British off-licence) and also at most supermarkets, although you'll still be able to drink at a restaurant or pub outside these hours.

There are no surprises when it comes to **soft drinks**, with all the usual names available. One unusual drink you might well encounter in the country's tearooms is locally produced rooibos (or redbush) tea, made from the leaves of an indigenous plant (see box, p.251).

Beer

Although South Africa is a major wine-producing country, **beer** is indisputably the national drink. It's as much an emblem of South African manhood as the braai and cuts across all racial and class divisions. South Africans tend to be fiercely loyal to their brand of beer, though they all taste pretty much the same, given that nearly all beer in the country is produced by the enormous **South African Breweries** monopoly. In fact, so big is SAB that in 2002 it bought Miller Brewing, the second-largest beer producer in the US, and formed SABMiller, one of the biggest brewers in the world. The advantage for South Africans was that a number of international labels became available to supplement the pretty undistinguished and indistinguishable local

WINING AND FINE DINING

Focused around the towns of Stellenbosch, Franschhoek, Paarl and Somerset West, The Western Cape **Winelands** (see p.164) has established itself as South Africa's culinary centre, where you'll find numerous fine dining restaurants in a small area. Many of these are on wine estates, and offer multi-course menus with wine pairings for each course – and, often, superb views too. Restaurants in the Winelands regularly win the majority of South Africa's **Top Restaurant Awards** (seven out of the top ten in 2013), as voted by *EatOut* magazine, which provides reliable restaurant reviews for establishments across South Africa (available from bookshops or online at ⓦeatout.co.za).

offerings dominated by Lion, Castle, Hansa and Carling Black Label lagers, which taste a bit thin and bland to a British palate, though they can be refreshing drunk ice-cold on a sweltering day. According to local beer aficionados, the SAB offerings are given a good run for their money by Windhoek Lager, produced by Namibian Breweries. Other widely available SAB offerings from their international subsidiaries are Peroni, Miller Genuine Draft, Grolsch and, the best of the lot, Pilsner Urquell.

In recent years, however, there has been a rapid growth in the number of **microbreweries** across the country, which produce **craft beers and ciders**. Brew Masters website (ⓦbrewmasters.co.za) lists all the breweries large and small throughout South Africa with a useful map, so that you can find out what local beers are brewed nearby.

Wine

South Africa is one of the world's top ten **winemaking** countries by volume. Despite having the longest-established New World winemaking tradition (going back over 350 years), this rapid rise has taken place within the past two post-apartheid decades. Before that, South Africa's stagnant and inbred wine industry produced heavy Bordeaux-style wines. After the arrival of democracy in 1994, winemakers began producing fresher, fruitier New World wines, though many aficionados still turned their noses up at them. It's over the last fifteen years that things have really started to rev up, with South African winemakers developing excellent wines that combine the best of the Old and New Worlds.

South Africa produces wines from a whole gamut of major cultivars. Of the **whites**, the top South African Sauvignon Blancs can stand up to the best the New World has to offer, and among the **reds** it's the blends that really shine. Also look out for red wine made from Pinotage grapes, a somewhat controversial curiosity unique to South Africa. **Port** is also made, with the best vintages from the Little Karoo town of Calitzdorp along the R62 (see p.189). There are also a handful of excellent **sparkling wines**, including Champagne-style, fermented-in-the-bottle bubbly, known locally as **methode cap classique** (MCC).

Wine is available throughout the country, although prices rise as you move out of the Western Cape. **Prices** start at under R30 a bottle, and you can get something pretty decent for twice that – the vast bulk of wines cost less than R100 – but you can spend upwards of R250 for a truly great vintage. All this means that anyone with an adventurous streak can indulge in a bacchanalia of sampling without breaking the bank.

The best way to sample wines is by visiting **wineries**, some of which charge a tasting fee. The oldest and most rewarding wine-producing regions are the **Constantia estates** in Cape Town (see p.107) and the region known as **the Winelands** around the towns of Stellenbosch (see p.164), Paarl (see p.171) and Franschhoek (see p.175), which all have well-established **wine routes**. Other wine-producing areas include **Robertson** (see p.181), the **Orange River** (see p.274) and **Walker Bay** (see box, p.202).

The media

South Africa lacks a strong tradition of national newspapers and instead has many regional publications of varying quality. Television delivers a mix of imported programmes and home-grown soaps heavily modelled on US fare, as well as the odd home-grown reality TV show and one or two watchable documentary slots. Radio is where South Africa best meets the needs of a diverse and scattered audience, and deregulation of the airwaves has brought to life scores of small new stations.

Newspapers

Of the roughly twenty daily **newspapers**, most of which are published in English or Afrikaans, the only two that qualify as nationals are *Business Day* (Ⓦbusinessday.co.za), which is a good source of serious national and international news, and the ANC-aligned *New Age* (Ⓦthenewage.co.za).

Each of the larger cities has its own English-language **broadsheet**, most of them published by South Africa's largest newspaper publisher, **Independent News & Media**. In Johannesburg, **The Star** (Ⓦthestar.co.za), the group's South African flagship, has a roughly equal number of black and white readers and offers somewhat uninspired Jo'burg coverage, padded out with international agency material. **Cape Times** (Ⓦcapetimes.co.za) and the tabloid **Cape Argus** (Ⓦcapeargus.co.za) follow broadly the same formula, as do the **Pretoria News** (Ⓦpretorianews.co.za), the **Herald** (Ⓦtheherald.co.za) in Port Elizabeth and the **Daily News** (Ⓦdailynews.co.za) in Durban.

The country's biggest-selling paper is the **Daily Sun**, a Jo'burg-based tabloid that taps into the concerns of township dwellers, with a giddy cocktail of gruesome crime stories, tales of witchcraft and the supernatural, and coverage of the everyday problems of ordinary people. Another Jo'burg tabloid, the **Sowetan** (Ⓦsowetan.co.za) has been going since the 1980s, but is a far more serious publication than the *Sun*. In Cape Town, the studiedly sleazy **Voice** attempts to emulate the *Sun* in the coloured community, with a downbeat mixture of crime, the supernatural and sex advice.

Unquestionably the country's intellectual heavyweight, the **Mail & Guardian** (Ⓦmg.co.za), published every Friday, delivers nonpartisan and fearless investigative journalism, but frequently struggles to escape its own earnestness.

Of the Sunday papers, The **Sunday Times** (Ⓦwww.sundaytimes.co.za), can attribute its sales – roughly a quarter million copies – to a well-calculated mix of investigative reporting, gossipy stories and rewrites of salacious scandal lifted from foreign tabloids, while **City Press** (Ⓦcitypress.co.za), which sells over half its copies in Gauteng, dishes up independently minded, politically savvy copy to its predominantly urban black readership.

However, the liveliest of all South Africa's news outlets is the boundary-breaking free online **Daily Maverick** (Ⓦdailymaverick.co.za), which is brim-full of news and analysis and boasts a stable of some of the country's most challenging and provocative columnists.

The easiest places to buy newspapers are corner stores and newsagents, especially the CNA chain. These outlets also sell **international publications** such as *Time*, *The Economist* and the weekly overseas editions of the British *Daily Mail*, the *Telegraph* and the *Express* – you'll also find copies of the daily and weekend international editions of the *Financial Times*.

Television

The **South Africa Broadcasting Corporation**'s three TV channels churn out a mixed bag of domestic dramas, sport, game shows, soaps and documentaries, filled out with lashings of familiar imports. SABC 1, 2 and 3 share the unenviable task of trying to deliver an integrated service, while having to split their time between the **eleven official languages**. English is the most widely used, with SABC 3 (Ⓦsabc3.co.za) broadcasting almost exclusively in the language, with a high proportion of British and US comedies and dramas, while SABC 2 (Ⓦsabc2.co.za) and SABC 1 (Ⓦsabc1.co.za) spread themselves thinly across all the remaining ten languages with a fair amount of English creeping in too. SABC 1, with its high proportion of sports coverage, has the most viewers.

South Africa's first and only free-to-air independent **commercial channel** e.tv (Ⓦetv.co.za) won its franchise in 1998 on the promise of providing a showcase for local productions, a pledge it has signally failed to meet.

There is no cable TV in South Africa, but **DSTV** (Ⓦdstv.co.za) offers a satellite television subscription service with a selection of sports, movies, news and specialist channels, some of which are piped into hotels.

Radio

Radio is a hugely popular medium among South Africans, who spend an average of three-and-a-half hours a day listening to broadcasts. National broadcaster the SABC operates a radio station for each of the eleven official language groups. The English-language service, SAfm (Ⓦsafm.co.za), is increasingly degenerating into tedious wall-to-wall talk shows interspersed with news. The SABC also runs 5FM Stereo, a national pop station broadcasting Top 40 tracks, while its Metro FM is targeted at black urban youth.

To get a taste of what makes South Africans tick, tune into the privately owned **Gauteng talk station 702** (in Jo'burg 92.7 FM and in Pretoria 106 FM; Ⓦ702.co.za) or its Cape Town sister station **CapeTalk** (567 AM; Ⓦcapetalk.co.za), both of which are a lot livelier than the state stations and broadcast news, weather, traffic and sports reports. Apart from these, there are scores of regional, commercial and community stations, broadcasting a range of music and other material, which makes surfing the airwaves an enjoyable experience, wherever you are in the country.

Festivals

South Africa has no shortage of events – there are more than eighty music festivals each year, nine of them over the Easter weekend alone. In addition, countless small towns host umpteen diverting minor events. Although Johannesburg and Cape Town tend to dominate, the country's two biggest cultural events, the National Arts Festival and the Klein Karoo Nasionale Kunstefees, both take place in small Karoo towns (Grahamstown and Oudtshoorn respectively). Once things get humming, they swell to twice their normal size.

JANUARY

Cape Town Minstrel Carnival Cape Town South Africa's longest and most raucous annual party brings over ten thousand spectators to watch the parade through the city centre on January 2 for the Tweede Nuwe Jaar or "Second New Year" celebrations. Brightly decked-out minstrel troupes parade, and vie in singing and dancing contests. Tickets can be reserved through Computicket (W computicket.com).

Maynardville Shakespeare Festival Cape Town W maynardville .co.za. A usually imaginative production of one of the Bard's plays is staged each year in the beautiful setting of the Maynardville Open Air Theatre in Wynberg.

FEBRUARY

Cape Town Pride Pageant W capetownpride.co.za. Series of gay-themed events over ten days, taking in a bunch of parties and a street parade.

MARCH

Cape Argus Pick 'n Pay Cycle Tour Cape Town W cycletour.co.za (see p.64). The largest, and most spectacular, individually timed bike race in the world, much of it along the ocean's edge, draws many thousands of spectators.

Cape Town International Jazz Festival Cape Town W capetownjazzfest.com. Initiated in 2000 as the Cape Town counterpart of the world-famous North Sea Jazz Festival, this event is held over the last weekend of the month and draws leading local and international performers.

APRIL

Afrika Burn Tankwa Karoo, Northern Cape W afrikaburn.com. South Africa's official spinoff of the Burning Man festival held in Nevada is a spectacular week-long festival of performance,

creativity, revelry and controlled pyromania in the Karoo desert.

Klein Karoo Nasionale Kunstefees Oudtshoorn, Western Cape W kknk.co.za. South Africa's largest Afrikaans arts and culture festival turns the otherwise dozy Karoo *dorp* of Oudtshoorn into one big jumping party with a significant English-language component.

Two Oceans Marathon Cape Town W twooceansmarathon.org .za. Another of the Western Cape's big sporting events is this 56-kilometre ultra-marathon, which bills itself as "the world's most beautiful marathon", with huge crowds lining the route to cheer on the participants.

Splashy Fen Music Festival Underberg, KwaZulu-Natal W www .splashyfen.co.za. Held at the beginning of the month, South Africa's oldest music festival draws thousands of punters to a beautiful farm in the Drakensberg foothills, with a spread of mainstream and alternative rock and pop and a kids' programme too.

Pink Loerie Mardi Gras Knysna, Western Cape W pinkloerie.co.za. Five-day gay pride celebration of parties, contests, cabaret, drag shows and performance in South Africa's oyster capital.

MAY

Franschhoek Literary Festival Franschhoek, Western Cape W flf .co.za. Three day celebration of books, writers and wine, featuring leading local and international writers, editors and cartoonists.

Good Food & Wine Show Cape Town W goodfoodandwineshow .co.za. Celebrity chefs from around the world cooking live is just one of the compelling attractions that make this the foodie event of the year. There are also hands-on workshops, delicious nibbles and wine as well as kitchen implements and books for sale.

Comrades Marathon Durban/Pietermaritzburg, KwaZulu-Natal W comrades.com. A national institution, held at the end of the month. The Comrades, run along the 80km between Durban and Pietermaritzburg, attracts around thirteen thousand runners, many of them international competitors.

JUNE

National Arts Festival Grahamstown, Eastern Cape (see box, p.319). The largest arts festival in Africa, with its own fringe festival – ten days of jazz, classical music, dance, cabaret and theatre spanning every conceivable type of performance.

Encounters South African International Documentary Film Festival Johannesburg and Cape Town W encounters.co.za. Fortnight-long showcase of documentary film-making from South Africa and the world.

Out in Africa, South African Gay & Lesbian Film Festival Cape Town and Johannesburg W oia.co.za. Purportedly the most popular movie festival in the country, screening gay- and lesbian-themed international and local productions over the first ten days of the month.

JULY

Knysna Oyster Festival Knysna, Western Cape W oysterfestival .co.za. Just over a week of carousing and oyster-eating along the Garden Route with lots of wine-tasting and other satellite events in between.

Good Food & Wine Show Gauteng Town W goodfoodandwineshow.co.za. See May.

AUGUST

Arts Alive Johannesburg ⓦ artsalive.co.za. Jo'burg's largest arts event features a month of dance, visual art, poetry and music at venues in Newtown, the cultural precinct in the inner city.

Cape Town Fashion Week ⓦ africanfashioninternational.com. Multiple shows over three days, showcasing new spring and summer collections of leading South African designers on the catwalk.

Oppikoppi Bushveld Festival Northam, North West Province ⓦ oppikoppi.co.za. South Africa's answer to Woodstock, Oppikoppi (Afrikaans for "on the hill") brings the bushveld hills alive with the sound of music, as some sixty local and foreign bands rock the *bundu* (outback) for three days and nights.

Joy of Jazz Johannesburg ⓦ joyofjazz.co.za. Jo'burg's flagship jazz festival offers three days of varied music.

SEPTEMBER

FNB Dance Umbrella Johannesburg ⓦ danceumbrella.co.za. The country's leading contemporary dance festival showcases a variety of local dance forms at the beginning of September.

Hermanus Whale Festival Hermanus, Western Cape ⓦ whalefestival.co.za. To coincide with the peak whale-watching season, the southern Cape town of Hermanus (see p.198) stages its annual festival over several days with plays, a craft market, a children's festival and live music.

OCTOBER

Good Food & Wine Show Durban ⓦ goodfoodandwineshow .co.za. See May.

Rocking the Daisies Darling, Western Cape ⓦ rockingthedaisies .com. South Africa's premier and biggest youth music festival showcases monster local and international acts. Held on the Cloof Wine Estate, where most people camp for all three days.

NOVEMBER TO MARCH

Kirstenbosch Summer Sunset Concerts Cape Town ☎ 021 799 8783. Popular concerts held on the magnificent lawns of the botanical gardens at the foot of Table Mountain. Performances begin at 5.30pm and cover a range of genres. Come early to find a parking place, bring a picnic and some Cape bubbly, and kick back. Tickets available at the gate.

DECEMBER

Mother City Queer Projects Cape Town (see box, p.148). A hugely popular party attracting thousands of gay revellers. Outlandish get-ups, multiple dancefloors and a mood of sustained delirium make this event a real draw.

Carols by Candlelight at Kirstenbosch Cape Town ☎ 021 799 8783. The botanical gardens' annual carol-singing and Nativity tableaux – staged on the Thursday to the Sunday before Christmas – is a Cape Town institution, drawing crowds of families with their picnic baskets. Gates open at 7pm and the singing kicks off at 8pm.

Franschhoek Cap Classique and Champagne Festival Franschhoek ⓦ franschhoekmcc.co.za. Popular three-day bacchanalia of bubbly sampling and gourmandizing in the Cape Winelands, with a vast selection of local and French sparkling wine on offer.

Activities and outdoor pursuits

South Africa's diverse landscape of mountains, forests, rugged coast and sandy beaches, as well as kilometres of veld and national parks, make the country supreme outdoor terrain. South Africans have been playing outdoors for decades, resulting in a well-developed infrastructure for activities, an impressive national network of hiking trails and plenty of operators selling adventure sports.

Hiking trails

South Africa has a comprehensive system of **footpaths** (inspired by the US Appalachian Hiking Trail). Wherever you are – even in the middle of Johannesburg – you won't be far from some sort of trail. The best ones are in wilderness areas, where you'll find **waymarked paths**, from half-hour strolls to major hiking expeditions of several days that take you right into the heart of some of the most beautiful parts of the country.

Overnight trails are normally well laid out, with painted route markers, and campsites or huts along the way. Numbers are limited on most, and many trails are so popular that you may need to book months (up to eleven months in some cases) in advance to use them.

There are also **guided wilderness trails**, where you walk in game country accompanied by an armed guide. These walks should be regarded as a way to get a feel for the wild rather than actually see any wildlife, as you'll encounter far fewer animals on foot than from a vehicle. Specialist trails include mountain biking, canoeing and horseback trails, while a handful of trails have been set up specifically for people with disabilities, mostly for the visually impaired or those confined to wheelchairs.

Watersports

South Africa has some of the world's finest **surfing** breaks. The country's perfect wave at Jeffrey's Bay was immortalized on celluloid in the 1960s cult movie *Endless Summer*, but any surfer will tell you that there are equally good, if not better, breaks all the way along the coast from Namibia to Mozambique.

Surfers can be a cliquey bunch, but the South African community is among the friendliest in the world and, provided you pay your dues, you should find yourself easily accepted. Some of the world's top shapers work here, and you can pick up an excellent **board** at a fraction of the European or US price. **Boogie-boarding** and **body-surfing** make easy alternatives to the real thing, require less skill and dedication, and are great fun. **Windsurfing** (or sailboarding) is another popular sport you'll find at many resorts, where you can rent gear.

On inland waterways, South African holidaymakers are keen **speedboaters**, an activity that goes hand in hand with **waterskiing**. **Kayaking** and **canoeing** are also very popular, and you can often rent craft at resorts or national parks that lie along rivers. For the more adventurous, there's **whitewater rafting**, with some decent trips along the Tugela River in KwaZulu-Natal and on the Orange River.

Diving and snorkelling

Scuba diving is popular, and South Africa is one of the cheapest places in the world to get an internationally recognized open-water certificate. **Courses** start at around R3300 (including gear) and are available at all the coastal cities as well as a number of other resorts. The most rewarding diving is along the St Lucia Marine Reserve on the northern KwaZulu-Natal coast, which hosts one hundred thousand dives every year for its coral reefs and fluorescent fish.

You won't find corals and bright colours along the Cape coast, but the huge number of sunken vessels makes **wreck-diving** popular, and you can encounter the swaying rhythms of giant kelp forests. There are a couple of places along the southern Cape and Garden Route where you can go on **shark-cage dives** and come face to face with deadly great whites.

KwaZulu-Natal is also good for **snorkelling** and there are some underwater trails elsewhere in the country, most notable of which is in the Tsitsikamma National Park.

Other activities

Fishing is another well-developed South African activity and the coasts yield 250 species caught through rock, bay or surf angling. Inland you'll find plenty of rivers and dams stocked with freshwater fish, while trout fishing is extremely well established in Mpumalanga, the northern sections of the Eastern Cape and the KwaZulu-Natal Midlands.

There are ample opportunities for aerial activities. In the Winelands you can go **ballooning**, while **paragliding** offers a thrilling way to see Cape Town, by diving off Lion's Head and riding the thermals. More down-to-earth options include **mountaineering** and **rock climbing**, both of which have a huge following in South Africa. In a similar vein is **kloofing** (or canyoning), in which participants trace the course of a deep ravine by climbing, scrambling, jumping, abseiling or using any other means.

If you can't choose between being airborne and being earthbound, you can always bounce between the two by **bungee jumping** off the Gouritz River Bridge near Mossel Bay – the world's highest commercial jump.

Horseriding is a sport you'll find at virtually every resort, whether inland or along the coast, for trips of two hours or two days. Take your own hat, as not everyone provides them. **Birdwatching** is another activity you can do almost anywhere, either on your own, or as part of a guided trip with one of the several experts operating in South Africa. Among the best birdwatching spots are Mkhuze and Ndumo game reserves in KwaZulu-Natal.

Golf courses in South Africa are prolific and frequently in stunningly beautiful locations. Finally, you can **ski** at one or two resorts in the Eastern and Western Cape, gaining a quirky and unusual experience of Africa.

BEACH CONDITIONS

Don't expect balmy Mediterranean seas in South Africa: of its 2500km of coastline, only the stretch along the Indian Ocean seaboard of KwaZulu-Natal and the northern section of the Eastern Cape can be considered **tropical**, and along the entire coast an energetic surf pounds the shore. In Cape Town, sea bathing is only comfortable between November and March. Generally, the further east you go from here, the warmer the water becomes and the longer the **bathing season**. Sea temperatures that rarely drop below 18°C make the KwaZulu-Natal coast warm enough for a dip at any time of year.

A word of warning: dangerous **undertows** and **riptides** are present along the coast and you should try to bathe where lifeguards are present. Failing that (and guards aren't that common away from the main resorts out of season), follow local advice, never swim alone, and always treat the ocean with respect.

Spectator sports

South Africa is a nation obsessed by sport, where heights of devotion are reached whenever local or international teams take to the field. Winning performances, controversial selections and scandals commonly dominate the front as well as the back pages of newspapers, and it can be hard to escape the domination of sport across radio, television and advertising media. The major spectator sports are football, rugby and cricket, and big matches involving the international team or heavyweight local clubs are well worth seeing live.

Football

Football is the country's most popular game, with a primarily black and coloured following, and it is now starting to attract serious money.

The professional **season** runs from August to May, with teams competing in the **Premier Soccer League** (W thepsl.co.za) and a couple of knock-out cup competitions. Unlike rugby teams, football teams do not own their own grounds and are forced to rent them for specific fixtures. In Gauteng, the heartland of South African football, all the big clubs share the same **grounds**, which has prevented the development of the kind of terrace fan culture found elsewhere, and football **crowds** are generally witty and good-spirited. The very big games, normally involving Johannesburg's two big teams, **Kaizer Chiefs** and **Orlando Pirates**, simmer with tension, though violence is rare. Although Chiefs and Pirates are both Sowetan clubs, they have a nationwide following, and their derbies are the highlight of the PSL's fixture list. The dominance of these long-time Jo'burg rivals has been challenged in recent years by Pretoria-based Mamelodi Sundowns and SuperSport United, both of which are regular champions of the Premier Soccer League.

Games are played on weekday evenings (usually at 7.30pm or 8.30pm) and at 3pm on Saturdays. **Tickets** cost about R50 to watch top teams play.

The **national squad**, nicknamed Bafana Bafana (literally "boys boys" but connoting "our lads"), is imaginative and strong on spectacular athletic feats, but less impressive when it comes to teamwork and resilience. Indeed, at the 2010 World Cup, host Bafana delivered an entertaining draw against Mexico in the opening match, but against Uruguay suffered the worst defeat (3–0) for a host nation since 1970, and was eliminated in the group stages. Sadly, Bafana failed to even qualify for the 2014 World Cup in Brazil.

Rugby

Rugby is hugely popular with whites, though attempts to broaden the game's appeal among a black audience, have struggled. South Africa's victory against England at the 2007 World Cup final in Paris did for a brief spell bring the whole country together. The strength of emotion almost matched that shown in 1995 when South Africa hosted the event. Coming shortly after the advent of democracy, it attracted fanatical attention nationwide, particularly when the Boks triumphed and President **Nelson Mandela** donned a green Springbok jersey (long associated exclusively with whites) to present the cup to the winning side – as depicted in Clint Eastwood's 2009 film *Invictus*.

Following that, the goodwill dissipated, to be replaced by an acrimonious struggle to transform traditionally white sports (cricket and rugby) into something more representative of all race groups, particularly following the government's policy of enforcing **racial quotas** in national squads.

Despite these problems, the country's two World Cup victories in sixteen years testify to the fact that South Africa is very good at rugby, and you are likely to witness high-quality play when you watch either inter-regional or international games. The main domestic competition is the **Currie Cup**, with games played on weekends from March to October; admission to these matches starts at R50.

More recently this has been overshadowed by the **SuperRugby** competition, involving fifteen regional teams from **South Africa**, **New Zealand** and **Australia** with expansion mooted to eighteen teams from 2016, which will include a squad from **Argentina** and possibly from **Asia**. You'll catch a fair bit of SuperRugby action in the major centres of Johannesburg, Cape Town and Durban, though smaller places such as Port Elizabeth, East London and George sometimes get a look-in.

International fixtures involving the **Springboks** are dominated by visiting tours by northern-hemisphere teams and by the annual **Rugby Championship** competition, in which South Africa plays home and away fixtures against Australia, New Zealand and Argentina. These are normally played from July to September, and you will need to buy tickets well in advance.

Cricket

Cricket was for some years seen as the most progressive of the former white sports, with development programmes generating support and discovering talent among black and coloured communities. The sport was rocked to its foundations in 2000, however, when it was revealed that the South African national captain, the late **Hansie Cronje**, had received money from betting syndicates to influence the outcome of one-day matches. Cronje was banned for life, the credibility of the sport took a dive and the national team, the **Proteas** (formerly the Springboks), struggled for years to recover. In 2012 the South Africans finally achieved the number one test spot, becoming the only team to simultaneously win all three premier international competitions, including the One Day International (ODI) and Twenty20 (T20) cricket. In 2014, Australia beat them to a still-respectable second place in test cricket, while talented batsman Hashim Amla (ranked fourth in the world) made history as the first South African of colour to be appointed Proteas test captain.

The **domestic season** of inter-regional games runs from late-September to March, with the main competitions being the four-day **Sunfoil Series**, the series of one-day, fifty-overs matches, the **Momentum One Day Cup**, and the shorter twenty-overs **Ram Slam T20 Challenge**. The contests see six regional squads slogging it out for national dominance. Games are played throughout the week, and admission is from R60. In the international standings, South Africa is one of the world's top teams, and you stand a good chance of being around for an international test or one-day series if you're in the country between November and March. Expect to pay from R120 for an international, which are played in all the major cities.

Running and cycling

South Africa is very strong at long-distance **running**, a tradition that reached its apotheosis at the 1996 Atlanta Olympics when Josiah Thugwane won the marathon, becoming the first black South African to bag Olympic gold. The biggest single athletics event in South Africa, the **Comrades Marathon**, attracts nearly fifteen thousand participants, among them some of the world's leading international ultra-marathon runners. The ninety-kilometre course crosses the hilly country between Durban and Pietermaritzburg, with a drop of almost 800m

between the town and the coast. Run annually towards the end of May, the race alternates direction each year and is notable for having been non-racial since 1975, although it wasn't until 1989 that a black South African, Samuel Tshabalala, won it. Since then, **black athletes** have dominated the front rankings. Almost as well known is the **Two Oceans ultra-marathon**, which attracts ten thousand competitors each April to test themselves on the 56-kilometre course that spectacularly circuits the Cape Peninsula.

Traversing a 109-kilometre route, the **Pick 'n Pay Cape Argus Cycle Tour** also includes the Cape Peninsula in its routing. The largest – and most spectacular – individually timed cycle race anywhere, it attracts 35,000 participants from around the world each year in March.

Horse racing

You'll find huge interest among rich and poor South Africans in **horse racing**, with totes and tracks in all the main cities. Its popularity is partly due to the fact that for decades this was the only form of public gambling allowed in the country – on the pretext that it involved skill not chance. The highlight of the racing calendar is the **Durban July** held at Durban's Greyville racecourse. A flamboyant event, it attracts huge crowds, massive purses, socialites in outrageous headgear and vast amounts of media attention.

Parks, reserves and wilderness areas

No other African country has as rich a variety of parks, reserves and wilderness areas as South Africa. Hundreds of game reserves and state forests pepper the terrain, creating a bewildering but enticing breadth of choice. While there are dozens of unsung treasures among these, the big destinations amount to some two dozen parks geared towards protecting the country's wildlife and wilderness areas.

With a few exceptions, these are run by **Ezemvelo KZN Wildlife** (☏033 845 1000, ⓦwww .kznwildlife.com), which controls most of the public reserves in KwaZulu-Natal, and **South African National Parks** (☏012 428 9111, ⓦsanparks.org),

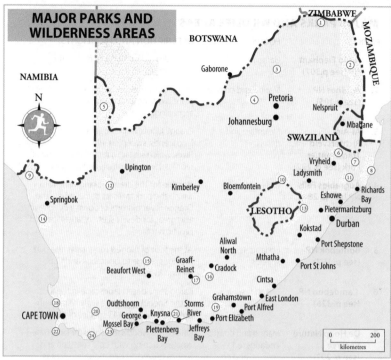

Addo Elephant NP	19	Golden Gate Highlands NP	10	Marakele NP	3
Agulhas NP	24	Hluhluwe-Imfolozi GR	11	Mkhuze GR	7
Ai-Ais Richtersveld Transfrontier Park	9	iSimangaliso Wetland Park	8	Mountain Zebra NP	16
Augrabies Falls NP	12	Ithala GR	6	Namaqua NP	14
Bontebok NP	20	Karoo National Park	15	Pilanesberg NP	4
Camdeboo NP	17	Kgalagadi Transfrontier Park	5	Table Mountain NP	22
De Hoop Nature Reserve	23	Kruger NP	2	Ukhahlamba Drakensberg Park	13
Garden Route NP	21	Mapungubwe NP	1	West Coast NP	18

which covers the rest of the country. In addition to the state-run parks there are **private reserves**, frequently abutting them and sharing the same wildlife population. Only some of the national parks are game reserves (see box, pp.66–67).

While most people come for South Africa's superb **wildlife**, don't let the **Big Five** (buffalo, elephant, leopard, lion and rhino) blinker you into missing out on the marvellous wilderness areas that take in dramatic landscapes and less publicized animal life. There are parks protecting marine and coastal areas, wetlands, endangered species, forests, deserts and mountains, usually with the added attraction of assorted animals, birds, insects, reptiles or marine mammals – South Africa is one of the top destinations in the world for land-based **whale watching**.

If you had to choose just one of the country's top three parks, **Kruger**, stretching up the east flank of Mpumalanga and Limpopo Province, would lead the pack for its sheer size (it's larger than Wales), its range of animals, its varied lowveld habitats and unbeatable game-viewing opportunities. After Kruger, the **Tsitsikamma** in the Western Cape attracts large numbers of visitors for its ancient forests, cliff-faced oceans and the dramatic Storms River Mouth as well as its Otter Trail, South Africa's most popular hike. For epic mountain landscapes, nowhere in the country can touch the **Ukhahlamba Drakensberg Park**, which takes in a series of reserves on the KwaZulu-Natal border with Lesotho and offers gentle hikes along watercourses as well as ambitious mountaineering for serious climbers.

The unchallenged status of Kruger as the place for sighting **elephants**, **lions** and casts of thousands of animals tends to put the KwaZulu-Natal parks in the shade, quite undeservedly. As well as offering the best places in the world for viewing **rhino**, these parks feel less developed than

MAJOR PARKS AND WILDLIFE AREAS

PARK	FOCUS	DESCRIPTION AND HIGHLIGHTS
1. **Addo Elephant NP (see p.307)**	Game reserve	The only Big Five national park in the southern half of the country
2. **Agulhas NP (see p.205)**	Marine and coastal	Rugged southernmost tip of Africa with rich plant biodiversity and significant archeological sites
3. **Ai-Ais-Richtersveld Transfrontier Park (see p. 292)**	Mountain and desert	Craggy kloofs, high mountains and dramatic landscapes, sweeping inland from the Orange River, which sustain a remarkable range of reptiles, birds, mammals and plant life
4. **Augrabies Falls NP (see p. 280)**	Desert reserve	Notable for the dramatic landmark from which the park takes its name, where the Orange River plummets down a deep ravine; also great for desert scenery, antelope and prolific birdlife
5. **Bontebok NP (see p. 197)**	Endangered species	At the foot of rugged mountains, the park provides refuge to bontebok and Cape mountain zebra
6. **Camdeboo NP (see p. 326)**	Desert reserve	Karoo semi-desert landscape in the foothills of the Sneeuberg range with 120m-high dolerite pillars plus 43 species of herbivore
7. **De Hoop Nature Reserve (see p. 207)**	Marine and coastal, endangered species, and coastal vegetation	One of the world's top spots for land-based whale watching with epic coastline and fynbos grazed by rare mountain zebras
8. **Garden Route National Park (see p. 218, p.224 & p.232)**	Marine and coastal/endangered species	Focused on three sections: wetlands and coast around Wilderness; Knysna's forests and lagoon; and Tsitsikamma's cliffs, gorges and ancient forests
9. **Golden Gate Highlands NP (see p. 437)**	Mountain enclave	Resort at the foot of rich sandstone formations in the heart of the Maluti Mountains
10. **Hluhluwe-Imfolozi GR (see p. 401)**	Game reserve	KwaZulu-Natal's hillier, smaller answer to Kruger is among the top African spots for rhinos
11. **Isimangaliso (see p. 404)**	Coastal wetland	Vast patchwork of wetlands, wilderness, coast and game reserves

Kruger, and often provide superior accommodation at comparable prices. Both Kruger and KwaZulu-Natal parks offer guided wildlife trails and **night drives**, a popular way to catch sight of the elusive denizens that creep around after dark.

Also worth a mention is the **Addo Elephant National Park** in the Eastern Cape: it's the third largest national park in South Africa, and still being expanded. The only Big Five reserve in the southern half of the country, Addo has a lot else in its favour:

it has the most diverse **landscape** of any reserve in the country; it is a day's drive from Cape Town; and it is the only major game reserve in the country that is **malaria-free**.

Park accommodation

Accommodation at national parks includes **campsites** (expect to pay R150–280 per tent); **safari tents** at some of the Kruger and KwaZulu-Natal

12.	**Ithala GR** (see p. 416)	Game reserve	Lesser-known small gem of a game reserve in mountainous country
13.	**Karoo NP** (see p. 193)	Desert reserve	Arid mountainous landscape with fossils, herbivores and wild flowers in spring
14.	**Kgalagadi Transfrontier Park** (see p. 278)	Desert/game reserve	Remote desert with rust-red dunes, desert lions, shy leopards and thousands of antelope
15.	**Kruger NP** (see p. 539)	Game reserve	The largest, best-stocked and most popular game reserve in the subcontinent
16.	**Mapungubwe NP** (see p. 572)	Archeology/game reserve	World Heritage Site listed for its significance as the location of a highly developed Iron Age culture. Also noted for its landscape and biodiversity, which supports a large variety of mammals
17.	**Marakele NP** (see p. 566)	Game reserve	Striking landscape of peaks, plateaus and cliffs, home to lions, elephants, rhinos and a variety of other mammals
18.	**Mkhuze GR** (see p. 408)	Game/bird reserve	Top birding venue and excellent for rhinos and other herbivores, plus walks in wild fig forest
19.	**Mountain Zebra NP** (see p.323)	Endangered species	Dramatic hilly landscape in otherwise flat country with rare mountain zebras and other herbivores
20.	**Namaqua NP** (see p.285)	Marine and coastal	Mountainous and coastal region renowned for its estimated 3500 plant varieties, among them beautiful spring wildflowers
21.	**Pilanesberg NP** (see p.508)	Game reserve	Mountain-encircled grassland trampled by the Big Five, accessible from Johannesburg
22.	**Table Mountain NP** (see p.108)	The natural areas of the peninsula	Extraordinarily rich and diverse flora and fauna that thrives in the wilderness that is Cape Town's back yard
23.	**Ukhahlamba Drakensberg Park** (see p.388)	Mountain reserve	A series of parks covering the highest, most stirring and most dramatic peaks in South Africa
24.	**West Coast NP** (see p.241)	Marine and coastal	Wetland wilderness with birding and watersports

restcamps (clusters of accommodation in game reserves, including chalets, safari tents, cottages and campsites; from R470 per tent); one-room **huts** with shared washing and cooking facilities (from R500); one-room en-suite **bungalows** with shared cooking facilities (from R900); and self-contained family **cottages** with private bath or shower and cooking facilities (from R1000). In national parks accommodation (excluding campsites) you're supplied with bedding, towels, a fridge and basic cooking utensils.

Some restcamps have a **shop** selling supplies for picnics or braais, as well as a **restaurant**.

The ultimate wildlife accommodation is in the **private game reserves**, most of which are around the Kruger National Park. Here you pay big bucks for accommodation, which is almost always luxurious, in large en-suite walk-in tents, or small thatched **rondavels**, or – in the larger and most expensive lodges – plush rooms with air conditioning. A couple of places have "bush-showers" (a hoisted bucket of

PARK FEES, RESERVATIONS AND ENQUIRIES

Fees given in our park accounts are generally conservation fees, payable daily. The most expensive places are Kruger National Park and Kgalagadi Transfrontier Park, for which foreign visitors pay a conservation fee of R264 per adult) followed by Addo Elephant National Park where the fee is R216. The majority of the rest charge R152, but some of the smaller parks charge a lot less.

As a rule of thumb, foreign visitors aged 12 and under pay half the adult rate; South African residents pay a quarter of the foreign adult fee, while citizens of the Southern Africa Development Community, to which many countries in the region belong, pay half the foreign adult fee.

Accommodation at most of South Africa's major national parks can be booked in advance (to stay in high season, do so several months in advance) through South African National Parks, except at Pilanesberg (see p.508) and the KwaZulu-Natal reserves, for which you book through Ezemvelo KZN Wildlife. Booking with South African National Parks by phone usually involves a long wait; reserving online is better (see p.64).

hot water with a shower nozzle attached) behind reed screens but open to the sky – one of the great treats of the bush is taking a shower under the southern sky. Some chalets or tents have gaslights or lanterns in the absence of **electricity**. Food is usually good and plentiful, and vegetarians can be catered for. Expect to pay upwards of R3000 per person per night, rising to the skies-the-limit at the most fashionable spots. High as these **prices** are, all meals and game drives are included, and as numbers are strictly limited, you get an exclusive experience of the bush.

Game viewing

Spotting game takes skill and **experience**. It's easier than you'd think to mistake a rhino for a large boulder, or to miss the king of the beasts in the tall grass – African game has, after all, evolved with **camouflage** in mind. Don't expect the volume of animals you get in wildlife documentaries: what you see is always a matter of **luck**, patience and skill. If you're new to the African bush and its wildlife, consider shelling out for at least two nights at one of the luxurious lodges on a private reserve (for example, those abutting Kruger); they're staffed by well-informed **rangers** who lead game-viewing outings in open-topped 4WDs.

The section on Kruger National Park (see p.539) gives more advice on how to go about spotting game and how to enjoy and understand what you do see – whether it's a brightly coloured lizard in a rest camp, head-butting giraffes at a waterhole or dust-kicking rhinos. Numerous **books** are available that can enhance your visit to a game reserve – especially if you plan a self-drive safari (see below).

Self-drive safaris

The least expensive way of experiencing a game park

is by **renting a car** and driving around a national park, taking advantage of the self-catering and camping facilities. You'll have the thrill of spotting game at your own pace rather than relying on a ranger, and for people with **children** a self-drive safari is the principal way to see a game reserve, as most of the upmarket lodges don't admit under-12s. The disadvantage of self-driving is that you can end up jostling with other cars to get a view, especially when it comes to lion-watching. Also, you may not know what animal signs to look for, and unless you travel in a minibus or 4WD vehicle you're unlikely to be high enough off the ground to be able to see across the veld.

The KwaZulu-Natal game reserves – foremost among them Hluhluwe-Imfolozi, Mkhuze and Ithala – offer rewarding opportunities for **self-drive touring**, as does the Pilanesberg Game Reserve in North West Province, while the remote Kgalagadi Transfrontier Park that stretches across the border into Botswana promises truly exciting wilderness driving. You might choose to cover a route that combines the substantial Kruger National Park with the more intimate reserves of KwaZulu-Natal province.

If you plan to self-drive, consider investing in good animal and bird **field guides**, and a decent pair of **binoculars** – one pair per person is recommended. Finally, whether you're cooking or not, it's worth taking a flask for tea and a cool bag to keep water cold.

Escorted safaris

It's possible to book places on a **safari excursion** – such packages are often organized by backpackers' lodges located near reserves, and occasionally by hotels and B&Bs. On the downside, these don't give you the experience of waking up in the wild, and entail spending considerably more time on the road than if you were based inside a reserve. But during South African school holidays, when Kruger, for example, is booked to capacity, you may have no other option.

Mostly, you get what you pay for as regards game-viewing packages. Be wary of any cheap deals on "**safari farms**" in the vicinity of Kruger. These are generally fine if you want to see animals in what are essentially huge zoos and make an acceptable overnight stop en route to Kruger, but are no substitute for a real wilderness experience – sooner or later you hit fences and gates on your game drive. Some of the better places in this category are listed in the relevant chapters.

Safaris on private reserves

If you choose well, the ultimate South African game experience has to be a **private reserve**. You can relax while your game-viewing activities are organized, and because you spend time in a small group you get a stronger sense of the wild than you ever could at one of the big Kruger restcamps. Best of all, you have the benefit of knowledgeable **rangers**, who can explain the terrain and small-scale wildlife as they drive you around looking for game.

Privately run safari lodges in concessions inside Kruger and some other national parks, such as Addo, operate along similar lines. The smaller private reserves accommodate between ten and sixteen guests; larger **camps** often cater for two or three times as many people, and resemble hotels in the bush. Many safari lodges have their own **water-holes**, overlooked by the bar, from which you can watch animals drinking. Nowhere are the private reserves more developed than along the west flank of the Kruger, where you'll find the top-dollar prestigious lodges as well as some places offering better value.

A typical day at a private camp or lodge starts at **dawn** for tea or coffee followed by guided **game viewing** on foot, or driving. After a mid-morning brunch/breakfast, there's the chance to spend time on a **viewing platform** or in a **hide**, quietly watching the passing scene. Late-afternoon game viewing is a repeat of early morning but culminates with **sundowners** as the light fades, and often turns into a **night drive** with spotlights out looking for nocturnal creatures.

Prices, which include accommodation, meals and all game activities, vary widely. The ultra-expensive camps offer more luxury and social cachet, but not necessarily better game viewing. You might find the cheaper camps in the same areas more to your taste, their plainer and wilder atmosphere more in keeping with the bush.

Health

You can put aside most of the health fears that may be justified in some parts of Africa; run-down hospitals and bizarre tropical diseases aren't typical of South Africa. All tourist areas boast generally high standards of hygiene and safe drinking water. The only hazard you're likely to encounter, and the one the majority of visitors are most blasé about, is the sun. In some parts of the country there is a risk of malaria, and you will need to take precautions.

Public hospitals in South Africa are fairly well equipped, but they face huge pressures under which their attempts to maintain standards are unfortunately buckling. Expect **long waits** and frequently indifferent treatment. **Private hospitals** or clinics, which are well up to British or North American standards, are usually a better option for travellers. You're likely to get more personal treatment, though you will have to pay, so although the **costs** are nowhere near as high as in the US, make sure you're adequately insured (see p.75). Private hospitals are listed in the town and city listings throughout the Guide.

Dental care in South Africa is well up to British and North American standards, and is less expensive. You'll find dentists in all the cities and most smaller towns, listed after doctors at the beginning of each town's listings in the telephone directory.

Inoculations

Although no specific **inoculations** are compulsory if you arrive from the West, it's wise to ensure that your **polio** and **tetanus** vaccinations are up to date. A **yellow fever** vaccination certificate is necessary if you've come from a country where the disease is endemic, such as Kenya, Tanzania or tropical South America.

In addition to these, depending on which parts of the country you're visiting, the Hospital for Tropical Diseases in London recommends a course of shots against **typhoid** and an injection against **hepatitis A**, both of which can be caught from contaminated food or water. This is a worst-case scenario, however, as typhoid is eminently curable and few visitors to South Africa ever catch it.

Vaccination against **hepatitis B** is essential only for people involved in health work; the disease is spread by the transfer of blood products, usually dirty needles.

It's best to start organizing to have jabs **six weeks** before departure. If you're going to another African country first and need the yellow fever jab, note that a yellow fever certificate only becomes valid ten days after you've had the shot.

MEDICAL RESOURCES FOR TRAVELLERS

Canadian Society for International Health ☎ 613 241 5785, ⓦ csih.org. Extensive list of travel health centres.

CDC ☎ 1 800 232 4636, ⓦ cdc.gov/travel. Official US government travel health site.

Hospital for Tropical Diseases Travel Clinic ⓦ thehtd.org. London-based hospital specializing in travel-related diseases.

International Society for Travel Medicine ☎ 1 404 373 8282, ⓦ istm.org. Has a full list of travel health clinics.

MASTA (Medical Advisory Service for Travellers Abroad) ⓦ masta.org. For information on the nearest UK travel clinic.

The Travel Doctor – TMVC ☎ 1300 658 844, ⓦ tmvc.com.au. Lists travel clinics in Australia and New Zealand.

Travel Doctor ☎ 0861 300 911, ⓦ traveldoctor.co.za. Lists travel clinics in South Africa.

Tropical Medical Bureau ⓦ tmb.ie. Travel clinics in Ireland.

Stomach upsets

Stomach upsets from food are rare, and salad and ice are both perfectly safe. As anywhere, though, don't keep food for too long, and wash fruit and vegetables as thoroughly as possible.

If you do get a stomach bug the best cure is lots of **water** and **rest**. Papayas – the flesh as well as the pips – are a good tonic to offset the diarrhoea. Otherwise, most chemists stock name-brand anti-diarrhoea remedies, such as Lomotil.

Avoid taking **antibiotics** at the first sign of illness. Instead keep them as a last resort – they don't work on viruses and annihilate your "gut flora" (most of which you want to keep), making you more susceptible next time round. Most tummy upsets will resolve themselves if you adopt a sensible **fat-free diet** for a couple of days, but if they do persist without improvement (or are accompanied by other unusual symptoms), then see a **doctor** as soon as possible.

The sun

The **sun** is likely to be the worst hazard you'll encounter in Southern Africa, particularly if you're fair-skinned.

Short-term effects of **overexposure** to the sun include burning, nausea and headaches. Make sure you wear adequate **sunscreen** and you don't stay too long in the sun – especially when you first arrive.

Take particular care with **children**, who should ideally be kept well covered at the seaside, preferably with UV-protective sun suits. Don't be lulled into complacency on cloudy days, when UV levels can still be high.

Bilharzia

One ailment that you need to take seriously throughout sub-Saharan Africa is **bilharzia** (schistosomiasis), carried in most freshwater lakes and rivers in South Africa except in the mountains. Bilharzia is spread by tiny, parasitic worm-like flukes which leave their water-snail hosts and burrow into human skin to multiply in the bloodstream; they then work their way to the walls of the intestine or bladder, where they begin to lay **eggs**.

The chances are you'll avoid bilharzia even if you swim in a suspect river, but it's best to avoid **swimming** in dams and rivers where possible. If you go **canoeing** or can't avoid the water, have a test for bilharzia when you return home.

Symptoms may be no more than a feeling of lassitude and ill health. Once the infection is established, abdominal pain and blood in the urine and stools are common. Fortunately, bilharzia is easily and effectively treatable.

Malaria

Most of South Africa is free of **malaria**, a potentially lethal disease that is widespread in tropical and subtropical Africa, where it's a major killer. However, **protection** against malaria is essential if you're planning to travel to any of these areas: northern and northeastern Mpumalanga, notably the Kruger National Park; northern KwaZulu-Natal; or the border regions of North West and Limpopo provinces. The highest **risk** is during the hot, rainy months from November to April. The risk is reduced during the cooler, dry months from May to October, when some people decide not to take prophylactic medication.

Malaria is caused by a parasite carried in the saliva of the female anopheles mosquito. It has a variable incubation period of a few days to several weeks, so you can become ill long after being bitten. The first symptoms of malaria can be mistaken for **flu**, starting off relatively mildly with a variable combination that includes fever, aching limbs and shivering, which come in waves, usually beginning in the early evening. Deterioration can be rapid as the parasites in the bloodstream proliferate. Malaria is not **infectious**, but can be fatal if not treated quickly: get medical help without delay if you go down with flu-like symptoms within a week of entering or three months of leaving a malarial area.

Doctors can advise on which kind of **antimalarial tablets** to take. It's important to keep to the prescribed dose, which covers the period before and after your trip. Consult your **doctor** or **clinic** several weeks before you travel, as you should start taking medication a week or two before entering the affected region – depending on the particular drug you're using.

Whatever you decide to take, be aware that no antimalarial drug is totally effective – your only sure-fire protection is to **avoid getting bitten**. Malaria-carrying mosquitoes are active between **dusk** and **dawn**, so try to avoid being out at this time, or at least cover yourself well. Sleep under a **mosquito net** when possible, making sure to tuck it under the mattress, and burn **mosquito coils** (which you can buy everywhere) for a peaceful, if noxious, night. If you have access to a power supply, electric mosquito-destroyers which you fit with a pad every night are less pungent than mosquito coils. Mosquito "buzzers" are useless. Whenever the mosquitoes are particularly bad – and that's not often – cover your exposed parts with **insect repellent**; those containing diethyltoluamide (DEET) work well. Other locally produced repellents such as Peaceful Sleep are widely available.

Bites and stings

Bites, **stings** and **rashes** in South Africa are comparatively rare. **Snakes** are present, but hardly ever seen as they move out of the way quickly. The sluggish puff and berg adders are the most dangerous, because they often lie on paths and don't move when humans approach. The best **advice** if you get bitten is to note what the snake looked like and get yourself to a clinic or hospital. Most bites are not fatal and the worst thing you can do is to panic: desperate measures with razor blades and tourniquets risk doing more harm than good.

Tick-bite fever is occasionally contracted from walking in the bush, particularly in long wet grass. The offending ticks can be minute and you may not spot them. **Symptoms** appear a week later – swollen glands and severe aching of the bones, backache and fever – with the disease running its course in three or four days. Ticks you may find on yourself are not dangerous – just make sure you pull out the head as well as the body (it's not painful). A good way of removing small ones is to smear **Vaseline** or grease over them, making them release their hold.

Scorpion stings and **spider bites** are painful but almost never fatal, contrary to popular myth. Scorpions and spiders abound, but they're hardly ever seen unless you turn over logs and stones. If you're collecting wood for a campfire, knock or shake it before picking it up. Another simple **precaution** when camping is to shake out your shoes and clothes in the morning before you get dressed.

Rabies is present throughout Southern Africa, with **dogs** posing the greatest risk, although the disease can be carried by other domestic or wild animals. If you are bitten you should go immediately to a clinic or hospital. Rabies can be treated effectively with a course of **injections**.

Sexually transmitted diseases

HIV/AIDS and venereal diseases are widespread in Southern Africa among both men and women, and the danger of catching the virus through sexual contact is very real. Follow the usual precautions regarding **safer sex**. There's no special risk from medical treatment in the country, but if you're travelling overland and you want to play it safe, take your own needle and transfusion kit.

Tuberculosis

TB is a serious problem in South Africa, but most travellers are at low risk. At higher risk are healthcare workers, long-term travellers and anyone with an impaired immune system, such as people infected with HIV. A **BCG vaccination** is routinely given to babies in South Africa, but its use elsewhere varies. Take medical advice on the question of **immunization** if you feel there may be a risk.

Crime and personal safety

Despite horror stories of sky-high crime rates, most people visit South Africa without incident; be careful, but don't be paranoid. This is not to underestimate the issue – crime is probably the most serious problem facing the country. However, once you realize that crime is disproportionately concentrated in the poor African and coloured townships, the scale becomes less terrifying. Violent crime is a particular problem not just in the townships but

SAFETY TIPS

IN GENERAL:

- Dress down and try not to look too like a tourist.
- Avoid wearing expensive jewellery and watches or carrying a camera openly in cities.
- Leave your designer shades at home – they are sometimes pulled off people's faces.
- If you are accosted, remain calm and cooperative.

WHEN ON FOOT:

- Grasp bags firmly under your arm.
- Don't carry excessive sums of money on you.
- Don't put your wallet in your back trouser pocket.
- Always know where your valuables are.
- Don't leave valuables exposed (on a seat or the ground) while having a meal or drink.
- Don't let strangers get too close to you – especially people in groups.
- In big cities, travel around in pairs or groups.

ON THE ROAD:

- Lock all your car doors, especially in cities.
- Keep rear windows sufficiently rolled up to keep out opportunistic hands.
- Never leave anything worth stealing in view when your car is unattended.

AT ATMS:

Cash machines are favourite hunting grounds for con men. Never underestimate their ability and don't get drawn into any interaction at an ATM, no matter how well-spoken, friendly or distressed the other person appears. If they claim to have a problem with the machine, tell them to contact the bank. Don't let people crowd you or see your personal identification number (PIN) when you withdraw money; if in doubt, go to another machine. Finally, if your card gets swallowed, report it without delay.

WHEN PAYING WITH A CARD:

- Never let your plastic out of your sight.
- At a restaurant, ask for a portable card reader to be brought to your table.
- At the till, keep an eye on your card.

---

also in Johannesburg, where the dangers are the worst in the country.

Protecting property and "**security**" are major national obsessions, and it's difficult to imagine what many South Africans would discuss at their dinner parties if the problem disappeared. A substantial percentage of middle-class homes subscribe to the services of armed private security firms. The other obvious manifestation of this obsession is the huge number of **alarms**, high walls and electronically controlled gates you'll find, not just in the suburbs, but even in less deprived areas of some townships. **Guns** are openly carried by police – and often citizens.

If you fall victim to a **mugging**, you should take very seriously the usual advice not to resist and do as you're told. The chances of this happening can be greatly minimized by using common sense and following a few simple rules (see box above).

Drugs and drink-driving

Dagga (pronounced like "dugger" with the "gg" guttural, as in the Scottish pronunciation of "loch") is **cannabis** in dried leaf form, South Africa's most widely produced and widely used drug. Grown in hot regions like KwaZulu-Natal (the source of Durban Poison), Swaziland (Swazi Gold) and as a cash crop in parts of the former Transkei, it is fairly easily available and the quality is generally good – but this doesn't alter the fact that it is **illegal**. If you do decide to partake, take particular care when scoring, as visitors have run into trouble dealing with unfamiliar local conditions.

Strangely, for a country that sometimes seems to be on one massive binge, South Africa has laws that prohibit **drinking** in public – not that anyone pays any attention to them. The drink-drive laws are routinely and brazenly flouted, making the country's

roads the one real danger you should be concerned about. People routinely stock up their cars with booze for long journeys, and even at filling stations you'll find places selling liquor. Levels of alcohol consumption go some way to explaining why during the Christmas holidays over a thousand people die in an annual orgy of carnage on the roads.

Sexual harassment

South Africa's extremely high incidence of **rape** doesn't as a rule affect tourists. However, at heart the majority of the country's males, regardless of race, hold on to fairly **sexist attitudes**. Sometimes your eagerness to be friendly may be taken as a sexual overture – always be sensitive to potential crossed wires and unintended signals.

Women should avoid travelling on their own, nor should they hitchhike or walk alone in deserted areas. This applies equally to cities, the countryside or anywhere after dark. Minibus taxis should be ruled out as a means of transport after dark, especially if you're not sure of the local geography.

The police

Poorly paid, shot at (and frequently hit), underfunded, badly equipped, barely respected and demoralized, the police in South Africa keep a low profile. If you

ever get stopped, at a **roadblock** for example (one of the likeliest encounters), always be courteous. And if you're driving, note that under South African law you are required to carry your driver's **licence** at all times.

If you are **robbed**, you need to report the incident to the police, who should give you a case reference for insurance purposes – though don't expect too much crime-cracking enthusiasm, or to get your property back.

Travel essentials

Climate

Although South Africa is predominantly a dry, sunny country, bear in mind that the chart below shows average maximums. **June and July** temperatures can drop below zero in some places; be prepared for average minimums of 4°C in Johannesburg, 7°C in Cape Town and 11°C in Durban.

Costs

The most expensive thing about visiting South Africa is getting there. Once you've arrived, you're likely to find it a relatively **inexpensive** destination. How cheap will depend partly on exchange rates at

AVERAGE DAILY MAXIMUM TEMPERATURES

CAPE TOWN

	Jan	Feb	Mar	Apr	May	Jun	Jul	Aug	Sep	Oct	Nov	Dec
Max (°C)	27	27	26	23	20	19	17	18	19	22	24	26
Max (°F)	81	81	79	73	68	66	63	64	66	72	75	79

DURBAN

	Jan	Feb	Mar	Apr	May	Jun	Jul	Aug	Sep	Oct	Nov	Dec
Max (°C)	27	28	27	26	24	23	22	22	23	24	25	26
Max (°F)	81	82	81	79	75	73	72	72	73	75	77	79

JOHANNESBURG

	Jan	Feb	Mar	Apr	May	Jun	Jul	Aug	Sep	Oct	Nov	Dec
Max (°C)	26	26	24	22	19	16	16	20	23	25	25	26
Max (°F)	79	79	75	72	66	61	61	68	73	77	77	79

SKUKUZA (KRUGER NATIONAL PARK)

	Jan	Feb	Mar	Apr	May	Jun	Jul	Aug	Sep	Oct	Nov	Dec
Max (°C)	31	31	30	29	27	25	25	26	29	29	30	30
Max (°F)	88	88	86	84	81	77	77	79	84	84	86	86

MASERU (LESOTHO)

	Jan	Feb	Mar	Apr	May	Jun	Jul	Aug	Sep	Oct	Nov	Dec
Max (°C)	20	17	14	11	9	7	7	9	11	14	17	20
Max (°F)	68	63	57	52	48	45	45	48	52	57	63	68

the time of your visit – in the decade after becoming fully convertible (after the advent of democracy in South Africa) the rand has seen some massive fluctuations against sterling, the dollar and the euro.

When it comes to daily budgets, your biggest expense is likely to be **accommodation**. If you're willing to stay in backpacker dorms and self-cater, you should be able to sleep and eat for under £25/$45/€30 per person a day. If you stay in B&Bs and guesthouses, eat out once a day, and have a snack or two, you should budget for at least double that. In luxury hotels expect to pay upwards of £150/$255/€190 a day, while luxury safari lodges in major game reserves charge from £200/$360/€260 a day to several times that. **Extras** such as car rental, outdoor activities, horseriding and safaris will add to these figures substantially. While most museums and art galleries impose an **entry fee**, it's usually quite low: only the most sophisticated attractions charge more than £2/$3.50/€2.50.

Electricity

South Africa's electricity supply runs at 220/230V, 50Hz AC. **Sockets** take unique round-pinned plugs; see ⓦkropla.com for details. Most hotel rooms have sockets that will take 110V electric shavers, but for other appliances US visitors will need an **adaptor**.

Emergencies

Police and **fire** ☎1011; **ambulance** ☎10177; **Netcare 911** private hospital network ☎082 911.

Entry requirements

Nationals of the US, Canada, Australia, New Zealand, Japan, Argentina and Brazil don't require a **visa** to enter South Africa. Most EU nationals don't need a visa, with the exception of passport holders from Bulgaria, Croatia, Estonia, Latvia, Lithuania, Romania and Slovenia, who need to obtain one at a South African diplomatic mission in their home country.

As long as you carry a passport that is valid for at least six months and with at least two empty pages you will be granted a **temporary visitor's permit**, which allows you to stay in South Africa for up to ninety days for most nationals, and 30 days for EU passport holders from Cyprus, Hungary, Poland and Slovakia. All visitors should have proof of a valid return ticket; without one, you may be required to pay the authorities the equivalent of your fare home (the money will only be refunded through a

lengthy process, after you have left the country). Visitors may also need to prove that they have sufficient funds to cover their stay.

Applications for **visa extensions** must be made at one of the main offices of the Department of Home Affairs, where you will be quizzed about your intentions and funds. In Cape Town, go to 56 Barrack St (☎021 468 4500); in Johannesburg, the office is at the corner of Plein and Harrison streets (☎011 639 4000). The Department also has offices in a number of other towns – check in the telephone directory or on its website (ⓦhome -affairs.gov.za), and make sure that the office you're intending to visit is able to grant extensions.

SOUTH AFRICAN DIPLOMATIC MISSIONS ABROAD

Australia corner of State Circle and Rhodes Place, Yarralumla, Canberra, ACT 2600 ☎02 627 2 7300, ⓦsahc.org.au.
Canada 15 Sussex Drive, Ottawa, Ontario K1M 1M8 ☎613 744 0330, ⓦsouthafrica-canada.ca.
Netherlands 40 Wassenaarseweg 2596 CJ, The Hague ☎070 392 4501, ⓦzuidafrika.nl.
New Zealand c/o the High Commission in Australia, see above, ⓦsahc.org.au/consular_new-zealand.htm.
UK Consular Section South Africa House, Trafalgar Square, London WC2N 5DP ☎021 7451 7299, ⓦsouthafricahouseuk.com.
US 3051 Massachusetts Ave, NW Washington, DC 20008 ☎202 232 4400, ⓦsouthafrica-newyork.net/homeaffairs/index.htm.
Consulates: 333 E 38th St, 9th floor, New York, NY 10016 ☎212 213 4880; 6300 Wilshire Blvd, Suite 600, Los Angeles, CA 90048 ☎323 651 0902.

Gay and lesbian travellers

South Africa has the world's first gay- and lesbian-friendly constitution, and Africa's most developed and diverse gay and lesbian scene. Not only is homosexuality **legal** for consenting adults of 18 or over, but the constitution outlaws any **discrimination** on the grounds of sexual orientation. Outside the big cities, however, South Africa is a pretty **conservative** place, where open displays of public affection by gays and lesbians are unlikely to go down well; many whites will find it un-Christian, while blacks will think it un-African.

South African Tourism, on the other hand, is well aware of the potential of pink spending power and actively woos **gay travellers** – an effort that is evidently paying off, with Cape Town ranking among the world's top gay destinations. The city is South Africa's – and indeed, the African continent's – gay capital. Like many things in the city, Cape Town's gay scene (see box, p.148) is white dominated, though there are a few gay-friendly **clubs** starting to emerge in the surrounding townships. The gay scene is a lot more multiracial in Johannesburg, especially in the clubs, while the Pretoria gay and lesbian scene has grown enormously over the past few years. There are also gay scenes in Port Elizabeth and Durban and you'll find a growing number of gay-run or gay-friendly establishments in small towns all over the country. There are **gay pride** festivals in Cape Town in February–March (**W** capetownpride.org) and in Jo'burg in September. The online **gay lifestyle magazine** Mamba (**W** mambaonline.com) is a useful resource for information about this and other gay events and organizations across the country, including the **South African Gay and Lesbian Film Festival** (**W** oia.co.za), which takes place in Cape Town and Johannesburg at the end of May.

Insurance

It's wise to take out an **insurance** policy to cover against theft, loss and illness or injury prior to visiting South Africa. A typical travel insurance policy usually provides cover for the loss of baggage, tickets and – up to a certain limit – cash or cheques, as well as cancellation or curtailment of your journey. Most of them exclude so-called dangerous sports unless an extra **premium** is paid: in South Africa this can mean scuba diving, white-water rafting, windsurfing, horseriding, bungee jumping and paragliding. In addition to these, check whether you are covered by your policy if you're hiking, kayaking, pony trekking or game viewing on safari, all activities people commonly take part in when visiting South Africa. Many policies can be chopped and changed to exclude **coverage** you don't need – for example, sickness and accident benefits can often be excluded or included at will. If you do take medical coverage, ascertain whether benefits will be paid as treatment proceeds or only after you return home, and if there

is a 24-hour medical emergency number. When securing baggage cover, make sure that the per-article limit will cover your most valuable possession. If you need to make a **claim**, you should keep receipts for medicines and medical treatment, and in the event you have anything stolen, you must obtain an official statement from the **police**.

Internet

Finding somewhere to access the **internet** will seldom be a problem in South Africa: cybercafés are found even in relatively small towns, and most backpacker hostels and hotels have internet and email facilities. Expect to pay R10–25 an hour for online access. If you are carrying your own computer or palm-top device you'll also be able to take advantage of the **wireless hotspots** at airports, cafés, malls and accommodation.

Mail

The deceptively familiar feel of South African post offices can lull you into expecting an efficient British- or US-style service. In fact, post within the country is slow and unreliable, and money and valuables frequently disappear en route. Expect domestic delivery times from one city to another of about a week – longer if a rural town is involved at either end. **International airmail** deliveries are often quicker, thanks to the city's direct flights to London. A letter or package sent by surface mail can take up to six weeks to get from South Africa to London.

Most towns of any size have a **post office**, generally open Monday to Friday 8.30am to 4.30pm and Saturday 8 to 11.30am (closing earlier in some places). The ubiquitous private **PostNet** outlets (**W** postnet.co.za) offer many of the same postal services as the post office and more, including **courier services**. Courier companies like FedEx

(☎0800 033 339, ⦿fedex.com/za) and DHL (☎086 034 5000, ⦿dhl.co.za) are far more reliable than the mail, though they are more expensive and available only in the larger towns.

Stamps can be bought at post offices and also from newsagents, such as the CNA chain, as well as supermarkets. Postage is relatively inexpensive – it costs about R6 to send a postcard by airmail to anywhere in the world, while a small letter costs about R7 to send. You'll find **poste restante** facilities at the main post office in most larger centres, and in many backpackers hostels.

Maps

Many **place names** in South Africa were changed after the 1994 elections – and changes are still being made – so if you buy a **map** before leaving home, make sure that it's up to date. Bartholomew produces an excellent map of South Africa, including Lesotho and Swaziland (1:2,000,000), as part of its World Travel Map series. Also worth investing in are MapStudio's "Miniplan" maps of major cities such as Cape Town, Durban and Pretoria: these are a convenient size and have useful details, such as showing hotels, cinemas, post offices and hospitals. **MapStudio** also produces good regional maps, featuring scenic routes and street maps of major towns, and a fine Natal Drakensberg map which shows hiking trails, picnic spots, campsites and places of interest.

South Africa's motoring organization, the **Automobile Association** (AA; see p.52), sells a wide selection of good regional maps (free to members) that you can pick up from its offices.

For travel around the Western Cape (including the Cape Peninsula) and the Eastern Cape's Wild Coast, the most accurate, up-to-date and attractive touring and hiking maps – the best bar none – are those produced by local cartographers **Slingsby Maps** (⦿slingsbymaps.com), which you can buy from bookshops.

Money

South Africa's currency is the **rand** (R), often called the "buck", divided into 100 **cents**. Notes come in R10, R20, R50, R100 and R200 denominations and there are coins of 5, 10, 20 and 50 cents, as well as R1, R2 and R5. At the time of writing, the **exchange rate** was hovering at around R18 to the pound sterling, R11 to the US dollar, R15 to the euro and R10 to the Australian dollar.

All but the tiniest settlement will have a **bank** where you can change money swiftly and easily.

Banking hours are Monday to Friday 9am to 3.30pm, and Saturday 9am to 11am; the banks in smaller towns usually close for lunch. In major cities, some banks operate **bureaux de change** that stay open until 7pm. Outside banking hours, some hotels will change money, although this entails a fairly hefty **commission**. You can also change money at branches of American Express and Rennies Travel.

Cards and travellers' cheques

Credit and **debit cards** are the most convenient way to access your funds in South Africa. Most international cards can be used to withdraw money at **ATMs**. Plastic can come in very handy for hotel bookings and for paying for more mainstream and upmarket tourist facilities, and is essential for car rental. **Visa** and **Mastercard** are the cards most widely accepted in major cities.

Travellers' cheques make a useful backup as they can be replaced if lost or stolen. American Express, Visa and Thomas Cook are all widely recognized brands; both US dollar and sterling cheques are accepted in South Africa.

Travellers' cheques and plastic are useless if you're heading into remote areas, where you'll need to carry **cash**, preferably in a safe place, such as a leather pouch or waist-level money belt that you can keep under your clothes.

Opening hours and holidays

The **working day** starts and finishes early in South Africa: shops and businesses generally open on **weekdays** at 8.30am or 9am and close at 4.30pm or 5pm. In small towns, many places close for an hour over **lunch**. Many shops and businesses close around noon on Saturdays, and most shops are closed on Sundays. However, in every neighbourhood, you'll find small shops and supermarkets where you can buy groceries and essentials after hours. Some establishments have different opening times in summer (April to August) and winter (September to March).

School holidays in South Africa can disrupt your plans, especially if you want to camp, or stay in the national parks and the cheaper end of accommodation (self-catering, cheaper B&Bs, etc), all of which are likely to be booked solid during those periods. If you do travel to South Africa over the school holidays, book your accommodation well in advance, especially for the national parks.

The longest and busiest holiday period is **Christmas** (summer), which for schools stretches over most of December and January. Flights and train berths can be hard to get from December 16 to January 2, when many business and offices close for their annual break. You should book your **flights** – long-haul and domestic – as early as six months in advance for the Christmas period. The inland and coastal provinces stagger their school holidays, but as a general rule the remaining school holidays roughly cover the following periods: Easter, mid-March to mid-April; winter, mid-June to mid-July; and spring, late September to early October. Exact **dates** for each year are given on the government's information website: ⓦinfo.gov.za/aboutsa/schoolcal.htm.

Phones

South Africa's **telephone** system, dominated by Telkom, generally works well. Public phone booths are found in every city and town, and are either coin- or card-operated. While international calls can be made from virtually any phone, it helps to have a **phone card**, as R20 won't last much more than a minute or two. Phone cards come in R20, R50, R100 and R200 denominations, available at Telkom offices, post offices and newsagents.

Mobile phones (referred to locally as cell phones or simply cells) are widely used in South Africa, with more mobiles than landlines in use. The competing networks – Vodacom, MTN, Cell C and VirginMobile – cover all the main areas and the national roads connecting them.

You can use a GSM/tri-band phone from outside the country in South Africa, but you will need a **roaming** agreement with your provider at home, which is likely to be expensive. A far cheaper alternative is to buy a **local SIM card** that replaces your home SIM card while you're in South Africa (check first that your phone isn't locked to your home network). The local SIM card contains your South African phone number, and you pay for airtime. Inexpensive starter packs (R100 or less) containing a SIM card and some airtime can be bought from the ubiquitous mobile phone shops and a number of other outlets, including supermarkets and the CNA chain of newsagents and supermarkets.

Another option is to **rent** a South African SIM card or a phone and SIM card when you arrive, via a company such as **Vodashop Renta Fone** (ⓦrentafone.net). Cards start at R5 a day and phones at R7. Phones (and GPS) rental can also be arranged with your car rental. Avis, Budget, Hertz and National all offer this, as does the Baz backpacker bus (see p.49).

CALLING HOME FROM SOUTH AFRICA

To dial out of South Africa, the international access code is ☎ 00. Remember to omit any initial zero in the number of the place you're phoning.

Australia international access code + 61
New Zealand international access code + 64
UK international access code + 44
US and Canada international access code + 1
Republic of Ireland international access code + 353

Taxes

Value-added tax (**VAT**) of fourteen percent is levied on most goods and services, though it's usually already included in any quoted price. Foreign visitors older than seven can claim back VAT on goods over R250. To do this, you must present an official tax receipt with your name on it for the goods, a non-South African passport and the purchased goods themselves, at the **airport** just before you fly out. You need to complete a VAT refund control sheet (VAT 255), which is obtainable at international airports. For further information contact the VAT Refund Administrator (☎011 394 1117, ⓦtaxrefunds.co.za).

Time

There is only one **time zone** in South Africa, two hours ahead of GMT year-round. If you're flying from anywhere in Europe, you shouldn't experience any jet lag.

Tipping

Ten to fifteen percent of the tab is the normal **tip** at restaurants and for taxis – but don't feel obliged to tip if service has been shoddy. Bear in mind that many of the people who'll be serving you rely on tips to supplement a meagre wage on which they support huge extended families. **Porters** at hotels normally get about R10 per bag. At South African garages and filling stations, someone will always be on hand to fill your vehicle and clean your windscreen, for which you should tip around R5–10. It is also usual at **hotels** to leave some money for the person who services your room. Many establishments, especially private game lodges, take (voluntary) communal tips when you check out – by far the fairest system, which ensures that all the low-profile staff behind the scenes get their share.

Tourist information

Given South Africa's booming tourism industry, it's not surprising that you'll have no difficulty finding **maps**, **books** and **brochures** before you leave. South African Tourism, the official organization promoting the country, is reasonably efficient: if there's an office near you, it's worth visiting for its free maps and **information** on hotels and organized tours. Alternatively, check its **website** ⓦ southafrica.net.

In South Africa itself, nearly every town, even down to the sleepiest *dorp*, has some sort of **tourist office** – sometimes connected to the museum, municipal offices or library – where you can pick up local maps, lists of B&Bs and travel advice. In larger cities such as Cape Town and Durban, you'll find several branches offering everything from hotel bookings to organized safari trips. We've given opening hours of tourist offices in the Guide, though they generally adhere to a standard schedule of Monday to Friday 8.30am to 5pm, with many offices also open on Saturdays and Sundays. In smaller towns some close between 1pm and 2pm, while in the bigger centres some have extended hours.

In this fast-changing country the best way of finding out what's happening is often by word of mouth, and for this, backpacker **hostels** are invaluable. If you're seeing South Africa on a budget, the useful notice boards, constant traveller traffic and largely helpful and friendly staff in the hostels will greatly smooth your travels.

To find out what's on, check out the entertainment pages of the daily **newspapers** or better still buy the *Mail & Guardian*, which comes out every Friday and lists the coming week's offerings in a comprehensive pullout supplement.

TRAVEL ADVISORIES

Australian Department of Foreign Affairs ⓦ dfat.gov.au.
British Foreign & Commonwealth Office ⓦ fco.gov.uk.
Canadian Department of Foreign Affairs ⓦ international.gc.ca.
Irish Department of Foreign Affairs ⓦ foreignaffairs.gov.ie.
New Zealand Ministry of Foreign Affairs ⓦ mfat.govt.nz.
US State Department ⓦ state.gov.

Travellers with disabilities

Facilities for **disabled travellers** in South Africa are not as sophisticated as those found in the developed world, but they're sufficient to ensure you have a satisfactory visit. By accident rather than design, you'll find pretty good **accessibility** to many buildings, as South Africans tend to build low (single-storey bungalows are the norm), with the result that you'll have to deal with fewer **stairs** than you may be accustomed to. As the car is king, you'll frequently find that you can drive to, and park right outside, your destination. There are organized **tours** and **holidays** specifically for people with disabilities, and activity-based packages for disabled travellers to South Africa are increasingly available. These packages allow wheelchair-bound visitors to take part in safaris, sport and a vast range of adventure **activities**, including whitewater rafting, horseriding, parasailing and zip-lining. Tours can either be taken as self-drive trips or as packages for large groups. The contacts below will be able to put you in touch with South Africa travel specialists.

USEFUL CONTACTS

ⓦ **access-able.com** US-based website aimed at travellers with disabilities that includes some useful information about South Africa.
ⓦ **disabledtravel.co.za** Website of occupational therapist Karin Coetzee aimed at disabled travellers with listings of accommodation, restaurants and attractions personally evaluated for accessibility, as well as useful links to everything from car rental and tours to orthopedic equipment.
ⓦ **flamingotours.co.za** Flamingo Tours and Disabled Ventures specializes in tours for tourists with special needs.
ⓦ **sanparks.org/groups/disabilities/general.php** Lists the wheelchair and mobility-impaired access and facilities that are available at South African National Parks.

Travelling with children

Travelling with **children** is straightforward in South Africa, whether you want to explore a city, relax on the beach, or head for the tranquility of the mountains. You'll find local people friendly, attentive and accepting of babies and young children. The following is aimed mainly at families with under-5s.

Although children up to 24 months only pay ten percent of the adult **airfare**, they get no seat or baggage allowance. Given this, you'd be well advised to secure bulkhead seats and reserve a basinet or sky cot, which can be attached to the bulkhead. **Basinets** are usually allocated to babies under six months, though some airlines use weight (under 10kg) as the criterion. From October 2014, parents travelling into South Africa with children may be asked to show the child's full **birth certificate**, and where only one parent is accompanying, parental or legal consent may be needed, such as an affidavit from the other parent or a court order. There are other requirements for **children travelling unaccompanied** or with adults who are not their parents: for further information, contact the South African Department of Home Affairs (🖤 dha.gov.za).

Given the size of the country, you're likely to be **driving** long distances. Aim to go slowly and plan a route that allows frequent stops – or perhaps take trains or flights between centres. The Garden Route, for example, is an ideal drive, with easy stops for picnics, particularly on the section between Mossel Bay and Storms River. The route between Johannesburg and Cape Town, conversely, is tedious.

Game viewing can be boring for young children, since it too involves a lot of driving – and disappointment, should the promised beasts fail to put in an appearance. Furthermore, of course, toddlers won't particularly enjoy watching animals from afar and through a window. If they are old enough to enjoy the experience, make sure they have their own **binoculars**. To get in closer, some animal parks, such as Tshukudu near Kruger, have semi-tame animals, while snake and reptile parks are an old South African favourite.

Family accommodation is plentiful, and hotels, guesthouses, B&Bs and a growing number of backpacker lodges have rooms with extra beds or interconnecting rooms. Kids usually stay for half-price. Self-catering options are worth considering, as most such establishments have a good deal of space to play in, and there'll often be a **pool**. A number of resorts are specifically aimed at families with older children, with suitable activities offered. The pick of the bunch is the **Forever** chain (🖤 fore versa.co.za), which has resorts in beautiful settings, including Keurboomstrand near Plettenberg Bay,

and two close to the Blyde River Canyon in Mpumalanga. Another excellent option is full-board family hotels, of which there are a number along the Wild Coast (see p.336), with playgrounds and canoes for paddling about lagoons, and often **nannies** to look after the kids during meals or for the whole day. Note that many **safari camps** don't allow children under 12, so you'll have to self-cater or camp at the national parks and those in KwaZulu-Natal.

Eating out with a baby or toddler is easy, particularly at an outdoor venue where they can get on unhindered with their exploration of the world. Some restaurants have highchairs and offer small portions. If in doubt, try the ubiquitous family-oriented **chains** such as Spur, Nando's or Wimpy.

Breast-feeding is practised by the majority of African mothers wherever they are, though you won't see many white women doing it in public. Be discreet, especially in more conservative areas – which is most of the country outside middle-class Cape Town, Johannesburg or Durban. There are relatively few **baby rooms** in public places for changing or feeding, although the situation is improving all the time and you shouldn't have a problem at shopping malls in the cities. You can buy disposable **nappies** wherever you go (imported brands are best), as well as wipes, bottles, formula and dummies. High-street chemists and the Clicks chain are the best places to buy baby goods. If you run out of **clothes**, the Woolworths chain has good-quality stuff, while the ubiquitous Pep stores, which are present in even the smallest towns, are an excellent source of cheap, functional clothes.

Malaria (see p.70) affects only a small part of the country, but think carefully about visiting such areas as the preventatives aren't recommended for under-2s. Avoid most of the major **game reserves**, particularly the Kruger National Park and those in KwaZulu-Natal, North West and Limpopo provinces, and opt instead for malaria-free reserves – Addo Elephant National Park in the Eastern Cape is an excellent choice. Malarial zones carry a considerably reduced risk in winter, so if you are set on going, this is the best time.

USEFUL CONTACTS

🖤 **capetownkids.co.za** Resources for parents and children in Cape Town.

🖤 **jozikids.co.za** Resources for parents and children in Johannesburg.

🖤 **kidscantravel.com** A useful website for planning a family holiday with lists of child-friendly accommodation.

Cape Town and the Cape Peninsula

VIEW OF LION'S HEAD AND THE TWELVE APOSTLES

1

Cape Town and the Cape Peninsula

Cape Town is Southern Africa's most beautiful, most romantic and most visited city. Its physical setting is extraordinary, something its pre-colonial Khoikhoi inhabitants acknowledged when they referred to Table Mountain, the city's most famous landmark, as Hoerikwaggo – the mountains in the sea. Even more extraordinary is that so close to the national park that extends over much of the peninsula, there's a pumping metropolis with a nightlife that matches the city's wildlife. You can swim with penguins at Boulders Beach and see the tip of the continent at Cape Point, take lunch at an Atlantic seaboard bistro, tipple at a Constantia wine estate in the afternoon, and party the night away in a Long Street club. All in a Cape Town day.

More than a scenic backdrop, **Table Mountain** is the solid core of Cape Town, dividing the city into distinct zones with public gardens, wilderness, forests, hiking routes, vineyards and desirable residential areas trailing down its lower slopes. Standing on the tabletop, you can look north for a giddy view of the **city centre**, its docks lined with matchbox ships. To the west, beyond the mountainous Twelve Apostles, the drop is sheer and your eye sweeps across Africa's priciest real estate, clinging to the slopes along the chilly but spectacularly beautiful **Atlantic seaboard**. To the south, the mountainsides are forested and several historic vineyards and the marvellous Botanical Gardens creep up the lower slopes. Beyond the oak-lined suburbs of Newlands and Constantia lies the warmer **False Bay seaboard**, which curves around towards **Cape Point**. Finally, relegated to the grim industrial east, are the coloured **townships** and black **ghettos** – a stark introduction to Cape Town when driving in from the airport towards the alluring Table Mountain, and an immediate reminder that you are visiting an unequal, divided city.

To appreciate Cape Town you need to spend time **outdoors**, as Capetonians do: they hike, picnic or sunbathe, often choose mountain bikes in preference to cars,

LONG STREET NIGHTLIFE

Highlights

❶ The Bo-Kaap One of Cape Town's oldest residential areas, its streets characterized by colourful nineteenth-century Cape Dutch and Georgian terraces. **See p.99**

❷ National Gallery Check out the sculpture *Butcher Boys* by Jane Alexander, the epitome of menace and brutality. **See p.94**

❸ Robben Island The infamous island prison where Nelson Mandela lived for nearly two decades. **See p.102**

❹ Kirstenbosch Gardens Picnic or hike in one of the world's loveliest gardens with its matchless rear wall – Table Mountain. **See p.106**

❺ Rotate up Table Mountain The revolving cable car is the city's best route to breathtaking views, without getting short of breath. **See p.108**

❻ Swim with penguins Boulders Beach offers wonderful bathing and is home to a colony of African penguins. **See p.122**

❼ Cape Point The dramatically rocky southernmost section of the Cape Peninsula offers spectacular views and walks. **See p.124**

❽ Township tour See where most Capetonians live and visit the vibrant Langa Quarter. **See p.126**

❾ Long Street nightlife Party till the early hours along the city centre's café, pub and nightclub strip. **See p.145**

HIGHLIGHTS ARE MARKED ON THE MAP ON P.84

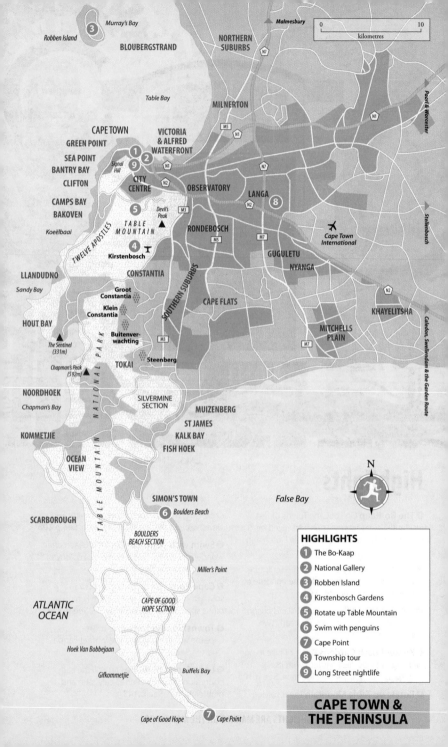

Murray's Bay

③ Robben Island

BLOUBERGSTRAND

Malmesbury

NORTHERN
SUBURBS

N7

Table Bay

MILNERTON

M5

N1

CAPE TOWN

GREEN POINT

VICTORIA
& ALFRED
WATERFRONT

N1

N7

SEA POINT

① ②

N1

Pearl & Worcester

BANTRY BAY

⑨

Signal
Hill

CLIFTON

CITY
CENTRE

N2

OBSERVATORY

LANGA

⑧

CAMPS BAY

BAKOVEN

⑤

Devil's
Peak

M3

RONDEBOSCH

Koeëlbaai

TABLE
MOUNTAIN

N2

Cape Town
International

TWELVE APOSTLES

④

Kirstenbosch

M5

GUGULETU

Stellenbosch

LLANDUDNO

CONSTANTIA

NYANGA

Sandy Bay

Groot
Constantia

SOUTHERN SUBURBS

N2

Klein
Constantia

CAPE FLATS

KHAYELITSHA

HOUT BAY

Buitenver-
wachting

M3

MITCHELLS
PLAIN

The Sentinel
(331m)

Steenberg

M7

TOKAI

Chapman's Peak
(592m)

NOORDHOEK

SILVERMINE
SECTION

MUIZENBERG

Chapman's Bay

ST JAMES

KOMMETJIE

KALK BAY

FISH HOEK

Caledon, Swellendam & the Garden Route

NATIONAL PARK

OCEAN
VIEW

N

SIMON'S TOWN

False Bay

SCARBOROUGH

⑥ Boulders Beach

TABLE MOUNTAIN

BOULDERS
BEACH SECTION

Miller's Point

ATLANTIC
OCEAN

CAPE OF GOOD
HOPE SECTION

Hoek Van Bobbejaan

Gifkommetjie

Buffels Bay

Cape of Good Hope

⑦ Cape Point

0   10
kilometres

HIGHLIGHTS

① The Bo-Kaap
② National Gallery
③ Robben Island
④ Kirstenbosch Gardens
⑤ Rotate up Table Mountain
⑥ Swim with penguins
⑦ Cape Point
⑧ Township tour
⑨ Long Street nightlife

CAPE TOWN &
THE PENINSULA

and turn **adventure activities** into an obsession. Sailboarders from around the world head for Table Bay for some of the world's best windsurfing, and the brave (or unhinged) jump off Lion's Head and paraglide down close to the Clifton beachfront. But the city offers sedate pleasures as well, along its hundreds of paths and 150km of beaches.

Cape Town's rich urban texture is immediately apparent in its varied **architecture**: an indigenous Cape Dutch style, rooted in northern Europe, seen at its most diverse in the Constantia wine estates, which were influenced by French refugees in the seventeenth century; Muslim dissidents and slaves, freed in the nineteenth century, added their minarets to the skyline; and the English, who invaded and freed these slaves, introduced Georgian and Victorian buildings. In the tightly packed terraces of the present-day Bo-Kaap and the tenements of District Six, coloured descendants of slaves evolved a unique, evocatively Capetonian brand of jazz, which is well worth catching live if you can.

Brief history

San hunter-gatherers, South Africa's first human inhabitants, moved freely through the Cape Peninsula for tens of millennia before being edged into the interior some two thousand years ago by the arrival of sheep-herding **Khoikhoi** migrants from the north. Over the following 1600 years, the Khoikhoi held sway over the Cape pastures. **Portuguese** mariners, in search of a stopoff point en route to East Africa and the East Indies, first rounded the Cape in the 1480s, and named it Cabo de Boa Esperanza (Cape of Good Hope), but their attempts at trading with the Khoikhoi were short lived.

The Cape goes Dutch

The Europeans did not seriously attempt to create a permanent stopping-off point at the Cape until the **Dutch East India Company** (VOC) cruised into Table Bay in 1652 and set up shop. The VOC, the world's largest corporation at the time, planned little more than a halfway house, to provide fresh produce to their ships trading between Europe and the East. Their small landing party, led by **Jan van Riebeeck**, built a mud fort where the Grand Parade now stands and established **vegetable gardens**, which they hoped to work with indigenous labour.

The Khoikhoi were understandably none too keen to swap their freedom for a nine-to-five job, so Van Riebeeck began to import **slaves** in 1658, first from West Africa and later the East Indies. The growth of the Dutch settlement alarmed the Khoikhoi, who in 1659 tried to drive the Europeans out; however, they were defeated and had to cede the peninsula to the colonists. By 1700, the settlement had grown into an urban centre, referred to as "Kaapstad" (Cape Town).

During the early eighteenth century, Western Cape Khoikhoi society disintegrated, **German** and **French** religious refugees swelled the European population, and slavery became the economic backbone of the colony, now a minor colonial village of canals and low, whitewashed, flat-roofed houses. By 1750, however, Cape Town was a town of over a thousand buildings, with 2500 inhabitants.

WINDY CITY

Weather is an abiding obsession of Capetonians, particularly the **southeaster**, the cool summer wind that blows in across False Bay. It can singlehandedly determine the kind of day you're going to have, and when it gusts at over 60km/h you won't want to be outdoors, let alone on the beach. Conversely, its gentler incarnation as the so-called **Cape Doctor** brings welcome relief on humid summer days, and lays the famous cloudy tablecloth on top of Table Mountain.

1

Goodbye slavery, hello segregation

In 1795, **Britain**, deeply concerned by Napoleonic expansionism, grabbed Cape Town to secure the strategic sea route to the East. This displeased the settlement's Calvinist Dutch burghers, but was better news for the substantially Muslim slave population, as Britain ordered the **abolition of slavery** in 1834. The British also allowed **freedom of religion**, and South Africa's first mosque was soon built by freed slaves, in Dorp Street in the Bo-Kaap.

By the turn of the nineteenth century, Cape Town had become one of the most cosmopolitan places in the world and a seaport of major significance, growing under the influence of the British Empire. The Commercial Exchange was completed in 1819, followed by department stores, banks and insurance company buildings. In the 1860s the docks were begun, Victoria Road was built from the city to Sea Point, and the suburban railway line to Wynberg, one of the southern suburbs, was laid. Since slavery had been abolished, Victorian Cape Town had to be built by **convicts** and prisoners of war transported from the colonial frontier in the Eastern Cape (see p.300). Racial segregation wasn't far behind, and an outbreak of bubonic plague in 1901 gave the town council a pretext to establish **N'dabeni**, Cape Town's first black location, near Maitland.

In 1910, Cape Town was drawn into the political centre of the newly federated South Africa when it became the **legislative capital** of the Union (see p.641). Africans and coloureds, excluded from the cosy deal between Boers and the British, had to find expression in the workplace. In 1919, they flexed their collective muscle on the docks, forming the mighty **Industrial and Commercial Workers Union**, which boasted two hundred thousand members in its heyday.

Competing nationalisms

Increasing industrialization brought an influx of black workers to the city, who were housed in the locations of **Guguletu** and **Nyanga**, built in 1945. Three years later, the whites-only National Party came to power, promising a fearful white electorate that it would reverse the flow of Africans to the cities. In Cape Town it introduced a policy favouring coloureds for employment, rather than Africans, and among Africans, only men who had jobs were admitted to Cape Town (the women were excluded altogether), and the construction of family accommodation for Africans was forbidden.

Langa township, a few kilometres east of the city's southern suburbs, became a stronghold of the exclusively black **Pan Africanist Congress** (PAC), which organized a peaceful anti-pass demonstration in Cape Town on April 8, 1960. During the demonstration, police fired on the crowd, killing three people and wounding many more. As a result, the government declared a state of emergency and banned anti-apartheid opposition groups, including the PAC and ANC.

In 1966, the notorious **Group Areas Act** was used to uproot whole coloured communities from District Six and move them to the desolate **Cape Flats**. Here, rampant gangsterism took root and remains one of Cape Town's most pressing problems today. To compound the issue, the National Party stripped away coloured representation on the town council in 1972.

Resistance resumes

Eleven years later, at a huge meeting on the Cape Flats, the extra-parliamentary opposition defied government repression and re-formed as the **United Democratic Front**, heralding a period of intensified opposition to apartheid. In 1986, one of the major pillars crumbled when the government was forced to scrap influx control; blacks began pouring into Cape Town seeking work and erecting shantytowns, making Cape Town one of the fastest-growing cities in the world. On February 11, 1990, the city's history took a neat twist when, just hours after being released from prison, **Nelson**

THE LANGUAGE OF COLOUR

It's striking just how un-African Cape Town looks and sounds. Halfway between East and West, Cape Town drew its population from Africa, Asia and Europe, and traces of all three continents are found in the genes, language, culture, religion and cuisine of South Africa's coloured population. **Afrikaans** (a close relative of Dutch) is the mother tongue of more than half the city's population. Having said that, a substantial number of Capetonians are born English-speakers and **English** punches well above its weight as the local lingua franca, which, in this multilingual society, virtually everyone can speak and understand.

Afrikaans is the mother tongue of a large proportion of the city's **coloured** residents, as well as many whites. The term "coloured" is contentious, but in South Africa it doesn't have the same tainted connotations as in Britain and the US, referring simply to South Africans of mixed race. Most brown-skinned people in Cape Town (over fifty percent of Capetonians) are coloureds, with Asian, African and Khoikhoi ancestry.

Mandela made his first public speech from the balcony of City Hall to a jubilant crowd spilling across the Grand Parade, the very site of the first Dutch fort. Four years later, he entered the formerly whites-only Parliament, 500m away, as South Africa's first democratically elected president.

Transformation

One of the anomalies of the 1994 election was that while most of South Africa delivered an **ANC landslide**, the Western Cape returned the **National Party**, the party that invented apartheid, as its provincial government. Politics in South Africa were not, it turned out, divided along a faultline that separated whites from the rest of the population as many had assumed; the majority of coloureds had voted for the party that had once stripped them of the vote, regarding it with less suspicion than they did the ANC. The Western Cape and its capital have consistently bucked South Africa's national trend of overwhelming ANC dominance. Since 2006 both have been governed by the liberal Democratic Alliance (DA), which maintains Cape Town as the city in the country with the least corruption and best infrastructure and facilities, though there have been violent protests in the townships about non-delivery of services. The city also suffers from a slew of other problems – poverty, unemployment, rampant crime and high infection rates for HIV and TB – with housing one of the biggest issues facing the metropolis (and, indeed, the whole of South Africa). Planners project that within the next twenty years the city's **population** will grow from its present 3.5 million to anywhere between five and seven million inhabitants. Cape Town remains a divided city, and one where inequality is extreme.

The City Centre

Strand Street marks the edge of Cape Town's original beachfront (though you'd never guess it today), and all urban development to its north stands on reclaimed land. To its south is the **Upper City Centre**, containing the remains of the city's 350-year-old historic core, which has survived the ravages of modernization and apartheid-inspired urban clearance, and emerged with enough charm to make it South Africa's most pleasing city centre. The entire area from Strand Street to the southern foot of the mountain is a collage of Georgian, Cape Dutch, Victorian and twentieth-century architecture, as well as being the place where Europe, Asia and Africa meet in markets, alleyways and mosques. Among the drawcards here are **Parliament**, the **Company's Gardens** and many of Cape Town's major **museums**. North of Strand Street to the shore, the **Lower City Centre** takes in the still-functional **Duncan Dock**.

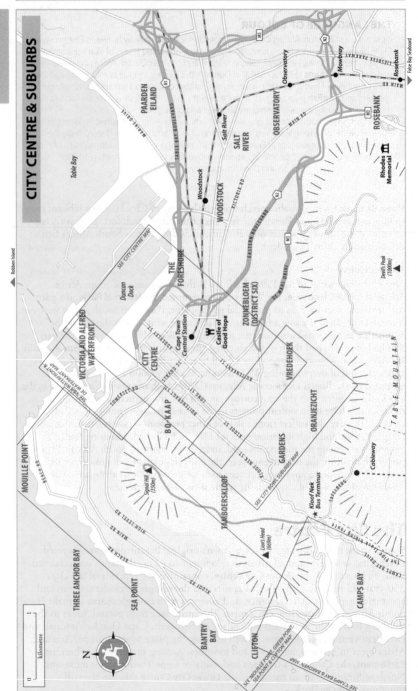

CITY CENTRE & SUBURBS

Robben Island

MOUILLE POINT

Table Bay

PAARDEN EILAND

Salt River

Woodstock

Mowbray

Rosebank

Observatory

OBSERVATORY

SALT RIVER

WOODSTOCK

ROSEBANK

Rhodes Memorial

Devil's Peak (1000m)

THE FORESHORE

Duncan Dock

VICTORIA AND ALFRED WATERFRONT

CITY CENTRE

Cape Town Central Station

Castle of Good Hope

ZONNEBLOEM (DISTRICT SIX)

VREDEHOEK

BO-KAAP

Signal Hill (350m)

TAMBOERSKLOOF

GARDENS

ORANJEZICHT

TABLE MOUNTAIN

Cableway

Lion's Head (669m)

Kloof Nek Bus Terminus

the Pipe Track hiking route

SEA POINT

THREE ANCHOR BAY

BANTRY BAY

CLIFTON

CAMPS BAY

SEE CAMPS BAY & BAKOVEN MAP

SEE MOUILLE POINT, GREEN POINT, SEA POINT & CLIFTON MAP

SEE CITY BOWL SUBURBS' MAP

SEE CITY CENTRE MAP

SEE SEA POINT & WATERFRONT & DE WATERKANT MAP

N

0   1   kilometre

Table Bay Seaboard

The Upper City Centre

Adderley Street, running from the train station in the north to the Gardens in the south, is the obvious orientation axis here. To its east, and close to each other just off Strand Street, are the **Castle of Good Hope**, the site of **District Six**, the **Grand Parade** and the **City Hall**. The district to the west of Adderley Street is the closest South Africa gets to a European quarter – a tight network of streets with cafés, buskers, bookshops, street stalls and antique shops congregating around the pedestrianized **St George's Mall** and **Greenmarket Square**. The **Bo-Kaap**, or Muslim district, three blocks further west across Buitengragt (which means the Outer Canal, but is actually a street), exudes a piquant contrast to this, with its minarets, spice shops and cafés selling curried snacks.

Southwest of Adderley Street, where it takes a sharp right into Wale Street, is the symbolic heart of Cape Town, with **Parliament**, museums, archives and De Tuynhuys – the Western Cape office of the President – arranged around the **Company's Gardens**.

Adderley Street

Once the place to shop in Cape Town, **Adderley Street**, lined with handsome buildings from several centuries, is still worth a stroll today. Its attractive streetscape has been blemished somewhat by a series of large 1960s and 1970s shopping centres but, just minutes from crowded malls, among the streets and alleys around Greenmarket Square, you can still find some human scale and historic texture. One of the ugliest buildings erected in the 1970s is the **Golden Acre** shopping complex, dominating the north end of Adderley Street – this area around Cape Town station is a hub for much of Cape Town's public transport.

The Slave Lodge

On the corner of Adderley and Wale streets • Mon–Sat 10am–5pm • R30 • ☎ 021 467 7229, ⓦ iziko.org.za/museums/slave-lodge

The Slave Lodge was built in 1679 to house the human chattels of the Dutch East India Company (VOC) – the largest single slaveholder at the Cape – and by the 1770s, almost a thousand slaves were held here. Under VOC administration (see p.85), the lodge also became the Cape Colony's main brothel, its doors thrown open to all comers for an hour each night. In 1810 the British administration decided to use the lodge as the Supreme Court, a function it retained for over a century. To clear out the government-owned slaves, it auctioned most off to private individuals, while the remaining two hundred were moved to smaller accommodation in the Company's Gardens, where they remained until they were freed in 1827, nearly ten years earlier than the rest of the slaves at the Cape. From 1914, the building was used as government offices, and now houses an exhibition, still evolving, about slavery.

THE NAMING OF ADDERLEY STREET

Although the Dutch used Robben Island as a political prison (see p.102), the South African mainland only narrowly escaped becoming a second Australia, a **penal colony** where British felons and enemies of the state could be dumped. By the 1840s, "respectable Australians" were lobbying for a ban on the transportation of criminals to the Antipodes, and the British authorities responded by trying to divert convicts to the Cape.

In 1848, the British ship *Neptune* set sail from Bermuda for Cape Town with a cargo of 282 prisoners. When news of its departure reached Cape Town there was outrage; five thousand citizens gathered on the Grand Parade the following year to hear prominent liberals denounce the British government. When the ship docked in September 1849, governor Sir Harry Smith forbade any criminal from landing while, back in London, politician **Charles Adderley** successfully addressed the House of Commons in support of the Cape colonists. In February 1850, the *Neptune* set off for Tasmania with its full complement of convicts, and grateful Capetonians renamed the city's main thoroughfare **Adderley Street**.

1

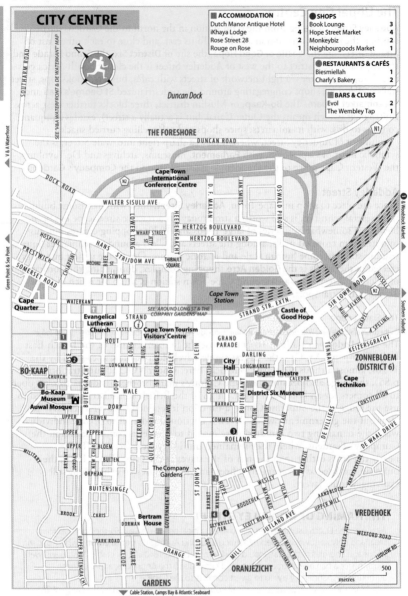

CITY CENTRE

■ ACCOMMODATION	
Dutch Manor Antique Hotel	3
iKhaya Lodge	4
Rose Street 28	2
Rouge on Rose	1

● SHOPS	
Book Lounge	3
Hope Street Market	4
Monkeybiz	2
Neighbourgoods Market	1

● RESTAURANTS & CAFÉS	
Biesmiellah	1
Charly's Bakery	2

■ BARS & CLUBS	
Evol	2
The Wembley Tap	1

Duncan Dock

THE FORESHORE

DUNCAN ROAD

Cape Town International Conference Centre

WALTER SISULU AVE

HERTZOG BOULEVARD

HERTZOG BOULEVARD

Cape Town Station

Cape Quarter

Evangelical Lutheran Church

Cape Town Tourism Visitors' Centre

Castle of Good Hope

BO-KAAP

Bo-Kaap Museum

Auwal Mosque

City Hall

GRAND PARADE

Fugard Theatre

District Six Museum

ZONNEBLOEM (DISTRICT 6)

Cape Technikon

The Company Gardens

ROELAND

Bertram House

VREDEHOEK

ORANJEZICHT

GARDENS

▼ Cable Station, Camps Bay & Atlantic Seaboard

0 ——— 500
metres

Long Street

Parallel to Adderley Street, buzzing one-way **Long Street** is one of Cape Town's most diverse thoroughfares, best known as the city's **main nightlife strip**. When it was first settled by Muslims some three hundred years ago, Long Street marked Cape Town's boundary; by the 1960s, it had become a sleazy thoroughfare of drinking holes and whorehouses. Miraculously, it's all still here, but with a whiff of gentrification and a rather boring section of discount furniture shops and fast-food joints; it deserves

1

SLAVERY AT THE CAPE

For nearly two centuries – more than half Cape Town's existence as an urban settlement – the city's economic and social structures depended on **slavery**. Although it was officially **abolished** at the Cape in 1838, its legacy lives on in South Africa. The country's coloured inhabitants, who make up fifty percent of Cape Town's population, are largely descendants of slaves and indigenous Khoisan people, and some historians argue that apartheid was a natural successor to slavery.

By the end of the eighteenth century, the almost 26,000-strong slave population of the Cape exceeded that of the free burghers (citizens, mostly of European extraction). Despite the profound impact this had on the development of social relations in South Africa, it remained one of the most neglected topics of the country's history, until the publication in the 1980s of a number of studies on slavery. There's still a reluctance on the part of most coloureds to acknowledge their slave origins.

Few, if any, slaves were captured at the Cape for export, making the colony unique in the African trade. Paradoxically, while people were being captured elsewhere on the continent for export to the Americas, the Cape administration, forbidden by the VOC from enslaving the local indigenous population, had to look further afield. Of the 63,000 slaves imported to the Cape before 1808, most came from East Africa, Madagascar, India and Indonesia, representing one of the broadest cultural mixes of any slave society. This diversity initially worked against the establishment of a unified group identity, but eventually a **Creolized culture** emerged which, among other things, played a major role in the development of the Afrikaans language.

exploration from the Wale Street junction towards Table Mountain.

Mosques still coexist with bars, *dagga* (weed) is readily available, and antique dealers, craft shops, bookshops and cafés do a good trade. The street is packed with backpacker hostels and a couple of upmarket hotels, though it can be very noisy into the early hours from the nightclubs. At night it's safe enough to pub or club crawl, and you'll always be able to find taxis.

Long Street Baths

Long and Orange streets • **Pool** daily 7am–7pm • R18 • **Turkish baths** Men Tues 1–7pm, Wed & Fri 8am–7pm, Sun 8am–noon; Women Mon, Thurs & Sat 9am–6pm • R40/hour • ☎ 021 400 3302

The **Long Street Baths** is an unpretentious and relaxing historic Cape Town institution, established in 1908 in an Edwardian building. Though shabby, it is a great place to do some lengths, or to get thoroughly clean in the Turkish baths (open to men and women at separate times).

Palm Tree Mosque

185 Long St • Not open to the public

An unmistakable landmark, just south of where Long Street crosses Leeuwen Street, the **Palm Tree Mosque** is fronted by a lone palm tree, its fronds caressing the upper storey. Significant as the only surviving eighteenth-century house in the street, it was bought in 1807 by members of the local Muslim community, who turned the upper floor into a mosque and the lower floor into living quarters.

Pan African Market

76 Long St • Oct–April Mon–Fri 8.30am–5.30pm & Sat 9am–3.30pm, May–Sept Mon–Fri 9am–5pm & Sat 9am–3pm • ⓦ panafrica.co.za

One of Cape Town's most intriguing places for African crafts, and one of the easiest to miss, is the **Pan African Market**, towards the north end of Long Street. Its inconspicuous frontage belies the three-floor warren of passageways and rooms that burst at the seams with traders selling vast quantities of art and artefacts from all over the continent. With a team of in-house seamstresses at the ready, this is also the place to get kitted out in African garb.

1

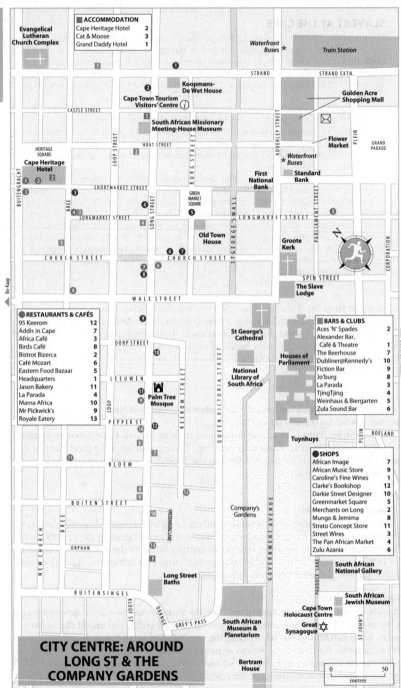

ACCOMMODATION
Cape Heritage Hotel	2
Cat & Moose	3
Grand Daddy Hotel	1

Evangelical Lutheran Church Complex

Waterfront Buses

Train Station

STRAND

STRAND EXTN.

Koopmans-De Wet House

Cape Town Tourism Visitors' Centre (i)

CASTLE STREET

Golden Acre Shopping Mall

ADDERLEY STREET

South African Missionary Meeting-House Museum

HOUT STREET

Flower Market

LOOP STREET

BURG STREET

PLEIN

GRAND PARADE

HERITAGE SQUARE

Cape Heritage Hotel

BUITENGRACHT

Waterfront Buses

First National Bank

Standard Bank

SHORTMARKET STREET

BREE

GREEN MARKET SQUARE

LONGMARKET STREET

ST GEORGE'S MALL

LONGMARKET STREET

LONG STREET

Old Town House

Groote Kerk

PARLIAMENT STREET

CORPORATION

CHURCH STREET

CHURCH STREET

SPIN STREET

The Slave Lodge

N

WALE STREET

Bo-Kaap

District Six Museum

RESTAURANTS & CAFÉS
95 Keerom	12
Addis in Cape	7
Africa Café	3
Birds Café	8
Bistrot Bizerca	2
Café Mozart	6
Eastern Food Bazaar	5
Headquarters	1
Jason Bakery	11
La Parada	4
Mama Africa	10
Mr Pickwick's	9
Royale Eatery	13

DORP STREET

St George's Cathedral

Houses of Parliament

National Library of South Africa

BARS & CLUBS
Aces 'N' Spades	2
Alexander Bar, Café & Theatre	1
The Beerhouse	7
Dubliner@Kennedy's	10
Fiction Bar	9
Jo'burg	8
La Parada	3
TjingTjing	4
Weinhaus & Biergarten	5
Zula Sound Bar	6

LEEUWEN

Palm Tree Mosque

LOOP

KEEROM STREET

QUEEN VICTORIA STREET

PEPPER ST

BLOEM

Tuynhuys

PLEIN

ROELAND

SHOPS
African Image	7
African Music Store	9
Caroline's Fine Wines	1
Clarke's Bookshop	12
Darkie Street Designer	10
Greenmarket Square	5
Merchants on Long	2
Mungo & Jemima	8
Strato Concept Store	11
Street Wires	3
The Pan African Market	4
Zulu Azania	6

BUITEN STREET

BREE

ORPHAN

NEW CHURCH

WEDDERBURG LANE

Company's Gardens

GOVERNMENT AVENUE

South African National Gallery

South African Jewish Museum

PADDOCK LANE

Cape Town Holocaust Centre

Great Synagogue

ST JOHN'S

BUITENSINGEL

KLOOF ST

Long Street Baths

ORANGE

GREY'S PASS

South African Museum & Planetarium

CITY CENTRE: AROUND LONG ST & THE COMPANY GARDENS

Bertram House

0	50
	metres

South African Missionary Meeting-House Museum

40 Long St, on the corner of Hout St • Mon–Fri 9am–4pm • Free

The **South African Missionary Meeting-House Museum** was the first missionary church in the country, where slaves were taught literacy and instructed in Christianity. This exceptional building, completed in 1804 by the South African Missionary Society, has one of the most beautiful frontages in Cape Town. Inside, an impressive Neoclassical timber **pulpit** perches high above the congregation on a pair of columns, framing an inlaid image of an angel in flight.

Greenmarket Square

Turning east from Long Street into Shortmarket Street, you'll skim the edge of **Greenmarket Square**, which is worth a little exploration to take in the cobbled streets, the market and the grand buildings. As its name suggests, the square started as a vegetable market, though it's now home to a flea market selling crafts, jewellery and hippie clobber.

Michaelis Collection at the Old Town House

Old Town House, Greenmarket Square • Mon–Fri 10am–5pm, Sat 10am–4pm • R20 • ☎ 021 481 3933, ⓦ iziko.org.za

On the western side of Greenmarket Square are the solid limewashed walls and small shuttered windows of the **Old Town House**, entered from Longmarket Street. Built in the mid-1700s, this beautiful example of Cape Dutch architecture houses the **Michaelis Collection** of predominantly minor but still significant Dutch and Flemish portrait, townscape, interior and landscape paintings.

St George's Mall

East of Greenmarket Square is **St George's Mall**, a pedestrianized road that runs northeast from Wale Street to Thibault Square, near the train station. Coffee shops, snack bars and lots of street traders and buskers make this a more pleasant route between the station and Company's Gardens than Adderley Street.

Church Street

Crossing St George's Mall towards its southern end, **Church Street** and the surrounding area abound with antique dealers, selling Africana and bric-a-brac. The pedestrianized section, between Long Street and Loop Street, is a pleasant area where the smell of coffee pervades the art galleries, and you can rest your legs at one of the outdoor tables at *Café Mozart* (see p.139).

Bree Street

Dotted with design and boutique shops and humming with restaurants and bars, **Bree Street** has become the new stomping ground for hipsters and well-heeled Capetonians. The conversion of the old buildings into new shops, restaurants and cafés has enhanced the lovely architecture that may have been overlooked in the past, and sparked the reclamation of the pavements by pedestrians. The intersection with Longmarket Street is the best spot to get a feel for this vibrant road.

St George's Cathedral

Wale street • Mon–Fri 8.30am–4.30pm, Sat 8am–12.30pm • Free • Church services Mon–Fri at 7.15am, also Tues–Thurs at 8am & 4pm, Wed at 10am & Sat 8am; Sun Mass at 9.30am • ⓦ sgcathedral.co.za

St George's Cathedral is interesting as much for its history as for its Herbert Baker Victorian Gothic design; on September 7, 1986, **Desmond Tutu** hammered on its doors, symbolically demanding to be enthroned as South Africa's first black archbishop. Three years later, he heralded the last days of apartheid by leading thirty thousand people from the cathedral to the City Hall, where he coined his now famous slogan for the new order: "We are the rainbow people!" he told the crowd, "We are the new people of South Africa!"

1

The crypt beneath the cathedral houses a decent café as well as hosting jazz and other concerts (ⓦ thecryptjazz.com).

Government Avenue and around

A stroll down pedestrianized **Government Avenue**, the southwest extension of Adderley Street, makes for one of the most serene walks in central Cape Town. This oak-lined boulevard runs past the rear of Parliament through the gardens, and its benches are frequently occupied by snoring tramps.

National Library of South Africa

5 Queen Victoria St • Mon, Tues, Thurs & Fri 9am–6pm, Wed 10am–5pm • Free • ⓦ nlsa.ac.za

At the northern end of Government Avenue, the **National Library** of **South Africa** houses one of the country's best collections of antiquarian historical and natural history books, covering Southern Africa. Built with the revenue from a tax on wine, it opened in 1822 as one of the first free libraries in the world.

Company's Gardens

Queen Victoria St

Stretching from the South African Library to the South African Museum, the **Company's Gardens** were the initial *raison d'être* for the Dutch settlement at the Cape. Established in 1652 to supply fresh greens to Dutch East India Company ships travelling between the Netherlands and the East, the gardens were initially worked by imported slave labour. At the end of the seventeenth century, the gardens were turned over to botanical horticulture for Cape Town's growing colonial elite. Ponds, lawns, landscaping and a crisscross web of oak-shaded walkways were introduced. Today the gardens are full of local plants, the result of long-standing European interest in Cape botany, and are a pleasant place to meander, featuring a pleasantly shady outdoor café.

Tuynhuys

About fifty metres south of the South African Library along Government Avenue, you'll see the grand buildings and tended flowerbeds of **Tuynhuys**, the Cape Town office (but not residence) of the president (closed to the public). Originally a Dutch building, it was remodelled during the governorship of **Lord Charles Somerset** (1814–26). The energy Somerset put into implementing an official policy of Anglicization at the Cape was matched only by his private obsession with architecture. Among the features he introduced to the building was the veranda sheltering under an elegantly curving canopy, supported on slender iron columns.

South African National Gallery

Government Avenue, Company's Gardens • Daily 10am–5pm • R30 • ⓦ iziko.org.za/museums/south-african-national-gallery

The **South African National Gallery** is an essential port of call for anyone interested in the local art scene, and includes a small but excellent permanent collection of contemporary South African art. Be sure to take in Jane Alexander's sculpture *Butcher Boys*, which figuratively portrays South Africa's inherent menace and violence.

You'll also find a fine display of traditional works from the southeast of the continent, based around a small collection donated by the German government. The exhibits, which include beadwork, carvings and craft objects, were chosen for their aesthetic qualities and rarity, and represent the gallery's policy of focusing on neglected parts of South Africa's heritage. In addition, another room contains minor works by British artists including George Romney, Thomas Gainsborough and Joshua Reynolds, as well as some Pre-Raphaelite paintings.

CLOCKWISE FROM TOP LEFT OSTRICH EGGS FOR SALE; THE CLOCK TOWER (P.102); CITY HALL AND THE GRAND PARADE (P.98) >

1

South African Jewish Museum
88 Hatfield St • Sun–Thurs 10am–5pm, Fri 10am–2pm • R50 • ⓦ sajewishmuseum.co.za

The **South African Jewish Museum** is partially housed in South Africa's first synagogue, built in 1863. One of Cape Town's most ambitious and successful permanent exhibitions, it tells the story of South African Jewry from its beginnings over 150 years ago to the present – a narrative that starts in the Old Synagogue, from which visitors cross, via a gangplank, to the upper level of a new two-storey building, symbolically re-enacting the arrival by boat of the first Jewish immigrants at Table Bay in the 1840s. Multimedia interactive displays, models and Judaica artefacts follow three threads: "**Memories**", looking at the roots and experiences of the immigrants; "**Reality**", covering their integration into South Africa; and "**Dreams**", examining a diversity of views about the role of Jews in South Africa, their relationship to Israel and their position in the world.

The **basement level** houses a wonderfully executed walk-through reconstruction of a Lithuanian village (most South African Jews have their nineteenth-century roots in Lithuania). A good restaurant, shop and auditorium are also housed in the museum complex.

Cape Town Holocaust Centre
88 Hatfield St • Mon–Thurs & Sun 10am–5pm, Fri 10am–1pm • Free • ⓦ ctholocaust.co.za

Opened in 1999, the **Holocaust Exhibition** is one of the most moving and brilliantly executed museums in Cape Town. Housed upstairs in the Holocaust Centre (in the same complex as the Jewish Museum), it resonates sharply in a country that only recently emerged from an era of racial oppression – a connection that the exhibition makes explicitly. Exhibits trace the history of anti-Semitism in Europe, culminating with the Nazis' Final Solution; they also look at South Africa's Greyshirts, who were motivated by Nazi propaganda during the 1930s and were later absorbed into the National Party. The story is told through text, photographs, artefacts (such as a concentration camp uniform), film clips, soundtracks, multimedia and interactive video.

The Great Synagogue
88 Hatfield St (entrance through same gate as Jewish Museum) • Mon 10am–1pm, Tues–Thurs & Sun 10am–4pm

The **Great Synagogue** is one of Cape Town's outstanding religious buildings. Designed by the Scottish architects Parker & Forsyth and completed in 1905, its facade features two soaring towers after the style of central European Baroque churches. The interior is dominated by an impressive copper-clad dome that arches over an alcove containing religious objects and beautifully decorated with golden mosaics.

The South African Museum
25 Queen Victoria St • Daily 10am–5pm • R30 • ⓦ iziko.org.za/museums/south-african-museum

The nation's premier museum of natural history and human sciences, the **South African Museum**, west of Government Avenue, is notable for its **ethnographic galleries**, which contain some very good displays on the traditional arts and crafts of several African groups and some exceptional examples of rock art. Upstairs, the **natural history galleries** display mounted mammals, dioramas of prehistoric Karoo reptiles, and Table Mountain flora and fauna. A highlight is the four-storey "whale well", in which a collection of beautiful whale skeletons hang like massive mobiles, accompanied by the eerie strains of their song.

The Planetarium
25 Queen Victoria St • Shows daily 11am–3pm & also Tues 8pm, closed first Mon of month outside school holidays • R40 • ⓦ iziko.org.za /museums/planetarium

The **Planetarium**, attached to the South African Museum, is recommended if you want to see the constellations of the southern hemisphere, accompanied by informed

1

commentary. There's also a changing programme of shows covering topics such as San sky myths. Leaflets at the museum provide a list of forthcoming attractions (or check the website), and you can buy a monthly chart of the current night sky.

Bertram House

Hiddingh Campus, Orange St • Mon & Fri 10am–5pm • Donation requested • ⓦ iziko.org.za/museums/bertram-house

At the southernmost end of Government Avenue, you'll come upon **Bertram House**, whose beautiful two-storey brick facade looks out across a fragrant herb garden. Built in the 1840s, the museum is significant as the only surviving brick Georgian-style house in Cape Town, and displays typical furniture and objects of a well-to-do colonial British family in the first half of the nineteenth century.

Bertram House was extensively restored to its current state in the 1980s (and again in 2010): imported face brick and Welsh slate were used to re-create the original facade, while the interior walls were redecorated in their earlier dark green and ochre, based on the evidence of paint scrapings. The reception rooms are decorated in the Regency style, while the porcelain is predominantly nineteenth-century English.

Houses of Parliament

Parliament St • National Assembly tours Mon–Fri on the hour 9am–noon • Free • Book one week in advance for tours & bring passport or ID • ☎ 021 403 2266, ✉ tours@parliament.gov.za, ⓦ parliament.gov.za

South Africa's **Houses of Parliament** are a complex of interlinking buildings, with labyrinthine corridors connecting hundreds of offices, debating chambers and miscellaneous other rooms. Many of these are relics of the 1980s reformist phase of apartheid when, in the interests of racial segregation, there were three distinct legislative complexes sited here to cater to different "races".

The original wing, completed in 1885, is an imposing Victorian Neoclassical building that first served as the legislative assembly of the Cape Colony. After the Boer republics and British colonies amalgamated in 1910, it became the parliament of the Union of South Africa. This is the old parliament, where over seven decades of repressive legislation, including apartheid laws, were passed.

The new chamber was built in 1983 as part of the **tricameral parliament**, P.W. Botha's attempt to avert majority rule by trying to co-opt Indians and coloureds – but in their own separate debating chambers. The tricameral chamber, where the three non-African races on occasions met together, is now the **National Assembly**, where you can watch sessions of parliament. One-hour **tours** leave from the Plein Street entrance to Parliament; this is also where you buy day tickets to the debating sessions, the most interesting of which is Question Time (Wed from 3pm) when ministers are quizzed by MPs.

Castle of Good Hope

Buitenkant & Darling sts, opposite the Grand Parade • **Castle** Daily 9am–4pm • R30 • **Guided tours** 11am, noon & 2pm • Free • ⓦ castleofgoodhope.co.za

From the outside, South Africa's oldest official building looks somewhat miserable, and its position on Darling Street, behind the train station and city-bus terminal, does nothing to dispel this. Nevertheless, the **Castle of Good Hope** is well worth the entrance fee; inside, a meticulous ten-year restoration has returned the decor to the British Regency style introduced in 1798. But the Castle has also shaken off a dour historical image, and has some **fine contemporary exhibitions**; check the website for current shows.

Completed in 1679, the castle replaced Van Riebeeck's earlier mud and timber fort, which stood on the site of the Grand Parade. It was built in accordance with seventeenth-century European principles of fortification, comprising strong bastions from which the outside walls could be protected by crossfire. For 150 years, the castle remained the symbolic heart of the Cape administration, a prison and a site where slaves were bought and sold – the centre of social and economic life.

1

Inside the castle are three interesting collections. The **Military Museum** has displays on the conflicts that dogged the early settlement; the **Secunde's House** has furnishings, paintings and *objets d'art* that filled the living space of the deputy governor; and the **William Fehr Collection**, one of the country's most important exhibits of decorative arts, includes paintings of the settlement, eighteenth- and nineteenth-century Dutch and Indonesian furniture, and seventeenth- and eighteenth-century Chinese and Japanese porcelain.

Guided tours take you to the prison cells and dungeons, where you can still see the touching centuries-old graffiti carved into the walls by prisoners, and visit the inner courtyard where families of slaves would stand together as they were divided, bought and sold.

The Grand Parade and the City Hall

The **Grand Parade** is a large open area, to the west of the Castle of Good Hope, which was originally built for military parades, but has since been used for markets, parking and political rallies.

The Grand Parade appeared on TV screens throughout the world on February 11, 1990, when 100,000 people gathered to hear **Nelson Mandela** make his first speech after being released from prison, from the balcony of the adjoining **City Hall**. A slightly fussy Edwardian building dressed in Bath stone, City Hall manages, despite its drab surroundings, to look impressive against Table Mountain.

District Six

South of the castle, in the shadow of Devil's Peak, is a vacant lot shown on maps as the suburb of **Zonnebloem**. Before being demolished by the apartheid authorities, it was an inner-city slum known as **District Six**, an impoverished but lively community of 55,000 predominantly coloured people. Later mythologized as the erstwhile soul of Cape Town, the district harboured a rich cultural life in its narrow alleys and crowded tenements.

In 1966, apartheid ideologues declared District Six a **White Group Area** and the bulldozers moved in, taking fifteen years to drive its presence from the skyline, leaving only the mosques and churches. But, in the wake of the demolition, international and domestic outcry was so great that the area was never developed apart from a few luxury town houses on its fringes and the hefty Cape Technikon, a college that now occupies nearly a quarter of the former suburb. After years of negotiation, a few of the original residents have moved back under a scheme to develop low-cost housing in the district.

District Six Museum

25a Buitenkant St • Mon–Sat 9am–4pm • R30 • Ⓦ districtsix.co.za

Few places in Cape Town speak more eloquently of the effect of apartheid on the day-to-day lives of ordinary people than the **District Six Museum**. Situated on the northern boundary of District Six, on the corner of Buitenkant and Albertus streets, the museum occupies the former **Central Methodist Mission Church**, which offered solidarity and ministry to the victims of forced removals right up to the 1980s, and became a venue for anti-apartheid gatherings. Today, it houses a series of fascinating displays that include everyday household items and tools of trades, such as hairdressing implements, as well as documentary photographs, which evoke the lives of the individuals who once lived here. Occupying most of the floor is a huge map of District Six as it was, annotated by former residents, who describe their memories, reflections and incidents associated with places and buildings that no longer exist. There's also an almost complete collection of original street signs, secretly retrieved at the time of demolition by the man entrusted with dumping them into Table Bay. Their **coffee shop** sells snacks, including traditional, syrupy *koeksisters*.

1

The Bo-Kaap

On the slopes of Signal Hill, the **Bo-Kaap** is one of Cape Town's oldest and most fascinating residential areas. Its streets are characterized by brightly coloured nineteenth-century Dutch and Georgian terraces, which conceal a network of alleyways that are the arteries of its **Muslim community**. The Bo-Kaap harbours its own strong identity, made all the more unique by the destruction of District Six, with which it had much in common. A particular dialect of Afrikaans is spoken here, although it is steadily being eroded by English. Some long-time residents have sold off family properties, and a number of trendy outsiders have moved in, starting up guesthouses that capitalize on the outstanding central city position, and views of Table Mountain.

Bo-Kaap residents are descended from dissidents and slaves imported by the Dutch in the sixteenth and seventeenth centuries. They became known collectively as **Cape Malay**, although most originated from Africa, India, Madagascar and Sri Lanka, with less than one percent actually from Malaysia.

The easiest way to get to the Bo-Kaap is by foot along Wale Street, which trails up from the south end of Adderley Street and across Buitengragt, to become the main drag of the Bo-Kaap.

Bo-Kaap Museum

71 Wale St • Mon–Sat 10am–5pm • R20 • ⓦ iziko.org.za/museums/bo-kaap-museum

One of the best introductions to Bo-Kaap history and traditions is the **Bo-Kaap Museum**, near the Buitengragt end of Wale Street. It consists mainly of the family house and possessions of Abu Bakr Effendi, a nineteenth-century religious leader brought out from Turkey by the British in 1862 as a mediator between feuding Muslim factions. He became an important member of the community, founded an Arabic school and wrote a book in the local vernacular – now regarded as possibly the first book to be published in what can be recognized as Afrikaans. The museum also displays exhibits exploring the local brand of Islam, which has its own unique traditions and nearly two dozen *kramats* (shrines) dotted about the peninsula.

Auwal Mosque

43 Dorp St

One block south of the museum is the **Auwal**, South Africa's first official mosque, founded in 1795 by Tuan Guru, a Muslim activist. Ten more mosques, whose minarets give spice to the quarter's skyline, now serve the district's ten thousand residents. Very little of the mosque's original structure remains and it blends in with the single-storey Georgian terraced houses it abuts, distinguished only by its large minaret.

De Waterkant

South of the V&A Waterfront and rubbing up against the west side of the city centre and Bo-Kaap is **De Waterkant**, with attractive Georgian terraced streets, some great restaurants and coffee spots and, notably, the pink square – the city's self-proclaimed gay quarter with clubs, pubs and saunas. With its elevated setting, cobbled streets,

BO-KAAP TOURS

The best way to explore Bo-Kaap is by joining one of the **walking tours** of the district that also take in the Bo-Kaap Museum. The most reliable is run by Bo-Kaap Guided Tours (☎ 021 422 1554, ⓦ bokaapcookingtour.co.za; R350, including entrance to the museum), a two-hour trip that is led by residents of the area, whose knowledge goes beyond the standard tour-guide script; the tour starts at the Bo-Kaap Museum and includes Cape Malay snacks. The same outfit also offers a similar tour that ends at the house of a Bo-Kaap resident for lunch, and where you get to help prepare and cook a typical delicious Cape Malay meal (R600; book at least two days in advance).

1

attractive terraces and harbour views, De Waterkant is a good district to simply wander and browse.

Strand Street

A major artery from the N2 freeway to the central business district, **Strand Street** neatly separates the upper from the lower city centre. Between the mid-eighteenth and mid-nineteenth centuries, it was one of the most fashionable streets in Cape Town because of its proximity to the shore. Its former cachet is now only discernible from a handful of quietly elegant national monuments left standing amid the roar of traffic.

Evangelical Lutheran Church

Corner of Buitengragt and Strand St • Mon, Wed & Fri 9am–noon • Free

Converted in 1785 from a barn, the **Evangelical Lutheran Church**'s facade includes Classical details such as a broken pediment perforated by the clock tower, as well as Gothic features like arched windows. Inside, the magnificent **pulpit**, supported by two life-size Herculean figures, is one of Cape Dutch architect Anton Anreith's masterpieces. The establishment of a Lutheran church in Cape Town in the late eighteenth century struck a significant blow against the extreme religious intolerance that was rife in the city. Previously, Protestantism had been the only form of worship allowed, with the Dutch Reformed Church holding an absolute monopoly over saving people's souls.

Koopmans-De Wet House

35 Strand St • Mon–Fri 10am–5pm • R20 • ⓦ iziko.org.za/museums/koopmans-de-wet-house

Sandwiched between two office blocks, **Koopmans-De Wet House** is an outstanding eighteenth-century pedimented Neoclassical town house and museum, accommodating a very fine collection of antique furniture and rare porcelain. The earliest sections of the house were built in 1701 by **Reyner Smedinga**, a well-to-do goldsmith who imported the building materials from Holland. The house changed hands more than a dozen times over the following two centuries, with minor additions made in the 1760s and a second storey added between 1774 and 1790. In 1806, it came into the hands of the De Wet family, eventually becoming the home of **Marie Koopmans-De Wet** (1834–1906), a prominent figure on the Cape social and political circuit.

The house represents a fine synthesis of Dutch elements (sash windows and large entrance doors) with the demands of local conditions; the huge rooms, lofty ceilings and shuttered windows reflect the high summer temperatures, while the front *stoep* has plastered masonry seats at each end. The **lantern** in the fanlight of the entrance to the house was a feature of all Cape Town houses in the eighteenth and early nineteenth centuries, its purpose to shine light onto the street and thus hinder slaves from gathering at night to plot.

The V&A Waterfront

ⓦ waterfront.co.za • The V&A Waterfront is served by MyCiTi bus routes #A01 from the airport, #104 from Sea Point and #106 from Camps Bay, as well as The Cape Town Sightseeing Bus, which runs two routes around the city's main sights and drops you outside the Two Oceans Aquarium (see p.128 for full route details)

The **Victoria and Alfred Waterfront**, known simply as the Waterfront, is Cape Town's original Victorian harbour and incorporates the city's most popular central shopping area – a busy complex of shops, restaurants, cinemas, waterside walkways and a functioning harbour. The retail focus is an enormous flashy **mall** (daily 9am–9pm) on two levels, extending along Quays Five and Six. The restaurants and cafés on the mall's east side, with their outdoor seating, have fabulous views of Table Mountain across the busy harbour. On the west side of the wharf, the **Red Shed Craft Workshop** (Mon–Sat 9am–9pm, Sun 10am–9pm; ☎021 408 7847) houses craft workers such as

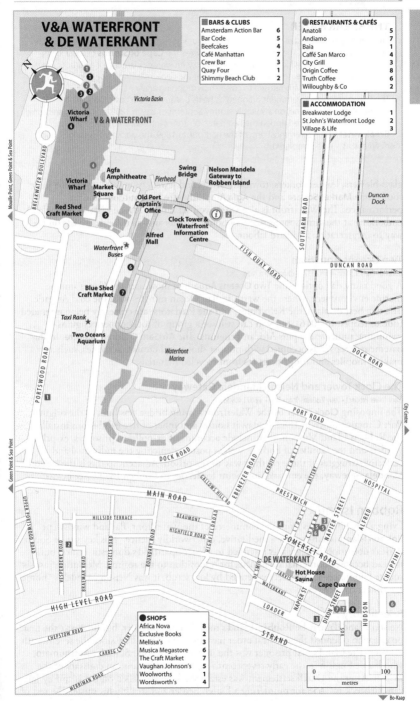

V&A WATERFRONT & DE WATERKANT

BARS & CLUBS

Amsterdam Action Bar	6
Bar Code	5
Beefcakes	4
Café Manhattan	7
Crew Bar	3
Quay Four	1
Shimmy Beach Club	2

RESTAURANTS & CAFÉS

Anatoli	5
Andiamo	7
Baia	1
Caffé San Marco	4
City Grill	3
Origin Coffee	8
Truth Coffee	6
Willoughby & Co	2

ACCOMMODATION

Breakwater Lodge	1
St John's Waterfront Lodge	2
Village & Life	3

SHOPS

Africa Nova	8
Exclusive Books	2
Melissa's	3
Musica Megastore	6
The Craft Market	7
Vaughan Johnson's	5
Woolworths	1
Wordsworth's	4

Map labels: Victoria Basin, Victoria Wharf, V & A WATERFRONT, Mouille Point, Green Point & Sea Point, Green Point & Sea Point, BREAKWATER BOULEVARD, Agfa Amphitheatre, Pierhead, Swing Bridge, Nelson Mandela Gateway to Robben Island, Victoria Wharf, Market Square, Old Port Captain's Office, Red Shed Craft Market, Clock Tower & Waterfront Information Centre, Alfred Mall, Waterfront Buses, Blue Shed Craft Market, Taxi Rank, Two Oceans Aquarium, Waterfront Marina, PORTSWOOD ROAD, FISH QUAY ROAD, SOUTHARM ROAD, Duncan Dock, DUNCAN ROAD, DOCK ROAD, PORT ROAD, DOCK ROAD, City Centre, GALLOWS HILL RD, EBENEZER ROAD, CARBITE, PRESTWICH, BENNETT, BATTERY, HOSPITAL, MAIN ROAD, HILLSIDE TERRACE, BEAUMONT, HIGHFIELD ROAD, HIGHFIELD ROAD, UPPER PORTSWOOD ROAD, VESPERDENE ROAD, BRAEMAR ROAD, WESSELS ROAD, BOUNDARY ROAD, LIDDLE, COBERN, NAPIER STREET, ALFRED, SOMERSET ROAD, CHIAPPINI, DE WATERKANT, DE SMIDT, JARVIS, NAPIER ST, Hot House Sauna, Cape Quarter, WATERKANY, DIXON STREET, HUDSON, HIGH LEVEL ROAD, CHEPSTOW ROAD, CARREG CRESCENT, LOADER, VOS, STRAND, MERRIMAN ROAD, Bo-Kaap

0   100
metres

THE BREAKWATER

Throughout the first half of the nineteenth century, arguments raged in Cape Town over the need for a proper dock. The Cape was often known as the **Cape of Storms** because of its tempestuous weather, which left Table Bay littered with wrecks. Clamour for a harbour grew in the 1850s with the increase in sea traffic arriving at the Cape, reaching its peak in 1860, when Lloyd's insurance company refused to cover ships dropping anchor in Table Bay.

The British colonial government dragged its heels because of the costs involved, but eventually conceded and, on a suitably stormy September day in 1860, at a huge ceremony, the teenage Prince Alfred tipped the first batch of stones into Table Bay to begin the **Breakwater**, the westernmost arm of the harbour. In 1869, the dock – consisting of two main basins – was completed.

glass-blowers, leatherworkers, township artists and jewellery-makers under one huge roof, while **Market Square** and the **Agfa Amphitheatre** host outdoor musical performances. The Waterfront is also where you set sail for Robben Island (see below), embarking at the same spot as many of South Africa's anti-apartheid activists on their way to incarceration and hard labour.

Two Oceans Aquarium

Dock Rd • Daily 9.30am–6pm • R125 • ⓦ aquarium.co.za

A good rainy day option, the **Two Oceans Aquarium** showcases the Cape's unique marine environment, where the warm Indian Ocean mingles with the cold Atlantic. The two best displays, the Kelp Forest and the Predators, are currently being upgraded (due to reopen in 2016), but you can still see a group of rockhopper penguins swimming underwater, plus African Penguins. The **AfriSam Children's Centre**, in the basement, keeps kids occupied with puppet shows and creative activities, such as making mobiles and fridge magnets from recycled materials.

The Clock Tower and Nelson Mandela Gateway

Clock Tower Precinct • Daily 7.30am–9pm • Free • ⓣ 021 409 5100

The imposing **Clock Tower** by the Waterfront's swing bridge was built as the original Port Captain's office in 1882. Today, it houses a number of free exhibitions installed by the Robben Island Museum that include accounts of ex-political prisoners, ex-prison warders and the families of both, as well as posters depicting the individual and collective struggles of those on their way to the prison. Adjacent to this is the **Nelson Mandela Gateway**, the embarkation point for ferries to Robben Island (see below).

Robben Island

Lying a few kilometres from the commerce of the Waterfront, flat and windswept **Robben Island** is suffused by a meditative, otherworldly silence. This key site of South Africa's liberation struggle was intended to silence apartheid's domestic critics, but instead became an international focus for opposition to the regime. Measuring just six square kilometres and sparsely vegetated by low scrub, it was Nelson Mandela's "home" for almost twenty years.

Brief history

Nelson Mandela may be Robben Island's most famous prisoner, but he wasn't the first: people who offended the political order have been banished here since the seventeenth century. The island's first prisoner was the indigenous Khoikhoi leader **Autshumato**, who learnt English in the early seventeenth century and became an emissary of the British. After the Dutch settlement was established, he was jailed on the island by Jan van Riebeeck in 1658 for murdering a Dutch herder and stealing his cattle. The rest of

1

the seventeenth century saw a succession of East Indies political prisoners exiled here for opposing Dutch colonial rule.

During the nineteenth century, the **British** used the island as a dumping ground for deserters, criminals and political prisoners. Captured **Xhosa leaders** who defied the empire during the Frontier Wars of the early to mid-nineteenth century were transported by sea from the Eastern Cape to be imprisoned here. In 1846, the island's brief was extended to include a whole range of the **socially marginalized**; criminals and political detainees were joined by vagrants, prostitutes, lunatics and the chronically ill. In the 1890s, a leper colony existed alongside the social outcasts. Lunatics were removed in 1921 and the lepers in 1930.

Robben Island's greatest era of notoriety began in 1961, when it was taken over by the **Prisons Department**. When Nelson Mandela arrived, it had become a maximum security prison, and inmates were only allowed to send and receive one letter every six months. Harsh conditions, including routine beatings and forced hard labour, were exacerbated by the geographical location: icy winds routinely blow in from the South Pole, and inmates wore only shorts and flimsy jerseys. Like every other prisoner, Mandela slept on a thin mat on the floor and was kept in solitary confinement in a cell measuring two metres square for sixteen hours a day.

Amazingly, the prisoners found ways of **protesting**, through hunger strikes, publicizing conditions when possible (by visits from the International Committee of the Red Cross, for example) and, remarkably, by taking legal action against the prison authority to stop arbitrary punishments. They won improved conditions over the years, and the island also became a university behind bars, where people of different political views and generations met; it was not unknown for prisoners to give academic help to their warders. The last political prisoners were released from Robben Island in 1991 and the remaining common-law prisoners were transferred to the mainland in 1996. A year later, the island was established as a museum, becoming a **UNESCO World Heritage Site** in 1999.

The island

The ferry trip from the Waterfront takes about half an hour. On arrival you are taken on a **bus tour** around the island and a **tour of the prison**. The bus tour stops off at several historical landmarks, the first of which is a beautiful shrine built in memory of Tuan Guru, a Muslim cleric from present-day Indonesia who was imprisoned here by the Dutch in the eighteenth century. On his release, he helped to establish Islam among slaves in Cape Town. The tour also passes a **leper graveyard** and **church** designed by Sir Herbert Baker.

Robert Sobukwe's house is perhaps the most affecting relic of incarceration on the island. It was here that Sobukwe (see box, p.325), leader of the Pan Africanist Congress (a radical offshoot of the ANC), was held in solitary confinement for nine years. No other political prisoners were allowed to speak to him, but he would sometimes gesture his solidarity with them by letting sand trickle through his fingers as they walked past. After his release in 1969, Sobukwe was restricted to Kimberley under house arrest, until his death from cancer in 1978.

ROBBEN ISLAND TOURS

A number of vendors at the Waterfront sell tickets for cruises, which may go close to Robben Island, but only the official ones sold at the **Nelson Mandela Gateway** will get you onto it (☎ 021 413 4219, ⦿ robben-island.org.za; R250, including boat trip, entry to the island, and 3hr 30min tour). Bookings must be made well in advance with a credit card as the boats are often full, especially around December and January. Boats leave daily at 9am, 11am, 1pm & 3pm, though all trips are weather dependent, and the tours are of variable quality, depending on the guide, but it is fascinating to look round the island and visit Mandela's cell.

1

Another stopoff is the **lime quarry** where Nelson Mandela and his fellow inmates spent countless hours of hard labour.

The Maximum Security Prison

The **Maximum Security Prison**, a forbidding complex of unadorned H-blocks on the edge of the island, is introduced with a tour through the famous **B-Section**; you'll be guided by a former inmate, after which you can wander freely. **Mandela's cell** has been left exactly as it was, without embellishments or display, but the rest are locked and empty.

In the nearby **A-Section**, the Cell Stories exhibition skilfully shows the sparseness of prison life, with the tiny isolation cells containing personal artefacts loaned by former prisoners, plus quotations, recordings and photographs.

Towards the end of the 1980s, cameras were sneaked onto the island, and inmates took snapshots of each other, which have been enlarged to almost life size and mounted as the **Smuggled Camera Exhibition** in the D-Section communal cells. The **Living Legacy** tour in F-Section involves ex-political prisoner guides describing their lives here and answering questions.

The southern suburbs

Away from Table Mountain and the city centre, the bulk of Cape Town's residential sprawl extends east into South Africa's interior. It's here that the **southern suburbs**, the formerly whites-only residential areas, stretch out down the east side of Table Mountain, ending at Muizenberg on the False Bay coast, with Claremont and Newlands acting as the central pivotal point. The area offers a quick escape from the city into forests, gardens and vineyards, all hugging the eastern slopes of the mountain and its extension, the Constantiaberg.

The quickest way of reaching the southern suburbs **by car** from the city centre, Waterfront or City Bowl suburbs is via the M3 highway. Alternatively, you can travel **by train** from Cape Town Station to Woodstock, Salt River, Observatory, Mowbray, Rosebank and Rondebosch, as well as all the stations southwards to Fish Hoek and Simon's Town, while the hop-on, hop-off sightseeing **buses** (see p.128) serve Kirstenbosch, the Constantia wine estates and Hout Bay.

Woodstock and Salt River

Windblown and gritty, **Woodstock** and **Salt River** are Cape Town's oldest suburbs, and closest to the heart of the industrial city. Old folk conversing on their *stoeps*, keeping an eye on children running around the crumbling streets, gives a hint of what Cape Town must have been like before the forced evictions to the Cape Flats of the 1970s and 1980s. Slowly but surely, however, these predominantly working-class coloured areas are being gentrified into Cape Town's premier design district, with clusters of design shops, artisan coffee houses and art galleries sitting alongside car dealers and second-hand furniture shops. The two suburbs blend imperceptibly, though Salt River remains poorer and more industrial, while Woodstock's pretty old Victorian houses have been snapped up by new arrivals and renovated.

Albert Road is the best place to head in Woodstock, with the **Old Biscuit Mill** hosting a terrific Saturday morning organic and artisanal food market (see p.155). It's also home to two of Cape Town's best contemporary restaurants, *Test Kitchen* (see p.142) and *Pot Luck Club* (see p.142), while the **Woodstock Exchange** (see p.155) is worth a visit for its mixture of shops and creative art and craft studios. For a further selection of the most interesting names in the area, check out ⓦmondaydesign.co.za/Woodstock-design-district.

Observatory

Abutting the southern end of Woodstock, **Observatory** is generally regarded as Cape Town's bohemian hub, a reputation fuelled by its proximity to the University of Cape Town, Groote Schuur Hospital Medical School and a number of NGOs. The refreshingly unrestored peeling arcades on Observatory's Lower Main Road, and the streets off it, have some nice places to chill or party. The huge Groote Schuur Hospital, which overlooks the freeway that sweeps through Observatory, was the site of the world's first heart transplant in 1967.

The Irma Stern Museum
Cecil Rd, Rosebank • Tues–Sat 10am–5pm • R10 • ⓦ irmastern.co.za

Irma Stern (see box below) is acknowledged as one of South Africa's pioneering artists of the twentieth century, more for the fact that she brought modern European ideas to the colonies than for any huge contribution she made to the art world. The **UCT Irma Stern Museum** was the artist's home for 38 years until her death in 1966 and is worth visiting if only to see Stern's collection of Iberian, African, Oriental and ancient artefacts. The whole house, in fact, reflects the artist's fascination with exoticism, starting with her own Gauguinesque paintings of "native types", the fantastic carved doors she brought back from Zanzibar, and the very untypical garden that brings a touch of the tropics to Cape Town with its exuberant bamboo thickets and palm trees.

The Rhodes Memorial
Rhodes Ave, Rondebosch • Restaurant and tea garden daily 9am–5pm • ⓦ rhodesmemorial.co.za • Reached via a signposted road that spurs northwest off the M3

The suburb of Rondebosch is home to the University of Cape Town (UCT), whose nineteenth-century buildings, handsomely festooned with creepers, sit grandly on the mountainside, overlooking Main Road and the M3 highway. Next to the campus, the conspicuous **Rhodes Memorial**, built to resemble a Greek temple, celebrates Cecil Rhodes with a sculpture of a wildly rearing horse and the empire-builder's bust planted at the top of a towering set of stairs. Herds of wildebeest and zebra nonchalantly graze on the slopes around the Memorial, and its **restaurant** offers terrific views of Cape Town. Below the Memorial, alongside the M3, you'll see the incongruous Mostert's Mill, a windmill built two centuries ago when the landscape was planted with wheat fields.

Newlands and Claremont
South of Rondebosch are some of Cape Town's most established, genteel suburbs, including **Newlands**, that almost merges with Rondebosch and is home to the city's famous rugby and cricket stadiums. South of Newlands, the well-heeled suburb of

---

IRMA STERN

Born in a backwater town in South Africa in 1894 to German–Jewish parents, Irma Stern studied at Germany's Weimar Academy. In reaction to the academy's conservatism, she adopted **expressionist distortion** in her paintings, some of which were included in the Neue Sezession Exhibition in Berlin in 1918. Stern went on several expeditions into Zanzibar and the Congo in the 1940s and 1950s, where she found the source for her intensely sensuous paintings, which shocked South Africa at the time.

Although Stern's work was appreciated in Europe, when she returned to South Africa after World War II critics claimed that her style was simply a cover for technical incompetence. South African art historians now regard her as the towering figure of her generation. One of her most famous works is the much reproduced *The Eternal Child* (1916), a simple but vibrant portrait of a young girl, while *The Wood Carriers* (1951) uses raw ochres, browns and oranges to create an exoticized portrayal of a pair of African women.

Claremont is an alternative focus to the city centre for shopping and entertainment, with a cinema and plenty of shops at **Cavendish Square Mall**.

Bishopscourt and Wynberg

A little further south, beyond the signpost to Kirstenbosch Gardens, **Bishopscourt**, as its name suggests, is home to the Anglican bishop of Cape Town, and full of luxurious mansions with enormous grounds. Further south still, the suburb of **Wynberg** is known for its Maynardville Shakespearean open-air theatre (see p.151) and the quaint row of shops and restaurants in Wolfe Street known as **Little Chelsea**. By contrast, Wynberg's Main Road offers a distinctly less genteel shopping experience, an interesting stroll past street vendors and fabric shops, as well as food outlets catering to the large number of workers travelling between Wynberg and Khayelitsha.

Kirstenbosch National Botanical Gardens

Rhodes Drive, signposted off the M3 close to Newlands • Daily: April–Aug 8am–6pm; Sept–March 8am–7pm • R47 • Free walking tours (Mon–Sat at 10am) and shuttle-car tours (every hour on the hour; R50) depart from Visitors Centre, Gate 1 • Served by The Blue Mini Peninsula Tour bus (see p.128) from the Waterfront; alternatively a taxi from the centre of town will cost around R175

Thirteen kilometres south of the city centre, the unmissable **Kirstenbosch National Botanical Garden** was established in 1913, and is one of the planet's great natural treasure houses. In 2004 it became the first botanical garden in the world to be granted UNESCO World Heritage status, in recognition of the international significance of its Fynbos vegetation (see box below) and the Cape plant kingdom that predominates here, attracting botanists from all over the world. Allow a good couple of hours to visit the garden, which has signboards and paved paths to guide you through its highlights, and labels to identify the trees and plants.

The most exciting feature is the **Boomslang Tree Canopy Walkway**, a raised steel-and-timber path that snakes its way up and through the trees of the **Arboretum**, providing panoramic views of the garden and surrounding mountains. Another interesting route is via the **Fragrance Garden** and adjacent **Braille Trail** created for blind visitors, with information signs in Braille and an abundance of aromatic and textured plants.

The garden trails off into **wild vegetation** covering a huge expanse of the rugged eastern slopes and wooded ravines of Table Mountain – the setting is breathtaking. Two popular paths, Nursery Ravine and Skeleton Gorge (see p.111), lead off from the **Contour Path** above Kirstenbosch; while the garden itself is safe from crime, if you are hiking up the slopes, or along the Contour Path to Constantia Neck or

---

FYNBOS

Early Dutch settlers were alarmed by the lack of good timber on the Cape Peninsula's hillsides, which were covered by nondescript, scrubby bush they described as *fijn bosch* (literally "fine bush") and which is now known by its Afrikaans name **fynbos** (pronounced "fayn-bos"). The settlers planted exotics, like the oaks that now shade central Cape Town, and over the ensuing centuries their descendants established pine forests on the sides of Table Mountain in an effort to create a landscape that fulfilled their European idea of the picturesque. It's only relatively recently that Capetonians have come to claim *fynbos* proudly as part of the peninsula's heritage. Amazingly, many bright blooms in Britain and the US, including varieties of geraniums, freesias, gladioli, daisies, lilies and irises, are hybrids grown from indigenous Cape plants.

Fynbos is remarkable for its astonishing variety of plants, its 8500 species making it one of the world's biodiversity hot spots. The Cape Peninsula alone, measuring less than 500 square kilometres, has 2256 plant species (nearly twice as many as Britain, which is five thousand times bigger). The four basic types of *fynbos* plants are **proteas** (South Africa's national flower); **ericas**, amounting to six hundred species of heather; **restios** (reeds); and **geophytes**, including ground orchids and the startling flaming red disas, which can be seen in flower on Table Mountain in late summer.

Newlands Forest and Rhodes Memorial, the usual safely precautions should be followed.

Facilities in the garden include an outdoor **coffee shop** (open daily for breakfast, lunch and teas), a **tea room** and a **restaurant** with a fire for winter days. In summer, however, one of the undoubted delights is to bring a picnic for the Sunday evening **open-air concert**, where you can lie back on the lawn, sip Cape wine and savour the mountain air and sunsets.

Constantia and its winelands

South of Kirstenbosch lie the elegant suburbs of **Constantia** and the Cape's oldest **winelands**. Luxuriating on the lower slopes of Table Mountain and the Constantiaberg, with tantalizing views of False Bay, the winelands lie off the M3, an easy thirty-minute drive from town.

The winelands started cultivated life in 1685 as the farm of **Simon van der Stel**, the governor charged with opening up the fledgling Dutch colony to the interior. Thrusting himself wholeheartedly into the task, he selected for his own use an enormous tract of the choicest land set against the Constantiaberg, the section of the peninsula just south of Table Mountain. He named the estate after his daughter Constancia, and this is now (with a minor change of spelling) the name of Cape Town's most prestigious residential area. Constantia grapes have been used for wine-making since Van der Stel's first output in 1705. After his death in 1712, the estate was divided up and sold off as the modern **Groot Constantia**, **Klein Constantia** and **Buitenverwachting**. All three estates are open to the public and offer tastings; they're definitely worth visiting if you aren't heading to the Winelands proper.

Groot Constantia

Groot Constantia Rd • **Grounds** Daily 9am–6pm • Free • **Cellar tours** Daily 10am–4pm on the hour • R40, including five wines to taste and a souvenir glass; booking essential • **Wine tasting** Daily 9am–5.30pm • R30 • ☎ 021 794 5128, ⓦ grootconstantia.co.za • Served by the Blue Mini Peninsula Tour bus (see p.128) from the Waterfront

Groot Constantia is the largest wine estate in Constantia and the one most geared to tourists. Its big pull is that it retains the rump of Van der Stel's original estate, as well as the original buildings, though its portrayal of life in a seventeenth-century colonial chateau makes scant reference to the slave labour that underpinned its operations. The **manor house**, a quintessential Cape Dutch building, was Van der Stel's original home, modified at the end of the eighteenth century by the French architect Thibault. Walking straight through it, down the ceremonial axis, you'll come to the cellar, fronted with a carved pediment, depicting a riotous bacchanalia, which represents fertility. The substantial grounds of Groot Constantia are serene and orderly, and make for good walks among the vines.

Klein Constantia

Klein Constantia Rd • Mon–Fri 9am–5pm, Sat 9am–3pm • Free • ⓦ kleinconstantia.com

Smaller than Groot Constantia, **Klein Constantia** offers free wine tastings in less regimented conditions than at the bigger estate and, although the buildings are far humbler, the setting is equally beautiful. Klein Constantia has a friendly atmosphere and produces some fine wines. Something of a curiosity is its **Vin de Constance**, the re-creation of an eighteenth-century Constantia wine that was a favourite of Napoleon, Frederick the Great and Bismarck. It's a delicious dessert wine, packaged in a replica of the original bottle, and makes a unique souvenir.

Buitenverwachting

Klein Constantia Rd • **Buildings** Mon–Fri 9am–5pm, Sat 10am–3pm • Free • **Picnic lunches** Late Nov–March noon–4pm • R135 per head; booking essential • ☎ 021 794 5190, ⓦ buitenverwachting.co.za

Buitenverwachting (roughly pronounced "bay-tin-fur-vuch-ting" with the "ch" as in the Scottish rendition of loch) is a bucolic place in the middle of the suburbs, with sheep and cattle grazing in the fields as you approach the main buildings, making it an inviting spot for a picnic lunch or an amble. The architecture and setting at the foot of the Constantiaberg are as good reasons to come here as the estate's impressive list of top-ranking wines, among them the classy Christine, an outstanding Bordeaux blend that has retained its edge for years. Overlooking the vineyards and backing onto the garden, the homestead was built in 1794 and features an unusual gabled pediment broken by an urn motif.

Table Mountain

Table Mountain, a 1087-metre flat-topped massif with dramatic cliffs and eroded gorges, dominates the northern end of the Cape Peninsula. Its north face overlooks the city centre with the distinct formations of **Lion's Head** and **Signal Hill** to the west and **Devil's Peak** to the east. The west face is made up of a series of gable-like formations known as the **Twelve Apostles**; the southwest face towers over Hout Bay and the east face over the southern suburbs. The mountain is a compelling feature in the middle of the city, a wilderness where you'll find wildlife and 1400 species of flora. Indigenous mammals include baboons, dassies (see box, p.110) and porcupines.

Reckoned to be the most-climbed massif in the world, Table Mountain has suffered under the constant pounding of **hikers** – although the damage isn't always obvious. Every year the mountain strikes back, taking its toll of lives. One of the commonest causes of difficulties is people losing the track (often due to sudden mist falling) and becoming trapped. If you plan to tackle one of its hundreds of walks or climbs, go properly prepared, or take a **full-day guided hike** tailored to your level of fitness (see p.152). You may choose to come back the easy way by cable car, or partially abseil.

The cable car

Cars leave from the lower cableway station on Tafelberg Road daily every 10–15min: Jan & Dec 8am–9pm; Feb & March 8.30am–7.30pm; April 8.30am–5.30pm; May–Oct 8am–6pm; Nov 8am–7pm • R215 return • The schedule can be disrupted by bad weather or maintenance work; for up-to-date information, call ☎ 021 424 8181, or check ⓦ tablemountain.net • From V&A Waterfront, the Red City Centre Tours bus (p.128) and MyCiTi buses #106 & 107 serve the cableway; alternatively take a metered taxi , or a minibus taxi from Adderley St. Drivers can park along Tafelberg Rd.

The least challenging, but certainly not least interesting, way up and down the mountain is via the highly popular **cable car** at the western table, which offers dizzying views across Table Bay and the Atlantic. The state-of-the-art Swiss system is designed to complete a 360-degree rotation on the way, giving passengers a full panorama. You can make a real outing of it by going up for breakfast or a sunset drink and meal at the vamped-up eco-restaurant; the upper station is an incomparable spot to watch the sun go down.

SACRED CIRCLE

A number of **Muslim holy men and princes** were exiled from the East Indies by the Dutch during the late seventeenth and early eighteenth centuries and brought to the Cape, where some became revered as **auliyah** or Muslim saints. The **kramats**, of which there are nearly two dozen in the province, are their burial sites, shrines and places of pilgrimage. The Signal Hill *kramat* is a shrine to **Mohamed Gasan Galbie Shah**, a follower of Sheik Yusuf, a Sufi scholar, who was deported to the Cape in 1694 with a 49-strong retinue. According to tradition, he conducted Muslim prayer meetings in private homes and slave quarters, becoming the founder of Islam in South Africa. **Sheik Yusuf**'s *kramat* on the Cape Flats is said to be one of a sacred circle of six *kramats*, including one on Robben Island, that protect Cape Town from natural disasters.

1

> ## DASSIES
>
> The outsized fluffy guinea pigs you'll encounter at the top of Table Mountain are **dassies** or hyraxes (*Procavia capensis*), which, despite their appearance, aren't rodents at all, but the closest living relatives of elephants. Their name (pronounced like "dusty" without the "t") is the Afrikaans version of *dasje*, meaning "little badger", a name given to them by the first Dutch settlers. Dassies are very widely distributed, having thrived in South Africa with the elimination of predators, and can be found in rocky habitats all over the country, often warming themselves in groups in the early morning sun, as they have poor body temperature control.

Walks and viewpoints

Climbing the mountain will give you a greater sense of achievement than being ferried up by the cable car, but proceed with extreme caution: it may look sunny and clear when you leave, but conditions at the top could be very different. There are fabulous hikes up and along Table Mountain (see p.152), but they are best done guided, both for mountain safety and because there have been some occasional and random muggings of tourists.

Signal Hill and Lion's Head

From the roundabout at the top of Kloofnek, a road leads all the way along **Signal Hill** to a car park and lookout, with good views over Table Bay, the docks and the city. A cannon was formerly used for sending signals to ships at anchor in the bay, and the Noon Gun, still fired from its slopes daily, sends a thunderous rumble through the Bo-Kaap and city centre below. Halfway along the road is a sacred Islamic *kramat* (see box), one of several dotted around the peninsula that protect the city. You can also walk up **Lion's Head**, a non-strenuous hour-long hike that seems to bring out half the population of Cape Town every full moon, but it should always be done in a group: Google "Lions Head full moon" for dates and details.

Platteklip Gorge

The first recorded ascent to the summit of Table Mountain was by the Portuguese captain Antonio de Saldanha, in 1503. He wisely chose **Platteklip Gorge**, the gap visible from the front table (the north side), which, as it turned out, is the most accessible way up. A short and easy extension will get you to Maclear's Beacon which, at 1086m, is the highest point on the mountain. The Platteklip route starts at the lower cableway station and ends at the upper station, so you can descend in a car.

From the lower station, walk east along Tafelberg Road until you see a sign pointing to Platteklip Gorge. A steep fifteen-minute climb brings you onto the **Upper Contour Path**. About 25m east along this, take the path indicated by a sign reading Contour Path/Platteklip Gorge. The path zigzags from here onwards and is very clear. The gorge is the biggest cleavage on the whole mountain, leading directly and safely to the top, but it's a very steep slog that will take two to three hours in total if you're reasonably fit. Once on top, turn right and ascend the last short section onto the **front table** for a breathtaking view of the city. A sign points the way to the upper cableway station – a fifteen-minute walk along a concrete path thronging with visitors.

Maclear's Beacon

Maclear's Beacon is about 35 minutes from the top of the Platteklip Gorge on a path leading eastward, with white squares on little yellow footsteps guiding you all the way. The path crosses the front table with Maclear's Beacon visible at all times. From the top you'll get views of False Bay and the Hottentots Holland Mountains to the east.

Skeleton Gorge and Nursery Ravine

You can combine a visit to the gardens at Kirstenbosch (see p.106) with an ascent up Table Mountain via one route and a descent down another, ending at the Kirstenbosch National Botanical Gardens' restaurant for tea. Starting at the restaurant, follow the **Skeleton Gorge** signs, which lead you onto the **Contour Path**. At the Contour Path, a plaque indicates that this is **Smuts' Track**, the route favoured by Jan Smuts, the Boer leader and South African prime minister. The plaque marks the start of a broad-stepped climb up Skeleton Gorge, involving wooden steps, stone steps, wooden ladders and loose boulders. Be prepared for steep ravines and difficult rock climbs – and under no circumstances stray off the path. This route requires reasonable fitness, and takes about two hours.

Skeleton Gorge is not recommended for the descent, as it can be very slippery; rather use **Nursery Ravine**. At the top of Skeleton Gorge, walk a few metres to your right to a sign indicating **Kasteelspoort**. It's just 35 minutes from the top of Skeleton Gorge along the Kasteelspoort path to the head of Nursery Ravine. The descent returns you to the 310-metre Contour Path, which leads back to Kirstenbosch. This entire walk lasts about five hours.

The Atlantic seaboard

Table Mountain's steep drop into the ocean along much of the western peninsula forces the suburbs along the **Atlantic seaboard** into a ribbon of developments clinging dramatically to the slopes. The sea washing the west side of the peninsula can be very chilly, far colder than on the False Bay seaboard. Although not ideal for bathing, the Atlantic seaboard offers mind-blowing views from some of the most incredible coastal roads in the world, particularly beyond **Sea Point**, and there are opportunities for whale-spotting. The coast itself consists of a series of bays and white-sanded beaches edged with smoothly sculpted bleached rocks; inland, the Twelve Apostles, a series of rocky buttresses, gaze down onto the surf. The beaches are ideal for sunbathing, or sunset picnics – it's from this side of the peninsula that you can watch the sun sink into the ocean, creating fiery reflections on the sea and mountains behind as it slips away. Make the most of the views, and beautiful people-watching, in some of the city's trendiest outdoor cafés and bars.

Mouille Point and Green Point

Just to the west of the V&A Waterfront, Mouille Point and its close neighbour, Green Point, are among the suburbs closest to the city centre. **Mouille** (moo-lee) **Point** is known principally for its squat rectangular Victorian lighthouse, commissioned in the 1820s, and painted like a children's picture-book lighthouse, with diagonal red and white stripes.

Mouille Point merges with the larger suburb of **Green Point**, which continues both inland from it and west along the ragged Atlantic shore. Green Point's proximity to the Waterfront – an easy ten-or-so minutes' walk away – and its position along the coast has turned it into a humming area of good accommodation and cafés.

BUSES ALONG THE ATLANTIC SEABOARD

The Blue Mini Peninsula Tour bus (see p.128) runs along the **Atlantic Seaboard Coast**, stopping at Hout Bay World of Birds, Mariner's Wharf, Imizamo Yethu township, Camps Bay, Bantry Bay, Sea Point and Green Point, while the Red City Centre Tour (see p.128) serves Camps Bay, Bantry Bay, Sea Point and Green Point. MyCiTi buses #106 and #107 run from the Waterfront to Camps Bay, while buses #104 and #105 run from the Civic Centre, close to Cape Town Station, to Sea Point.

CAPE TOWN STADIUM

Described by British architecture critic Jonathan Glancey as "a stunning white apparition … in a sublime setting", **Cape Town Stadium**, on Fritz Zonneneberg Rd in Green Point, was arguably the jewel in South Africa's 2010 World Cup crown. The towering, 68,000-seater stadium relies on natural light, and at night the open-meshed roof resembles an ethereal UFO. Controversy surrounded its high building costs, which were funded by taxpayers, while the revelation of **corruption** during the tender process for its construction further tainted the stadium's reputation. Today, local teams use the stadium for **football matches** and it also hosts **concerts** by mainstream international artists: tickets for both can be bought at ⓦ computicket.com/web/sport/soccer.

Sea Point

West along Main Road, Green Point merges with **Sea Point**, a cosmopolitan area crammed with apartment blocks, the odd Victorian house, tourist accommodation and restaurants. The Sea Point promenade is the best way to appreciate the rocky coastline and salty air, along with pram-pushing mothers, grannies, power walkers and joggers. People picnic or play ball games on the grassy parkland beside the walkway. The restaurants and shops are along Main Road, a busy thoroughfare, one block nearer Lion's Head than the Promenade.

Sea Point Pavilion Swimming Pool

Lower Beach Rd • Daily: May–Nov 9am–5pm; Dec–April 7am–7pm • R20

At the westernmost end of Sea Point Promenade, a series of four unheated saltwater, chlorine **pools** are set alongside the crashing surf in a stunning location. The largest of the four pools is Olympic-sized, making it a popular training tank for many of Cape Town's long-distance swimmers. There are also two kids' splash pools and a fully equipped diving pool.

Bantry Bay

At the westernmost edge of Sea Point lies **Bantry Bay**, combining the density of Sea Point with the wealth of the Atlantic suburbs; mansions rake back from the Atlantic

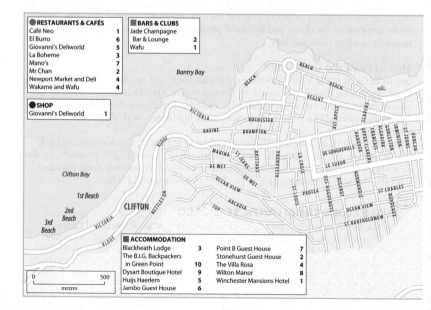

● RESTAURANTS & CAFÉS	
Café Neo	1
El Burro	6
Giovanni's Deliworld	5
La Boheme	3
Mano's	7
Mr Chan	2
Newport Market and Deli	4
Wakame and Wafu	4

■ BARS & CLUBS	
Jade Champagne	
Bar & Lounge	2
Wafu	1

● SHOP	
Giovanni's Deliworld	1

■ ACCOMMODATION			
Blackheath Lodge	3	Point B Guest House	7
The B.I.G. Backpackers		Stonehurst Guest House	2
in Green Point	10	The Villa Rosa	4
Dysart Boutique Hotel	9	Wilton Manor	8
Huijs Haerlem	5	Winchester Mansions Hotel	1
Jambo Guest House	6		

0 ____ 500
metres

shore on steep slopes, guarded by the granite boulders of Lion's Head. The upmarket resort hotels and self-catering apartment blocks are just far enough for comfort from the hubbub of Sea Point, but close enough should you want to walk to a restaurant.

Clifton

Fashionable **Clifton**, on the next cove along Victoria Road (the M6) from Bantry Bay, sits on the most expensive real estate in Africa, studded with fancy seaside apartments and four sandy **beaches**, reached via steep stairways separated by clusters of granite boulders. The sea here is good for surfing and safe for swimming, but bone-chillingly cold. Bring your own refreshments as there's only one overpriced café, although adjacent Camps Bay (see below) is packed with them. The beaches here are sheltered from the wind and popular with muscular ball-players and families alike, and are especially recommended on summer evenings to enjoy the sunset and cool of the day.

Camps Bay

The suburb of **Camps Bay** climbs the slopes of Table Mountain and is scooped into a small amphitheatre, bounded by the Lion's Head and the Twelve Apostles sections of the Table Mountain range. This, and the airborne views across the Atlantic, makes it one of the most desirable places to live in Cape Town. The main drag, Victoria Road, skirts the coast and is packed with trendy restaurants, a couple of nightspots and some upmarket accommodation, while the wide sandy is enjoyed by families of all shapes and colours. However, the beach is exposed to the southeaster, and there's the usual Atlantic chill and an occasional dangerous backwash.

Llandudno

There's little development between Camps Bay and the exclusive cove of **Llandudno**, 20km from Cape Town along Victoria Road (not served by public transport). Here a steep and narrow road winds down past smart homes to the shore, where the sandy

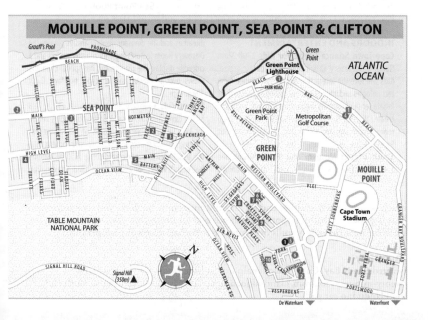

MOUILLE POINT, GREEN POINT, SEA POINT & CLIFTON

1

CAPE TOWN FOR KIDS

Cape Town is an excellent place to travel with children, with plenty of outdoorsy activities. A good **website** for finding out what's on is Cape Town Kids (ⓦcapetownkids.co.za). For **babysitters**, or even nannies, to accompany you on trips, try Sitters4U (ⓣ083 691 2009, ⓦsitters4u.co.za) or Super Sitters (ⓣ021 552 1220, ⓦsupersitters.net). Car rental companies will provide **child seats**, if booked in advance.

BEACHES AND SWIMMING POOLS

Cape Town's **beaches** are a classic summer weekend family outing, though the water is not warm. Most beaches are pretty undeveloped, so it's best to take what you need in the way of food and drinks with you. Get to the beach as early as possible to leave by 11am when the sun gets too strong, and to avoid the wind which often gusts up in the late morning.

On the False Bay seaboard, **Boulders Beach** (see p.122) is one of the few beaches to visit when the southeaster is blowing, and gorgeous at any time. It has safe, flat water, making it ideal for kids – and its resident penguin-breeding colony is an added attraction. **Fish Hoek** (see p.121) is one of the best peninsula beaches, with a long stretch of sand and a playground. The paved Jager's Walk which runs along the rocky coast here is suitable for pushchairs. **St James** (see p.120) boasts a safe tidal pool with a small sandy beach and photogenic bathing boxes, though it is seriously overcrowded on summer weekends. From here you can walk to Muizenberg along a pushchair-friendly coastal pathway.

The **Atlantic seaboard** is too cold for swimming, but does have some lovely stretches of sand, boulders and rock pools – and astonishing scenery. The beaches here are excellent for picnics, and on calm summer evenings idyllic at sunset. The closest stretch of coast to the centre ideal for prams – and rollerblading – is the paved **Sea Point promenade**, stretching 3km from the lighthouse in Mouille Point to Sea Point Pavilion, with the draw of playgrounds en route. The tidal pool and small rock pools of **Camps Bay** (see p.113) make this popular beach very child-friendly, and it's easily reached from the centre by car or bus. Finally, the six-kilometre stretch of white sand from **Noordhoek** to **Kommetjie** (see p.118) provides fine walking and horseriding opportunities, with stupendous views of Chapman's Peak. It has a sheltered area among the rocks on the Noordhoek side. If you're heading for Kommetjie you can go camel-riding at Imhoff Farm Village (see opposite).

As regards child-friendly swimming pools, **Newlands Pool** (see p.153) has a toddlers' pool and a little playground in large grounds, while the marvellous **Sea Point Pool** at Sea Point Pavilion (see p.112) has two paddling pools for children, and lawns to laze on.

INDOORS AND ENTERTAINMENT

Cape Town Science Centre for Kids 370B Main Road, Observatory ⓣ021 300 3200, ⓦctsc.org.za. Kids will love the interactive displays on science, new technologies and inventions here, which appeal to their innate sense of curiosity with things to touch, push and create. Highlights include a miniature train, a Lego room and a life size space shuttle. R40. Mon–Sat 9am–4.30pm, Sun 10am–4.30pm.

South African Museum and Planetarium See p.96. The four-storey whale well, African animal dioramas and the dinosaur displays always please. The Discovery Room features live ants, massive spiders and a crocodile display. The planetarium has special children's shows over weekends and in school holidays. Daily 10am–5pm.

Planet Kids 3 Wherry Rd, Muizenberg ⓣ021 788 3070, ⓦplanetkids.co.za. A great indoor play centre for kids up to 12, which is loads of fun, as well as offering healthy snacks and a calmer environment than the usual plastic, sugar-crazed scene (R30/hr, parents free entry). With good assistants on hand, you can drop

beach is punctuated at either end by magnificent granite boulders and rock formations. This is a good sunbathing spot and a choice one for bring-your-own sundowners. The small car park frequently spills over into the suburban streets at peak periods.

Sandy Bay

Isolated **Sandy Bay**, Cape Town's main nudist beach, can only be reached via a twenty-minute walk from Llandudno; a signposted path leads from the south end of the Llandudno car park.

off your child for an hour, or have tea and a home-bake while you wait. All abilities welcome, with facilities for kids with special needs. Wed–Sun 10am–6pm.

Ratanga Junction Century City, signposted off N1 ☎ 021 550 8504, ⓦ ratanga.co.za. Popular and safe theme park with thrilling rides such as the Cobra, Crocodile Gorge and Monkey Falls. An easy and fun day out for parents as well as kids. Don't bring your own food – everything must be purchased on site. It's only open during Cape school holidays, so call beforehand. The entry price gives you unlimited rides (R172, younger kids R85, R60 for non-riders). Sat & Sun 10am–5pm.

Scratch Patch and Mineral World Dido Valley Rd, off Main Rd, Simon's Town ☎ 021 786 2020, and V&A Waterfront ☎ 021 419 9429. Over-3s can search for jewels, filling a bag with the reject polished gemstones that literally cover the floor. At the Simon's Town venue you can also see one of the world's biggest gemstone tumbling plants in operation (Mon–Fri only). Simon's Town daily 8.30am–4.45pm; V&A daily 9am–6pm.

Two Oceans Aquarium See p.102. One of Cape Town's most rewarding museums, the aquarium features loads to interest a wide range of ages. As well as looking at the weird and wonderful sea creatures, children can handle a few species in the touch pool – sometimes this includes a small shark or sea urchins – while older kids can learn about marine ecology on computer terminals. Daily 9.30am–6pm.

OUTDOORS AND PICNICS

Blue Train Park Beach Rd, Mouille Point ☎ 084 314 9200, ⓦ thebluetrainpark.com. Take a trip on Cape Town's only miniature train for a view of the sea, passing ships and Robben Island. There's also plenty to wear kids out afterwards in the park with a jungle gym, a climbing rock, outdoor obstacles, basketball court, mini oval cement track and toddler push-bike track. Tues–Sun 9.30am–6pm.

The Deer Park Cafe 2 Deerpark Drive, Vredehoek ☎ 021 462 6311. The most central outdoor family venue, on the edge of a small park (sadly no deer) with swings and slides, and views across the suburb to Table Bay. There is a kids' menu, plus imaginative food for

adults, with plenty of fresh stuff. Daily 8am–8pm.

Green Point Urban Park Beach Rd, entrance opposite Green Point lighthouse. Offering vistas over the city and stadium, this grassy park has an educational biodiversity garden, tracks for jogging and cycling, a play park for small children and an outdoor gym for those a little older. Trees offer shade for picnics. Free entry. Daily 7am–7pm.

Imhoff Farm Village Kommetjie Rd, opposite the Ocean View turn-off ☎ 021 783 4545, ⓦ imhofffarm .co.za. Activities here include camel rides, horseriding on the beach, paintball, a farmyard petting zoo and a reptile park. There's also a good café, restaurant and farmers' shop with fabulous cheeses. Daily 9am–5pm.

Kirstenbosch National Botanical Gardens See p.106. Top of the list for a family outing, with extensive lawns for running about, trees and rocks to climb and streams to paddle in. There's no litter, no dogs, it's extremely safe and you can push a pram all over the walkways; it's also great for picnics or to have tea outdoors at the café. For older kids there are short waymarked walks.

Noordhoek Farm Village See p.118. A small, grassy green, surrounded by cafés, a bakery, crafts stores and a gift shop, with gentle country charm. At weekends you can grab a coffee and listen to live music at *Café Roux* while the children run around in the adjacent play park. Daily 9am–5pm.

Oude Molen Eco Village Alexandra Rd, Pinelands ☎ 021 447 8226. A working model of a sustainable eco-village in a suburban area. You can sample home-grown organic produce and wood-fired bread at the *Millstone Farmstall and Café* before taking the kids to play in the garden tree house, swing and play area. Children are encouraged to feed the horses and pigs nearby. Tues–Sun 8am–5pm.

Silvermine Nature Reserve See p.121. A good place to see *fynbos* vegetation at close quarters and stroll around the lake and picnic with small children; however, it is exposed, and not recommended in heavy winds or mist. For older children there are some mountaintop walks with relatively gentle gradients, which give spectacular views.

In the apartheid days, the South African police went to ingenious lengths to trap nudists, but today the beach is relaxed, so feel free to come as undressed as feels comfortable. It's a prime gay cruising spot too.

Hout Bay

Although no longer the quaint fishing village it once was, **Hout Bay** still has a functioning fishing harbour and is the centre of the local crayfish industry. Some 20km from the centre, it's a favourite day outing, and despite ugly modern

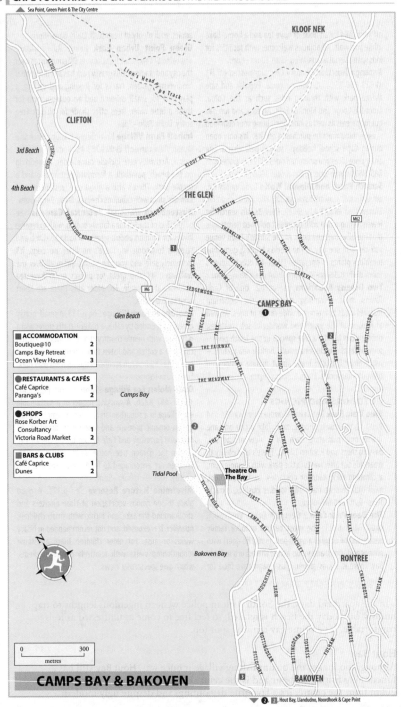

▲ Sea Point, Green Point & The City Centre

KLOOF NEK

CLIFTON

Lion's Head Pipe Track

3rd Beach

4th Beach

THE GLEN

CAMPS BAY ❶

Glen Beach

■ ACCOMMODATION	
Boutique@10	2
Camps Bay Retreat	1
Ocean View House	3

● RESTAURANTS & CAFÉS	
Café Caprice	1
Paranga's	2

● SHOPS	
Rose Korber Art	
Consultancy	1
Victoria Road Market	2

■ BARS & CLUBS	
Café Caprice	1
Dunes	2

Camps Bay

Theatre On The Bay

Tidal Pool

Bakoven Bay

RONTREE

BAKOVEN

0 ——— 300
metres

CAMPS BAY & BAKOVEN

1

DUIKER ISLAND CRUISES

The best way to take in the dramatic sea and mountain landscape is on a short cruise from Hout Bay harbour to **Duiker Island**, sometimes called "seal island" because it's home to a massive **colony** of South African, or Cape, seals, the largest of the fur seals. Of the operators that run tours (10 daily departures all year round; 45 min; R65) Nauticat (☎021 790 7278, ⓦnauticatcharters.co.za) is one of the best, with glass-bottomed boats that allow you to see the seals and kelp underwater.

---

development and a growing shantytown, the natural setting is spectacular, with the Sentinel and Chapman's Peak defining the entry to the bay. Highly unusual for Cape Town with its legacy of apartheid town planning, poor black areas nose right up to wealthy white ones.

ImiZamo Yethu township

As you head towards Constantia Nek from Hout Bay, you come to the township of **ImiZamo Yethu**, a tightly packed shackland settlement crawling up the hillside. ImiZamo Yethu was first settled during the late 1980s, the dying days of apartheid, by Xhosa job seekers from Willowvale in the rural Eastern Cape. Its population is now estimated at between twelve and thirty thousand. Although conditions are pretty dire (the highest levels of *E. Coli* ever recorded in South Africa were found in the Disa River which flows through the settlement), it is an easy township for visitors to visit and feel welcome.

World of Birds

Valley Rd • Daily 9am–5pm • R85 • Monkey jungle daily 11.30am–1pm & 2–3.30pm • Penguin feeding at 11.30am & 3.30pm • Pelican feeding at 12.30pm • Birds of prey feeding at 4.30pm • ⓦ worldofbirds.org.za

The **World of Birds** is home to more than three thousand birds, housed in surprisingly pleasant and peaceful walk-through aviaries, and four hundred animals in cages; allow at least two hours for a visit. The birds include indigenous species such as cranes, vultures, ostriches and pelicans, as well as a number of feathered exotics. The large walk-in monkey jungle includes among its inhabitants cute squirrel monkeys that visitors can handle and play with. There's a café serving light lunches, or you can picnic at the Flamingo Terrace. Children are well catered for with a couple of playground areas, and the setting with lush gardens and a mountainous backdrop makes for a very tranquil outing.

Chapman's Peak Drive

Toll charge R40 • ☎ 021 791 8222, ⓦ chapmanspeakdrive.co.za

Thrilling **Chapman's Peak Drive**, a 9km route with 114 curves, is one of the world's best ocean drives, winding along a cliff-edge to Noordhoek. There are a number of safe viewpoints along the route, some of which have picnic sites, so bring a snack and refreshments and stop to enjoy the spectacular view. The road is occasionally closed wing to rockfalls, so it's advisable to phone or check the website in advance.

TOURS OF IMIZAMO YETHU

Although it is unsafe to wander into ImiZamo Yethu alone, you can take a fun, two-hour **walking tour** (daily at 10.30am, 1pm & 4pm; R75; ☎083 719 4870, ⓦ suedafrika.net/ imizamoyethu) with enthusiastic and accomplished guide Afrika Moni, who knows the place and its history inside out. He walks you through his home township, stopping to chat to proprietors of informal "spaza" shops, sipping traditional beer at a *shebeen*, as well as popping into shacks and brick houses. Tours start from the police station at the entrance to the township, where there are reserved parking places for visitors; the Blue Mini Peninsula Tour bus (see p.128) stops here too.

1

Noordhoek

A desirable settlement at the southern end of Chapman's Peak Drive, 25km from the city centre, **Noordhoek** consists of smallholdings and riding stables in a gentle valley planted with oaks, the centre of which is the Farm Village. When Chapman's Peak is closed, Noordhoek is accessible via the M3 south over Oukaapseweg.

Noordhoek beach

On the right as you come in from Chapman's Peak is the unobtrusive sign for **Noordhoek Beach**, whose immense, white, kelp-strewn sands stretch towards Kommetje. Each morning at 7.15am, **racehorses** gallop along the sand, while, at other times, amateur riders (see p.153) share the wide beach with local dog walkers. The sea is cold, wild and spectacular, framed by Chapman's Peak, though strong winds can sometimes turn the beach into a sandblaster. The nearby *Monkey Valley Resort* (see p.137) welcomes non-residents for reasonably priced meals with great views, its groves of milkwood trees offering shelter from the wind.

Noordhoek Farm Village

Village Lane • Daily 9am–5pm • Free • ☏ 021 789 2812, ⓦ noordhoekvillage.co.za

The **Noordhoek Farm Village**, close to the signposted entrance to Chapman's Peak drive, is an excellent place for refuelling or entertaining children. It has one of Cape Town's best restaurants, *The Foodbarn* (see p.143) and there's also a sushi restaurant, a café, deli and pub, as well as a children's playground and several craft shops.

Kommetjie

Although only a few kilometres' walk south of Noordhoek along the beach, getting to the tiny settlement of **Kommetjie** by road involves a detour inland to avoid the wetlands. Facilities are limited and one of the main reasons to come here is for the superb walks, either around the rocky shore near Slangkop lighthouse, or across the extensive sands of Long Beach back towards Noordhoek.

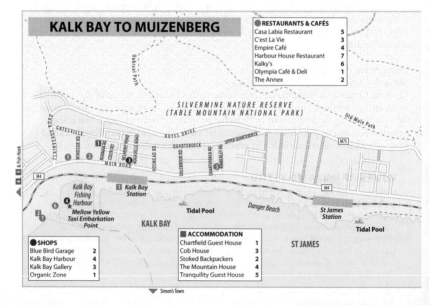

Scarborough

The developing and idyllic village of **Scarborough** is the most far-flung settlement along the peninsula, with turquoise, cold water and white sands. The drive here from Simon's Town is an easy and lovely one, winding over the spine of the peninsula and on to Cape Point.

The False Bay seaboard

In summer the waters of **False Bay** are several degrees warmer than those on the Atlantic seaboard, which is why Cape Town's oldest and most popular seaside development is along this flank of the peninsula. A series of village-like suburbs, backing onto the mountains, each served by a Metrorail station, is dotted all the way south from **Muizenberg**, through **St James**, **Kalk Bay**, **Fish Hoek** and down to **Simon's Town**. Each has its own character with restaurants, shops and places to stay, while Simon's Town, one of South Africa's oldest settlements, is worth taking in as a day-trip and makes a useful base for visiting the Cape of Good Hope section of the **Table Mountain National Park** and **Cape Point** (see p.124).

ARRIVAL AND DEPARTURE   FALSE BAY SEABOARD

By car From central Cape Town, the best route is along the M3 south to Muizenberg. Boyes Drive, a high-level alternative to Main Rd, runs for about 5km between the suburbs of Lakeside at the southern end of the M3 and Kalk Bay, and offers spectacular views.

By train The train ride to Simon's Town is reason enough to visit, with most stations from Muizenberg onwards

situated close to the shore. From Cape Town, Metrorail (☎021 449 6478, ⓦwww.metrorail.co.za) trains run to Simon's Town (Mon–Fri 5am–7pm 2 hourly, Sat & Sun 1 hourly; 1hr 15min; R15), with more frequent trains to Fish Hoek (3 hourly; 58min; R13). Both routes run via Muizenberg (48min; R13), St James (51min; R10) and Kalk Bay (53min; R10).

Muizenberg

Now a bit run down, **Muizenberg** was once South Africa's most fashionable seaside resort, with brightly coloured bathing boxes along the beach reminding visitors of its

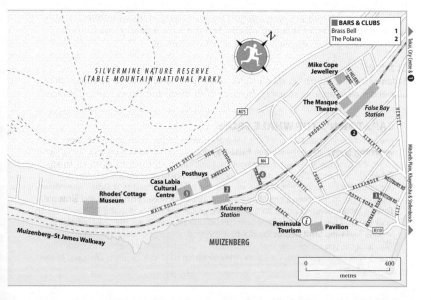

1

ALL ABOARD

These beachfront surf shops offer surfing lessons and equipment rental for those who want to try their skills on Muizenberg's breakers.

Gary's Surf School 34 Balmoral Building, Beach Rd • 021 788 9839, ⓦ garysurf.com. R380 for a two-hour lesson including gear rental.

Surf Shack Muizenberg Corner, Beach Rd • 021 788 9286, ⓦ surfshack.co.za. R330 for a 90min lesson, or four lessons for R1100.

more elegant heyday. However, nothing detracts from its long, safe and fabulous beach, which shelves gently, making it the most popular spot along the peninsula for swimming. It was also nominated one of the world's top twenty surfing villages by National Geographic, and the beachfront has several surf shops offering lessons and equipment rental (see box above), as well as a couple of cafés. Make sure you don't take valuables, including car keys, onto Muizenberg beach – leave them with one of the staff at the beachfront surf shops, who will happily look after them.

The Historical Mile

A short stretch of the shore, starting at Muizenberg station, is known as the **Historical Mile**, dotted with a run of notable buildings. **Muizenberg Station**, an Edwardian-style edifice completed in 1913, with its lovely ornate clock tower, is now a National Monument, while the **Posthuys** is a rugged whitewashed and thatched building dating from 1673 and a fine example of the Cape vernacular style – and purportedly the oldest European building in South Africa. **Rhodes' Cottage Museum**, 246 Main Road (Tues–Sun 10am–1pm & 2–5pm; free), was bought in 1899 by the millionaire empire builder who died here in 1902, and contains some personal memorabilia and period furniture.

Casa Labia Cultural Centre

192 Main Rd • Tues–Sun 10am–4pm • Free • ☎ 021 788 6068, ⓦ casalabia.co.za

The most idiosyncratic of the buildings along the Historical Mile, **Casa Labia** was completed in 1930 as the residence of the Italian consul, Count Natale Labia. Built in the eighteenth-century Venetian style, it's a glorious piece of architectural bling on Main Road and worth popping into just for the *palazzo*'s film-set **interiors**. It also houses a **cultural centre** that puts on concerts and talks, a **gallery** that features contemporary South African art, and a rather opulent café.

St James

St James is more upmarket than neighbouring Muizenberg, its mountainside homes accessed mostly up long stairways between Main Road and Boyes Drive. The best

CAPE TOWN'S TOP WHALE SPOTS

The commonest whales around Cape Town are southern rights, and the best **whale-watching spots** are on the warmer **False Bay** side of the peninsula from August to October. Along the False Bay seaboard, whale signboards indicate good places for sightings. **Boyes Drive**, running along the mountainside behind Muizenberg and Kalk Bay, provides an outstanding vantage point, and there are often whales off the coast at St James. Alternatively, sticking close to the shore along Main Road, the stretch between **Fish Hoek** and **Simon's Town** is recommended, with a particularly nice spot above the rocks at the south end of Fish Hoek Beach. Even better vantage points can be found further down the coast between Simon's Town and **Smitswinkelbaai**, where the road goes higher along the mountainside. Without a car, you can get the train to Fish Hoek or Simon's Town and whale-spot from the Jager's Walk beach path that runs along the coast from Fish Hoek to Sunny Cove, just below the railway line.

1

reason to hop off the train here is for the **sheltered tidal pool** and the twenty-minute walk along the **paved coastal path** that runs along the rocky shore to Muizenberg – one of the peninsula's easiest and most rewarding walks, with panoramas of the full sweep of False Bay. Look out for seals and, in season, whales.

The compact St James beach draws considerable character from its much-photographed Victorian-style bathing boxes, whose bright, primary colours catch your eye as you pass by road or rail. The beach tends to be overcrowded at weekends and during school holidays; occasionally, African Christian groups carry out jubilant baptising ceremonies here, early on Sunday mornings, wading fully dressed into its waters.

Kalk Bay

One of the most southerly of Cape Town's suburbs, **Kalk Bay** centres around a lively working harbour with wooden fishing vessels, mountain views, and a strip of shops packed with collectibles, antique shops, trendy coffee shops and excellent restaurants. Kalk Bay somehow managed to slip through the net of the Group Areas Act, making it one of the few places on the peninsula with an intact coloured community, and Kalk Bay and the larger Hout Bay are the only harbour settlements still worked by coloured fishermen. It is well known for its artistic and alternative community too, living up cobbled streets, and there is a fair bit of visitor accommodation available.

The village is arranged around the small docks, where you can watch the boats come in; you can also buy fresh fish, which are flung onto the quayside, sold in spirited auctions, gutted for a small fee and the innards then thrown to waiting seals. Kalk Bay is busiest on Saturdays and Sundays when Capetonians descend to breakfast or lunch at one of the excellent cafés, wander the shops and harbour, or have a drink at the water's edge.

Silvermine Nature Reserve

Ou Kaapse Weg, signposted at the southern end of the M3 • Daily: May–Sept 8am–5pm; Oct–April 7am–6pm • R40

Part of the Table Mountain chain, the beautiful **Silvermine Nature Reserve** offers walks with fabulous views of both sides of the peninsula, and a lake to swim in and picnic by. At the entrance, you'll be given a sketchy map of the reserve with the walks marked on, though the accurate *Slingsby Silvermine & Hout Bay Map* (⊚slingsbymaps.com) is by far the best map of the reserve.

Fish Hoek

South of Kalk Bay, **Fish Hoek** boasts one of the peninsula's finest family **beaches** along the False Bay coast. The best and safest swimming is at its southern end, where the surf is moderately warm, tame and much enjoyed by boogie boarders. Thanks to the beach, there's a fair amount of accommodation (see p.138), but this is otherwise one of the dreariest suburbs along the False Bay coast. An obscure bylaw banning the sale of alcohol in supermarkets or bottle stores boosts the town's image as the Mother Grundy capital of the peninsula.

Simon's Town

The country's third-oldest European settlement, and also South Africa's principal naval base, **Simon's Town** isn't the hard-drinking, raucous place you might expect. It's exceptionally pretty, with a near-perfectly preserved historic streetscape, slightly marred

---

FALSE BAY WATER TAXI

In summer, **the Mellow Yellow Water Taxi** runs across False Bay from Kalk Bay to Simon's Town (☎073 473 7684, ⊚watertaxi.co.za; R100 one-way, R150 return). The trip is highly recommended, and one of the few ways to get on the water in False Bay; book ahead as the boat only goes if there are enough people and weather conditions are favourable.

1

on the ocean side by the domineering **naval dockyard**. On the other hand, glimpses of naval squaddies square-bashing behind the high walls or strolling to the station in their crisp white uniforms are part of the place's distinct character. Just 40km from Cape Town, roughly halfway down the coast to Cape Point, Simon's Town is a favourite stop-off point on peninsula tours, but it's also a good option for a holiday base, with sweeping vistas of False Bay and the Hottentots Holland Mountains. A few kilometres to the south is **Boulders Beach**, with its colony of cute **African penguins** – reason enough alone for a Simon's Town visit.

Brief history

Founded in 1687 as the winter anchorage of the Dutch East India Company, Simon's Town was one of several places in and around Cape Town modestly named by **Governor Simon van der Stel** after himself. Its most celebrated visitor was Lord Nelson, who convalesced here as a midshipman while returning home from the East in 1776. Nineteen years later, the British sailed into Simon's Town and occupied it as a bridgehead for their first invasion and occupation of the Cape. They left after just seven years, only to return in 1806. Simon's Town remained a British base until 1957, when it was handed over to South Africa.

There are fleeting hints, such as the occasional mosque, that the town's predominantly white appearance isn't the whole story. In fact, the first **Muslims** arrived from the East Indies in the early eighteenth century, imported as slaves to build the Dutch naval base. After the British banning of the slave trade in 1807, ships were compelled to disgorge their human cargo at Simon's Town, where one district became known as Black Town. In 1967, when Simon's Town was declared a White Group Area, there were 1200 well-established coloured families living here, who were descended from these slaves. By the early 1970s, the majority had been forcibly removed under the Group Areas Act to the township of Ocean View, whose inspiring name belies its desolation.

Simon's Town Museum

Court Rd • Mon–Fri 10am–4pm, Sat 10am–1pm • R20 • Ⓦ simonstown.com/museum

The building now housing the **Simon's Town Museum** was once the Old Residency, built in 1772 for the Governor of the Dutch East India Company, and has also served as the slave quarters (the dungeons are in the basement) and town brothel. The museum's motley collection includes maritime material and an inordinate amount of information and exhibits on Able Seaman Just Nuisance, a much-celebrated seafaring Great Dane. He enjoyed drinking beer with the sailors he accompanied into Cape Town, and was adopted as a mascot by the Royal Navy during World War II.

Jubilee Square and St George's Street

In the centre of Simon's Town, a little over 1km south of the station, lies **Jubilee Square**, a palm-shaded car park just off St George's Street. Flanked by some cafés and shops, the street has on its harbour-facing side a broad walkway with a statue of the ubiquitous Able Seaman Just Nuisance and a few curio sellers. A couple of sets of stairs lead down to the **Marina**, a modest development of shops and restaurants set right on the waterfront.

Boulders Beach and the Penguin Reserve

2km from Simon's Town Station • Daily: Feb–March 8am–6.30pm; April–Sept 8am–5pm; Oct–Nov 8am–6.30pm; Dec–Jan 7am–7.30pm • R53 • HGTS Tours (☎ 021 786 5243) runs a taxi service from Simon's Town Station to Boulders Beach (one-way R40).

Boulders Beach takes its name from the huge granite rocks, which create a cluster of little coves with sandy beaches and clear sea pools that are gorgeous for swimming. However, the main reason people come to Boulders' fenced seafront reserve is for the **African penguins** (formerly known as jackass penguins). African penguins usually live

---

SPOTTING MARINE LIFE IN FALSE BAY

False Bay is one of the best places in the country to see **Great White Sharks**, and you can also go **whale-watching** and visit **seals**. One of the best shark trip operators is **Apex Shark Expeditions** (☎ 021 786 5717, ⓦ apexpredators.com; Feb–March R1750, April–May R1900, June–Aug R2400), run by naturalists Chris and Monique Fallows, who have worked with National Geographic and the BBC. They run a range of marine trips from Simon's Town pier, including shark-cage diving. Their emphasis is on observing the sharks' behaviour, and that of other marine creatures that you'll encounter on the trip out to Seal Island. Passengers numbers are strictly limited to twelve, and you get twenty to thirty minutes in the cage. The long-established **Simon's Town Boat Company** (☎ 083 257 7760, ⓦ boatcompany.co.za) runs whale-watching trips (R750), plus cruises around Cape Point (R550) and tours to Seal Island (R400). It also offers guided history tours that include a visit to the Naval Dockyard and a **tour of a submarine** (R80).

---

on islands off the west side of the South African coast, and the Boulders birds form one of only two mainland colonies in the world. This is also the only place where the endangered species are actually increasing in numbers, and provides a rare opportunity to get a close look at them.

Access to the Boulders reserve is through two gates, one at the Boulders Beach (eastern) end, off Bellevue Road, and the other at the **Seaforth Beach** (western) side, off Seaforth Road. Both entrances are signposted along Main Road between Simon's Town and Cape Point. At Seaforth, there's a small visitors' centre and deck, from which two boardwalks lead to either end of Foxy Beach where you'll see hundreds of penguins. Most people walk from Seaforth to Boulders, looking at all the penguins in the bushes along the paths, where there are masses of burrows for nesting. At Seaforth itself, there is safe swimming on the beach, which is bounded on one side by the looming grey mass of the naval base. While there are no facilities of any kind on Boulders Beach, there is a restaurant with outdoor seating and fresh fish on the menu at both Seafront and Boulders beach entrances.

Cape of Good Hope

Daily: April–Sept 7am–5pm; Oct–March 6am–6pm • R105 • ☎ 021 780 9526, ⓦ tmnp.co.za, ⓦ capepoint.co.za

Most people come to the **Cape of Good Hope section** of the Table Mountain National Park to see the southernmost tip of Africa at **Cape Point**. In fact, the continent's real tip is at Cape Agulhas, some 300km southeast of here (see p.205), but Cape Point is a lot easier to get to and a hugely dramatic spot. The reserve sits atop massive sea cliffs with huge views, strong seas and, when it's blowing southeast, gales that whip off caps and sunglasses as visitors gaze southwards from the old lighthouse buttress.

From the car park, the famous viewpoint is a short, steep walk up a series of stairs to the original lighthouse. A **funicular** (R52 return) runs to the top, where there's a curio shop.

ARRIVAL AND INFORMATION   CAPE OF GOOD HOPE

By guided tour There's no public transport to the reserve, but numerous tours take it in as part of a package of peninsula highlights (see p.130). Day Trippers (☎ 021 511 4766, ⓦ daytrippers.co.za) runs fun tours from Central Cape Town for R630 (including a picnic lunch), some of which give you the option of cycling part of the way. However you get there, go as early as you can in the day – the chances of the crowds and of the wind gusting up increase as the day progresses.

Tourist information Buffelsfontein Visitors' Centre, 8km from the entrance gate, has attractive displays about the local fauna and flora as well as video screenings on the ecology of the area (daily 7.30am–5pm).

1

FURRY FELONS

Baboons may look amusing, but be warned: they can be a menace. Keep your car windows closed, as it's not uncommon for them to invade vehicles, and they're adept at swiping picnics. You should lock your car doors even if you only plan to get out for a few minutes as there are growing reports of baboons opening unlocked car doors while the vehicle owner's back is turned. Avoid unwrapping food or eating or drinking anything if baboons are in the vicinity. Feeding them is illegal and provocative and can incur a fine. Authorized baboon-chasers are in evidence in several places, warding them off.

Cape Point and around

Cape Point is the treacherous promontory of rocks, winds and swells braved by navigators since the Portuguese first "rounded the Cape" in the fifteenth century. Plenty of wrecks lie submerged off its coast, and at **Olifantsbos** on the west side you can walk to a US ship sunk in 1942, and a South African coaster that ran aground in 1965. The **Old Lighthouse**, built in 1860, was too often dangerously shrouded in cloud, and failed to keep ships off the rocks, so another was built lower down in 1914. It's not always successful in averting disasters, but is still the most powerful light beaming onto the sea from South Africa.

Walking

Most visitors make a beeline for Cape Point, seeing the rest of the reserve through a vehicle window, but walking is the best way to appreciate the dramatic landscape and **flora**.

There are several waymarked **walks** in the Cape of Good Hope Nature Reserve. If you're planning a big hike it's best to set out early, and take plenty of water, as shade is rare and the wind can be foul. One of the most straightforward **hiking routes** is the signposted forty-minute trek from the car park at Cape Point to the more westerly **Cape of Good Hope**. For exploring the shoreline, a clear path runs down the Atlantic side, which you can join at **Gifkommetjie**, signposted off Cape Point Road. From the car park, several sandy tracks drop quite steeply down the slope across rocks, and through bushes and milkwood trees to the shore, along which you can walk in either direction.

The beaches

A single main road runs from the Cape Point entrance to the car park, restaurant and funicular. A number of roads branch off this, each leading to one of the series of beaches on either side of the peninsula. The sea is too dangerous for swimming, but there are safe tidal pools at the **Buffels Bay** and **Bordjiesrif beaches**, which are adjacent

CAPE FAUNA

Along with indigenous plants and flowers, you may well spot some of the animals living in the *fynbos* habitat on Cape Point. **Ostriches** stride through the low *fynbos*, and occasionally **African penguins** come ashore. A distinctive bird on the rocky shores is the **black oystercatcher** with its bright red beak, jabbing limpets off the rocks. You'll also see **Cape cormorants** in large flocks on the beach or rocks, often drying their outstretched wings. Running up and down the water's edge, littered with piles of shiny brown *Ecklonia* kelp, are **white-fronted plovers** and **sanderlings**, probing for food left by the receding waves.

As for mammals, **baboons** lope along the rocky shoreline, while grazing on the heathery slopes you'll see **bontebok**, **eland** and **red hartebeest**, as well as **Cape rhebok** and **grysbok**. If you're very lucky, you may even see the rare **Cape mountain zebras**. What you will undoubtedly see are rock agama lizards, black zonure lizards and rock rabbits (*dassies*).

1

to each other, midway along the east shore. Both have braai stands, but more southerly Buffels Bay is the nicer, with big lawned areas and some sheltered spots to have a picnic.

The Cape Flats and the townships

East of the northern and southern suburbs, among the industrial smokestacks and the windswept **Cape Flats**, reaching well beyond the airport, is Cape Town's largest residential quarter, taking in the **coloured districts**, **African townships** and shantytown **squatter camps**. The Cape Flats are exactly that: flat, barren and populous, exclusively inhabited by Africans and coloureds in separate areas, with the M5 acting as a dividing line between it and the largely white southern suburbs.

Brief history

The African townships were historically set up as dormitories to provide labour for white Cape Town, not as places to build a life, which is why they had no facilities and no real hub. The **men-only hostels**, another apartheid relic, are at the root of many of the area's social problems. During the 1950s, the government set out a blueprint to turn the tide of Africans flooding into Cape Town. No African was permitted to settle permanently in the Cape west of a line near the Fish River, the old frontier over 1000km from Cape Town; women were entirely banned from seeking work in Cape Town and men prohibited from bringing their wives to join them. By 1970 there were ten men for every woman in Langa.

In the end, apartheid failed to prevent the influx of work-seekers desperate to come to Cape Town. Where people couldn't find legal accommodation they set up **squatter camps** of makeshift iron, cardboard and plastic sheeting. During the 1970s and 1980s, the government attempted to demolish these and destroy anything left inside – but no sooner had the police left than the camps reappeared, and they are now a permanent feature of the Cape Flats. One of the best known of all South Africa's squatter camps is **Crossroads**, whose inhabitants suffered campaigns of harassment that included killings by apartheid collaborators and police, and continuous attempts to bulldoze it out of existence. Through sheer determination and desperation its residents hung on, eventually winning the right to stay. Today, the government is making attempts to improve conditions in the shantytowns by introducing electricity, running water and sanitation, as well as building tiny brick houses to replace the shacks. In addition, several new projects are under way to encourage tourists into the townships, which highlight positive social and economic development and responsible tourism.

Langa

The oldest and most central township, **LANGA** lies off the N2, between the largely white suburb of Pinelands and the airport. In this relentlessly grey and littered place, without

---

VISITING THE TOWNSHIPS

Visiting the townships under your own steam is not recommended – besides the potential threat of opportunistic crime, road signs are very poor and opening and closing times erratic, so it's hard to find your own way around to the places listed. The best way to visit any of the township projects is on a **tour**, either with Coffeebeans Routes (☎021 424 3572, ⓦcoffeebeansroutes.com; see p.131), which safely navigates visitors through the sprawling and disorientating townships, or Real Cape Tours (☎082 885 8945, ⓦfacebook.com/realcape; see p.131). It's possible, too, to gain a deeper understanding of the daily lives of the majority of South Africans by **staying overnight** in a B&B at one of the townships (see box, p.135), or by visiting the townships' first artisan coffee shop (see p.143).

THE TOWNSHIP WINERY

Cape Town's first township- and black-owned winery, **The Township Winery,** is situated in Philippi, an area where patches of farmland exist amid mass housing. The winery aims to increase community ownership by giving hundreds of individual homesteads Sauvignon Blanc vines to grow at their own homes, which will go towards the production of a wine called "Township Winery" (Ⓦ townshipwinery.com). Once the project is more established, they plan to run tours and tastings.

the tiniest patch of green relief, you'll find a vibrant street life, with hairdressers galore and people selling sheep and goats' heads and other meaty treats. It's also home to the **Langa Quarter,** Harlem St (Mon–Sun 9am–4pm; Ⓦ facebook.com/ikhayalelanga), a new project focused around eight streets in Langa, which aims to create an alternative tourism hub to the city centre. In Rhubusana Street, several homes have been turned into galleries, where you can walk around looking at the art works and meeting local people. The best way to visit the area is with Coffeebeans Routes (see p.131).

Langa Heritage Museum
Washington St • Mon–Sat 9am–4pm • Free • ☎ 021 694 8320

The **Langa Heritage Museum** is the only museum in Cape Town's townships. It is dedicated to the *dompas* or pass system, which during apartheid years required black citizens to carry a pass to enter "white-only" areas for work. The modest and rather austere museum is located in the Old Pass Court where people were tried for transgressing the pass laws.

Mitchell's Plain

South of the African ghettoes is **Mitchell's Plain**. Populated by Cape Coloureds, the area stretches down to the False Bay coast (you'll skirt Mitchell's Plain if you take the M5 to Muizenberg). More salubrious than any of the African townships, Mitchell's Plain reflects how, under apartheid, lighter skins meant better conditions, even if you weren't quite white. But for coloureds, the forced removals were no less tragic, many being summarily forced to vacate family homes because their suburb had been declared a White Group Area. Many families were relocated here when District Six was razed (see p.98), and their communities never fully recovered – one of the symptoms of dislocation and poverty is the violent gangs and drug culture that have become an everyday part of Mitchell's Plain.

Gugulethu

The township of **Gugulathu** (known to locals as Gugs) is home to two memorials, both best visited on a Coffeebeans Routes tour (see p.131). Consisting of seven solid, powerful granite statue-like constructions, the **Gugulethu Seven Memorial** is dedicated to the struggle and death of members of an anti-apartheid group who were shot and killed by members of the South African Police force in 1986. The nearby **Amy Bielh Memorial** (Ⓦ amybiehl.co.za) marks the spot where Amy, a white American anti-Apartheid activist, was murdered by local residents in 1993, at the age of 26: the monument is a moving tribute to her courageous, all-too-short life.

ARRIVAL AND DEPARTURE   CAPE TOWN AND THE CAPE PENINSULA

BY PLANE

Cape Town International Airport Cape Town's international and domestic airport (CPT; Ⓦ acsa.co.za) lies 22km east of the city centre, and is served by all South Africa's domestic airlines, plus a variety of

international ones (see p.47). Its bureau de change opens to coincide with international arrivals, and there are also ATMs here and a tourist information desk. The major car rental firms have desks inside the international terminal; prebooking a vehicle is essential, especially during the

1

week and over the mid-December to mid-January and Easter peak seasons.

Taxis into the city Metered 24-hour taxis operated by Touch Down Taxis (☎021 919 4659), an association of independent cab companies officially authorized by the airport, wait in ranks outside both terminals and charge around R250 for the trip into the city.

Buses into the city The cheapest transport from the airport to the centre is the MyCiTi bus (every 20min; 4.20am–9pm; R60–70; ☎0800 65 64 63, ⓦmyciti.org.za) which goes to the Civic Centre on Hertzog Boulevard, opposite the central train and bus station with comprehensive connections further afield (see below). More expensive but considerably more convenient are the door-to-door shuttle services such as Centurion (☎086 111 5388), ⓦcenturiontours.co.za) .

BY TRAIN

Cape Town Station The city's mainline train station is in the centre of town on the corner of Strand and Adderley streets, with three trains a week between Cape Town and Johannesburg (26 hours), stopping at Matjiesfontein (5hr), Kimberley (16hr 30min) and Bloemfontein (23hr); book online at Shosholoza Meyl (ⓦshosholozameyl.co.za). The luxury Blue Train (ⓦwww.bluetrain.co.za) and Rovos Rail (ⓦrovos.com) services also stop here (see p.50).

BY BUS

Intercity buses Serving most towns in the country between them, South Africa's three intercity bus companies are Greyhound (☎083 915 9000, ⓦgreyhound.co.za), Intercape (☎021 380 4400, ⓦintercape.co.za) and Translux (☎086 158 9282, ⓦtranslux.co.za). Intercape and Translux buses arrive on the northeastern side of the main train station, off Adderley Street, while Greyhound buses arrive on the northwestern side of the station in Adderley Street itself. For a single fare from Cape Town, expect to pay around R270 to Paarl, R360 to Mossel Bay, and R450 to Port Elizabeth.

Baz Bus The useful hop-on/hop-off Baz Bus (☎0861 229 287, ⓦbazbus.com) runs daily between Cape Town and Port Elizabeth in both directions, via Mossel Bay, George, Knysna, Plettenberg Bay, Storms River and Jeffrey's Bay, with other stops possible along the N2. The service is aimed at backpackers, with buses stopping off at hostels en route. The Cape Town to Port Elizabeth fare is R1550 one-way, though it's better value to buy a pass, available in seven-day (R1700), fourteen-day (R2700) and 21-day (R3300) versions. Book online, through hostels, at Cape Town central tourist office (see p.131), or at the central Baz office, 32 Burg St, Cape Town.

SA Connection Faster and less cumbersome than the large Intercity buses, SA Connection (☎086 110 2426, ⓦsaconnection.wozaonline.co.za) is a daytime mini-bus shuttle service linking Cape Town (Claremont) along the Garden Route with Port Elizabeth and East London (3–4 weekly; R750).

GETTING AROUND

Although Cape Town's city centre is compact enough to get around on foot, many of the major attractions are spread along the considerable length of the peninsula and require transport to get there. Between them, the MyCiTi rapid bus service and Metrorail, a single train line down the peninsula, offer a relatively comprehensive trunk service that covers much of Cape Town, while the two Cape Town Sightseeing Bus routes are useful for visiting the city's main tourist sights. All rail, most bus transport (both intercity and from elsewhere in the city) and most minibus taxis converge around the main train station and the Golden Acre shopping complex, at the junction of Strand and Adderley streets in the heart of Cape Town: it's a confusing muddle, but everything you need for your next move is within two or three blocks of here, including tourist information (see p.131).

BY BUS

MyCiTi Bus A safe commuter system, MyCiTi Bus (☎080 065 6463, ⓦmyciti.org.za) runs daily from 5am to 10pm, with stations along dedicated trunk roads, emulating a rail system. Frequent buses reliably serve the city centre, City Bowl suburbs, Atlantic Seaboard and Northern Suburbs, with buses every 10–20 minutes during peak periods (6.30–8.30am & 4–6pm) and every 20–30 minutes during the off-peak period and at weekends. Importantly it is the only safe public transport option in the evening. Cash is not accepted on the buses, so you'll need a myconnect card, which you can preload with credit; cards can be bought for R25 from MyCiTi stations as well as at the airport and visitor information centres in town, and can be refunded after your stay (you'll need to show your receipt). When you board the bus, tap your card against validators marked "in", and again on one marked "out" when you get off. Fares range from R5 for routes within the city centre, to R10 from the centre to Hout Bay or Table View and R60 to the airport. The MyCiTi website has user-friendly and up-to-date information on fares, routes and timetables.

Cape Town Sightseeing Bus The open-top, hop-on, hop-off red Cape Town Sightseeing Buses (☎021 511 6000, ⓦcitysightseeing.co.za ; 1-day ticket R150, children R70) leave from the Two Oceans Aquarium at the Waterfront, and run along two useful routes, with the Red Tour visiting the main city centre attractions, and the Blue Tour heading to sights along the peninsula. The buses are a convenient and fun way to travel with headphone commentary on two channels – one for adults and another

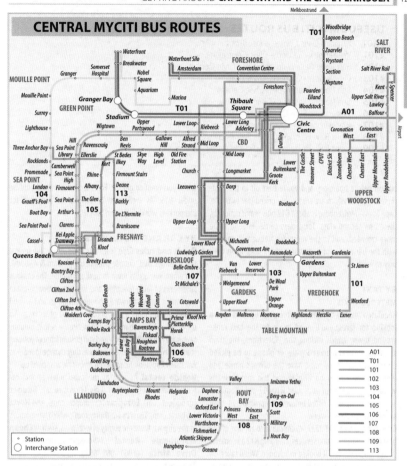

CENTRAL MYCITI BUS ROUTES

for children featuring the voices of Blatjan Baboon and Madisa Mongoose among others. The Blue Mini Peninsula Tour (daily 9am–3.25pm: May to mid-Sept every 35min; mid-Sept to early May every 20–25min) stops at Cape Town Tourism in Burg Street, *The Mount Nelson Hotel*, Kirstenbosch, World of Birds, Imizamo Yethu Township, Mariner's Wharf in Hout Bay, Camps Bay and Sea Point. The Red City Centre Tour (daily 9am–5.15pm: May to mid-Sept every 20min; mid-Sept to April every 15min) stops at Cape Town Tourism, St George's Cathedral, SA Museum, Jewish Museum, District Six Museum, Castle of Good Hope, Gold Museum, Cableway, Camps Bay and Sea Point.

BY TRAIN

Metrorail Cape Town's suburban overground train service is run by Metrorail (☎ 080 065 64 63, ⓦ www .capemetrorail.co.za). Three lines run east from Cape Town

station to Strand (through Bellville), to the Cape Flats, and to the outlying towns of Stellenbosch and Paarl, though these journeys aren't recommended, as they run through some less safe areas of the Flats. The service to the False Bay seaboard from Cape Town station, however, is one of the great urban train journeys of the world, reaching the coast at Muizenberg and continuing south to Simon's Town, sometimes so spectacularly close to the ocean that you can feel the spray and peer into rock pools. The trains are regular, though not especially reliable and you should avoid boarding an empty carriage. Several trains an hour run as far as Fish Hoek (Mon–Fri 5am–8pm roughly every 15min, Sat 6.20am–6.45pm every 20min, Sun 5.50am–6.30pm roughly hourly, though more frequently in summer), with services onto Simon's Town every forty to sixty minutes. Note that there are no signposts to stations on the streets. Tickets must be bought at the

USEFUL MYCITI BUS ROUTES

#A01	Airport–Civic Centre–Waterfront
#101	Vredehoek–Gardens–Civic Centre
#102	Salt River Rail–Walmer Estate–Civic Centre
#103	Oranjezicht–Gardens–Civic Centre
#104	Sea Point–Waterfront–Civic Centre
#105	Sea Point–Fresnaye–Civic Centre
#106	Waterfront Silo–Civic Centre–Camps Bay (clockwise)
#107	Waterfront Silo–Civic Centre–Camps Bay (anti-clockwise)
#108	Hout Bay–Hangberg–Sea Point–Civic Centre
#109	Hout Bay–Imizamo Yethu–Sea Point–Civic Centre

station before boarding, and you're best off in the first-class carriages, which are reasonably priced (for example, Cape Town–Muizenberg is about R12 one-way); curiously, there's no second class. Third class carriages tend to be more crowded, and in the mornings frequently ring out with the harmonies of domestic workers singing on their way to work.

BY TAXI

METERED TAXIS

Regulated metered taxis don't cruise up and down looking for fares; you'll need to go to the taxi ranks around town, which include the Waterfront, the train station and Greenmarket Square, or phone to be picked up (see below). Taxis must have the driver's name and identification clearly on display and the meter clearly visible. Fares work out at around R10–12 per kilometre. The three companies listed below run a prompt, 24-hour service, seven days a week.

City Cabs 📞 021 202 2222, 🌐 citycabsa.co.za. One of the best radio controlled taxi services, charging R12 a kilometre with a minimum fee, if booked in advance. When taken off the street you can usually bargain and get extremely competitive fares.

Excite Taxis 📞 021 448 4444, 🌐 excitetaxis.co.za. Fares are R9 a kilometre within the city centre to southern suburbs, but there may be an additional charge for further flung destinations.

Rikkis 📞 0861 745 547, 🌐 rikkis.co.za. One of the cheapest operators in Hout Bay and the southern suburbs: fares are R10 a zone, so a ride from the Waterfront to the City Bowl, for example, would set you back about R60. After 10pm there is an extra charge of R80.

MINIBUS TAXIS

Minibus taxis are cheap, frequent and bomb up and down the main routes at tearaway speeds. They can be hailed from the street – you'll recognize them from the hooting, booming music and touting – or boarded at the central taxi rank, adjacent to the train station. Once you've boarded, pay the assistant, who sits near the driver, and tell him

when you want to get off. Fares for most trips should be under R15. As well as risky driving, be prepared for pickpockets working the taxi ranks.

BY CAR AND MOTORBIKE

Roads and rules Cape Town has good roads and several fast freeways that, outside peak hours (7–9am & 4–6pm), can whisk you across town in next to no time. The obvious landmarks of Table Mountain and the two seaboards make orientation straightforward, though driving in and around Cape Town presents a few peculiarities all of its own. An unwritten rule of the road on the peninsula is that minibus taxis have the right of way – and will push in front of you and routinely run through amber lights as they change to red – as will many Capetonians, to whom amber means speed up.

Vehicle rental As well as the usual international car rental companies, such as **Avis** (🌐 avis.co.za), **Budget** (🌐 budget.com), **Europcar** (🌐 europcar.com), and **Hertz** (🌐 hertz.com) **Thrifty** (🌐 thrifty.com), which have offices at the airport, there are plenty of local ones, such as **Cheap Motorhome Rental** (🌐 cheapmotorhomes.co.za), **Drive Africa** (📞 061 066 8578, 🌐 driveafrica.co.za), **Tempest** (📞 11 552 3900, 🌐 tempestcarhire.co.za) and **Vineyard Car Hire** (🌐 vineyardcarhire.co.za), some of which will come and meet you at the airport, if you book in advance. Alternatively, you can rent scooters (daily 9am–11pm, 🌐 capetownscooter.co.za) for around R220 a day, or more powerful BMW and Harley Davidson bikes with full protective gear from Cape Bike Travel at 125 Buitengracht (📞 084 606 4449, 🌐 capebiketravel.com) for R1200 a day, including comprehensive insurance and helmet.

BY GUIDED TOUR

Cape Town is awash with guided tours, which can often be the best way to get under the skin of the city. As well as general tours that take in all the main sights, a number of smaller companies offer niche cultural tours; the most popular of these are township tours, which are the safest way to visit the African and coloured areas that were created under apartheid.

WALKING TOURS

One of the best way to get to grips with the orientation of the city is on a walking tour through central Cape Town. Tours run by the two companies below depart mid-morning daily, except Sundays, from the Visitor Information Centre in Burg Street, and last roughly three hours. You need to book in advance. Alternatively, check out Voice Maps (ⓦvoicemap.me), where you can download an app walking tour of various areas in the city, narrated by local Capetonians who are knowledgeable and passionate about their own districts.

Cape Town on Foot ☎021 462 4252, ⓦwanderlust .co.za. Run by an ex-teacher and writer, the tours (R200 per person) take in the city centre as well as the Bo-Kaap, and can be taken in English or German.

Footsteps to Freedom ☎083 452 1112, ⓦfootstepstofreedom.co.za. Runs a tour (R220 per person) that takes in the historical sights and buildings of the city with a conscious politico/socio slant.

GENERAL TOURS

Cape Convoy ☎021 531 1928, ⓦcapeconvoy.com. Tours in a canopied Land-Rover with a passionate and fun Brit, Rob Salmon, who offers a reduced rate (R1000) if you book the two most popular tours: the full-day Cape Point and the Table Mountain and Robben Island tour. Trips can also be arranged to the Winelands and to the nearest safari park to see some wildlife, a couple of hours out of Cape Town.

Day Trippers ☎021 511 4766, ⓦdaytrippers.co.za. An excellent company if you want an active Peninsula and

Cape Point day tour that will include cycling and hiking. One can go further afield to hike and cycle in the Cederberg, Little Karoo and Winelands.

CULTURAL TOURS

Andulela Tours ☎021 418 3020, ⓦandulela.com. Fabulous selection of under-the-skin tours, which could get you drumming, bead-making or cooking in the African townships, visiting the homes of well-known Cape Jazz musicians, cooking Cape Malay food in the Bo-Kaap, going on a soccer tour, or learning about baboons with a conservationist at Cape Point. They can also take you further afield to the Cederberg to look at rock art.

Bonani Our Pride ☎021 531 4291, ⓦbonanitours .co.za. Recommended tours where you meet local people as well as visit sights of political significance in the townships. It offers township evening tours, gospel tours to Xhosa churches on a Sunday morning, and Xhosa folklore tours.

★**Coffeebeans Routes** ☎021 424 3572, ⓦcoffeebeansroutes.com. Run by Iain Harris, Coffeebean Routes is a pioneer in creative tourism in the townships, and the place to go to for music and cultural tours including the Cape Jazz Safari, the Township Futures tour, plus tours based around cuisine and fashion.

The Real Cape ☎082 885 8945, ⓦfacebook.com /realcape. Full and half-day cultural and historical tours, run by Chris, a development economist, who pulls no punches when examining the contrast of poverty and privilege in South Africa.

INFORMATION

Tourist Information The main Cape Town Tourism Visitor Centre is in the city centre, at The Pinnacle, Burg & Castle streets (daily 8am–6pm; ☎021 487 6800, ⓦcapetown .travel), and runs a comprehensive booking service for accommodation, activities and national parks; it also has a coffee shop, bookshop and cybercafé, and dishes out lots of brochures and cheap city maps. Cape Town Tourism also runs smaller bureaux at the airport (☎021 934 1949), the V&A Waterfront (☎021 408 7600) and the Lower Cableway (☎021 422 1075).

Events listings To find out what's on, check listings websites such as Cape Town Magazine (ⓦcapetownmagazine.com) or

What's On in Cape Town (ⓦwhatsonincapetown.com). Alternatively, look at the entertainment pages of the daily newspapers, or the excellent events listings in the *Mail & Guardian*'s Friday supplement, which injects some attitude into its reviews and listings.

Maps If you're planning to explore beyond the city centre, buy a detailed street atlas from any bookshop (see p.154). MapStudio's *A to Z Streetmap* is the cheapest; it's adequate for the centre and most of the suburbs, but doesn't cover Simon's Town. The best detailed maps of the peninsula and large parts of the Western Cape and beyond are Slingsby Maps (see p.76).

ACCOMMODATION

Cape Town has plenty of accommodation to suit all budgets, though booking ahead is recommended, especially over the Christmas holidays (mid-Dec to mid-Jan) – Cape Town Tourism's efficient **accommodation booking** service (ⓦcapetown.travel) can help. Cape Town is a long peninsula and there are many different locations all with hotly debated advantages and varying physical beauties. You'll need to choose whether you want to be central, with nightlife on your doorstep, or would prefer a quieter setting closer to the ocean, in which case you'll travel further to get into the city. The greatest concentration of accommodation is in the City Centre, City Bowl and the Atlantic seaside strip as far as Camps Bay. One of the few ways to experience black South Africa here is to stay in one of the African townships.

1

CITY CENTRE

Cape Town's liveliest streets are Long Street and Bree Street. There are a number of backpacker lodges and a couple of hotels on Long St itself, plus several places east of Long St around the museum complex and the Company's Gardens. From here you can walk to all the museums, trawl Cape Town's best nightlife spots, and find transport easily to the Waterfront. Expect rooms fronting Long St to be noisy.

★**Cape Heritage Hotel** 90 Bree St ☎ 021 424 4646, ⍟ capeheritage.co.za; map p.92. An exceptionally stylish, elegant and tastefully restored boutique hotel in a row of houses dating from 1771, in Cape Heritage Square, just below the Bo-Kaap. The rooms are spacious and decorated with contemporary handcrafted objects and original paintings. The service is charming. R2100

Cat & Moose 305 Long St ☎ 021 423 7638, ⍟ catandmoose.co.za; map p.92. The most stylish of the Long Street backpackers, housed in an eighteenth-century building a couple of doors from the steam baths at the south end of the city centre. Timber floors, rugs, earthy reds and ochres as well as some African masks imbue it with a warm ethnic feel, as do the humble communal cooking and eating areas. The rooms are arranged around a leafy courtyard, which contains a small plunge pool. The double rooms are among the most affordable in town. Dorm R140, double R410

Dutch Manor Antique Hotel 158 Buitengracht, Bo Kaap ☎ 21 422 4767, ⍟ dutchmanor.co.za; map p.90. Travel back in time to a town house meticulously filled with period furniture, lavish tapestries and four-poster beds. Bathrooms and breakfast room are spotless and modern, and there's a small balcony overlooking the street. Very central location in the City Bowl; off-street parking available. R1600

Grand Daddy Hotel 38 Long St ☎ 021 424 7247, ⍟ granddaddy.co.za; map p.92. The *Grand Daddy* features seven retro-cool American Airstream trailers, decorated by local artists, that sit on the roof and are linked by wooden walkways. You can stay in one of these snug trailers on the rooftop, or in one of the hotel's double rooms, which are also imaginative, colourful and funky, and have queen-sized beds. R1910

iKhaya Lodge Wandel St, Dunkley Square ☎ 021 461 8880, ⍟ ikhayalodge.co.za; map p.90. This guesthouse is on a pretty square, right by the Company's Gardens and the museums, and close to trendy places to eat. En-suite rooms in the main lodge building have balconies overlooking the square, while a few luxury lofts boast ethnically inspired decor and separate double rooms. Offers 24hr reception, satellite TV and wi-fi throughout. Double R995, loft R1900

Rose Street 28 28 Rose St, Bo Kaap ☎ 021 424 3813, ⍟ rosestreet28.co.za; map p.90. The most affordable and best value for money B&B in town. There are three jointly managed separate town houses, centrally located on trendy Rose St, each containing three en-suite double rooms with shared kitchenette and courtyard. Houses vary slightly, though all bedrooms are compact, basic doubles. R690

Rouge on Rose 25 Rose St, at Hout St ☎ 021 426 0298, ⍟ rougeonrose.co.za; map p.90. Nine modern, comfortable suites in a Bo-Kaap guesthouse, on an increasingly gentrified street, with great views across to Signal Hill or the city. It has convenient microwave and self-catering basics if you fancy a night in, and there's free wi-fi. R1500

V&A WATERFRONT AND DE WATERKANT

Accommodation here tends to be upmarket; there are, however, a couple of reasonably priced places to stay. Staying at the Waterfront is a good idea if you like shopping in a self-contained safe area, and you want to walk to restaurants and cafés, with transport readily available. On a hillside, less than 1km from the Waterfront, adjacent to the Bo-Kaap and a short hop to Green Point or the city centre, De Waterkant is a desirable place to stay, full of restored Victorian terraces on narrow, well-kept cobbled streets.

Breakwater Lodge Portswood Rd, Waterfront ☎ 021 406 1911 (ask for Lodge Reservations), ⍟ breakwaterlodge.co.za; map p.101. The most affordable place to stay in the Waterfront, this hotel is linked to Cape Town University's Graduate School of Business. It's pretty characterless and rates do not include breakfast; choose it only if the location is what matters most. R1350

St John's Waterfront Lodge 6 Braemar Rd ☎ 021 439 1404, ⍟ stjohns.co.za; map p.101. The closest hostel to the Waterfront (a 15min walk away), *St John's* is well run by friendly and helpful staff. Accommodation comes in dorms and private doubles, and communal facilities include a swimming pool, a great garden, an outdoor BBQ area, free wi-fi, a laundry service machine and a travel centre. Dorm R150, double R550

★ **Village and Life** Reception at 1 Loader St, De Waterkant ☎ 021 409 2500, ⍟ villageandlife.com; map p.101. These attractively restored historic cottages are adjacent to the Bo-Kaap and less than 1km from the Waterfront, Green Point and city centre. The luxury cottages in Waterkant, Loader, Dixon and Napier streets have up to three bedrooms; some have garages, swimming pools and roof gardens with harbour or mountain views. The company also has self-catering apartments for rent in the Waterfront itself. One-bedroomed cottage R1950

CITY BOWL SUBURBS

The City Bowl suburbs are a popular choice for accommodation as they are central but quieter and leafier than the immediate city centre, especially the further up

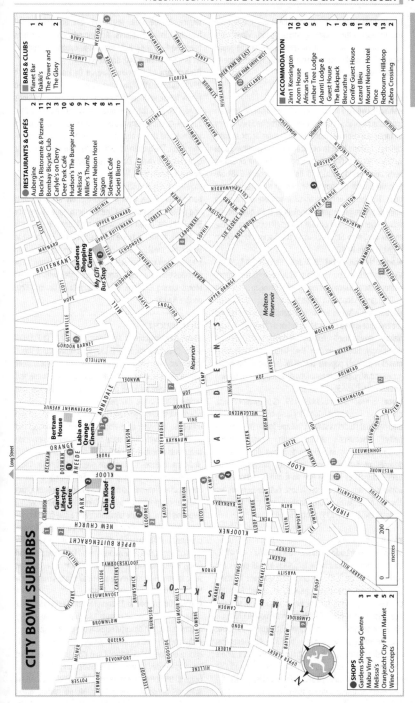

CITY BOWL SUBURBS

■ BARS & CLUBS

Planet Bar	1
Rakiki's	2
The Power and The Glory	2

■ ACCOMMODATION

2inn1 Kensington	12
Acorn House	10
African Sun	6
Amber Tree Lodge	5
Ashanti Lodge & Guest House	7
The Backpack	9
Blencathra	8
Conifer Guest House	8
Lezard Bleu	11
Mount Nelson Hotel	3
Once	4
Redbourne Hildrop	13
Zebra Crossing	2

● RESTAURANTS & CAFÉS

Aubergine	2
Bacini's Ristorante & Pizzeria	11
Bombay Bicycle Club	12
Carlyle's on Derry	3
Deer Park Café	10
Hudson's The Burger Joint	6
Melissa's	9
Miller's Thumb	7
Mount Nelson Hotel	4
Saigon	8
Sidewalk Café	5
Societi Bistro	1

● SHOPS

Gardens Shopping Centre	3
Mabu Vinyl	1
Melissa's	4
Oranjezicht City Farm Market	5
Wine Concepts	2

the mountainside you go, and the more comfortable guesthouses often have gardens, good views and swimming pool. A few backpacker lodges can be found along Kloof St, the continuation of Long St and home to some great cafés and restaurants.

GARDENS

Ashanti Lodge 11 Hof St ☎ 021 423 8721, ⓦ ashanti .co.za; map p.133. This massive, refurbished two-storey Victorian mansion has marbling and ethnic decor, soaring ceilings, a nicely kept front garden and a swimming pool with sun terrace. The private rooms (with twin or double beds and shared bath) and dorms (sleeping 6–8) are furnished with custom-made wrought-iron bunks and beds. The bar is very lively, so if you are not a party animal, you might want to book in at their guesthouse, which offers en-suite private rooms (R1000), round the corner on Union St; check-in at the backpackers. Dorm R190, double R650

Mount Nelson Hotel 76 Orange St ☎ 021 483 1000, ⓦ mountnelson.co.za; map p.133. Cape Town's *grande dame*: a fine and famous high colonial Victorian hotel, built in 1899 (and extended in the late 1990s). Perfectly located, the building is set in extensive established gardens, and the entrance is via a majestic palm-lined colonnade. *Mount Nelson* takes itself terribly seriously and charges accordingly. Rooms are not that large, but its location makes it a highly popular choice for internationals in the movie industry, parliamentarians or anyone who is staying on expenses. R7565

Once 73 Kloof St ☎ 0214246169, ⓦ stayatonce.com; map p.133. This hostel is ideal for long-term volunteers or international students staying in Cape Town, who can get hefty discounts (R3800/month room only). Accommodation is in modern four-bed dorms, twins, doubles or family rooms, all with private en-suite bathrooms. Rates include free wi-fi and breakfast at the adjacent trendy coffee shop, whose outside benches are always filled with those soaking up the Kloof St atmosphere. Dorm R235, double R850

TAMBOERSKLOOF

★ **Amber Tree Lodge** 10 Kloof Nek Rd ☎ 021 422 4126, ⓦ ambertreelodge.co.za; map p.133. A small owner-run backpacker lodge, with a lounge that's draped in warm tapestries and opens onto a peaceful courtyard. Four-bed dorm rooms are light, and the wooden bunks are spacious and solid. Dorm R180, twin R750, family room R1200

★ **The Backpack** 74 New Church St ☎ 021 423 4530, ⓦ backpackers.co.za; map p.133. An excellent backpackers made up of four interconnected houses, where the interior has a spacious maze-like effect. It's walkable from the City Bowl suburbs and the city centre, and has the best communal and outdoor space in the area – a pool

terrace, lounge area, restaurant, bar and garden, all furnished in bold colours. Accommodation is in dorms (sleeping 4–8) and private rooms; some rooms are suitable for families. Dorm R240, double R1200

Blencathra 4 Cambridge Ave, at De Hoop ☎ 021 424 9571, ⓦ blencathra.co.za; map p.133. A large relaxed family house with stunning views on the slopes of Lion's Head, 2km from the city centre and 4km from the Atlantic. The self-catering rooms are peaceful and spacious; four are en suite, and there's also an en-suite four-person women-only dorm. The garden has seating, a swimming pool and a cute twin-bed chalet. Dorm R180, double R900

Zebra Crossing 82 New Church St ☎ 021 422 1265, ⓦ zebra-crossing.co.za; map p.133. A no-frills backpacker lodge, with a child-friendly attitude, wi-fi and off-street parking. On the northern edge of the City Bowl suburbs, it's an easy walk to the Kloof St restaurants and pubs, as well as those in the city centre. The café-bar serves full meals and decent coffee, and there are two pleasant terraces beneath vines. Accommodation is in spacious dorms, a double and a few singles, with the best rooms taking in views of the mountain. Dorm R120, double R420

ORANJEZICHT

2Inn1 Kensington 21 Kensington Crescent ☎ 021 423 1707, ⓦ 2inn1.com; map p.133. On a broad, quiet street, these two adjacent renovated houses with bright, sleek furnishings and quiet music drifting over the lounge and dining area give off a feel of a welcoming, private café. The building backs onto a 10m pool and deck area with sunbeds, where guests can enjoy complimentary beer, wine, tea and coffee at sundowner time. Rooms have private terraces and are equipped with all the usual mod cons, plus there are spa treatments available on site. R1900

★ **Acorn House** 1 Montrose Ave ☎ 021 461 1782, ⓦ acornhouse.co.za; map p.133. Set among a row of guesthouses high on the hill towards Table Mountain, this 100-year-old residence has maintained its grandeur with a sweeping lawn, colonial furnishings and a sun-filled lounge room, and added the comforts of a pool, breakfast room, courtyard and Nespresso machine. Rooms at the front offer great city views, while the back shows off Table Mountain, and family rooms have their own private courtyards. Excellent value for money, great service and small touches make a stay here personal and memorable. R1400

Conifer Guest House 1 Jagersfontein Lane ☎ 021 461 3762, ⓦ conifer.co.za; map p.133. Situated on a leafy narrow street, this peaceful guesthouse is lovely and quiet, with a homely feel, wooden floors and white linen. There is also an outdoor breakfast area, gas BBQ and one excellent value-for-money family room (R1550). R1150

Lezard Bleu 30 Upper Orange St ☎ 021 461 4601, ⓦ lezardbleu.co.za; map p.133. This guesthouse offers seven en-suite rooms, furnished with maple beds and cupboards in a spacious open-plan 1960s house. The cosy lounge is perfect for reading, opening onto an outside deck, while each bedroom backs onto the garden and swimming pool. It even boasts its own treehouse room. R1330

Redbourne Hilldrop 12 Roseberry Ave ☎ 021 461 1394, ⓦ redbourne.co.za; map p.133. This small four-room B&B oozes hospitality and a quiet charm. It has a modern exterior, while the interior, with high ceilings and wooden floors, is appointed with antique furniture. There's an outside plunge pool and a small breakfast room with a panoramic view of the city. Hefty off-season discounts are available. R1375

VREDEHOEK

African Sun 3 Florida Rd ☎ 021 461 1601, ⓔ afpress@ iafrica.com; map p.133. A small self-catering apartment, attached to a family house a little over 1km from the city centre. Furnished with pared-back ethnic decor, it's run by

friendly, well-informed owners, who are both well-known published writers. They also offer literary evenings and tours. Good value. R650

SOUTHERN SUBURBS

Cape Town's gracious southern suburbs – Rosebank, Claremont, Newlands and Rondebosch, on the forested side of the mountain – are home to Kirstenbosch Gardens as well as the fine Newlands cricket and rugby grounds, Groote Schuur hospital and the University of Cape Town. Observatory is a few minutes' drive from the city centre and offers buzzing cafés, a couple of backpacker lodges and reasonable nightlife.

African Heart 27 Station Rd, Observatory ☎ 0761183213, ⓦ backpackersincapetown.co.za. This uniquely designed hostel is set in a Victorian house with wooden floors, comfy couches and bold murals and mosaics. There are several chillout areas and an outdoor

---

AFRICAN TOWNSHIP HOMESTAYS

One of the best ways to get a taste of the African townships is to spend a night with one of the growing number of township residents offering **B&B accommodation**. You'll encounter the warmth of *ubuntu* – traditional African hospitality – by staying with a family with whom you'll eat breakfast and dinner; they will often take you around their local area to *shebeens* (unlicensed bars), music venues, church or just to meet the neighbours.

Some B&Bs will send someone to collect you from the airport; if you're driving, they'll give you detailed directions or meet you at a convenient and obvious landmark. **Prices** are R480–600 per double, which is considerably cheaper than in the centre of Cape Town, and you'll get to experience something a little different. As well as the places listed below, **booking** can be made through Cape Tourism Centre in Langa (☎ 021 695 4981, ⓦ capetowntravel.co.za).

KHAYELITSHA

Kopanong B&B C329 Velani Crescent ☎ 021 517 4206 or 082 476 1278, ⓦ kopanong-township.co.za. One of the most dynamic B&B operations in Khayelitsha, run by the tireless Thope Lekau, who is on a mission to help her guests engage with township life. This former NGO worker will treat you to a history of the township, introduce you to local music and dish up a traditional family breakfast. A traditional dinner is available on request, as is a guided tour.

Majoro's 69 Helena Crescent ☎ 082 537 6882, ⓦ mycapetownstay.com/MajorosBB. The charming Maria Maile hosts guests in her family home, which has three rooms that share a bath and toilet. Dinner includes traditional dishes such as *mielie pap* (maize porridge), or you can choose to eat in a neighbouring restaurant after which you can watch TV with the family or visit the local tavern. The next day you'll be treated to an English breakfast of sorts, which may include bacon and egg alongside fish cakes, sausages and home-made steamed bread.

Malebo's 18 Mississippi Way ☎ 021 361 2391. This

B&B consists of five rooms, which share bath and toilet facilities, in the welcoming home of Lydea Masoleng and her husband. In the morning you'll be served a continental breakfast; dinners, which combine Western dishes with traditional African food, are available on request. You're welcome to join your hosts on outings to a *shebeen* or, on Sunday, to church.

LANGA

Ma Neo's 30 Zone 7 St ☎ 021 694 2504, ⓔ maneo@ absamail.co.za. Friendly hostess Thandiwe Peter offers accommodation in two rooms outside the house and one inside the family home, in Cape Town's oldest township, and the closest to the city centre; most guests drive here. She will take guests to some of the township highlights, including a local *shebeen*.

Nombulelo's Guesthouse 9 Harlem St ☎ 072 827 5228, ⓔ sicamba.nombulelo@gmail.com. This is a great place to stay, with friendly service courtesy of the lovely owner, Nombulelo. It's close to *Ace's* tavern and the homes that collectively make up Langa township's art galleries (see p.127).

braai, plus reduced rates for long termers (R5200/month including meals). Dorm R130, double R440

Carmichael House 11 Wolmunster Rd, Rosebank ☎021 689 8350, ⓦcarmichaelhouse.co.za. A two-storey guesthouse, close to the University of Cape Town, in a building that dates from the early twentieth century and contains six big rooms. There's a peaceful garden, a swimming pool and secure parking, plus wi-fi or the use of a laptop at reception to check your email. R1360

★ **The Vineyard** Colinton Rd, on the corner of Protea Rd, Newlands ☎021 657 4500, ⓦvineyard.co.za. In a restored 1799 country villa, decorated in a contemporary style, this is one of the city's top stays, with luxurious good-value rooms. The extensive gardens are like those of a peaceful country estate, with an outstanding panorama of the forested slopes of Table Mountain. Has a spa and large heated swimming pool – a great choice for a pampered stay. R2550

ATLANTIC SEABOARD

Down the Atlantic seaboard lie the seaside suburbs of Mouille Point, Green Point, Three Anchor Bay and Sea Point. Historically Cape Town's hotel and high-rise land, this is packed with a range of accommodation, making it a good choice if you want to be on the coast, but close to the city centre. South from Sea Point along Victoria Drive, the well-heeled mountainside suburb of **Camps Bay** has soaring views over the Atlantic, while being close to the city centre, and with its own restaurants and shops. Though nearby **Llandudno** lacks shops or restaurants, it can boast similar vistas and a supremely beautiful beach with clusters of granite boulders at either end. **Hout Bay** is the main urban concentration along the lower half of the peninsula, with a harbour, pleasant waterfront development and the only public transport beyond Camps Bay. South of Hout Bay is the posh and semi-rural settlement of **Noordhoek**, close to Table Mountain National Park, with good horseriding, beach walks and surfing.

GREEN POINT

★ **The B.I.G. Backpackers in Green Point** 18 Thornhill Rd ☎021 434 0688, ⓦbigbackpackers.co.za; map pp.112–113. A backpacker lodge with a light, clean, modern, rustic feel, which caters for a quieter crowd looking for a short-term home from home. It has a fully equipped self-catering kitchen, braai area, two comfy lounge rooms, a TV room and a sunny outside garden with a plunge pool. Four-bed dorms are light and spacious and have private balconies. Prices include free coffee. Dorm R200, double R800

Dysart Boutique Hotel 17 Dysart Rd ☎021 439 2832, ⓦdysart.de; map pp.112–113. This luxury boutique hotel is styled in afro chic, with a polished yet natural-looking interior. Each of the six rooms boasts a private balcony, flat-screen TV and mini-bar. The real draw, however, is outside – two infinity pools, and wooden decking with sunbeds, umbrellas and tables make this the perfect spot for relaxing with a cocktail. R2100

Jambo Guest House 1 Grove Rd ☎021 439 4219, ⓦjambo.co.za; map pp.112–113. In a quiet cul-de-sac off Main Rd, this small, atmospheric establishment offers four luxury en-suite rooms and one garden suite. The lush, leafy exterior and enclosed garden with a pond are delightfully soothing, and the service is excellent. R1500

Point B Guest House 14 Pine Rd ☎021 434 0902, ⓦpointb.co.za; map pp.112–113. Set in a 1900s house, with slightly out-dated decor, wicker furniture and a comfortable lounge room overlooking the garden. Upstairs are two modern rooms with small balconies, and the downstairs rooms lead onto private patios. Outside is a communal leafy garden courtyard, where guests can lounge on the wooden decking, sun beds, or in the mosaic plunge pool. Great personal service. R1300

Wilton Manor 15 Croxteth Rd ☎021 434 7869, ⓦwiltonguesthouses.co.za; map pp.112–113. This beautifully renovated Victorian guesthouse is set on on a quiet street, close to the city centre. Outside is a spacious and sunny deck with a homely atmosphere, breakfast tables and a plunge pool to cool off in. R1500

SEA POINT

★ **Blackheath Lodge** 6 Blackheath Rd ☎021 439 2541, ⓦblackheathlodge.co.za; map pp.112–113. Down a quiet backstreet, but close to the Sea Point action, this superb owner-run guesthouse in a Victorian home has sixteen large and airy rooms (some with views of Lion's Head and sea views), and the king-sized beds are the most comfortable in Cape Town. Breakfast is served on a courtyard-garden deck overlooking the pool and bar. R1850

Huijs Haerlem 25 Main Drive ☎021 434 6434, ⓦhuijshaerlem.co.za; map pp.112–113. This elegant and friendly guesthouse is made up of two adjacent houses furnished with Dutch antiques. Each of its eight rooms has a sea view, a vista of Signal Hill or overlooks the lovely garden. R1450

★ **Stonehurst Guest House** 3 Frere Rd ☎021 434 9670, ⓦstonehurst.co.za; map pp.112–113. An airy tin-roofed Victorian residence with original fittings and furnished with an attractive mixture of antiques collected by the friendly antique-dealer owner, Jan. There's a pleasant front garden, a kitchen for self-catering and a guest lounge. Most rooms are en suite, and some have balconies. Great value and location, a couple of streets back from busy Main Rd. R850

The Villa Rosa 277 High Level Rd ☎021 434 2768, ⓦvilla-rosa.com; map pp.112–113. A friendly eight-room guesthouse in a brick-red two-storey Victorian house on the lower slopes of Signal Hill, two blocks from the beachfront promenade. Decorated with simplicity and style, all rooms have TVs, phones and safes, but only some, on the upper floor, have sea views. R975

★**Winchester Mansions Hotel** 221 Beach Rd ✆ 021 434 2351, ⓦ www.winchester.co.za; map pp.112–113. In a prime spot across the road from the seashore, this 1920s hotel has an atmosphere straight from the pages of an Agatha Christie book, though the best rooms are fresh and contemporary. A cool Italianate courtyard restaurant is overlooked by balconies draped in luxuriant creepers. There's a good restaurant, too. R2500

CAMPS BAY AND BAKOVEN

★**Boutique@10** 10 Medburn Rd, Camps Bay ✆ 021 438 1234, ⓦ boutique10.co.za; map p.116. Like staying in a friend's lavishly appointed house, this owner-managed guesthouse has four comfortable rooms, each with unique decor. Restored with reclaimed timber from an old hotel, the light and airy open-plan lounge and kitchen opens onto decking, complete with sun beds, plunge pool and a stunning view of the Atlantic Ocean and Lion's Head. R2200

Camps Bay Retreat 7 Chilworth Rd, Camps Bay ✆ 021 437 8300, ⓦ campsbayretreat.co.za; map p.116. The secluded Earls Dyke mansion house, set on a four-acre nature reserve in the middle of Camps Bay, is just a 5min walk from the beach. The rooms are spacious with plush colonial furnishings, as are the main hotel foyer, lounge, reading room and fine-dining restaurant and bar. The bar, on the veranda above a gentle sweeping lawn, has good views of the Atlantic. There's also a spa, three swimming pools (including one that looks like a natural mountain pool) and tennis courts. R4000

Ocean View House 33 Victoria Rd, Bakoven ✆ 021 438 1982, ⓦ oceanview-house.com; map p.116. A river runs through the grounds of this family-run, eccentrically blue-and-yellow boutique hotel, set in a gorgeous garden that borders a *fynbos* reserve. The fourteen spacious rooms are comfortable and stylishly furnished with either mountain or sea views. R1950

HOUT BAY, LLANDUDNO AND NOORDHOEK

★**Hout Bay Hideaway** 37 Skaife St, Hout Bay ✆ 021 790 8040, ⓦ houtbay-hideaway.com. An outstanding guesthouse bursting with luxurious touches – Persian rugs, Art Deco armchairs and huge beds. Each of the four rooms has a mountain or sea view and outdoor decks where breakfast is served. At the back, there's a saltwater infinity pool in a *fynbos* garden that disappears onto the mountainside. R1650

★**Houtkapperspoort** Hout Bay Main Rd, around 5km from Hout Bay and 15km from the city centre ✆ 021 794 5216, ⓦ houtkapperspoortresort.co.za. These rustic

one- and two-bedroom, stone-and-brick self-catering cottages are close to Constantia Nek, right by the Table Mountain Nature Reserve. You can follow paths from the estate straight up the mountain slopes, play tennis or take a dip in the solar-heated pool. R1600

Monkey Valley Resort Mountain Rd, Noordhoek ✆ 021 789 8000, ⓦ monkeyvalleyresort.com. Spread over several acres of Chapman's Peak, some 40km south of the city centre, is an attractive group of mainly wooden-and-thatched chalets. Overlooking Noordhoek Beach, the site is surrounded by indigenous vegetation, though the only monkeys you'll find are in the name. You can eat in the restaurant, self-cater or stay on a B&B basis, in a variety of accommodation options, depending on the size of the group. Double R1500, self-catering cottage R2130

Sunbird Mountain Retreat & Lodge Boskykloof Rd, Hout Bay ✆ 021 790 7758, ⓦ sunbirdlodge.co.za. Four pleasant, spacious self-catering apartments and a guesthouse that includes a family unit, all nestled in a forest high up on the mountainside. Every room has a great view, and there's a secluded swimming pool. Double R1200, apartment R800

★**Sunset on the Rocks** 11 Sunset Ave, Llandudno ✆ 021 790 2103, ⓦ sunsetontherocks.co.za. This is a magical hideaway on one of the loveliest coves on the peninsula; three compact, self-contained flats sit in the midst of a wonderful *fynbos* garden belonging to charming proprietors Brian and Helen Alcock. Llandudno itself has no shops and restaurants, but Hout Bay is only 10min away by car. R800

Tintswalo Atlantic Chapmans Peak Drive, Hout Bay ✆ 011 300 8888, ⓦ www.tintswalo.com/atlantic. A stunning luxury lodge in a spectacular and isolated location on the rocks below Chapman's Peak, within Table Mountain Reserve. The large bedrooms have ocean views and are unique in style. Two large decking areas, with a heated jacuzzi and saltwater pool, lounge, bar, restaurant and wine cellar are all at guests' disposal, and someone from the lodge will pick you up from Chapmans Peak Drive by landrover. R8520

FALSE BAY SEABOARD

This is the area to look in if you want to swim every day, surf and walk on the beach, as well as enjoy excellent eateries, but with the city centre just 20km away by car, and connected by train during the day. Muizenberg, the oldest of Cape Town's seaside suburbs, was once hugely popular, though is now a bit run down. To its south is salubrious St James, while the jewel in the crown is Kalk Bay with its working harbour, quirky shops and arty cafés. Fish Hoek, further south, is recommended for its beach, while Simon's Town, 45 minutes' drive from the city, is regarded by many as a separate village, which it originally was, although it's definitely part of the metropolis now. There are far fewer guesthouses than on the Atlantic side, so self-catering apartments are popular, especially in Kalk Bay: check ⓦsafarinow.com or Peninsula Tourism (ⓦcapetown.travel).

MUIZENBERG

★**Cob House** 13 Watson Rd, Muizenberg ☎021 788 6613, ⓦcobhouse.co.za; map pp.118–119. The greenest B&B in Cape Town, *Cob House* is run by an exceptionally friendly family and set just 200m from the beach. There is one comfy guest room that sleeps up to four, and the rate includes a room-service organic breakfast. The owner, Simric Yarrow (teacher, storyteller and musician), also runs excellent tours around the city (ⓦoffbeatcapetown .yolasite.com). Double R̲7̲5̲0̲, family R̲9̲5̲0̲

Stoked Backpackers 175 Main Rd, Muizenberg ☎082 679 3651, ⓦstokedbackpackers.com; map pp.118–119. Vibey, well-run backpackers next to the station, over the railway line from Surfers Corner. Surfing or kite-surfing lessons can be arranged, as well as Cape Point trips or wine tasting in Stellenbosch. The best en-suite rooms (worth the extra cost) are on the upper levels with sunrise sea views, and when there is no wind, the upstairs terrace area that overlooks the beach is stunning. Dorm R135, double R̲5̲5̲0̲

FISH HOEK AND KALK BAY

★**Chartfield Guest House** 30 Gatesville Rd, Kalk Bay ☎021 788 3793, ⓦchartfield.co.za; map pp.118–119. This well-kept, rambling house sits halfway up the hill overlooking the harbour, with terrific sea views from some rooms. It's just a hop and a skip down the cobbled road or steps to some of the city's finest restaurants. Double R̲9̲0̲0̲, 3-bed self-catering cottage R̲2̲0̲0̲0̲

The Mountain House 7 Mountain Rd, Clovelly ☎083 455 5664, ⓦthemountainhouse.co.za; map pp.118–119. Beautiful self-catering accommodation equidistant between Fish Hoek and Kalk Bay. Built in the garden of local architect Carin Hartford, the two-bedroom cottage has windows on all sides to capitalize on the incredible mountain setting, and the living space flows out to a timber deck. R̲1̲0̲5̲0̲

Tranquility Guest House 25 Peak Rd, Fish Hoek ☎021 782 2060, ⓦtranquil.co.za; map pp.118–119. This warm and welcoming place, within walking distance of the beach, is on Fish Hoek mountainside and offers good ocean views. There are four cosy B&B en-suite rooms, plus a self-catering apartment with its own entrance for the same price. Guests can soak in the outdoor jacuzzi. R̲1̲2̲0̲0̲

SIMON'S TOWN AND AROUND

Blue Bay 48 Palace Hill Rd ☎021 786 1700, ⓦbbay .co.za. A luxurious self-catering house with stupendous ocean views and a tranquil ambience, 1km from the centre of Simon's Town. With one double and two twin rooms, the place is rented as a whole. 2–3 people R̲9̲0̲0̲, 6 people R̲1̲8̲0̲0̲

Bosky Dell Cottages 5 Grant Rd, Boulders Beach ☎021 786 3906, ⓦboskyonbouldersbeach.co.za. Overlooking the granite rocks and coves of Boulders Beach, this former farmhouse offers five simple but comfortable self-catering cottages. A path runs down to the beach, and there are wide lawns from which to enjoy the stupendous views. R̲8̲0̲0̲

Simon's Town Backpackers 66 St George's St ☎021 786 1964, ⓦcapepax.co.za. Conveniently located in the heart of Simon's Town, within walking distance of the station, this boutique backpacker joint offers bunk-bed dorms and fairly spacious doubles, plus there's a large balcony with a view of the waterfront. You can rent bicycles here and ride to Cape Point, or arrange a kayak tour to paddle past the penguin colony. Dorm R̲1̲9̲0̲, double R̲3̲8̲0̲

Topsail House 176 St George's St ☎021 786 5537, ⓦtopsailhouse.co.za. An old convent converted into a backpacker lodge, with more space than average, though the place is a tad staid. There are various accommodation options including an extraordinary bedroom in a chapel, though the en-suite doubles upstairs are the nicest. R̲7̲5̲0̲

EATING

Eating out is one of the highlights of visiting Cape Town, and the city is home to a large number of relaxed and convivial restaurants, which generally serve imaginative food of a high standard. Prices are inexpensive compared with much of the developed world, and you can eat innovative food by outstanding chefs in upmarket restaurants for the kind of money you'd spend on a pizza back home. This is the place to splash out on whatever takes your fancy, and you'll find the quality of meat and fish very high, with many vegetarian options available as well. There are a couple of restaurants dedicated to **Cape** or **African Cuisine** (see box, p.140), though other genres are done a lot better. You can expect fresh **Cape fish** at every good restaurant as well as seafood from warmer waters – try one of the delicious Cape fish like Yellow Tail, which is not endangered. Also check out the fun **neighbourhood markets**, where you can get a drink and something tasty to eat from a stall (see p.154).

CITY CENTRE

95 Keerom 95 Keerom St ☎021 422 0765, ⓦ95keerom.com; map p.92. Flash, fabulous and expensive, *95 Keerom* offers fresh and light Italian nouvelle cuisine, with dishes such as grilled beef, butternut ravioli and seared tuna (average mains R220). In 2013, chef

Giorgio Nava won gold in the Pasta World Championship in Italy with his broccoli and anchovy pasta primi (R70). Mon–Sat 6.30–9.30pm.

★**Addis in Cape** 41 Church St ☎021 424 5722, ☻addisincape.co.za; map p.92. This friendly restaurant has a lovely laidback atmosphere. You'll find delicious traditional Ethiopian dishes on the menu, such as spicy red lentils (R109), served on yummy *injera* (sourdough flatbread) to soak up the flavours and eat with your fingers (R110). Mon–Sat noon–10.30pm.

Africa Café 108 Shortmarket St, Cape Heritage Square ☎021 422 0221, ☻africacafe.co.za; map p.92. Probably the best tourist restaurant in Cape Town for African cuisine, with a fantastic selection of dishes from across the continent. Given that you're served a communal feast of sixteen dishes, and that you can have as many extra helpings as you like, the R250-per-head price tag is pretty reasonable. Booking essential. Mon–Sat 6–10.30pm.

Biesmiellah 2 Wale St, at Pentz St, Bo-Kaap ☎021 423 0850, ☻biesmiellah.co.za; map p.90. This is one of the oldest restaurants for traditional Cape cuisine; rather than a sit-down meal, join local residents in the queue for their takeaway samosas and delicious savoury wraps called *salomes* (R48). There are plain veg or bean ones for vegetarians, but the most popular remain prawn or mutton. Mon–Sat 7.30am–10pm.

Birds Café 127 Bree St ☎021 426 2534, ☻facebook .com/BirdsCafe; map p.90. There are long communal tables in this airy, central venue, where you can happily check your emails over a cappuccino. The cakes – especially the carrot (R40) – are recommended, as is the Birds' nest warm salad with a poached egg nesting on steamed broccoli and mushrooms (R60), and everything is served on local pottery. Mon–Fri 7am–5pm, Sat 8am–2pm.

★**Bistrot Bizerca** 98 Shortmarket St, Heritage Square ☎021 423 8888, ☻bizerca.com; map p.92. A gourmet bistro with a modern, funky feel and consistently good reputation. The food, from French chef Laurent Deslandes, is light, elegant and creative, and made using local ingredients, with delightful meat and fish choices (mains R150) and impressive desserts. Not cheap, but worth every penny, and the service is excellent. Booking essential. Mon–Fri noon–2.30pm & 6–10pm, Sat 6–10pm.

★**Café Mozart** 37 Church St ☎021 424 3774, ☻themozart.co.za.com; map p.92. Sit under trees in a handsome street, or in the colourful and attractive interior with quirky antique pieces, for hearty breakfasts, high teas or a good glass of wine. Their "table of love" (R45) is a mix of fresh salads and breads, which make up a delicious and healthy lunch. Mon–Fri 7am–4pm, Sat 9am–3.30pm.

Charly's Bakery 38 Canterbury St, District Six ☎021 461 5181, ☻charlysbakery.co.za; map p.90. Don't be fooled by the plain decor and modest location – you'll find people queuing out of the door for the most spectacular

and decorative cakes in Cape Town, such as the red velvet cupcakes or wheat- and gluten-free lemon meringue cupcakes (both R20). They also do breakfasts and light lunches (around R50). Tues–Fri 8am–5pm, Sat 8.30am–2pm.

Eastern Food Bazaar The Wellington, Darling St ☎021 461 2458, ☻easternfoodbazaar.co.za; map p.92. Cheap, canteen-style restaurant with an Indian and Cape Malay menu (mains R30). You queue up to order, and there are often long waits at lunchtime. It is busy, lively and portions are huge, with *faloodas* and *lassis* made fresh on site. No alcohol is permitted. Daily 11am–10pm.

Headquarters Heritage Square, 100 Shortmarket St ☎021 424 6373, ☻hqrestaurant.co.za; map p.92. There is only one thing on the menu here – prime free-range Namibian sirloin steak and butter sauce with perfect matchstick chips and salad (R175). On Friday nights, a DJ plays relaxing beats; things hot up around 10.30pm, when the tables are pushed back for dancing. There are two dinner sittings (at 6pm and 8.30pm), and on Mon evenings you get two meals for the price of one. Booking always essential. Mon–Sat 12.30–10.30pm.

★**Jason Bakery** 185 Bree St ☎021 021 424 5644, ☻jasonbakery.com; map p.92. With an unswerving local following, Jason is renowned for his pastries, pies and sourdough rye bread. Among the imaginative offerings at this fashionable spot, braised pork belly and apple pie (R40) is a favourite, while bangers and mash pie sometimes features on the daily-changing menu. Bacon croissants and excellent coffee are standard breakfast fare, and Sat is the bonanza baking day, when Jason tweets his specials. For lunch, the most popular sandwich is chicken Caesar on rye (R60). Mon–Fri 7am–3.30pm, Sat 8am–2pm.

La Parada 107 Bree St ☎021 426 0330, ☻107bree .co.za; map p.92. This restaurant serves the most authentic tapas in South Africa on long, wooden communal tables – it's moderately priced, too (R18–48). You'll also find craft beer, reasonable cocktails and a bustling, noisy atmosphere. There is an identical sister restaurant in Main Rd, Kalk Bay. Daily noon–2am.

Mama Africa 178 Long St ☎021 424 8634, ☻mamaafricarestaurant.co.za; map p.92. With food from around the continent, the menu here includes a mixed grill of springbok, impala, kudu, ostrich and even crocodile (mains R170). You can also sit at the 12m-long bar – in the form of a green mamba – and listen to live marimba music. Mon–Sat 6.30–11pm, Tues–Fri also 11am–4pm.

Mr Pickwick's Café and Bar 2 Greenmarket Place, 54 Shortmarket St; map p.92. The number one place for cheap, early breakfasts, or midnight munchies, every day of the year. Hearty and cheap "tin-plate" meals, including a challenging range of hot and cold foot-long sandwiches (R50) are dished out even after the pubs close, as are decadent milkshakes. Daily 7am–2am.

AFRICAN FOOD

Around the centre of Cape Town you will find a couple of restaurants offering African food, but these are geared towards tourists – you would never find a full-blooded Xhosa worker eating in Long Street. The best way to experience the African food is by staying in a B&B in the **townships** (see box, p.126), or by taking a tour that includes an organized township meal or a drink in a *shebeen* (see p.57).

You are not going to find authentic places to eat and drink if you just drive about in the townships, which would be unwise and unsafe in any event, but there is one notable exception, *Mzoli's*.

Mzoli's Shop 3, NY 115, Gugulethu ☏ 021 638 1355. In the closest township to the centre, and within easy driving distance, *Mzoli's* is often full of tourists, but you will get the real thing food-wise – Jamie Oliver adored its tasty barbecued meat (*tshisanyama* – "chi-san-knee-yama"), which ranges from chops, *boerewors* sausage, cuts of beef and lamb served with dumplings, *pap* (thick maize porridge), meat sauce and *chakalaka*, a tomato salad. A meal will set you back about R50, and you'll need to call first for reservations and directions. Not suitable for vegetarians or those with small appetites. Daily 9am–6pm.

Royale Eatery 273 Long St ☏ 021 422 4536, ⓦ royaleeatery.com; map p.92. A hip hangout serving inexpensive gourmet burgers, with unusual combinations such as brie or roasted vegetables. Choose from lamb, beef, chicken and seven vegetarian patties including tofu. The Miss Piggy burger with bacon and guacamole (R75) is a favourite. It's usually packed, so book ahead, especially for a balcony seat with street views. Mon–Sat noon–10.30pm.

V&A WATERFRONT AND DE WATERKANT
THE WATERFRONT
Baia Upper Level, Quay 6 ☏ 021 421 0933, ⓦ baiarestaurant.co.za; map p.101. Sit on the terraced balcony and take in the views of Table Mountain while dining on masterfully cooked fresh fish and seafood; there's line-fish papillote (baked in a parchment paper parcel with tomato, courgettes, fennel and thyme; R150), or grilled *kingklip* is recommended if you want something simpler (R170). Booking essential, especially for dinner. Daily noon–11pm.

Caffé San Marco Piazza level, Victoria Wharf ☏ 021 418 5434, ⓦ sanmarco.co.za; map p.101. This coffee shop and bar with outdoor seating offers an all-day breakfast menu, good sandwiches on Italian breads, wraps and fresh salads. The grilled calamari with garlic and chilli is delicious (R90), and they sell eighteen flavours of ice cream and sorbet. Daily 8am–11pm.

City Grill Shop 155, Victoria Wharf ☏ 021 421 9820, ⓦ citygrill.co.za; map p.101. An excellent, if rather touristy and pricey steakhouse, celebrating the meaty heart of South African cuisine. Their ostrich kebab (R195) is recommended, and you can't go wrong with a full-blooded rump steak (R150), or a biltong and dry sausage appetizer (R79). The wine list is excellent, with 150 vintage wines to choose from, and there are good sea views which you can enjoy from outdoor tables under umbrellas. Daily 9.30am–11pm.

Truth Coffee 36 Buitenkant St ☏ 021 200 0440, ⓦ truthcoffee.com; map p.101. These artisan coffee roasters supply some of the best restaurants in Cape Town and serve a great cup of coffee (R18) in a venue with a chic industrial design built around a cast-iron vintage roaster drum. It's worth going for the "steampunk" décor alone, but eat elsewhere. Mon–Fri 7am–6pm, Sat 8am–6pm, Sun 8am–2pm.

Willoughby & Co Shop 6182, Lower Level, Victoria Wharf ☏ 021 418 6115, ⓦ willoughbyandco.co.za; map p.101. Despite a lack of sea views, this is hands down the best fish restaurant at the Waterfront, serving fantastic sushi and seafood (mains around R160) in a lively atmosphere. Daily noon–11pm.

DE WATERKANT
★**Anatoli** 24 Napier St ☏ 021 419 2501, ⓦ anatoli.co.za; map p.101. This Turkish restaurant, a little on the pricey side but bursting with personality, is set in an early twentieth-century warehouse. It's great for vegetarians, and the excellent meze includes delicious Greek vine-wrapped *dolmades* (R40), with at least twenty others to choose from on a starters platter. For meat eaters, look no further than the kebabs and rice (R135). *Anatoli* also serves superb desserts, such as pressed dates topped with cream (R50). Mon–Sat 6.30–10.30pm.

★**Origin Coffee** 28 Hudson St ☏ 021 421 1000, ⓦ originroasting.co.za; map p.101. These coffee devotees serve home-roasted beans from across Africa and beyond to Asia and Latin America, and their range of teas is equally appealing. Although you can complement your drink with a little something to eat, food is secondary to the quality of the drinks (R70). Mon & Wed–Fri 7am–5pm, Tues 7am–3pm, Sat & Sun 9am–2pm.

CITY BOWL SUBURBS

Aubergine 39 Barnet St, Gardens ☏021 465 4909, ⓦaubergine.co.za; map p.133. An unbeatable choice for an elegant five-star dinner, with a garden to sit in and enjoy the top-quality Afro-Asian cooking of chef Harald Bresselschmidt. Expensive, but memorable, with a strong emphasis on fresh and local foods. Vegetarians can also find an inspired selection. A three-course menu will set you back R435, or R600 with wine. Mon–Sat 6–10pm, Wed–Fri also noon–2pm.

Bacini's Ristorante & Pizzeria 177 Kloof St, Gardens ☏021 423 6668, ⓦbacini.co.za; map p.133. A reliable, bustling Italian restaurant, serving dishes such as a delicious wood-fired ricotta, spinach, aubergine and sundried tomato pizza (R85). Daily noon–10.30pm.

★**Bombay Bicycle Club** 158 Kloof St, Gardens ☏021 423 6805, ⓦthebombay.co.za; map p.133. Don't expect Indian cuisine here, but do expect a great place for a fun evening out. There are things to play with in every area, whether you're sitting at a table with swings, or wearing silly hats. Food includes grills, soups, pastas and carpaccios (average mains R150). Booking essential, as it's often full. Mon–Sat 6–11pm (bar from 4pm).

Carlyle's on Derry 17 Derry St, Gardens ☏021 461 8787, ⓦcarlyles.co.za; map p.133. A friendly place where you'll need to book in advance for a table. From 6pm they serve a great selection of thin-based, gourmet pizzas such as fig and blue cheese, Thai chicken and coriander, or lemon-infused ham and rocket (R80). They also serve meat dishes (R95–130), pasta (R60–85) and salads (R45–85). Daily 5.30–10.30pm.

Deer Park Café 2 Deer Park Drive, Vredehoek ☏021 462 6311; map p.133. On the lower slopes of Table Mountain and with an enclosed park sloping below outdoor tables, this is the best central place to take children – and there's plenty for them on the menu, such as ciabatta french toast (R56). It's a great place for adults, too – not only for the setting, but for fresh, well-priced food. For lunch, the toasted ciabatta with a selection of hummus, feta, roasted peppers, olive tapenade and basil pesto is a winner (R70). Daily 8am–8pm.

Hudson's The Burger Joint 69 Kloof St, Gardens ☏021 426 5974, ⓦtheburgerjoint.co.za; map p.133. A good place for gourmet burgers (R38–88), with trendy young patrons, loud rock music, craft beer, home-made lemonade and Bar One milkshakes (R40). Besides a huge choice of burgers, there are also decent salads, such as "The Good Girl" – butternut squash with feta (R60). Daily noon–11pm.

Miller's Thumb 10b Kloof Nek Rd, Tamboerskloof ☏021 424 3838, ⓦmillersthumb.co.za; map p.133. In a house on a residential street, this restaurant makes consistently good seafood dishes, with a selection of line fish prepared in a variety of ways and served in a cheerful environment. For those not into fish, they also do juicy steaks (R120). Mon & Sat 6.30–10.30pm, Tues–Fri 12.30–2pm & 6.30–10pm.

Mount Nelson Hotel 76 Orange St, Gardens ⓦmountnelson.co.za; map p.133. Colonial-style afternoon tea, in Cape Town's oldest and most gracious hotel is a culinary highlight of the city. The large tea tables are piled high with hot and cold pastries, classic savouries like smoked salmon sandwiches and scrumptious cakes. You won't need dinner after the R235 feast you get here. Book in advance online; there's a smart-casual dress code. Tea at 1.30pm & 3.30pm.

★**Saigon** 72 Kloof St, at Camp St, suburb ☏021 424 7670; map p.133. Authentic Vietnamese food and sushi, with impeccable service. The chicken with cashew nuts is very tasty, as is the duck curry (mains around R90). The best spot to sit is close to the large windows which frame Table Mountain. Daily noon–2.30pm & daily 6–10.30pm. Closed lunchtime Sat.

★**Sidewalk Café** 33 Derry St, Vredehoek ☏021 461 2839, ⓦsidewalk.co.za; map p.133. This modern, funky café has large windows and an enticing and imaginative menu featuring healthy and fresh or decadent dishes (mains around R110). Vegetarians do well, too – the grilled field mushrooms, roasted aubergine, olives, halloumi and harissa-mayo sandwich with salad is a good choice for a light lunch. Free wi-fi. Mon–Sat 8am–10.30pm, Sun 9am–2pm.

★**Societi Bistro** 50 Orange St, Gardens ☏021 424 2100, ⓦsocieti.co.za; map p.133. A little pricey, this friendly bistro offers good Italian-style food, in a lovely restored building and garden, with a fireplace for winter evenings. The risotto here is always a hit (R112), and starters include ox tongue (R55), chicken liver parfait (R58) and beetroot carpaccio (R39). There is always a vegan dish on the menu, too, such as quinoa curry with seasonable vegetables, sambals and roti (R83). Mon–Sat noon–10pm.

SOUTHERN SUBURBS

Catharina's Steenberg Estate, Constantia ☏021 713 2222, ⓦsteenberghotel.com. This restaurant, on a lovely wine estate and serving beautifully presented food, is ideal for special (though not stiflingly formal) occasions. The evenings here are cosy, and you can lounge on the comfy bar sofas while sipping champagne made on the estate. During the day, there are views through large glass walls onto the vineyard. Seafood and venison regularly feature on the menu, or try the rich potato gnocchi with asparagus, peas, artichokes and a creamy parmesan sauce (R105). Daily 7am–10am & 11am–11pm.

Chandani 85 Roodebloem Rd, Woodstock ☏021 447 7887, ⓦchandani.co.za. You won't do better in Cape Town for Indian cuisine than *Chandani*, which specializes in

North Indian food. It's great for vegetarians, with plenty of paneer dishes – the house speciality is a mashed version with onions, peas and spices (R80). The restaurant is set in a tastefully restored Victorian house, in a gritty neighbourhood. Mon–Sat noon–3.30pm & 7–10pm.

Common Ground Café 23 Milner Rd, Rondebosch ☎ 021 686 0154. Attached to a church, this is an unlikely contender for the best coffee in town, but the baristas are true artists who take their business seriously. They also offer among the most reasonably priced breakfasts in town (R43) and have a small sandwich menu and pay-by-weight lunchtime buffet. The atmosphere is relaxed – there are sofas to recline on – and the views of Devil's Peak across Rondebosch Common are lovely. Mon–Fri 7am–4pm, Sat 8am–2pm, Sun 8.30am–2pm & 5.30–8.30pm.

Kirstenbosch Tea Room Restaurant Rhodes Drive, Newlands ☎ 021 797 4883, ⓦ ktr.co.za. The gorgeous garden setting and the pleasing, Cape country food – particularly the pickled fish (R106) or home-made burgers (R95) – is the draw here. They have some good options for vegetarians and you can order a gourmet picnic (R160/person) and even rent a picnic blanket (R30). Daily 8.30am–5pm.

★ **The Kitchen** 111 Sir Lowry Rd, Woodstock ☎ 021 462 2201. Run by Karen Dudley, *The Kitchen* uses the freshest ingredients to create fabulous, inventive sandwiches. Karen's "love sandwiches" on artisanal bread (R45) are especially popular, and there is an ever-changing range of salads. This is one of the best and cheapest places in town, especially if you are vegetarian, for a casual, lively, good-value lunch. The service here is fast and efficient, and the whole place buzzes; it's not a place to linger. Mon–Fri 8am–4pm.

★ **Pot Luck Club** Top Floor, Silo Building, Old Biscuit Mill, Albert Rd, Woodstock ☎ 021 447 0804, ⓦ thepotluckclub.co.za. Set in a remarkable venue, this place is all about inventive, expensive and tasty tapas dishes (around R80 each). The menu is arranged according to sweet, salty, bitter and *umami* flavours; order several, and share with friends. Sweet tapas, such as bean-paste-glazed beef short rib with a steamed bun and pickles (R95), is not to be confused with a "sweet ending", such as pecan pie with celeriac ice cream (R60). You'll need to book a few weeks in advance and will be allocated a seating time. Mon–Sat noon–2.30pm & 6.30–10pm, Sun 11.30am–2.30pm.

★ **Test Kitchen** Old Biscuit Mill, 375 Albert Rd, Woodstock ☎ 021 447 2337, ⓦ thetestkitchen.co.za. At South Africa's top, award-winning fine-dining contemporary restaurant, you'll be overwhelmed by the sensual feast of tastes, smells and colours provided by the creative mastery of Chef Luke Dale Roberts. The food on the ever-changing menu, such as confit duck leg with mushroom and liver stuffing, assorted onions, truffle-and-*foie-gras* egg and duck liver *jus* (R160), is innovative, often with unusual ingredients and combinations of flavours that you can enjoy in an industrial-style setting with a casual ambience. You may need to book months in advance. Tues–Sat 12.30–2pm & 7–9pm.

ATLANTIC SEABOARD
GREEN POINT

El Burro 81 Main Rd, Green Point ☎ 021 433 2364, ⓦ elburro.co.za; map pp.112–113. This fun, casual spot offers Mexican food without too much cheese and grease (mains R100), plus a good view from the balcony of Green Point Stadium. There are plenty of veggie options, and the butternut enchilada is delicious (R65). Mon–Sat noon–11.30pm.

★ **Giovanni's Deliworld** 103 Main Rd ☎ 021 434 6893; map pp.112–113. With both indoor and pavement seating (good for people-watching), this lively Italian deli and coffee shop is right across from the Stadium and has its own screen for watching sports. It offers delicious coffee, excellent made-to-order sandwiches, salads and dips and good prepackaged meals (R45–65). Daily 8am–9pm.

Mano's 39 Main Rd ☎ 021 434 1090, ⓦ mano.co.za; map pp.112–113. Popular with model-types and generally beautiful people, this place serves seafood, grills and pasta from a mixed menu that includes fish 'n' chips, Prego rolls and *penne arrabiata* (all around R70), as well as exciting salads, and one of the best *crème brûlées* in town (R60). After dinner, the party continues in *Jade* champagne bar upstairs (see p.149). Mon–Sat noon–10pm.

MOUILLE POINT

Café Neo 129 Beach Rd ☎ 021 433 0849; map pp.112–113. *Neo* serves deli-style food with a Greek influence (mains around R50–70). Tasty breakfast options include Greek yoghurt with nuts and honey, or porridge with berries, and at other times there are meze platters, salads and sandwiches. Vegetarians can do well here, and the umbrella-shaded outdoor seating offers views of either Green Point stadium or the lighthouse. Daily 7am–7pm.

★ **Newport Market and Deli** 47 Beach Rd ☎ 021 439 1538, ⓦ newportdeli.co.za; map pp.112–113. This light, airy deli, with views onto Table Bay, serves coffee, excellent sandwiches (around R60), tasty salads such as watermelon & feta (R60), and hot dishes like macaroni cheese (R56) or chicken burgers (R45–75). The interesting smoothies, such as pawpaw, mixed berries and mango (R32), make a welcome change from breakfast fry-ups and toasted sandwiches. Daily 7am–10pm.

Wakame and Wafu 47 Beach Rd ☎ 021 433 2377, ⓦ wakame.co.za; map pp.112–113. Specializing in Asian-fusion food, *Wakame* serves formal meals such as top-notch sesame crusted seared tuna (R130), plus killer desserts – try the chocolate and banana spring rolls – and every table has a view of the ocean. Upstairs, *Wafu*, offers a tapas and dim sum menu, and is a great sundowner spot, where you can soak up the best sea views in Cape Town, classic Martini in hand (R45). Both places have their own sushi bar, too, where six salmon roses will set you back R75. Booking essential. Daily noon–3pm & 6–10pm.

SEA POINT

La Boheme Wine Bar & Bistro 341 Main Rd ⊕021 434 6539, ⓦlabohemebistro.co.za; map pp.112–113. Enjoyable and inexpensive, with a menu full of interesting, well-presented rural French food and lovely wines by the glass – there are at least sixty to choose from. Dishes (around the R85 mark) include ostrich meatballs with tagliatelli and potato gnocchi. There's pavement seating, while their sister espresso and tapas bar next door is great for a small bite to eat and serves fantastic coffee (R80). Daily 8.30am–9.30pm.

Mr Chan 178a Main Rd ⊕021 439 2239, ⓦmrchan .co.za; map pp.112–113. This worthwhile Chinese restaurant has been serving happy customers for the last twenty years with excellent Hong Kong-style beef, prawns, roast duck and, for vegetarians, braised bean curd and mixed vegetables. Lunch specials are R65, dinner set menus R150. Daily noon–2.30pm & 6–10.30pm.

CAMPS BAY, HOUT BAY AND NOORDHOEK

Café Caprice 37 Victoria Rd, Camps Bay ⊕021 438 8315, ⓦcafecaprice.co.za; map, p.116. Directly opposite Camps Bay beach (though the tables are on the pavement, not on the beach itself), this lively, albeit pretentious, Mediterranean-style restaurant is a great place to soak up street life, sunshine and sunsets. You can get nibbles like hummus and pita (R42), or more substantial fish or meat dishes, or just a drink. Daily 9am–midnight.

Café Roux Noordhoek Farm Village ⊕021 789 2538, ⓦcaferoux.co.za. This chilled-out café sells wholesome and healthy food with a contemporary feel, plus live music on Sun afternoons and some weekday evenings. They serve breakfasts (from R45), gourmet sandwiches (from R70), burgers (from R75) and other simple fare, with a menu (and garden) that caters to children. Sit under umbrellas with your "crazy duck" salad (R92) or have tea after doing Chapman's Peak, and gaze at the surrounding mountains. Daily 8.30am–11am & noon–5pm.

★**The Foodbarn** Noordhoek Farm Village ⊕021 789 1390, ⓦthefoodbarn.co.za. Excellent gourmet French food from acclaimed chef, Franck Dangereux, at reasonable prices – though service is slow. Children are welcome, and you can sit on a sunny veranda in beautiful surroundings. Starters feature spicy fish soup (R72), and there are some interesting meats on the menu, such as grilled springbok

rump with turnip tatin (R165). Each dish is paired with a wine, so you may need a taxi home after a lingering lunch. Booking essential. Daily noon–3pm, Wed–Sat also 7–9.30pm.

★**Kitima** 140 Main Rd, Hout Bay ⊕021 790 8004, ⓦkitima.co.za. Cape Town's best Asian Fusion restaurant, with a Thai slant, in a lovely Cape Dutch Manor House. The food couldn't be fresher and is prepared in front of your eyes, with sushi and sashimi, dim sum and a plethora of seafood and meat stir-fries and curries, such as salmon *panang* (R125) or ostrich with lemongrass (R125). Don't miss the sumptuous Sunday buffets (R250), for which you'll definitely need to book. Tues–Sat noon–10.30pm, Sun noon–3pm.

La Cuccina Food Store Victoria Mall, Victoria Rd, Hout Bay ⊕021 790 8008. This high-quality deli and café is set in pleasant surroundings, and the delicious food compensates for the lack of sea views. At lunchtime, there's a tasty buffet of quiches, salads and lasagne, sold by weight (R16/100g). The breakfasts are great, too. Daily 7am–5pm.

Paranga Shop 1, The Promenade, Victoria Rd, Camps Bay ⊕021 438 0404, ⓦparanga.co.za; map, p.116. Popular hangout at the beach, a place to see and be seen while you pick at expensive salads, seafood, pasta or sushi. There's a variety of sparkling wines and champagnes on offer including the South African Pongracz (R60), plus all sorts of wines, whiskeys and cocktails. Daily 9am–midnight.

Wharfette Bistro The Harbour, Hout Bay ⊕021 790 1100, ⓦmarinerswharf.com. A relaxed, well-run and popular seafood restaurant, decorated with nostalgic photographs and memorabilia from Cape Town's passenger liner days. The views of the harbour from the terrace seating outshine the food, but it's a fine spot for fish 'n' chips (R55) and a cold beer. Daily 10am–9pm.

THE TOWNSHIPS

Department of Coffee Next to Khayletisha Station, Khayelitsha ⊕073 300 9519, ⓦtwitter.com /Dpmofcoffee. More intrepid travellers can visit independently the first artisan coffee house in a township, where you can get real coffee, hot chocolate, orange juice or muffins for under R10, and sit at the outdoor seating beneath orange umbrellas. Mon–Fri 6am–6pm, Sat 8am–3pm.

FALSE BAY SEABOARD

MUIZENBERG

Casa Labia Café 192 Main Rd ⊕021 788 6068, ⓦcasalabia.co.za; map pp.118–119. Contemporary Italian food and English-style high teas in seafront *palazzo* surroundings, furnished with oil paintings, antiques and beautiful table linen. Set breakfasts

1

include pancakes, eggs, pancetta, sausages, mushrooms, tomatoes, sweet potato toast with jam and coffee or tea, all for R155. There's usually a good art exhibition upstairs, and the small craft shop sells carefully chosen pieces. Courtyard dining comes with mountain views. Tues–Sun 10am–4pm.

Empire Café 11 York Rd ☎021 788 1250, Ⓦempirecafe.co.za; map pp.118–119. Enjoy good coffee and fresh pastries while you gaze at passing trains and the blue ocean beyond, or work at your computer, and use free the wi-fi. Their tasty pastas (R50) make a wholesome lunch, and your waiter may slide down the banisters to despatch your order, though it's rather slower bringing the goods up. Daily 7am–4pm, Sun from 8am.

KALK BAY

★**The Annex** 124 Main Rd, above Kalk Bay Books ☎021 788 2453, Ⓦtheannex.co.za; map pp.118–119. The best outdoor venue in Kalk Bay, with tables on a terrace giving superb views over the harbour and bay beyond. The food is terrific – eggs Benedict on home-baked ciabatta (R45) is a firm favourite – and there's a deli downstairs. As the owner is a wine maker, expect an informed and interesting selection of Cape wines. Daily 8am–9pm, Sat & Sun from 7am.

C'est La Vie 20 Main Rd, opposite Dale Brook Pool ☎083 676 7430; map pp.118–119. Unassuming and tiny French-styled bakery, which offers pavement breakfasts (R45), real baguettes and orange juice, croissants and excellent coffee. Wed–Sun 7am–3pm.

Harbour House Restaurant On the harbour ☎021 788 4133, Ⓦharbourhouse.co.za; map pp.118–119. This memorable venue serves seafood and Mediterranean food, in a spectacular setting on the breakwater of Kalk Bay harbour. The Mozambique tiger prawns (R195) are worth a try, but there is also lamb and beef on the menu, plus some vegetarian options. Portions are small, but rich and beautifully presented. Booking is essential and you'll have to choose one of two sitting times. Daily noon–4pm & 6–10pm.

Kalky's On the harbour ☎021 788 1726; map pp.118–119. For years, this unpretentious eatery has been serving the fishing community the best fish 'n' chips on the peninsula (R56) plus great-value seafood platters. Fish is hauled off the boats and straight into the frying pan; wait a bit longer and you can have your catch grilled. Daily 10am–7pm.

★**The Olympia Café & Deli** Main Rd ☎021 788 6396, Ⓦfacebook.com/OlympiaCafeKalkBay; map pp.118–119. Always buzzing, a tad scruffy and with views of the harbour, *Olympia* offers great coffee accompanied by their own freshly baked goods, while lunch menus often feature local fish and mussels (mains around R100). They don't take bookings, so arrive early for dinner or join the queue.

Their bakery is round the corner, where you can get bread, pastries, excellent take-away coffee and sandwiches. Daily 7am–9pm, bakery till 5pm.

SIMON'S TOWN AND THE DEEP SOUTH

Black Marlin Main Rd, south of Simon's Town ☎021 786 1621, Ⓦblackmarlin.co.za. Every kind of sea denizen, apart from the restaurant's namesake, is on the menu at this popular place on the road to Cape Point. The food is fine, but it's the clifftop views from the outdoor tables that are the main appeal – especially when there are whale sightings. Catch of the day costs R119, and weekend breakfasts are very cheap – scrambled egg on toast is R25. Daily noon–10pm, Sat & Sun from 9am.

★**Blue Water Café** Imhoff Farm, Kommetjie Rd, opposite the Ocean View turn-off ☎021 783 2007, Ⓦimhofffarm.co.za. This is the best restaurant to stop at on the Cape Point round route – the menu offers surprisingly good fish (mussels R90), pasta (R86), wood-fired pizzas (R70) and wines, as well as breakfasts and teas. Set in a handsome Cape Dutch homestead, there are good views onto the wetlands and ocean beyond, and there's a fire in winter. Service is attentive, and you can book a table outdoors next to a large lawn, where children can play. Tues 9am–5pm, Wed–Sun 9am–9pm.

Camel Rock Main Rd, Scarborough ☎021 780 1122. A local hangout that makes scant effort to cater to tourists, this homely joint is the only place for a beer and bite in Scarborough, serving unexceptional seafood dishes (R105). Wed–Mon 11am–9pm.

Salty Sea Dog 2 Wharf St, Waterfront, Simon's Town ☎021 7861918, Ⓦsaltyseadog.co.za. There's nothing fancy about this small restaurant on the wharf, but they do plain old fish 'n' chips (R40) extremely well, and they serve beer and wine. With indoors and alfresco seating, it makes a great lunch stop on an outing to Cape Point. Mon–Sat 8.30am–9pm, Sun (takeaways only) 8.30am–4.30pm.

Tibetan Teahouse 2 Harrington Rd, Seaforth Beach ☎021 786 1544. Traditional Tibetan recipes are served from a completely vegetarian menu, with offerings such as yak-free lentil stew (R60). You'll find the venue signalled by its prayer flags, close to Boulders Beach and on the way to Cape Point. Tues–Sun 10am–5pm.

Two Oceans Cape Point ☎021 702 0703, Ⓦtwo-oceans.co.za. The star of the show at this seafood-focused restaurant is the sublime view from its alfresco deck, taking in False Bay and its mountains – this is a great place to see whales in season. There's a large fish and seafood menu including the "smack of sea" antipasti, with mackerel, prawns, cured trout, Cape Yellowtail, crispy squid heads, pickled mussels and *snoek* paté (R230), plus sushi and some meaty options. Daily 9am–4pm.

BARS AND CLUBS

Being a hedonistic city – especially in the summer – Cape Town has plenty of great places to drink and party, especially along **Long Street** where it's safe and busy, and there are taxis to get you home. In the summer, the Atlantic Seaboard, notably **Camps Bay**, is a great option, especially for sundowners. When the dust has settled after Saturday's hedonism, Sunday nights are notably quiet, though there are a couple of welcoming options. Most liquor **licences** stipulate that the last round is served at 2am, but this is far from strictly followed; bars often stay open until the last customer leaves. Laws prohibit the sale of alcohol in shops from 6pm on Saturday and all day Sunday. Drink **prices** obviously depend on the venue – a beer in a sports bar might set you back R18, while local craft brews cost upwards of R45. A smart bar will charge up to R65 for a cocktail, while glasses of delicious Cape wine begin at R40. **Clubs** get going after 10pm and are pretty international in flavour, with **DJs** mixing house hits you're bound to recognize. Some may have a **cover charge**, but this is usually only when they have live music on and it's never more than R100. It's not a good idea to walk around late at night, so take a **taxi number** out with you (see p.130). Many bars and clubs offer food as well. When it comes to **live music**, the best-known South African musicians are sadly better appreciated, and better paid, abroad than in their own country. If anyone good is in town, you will pick that up on posters or in a listings magazine. Cape Town is known for its brand of Cape Jazz, but there is nowhere regular to pick that up, though the best jazz event of the year happens in late March at the annual **Cape Town International Jazz Festival**. The Baxter and Artscape (see p.150) are both likely venues for any good musical offerings.

CITY CENTRE
LONG STREET AND BREE STREET

Aces 'N' Spades 62 Hout St ☎021 424 1620, ⓦacesnspades.com; map p.92. This place is usually jam-packed from the bar (bottled beers R20), where chic meets grunge, to the heaving dance floor where rock'n'roll music sets the tempo for enthusiastic dancing. A safe bet for a great night out, if you don't mind a mass of bodies and a croaky voice in the morning. Mon–Sat 7pm–2am.

The Beerhouse 223 Long St ☎021 424 3370, ⓦbeerhouse.co.za; map p.92. With a menu of 20 taps and 99 bottles, 75 percent of which are local craft brews, it's no wonder a whole day can go by at this modern "beer hall" without moving from the large balcony overlooking Long St. It's quite expensive (pint R40–70) and not conducive to thoughtful beer tasting, but the large tables are perfect for groups. Daily noon–late.

Dubliner @ Kennedy's 251 Long St ☎021 424 1212, ⓦdubliner.co.za; map p.92. Crammed, wildly popular traditional Irish pub with Guinness and pilsner on tap (R28), pub meals from lunch until midnight daily, and live music from 10pm every night. Other features include flat screens for sporting events and a pool table. Cover charge R60–70 Fri & Sat. Daily 11am–4am.

Fiction Bar 226 Long St ⓦfictionbar.com; map p.92.

Fiction hosts stand-out electronic music nights and high-quality local and international DJs; the likes of Skrillex, Diplo, Pendulum and Noisia have popped in for impromptu sideshows. Lose yourself on the energetic dance floor then head out to the balcony overlooking Long Street to recover. Bottled beers R18; cover charge R30–60. Tues–Sat 10pm–4am.

Jo'burg 218 Long St ☎021 422 0142; map p.92. A good, if crowded, place to hang out, grooving to a fresh soundtrack or playing pool against one of the local patrons. Many people end up here during a night out on Long St, and it's one of the few places open on Sun nights. Cool off on the open-air patio outside. Bottled beer R18. Mon–Sat noon–4am, Sun 6pm–4am.

★ **La Parada** 107 Bree St ☎021 426 0330; map p.92. With its open windows, vibrant atmosphere and creative Spanish tapas menu, *La Parada* is a highlight of the hip bars on Bree and the long, sociable tables are filled with well-heeled Capetonians from lunch through to late. Cocktails are R55–65, while a glass of wine will set you back R35. No bookings. Daily noon–2am.

★ **TjingTjing** 165 Longmarket St ☎021 422 4374, ⓦtjingtjing.co.za; map p.92. This rooftop cocktail bar is a low-key favourite for trendy young professionals with its upbeat soundtrack and mouth-watering cocktail menu

NEW YEAR, NEW YEAR – SO GOOD THEY DO IT TWICE

A long-standing tradition in Cape Town is **Tweede Nuwe Jaar** (second New Year) on January 2 – until recently an official public holiday. Historically, this was the only day of the year slaves were allowed off, and the day has persisted as a holiday of epic proportions. *Tweede Nuwe Jaar* sees Cape Minstrels from the coloured community dancing through the streets of the city centre performing a traditional form of singing and riotous banjo playing, with each troupe dressed in matching outfits, often featuring outrageous colour combinations. Some roads in the centre are blocked off during the day for the festivities, which process through the city and end up at Green Point Stadium.

1

TOP FIVE SUNDOWNER SPOTS

Cape Town has some great places to kick back with a cocktail and admire the vista. Here is our pick of the best with waterfront views.

Alba Cocktail Lounge, Waterfront
See below
Brass Bell, Kalk Bay See below

Paranga, Camps Bay See p.143
Polana, Kalk Bay See p.149
Wafu, Mouille Point See p.142

(R50–65) – expect unusual ingredients such as *fynbos*, candyfloss vodka and balsamic vinegar. Tues–Fri 4pm–2am, Sat 6.30pm–2am.

Weinhaus & Biergarten 110 Bree St ☎021 422 2770, ⊕biergarten.co.za; map p.92. For a great atmosphere and outdoor seating in the inner city, there is nowhere better: sample delicious craft beer brewed in Europe (R45 a pint) in *Biergarten* or a wide selection of wines at *Weinhaus*. Smack bang in the middle of the rejuvenated Bree St precinct, this is a popular place for after-work drinks with plenty more trendy wine bars in the vicinity. Tues–Thurs & Sat 3–11pm, Fri noon–11pm.

Zula Sound Bar 194 Long St ☎021 424 2442, ⊕zulabar.co.za; map p.92. Live, local talent of variable quality (music, comedy and the odd poetry reading) is showcased here every night, while the well-priced restaurant serves nachos, salads, chicken wings and burgers alongside Cape wines and tap beers (R30). There's also a balcony and a games room. Cover charge R20–R100. Tues–Sun 11am–4am.

ELSEWHERE IN THE CITY CENTRE

Alexander Bar, Café & Theatre 76 Strand St, ☎021 300 1088, ⊕alexanderbar.co.za; map p.92. Handsomely furnished in old world decor, this is a good spot for a quiet conversation or nightcap and a much needed addition to Cape Town's social scene. Old rotary phones in the bar allow you to call the table next to you while sipping a single malt (R40). Upstairs is an intimate theatre space which hosts music, comedy and plays. Mon–Sat 11am–1am.

Evol 69 Hope St ☎021 465 4918; map 90. Named after a Sonic Youth album, this is the best club in town to hear DJs mix alternative, electro, punk and indie music for a committed crowd. Good dancing, open late into the night, but in a grungy and slightly dingy venue. Bottled beer R18; Cover charge R20. Mon–Sat noon–4am.

The Power and The Glory 13d Kloof Nek Rd ☎021 422 2108; map p.133. On any night of the week "PnG's" is a magnet for hipsters sporting neatly trimmed beards, checked shirts, red lipstick and vintage dresses. The well-styled bistro, kitted out with old-school metal chairs and botanical drawing prints, serves coffee during the day then blends seamlessly with a smoking room and cosy bar serving craft beers (pint R45) at night. Mon–Sat 8am–2am.

Rafiki's 13b Kloof Nek Rd, Tamboerskloof ☎021 426 4731, ⊕rafikis.co.za; map p.133. A laidback bar with a wraparound veranda where you can hang out all day slowly getting sozzled, cheering on sports teams on the big screen or using the free wi-fi. There are roaring fires in winter, and it's popular with students, backpackers and locals alike. Try their chilli-poppers, everything-on-it pizzas and a house cocktail (R45). Daily 11am–2am.

V&A WATERFRONT

Alba Cocktail Lounge Pierhead, above the Hilderbrand Restaurant ☎021 425 3385, ⊕albalounge .co.za; map p.101. Cocktails and snacks in a stunning setting, equipped with sofas and fireplace for winter, looking out over the Waterfront. In summer, enjoy an Albatizer (made with JellyTots and Apple Sourz; R30) on the outdoor deck. Live music twice a week; DJ daily 5pm to close. Daily 11am–1am.

Quay Four Tavern Quay Four ☎021 419 2008, ⊕quay4.co.za; map p.101. Established nearly twenty years ago, the *Tavern* is an old favourite with tourists and locals alike. Watch the world go by with a drink on the terrace overlooking the V&A (pint tap beer R30), share a hearty pub meal with friends or catch the nightly free live music. Daily 11am–2am.

Shimmy Beach Club 12 South Arm Rd ⊕shimmybeachclub.com; map p.101. With a private beach, outdoor deck and an infinity plunge pool, the luxurious *Shimmy Beach Club* is draped with beautiful people day and night. Completing the flashy set-up are an upmarket restaurant, indoor dance floor, expensive cocktail menu (R40–60) and live local and international electronic music acts every Sun during summer. Cover charge R100–250. Daily 11am–2am.

SOUTHERN SUBURBS

Brass Bell Kalk Bay station, Main Rd, Kalk Bay ☎021 788 5455, ⊕brassbell.co.za; map pp.118–119. The *Brass Bell* has arguably the best location on the peninsula, with False Bay's waves breaking against the wall of its outdoor terrace. It's a fantastic watering hole, serving a range of wines by the glass (R30) and tap beers (pint R28–35), plus decent fish 'n' chips. Daily 11am–10pm.

1

GAY AND LESBIAN CAPE TOWN

Cape Town is South Africa's – and indeed, the African continent's – gay capital. The city has always had a vibrant gay culture, attracting gay travellers from across the country and the globe. Cape Town's **gay village**, with B&Bs, guesthouses, pubs, clubs, cruise bars and steam baths, is concentrated along the entertainment strips of Somerset Road and the inner-city suburbs of Green Point, Sea Point and, particularly, the chic De Waterkant, adjacent to the centre. Despite South Africa's liberal constitution legalizing same-sex marriages, outside the city attitudes remain conservative and there is a great deal of homophobia.

Cape Town hosts a hugely popular annual **gay costume party**, organized by Mother City Queer Projects (**w** mcqp.co.za), a ten-day festival held each December the week before Christmas. People dress as outrageously as possible according to the official yearly theme (past ones have included Kitchen Kitsch and Space Cowboys) and the event seeks to rival Sydney's Mardi Gras. There's also an annual **gay pride festival** in February (**w** capetownpride.org).

RESOURCES AND INFORMATION

Besides the South African gay **websites** and resources listed on p.74, **w** gaynetcapetown .co.za is aimed specifically at gay and lesbian travellers to Cape Town, with restaurants and gay accommodation listings, as well as information about HIV/AIDS, while **Health4Men** at 24 Napier St, in the De Waterkant (**t** 021 421 6127, **w** health4men.co.za) provides free sexual health services to men.

The best **listings** magazine is *Out Africa Magazine*, available from the bars and restaurants in De Waterkant, and from GAP Leisure (**w** gapleisure.com), on the corner of Napier and Waterkant streets, an agency that specializes in finding gay accommodation in the De Waterkant and countrywide. Though there are many **lesbians** living in Cape Town, there are no dedicated lesbian bars or clubs. Make it Sexy Sisters (**t** 083 760 8499, **w** facebook .com/MISSmakeitsexysisters.com) hosts regular themed parties for women every month or two at different venues with lesbian DJs and performers.

BARS

Amsterdam Action Bar 12 Cobern St, off Somerset Rd, De Waterkant; map p.101. Old-school gay bar with a more mature crowd, some Leather Men and Bears, no disco and a pool table. Daily 4pm till late.

Bar Code 18 Cobern St, De Waterkant **t** 021 421 5305, **w** leatherbar.co.za; map p.101. A men-only leather, uniform and jeans bar with darkrooms and an outdoor deck. It's worth finding out what the evening's dress code is beforehand, in case they're having a themed night. Entrance R50. Sun–Thurs 10pm–2am, Fri & Sat 10pm–4am.

Beefcakes 40 Somerset Rd, Green Point **t** 021 425 9019, **w** beefcakes.co.za; map p.101. A seriously camp burger bar, with pink flamingo wallpaper and feathers, where you can create your own delicious burger, and wear a sequined cowboy hat. There is a range of live entertainment from Drag Divas to "Bitchy Bingo", on varying nights. Great for cocktails. Mon–Sat noon till late.

Café Manhattan 74 Waterkant St, De Waterkant, and 247 Main Rd, Sea Point **w** manhattan.co.za; map p.101. A buzzing bar-restaurant chain with an affordable and largely meat-orientated menu. The De Waterkant branch has an attractive terrace beneath oak trees, while the Sea Point branch is ideal for people-watching on a busy street. Always bustling and lively, and welcoming of all genders and orientations, though it is primarily a gay venue. Daily 10am–2am.

Crew Bar 30 Napier St, Green Point **t** 081 813 2243, **w** facebook.com/CrewBarCapeTown; map p.101. Stylish bar with topless barmen and sexy go-go dancers. The verandas are packed in the summer, and it's a good choice for a party. Small cover charge. Daily 7pm–4am.

SAUNA

The Hothouse 18 Jarvis St, Green Point **w** hothouse .co.za. A luxurious, men-only pleasure and relaxation complex, and the only one of its kind in Cape Town, with jacuzzis and steam rooms, as well as a sundeck boasting superb views. There's also a bar (complete with fireplace). Entrance R110–140 depending on days and times. Mon–Wed noon–2am, Thurs noon–4am, Fri–Sun noon–6am.

Foresters' Arms 52 Newlands Ave, Newlands ☎ 021 689 5949, ⒲ forries.co.za. Preppy students and professionals gather to quaff beer (bottles R18) at this large, very popular wood-panelled pub, with a beautiful hedged-in courtyard where you can grab a bench for a lazy afternoon pint. Mon–Thurs & Sat 9am–11pm, Fri 9am–midnight, Sun 9am–9pm.

The Polana Kalk Bay Harbour, off Main Rd, Kalk Bay ☎ 021788 7162, ⒲ harbourhouse.co.za/ polana; map pp.118–119. *The Polana* has a spectacular setting right on the rocks. Local wines feature heavily on the drinks list (from R25 a glass) and there's also a short tapas menu; the only drawback is that smoking is allowed in the drinks/lounge area. There's often live music and dancing Sun evenings. Daily 6–10.30pm.

Tiger Tiger 103 Main Rd, Claremont ☎ 021 863 2220, ⒲ tigertiger.co.za. *Tiger Tiger* is reliable for parties, with six bars and a spacious dancefloor pumping commercial music out of a state-of- the-art sound system; Sat nights are good. Cover charge R50; bottled beers R18. Thurs–Sat 8pm–4am.

ATLANTIC SEABOARD

Café Caprice 37 Victoria Rd, Camps Bay ☎ 021 438 8315, ⒲ cafecaprice.co.za; map p.116. This beach-facing hangout, popular with tanned and gorgeous celebs and wannabes, is just right for cocktails (R55). Families are welcome during the day for breakfast and lunch, but the pace increases at sunset and pavement tables are like gold dust. Daily 9am–late.

Dunes 1 Beach Rd, Hout Bay ☎ 021 790 1876, ⒲ dunesrestaurant.co.za; map p.116. Right on Hout Bay beach, this is a popular hangout for families, especially on sunny weekend afternoons. Drinks include tap beer (R28) and cocktails (from R40). Daily 9am–10pm.

Jade Champagne Bar 39 Main Rd above *Manos Restaurant*, Green Point ☎ 021 439 4108, ⒲ jadelounge.co.za; see map pp.112–113. Classy lounge-bar with nightly DJs, plush sofas, chandeliers and a semi-enclosed balcony to relax on with a cocktail (R55). Over 23s only; reservations recommended. Wed–Sat 8pm–2am.

ALL ABOUT THE BEER

The bulk of South Africa's **beer** production is monopolized by the huge South African Breweries (SAB), one of the world's largest beer makers and the oldest brewery in Africa; it runs excellent tours of its brewery at 3 Main Road, Newlands (Mon–Thurs at 10am, noon & 2pm, Fri at 10am, noon, 2pm & 4pm, Sat at 10am & noon, also Tues & Wed at 6pm; R50; ☎ 021 658 7440, ⒲ newlandsbrewery.co.za), which include a beer tasting and two free drinks. However, like much of the world, South Africa has seen a recent renaissance in the popularity of **microbreweries** with many – including Jack Black, Boston, Darling Brew, Mitchell's and Cape Brewing Company – making excellent versions of popular American and European beer styles like weis, IPA, amber and pale ales. One interesting trend to watch out for are the beer-wine hybrids and experimental beers aged in wine barrels, which are currently being produced by microbreweries such as Devil's Peak and Triggerfish.

To take a dip into the world of **craft beer** in South Africa and find out about the latest festivals, check ⒲ thecraftbeerproject.co.za. Below are our top three places in Cape Town to sample craft beer.

★ **Banana Jam Cafe** 157 2nd Avenue, Kenilworth ☎ 021 674 0186, ⒲ bananajamcafe.co.za; map p.101. Although not centrally located, this Caribbean-themed restaurant is the place to go for a relaxed introduction to the spectrum of South African beer, with help from their knowledgeable staff. It has an ever-increasing selection of local and imported beers, most of which are exclusive, plus weekly guest beers (pint R36–45) – try the six-sample tasting plate. Daily 11am–late.

Devil's Peak Taproom 95 Durham Ave, Salt River ☎ 021 200 5818, ⒲ devilspeakbrewing.co.za. Sample the entire Devil's Peak range in their chic,

colonial-style bar-restaurant, directly adjacent to the brewery (pint R30–45), where the magic happens. As well as an excellent regular menu it also offers beer and food pairing. Tues–Sat noon–10pm.

The Wembley Tap 80 McKenzie St, Gardens ☎ 021 300 0946, ⒲ wembleytap.co.za; map p.90. Handily-located in the city centre, *The Wembley Tap* offers thirty local and imported beers on tap (pint R38–45), plus some exclusives, in minimal, industrial surroundings. There's also a large beer garden and menu of stomach-lining pizzas. Mon 4–11pm, Tues & Wed noon–midnight, Thurs–Sat noon–1am.

1

CAPE TOWN JAZZ AND GHOEMA

One of Cape Town's musical treasures is **Cape jazz**, a local derivative of the jazz genre with distinctive African flavours. Its greatest exponent is the internationally acclaimed **Abdullah Ibrahim**. Born and raised in District Six, Ibrahim is a supremely gifted pianist and composer, who has for decades produced a hypnotic fusion of African, American and Cape idioms. Some of his renowned recordings include *Mannenberg* and *African Marketplace*, combining the fluttering rhythms of *ghoema* – traditional Cape carnival music – with the call-and-answer structure of African gospel. Other Cape Jazz legends include a triumvirate of distinctive saxophonists: the late Basil Coetzee, a phenomenal tenor saxophonist; Robbie Jansen, alto player with a raunchy and original style; and Winston Mankunku, schooled on Coltrane and Wayne Shorter, with his unique brand of African inflections. The annual **Cape Town International Jazz Festival** (April; ⓦ capetownjazzfest.com) features some of the world's most renowned musicians.

Ghoema is the rhythm played on a *ghoema* drum, a sound that, for many generations, has been the basis for the popular *moppies* (comic songs) and *ghoemaliedjies* (picnic songs). The term *ghoema* comes from the barrel-shaped drum made out of a tin can without a bottom. Cape Town's colourful minstrel troops occupy the streets of the city over New Year, when the hugely popular Rio-style *nagtroepe* (literally night-time marchers) with their armies of spectators fill the city's streets from January 1 onwards, while *ghoema* troupes compete for honours in festival gatherings. Catch the Christmas Bands and Malay Choirs in this same season for **marching music** in the city.

ENTERTAINMENT

There is a satisfying range of dramatic and musical performances on offer in Cape Town that are easily accessed as theatres are scarcely full, and very affordable compared with London or New York. Despite the virtual lack of arts funding by the government, there is a creative and lively arts scene. Check out the offerings at the major arts venues, the **Baxter**, **Artscape** and the **Fugard Theatre**, where you are likely to find something appealing, either a play, a classical concert, opera, contemporary dance or comedy. The daily *Cape Times* and *Argus* carry listings and reviews.

CLASSICAL MUSIC AND AFRICAN OPERA

Classical music has a relatively small but faithful following, with symphony concerts at the City Hall and Baxter Theatre. There are free lunchtime concerts, often showcasing the work of students from Cape Town University's South African College of Music, on Thursdays at 1pm; these take place at the Baxter Theatre (ⓦ baxter .co.za) or at the college itself (ⓣ 021 650 2640, ⓦ web.uct .ac.za/depts/sacm). Many recitals by visiting soloists and chamber ensembles are put on by an organization called Cape Town Concert Series (ⓦ ctconcerts.co.za), and there are regular and excellent performances in different churches by Cape Town's only Baroque ensemble, Camerata Tinta Barocca (ⓦ ctbmusic.co.za). It's a treat to catch one of the performances by Cape Town Opera (ⓦ capetownopera .co.za) to hear black South Africans, who dominate opera in South Africa, injecting some powerful new voices and energy into a programme that still predominantly features European works.

THEATRES

Tickets for all of the venues and performances listed are available from Computicket (ⓣ 083 915 8000, ⓦ computicket.com), and you'll find most ticket prices very reasonable at R90–250.

African Dance Theatre Moyo, Clocktower V&A Waterfront ⓣ 021 424 9513, ⓦ theafricandance theatre.co.za. Although aimed at tourists, the African Dance Theatre gives a snapshot into African dance culture with enthralling performances of warrior dances and township inventions like the gumboot dance, pantsula and kwela.

Artscape D.F. Malan St. Foreshore ⓣ 021 410 9838, ⓦ artscape.co.za. Cape Town's most central and largest arts venue, where major productions are staged. Catch contemporary dance, ballet or opera, with some adventurous new dramas appearing periodically. Don't be intimidated by the monumental 1970s apartheid architecture.

Baxter Theatre Centre Main Rd, Rondebosch ⓣ 021 685 7880, ⓦ baxter.co.za. This mammoth brick theatre complex – its design inspired by Soviet Moscow's central train station – is the cultural heart of Cape Town, mounting an eclectic programme of innovative plays, comedy festivals, jazz and classical concerts and kids' theatre. It's the first place to check out what's on when you hit town.

Fugard Theatre Caledon St, District Six ⓣ 021 461 4554, ⓦ thefugard.com. On the east side of central Cape Town in the old District Six, the Fugard Theatre runs a cross-section of interesting productions in a stylishly renovated

CAPE TOWN'S THEATRE SCENE

Athol Fugard is the best known South African playwright internationally. Some of his finest plays include the critically acclaimed *Bosman and Lena* and *Master Harold and the Boys* and he is still producing some fine work today with a steady trickle of innovative plays. More controversial is the brilliant **Brett Bailey**, a white man more "township" than many blacks, who creates electrifying, chaotic visual and physical theatre with his company **Third World Bunfight** (W thirdworldbunfight.co.za). The company puts on theatre productions, installations, house music shows and opera, mostly concerned with the post-colonial landscape of Africa. You're as likely to catch Bailey's works in Europe, however, as you are in Cape Town. The city's most famous son is Cape Town-born RSC actor **Sir Anthony Sher**, who appears here every other year in some fabulous productions.

As for **musicals**, **David Kramer** and the late **Taliep Petersen** produced several hit shows, although Kramer is best known for his show *Kitaar Blues*, sung in Afrikaans with township and Cape rhythms. He doesn't perform often now (W davidkramer.co.za), but the soundtrack to *Kitaar Blues* is on sale at the African Music Store, 134 Long St, or at W khalahari.net or.

church – it has a particularly nice ambience for a pre- or post-show drink.

Maynardville Open Air Theatre Piers/Wolfe St, Wynberg W maynardville.co.za. Every year in Jan and Feb, an imaginative production of a Shakespeare play is staged by the cream of Cape Town's actors and designers under the summer stars in Maynardville Park.

Theatre On The Bay Camps Bay W theatreonthebay .co.za. Known for taking headline shows from overseas and adapting them to the local stage using South African actors, Theatre On The Bay puts on Liberace-esque performances of drama, musicals, comedy, cabaret, music and dance.

COMEDY

★ **Evita se Perron** Darling Station, Arcadia Rd, Darling T 022 492 2831, W evita.co.za. An hour's drive north of Cape Town, on the R27, the town of Darling is well worth visiting for its camply converted train station, which hosts the satirical shows of Pieter Dirk Uys. It makes for a great day out, and is a highlight of a stay in South Africa; check the website for dates.

Jou Ma Se Comedy Club The Pumphouse, V&A Waterfront T 021 418 8880, W joumasecomedy.com. A dedicated comedy venue in Cape Town, run by comedian Kurt Skoonraad, which features up and coming South African comedians as well as established acts such as Rob Van Vuuren. Tickets cost R95, and their

website also carries information about other comedy events and clubs in the city.

On Broadway 44 Long St T 021 424 1194, W onbroadway.co.za. One of the few venues committed to the city's small cabaret scene is this fun bar-restaurant with live performances, comedy and music playing to a big crowd nightly. Ticket prices are lower than at mainstream venues. Daily 6.30pm–late.

CINEMAS

Galileo Open Air Cinema W thegalileo.co.za. Catch an all-time classic film under the stars at three locations across the city – sunset over the Kirstenbosch Gardens or at the Waterfront are both pretty spectacular backdrops. Nov–April; tickets R70–100.

★ **Labia** 69 Orange St T 021 424 5927, W labia.co.za. The retro Labia (Lah-bia) shows an intelligent mix of art films, cult classics and new releases, and is Cape Town's only independent cinema. Tickets R40.

Pink Flamingo Grand Daddy Hotel, 38 Long Street W granddaddy.co.za/pinkflamingo. The urban rooftop setting, complete with vintage airstream trailers, makes this a great option for open-air cinema. Mondays at sunset; tickets R90.

Ster-Kinekor Cinema Nouveau Waterfront T 082 16789, W sterkinekor.com. A reliable art-house cinema that shows films three times a day. Tickets R65–90.

OUTDOOR ACTIVITIES AND SPORTS

One of Cape Town's most remarkable features is the fact that it melds with the Table Mountain National Park, a patchwork of mountains, forests and coastline – all on the city's doorstep. There are few, if any, other cities in the world where outdoor pursuits are so easily available and affordable. You can try activities such as sea kayaking, abseiling, rock climbing and scuba diving for little more than the price of a night out back home. Alternatively, just let everyone else get on with it while you sink a few beers and watch the cricket, rugby or football – to find out what major fixtures are on, and to book for them, check W computicket.com.

1

CAPE TOWN'S FILM FESTIVALS

Although Cape Town is booming as a film-production centre, local feature films are scarce, though some excellent documentaries are produced. There are several film festivals of note: the **South African International Documentary Festival** (Ⓦ encounters.co.za) in June or July features riveting South African documentaries as well as award winning international films; the **TRI Continental Film Festival** (Ⓦ 3continentsfestival.co.za) in August or September has a strong developing world socio-political emphasis; the **AFDA Experimental Film Festival** (Ⓦ afda.co.za/festivals.php) in November shows short films by graduates of South Africa's leading film school; while the **Cape Town & Winelands Film festival** (Ⓦ films-for-africa.co.za) in early November shows screenings of around thirty new South African short films and documentaries.

SPECTATOR SPORTS

Cricket Keenly followed by a wide range of Capetonians. The city's cricketing heart is at Newlands Cricket Ground (also known after its sponsors as Sahara Park), 61 Campground Rd, Newlands (Ⓣ 021 657 2003, Ⓦ cricket .co.za). One of the most beautiful grounds in the world, Newlands nestles beneath venerable oaks and the elegant profile of Devil's Peak, and plays host to provincial, test and one-day international matches.

Football Though football matches aren't as well attended as cricket or rugby fixtures, Cape Town football is burgeoning with talent and has become more prominent since the 2010 World Cup. The dusty streets of the Cape Flats have produced superb young footballers such as Benni McCarthy (Porto, Ajax Amsterdam, Celta Vigo) and Quinton Fortune (Atletico Madrid, Manchester United). The most ambitious and professional club in the city is Ajax (pronounced "I-axe") Cape Town (Ⓦ ajaxct.co.za), jointly owned by its Amsterdam namesake. The most exciting games to attend are those between a local outfit and one of the Soweto glamour teams, Orlando Pirates and Kaizer Chiefs. Matches take place at the Green Point Stadium; Athlone Stadium, off Klipfontein Rd, Athlone; and Newlands Rugby Stadium (see below).

Rugby The Western Cape is one of the world's rugby heartlands, and the game is followed religiously here. Provincial, international and Super 12 contests are fought on the hallowed turf of Newlands Rugby Stadium, Boundary Rd, Newlands (Ⓣ 021 659 4600, Ⓦ wprugby.co.za).

PARTICIPATION SPORTS AND OUTDOOR ACTIVITIES

Abseiling You can abseil off Table Mountain with Abseil Africa (Ⓣ 021 424 4760, Ⓦ abseilafrica.co.za) for around R700. A guided summit walk up Platteklip Gorge costs R250.

Birdwatching The peninsula boasts up to four hundred different species of birds, with open-water boat trips virtually guarantee sightings of four species of albatross. Good places for birdwatching include Lion's Head,

Kirstenbosch Gardens and the Cape of Good Hope Nature Reserve, as well as at Kommetjie and Hout Bay; you can find out about birding trips in Cape Town from Birding Africa (Ⓣ 021 531 9148, Ⓦ www.birdingafrica.com), and about boat tours from Anne Grey (Ⓣ 083 311 1140, Ⓦ annealbatross.org).

Cycling Cycling is popular all over the peninsula, and is a great way to take in the scenery, though be very vigilant about intolerant car drivers. Africa's biggest social bike ride, the Moonlight Mass (Ⓦ moonlightmass .co.za), heads out once a month at 9pm from the Green Point Circle: this casual night ride began on Twitter to promote cycling, and has been gaining popularity ever since. The annual, spectacular Argus Cycle Tour, in March, travels 109km around the peninsula with forty thousand riders: for details contact Pedal Power Associates (Ⓣ 021 689 8420, Ⓦ cycletour.co.za), which also organizes fun rides from Sept to May. Mountain bikes can be rented from Downhill Adventures, Shop 10 Overbeek Building, on the corner of Kloof and Orange streets (Ⓣ 021 422 0388, Ⓦ downhilladventures.co.za), for R200 a day. It also offers organized cycle outings that include trips to Cape Point, the Winelands and a Table Mountain descent.

Golf The Milnerton golf course, Bridge Rd, Milnerton (Ⓣ 021 552 3108 Ⓦ milnertongolf.co.za), is tucked in between a lagoon and Table Bay, and boasts classic views of Table Mountain. Another popular course is at Westlake Golf Club, Westlake Ave, Lakeside (Ⓣ 021 788 2020, Ⓦ westlakegolfclub.co.za), at the end of the M3 at the southern end of the Constantia Valley.

Gyms Virgin Active clubs (Ⓣ 086 020 0911, Ⓦ virginactive .co.za) runs upmarket, well-appointed gyms dotted around the peninsula, all with large swimming pools and spotless changing rooms; phone for visitor rates.

Hiking The safest and most accessible places to walk are Kirstenbosch Gardens and the Sea Point promenade, Muizenberg, Fishhoek or Noordhoek beaches. For hikes up Table Mountain, Silvermine Reserve or Cape Point area, contact experienced mountaineer, rock climber and surfer

Mike Wakeford (☎083 402 0288 ⓦguidedbymike.co.za; half-day hike R950, full day R1600), or Margie Curran, a registered Table Mountain Guide (☎021 715 6136, ⓦtablemountainwalks.co.za), who offers a classic Table Mountain ascent for R800.

Horseriding Horse Trail Safaris, Indicator Lodge, Skaapskraal Rd, Ottery (east of Wynberg across the M5; ☎021 703 4396, ⓦhorsetrailsafaris.co.za), offers riding through the dunes to the coast, though you are only on the actual beach for ten minutes. Sleepy Hollow Horse Riding, Sleepy Hollow Lane, Noordhoek (☎021 789 2341 or ☎083 261 0104, ⓦsleepyhollowhorseriding .co.za), covers the spectacular Noordhoek Beach, as does Imhoff Farm (☎082 774 1191). They all charge abour R450 for two hours.

Kayaking Real Cape Adventures (☎021 790 5611 or ☎082 556 2520, ⓦseakayak.co.za) offers a range of half- or full-day sea-kayaking packages that include trips around Cape Point, to the penguin colony at Boulders Beach and around Hout Bay. Downhill Adventures, on the corner of Kloof and Orange sts in the city centre (☎021 422 0388, ⓦdownhilladventures. co.za), offers trips from Mouille Point or Simon's Town from R500 per half-day.

Kiteboarding Surf Store Muizenberg (☎021 788 5055, ⓦsurfstore.co.za) offers full day lessons (R1290) as well as stand-up paddle boarding, though the prime kiteboarding spot is out of town at Langebaan (see "Windsurfing", below)

Mountain biking Day Trippers (☎021 511 4766, ⓦdaytrippers.co.za) offers mountain-bike tours, including one from Scarborough to Cape Point. Downhill Adventures ("Cycling", opposite) offers similar tours, including Tokai Forest.

Paragliding Cape Town has great air thermals for paragliding: the usual spot is from Lion's Head, drifting down to Camps Bay. Cape Town Tandem Paragliding (☎076 892 2283, ⓦparaglide.co.za) offers tandem jumps from R950. Wallend-Air School (☎021 762 2441, ⓦwallendair.com), run by Peter Wallend (one of SA's paragliding champs), offers courses to get your paragliding licence.

Rock climbing High Adventure (☎021 689 1234 or ☎082 437 5145, ⓦhighadventure.co.za) will take you to some unusual and unique locations depending on your ability; packages are tailor-made, for a minimum of two people. Try also Mike Wakeford (see "Hiking", opposite). For an indoor climbing wall, try City Rock Indoor Climbing Centre, 21 Anson Rd, Observatory (☎021 447 1326, ⓦcityrock.co.za).

Running The best places to jog are up the mountain tracks of Newlands Forest, and along the Sea Point Promenade. The Two Oceans Marathon, every Easter Saturday (ⓦtwooceansmarathon.org.za), is an international event, where athletes run the arduous 56km marathon around the peninsula.

Sandboarding Downhill Adventures (see "Mountain biking", above) is the pioneer of this ski-related adventure sport. Boards, boots and bindings are provided, as well as expert instruction for beginners. Sunscene Outdoor Adventures (☎021 783 0203, ⓦsunscene.co.za) offers sandboarding as well as surfing, and is good at teaching kids. Expect to pay from R650 for a day's sandboarding, or try a sandboarding-plus-surfing combo (R900), or sandboarding and paragliding (R2000).

Scuba diving While the Cape waters are cold, they're also good for seeing wrecks, reefs and magnificent kelp forests. Down South Scuba Muizenberg (☎021 788 7616, ⓦdownsouthscuba.co.za), offers PADI courses and dive trips to see cow sharks for those with a licensce, as well as wrecks and caves.

Skydiving The ultimate way to see Table Mountain and Robben Island is from a tandem jump 3000m up; contact Skydive Cape Town, situated 20min from Cape Town along the R27 West Coast Rd (☎082 800 6290, ⓦskydivecapetown.za.net; R1550).

Surfing Top surfing spots include Big Bay at Bloubergstrand (competitions are held here every summer), Llandudno, Muizenberg and Long Beach near Kommetjie and Noordhoek. Muizenberg is the best place to learn to surf; try Gary's or Surf Shack (see box, p.120). For information on competitions and surfing in South Africa, including what the waves are up to, check ⓦwavescape.co.za.

Swimming Sea swimming is best on the warmer side of the peninsula at Muizenberg, St James and Fish Hoek beaches. For pools, try Long St Baths, Long St (☎021 400 3302; daily 7am–7pm; R20), Cape Town's only public heated indoor pool; or Newlands Swimming Pool, corner of Main and San Souci roads, Newlands (☎021 671 2729; summer daily 10am–6pm; R15), an Olympic-sized chlorinated outdoor pool. The unheated, ocean-side Sea Point Swimming Pool on Beach Rd (☎021 434 3341; summer daily 7am–7pm, winter daily 9am–5pm; R20) is an Olympic-sized chlorinated seawater pool, with lawns to laze on.

Windsurfing and kitesurfing While most Capetonians moan about the howling southeaster in summer, it's heaven if you're into windsurfing; Langebaan, a 75min drive north of town, is one of the best spots, as the enormous lagoon offers better conditions than the choppier ocean around Cape Town, which has a bigger swell. Cape Sport Centre, Langebaan (☎022 772 1114, ⓦcapesport.co.za), offers a variety of watersports and has accommodation along the same street. Prices for windsurfing start at R600 for a lesson and two hours on the water; a two-day kitesurfing package costs from R2400, including gear and instruction.

1

SHOPPING

The **V&A Waterfront** is the city's most popular shopping venue; it has a vast range of shops, the setting on the harbour is lovely and there's a huge choice of places to eat and drink. Nearby, the **Cape Quarter**, accessed off Somerset Road in Green Point, is smaller and more exclusive. While most South African malls tend to follow the American model, offering a safe, sterile indoor environment for browsing, banking and eating, the city centre itself offers variety: **Long Street** is good for crafts, antiques and secondhand books, while **Bree Street and Kloof Steet** are perfect for unique designer goods. For something edgier, the increasingly gentrified fringe suburbs of **Woodstock** and **Salt River** boast clusters of cutting-edge design shops, markets and some of the best restaurants and cafés in the city. Cape Town's Green Map (ⓦ greenmap.org) is a great source of information about ethical shopping, organic markets, delis and health shops.

BOOKS

★ **Book Lounge** 71 Roeland St ⓦ booklounge.co.za; map p.90. The most congenial central bookshop, with comfy sofas and a downstairs café, stocks an excellent selection of local books and an imaginative list of imported titles, as well as running evening events with local intellectuals and writers. Mon–Fri 8.30am–7.30pm, Sat 9.00am–5pm, Sun 10am–4pm.

Clarke's Bookshop 199 Long St ⓦ clarkesbooks.co.za; map p.92. The best place in Cape Town for South African books has well-informed staff who can help you find what you want among the huge selection of local titles covering literature, history, politics, natural history and the arts. It also deals in collectors' editions of South African books. Mon–Fri 9am–5pm, Sat 9.30am–1pm.

Exclusive Books Victoria Wharf, V&A Waterfront ⓦ exclus1ves.co.za; map p.101. Though small by British and American standards, the reasonably well-stocked shelves include magazines and a wide choice of coffee-table books on Cape Town and South African topics. There are other branches at V&A, Cavendish Square and Constantia Village Shopping Centre (check the website for their opening times). Mon–Sat 9am–10.30pm, Sun 9am–9pm.

Kirstenbosch Shop Kirstenbosch National Botanical Gardens (see p.106). A good selection of natural-history books, field guides and travel guides covering southern Africa, as well as a range of titles for kids. You don't need a Gardens ticket to browse. Daily 9am–6pm; open until 7pm in summer.

Wordsworth's Books V&A Waterfront; ⓦ wordsworth .co.za; map p.101. A good general bookshop, with a specialist travel section; it also has stores in Gardens Shopping Centre and Sea Point. Daily 9am–9pm.

CERAMICS

Art In The Forest Off Constantia Nek Circle, Rhodes Drive, Constantia Nek ☎ 021 794 0291, ⓦ artintheforest.com. Perched within a hillside forest with sweeping views, this is a thriving ceramic centre and gallery representing leading South African ceramicists. All profits support their outreach programmes for vulnerable children. Mon–Fri 9am–4.30pm, Sat 10am–3pm.

Clementina Ceramics The Old Biscuit Mill 375 Albert Road, Woodstock ⓦ clementina.co.za. Specializing in colourful ceramics and tableware by Clementina van der Walt, the shop also stocks unusual cards and other designer crafts. Mon–Fri 9am–5pm, Sat 9am–3pm.

CRAFT MARKETS

Greenmarket Square Burg St; map p.92. City-centre open-air market on a cobbled square where you can pick up loads of presents to take home, from all over the continent. It's also the best place in town for colourful handmade Cape Town hippy gear and Tanzanian beach wraps (*kikois*). Mon–Sat 9am–4pm.

The Pan African Market 76 Long St; map p.92. A multicultural hothouse of township and contemporary art, artefacts, curios and crafts. There's also a café specializing in African cuisine, a bookshop, a Cameroonian hairbraider and a West African tailor. Mon–Fri 9am–5pm, Sat 9am–3pm.

Victoria Road Market Camps Bay; map p.116. Carvings, beads, fabrics and baskets sold from a roadside market spectacularly sited on a clifftop overlooking the Atlantic. Daily 9am–5pm.

CRAFT SHOPS

Africa Nova Cape Quarter, Waterkant St, De Waterkant ⓦ africanova.co.za; map p.101. A better-than-average selection of ethnic crafts and curios as well as contemporary African textiles and artwork, with an emphasis on the individual and handmade. Mon–Sat 10am–5pm, Sun (summer only) 10am–2pm.

African Image Corner Church/Burg St, City Centre; map p.92. One of the best places for authentic traditional and contemporary African arts and crafts, from fabrics and antique sculpture to pieces using recycled materials and South African beadwork. Mon–Fri 9am–5pm, Sat 9am–1pm.

Ethno Bongo Main Rd, Hout Bay ⓦ dolceandbanana .com. A charming shop selling wonderful and well-priced crafts, jewellery and accessories. They use natural materials, gemstones, shells and reclaimed wood, and also sell ethnic clothing – highly recommended for unique gifts and souvenirs. Mon–Fri 9.30am–5.30pm, Sat 9.30am–4pm, Sun 10am–2pm.

Monkeybiz 43 Rose St, Bo-Kaap ⓦmonkeybiz.co.za; map p.90. Colourful animals and beaded figures made at a non-profit income-generating project. Good place to buy quality craft work which is uniquely South African and helps a good cause. Mon–Fri 9am–5pm, Sat 9am–1pm.

Rose Korber Art Consultancy 48 Sedgemoor Rd, Camps Bay ☎021 438 9152, ⓦrosekorberart.com; map p.116. This should be the first stop for the serious collector, with an exceptional selection of contemporary arts and crafts, including ceramics and beadwork from around the continent. Mon–Fri 9am–5pm, Sat & Sun by appointment.

Street Wires 77 Upper Shortmarket St, Bo-Kaap ⓦstreetwires.co.za; map p.92. Large range of wire and beadwork, made in the studio of their orange-coloured premises, where you can buy small beaded animals or beautiful tableware and lamps. Mon–Fri 9am–5pm, Sat 9am–1pm.

Wola Nani 9 Drake Street, Observatory ⓦwolanani .co.za. A long-established non-profit organization, Wola Nani supports crafters whose works include recycled papier maché bowls, jewellery, lampshades, designer light bulbs, beadwork and recycled magazine mirrors. Mon–Fri 8.30am–4.30pm.

Woodstock Exchange 66 Albert Rd, Woodstock ☎021 486 5999, ⓦwoodstockexchange.co.za. An interesting centre for creative collectives, beautiful leather workshops and work-friendly cafés filled with Capetonian freelancers. Mon–Fri 8am–5pm, Sat 8am–2pm.

FOOD AND DRINK

The most convenient supermarkets in central Cape Town are the Pick 'n Pay (daily 8am–10pm) and Woolworths (daily 9am–9pm), both in the V&A Waterfront, and with far longer trading hours than anywhere else in the city.

DELIS

Andiamo Cape Quarter Dixon St, De Waterkant ☎021 421 3687 ⓦandiamo.co.za; map p.101. Italian deli where you can select from meats, cheeses, salads, dips, meze and fresh breads to take on your mountain walk. Phone ahead and they'll put the picnic together for you. Mon–Fri 7am–11pm, Sat & Sun 9am–11pm.

Giovanni's Deliworld 103 Main Rd, Green Point; map pp.112–113. Excellent breads and Italian foods to take away, plus the option of sitting down for a pavement coffee with a view of Green Point Stadium. Daily 8.30am–9pm.

Melissa's Waterfront ⓦmelissas.co.za; map p.101. Highly delectable imported and local specialities at a popular gourmet deli with the option of eating in. It's not cheap, but always worth it. Branches also on Kloof St, Gardens and in Constantia Village. Daily 7.30am–10pm, Sat & Sun 9am–10pm.

Organic Zone Lakeside Shopping Centre, Main Rd, Lakeside ⓦorganiczone.co.za; map pp.118–119. Always fresh and well-stocked organic fruit and veg, as well as grains, honey, breads and dairy products. Reasonably priced for quality. Mon–Fri 8.15am–6pm, Sat & Sun 8.15am–5pm.

FRESH FISH

Fish Market Mariner's Wharf, Hout Bay Harbour. Fresh seafood from South Africa's original waterfront emporium, but slicker and less atmospheric than Kalk Bay Harbour. Mon–Fri 9am–5.30pm, Sat & Sun 9am–6pm.

Kalk Bay Harbour Harbourside, Kalk Bay; map pp.118–119. Buy fresh fish directly from the fishermen and have it gutted and scaled on the spot. Your best bet is lunchtime, especially at weekends, though catches are dependent on several factors including the weather and rough seas, so you may not get any.

LOCAL FOOD MARKETS

Blue Bird Garage Market 39 Albertyn Road, Muizenberg ☎082 331 2471; map pp.118–119. A lively Friday night institution in the south, with stalls selling reasonably priced food, wine and craft beer, often accompanied by live music, all in a former aeroplane hangar next to the railway line. Fri 4–10pm.

Hope Street (City Bowl) Market 14 Hope St ⓦcitybowlmarket.co.za; map p.90. This weekly market is becoming a regular social affair for young locals. Entering the market hall is a sensory experience, its jam-packed stalls laden with everything from handmade jewellery, vintage clothing to curries, burgers and a live band on stage. Take your pick from the mouth-watering options then grab a spot at one of the communal tables. Thurs 4.30–8.30pm, Sat 9am–2pm.

Hout Bay Market Bay Harbour 31 Harbour Rd, Hout Bay ☎082 570 5997, ⓦbayharbour.co.za. Situated in an old fish factory, this cavern-like hall might have had humble beginnings but today it's a different picture. Stalls sell African crafts and local designer clothes alongside a host of artisan food traders – some even offering oysters and champagne – and live acoustic acts. Fri 5–9pm, Sat & Sun 9.30am–4pm.

Neighbourgoods Market Old Biscuit Mill, 373–375 Albert Rd (off Lower Main Rd); map p.90. This Victorian warehouse is one of the best places to head for a foodie experience, while marvelling at the array of artisanal cheese, wood-fired bread, coffee, beer, fresh flowers, fruit and veg on offer. It's not cheap, but it sells the best produce of its kind in the Cape, as well as exceptional local designer crafts, home wares and clothing. Sat 9am–2pm.

Oranjezicht City Farm Market Upper Orange St ⓦozcf.co.za. City Bowl locals get fabulously fresh

1

organic produce, bread and coffee here on a Saturday morning while browsing a small selection of local crafts. This thriving, non-profit urban farm was started on disused ground that was once part of an eighteenth century estate. Sat 9am–2pm, though produce sells out fast.

WINE

Caroline's Fine Wines 62 Strand St; King's Warehouse, V&A Waterfront ⓦ carolineswine.com; map p.92. Caroline Rillema has been in the wine business since 1979 and stocks the Cape's finest and most exclusive wines. Mon–Fri 9am–5.30pm, Waterfront also Sat 9am–1pm.

Vaughan Johnson's Dock Rd, V&A Waterfront ⓦ vaughanjohnson.co.za; map p.101. One of Cape Town's best-known wine shops, selling a huge range of labels from all over the country, though it can be a bit pricey. Mon–Fri 9am–6pm, Sat 9am–5pm, Sun 10am–5pm.

Wine Concepts Gardens Lifestyle Centre, Kloof St ⓦ wineconcepts.co.za; map p.133. An excellent selection of South African and foreign wines from a knowledgeable and helpful outfit. Mon–Fri 10am–6pm, Sat 9am–6pm.

MALLS AND SHOPPING CENTRES

Blue Route Mall Tokai Rd, Tokai. Major retailers and supermarkets are represented at this handy mall for those staying in Constantia or along the False Bay. Mon–Sat 9am–7pm, Sun 9am–5pm.

Cavendish Square Mall Claremont station, Vineyard Rd, Claremont. An upmarket multistorey complex, which the major shopping focus for the southern suburbs. Mon–Sat 9am–7pm, Sun 10am–5pm.

Constantia Village Shopping Centre Main Rd, Constantia. A small exclusive mall including two large supermarkets, a post office and general, practical shopping facilities. Mon–Fri 9am–5pm, Sat 9am–5pm, Sun 9am–2pm.

Gardens Shopping Centre Mill St, Gardens; map p.133. Very close to the Company's Gardens and city centre, this is a good sized mall with every shop you might need including two large supermarkets, a bookstore, pharmacy, optometrist and, surprisingly, local south African craft and fashion stores. Mon–Fri 9am–7pm, Sat 9am–5pm, Sun 9am–2pm.

V&A Waterfront map p.101. It would be possible to visit Cape Town and never leave the Waterfront complex, which has a vast range of upmarket shops packed into the Victoria Wharf Shopping Centre, including outlets of all the major South African chains, selling books, clothes, food and crafts, as well as two cinemas, one showing art-house films. Daily 9am–9pm.

MUSIC

African Music Store 134 Long St ⓦ africanmusicstore .co.za; map p.92. Small, upbeat and centrally located shop specializing in African music from around the continent. It also has a modest collection of instruments, such as shakers and thumb pianos. Mon–Fri 9am–6pm, Sat 9am–2pm.

Mabu Vinyl 2 Rheede St, Gardens ⓦ mabuvinyl.co.za; map p.133. The aficionado's choice for a great selection of secondhand CDs, vinyl and, even cassettes, of many genres. Since *Searching for Sugarman* won an Oscar, it has made a splash with tourists who pop by to see a part of Rodriguez history. Mon–Fri 9am–7pm, Sat 9am–6pm, Sun 11am–3pm.

Musica Megastore V&A Waterfront ⓦ musica.co.za; map p.101. A megastore by international standards, with one of the best ranges of African music in the city, plus classical and jazz, pop and rock, and DVDs and video games. Daily 9am–9pm.

DIRECTORY

Banks and exchange Main bank branches with ATMs are easy to find in the shopping areas of the city. For currency exchange try one of the following: American Express, Shop 11a, Alfred Mall, Waterfront (Mon–Fri 9am–7pm, Sat 9am–5pm, Sun 9am–5pm); Rennies Foreign Exchange, Victoria Wharf, V&A Waterfront (Mon–Sat 9am–9pm, Sun 10am–9pm); or Master Currencies, Cape Town International Airport (Mon–Sun 6.30am–10pm).

Consulates Canada 19th Floor, South African Reserve Bank building, 60 St George's Mall (ⓣ 021 423 5240); Netherlands 100 Strand St (ⓣ 021 421 5660); UK 15th Floor, Southern Life Centre, 8 Riebeek St (ⓣ 021 405 2400).

Hospitals The two largest private hospital groups, Netcare (emergency response ⓣ 082 911, ⓦ netcare.co.za) and

Medi-Clinic (emergency response operated by ER24 ⓣ 084 124, ⓦ mediclinic.co.za), have hospitals all over the Cape Peninsula. Cape Town Medi-Clinic, 21 Hof St, Oranjezicht (ⓣ 021 464 5500; emergency ⓣ 021 464 5555), is close to the city centre in the middle of the City Bowl; Christiaan Barnard Memorial Hospital, 181 Longmarket St (ⓣ 021 480 6111), is Netcare's most central private hospital; and Constantiaberg Medi-Clinic Burnham Road, Plumstead in the southern suburbs (ⓣ 021 799 2911; emergency ⓣ 021 799 2196), is the closest private hospital to the False Bay seaboard. The state ambulance emergency number is ⓣ 10177. For more routine medical care, there are over two dozen private Medicross medical centres (ⓦ www.medicross .co.za) across the Western Cape, which are not open 24 hours, but operate extended hours.

Laundry Most backpacker hostels have laundry facilities, while guesthouses, hotels and B&Bs usually offer a laundry service for a charge.

Mobile phone rental Available at the airport from Vodashop Rentafone (ⓦ rentafone.net) or Cellucity (ⓦ cellucity.co.za), where you can also buy a local SIM card, or from the Cellucity, Shop 6193, V&A Waterfront (ⓣ 021 418 1300).

Pharmacies Chemists with extended opening hours include Hypermed Pharmacy, corner York and Main roads, Green Point (Mon–Fri 8.30am–7pm, Sat & Sun 9am–7pm; ⓣ 021 434 1414) and Sunset Pharmacy, Sea Point Medical Centre, Kloof Rd, Sea Point (daily 8.30am–9pm; ⓣ 021 434 3333). Homeopathic remedies are available from White's Chemist, 61 Plein St (Mon–Fri 8am–5pm, Sat 8am–12.30pm; ⓣ 021 465 3332).

Police The central police station is on Caledon Square, Buitenkant St. For emergencies, call ⓣ 10 111.

Post office The main post office is on Parliament St (Mon, Tues, Thurs & Fri 8am–4.30pm, Wed 8.30am–4.30pm, Sat 8am–noon).

The Western Cape

OSTRICH FARM, OUDTSHOORN

The Western Cape

The most mountainous and arguably the most beautiful of South Africa's provinces, the Western Cape is also the most popular area of the country for foreign tourists. Curiously, it's the least African province. Visitors spend weeks here without exhausting its attractions, but frequently leave slightly disappointed, never having quite experienced an African beat. Of South Africa's nine provinces, only the Western Cape and the Northern Cape don't have an African majority; one person in five here is African, and the largest community, making up 55 percent of the population, are coloureds – people of mixed race descended from white settlers, indigenous Khoisan people and slaves from the East.

Although the Western Cape appears to conform more closely to the developed world than any other part of the country, the impression is strictly superficial. Behind the prosperous feel of the Winelands and the Garden Route lies the reality of people living in poverty in shacks on the outskirts of well-to-do towns, and on farms where nineteenth-century labour practices prevail, despite the end of apartheid. Nevertheless, you can't fail to be moved by the sensuous beauty of the province's mountains, valleys and beaches. **The Winelands**, less than an hour from Cape Town, are all about eating, drinking and visual feasting on gabled homesteads among vineyards backed by slatey crags.

The best-known feature of the Western Cape is the **Garden Route**, a drive along the N2 that extends between Cape Town and Port Elizabeth (see p.300). **Public transport** along the Garden Route is better than anywhere in the country, partly

DE HOOP NATURE RESERVE

Highlights

❶ Wine estate lunches Eat alfresco and quaff fine vintages at the top restaurants in South Africa, while gazing out at beautiful vineyards and mountains. **See p.164**

❷ Route 62 This mountainous inland route takes you via dozy villages, across spectacular passes and through semi-desert. **See p.174**

❸ De Hoop Nature Reserve Massive dunes and edge-to-edge whales make this the most exciting coastal nature reserve in the country. **See p.207**

❹ Ocean safaris Learn about whales and dolphins on an excursion around Plettenberg Bay. **See p.231**

❺ Storms River Mouth A dramatic section of coast, where hillside forests drop away to rocky coastline and the Storms River surges out of a gorge into the thundering ocean. **See p.234**

❻ Seafood Feast on endless courses of fish and lobster at one of the casual beachside eating places along the West Coast. **See p.237**

❼ Oudrif An exceptional and remote retreat lodge on the edge of a gorge in the dry and dramatic redstone back country of the Cederberg. **See p.252**

HIGHLIGHTS ARE MARKED ON THE MAP ON PP.162–163

because the route is a single stretch of freeway, and tour operators have turned it into the country's most concentrated strip for packaged **adventure sports** and **outdoor activities**.

To the east of the Winelands, the **Breede River Valley** is a region usually bypassed along the N1 en route to Johannesburg, but featuring among its functional fruit-farming towns are some hideaways favoured by Capetonians as weekend retreats. Though the region was neglected by visitors in the past, some creative marketing has

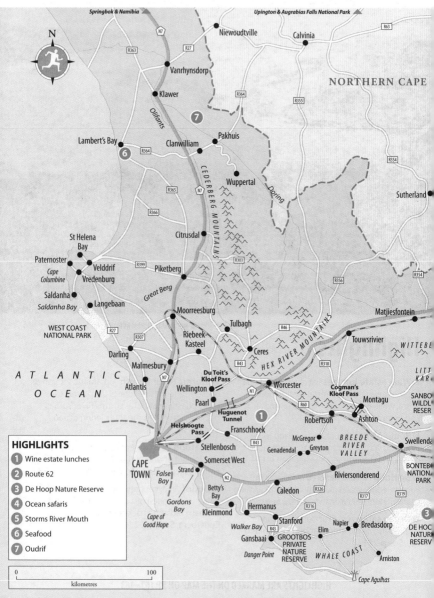

HIGHLIGHTS

1. Wine estate lunches
2. Route 62
3. De Hoop Nature Reserve
4. Ocean safaris
5. Storms River Mouth
6. Seafood
7. Oudrif

0   100

kilometres

now literally put it on the map as **Route 62**, most of which consists of the intriguing eponymous back road tracing its way through the interior, linking **Little Karoo** towns between Cape Town and Port Elizabeth.

The **Overberg** – roughly the area between Arniston and Mossel Bay along the coast, and inland to Swellendam – is another region that remains hidden behind the mountains. West of here, the **Whale Coast** is the best area in the country for shore-based whale-watching, and a couple of pleasant coastal towns lie off the main routes.

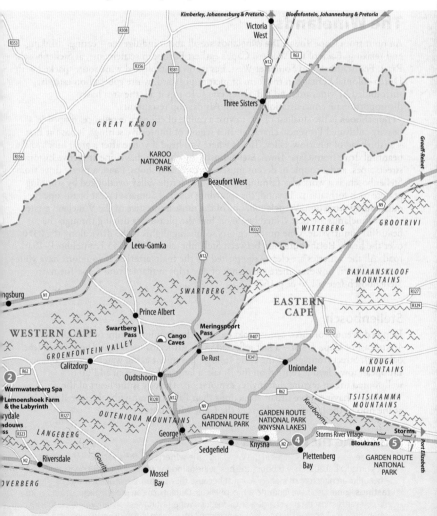

WESTERN CAPE

North of Cape Town, the less popular, remote and windswept **West Coast** is usually explored during the wild-flower months of August and September, when visitors converge on its centrepiece, the West Coast National Park. Its other major draw, 200km north of Cape Town on the N7, is the Cederberg, a rocky wilderness with hikes and hidden rock-art sites – the work of indigenous **San people**, who were virtually extinguished in the nineteenth century.

The Winelands

An hour from Cape Town, **The Winelands** are all about indulgence – eating, drinking and relaxing. Each of the Western Cape's earliest European settlements, at Stellenbosch, Paarl, Franschhoek and Somerset West, has its own established wine route, packed with Dutch colonial heritage in the form of picture-postcard, white gabled homesteads, surrounded by vineyards and tall, slatey crags. To top it all, the area has a disproportionate concentration of South Africa's top restaurants.

Franschhoek is the smallest of the towns: a centre of culinary excellence, draped in a heavily cultivated Provençal character. In a region of impressive settings, it has the best – at the head of a narrow valley. This is where you head if you're after a great lunch and a beautiful drive from Cape Town. **Stellenbosch**, by contrast, has some attractive historical streetscapes, and a couple of decent museums, cafés and shops. **Paarl**, a pretty drive from Stellenbosch, is a workaday farming town set in a fertile valley overlooked by stunning granite rock formations. Beyond, the sprawling town of **Somerset West** boasts one outstanding attraction, **Vergelegen**, one of the most impressive of the Wineland estates.

The Winelands are best visited by car, as half the pleasure is driving through the beautiful countryside. One of the region's scenic highlights is the drive along the **R310** over the heady **Helshoogte Pass** between Stellenbosch and the R45 Franschhoek–Paarl road. All the wineries are clearly signposted off the main arteries. If you don't have your own transport, however, there are plenty of day-trips available from Cape Town or Stellenbosch (see p.130 & p.167)

Stellenbosch

Dappled avenues of three-century-old oaks are the defining feature of **STELLENBOSCH**, 46km east of Cape Town – a fact reflected in its Afrikaans nickname *Die Eikestad* (the oak city). Street frontages of the same vintage, pavement cafés, water furrows and a European town layout centred on the Braak, a large village green, add up to a well-rooted urban texture that invites exploration. The city is the heart of the Winelands, having more urban attractions than Paarl or Franschhoek, as well as being at the hub of the largest and oldest of the Cape **wine routes**.

TACKLING THE WINELANDS

Of the several hundred estates in the Winelands, the **wineries** in our selection were picked not primarily because they produce the best wine (although some do), but for general interest – beautiful architecture or scenery – or just because they are fun. While all the wineries offer **tastings**, some also have fantastic, atmospheric restaurants, or can provide picnics to enjoy in the vineyards; most estates charge a small fee for a wine-tasting session (anywhere up to R40). When visiting, choose an area to explore and don't try to cram in too many wineries in a day unless you want to return home in a dizzy haze; note, too, that several wineries are closed on Sundays, or have shorter opening hours in winter.

The definitive and widely available John Platter's **South African Wine Guide** (also available as an iPhone app) is a useful companion, which provides ratings of the produce of pretty well every winery in the country.

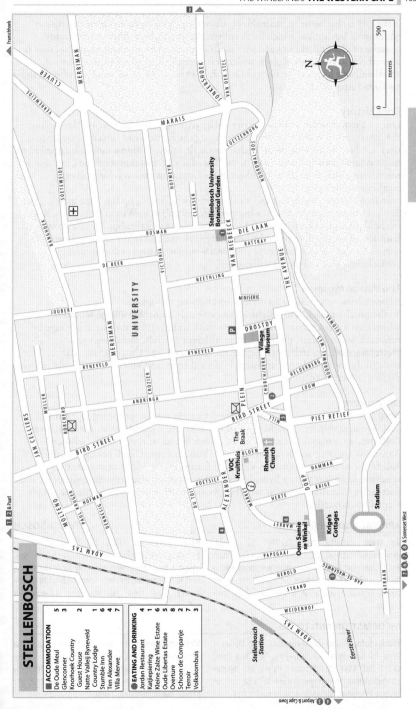

STELLENBOSCH

■ ACCOMMODATION
De Oude Meul	5
Glenconner	3
Knorhoek Country Guest House	2
Natte Valleij Ryneveld Country Lodge	1
Stumble Inn	6
Ten Alexander	4
Villa Merwe	7

● EATING AND DRINKING
Jordan Restaurant	4
Katjiepiering	1
Kleine Zalze Wine Estate	6
Oude Libertas Estate	5
Overture	8
Schoon de Companje	2
Terroir	7
Volkskombuis	3

The city is also home to Stellenbosch University, Afrikanerdom's most prestigious educational institution, which helps enliven the atmosphere. But even the heady promise of plentiful alcohol and thousands of students hasn't changed the fact that at heart this is a conservative place, which was once the intellectual engine room of apartheid, and fostered the likes of Dr H.F. Verwoerd, the prime minister who dreamed up Grand Apartheid.

Brief history

One of **Simon van der Stel**'s first actions after arriving at the Cape in 1679 to assume the governorship was to explore the area along the Eerste River (literally "the first river"), where he came upon an enchanting little valley. Within a month it appeared on maps as Stellenbosch ("Stel's bush"), the first of several places around the Cape that he was to name after himself or members of his family; another was Simonsberg overlooking the town.

Charged by the Dutch East India Company with opening up the Cape interior, Van der Stel soon settled the first **free burghers** in Stellenbosch. Within eight years, sixty freehold grants had been made and within two decades Stellenbosch was a prosperous, semi-feudal society dominated by landowners. By the end of the century there were over a thousand houses and some substantial burgher estates in and around Stellenbosch, many of which still exist.

The Village Museum

18 Ryneveld St • Mon–Sat 9am–5pm, Sun Sept–Feb 10am–4pm & March–Aug 10am–1pm • R25

Stellenbosch's museum highlight is the extremely enjoyable **Village Museum**, which cuts a cross section through the town's architectural and social heritage by means of four adjacent dwellings from different periods, including the **Blettermanhuis**, an archetypal eighteenth-century Cape Dutch house. They're beautifully conserved and furnished in period style, and you'll meet the odd worker dressed in period costume.

Dorp Street

Dorp Street, Stellenbosch's best-preserved historic axis, is well worth a stroll just to soak in the ambience of buildings, gables, oaks and roadside water furrows. **Krige's Cottages**, an unusual terrace of historic town houses at nos. 37–51, between Aan-de-Wagenweg and Krige Street, were built as Cape Dutch cottages in the first half of the nineteenth century; Victorian features were added subsequently, resulting in an interesting hybrid, with gables housing Victorian attic windows and decorative Victorian verandas with filigree ironwork fronting the elegantly simple Cape Dutch facades.

ARRIVAL AND DEPARTURE   STELLENBOSCH

By train Metrorail trains (☎0800 65 64 63, ⓦwww.capemetrorail.co.za) travel between Cape Town and Stellenbosch roughly every ninety minutes during the day, and take about an hour, but use this line, which travels through rough areas of the Cape Flats, with caution.

By bus The Baz Bus (☎0861 229 287, ⓦbazbus.co.za) runs daily from Cape Town to Somerset West, 50km east, where it drops passengers off at the BP filling station next to the *Lord Charles Hotel*. Some hostels run shuttle services from there, but you must arrange this beforehand.

INFORMATION AND TOURS

Tourist information The tourist office, at 36 Market St (Mon–Fri 8am–5pm, Sat 9am–2pm, Sun 9am–2pm; ☎021 883 3584, ⓦstellenbosch.travel), can reserve accommodation, though you'll need to book well in advance in summer, when rooms can be hard to find.

Walking tours Leaving from the tourist office in the morning and afternoon, a walking tour is a great way to see the architectural highlights and get a feel of the town (by appointment with Sandra ☎021 887 9150; R100 per person; minimum of six in a group).

WINE TOURS

If you want to visit the vineyards, ask at the tourist office, which represents a number of wine tour operators and can steer you towards the right one, depending on your time and budget. Expect to pay a minimum of R350 for a half-day tour and R550 for a full-day tour, including tasting fees. Recommended companies include:

Bikes n Wines ☎ 074 186 0418, ⓦ bikesnwines.com. If you are feeling energetic, you can tour the vineyards by bicycle with Bikes n Wines which do a half-day tour (R550) and an overnight mountain bike trail option (R1950).

Easy Rider Wine Tours ☎ 021 886 4651, ⓦ winetour .co.za. Based at *Stumble Inn* backpacker lodge (see below), Easy Rider Wine Tours offers packages to four wineries (R500), with lunch at Franschoek thrown in.

Equine Sport Centre ☎ 071 597 2546, ⓦ equinesportcentre.co.za. Explore the vineyards on horseback, with rides at Morgenhof, Knorhoek and Remhoogte Wine Estates. Suitable for beginners or experienced riders, with capable lead riders and well-schooled horses. Shorter rides cover one wine estate (R220), half-day rides cover two (R600) and full-day outings (R900) visit all three estates – with stops for tastings and great views of the sea and Table Mountain on some rides.

The Vine Hopper ☎ 084 492 4992, ⓦ vinehopper .co.za. A convenient hop-on-hop-off bus, which stops at a dozen wineries, including the Van Ryn's Brandy Cellar. Call in advance for their days and routes, which vary depending on the season and demand (day-ticket R240).

ACCOMMODATION

Banghoek Place 193 Banghoek Rd ☎ 021 887 0048, ⓦ banghoek.co.za. Slightly more upmarket sister hostel to the *Stumble Inn* (see below), with mostly en-suite double, twin and triple rooms that offer terrific value, plus three small dorms. Discount packages available that include two nights' accommodation plus a wine tour. Dorm R150, double R500

De Oude Meul 10a Mill St (off Dorp St) ☎ 021 887 7085, ⓦ deoudemeul.com. Located in the middle of town on a fairly busy street, above an antique shop, these pleasant rooms are good value. Ask for one at the back to ensure a quiet night's sleep. R1000

Glenconner Jonkershoek Rd, 4km from the centre ☎ 021 886 5120 or ☎ 082 354 3510, ⓔ glenconner@ icon.co.za. Both self-catering and B&B options are available at these pretty farm cottages with horses grazing in the fields below. The tranquil valley setting is spectacular, close to the walks in the Jonkershoek Nature Reserve. Breakfast can be taken under an old oak tree. R750

Knorhoek Country Guest House Knorhoek Wine Estate, off the R44, 7km north of town ☎ 021 865 2114, ⓦ knorhoek.co.za. With a bucolic setting in a snug valley, these old farm buildings have been turned into modern guest rooms and cottages. Each has a sunny patio, lawn and a feeling of calm luxury, plus guests can wander the gardens and vineyard. Double R900, cottage R1250

Natte Valleij On the R44, 12km north of town ☎ 021 875 5171, ⓦ nattevalleij.co.za. Guests have a choice of a large cottage sleeping six, a smaller one-bedroom unit attached to an old wine cellar or an en-suite room with its own entrance. There's a swimming pool, and breakfast (included) is served on the veranda. R720

Ryneveld Country Lodge 67 Ryneveld St ☎ 021 887 4469, ⓦ ryneveldlodge.co.za. Gracious late-nineteenth-century building, now a National Monument and furnished with Victorian antiques. The rooms are spotless, with the two best ones upstairs leading onto a wooden deck. There are also two family cottages, which sleep up to four, and a pool. R1400

Stumble Inn 12 Market St ☎ 021 887 4049, ⓦ stumbleinnstellenbosch.hostel.com. The town's best and longest-standing hostel, spread across two houses that date from the turn of the last century and are run by friendly, switched-on staff. Just down the road from the tourist office, the hostel is also noted for its good-value tours. Dorm R130, double R370

Ten Alexander 10 Alexander St ☎ 021 887 4414, ⓦ 10alexander.co.za. This guesthouse is functional, quiet and pleasant, and very well run by its chatty owner. The rooms are small and spotless, plus there's a nice garden and pool. It also has self-catering facilities. R1120

Villa Merwe 6 Cynaroides Rd, Paradyskloof ☎ 021 880 1185, ⓦ villamerwe.co.za. Two immaculate and comfortable rooms in the owner's modern house, each with its own entrance and bathroom. There's a lounge, pool and garden, and it's just a 5min drive from the centre. R900

EATING

Lunch or dinner at a vineyard is one of best eating experiences in South Africa, and almost every wine estate has a restaurant or does prebooked picnics. Several of the **vineyard restaurants** are among the top ten in the country, so you'll need to reserve a table weeks or months in advance, particularly in the summer. Stellenbosch town has some appealing **pavement cafés**, especially down Church Street, while in the evenings the student presence ensures a relaxed (and occasionally) raucous drinking culture. On Saturday mornings (9am–2pm), it's worth visiting the fabulous and very popular **farmers' market** (ⓦslowmarket.co.za) in the Oude Libertas Estate grounds, off the R310 just south of the centre, where you'll find a range of locally produced and organic food to eat and take away, including breads, cheeses, meats, vegetables, fruit, beers and estate wines.

Jordan Restaurant Jordan Wine Estate, 11.5km west of Stellenbosch, off the R310 ☎021 881 3612, ⓦjordanwines.com. One of the country's top chefs rules the roost here and never fails to please. Expect exquisite food, service and wines, which can be enjoyed on a deck overlooking a lake and distant mountains. The reasonably priced set menu is based on seasonal ingredients (R275 for two courses, R320 for three) and you can even visit the cheese tasting room in-between courses. Next to the restaurant is the *Bakery at Jordan* (ⓦthebakery.co.za), which does interesting breakfasts, lighter meals and cheese and charcuterie platters (R120). Restaurant summer Sun–Wed noon–3pm, Thurs–Sat noon–3pm & 6.30pm onwards; winter Wed, Sat & Sun noon–3pm, Thurs & Fri noon–3pm & 6.30pm onwards; Bakery daily 8.30am–3.30pm.

Katjiepiering Botanical Gardens, corner of Neetling & Van Riebeeck ☎021 808 3054. Set under shady trees in a tranquil garden, this café offers a wonderful respite on a hot day. Reasonably priced dishes include an excellent mince-based *bobotie* (R60), and the salads are generous. Daily 8am–5pm.

Overture Hidden Valley Wine Estate, Annandale Rd ☎021 880 2646, ⓦdineatoverture.co.za. Top of the town in more ways than one, *Overture* looks down from the hills into the Annandale Valley – and it consistently wins awards as one of the country's top restaurants. Based on classical French cuisine, the dishes are made from scratch with fresh ingredients and interesting contemporary twists. Select three courses (R370) or sample the works with the six-course tasting menu (R600). Book way in advance. Wed & Sun noon–3pm, Thurs–Sat noon–3pm & 7–10.30pm.

★**Schoon de Companje** Corner of Bird & Church streets ☎021 883 2187, ⓦdecompanje.co.za. A café combined with a deli, with various nooks to settle down in and good coffee and croissants. The pavement seating is one of the big draws in summer, as are the artisan ice creams and locally brewed Stellenbrau craft beer. Tues–Sat 7.30am–7pm, Sun 8am–3pm.

Terroir Kleine Zalze Wine Estate, Strand Rd (R44) ☎021 880 8167, ⓦwww.kleinezalze.com. Some 8km from Stellenbosch on a wine and golf estate, *Terroir* has a

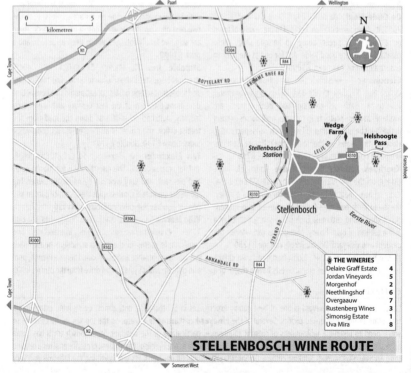

🍷 THE WINERIES	
Delaire Graff Estate	**4**
Jordan Vineyards	**5**
Morgenhof	**2**
Neethlingshof	**6**
Overgaauw	**7**
Rustenberg Wines	**3**
Simonsig Estate	**1**
Uva Mira	**8**

STELLENBOSCH WINE ROUTE

WINERIES AROUND STELLENBOSCH

Stellenbosch was the first locality in the country to launch a **wine route**, in 1971, and although the region is home to only a fraction of South Africa's vineyards, its wine route is the most extensive in the country, with almost three hundred establishments.

Delaire Graff Estate On the Helshoogte Pass, 6km east of Stellenbosch along the R310 to Franschhoek ☎ 021 885 8160, ⊚ delaire.co.za. The highly regarded *Delaire Graff* restaurant has possibly the best views in the Winelands, looking through pin oaks across the Groot Drakenstein and Simonsig mountains and down into the valley. The wines are outstanding; the majority are being white, but they also produce a great red blend. A tasting of three wines costs R50, or you can go for a food and wine pairing class with a tutor (book in advance; R150). Mon–Sat 10am–5pm, Sun 10am–4pm; restaurant Wed–Sat & Mon noon–2.15pm & 6.30–9pm, Tue & Sun noon–2.15pm.

Jordan Vineyards 11.5km west of Stellenbosch off the R310 ☎ 021 881 3612, ⊚ jordanwines.com. A pioneer among the new-wave Cape wineries, Jordan's hi-tech cellar and modern tasting room is complemented by its friendly service. The drive there is half the fun, taking you into a *kloof* bounded by vineyards that get a whiff of the sea from both False Bay and Table Bay, which has clearly done something for its output – it has a list of outstanding wines as long as your arm and a highly rated restaurant (see opposite). Tasting R35 for six wines, refundable with purchases. Daily 9.30am–4.30pm.

Morgenhof 4km north of Stellenbosch on the R44 ☎ 021 889 551, ⊚ morgenhof.com. French-owned chateau-style complex on the slopes of the vine-covered Simonsberg, owned by Anne Cointreau-Huchon (granddaughter of the founder of Remy Martin cognac). Morgenhof has a light and airy tasting room with a bar, and delicious light lunches are served outside, topped off with ice cream on the lawns. They produce the excellent Morgenhof Estate red blend and a couple of brilliant whites (including a Chenin Blanc, Chardonnay and Sauvignon Blanc) under the same label, while the Fantail range is their second, more affordable label. Tasting R25 for five wines. Daily 9am–5.30pm; restaurant daily 9am–4pm.

Neethlingshof 6.5km west of Stellenbosch on Polkadraai Rd (the R306) ☎ 021 883 8988, ⊚ neethlingshof.co.za. Centred around a beautifully restored Cape Dutch manor dating from 1814, and reached down a kilometre-long avenue of stone pines, Neethlingshof's first vines were planted in 1692. There's a restaurant, and for R70 you can try their "flash food" light lunch – pairings of five wines with bite-sized delicacies (booking essential). The estate has two labels: Premium and Short Story reserve range, which consists of a Pinotage, a red blend and a flagship Noble Late Harvest white. Tasting R30 for six wines. Mon–Fri 9am–5pm, Sat & Sun 9am–3.30pm; restaurant Mon–Sat 9am–8.30pm, Sun 9am–3.30pm.

Overgaauw 6.5km west of Stellenbosch, off the M12 ☎ 021 881 3815, ⊚ overgaauw.co.za. Notable for its elegant Victorian tasting room, this pioneering estate was the first winery in the country to produce Merlots, and it's still the only one to make a wine with Sylvaner grapes, a well-priced, easy-drinking dry white. Tasting R20 for six wines, refundable upon purchase. Mon–Fri 9am–noon & 1–4pm, Sat 10am–2pm.

Rustenberg Wines off Lelie Rd, Ida's Valley ☎ 021 809 1200, ⊚ rustenberg.co.za. One of the closest estates to Stellenbosch, Rustenberg is also one of the most alluring, reached after a drive through orchards, sheep pastures and tree-lined avenues. An unassuming working farm, whose first vines were planted in 1692, it has a romantic pastoral atmosphere, in contrast to its architecturally stunning tasting room in the former stables. Their high-flyers include the Peter Barlow Cabernet Sauvignon, John X Merriman red blend and Five Soldiers Chardonnay. Tasting R25 for six wines, refundable upon wine purchase. Mon–Fri 9am–4.30pm, Sat 10am–3.30pm.

Simonsig Estate 9.5km north of Stellenbosch, off Kromme Rhee Rd, which runs between the R44 and the R304 ☎ 021 888 4900, ⊚ simonsig.co.za. This winery has a relaxed outdoor tasting area beneath vine-covered pergolas, offering majestic views back to Stellenbosch of hazy stone-blue mountains and vineyards. The first estate in the country to produce a bottle-fermented bubbly some three decades back, it also produces a vast range of first-class still wines. Tasting R30 for five wines and a bubbly. Mon–Fri 8.30am–5pm, Sat 8.30am–4pm, Sun 10am–3pm.

★ **Uva Mira** About 8km south of Stellenbosch, off Annandale Rd, which spurs off the R44 ☎ 021 880 1683, ⊚ uvamira.co.za. Enchanting boutique winery that's worth visiting just for the winding drive halfway up the Helderberg. The highly original tasting room, despite being fairly recently built, gives the appearance of a gently decaying historic structure, and there are unsurpassed views from the deck across mountainside vineyards to False Bay some 50km away – on a clear day you can even see Robben Island. Check out their international award-winning 2005 Chardonnay and their flagship Bordeaux-style red blend. Tasting R30 for three wines. Daily 10am–4.30pm, Sat & Sun 10am–4pm.

2

surprisingly relaxed dining room (for a nationally fêted restaurant) and tables outside under shady oaks. The expensive French-inspired menu is based as far as possible on local seasonal produce, with signature dishes that include a prawn risotto starter (R115) and kingklip with squid and mussels (R195). Mon–Sat noon–2.30pm & 6.30–9.30pm, Sun noon–2.30pm.

Volkskombuis Aan-de-Wagenweg Off Dorp St ☎ 021 887 2121, ⓦ volkskombuis.co.za. Popular spot on the banks of the Eerste River, in a beautiful seventeenth-century Cape Dutch house. If you want to sample traditional Cape cuisine then this is the place to head, with dishes including including *bobotie* and braised oxtail (R140). Daily noon–3pm & 6pm onwards.

Somerset West and around

The only compelling reasons to trawl out to the unpromising town of **SOMERSET WEST**, 50km east of Cape Town along the N2, are for **Vergelegen** on Lourensford Road, and its immediate neighbour **Morgenster**, which are officially part of the Helderberg wine route, but can easily be visited from Stellenbosch, just 14km to the north.

Vergelegen

Daily 9.30am–4pm • R10 • Wine tasting R30 for six wines • ☎ 021 847 1346, ⓦ vergelegen.co.za

An architectural treasure as well as producing a stunning range of wines, **Vergelegen** represents a notorious episode of corruption at the Cape in the early years of Dutch East India Company rule. Built by Willem Adriaan van der Stel, who became governor in 1699 after his father Simon retired, the estate formed a grand Renaissance complex in the middle of the wild backwater that was the Cape at the beginning of the eighteenth century. Willem Adriaan acquired the land illegally and used Company slaves and resources to build Vergelegen and farm vast tracts of surrounding land. He also abused his power as governor to corner most of the significant markets at the Cape. When the Company became aware of this, they sacked Willem Adriaan and ordered Vergelegen to be destroyed. It's believed that the destruction wasn't fully carried out and the current building is thought to stand on the original foundations.

Vergelegen was the only wine estate visited by Britain's Queen Elizabeth II during her 1995 state visit to South Africa – a good choice, as there's enough here to occupy even a monarch for an easy couple of hours. The **interpretive centre**, just across the courtyard from the shop at the building entrance, provides a useful history and background to the estate. Next door, the **wine-tasting centre** offers professionally run sampling with a brief talk through each label. The **homestead**, which was restored in 1917 to its current state by Lady Florence Phillips, wife of a Johannesburg mining magnate, can also be visited. The massive grounds, planted with chestnuts and camphor trees and with ponds around every corner, make this one of the most serene places in the Cape.

EATING AND DRINKING   VERGELEGEN

★ **Vergelegen** ☎ 021 847 1346, ⓦ vergelegen.co.za. One of the best ways to enjoy the surroundings at Vergelegen is to order a gourmet picnic basket (R195 per person; summer only), which will be laid out under the camphor trees, complete with checked table cloth and wicker basket. *The Stables* offers breakfast, lunch and coffees in a bistro environment, while *Camphors*

Restaurant is one of the top Winelands eating experiences – the seasonal menu might include steak tartare from their own Nguni cattle (R375 for three courses, and R275 for two). The Stables daily 9.30am–4pm; Camphors Restaurant Wed, Thurs & Sun noon–2.30pm, Fri & Sat noon–2.30pm & 6.30–9pm.

Morgenster

Mon–Sun 10am–5pm • R45 for wine tasting, R20 for olive oil tasting • ☎ 021 852 1738, ⓦ morgenster.co.za

Vergelegen's immediate neighbour, **Morgenster** sits in an exquisite rustic setting and has a tasting room whose veranda looks onto a lovely lake with hazy mountains in the distance. As well as producing two stellar blended reds, the estate offers the unusual addition of olive tasting, with three types of olive, three types of oil (including an award-winning cold-pressed extra virgin olive oil) and some delicious olive paste.

Paarl

Although **PAARL** is attractively ensconced in a fertile valley brimming with historic buildings, at heart it's a parochial *dorp*, lacking the sophistication of Stellenbosch or the striking setting of Franschhoek. It can claim some virtue, however, from being a prosperous farming centre that earns its keep from the agricultural industries – grain silos, canneries and flour mills – on the north side of town, and the cornucopia of grapes, guavas, olives, oranges and maize grown on the surrounding farms.

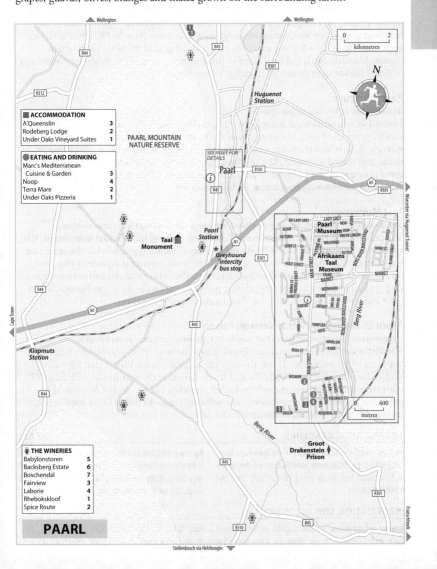

ACCOMMODATION

A'Queenslin	3
Rodeberg Lodge	2
Under Oaks Vineyard Suites	1

EATING AND DRINKING

Marc's Mediterranean Cuisine & Garden	3
Noop	4
Terra Mare	2
Under Oaks Pizzeria	1

THE WINERIES

Babylonstoren	5
Backsberg Estate	6
Boschendal	7
Fairview	3
Laborie	4
Rhebokskloof	1
Spice Route	2

PAARL

2

Brief history

In 1657, five years after the establishment of the Cape settlement, a party led by **Abraham Gabbema** arrived in the Berg River Valley to look for trading opportunities with the Khoikhoi, and search for the legendary gold of Monomotapa. With treasure on the brain, they awoke after a rainy night to see the silvery dome of granite dominating the valley, which they dubbed Peerlbergh (pearl mountain); in its modified form, **Paarl**, became the name of the town.

Thirty years later, the commander of the Cape, Simon van der Stel, granted strips of the Khoikhoi lands on the slopes of Paarl Mountain to French Huguenot and Dutch settlers. By the time Paarl was granted town status in 1840, it was still an outpost at the edge of the Drakenstein Mountains, a flourishing wagon-making and last-stop provisioning centre. The town holds deep historical significance for the two competing political forces that forged modern South Africa. **Afrikanerdom** regards Paarl as the hallowed ground on which their language movement was born in 1875 (see box opposite), while the **ANC** and everyone else remember it as the place from which Nelson Mandela made the final steps of his long walk to freedom, when he walked out of **Groot Drakenstein Prison** (then called Victor Verster) in 1990.

Paarl Museum

303 Main St • Mon–Fri 9am–4pm, Sat 9am–1pm • R5

Housed in a handsome, thatched Cape Dutch building with one of the earliest surviving gables (1787), the contents of the **Paarl Museum** don't quite match up to its exterior. It does include some reasonably enlightening panels on the architecture of the town, and several eccentric glass display cases of Victorian bric-a-brac. There's also some coverage of the indigenous Khoisan populations of the area and the changes that came with European colonization, including slavery.

Taal Monument

Daily 9am–5pm • Free • To get here, drive south along Main St and follow the signs to your right up the slope of the mountain

The only other sight of any interest in Paarl itself is the grandiose **Taal Monument**, the apartheid-era memorial to the Afrikaans language, standing just outside the centre on top of Paarl Mountain. The monument used to be as important a place of pilgrimage for Afrikaners as the Voortrekker Monument in Pretoria. From the coffee and curio shop you can admire a truly magnificent panorama across to the Cape Peninsula and False Bay in one direction and the Winelands ranges in the other.

Groot Drakenstein (Victor Verster) Prison

Roughly 9km south of the N1 as it cuts through Paarl, along the R301 (the southern extension of Jan van Riebeeck St)

The **Victor Verster Prison**, renamed **Groot Drakenstein** in 2000, was Nelson Mandela's last place of incarceration. It was through the gates at Victor Verster that he walked to his freedom on February 11, 1990, and it was here that the first images of him in 27 years were broadcast (under the Prisons Act, not even old pictures of him could be published during his incarceration). The working jail looks rather like a boys' school fronted by rugby fields beneath hazy mountains.

ARRIVAL AND DEPARTURE   PAARL

By bus Daily Greyhound intercity buses from Cape Town (1hr) stop at the Monument Shell Garage, on the corner of Main Road and South Street, about 2km from the tourist office.

By train Metrorail and Spoornet services from Cape Town (18 daily; 1hr 15min) pull in at Huguenot Station in Lady Grey Street at the north end of town, near to the central shops. Use the trains with caution.

INFORMATION AND ACTIVITIES

Tourist information The tourist office, on the corner of Main and Plantasie streets (Mon–Fri 8am–5pm, Sat 9am–1pm & Sun 10am–1pm; ☎021 872 4842, ⓦ paarlonline.com), has a good selection of maps,

2

THE HISTORY OF AFRIKAANS

Afrikaans is South Africa's third mother tongue, spoken by fifteen percent of the population and outstripped only by Zulu and Xhosa. English, by contrast, is the mother tongue of only nine percent of South Africans.

Signs of the emergence of a new Southern African dialect appeared as early as 1685, when a Dutch East India Company official from the Netherlands complained about a "distorted and incomprehensible" version of Dutch being spoken around modern-day Paarl. By absorbing English, French, German, Malay and indigenous words and expressions, the language continued to diverge from mainstream Dutch, and by the nineteenth century was widely used in the Cape by both white and coloured speakers, but was looked down on by the elite.

In 1905, **Gustav Preller**, a young journalist from a working-class Boer background, set about reinventing Afrikaans as a "white man's language". He aimed to eradicate the stigma of its "coloured" ties by substituting Dutch words for those with non-European origins. Preller began publishing the first of a series of populist magazines written in Afrikaans and glorifying Boer history and culture. Pressure grew for the recognition of Afrikaans as an official language, which came in 1925.

When the **National Party** took power in 1948, its apartheid policy went hand in hand with promoting the interests of its Afrikaans-speaking supporters. Afrikaners were installed throughout the civil service and filled most posts in the public utilities. Despite there being more coloured than white Afrikaans speakers, the language quickly became associated with the apartheid establishment. This led directly to the **Soweto uprising** of 1976, when the government attempted to enforce Afrikaans as the sole medium of instruction in African schools. At the same time, the repression of the 1970s and 1980s and the forced removals under the Group Areas Act led many coloured Afrikaans speakers to adopt English in preference to their tainted mother tongue.

There are few signs that Afrikaans will die out, though. Under the new constitution, existing language rights can't be diminished, which effectively means that Afrikaans will continue to be almost as widely used as before. But it is now as much with coloured as white people that the future of the **taal** (language) rests.

including the wine routes, and can help with booking accommodation.

Horse and quad-bike trails Based at the Rhebokskloof wine estate (see box, p.179), Wine Valley Horse Trails (☏021 869 8687 or ☏083 226 8735, ⓦhorsetrails-sa. co.za) offers one- to four-hour equestrian trails for novices and experts through the surrounding countryside. Prices start from R300 for a one-hour trail. Longer trails are restricted to experienced riders, but a half-day package (R650) of a ride plus a wine tasting at the estate is available to novices. They also rent out quad-bikes, which start at R250 for a half-an hour trail.

ACCOMMODATION

A'Queenslin 2 Queen St ☏021 863 1160, ✉aqueenslin@telkomsa.net. Two large en-suite rooms with their own entrances and private garden spaces, plus three doubles that share a bathroom, in a split-level family home in a quiet part of town, bounded on one side by vineyards and towered over by Paarl Rock. Limited self-catering is possible – there's a fridge and microwave – or opt for a full English breakfast (R65 extra). R700

Rodeberg Lodge 74 Main St ☏021 863 3202, ⓦrodeberglodge.co.za. Plain period furnishings give the en-suite rooms in this huge, centrally located and well-run Victorian townhouse a cool, spacious feel. Ask for a room at the back, if traffic noise bothers you. R850

Under Oaks Vineyard Suites Off the R45, 8km north of Paarl ☏021 869 8535, ⓦunderoaks.co.za. Good value, luxurious rooms, with comfy beds and plush linen, in a purpose-built, modern guesthouse on a vineyard overlooking the wide, fertile valley towards Wellington. Breakfast is served in a historic wine estate dining room overlooking pastures, and there's an on-site pizzeria for dinner (see p.175). You can try the flagship Sauvignon Blanc or Cabernet Sauvignon at their adjoining boutique winery. R1200

EATING AND DRINKING

A working town, Paarl has none of the Winelands foodie pretensions of Franschhoek or Stellenbosch, but you'll find a number of places along the main street for a decent coffee or a meal, as well as a couple of outstanding places on the surrounding vineyards.

Marc's Mediterranean Cuisine & Garden 129 Main St ☎021 863 3980, ⓦmarcsrestaurant.co.za. One of Paarl's most popular casual restaurants, *Marc's* dishes up a moderately priced, simple but tasty menu that includes paella, Lebanese meze (R120), couscous, seafood and lamb, served in a converted historic house with a large outdoor area dotted with sun umbrellas and lemon trees. Mon–Sat 10am–2.30pm & 6.30–9.30pm.

Noop 127 Main St ☎021 863 3925, ⓦnoop.co.za. This super-cool pavement wine bar has a dauntingly long menu and equally extensive list of wines by the glass. They have some great takes on simple favourites

2

WINERIES AROUND PAARL

There are a couple of notable wineries in Paarl itself, but most are on farms in the surrounding countryside. Boschendal, one of the most popular of these, is officially on the Franschhoek wine route (see box, p.178), but is in easy striking distance of Paarl. Most of the wineries have a restaurant, generally of a high standard, and some have beautiful rooms to stay in, often a more appealing option than staying in central Paarl.

★**Babylonstoren** Simondium Rd ☎021 863 3852, ⓦbabylonstoren.com. Popular with tourists, and for good reason, Babylonstoren is beautifully set against the high Drakenstein mountains, with extensive gardens, ducks, chickens and olive trees as well as many acres of vineyard; there's also a shop selling South African cookery books and upmarket crafts. Of the two restaurants on the wine estate, the *Green House* is less formal while *Babel* is known for more traditional South African food. Entry to the estate costs R10. Estate daily 9am–5pm; *Green House* daily 10am–4pm; *Babel* Wed–Sun noon–4pm, Fri & Sat 6.30–8.30pm.

Backsberg Estate 22km south of Paarl on Simondium Rd (WR1) ☎021 875 5141, ⓦbacksberg .co.za. Notable as the first carbon-neutral wine estate in South Africa, Backsberg produces some top-ranking red blends and a delicious Chardonnay in its Babylons Toren and Black Label ranges. Outdoor seating, with views of the rose garden and vineyard on the slopes of the Simonsberg, makes this busy estate a nice place to while away some time. There's also a restaurant and a maze. Tasting R15 for five wines. Tasting and restaurant Mon–Fri 9am–3.30pm, Sat & Sun 9am–3.30pm.

The Fairview Estate Suid Agter Paarl Rd, on the southern fringes of town ☎021 863 2450, ⓦfairview.co.za. One of the most fun of the Paarl estates (especially for families), with a resident population of goats who clamber up the spiral tower, featured in the estate's emblem, at the entrance. A deli sells breads and preserves, and you can also sample and buy the goats', sheep's and cows' cheeses made on the estate (R15), while wine tasting costs R25 for six wines and a cheese selection. Fairview is an innovative, family-run place, but it can get a bit hectic when the tour buses roll in. The *Goatshed* restaurant offers a cheese platter (R65) and is well known for its Sunday lunch. Tasting and restaurant daily 9am–5pm.

Laborie Taillefert St ⓦlaboriewines.co.za. One of the most impressive Paarl wineries, all the more remarkable for being right in town. The beautiful manor is fronted by a rose garden, acres of close-cropped lawns, historic buildings and oak trees – all towered over by the Taal Monument. There's a truly wonderful tasting room with a balcony that juts out over the vineyards trailing up Paarl Mountain, as well as a great restaurant with terrace seating offering good views. Their flagship is the Jean Taillefert Shiraz, while the Pineau de Laborie, a dessert wine made from pinotage grapes laced with Pinotage brandy, is also worth a try. Tasting R25. Mon–Sat 9am–5pm, Sun 11am–5pm.

Rhebokskloof Signposted off the R45, 11.5km northwest of Paarl ☎021 869 8386, ⓦrhebokskloof .co.za. A highly photogenic wine estate, and a great place to bring kids, Rhebokskloof sits at the foot of sculptural granite *koppies* overlooking a lake with a shaded terrace for summer lunches and gourmet meals. Meat is the house speciality, with exciting combinations of flavours, and the Sunday lunch buffets (R185) are tremendously popular. It's also a good place for afternoon teas, and they can prepare picnics on the lawns outside (R295 for two). In terms of wine, Shiraz is where they make their mark. Wine tasting R15 for five wines. Mon–Fri 9am–5pm, Sat & Sun 9am–3pm; restaurant daily 9am–5pm, dinner by reservation only Friday 6pm onwards.

Spice Route Suid Agter Paarl Rd ☎ 021 863 5222, ⓦspiceroute.co.za. The Spice Route farm offers unusual tastings drawn from several artisanal producers who are based in different buildings on the same estate. You can try beer and biltong at the Cape Brewing Company, hand-made chocolate and wine pairing at the *DV Artisan Chocolate, Roastery and Expresso Bar* (R100), or local grappa at *La Grapperia Pizza and Tapas Bar*, the only place open in the evening after 5pm. Other residents include an art gallery, glass blowers and farm shop. It is popular with groups, so book tastings in advance. Daily 11am–5pm.

such as burgers, pasta, pizza and steaks (R95). Mon–Sat 11am–9.30pm.

★**Terra Mare** 90a Main St ☎ 021 863 4805. Italian- and Mediterranean-influenced dishes, using local ingredients and cooked with considerable flair – try the three mushroom risotto to start (R85) and limoncello sorbet for dessert (R45). The glass and steel restaurant has great sweeping views of the Paarl Valley. Mon–Sun 11am–2pm & 6–10pm.

Under Oaks Pizzeria *Under Oaks Vineyard Suites,* Off the R45, 8km north of Paarl ☎ 021 869 8962. The best thing about eating a delicious wood-fired pizza here, while drinking wine from grapes grown on the farm, is the setting beneath majestic oak trees. There's a relaxed vibe, too, with children running about on the lawns, and it's very popular with local families. Tues–Sat 11.30am–8.30pm, Sun noon–3.30pm.

Franschhoek

If eating, drinking and sleeping is what the Winelands is really about, then **FRANSCHHOEK**, 33km from Stellenbosch and 29km from Paarl, is the place that does it best. Its late Victorian and more recent Frenchified rustic architecture, the terrific setting (hemmed in on three sides by mountains), the vineyards down every other backstreet, and some vigorous myth-making have created a place you can really lose yourself in, a set piece that unashamedly draws its inspiration from Provence.

Between 1688 and 1700, about two hundred **French Huguenots**, desperate to escape religious persecution in France, accepted a Dutch East India Company offer of passage to the Cape and the grant of lands. They made contact with the area's earliest settlers, groups of **Khoi herders**, whom the white settlers gradually dispossessed. By 1713 white hegemony was established and the area was known as *de france hoek*. Though French-speaking died out within a generation, many of the estates are still known by their original French names. Franschhoek itself occupies parts of the original farms of La Cotte and Cabriere and is relatively young, having established around a church built in 1833.

The Huguenot Museum and the monument

Lambrechts Rd • Sun–Thurs 9am–5pm & Sun 2–5pm • R10

If you drive through Franschhoek, you can't really miss the **Huguenot Memorial Museum** because it's adjacent to the town's most obvious landmark, the **Huguenot Monument**, in a prime position at the head of Huguenot Road, the main road through

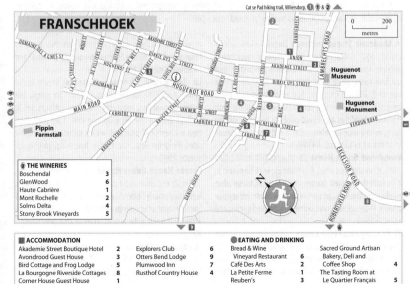

FRANSCHHOEK

THE WINERIES

Boschendal	3
GlenWood	6
Haute Cabrière	1
Mont Rochelle	2
Solms Delta	4
Stony Brook Vineyards	5

■ ACCOMMODATION				● EATING AND DRINKING			
Akademie Street Boutique Hotel	2	Explorers Club	6	Bread & Wine		Sacred Ground Artisan	
Avonwood Guest House	3	Otters Bend Lodge	9	Vineyard Restaurant	6	Bakery, Deli and	
Bird Cottage and Frog Lodge	5	Plumwood Inn	7	Café Des Arts	2	Coffee Shop	4
La Bourgogne Riverside Cottages	8	Rusthof Country House	4	La Petite Ferme	1	The Tasting Room at	
Corner House Guest House	1			Reuben's	3	Le Quartier Français	5

town. The monument consists of three skinny, interlocking arches symbolizing the Holy Trinity, while the museum provides comprehensive coverage of Huguenot history and culture, and of their contribution to modern South Africa.

Museum van de Caab

Solms Delta Wine Estate,12km north of Franschhoek along the R45 • Sun–Thurs 9am–5pm, Fri & Sat 9am–6pm • Free • ⓦ solms-delta.co.za

The highly recommended **Museum van de Caab** gives a condensed and riveting slice through South African vernacular history as it happened on the farm and its surroundings. Housed alongside the atmospherically understated tasting room in the original 1740s gabled Cape Dutch cellar, the display begins with Stone Age artefacts found on the site and goes on to trace the arrival of the aboriginal Khoisan people, their colonization by Europeans, the introduction of slavery and how this eventually evolved into the apartheid system, and its eventual demise.

INFORMATION AND ACTIVITIES   FRANSCHHOEK

Information Just north of the junction with Kruger Street, the tourist office, at 62 Huguenot Rd (Mon–Fri 8am–5pm, Sat 9am–5pm, Sun 9am–4pm; ☎021 876 2861, ⓦ franschhoek.org.za), has some excellent maps of the village and its winelands.

Hiking The best hike in the vicinity is the Cat se Pad (Cat's Path), which starts on your left just under a kilometre from the museum as you head out of town up the Franschhoek Pass. The walk leads though *fynbos* to the mountains surrounding the valley, with good views en route. The first two-kilometre section gets you to the top of the pass, and you can keep going for another 10km in the direction of Villiersdorp (though you don't actually reach it).

Equestrian wine tours Paradise Stables, Roberstsvlei Rd (☎021 876 2160 or ☎084 586 2160, ⓦ paradisestables .co.za), runs horse-rides to Rickety Bridge and Mont Rochelle wineries (Mon–Sat at 8.45am & 1.15pm; 2hr 30min in the saddle, with a 30–45min stop at each winery; R700); wine tasting is included in the price, though lunch is not. If you want to simply ride, they have outrides for R200 an hour (Mon–Sat at 7.30am & 5.45pm) on well-behaved Arabian horses, ridden with halters. The farm where the ride begins also has a couple of reasonably priced cottages for rent (R400).

ACCOMMODATION

On the whole, guesthouse accommodation in Franschhoek is pricey, though the rooms are of high quality and frequently in unparalleled settings; some of the wine estates outside town also offer luxury rooms. Budget accommodation is hard to find, but there are a couple of reasonably priced self-catering cottages and a backpackers' hostel. In summer, accommodation is at a premium, so book as far ahead as possible.

★**Akademie Street Boutique Hotel** 5 Akademie St ☎082 517 0405, ⓦ aka.co.za. Luxury guesthouse offering total privacy in its tastefully decorated and spacious suites set in beautiful gardens. Facilities include free wi-fi, DVDs, a fridge stocked with free drinks and a long, saltwater swimming pool. Gourmet breakfasts with regional specialities are served poolside by the charming hosts, who'll happily recommend a restaurant for dinner and book a table for you. R4100

Avondrood Guest House 39 Hugenot St ☎021 876 2881, ⓦ avondrood.com. A guesthouse with six rooms in a beautifully restored home, which gets accolade after accolade for the level of comfort and aesthetic experience offered. There are extensive lawns, a manicured garden and a pool. R2500

Bird Cottage and Frog Lodge Verdun Rd, 4.5km from town ☎021 876 2136, ⓔ grahamh@radionet.co.za. Two artistically furnished cottages that each sleep four, surrounded by beautiful indigenous gardens near the

mountains. It's as remote as you'll get this close to Franschhoek as well as being thoroughly laidback and exceptional value. R700

La Bourgogne Riverside Cottages Excelsior Rd ☎021 876 3245, ⓦ labourgogne.co.za. Six simply but tastefully furnished converted labourers' cottages set in gardens along a river on a working farm. They press their own oil here and produces wines, including the highly rated Progeny Sémillon; there's free wine tasting for guests. R900

Corner House Guest House 5 Union St ☎021 876 4729, ⓦ thecornerhouse.co.za. One of Franschhoek's few moderately priced guesthouses, the Dutch-run *Corner House* offers six bright and spotless rooms, and a pretty garden with a pool. They're also pet-friendly. R800

★**Explorers Club** Cook's Cottage Corner ☎021 876 4729, ⓦ explorersclub.co.za. A quartet of centrally located self-catering houses, each sleeping 2–10 people

2

and located in a great part of Franschoek, close to vineyards and restaurants. All the properties are luxurious, modern and tasteful, and two have their own pool. R2500

Otters Bend Lodge Dassenberg Rd ☏ 021 876 3200, ⓦ ottersbendlodge.co.za. Rustic lodge with double and twin-bedded cabins, dorms and camping on the lawn, five minutes' drive from town. It's surrounded by orchards and vineyards, and there's an inviting communal area,

complete with a roaring fire in winter, a well-equipped kitchen and an outside braai area. Camping R150, dorm R150, double R450

Plumwood Inn 11 Cabriere St ☏ 021 876 3883, ⓦ plumwoodinn.com. Excellent boutique guesthouse with smart, clean and modern furnishings. They've paid close attention to detail throughout – from the custom-made cotton tablecloths to the luxurious beds and bathrooms, and the impeccable service. R1400

WINERIES AROUND FRANSCHHOEK

Franschhoek's wineries are small enough and sufficiently close together to make it a breeze to visit two or three in a morning. Heading north through town from the Huguenot Monument, you'll find most of the wineries signposted off Huguenot Rd and its extension, Main Rd; the rest are off Excelsior Rd and the Franschhoek Pass Rd.

Boschendal Pniel Rd, just after the junction of the R45 and R310 to Stellenbosch ⓦ boschendalwines .com. One of the world's longest-established New World wine estates, Boschendal draws busloads of tourists – around 200,000 visitors a year – with its impressive Cape Dutch buildings, tree-lined avenues, beautiful gardens, restaurants and cafés and, of course, wines. Of their six labels, the Pavilion range delivers high-class, well-priced plonk (Shiraz–Cabernet Sauvignon, Rosé and a white blend), while the top ranges include wines such as the Cecil John Reserve Shiraz and Sauvignon Blanc. Tastings cost R30. Try their famous picnic baskets (R165 per person) on the extensive lawns. Daily 9am–4.30pm.

GlenWood Robertsvlei Rd, signposted off the R45 ☏ 021 876 2044, ⓦ glenwoodvineyards.co.za. Small winery in a beautiful setting that produces outstanding wines year after year. Although only ten-or-so minutes' drive from the village, it feels surprisingly remote, and vineyard and cellar tours are frequently conducted by the owner. Their flagship wines are the Grand Duc Chardonnay and Grand Duc Syrah. Tasting R30. The restaurant, *Le Bon Vivant*, is good too, serving simple bistro food in a dramatic setting, but must be booked in advance. Estate Mon–Fri 11am–4pm, Sept–April also open Sat & Sun 11am–3pm; restaurant Thurs–Tues noon–3pm.

Haute Cabrière About 2km from town along the Franschhoek Pass Rd ☏ 021 876 8500, ⓦ cabriere .co.za. Atmospheric winery notable for its Pinot Noirs and colourful wine-maker Achim von Arnim, whose presence guarantees an eventful visit; try to catch him or, more commonly now, his son Takuan, when they demonstrate *sabrage* – slicing off the upper neck of a bubbly bottle with a French cavalry sabre. Cabrière is also noted for its top-notch Pierre Jourdan range of sparkling wines. Tasting R30 for five wines and R60 for

five bubblies. Mon–Fri 9am–5pm, Sat 10am–4pm, Sun 11am–4pm.

★ **Mont Rochelle** Dassenberg Rd ☏ 021 876 2770, ⓦ montrochelle.co.za. Set against the Klein Dassenberg, Mont Rochelle has one of the most stunning settings in Franschhoek and an unusual cellar in a converted nineteenth-century fruit-packing shed, edged by eaves decorated with fretwork, stained-glass windows and chandeliers. Chardonnay is what they do best here, but don't overlook their stellar Sauvignon Blanc and Syrah. Tasting R30. The estate also has comfortable accommodation and two restaurants, and picnics are available (R290 for two). Daily 10am–6pm.

★ **Solms Delta** 13km north of Franschhoek along the R45 ☏ 021 874 3937, ⓦ solms-delta.co.za. Pleasantly bucolic Solms Delta produces unusual and consistently outstanding wines, which, on a summer's day, you can taste beneath ancient oaks at the edge of the vineyards with a picnic (R290 for two people). Half the profits from the wines produced go into a trust that benefits residents of the farm and the Franschhoek Valley. The Solms-Wijn de Caab range includes the excellent Hiervandaan (an unusual blend dominated by Shiraz, and including Carignan, Mourvèdre and Viognier grapes) and the even more highly rated Amalie (vine-dried Grenache Blanc and Viognier). Tasting R20 for six wines. Daily 9am–5pm.

Stony Brook Vineyards About 4km from Franschhoek, off Excelsior Rd ☏ 021 876 2182, ⓦ stonybrook.co.za. Family-run boutique wine estate, with just 140,000 square metres of vineyards, that produces first-rate wines, including the acclaimed flagship Ghost Gum Cabernet Sauvignon, which takes its name from a magnificent old tree outside the house and informal tasting room. Tastings are convivial affairs conducted by the owners and are by appointment only (R35). Mon–Fri 10am–5pm, Sat 10am–1pm.

Rusthof Country House 12 Huguenot St ☎ 021 876 3762, ⓦ rusthof.com. Modern eight-roomed guesthouse along the main drag (although it doesn't feel like it) and close to some of Franschhoek's top restaurants. The rooms open onto a rose garden, and the service is good; there are also a couple of family rooms. **R2060**

EATING AND DRINKING

Eating and drinking is what Franschhoek is all about, and its **restaurants** rate among the country's best. Franschhoek's cuisine tends to be French-inspired, with an emphasis on local ingredients. Restaurants in town are concentrated along Huguenot Rd, but there are a number of excellent more rustic alternatives in the surrounding wine estates, several of which do picnics in their beautiful grounds. Booking is essential, particularly for the smarter restaurants, and winter opening hours may be reduced. Every Saturday (9am–2pm) there is a farmers' market in the churchyard on Main Rd.

Bread & Wine Vineyard Restaurant Moreson Farm, Happy Valley Rd ☎ 021 876 3692, ⓦ moreson.co.za. Signposted off the R45 and surrounded by lemon groves and vineyards, this is a genial and child-friendly restaurant, specializing in home-cured charcuterie (R75) and the estate's own wines. It's regularly rated among the top twenty restaurants in the country. Daily noon–3pm.

Café Des Arts 7 Reservoir St, next to the library ☎ 021 876 2952, ⓦ cafedesarts.co.za. The service and food are consistently good here, with unfussy but flavoursome dishes – the *teriyaki* pork belly with stir-fried noodles is recommended (R110). It's a relaxed spot, also good for coffee and something delicious from their small bakery. Mon–Sat 8am–3pm & 6.30–10pm.

La Petite Ferme Franschhoek Pass Rd ☎ 021 876 3016, ⓦ lapetiteferme.co.za. With gorgeous views across a vineyard-covered valley, this restaurant has won awards galore – slow roasted lamb has been on the menu for thirty years and never fails to please (R162). Lunches are served with wines from the restaurant's cellar. Friday night sundowners are a summer highlight, with live music on the lawn. Daily noon–4pm, plus dinner from 6.30pm on Fridays in summer.

Reuben's 19 Huguenot Rd ☎ 021 876 3772, ⓦ reubens .co.za. Centrally situated restaurant with a modern interior, shady courtyard and trendy bar area where an old Dakota wing serves as the counter. Good for a lazy lunch in summer under the cooling mist spray. The menu is modern French cuisine with cosmopolitan influences – venison features big and there's always poultry, lamb, pork, seafood and a vegetarian option such as potato gnocchi (R110). Daily noon–3pm & 7–9pm.

★ **Sacred Ground Artisan Bakery, Deli and Coffee Shop** 36 Huguenot St ☎ 021 876 2759. An affordable place that serves excellent sandwiches, such as the "veg patch" with mushrooms, olives, pesto and cheese (R50), as well as fresh pastries, pies and coffee. Mon–Sun 7am–6pm.

★ **The Tasting Room at Le Quartier Français** 16 Huguenot Rd ☎ 021 876 2151, ⓦ lqf.co.za. The place that made Franschhoek synonymous with food years ago and still today one of South Africa's best restaurants, skippered by Margot Janse – Africa's only female Grand Chef. Formal evening meals have a contemporary, global flavour and you need to book months in advance (R850 for an eight-course menu). There's also an appealing lounge bar serving breakfast, craft beer, local wines and exceptionally good tapas, with dishes like prawn popcorn, wildebeest doughnuts and gruyere oreos. Restaurant Tues–Sat 7–10pm; bar daily 7am–11pm.

Route 62 and the Little Karoo

One of the most rewarding journeys in the Western Cape is the **mountain route** from Cape Town to Port Elizabeth, which runs largely along the R62, and thus is often referred to as **Route 62**. Less known than its coastal counterpart, the Garden Route (see p.208), this trip takes you through some of the most dramatic mountain passes in the country and crosses a frontier of *dorps* and drylands. This "back garden" of the Little Karoo is in many respects more rewarding than the Garden Route, being far less developed, with spectacular landscapes, quieter roads and some great small towns to visit.

The most likeable of these towns are the historic spa town of Montagu, rural and arty Barrydale, and the port capital Calitzdorp. Oudtshoorn and the Cango Caves mark the convergence of the mountain and coastal roads; over the most dramatic of all passes in the Cape – the unpaved **Swartberg Pass**, 27km of spectacular switchbacks and zigzags through the Swartberg Mountains – is **Prince Albert**, a Karoo village whose spare beauty and remarkable light make it popular with artists.

2

PASSES AND POORTS OF THE LITTLE KAROO

The Little Karoo is hemmed in by a gauntlet of rugged mountains and steep-sided valleys (or *poorts*) that for centuries made this area virtually impassable for wheeled transport. In the nineteenth century, the British began to tackle the problem and dozens of passes were built through the Cape's mountains, 34 of which were engineered by the brilliant road-builder Andrew Geddes Bain and his son Thomas. In fact, whatever the Little Karoo lacks in museums and art galleries is amply compensated for by the towering drama of these Victorian masterpieces. We've listed a selection of some of the best of the passes below.

Cogman's Kloof Pass Between Ashton and Montagu. A five-kilometre route that's at its most dramatic as it cuts through a rock face into the Montagu Valley.

Gamkaskloof Pass Also called Die Hel (The Hell; see box, p.191), reached from the summit of the Swartberg Pass. Arguably the most awesome of all the passes, leading into a dramatic and lonely valley, all on gravel.

Meiringspoort A tarred road through a gorge in the Swartberg, which can be taken to reach Prince Albert. The road keeps crossing a light-brown river, while huge slabs of folded and zigzagging rock rise up on either side.

Prince Alfred's Pass On the R339, between the N2, just east of Knysna, and Avontuur on the R62. A dramatic dirt road twisting through mountains, past a few isolated apple farms.

Swartberg Pass Between Oudtshoorn and Prince Albert. Over-the-Swartberg counterpart of Meiringspoort, with 1:7 gradients on narrow untarred roads, characterized by precipitous hairpins.

From Prince Albert, the hinterland of the **Great Karoo** opens up, the semi-desert that covers one-third of South Africa's surface. The fruit farms of the **Little Karoo** spread out into treeless plains, vegetated with low, wiry scrub, and dotted with flat-topped hills. The best of the Karoo can be found in the **Karoo National Park**, while, in **Sutherland**, the clear, clean air provides some of the best stargazing opportunities in the world.

Worcester

The best part of the journey from Cape Town to **WORCESTER**, 110km east, is the **Huguenot Toll Tunnel** on the N1, burrowing through high mountains that give onto a magnificent valley. A relatively large town for this part of the world, Worcester is an agricultural centre with a number of factories and smelly chicken farms. It's at the centre of a wine-making region, consisting mostly of cooperatives bulk-producing the plonk that makes up about a fifth of the national output. J.M. Coetzee, South Africa's most acclaimed writer internationally, grew up here, though there's no museum or anything to celebrate his work, and the main reason to stop is to visit the peaceful botanical gardens.

Karoo Desert Botanic Gardens

On the N1As you enter Worcester • Daily 7am–7pm • R20 • Restaurant daily 9am–5pm • ☎ 023 347 0785 ⓦ sanbi.org/gardens /karoo-desert

Entering Worcester from Cape Town, you'll see signs to the **Karoo Botanic Gardens**, a sister reserve to Cape Town's Kirstenbosch, known for its show of indigenous spring flowers and succulents. The best time to visit the gardens is from late July to early September when purple, orange and yellow flowers bloom here in profusion. Three hiking trails meander through large wild areas, full of desert plants and prickly blooms, and in winter, snow caps the dramatic backdrop of the Hex River mountain range. The pleasant *Kokerboom* restaurant serves light meals, looking out over the gardens onto an attractive mountain backdrop.

Worcester Museum

Just outside the centre of town at Kleinplasie – to get here, head east along High St and turn right onto the road to Robertson • Mon–Sat 8am–4.30pm, Sun 10am–3pm • R20

The absorbing **Worcester Museum** depicts life on the Karoo frontier between 1690 and 1900, and is made up of about two dozen reconstructed buildings, with staff in old-style workshops engaged in crafts and home industries. Look out for the corbelled shepherd's hut, which represents a vernacular style unique to the Karoo, using domed stone roofs rather than beam and lintel construction – a response to the dearth of timber in the treeless expanse.

Robertson

ROBERTSON is the largest town in the attractive stretch of the Breede River Valley, known locally as the Robertson Valley. The acidity level of the soil is ideal for growing grapes – indeed, the Robertson Valley is responsible for some ten percent of South Africa's vineyards – but irrigation is necessary as the climate is hot and dry. The best wines here tend to be Chenin Blancs and Colombards, and some good Muscadels are made too.

The only conceivable reason for visiting this fruit-picking town is to taste and buy wine, which tends to be cheaper than around the winelands closer to Cape Town, and very good.

ARRIVAL AND INFORMATION   ROBERTSON

By car Some 160km from Cape Town, Robertson is best approached via the N1. There's no public transport to the town.

Information The tourist office is on Voortrekker St (Mon–Fri 8am–5pm, Sat 9am–2pm, Sun 10am–2pm; ☎ 023 626 4437, ⓦ robertsontourism.co.za).

WINERIES IN AND AROUND ROBERTSON

The Robertson Valley's **wine route** extends to McGregor in the south and to Bonnievale in the east; we've picked out the best of its nearly three dozen wineries, all of which are free to visit, and most offer free tastings too . If you don't have time to meander, you can purchase wine from **La Verne Wine Boutique** (Mon–Thurs 9am–5.30pm, Fri 9am–6pm, Sat 9am–5pm, ⓦ lavernewines.co.za), situated in a converted railway cottage, next to the Robertson Art Gallery as you enter town from the west on the R60, which represents most of the local wine cellars. You can taste wine here, as well as buy by the case or just the odd bottle. La Verne sells online too, and can deliver anywhere in South Africa.

Bon Courage Roughly 10km southeast of Robertson along the R317 ⓦ boncourage.co.za. Producer of some great sweet whites, especially Muscadel, with a tasting room in a beautiful old homestead along the Breede River. Its *Café Maude* serves breakfast and light lunches. Mon–Fri 8am–5pm, Sat 9am–3pm.

De Wetshof About 12km southeast of town along the R317 ⓦ dewetshof.com. Top-notch estate with photogenic mountain and vineyard views, producing several excellent wines, including its flagship Bateleur Chardonnay. Mon–Fri 8.30am–4.30pm, Sat 9.30am–1pm.

Graham Beck About 7km west of Robertson along the R60 ⓦ grahambeckwines.co.za. A modern, high-flying estate making an international splash, with orders from British supermarket giants for its vast range of reds and whites, many of them in the top rank. The tasting room is daringly modern. Mon–Fri 9am–5pm,

Sat 10am–4pm.

Robertson Winery In town, just off the R60 ⓦ robertsonwinery.co.za. Producer of some good-value and highly drinkable Chardonnays and Colombards, sold cheaper here than in the shops. Mon–Fri 8am–5pm, Sat & Sun 9am–3pm.

Springfield A few kilometres southeast of Robertson on the R317 ⓦ springfieldestate.com. Stellar estate that produces a range of really outstanding reds and whites, a number of which are among South Africa's frontrunners. Mon–Fri 8.30am–5pm, Sat 9.30am–4pm.

Van Loveren 15km northwest of Bonnievale along the R317 ⓦ www.vanloveren.co.za. Wine tasting in a lovely garden at a winery known for its hugely quaffable wines, including River Red, South Africa's classic plonk , which offers consistently good value. Mon–Fri 8.30am–5pm, Sat 9.30am–3.30pm, Sun 11am–3pm.

ACCOMMODATION

The Lemontree House 2 Church Street ☎023 626 1384, ⓦlemontreehouse.co.za. A restored Victorian house with comfortable rooms furnished in a tasteful cottagey style. The beautiful garden with oak and pecan trees and a salt-water pool, plus a cosy fireplace in winter, add to the feeling of peace and tranquillity here. R700.

Robertson Backpackers 4 Dordrecht Ave ☎023 626 1280, ⓦrobertsonbackpackers.co.za. In a spacious Victorian house, this is one of the best backpackers in the Western Cape, with its own reasonably priced wine tour (R250 per person), a fireplace for chilly winter nights and a nice garden. They also run a good river-rafting trip. Camping R60, dorm R100, double R330

McGregor

McGregor is an attractive place, with thatched, whitewashed cottages glaring in the summer daylight amid the low, rusty steel-wool scrub, vines and olive trees, and a quiet, relaxed atmosphere that has attracted a small population of spiritual seekers and artists. It makes a great weekend break from Cape Town, with a couple of decent restaurants, plenty of well-priced accommodation, and a beautiful retreat centre that offers reasonably priced massage. Spending the day wine tasting in the environs is another attraction, as long as it's not a Sunday when almost everything is closed.

McGregor gained modest prosperity in the nineteenth century by becoming a centre of the whipstock industry, supplying wagoners and transport riders with long bamboo sticks for goading oxen. There aren't too many ox-drawn wagons today, and tourism, though developing, is still quite limited. A great draw is to walk the **Boesmanskloof Traverse** (see box, p.195), which starts 14km from McGregor and crosses to Greyton on the other side of the mountain. From McGregor you can walk a section of the trail, hiking to the main waterfall and back to the trailhead – a beautiful three- to four-hour round hike through the river gorge (*kloof* in Afrikaans).

ARRIVAL AND INFORMATION MCGREGOR

By car McGregor, 180km from Cape Town and 21km south of Robertson, is at the end of a minor road signposted off the R60. Don't be tempted by an approach from the south which may look like a handy back route – you'd need a 4WD for this. Allow two and a half hours for the drive from Cape Town along the N1, turning onto the R62 at Worcester for Robertson.

Information The tourist office on Voortrekker St (Mon—Sat 9am—1pm & 2—4.30pm, Sun 9am—1pm; ☎023 625 1954, ⓦtourismmcgregor.co.za) can book accommodation and issue permits for walking the whole Boesmanskloof Traverse or simply for the waterfall section (R30). They will also direct you to artists' studios in town, to massage and yoga classes, and give you times of the daily meditation sessions at *Temenos Retreat* (see below).

ACCOMMODATION

The Barn Grewe St ☎076 411 9477, ⓦthebarnmcgregor .co.za. Beautifully restored self-catering barn sleeping six in three rooms, with a Victorian bath, antique Cape furniture, fireplace and wood-burning stove. Rates drop to R950 for two people. R1350

Green Gables Country Inn 7 Smith St ☎023 625 1626, ⓦgreengablescountryinn.co.za. Reasonably priced country accommodation on the edge of town, with a swimming pool, an English-style pub and a restaurant (see opposite). The decor is cosy if slightly cluttered, and service is warm and personal. R700

The Old Village Lodge Voortrekker St ☎023 625 1692, ⓦoldvillagelodge.co.za. Upmarket B&B in a Victorian cottage on the main road, with a pretty garden, swimming pool and rooms furnished in an elegant and comfortable country style. R900

Rhebokskraal Farm Cottages 2km south of town ☎082 896 0429, ⓦrhebokskraalolives.co.za. Secluded cottages, each on a different part of this beautiful fruit, olive and grape farm, which is within easy reach of the restaurants in town. R500

★**Tanagra Guest Wine Farm** 4.5km northeast of McGregor, towards Robertson ☎023 625 1780, ⓦtanagra-wines.co.za. Idyllic wine farm with stylish, light and airy cottages, all with private verandas and mountain views. One cottage is totally off the grid, with a private plunge pool, hammocks and a fireplace. There are walking trails on the farm itself or in the adjoining Vrolijkheid Nature Reserve. Breakfast is available for an extra R125 per person. R700

★**Temenos Country Retreat** On the corner of Bree and Voortrekker streets ☎023 625 1871, ⓦtemenos

.org.za. Retreat centre with cottages dotted about beautiful gardens, with a lap-length swimming pool, library and meditation spaces. It's safe and peaceful – an ideal place for solo women. **R700**

Whipstock Farm 7km southwest of McGregor, towards Boesmanskloof ☎073 042 3919,

ⓦ whipstock.co.za. Farm accommodation in a Victorian house with five cottages, each with white-washed walls, wooden beams, a fridge and tea-making facilities. Meals are served communally in a large dining room with a fireplace. It's ideal for families wanting a nature-based holiday. **R440**

EATING AND DRINKING

Deli Girls Voortrekker St. Great for picnic supplies, with smoked fish, cheese, chocolate and other tempting goodies on offer. You can sit on the back porch to savour home-made dishes, such as cottage pie and salad, tandoori pork chop or a rich cheesy pasta and veg bake with salad (R50). Daily 9am–4.30pm.

Green Gables Country Inn 7 Smith St ☎023 625 1626, ⓦgreengablescountryinn.co.za. Alfresco dinners on the terrace overlooking vineyards and the village, with a cosy dining room and a fireplace for winter nights. There are generally three simple but good quality dishes on the menu, such as chicken curry, fish and chips and lamb shank (R90). Booking essential. Wed, Fri & Sat 6–10pm.

Karoux Restaurant Voortrekker St ☎023 625 1421. Intimate restaurant serving gourmet food you wouldn't expect to find in a sleepy village, such as crispy duck with exotic mushroom wontons, and free range chicken liver parfait with truffled blueberry vinaigrette (R60). Booking essential. Mon & Fri–Sun 7–10pm.

★**Tebaldi's at Temenos** On the corner of Bree and Voortrekker streets ☎023 625 1871, ⓦ temenos.org .za. Breakfasts and salad lunches served in a tranquil garden setting, or on the street-facing *stoep*. The coq au vin, served on a bed of creamy mash, is recommended (R90). Tues & Sun 9.30am–3.30pm, Wed–Sat 9.30am–3.30pm & 7–9.30pm.

Montagu

As you approach **Montagu**, soaring mountains rise up in vast arches of twisted strata that display reds and ochres; in spring, the town, known for its fruit growing, is full of peach and apricot blossoms. Montagu is certainly very pleasing, with sufficient Victorian architecture to create an historic character, and worth a night at least.

The town was named in 1851 after **John Montagu**, the visionary British Secretary of the Cape, who realized that the colony would never develop without decent communications and was responsible for commissioning the first mountain passes connecting remote areas to Cape Town. The grateful farmers of Agter Cogman's Kloof (literally "behind Cogman's Kloof") leapt at the chance of a snappier moniker for their village and named it after him.

Montagu is best known for its **hot springs**, but serious **rock climbers** come for its cliff faces, which are regarded as among the country's most challenging. You can also explore the mountains on a couple of trails or, easiest of all, on a tractor ride onto one of the peaks. Montagu is also conveniently positioned for excursions along both the Robertson and Little Karoo **wine routes** (see p.181). On Saturday mornings, don't miss the local **farmers' market** at the church, where you can get local olives and olive oil, bread, cheese, almonds and dried fruit from the surrounding farms – all exceptionally well priced. In summer bags of peaches and apricots are often sold from backyards or along the roadside, for next to nothing

Montagu Springs Resort

About 3km northwest of town on the R318 • Daily 8am–11pm • R100 • ☎023 614 1050, ⓦ www.montagusprings.co.za

Montagu's main draw is the **Montagu Springs Resort**; several chlorinated open-air pools of different temperatures and a couple of jacuzzis are spectacularly situated at the foot of cliffs – an effect spoilt by the neon lights of a hotel complex and fast-food restaurant. It's a fabulous place to take kids, though at weekends it becomes a mass of splashing bodies. If you want a quiet time, go first thing in the morning or last thing at night. The temperatures in winter are not hot enough to be entirely comfortable, when you're better off heading to the springs at Caledon (see box, p.193) or Warmwaterberg (see box, p.185), which are much hotter and quieter.

2

ARRIVAL AND INFORMATION

By car Montagu is 190km from Cape Town, via the N1. The approach from the south through Cogman's Kloof Gorge numbers among the most dramatic arrivals in the country.
By shuttle bus Danie (☎ 072 750 3125) runs a very reasonably priced shuttle service between Montagu and

MONTAGU

Cape Town, but you'll need to fit in with his schedule (R160).
Information The tourist office is at 24 Bath St (Mon–Fri 8am–6pm, Sat 9am–5pm, Sun 9.30am–5pm; ☎ 023 614 2471, ⓦ montagu-ashton.info).

ACCOMMODATION

★**Aasvoelkrans** 1 Van Riebeeck St ☎ 023 614 1228, ⓦ aasvoelkrans.co.za. Four imaginative garden rooms in a guesthouse on a farm, in a pretty part of town. Arabian horses graze in the surrounding fields, and there's also a two-bedroomed self-catering cottage suitable for a family or larger group. R900
De Bos Guest Farm 8 Brown St ☎ 023 614 2532, ⓦ debos.co.za. Lovely shady camping pitches, dorms, basic en-suite doubles and family bungalows on a farm at the western edge of town, close to the spectacular twisted mountain slopes. There are hikes on the doorstep, and it's also popular with rock climbers who bring their own kit to tackle climbs in the area. Camping R60, dorms R90, doubles R360
Montagu Rose Guest House 19 Kohler St ☎ 023 614 2681, ⓦ montagurose.co.za. A well-run guesthouse in a modern home. All the rooms have baths and mountain views, one is wheelchair friendly, and there is a family room for four, too. R700
Montagu Springs Signposted off the R62, west of

town ☎ 023 614 1050, ⓦ www.montagusprings.co.za. Large, milling resort with fully equipped self-catering chalets, some more luxurious than others, sleeping four. The only reason to stay here is if you are travelling with children and want to have endless access to the pools and playing areas. Prices are roughly a third lower during the week. Self-catering for a family at the weekend R940
Mystic Tin 38 Bath St ☎ 082 572 0738, ⓦ themystictin .co.za. Two reasonably priced family rooms and two garden rooms, simply but stylishly furnished in a rustic/ ethnic manner. R520
★**Squirrel's Corner** On the corner of Bloem and Jouberts streets ☎ 023 614 1081, ⓦ squirrelscorner.co.za. A reasonably priced B&B situated two blocks from the main road, with four comfortable, spotless en-suite rooms in a friendly family house, as well as an African-themed garden suite. They make a delicious omelette for breakfast plus local fruits and preserves, and you will be greeted with a glass of Montagu muscadel on arrival. R600

EATING AND DRINKING

Die Stal 8km out of town on the R318 ☎ 082 324 4318. A pleasant café/restaurant on a farm where you can sit on the porch and view the surrounding orchards and farmlands. It serves breakfast, lunches and teas – a hearty favourite is lamb rump (R105), while vegetarians may opt for the ploughman's platter (R85). Tues–Sun 9am–5pm.
★**Mystique Tin** 38 Bath St ☎ 082 572 0738, ⓦ themystictin.co.za. Table-cloths, candlelight and a winter fire-place provide a cosy yet casual environment to sample South African specialities cooked with flair, with twists of flavour from other cuisines. The ostrich herb meat balls served with roasted almonds and potato bread are worth a go (R92) and there are a couple of appealing vegetarian options, all accompanied by hand-crafted beers brewed in their Karoo

microbrewery. Wed–Mon 5pm–9.30pm.
Simply Delicious Restaurant Four Oaks Guesthouse, 46 Long St ☎ 023 614 3483, ⓦ four-oaks.co.za. In the shady courtyard of a handsome 1860 thatched house, this restaurant makes a good stop for a light lunch or dinner. The steak with seasonable vegetables (R100) is good, while vegetarians can get a veg wrap for lunch (R55). Summer daily 12.30–2.30pm & 7–9pm; winter Mon–Sat 12.30–2.30pm & 6.30–9pm.
Ye Olde Tavern 22 Church St ☎ 023 614 2398. Oddly named restaurant in the dry Karoo, serving South African specialities, such as bobotie (R80), as well as salads, burgers, pizza and pasta with indoor or outdoor seating to enjoy the warm summer nights. Booking advisable. Mon–Sat 6–10pm

---

MONTAGU ACTIVITIES

Montagu's tourist office (see above) can provide maps for three **hikes** that begin from the Old Mill at the north end of Tanner Street. Two are full-day hikes, while the shortest is the **Lover's Walk**, a stroll of just over 2km that follows the Keisie River through Bath Kloof (or Badkloof) to the hot springs.

The less energetic may prefer a recommended three-hour **tractor ride** (Wed & Sat at 10am & 2pm; R110; ☎ 023 614 3012) up the **Langeberg Mountains**. The tractor leaves from Protea Farm, which is 29km from Montagu along the R318 Koo/Touws River road. Remember to take warm clothes in the cooler months.

Barrydale and around

BARRYDALE, 240km from Cape Town, is perfect for a couple of days of doing very little other than experiencing small-town life in the Little Karoo. There's a distinctly rural feel about the town: vineyards line the main road, farm animals are kept on large plots of land behind dry-stone walls, and you'll find fig, peach and quince trees thriving in the dryness. Unsurprisingly, the town's beauty and tranquillity have made it an artists' haven – Van Riebeeck Street, the main drag, has more pedestrians than cars, and is dominated by an ivory church. West of town you'll find big game – and correspondingly high rates – at the magnificent **Sanbona Wildlife Reserve**, though day visitors are not accepted. To the east, you can totally relax at the **Warmwaterberg hot springs**.

Sanbona Wildlife Reserve

Twenty kilometres west of Barrydale off the R62 · R7800 per person per night at a lodge including meals and two game drives · ☎ 028 572 1365, ⓦ sanbona.com

An amalgamation of 21 farms that together create a massive wilderness area, **Sanbona Wildlife Reserve** is set in gorgeous landscape – rocky outcrops, mountains and semi-desert vegetation with two luxurious all-inclusive lodges. *Dwyka Tented Lodge* has the more spectacular setting and is closer to where most of the game can be found, while *Gondwana Family Lodge* is great if you are travelling with children. Although the game is sparser here than in the major parks such as Kruger, it is the only place in the Western Cape with free-roaming lions and cheetahs, and there's also a herd of elephants. A two-night stay is recommended and day visitors are not allowed – check for specials and cheaper winter rates.

ARRIVAL AND INFORMATION

BARRYDALE

By car Allow three and a half hours for the journey from Cape Town, either via the N1 and R62, or on the N2, and cutting inland on the R324 just east of Swellendam for the lovely drive through Suurbraak and the Tradouw Pass. Both routes are equally recommended for the scenery and ease of travel.

Information There's a tiny visitor information centre (Mon–Fri 9am–5pm, Sat & Sun 9am–2pm ☎ 028 572 1572, ⓦ barrydale.co.za) on the R62 at the entrance to the village.

ACCOMMODATION

InKaroo Cottage 2 Bain St near the cemetery ☎ 028 572 1344. Beautifully restored and furnished in a contemporary style, this self-catering Karoo farmhouse cottage sleeps 4–6 people. It has dry-stone walls and seating at the back of the house under vines, with sunset views onto the mountains. R600

★**Tradouw Guest House** 46 van Riebeeck St ☎ 028 572 1434, ⓦ tradouwguesthouse.co.za. One of the best accommodation options along the R62, Leon and Denis' friendly *Tradouw Guest House* has four simple, homely rooms with sash windows, and thick white cotton sheets and blankets. The rooms open onto a courtyard shaded by vines where you can breakfast, while two are accessed from the appealing large garden. There's a roaring fire in the lounge in winter. R700

WARMWATERBERG SPA

Thirty kilometres east of Barrydale (just beyond Ronnie's Sex Shop), **Warmwaterberg Spa** (daily 8am–6pm; ☎ 028 572 1609, ⓦ warmwaterbergspa.co.za; day visitors R40) is a Karoo farm blessed with natural hot water siphoned into two outdoor, unchlorinated hot pools and surrounded by lush green lawns and lofty palms. Primarily aimed at South Africans, it gets rather crowded and noisy during school holidays and at weekends. Indeed, the best time of day to enjoy the baths is after dark, when the steam rises into the cold, starry Karoo sky. The farm is attractively set, with mountain vistas to gaze at from the baths and fantastic bird life drawn by this oasis amid the desert landscape. There's basic, reasonably priced, self-catering **accommodation** here – in wooden cabins or rooms in the main farmhouse, each with an indoor spa bath (R640). There are also some camping pitches (R325), a bar and a restaurant serving dinners and breakfasts.

2

2

EATING

Blue Cow Signposted off the eastern side of the R62. The setting, overlooking fields and a dam, is restful and they do pleasant cakes, milkshakes and light meals (R60). A good place to stop if you're travelling with children and they need to run around. Mon–Sat 8am–5pm.

Clarke of the Karoo Mud Gallery, on R62 ☏ 028 572 1017, ⓦ clarkeofthekaroo.co.za. A great option for tasty steaks, *bobotie* and other hearty country fare, with a starter provided on the house. Their Karoo lamb curry and venison burger on ciabatta are recommended (R90). Thurs–Tues 8am–5pm, Wed 6–9pm.

Jam Tarts on R62 ☏ 028 572 1017. The best place along

the R62 for coffee and light meals, such as delicious soups and pizzas, is *Jam Tarts*, where you can also pick up local olives and delicious jams with funky labels. Tues–Sun 8am–4.30pm, Mon 6–9pm.

★**Mez Karoo Kitchen** Van Riebeeck St ☏ 082 077 5980. Excellent and reasonably priced Mediterranean food, such as light tapas meals and a Greek lamb speciality (R110). The bright-pink rose-water ice cream served with pistachios and fresh mint is delightful. Tables are in Michelle's cosy kitchen in her home, though there are some outside seats too. Book ahead. Thurs–Sat 6–10pm, Sun 1–3pm.

SHOPPING

Arts and crafts Unsurprisingly for an artistic community, Barrydale has some interesting art and craft shops, such as the Mud Gallery, on the R62 (Mon–Fri 9am–5pm, Sat & Sun 9am–1pm; ☏ 028 572 1950, ⓦ mud.co.za), and Magpie Studio, 27 Van Riebeeck Street (Tues–Fri 10am–5pm, Sun 9am–1pm; ☏ 028 572 1997, ⓦ magpieartcollective.com), which makes

colourful light fittings and chandeliers from recycled materials – Michelle Obama even ordered one for the White House.

Wine There are a couple of wine outlets that are worth a visit for tasting and buying, particularly the Southern Cape Winery in Van Riebeeck Street (Mon–Fri 9am–5pm, Sat 9am–1pm; ☏ 028 572 1012).

Oudtshoorn

OUDTSHOORN, 420km from Cape Town and an arid, mountainous 180km from Barrydale, styles itself as the ostrich capital of the world; the town's surrounds are indeed crammed with ostrich farms, several of which you can visit, and the local souvenir shops keep busy dreaming up 1001 tacky ways to recycle ostrich parts as comestibles and souvenirs. The town's main interest visually lies in its Victorian and Edwardian sandstone buildings, some of which are unusually grand and elegant for a Karoo dorp, while it also makes a good base for visiting the nearby **Cango Caves** (see p.188).

Brief history

Oudtshoorn started out as a small village named after Geesje Ernestina Johanna van Oudtshoorn, wife of the first civil commissioner for the nearby town of George. By the 1860s **ostriches**, which live in the wild in Africa, were being raised in the ideal conditions of the Oudtshoorn Valley. The quirky Victorian fashion for large feathers had turned the ostriches into a source of serious wealth, and by the 1880s hundreds of thousands of kilos of feathers were being exported. Despite this economic boom, the labourers – mostly coloured descendants of the Outeniqua and Attaqua Khoikhoi and trekboers – received derisory wages supplemented by rations of food, wine, spirits and tobacco. In the early twentieth century, the most successful farmers and traders built themselves feather palaces, ostentatious sandstone Edwardian buildings that have become the defining feature of Oudtshoorn.

C.P. Nel Museum

Corner of Baron van Reede St and Voortrekker Rd • Mon–Fri 8am–5pm, Sat 9am–1pm • R15

The **C.P. Nel Museum** is a good place to start your explorations. A handsome sandstone building, it was built in 1906 as a boys' school, but now houses an eccentric collection of items relating to ostriches.

Le Roux Town House

Corner of Loop and High streets • Mon–Fri 9am–5pm • R15

Le Roux Town House is a perfectly preserved family town house, and the only one of the

2

OSTRICH TOURS

Many people come to Oudtshoorn to see, or even ride, **ostriches**, which are raised locally for their low-cholesterol meat. You don't actually have to visit an ostrich farm to view Africa's biggest bird, as you're bound to see flocks of them while driving past farms in the vicinity. A number of show farms offer **tours** (45–90min), which include the chance to sit on an ostrich and the spectacle of jockeys racing the birds. Best of the bunch is **Cango Ostrich and Butterfly Farm** (❶044 272 4623; tours every 30min; R70), on the main road between Oudtshoorn and the Cango Caves, which takes only one group of visitors (or individuals) at a time.

much-vaunted feather palaces that is open to the public to look round. The beautiful furnishings were all imported from Europe between 1900 and 1920, and there is plenty to stroll around and admire.

★Buffelsdrift Game Lodge

7km from Oudtshoorn on the Cango Caves road • Free entry ; elephant interactions R210 per adult, and R30 for a bucket of food • ❶044 272 0106, ⓦ buffelsdrift.com

At the **Buffelsdrift Game Lodge**, you get to stroke **elephants** under the guidance of their handlers, and watch them training and at play (book ahead for elephant interactions daily at 10am, 11am, 1pm & 2pm). From the lodge's restaurant (see p.188) on the large dam, you can often see hippos, and may be lucky enough to spot other animals, such as antelope, coming to drink. There is safari-style accommodation too (see below).

ARRIVAL, INFORMATION AND TOURS   OUDTSHOORN

By bus Intercity buses pull in at Queens Mall, off Voortrekker St, where you'll also find the Pick 'n Pay supermarket and chemist. It's a six-hour drive from Cape Town, one-and-a-half hours from George, and fourteen hours from Gauteng, all routes that are served by national coach companies. A daily shuttle from George collects guests for *Backpacker's Paradise* (see below).
Information The tourist office, at 80 Voortrekker St, in front of the library (Mon–Fri 8.30am–5pm, Sat 9.30am–12.30pm; ❶044 279 2532, ⓦ oudtshoorn.com) is good for information about the caves, ostrich farms and local accommodation.
Tours *Backpacker's Paradise* (see below) rents out bikes and also arranges spectacular adventurous cycling trips down the Swartberg Pass, with motor vehicle backup.

ACCOMMODATION

Oudtshoorn has a number of large **hotels** catering mainly to tour buses, plus plenty of good-quality B&Bs and guesthouses, a centrally located campsite with chalets, and one of the country's best-run backpacker lodges. Some of the nicest places to stay are in the attractive countryside en route to Cango Caves. You'll need to book months in advance if you want to stay during the Easter holidays, when the week-long **Klein Karoo Nasionale Kunstefees** (KKNK; ⓦ absakknk.co.za), a major arts festival, mostly in Afrikaans, takes place.

Backpacker's Paradise 148 Baron van Reede St ❶044 272 3436, ⓦ backpackersparadise.net. A well-run two-storey hostel along the main drag, with three-quarter beds, en-suite doubles and family rooms as well as dorms. There are nightly ostrich and veg-friendly braais, and a daily shuttle from the Baz Bus drop-off in George to the hostel. The on-site adventure centre organizes cycle trips in the Swartberg Pass and there's a daily shuttle to the Cango Caves, ostrich farm and wildlife ranch, as well as horse-riding. Camping R70, dorm R130, double R400

Berluda On the R328, 15km from Oudtshoorn, en route to Cango Caves ❶044 272 8518, ⓦ berluda.co.za. An avenue of trees leads up to a fairly modern-looking farmhouse with five bedrooms and two self-catering

cottages in a well-established garden. The friendly owners can organize ostrich farm tours on their property 8km away, and there is a pool to cool off in. R1260

Buffelsdrift Game Lodge 7km from town on the road to the caves ❶044 272 0106, ⓦ buffelsdrift.com. The town's top stay, with luxurious en-suite safari tents overlooking a large dam where hippo lurk. Breakfast, served in the grand thatched dining area, is included, and game drives or horseback rides to view rhino, buffalo, elephant, giraffe and various antelope can be included in a package, or paid for separately (see above). R2500

★ De Oue Werf Signposted off the R328 to Cango Caves, 12km north of Oudtshoorn ❶044 272 8712, ⓦ ouewerf .co.za. Luxurious and well-priced garden rooms on a working farm, run by the very welcoming sixth generation of the family. Green lawns run down to a dam, which has a swinging slide and raft to play on, and lots of birdlife. A great option if you're visiting the caves and want to stay in the country. R1120

★ **Gum Tree Lodge** 139 Church St ☎ 044 279 2528, ⓦ gumtreelodge.co.za. A few minutes' walk from the town centre, this peaceful B&B fronts onto a river with good birdlife, and boasts a pool and deck and a well-stocked pub. The five rooms have modern bathrooms, a/c and TV and there's also a two-roomed self-catering cottage sleeping four. Double R830, cottage R1250

Kleinplaas Holiday Resort 171 Baron van Reede St ☎ 044 272 5811, ⓦ kleinplaas.co.za. Well-run, shady camping pitches plus fully equipped self-catering brick chalets, conveniently close to town, with a swimming pool and launderette. The knowledgeable owners will show you the ropes, and can also provide breakfast. Camping R275, chalet R785

EATING AND DRINKING

Bello Cibo 145 Baron van Reede St ☎ 044 272 3245. Relaxed and reasonably priced Italian place with indoor and outdoor seating, making it a good choice for children. Besides pizza and pasta, there are some creative ostrich (R65) dishes. Booking advisable. Mon–Sat 5–11pm.

Buffelsdrift Game Lodge 7km out of town towards Cango Caves ☎ 044 272 0106, ⓦ buffelsdrift.com. Have a great breakfast buffet or lunch on a wooden deck overlooking the waterhole, and do a spot of game viewing at the same time. Local specialities include *roesterkoek* – delicious sandwiches roasted on the coals

(R90). The lodge is open to non-guests for meals, and you could combine it with an elephant encounter or other game activity. Daily 7am–3pm.

Café Brulé *Queen's Hotel*, 5 Baron van Reede St ☎ 044 279 2414, ⓦ queenshotel.co.za. The nicest café in town is in the restored *Queen's Hotel*, which has a rather grand, colonial ambience. Drop in for a generous cooked breakfast, a light lunch such as ostrich burger (R60), or a cappuccino overlooking the main street. They make their own pastries and breads too, and there is a deli counter if you're putting together a picnic. Mon–Fri 7am–5pm, Sat & Sun 7am–4pm.

Cango Caves

30km from Oudtshoorn • Daily 9am–4pm • R80 • ☎ 044 272 7410, ⓦ cangocaves.co.za • From Oudtshoorn, head north for 30km along the signposted, scenic, quiet R328, which continues on to Prince Albert via the majestic Swartberg Pass

The **Cango Caves** number among South Africa's most popular attractions, drawing a quarter of a million visitors each year to gasp at their fantastic cavernous spaces, dripping rocks and rising columns of calcite. In the two centuries since they became known to the public, the caves have been seriously battered by human intervention, but they still provide a stunning landscape growing inside the Swartberg foothills. Don't go expecting a serene and contemplative experience, though: the only way of visiting the caves is on a **guided tour** accompanied by a commentary.

Brief history

San hunter-gatherers sheltered in the entrance caves for millennia before white settlers arrived, but it's unlikely that they ever made it to the lightless underground chambers. **Jacobus van Zyl**, a Karoo farmer, was probably the first person to penetrate beneath the surface, when he slid down on a rope into the darkness in July 1780, armed with a

---

CAVE TOURS

The only way to visit the caves is on a guided tour leaving from the **visitors' complex,** where you'll find some interesting displays about the geology, people and wildlife connected with the caves, a decent restaurant and a souvenir shop. You can chose from two types of tour that leave hourly: the **Standard Tour** (on the hour; 1hr; R80) visits the first six chambers, but far more interesting is the **Adventure Tour** (on the half-hour; 90min; R100), which takes you through the first six chambers then on into the deeper sections, where the openings become smaller and smaller. Squeezing through tight openings with names like **Lumbago Walk**, **Devil's Chimney** and **The Letterbox** is a more authentic experience, but not recommended for the overweight or claustrophobic, and you should wear oldish clothes and shoes with a good grip to negotiate the slippery floors.

lamp. Over the next couple of centuries the caves were explored and pillaged by a growing number of vistors, some of whom were photographed cheerfully carting off wagonloads of limestone columns.

In the 1960s and 1970s the caves were made accessible to mass visitors when a **tourist complex** was built, the rock-strewn floor was evened out with concrete, ladders and walkways were installed, and the caverns were subsequently turned into a kitsch extravaganza with coloured lights, piped music and an indecipherable commentary that drew hundreds of thousands of visitors each year. Under the premiership of Dr Hendrik Verwoerd, the arch-ideologue of racial segregation, a separate "non-whites" entrance was hacked through one wall, resulting in a disastrous through-draft that began dehydrating the caves. Fortunately, the worst excesses have now ended; concerts are no longer allowed inside the chambers, and the coloured lights have been removed.

Calitzdorp

The small Karoo village of **CALITZDORP** hangs in a torpor of midday stillness, with its attractive, unpretentious Victorian streets and handful of wineries. There's little to do here, apart from have coffee, taste some port at one of Calitzdorp's modest **wineries** (see box below), buy some olives and wander through the streets.

ARRIVAL AND INFORMATION

CALITZDORP

By car Calitzdorp is 370km from Cape Town, 50km east of Oudtshoorn on the R62. If you're driving from Cape Town, allow five hours with a lunch stop. If you are travelling between Cape Town and Port Elizabeth along the R62,

Clitzdorp makes a good halfway, overnight stop.
Information The tourist office is at the Shell Garage on Voortrekker Street (Mon–Fri 9am–5pm, Sat 8am–1pm; ☎044 213 3775, ⓦcalitzdorp.org.za).

ACCOMMODATION

Die Dorpshuis 4 Van Riebeek St, opposite the church ☎044 213 3453, ⓦdiedorpshuis.co.za. Exceptional value, airy, no-frills rooms in a nineteenth-century house. There is an on-site restaurant that serves up reasonably priced sandwiches, teas and light meals as well as heavier traditional Karoo food, such as stews and lamb. **R600**
Port-Wine Guest House On the corner of Queen and Station streets ☎044 213 3131, ⓦportwine.net. The smartest and most comfortable guesthouse in town, in a renovated early nineteenth-century homestead with local

paintings on the walls, and a veranda overlooking the Boplaas Estate. There is a pool and rose garden at the back, too. **R850**
Welgevonden Guesthouse St Helena Rd ☎044 213 3642, ⓦwelgevondenguesthouse.co.za. A comfortable country-style guesthouse, on a smallholding adjacent to the Boplaas wines estate, 300m from the main road. The four en-suite bedrooms, set in an 1880 outbuilding, are furnished with brass or wooden bedsteads, patchwork quilts and wooden family heirloom furniture. **R640**

The Groenfontein Valley

A circuitous minor route diverts off the R62, just east of Calitzdorp, and drops into the highly scenic **Groenfontein Valley**. The narrow dirt road twists through the Swartberg foothills, past whitewashed Karoo cottages and farms and across brooks, eventually

SOUTH AFRICAN PORT

Some of South Africa's best **ports** are produced at Calitzdorp's wineries, signposted down side roads, a few hundred metres from the centre of town. The most highly recommended is **Die Krans Estate** (Mon–Fri 9am–5pm, Sat 9am–3pm; free; ☎044 213 3314, ⓦdekrans.co.za), where you can sample the wines and ports – its vintage reserve port is reckoned to be among the country's top three – and stretch your legs on a thirty-minute vineyard walk in lovely countryside. **Boplaas Estate** (Mon–Fri 9am–5pm, Sat 9am–3pm; free tasting; ☎044 213 3326, ⓦboplaas .co.za) also produces some fine, award-winning ports and is worth a visit to see its massive reed-ceiling tasting room, which looks like a cantina that fell off the set of a spaghetti western.

joining the R328 to Oudtshoorn. Winding through these back roads is also an option to reach the Cango Caves (see p.188) and Prince Albert (see below), and is one of the best drives you'll ever do in South Africa. Many of the roads are unsealed but are perfectly navigable in an ordinary car if taken slowly.

ACCOMMODATION — THE GROENFONTEIN VALLEY

2

Kruis Rivier Guest Farm 17km off the R62 (signposted turn off 14km east of Calitzdorp) 044 213 3788, kruisrivier.co.za. Homely, simply furnished cottages beneath the mountains, with lovely streams and waterfalls. It makes an excellent base for hiking, and the owners will also do breakfast on request and provide braai packs, home-made bread and wood. **R400**

Red Stone Hills 6km off the R62 (signposted turn-off 14km east of Calitzdorp) 044 213 3783, redstone.co.za. Four lovely period-furnished Victorian cottages on a working farm in a landscape full of red rock formations. The owners can provide breakfast and dinner on request. Besides walking and cycling trails, there is birdwatching and the four horses on the farm can be ridden. **R580**

★ **The Retreat at Groenfontein** 20km northeast of Calitzdorp and 59km northwest of Oudtshoorn 044 213 3880, groenfontein.com. This isolated Victorian colonial farmstead borders the 2300-square-kilometre Swartberg Nature Reserve, an outstandingly beautiful area of gorges, rivers and dirt tracks. Accommodation is in comfortable en-suite rooms, each with its own fireplace, and rates include full board with vegetarians well catered for – the hospitable and helpful owners turn every evening into a fine dinner party. **R1420**

Prince Albert and around

Isolation has left intact the traditional rural architecture of **PRINCE ALBERT**, an attractive little town 70km north of Oudtshoorn, across the loops and razorbacks of the Swartberg Pass – one of the most dramatic drives imaginable. Although firmly in the thirstlands of the South African interior, on the cusp between the Little and Great Karoo, Prince Albert is all the more striking for its perennial **spring**, whose water trickles down furrows along its streets – a gift that propagates fruit trees and gardens.

The town's essence is in the fleeting impressions that give the flavour of a Karoo *dorp* like nowhere else: the silver steeple of the Dutch Reformed **church** puncturing a deep-blue sky, and residents sauntering along or progressing slowly down the main street on squeaky bikes. The town is also known for its paintings and art works by local artists and **mohair products**, such as rugs, socks, scarves and other garments.

ARRIVAL AND DEPARTURE — PRINCE ALBERT

By car From Cape Town allow 5–6 hours for the 420km trip. The fastest and least scenic route is along the N1, past Laingsburg, and involves no mountain passes (turn off onto the Price Albert Road), though the most scenic route is along the R62 to Calitzdorp or Oudsthoorn, and along the R328 over Swartberg, the mighty, gravelled mountain pass that offers some of the best views in the Western Cape.

By train Trains between Cape Town and Johannesburg (Wed, Fri & Sun; Shosholoza Meyl 086 000 8888) stop at Prince Albert Road station, 45km from the hamlet. Be warned that the trains are often late, and Prince Albert Road station has absolutely no facilities. Arrange to be collected by your guesthouse, or book a taxi in advance through Billy van Rooyen (072 337 3149).

By bus Greyhound buses (083 915 9000, greyhound.co.za) stop daily at Prince Albert Road Station, on the N1, on its Cape Town to Johannesburg run, but you will need to arrange to be picked up (see "by train", above) for the 45km journey to Prince Albert.

INFORMATION AND ACTIVITIES

Information The tourist office on Church Street (Mon–Fri 9am–5pm, Sat 9am–noon; 023 541 1366, princealbert.org.za) has maps with accommodation, restaurants and craft shops, and can point you to other activities in the area, such as olive oil tasting or trips to the largest fig farm in South Africa.

Stargazing tours The Karoo sky is heaven for astronomers because of the lack of light pollution, and you get some of the Southern Hemisphere's sharpest views of the firmament from here. One of the most exciting things to do in Prince Albert is to watch the night skies with resident astronomer Hans Daehne (new moon only; R300 for a lecture and viewing; 072 732 2950, astrotours.co.za); book well in advance.

ACCOMMODATION

Dennehof Guest House Off Christina de Wit St, on the outskirts of town ☎ 023 541 1227, ⓦ dennehof.co.za. Five rooms – the best two with spa baths – in a homestead that is a national monument and one of the town's top stays. They can organize hiking and mountain-biking trips – you're driven up the Swartberg, and descend the terrifying 18km on your own two wheels (R250) – or will rent you a bike for a more sedate day's riding around town (R100). R1060

Karoo Lodge 66 Church St ☎ 023 541 1467 or ☎ 082 692 7736, ⓦ karoolodge.com. You'll find reasonably priced, spacious accommodation at this B&B, run by a hospitable couple. Each of the suites, complete with pure cotton sheets and goose down duvets, leads onto the pool and garden filled with crimson bougainvillea. R980

Karoo Views Margrieta Prinsloo Rd ☎ 023 541 1929, ⓦ karooview.co.za. Upmarket, comfortable self-catering in four modern Karoo-style cottages on the edge of town with views of the Swartberg and surrounding countryside, but close enough to walk into town. R850

Mai's Guest House 81 Church St ☎ 023 541 1188, ⓦ maisbandb.co.za. A comfortable, restored nineteenth-century house with great linen, a/c, a pool and lots of cats. A fabulous breakfast is served under the vines, dished up by the full-of-beans Irish owner. R900

★ **Onse Rus** 47 Church St ☎ 023 541 1380, ⓦ onserus .co.za. Cool, thatched B&B rooms attached to a restored Cape Dutch house, with welcoming and informed owners who serve you tea and cake on arrival. Breakfasts include delicious home-made muesli and local yoghurt, as well as the usual eggs. You can also arrange to visit their nearby farm and labyrinth during the day, for a picnic. R950

EATING

Café Photo Albert 44 Church St ☎ 023 541 1030. You can tuck into local dishes with a Swiss twist on the veranda of this café, such as Swiss pie with biltong (R70). It's also a good spot for a cup of Italian coffee and a freshly made waffle. You'll need to bring your own wine for dinner. Tues–Sun 9am–10pm.

★ **Gallery Cafe** 57 Church St ☎ 023 541 1197. Imaginative dishes cooked by passionate chef Brent, who creates a relaxed ambience above the Prince Albert Gallery, with balcony seating – the first choice for a meal in Prince Albert. Vegetarians and vegans are catered for, there are delightful starters, meat dishes including kudu (R110), springbok and chicken and homemade ice creams: book in advance. Daily 6pm–10pm.

Ladida Coffee Shop At the southern end of Church St. You can sit on the veranda and try home-made ginger beer or coffee with a fig and blue cheese burger (R70) while using the free wi-fi. There is plenty to buy by way of snacks, excellent dried fruit and rusks, as well as local olives that are among the best in South Africa. Mon, Wed–Fri 8am–4pm, Sat & Sun 8am–3pm.

SHOPPING

Gay's Guernsey Dairy Christina de Wit Street, southern end of town ☎ 023 541 1274, ⓦ gaysguernseydairy .yolasite.com. Fantastic, award-winning home-made cheeses, which you can taste before buying, as well as yoghurts and cream. If you're travelling with children, you can take them to watch the milking at sunrise, and walk around

---

GO TO HELL

Prince Albert is one of the best places to begin a trip into the valley of **Die Hel** (also known as Hell, The Hell or Gamkaskloof), part of the Swartberg Nature Reserve. With the Gamka River running through it, the 20km-long fertile valley is a deep cleft between the towering Swartberg mountains that appeals for its silence, isolation and birdlife. The valley was only opened up to road transport in 1962, and still has no electricity supply, petrol, ATMs, cell phone reception or shops.

Although it doesn't look far on the map, you'll need to allow two-and-a-half hours from Port Albert to make the spectacular but tortuous **drive** into it along a dirt road. A 4WD isn't needed, but you shouldn't attempt the drive in December or January without air conditioning. Alternatively, Lisa from *Onse Rus* B&B (see above) organizes **tours** for a minimum of two people, and will pick you up if you want to hike a section of the road (4–12km).

There's **accommodation** at spick-and-span *Nature Conservation Camping and Cottages* (☎ 021 483 0190, ⓦ capenature.co.za/reserves/swartberg-nature-reserve; camping R220; cottage R520), as well as a **restaurant** (daily 7am–8pm), which serves good home cooking and will make up picnic baskets. The restaurant owner, Annetje Joubert, also offers self-catering and camping accommodation and runs informal historical tours of the area (☎ 023 541 1107, ⓦ gamkaskloof.co.za; camping R200, cottage R250/person, tours R50).

the farm looking at the animals. Mon–Fri 7–9am, 10am–noon & 4–6pm, Sat & Sun 7–10am & 4.30–6pm.

Karoo Looms 55 Church St ☎ 023 541 1363, ⓦ karooweavery.co.za. The best place for mohair carpets and rugs with bright, funky designs. Also look out for cotton bath mats off the looms. Mon–Fri 9am–5pm, Sat 9am–1pm.

Prince Albert Gallery 57 Church St ⓦ princealbertgallery .co.za. Out of a number of shops on Church Street, this is the best place to look for artworks and crafts, sculpture, beadwork, jewellery and ceramics. Mon–Fri 9am–4pm, Sat 9am–2pm, Sun 10am–1pm.

2 Matjiesfontein

One of the quirkier manifestations of Victorian colonialism lies 250km northeast of Cape Town at the historic village of **MATJIESFONTEIN** (pronounced "Mikey's-fontayn"). Little more than two dusty streets beside a train track, the village resembles a film set rather than a Karoo *dorp*: every building, including the grand train station, is a classic period piece, with tin roofs, pastel walls, well-tended gardens and Victorian frills. At the eastern end of the main street is the centrepiece, the *Lord Milner*, a hotel decked out with turrets and balconies and fountains by the entrance. If you're passing by, make sure you stop at least for a look around.

The origins of this curious place lie in the tale of a young Scottish entrepreneur, **Jimmy Logan**, who came to Cape Town to work on the railways. He built Matjiesfontein as a health resort – making much play of the clean Karoo air – and it became a gathering point for the wealthy and influential around the turn of the last century. Today the village does brisk trade as a treasured relic.

ACCOMMODATION   MATJIESFONTEIN

Lord Milner ☎ 023 561 3011, ⓦ matjiesfontein.com. Inside the *Lord Milner*, there are huge portraits on the wall, grand staircases, polished brass fittings and, perhaps taking the theme a touch too far, rather surly service from waitresses dressed in black and white, with doilies on their heads. There's also a dimly lit dining room and an aged and creaking bar. R1300

Sutherland

Remote **SUTHERLAND**, fearfully known to South Africans as the coldest spot in the country and featured on every weather report, is actually most notable for its clear, unpolluted skies, and for being one of the handful of places in the world where scientists can study Deep Space. You can visit the Observatory here, which is actually a hilltop covered with huge silver domes, housing massive telescopes where experts from all over the world spend freezing nights, extending human knowledge. The largest telescope here is **SALT** (the **South African Large Telescope**), the second-largest telescope in the southern hemisphere.

Observatory

18km east of Sutherland • Tours Mon–Sat at 10.30am & 2.30pm • R60 • Night tours Mon, Wed, Fri & Sat ; the time depends on the season • R80 • Book tours in advance; punctuality essential • Sat 9am–3pm shorter tours leave on the hour which do not need advance booking • R60 • ☎ 023 571 2436, ⓦ saao.ac.za

Day-time tours of the Observatory start from the informative visitors' centre and take you to see the massive **SALT** – an extremely valuable machine behind protective glass, which is powerful enough, with its 91 hexagonal mirrors, to be able to see just one candle were it placed on the moon. Only scientists at the Observatory actually get to look through SALT, though the night tours provide smaller telescopes for visitors and an interesting talk on the stars.

ACCOMMODATION AND EATING   SUTHERLAND

Halley se Kom Eet *Sterland Boerdery*, 1km before you reach Sutherland on the R345 ☎ 023 571 1405. Modest coffee shop serving muffins and toasted sandwiches (R50), and a set menu (R140) for dinner (advance booking only),

which finishes by 8pm, so that you can attend the stargazing talk. Vegetarians can be catered for, with notice. Mon, Wed–Fri 9am–4pm, Sat 9am–noon, plus Mon–Sat 6–8pm.
★**Kambrokind B&B** 19 Piet Retief St ☎ 023 571 1405, ⓦ sutherlandinfo.co.za. Comfortable and warm rooms in

a house whose owner, amateur astronomer Jurg Wagener, sets up telescopes for guests and gives a nightly stargazing talk, at the nearby *Sterland Boerdery*. He can also book self-catering accommodation for the same price on nearby *Middelfontein Farm*, 1.3km away on the RR354. R800

Karoo National Park

The entrance gate is 2km south of Beaufort West, with the reception by the Rest Camp, 10km into the park • R144 • Gate daily 5am–10pm • Reception daily 7am–7pm • ☎ 023 415 2828, ⓦ sanparks.org/parks/karoo

Karoo National Park's attraction is in its mountainous, spare landscape and the serene atmosphere – and it scores highly as a place to break the long drive between Johannesburg and Cape Town. Near the main restcamp there is an environmental **education centre**, along with three **trails**: an 11km day-walk; a short but informative tree trail; and an imaginative fossil trail (designed to accommodate wheelchairs and incorporating Braille boards), which tells the fascinating 250-million-year geological history of the area and shows fossils of the unusual animals that lived when the Karoo was a vast inland sea. While there are some **black rhino**, big game is limited, although there are some impressive raptors, including the **black eagle**.

ACCOMMODATION | **KAROO NATIONAL PARK**

★**Main Rest Camp** 10km into park ☎ 023 415 2828, ⓦ sanparks.org/parks/karoo. Thirty fully equipped chalets and cottages strung out on either side of the main complex, all positioned with lovely outlooks onto the Karoo landscape. There's a pool nearby, plus a shop selling basic foodstuffs and a restaurant (daily breakfast and dinner included in the rate), which is open to day visitors too. The campsite is hidden away over a rise. Camping R215, double R1010

★**Matoppo Inn** On the corner of Bird and Meintjies streets, Beaufort West ☎ 023 415 1055, ⓦ matoppoinn.co.za. Elegant rooms with brass beds and antique furniture, as well as standard rooms with more modern furnishings, in the town's old *drostdy*, or magistrate's house. The gardens are beautiful – it's a green oasis in the deserty Karoo – and there's a pool, good food all day, and a tranquil atmosphere. R780

The Overberg interior and the Whale Coast

East of the Winelands lies a vaguely defined region known as the **Overberg** (Afrikaans for over the mountain). In the seventeenth century, when Stellenbosch, Franschhoek and Paarl were remote outposts, everywhere beyond them was, to the Dutch settlers, a fuzzy hinterland drifting off into the arid sands of the Karoo.

Of the two main routes through the Overberg, the **N2** strikes out across the interior, a four- to five-hour stretch of sheep, wheat and mountains. North of the N2 is **Greyton**, a charming, oak-lined village used by Capetonians as a relaxing weekend retreat, and the starting point of the **Boesmanskloof Traverse** – a terrific two-day trail across the mountains into the Karoo. The historic Moravian mission station of **Genadendal**, ten minutes down the road from Greyton, has a strange Afro-Germanic ambience that offers a couple of hours' pleasant strolling. **Swellendam**, with its well-preserved streetscape with serene Cape Dutch buildings and superb country museum, is favoured for the first night's stop on a Garden Route tour.

CALEDON SPA

The thermal springs at **Caledon Spa and Casino** (Tues–Sun 10am–7pm; R150; ☎ 028 214 5100), signposted off the N2, make a fun day-trip out of Cape Town, or a restorative stop off the N2. The Victorians built a pool filled with steamy, naturally brown water where the Khoi people had once had wallowing holes, and now there is a series of pools of varying temperatures to luxuriate in. There's also a steam room and sauna, but bring your own towel and robe.

The real draw of the area is the **Whale Coast**, close enough for an easy outing from Cape Town, yet surprisingly undeveloped. The exception is popular **Hermanus**, which owes its fame to its status as the whale-watching capital of South Africa. The whole of this southern Cape coast is, in fact, prime territory for land-based whale-watching. Also along this section of coast is **Cape Agulhas**, the southernmost point on the continent, where rocks peter into the ocean. Nearby, and more exclusive, is **Arniston**, one of the best-preserved fishing villages in the country, and a little to its east the **De Hoop Nature Reserve**, an exciting wilderness of bleached dunes, craggy coast and more whales.

Greyton

Tucked away at the edge of the Riviersonderend (meaning "river with no end") Mountains, the small, peaceful village of **GREYTON** is a favourite weekend destination for Capetonians, based around a core of Georgian and Victorian buildings, shaded by grand old oaks. It offers good guesthouses, cafés, restaurants and places to walk, most notably the **Boesmanskloof Traverse** hike, which crosses the mountains to a point 14km from McGregor.

ARRIVAL AND INFORMATION   GREYTON

By car Greyton is 145km from Cape Town, a journey of around two to two and a half hours. The best route is to turn off the N2, just west of Caledon, and follow the signposted, sealed R406 for 30km – ignore any other signs to Greyton on the N2 as they are for unsealed, difficult roads.

Information The tourist office is at 29 Main St, along the main road as you come into town (Mon–Fri 8am–5pm, Sat 9am–2pm; ☎ 028 254 9414, ⓦ greytontourism.com), and has lists and pictures of the many self-catering cottages in the region.

ACCOMMODATION

Anna's Cottages 1 Market St ☎ 084 764 6012, ⓦ greyton-accommodation.com. Chose from a treehouse with an oak tree growing though it, complete with bath, or three lovely self-catering garden cottages, all attractively and eclectically furnished. Mark Cottage is a large space with two double-bed alcoves, indoor and outdoor cooking facilities, fairy lights and fireplaces. Cottage R600, treehouse R800

High Hopes 89 Main Rd ☎ 028 254 9898, ⓦ highhopes .co.za. One of the best B&Bs in town, in a beautiful country-style home set in large gardens with a swimming pool. There are four rooms, plus a self-contained unit with a kitchen, which can be taken on a B&B or self-catering basis. They offer a variety of therapies, including massage, and rent out bikes, too. R1100

EATING

The town has a short Saturday **market** at the corner of Main Road and Cross Market Street, opposite the church (10am–noon), to which locals bring their produce, including organic vegetables, fabulous and well-priced cheeses, decadent cakes, breads, biscuits and preserves.

Abbey Rose Main Rd ☎ 028 254 9470. A nice garden and street-side setting, with a delightful rose garden and hearty but uncomplicated food – try the oxtail stew (R120) and the malva pudding (R36). Tues 4–10pm, Thurs 11.30am–3pm, Fri & Sat 11.30am–3pm & 6–10pm, Sun 9am–3pm.

Oak and Vigne Café DS Botha St ☎ 028 254 9037. An extremely popular restaurant in an old cottage with an oak-shaded terrace. Fresh bread and croissants are baked daily, plus cooked breakfasts (R50) and good cocktails, such as the Greyton Mule (vodka, ginger beer and lime; R35), though service can be slow. Mon–Sun 8am–5pm.

★**Peccadillo's** 23 Main Rd ☎ 028 254 9066. With a reputation for the best fine dining in town, *Peccadillo's*

serves food with a strong Mediterranean influence – try the local trout dishes, pork belly or wood-fired pizza (R82). A good place to try boutique wines, since the British owner is a wine buff. Thurs–Mon noon–3pm & 6.30–10pm.

★**Searle's Trading Post** 36 Main Rd ☎ 028 254 9550, ⓦ searles.co.za. This rambling establishment has the most appealing vibe in town, with a variety of places to sit indoors and outdoors, a pub, eclectic antiques and kitchenware for sale, and the odd cat lounging on a sofa. Besides the warmth and visual appeal, the food is excellent and well priced, including thin-crust pizzas (R70) and country dishes like roasted pork belly with onions, green beans and sweet potato wedges (R95). Summer Tues–Sat 9am–10pm, Sun 9am–5pm.

THE BOESMANSKLOOF TRAVERSE

The 14km **Boesmanskloof Traverse** takes you from Greyton across the Riviersonderend mountain range to the glaring Karoo scrubland around the town of McGregor (see p.182). No direct roads connect the two towns; to drive from one to the other involves a circuitous two-hour journey.

The classic way to cover the Traverse is to walk from Greyton to **Die Galg** (14km from McGregor), where people commonly spend the night, returning the same way to Greyton the following day. The Traverse rises and falls a fair bit, so you'll have to contend with a lot of strenuous uphill walking. If you're based in Greyton and don't want to do the whole thing, walk to **Oak Falls**, 9km from Greyton, and back. Composed of a series of cascades, it's the highlight of the route, its most impressive feature being a large pool where you can rest and swim in cola-coloured water.

TRAIL PRACTICALITIES

You're free to walk the first 5km of the trail and back, but you'll need a permit (R40 per person per day) to walk to Oak Falls or Die Galg, or to complete the whole route from Greyton to Die Galg: book in advance at the Greyton tourist office (see opposite).

Genadendal

Just 6km from Greyton, **GENADENDAL**, whose name means "valley of grace", was founded in 1737 by Moravians, and some of the ochre and earthy-pink architecture hints at Central European influences. The village's focus is around **Church Square**, dominated by a very Germanic church building dating from 1891. The eighteenth-century bell outside became the centre of a flaming row, when missionary Georg Schmidt annoyed the local white farmers by forming a small Christian congregation with impoverished Khoi – who were on the threshold of extinction – and giving refuge to maltreated labourers from local farms. What really annoyed the farmers was the fact that while they, white Christians, were illiterate, Schmidt was teaching native people, whom they considered uncivilized, to read and write. The Dutch Reformed Church, under the control of the Dutch East India Company, waded in when Schmidt began baptizing converts, and prohibited the mission from ringing the bell which called the faithful to prayer.

In 1838, the mission established the first teacher training college in the country, which the government closed in 1926, on the grounds that coloured people didn't need tertiary education and should be employed as workers on local farms – a policy that effectively ground the community into poverty. In 1995, in recognition of the mission's role in education, Nelson Mandela renamed his official residence in Cape Town "Genadendal".

Swellendam

SWELLENDAM is an attractive historic town at the foot of the Langeberg, 220km from Cape Town. With one of the best country museums in South Africa, it's a congenial stop along the N2 between Cape Town and the Garden Route. And because of its ample supply of good accommodation and its position – poised between the coastal De Hoop Nature Reserve and the Langeberg – it's a suitable base for spending a day or two exploring this part of the Overberg, with the Bontebok National Park, stomping ground of an attractive type of antelope, close at hand to the south. The town is built along a very long main road with no traffic lights; it's most attractive at either end, with a mundane shopping area in the middle. The eastern end is dominated by the museum complex, which serves as a tourist centre of sorts.

Brief history

South Africa's third-oldest white settlement, Swellendam was established in 1745 by Baron Gustav van Imhoff, a visiting Dutch East India Company bigwig. He was deeply concerned about the "moral degeneration" of burghers who were trekking further and further from Cape Town and out of Company control. Of no less concern to the Baron was the loss of revenue from these "vagabonds" who were neglecting to pay the Company for the right to hold land and were fiddling their annual tax returns. The town grew into a prosperous rural centre known for its wagon-making, and for being the last "civilized" port of call for *trekboers* heading out into the interior. The income generated from this helped build Swellendam's gracious homes, many of which went up in smoke in a fire in 1865, which razed much of the town centre.

Oefeningshuis
36 Voortrek St

The only building in the centre to survive the town's 1865 fire was the Cape Dutch-style **Oefeningshuis**. Built in 1838, it was first used as a place for religious activity, then as a school for freed slaves and has surreal-looking clocks with frozen hands carved into either gable end, below which there's a real clock.

Dutch Reformed church
Voortrek St

The imposing **Dutch Reformed church**, dating from 1910, incorporates Gothic windows, a Baroque spire, and Cape Dutch gables into a wedding cake of a building that agreeably holds its own, against the odds, and certainly still draws a good crowd on Sundays.

Drostdy Museum
18 Swellegrebel St • Mon–Fri 9am–4.45pm, Sat & Sun 10am–3.45pm • R20

On the east side of town, a short way from the centre, is the excellent **Drostdy Museum**, a collection of historic buildings arranged around large grounds, with a lovely nineteenth-century Cape garden. The centrepiece is the *drostdy* itself, built in 1747 as the seat of the *landdrost*, a magistrate-cum-commissioner sent out by the Dutch East India Company to control the outer reaches of its territory. The building conforms to the beautiful limewashed, thatched and shuttered Cape Dutch style of the eighteenth century, but the furnishings are of nineteenth-century vintage.

ARRIVAL AND INFORMATION   SWELLENDAM

By car Swellendam is 220km (about 3hrs drive) from Cape Town, on the N2, and 533km from Port Elizabeth, 7hrs drive up the Garden Route.

By bus Coaches, including the Baz Bus, run between Cape Town and Port Elizabeth via Swellendam, dropping off at the *Swellengrebel Hotel*, in the centre of town.

Information The tourist office, 22 Swellengrebel St, in one of the museum buildings (Mon–Fri 9am–5pm, Sat & Sun 9am–2pm; ☎028 514 2770, ⓦswellendamtourism .co.za).

ACCOMMODATION

★**Augusta de Mist** 3 Human St ☎028 514 2425, ⓦaugustademist.com. A 200-year-old homestead with three beautifully renovated cottages, two garden suites and a family unit, all with percale linen, and altogether luxurious and stylish. There's a rambling terraced garden and pool, plus a good restaurant on site, though you need to book meals in advance. R1200

★**Cypress Cottage** 3 Voortrek St ☎028 514 3296, ⓦcypress-cottage.co.za. The seven charming rooms here are great value, and decorated with antiques. The grand house is one of the oldest in town and the friendly owner is a brilliant gardener. R700

HORSERIDING IN SWELLENDAM

At the eastern edge of town, **Two Feathers Horse Trails** (☎082 494 8279, ⓦswellendambackpackers.co.za; 90min rides R350; day-trips for experienced riders R1500) offers good riding in the mountains or forests in the Marloth reserve, securely seated in a western-style saddle.

Eenuurkop Huisie 8km from town on the Ashton Rd ☎028 514 1447, ⊛eenuurkop.co.za. Two self-catering cottages, one with three bedrooms, the other with one, in a stunning setting with great views and access to mountain walks. R800

Hermitage Huisies 3km from town on R60 to Ashton ☎028 514 2308 or ☎082 380 2080, ⊛wildebraam.co.za. Two restored labourers' self-catering cottages, sleeping four or five people, plus a flat for two, on a berry farm, with a duck pond and grazing sheep and horses, ideal for families. The farm next door, *Wildebraam* (same contact details), has two more upmarket cottages. If you want to ride, you can arrange in advance to be taken up the mountain, plus there is berry picking in Nov & Dec, and a liquor-tasting cellar at *Wildebraam*. R530

Lulu's B&B 10 Voortrek St ☎028 514 2202 or ☎082 343 4648. A well-run and centrally located B&B with three en-suite rooms and a self-catering loft apartment (sleeping up to eight people) above. It is the cheapest place in town, but don't expect an elegant guesthouse. R400

Swellendam Backpackers 5 Lichtenstein St ☎028 514 2648 or ☎082 494 8279, ⊛swellendambackpackers .co.za. Swellendam's only hostel is a friendly place, well situated near the Marloth Nature Reserve, and close to the Drostdy Museum, with a large campsite, dorms and decent doubles. Staff can arrange activities including horseriding and hiking permits for Marloth. Children are welcome, as there's lots of space, and there is a convenient on-site bar. Dorm R130, double R410

Swellendam Country Lodge 237 Voortrek St ☎028 514 3629, ⊛swellendamlodge.com. Six garden rooms with separate entrances, reed ceilings and elegant, uncluttered decor in muted hues. There's a veranda for summer days, as well as a swimming pool and well-kept garden. R960

EATING

De Companjie 5 Voortrek St ☎083 399 0299, ⊛decompanjie.co.za. Set in a pleasing historic building that also functions as a lovely guesthouse. It offers breakfasts, salad-based lunches, good teatime eats and hearty dinners, such as steaks (R130) and venison dishes. Wed–Sat 9am–9pm, Sun noon–9pm.

The Old Gaol Coffee Shop Church Square, 8a Voortrek St ☎028 514 3847. A great place where you can get milk tart in a copper pan and *roosterkoek*, traditional bread made on an open fire, with nice fillings (R50). A great choice for kids, with an outdoor play area. Mon, Tues, Sat & Sun 8.30am–5pm, Wed–Fri 8.30am–10pm.

Woodpecker Deli 270 Voortrek St ☎028 514 2924. A casual and reasonably priced restaurant that serves tasty pizzas (R80), pasta, soups and burgers, rather than traditional South African meals. Mon–Sat 11.30am–9pm, Sun 11.30am–5pm.

Bontebok National Park

Just 6km south of Swellendam along the Breede River • Daily: May–Sept 7am–6pm; Oct–April 7am–7pm • R80, overnight visitors free entry • ☎028 514 2735, ⊛sanparks.org/parks/bontebok

Bontebok National Park is a compact 28-square-kilometre reserve at the foot of the Langeberg range that makes a relaxing overnight stop between Cape Town and the Garden Route. The park was established in 1931 to save the Cape's dwindling population of bontebok, an attractive antelope with distinctive cappuccino, chocolate-brown and white markings on its forehead and hindquarters. By 1930, hunting in the area had reduced the number of animals to a mere thirty. Their survival has happily been secured and there are now three hundred of them in the park, as well as populations in other game and nature reserves in the province. There are no big cats in the park, but **mammals** you might encounter include rare Cape mountain zebra, red hartebeest and grey rhebok, and there are more than 120 **bird species**. It's also a rich environment for **fynbos**, with nearly five hundred species here, including erica, gladioli and proteas. Apart from game viewing, there are opportunities to swim in the Breede River, hike a couple of short nature trails and fish.

ACCOMMODATION   BONTEBOK NATIONAL PARK

★**Bontebok National Park** ☎028 514 2735, ⊛san parks.org/parks/bontebok. Self-catering accommodation is available in ten, fully equipped chalets, the best of which have river views. There is also a campsite with very clean washing facilities – the pitches without electricity are cheaper. Camping R220, chalet R910

Pringle Bay and Betty's Bay

The coastal drive along the R44 from Cape Town to Hermanus is spectacular – one of the most beautiful drives in the country – though this stretch is home to a series of rather unattractive, ever developing settlements, including **Pringle Bay** and **Betty's Bay**. The main reason to visit Betty's Bay is for its Botanical Gardens (see below) and its colony of African (jackass) penguins, at **Stony Point Penguin Colony** (daily sunrise–sunset; R20), which can be seen from the well-signposted wooden boardwalk.

2

Harold Porter National Botanical Garden

Off the R44, Betty's Bay • Mon–Fri 8am–4.30pm, Sat & Sun 8am–5pm • R20 • ☎ 028 272 9311

Harold Porter National Botanical Garden is a wild sanctuary of coastal and montane *fynbos* that makes a good stop along the R44, if only to picnic or have tea at its outdoor café. The relatively compact botanical garden extends over two square kilometres from the mountains, through marshland down to coastal dunes. Once here, you'll probably get lured at least some of the way up the *kloof* that runs through the reserve; as you get higher up, you're treated to sea views in one direction and rugged mountains in the other.

Although wildlife in the form of small **antelope**, **baboons** and **leopards** is present, they are rarely sighted and it's more worthwhile to look out instead for the birds and blooms. Four **trails** of between one and three hours meander through the gardens, but you can just as easily take yourself off on an impromptu stroll, up and across the red-stained waters (the colour stems from phenols and tannins leaching from the *fynbos*) running through Disa Kloof.

ACCOMMODATION AND EATING   PRINGLE BAY AND BETTY'S BAY

★**Hook, Line and Sinker** Off Pass Rd, Pringle Bay ☎ 028 273 8688. The best place to eat in the area is run by a husband-and-wife team in their own home. There is only seasonal fish and steak on the menu, cooked on an open fire by larger-than-life Stephan, who has spent years deep-sea diving along the West Coast. Prices are moderate, and you won't eat better fish in the country; you can also buy the catch of the day to take home (R70).

Reservations essential. Mon 7pm til late, Tues–Sun noon–5pm & 7pm til late.
★**Moonstruck on Pringle Bay** 264 Hangklip Rd, Pringle Bay ☎ 028 273 8162, ⓦ moonstruck.co.za. This romantic and palatial modern guesthouse has four huge rooms with sea-facing balconies. It's a short walk from the guesthouse to a bay with good swimming. **R1700**

Hermanus

On the edge of rocky cliffs and backed by mountains, **HERMANUS**, 112km east of Cape Town, sits at the northernmost end of Walker Bay, an inlet whose protective curve attracts calving whales as it slides south to the promontory of Danger Point. From about July, southern right whales (see box, p.200) start appearing in the warmer sheltered bays of the Western Cape, and the town trumpets itself as the **whale capital** of South Africa. To prove it, an official whale crier (purportedly the world's only one) struts around armed with a mobile phone and a dried kelp horn through which he yells the latest sightings. There's even an annual **whale festival** during the last week in September, when the town puts on events ranging from ecology talks to classical recitals – in fact, anything with a whale connection, however tenuous (check ⓦ whalefestival.co.za for details).

There is still the barest trace of a once-quiet cliff-edge fishing village around the historic harbour and in some understated seaside cottages, but for the most part the town has gorged itself on its whale-generated income. An almost continuous five-kilometre cliff path through coastal *fynbos* hugs the rocky coastline from the old harbour to Grotto Beach in the eastern suburbs, and it's from this path that you will spot whales.

Main Road, the continuation of the R43, meanders through Hermanus, briefly becoming Seventh Street. Market Square, just above the old harbour and to the south

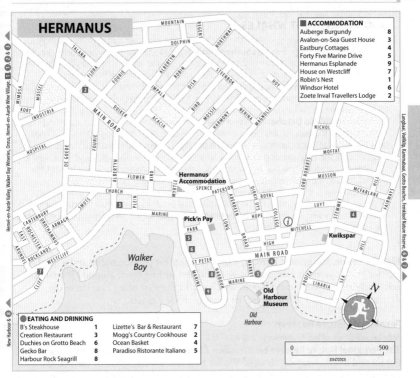

HERMANUS

ACCOMMODATION

Auberge Burgundy	8
Avalon-on-Sea Guest House	3
Eastbury Cottages	4
Forty Five Marine Drive	5
Hermanus Esplanade	9
House on Westcliff	7
Robin's Nest	1
Windsor Hotel	6
Zoete Inval Travellers Lodge	2

EATING AND DRINKING

B's Steakhouse	1	Lizette's Bar & Restaurant	7
Creation Restaurant	3	Mogg's Country Cookhouse	2
Duchies on Grotto Beach	6	Ocean Basket	4
Gecko Bar	8	Paradiso Ristorante Italiano	5
Harbour Rock Seagrill	8		

of Main Street, is the closest thing to a centre, and it's here you'll find the heaviest concentration of restaurants, craft shops and flea markets – the principal forms of entertainment in town when the whales are taking time out.

Old Harbour Museum

At the Old Harbour • Mon–Sat 9am–4.30pm, Sun noon–4pm • R20

The **Old Harbour Museum**, just below Market Square, is home to some uncompelling displays, among which you'll find lots of fishing tackle and sharks' jaws. Outside, a few colourful boats, used by local fishermen from the mid-eighteenth to mid-nineteenth centuries, create a photogenic vignette in the tiny harbour.

New Harbour

A couple of kilometres west of town along Westcliff

The **New Harbour** is a working fishing harbour, dramatically surrounded by steep cliffs, projecting a gutsy counterpoint to the more manicured central area. The whales sometimes enter the harbour – and there's nowhere better to watch them than from the *Harbour Rock* (see p.202).

Beaches and swimming

Just below the *Marine Hotel* on Marine Drive, a beautiful tidal pool offers the only sea swimming around the town centre's craggy coast. For sandy beaches, you have to head out east to the suburbs, where you'll find a decent choice, starting with secluded Langbaai, closest to town, a cove beneath cliffs at the bottom of Sixth Avenue that has a narrow strip of beach and is excellent for swimming. Voelklip, at the bottom of

2

SOUTHERN RIGHT WHALES

All nine of the great whale species of the southern hemisphere pass by South Africa's shores, but the most commonly seen are **southern right whales** (their name derives from being the "right" one to kill because of their high oil and bone yields and the fact that, conveniently, they float when dead). Southern right whales are black and easily recognized from their pale, brownish callosities. These unappealing patches of raised, roughened skin on their snouts and heads have a distinct pattern on each animal, which helps scientists keep track of them.

Female whales come inshore to calve in sheltered bays, and stay to nurse their young for up to three months. **July to October** is the best time to see them, although they start appearing in June and some stay around until December. When the calves are big enough, the whales head off south again, to colder, stormy waters, where they feed on enormous quantities of plankton, making up for the nursing months when the females don't eat at all. Though you're most likely to see females and young, you may see males early in the season boisterously flopping about the females, though they neither help rear the calves nor form lasting bonds with females.

What gives away the presence of a whale is the **blow or spout**, a tall smoky plume which disperses after a few seconds and is actually the whale breathing out before it surfaces. If luck is on your side, you may see whales **breaching** – the movement when they thrust high out of the water and fall back with a great splash.

Eighth Avenue, has grassed terraces, which are great for picnics, toilets and a nearby café for tea. Adjacent is Kammabaai, with the best surfing break around Hermanus, and 1km further east, Grotto Beach, which marks the start of a 12km curve of dazzlingly white sand that stretches all the way to De Kelders.

Fernkloof Nature Reserve

On the east side of town, off Main Rd on Theron St • Daily dawn–dusk • Free

The **Fernkloof Nature Reserve** encompasses fifteen square kilometres of mountainous terrain and offers sweeping views of Walker Bay. It has some 40km of **waymarked footpaths**, including a 4.5-kilometre circular nature trail. Visiting is an excellent way to get close to the astonishing variety of delicate *fynbos* (over a thousand species have been identified in the reserve), much of it flowering species that attract scores of birds, including the brightly coloured sunbirds and sugarbirds endemic to the area.

ARRIVAL AND INFORMATION   HERMANUS

By car The most direct route to Hermanus, 125km from Cape Town, is to take the N2 then head south onto the R43 at Bot River (a 1hr 30min drive), though the winding road that leaves the N2 just before Sir Lowry's Pass, hugs the coast from Strand and is one of the most scenic coastal drives in South Africa (2hr).

By bus The Baz Bus (☎ 021 422 5202, ⊛ bazbus.com) from Cape Town and Port Elizabeth drops off at Bot River 34km north east of Hermanus on the R43, from where you can arrange to be collected by your hostel. Two shuttles – Bernadus (☎ 028 316 1093 or ☎ 083 658 7848) and Splash

(☎ 028 316 4004) – also ply the route between Hermanus and Cape Town (1hr 30min) operating on demand, so you need to book in advance: a single journey from the centre of Cape Town costs R400 per person.

Information The helpful tourist office, at the old station building in Mitchell Street (Mon–Sat: Sept–April 8am–6pm; May–Aug 9am–5pm & Sun 9am–2pm; ☎ 028 312 2629, ⊛ hermanus.co.za), provides maps and brochures about the area, and can book accommodation, whale-watching, and shark-cage diving trips.

ACCOMMODATION

Auberge Burgundy 16 Harbour Rd ☎ 028 313 1201, ⊛ auberge.co.za. A Provençal-style country house in the town centre, close to the water, with a stylish Mediterranean atmosphere and a lavender garden. The rooms are light and airy and decorated with imported French fabrics. R1400

Avalon-on-Sea Guest House 1 Marine Drive ☎ 028

312 1258, ⊛ avalononsea.co.za. Within walking distance of the town centre and right on the cliff path, this seafront house has five rooms, three of which have sea views. Expect comfort but not masses of style. R900

Eastbury Cottages 36 Luyt St ☎ 028 312 1258, ⊛ eastburycottage.co.za. Four very reasonably priced, fully equipped self-catering cottages, near the centre of town. Prices vary depending on group size, and breakfast can be ordered for an extra R70. R580

Forty Five Marine Drive 45 Marine Drive ☎ 028 312 3610, ⓦ 45marinehermanus.com and ⓦ hermanuses planade.com. Cliffside self-catering apartments of varying sizes, with terrific views across the bay. They also have some seafront backpacker apartments, duplex units and cottages further along Marine Drive at *Hermanus Esplanade*, which are more affordable and child-friendly. In December, both properties are booked up months in advance. *Forty Five Marine Drive* R900; *Hermanus Esplanade* R250

House on Westcliff 96 Westcliff Rd ☎ 028 313 2388, ⓦ westcliffhouse.co.za. This homely B&B is situated just out of the centre near the new harbour and boasts six bedrooms in a classic Cape-style house with a protected, tranquil garden and a solar-heated pool and jacuzzi. All rooms are en suite and have their own entrance off the garden, and there is also a three-bed family room. R900

Robin's Nest 10 Meadow Ave ☎ 028 316 1597,

ⓔ leonie.b@telkomsa.net. Three fully equipped, plain, self-catering studio flats above a garage in a garden, 4km west of the centre. Reached through the Hemel-en-Aarde shopping village, these purpose-built, two-storey flats sleep two and have good mountain views. R680

Windsor Hotel 49 Marine Drive ☎ 028 312 3727, ⓦ windsorhotel.co.za. This oldish, but popular seafront hotel offers a range of accommodation right on the cliff edge. It's ideally situated in the centre of Hermanus and guests can enjoy sea views from the dining room, lounges and several of the bedrooms. R1360

Zoete Inval Traveller's Lodge 23 Main Rd ☎ 028 312 1242, ⓦ zoeteinval.co.za. A quiet and relaxing hostel, with a distinct lack of party vibe, comprising dorms, doubles and family suites, with extras like good coffee, a jacuzzi (nice even in the rain) and fireplace. They can organize extra baby beds, tours and outings, and transport to and from the Baz Bus drop-off in Bot River. Dorm R120, double R400, family room R750

EATING AND DRINKING

Seafood is the obvious thing to eat in Hermanus – and you'll find plenty of restaurants serving it – though the views are generally better than the food: book well ahead at weekends and in summer. Alternatively, the nearby wine estate valley of Hemel-en-Aarde, west of town, has some decent restaurants. Hermanus harbour is the place to pick up fish and chips, or head to the **market** at the Hermanus Cricket Grounds (Sat 8am–noon; ⓦ hermanus.co.za/hermanus-market) for excellent Bot River cheeses as well as fresh pasta, pesto, muffins, hummus and baked goods.

HERMANUS

Dutchies on Grotto Beach 10th Avenue, Grotto Beach, Voëlklip ☎ 028 314 1392, ⓦ dutchies.co.za. The

only place to eat on the beach, and a good one at that. There isn't much Dutch character to the menu, but the management and service sparkle. Prices are reasonable – a

WHALE-WATCHING BY LAND, SEA AND AIR

The Southern Cape provides some of the easiest and best places in the world for **whale-watching,** with the graceful creatures easily visible from the shore, if you come at the right time of year. In Hermanus, the best **land-based vantage points** are the concrete cliff paths that ring the rocky shore from New Harbour to Grotto Beach. There are interpretation boards at three of the most popular viewpoints (Gearing's Point, Die Gang and Bientang's Cave), though these are also the most congested spots – during the whale season, the paths can be lined two or three deep with people. Aficionados claim that De Kelders (see p.204), some 39km east of Hermanus, is better, while De Hoop Nature Reserve (see p.207), east of Arniston, is reckoned to be the ultimate place along the southern African coast for whale-watching.

If you prefer to view the whales from the water, note that several operators run **boat trips** from Hermanus, all offering a similar service. Boats must give a fifty-metre berth to whales, but if a whale approaches a boat, the boat may stop and watch it for up to twenty minutes. Hermanus Whale Cruises (☎ 028 313 2722, ⓦ hermanus-whale-cruises.co.za) runs a two-hour boat trip for 87 passengers four times daily from the New Harbour (June–Dec; R650). Further around Walker Bay in Kleinbaai, Marine Dynamics and Dyer Island Cruises, on Geelbek St (☎ 028 384 0406, ⓦ whalewatchsa.com), runs whale cruises daily at 9.15am, 11.45am & 2.15pm (2hr 30min; R900) in the Dyer Island area, with a marine biologist on board.

Perhaps the ultimate way to spot whales is **from the air**. Evan Austin, based in Hermanus (African Wings; ☎ 028 312 2701, ⓦ africanwings.co.za), flies a maximum of three people in a small plane over the bay to view whales, dolphins, sharks and other sea life. Flights range from thirty minutes (R3200) to an hour (R6000), and guarantee whale sightings in season, with the chance to observe mothers and baby whales interacting.

healthy breakfast (hot drink, fresh orange juice, fruit salad, Greek yoghurt and muesli) will set you back just R50, while a Dutch cheese sandwich is R52. Book ahead, especially to get outdoor seating. Daily 8am–9pm.

Gecko Bar New Harbour ☎ 028 312 2920. The large and noisy *Gecko Bar* has great sea views and serves excellent cocktails (R30–50), pizzas and burgers. It's always packed and has occasional live music (smoking is permitted). Daily 12.30pm till late.

★**Harbour Rock Seagrill** New Harbour ☎ 028 312 2920. This busy and fairly upmarket restaurant serves seafood with stunning views. Two favourite dishes are the seafood risotto and the local kabeljou fish (both R135). Daily 12.30–3pm & 6.30–10pm.

★**Lizette's Bar & Restaurant** 20 8th Street, Voelklip ☎ 028 314 0308, ☜ lizetteskitchen.com. Well-known chef Lizette Crabtree cooks up a storm in this spacious restored house, which has plenty of outdoor seating, a play area for kids, water bowls for dogs and a cosy interior. With her experience of cooking in the east, you can expect some flavoursome noodles, and broths such as Vietnamese Pho Bo (R60), as well as Moroccan dishes, some South African favourites with a twist, and burgers. Take-aways available, too. Mon–Thurs 9am–10pm, Fri & Sat 9am–11pm, Sun 9am–4pm.

Ocean Basket Fashion Square, 137 Main Rd ☎ 028 312 1313. Part of a reasonably priced and consistently reliable seafood chain, this restaurant is popular thanks in no small part to its fabulous setting, serving up fish and chips and a seafood platter for two (R220). Daily 11.30am–2.30pm & 6–9pm.

Paradiso Ristorante Italiano 83 Marine Drive ☎ 028 313 1153. Situated behind the village square, near the water in a zone of tourist restaurants, this reliable Italian place serves seafood dishes and chicken, alongside delicious pizza (R80) and pasta. Lunchtime pizzas, with just two toppings, are cheaper (R60). Mon–Sun 11am–9pm.

HEMEL-EN-AARDE

B's Steakhouse Hemel-en-Aarde Village, 5km from Hermanus, on the R43 ☎ 028 316 3625. A friendly and buzzing independent steakhouse serving brilliantly prepared, reasonably priced, slabs of beef (R130). Its formidable wine list and child-friendliness makes it an obvious choice for families, and they get endless repeat visits. Tues–Sun 6.30–10pm.

★**Creation Restaurant** Hemel-en-Aarde Valley, 23km from Hermanus, along the R320 to Caledon ☎ 028 212 1107, ☜ creationwines.com. A fabulous contemporary, elegant – yet informal – restaurant with tables, both inside and out, looking onto the *fynbos*-clad mountains. The antipasto dishes and canapés are sublime, and the food is created to complement the wines (food and wine pairing R125). Children are well catered for, with their own tasting menu of five dishes paired with five surprise drinks (R75). Daily 11am–4pm.

★**Mogg's Country Cookhouse** Hemel-en-Aarde Valley, 12km from Hermanus along the R320 to

---

WINE ROUTE 320

Running along the Hemel-en-Aarde Valley, **Wine Route 320** visits several small wineries dotted along the R320 to Caledon, which branches off the main coastal road, 2km west of Hermanus. Some of South Africa's top **wines** come from these vineyards, which are worth visiting for their first-class wines and intimate tasting rooms, with views of the stark scrubby mountains just inland. They are also known as the Walker Bay wineries after the nearby coast, whose sea breezes influence the kind of grapes grown and wines produced.

Hamilton Russell Winery 8km along the R320 ☎ 028 312 3595, ☜ hamiltonrussellvineyards.com. The longest established of the Walker Bay wineries, Hamilton Russell produces some of South Africa's priciest wines. They are especially known for their Pinot Noir and Chardonnay. Mon–Fri 9am–5pm, Sat 9am–1pm.

Bouchard Finlayson 10km along the R320 ☎ 028 312 3515, ☜ bouchardfinlayson.co.za. This establishment has a formidable reputation, and produces a wide range of wines, including a dry white blend, Blanc de Mer, and its flagship, award-winning Galpin Peak Pinot Noir, grown on the slopes of Galpin peak. Mon–Fri 9.30am–5pm, Sat 9.30am–12.30pm.

Ataraxia Wines 19km along the R320 ☎ 028 212 2007, ☜ ataraxiawines.co.za. Contemporary and stylish, this newish winery offers mountain views from its wine-tasting lounge, which is built like a chapel to contemplate the heavenly wines. Mon–Fri 9am–4pm, Sat 10am–5pm.

★**Creation** 23km along the R320 ☎ 028 212 1107, ☜ www.creationwines.com. The best of the wineries, Creation produces fabulous wines and is known for its gourmet food and wine pairings (daily 11am–4pm), as well as chocolate- and tea-tasting. Its best wines are the Creation Syrah and Syrah Grenache which are dark, fruity and aromatic. A wine tutor will help you to appreciate their complex and delicious wines, all served in the most elegant imported glassware. Book well in advance at weekends. Daily 10am–5pm.

Caledon ☏ 076 314 0671, ⓦ moggscookhouse.com. In an unlikely location for such a successful restaurant – a farm cottage – with superb views across the valley, *Mogg's* is an intimate place that's always full and unfailingly excellent. It serves whatever takes the fancy of chefs Jenny Mogg and her daughter Julia, but might include such dishes as pan-fried fish on red pepper risotto, or chicken breast topped with marinated mozzarella, cherry tomatoes and pesto (R90–125) Booking is essential and children are welcome. Wed–Sun noon–2.30pm

Stanford

East of Hermanus, the R43 takes a detour inland around the attractive Klein River Lagoon, past the pretty riverside hamlet of **STANFORD**. Despite its proximity to hyped-up Hermanus, this historic village, established in 1857, has become something of a refuge for arty types seeking a tranquil escape from the urban rat race. Stanford's principal attraction is its streetscape of simple **Victorian architecture** that includes limewashed houses and sandstone cottages – as well as an Anglican church – with thatched roofs that glow under the late afternoon sun. The town's northern boundary is the attractive **Klein River**, where rich birdlife lives in and among the rustling reed beds lining the riverbanks, and you stand a chance of spotting the flashy malachite kingfisher.

Birkenhead Brewery

Just across the R43 from Stanford along the R326 • **Beer and wine tasting** daily 11am–5pm • **Lunch** Wed–Sun 11am–4pm • ☏ 028 341 0013, ⓦ walkerbayestate.com

Although **Birkenhead Brewery** bills itself as a "craft brewery estate", the gleaming stainless-steel pipes and equipment inside soon dispel any images of bloodshot hillbillies knocking up a bit of moonshine on the quiet. This is a slick operation and a great place to go for a pub lunch or to sample delicious craft beers and wines.

ARRIVAL, INFORMATION AND TOURS · STANFORD

By car Stanford is 173km from Cape Town. Take the Hermanus turning from the N2 (about 90km from Cape Town), and follow the R43 for another 33km through Hermanus to Stanford.

Information The tourist office, on Main Road (Mon–Thurs 8.30am–4.30pm, Fri 8.30am–5pm, Sat 9am–4pm, Sun 9am–1pm; ☏ 028 341 0340, ⓦ stanfordtourism.co.za), can help with booking accommodation, and provide a brochure for a walking tour of the village that takes in various historical houses.

Boat trips The Klein River can be explored on a boat trip or by renting a kayak and setting off on your own (for both, contact Ernie ☏ 083 310 0952; boat trip R100; canoe and kayak rental R100).

ACCOMMODATION

B's Cottage 17 Morton St ☏ 028 341 0430, ⓦ stanford -accommodation.co.za. A small, open-plan, self-catering thatched house, sleeping two upstairs, and one on the couch in the downstairs living room, with an English-style country garden. It's popular and central, so book well ahead. R600

Klein River Cottage On the R326, 7km from Stanford ☏ 028 341 0693, ⓦ kleinrivercheese.co.za/cottage .php. On the Klein River Cheese Farm (p.204), this charming three-bedroomed/two-bathroomed Victorian cottage is right on the river, and has a fireplace for the winter. There's a minimum stay of two nights. R600

Mosaic Farm 10km from Stanford centre, exit from Queen Victoria St ☏ 028 313 2814, ⓦ mosaicfarm.net. In a natural setting with access to a wild part of the lagoon, this farm has 4km of lagoon frontage, with stone, canvas and thatch self-catering chalets, plus the luxury full-board lagoon-side safari camp *Lagoon Lodge* on the same site (R4800). Cruises, nature walks, canoeing and 4X4 excursions to the beach are all available. Chalets R800

★ **Stanford River Lodge** 4km from Stanford centre, exit from Queen Victoria St ☏ 028 341 0444 or ☏ 082 378 1935, ⓦ stanfordriverlodge.co.za. Sunny, spacious and modern self-catering cottages with river and mountain views. It's a lovely, upmarket place with river swimming and canoeing in summer. Owners John and Valda Finch can provide a breakfast basket for a bit extra. R750

EATING

★ **Madres Ktchen** Robert Stanford Estate, 1km west of Stanford ☏ 028 341 0647. The best place for breakfast, while the fabulous lunches include platters of home-made bread, pâtés and cheeses, plus herbs and veggies from the garden, complemented by wines from their own estate (R105). It is great for children, with lawns, a jungle gym and ducks to feed. Thurs–Tues 8am–4pm.

★ **Mariana's Bistro and Home Deli** Du Toit St ☎ 028 341 0272. The innovative and reasonably priced country food served at this Victorian cottage is good enough to draw Cape Town gourmands out for a long lazy lunch. Food and wines are local, and many of the vegetables are picked from the garden of the warm and engaged owners (mains average R110). You'll need to book a couple of months beforehand, though, and ask for a table on the stoep. No children under 10. Thurs–Sun noon–4pm.

SHOPPING

Klein River Cheese Farm 2km beyond Birkenhead Brewery, and 7km from Stanford on the R326 ☎ 028 41 0693, ⓦ kleinrivercheese.co.za. Sample tastings of its famous Gruyere, Leiden, Colby and Dando cheeses, or buy a picnic basket to eat under the trees next to the river (picnics Sept 15 to May 15 daily 11am–3pm; reserve ahead). Mon–Fri 9am–5pm, Sat 9am–1pm.

Raka 17km from town along the R326 ☎ 028 341 0676, ⓦ rakawine.co.za. Sells Stanford's best wine, and also offers wine tastings. Mon–Fri 9am–4.30pm, Sat 10am–2.30pm.

Gansbaai and De Kelders

GANSBAAI, 39km from Hermanus, is a workaday place, economically dependent on its fishing industry and the seafood canning factory at the harbour, which gives the place a gutsier feel than the surrounding holidaylands, but there's little reason to spend time here unless you want to engage in **great white shark safaris** (see box opposite), Gansbaai's other major industry. It is an appropriately competitive and cut-throat business, with operators engaged in a blind feeding frenzy to attract punters.

DE KELDERS, a couple of kilometres further east, is a suburb of Gansbaai. The De Kelders holiday homes and mansions are for the most part bland and ostentatious, but its rocky coast provides outstanding whale-watching and there is access to a beautiful, long sandy beach at the Walker Bay Nature Reserve, known by everyone as "Die Plat", where you can clamber over rocky sections and walk for many kilometres. Swimming is rather dangerous though, so it is best not to venture in more than knee-high.

ARRIVAL AND INFORMATION
GANSBAAI AND DE KELDERS

By car Take the Hermanus off-ramp from the N2 (about 90km from Cape Town), and follow the R43 for another 85km through Hermanus and Stanford.

Information The tourist office is at Great White Junction, Kapokblom St (Mon–Fri 8.30am–5pm, Sat 9am–4pm, Sun 10am–2pm; ☎ 028 384 1439, ⓦ gansbaaiinfo.com).

ACCOMMODATION

Ama-Krokka 28 Vyfer St, De Kelders ☎ 028 384 2776, ⓦ ama-krokka.co.za. While there are no sea views from the rooms, this homely B&B is just 500m from the beach and has a pool. The two suites have their own patio, and a microwave so you can have a stab at self-catering. R1100

Cliff Lodge 6 Cliff St, De Kelders ☎ 028 384 0983, ⓦ clifflodge.co.za. A stylish seafront guesthouse, perched on the cliffs of De Kelders, with breathtaking views from all four luxurious bedrooms and the spacious penthouse suite, plus a deck for whale-watching and a pool. R2200

★ **Crayfish Lodge** Killarney St, De Kelders ☎ 028 384 1898, ⓦ crayfishlodge.net. This is the top stay in town; a palatial guesthouse with sea views and an individual patio or courtyard for all five rooms. If you're treating yourself, go for the upstairs suites with jacuzzis (R3000). A path leads down to a rocky beach with a channel for bathing, and there's a heated swimming pool. R2200

EATING AND DRINKING

Benguela On corner of Church & Harbour streets, Gansbaii ☎ 028 384 2120. Smartish restaurant on a working harbour, offering beautifully presented plates of seafood, meat or vegetarian dishes (R90). Surprisingly, the meat dishes surpass the fish. The desserts are recommended, prices reasonable and the host, Jonathan, is welcoming and friendly. Daily 11am–2pm & 7–10pm.

Coffee on the Rocks Cliff St De Kelders ☎ 028 384 2017. A small bistro that does great coffee, cakes and light meals, with a deck in an unsurpassed position for whale-watching; also a good choice for leisurely Sunday roasts (R85). Booking is essential. Wed–Sun 10am–5pm.

Gansbaai Fisheries Gansbaai Harbour. Enjoy over-the-counter traditional fresh fish and chips (R50), while you

2

DYER ISLAND AND SHARK ALLEY

How a black American came to be living on an island off South Africa in the early nineteenth century is something of a mystery. But, according to records, **Samson Dyer** arrived here in 1806 and made a living collecting guano on the island that subsequently took his name. **Dyer Island** is home to substantial **African penguin** and **seal breeding colonies**, both of which are prized morsels among great white sharks. So shark-infested is the channel between the island and the mainland at some times of year that it is known as **Shark Alley**, and these waters are used extensively by operators of **great white shark viewing trips**. If you go on a trip, you'll be safely contained within a sturdy boat or cage, and do not need to be able to dive.

Marine Dynamics and Dyer Island Cruises Geelbek St, Gansbaai ☎028 384 0406, ⓦwhalewatchsa.com. Whale cruises daily at 9.15am, 11.45am & 2.15pm (2hr 30min; R900) in the Dyer Island area, with a marine biologist on board, as well as shark-cage diving trips (R1500). They also do day-trips from Cape Town (R1850) or Hermanus (R1600); you need to book and pay in advance.

watch the fishing boats come in at the gritty harbour. The best place to sample local fish straight off the boats. Daily 9am–5pm.

★**Grootbos Nature Reserve** 10km from Gansbaai ☎028 384 8008, ⓦgrootbos.com. This delightful eco-lodge is one of the culinary highlights of the area, offering fine-dining traditional cuisine with a modern twist. They only have a set menu, which is very reasonable for the quality; a three-course lunch costs R235, while the five-course dinner is R395. Daily 1–3pm & 6.30–9pm.

Cape Agulhas

Along the east flank of the Danger Point promontory, the rocky and shallow coastline with heavy swells and strong currents makes this one of South Africa's most treacherous stretches of coast – one that has claimed over 250 wrecks and around 2500 lives. Its rocky terrain also accounts for the lack of a coastal road from Gansbaai to **Cape Agulhas**, the southernmost tip of Africa.

The actual tip of the continent is marked by a rock and plaque about 1km from the landmark of Agulhas lighthouse, towards Suiderstrand. Following the dirt road to **Suiderstrand** itself takes you to some beautiful, undeveloped beaches with rock pools to explore, and is definitely the best part of Agulhas.

L'AGULHAS, the rather windblown settlement associated with the southern tip, consists of a small collection of holiday houses and a few shops. It's a much quieter coastal destination than anywhere along the Garden Route, though. The centre of Agulhas, if you can call it a centre, is along Main Road, where you'll find a couple of restaurants, a small supermarket and a craft shop. **Struisbaai**, about 6km east of Agulhas, off the R319, with an attractive harbour and fabulous, long sandy beaches ideal for swimming, is little more than a small collection of holiday homes.

Agulhas Lighthouse

Daily 9am–4.30pm • R25

The red and white **Agulhas Lighthouse**, commissioned in 1849, offers vertiginous views from its top, reached by a series of steep ladders. The appeal of lonely lighthouses on rocky edges beaming out signals to ships at night is explored here through some interesting exhibits about lighthouses around South Africa.

ARRIVAL, INFORMATION AND TOURS   CAPE AGULHAS

By car Agulhas is 230km from Cape Town. Take the N2 to Caledon (115km), then the R316 to Bredasdorp, where the road splits; the more westerly branch (the R319) continues 43km on to Agulhas. The drive takes you through rolling farmlands where you are almost certain to see South Africa's national bird, the elegant and endangered blue crane, feeding in the fields.

Information The tourist office at Agulhas Lighthouse

2

ELIM MISSION STATION

Some 40km northwest of Agulhas, the Moravian mission station of **ELIM** was founded in 1824, its streets lined with thatched, whitewashed houses and fig trees. This central area is the most attractive part of the village, though the rest of it feels rather run-down and forsaken. **Tours**, arranged by Elim tourist office in Church Street (Mon–Sat 9am–12.30pm & 1.30–5pm; ☎028 482 1806) take in the oldest house in the settlement, the church, the restored water mill where wheat is still ground, and the pottery studio. There's also a **memorial** commemorating the emancipation of slaves in 1834, the only such monument in South Africa; its presence reflects the fact that numerous freed slaves found refuge in mission stations like Elim.

(Mon–Sun 9am–5pm; ☎028 435 7185, ⓦ discover capeagulhas.co.za) provides an excellent free guidebook *Discover Cape Agulhas*, with a map of the vineyards and wineries in the area.

Tours Derek Burger of Tip of Africa Safaris (☎082 774 4448, ⓦ tipofafricasafaris.com) offers reliable tours from Cape Agulhas in his comfortable Land Cruiser to De Hoop (R1000) and other remote parts of the coast.

ACCOMMODATION

Agulhas Ocean Art House Main Rd ☎028 435 7503, ⓦ capeagulhas-arthouse.com. A striking modern building with six rooms, each furnished in a contemporary style and with a balcony boasting either sea or mountain views. There's also an on-site café and an art gallery that displays local paintings, photography and sculpture. R2000

Cape Agulhas Backpackers On the corner of Duiker and Main roads ☎082 372 3354, ⓦ capeagulhas backpackers.com. The only budget place around Agulhas has camping, dorms and doubles, all with good bedding, plus a pool and garden. It's run by a couple who can organize boating, surfing lessons, kiteboarding, horse-riding and other activities around Struisbaai. Pick-ups from Botrivier or Swellendam can be arranged. Camping R70, dorm R120, double R350

★**Pebble Beach** Suiderstrand, follow signs to the

Southern Tip of Africa, and then the signs for Suiderstand, 4km beyond ☎028 435 7270 or ☎082 774 5008, ⓦ pebble-beach.co.za. Uniquely positioned on the edge of Agulhas National Park, with kilometres of undeveloped beach to the west, and the scent of *fynbos* wafting in from the dunes. A modern, thatched house, this sea-facing guesthouse has three en-suite rooms, all with white beds and wooden floors. The upstairs bedroom features a bath and large balcony with sea views. R1050

Southermost B&B On the corner of Van Breda and Lighthouse streets ☎028 435 6565, ⓦ southermost .co.za. A well-loved and rather dilapidated historic beach cottage, run by the welcoming Meg, with an indigenous garden sloping down to the water's edge. It is an easy walk from here to the centre to get an evening meal. Closed in winter. R700

EATING

Agulhas Seafoods Main Rd ☎028 435 7207. The best fish and chips (R55) in the region – people even travel from as far as Cape Town to enjoy them. As well as local fish, they also serve calamari. Mon–Sat 10am–7pm, Sun 10am–3pm.

Twisted Fork Restaurant and Bar 184 Main Rd ☎028 435 6291. This is the place to go for a night out at the pub, and the food is not bad either. The Thai chicken

and prawn curry is recommended (R95), and the catch of the day is served with excellent chips. Daily 11am–2am.

Zuidste Kaap 99 Main Rd ☎028 435 7838. Straightforward, no-frills cooking in this elegant thatched restaurant. It has a lovely ambience with an airy, open feel, though no sea views. Recommended dishes include stuffed chicken breasts and locally caught line fish (R135). Mon–Fri 12–10pm, Sat & Sun 11am–9pm.

Arniston

After the cool deep blues of the Atlantic to the west, the azure of the Indian Ocean at **ARNISTON** is startling, made all the more dazzling by the white dunes interspersed with rocky ledges. If you want nothing more than beach life, this is one of the best places to stay in the Overberg. The colours may be tropical, but the wind can howl unpredictably here, as anywhere else along the Cape coast, and when it does, there's nothing much to do. The village is known to locals by its Afrikaans name, Waenhuiskrans ("wagon-house cliff"), after a cliff containing a huge cave 1500m south of town, which *trekboers* reckoned was spacious enough for a wagon and span of oxen. The English name derives from a British ship, the *Arniston*, which hit the rocks here in 1815.

The shallow seas, so treacherous for vessels, provide Arniston with safe swimming waters. You can swim next to the slipway or at **Roman Beach**, the main swimming beach, just along the coast as you head south from the harbour. Apart from sea bathing, the principal attraction is **Kassiesbaai**, a district of starkly beautiful limewashed cottages, now declared a National Monument and home to coloured fishing families that have for generations made their living here. Although it is a living community, Kassiesbaai is also a bit of a theme park for visitors stalking the streets with their cameras. Heading north through Kassiesbaai at low tide, you can walk along an unspoilt beach for 5km.

Heading south of the harbour for 1500m along spectacular cliffs, you'll reach the vast **cave** after which the town is named. From the car park by the cave, it's a short signposted walk down to the *fynbos*-covered dunes and the cave, which can only be reached at low tide. The rocks can be slippery and have sharp sections, so be sure to wear shoes with tough soles and a good grip.

2

ARRIVAL AND DEPARTURE   ARNISTON

By car The town is reached on the R316, 24km southeast of Bredasdorp, and 220km from Cape Town. There's no

public transport to Arniston.

ACCOMMODATION

Arniston Lodge 23 Main Rd ☎028 445 9175, ⓦarnistonlodge.co.za. In the residential area of town, this B&B has four rooms in a two-storey thatched house with a pool. The upstairs rooms have sea views and better bathrooms than those downstairs. R̲1̲1̲9̲0̲

Arniston Resort Signposted 300m from the centre along the main road into Arniston ☎028 445 9620. You can pitch your own tent or stay in one of the four- or six-bed en-suite rather plain and functional bungalows here. The cheaper, older ones don't provide linen, and you'll pay a bit more to have all the mod cons including TV. The place can get crowded and very noisy at weekends and in peak season. R̲4̲8̲0̲

Arniston Seaside Cottages Huxham St, signposted as

you arrive from Bredasdorp ☎028 445 9772, ⓦarnistonseasidecottages.co.za. A series of attractive and modern self-catering places built in the style of traditional fisherman's cottages with limewashed walls and thatched roofs. Clean and bright, they're in a good position just a few minutes' walk from the beach and come fully equipped. R̲6̲4̲0̲

★**Arniston Spa Hotel** Beach Rd ☎028 445 9000, ⓦarnistonhotel.com. Dominating the seafront, this luxurious spa hotel boasts every comfort, including a spa with massage and beauty treatments. The best rooms have a balcony with sea views, or a fireplace. It is one of the best-set beach hotels in the country, and the only one in town. R̲2̲1̲5̲0̲

EATING AND DRINKING

Arniston Hotel Beach Rd. Pleasing fresh fish dinners (R120), with outdoor seating to take in the sea views. It's also home to the town's only bistro bar, which serves burgers and the like and has sport on TV. Daily 11am–9.30pm.

★**Willeen's Meals** Arts and Crafts House C26, Kassiesbaai ☎028 445 9995. An authentic fisherman's

cottage where you'll be served traditional Cape Malay meals, such as *bobotie*, a seafood platter (R150) or fried fish, by family members. They have a BYO booze policy, though soft drinks are available. You can also just have tea and scones in the garden while enjoying the sea views. Daily 8am–10pm.

De Hoop Nature Reserve

Daily 7am–6pm • R40

De Hoop is the **wilderness highlight** of the Western Cape and one of the best places in the world for land-based whale-watching from July to October, with the greatest numbers of whales to be seen in August and September. There's no need to take a boat or use binoculars; in season you'll see whales blowing or breaching – leaping clear of the water – or perhaps slapping a giant tail. Although the reserve could technically be done as a day-trip from Agulhas, Arniston or Swellendam, you'll find it far more rewarding to come here for a night or more. The **Whale Trail** hike is one of South Africa's best walks and among the finest wildlife experiences in the world (6 days; 54km).

The breathtaking coastline is edged by bleached sand dunes standing 90m high in places, and rocky formations that at one point open to the sea in a massive craggy arch. The flora and fauna are impressive, too, encompassing 86 species of mammal, 260 different birds and 1500 varieties of plants. Inland, rare **Cape mountain zebra**, **bontebok** and other **antelope** congregate on a plain near the reserve accommodation.

ARRIVAL AND INFORMATION   DE HOOP NATURE RESERVE

By car The quickest route from Cape Town is along the N2; De Hoop is signposted off it, 13km west of Swellendam. From the Overberg, take the signposted dirt road that spurs off the R319 as it heads out of Bredasdorp, 50km to its west.

By tour You can take a full-day tour from Agulhas or Arniston with Derek Burger of Tip of Africa Safaris (☎ 082

774 4448, ⓦ tipofafricasafaris.com; R1000), who will take you on the dirt roads in his comfortable Land Cruiser.

Information The information office (daily 7am–6pm; ☎ 028 542 1114) is at De Opstel, a twenty-minute drive from the coast. Next door is the reserve's only restaurant, and a small shop that only sells basics, so stock up before you come, in Swellendam or Bredasdorp.

ACCOMMODATION AND EATING

★**De Hoop Cottages** ☎ 021 422 4522, ⓦ dehoopcollection.co.za. All accommodation within the National Park is booked through the De Hoop Collection, and ranges from camping to luxurious cottages, with smaller places for two people, and larger houses for a group. Camping is the cheapest option, since none of the cottages are especially cheap, though all are appealing and comfortable. Camping R295, cottage R800

Fig Tree On the reserve, close to the information office ☎ 028 542 1254. De Hoop's only restaurant uses local ingredients and Elim wines, with good-value set-menu dinners, often including fish (R200). Picnics can be ordered, and there is a lovely place to sit outdoors with a

sundowner after a day at the beach. Reservations are required, especially in winter. Daily 8–11am, noon–3pm & 7–9pm.

Verfheuwel Farm, Potberg Road, in the direction of Malgas, 14km from the entrance to the reserve ☎ 028 542 1038 or ☎ 082 767 0148, ⓦ verfheuwelguestfarm.co.za. This farm cottage accommodation, attached to the main farmhouse, is run by hospitable Afrikaner farming folk, and sleeps a couple, with beds in the living area for children. The garden is beautiful and has a swimming pool, and the owners will bring dinner to your cottage if you book in advance. R700

The Garden Route

The **Garden Route**, a slender stretch of coastal plain between Mossel Bay and Storms River Mouth, has a legendary status as South Africa's paradise – reflected in local names such as **Garden of Eden** and **Wilderness**. This soft, green, forested swath of nearly 200km is cut by rivers from the mountains to the north, tumbling down to its southern rocky shores and sandy beaches.

The Garden Route coast is dominated by three inlets, of which the closest to Cape Town is **Mossel Bay**, an industrial centre of some charm that marks the official start of the Garden Route. Next is **Knysna**, with a well-rooted urban character but no beach. A major draw here is the **Knysna forest**, covering some of the hilly country around Knysna, the awe-inspiring remnants of once vast ancient woodlands. Knysna's eastern neighbour, **Plettenberg Bay**, has good swimming beaches, while all the towns offer a plethora of outdoor activities, from hiking in forests, to marine safaris or exploring deep river gorges on a tube.

Between the coastal towns are some ugly modern holiday developments, but also some wonderful empty beaches and tiny coves, such as **Victoria Bay** and **Nature's Valley**. Best of all is the **Tsitsikamma** section of the Garden Route National Park, which has it all – indigenous forest, dramatic coastline, the pumping **Storms River Mouth** and South Africa's most popular hike, the **Otter Trail**.

FROM TOP LEFT SOUTHERN RIGHT WHALE (BOX, P.200); CAPE MOUNTAIN ZEBRA (P.42); BONTEBOKS(P.32) – ALL DE HOOP NATURE RESERVE (BOX, P.207) >

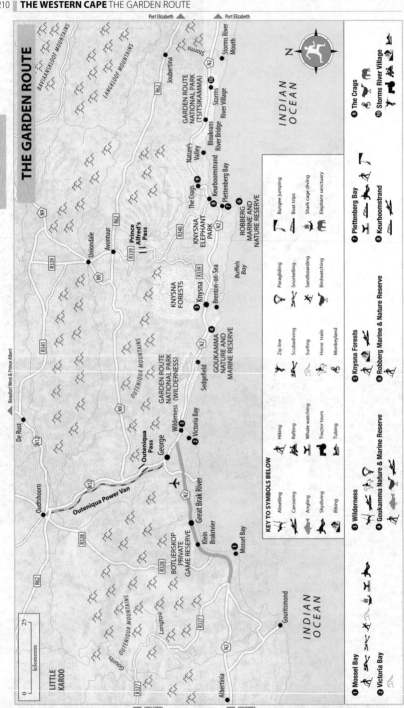

THE GARDEN ROUTE

KEY TO SYMBOLS BELOW

Abseiling · Hiking · Paragliding · Bungee jumping

Canoeing · Rafting · Zip line · Boat trips

Angling · Whale watching · Scubadiving · Shark cage diving

Skydiving · Tractor tours · Surfing · Snorkelling · Elephant sanctuary

Biking · Tubing · Horse trails · Sandboarding

Monkeyland · Birdwatching

1 Mossel Bay
2 Victoria Bay
3 Wilderness
4 Goukamma Nature & Marine Reserve
5 Knysna Forests
6 Robberg Marine & Nature Reserve
7 Plettenberg Bay
8 Keurboomstrand
9 The Crags
10 Storms River Village

Brief history

Khoi herders who lived off the Garden Route's natural bounty considered the area a paradise, calling it *Outeniqua* (the man laden with honey). Their Eden was quickly destroyed in the eighteenth century with the arrival of Dutch **woodcutters**, who had exhausted the forests around Cape Town and set about doing the same in Outeniqua, killing or dispersing the Khoi and San in the process. Birds and animals suffered too from the encroachment of Europeans. In the 1850s, the Swedish naturalist Johan Victorin shot and feasted on the species he had come to study, some of which, including the endangered *narina trogon*, he noted were both "beautiful and good to eat".

Despite the dense appearance of the area, what you see today are only the remnants of one of Africa's great **forests**; much of the indigenous hardwoods have been replaced by exotic pine plantations, and the only milk and honey you'll find now is in the many shops servicing the Garden Route coastal resorts.

2

GETTING AROUND

THE GARDEN ROUTE

By air The airport at George, the largest town on the Garden Route, is served by daily scheduled flights from Johannesburg and Cape Town.

By Baz Bus The daily Baz Bus (☎ 0861 229 287, ⓦ bazbus .co.za) between Cape Town and Port Elizabeth picks up passengers in Cape Town at 7.15–8.30am and Port Elizabeth at 6.45–7.30am. It provides a door-to-door service within the central districts of all the towns along the way, and will happily carry outdoor gear, such as surfboards or mountain bikes. Although the buses take

standby passengers if there's space available, you should book ahead to secure a seat.

By intercity bus Intercape, Greyhound and Translux intercity buses from Cape Town and Port Elizabeth stop at Mossel Bay, George, Wilderness, Sedgefield, Knysna and Storms River (the village, but not the Mouth, which is some distance away). They are better and cheaper than the Baz Bus for more direct journeys, though these the buses often don't go into the town, but let passengers off at petrol stations on the highway instead.

Mossel Bay

MOSSEL BAY, a midsized town 397km east of Cape Town, gets a bad press, mainly because of the huge industrial facade it presents to the N2. Don't panic – the historic centre is a thoroughly pleasant contrast, set on a hill overlooking the small working harbour and bay, with an interesting museum and safe swimming beaches.

Mossel Bay bears poignant historical significance as the place where indigenous Khoi cattle herders first encountered Europeans in a bloody spat. A group of Portuguese mariners under captain **Bartholomeu Dias** set sail from Portugal in August 1487 in search of a sea route to India, and months later rounded the Cape of Good Hope. In February 1488, they became the first Europeans to make landfall along the South African coast, when they pulled in for water at an inlet they called Aguado de Saó Bras ("watering place of St Blaize"), now Mossel Bay. The Khoikhoi were organized into distinct groups, each under its own chief and each with territorial rights over pastures and water sources. The Portuguese, who were flouting local customs, saw it as "bad manners" when the Khoikhoi tried to drive them off the spring. The Portuguese retaliated with crossbow fire that left one of the herders dead.

Bartholomeu Dias Museum Complex

1 Market St • Maritime Museum Mon–Fri 9am–4.45pm, Sat & Sun 9am–3.45pm • R20; Dias caravel R20 extra

Mossel Bay's main urban attraction is the **Bartholomeu Dias Museum Complex**, housed in a collection of historic buildings within a couple of minutes' walk of each other and well integrated into the small town centre. The highlight is the **Maritime Museum**, a spiral gallery with displays on the history of European, principally Portuguese, seafaring, arranged around a full-size replica of Dias' original caravel. The ship was built

2

in Portugal and sailed from Lisbon to Mossel Bay in 1987 to celebrate the five-hundredth anniversary of Dias' historic journey.

The **Post Office Tree**, just outside the Maritime Museum, purportedly may be the very milkwood under which sixteenth-century mariners left messages for passing ships in an old boot. You can post mail here in a large, boot-shaped letterbox and have it stamped with a special postmark. Of the remaining exhibitions, the **Shell Museum and Aquarium**, next to the Post Office Tree, is the only one worth taking time to visit. This is your chance to see some of the beautiful shells found off the South African coast, as well as specimens from around the world.

The Point and St Blaize Lighthouse

East of the harbour, the coast bulges south towards the **Point**, which has several restaurants and a popular bar/restaurant (see p.214) with a deck at the ocean's edge, from which you may see dolphins cruising past.

A couple of hundred metres to the south at the top of some cliffs, the **St Blaize Lighthouse**, built in 1864, is still in use as a beacon to ships. Below it, the **Cape St Blaize Cave** is both a marvellous lookout point and a significant archeological site. A boardwalk leads through the cave past three information panels describing the history of the interpretation of the cave, where in 1888 excavations uncovered stone tools and showed that people had been using the cave for something close on 100,000 years. The path leading up to the cave continues onto the Cape St Blaize trail (see box opposite).

ARRIVAL AND INFORMATION   **MOSSEL BAY**

By bus Of all the buses, only the daily Baz Bus comes right into town, dropping you off at *Mossel Bay Backpackers* and *Park House Lodge*. The intercity buses stop at Shell Voorbaai Service Station, 7km from the centre, at the junction of the national highway and the road into town: 24/7 Taxi (☏ 082 932 5809) will take you into town from the bus stop.

Destinations (intercity buses) Cape Town (6–7 daily; 5hr 30min); Durban (daily; 18hr 30min); George (6–7 daily;

45min); Johannesburg (1–2 daily; 14hr); Knysna (6–7 daily; 1hr 15min); Oudtshoorn (1–2 daily; 1hr 15min); Plettenberg Bay (6–7 daily; 2hr 15min); Port Elizabeth (6–7 daily; 4hr 30min); Pretoria (1–2 daily; 15hr).

Information The tourist office is on the corner of Church and Market streets (Mon–Fri 8am–6pm, Sat & Sun 9am–4pm; ☏ 044 691 2202, ⓦ visitmosselbay.co.za), with shelves of brochures about Mossel Bay and the rest of the Garden Route, and a map of the town.

ACCOMMODATION

While there is no shortage of accommodation in Mossel Bay itself, you may prefer to stay out of town in more rural surroundings. There are a couple of good options just off the R328 towards Oudtshoorn, which takes you over the forested coastal mountains of Robinson Pass into the desiccated Little Karoo, passing some great scenery en route.

MOSSEL BAY

Edward Charles Manor Hotel 1 Sixth Ave ☏ 044 691 2152, ⓦ edwardcharles.co.za. An upmarket two-storey guesthouse in a central location overlooking Santos Beach with a swimming pool. There are fifteen en-suite rooms and a courtesy shuttle to take you to town. R1150

Mossel Bay Backpackers 1 Marsh St ☏ 044 691 3182, ⓦ mosselbaybackpackers.co.za. Well-run lodge with squeaky clean rooms, just 300m from the sea. There's a swimming pool, garden and football table, and they can also book adventure activities. Dorm R170, double R440

Park House Lodge 121 High St ☏ 044 691 1937, ⓦ parkhouse.co.za. Top-notch budget accommodation in twenty rooms distributed across three buildings, one of

which is a beautiful nineteenth-century sandstone manor house. Some rooms have private entrances leading onto the lush garden. Dorm R170, double R780

Protea Hotel Mossel Bay Bartholomeu Dias Museum Complex, Market St ☏ 044 691 3738, ⓦ proteahotels .com/mosselbay. Opposite the tourist office, in an old Cape Dutch manor house, this quaint place in the town centre overlooks Santos Bay and the harbour. Breakfast is served at the nearby *Café Gannet*, Mossel Bay's nicest restaurant (see p.214). R1535

OUT OF TOWN: ALONG THE R328

Eight Bells Mountain Inn 35km from Mossel Bay on the R328 ☏ 044 631 0000, ⓦ eightbells.co.za. A firm favourite with well-heeled families wanting a fully catered

ACTIVITIES AROUND MOSSEL BAY

Mossel Bay is a springboard for popular **activities**, including skydiving, surfing instruction, sandboarding and deep-sea fishing, all of which can be booked through the Garden Route Adventure Centre at *Mossel Bay Backpackers* (☎044 691 3182, ⊛gardenrouteadventures .com).

DIVING AND SNORKELLING

There are several rewarding diving and snorkelling spots around Mossel Bay, though these aren't tropical seas, so don't expect clear warm waters, but with visibility usually between 4m and 10m you stand a good chance of seeing octopus, squid, sea stars, soft corals, pyjama sharks and butterfly fish.

Electro Dive ☎082 561 1259, ⊛www.electrodive .co.za. This outfit rents out gear and runs shore- and boat-based dives to local reefs and wrecks (R240–400 including kit) plus guided snorkelling trips (R220). It also offers Open Water certification courses (around R3800), a scuba crash course (R800) and one-off dives (R400).

HIKING

On the mainland you can check out the coast on the St Blaize hiking trail, an easy fifteen-kilometre walk (roughly 4hr each way) along the southern shore of Mossel Bay; a map is available from the tourist office. The route starts from the Cape St Blaize Cave, just below the lighthouse at the Point, and heads west as far as Dana Bay, taking in magnificent coastal views of cliffs, rocks, bays and coves.

SANDBOARDING AND SURFING

Mossel Bay is one of the best places in the country for sandboarding: the dunes are big, the sand is moist and fine and you pay roughly half what you would in Cape Town. The so-called "Dragon Dune", at 320m, is the longest runnable stretch of sand in the country – the dune tends to run faster during the winter months.

Billeon Surf and Sandboarding Surf Factory, Fields St ☎082 97 11 405, ⊛billeon.com. Runs trips to the "Dragon Dune", which are suitable for all

levels, from beginner to extreme. They also offer surfing instruction, and Mossel Bay has a good beach break suitable for novices (R350 per person for 2hr). All gear is included in the price for both sandboarding and surfing (R380 per person for 3hr; group discounts available).

SKYDIVING

Skydive Mossel Bay Mossel Bay Airfield ☎044 695 1771, ⊛skydivemosselbay.com. For the ultimate adrenaline junkies, Skydive Mossel Bay offers tandem skydives from 3000m (R2000) and skydiving courses.

SHARK ENCOUNTERS

White Shark Africa Corner of Church and Market streets ☎044 691 3796, ⊛whitesharkafrica.com. One of South Africa's better shark-cage operations, they'll let you watch from a boat or go underwater in a cage for R1300. The best months for sightings are March to November, but at no time are encounters guaranteed.

WHALE-WATCHING AND SEAL ISLAND CRUISES

The Romonza ☎044 690 3101, ⊛mosselbay.co.za. A medium-sized yacht, the *Romonza* runs cruises from the yacht marina in the harbour around Seal Island (hourly 10am–3pm; adults R145, children R70), about 10km northwest of Santos Beach, to see the African penguin and seal colonies. It's also the only registered boat in Mossel Bay allowed to run boat-based whale-watching cruises (2–3hr; adults R660, children R400). As elsewhere along this coast, the whale season is variable with southern rights appearing from June till late October. If you're extremely lucky, you may also see a humpback whale.

---

hotel-style holiday, with all sorts of activities laid on for children, including horseriding, swimming, tennis and walking. The atmosphere is friendly and it's superbly run. Out of school holidays it remains a restful place to stay with lovely gardens and extensive grounds, close to the top of the Robinson Pass. R1200

★**Outeniqua Moon Percheron Stud and Guest Farm** 23km from Mossel Bay on the R328, just below the Robinson Pass ☎044 631 0093 or ☎082 564 9782, ⊛outeniquamoon.co.za. Comfortable, classy

self-catering, B&B or full-board accommodation in four colonial cottages or bedrooms on a working farm with beautiful views of the Outeniqua mountains. You can swim laps in the 25m ozone pool, explore the farm's 100 hectares of forest, or spend some time with the huge, serene draft horses, petting foals or taking a carriage ride (R80 per person including tea and cake; 45min). If you eat here, prepare to be spoilt with home-made bread and other farm delights. Double R1300, two-bedroom self-catering cottage R1000

EATING AND DRINKING

Café Gannet Market St ☎ 044 691 1885, ⓦ oldposttree .co.za. Close to the Bartholomeu Dias Museum Complex, Mossel Bay's smartest restaurant serves straightforward seafood dishes, such as grilled sole (R165), at a moderate price in a stylish garden with glimpses across the harbour; it's a good spot for sundowners. Daily 7.30am–10pm.

Delfino's Espresso Bar and Pizzeria Point Village ☎ 044 690 5247. Serves pasta (R65), pizza and steak as well as decent coffee all at reasonable prices, and with great views of the sea. Daily 7am–11pm.

★**Kai** 4 Mossel Bay Harbour ☎ 079 980 3981, ⓦ kaai4 .co.za. Relaxed, rustic, open-air beach restaurant, with sprawling picnic tables in a stunning location right on the beach, where you can watch your seafood cook on an open fire (R85). Although the menu is small, the servings are large and good value for money. Daily 10am–10pm (closed when raining).

King Fisher Point Village ☎ 044 690 6390, ⓦ thekingfisher.co.za. A relaxed joint that, as its name suggests, specializes in seafood, from humble fish and chips to lobster thermidor and everything in between (mains average around R120). There's also a kids' menu. Its elevated position above *Delfino's* means it has excellent views. Daily 11am–11pm.

Botlierskop Private Game Reserve

22km from Mossel Bay, off the R328 • ☎ 044 696 6055, ⓦ botlierskop.co.za

While there is nothing wild about it, **Botlierskop Private Game Reserve** works hard to provide a safari atmosphere, and you will usually (although not always) get to see lions in their huge enclosure – there's also a good chance of spotting rhinos, elephants, giraffes and antelope. Day visitors are welcome to visit and take one of the professionally put together packages, which include a number of activities, such as game drives (R420; 3hr); elephant rides (R520; 30min) and horse rides (R270; 1hr); all activities must be booked in advance.

ACCOMMODATION   BOTLIERSKOP PRIVATE GAME RESERVE

Botlierskop Private Game Reserve 22km from Mossel Bay ☎ 044 696 6055, ⓦ botlierskop.co.za. The luxury tented accommodation here has a real safari vibe, with decks and outdoor seating. There's a lovely pool, a spa and two restaurants, one of which has great views over the river. Half board, including a game drive R2400/person

George

There's little reason to visit **GEORGE**, unless you need what a big centre offers – airport, hospital and shops – and it does lie conveniently halfway between Cape Town and Port Elizabeth. A large inland town, surrounded by mountains, George is a 5km detour northwest off the N2, and 9km from the nearest stretch of ocean at Victoria Bay. Sadly, all that's left of the forests and quaint character that moved Anthony Trollope, during a visit in 1877, to describe it as the "prettiest village on the face of the earth" are some historic buildings, of which the beautiful Dutch Reformed Church in Davidson Street is the most notable. Other than that, George's claim to recent fame (or notoriety) is that it was the parliamentary seat of former State President **P.W. Botha** (see box opposite), the last of South Africa's apartheid hardliners.

ARRIVAL AND DEPARTURE   GEORGE

By car George is 531km from Cape Town (allow 6 hours for the journey) and 66km northeast of Mossel Bay.

By plane Kulula and SAA have daily flights (1hr 50min) between Johannesburg and the small George airport, 10km west of town on the N2. SAA also flies here daily from Cape Town (50min).

By bus Intercape, Translux and Greyhound intercity buses pull in at George station, adjacent to the railway museum on their routes between Cape Town and Port Elizabeth. The Baz Bus drops off at *Outeniqua Backpackers* on Merriman St on its daily run between Cape Town and Port Elizabeth.

Destinations Cape Town (6–7 daily; 6hr); Durban (1 daily; 18hr); Johannesburg (1–2 daily; 15hr); Knysna (6–7 daily; 1hr); Mossel Bay (6–7 daily; 45min); Oudtshoorn (3–4 daily; 1hr 30min); Plettenberg Bay (6–7 daily; 1hr 30min); Port Elizabeth (6–7 daily; 4hr 30min); Pretoria (1–2 daily; 16hr).

2

PRESIDENT BOTHA AND APARTHEID'S LAST STAND

Pieter Willem Botha was the last and most rabid of South Africa's apartheid enforcers. A National Party hack from the age of 20, Botha worked his way up through the ranks, becoming an MP in 1948 and subsequently **Minister of Defence**, a position he used in 1978 to unseat Prime Minister John Vorster. Botha set about streamlining apartheid, modifying his own role from that of a British-style prime minister, answerable to parliament, to one of an executive president taking vital decisions in the secrecy of a President's Council heavily weighted with army top brass.

Informed by the generals that apartheid couldn't be preserved purely through force, Botha embarked on his **Total Strategy**, reforming peripheral aspects of apartheid while fostering a black middle class as a buffer against the ANC. He also pumped vast sums into building an enormous military machine that crossed South Africa's borders to bully or crush neighbouring countries harbouring anti-apartheid activists. At home, security forces were free to murder, maim and torture **opponents of apartheid**.

Botha blustered on through the late 1980s, while his bloated military sucked the state coffers dry. Even National Party stalwarts realized that his policies were leading to ruin, and in 1989, when he suffered a stroke, the party was quick to replace him with **F.W. de Klerk**, who swiftly announced reforms.

Botha lived out his unrepentant retirement near George, declining ever to apologize for the political crimes committed by his administration. Curiously, when he died in 2006, he was given an uncritical, high-profile state funeral, broadcast on national television and attended by members of the government, including then-president, Thabo Mbeki.

ACCOMMODATION

10 Caledon Street 10 Caledon St ☎044 873 4983, ⊛10caledon.co.za. An easy walk to the city centre, this spotless guesthouse on a quiet street is the pick of the mid-priced B&Bs, featuring balconies with mountain views and a garden. The owners are superb hosts and provide an excellent breakfast. R850

Die Waenhuis 11 Caledon St ☎044 874 0034, ⊛diewaenhuis.co.za. Mid-nineteenth-century home that has retained its period character with eleven spacious en-suite rooms, a beautiful garden and gracious hosts. English breakfasts are served in a sunlit dining room. R850

Mount View Resort & Lifestyle Village York St ☎044 874 5205, ⊛mountviewsa.co.za. Modern complex that lacks much character, but offers great value one-, two- and three-bedroom en-suite chalets

and rondavels. The gardens are well kept and pleasant and the complex also houses a wellness and beauty salon, a ten-pin bowling alley and a pool hall. Rondavels R390, chalets R1180

Oakhurst Hotel Corner of Meade & Cathedral streets ☎044 874 7130. Charming, centrally located manor house with a country feel, green lawns, and a peaceful garden with pool. There's a lovely dining area and views of the Outeniqua mountains, too. R1000

Outeniqua Backpackers 115 Merriman St ☎082 316 7720, ⊛outeniqua-backpackers.com. Friendly hostel in a bright and airy suburban house with comfortable dorms and doubles, some with mountain views. There's a swimming pool, and they provide free airport pick-ups. The Baz Bus pulls in here. Dorm R140, double R500

EATING AND DRINKING

Kafe Serefe 60 Courtenay St ☎044 884 1012. Hugely popular venue that serves South African cuisine with a Turkish twist. Meat is the speciality, with dishes such as sirloin steak with blue cheese sauce, walnuts and figs, or pork with goat's cheese and fig sauce (R90). There's also a good choice of mezze, plus belly dancing on Wednesday and Friday nights. Mon–Fri 9am–4.30pm & 6.30–11pm, Sat 6–11pm.

La Capannina 122 York St ☎044 874 5313. Italian restaurant where you eat excellent pizzas and pasta, as well as dishes like beef fillet on a bed of polenta, plus

distinctly un-Italian fare such as ostrich jambalaya with a hint of curry (R85). Mon–Fri noon–10pm, Sat & Sun 6–10pm.

The Old Town House Corner of York and Market streets ☎044 874 3663. There's a lovely ambience in this historic town house, where the food is well cooked with attention to detail in an intimate setting. Although they specialize in venison and beef, vegetarians are well catered for and the baked pasta is delicious (R65). Mon–Fri noon–3pm & 6–10pm, Sat 6–10pm.

Victoria Bay

Some 9km south of George and 3km off the N2 lies the minuscule hamlet of **VICTORIA BAY**, on the edge of a small sandy beach wedged into a cove between cliffs, with a grassy sunbathing area, safe swimming and a tidal pool. During the December holidays and over weekends, the place packs out with day-trippers, and rates as one of the top **surfing** spots in South Africa. Because of the cliffs, there's only a single row of buildings along the beachfront, home to some of the most dreamily positioned guesthouses along the coast (and, therefore, some of the priciest).

ARRIVAL AND DEPARTURE
VICTORIA BAY

By car Arriving by car, you'll encounter a metal barrier as you drop down the hill to the bay, and you'll have to try and park in the car park, which is frequently full (especially in summer). If you're staying at one of the B&Bs, leave your car at the barrier and collect the key from your lodgings to gain access to the private beach road.

By bus The daily Baz Bus provides the only public transport to Victoria Bay, dropping passengers at the *Victoria Bay Surf Lodge*.

ACCOMMODATION

Land's End Guest House The Point, Beach Rd ☎ 044 889 0123, ⊛ vicbay.com/lands-end. En-suite rooms in what claims to be "the closest B&B to the sea in Africa", as well as self-catering accommodation a few doors away at *Bay House*, which sleeps four, and *Sea Cottage*, which sleeps five. **R1300**

Sea Breeze Holiday Resort Along the main road into the settlement ☎ 044 889 0098, ⊛ seabreezecabanas .co.za. A variety of budget self-catering accommodation, including modern two-storey holiday huts and wooden chalets, sleeping two, four or eight people. The huts have no sea views, but it's an easy stroll to the beach. **R660**

VicBay Safari Backpackers Victoria Bay Rd ☎ 044 889 0113, ⊛ vicbaysurfari.co.za. Predominately a surfers' lodge, but with all home comforts including wi-fi, DSTV, a self-catering kitchen and BBQ areas. There's also a trampoline, pool table, table tennis, volleyball and shuttles to the beach and George. The lodge offers surf camps and full- or half-day surf lessons for all levels at the easy, local right-hand point break. Dorm **R180**, double **R750**, family room **R1100**

EATING

There are no food shops or restaurants at Victoria Bay, so you'll need to bring your own supplies. However, there is a marvellous delivery service, run by Mr Delivery in George (☎ 044 873 6677), which will collect pre-ordered takeaways from George, as well as groceries bought on line at Pick 'n' Pay, and even DVDs.

Wilderness

East of Victoria Bay, across the Kaaimans River, the beach at **WILDERNESS** is so close to the N2 that you can pull over for a quick dip and barely interrupt your journey, though you'll struggle to find African wilderness among the sprawl of retirement homes, holiday houses and thousands of beds for rent in the vicinity. The beach, renowned for its long stretch of sand, is backed by tall dunes, blighted by holiday houses. Once in the water, stay close to the shoreline: the coast here is notorious for its unpredictable currents.

The main attraction, though, is the Wilderness section of the Garden Route National Park (see p.218), whose river is lovely to paddle along, with good bird-spotting.

ARRIVAL AND INFORMATION
WILDERNESS

By bus Greyhound, Intercape and Translux buses running between Cape Town and Port Elizabeth stop at the Caltex Garage, on the corner of South St and the N2. The daily Baz Bus stops at Fairy Knowe Backpackers.

Destinations Cape Town (6–7 daily; 7hr 40min); Knysna (6–7 daily; 40min); Mossel Bay (6–7 daily; 1hr); Plettenberg Bay (6–7 daily; 1hr 10min); Port Elizabeth (6–7 daily; 4hr 30min); Sedgefield (6–7 daily; 20min);

Storms River Bridge (6–7 daily; 2hr).

Information The tourist office is in Milkwood Village Mall, Beacon Road, off the N2 opposite the Caltex Garage (Mon–Fri 7.45am–4.30pm, Sat 9am–1pm; ☎ 044 877 0045, ⊛ george.org.za).

Services Wilderness's tiny village centre, on the north side of the N2, has a petrol station and a few shops.

ACCOMMODATION

Beach House Backpackers Western Rd ☏ 044 877 0549, ⓦ wildernessbeachhouse.com. Set on the hill, with ocean views from hammocks on the terrace, *Beach House Backpackers* has very basic dorm rooms and doubles with a communal kitchen. Internet availability is sketchy, and no alcohol can be brought from outside. Cooking classes, surf lessons and board rental are available. Dorm R150, double R450

Fairy Knowe Backpackers 6km from the village, follow signs from the N2 east of Wilderness ☏ 044 877 1285, ⓦ wildernessbackpackers.com. The oldest home (built in 1897) in the area, with a wraparound balcony and set in the quiet woodlands near the Touw River, though nowhere near the sea. In peak season it gets busy and can be very noisy near the bar. The Baz Bus drops off here. Dorm R130, double R480

Island Lake Holiday Resort Lakes Rd, 2km from the Hoekwil/Island Lake turn-off on the N2 ☏ 044 877 1194, ⓦ islandlake.co.za. Camping and self-catering rondavels that sleep four on one of the quietest and prettiest spots on the lakes. The rondavels are basic one-roomed affairs with kitchenettes equipped with hotplates, microwaves and utensils, though the washing and toilet facilities are communal. Camping R220, rondavel R430

Mes-Amis Homestead Buxton Close, signposted off the N2 on the coastal side of the road, directly opposite the national park turn-off ☏ 044 877 1928, ⓦ mesamis .co.za. Nine double rooms, each with its own terrace, offering some of the best views in Wilderness. The rooms are elegantly furnished with crisp white bedding and curtains, plus luxurious touches such as bathrobes and espresso machines in each room. R1400

★ **Palms Wilderness Retreat** Owen Grant Rd ☏ 044 877 1420, ⓦ palms-wilderness.com. With lush tranquil gardens, a pool, spa and lots of private outdoor seating for curling up with a book, you will find plenty here to help you relax and unwind. Rooms with thatched roofs are stylishly decorated, equipped with coffee and tea stations and there is a plush guest lounge with satellite TV and a small library. R1900

Wilderness Bush Camp Heights Rd (follow Waterside Rd west for 1600m up the hill) ☏ 044 877 1168, ⓦ boskamp.co.za. Six self-catering timber units with loft bedrooms, thatched roofs and ocean views. The camp, set on a hillside amid *fynbos* wilderness, is part of a conservation estate that you're free to roam around. R650

EATING

The Girls George Rd ☏ 044 877 1648, ⓦ thegirlsrestaurant.co.za. Deservedly one of the most popular restaurants in the village, *The Girls* fuses classic French dishes, such as steak tartare, with North African and Middle Eastern influences. The prawns are fantastic, they do a mean steak (R150) and vegetarians get a decent look in. Tues–Sun 6pm–late.

Salinas Beach Restaurant Corner of N2 and Zundorf Lane ☏ 044 877 001. An easy stop-off on the N2 with a great view over the beach from tables under umbrellas on the terrace. They're known for fresh fish brought in from Mossel Bay or Knysna, good cocktails (R40) and excellent cheesecake. Daily 11am–10pm.

Serendipity Freesia Ave ☏ 044 877 0433, ⓦ serendipitywilderness.com. A fine-dining restaurant on the banks of the Touw River Lagoon, where a husband-and-wife team cook fabulous meals, with Asian, Mediterranean and South African influences. There's a seasonal five-course set menu (R380), while vegetarians may be tempted by the twice-baked goat's cheese soufflé or aubergine and pumpkin roulade. Book well ahead. Mon–Sat 7pm–late.

Zuchini Timberlake Organic Village ☏ 044 882 1240, ⓦ zucchini.co.za. This restaurant cooks with veg from its own organic gardens and sources free-range or organic meat. The simple, but tasty, meals come in large portions – dishes include gourmet burgers such as the "Dronk Bok" which is topped with brandy-soaked pears (R80), crème fraîche and home-made nut-brittle. Drinks include thirteen types of locally brewed craft beer and sulphur-free wine. Phone before you go as opening times change according to seasons. Mon–Wed 9am–5pm, Thurs–Sun 9am–9pm.

ACTIVITIES IN AND AROUND WILDERNESS

Abseiling, canoeing and kloofing Eden Adventures (☏ 044 877 0179 or ☏ 083 628 8547, ⓦ eden.co.za) offers daily kloofing adventures (8am–1pm, R500) and abseiling (1.30–4.30pm, R500); a full day taking in both activities costs R850. They also rent out two-seater canoes (R50/hr), so that you can explore the Touw River.

Horse Trails Black Horse Trails 19km into the mountains, up the Hoekwil Rd (☏ 082 494 5642, ⓦ blackhorsetrails.co.za) runs mountain and forest horseriding tours using bitless bridles (R275 for 90min or R425 for 3hr).

Paragliding To see it all from the air, sign up with the recommended Cloudbase Paragliding Adventures (☏ 044 877 1414, ⓦ cloudbase-paragliding.co.za) for a tandem paragliding jump that starts from R450 for a minimum of fifteen minutes. You'll only be taken up when the weather offers absolutely safe conditions. They also offer a one-day introductory course for R950.

2

Garden Route National Park: Wilderness Section

Reception Daily 7am–5.30pm • R100 • ☎ 044 877 0046, ⓦ sanparks.org • From the N2, follow road signs to Wilderness National Park to get to the Reception and Ebb and Flow restcamps. For the Western access to the park, drive through the town of Wilderness, across the bridge and turn right for Reception.

Stretching east from Wilderness village is the **Wilderness National Park**, the least aptly named national park in South Africa, as it never feels very far from the rumbling N2. Although the park takes in beach frontage, it's the **forests** you should come for, as well as the 16km of inland waterways; the variety of habitats here includes coastal and montane *fynbos* and wetlands, attracting 250 species of **birds** – as well as many holidaymakers. There are five waymarked **hiking trails** in the Wilderness Section of between two and five kilometres. A map of the trails, which also shows the location of three bird hides, is available at reception or you can download it from the SANParks website (see above). Alternatively, you can rent a **canoe** from Eden Adventures (see box, p.217) and navigate the **Touw River** from the restcamp down to the beach.

ACCOMMODATION   WILDERNESS NATIONAL PARK

The park has two restcamps, *Ebb and Flow North* and *Ebb and Flow South*, both on the west side of the park; they can be booked at ⓦ sanparks.org/parks/garden_route/camps/wilderness.

Ebb and Flow North Right on the river, this restcamp is cheap, old-fashioned and away from the hustle. It offers camping, fully equipped two-person rondavels with their own showers as well as rondavels with communal washing and toilet facilities. Camping **R270**, rondavel **R270**

Ebb and Flow South This site has camping and modern accommodation in spacious log cottages on stilts plus brick bungalows for up to four people (with private kitchen and bathroom). There are also en-suite forest huts with communal kitchens that sleep two. Camping **R240**, hut **R625**, bungalow **R1235**

Goukamma Nature Reserve

Daily 7.30am–4pm • R40, free entry for overnight visitors • ☎ 044 383 0042

An unassuming sanctuary of around 220 square kilometres, **Goukamma Nature Reserve** starts near Sedgefield and stretches east to Buffalo Bay (also known as Buffels Bay). The reserve's boundaries take in the freshwater **Groenvlei Lake** and approximately 18km of beach frontage, as well as some of the highest vegetated dunes in the country. The landscape is good for walking, as it's covered with coastal *fynbos* and dense thickets of milkwood, yellowwood and candlewood trees.

Because of the diversity of coastal and wetland habitats, over 220 different kinds of **birds** have been recorded in the reserve, including fish eagles, Knysna louries, kingfishers and very rare African black oystercatchers. Away from the water, you stand a small chance of spotting one of the area's **mammals**, including bushbuck, grysbok, mongoose, vervet monkeys, caracals and otters.

ARRIVAL AND DEPARTURE   GOUKAMMA NATURE RESERVE

By car Two roads off the N2 provide access to the reserve, though there are no public roads within the reserve itself. The entrance is accessed from the Buffalo Bay side along Buffalo Bay road, and the reserve office is halfway down

here. On the western side, a dirt road runs down to Platbank Beach taking you past the tiny settlement of Lake Pleasant on the south bank of Groenvlei Lake, which consists of little more than a hotel and holiday resort.

ACCOMMODATION

There are two fully equipped bush camps on the Groenvlei side of the reserve and three thatched rondavels on the east side; all can be booked through CapeNature (☎ 021483 0000, ⓦ capenature.co.za). Alternatively, the privately run *Teniqua Treetops* camp is just outside the park, but close enough to explore the area.

★**Teniqua Treetops** 23km northeast of Sedgefield ☎ 044 356 2868, ⓦ teniquatreetops.co.za; map p.225.

A unique and romantic retreat beneath the boughs of virgin forest between Sedgefield and Knysna, that includes 4km

---

ACTIVITIES IN GOUKAMMA NATURE RESERVE

Apart from **angling** and **birdwatching**, the Goukamma offers a number of self-guided activities, including safe **swimming** in Groenvlei Lake. There are also several day-long **hiking** trails that enable you to explore the reserve's different habitats. A beach walk, which takes around four hours one way, traverses the 14km of crumbling cliffs and sands between the Platbank car park on the western side of the reserve and the Rowwehoek one on the eastern side. Alternatively, you can go from one end of the reserve to the other via a slightly longer inland trek across the dunes. There's also a shorter circular walk from the reserve office through a milkwood forest.

Alternatively, you can **canoe** on the Goukamma River on the eastern side of the reserve; a limited number of canoes can be hired from the reserve office during the week or at the gate over the weekend (single canoes R60 a day; double canoes R100).

---

of woodland walks and a river with pools for swimming. Luxury tents are raised on timber decks, and one unit is wheelchair accessible. As well as being a chilled-out hideout, this is a fascinating example of sustainable living in practice: not a single tree was felled to build *Teniqua*; recycled materials were used where possible; water is gravity fed; showers are solar-heated; and toilets use a dry composting system that preserves water. R1660

Knysna

KNYSNA (pronounced "nize-na"), 102km east of Mossel Bay, stands at the hub of the Garden Route. Its lack of ocean beaches is compensated for by its hilly setting around the **Knysna lagoon**, its handsome **forests**, good opportunities for **adventure sports** and a pleasant **waterfront development**. If you're looking for somewhere quiet or rural, Knysna is not for you – it is busy yet sophisticated, with good restaurants and ever-burgeoning housing developments.

Knysna wraps around the lagoon, with its oldest part – the **town centre** – on the northern side. Here, a small historic core of Georgian and Victorian buildings gives the town a distinctive character that is enhanced by coffee shops, craft galleries, street traders and a modest nightlife. The lagoon's narrow mouth is guarded by a pair of steep rocky promontories called **The Heads**, the western side being a private nature reserve and the eastern one an exclusive residential area (confusingly, also called The Heads), along dramatic cliffs above the Indian Ocean. Although you can swim in the lagoon, there's no sea beach at Knysna – the closest one is 20km from town at Brenton-on-Sea.

Brief history

At the beginning of the nineteenth century, the only white settlements outside Cape Town were a handful of towns that would have considered themselves lucky to have even one horse. Knysna, an undeveloped backwater hidden in the forest, was no exception. The name comes from a Khoi word meaning "hard to reach", and this remained its defining character well into the twentieth century. One important figure was not deterred by the distance – **George Rex**, a colonial administrator who placed himself beyond the pale of decent colonial society by taking a coloured mistress. Shunned by his peers in Britain, he headed for Knysna in the early 1800s in the hope of making a killing exporting hardwood from the lagoon.

When Rex died in 1839, Knysna had become a major **timber centre**, attracting white labourers who felled trees with primitive tools for miserly payments, and looked set eventually to destroy the forest. The forest narrowly escaped devastation by far-sighted and effective conservation policies introduced in the 1880s.

By the turn of the twentieth century, Knysna was still remote, and its forests were inhabited by isolated and inbred communities made up of the impoverished descendants of the woodcutters. As late as 1914, if you travelled from Knysna to

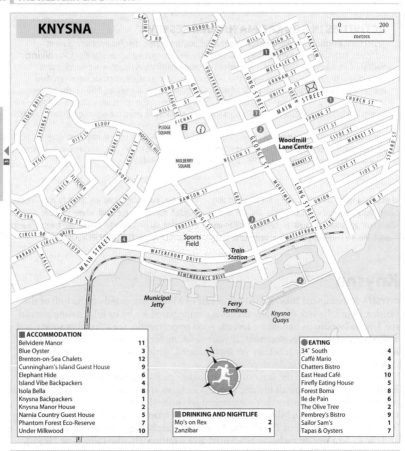

KNYSNA

0 — 200 metres

ACCOMMODATION

Belvidere Manor	11
Blue Oyster	3
Brenton-on-Sea Chalets	12
Cunningham's Island Guest House	9
Elephant Hide	6
Island Vibe Backpackers	4
Isola Bella	8
Knysna Backpackers	1
Knysna Manor House	2
Narnia Country Guest House	5
Phantom Forest Eco-Reserve	7
Under Milkwood	10

DRINKING AND NIGHTLIFE

Mo's on Rex	2
Zanzibar	1

EATING

34° South	4
Caffé Mario	4
Chatters Bistro	3
East Head Café	10
Firefly Eating House	5
Forest Boma	8
Ile de Pain	6
The Olive Tree	2
Pembrey's Bistro	9
Sailor Sam's	1
Tapas & Oysters	7

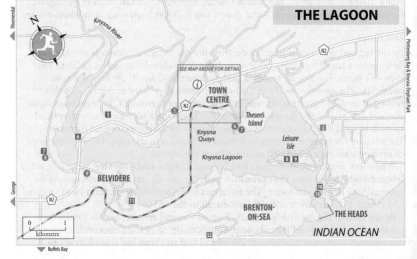

THE LAGOON

SEE MAP ABOVE FOR DETAIL

TOWN CENTRE

Knysna River

Thesen's Island

Knysna Quays

Leisure Isle

Knysna Lagoon

BELVIDERE

BRENTON-ON-SEA

THE HEADS

INDIAN OCEAN

0 — 1 kilometre

Buffels Bay

Rheenendal

George

Plettenberg Bay & Knysna Elephant Park

George you would have to open and close 58 gates along the 75-kilometre track. Fifteen years on, the passes in the region proved too much for **George Bernard Shaw**, who did some impromptu off-road driving and crashed into a bush, forcing Mrs Shaw to spend a couple of weeks in bed at Knysna's *Royal Hotel* with a broken leg.

Knysna Quays and Thesen's Island

About 500m south of Knysna Tourism, at the end of Grey Street

2

Knysna Quays, the town's waterfront complex and yacht basin, was built at the end of the 1990s; the elegant two-storey steel structure with timber boardwalks resembles a tiny version of Cape Town's V&A Waterfront. Here you'll find a mix of hotels, shops and a couple of good eating places, some with outdoor decks, from which you can watch yachts drift past. Further stylish shops and places to eat, at the edge of the lapping lagoon, can be found on **Thesen's Island**, reached by a causeway at the south end of Long Street.

Leisure Isle and Eastern Head

The main reasons to head for **Leisure Isle**, off the eastern suburbs, are the excellent swimming in the lagoon and the views out to sea through the gap between The Heads. The best bathing spots are along the southern shore of the island, particularly the western section along Bayswater Drive, though the swimming is only good around high tide in summer. Continuing south along George Rex Drive brings you to the web of roads winding through the small suburban areas of The Heads.

ARRIVAL AND INFORMATION

KNYSNA

By car Knysna is 491km and six hours' drive from Cape Town on the N2, which merges with Knysna's Main Street as it enters the town.

By Bus The Baz Bus drops off at *Knysna Backpackers* (see below), while Intercape and Translux buses drop passengers at the old train station in Remembrance Avenue opposite Knysna waterfront; Greyhound buses stop at the Toyota Garage, 9 Main Rd.

Destinations Cape Town (6–7 daily; 7hr); Durban (daily;

17hr); George (6–7 daily; 1hr); Johannesburg (1–2 daily; 16hr); Mossel Bay (6–7 daily; 1hr 15min); Oudtshoorn (1–2 daily; 2hr); Plettenberg Bay (6–7 daily; 1hr 30min); Port Elizabeth (6–7 daily; 4hr 30min); Pretoria (1–2 daily; 17hr); and all Garden Route towns along the N2.

Information Knysna Tourism, 40 Main St (Mon–Fri 8am–5pm, Sat 8.30am–1pm; ☎ 044 382 5510, ⓦ visitknysna.co.za), provides maps and can book activities and accommodation around Knysna.

ACCOMMODATION

The best places to stay in Knysna are well away from the N2 main road, with views of the lagoon and The Heads. Out of town there are some excellent establishments as well as some reasonably priced self-catering cottages right in the forest. For somewhere quieter, make for the western edge of the lagoon at Brenton-on-Sea, which has a spectacular beach.

TOWN CENTRE AND KNYSNA QUAYS

Island Vibe Backpackers 67 Main Rd ☎ 044 382 1728, ⓦ islandvibe.co.za; map opposite. Part of the popular *Island Vibe Backpackers* group that is situated along the Garden Route, this branch has a good location, swimming pool and a deck. The facilities are not plush but it is a decent cheap option and an excellent place to sign up for some adventure activities. Dorm R140, double R480

Knysna Backpackers 42 Queen St ☎ 044 382 2554, ⓦ knysnabackpackers.co.za; map opposite. Spotless, well-organized hostel in a large, rambling and centrally located Victorian house that has been declared a National Monument. This tranquil establishment has five rooms rented as doubles (but able to sleep up to four people) and

a dorm that sleeps eight. Dorms R140, double R380

Knysna Manor House 19 Fichat Street ☎ 044 382 5440, ⓦ knysnamanor.co.za; map opposite. A centrally located hundred-year-old house with yellow wood floors and colonial furnishings. It is good value for money although a little dated in style. There are twin, double and family rooms as well as a swimming pool and garden. R870

LEISURE ISLE AND THE HEADS

Cunningham's Island Guest House 3 Kingsway, Leisure Isle ☎ 044 384 1319, ⓦ islandhouse.co.za; map opposite. Purpose-built two-storey, timber-and-glass guesthouse with eight suites, decked out in dazzling white

2

KNYSNA CRUISES

One of the most pleasant trips from Knysna is a **cruise** across the lagoon to The Heads. Knysna Featherbed Company (☎044 382 1693, ⓦknysnafeatherbed.com) runs a number of trips a day from Knysna Quays to The Heads; the shortest takes 75 minutes (R110). For travel beyond The Heads, you can take a sailing trip (1hr 30min; R340) or a sunset cruise (2hr 30min; R655) with delicious food and wine. The only way to reach the private **Featherbed Nature Reserve** on the western side of the lagoon is on a four-hour Featherbed Nature Tour (R530), which includes the boat there, a 4WD shuttle to the top of the western Head and a buffet meal; a slightly shorter version (3hr 45min; R400) excludes the meal. **Bookings** are essential, and can be made at the kiosk on the north side of Knysna Quays; **departures** are from Waterfront Jetty and the municipal jetty on Remembrance Avenue, 400m west of the quays and station.

---

relieved by a touch of blue and some ethnic colour (stripy cushions and African baskets). Each room has its own entrance leading to the garden, which has a swimming pool shaded by giant strelitzias. Stylish and comfortable, its only drawback is the lack of views. R895

Under Milkwood George Rex Drive, The Heads ☎044 384 0745, ⓦmilkwood.co.za; map p.220. Luxury self-catering accommodation on the lagoon at the foot of The Heads with its own private beach – safe for swimming – and terrific views of the mountains and water. Three two-bedroom self-catering units, with their own sundecks, are surrounded by milkwood trees; rates vary depending on the location, and there are hefty off-season discounts. R1459

WEST OF TOWN

Blue Oyster Corner of Rio & Stent streets ☎044 382 2265, ⓦblueoyster.co.za; map p.220. Hospitable three-storey, vaguely Greek-themed B&B set high on one of the hills that rises up behind Knysna, offering fabulous panoramas across the lagoon to The Heads. The four comfortable double rooms, of which the ones on the top floor have the best views, are done out in white and blue. R1000

Elephant Hide Off Knysna Cherry Lane ☎044 382 0426, ⓦelephanthide.co.za; map p.220. Overlooking the Lagoon, 3km from the town centre, this peaceful guesthouse has seven rooms, each lavishly styled with warm and earthy textures and tones. The lagoon suites are a honeymooner's dream, with a spa bath and floor-to-ceiling windows overlooking the lagoon, as well as a private balcony and a king-sized bed. The guesthouse has a spacious communal lounge and a fireplace for winter, and there's a dreamy swimming pool and deck area to laze on in the summer. R1960

Isola Bella 21 Hart Lane, Leisure Isle ☎044 384 0049, ⓦisolabella.co.za; map p.220. You can't help but gasp at the views of The Heads through the huge windows of this imposing guesthouse at the lagoon's edge. You'll either love or loathe the mildly operatic decor – repro furniture, lots of oil paintings and some floral fabrics. Either way, the

rooms are undeniably luxurious. Breakfast is served on the spectacularly positioned balcony overlooking the water. Double R1850, self-catering studio R950

★**Narnia Country Guest House** Signed off Welbedacht Lane, 3km west of Knysna ☎044 382 1334, ⓦnarnia.co.za; map p.220. On a hillside with distant views of the lagoon, this is a fun stone and rough-hewn timber farmhouse in a glorious garden. Decorated in a rustic-chic style, the comfortable, semi-detached two-bedroom cottage downstairs has a lounge, fireplace and kitchenette, while the Pool House sleeps three and leads out onto a large pool with a deck and lovely views. Walks on the property include one down to a small lake. R1500

Phantom Forest Eco-Reserve Phantom Pass Rd, west of town off the N2 ☎044 386 0046, ⓦphantomforest .com; map p.220. Breathtaking, tranquil forest lodge making extensive use of timber and glass, set on a hill in indigenous forest, with fabulous lagoon views. African fabrics and pure cotton linen reinforce the sense of unbridled luxury. Timber boardwalks wind through the forest to connect the suites to the main buildings, which feature a safari-style dining room, an open-air hot tub, a massage suite and a jacuzzi. The swimming pool teeters on the edge of the hill, cocooned by vegetation, with vervet monkeys frolicking in the forest canopy. R4274

THE FOREST

★**Forest Edge Cottages** Rheenendal turn-off, 16km west of Knysna on the N2 ☎082 456 1338, ⓦforestedge.co.za; map p.225. Ideal if you want to be close to the forest itself, these traditional two-bedroom woodcutters' cottages have verandas built in the vernacular tin-roofed style. Self-contained, fully equipped and serviced, they sleep four, while the luxury ones (an extra R300) have free wi-fi, satellite TV and a fireplace. You can also sample produce from the organic vegetable garden and local honey, or collect fresh eggs from the farm's chickens. Forest walks and cycling trails start from the cottages. R750

Southern Comfort Western Horse Ranch 3km along the Fisanthoek Rd, 17km east of Knysna en route to

TOWNSHIP TOURS AND HOMESTAYS

Get a taste of Knysna's townships by joining one of the warts-and-all tours run by **Eco Afrika** (tours daily at 10am & 2pm; R400; booking essential; ☎082 558 9104, ⓦeco-afrika-tours.co.za), that visit five areas, where you'll be given some historical background and get a chance to walk around and chat to people. You can include lunch with a township family as part of the package for an R50.

Eco Afrika can also arrange **homestays** in a shanty town within the townships, where you stay with a family in a corrugated iron shack (R150). The tour operator will drop you off and pick you up the next morning.

Plettenberg Bay ☎044 532 7885, ⓦschranch.co.za; map p.225. Affordable and suitable for large groups, the accommodation here is in very basic double rooms and dorms, on a farm adjacent to the eastern section of the Knysna forest. There are plenty of activities, including horseriding (at 8.30am & 2.30pm; one-hour ride R270, two-hour ride R370), quad-biking (4km; R270) and massages for the saddle-weary. You can self-cater or eat here. Dorm R130, double R300

BELVIDERE AND BRENTON-ON-SEA

Belvidere Manor Duthie Drive, Belvidere Estate ☎044 387 1055, ⓦbelvidere.co.za; map p.220. A collection of tin-roofed reproduction Victorian cottages, nicely positioned on the water's edge. This is the only accommodation in this exclusive leafy area, with its lush gardens and replica Norman church, built in the 1850s. R2400

Brenton-on-Sea Chalets C.R. Swart Drive, Brenton beachfront ☎044 381 0081, ⓦbrentononsea.net; map p.220. A 15min drive from Knysna and overlooking the long curve of Brenton beach, which swings round to Buffels Bay, these three-bedroom, self-catering chalets sleep six people, and are well equipped and comfortably furnished. R980

EATING

Knysna has a lot of good restaurants catering to a wide range of palates, though in summer and holiday periods you'll need to book ahead. There are also one or two excellent coffee shops in town, and no shortage of tempting delis, where you can make up a picnic to take into the surrounding forests, waterways and beaches.

34° South Knysna Quays ☎044 382 7331, ⓦ34-south .com; map p.220. An outstanding deli, café, restaurant, bar and sushi bar selling imported groceries and home-made food. The extensive menu includes seafood in all its guises – from *peri-peri* calamari heads to a Thai red curry mussel pot (R95) and tempura calamari hand rolls (R32). From here you can watch the drawbridge open to let yachts sail through. Daily 8.30am–10pm.

Caffé Mario Knysna Quays ☎044 382 7250; map p.220. An intimate Italian waterside restaurant with outdoor seating, and *paninoteca* and *tramezzini* on its snack menu as well as great pizza (R70) and pasta. The food is consistently good value. Daily 7.30am–10pm.

Chatters Bistro Corner of Gray & Gordon streets ☎044 382 0203, ⓦchattersbistro.co.za; map p.220. With an enclosed garden, a fireplace in winter and eighty wines on the drinks list, this is the place to go in Knysna for superb thin and crispy pizzas (with wheat and gluten-free bases available) and pastas (R70). Tues–Sun noon–9.30pm.

East Head Café 25 George Rex Drive ☎44 384 0933, ⓦeastheadcafe.co.za; map p.220. Very popular café with an outdoor area, panoramic views of the Knysna heads and a kids' playground. Try their simple, delicious seafood dishes (R80), classic wraps and salads, or a killer mojito. Note they don't take bookings and parking can be tricky. Daily 8am–3.30pm.

Firefly Eating House 152a Old Cape Rd ☎044 382 1490, ⓦfireflyeatinghouse.com; map p.220. Relaxed little bistro whose fiery-red decor and sparkling fairy lights match the mid-priced spicy menu. Delicious tapas-style dishes draw their inspiration from Malaysia, Thailand and East and South Africa (R45). Recommended if you like it hot. Tues–Sun 6–10pm.

Forest Boma Phantom Forest Eco-Reserve, Phantom Pass Rd ☎044 386 0046; map p.220. Eating is secondary to the setting here, among the most beautiful in South Africa, in a forest with views of the whole estuary. The six-course pan-African set menu (R400) ranges from kudu and prune *sosatie* (spicy skewered mince) with herb polenta, to pan-fried ostrich in black cherry sauce, and tempting desserts such as brandy snap baskets. Booking essential. Daily 6.30–8.30pm.

★**Ile de Pain** Thesen Island ☎044 302 5707, ⓦiledepain.co.za; map p.220. A trendy restaurant in an artisan bakery that serves salads, baguettes, oysters and pasta dishes. Try the crusty wood-fired bread with butter and preserves for breakfast, or opt for one of the delicious pastries with coffee (R60). Tues–Sat 8am–3pm, Sun 9am–1.30pm.

2

The Olive Tree 12 Wood Mill Lane, Main Rd; map p.220. This local favourite offers bistro dining, with fresh ingredients and Mediterranean-influenced dishes, all beautifully presented (mains average R130). It's great for vegetarians. Mon–Sat 6–10pm.

Pembrey's Bistro Brenton Rd, Belvidere ☏044 386 0005, ⓦpembreys.co.za; map p.220. Small, unpretentious and highly rated restaurant that fuses country cooking with haute cuisine. You'll usually find ostrich, springbok and duck confit with sauces such as balsamic caramelized peaches (R160) on the daily changing menu. The help-yourself Mediterranean-inspired salad buffet, with herbs from the garden, is a winner and appetising starters range from fresh crab and dill ravioli (R85) to veggie friendly options. Wed–Sun 6.30pm–late.

★**Sailor Sam's** Main Rd, opposite the post office ☏044 382 6774; map p.220. A warm-hearted, old-fashioned chippy that offers incredible value, brilliant fish and chips and the cheapest oysters in town (R10 per oyster). Don't tell a soul, but the delicious shellfish aren't local; they're shipped in from the West Coast. Mon–Sat 11am–8.30pm, Sun 11am–3pm.

Tapas & Oysters Thesen Island ☏044 382 7196, ⓦtapasknysna.co.za; map p.220. This is a hip local hang-out with live music on Wed and Fri accompanied by half-price drinks. Inside, it is open and airy with floor-to-ceiling windows and a wrap-around deck, right on the harbour. Sushi is on the menu, as well as both Spanish and South African tapas, including a traditional pickled fish dish, *frikkadelletjies* (meatballs) and smoked snoek (R40). Daily 11am–11pm.

DRINKING AND NIGHTLIFE

Mo's on Rex George Rex Drive ☏044 384 0493; map p.220. A lively, local hang out with loads of atmosphere and a big outdoor beer garden. The restaurant is good value for money too, serving up pizzas (R50) and ribs. Mon–Sat noon–late.

Zanzibar Corner of St George's and Main streets ☏044 382 0386; map p.220. Knysna's longest-established nightclub occupies the premises of the Old Barnyard Theatre and blends everything from pop to commercial house and beyond. It continues with the Barnyard's tradition of occasional live acts that include bands, cabaret and comedy (spirit + mixer R35). Daily noon–2am.

DIRECTORY

Emergencies General emergency number from landline ☏107, from mobile phone ☏112; Police ☏044 302 6600; National Sea Rescue ☏082 990 5956.

Hospital Life Knysna Private Hospital, Hunters Drive (☏044 384 1083), is well run and has a casualty department open to visitors.

Mountain bike rental Knysna Cycle Works, 20 Waterfront Drive (☏044 382 5151, ⓦknysnacycles.com) rents out bikes (from R170/day) and provides maps and information about trails in the Harkerville Forest, which is a brilliant area to explore.

The Knysna forests

The best reason to come to Knysna is for its **forests**, shreds of a once magnificent woodland that was home to **Khoi** clans and harboured a thrilling variety of wildlife, including **herds of elephants**. The forests attracted European explorers and naturalists, and in their wake woodcutters, gold-diggers and businessmen such as George Rex (see p.219), all bent on making their fortunes here.

The French explorer **Francois Le Vaillant** was one of the first Europeans to shoot and kill an elephant in the forest. The explorer found the animal's feet so delicious that he pronounced: "Never can our modern epicures have such a dainty at their tables." Two hundred years later, all that's left of the Khoi people are some names of local places, while the legendary Knysna elephants have fared little better and are teetering on the edge of extinction.

> **EXPLORING THE FORESTS**
> **Knysna Forest Tours and Mountain Biking Africa** (Tony Cook ☏082 783 8392, ⓦmountainbikingafrica.co.za or ⓦknysnaforesttours.co.za) runs guided forest and coastal **hikes**, **trail-running**, **mountain biking** and **canoe trips** in the area, as well as birdwatching and fly fishing. You can also combine two activities into a full-day trip. Half-day hikes start at R495 per person, and biking trips at R580 including refreshments.

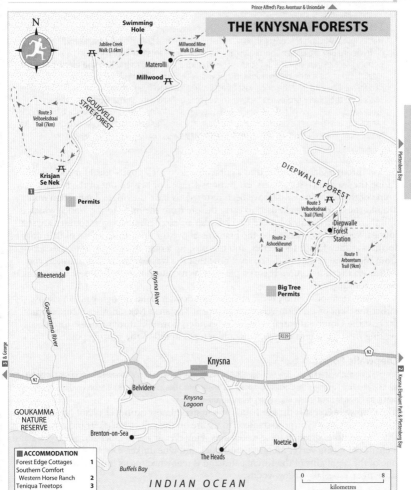

THE KNYSNA FORESTS

N

Prince Alfred's Pass Avontuur & Uniondale

Swimming
Hole

Jubilee Creek
Walk (3.6km)

Millwood Mine
Walk (3.6km)

Materolli

Millwood

GOUDVELD
STATE FOREST

Route 3
Velboeksdraai
Trail (7km)

**Krisjan
Se Nek**

1

Permits

DIEPWALLE FOREST

Route 3
Velboeksdraai
Trail (7km)

Diepwalle
Forest
Station

Route 2
Ashoekheunel
Trail

Route 1
Arboretum
Trail (9km)

Rheenendal

Knysna River

**Big Tree
Permits**

Goukamma River

R339

N2

Knysna

Belvidere

*Knysna
Lagoon*

GOUKAMMA
NATURE
RESERVE

Brenton-on-Sea

Noetzie

ACCOMMODATION
Forest Edge Cottages   1
Southern Comfort
  Western Horse Ranch   2
Teniqua Treetops   3

Buffels Bay

The Heads

INDIAN OCEAN

0   8
kilometres

2

Plettenberg Bay

Knysna Elephant Park & Plettenberg Bay

George

Goudveld State Forest

Just over 30km northwest of Knysna • Daily sunrise–sunset • R100 • Follow the N2 west from Knysna toward George, turning right onto Rheenendal Rd just after the Knysna River, and continue for about 25km, following the Bibby's Koep signposts until the Goudveld sign

The beautiful **Goudveld State Forest** is a mixture of plantation and indigenous woodland. It takes its name from the gold boom (*goudveld* is Afrikaans for goldfields) that brought hundreds of prospectors to the mining town of **Millwood** in the 1880s. The boom was short-lived, and bust followed in 1890 after most of the mining companies went to the wall. Today, the old town is completely overgrown, apart from signs indicating where the old streets stood. The forest itself is still lovely, featuring tall, indigenous trees, a delightful valley with a stream, and plenty of swimming holes and picnic sites.

Hiking in the Goudveld

A number of clearly **waymarked hikes** traverse the Goudveld. The most rewarding (and easy going) is along **Jubilee Creek**, which traces the progress of a burbling brook for

2

THE KNYSNA ELEPHANTS

Traffic signs warning motorists about elephants along the N2 between Knysna and Plettenberg Bay are rather optimistic: there are few elephants left and, with such a large forest, sightings are extremely rare. But such is the mystique attached to the **Knysna elephants** that locals tend to be a little cagey about just how few they number. By 1860, the thousands that had formerly wandered the once vast forests were down to five hundred, and by 1920 (twelve years after they were protected by law), there were only twenty animals left – the current estimate is three. Loss of habitat and consequent malnutrition, rather than full-scale hunting, seems to have been the principal cause of their decline. The only elephants you're guaranteed to see near Knysna are at the **Elephant Sanctuary** (see p.232), near Plettenberg Bay.

3.5km through giant woodland to a gorgeous, deep rock pool – ideal for cooling off. Along the way you'll see miners' excavations scraped or blasted out of the hillside. Some of the old mine works have been restored, as have the original **reduction works** around the cocopan track, used to carry the ore from the mine to the works, which is still there after a century. Jubilee Creek is also an excellent place to encounter **Knysna louries**; keep an eye focused on the branches above for the crimson flash of their flight feathers as they forage for berries. You can pick up a **map** directing you to the creek from the entrance gate to the reserve; note that the waymarked trail is linear, so you return via the same route. There's a pleasant **picnic site** along the banks of the stream at the start of the walk.

A more strenuous option is the circular **Woodcutter Walk**, though you can choose either the 3km or the 9km version. Starting at **Krisjan se Nek**, another picnic site not far past the Goudveld entrance gate, it meanders downhill through dense forest, passing through stands of tree ferns, and returns uphill to the starting point.

Diepwalle Forest

Just over 20km northeast of Knysna • daily 6am–6pm • R100 • From Knysna, follow the N2 east towards Plettenberg Bay, turning left onto the R339 after 7km. Continue in the direction of Avontuur and Uniondale for 17km, when you'll reach the signposted turn-off on your right to the Diepwalle Forest Station, where there's designated parking

The **Diepwalle Forest** is the last haunt of Knysna's almost extinct elephant population. The only elephants you're guaranteed to see are on the painted markers indicating the three main hikes through these woodlands. However, if you're quiet and alert, you stand a chance of seeing vervet monkeys, bushbuck and blue duiker. Diepwalle (deep walls) is one of the highlights of the Knysna area and is renowned for its impressive density of huge trees, especially **yellowwoods**.

Hiking in Diepwalle

Diepwalle's **Elephant Walk** consists of three looped hiking routes covering 7km, 8km and 9km of terrain respectively. They pass through flat to gently undulating country covered by indigenous forest and montane *fynbos*. If you're moderately fit, the hikes should each take three to three-and-a-half hours. All three loops start and end at the **Diepwalle Forest Station** (see above).

The 9km **Route 1**, marked by black elephants, descends through an **arboretum** to a stream edged with tree ferns. Across the stream you'll come to the much-photographed **Big Tree**, a six-hundred-year-old Goliath yellowwood. The easy 8km **Route 2**, marked by white elephants, crosses the Gouna River, where there's a large pool allegedly used by real pachyderms. Most difficult of the three hikes is the rewarding 7km **Route 3**, marked by red elephants, which passes along the foothills of the Outeniquas. Take care here to stick to the elephant markers, as they overlap with a series of painted footprints marking the Outeniqua Trail, for which you need to have arranged a permit to use. Just before the Veldboeksdraai picnic site stands another mighty yellowwood regarded by some as the most beautiful in the forest.

Plettenberg Bay

Over the Christmas holidays, tens of thousands of residents from Johannesburg's wealthy northern suburbs decamp to **PLETTENBERG BAY** (usually called Plett), the flashiest of the Garden Route's seaside towns. Plett's town centre, at the top of the hill, consists of a conglomeration of supermarkets, swimwear shops, estate agents and restaurants largely aimed at the holiday trade. It's wise to give it a miss during peak season, when accommodation is scarce and prices high.

Yet during low season the banal suburban development on the surrounding hills somehow doesn't seem so bad because the bay views really are stupendous. Further afield, the deep-blue **Tsitsikamma Mountains** drop sharply to the inlet and its large estuary, providing a constant vista to the town and its suburbs. The bay curves over several kilometres of white sands separated from the mountains by forest, which makes this a green and temperate location with rainfall throughout the year.

Southern right whales appear every winter, and are a seriously underrated attraction, while **dolphins** can be seen throughout the year, hunting or riding the surf, often in substantial numbers. **Swimming** is safe, and though the waters are never tropically warm they reach a comfortable temperature between November and April. On the east of the bay lies the seaside resort of **Keurboomstrand** and beyond that **The Crags** (both of them more or less suburbs of Plett) with its trio of wildlife parks: Monkeyland, Birds of Eden and the Elephant Sanctuary, all worth a visit, especially if you're travelling with children.

ARRIVAL AND INFORMATION

PLETTENBERG BAY

By car Plettenberg Bay is 33km east of Knysna, 520km from Cape Town and 1 140km from Johannesburg.
By bus The Baz Bus drops passengers off at accommodation in town, while Intercape, Greyhound and Translux intercity buses stop at the Shell Ultra City petrol station, just off the N2 in Marine Way, 2km from the town centre.
Destinations Cape Town (6–7 daily; 7hr 30min); Durban

(daily; 16hr); George (6–7 daily; 1hr 30min); Knysna (6–7 daily; 1hr 30min); Mossel Bay (6–7 daily; 2hr 15min); and Port Elizabeth (6–7 daily; 2hr 30min).
Information The tourist office, Shop 35, Mellville Corner, Main Street (Mon–Fri 9am–5pm, Sat 9am–1pm; ☎044 533 4065, ⊚plettenbergbay.co.za), has maps of the town and may be able to help with booking accommodation.

ACCOMMODATION

IN TOWN
Albergo for Backpackers 8 Church St ☎044 533 4434, ⊚albergo.co.za. Self-catering backpackers, with friendly staff, a nice garden area, free wi-fi, a TV room and a pool table. They can also book adventure activities and have free bodyboards and rent out canoes. It's very popular and can get noisy in high season. Camping R100, dorm R175, double R550
Amakaya Backpackers 15 Park Lane ☎044 533 4010, ⊚amakaya.co.za. Close to town and the beach, this place is well set up for backpackers with communal lounge areas, an outside fire pit and hammocks to while away your time. They also boast an upstairs veranda with a bar and

swimming pool with views of the lagoon and mountains. Minimum stay of two nights at weekends. Dorm R175, double R480
Nothando Backpackers 5 Wilder St ☎044 533 0220, ⊚nothando.com. Top-notch child-friendly hostel run by a former teacher. A 5min walk from Plett's main drag, this suburban home has seven doubles and three dorms. A good breakfast is available for an extra R50. Dorm R160, double R500, family room R820

WEST TO ROBBERG
Anlin Beach House 33 Roche Bonne Ave ☎044 533 3694, ⊚anlinbeachhouse.co.za. Stylish and comfortably

---

PLETT'S BEACHES

Visitors principally come to Plett for its beaches – and there's a fair choice. Beacon Island Beach, or **Main Beach**, right at the central shore of the bay, is where the fishing boats and seacats anchor a little out to sea. The small waves here make for calm swimming, and it's an ideal family spot. **Lookout Beach** is one of the nicest stretches of sand for bathers, or sun lizards, and has a marvellously located restaurant (see p.230), from which you can often catch sight of **dolphins** cruising into the bay. From here you can walk for several kilometres down the beach towards Keurbooms and the **Keurbooms Lagoon**.

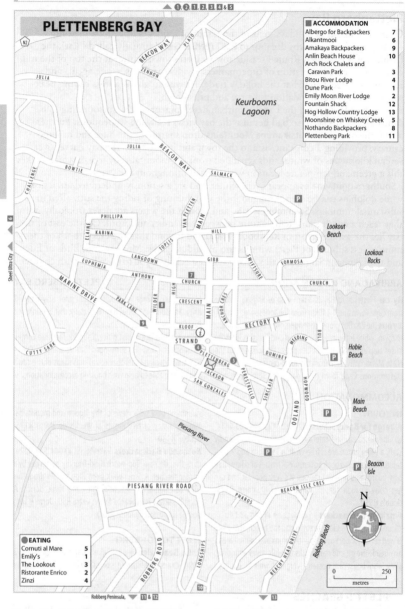

PLETTENBERG BAY

2

N2

JULIA

BEACON WAY

PLATO

ZENNON

Keurbooms
Lagoon

JULIA

BEACON WAY

SALMACK

CHALLENGE

BOWTIE

Steel Ultra City

6

PHILLIPA

ELAINE

KARINA

VAN PLETTEN

MAIN

HILL

Lookout
Beach

3

Lookout
Rocks

EUPHEMIA

LANGDOWN

TOPLIS

GIBB

SWIFTSURE

FORMOSA

ANTHONY

HIGH

CHURCH

CHURCH

MARINE DRIVE

PARK LANE

WILDER

8

CRESCENT

MAIN

ANCHOR CRES

RECTORY LA

BULL

7

9

KLOOF

i

STRAND

4

PLETTENBERG

5

DUMINEY

WEEDING

Hobie
Beach

CUTTY SARK

JACKSON

SAN GONZALES

PERESTRELLO

SINCLAIR

GOOMOOH

OOLAND

Main
Beach

Piesang River

P

P

Beacon
Isle

PIESANG RIVER ROAD

PHAROS

BEACON ISLE CRES

N

ROBBERG ROAD

LONGSHIPS

BEACHY HEAD DRIVE

Robberg Beach

0   250
metres

Robberg Peninsula, ▼ ⓫ & ⓬   ▼ ⓭

■ ACCOMMODATION

Albergo for Backpackers	7
Alkantmooi	6
Amakaya Backpackers	9
Anlin Beach House	10
Arch Rock Chalets and Caravan Park	3
Bitou River Lodge	4
Dune Park	1
Emily Moon River Lodge	2
Fountain Shack	12
Hog Hollow Country Lodge	13
Moonshine on Whiskey Creek	5
Nothando Backpackers	8
Plettenberg Park	11

● EATING

Cornuti al Mare	5
Emily's	1
The Lookout	3
Ristorante Enrico	2
Zinzi	4

kitted out garden studios, luxury suites with kitchenettes and a larger family unit with three bedrooms and a kitchen in a garden setting close to Robberg Beach. The accommodation is serviced daily. **R1900**

★**Fountain Shack** Robberg Nature Reserve ☎ 021 483 0190, ⓦ capenature.co.za/reserves/robberg -nature-reserve. An isolated, renovated wooden cottage sleeping eight, with no electricity and beautifully set above the ocean. There is no vehicle access – you need to walk for two hours to reach it – though linen, cooking facilities and cutlery is provided, so just bring your own food. **R1300**

Plettenberg Park Near the end of Robberg Rd ☎ 044 533 9067, ⓦ plettenbergpark.co.za. Perched on the Robberg cliff edge, this stupendously located and very pricey luxury boutique hotel has seven suites with sea views, while the remaining three look onto a beautiful little lake surrounded by *fynbos*. A set of meandering timber steps leads down from the pool deck to an isolated private beach below with a lovely natural rock pool. R7834

KEURBOOMSTRAND AND EAST OF PLETT
Arch Rock Chalets and Caravan Park Arch Rock ☎044 535 9409, ⬆archrock.co.za. Seventeen fully-equipped chalets, with one or two bedrooms, in the best position at Keurbooms, right on the beach. Apart from the forest chalets and log cabins, which are set back among trees (R600), the rest have sea views. Camping R150, chalet R1100

Bitou River Lodge Bitou Valley Rd (the R340), about 4km from the N2 ☎044 535 9577, ⬆bitou.co.za. Great value in a lovely spot on the banks of the Bitou River, this intimate establishment has five comfortable but unfussy bedrooms that overlook a pretty garden with a lily pond. Rates includes the use of canoes on the river. R1450

Dune Park Keurboomstrand Rd, leading off the N2 and running along the shore to Keurbooms ☎044 535 9606, ⬆dunepark.co.za. Luxury hotel whose airy bedrooms are simple and stylish, with crisp white linen. Two-bedroom self-catering cottages built on top of high dunes provide great views (R1500) within spitting distance of the sea. R850

Emily Moon River Lodge Rietvlei Rd, off the N2 (turn off at Penny Pinchers) ☎044 533 2982, ⬆emilymoon.co.za. This highly imaginative and luxurious lodge, perched on a ridge looking across the Bitou Wetlands, is owned by a dealer in ethnic art. The place is not only littered with Batonga sculptures and Swazi crafts, it has in places been constructed out of artworks, such as the intricate Rajastani arched screen that is the entrance to the magnificently sited restaurant. Each of its chalets jetties out of the hillside to offer views from a private deck (and bathroom) of the oxbowing Bitou, along which small game can occasionally be seen. There is a family suite that sleeps four where children get a discounted rate. R2980

★ **Hog Hollow Country Lodge** Askop Rd, 18km east of Plettenberg Bay (turn south off the N2 at the signpost) ☎044 534 8879, ⬆hog-hollow.com. A touch of luxury on a private reserve where each of the chalets, done out in earthy colours and spiced up with African artefacts, has a its own wooden deck with vistas across the forest and Tsitsikamma Mountains; superb food is served as well. From here, you can hike for a couple of hours through forest to Keurbooms beach, or drive there in 15min. R3112

Moonshine on Whiskey Creek 14km east of Plettenburg Bay along the N2, signposted north of the N2 ☎044 534 8515 or ☎072 200 6656, ⬆whiskeycreek.co.za. Fully equipped bungalows, three wooden cabins and one creatively renovated labourer's cottage (R720), nestled in indigenous forest, with a children's play area. One of the best reasons to come here is the access to a secluded natural mountain pool and waterfall at the bottom of the nearby gorge. Note they don't take credit cards. R1440

EATING AND DRINKING

Restaurants come and go in Plett at a similar lick to the tides, but one or two long-standing establishments have managed to remain afloat. Locally caught fresh fish is the thing to look out for and, because the town is built on hills, many restaurants have terrific views.

WHALING AND GNASHING OF TEETH

For conservationists, the monumental 1970s eyesore of *Beacon Island Hotel*, on a promontory on the southern side of the Piesang River mouth, may not be such a bad thing, since previously it was the site of a whale-processing factory established in 1806 – one of some half-dozen such plants erected along the Western Cape coast that year. Whaling continued at Plettenberg Bay until 1916. Southern right whales were the favoured species, yielding more oil and **whalebone** – an essential component of Victorian corsets – than any other. In the nineteenth century, a southern right would net around three times as much as a humpback caught along the Western Cape coast, leading to a rapid decline in the southern right population by the middle of the nineteenth century. In 1913, Plettenberg Bay was the site of one of seventeen shore-based and about a dozen floating factories between West Africa and Mozambique, which that year between them processed a mammoth ten thousand whales.

Inevitably, a rapid decline in populations began: by 1918, all but four of the shore-based factories had closed owing to lack of prey. The remaining whalers now turned their attention to fin and blue whales. When the South African fin whale population became depleted by the mid-1960s to twenty percent of its former size, they turned to sei and sperm whales. When these populations declined, the frustrated whalers started hunting minke whales, which at 9m in length are too small to be a viable catch. In 1979 the South African government banned all whaling activity.

2

WHALE- AND DOLPHIN-WATCHING VIEWPOINTS IN PLETTENBERG BAY

Elevated ocean panoramas give Plettenberg Bay some **outstanding viewpoints** for watching southern right whales between June and October. An especially good vantage point is the area between the wreck of the *Athene* at the southern end of Lookout Beach and the Keurbooms River. The Robberg Peninsula is also excellent, looming protectively over this whale nursery and giving a grandstand view of the bay. Other good viewpoints in town are from Beachy Head Road at Robberg Beach; Signal Hill in San Gonzales Street past the post office and police station; *Beacon Island Hotel* on Beacon Island; and the deck of the restaurant *The Lookout* (see below) on Lookout Beach. Outside Plett, the Kranshoek viewpoint and hiking trail offers wonderful whale-watching points along the route; to get there, head for Knysna, take the Harkerville turn-off, and continue for 7km .

Emily's Rietvlei Rd, off the N2 (turn off at Penny Pinchers) ☎ 044 533 2982. Boutique restaurant attached to *Emily Moon's Lodge* that many regard as the best in the area, offering stunning views of the Bitou Wetland and classical French cuisine with an edge. The menu is based on what seasonal ingredients are locally available each day, but there's always a choice of five or six starters and mains with a small range of desserts. The fillet of sole is a good fish choice (R150). Booking essential, especially for a table on the deck. Mon 6.30–10pm, Tues–Sun noon–3pm & 6.30–10pm.

The Lookout Lookout Beach ☎ 044 533 1379, ⓦ lookout.co.za. There are marvellous bay views at this bar-restaurant, with umbrellas and outdoor tables. The menu focuses on seafood, including crayfish, and they also do good chargrilled steaks (R130), poultry, pasta, salads and

breakfasts. Daily 9am–9pm.

Ristorante Enrico Main Beach, Keurboomstrand ☎ 044 535 9818. Casual restaurant right on the beach with a holiday vibe, where you can eat outside and enjoy the sea breeze. It serves mid-priced Italian standards, such as thin-based pizzas, pasta and veal (R90). Summer daily noon–10pm; winter Tues–Sun noon–10pm.

Zinzi *Hunter's Country House*, off the N2, 10km west of Plett ☎ 044 501 1111, ⓦ zinzi.hunterhotels.com. The food here has distinctly international flavours with an African influence – you'll find such delights as Asian pork belly, wild mushroom risotto with truffle oil (R90) and rooibos pannacotta with Cape gooseberry compote for dessert. It's unstuffy, with fair prices and a welcoming attitude to children. Daily noon–2.30pm & 6–9.30pm.

Robberg Marine and Nature Reserve

Robberg Rd • Daily Feb–Nov 7am–5pm; Dec & Jan 7am–8pm; R40 • ☎ 021 483 0190, ⓦ capenature.co.za/reserves/robberg -nature-reserve

One of the Garden Route's nicest walks is the four-hour, nine-kilometre circular route around the spectacular rocky peninsula of **Robberg**, 8km southeast of Plett's town centre. Here you can completely escape Plett's development and experience the coast in its wildest state, with its enormous horizons and lovely vegetation. Much of the walk takes you along high cliffs, from where you can often look down on seals surfacing near the rocks, dolphins arching through the water and, in winter, whales further out in the bay. If you don't have time for the full circular walk, note there is a shorter two-hour hike and a thirty-minute ramble, a map is provided at the entrance gate. There is one rustic hut, *Fountain Shack*, to stay overnight (see p.228).

Keurboomstrand

Some 14km east of Plettenberg Bay by road, across the Keurbooms River, is the uncluttered resort of **KEURBOOMSTRAND** (Keurbooms for short), little more than a suburb of Plett, sharing the same bay and with equally good beaches, but less safe for swimming. The best place to take the waves is at **Arch Rock**, in front of the caravan park, though **Picnic Rock beach** is also pretty good. A calm and attractive place, Keurbooms has few facilities; and if you're intending to stay here you should stock up in Plett beforehand. One of Keurbooms' highlights is **canoeing** up the river (see box opposite).

ACTIVITIES AND TOURS AROUND PLETTENENBURG BAY

BOAT TRIPS
Keurbooms River Ferries Signposted on the east side of the Keurbooms River Bridge ☏ 083 254 3551, ⓦ ferry.co.za. This company runs daily guided boat trips upriver (at 11am, 2pm & sunset; R150) with knowledgeable guides skilled at spotting rare birds – the indigenous forest comes right down to the water's edge. Park entrance fee is R40 per person.

BUNGEE JUMPING
Bloukrans Bungy ☏ 042 281 1458, ⓦ faceadrenalin.com. The world's highest commercial bungee jump launches off the 216-metre Bloukrans River Bridge and costs R790 (excluding pictures or video) for the seven-second descent. For the less brave, there's a bridge walk over the jump site (R100).

CANOEING
CapeNature On the east side of the Keurbooms River Bridge along the N2 ☏ 044 533 2125. This outfit rents out fairly basic canoes, so that you can explore the river yourself (R120 per day for a two-person canoe).

HIKING
If you're keen on walking and the outdoors, you'll find a couple of excellent hikes around Plett, which tend to get less busy than the more popular trails around Tsitsikamma National Park (see p.232). The waymarked hikes listed below are two to five days long: for permits and bookings contact ☏ 044 302 5606 or ☏ 044 302 5600 and ⓔ reservations @samparks.org.

Harkerville Coastal Trail Starts and ends at Harkerville Forestry Station, 12km west of Plettenberg Bay, signposted off the N2: R212 per person plus daily conservation fee R25. Close to the roads, this circular two-day trail of 26.5km doesn't feel as remote as the Otter Trail (see box, p.236) but is a good second-best, taking in magnificent rocky coastline, indigenous forest and *fynbos*. Lots of rock scrambling and some traversing of exposed, narrow ledges above the sea is required, so don't attempt it if you're unfit or scared of heights. Monkeys, baboons and fish eagles are commonly seen, and you may also spot dolphins or whales.

Outeniqua Trail Starts at the old forest station at Beervlei (where there are eight overnight huts; directions are given when you book), and ends at Harkerville Forestry Station, 12km west of Plettenberg Bay; R73 per person per day. This

108km hike takes seven days (though shorter versions are possible), and takes you through indigenous forest, including giant yellowwood trees, pine plantations and gold-mining remains at Millwood in the Goudveld State Forest.

CLIMBING AND KLOOFING
GoVertical Mountaineering Adventures ⓦ govertical.co.za, ☏ 082 731 4696. Kloofing (also known as canyoning) is the most adventurous way of exploring the deep river gorges between Knysna and Plett. GoVertical can teach the basics of rock-climbing and take experienced climbers out; prices depend on the size of the group, and are given when you enquire.

SKYDIVING
Skydive Plettenberg Bay ☏ 082 905 7440, ⓦ skydiveplett.com. If you fancy an adrenaline rush, you can go tandem skydiving (no experience required) with these guys, who charge R1850 for a 10,000ft jump; a DVD or video of the event is an optional extra.

TOWNSHIP TOURS
Ocean Blue Central Beach ☏ 044 533 5083 or ☏ 083 701 3583, ⓦ oceanadventures.co.za. Ocean Blue arranges relaxed tours into Plett's township with a guide who is a member of the host community. Trips cost R200 per person and the profits go into a development trust, which among other things pays teachers' salaries and funds a crèche.

WHALE AND DOLPHIN WATCHING
Dolphin Adventures Central Beach ☏ 083 590 3405, ⓦ dolphinadventures.co.za. Sea kayaking is one of the best ways to see whales, and this outfit runs unforgettable trips with experienced and knowledgeable guides in two-person kayaks (2hr–2hr 30min, R250; children R150, including all equipment). Alternatively, you can just rent a canoe and go out on your own (1hr R100; 2hr R150).
Ocean Blue Central Beach ☏ 044 533 4897 or ☏ 083 701 3583, ⓦ oceanadventures.co.za. A licensed outfit that offers sea-kayaking (R250) and boat-based whale-watching (R700) tours.
Ocean Safaris Shop 3, Hopwood St ☏ 044 533 4963, ⓦ oceansafaris.co.za. Tailor-made cruises from a licensed whale-watching company. Whale-watching by boat (R680) virtually guarantees sightings between July and September. Out of whale season, it's still worth going out to see dolphins and seals (R420).

2

The Crags

The Crags, 2km east of Keurboomstrand, comprises a collection of smallholdings along the N2, a bottle store and a few other shops on the forest edge, but the reason most visitors pull in here is for the **Elephant Sanctuary**, **Monkeyland** and **Birds of Eden**. To get to all three attractions from Keurbooms, look out for the BP petrol station, then take the Monkeyland/Kurland turn-off and follow the Elephant Sanctuary/Monkeyland signs for 2km.

Elephant Sanctuary

Monekyland Rd, 19km east Plettenberg Bay off the N2 • Daily 8am–5pm • Trunk-in-Hand programme daily at 7.30am • R475; elephant ride R475; elephant brush-down R575 • ☎ 044 534 8145, ⓦ elephantsanctuary.co.za

The **Elephant Sanctuary** offers a chance of close encounters with its half-dozen pachyderms, all of whom were saved from culling in Botswana and Kruger National Park. On the popular one-hour Trunk-in-Hand programme, which includes an informative talk about elephant behaviour, you get to walk with an elephant, holding the tip of its trunk in your hand and also to feed and interact with it. You can also go on fifteen-minute elephant-back rides and help to brush down the elephants.

Monkeyland

400m beyond the Elephant Sanctuary • Daily 8am–5pm • Tours R160; combined ticket with Birds of Eden R260 ; entry to the viewing deck is free • ⓦ monkeyland.co.za

Monkeyland brings together primates from several continents, all of them orphaned or saved from a dismal life as pets. **Guides** take visitors on informative walks to experience indigenous forest and enjoy chance encounters with creatures such as ringtail lemurs from Madagascar and squirrel monkeys from South America. All the primates are free to move around the reserve, looking for food and interacting with each other and their environment in as natural a way as possible.

One of the sanctuary's highlights is crossing the Indiana Jones-esque **rope bridge** (at 128m, it's purportedly the longest such bridge in the southern hemisphere) spanning a canyon to pass through the upper reaches of the forest canopy, where a number of species spend their days. For **refreshments** or meals, there's a restaurant with a forest deck at the day lodge.

Birds of Eden

Daily 8am–5pm • R160; combined ticket with Monkeyland R260 • ⓦ birdsofeden.co.za

Under the same management as Monkeyland and right next door, **Birds of Eden** is a huge bird sanctuary. Great effort was taken to place netting over a substantial tract of forest with as little impact as possible. As with Monkeyland, most of Birds of Eden's charges were already living in cages and are now free to move and fly around within the confines of the large enclosure (so large in fact that you can easily spend an hour slowly meandering along its winding, wheelchair-friendly, wooden walkway).

Although it has been criticized for cutting off local birds from their traditional turf and disrupting some migration routes, the result is remarkable, with little lakes, waterfalls and a **suspension bridge** along the way. Most of the birds are exotics, some impossibly brightly coloured (such as the incandescent scarlet ibis from South America and golden pheasant from China), but you'll also see a number of locals, such as the Knysna lourie and South Africa's national bird, the blue crane. Watch out for the cheeky cockatoos that may alight on your shoulder and steal buttons from your shirt. A **restaurant** by one of the lakes sells light meals and drinks.

Tsitsikamma

The **Tsitsikamma section** of the Garden Route National Park, roughly midway between Plettenberg Bay and Port Elizabeth, is the highlight of any Garden Route trip, extending for 68km along a narrow belt of coast, with dramatic foamy surges of rocky coast, deep river gorges and ancient hardwood forests clinging to the edge of tangled, green cliffs. Don't pass up its main attraction, **Storms River Mouth**, the most dramatic estuary on this exhilarating piece of coast. Established in 1964, Tsitsikamma is also South Africa's oldest marine reserve, stretching 5.5km out to sea, with an **underwater trail** open to snorkellers and licensed scuba divers.

Tsitsikamma itself has two sections: **Nature's Valley** in the west and **Storms River Mouth** in the east. Each section can only be reached down a winding tarred road from the N2 (apart from hiking, there's no way of getting from one to the other through the park itself). Nature's Valley incorporates the most low-key settlement on the Garden Route, with a fabulous sandy beach stretching for 3km. South Africa's ultimate hike, the five-day **Otter Trail** (see box, p.236), connects the two sections of the park.

The nearest settlement to Storms River Mouth, some 14km to its north at the top of a steep winding road, is the confusingly named **Storms River Village**, which is outside the national park and some distance from any part of the river, but makes a convenient base for adventure activities in the vicinity and day-trips down to Storms River Mouth.

Nature's Valley

Nature's Valley, at the western end of the Tsitsikamma section of the Garden Route National Park, extends inland into a rugged and hilly interior incised with narrow valleys and traversed by a series of footpaths. It also incorporates a pleasingly old-fashioned settlement on the stunningly beautiful Groot River Lagoon with 20km of beach. Bypassed by the N2, and by intercity buses and tour parties, Nature's Valley is the supreme destination if you're after a relaxed retreat along the Garden Route.

Walks

There are plenty of good **walks** at Nature's Valley, many starting from the national park campsite, 1km north of the village, where you can pick up maps and information about birds and trees. One of the loveliest places to head for is **Salt River Mouth**, 3km west of Nature's Valley, where you can swim and picnic – though you'll need to ford the river at low tide. This walk starts and ends at the café at Nature's Valley. Also recommended is the circular 6km **Kalanderkloof Trail**, which starts from the national park campsite, ascends to a lookout point, and descends via a narrow river gorge graced with a profusion of huge Outeniqua yellowwood trees and Cape wild bananas.

ARRIVAL AND INFORMATION   NATURE'S VALLEY

By car Nature's Vally is 29km east of Plettenberg Bay, down the lovely winding Groot River pass (along which you'll often encounter baboon troops).
By bus The Baz Bus drops off here at the *Wild Spirit Lodge*, 8km from the ocean.

Information Nature's Valley Trading Store, on the corner of Forest and St Michael streets (📞 044 531 6835, 🌐 www.cyberperk.co.za/naturesvalley), is effectively the village centre and acts as an informal but excellent information bureau.

ACCOMMODATION

Accommodation in Nature's Valley itself is pretty limited, which contributes to its low-key charm, but you'll find some choice options on the road leading off the N2 into the village, just before the switchbacks begin. If you're self-catering, contact Meyer van Rooyen (📞 082 772 2972), who handles a number of houses in and around Nature's Valley, and make sure you stock up on provisions before you get here, since local supplies are basic.

Four Fields Farm Nature's Valley Rd, 3km from the N2 along the R102 and 8km from Nature's Valley 📞 044 534 8708, 🌐 fourfields.co.za. A welcoming and unpretentious former dairy farm, less than 10min drive from the sea. The self-catering farm house has four bedrooms, simply furnished with beautiful old pieces and

French doors leading to their own private decks, which in turn open onto a much-loved garden surrounded by fields. An additional flat sleeps four (R1100) and another sleeps a couple (R660). R1760
Lily Pond Lodge 102 Nature's Valley Rd, 3km from the N2 along the R102 and 6km from Nature's Valley

☎044 534 8767, ⊕lilypond.co.za. Probably the most memorable accommodation in Nature's Valley, this luxury lodge has four en-suite rooms with patio doors opening onto private terraces, plus sound systems, TVs and wi-fi, while the two spacious luxury suites also have their own lounge, under-floor heating and king-sized beds. There are three even more luxurious garden suites and a honeymoon suite that has its own private garden. R1500

★ **Nature's Valley Restcamp** 1km to the north of the village. Book through South African National Parks (☎044 531 6700, ⊕sanparks.org/parks/garden_route/camps/natures_valley) or, if you're already in Nature's Valley, the camp supervisor on ☎044 531 6700. Campsites tucked into indigenous forest, plus basic two-person forest huts with communal ablution facilities. Camping R190, hut R450

Rocky Road Backpackers 1.5km from the N2 along the R102, 12km from Nature's Valley ☎072 270 2114, ⊕rockyroadbackpackers.com. A tranquil backpacker retreat with landscaped gardens, set on a large forested property. It has all home comforts including free wi-fi, an outdoor pizza oven, forest bathroom and a highly social

Friday braai night. There is a range of sleeping options, the most appealing being the luxury tents with soft bedding and electric blankets. Camping R80, luxury tent R140, dorm R120, double R600

Tranquility Lodge 130 Saint Michael's St ☎044 531 6663, ⊕tranquilitylodge.co.za. If Nature's Valley has a centre, then this comfortable lodge, next to the village's only shop, is bang in the middle of it. A two-storey brick and timber building set in a garden that feels as if it's part of the encroaching forest, it is just 50m from the beach. Breakfast is served on an upstairs deck among the treetops. All rooms are en suite and there's also a larger honeymoon suite (R2400) with a spa bath, double shower, fireplace and private deck. R1300

Wild Spirit Lodge and Backpackers Nature's Valley Rd, 8km from Nature's Valley ☎044 534 8888, ⊕wildspiritlodge.co.za. This lodge has an alternative focus, with accommodation in dorms in three two-storey garden cottages. There's free wi-fi, a kitchen for self-catering, a yoga and meditation room, book exchange, live music and drumming nights, and a big outdoor braai. Camping RR80, dorm R120, double R400

EATING AND DRINKING

Nature's Valley Trading Store Forest and St Michael streets ☎044 531 6835, ⊕www.cyberperk.co.za/naturesvalley. The only place in the village that does food and booze is a pretty informal and convivial spot for

seafood, steaks, burgers and toasted sandwiches, and provides the only nightlife in the village – a large-screen TV – apart from gazing at the stars. Daily 9.30am–8.45pm.

Storms River Mouth

55km east of Plettenberg Bay • Daily 7am–7.30pm • R108 • ☎042 281 1607

In contrast to the languid lagoon and long soft sands of Nature's Valley, **Storms River Mouth** presents the elemental face of the Garden Route, with the dark Storms River surging through a gorge to battle with the surf. Don't confuse this with **Storms River Village** just off the N2, which is nowhere near the sea, but right in the forest. Storms River Mouth lies 18km south of Storms River Bridge, on the N2. Most people stop at the bridge to gaze into the deep river gorge and fill up at the most beautifully located service station in the country. Even if your time is limited and you can't spend the night, it's worth detouring the 18km down to Storms River Mouth to gaze at the coastline.

Walking is the main activity at the Mouth, and at the visitors' office at the restcamp you can get **maps** of short, waymarked coastal trails that leave from here. Most rewarding is the **three-kilometre hike** west from the restcamp along the start of the Otter Trail to a fantastic **waterfall** pool at the base of fifty-metre-high falls. Less demanding is the kilometre-long **boardwalk stroll** from the restaurant to the suspension bridge to see the river mouth. On your way to the bridge, don't miss the dank *strandloper* (beachcomber) **cave**. Hunter-gatherers frequented this area between five thousand and two thousand years ago, living off seafood in wave-cut caves near the river mouth. A modest display shows an excavated midden, with clear layers of little bones and shells. **Swimming** at the Mouth is restricted to a safe and pristine little sandy bay below the restaurant, with a changing hut, though conditions can be cold in summer if there are easterly winds and cold upwellings of deep water from the continental shelf.

RIGHT KNYSNA LAGOON (P.219) >

2

NATURE'S VALLEY AND STORMS RIVER HIKES

Dolphin Trail This is the Garden Route's luxury, portered trail. The terrain through the Tsitsikamma National Park is breathtaking, covering the rugged coastal edge and the natural forest. The trail starts at Storms River Mouth and ends at Sandrif River Mouth, covering a distance of 20km over three and a half days. The price (R4990 per person) includes food, accommodation and permits, a guide, a boat trip up the Storms River Gorge and a 4WD through the Storms River Pass: book through the Fernery ☎ 042 280 3588, ⊕ dolphintrail.co.za.

Otter Trail The Otter Trail is South Africa's flagship hike; it is simply magnificent hiking along a pristine stretch of coastline and forest where there is no habitation or vehicle access. You need to be fit for the steep sections, and an experienced hiker – you carry everything from hut to hut, and you need to be able to manage deep river crossings. It starts at Storms River Mouth and ends at Nature's Valley (distance 42km; duration five days), and the maximum number of people on the trail is twelve; book through South African National Parks at least twelve months in advance (R925 plus park conservation fees of R600 per person; ☎ 012 428 911, ⊕ sanparks.org).

Tsitsikamma Trail An inland hike through indigenous forest, long stretches of open *fynbos* and the Tsitsikamma mountain range. Five overnight huts accommodate 24 people and it is a fairly strenuous hike (around 60km), although you won't cover more than 17km or so per day. It starts at Nature's Valley and ends at Storms River Bridge (R135 per person per night, with porterage available for additional R800 per day); book through MTO Ecotourism (☎ 042 281 1712, ⊕ mtoecotourism.co.za/tsitsikama.htm).

ACCOMMODATION AND EATING   STORMS RIVER MOUTH

Storms River Mouth Restcamp ☎ 042 281 1607, ⊕ sanparks.org/parks/garden_route/camps/storms _river. Sited on tended lawns, *Storms River Mouth Restcamp* is poised between a craggy shoreline of black rocks, pounded by foamy white surf, and steeply raking forested cliffs. It has a variety of accommodation options, not especially nice and rather modest and worn, but all with sea views and the ever-present sound of the surging surf. Advance booking is essential (see p.68) and you may have to take whatever is available, as its location makes it understandably popular. Two units have disabled access. Camping R345, forest hut R565, chalet R1100

Tsitsikamma Restaurant The only place to eat at Storms River Mouth has such startling views that it can be forgiven its mediocre fare of English breakfasts, toasted sandwiches, burgers, pastas and steak, and indifferent service. They have reasonable range of seafood dishes (R100), however, and you can get a drink out on the wooden deck. Daily 8.30am–10pm.

Storms River Village

About a kilometre south of the national road, **STORMS RIVER VILLAGE** is a tranquil place crisscrossed by a handful of dirt roads and with about forty houses, enjoying mountain views. Its main attraction is as a centre for adventure activities, of which the **Canopy Tour** is the main drawcard. It also makes a lovely, forested easily accessible place to overnight, if you're travelling from Cape Town (579km west) to Port Elizabeth (179km east).

ACCOMMODATION   STORMS RIVER VILLAGE

★**The Armagh** Fynbos Ave ☎ 042 281 1512, ⊕ thearmagh.com. A hospitable and very comfortable guesthouse with excellent bathrooms and bed linen, in a beautiful garden that drifts off into the *fynbos*. There are two budget rooms, four standard ones, a garden cottage and an ultra luxurious and very private honeymoon room, all of which open onto the garden. There's a nice swimming pool and a decent restaurant. R1300

★**At the Woods Guest House** 49 Formosa St, along the main drag into town ☎ 042 281 1446, ⊕ atthewoods.co.za. The nicest place in town, this friendly, modern guesthouse has traditional reed ceilings and large, comfortable rooms with king-sized beds and French doors that open onto garden verandas, or, upstairs, onto private decks with mountain views. Three-course home-cooked dinners can be arranged, and there's a nice communal lounge with a fireplace where you can use the internet. R990

Tsitsikamma Backpackers 54 Formosa St ☎ 042 281 1868, ⊕ tsitsikammabackpackers.co.za. Well-run hostel that claims environmentally friendly and fair-trade credentials. The accommodation here includes luxury tents set in a beautiful garden. You can self-cater or order a reasonably priced breakfast or dinner, and there's a bar. They offer a

2

STORMS RIVER ACTIVITIES

BOAT TRIP

SANParks ☎ 042 281 1607. Runs boat trips about 1km up Storms River for up to twelve people (R115 for 30min, plus R84 conservation fee). Book at the dive shop, just beneath the restaurant, which is also where the trips leave from.

CANOPY TOUR

Storms River Adventures ☎ 042 281 1836, ⓦ stormsriver.com. The Storms River Adventures Canopy Tour (R495) through the treetops gives a bird's eye view of the forest as you travel 30m above ground along a series of interconnected cables attached to the tallest trees. The system has been constructed in such a way that not a single nail has been hammered into any tree.

MOUNTAIN BIKING

A 22km mountain trail winds through the forest on the edge of the village and offers terrific views of the river gorge and coastline. *Tsitsikamma Backpackers* rents out mountain bikes for the day (R220).

TOURS

Woodcutters' Journey ☎ 042 281 1836, ⓦ stormsriver.com. A relaxed jaunt that takes you down through the forest to the river along the old Storms River Pass in a specially designed trailer, drawn by a tractor (teatime trip R200; lunchtime trip R250). The trip is run by Storms River Adventures, which has its headquarters next to the Storms River Village post office.

TUBING

Tube 'n Axe Backpackers ☎ 042 281 1757, ⓦ tubenaxe.co.za. *Tube 'n Axe Backpackers* runs trips down the Storms River gorge, where you ride the river and its rapids buoyed up by a small inflatable during the high-water season, which is generally winter (half-day R490; full-day R800).

ZIPLINE

Tsitsikamma Falls Adventures ☎ 072 030 4367, ⓦ tsitsikammaadventure.co.za. A faster, higher alternative to the Canopy Tour, geared more to adrenaline junkies, this zipline tour across the Kruis River (R380) crisscrosses an awesome ravine, zipping over three waterfalls. At times, it is 50m above the ground and the longest slide measures 211m.

shuttle service to the Storms River Mouth (R100 per person; minimum three passengers), and pick up guests for free from the Storms River Bridge. Tent R340, dorm R160, double R470

Tsitsikamma Village Inn Darnell St, along the road into the village and left at the T-junction ☎ 042 281 1711, ⓦ tsitsikammahotel.co.za. A charming, old-fashioned and well-run hotel in the village amid the trees and with a well-tended garden. It has 49 rooms in eleven cottage units, and a pub and restaurant on the premises. R990

Tube 'n Axe Backpackers Corner of Darnell and Saffron streets ☎ 042 281 1757, ⓦ tubenaxe.co.za. A wacky place that works hard to compete with the bright lights of Knysna and Plett by offering drumming nights, a pool table and loads of laughs. Accommodation, besides the usual dorms and doubles, includes two-person elevated tents. Camping R85, elevated tent R300, dorm R150, double R480

EATING

De Oude Martha *Tsitsikamma Village Inn*, Darnell St ☎ 042 281 1711, ⓦ tsitsikammahotel.co.za. Perfectly acceptable, if unexceptional, hotel restaurant that serves unpretentious breakfasts, lunches and dinners (mains average R160), but the best thing about it is the cosy pub with a welcoming fireplace on damp winter nights. Daily 7am–9pm.

Rafters *The Armagh*, Fynbos Ave ☎ 042 281 1512, ⓦ thearmagh.com. Cape Muslim sweet and mild curries feature big on the menu (R115), and there's an emphasis on using local products. South African cuisine is prepared using garden greens in the salads, fish from Plettenberg Bay, and meat sourced from nearby. Daily 8am–9pm.

The West Coast

The **West Coast** of South Africa – remote, windswept and bordered by the cold Atlantic – demands a special appreciation. For many years the black sheep of Western Cape tourism, it has been set upon by developers who seem all too ready to spoil the bleached, salty emptiness that many people have just begun to value. The sandy soil and dunes harbour a distinctive coastal *fynbos* vegetation, while the coastline is almost devoid of natural inlets or safe harbours, with fierce southeasterly summer winds and dank winter fogs, though in spring **wild flowers** ever-miraculously appear in the veld. The southern 200km of the region, by far the most densely populated part of the coast, has many links to Namaqualand to the north (see p.282) – not least the flowers.

Outside the flower months of August and September, this part of the West Coast has a wide range of attractions, particularly in summer when the lure of the sea and the cooler coast is strong. The area is well known for its variety of activities, most popularly watersports, hiking and some excellent **birdwatching** (see box below).

A highlight of a number of West Coast towns is the casual but sumptuous **seafood** feast served in **open-air restaurants**, with little more than a canvas shelter held up with driftwood and lengths of fishing twine or a simple wind-cheating brush fence as props. Here, you can savour endless courses of West Coast delicacies right by the ocean, in the style of a beach braai – one of the undisputed highlights of any holiday to South Africa.

Swartland

The N7 highway north from Cape Town leads quickly into the pleasing and fertile **Swartland** landscape. Swartland means "black country", but while the rolling countryside takes on some attractive hues at different times of year, it's never really black. The accepted theory is that before the area was cultivated, the predominant vegetation was a grey-coloured bush called **renosterbos** (rhinoceros bush) which, seen from the surrounding ranges of hills, gave the area a complexion sufficiently dark to justify the name.

Bordered to the west by the less fertile coastal strandveld and to the east by the tall mountain range running from Wellington to the Cederberg, Swartland is known best as a wheat-growing area, although it also supports dairy farms, horse studs, tobacco crops and vineyards famous for earthy red wines. The N7 skirts a series of towns on its way north, including the largest in the region, **Malmesbury**. If you're travelling south towards Cape Town, look out for some unusual views of Table Mountain, and also for tortoises, which you should take care to avoid as they cross the road.

BIRDWATCHING ON THE WEST COAST

The **West Coast** is a twitchers' dream, where you can tick off numerous wetland species. The most rewarding viewing time is just after **flower season** in early summer, which heralds the arrival of around 750,000 migrants on their annual pilgrimage from the northern hemisphere, many from as far off as the Arctic Circle. They spend about eight months fattening up on delicacies from the tidal mudflats before their arduous journey back to their breeding grounds. **Langebaan** in the West Coast National Park is the best place in the country for such sightings and is considered the fifth most important wetland in the world, hosting over 250 bird species, more than a quarter of South Africa's total. The Berg River estuary and saltworks at **Velddrif** are another vital feeding ground for waders.

The coastal lake of **Verlorenvlei**, meaning "the lost marsh", is one of the most important wetlands in South Africa; it stretches 13.5km from its mouth at Eland's Bay (25km south of Lambert's Bay) to its headwaters near Redelinghuys. Look out here for the purple gallinule, a colourful, shy wader, and the African marsh harrier, a raptor that may be declining in numbers. Here species more fond of arid conditions merge with the waders, and there have been some rare sightings including a black egret and a palm-nut vulture. At **Bird Island**, Lambert's Bay, a sunken hide makes it convenient to view the garrulous behaviour of the breeding colony of Cape gannets.

Darling and around

The small country town of **DARLING** is famous for its rolling countryside, vineyards and dairy products, as well as displays of wild flowers in spring. The town boasts some handsome old buildings and is something of an **artists' colony**, though it's far better known as the home of one of South Africa's best-loved comedians, **Pieter Dirk-Uys**, who regularly performs here at weekends.

Evita se Perron

At the old train station in the centre of town • Tues–Sun 10am–4pm • ☎ 022 492 3930, ⓦ evita.co.za

Pieter Dirk-Uys, South Africa's most famous comedian, has established his best-known and loved character, **Evita Bezuidenhout** (South Africa's answer to Dame Edna Everidge), as the hostess of a weekend cabaret show here. Taking in lunch and a show here is one of the best days out from Cape Town you can have. Book in advance.

!Khwa Ttu San Culture and Education Centre

Some 20km west of Darling, along the R27, 70km from Cape Town • Mon–Sun 9am–5pm • Free • Tours daily at 10am & 2pm; R240 • ☎ 022 492 2998, ⓦ www.khwattu.org

If you'd like some knowledge and contact with "bushmen" or San, **!Khwa Ttu San Culture and Education Centre** is the place to go. The centre is run by descendants of Northern Cape San people in partnership with a Swiss NGO, with profits returned to San communities. There is an excellent exhibition of photographs, authentic crafts for sale and a restaurant, all appealingly situated on a hilltop. With a couple of hours in hand, you can take one of their tours to a replica San village and see tracking and hunting techniques. It's also possible to stay overnight here (see below).

ARRIVAL AND INFORMATION   DARLING AND AROUND

By car Darling is easily reached from Cape Town (75km away) on a day-trip, via the coastal R27 route.

Information The tourist office on Pastorie St (Mon–Fri 9am–1pm & 2–4pm, Sat & Sun 10am–3pm; ☎ 022 492 3361, ⓦ darlingtourism.co.za) can book accommodation in Darling and on surrounding farms.

ACCOMMODATION

Darling Lodge 22 Pastorie St ☎ 022 492 3062, ⓦ darlinglodge.co.za. A restored Victorian house, with six en-suite rooms. There's a pool with three rooms around it, and a garden big enough to relax and lose yourself in. **R980**

!Khwa Ttu San Culture and Education Centre Some 20km west of Darling, along the R27 ☎ 022 492 2998, ⓦ www.khwattu.org. Accommodation comprises a tented camp, with communal facilities, and a two-bedroomed self-catering house with a fireplace inside. The centre, on a lovely farm, makes a good base for an exploration of Darling and the West Coast National Park. Tented camp **R250**, house **R960**

★ **Trinity Guest Lodge** 19 Long St ☎ 022 492 3430, ⓦ trinitylodge.co.za. A charming Victorian guesthouse set in gracious large grounds, with wooden shutters and a verandah. It offers a two-night package (R1500 pp) that includes a ticket to a Pieter Dirk-Uys show at Eva se Perron (see above), and a wine tasting and lunch at the historic Groote Post Wine Estate just out of town. **R800**

WEST COAST FLOWERS

During August and September you'll see **wild flowers** across the West Coast region, with significant displays starting as far south as **Darling**. Excellent flowers are also found in the **West Coast National Park** and the hazy coastal landscapes around **Cape Columbine** and **Lambert's Bay**, while inland **Clanwilliam** is the centre of some good routes. An incredible four thousand flower species are found in the region, most of them members of the daisy and mesembryanthemum groups. For up-to-date advice and guidance, contact the helpful tourist offices in Darling, Saldanha and Clanwilliam; for further tips on flower-viewing, see box, p.283.

2

EATING

Bistro Seven Restaurant and Coffee Bar 7 Main Rd ☎ 022 492 3626, ⓦ bistrosevendarling.com. Bakery and coffee shop that serves cakes, tarts, pasties and sandwiches. Evening meals include steaks, line fish, salads and Malay beef curry (R90), and there's also a lively sports bar. Bistro Wed–Mon 11am til late; Bar Mon & Wed–Fri open from 5pm, Sat & Sun from noon.

Cloof Winery Twenty minutes' drive from Darling towards Malmesbury on R315 ☎ 022 492 2839, ⓦ cloof.co.za. Reasonably priced light lunches including Caesar salad, chicken wrap and butternut ravioli (R85),

plus a children's menu, and Sunday lunches in the summer; book in advance. Tues–Sat 11am–3pm.

★ **Hilda's Kitchen** Groote Post Wine Estate, Darling Hills Rd, off the R27 ☎ 022 492 2825 ⓦ www .grootepost.com. Modern, award-winning country cooking including hearty soups, fish cakes with Asian flavours, and rich lamb pie (R90), in a beautiful eighteenth-century house, complemented by wines from the estate; booking essential. Children are welcome to roam in the extensive grounds. Wed–Sun noon–2.30pm.

Langebaan

Once the home to the largest whaling station in the southern hemisphere, and for a while Cape Town's long-haul passenger flight terminus (when seaplanes from Europe touched down on the lagoon during World War II), **LANGEBAAN** now sells itself as the gateway to the **West Coast National Park**, though it has become depressingly overdeveloped. If you're after a small-town West Coast experience, Paternoster (see p.242) is a better bet. However, if you want to spend time in the small but precious West Coast National Park itself, where there is almost zero accommodation, or if you're into windsurfing, kitesurfing or sailing and have been wondering how to harness the big southeasterly summer winds, the excellent conditions here mean Langebaan could be just your thing. Right off the beach the water is flat, the sailing winds – as the ragged flags above the centre testify – anywhere from fresh to fearsome and, unless you catch a fast-running tide out towards the Atlantic, it's all reasonably safe.

ARRIVAL AND INFORMATION
LANGEBAAN

By bus A daily bus, run by Elwierda (☎ 0861 001 094, ⓦ elwierda.com), leaves Cape Town Station at 5pm; the journey takes 2hr. Book in advance.

Information The tourist office is in the municipal building on Bree St (Mon–Fri 9am–5pm, Sat 9am–2pm; ☎ 022 772 1515, ⓦ langebaaninfo.com).

ACCOMMODATION

Friday Island Next to Cape Sport, on the beach ☎ 022 772 2506, ⓦ fridayisland.co.za. Perfect for watersports' enthusiasts wanting a more upmarket place to stay, it has fresh and light units with small kitchenettes, wooden decks and outdoor courtyards opening from the bathroom to hang up wet gear. Sea view rooms cost an extra R300 or so.

There's also an in-house restaurant and pub. R720

Puza Moya On the corner of North and Suffern streets ☎ 022 772 1114, ⓦ capesport.co.za. Cheerful en-suite rooms with a shared kitchen and courtyard for braais. A good option if you like to socialize in a relaxed environment after an active day. R600

EATING

★ **Die Strandloper Restaurant and Beach Bar** On the beach just beyond the Cape Sport Centre on the

road to Saldanha ☎ 022 772 2490 or ☎ 083 227 7195. A good example of the West Coast's lively open-air

---

HITTING THE WATER IN LANGEBAAN

If you want to try your hand at any of the **watersports** on offer in Langebaan, the friendly Cape Sport Centre (98 Main St; daily 9am–5pm; ☎ 022 772 1114, ⓦ capesport.co.za), on the beach on the northern edge of town, is the place to head to for **windsurfing**, **hobiecat sailing** and **kitesurfing** tuition. **Sailing courses** on the Langebaan Lagoon are run by Ocean Sailing Academy based in Cape Town (☎ 082 891 4477, ⓦ oceansailingacademy .co.za).

seafood restaurants, with sand beneath your feet and fishing nets above. Committed to sustainable seafood, this is a good place to try West Coast fish delicacies like *harders* and dried *snoek*: it's R250 for a ten-course set menu, and booking is essential. Mid-Jan to mid-Nov Sat & Sun 12.30–3.30pm; mid-Nov to mid-Jan daily 12.30–3.30pm & 6.30–9.30pm.

Kalmer Karma Sports Bar 98 Main Rd ✆ 022 772 707 9116, ✇ facebook.com/kalmerkarma. In a beautiful location on the beach with tables outside, this is the best place in town for sundowners. There's a good selection of craft beers (R45) on offer, as well as pub meals, with fish often on the menu. Wed–Sun 11am–11pm.

Pearly's On the main beach. Crowded eating, drinking and ogling spot with outside tables, in a great location for watching the sunset, and enjoying uncomplicated pizza, pasta (R90), seafood or grilled steak. Daily 9.30am–midnight.

West Coast National Park

Daily: April–Aug 7am–6pm; Sept–March 7am–7pm • R120 • ✆ 022 772 2144

The **West Coast National Park** is one of the best places to savour the charm of the West Coast, which elsewhere is being devoured by housing developments. The park protects over forty percent of South Africa's remaining pristine strandveld and 35 percent of the country's salt marshes, and incorporates most of Langebaan Lagoon and a Y-shaped area of land immediately around and below it.

Much of the park's appeal lies in uplifting views over the still lagoon to an olive-coloured, rocky hillside, the sharp, saline air, and the calling gulls and Atlantic mists vanishing in the harsh sunlight. This isn't a game park – a few larger antelope are located in the Postberg section of the park, an area open only during the spring flower season – but there are huge numbers of **birds**, including some seventy thousand migrating waders, ostriches and tortoises galore. A number of well-organized interpretive walking trails lead through the dunes to the long, smooth, wave-beaten Atlantic coastline, offering plenty of opportunity to learn about the hardy *fynbos* vegetation that so defines the look and feel of the West Coast region. The best time to visit the park is in **spring**, when the sun is shining and the flowers are out, although this is, inevitably, also the busiest period. Like much of the West Coast, the national park is chilly and wet in winter, and hot and wind-blasted in summer.

On the southern tip of the lagoon is the effective centre – a large old farmhouse called **Geelbek**. From here, continue up the peninsula on the western side of the lagoon and you'll pass the entrance to **Churchhaven**, a tiny exclusive and beautiful village (gated to prevent day visitors), and two signposted beaches with picnic areas, Priekstool and Kraalbaai.

A little further on is the demarcated **Postberg area**, open only during flower season (see box, p.239), but worth visiting at that time to see **zebra**, **gemsbok** and **wildebeest** wandering through fields of wild flowers.

ARRIVAL AND INFORMATION   WEST COAST NATIONAL PARK

By car The park is 90km from Cape Town, and there are two entrance gates to the park: one on the R27, roughly 10km north of the turning to Yzerfontein, and the other south of Langebaan. The park isn't huge – if you're driving you'll cover the extent of the roads in a couple of hours.

Information Staff at the Geelbek Information Centre in the Geelbek Cape Dutch House (Mon–Fri 8.30am–4pm, Sat & Sun 9am–1pm) can direct you to the bird hides nearby, or give you information about walks in the area.

ACCOMMODATION AND EATING

★**Churchhaven Beach Houses** Churchhaven ✆ 021 790 0972, ✇ perfecthideaways.co.za. A couple of stunning, if very pricey, self-catering beach houses (sleeping 2–10) in sought-after Churchhaven. They are contemporary in design, with top-quality beds and linen, and secluded outdoor showers and patios with incomparable views. R4500 per night, per house.

Duinepos 1km from Geelbek (signposted) ✆ 022 707 9900, ✇ duinepos.co.za. Eleven self-catering chalets, set in *fynbos*, but with no access to the water because of bird breeding. There's a swimming pool on site, or lagoon swimming at Priekstool or Kraalbaai, some 12–15km away. R800

Geelbek Restaurant Geelbek ☎ 022 772 2134. Magnificent setting in a graceful Cape Dutch building on the lagoon, where you can sit outside and see flamingos if you are lucky. South African dishes, such as *bobotie* (R90), ostrich burgers, *snoek* salad and Cape Malay curries, are the speciality, though the surroundings are more appealing than the food. Booking essential during flower season. Daily 9am–5pm.

Vredenburg

North of Saldanha lies a sizeable inland farming centre, **VREDENBURG**, an unremarkable town in a featureless setting. However, it's a usefeul place to visit for its well-stocked supermarkets and is a good place to buy fuel, since many of the smaller towns nearby don't have filling stations.

West Coast Fossil Park

About 10km southeast of Vredenburg, on the R45 • Mon–Fri 8am–4pm, Sat & Sun opening times vary, so phone first • R20 • Guided tours daily; phone to check times and book, R60 • ☎ 022 766 1606, ⦿ fossilpark.org.za

Founded in 1998 on the site of a decommissioned phosphate mine, and still being developed, the interesting **West Coast Fossil Park** is a relatively low-key affair, but highly recommended nevertheless. Displays include thousands of fossils and modern animal bones, as well as information panels about the extinct species dating back about five million years ago that were found on site. Finds include fossils from sabre-toothed cats, two species of extinct elephant, and sivatheres – long-horned, short-necked, giraffe-like browsers. Perhaps strangest of all are the extinct giant bears, *Agriotherium africanum*, which weighed in at 750kg (compared to 150kg for a large lion), making them the heftiest predators – and the only known bears – to have roamed sub-Saharan Africa in the past 65 million years. The guided tours are recommended, though you can wander around by yourself.

ARRIVAL AND INFORMATION   VREDENBURG

By bus A daily bus, operated by Elwierda (☎ 086 100 1094, ⦿ elwierda.com), leaves Cape Town Station for Vredenberg at 5pm; the return journey leaves Vredenberg for Cape Town at 5.50am. The journey time from Cape Town is 3hr.

Information The West Coast Peninsula Tourism Bureau is in the Atrium Building on Main Rd (Mon–Fri 9am–5pm; ☎ 022 715 1142, ⦿ capewestcoastpeninsula .co.za).

ACCOMMODATION

Windstone Backpackers Just past the main crossroads of the R45 from Vredenburg and the R27 from Cape Town ☎ 022 766 1645 or ☎ 083 477 1756, ⦿ windstone.co.za. With four- and six-bed dorms, some doubles, and a family room, *Windstone* makes a friendly base for exploring the region. The owners also run a horseriding centre, with rides in the adjoining fossil park and nature reserve (☎ 073 210 6050; R250). Dorm R130, double R330

Paternoster

The best of the West Coast is to be found at the village of **PATERNOSTER**, a favourite weekend seaside destination for Capetonians. Small-scale angling and crayfish netting is the principal economic activity of the village, and most of the fishermen live in the whitewashed cottages of the coloured district to the west of the hotel. When they're not out at sea, their small, brightly painted boats lie beached at the water's edge.

Unfortunately, Paternoster has become a bit of a building site of late, with lots of people building houses in this idyllic spot, and it's also developed a reputation for opportunistic theft from unsuspecting tourists. Nevertheless the coast itself is beautiful, saved from development by the Columbine Nature Reserve, 3km to the west (see below), where huge waves smash against large granite rocks as smooth as whales' backs.

Columbine Nature Reserve

3km to the west of Paternoster, along an unpaved road • Nature reserve daily sunrise to sunset • R20 • Columbine lighthouse tours on request • R15 • ☎ 022 752 2705

A small area set aside to conserve the sandveld-*fynbos* heathland indigenous to the region, the **Columbine Nature Reserve** makes a stunning change from the salty flats that typify the West Coast. Large vegetated dunes sweep down to a shoreline of massive pink granite boulders and little coves, with beaches that are blue-tinged, a result of mussel shells being washed up and finely crushed into the sands. It's best to park at **Tieties Bay** (camping is allowed here, right by the ocean), from where you can simply follow the marked path over the rocks and along the dunes to explore the area.

Besides rambling, there are some excellent coastal **hikes** through the reserve, including two long day-trails: Vredenburg tourist office (see opposite) can provide details of these. Along the road from Paternoster to the reserve you'll pass the **Cape Columbine lighthouse**, built in 1936 on Castle Rock. Usually the first lighthouse to be sighted by ships from Europe rounding Africa, it emits a single white flash every fifteen seconds.

ARRIVAL AND INFORMATION   PATERNOSTER

By car Paternoster is 15km northwest of Vredenburg and 160km from Cape Town, on the R27.

By bus The daily Elwierda Bus (☎ 0861 001 094, ⓦ elwierda.com), which runs between Cape Town and Saldanha, stops at nearby Vredenberg (see opposite).

Information The tourist office is next to the fish market at the beach, signposted from the main road as you enter town (Mon–Fri 9am–5pm, Sat 10am–3pm; ☎ 022 752 2323, ⓦ capewestcoastpeninsula.co.za).

ACCOMMODATION

Baywatch Villa Collection 8 Ambyl Rd ☎ 022 752 2039, ⓦ baywatchvilla.co.za. Five luxurious self-catering thatched fisherman-style cottages, just two minutes' walk from Long Beach, in the quiet part of town to the north. **R990**

Beach Camp Signposted from Paternoster in Cape Columbine Reserve ☎ 082 926 2267, ⓦ beachcamp .co.za. Right on the beach, in its own bay, *Beach Camp* has walk-in tents and small A-frames, some of which can sleep children. There's a bar where you can breakfast on the terrace, and fish braais are available if booked in advance. Otherwise, bring your own supplies to self-cater. They offer pick-ups from the Elwierda Bus, at Vredenburg. **R600**

Die Opstal Sonkwasweg ☎ 083 988 4645, ⓦ paternoster-villas.co.za. Three self-catering flats and a studio, all with separate entrances. The building is one row behind the beachfront properties, and it's cheaper than other options as it lacks beach views, though you can be on the beach within two minutes. **R800**

Light House Keeper Cottages Cape Columbine Reserve ☎ 021 449 2400. Self-catering is offered in three former lighthouse keepers' cottages around the lighthouse, on a prominent headland in the Cape Columbine reserve. The cottages are kitted out with all mod cons, and have two or three bedrooms. **R700**

Mosselbank On the corner of Trappieklip and Mosselbank streets ☎ 022 752 2027, ⓦ weskus.com. A hospitable B&B in a suburban development in the northern part of town, close to Long Beach. There are five en-suite rooms, some of which come with sea views. **R900**

★ **Oystercatchers' Haven** 48 Sonkwasweg ☎ 022 752 2193, ⓦ oystercatchershaven.com. A beautiful guesthouse with three romantic rooms, situated on the beach, on the edge of Columbine Reserve. The views are wonderful, and there's a swimming pool plus loungers close to the beach. **R1900**

★ **The Paternoster Dunes** 18 Sonkwas St ☎ 083 560 5600, ⓦ paternosterdunes.co.za. A gorgeous guesthouse with contemporary beachhouse-style rooms leading onto the sand, and everything designed to inspire and delight the senses. The pool, in the central courtyard, is protected from the wind. Make sure you have a seaview room, rather than a courtyard-facing one. **R1900**

SEA KAYAKING IN PATERNOSTER

An adventure highlight of Paternoster is guided **sea kayaking**. Kayak Paternoster (☎ 082 824 8917, ⓦ kayakpaternoster.co.za; no under 16s; closed in winter) runs one-hour trips (R200), which are as much about observing and learning about birds, whales, dolphins and seals as about paddling. The kayaks launch from the Main Beach, but won't go out if the swell is too big.

2

EATING AND DRINKING

Gaaitjie Off Sampson Rd ☏ 022 752 2242 ⊛ saltcoast .co.za. The top-notch chef here produces creative seafood-based dishes in a great beachside location – try the starter of crayfish cocktail (R80). Book in advance for a sea-facing table – you'll be provided with a rug for the chill sea breezes. The chef can produce something delicious on request for vegetarians. Thurs–Mon noon–3pm & 6–9pm; closed in winter.

Noisy Oyster St Augustine Rd ☏ 022 752 2196. You'll find creamy oysters and crayfish (R130), as well as meat dishes and vegetarian options, at this informal restaurant just off the main drag. What it lacks in setting, it makes up for in ambience and good food. Wed–Sat noon–3pm &

6–9pm, Sun noon–3pm; closed June & July.

Oep Ve Koep St Augustine Rd ☏ 022 752 2105. In a wind-sheltered garden, this is a good choice for imaginative lunches, such as mussel and lentil *bobotie* (R100), made by a talented chef who is inspired by local fare. It also serves local craft beers and wines. Summer daily 9.30am–2.30pm; winter Wed–Sun 9am–3pm.

Paternoster Hotel St Augustine Rd ☏ 022 752 2703. Known for their West Coast seafood platters (R460 for two), and if you book in advance they can organize a seafood braai. Check out the hotel's *Panties Bar*, whose roof is festooned with assorted knickers and the odd trophy bra. Daily 8am–9.30pm.

Velddrif

At the northern end of the R27 from Cape Town is **VELDDRIF**, a fishing town situated at the point where the Great Berg River meets the sea. Each year the Berg River **canoe marathon** (which starts near Ceres, 49km north of Worcester) ends here at a marina development called Port Owen. Over the last couple of decades, the town has outgrown its fishing industry origins and is now dominated by a modern suburbia of brick bungalows. However, the town's setting on the meandering Berg and the surrounding wetlands – as well as the vision of some locals, who have managed to stay the eager hand of the demolition crews – has resulted in Velddrif retaining a little of its historic character, and there is a wealth of **birdlife**, including pelicans and flamingos, along both banks of the river (see box, p.238).

In the quieter backwaters near the Velddrif bridge, you can still see individual fishermen in small boats landing catches of mullet or horse mackerel. The fish are then dried and salted to make *bokkoms*, known as a delicacy, but essentially a source of cheap protein for fishermen and farm workers on the West Coast. To see the rickety wooden jetties where the boats tie up, and the frames and sheds by the shore where *bokkoms* are strung up to dry, turn right at the roundabout just over the bridge coming into town on the R27, and after 1km or so take the first right-hand turn down to the riverside. Turning left over the same bridge takes you to Pelican Harbour, where a number of coffee and craft shops are housed in a renovated fishing factory.

INFORMATION AND TOURS   VELDDRIF

Information The tourist office is on Voortrekker Rd (Mon–Fri 8.30am–1pm, 2–5pm, Sat 9am–1pm; ☏ 022 783 1821, ⊛ tourismvelddrif.co.za).

Boat trips You can take a pleasant boat trip into the

wetlands with well-informed birder Dan Ahlers (☏ 082 951 0447; 60min trip R150), who takes excursions up the Berg River. He also leads bay cruises on which you stand a chance of seeing marine mammals.

ACCOMMODATION

★ **Kersefontein Guest Farm** 25km south of Velddrif on the Berg River ☏ 022 783 0850, ⊛ kersefontein .co.za. A highlight of the West Coast region, this is a working farm grazed by wild horses that dates back to the eighteenth century, and boasts several handsome Cape Dutch listed buildings, complete with antiques, some of which have been converted into stylish accommodation. Julian Melck, the eighth-generation owner, treats guests to lively tales of adventures on a South African farm. <u>R1280</u>

Kuifkopvisvanger 5km from town on the other side of the river ☏ 022 783 0818, ⊛ kuifkop.co.za. There are just seven charming, rustic fishermen's cottages here, with views of the river and marshlands. In addition, camping is available, and in the summer you can use the canoes to explore or swim in the river. Camping per person <u>R90</u>, cottage <u>R550</u>

Riviera 136 Voortrekker Rd ☏ 022 783 1137, ⊛ eigevis .com. The *Riviera* has double rooms, plus well-equipped self-catering chalets sleeping four (R780), each with a patio and set on the water's edge. There's also a restaurant and bar.

Flamingos and many other water birds can be seen from the restaurant/bar balcony, and the food is good. R800

EATING AND DRINKING

Eigevis Fish Shop Jameson St, close to the Laaiplek Hotel. If you're self-catering, this is the place to stock up on frozen seafood, including lobster, or to come for fresh fish and chips. Mon–Sat 9am–5pm.

The Laaiplek Hotel Jameson St ☎022 783 1116. A long-established old-fashioned harbour hotel, great for a drink with views of large boats, fish factories and cranes, as well as birds. They offer seafood and steaks and huge Sunday buffet lunches (R95). Mon–Sat 7.30am–9.30pm, Sun 7.30am–2.30pm.

★**Vishuis** About 3km west of Velddrif along the atmospheric riverside dirt road from the Velddrif bridge ☎022 783 1183. Housed in a restored traditional fish-drying factory, with outdoor seating offering views across the wetlands, *Vishuis* serves well-priced English breakfasts and excellent fish-and-chip lunches (R90). Book ahead for dinner. Summer Tues–Sat 9am–9pm, Sun 9am–3pm; winter Tues–Sat 10.30am–6pm, Sun 10am–3pm.

Elands Bay

Elands Bay (more commonly known as Elands) is a popular weekend destination, with a couple of guesthouses and restaurants, some fine bushman rock paintings on the south-side cliffs, and exceptional birdwatching. It's probably a place to catch before it's developed, though, like most of the West Coast, the water is freezing, and the coastline spare, windswept and harsh – the tide spewing mounds of kelp, shells and dried-out seal bones onto the deserted beaches. The spring flowers in this vicinity are also phenomenal.

Elands is divided into north and south sides by the **Verlorenvlei** ("lost wetland"), which supports over two hundred bird species. The nicer side is the south, where the surfers hang out. Above here, the Bobbejaanberg ridge runs into the sea. Where the road ends beneath the cliffs is the harbour, and the path up to a large cave with rock art, including some big eland and hundreds of handprints, which are thought to be connected to rites of passage – when adolescents imprinted their hands as they walked through the site.

ARRIVAL AND DEPARTURE   ELANDS BAY

By car It's a lonely 70km drive from Velddrif to Elands Bay, though the road is tarred all the way. It's approximately

200km from Cape Town (2hr 30min to drive).

ACCOMMODATION

Elands Bay Guest House 184 Kreef Rd, South Side ☎022 972 1755, ⍵elandsbayguesthouse.co.za. No frills self-catering accommodation, sleeping up to four people. It's principally geared to groups of surfers, with a communal kitchen and lots of wetsuits drying in the sun. R800

Elands Bay Hotel North Side Beachfront ☎022 972 1640, ⍵elandsbayhotel.co.za. Reasonably priced accommodation right at the beach, with double rooms

– go for the sea-facing ones with splendid views – as well as backpackers' rooms and camp sites. Camping per person R30, dorm R200, double R890

★**Vensterklip** 5km from Elands Bay ☎022 972 1340, ⍵vensterklip.co.za. A farm on the *vlei* with self-catering in restored, historic cottages, as well as camping, including tents for hire, and a good restaurant on site. Day visitors can rent kayaks to nose around the *vlei* (they are free for guests). Camping R120, cottage R700

EATING

Elands Bay Hotel North Side Beachfront. The only central option for reasonably priced seafood meals, grills and steak (R75), or pop in for a drink with brilliant views. Breakfasts are popular after a long surfing bout. Daily 8am–10pm.

Tin Kitchen Country Restaurant 5km from Elands

Bay ☎022 972 1340. The best bet for food, though only at weekends, serving meals using organic ingredients wherever possible, farm meat, local seafood and seasonal vegetables, in an old barn or outside in the garden. Friday nights are their popular and lively pizza nights (R80). Fri & Sat 9am–10pm, Sun 9am–3pm.

Lambert's Bay

The rather forlorn town of **LAMBERT'S BAY** is the only settlement of any note between Velddrif and Port Nolloth, the latter almost at the Namibian border. It's an important fishing port, although judging by the sights and sounds of the harbour even the fishermen have to stand aside for the impressive colony of **gannets** on **Bird Island**, in the centre of the bay.

Bird Island
Daily dawn–dusk • R30

It's possible to walk out to the island on the causeway for a closer look at the tightly packed, ear-piercing mass of petulant gannets from the bird hide, along with a few disapproving-looking penguins and cormorants, though viewing is not always guaranteed outside of breeding season. The bay plays host to a resident pod of around seven **humpback whales** during their breeding season from July to November. This is also the southernmost area ranged by **Heaviside's dolphins** – small, friendly mammals with wedge-shaped beaks (rather than the longer ones more commonly associated with dolphins), with a white, striped patterning reminiscent of killer whales. You may be lucky and view the cavorting mammals on trips from the fishing port.

ARRIVAL AND INFORMATION   LAMBERT'S BAY

By car Lambert's Bay is some 27km north of Elands Bay, and 70km due west of Clanwilliam by tarred road.
Information The tourist office is on Main Rd (Mon–Fri 9am–5pm, Sat 9am–12.30pm; ☎027 432 1000, ⓦ lambertsbay.co.za).

ACCOMMODATION

Donkieskraal Guest Lodge and Private Game Reserve Between Lambert's Bay and Clanwilliam ☎083 235 4717, ⓦdonkieskraal.co.za. A potato and game farm with chalets built right into the rocks to give a furnished cave experience, plus four safari tents nestling into the rocky hillside, and a campsite. While it's self-catering, the owner can provide meals on request. Camping R90, safari tent R500, chalet R800

Lamberts Bay Hotel Voortrekker St ☎027 432 1126, ⓦwww.lambertsbayhotel.co.za. Smack in the centre of town, this conventional and rather old-fashioned hotel offers neat and reasonably priced rooms, a swimming pool at the back, and help with organizing boat trips, and activities such as birding, beach riding or spring flower trips. R800

EATING

Isabella's Restaurant and Coffee Shop At the harbour ☎027 432 1177. A favourite choice, largely for its location right on the waterfront with tables and chairs outdoors to take in the harbour atmosphere and views. It offers the whole gamut of meals, from coffee and cake to fish and chips, prawns or a pot of mussels, but is renowned for its blowout cooked West Coast breakfast (R80). Daily 8am–9pm.
★**Muisbosskerm** Elands Bay Rd, 5km from Lamberts Bay ☎027 432 1017. The original West Coast open-air seafood restaurant scores on location – right on the edge of the ocean, on a deserted beach, and rated by many as one of the top ten things to do on a visit to South Africa. A massive buffet (R195) is on offer, with baked, smoked or grilled fish, potato bread cooked in a clay oven and traditional *waterblommetjie* stew, complete with Afrikaans *boeremusiek* in the background. It is not open every day (phone to check before coming), and you will need to book in advance. Lunch from 12.30pm, dinner from 6.30pm.

The Cederberg

A bold and jagged outcrop of the Western Cape fold escarpment, the **Cederberg range** is one of the most magical wilderness areas in the Western Cape. Rising with a striking presence on the eastern side of the Olifants River Valley, around 250km north of Cape Town, these high sandstone mountains and long, dry valleys manage to combine accessibility with remote harshness, offering something for hikers, campers, naturalists and rock climbers.

The **Cederberg Wilderness Area**, flanking the N7 between Citrusdal and Clanwilliam, was created to protect the silt-free waters of the Cederberg catchment area, but it also provides a recreational sanctuary with over 250km of hiking trails. In a number of places, the red-hued sandstone has been weathered into grotesque, gargoyle-like shapes and a number of memorable natural features. Throughout the area there are also numerous **San rock-art** sites, an active array of Cape mountain fauna, from baboon and small antelope to leopard, caracal and aardwolf, and some notable montane *fynbos* flora, including the gnarled and tenacious Clanwilliam cedar and the rare snow protea.

The Cederberg is accessed from Cape Town on the N7; the two main, though very small, towns of **Citrusdal** and **Clanwilliam** lie just off the highway near, respectively, the southern and northern tips of the mountain range, but are not in the mountains themselves, and are not the places to base yourself if you want to hike. The main road route into the Cederberg is along a dirt road marked **Algeria**, which branches off the N7 between the two towns; it's 18km from the turn-off to Algeria campsite. The eastern side of the Cederberg, known as the **Koue Bokkeveld**, is not accessed from the N7, but from the N1 and Ceres.

Citrusdal

North of Piketberg on the N7, a long, flat plain reaches out to the line of Olifantsrivierberg Mountains, which the highway crosses by way of the impressive **Piekenierskloof Pass**, forged in 1857 by the indomitable road engineer Thomas Bain. CITRUSDAL appears in the rolling countryside of the Olifants River Valley, with the dramatic mountainscape of the Cederberg behind, though it is bypassed by the N7. Strange as it may seem now, early Dutch explorers saw huge herds of elephants here as they travelled north towards Namaqualand, hence the river's name.

One of the principal attractions of this area is the natural **hot springs** 16km from Citrusdal, which you can visit as a day visitor or stay overnight (see below).

ARRIVAL AND INFORMATION   CITRUSDAL

By car Citrusdal is a couple of kilometres off the N7, 170km from Cape Town.

Information The tourist office, at 39 Voortrekker St

(Mon–Fri 8.30am–5pm, Sat 9am–noon; ☎022 921 3210, ⊕ citrusdal.info), has a comprehensive list of self-catering cottages and bed and breakfast accommodation in the area.

ACCOMMODATION

The Baths South off the road leading into Citrusdal from the N7, then 16km down a good tarred road ☎022 921 8026, ⊕ thebaths.co.za. A pleasantly old-fashioned, if rather rule-bound, mineral spa resort with one large hot pool (43˚C), a cold pool and several large indoor spa baths. Day visitors pay R80 to use the amenities, though guests get to use them for free. The place is set in a beautiful wooded glen with camping pitches, chalets and self-catering rooms in some large old stone buildings. There's also restaurant with passable

food, though most people self-cater. Camping R100, double R650

★**Petersfield Mountain Cottages** 4km from Citrusdal ☎022 921 3316, ⊕ petersfieldfarm.co.za. On a working rooibos and citrus farm, with some of the best self-catering cottages you'll find anywhere; each secluded cottage sleeps 2–4 people and has its own private pool. For weekends, you'll need to book a year in advance, and the minimum stay is two nights. The weekday rate is about R300 cheaper. Cottage R1200.

INTO THE MOUNTAINS

You have to **hike** to actually get into the Cederberg mountains themselves; short walks are possible from a few properties, but if you want to do any serious walking you should be properly equipped and experienced as this is rough country, and weather conditions can be harsh throughout the year.

One of the best ways to get into the mountains is with **professional mountaineer** Mike Wakeford, who offers tailor-made multi-day trekking trips that depart from Cape Town (☎079 722 9808, ⊕ guidedbymike.co.za). Prices depend on the number of people and days.

The Cederberg Wilderness Area

The main route into the Cederberg, and Algeria, the forest station that serves as a focal point for the area, heads east off the N7, 28km north of Citrusdal, and connects all the way towards Ceres in the east. The 710-square-kilometre **Cederberg Wilderness Area** features many designated trails, including the two main peaks, **Sneeuberg** (2027m) and **Tafelberg** (1969m), as well as the awesome rock formations of the huge **Wolfberg Arch** and **Cracks** in the southeast of the reserve, and a 30m-high freestanding pillar shaped like (and known as) the **Maltese Cross**, to its south.

ARRIVAL AND INFORMATION   THE CEDERBERG WILDERNESS AREA

By car The main route into the Cederberg is along Algeria Rd (clearly signposted to Algeria). It's a rough dirt road, but fine in an ordinary car if you take it fairly slowly. From Cape Town it is about 250km, and you'll need to allow three and a half hours.

Information You'll need permits to hike, which are easy and cheap to get from the CapeNature Office at Algeria campsite (daily 7.30am–7pm; ☎ 0861 227 362 8873, ⓦ www.capenature.org.za). An indispensable map *Exploring the Cederberg* (ⓦ slingsbymaps.com) has all the resorts, roads and distances marked on it, and is available from hiking shops.

ACCOMMODATION

Algeria Campsite 18km east on Algeria Rd, signposted off the N7 ☎ 0861 227 362 8873, ⓦ www .capenature.org.za. A pretty riverside site, with a gorgeous river pool and hikes leaving from the campsite itself into the surrounding mountains. It can be quite crowded and noisy during school hols but the kids will have a ball. There are also a couple of self-catering chalets here, and isolated cottages a few kilometres away, which have paraffin lamps rather than electricity. Camping R200, chalet R580

Jamaka Organic Farm Cottages and Campsite Signposted and accessed just before Algeria, on the Algeria Rd ☎ 027 482 2801, ⓦ jamaka.co.za. The campsite on this organic citrus and mango farm has a lovely setting, though for good hikes you will need to drive over to *Algeria Campsite*, and do the trails from there. If you want a roof over your head, note that the best of their reasonably priced cottages is the stone one next to the river. Camping R160, cottage R360

Kromrivier 50km south of Algeria ☎ 027 482 2807, ⓦ cederbergtourist.co.za. Fourteen fully equipped chalets, sleeping four: the more expensive ones come with their own baths. There are also camping pitches near river pools for swimming, plus a coffee shop on site if you don't feel like cooking, though you'll need to pre-order dinner by 4pm on the day. Camping R150, chalet R500

★ **Sanddrif** About 26km south of Algeria, along the same dirt road ☎ 027 482 2825, ⓦ cederbergwine .com. Fully equipped chalets with one to three rooms (bring your own bedding), on a farm with natural river pools and good walks, as well as camping. *Sanddrif* also sells permits for the classic walks on its property – the Maltese Cross, Wolfberg Arch and Cracks – and offers tasting sessions of the wines made from grapes grown on the farm. There is a shop selling basics, too. Camping R150, chalet R650

Koue Bokkeveld (South Eastern Cederberg)

The southeastern Cederberg mountain range, known as the **Koue Bokkeveld**, is remote and wild, with some wonderful places to stay. You'll need to be self-sufficient if you are self-catering, as there are no shops or cafés hereabouts, though all the places listed below have restaurants. The best way to approach this region is from Worcester on the N1: from here, take the R303 to Ceres, then turn right at Op de Berg to join the Algeria dirt road which heads north to eventually join the N7.

ACCOMMODATION   KOUE BOKKEVELD

Cederberg Oasis On the R303, 70km from Op de Berg and 62km east of Algeria ☎ 027 482 2819, ⓦ cederbergoasis.co.za. Backpackers' accommodation in basic rooms, doubles and dorms, plus camping on the lawn. It has a licensed restaurant, serving meals of gigantic proportions, though you'll need to prebook for dinner. The owner Gerrit will hand-draw you a map and sell you permits so that you can visit the nearby sandstone formations and rock art at Tanjieskraal and Stadsaal Caves. Camping for four R135, doubles R300

FROM TOP LEFT SUSPENSION BRIDGE, STORMS RIVER MOUTH (P.234); CANOPY TOUR, STORMS RIVER ADVENTURES (P.237); WOLFBERG ARCH, CEDERBERG WILDERNESS AREA >

2

> ## CEDERBERG ROCK ART
>
> The Cederberg has around 2500 known **rock-art sites**, estimated to be between one and eight thousand years old. They are the work of the first South Africans, hunter gatherers known as San or **Bushmen**, the direct descendants of some of the earliest Homo sapiens who lived in the Western Cape 150,000 years ago.
>
> One of the best ways to see the rock art is on a self-guided 4km walk from *Traveller's Rest Farm* (see p.252) along the Sevilla Trail, which takes in ten sites.
>
> Alternatively, you can take a half-day tour to the Warmhoek site near Clanwilliam, run by the excellent Living Landscape Project, 18 Park St in Clanwilliam (☎027 482 1911, ⓦcllp.uct.ac.za), and led by competent local guides. The project is the brainchild of archeologist John Parkington, from the University of Cape Town, whose books on rock art in the Cederberg (*The Mantis and the Moon* and *Cederberg Rock Paintings*) offer the best interpretation of the puzzling and beautiful images you'll see delicately painted on rocks and overhangs.

★ **Kamma** 52km from Op de Berg, off the R303 ☎021 872 4343, ⓦkaggakamma.co.za. A luxury lodge with some accommodation built into the rocks to resemble caves, plus nicer thatched chalets with verandas looking out onto natural veld. There are walks, game drives, and a good restaurant and bar, and guests can opt for a stargazing tour – their high-powered telescope, combined with no lights or pollution, lets you see clearly the moons of Jupiter. The rock art and rock formations on the property are magnificent – some of the best are in a rock shelter close to the large swimming pool. One of the highlights is the sundowner game drive followed by dinner around a fire beneath the stars. They offer an all-inclusive rate including meals and activities (R2483 per person), or you can just opt for bed and breakfast. Camping per person R60, double R2800

★ **Mount Ceder** On the R303, 42km from Op de Berg ☎023 317 0113, ⓦmountceder.co.za. A very comfortable mountain retreat with self-catering cottages, some of which have jacuzzis. The cottages are self-catering – some have mains electricity and sleep four, while others sleep two and are solar-powered. There are also three sought-after luxury camping pitches, each with its own ablutions and solar lighting. It's spectacularly set in a wide valley on an olive farm along a river with pools for swimming, and surrounded by fierce, rugged mountains. There's also a restaurant, and this is one of the few places in the Cederberg that offers horseriding (R250). Camping R300, cottages R800.

Clanwilliam

At the northern end of the Cederberg, **CLANWILLIAM** is an attractive and assured small town. It carries off with some aplomb its various roles as a base for the majestic Cederberg Wilderness Area, a centre for spring flowers, a service centre for surrounding farms, and the place to head for if you want to see good **rock art** within easy striking distance of Cape Town. Established in the last years of the eighteenth century, Clanwilliam is one of the older settlements north of Cape Town and features a number of historic buildings around town.

ARRIVAL AND INFORMATION CLANWILLIAM

By bus The daily Intercape bus from Cape Town to Windhoek stops 7km away at a garage on the N7, though there's no way of getting from there into town.

Information The tourist office on Main Rd (Mon–Fri 8.30am–5pm, Sat 8.30am–12.30pm; ☎027 482 2024, ⓦclanwilliam.info) sells permits for bouldering (see p.252).

ACCOMMODATION

Blommenberg Guest House 1 Graafwater Rd ☎027 482 1851, ⓦblommenberg.co.za. Opposite the garage as you come into Clanwilliam, this guesthouse has good-value rooms with pine beds and fittings set around a pleasantly shady courtyard garden and swimming pool. Four family-sized rooms on the veranda can be used for self-catering. R1020

Living Landscape 18 Park St ☎027 482 1911. Acceptable place to stay, and the only backpacker accommodation in the centre of Clanwilliam, with dorms in a suburban house next door to a community project. It is mostly geared towards school and university groups on rock-art projects. R100

Ndedema Lodge 48 Park St ☎027 482 1314,

ⓦ ndedemalodge.co.za. A romantic Victorian B&B with an upmarket feel, and a charming garden with a pool. Its four antique-filled rooms, two of which have canopied beds, come with cotton bedlinen, plush towels and dressing gowns. R1200

EATING

Nancy's Tea Room 33 Main Rd ☎ 027 482 2661. The outdoor garden here is a peaceful place for breakfast or lunch; they serve toasted sandwiches, savoury mince and cheddar melt (R50) and good coffee. Slightly heavier lunch dishes includes *bobotie*, one of the few things on the menu that doesn't come with chips. Mon–Sat 8am–4.30pm.

Olifants Huis 1 Main Rd ☎ 027 482 2301. The best choice for an evening meal, in a cosy Afrikaans-styled manor house, with a wood-fired pizza oven and a good reputation for steaks (R90). The chef uses local, seasonal ingredients to create interesting dishes such as ostrich fillets smoked over rooibos tea-leaves. Mon–Sat 5–9.30pm.

★**Yellow Aloes** 1 Park Rd ☎ 027 482 2018. Its setting on a veranda looking onto the garden and nursery makes this a charming place to enjoy a full bacon-and-egg breakfast (R70) or a light lunch. If you book in advance, they'll serve a romantic dinner beneath the trees (three courses R120). Daily 8am–5pm.

The Boskloof

About 1km east of Clanwilliam along the Pakhuis Pass road, a good dirt road heads south and drops into the **Boskloof**, through which the Jan Dissels River traces its course. Although less than 10km from the town, and 290km from Cape Town, the valley feels a very long way from anywhere and is a relaxed spot where you can spend time lolling about along the riverbank, swimming in its natural pools or just walking along the dirt road that twists through the mountains. From the valley you can hike up into the Cederberg Mountains on the **Krakadouw hiking trail**, which starts at **Krakadouw Cottages**, where you can buy permits. Hikes can last up to a week, though you can also do shorter day or half-day hikes along a section of the trail.

ACCOMMODATION   THE BOSKLOOF

Boskloof Swemgat Boskloof Rd, 13km from Clanwilliam ☎ 027 482 2522, ⓦ boskloofswemgat .co.za. Accommodation is in eight simple, self-catering cottages without a great deal of privacy, in an open, grassy area, right on the river. The draw of this place is the excellent river swimming and reasonable prices. R600

Klein Boschkloof Chalets Boskloof Rd, 9km from Clanwilliam ☎ 027 482 2441, ⓦ kleinboschkloof .co.za. A reasonably priced collection of 250-year-old Cape Dutch farm buildings converted into guest cottages. The thatched chalets stand in the middle of fragrant citrus groves, and are finished to a high standard, with cooking gear, bed linen and towels provided. Breakfast and dinner are available by prior arrangement. R700

ROOIBOS TEA

Few things in South Africa create such devotion or aversion as **rooibos** (literally, "red bush") **tea**. Still sown and harvested by hand on many farms, rooibos is a type of *fynbos* plant grown only in the mountainous regions around Clanwilliam and Nieuwoudtville. The caffeine-free, health tea brewed from its leaves is firmly entrenched alongside regular tea and coffee in South African homes, and now even comes as an espresso, known as Red Espresso, which you can buy in powdered form from supermarkets or order as a brew at an increasing number of cafés.

To see how the tea is grown and processed on a farm, take one of the **tours** offered by Elandsberg Eco Tours (☎ 027 482 2022, ⓦ elandsberg.co.za; R100), which leave from their premises 20km west of Clanwilliam, on the Lambert's Bay road. Alternatively, you can visit the country's main **rooibos tea processing factory** in Ou Kaapse Weg in Clanwilliam (☎ 027 482 2155), which shows videos of the manufacturing process (Mon–Fri at 10am, 11.30am, 2pm & 3.30pm), and sells rooibos tea and rooibos-inspired cosmetics.

Northern Cederberg and the Pakhuis Pass

The **R364** northeast from Clanwilliam winds over the **Pakhuis Pass**, a drive worth taking for its lonely roadside scenery and inspiring views. This area, called **Rocklands**, is said to be one of the two best places in the world for **bouldering**, so expect to see plenty of lithe climbers going to and from the graded routes, particularly in the milder winter months. Although you are below the Cederberg massifs, the rocks, rivers, valleys and sense of space make this area very appealing, with the added attraction of providing access to the finest rock art in the Western Cape (see p.250).

2

ACCOMMODATION   NORTHERN CEDERBERG AND THE PAKHUIS PASS

All the accommodation in this area is along the Pakhuis Pass Rd. The road is tarred, though it peters out beyond Bushman's Kloof into a network of dirt roads leading to farms.

Alpha Excelsior Guest Farm and Winery ☎ 027 482 2700, ⓦ alphaexcelsior.co.za. Three cottages, the nicest of which, Weaver, is nearest to the river and sleeps two; the others sleep more, and there's an attic room in one house with dorm beds, often taken up by rock climbers. The farm, run by friendly folk, has its own small winery too, with bottles for sale. Dorm R90, cottage R600

Bushman's Kloof ☎ 027 482 2627, bookings ☎ 021 437 9278, ⓦ bushmanskloof.co.za. A luxury lodge, which has won international hotel accolades, set in a wilderness area with game drives and rock art – there are more than 125 recorded rock art sites on the property. The rangers are trained in both wildlife guiding and rock-art interpretation. The rate includes all meals, game drives and guided rock-art trails. R8000

De Pakhuys Rocklands ☎ 027 482 1879, ⓦ depakhuys .co.za. Three large garden cottages of varying sizes on a rooibos farm, 26km from Clanwilliam, with marked hiking

trails, starting near the secluded campsite, plus a farm dam for swimming. The owners are exceptionally obliging and let guests use their swimming pool and braai facilities. The farm is also used by climbers, and sells permits for bouldering. Camping R60, cottage R800

★**Travellers Rest** ⓦ travellersrest.co.za. Twelve self-catering cottages in different locations on a passion fruit, rooibos and sheep farm, where there are plenty of walks. The accommodation is basic, but the landscape is stirring. Meals for groups can be pre-arranged and there is a farm stall which also serves daytime meals. The main attraction is the 4km Sevilla bushman painting trail, starting right beside the farm. The trail takes in nine separate rock-art sites, and provides an easy and varied introduction to rock art; if you're pushed for time, you can restrict yourself to the first six, which are the best. Horse trails can also be arranged, and there are river pools for summer swimming. R450

Wuppertal and the Biedouw Valley

One of the best drives you can do in the Western Cape is along the mountainous R364 dirt road, pretty awful and steep in parts, which winds through remote valleys to reach historic **WUPPERTAL**. Set deep in the tunefully named Tra-tra Valley, the Moravian

---

OUDRIF

An exceptional retreat lodge in the Cederberg back country, 48km from Clanwilliam along rough dirt roads, ★**Oudrif** (booking essential; ☎ 027 482 2397, ⓦ oudrif.co.za; R1700) occupies inspiring countryside in the transitional zone between the foothills of the mountains and the dry Karoo, with redstone gorges and a wide valley incised by the Doring River. Although there are wonderful **guided walks** through *fynbos* to San rock-art sites and paddling opportunities on the river, this is as much a place to chill out – the only rule enforced by the co-owner and manager Bill Mitchell, and his wife Janine, is that there are no rules. The multi-talented Mitchell is also a qualified chef and does all the cooking at this full-board establishment.

    Accommodation is in five straw-bale houses. The cream-coloured chalets have an uneven hewn quality that befits their isolation on the edge of the gorge that falls away to the Doring River. Each is stylishly equipped with retro furniture and has a double and a three-quarter bed; the power for lighting is provided by solar panels, and showers are heated.

mission station is one of the oldest in the Western Cape and, with a tiny collection of thatched cottages in the small centre and along the river, it remains one of the most untouched settlements in South Africa. Run by the church elders and with an entirely coloured population, the mission is famous for making **velskoene** (literally "hide shoes"), the suede footwear commonly known as *vellies* and part of Afrikaner national dress. You can see the shoes being made and, of course, buy them at the little shop at De Werf – the centre that clusters around the church.

On the way to Wuppertal you can turn into the **Biedouw Valley**, which only has traffic during the spring, when the valley floor is carpeted with flowers.

ACCOMMODATION

Enjolife Biedouw Valley Rd ☎ 027 482 2869, ⓦ soulcountry.info. The best reason to visit the Biedouw Valley is to stay at this isolated 200-year-old farmhouse, run by a young German couple who offer lovely self-catering chalets at backpacker prices. There's also camping, though the campsite is not so appealing. The emphasis here is on enjoying nature, and in the hot summer you can swim at the farm dam. Owing to its isolation, it's a place to spend a few days, rather than simply overnight. Access is only on dirt roads. Dinners can be booked on request and the owner, a former Lufthansa pilot, can arrange flights here. Camping R60, chalet R400

The
Northern
Cape

RICHTERSVELD TRANSFRONTIER PARK

The Northern Cape

The vast Northern Cape, the largest and most dispersed of South Africa's provinces, is not an easy region to tackle as a visitor. From the lonely Atlantic coast to Kimberley, the provincial capital on its eastern border with the Free State, it covers over one-third of the nation's landmass, an area dominated by heat, aridity, empty spaces and huge travelling distances. The miracles of the desert are the main attraction – improbable swaths of flowers, diamonds dug from the dirt and wild animals roaming the dunes.

The most significant of these surprises is the **Orange** (or Gariep) **River**, flowing from the Lesotho Highlands to the Atlantic where it marks South Africa's border with Namibia. The river separates the **Kalahari** and the **Great Karoo** – the two sparsely populated semi-desert ecosystems that fill the interior of the Northern Cape. On its banks, the isolated northern centre of **Upington** is the main town in the Kalahari region, the gateway to the magnificent **Kgalagadi Transfrontier Park** and the smaller **Augrabies Falls National Park**.

In **Namaqualand**, on the western side of the province, the brief winter rains produce one of nature's truly glorious transformations when in August and September the land is carpeted by a magnificent display of wild flowers. A similar display of blossoming succulents can be seen at the little-visited |Ai-|Ais/Richtersveld National Park, a mountain desert tucked around a loop in the Orange River either side of the Namibian border.

Despite these impressive natural attractions, most of the traffic to the Northern Cape is in its southeastern corner, through which the two main roads between Johannesburg and Cape Town, the **N1** and the **N12**, pass. However, given the uninspiring nature of this area, it isn't covered in this book. A less obvious way to get from Johannesburg to Cape Town involves taking the **N14** through Upington, passing the atmospheric old mission station at **Kuruman**, then driving on to **Springbok** and following the scenic **N7** down the coast. This route is around 400km longer than the N1 or N12 but, while the N14 has more than its fair share of long, empty landscapes, the sights along the way are more interesting.

Getting around by **public transport** can be a pain. While the main towns of Kimberley, Springbok and Upington lie on Intercape's bus routes (with connections to Windhoek in Namibia), many services arrive and depart at night and thus miss the scenery. Minibus taxis cover most destinations several times a day during the week, but are much reduced or nonexistent at weekends. Taxis don't serve the national parks (take an organized tour instead). Details of the most useful routes are given in the text.

Brief history
The history of the Northern Cape area is intimately linked to the **San**, South Africa's first people, whose hunter-gatherer lifestyle and remarkable adaptations to desert life

AUGRABIES FALLS

Highlights

❶ The Big Hole The vast hand-dug crater that dominates Kimberley is an awesome testament to South Africa's pioneer diamond hunters. **See p.262**

❷ Kgalagadi Transfrontier Park Discover lion, gemsbok and meerkat among the parched red sand dunes of the Kalahari. **See p.278**

❸ Augrabies Falls Marvel at South Africa's most powerful waterfall, where the Orange River thunders into an echoing gorge carved out of the desert. **See p.280**

❹ Driving down the N7 The province's most scenic drive stretches south from Springbok

through rocky mountains and peaceful dorps. **See p.282**

❺ Namaqualand flowers In August and September the veld bursts into colour with a superb natural floral display, and boasts a fascinating variety of unusual succulents year-round. **See p.283**

❻ |Ai-|Ais/Richtersveld National Park South Africa's only mountain desert, a hot, dry and forbidding place that can only be explored by 4WD or by drifting down the Orange River in an inflatable canoe. **See p.292**

HIGHLIGHTS ARE MARKED ON THE MAP ON PP.258–259

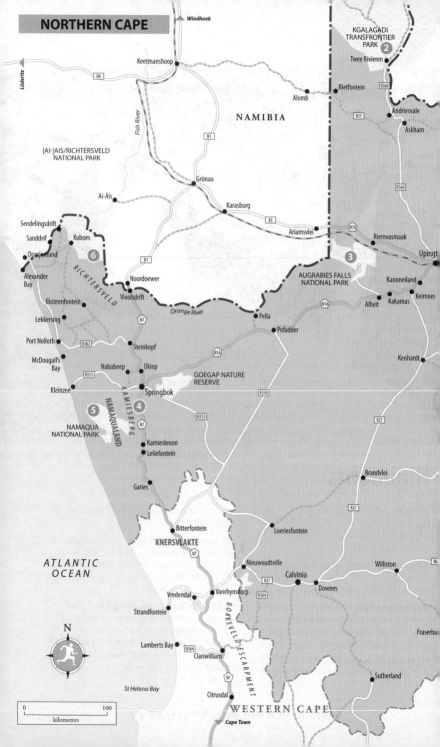

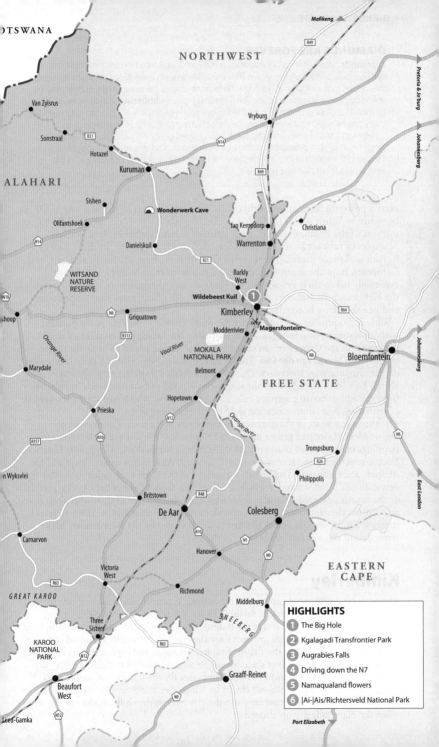

BOTSWANA

NORTHWEST

Mafikeng

R49

Pretoria & Jo'burg

Johannesburg

Van Zylsrus

Vryburg

N14

Sonstraal

R31

Hotazel

R49

KALAHARI

Kuruman

Sishen

Wonderwerk Cave

N14

Christiana

Olifantshoek

Jan Kempdorp

Danielskuil

Warrenton

R31

WITSAND
NATURE
RESERVE

Barkly West

N10

Wildebeest Kuil

①

KIMBERLEY

...shoop

N8

Griquatown

Modderrivier

Magersfontein

R313

R64

Vaal River

MOKALA
NATIONAL PARK

N8

Bloemfontein

Johannesburg

Marydale

Belmont

FREE STATE

East London

Prieska

Hopetown

N12

Orange River

N10

R357

Trompsburg

N6

R26

n Wyksvlei

Philippolis

Britstown

R48

De Aar

Colesberg

N10

N1

Carnarvon

Hanover

N9

Victoria
West

**EASTERN
CAPE**

R63

Richmond

GREAT KAROO

Middelburg

Three
Sisters

SNEEBERG

KAROO
NATIONAL
PARK

R63

N12

Beaufort
West

Graaff-Reinet

N9

Leed-Gamka

N12

Port Elizabeth

HIGHLIGHTS

① The Big Hole
② Kgalagadi Transfrontier Park
③ Augrabies Falls
④ Driving down the N7
⑤ Namaqualand flowers
⑥ |Ai-|Ais/Richtersveld National Park

DIAMONDS ARE FOREVER

Diamonds originate as carbon particles in the Earth's mantle, which are subjected to such high pressure and temperature that they crystallize to form diamonds. Millions of years ago the molten rock, or magma, in the mantle burst through weak points in the Earth's crust as volcanoes, and it is in the pipe of cooled magma – called **kimberlite**, after Kimberley – that diamonds are found. Finding kimberlite, however, isn't necessarily a licence to print money – in every one hundred tonnes there will be about twenty carats (4g) of diamonds.

The word "carat" derives from the carob bean – dried beans were used as a measure of weight. (Carat has a different meaning in the context of gold, where it is a measure of purity.) De Beers estimates that fifty million pieces of diamond jewellery are bought each year – which represents a lot of marriage proposals.

exert a powerful fascination. Although no genuine vestiges of the San way of life can be found in South Africa (only tiny pockets remain in the Namibian and Botswanan sections of the Kalahari desert), their heritage is most visible in the countless examples of **rock art** across the province, and, to a lesser extent, in their ancient legends and place names. The movement of Africans from the north and east, and Europeans from the southwest, drove the San from their hunting grounds and eventually led to their extinction; yet for both sets of newcomers, the semi-desert of the Karoo and the Kalahari at first appeared to offer little more than hopelessness and heartbreaking horizons.

What it did provide – wealth under the dusty ground – the Europeans pursued without restraint, beginning in 1685, soon after the Dutch first established their settlement in the Cape, with an expedition into Namaqualand to mine for copper led by **Governor Simon van der Stel**. The other Europeans who made an early impression on the province were **trekboers**, Dutch burghers freed from the employment of the Dutch East India Company in the Cape who wanted to find new lands to farm away from the authoritarian company rule, and **missionaries**, who established a framework of settlement and communication used by all who came after.

Within a few years of the discovery of **diamonds** in the area, a settlement of unprecedented size had grown up around Kimberley. The town soon boasted more trappings of civilization than most of the southern hemisphere, with public libraries, electric streetlights and tramways, as well as South Africa's first urban "location" for Africans and coloureds. The British authorities in the Cape were quick to annexe the new diamond fields – a move which didn't endear them to either the Orange Free State or the mainly coloured **Griqua** people, who both claimed this ill-defined region. It was no surprise, therefore, that at the outbreak of the **Anglo-Boer War** in 1899, rich and strategic Kimberley was one of the first towns besieged by the Boer armies. Many reminders of the war can still be seen in the area.

Kimberley

Although it's a provincial capital and the historic centre of production of one of the world's most valuable materials, **KIMBERLEY** itself is neither large nor glamorous. During the diamond rush, it was the fastest-growing city in the southern hemisphere and Cecil Rhodes held in his grip not only the fabulously wealthy diamond industry, but the heart and mind of the British Empire; yet status and sophistication have been draining from Kimberley ever since. Even the all-controlling De Beers Group (sometimes called the "grandfather" of Kimberley for the number of people it has directly and indirectly employed) closed its Kimberley mines in 2005 as part of a process to streamline the company, and the city lives in the chilly shadow of the day when the diamonds dry up altogether.

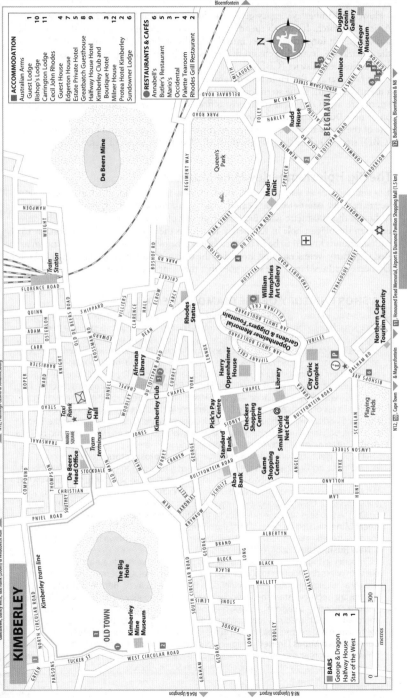

KIMBERLEY

3

However, Kimberley's legacy gives it an historic flavour few other cities in South Africa can match. It's worth spending a few hours seeking out some of the many old buildings, not forgetting to peer into the depths of the Big Hole just west of the centre, the remarkable, hand-dug chasm that takes up almost as much land area as the city's central business district (CBD).

The fact that the Big Hole is underground doesn't make orientation immediately easy; a useful landmark is the stern-looking skyscraper, **Harry Oppenheimer House** (often referred to as HOH), near the tourist office. Many of Kimberley's other main sights lie on or near **Du Toitspan Road**, which slices diagonally across the city centre and becomes one of the main arteries out of town to the southeast. The central business district (CBD) sits at Du Toitspan Road's northern end, to the south of Lennox Road.

The Big Hole: Kimberley Mine Museum

On the western side of the hole along West Circular Rd • **Museum** Daily 8am–5pm, last entry 4pm • R85 • **Tram** Every quarter past the hour from the City Hall, and on the hour from the Big Hole 9.15am–4.15pm • R10 • ☎ 053 839 4600, ⓦ thebighole.co.za

Although the 500-metre-wide **Big Hole**, just west of the city centre, is neither the only nor even the biggest hole in Kimberley, it remains the city's principal attraction. In 1871, with diamonds known to be in the area (see box below), a group of workers known as the Red Cap Party were scratching around at the base of **Colesberg koppie**, a small hill on the De Beers brothers' farm. The story goes that they sent one of their cooks to the top of the

---

A SHORT HISTORY OF THE DIAMOND FIELDS

The area now known as the **Diamond Fields** was once unpromising farmland, marked by occasional *koppies* inhabited by pioneer farmers and the Griquas, an independent people of mixed race. In 1866 this changed forever, when a 15-year-old boy noticed a shiny white pebble on the banks of the Orange River near Hopetown, about 120km southwest of Kimberley. Just as word of that discovery was spreading, another Hopetown resident, Schalk van Niekerk, acquired from a Griqua shepherd a massive 83.5-carat diamond. These two stones became known, respectively, as "**Eureka**" and "**The Star of South Africa**"; the latter was described at the time – with some justification – by the British Colonial Secretary as the "rock on which the future success of South Africa will be built". Certainly in the short term, the discoveries provoked wild optimism: thousands of prospectors made the gruelling trek across the Karoo to sift through the alluvial deposits along the banks of the Orange and Vaal rivers, and by 1873 there were an estimated fifty thousand people living in the area.

Although plenty of diamonds were found in the rivers, **prospectors** also began scratching around in the dry land between them, encouraged by tales of diamonds found in farmhouse bricks made from local earth. Two of the most promising "dry diggings" were on a farm owned by two brothers, Johannes Nicolas and Diederick Arnoldus de Beer. In 1871 the brothers sold the farm, which they had bought a few years previously for £50, to prospectors for the sum of £6300. The two sites subsequently became the **Kimberley Mine**, or Big Hole, and the **De Beers Mine**, situated on either side of the centre of Kimberley. The Big Hole was the focus of the most frenetic mining activity of the early years, and the shantytown that grew up around it, **New Rush**, was the origin of the present city.

Kimberley in those days was a heady, rugged place to live, with little authority or structure, but with prizes rich enough to attract bold men with big ideas. Of these, two very different, if equally ambitious, men rose to prominence in the new settlement. **Barney Barnato**, a flamboyant Cockney, established his power base at the Kimberley Mine, while **Cecil Rhodes** (see box opposite), a parson's son who had come out to join his brother in South Africa to improve his health, gradually took control of the De Beers Mine. The power struggle between the two men was intense, culminating in the formation in 1888 of the **De Beers Consolidated Mines Limited**, an agreement involving the transfer from Rhodes to Barnato of over £5 million, an astronomical sum in those days. This consolidation laid the foundation for De Beers' monopoly of the diamond industry in South Africa.

CECIL JOHN RHODES

When **Cecil Rhodes** first arrived in the Kimberley Diamond Fields he was a sickly 18-year-old, sent out to join his brother for the sake of his health. Soon making money buying up claims, he returned to Britain to attend Oxford University, where his illnesses returned and he was given six months to live. He came back out to South Africa, where he was able to improve both his health and his business standing, allowing him to return to Oxford and graduate in 1881. By that point he had already founded the **De Beers Mining Company** and been elected an MP in the **Cape Parliament**.

Within a decade, Rhodes controlled ninety percent of the world's diamond production and was champing at the bit to expand his mining interests north into Africa, with the British Empire in tow. With much cajoling, bullying, brinkmanship and obfuscation in his dealings with imperial governments and African chiefs alike, Rhodes brought the regions north of the Limpopo under the control of his **British South African Company** (BSAC). This territory – now Zimbabwe and Zambia – became known as **Rhodesia** in 1895, the same year as a Rhodes-backed invasion of the Transvaal Republic, the **Jameson Raid**, failed humiliatingly. Rhodes was forced to resign as prime minister of the Cape Colony, a post he had assumed in 1890 at the age of 37, while the Boers and the British slid towards war. He spent the first part of the war in besieged Kimberley, trying to organize the defences and bickering publicly with the British commander. A year after the end of the war, Rhodes died at Muizenberg near Cape Town, aged only 49 and unmarried; he was buried in the Matopos Hills near Bulawayo in Zimbabwe.

hill as a punishment for being drunk, telling him not to return until he'd found a diamond. The unnamed servant duly came back with a peace offering, and within two years there were over fifty thousand people in the area frantically turning Colesberg *koppie* inside out. In its heyday, tens of thousands of miners swarmed over the mine to work their 10-square-metre claim, and a network of ropes and pipes crisscrossed the surface; each day saw lives lost and fortunes either discovered or squandered. Once the mining could go no further from the surface, a shaft was dug to allow further excavations beneath it to a depth of over 800m. Incredibly, the hole was dug to a depth of 240m entirely by pick and shovel, and remains one of the largest manmade excavations in the world. By 1914, when De Beers closed the mine, some 22.6 million tonnes of earth had been removed, yielding over 13.6 million carats (2722kg) of diamonds.

The only official way to see the Big Hole is from inside the **Kimberley Mine Museum**, which you can reach either on foot or via a delightfully rickety, open-sided tram that runs from the City Hall. The museum gives a comprehensive insight into Kimberley's main claim to fame. The Big Hole itself is viewed from a suspended platform, from which you can peer down into nothingness. An informative film puts it all into context, as do other displays, from a re-creation of a nineteenth-century mineshaft to a vault full of real diamonds.

The Old Town

West Circular Rd • Daily 8am–5pm • Free

This impressive collection of **historic buildings**, many originating from the days of Rhodes and Barnato, is scattered around the entrance to the Mine Museum and can be wandered through without paying the museum entry fee. The old shops, churches, pub, banks and sundry other period institutions were moved here from the city centre when development and demolition threatened; now there's enough here to create a fairly complete settlement, and most of the fixtures, fittings and artefacts are genuine.

Diamond Dig

Daily 8am–5pm • R30

One of the more engaging features in the Old Town is an area where you can buy a bucket of **alluvial river diggings** and sift through it on old sorting tables, in the hope of finding one of the mock diamonds planted among the gravel. The rocks can be exchanged for various prizes, and the price of the bucket includes a shot at some old-fashioned ten-pin bowling as well.

Market Square and around

At the heart of the city centre is **Market Square**, dominated by the white, Corinthian-style City Hall (1899). During the early diamond days, the square was the hub of buying and selling, and still today around the square, the sense of movement and commerce is perpetuated by a large taxi rank and an assortment of scruffy but colourful stalls and traders. One block west of Market Square along the tramline, at **36 Stockdale St**, lies the head office of De Beers, a dignified but unremarkable old building (not open to the public) rather swallowed up by the city around it.

The Africana Library

63–65 Du Toitspan Rd · Mon–Fri 8am–12.45pm & 1.30–4.30pm · ☎ 053 830 6247, Ⓦ africanalibrary.co.za

The small but engrossing **Africana Library**, across the road from the Kimberley Club, specializes in historical material relevant to Kimberley and the Northern Cape including records by early European travellers and documentation and photos of the Anglo-Boer War (1899–1902). Opened in 1887 as the Kimberley Public Library, it retains many original features, and one of the librarians will show you around if you ask nicely.

The CBD

At the junction of Du Toitspan and Lennox roads stands a statue of **Cecil Rhodes** who sits astride a horse while peering at his map of Africa. The **CBD** area begins across Lennox Street, where the **Oppenheimer Memorial Gardens** contain a bust of mining magnate Sir Ernest Oppenheimer and the Diggers' Fountain; the latter depicts five miners holding aloft a massive sieve, and looks particularly impressive when floodlit after dusk. The tall building overlooking the gardens is **Harry Oppenheimer House** (HOH), the offices of De Beers' DTC (Diamond Trading Company; not open to the public), on the upper floors of which all of the company's South African-mined diamonds are assessed for caratage, colour, clarity and shape. To allow this to take place in the best natural light, the building faces south, with special windows to eliminate glare; there are no windows on the other faces other than small ones along the stairwell.

William Humphreys Art Gallery

On the opposite side of the gardens to HOH, in the Civic Centre · Mon–Fri 8am–4.45pm, Sat 10am–4.45pm, Sun & holidays 2–4.45pm · R5 · ☎ 053 831 1724, Ⓦ whag.co.za

The **William Humphreys Art Gallery**, one of South Africa's few top-notch art galleries, is an unexpected gem. Although dominated by European Old Masters when it opened in 1952, the collection has always moved with the times and now houses an impressively well-balanced representation of South African art, including both traditional and contemporary work and some excellent modern sculpture. The gallery was one of the first places in the world to display **San rock paintings** as works of art rather than anthropological museum pieces. At the back of the gallery is a very pleasant **tea room** (see p.268).

The Kimberley Club

70–72 Du Toitspan Rd · ☎ 053 832 4224, Ⓦ kimberleyclub.co.za

Not far southwest of Market Square is the two-storey **Kimberley Club**, founded in 1881 by the new settlement's movers and shakers. The club was modelled on London's gentlemen's clubs, but its colourful, enterprising members made the place dynamic rather than stuffy. Today it is a smart hotel (see p.267), and retains its original fixtures

KIMBERLEY TOURS

While the cessation of operations at the De Beers mines has brought to an end the fascinating underground tours of a working diamond mine, Kimberley still offers a series of informative and entertaining local tours. The **Diamantveld Visitor Centre** (see p.266) maintains a list of accredited guides; alternatively, contact the recommended **Diamond Tours Unlimited** (📞084 645 7754, 🌐diamondtours.co.za).

GHOST TOURS

If you're brave enough to hear the stories of restless spirits, or simply like the idea of poking around some of Kimberley's most interesting buildings after hours, join a **Ghost Tour** (R80) of the city. You'll be shown scenes of strange encounters at places such as the Africana Library, the Regimental headquarters and spooky Rudd House in Belgravia. Tours begin at 6pm at the Honoured Dead Memorial, and last three to four hours; book through Diamond Tours Unlimited (see above).

TOWNSHIP TOURS

Kimberley was the first settlement in South Africa to establish "locations" on its fringes to house the African and coloured labourers working in the mines. A tour of **Galeshewe**, named after a rebellious nineteenth-century chief, offers an insight into a typical modern South African township with its mix of shacks, simple government houses and the more ostentatious homes of locals-made-good. The tour takes in some alternative historic sights, including the grave of **Sol Plaatje** (see box, p.515) and the house where **Robert Sobukwe** (see box, p.325), founder of the Pan-African Congress, lived under house arrest after his release from Robben Island in 1969. Most tours finish with the post-apartheid **Northern Cape Provincial Legislature complex** – an extraordinary construction combining elements of traditional African design with silver polygonal slabs. Book through the Diamantveld Visitor Centre (see above).

3

and fittings such as the leather armchairs in the smoking lounge and marble in the hallway, and there are plenty of fine antiques. It's possible to look around or eat at the restaurant (see p.268), though you'll get a much less chilly welcome if you introduce yourself at the reception and respect the club's dress code, which includes no T-shirts or shorts in the dining room and bar.

Belgravia

Du Toitspan Rd

Belgravia, the residential suburb where most of Kimberley's wealthy families lived during the boom years, lies about 1km southeast of the CBD. The focus of the area is at the junction of Du Toitspan and Egerton roads, where you'll find the historic **Halfway House Pub** (see p.268). The pub takes its name from its location halfway between the De Beers and Bultfontein mines, and gained fame as a drive-in (or, in those days, ride-in) pub, a custom started by Cecil Rhodes who liked a tipple while in the saddle. Nowadays you can still drive up and blow your horn to attract the bartender.

McGregor Museum

Atlas Rd • Mon–Sat 9am–5pm, Sun 2–5pm • R20 • 📞 053 839 2717, 🌐 museumsnc.co.za

The fabulous **McGregor Museum**, named after an early mayor of Kimberley, is housed in a magnificent Victorian mansion. The highlight here is the extensive and imaginative Ancestors Display, which draws on archeological evidence to piece together an absorbing and – unusual still in South Africa – well-balanced exhibition on the various ancestral roots of today's inhabitants of the Northern Cape, going right back to evidence of the earliest hominids millions of years ago. There's also an evocative section on the siege of Kimberley; Cecil Rhodes himself stayed in two of the ground floor rooms here during the siege, which have been furnished in the style of the day.

Duggan-Cronin Gallery

Egerton Rd • Mon–Fri 9am–5pm • Donation • ☎ 053 839 2700

The **Duggan-Cronin Gallery**, adjacent to the McGregor Museum, includes over eight thousand endearingly unsophisticated photographs portraying the lifestyles of the indigenous people of South Africa between the two world wars. The majority were taken between 1904 and 1953 by Alfred Duggan-Cronin, a night watchman for De Beers.

Lodge Road houses

Lodge Rd • Arrange a guide from the McGregor Museum to visit Rudd House and Dunluce • R25 for each house

A trio of elegantly restored Belgravia houses, all on Lodge Road, are redolent of the atmosphere of old Kimberley and give a sense of the kind of wealth the city once attracted: **Rudd House** at no. 5 was the mansion of mining magnate and partner of Rhodes, Charles Dunnell Rudd; at no. 7, the Edwardian estate birthplace of Harry Oppenheimer, now the *Estate Private Hotel* (see opposite), was the family's last Kimberley home before they moved to Johannesburg in 1915; and **Dunluce** at no. 10 is an elegant late Victorian home, the former residence of one of the mayors of Kimberley.

ARRIVAL AND DEPARTURE   KIMBERLEY

By plane Kimberley's airport (☎ 053 838 3337, ⓦ acsa .co.za) lies 7km to the west of the city, along the N8 to Upington. South African Airways (☎ 053 838 3337, ⓦ flysaa.com), based at the airport, operate flights to Johannesburg and Cape Town. There's no regular transport into town, so phone for a taxi (see opposite). Most of the major car rental agencies are based at the airport, including Avis (☎ 053 851 1082), Budget (☎ 053 851 1182), Hertz (☎ 053 830 2200) and Tempest (☎ 053 851 1516).
Destinations: Cape Town (2–3 daily; 1hr 40min); Johannesburg (4–5 daily; 1hr 20min).

By bus Intercity buses stop outside the Diamantveld Visitor Centre, which is handy when arriving on overnight Greyhound and Translux services from Cape Town, but to be avoided on daytime departures from Cape Town or Jo'burg, which arrive at night when the place is deserted. You can either arrange for a hotel to pick you up, ask to be dropped off at one of the hotels along the N12 (Bishops Avenue) just south of the centre, or alight at the Shell Ultra City service station 6km north of town on the N12, which is a much safer place to call a taxi. Information and tickets for the four main intercity bus companies (Intercape, Greyhound, SA Roadlink and Translux) are available at the Tickets 4 Africa bureau inside the Diamantveld Visitor Centre (see below; Mon–Fri 8am–7.30pm, Sat 8am–12.30pm; ☎ 053 832 6040); most buses depart from just outside. Intercape,

Greyhound, Translux and SA Roadlink all have services to Jo'burg and Cape Town via Bloemfontein, and Intercape and Translux have services to Upington.
Destinations: Bloemfontein (daily; 2hr 15min); Cape Town (daily; 11hr 30min); Johannesburg (daily; 5hr 45min–7hr 5min); Upington (daily; 5hr 20 min).

By train The train station (☎ 053 838 2709, ⓦ shosholozameyl.co.za) is just off Quinn St on the northeastern edge of town. As services arrive and depart after dark, always get a taxi to and from your accommodation; they can be found outside the station.
Destinations: Beaufort West (4 weekly; 7hr 10min); Cape Town (4 weekly; 17hr 10min); Johannesburg (4 weekly; 8hr 30 min); Klerksdorp (4 weekly; 4hr 40min); Worcester (4 weekly; 14hr 40min).

By minibus taxi Minibus taxis operate from Pniel Rd (the northern extension of Bultfontein Rd), 1.5km from the tourist office. To be sure of a ride in daylight, arrive at 6.30am (7am winter); most destinations also have early afternoon departures, but on these you risk being dropped off at night. Services on all routes are reduced on Saturday, and often nonexistent on Sunday. Frequencies given below refer to weekdays. Except to Barkly West (for which you pay on board), fares are paid at an office on Pniel Road beside the long-distance rank.
Destinations: Barkly West (hourly; 30min); Kuruman (1–2 daily; 2hr 30min); Upington (3–4 daily; 5hr).

INFORMATION

Tourist offices The Diamantveld Visitor Centre is at 121 Bultfontein Rd (Mon–Fri 8am–5pm, Sat 8am–noon; ☎ 053 832 7298, ⓦ solplaatje.org.za). The staff can provide city plans, lists of places to stay, and information on local tours (see box, p.272), and give out maps for self-guided walking tours of Kimberley – the Belgravia Historical Walk

and the Great Kimberley North Walk. A few hundred metres southeast is the Northern Cape Tourism Authority, at 15 Dalham Rd (Mon–Fri 7.30am–4pm; ☎ 053 833 1434, ⓦ experiencenortherncape.com), which can provide more information about the province, particularly wildlife parks and reserves.

GETTING AROUND

On foot Central Kimberley is fairly walkable, but take taxis at night; note that around town, many street names are written on the curbside rather than on signs.

By taxi The main taxi rank is in Market Square, behind the City Hall; alternatively, call AA Taxis (☎ 053 861 4015).

ACCOMMODATION

The bulk of the town's hotels, guesthouses and B&Bs lie in the southern suburbs, most within a kilometre or two of the centre. The most atmospheric places – occupying historic buildings – are clustered in and around the upmarket Belgravia suburb.

HOTELS AND GUESTHOUSES

Australian Arms Guest Lodge At the Kimberley Mine Museum and Big Hole, entrance on Tucker St ☎ 053 832 1526, ⓦ australianarms.co.za. Perfectly located for visits to the museum and Big Hole, with thirteen themed rooms that are decorated with antiques in the style of an old mining boarding house. The atmospheric dining room serves meals, while the pub has a long wooden bar and original fittings. R880

Bishop's Lodge 9 Bishops Ave ☎ 053 831 7876, ⓦ bishopslodge.co.za. Close to the tourist office, this quiet, modern affair offers spotless twins and doubles, keenly priced self-catering apartments (R895), and a suite with wheelchair access. There's a swimming pool, but no meals except breakfast. Room R725, apartment R895

Carrington Lodge 60 Carrington Rd, at the corner with Oliver Rd ☎ 053 831 6448, ⓦ carringtonlodge .co.za. Friendly guesthouse on the edge of Belgravia with a colonial style wrap-around veranda, pool and pleasant garden with a braai area. The sixteen stylish rooms have a/c, while ramps provide good wheelchair access. R1040

Cecil John Rhodes Guest House 138 Du Toitspan Rd ☎ 053 830 2500, ⓦ ceciljohnrhodes.co.za. The most central of the historic guesthouses, built in 1895, with eight airy and elegantly furnished rooms with all mod cons, plus a shady tea garden facing the road. Dinner on request. R760

Edgerton House 5 Egerton Rd ☎ 053 831 1150, ⓦ edgertonhouse.co.za. An ornate Belgravia option in an attractive Edwardian house kitted out with crystal chandeliers and gold-plated bathroom fittings. There are thirteen elegant rooms, plus a pool and tea garden. R950

★ **Estate Private Hotel** 7 Lodge Rd ☎ 053 832 2668, ⓦ theestate.co.za. Five attractive wheelchair-friendly rooms with all mod cons in the Oppenheimers' lavish former Belgravia home, open to visitors by day (see opposite). There's also a pool, shady tea garden and restaurant. Excellent value given the quality and standard of service (it's also a chefs' and hospitality school). R850

Greatbatch Guesthouse 3 Egerton Rd ☎ 053 832 1113, ⓦ greatbatchguesthouse.co.za. Elegant guesthouse and backpackers within walking distance of the centre occupying the former home of the architect who created Dunluce (see opposite) and other notable Kimberley buildings. There are attractive, antique-filled rooms in the main house; the dorm is a little cramped, but quirky old miners' bunks make up for the lack of space. Dorm R180, double R600

Halfway House Hotel 229 Du Toitspan Rd, at the corner with Egerton Rd ☎ 053 831 6324, ⓦ halfwayhousehotel.co.za. Seven large and airy en-suite rooms around a paved beer garden behind the historic boozer. A handy place to crash after sampling the pub's nocturnal delights, but be prepared for noisy evenings. R595

Kimberley Club and Boutique Hotel 70–72 Du Toitspan Rd ☎ 053 832 4224, ⓦ kimberleyclub.co.za. This local landmark has been refurbished to include 21 spacious rooms, some with balconies and claw-foot baths. Best of all, staying gives you access to the historic members' bar. Book ahead for weekdays. R1170

Milner House 31 Milner St ☎ 053 831 6405, ⓦ milner house.co.za. Another Belgravia guesthouse, this one more modest and down-to-earth than the others, with six comfortable rooms decorated in refreshing whites, and a swimming pool set in a shady garden. R740

Protea Hotel Kimberley West Circular Rd ☎ 053 802 8200, ⓦ proteahotels.com. Perched on the edge of the Big Hole, Kimberley's *Protea* is of excellent quality and furnished with all the mod cons. Some effort has been made to make the place look suitably antique, with brick walls and a pool shaped like a cattle trough. R935

Sundowner Lodge 1 Bishops Ave ☎ 053 831 1145, ⓦ sundownerlodgekby.co.za. Within shouting distance of the tourist office, this friendly family-run place has a vaguely colonial feel and leafy peaceful gardens, and offers fourteen huge rooms in rows of chalets with verandas. R550

EATING, DRINKING AND NIGHTLIFE

There's little in the way of nightlife in Kimberley but the handful of historic pubs (use a taxi after dark) are atmospheric for a late night drink. The Flamingo Casino complex just out of town on Phakamile Mabije Road (the N12 towards Johannesburg; ☎ 053 830 2600, ⓦ suninternational.com) stays open until the early hours.

RESTAURANTS AND CAFÉS

Annabell's Du Toitspan Rd, next to Halfway House ☎ 053 831 6324. Offers a similar range of pub food to the *Halfway House* next door, but served at padded leather booths in a more elegant atmosphere, with a few pizzas and pasta dishes thrown in (around R59). The pleasant *Skybar* on the roof is a great place for sundowners. Restaurant Mon–Sat 6–10pm; Skybar Tues–Sat 6–10pm.

Butler's Restaurant Estate Private Hotel, 7 Lodge Rd ☎ 053 832 2668, ⓦ theestate.co.za. Kimberley's finest and most elegant restaurant in an atmospheric dining room with starched white linen, sliver and china. The menu offers South African dishes like springbok medallions or kingklip, often with a modern twist. Pricey (mains from R110), but recommended for a treat. Daily 6.30–10pm.

★**Mario's** 159 Du Toitspan Rd ☎ 053 831 1738, ⓦ marioskimberley.co.za. Bright, cheery and easy-going Italian place that's justifiably one of the most popular restaurants in town, with friendly staff and an extensive menu ranging from light lunches and pizzas to more elaborate meals (mains R55–135). There's also a good – if expensive – wine list. Mon–Fri noon–3pm & 6pm–late; Sat 6pm–late.

Occidental At the Kimberley Mine Museum and Big Hole, entrance on Tucker St, ☎ 053 830 4418. Unlike the other museum buildings in the Old Town, this is a fully functioning bar and restaurant with a good though small menu – try the excellent Karoo lamb chops (mains around R70). Mon–Fri 9am–7pm, Sat 9am–6pm, Sun 9am–5pm.

Palette Tearoom William Humphreys Art Gallery, Civic Centre. Modest little tearoom serving healthy food like fruit shakes, teas and fresh salads – a nice change from the meaty offerings you find elsewhere. Daily 10am–4pm.

Rhodes Grill Restaurant Kimberley Club, 70–72 Du Toitspan Rd ☎ 053 832 4224, ⓦ kimberleyclub.co.za. One of the town's most sophisticated restaurants, serving a mix of local and international dishes – everything from springbok steak to Thai curry – for unexpectedly reasonable prices (R70–140), along with a hefty wine list. The *Vitello Café* is a more informal spot for light meals on the front porch of the club. Restaurant daily 7–10am, noon–2.30pm & 6–9.30pm; café daily 11am–6pm.

BARS

George & Dragon 187 Du Toitspan Rd ☎ 053 833 2075. Popular English theme pub and sports bar. The food – from steaks to *bobotie* – tends to be rather hit or miss, but the portions are large and prices reasonable (mains around R70). Also features the town's best selection of draught beers. Daily 11am–late.

★**Halfway House** Corner of Du Toitspan and Egerton rds ☎ 053 831 6324, ⓦ halfwayhousehotel.co.za. Cecil Rhodes' old refreshment stop, known as "the Half" and still a favourite for its unpretentious atmosphere. There's a beer garden out the back with couches and free wi-fi and two pool tables. Also serves good, cheap British pub food (mains from R48). Mon–Sat 11am–2am.

Star of the West West Circular Rd, at the corner of North Circular Rd ☎ 053 832 6463. Kimberley's oldest pub (1873) remains a defiantly local dive, complete with eccentric locals propping up the bar. It also receives its fair share of tourists, who enjoy drinking a beer or eating a decent, cheap pub meal in the beer garden. Tends to host live bands on Fri or Sat nights. Daily 10am–late.

DIRECTORY

Banks Absa, corner of Bultfontein Rd and Long St, and Standard Bank, opposite Absa on Bultfontein Rd, have foreign exchange facilities.

Hospitals and doctors Best-equipped is the 24hr Medi-Clinic, 177 Du Toitspan Rd (☎ 053 838 1111, emergencies ☎ 0800 053 053, ⓦ mediclinic.co.za).

Internet access Small World Net Café, 42 Sidney St (☎ 053 831 3484; Mon–Fri 8am–6pm, Sat 9am–2pm).

Pharmacies Piet Muller Pharmacy, 52 Market Square (☎ 053 831 1787; Mon–Fri 8am–8.30pm, Sat 8am–1pm & 5.30–8.30pm, Sun 10am–12.30pm & 5.30–8.30pm); Medpark, 143 Du Toitspan Rd (☎ 053 831 1737; Mon–Fri 8am–6pm, Sat 8am–1pm).

Post The post office is on the eastern side of Market Square (Mon–Fri 8.30am–4.30pm, Sat 9am–noon).

Around Kimberley

A couple of interesting places lie on or near the R31, which runs northwest out of Kimberley in the direction of Kuruman: there is some fascinating San rock art at **Wildebeest Kuil**, while the area around Barkly West was where some of the first **diamond camps** sprang up in the 1860s. South of Kimberley along the N12, the mostly unremarkable landscape around Magersfontein was the setting for one of the most dramatic campaigns of the **Anglo-Boer War,** while one of South Africa's newest parks, **Mokala National Park,** is the nearest place to Kimberley to see wildlife in a natural bush environment.

RIGHT GEMSBOK IN KGALAGADI TRANSFRONTIER PARK (P.278) >

Wildebeest Kuil

Around 15km from Kimberley along the R31 road to Barkly West • Tues–Fri 8.30am–5.30pm, Sat & Sun 11am–4pm • R25 • ☎ 053 833 7069, ⓦ wildebeestkuil.itgo.com • Coming from Kimberley, you can catch one of the frequent minibus taxis to Barkly West and ask to be dropped at the signposted turning – the site is close by

Wildebeest Kuil is a small *koppie* of ancient andesite rock. This is an important rock-art site, unusual in that the images are engraved (rather than painted) and are found on loosely scattered rocks and small boulders, rather than cave walls or overhangs. A number of boardwalks have been built to allow access without disturbing the engravings. Under South Africa's programme of land restitution, ownership of the site has been given to the local !Xun and Khwe San communities, and trained guides (included in the price) are on hand to show you around. The visitor centre at the base of the *koppie* provides an introductory display and shows a video and there are some San crafts for sale.

Magersfontein

32km south of Kimberley along the N80 and then the gravel road to Modder River • Daily 8am–5pm • R30 • Contact MGregor Museum ☎ 053 839 2722, ⓦ museumsnc.co.za

The Anglo-Boer War battlefield at **Magersfontein** provides a poignant reminder of the area's blood-spattered past. This is where Boer forces put trench warfare into effect against British troops, with devastating results (see box below). Signs at the battlefield point the way to the **visitor's centre** and its small **museum**, which has some vivid exhibits, including an audiovisual re-creation of the battle. You can also hike up to various monuments situated on the western end of the line of hills. Out on the battlefield itself – now open veld with springbok grazing and the occasional car throwing up a plume of dust along the dirt road – the lines of **trenches** and other memorials can still be seen, including a pair of granite crosses marking the graves of Scandinavian soldiers who fought on the Boer side.

THE KIMBERLEY CAMPAIGN

At the outbreak of the **Anglo-Boer War**, the Boer forces identified diamond-rich Kimberley as an important strategic base and quickly besieged the city, trapping its residents, including Cecil Rhodes, inside. In response, the British deployed an army under **Lord Methuen** to relieve the city. The size of the army and lack of knowledge of the terrain compelled them to advance from the coast along the line of the railway so that a supply of troops, water, food and equipment could be ensured.

Methuen first encountered Boer forces at Belmont; this was followed by further battles at Graspan and the Modder River, from which the Boers made a tactical withdrawal to Magersfontein, a range of hills 30km south of Kimberley. Here the Boer generals, under the leadership of General Cronjé and the tactical direction of **Koos de la Rey**, decided to dig a line of trenches along the bottom of the *koppie* rather than defend the top of the ridge of hills, as was their usual tactic.

In the early hours of December 11, 1899, the British advanced on Magersfontein, fully expecting the enemy to be lined along the ridge. The British were led by the **Highland Regiment**, fresh from campaigns in North Africa and India, and considered the elite of the British army. Just before dawn, as they fanned out into attack formation, four thousand Boers in the trenches just a few hundred metres away opened fire. The use of trenches was, at that point, a rare tactic in modern warfare, and the element of surprise caused devastation in the ranks. Those not killed or wounded in the first volleys were pinned down by snipers for the rest of the day, unable to move in the coverless veld and suffering appallingly under the hot sun. The next day the British withdrew to the Modder River, and the relief of Kimberley was delayed for two months. The defeat was one in a series of three the British suffered within what became known as "Black Week", news of which sent shock waves through the British public, who had been expecting their forces to overrun the "crude farmers" before Christmas.

One of the most enjoyable ways of finding out more about the history of the area is to book a one-day battlefield tour with Steve Lunderstedt (☎083 732 3189) or Frank Higgo (☎082 963 6657), both enthusiastic and entertaining military historians. Their tours (around R1300 per group) provide a vivid picture of the campaign, with trips to battlefields, fortifications and gun positions, and walks to get a sense of the terrain and look for old shells and other evidence of the fighting. Alternatively, pick up a "Kimberley Meander" brochure from the tourist office in Kimberley (see p.266) for detailed self-drive directions.

Mokala National Park

Daily September–April 6am–7pm, May-August 7am–11pm • R138 • ☎ 053 204 0164, ⓦ sanparks.org

Opened in 2007, Mokala became the new home for animals relocated from the former Vaalbos National Park, which was de-proclaimed after a successful land claim by local people. Mokala is a Setswana name for the gnarly camelthorn tree (*Acacia erioloba*), which dominates the hilly, sandy landscape, and the park covers 19,611 hectares in the transition zone between the Karoo and Kalahari biomes. As such there is a good variety of plains game including both black and white rhino, buffalo, tsessebe, roan, eland, sable, giraffe, zebra, and blue and black wildebeest. There are no large cats or other predators, but Mokala's dolerite outcrops and riverine vegetation attracts a prolific number of raptors – you'll see plenty of pale chanting goshawks, martial eagles, and lappet-faced, white-backed and Cape vultures. At night, with the Kalahari sky full of stars, keep an eye open for Cape eagle owls in the camelthorns.

ARRIVAL AND INFORMATION   MOKALA NATIONAL PARK

By car The park lies roughly 70 km southwest of Kimberley. There are two entrances off the N12 towards Cape Town; the first turnoff is 37 km from Kimberley and leads 16 km to *Lilydale Rest Camp*, the second turnoff is 57 km from Kimberley at the Heuningneskloof Crossing and goes 21 km to the main reception and *Mosu Lodge*.

Information Both *Lilydale* and *Mosu* are 6 km from the park entrance gates. There are no shops but there is a restaurant at *Mosu Lodge* (daily 8–10am, noon–2pm & 6–9pm). Guided morning, sunset and night drives can be arranged at Mosu (from R220).

GETTING AROUND

By car Within the park a gravel road (26 km) links Lilydale and Mosu and there are several game-viewing circuits. A normal car is sufficient except after heavy rain when a 4WD

may be necessary. The closest fuel station is at Modderrivier, on the N12, 36km south of Kimberley.

ACCOMMODATION

Reservations for all accommodation should be made through South African National Parks in Pretoria (☎012 428 9111, ⓦ sanparks.org). For late bookings (under 48 hours) and camping contact the park direct (☎053 204 0164). Wheelchairs are accommodated in all the camps.

Lilydale Rest Camp The more rustic option in the park with nine self-catering chalets in a picturesque location on the Riet River in the north of the park, which will particularly appeal to birders. There's a swimming pool and pre-booked breakfasts are on offer. R600.

Mosu Lodge Comfortable, smart and well designed, Mokala's main camp has sixteen low stone and thatched

bungalows, some with kitchens, and facilities include a pool, communal television lounge, and a restaurant and bar. R855

Motswedi Camp Site About 10 km from *Mosu* in the south of the park, *Motswedi* offers six attractive camping sites, arranged in a half-moon around a waterhole and each with its own ablution and cooking facilities. You can eat at the *Mosu* restaurant but must pre-book dinner. R310

The Kalahari

While the Northern Cape has no shortage of dry, endless expanses, the most emotive by far is the **Kalahari**. The very name holds a resonance of sun-bleached, faraway spaces

KALAHARI TOURS

To save yourself driving the vast distances of the Kalahari region – and to take advantage of specialized knowledge of the area's distinctive flora, fauna, landscapes and climate – it's worth considering joining a **guided tour**. The following is a list of reliable, knowledgeable and well-organized tour operators offering a range of Kalahari-based tours, which incorporate a visit to **Augrabies Falls** and the **Kgalagadi Transfrontier Park**, although customized itineraries are also available. Prices start at around R4000–5000 per person for a three-day camping safari depending on numbers and what's included. These operators can also organize tours to the |Ai-|Ais/Richtersveld National Park (see p.292).

Diamond Tours Unlimited Kimberley ☎ 084 645 7754, ⓦ diamondtours.co.za.

Kalahari Outventures Augrabies Village ☎ 054 453 0001, ⓦ kalahari-adventures.co.za.

Kalahari Safaris Upington ☎ 054 332 5653, ⓦ kalaharisafaris.co.za.

Kalahari Tours and Travel Upington ☎ 054 338 0375, ⓦ kalahari-tours.co.za.

and the unknown vastness of the African interior, both harsh and magical. The name derives from the word *kgalagadi* (saltpans, or thirsty land), and describes the semi-desert stretching north from the Orange River to the Okavango Delta in northern Botswana, west into Namibia and east until the bushveld begins to dominate in the catchment areas of the Vaal and Limpopo rivers.

The Kalahari in the Northern Cape is characterized by surprisingly high, thinly vegetated red or orange sand dunes, scored with dry river beds and large, shimmering saltpans. Although this is, strictly speaking, semi-desert, daytime temperatures are searingly hot in summer and nights are numbingly cold in winter. North of the Orange, South Africa's longest river, the land is populated by tough, hard-working farmers and communities largely descended from the indigenous San hunter-gatherers and nomadic Khoi herders. For many land-users, there is an increasing realization that **eco-tourism** may be the only viable option on huge areas where stock farming and hunting provide at best a marginal living.

Upington, the main town in the area, stands on the northern bank of the Orange at the heart of an irrigated corridor of intensive wheat, cotton and, most prominently, grape farms. At the far end of the farming belt, about an hour's drive west, the Orange picks up speed, frothing and tumbling into a huge granite gorge at **Augrabies Falls**, the focus of one of the area's two national parks. The other is the undoubted highlight of this area, the **Kgalagadi Transfrontier Park**. A vast desert sanctuary rich in game and boasting a magnificent landscape of red dunes and hardy vegetation, it's well worth the long trek to get there.

Upington

As an inevitable focus of trips to Kgalagadi and Augrabies, as well as those to and from Namaqualand and Namibia, **UPINGTON**, just over 400km west of Kimberley, is a good place to stop for supplies, organize a park tour or onward accommodation, or simply draw breath. Situated on the banks of the Orange River (also called the Gariep River), central Upington is compact and easy to get around, with most of the activity on the three main streets running parallel to the riverbank. It can be a mellow spot, with plenty of greenery softening the arid landscape that surrounds it – a result of the irrigation that allows Upington to be surrounded by vineyards. However, the savage summer temperatures mean you probably won't want to linger too long.

Kalahari Oranje Museum

4 Schröder St • Mon–Fri 9am–12.30pm & 2–5pm, Sat 9am–noon • Free • ☎ 054 332 6064

The **Kalahari Oranje Museum** is housed in a church and mission station that was erected by the Reverend Schröder in 1875 – Upington was founded in 1884, nine years after Schröder started his mission. The domestic items and historic photographs on display offer a good insight into the resourcefulness and hardships of the first settlers in the largely inhospitable expanses of semi-desert that covers most of the Northern Cape. Outside is a life-sized bronze statue of a donkey working a horse mill; it symbolizes the contribution made by donkeys during the irrigation of the lower Orange River Valley in the 1920–30s.

The Orange River

Sakkie se Arkie cruise Sept–April daily 6pm, by prior arrangement in winter if the river is sufficiently high • R80 • ☎ 082 564 5447 or ☎ 082 575 7285, Ⓦ arkie.co.za

Upington's obvious highlight is the **Orange River**, but unless you're staying at one of the riverside guesthouses (see p.274), it tends to be hidden from view. The terrace behind *O'Hagan's Irish Pub* on Schröder Street (see p.275) is a good place to admire

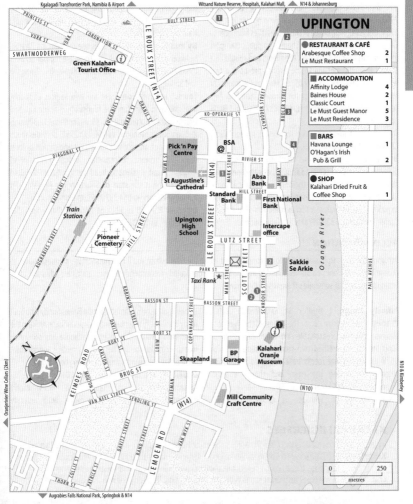

3

Kgalagadi Transfrontier Park, Namibia & Airport ▲   Witsand Nature Reserve, Hospitals, Kalahari Mall, ▲   N14 & Johannesburg

UPINGTON

● **RESTAURANT & CAFÉ**
Arabesque Coffee Shop   2
Le Must Restaurant   1

■ **ACCOMMODATION**
Affinity Lodge   4
Baines House   2
Classic Court   1
Le Must Guest Manor   5
Le Must Residence   3

■ **BARS**
Havana Lounge   1
O'Hagan's Irish
Pub & Grill   2

● **SHOP**
Kalahari Dried Fruit &
Coffee Shop   1

Green Kalahari Tourist Office

Pick 'n Pay Centre

St Augustine's Cathedral

BSA
@

Absa Bank

Standard Bank

First National Bank

Train Station

Upington High School

Pioneer Cemetery

Intercape office

Sakkie Se Arkie

Taxi Rank

Skaapland

BP Garage

Kalahari Oranje Museum

Mill Community Craft Centre

Oranjerivier Wine Cellars (2km)

N10 & Kimberley

Augrabies Falls National Park, Springbok & N14

0   250
metres

the river and its swans. Better still, take a two-hour sunset cruise with Sakkie se Arkie on its strange two-tier barge; it departs from the riverbank at the east end of Park Street.

The vineyards

Upington's **vineyards** produce mostly table grapes, as well as raisins and sultanas (important export crops for the region), though some wine is also made. Wine tasting is offered by Orange River Cellars (Mon–Fri 8am–5pm, Sat 9am–noon; free; ☏054 337 8800, ⊛ orangeriverwines.com) in the industrial estate 3km west of the town centre off Industria Street. Alternatively, you can sample or buy its output at *Le Must Restaurant* (see opposite), or at the Kalahari Dried Fruit & Coffee Shop (next to the Kalahari Oranje Museum on Schröder Street; Mon–Fri 8am–5pm, Sat 8am–1pm; ☏054 331 2430), which also sells other local produce, including dried fruit, olives and pickles.

ARRIVAL AND DEPARTURE

By plane Upington Airport is 7km north of town off the N10 towards the Kgalagadi Transfrontier Park (☏054 337 7900, ⊛acsa.co.za). South African Airways (☏054 332 2161, ⊛flysaa.com), based at the airport, flies from here to Cape Town and Johannesburg. There is no public transport from the airport but taxis meet the flights and should cost around R80–100; getting to the airport, pre-book a taxi with Oranje Taxis (☏054 339 0576). Most of the major car rental agencies are based at the airport, including Avis (☏054 332 4746/7), Budget (☏054 337 5200) and Hertz (☏054 337 3613).

Destinations: Cape Town (daily; 1hr 50min); Johannesburg (2–3 daily; 1hr 35min).

By bus The only major bus company operating from Upington is Intercape (☏054 332 6091, ⊛intercape.co.za); buses arrive and depart from their office on Lutz St. If you're likely to arrive at night, it's best to get your accommodation to pick you up or arrange a taxi to meet you off the bus – Oranje Taxis (☏054 339 0576) is a reliable option.

Destinations: Bloemfontein (daily; 7hr 30min); Cape Town (daily; 12hr); Johannesburg (daily; 10hr 50min); Kimberley (daily; 5hr 20min); Pretoria (daily; 11hr 15min); Windhoek, Namibia (daily; 11hr).

By minibus taxi Minibus taxis use the rank on Park St between Le Roux and Mark sts. There are regular services throughout the day (fewer on Sun) to Kimberley, Kuruman and Springbok.

Tourist information There are two sources of tourist information in Upington. The tourist office at the Kalahari Oranje Museum (see p.272; Mon–Fri 9am–12.30pm & 2–5pm, Sat 9am–noon; ☏054 337 2952) provides maps and brochures, an accommodation list and details of local tours. For regional information, including details of Augrabies and Kgalagadi, head to the Green Kalahari Tourist Office at the start of Swartmodder Rd (Mon–Fri 7.30am–4.30pm; ☏054 337 2952, ⊛upington.com).

Internet BSA, 58 Le Roux St (Mon–Fri 8am–5pm, Sat 8am–noon; ☏054 331 2689).

ACCOMMODATION

Accommodation in Upington tends to be concentrated along the river, where you'll find no shortage of guesthouses to choose from – the ones on Budler St and Murray Avenue are particularly recommended. Reservations are advisable at all times to ensure that someone's there when you arrive.

Affinity Lodge 4 Budler St ☏054 331 2101, ⊛affinityguesthouse.co.za. The largest of the riverfront choices, offering reasonable en-suite rooms in a functional white-washed two-storey building, all with DSTV and a/c. Many rooms have access to a common balcony overlooking the river, and there's a small swimming pool and braai area. **R750**

Baines House 80 Schröder St ☏054 332 1333, ⊛bainshouse.com. Named after the Baines family who built many of the major mountain road passes in South Africa in the nineteenth century, this smart guesthouse has six stylish rooms, a cosy lounge and bar with a fireplace and veranda, and a pretty garden with small swimming pool. **R680**

Classic Court 26 Josling St ☏054 332 6142, ⊛classiccourt.co.za. Reliable B&B with nicely decorated, good-value en-suite rooms with separate

---

KALAHARI KUIERFEES

In late September, *Die Eiland Resort*, across the river from Upington, plays host to the **Kalahari Kuierfees** (last Thursday to Saturday; ⊛kalahari-kuierfees.co.za). A chance for the local Afrikaner community to come together to celebrate their culture, language and food, the event combines flea markets and craft stalls with a triathlon, arts, live Afrikaner music and dance.

entrances, DSTV and wi-fi. No river views, but there is a tiny pool and it's close to the shops and restaurants in the new Kalahari Mall. **R600**

Le Must Guest Manor and Residence 12 Murray Ave & 14 Budler St ☎ 054 332 3971, ⓦ lemustupington.com. Two Cape Dutch houses on the riverbank with eighteen elegant, comfortable rooms between them and large gardens (the lavishly decorated *Residence* is more upscale), offering luxury and sophistication rarely encountered in the Northern Cape. **R1180**

EATING, DRINKING AND NIGHTLIFE

As the only large town for hundreds of kilometres, Upington seems like culinary heaven compared to the *dorps* you pass through to get here.

Arabesque Coffee Shop 24 Scott St, ☎ 054 331 3412. Pleasant café that offers a variety of coffees, teas, smoothies and fruit shakes; food includes English breakfasts, sandwiches, pancakes, cakes and tarts (R35–70). Its open late on some evenings for suppers of home-cooked *bobotie* or lasagne, and if it's warm there may be a braai in the garden. Mon & Tues 8am–5pm, Wed–Sat 8am–9pm.

Havana Lounge 35 Mark St ☎ 054 331 1398. Slick restaurant and bar with a leathery cigar lounge, offering decent cocktails and a Latin-flavoured tapas menu (R40–115). It also opens early for breakfasts and good coffees. Daily 8am–11pm.

★ **Le Must Restaurant** 11a Schröder St ☎ 054 332 6700. One of the most outstanding restaurants in the Northern Cape, offering the likes of slow-cooked oxtail and grilled pork cutlets and local delicacies such as *bobotie* spring rolls with sultana jelly (mains R90–115). Paired with a superb list of local wines and great service, it makes for an unexpectedly sophisticated dining experience. Mon–Fri noon–2pm, daily 7–10pm.

O'Hagan's Irish Pub & Grill 20 Schröder St ☎ 054 331 20050. The best place in town to down a beer, with real Guinness and a lovely terrace at the back overlooking the river. You'll find things like ostrich and springbok on the meat-heavy menu, but there's also a choice of lighter pastas and vegetarian meals (mains R70–150). Mon–Sat 8am–midnight, Sun 9am–11pm.

Kuruman

The Eye daily sunrise–sunset • R10

Around 265km east of Upington, lying near the border between the Northern Cape and North West Province, the historic settlement of **KURUMAN** is an important landmark along the main N14 route to and from Gauteng. The settlement grew up around **The Eye** ("Die Oog" in Afrikaans), a natural spring which, since time immemorial and through drought and flood, has consistently delivered twenty million litres a day of crystal-clear water. The Eye was the focal point for a rather unsettled Tswana clan called the **Batlhaping**, whose chief, Mothibi, first invited missionaries to live among his people in the early nineteenth century. It was a decision that led to the building of the famous **Mission Station** by Robert Moffat, and the establishment of Kuruman as the "Gateway to the Interior" of darkest Africa.

These days, Kuruman's centre is pretty scruffy, dominated by cut-price chain stores, faceless supermarkets and litter-strewn minibus-taxi ranks. You can visit **The Eye**, next to the tourist office, though there isn't much to look at: a moss-covered slab of rock dribbling water and a lily-covered pond surrounded by a high green fence. More interesting is the Moffat Mission Station, some 5km north of town (see below).

Moffat Mission Station

About 5km north of town, on Moffat Lane • Daily 8am–5pm • R10 • ☎ 053 712 1352

Kuruman's main attraction is **Moffat Mission Station**, where a large, often gruff, energetic Scot, Robert Moffat, and his demure but equally determined wife, Mary, established a mission (see box, p.276) where they lived for fifty years. During this time they produced and printed the first Tswana Bible, and saw their eldest daughter, also called Mary, married to the missionary/explorer David Livingstone. Charmingly overgrown and shaded by tall acacia and camelthorn trees, the atmospheric old village looks much as it did in the nineteenth century. It includes the Moffat homestead, with the original printing press on display, along with a collection of furniture, portraits and

THE MOFFATS AND THEIR MISSION

Robert and Mary Moffat, newly married envoys of the London Missionary Society, arrived in the Kuruman area in 1820, initially at a place rather charmingly mistranslated by early explorers as Lattakoo about 14km from Kuruman. As a former market gardener, however, Moffat soon saw the advantages of irrigating the flow of The Eye of Kuruman, and began to build his mission on the closest land wide and flat enough to plough.

Moffat didn't clock up too many converts – by the time he had built his eight-hundred-seater "Cathedral of the Kalahari", in 1838, he had just nine – but the challenge of preaching and establishing a school inspired him not only to learn the local language, which he did by living for a period in a remote Tswana village, but also to attempt the daunting task of **translating the Bible** into Tswana, which he then published on an imported iron printing press. The mission at Kuruman, meanwhile, carried on until the passing of the Group Areas Act of 1950, which brought about the end of the school and the church as a functioning place of (multiracial) worship.

a wagon used by the missionaries. In front of the homestead is the furrow that Robert dug to bring water from The Eye.

Witsand Nature Reserve

Halfway between Kuruman and Upington, reached by heading south off the N14 from Olifantshoek • Daily 8am–6pm • R50 • ☎ 083 234 7573, ⓦ witsandkalahari.co.za • For organized trips, contact Kalahari Safaris in Upington (see box, p.272)

The **Witsand Nature Reserve** is famous for its pristine white "roaring" dunes: in summer a curious rumbling sound occurs when the dunes, 9km in extent, are disturbed, possibly by ground water. While the reserve isn't exactly teeming with wildlife, it does have an abundance of desert bird species, and with patience you may also be rewarded by springbok, duikers and ground squirrels. It's also possible to stay here (see below).

ARRIVAL AND INFORMATION   KURUMAN

By bus The daily Intercape bus to Upington (3hr 30min) passes through Kuruman at 6.30pm, and at 11.25am to Jo'burg (7hr 20min) and Pretoria (8hr 20min) via Vryburg (7hr 20min), Klerksdorp and Potchefstroom. The buses stop at the Leach Caltex petrol station on Main St, 1.5km west of The Eye and tourist office (reservations ☎ 021 380 4400, ⓦ intercape.co.za); arrange in advance for your accommodation owners to pick you up.

By minibus taxi Minibus taxis are the only option to get

to Kimberley (2–3 daily; 2hr); they stop at the rank on Voortrekker St, just south of Main St. Minibus taxis for Upington (1–2 daily; 2hr 45min) leave from the sprawling taxi rank on Tsening Rd north of Main St – note, however, that services on all routes are reduced on Saturday and often nonexistent on Sunday.

Tourist information In the old *drostdy* (magistrate's house) on Main St just west of The Eye (Mon–Fri 9.30am–1pm & 2–4pm; ☎ 053 712 1001, ⓦ visitkuruman.co.za).

ACCOMMODATION

Die Mynhuis 10 Botha St ☎ 053 712 2546, ⓦ diemynhuis.co.za. Six rooms surrounding a garden, each with its own entrance and decor reminiscent of the mine after which it was named. There are also two larger family suites, with meals available on request. R700

Oude Werf Lodge 12 Winkel St ☎ 053 712 0117, ⓦ oudewerf-lodge.co.za. Modern lodge about 1.5 km north of the centre offering budget and double rooms with a bushman themed decor, a/c, fridge and DSTV, plus motel-style parking outside. There's a decent restaurant and friendly pub that's popular with the locals. R600

Red Sands Country Lodge In the Kuruman Hills, 15km along the N14 towards Upington ☎ 053 712 0033, ⓦ redsands.co.za. A pleasant option outside

weekends and school holidays (when it gets very busy). Besides camping facilities, they have characterful thatched stone rondavels and comfy self-catering chalets sleeping up to four. There's also a good German/South African restaurant for breakfast and dinner and a generous buffet lunch on Sunday, and the swimming pool has its own bar. Camping R95, rondavels & chalets R980

Witsand Nature Reserve Off the N14, between Kuruman and Upington ☎ 083 234 7573, ⓦ witsandkalahari.co.za. There are some superb self-catering air-conditioned chalets to stay in at the nature reserve, each sleeping up to six. A campsite is also available. There's a kiosk on site that stocks some dried and tinned food, alongside non-alcholic drinks; bring everything else with you. Camping R110, chalet R960

EATING

Eating out is limited in Kuruman, though there are branches of Spur (a franchise steakhouse), Wimpy and KFC on Main Street, and the Spar and Pick'n Pay supermarkets, both of which are also on Main Street, have takeaway counters.

Cappello 22 Main St, ☎ 053 712 3956. One of the better South African chain restaurants with a fairly long menu and a decent choice of wine and beers on tap. Light meals include sticky chicken wings and burgers, or the hungry can go for the large T-bone steaks or lamb shanks (R45–130). Mon–Sat 7am–11pm, Sun 10am–11pm.

DIRECTORY

Banks To change money, try Absa Bank at the corner of Main and Livingstone sts; other banks also have central branches.

Hospital On Main St, 1km east of the tourist office (☎ 053 712 8100).

Post office On Church St, two blocks north and one block west of the tourist office.

Tswalu Kalahari Reserve

On the R31, 100km northwest of Kuruman • ☎ 053 781 9311, reservations ☎ 011 274 2299, ☺ tswalu.com

The upmarket Tswalu Kalahari Reserve centres on an impeccably stylish game lodge not far from the tiny settlement of Sonstraal, northwest of Kuruman. Tucked under the 1500-metre Korannaberg Mountains, this is the largest privately owned game reserve in South Africa. Some R50 million was spent bringing over nine thousand head of game to this desert setting, including some highly endangered desert black rhino, sable, roan antelope and cheetah. The reserve is only accessible to overnight guests, and the price for accommodation (from R20,000 per couple) includes game drives, horseriding and full board.

Wonderwerk (Miracle) Cave

Along the R31 towards Danielskuil, 45km south of Kuruman • Daily 8am–5pm • R20 • ☎ 082 222 4777

This intriguing limestone **cave**, burrowing 139m into the hillside, is thought to be one of the longest-inhabited caves on Earth. A major archeological site, it has yielded important evidence of human occupation in various eras dating back over 800,000 years, including fossils, animal teeth, San rock paintings and engraved stones. There is a small visitor's centre on the site and three basic self-catering chalets sleeping up to four (from R375). Sometimes there are archeologists working in the cave, but if there's no one around, you'll have to ask at the farm for the gate to be unlocked.

KGALAGADI WILDLIFE

The open landscape of the Kgalagadi Transfrontier Park offers almost unobstructed game viewing and it is especially renowned for predator watching, with excellent chances of seeing cheetah, leopard, brown and spotted hyena and the black-maned Kalahari lion. These commonly have much darker manes than those found in the bushveld, and studies have shown their behavioural and eating patterns to be distinctively well adapted to the semi-desert conditions here. The park is also known for the seasonal movement of large herbivores such as blue wildebeest, springbok, eland and red hartebeest, but the star of the Kgalagadi show is the gemsbok, a beautiful, large, lolloping antelope with classically straight, V-shaped horns, which is a frequently spotted galloping across the plains and dunes. Birdwatchers will be well rewarded with some extravagant **birdlife** including vultures, eagles, the dramatic bateleur (which takes its name from the French word for an acrobatic tumbler), bustards and ostrich. There's also a good chance you'll see family groups of **meerkat**, a relative of the mongoose and squirrel, striking their characteristic pose of standing tall on their hind legs while looking round nervously for signs of danger.

3

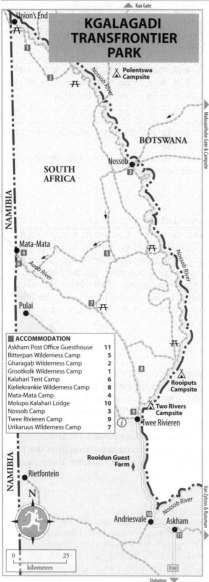

ACCOMMODATION

Askham Post Office Guesthouse	11
Bitterpan Wilderness Camp	5
Gharagab Wilderness Camp	2
Grootkolk Wilderness Camp	1
Kalahari Tent Camp	6
Kieliekrankie Wilderness Camp	8
Mata-Mata Camp	4
Molopo Kalahari Lodge	10
Nossob Camp	3
Twee Rivieren Camp	9
Urikaruus Wilderness Camp	7

Kgalagadi Transfrontier Park

Opening hours vary from month to month, roughly sunrise–sunset • R248 • ☎ 054 561 2000, ⊛ sanparks.org

Africa's first official transfrontier park, named **KGALAGADI TRANSFRONTIER PARK** after the ancient San name for the Kalahari (it's pronounced "kha-la-khadi", the kh as in the Scottish "loch"), is the result of the formalization of a long-standing joint management arrangement between South Africa's Kalahari-Gemsbok National Park and Botswana's neighbouring Gemsbok National Park. The local **Mier** and **San** communities have agreed that their land be jointly managed by themselves and South African National Parks, so that the land remains part of the wildlife sanctuary. The park is run as a single ecological unit and gate receipts are shared, although the tourist facilities in South Africa and Botswana are still run autonomously. Almost all visitors to the park will, however, encounter only the South African section, where most of the established tourist facilities are found.

Kgalagadi covers an area of over 37,000 square kilometres – nearly twice the size of Kruger National Park – and although the South African side is by far the smaller section, it still encompasses a vast 9500 square kilometres. Be prepared to clock up some serious mileage here; the game drive between the park entrance at **Twee Rivieren** and the **Mata-Mata restcamp** on the western edge of the reserve takes about two-and-a-half-hours. The park is bounded on its western side by the Namibian border, and to the south by the dry Auob River and a strip of land running parallel to this. The national boundary with **Botswana** follows the dry Nossob river bed, as does one of the few roads in the park. No fences exist along this line, allowing game undisturbed access to the ancient migration routes so necessary for survival in the desert. The main roads follow the river beds, and this is where the game – and their predators – are most likely to be. Water flows very rarely in the two rivers, but frequent boreholes have been drilled to provide water for the game. Larger trees such as camelthorn and witgat (shepherd's tree) offer a degree of shade and nutrition, and desert-adapted plants, including types of melon and cucumber, are a source of moisture for the animals.

WHEN TO VISIT THE KGALAGADI TRANSFRONTIER PARK

In a place where ground temperatures in the **summer** can reach a scorching 70°C, **timing your visit is everything**. The best period to be in the park is **between March and May**, when there is still some greenery left from the summer rain and the sun is not so intense. **Winter** can be very cold at night, while **spring**, though dry, is a pleasant time before the searing heat of summer.

Much of the park is dominated by **red sand dunes**, which, when seen from the air, lie strung out in long, wave-like bands. From a car, the perspective is different, as you are in the valley of the river bed, but this doesn't prevent the path from offering one of the finest **game-viewing** experiences in South Africa – not only for the animals, but for the setting, with its broad landscapes, the crisp light of morning and the huge open skies. The clear viewing and wonderful light are ideal for **photography**, as shown by the exhibition at the visitor centre at *Twee Rivieren Camp*.

ARRIVAL AND DEPARTURE   KGALAGADI TRANSFRONTIER PARK

By car Coming from Gauteng, the longer approach to the park is via the R31, which is surfaced only between Kuruman and Hotazel – the remainder is a long, bleak dirt road which should only be tackled in a sturdy vehicle. Alternatively, you can drive further along the N14 to Upington and turn onto the R360, which is surfaced the 265 km to the park entrance at *Twee Rivieren*. You can also access the park from Namibia through the Mata-Mata Gate and from Botswana through the Two Rivers, Mabuasehube and Kaa gates. Visitors wanting to exit the park via a different country from the one they entered from should note that all immigration controls must be done at Twee Rivieren and that a two night stay in the park is compulsory. Whichever way you get there, the journey is a hot and weary one, but you'll see plenty of the

classic red dunes of the Kalahari on the way. Fuel is available at Andriesvale and Askham on the R360 before Twee Rivieren, and at Twee Rivieren, Nossob and Mata-Mata camps, but note it is more expensive within the park than at the petrol stations outside.

By plane and tour The two alternatives to making the long drive to Kgalagadi from Gauteng or the Cape are to go on a package tour (see box, p.272), or to fly to Upington Airport from where you can pick up a hire car. As well as those listed on p.274, there are also companies in Upington that rent out 4WDs with camping equipment, which can be an affordable way to explore the park; try Desert 4x4 (☎054 332 1560, ⌨desert4x4.co.za) or Kalahari 4x4 (☎054 332 3098, ⌨kalahari4x4hire.co.za).

TOURIST INFORMATION AND ACTIVITIES

Tourist information The visitor's centre at *Twee Rivieren* (☎054 561 2000) has exhibitions and slide shows worth checking out.

Activities The focus in Kgalagadi Transfrontier Park is on self-guided game drives, but night and day game drives

and day walks can be booked on arrival at the *Nossob*, *Twee Rivieren* and *Mata-Mata* camps. Look out for details posted at the restcamp offices about what's happening on any given day. Rates are R180–310 per person depending on numbers and duration.

GETTING AROUND

By car The park roads are gravel. While you can travel in a normal car, bear in mind that the higher the clearance the better – a car packed with four adults might struggle. It's also a good idea to reduce the pressure in your tyres by about half a bar before setting off and to play the steering to maintain traction. You might find it's often easier to drive either side of

the "road" along tracks left by other drivers. If you're in a rental car, check the small print as it may exclude cover for damaged wheels, undercarriage and paintwork. In the event of a breakdown you just have to sit it out until someone else passes; a park vehicle patrols most roads each day. Entry to the Botswana side of Kgalagadi is only allowed by 4WD.

ACCOMMODATION

INSIDE THE PARK

It's vital to book park accommodation, even for campsites, as early as you can through South African National Parks in Pretoria (☎012 428 9111, ⌨sanparks .org). The park has a choice of cottages and camping in two broad types of site: fenced restcamps at *Twee Rivieren*, *Mata-Mata* and *Nossob*, which have electricity (even in

the campsites) and creature comforts such as kitchens, fans or air conditioning, braai areas and shops, and some of the units are wheelchair accessible; and six far more basic and remote unfenced wilderness camps, for which you need to be completely self-sufficient. It's worth staying at least a night at a park restcamp away from *Twee Rivieren* to taste the raw flavour of the desert. If time is limited, an excursion to *Mata-Mata* makes sense, but *Nossob*, although further off, is better for atmosphere and game viewing: as well as hearing the lions roaring at night, you'll probably have your best chance of seeing them in this area. The roads to *Nossob* and *Mata-Mata* follow river beds, and so are good for spotting game. On the Botswana side, facilities are limited to campsites at *Mabuasehube, Two Rivers, Rooiputs* and *Polentswa;* visitors here need to be completely self-sufficient. For reservations, contact the Botswana Parks Authority office in Gaborone (☎ 09 267 318 0774, ✉ dwnp@gov.bw).

Bitterpan Wilderness Camp A peaceful spot near the centre of the park on a 4WD trail between *Nossob* and *Mata-Mata* (access by 4WD only), with four unfenced reed cabins perched on the edge of a saltpan. R1140

Gharagab Wilderness Camp Four log cabins in an unfenced area in the remote far north, a four-hour drive from *Nossob* (access by 4WD), with elevated views onto a landscape of dunes and thornveld savannah. R1140

Grootkolk Wilderness Camp This unfenced desert camp near Union's End at the very northern tip of the South African section is in prime predator country; its four chalets come fully equipped with cooking supplies, linen and fans, and they're usually booked solid months in advance. R1270

★ **Kalahari Tent Camp** Guarded by an armed guide, this unfenced site has comfortable, fully equipped, self-catering tents built of sandbags and canvas (including one luxurious "honeymoon tent"), all decorated in desert tones with views over the Auob River. There's also a swimming pool. R1275

Kieliekrankie Wilderness Camp This is the closest wilderness camp to *Twee Rivieren* (41km), and is accessible to ordinary vehicles; it offers four unfenced cabins sunk into a red sand dune, providing lovely panoramic views of the desert. R1270

Mata-Mata Camp A fenced restcamp 120km northwest of *Twee Rivieren* on the Namibian border, at the end of the road that follows the course of the Auob River. Accommodation is in fully equipped family cottages (sleeping six), comfortable two-person bungalows and a campsite. Other amenities include a water hole lit up at

night, a shop and fuel. Camping R225, bungalow R730

Nossob Camp On the Botswana border, 160km north of *Twee Rivieren* along the Nossob River Rd, this is the most remote of the three fenced restcamps. It has fifteen simple chalets, better family-size guesthouses (sleeping four), a cottage and a campsite. There's also a supply shop, fuel, plus a predator information centre (the place is famed for nocturnal visits by lions). Camping R225, chalet R765

Twee Rivieren Camp The first, and most developed, of the three fenced restcamps, right by the entrance, offering over thirty pleasant self-catering chalets with thatched roofs and nice patio areas, a sizeable campsite (with or without electricity), a mediocre restaurant, a pool, fuel, and a shop selling souvenirs and simple foodstuffs. Camping R225, chalet R980

Urikaruus Wilderness Camp Roughly halfway between *Twee Rivieren* and *Mata-Mata*, with an attractive setting among camelthorn trees overlooking the Auob River; the four two-person cabins, all equipped with solar power and kitchen supplies, are built on stilts and connected by a plank walkway. R1270

OUTSIDE THE PARK

On the approach road to Kgalagadi there are a couple of places to stay. However, with morning being the best time for game viewing, staying en route to the park isn't really an option if you're on a tight schedule.

Askham Post Office Guesthouse 72km from Twee Rivieren, in Askham ☎ 082 494 4520, ✉ askhamk @mweb.co.za. This B&B offers three spacious and clean en-suite rooms and a self-catering flat for four on the site of the old post office. There's also a small coffee shop and craft shop; overnight guests can pre-order evening meals. R580

Molopo Kalahari Lodge 55km from Twee Rivieren, in Andriesvale ☎ 054 511 0008, ⊛ molopodge.co.za. A smart, well-run place with over fifty comfortable en-suite chalets around a pool, as well as luxury bush tents, campsites, a bar and a decent restaurant. It also has a filling station and a small shop selling, drinks, ice and meat for braais, and you can stop for coffee when driving towards the park. Camping R150, chalet R510

Augrabies Falls National Park

Daily 7am–7pm • R144 • ☎ 054 452 9200, ⓦ sanparks.org

One of the undoubted highlights of any trip to the Northern Cape is **AUGRABIES FALLS NATIONAL PARK**, 120km west of Upington. Roaring out of the barren semi-desert, sending great plumes of spray up above the brown horizon, the falls – still known by their Khoikhoi name, *Aukoerabis*, "the place of great noise" – are the most spectacular moment in the two-thousand-kilometre progress of the Orange River. At peak flow, the huge volume of water plunging through the narrow channel actually compares with the more docile periods at Victoria Falls and Niagara, although Augrabies lacks both the height and the soul-wrenching grandeur of its larger rivals. But in its eerie desert setting under an azure evening sky, the falls provide a moving and absorbing experience. The sides of the canyon are shaped like a smooth parabola, and there are many tales of curious visitors venturing too far to peer at the falls and sliding helplessly into the seething maelstrom below. Despite the odd miraculous survival, several dozen people have died here since the national park was created in 1966.

Visiting the park

The **falls** are viewed from behind a large fence, while a boardwalk allows wheelchair access to the viewpoint. To see more of the **gorge**, walk the short distance to **Arrow Point** or drive on the link roads round to Ararat or Echo Corner. The atmosphere is at its best near **sunset**, when the sun shines straight into the west-facing part of the gorge.

The fairly inhospitable **northern section** of the park covers 184 square kilometres on both sides of the river. The land is dry and harsh, with sparse plants typical of arid areas, such as kokerboom (quiver tree), camelthorn and Namaqua fig. The landscape is punctuated by various striking rock formations, notably **Moon Rock**, a huge dome of smooth, flaking granite rising out of the flat plains. If you drive on the (unsurfaced) roads in the park you'll probably spot some of the resident fauna – including eland, klipspringer and springbok – while you're likely to see dassie, mongoose and lizards around the falls and the camp.

The **best time to visit** Augrabies is from March to May, when the temperatures are slightly cooler and the river is at its maximum flow after summer rainfall up in the Lesotho catchment areas. With your own transport, the falls are easily visited as a day-trip from Upington, although there's plenty of reasonable accommodation both in the park itself and nearby.

Kakamas

The route to Augrabies from Upington is west along the N14, following the Orange River and its rich fringe of vineyards, orchards and alfalfa fields. Eighty kilometres southwest of Upington, **KAKAMAS** is the last town before the park and a handy base if you're driving. The settlement was founded in 1897 by the Dutch Reformed Church as a colony for livestock farmers rendered destitute by a prolonged drought; each farmer contributed manpower for a system of irrigation canals and tunnels, and was rewarded with a plot of irrigated land. Considered primitive by the experts of the day, their handiwork still funnels water to the land today and a number of still-working waterwheels can be spotted around the town.

ARRIVAL AND INFORMATION — AUGRABIES FALLS NATIONAL PARK

By car The well-signposted turnoff to the park is at Alheit on the N14, 10km west of Kakamas. From Alheit it is 39km to the park gate, along the R359. There is no public transport to the park, but most of the Kalahari tours out of Upington and elsewhere in the Northern Cape (see box, p.272) incorporate a visit to the falls.

Information The park's reception, just up the road from the entrance gate (daily 7am–7pm), has a shop, a self-service snack bar and a restaurant with views towards the gorge.

ACTIVITIES AT AUGRABIES FALLS

The circular **Dassie nature trail** is an easy 5km hike out from the main restcamp along the river and to Moon Rock; reception can provide maps. More challenging is the three-day **Klipspringer trail** (April 1 to Sept 30; R220), which involves two overnight stops at simple huts; advance booking is essential. **Night game drives** can also be booked at reception (R220), and there's a 94-kilometre **self-drive route** (4WD only) in the park's northwestern section for viewing plains game that takes about six hours to complete.

Perhaps more instantly gratifying is the "**Augrabies Rush**", a half-day trip on small rafts down 8km of increasingly swift river immediately above the falls, run by Kalahari Outventures (see box, p.272; R350 per person with a minimum of four). It also runs an overnight rafting trip taking you deep into the empty country upriver of the falls with a simple camp set up on the riverbank (R1495).

ACCOMMODATION

Augrabies Falls Backpackers Augrabies village, 11km before the park gate ☎072 515 6079, ⓦaugrabiesbackpackers.co.za. Rustic, laid-back country house 2km down a dirt road (follow the signs from the main road to the falls). The rooms are simple, but the owner is full of tips on local activities and runs balloon trips from March to December. Dorm R180, double R340

Augrabies Falls Lodge & Camp 3km before the gate ☎054 451 7203, ⓦaugfallslodge.co.za. Pared-down backpacker accommodation with a dorm and double rooms in a hotel set in grounds of palm trees conveniently close to the falls. There's also a campsite. Each site has its own bathroom, and there's a decent bar and restaurant. Camping R95, dorm R110, double R530

The Falls Guest House On the R359, 2km before the gate ☎082 928 7938, ⓦthefallsaugrabies.com. One of the more upmarket options in the area, this renovated farmhouse has four big, cool rooms and one family cottage, with nice furnishings and a generous veranda overlooking rows of vines. Dinners or braais can be arranged. R895

Kalahari Gateway Hotel 19 Voortrekker St, Kakamas ☎054 431 0838, ⓦkalaharigateway.co.za. Large and a

bit tired looking, with the stuffy atmosphere of a conference venue. The rooms are adequate, though, and there's a swimming pool, two bars and a restaurant as well as a few self-catering apartments. R950

National Park Chalets At the park reception, reservations through South African National Parks in Pretoria ☎012 428 9111, ⓦsanparks.org; for camping and late bookings, contact reception directly, ☎054 452 9200. A large camp with a number of comfortable brick chalets and family cottages (three of which are wheelchair accessible), within walking distance of the falls and with access to three swimming pools. There is also a campsite. You can either self-cater (the nearest supermarket is in Kakamas) or eat at the restaurant. Camping R195, chalet R815

Vergelegen Guesthouse & Restaurant About 3km east of Kakamas ☎054 431 0976, ⓦaugrabiesfalls .co.za. One of the most attractive guesthouses in the region with sixteen neat rooms (two self-catering) on a farm by the main road, complete with a swimming pool and an excellent restaurant offering a menu of interesting local dishes like lamb shank, biltong soup and springbok carpaccio. R940

Namaqualand

NAMAQUALAND is another Northern Cape region whose name conjures up images of desolation and magic. According to an oft-quoted saying about the area, in Namaqualand you weep twice: once when you first arrive and once when you have to leave. This is the land of Khoikhoi herders called the **Nama**: the Little Nama, who lived south of the Orange River, and the Great Nama, who lived north of the river in what is now Namibia. Sparsely populated, the region stretches south from the Orange to the empty **Knersvlakte** plains around Vanrhynsdorp, and from the **Atlantic coast** to the edge of the **Great Karoo**. Above all, Namaqualand is synonymous with the incredible annual display of brightly coloured **wild flowers** that carpet the landscape in August and September, one of South Africa's most compelling spectacles. Even outside flower season, swathes of orange, purple and white daisies emerge, and there is a tenacious beauty about this dry, empty landscape of mountain deserts, mineral-bearing granite hills and drought-defiant succulents.

The **N7** highway between Namibia and Cape Town cuts across Namaqualand, offering one of the most scenic drives in the country. At its northern end, at the junction with the dusty **N14** from Upington and the Kalahari, lies the region's capital, **Springbok**. This is the best base for flowers – the nearby **Namaqua National Park** provides reliable displays even in years of low rainfall, when displays elsewhere may be muted – and for visiting the Province's remote northwestern corner: the **Diamond Coast**, stretching from Port Nolloth to the Namibian border. The harsh but spectacular |Ai-|Ais/Richtersveld National Park stretches inland, bisected by the Orange River – rafting on which ranks high among the region's attractions.

Springbok

The semi-arid expanse of northern Namaqualand is where the Karoo merges into the Kalahari, and both meet the ocean. If it weren't for the discovery of copper in the 1600s, and more recently of alluvial and offshore diamonds washed down from the Kimberley area by the Orange River, the region might well not have acquired any towns at all. Fresh water is scarce, and its presence here ensured the survival of **SPRINGBOK**, the region's capital, after its copper mines were exhausted.

Attractively hemmed in by hills, Springbok is the main commercial and administrative centre of Namaqualand, and an important staging post at the junction of the N7 and N14 highways. Lying 381km southwest of Upington, and 119km south of the border with Namibia at Viooolsdrift, it makes a pleasant base for visiting northern Namaqualand's flower fields in August and September (see box below) or a springboard for visiting the coast, and it's a good place to arrange trips to the |Ai-|Ais/Richtersveld National Park (see p.292).

Springbok's main action is centred on the mound of granite boulders next to the taxi rank in the town centre. Called **Klipkoppie** ("rocky hill"), this was the site of a British fort blown up by General Jan Smuts' commando during the Anglo-Boer War. A few hundred metres up from Klipkoppie, at the back of town, a gash in the hillside marks the **Blue Mine**, the first commercial copper mine in South Africa, sunk in 1852. Recent activity here has been in search of gemstones – previously ignored in the frantic hunt for copper ore – and zinc. A short trail wends up to a good **viewpoint** over town. You'll find a good selection of gemstones for sale at *Springbok Lodge*, together with an excellent display of mineralogical specimens from all over the globe.

3

ARRIVAL AND DEPARTURE   SPRINGBOK

By car Coming from Upington, the N14 eventually becomes Voortrekker St, the town's main drag, and veers south at the taxi rank to rejoin the N7 for Cape Town.
By bus Intercape buses pick up and drop off next to the Engen garage on Voortrekker St (reservations ☎021 380

4400, ⓦintercape.co.za, or buy tickets at Shoprite, 200m back towards town).
Destinations: Cape Town (daily; 8hr 35min); Upington (daily; 4hr 40min); Windhoek, Namibia (daily; 12hr 30min).

VIEWING THE FLOWERS OF NAMAQUALAND

The seeds of the spectacular **flowers of Namaqualand** – daisies, aloes, gladioli and lilies – lie dormant under the soil through the droughts of summer, waiting for the rain that sometimes takes years to materialize. About four thousand floral species are found in the area, a quarter of which are found nowhere else on Earth. Although it's difficult to predict where the best displays will occur, for more or less guaranteed flowers you can head for the Skilpad section of **Namaqua National Park** (see p.285) or to the **|Ai-|Ais/Richtersveld National Park** (see p.300), with its ocean-mist-fed succulents.

One indication of where the displays will occur is **winter rainfall**; flowers follow the rain, so early in the season they will be out near the coast, moving steadily inland. **Temperature** is also a factor, meaning that on cool or cloudy days displays are muted.

PRACTICALITIES

Flower-viewing in Namaqualand involves a lot of driving, simply because the distances are so great. **Cycling** is an option, although it can be frustrating if the best displays turn out to be 20km away from where you're based. Book **accommodation** well in advance, either on a farm (ideal if you don't have your own transport, as you can walk around the farm's own flower fields) or in a town like Springbok. Note that accommodation rates can increase substantially during flower season. The following tactics are worth keeping in mind:
• Plan your route before heading out – your hosts may have inside information about the best spots on a particular day.
• The flowers only open up around 10am, so you have time for a good breakfast. Because flowers turn to face the sun, it's best to drive westwards in the morning and eastwards in the afternoon.
• Take lots of pictures, but don't pick the flowers.

FLOWER TOUR OPERATORS

Diamond Tours Unlimited 71 Jacobson Ave, Kimberley ☎084 645 7754, ⓦdiamondtours.co.za.

Kalahari Tours and Travel 12 Mazurka Curve, Upington ☎054 338 0375, ⓦkalahari-tours.co.za.

By minibus taxi Most minibuses leave from the taxi rank at Klipkoppie, and run to Cape Town (6hr) at around 11am every day except Saturdays and go via the other towns on the N7.

INFORMATION

Tourist information The helpful tourist office (Mon–Fri 8am–4.45pm, during flower season also Sat & Sun 8.30am–4pm; ☎ 027 712 8035, ⌨ namakwa-dm.gov.za), is on Voortrekker St 700m south of the taxi rank. Another source of local wisdom (and dour wit) is the *Springbok Lodge* on the corner or Voortrekker and Kerk sts. A hub for travellers and locals, it also sells an excellent selection of books, including plenty of titles on Namaqualand and its flowers, the history of copper mining and the Nama, the Richtersveld and rock art.

ACCOMMODATION

There's no shortage of rooms in Springbok, but you're still advised to book ahead in flower season (usually Aug–Sept) when room rates may be slightly higher.

★ **Annie's Cottage** 4 King St, signposted from Klipkoppie ☎ 027 712 1451, ⌨ springbokinfo.com. Extremely stylish, comfortable and colourful rooms in a restored colonial house decorated with local artwork, with a swimming pool under jacaranda trees. There are hiking and biking trails nearby, and the gregarious owner is a good source of information about where to see the best flowers. R1050

Elkoweru Guest House 1 Bree St ☎ 027 718 1202, ⌨ elkoweru.co.za. A modern two-storey guesthouse in vaguely Mediterranean style with a range of rooms from singles to family self-catering flats; plain and simple but each has DSTV, tea and coffee stations and a/c. Dinners on request. R550

Mountain View Guest House 2 Overberg Ave (turn-off is 100m south of the tourist office, from where it's another 1km along Overberg Ave) ☎ 027 712 1438, ⌨ mountview.co.za. Ten tasteful, colourfully African-themed rooms (two self-catering) in this stylish guesthouse, pleasantly situated on the fringe of the town, right by a short trail offering views over Springbok. R940

Naries Namaqua Retreat 27km west of town along the Kleinzee Rd (R355) ☎ 027 712 2462, ⌨ naries.co.za. A homely, comfortable place to stay, with stylish rooms in an atmospheric Cape Dutch farmhouse, plus a self-catering cottage and three luxurious dome-shaped suites nestled among the boulders nearby. No under-12s allowed in the main farmhouse or the suites. The candlelight dinners are a big draw, and hiking and horseriding can be arranged. Rates are for half board. R1860

Springbok Caravan Park 2km southeast of town along the R355 ☎ 027 718 1584, ⌨ springbokcaravan park.co.za. The closest campsite to town, *Springbok Caravan Park* is plain and shadeless but well maintained and attractively surrounded by boulders and quiver trees; along with tent sites, it offers four-bed chalets and a swimming pool. Camping R70, chalet R400

Springbok Lodge 37 Voortrekker St, entrance on Kerk St ☎ 027 712 1321, ⌨ springboklodge.com. Simple but characterful and good value, offering 48 rooms with or without kitchens, all in distinctive white and yellow buildings within walking distance of the reception office/curio shop and the restaurant. R460

EATING AND DRINKING

El Dago 39 Voortrekker St, just south of the taxi rank ☎ 027 718 1475. A family-friendly restaurant good for steaks, seafood and pizzas (R80–100), with a sunny street-facing balcony. Mon–Sat 11am–10pm.

Springbok Lodge Restaurant 37 Voortrekker St, entrance on Kerk St ☎ 027 712 1321. Vaguely reminiscent of an American diner from the 1950s, serving a large but mediocre selection of steak, fish and burger meals and local wines (mains R50–90). Mon–Sat 7am–10pm, Sun 8am–10pm.

Tauren Steakranch Hospital St, just north of the taxi rank ☎ 027 712 2717. Attractive African-style decor, serving steaks dished up in a number of adventurous ways – topped with snails, for instance, or flambéed in brandy (mains around R100). Mon–Sat noon–10pm.

Titbits Voortrekker St, across the road from Springbok Lodge ☎ 027 718 1455. The best place for a drink, notable for its impressive cocktail selection, which includes chocolate Martinis and a house special involving ice cream. They also serve food, mainly pasta and pizza (mains R50–80). Mon–Sat 8am–10pm, Sun noon–10pm.

DIRECTORY

Bank You can change money at all the banks in the centre including the Absa Bank, facing the taxi rank on Namakwa St.

Camping and 4WD hire Fully equipped 4WDs and camping gear can be rented from Richtersveld Challenge at 96 Voortrekker St, opposite the tourist office (☎ 027 718 1905, ✉ richtersveld.challenge@kingsley.co.za); another alternative is to rent 4WD from the companies in Upington (see p.274).

Internet access WS Computers on Lodge St, just east of the taxi rank (☎ 027 712 2127, Mon–Fri 8am–4pm).

Goegap Nature Reserve

Entrance on the R355, 15km east of Springbok • Daily 8am–6pm during flower season, otherwise 8am–4pm • R15 • ☎ 027 718 9906

The **Goegap Nature Reserve** proclaims itself to be "Namaqualand in miniature". With close to six hundred indigenous flower species, it is a popular destination during flower season, and a garden showcasing some of the unusual, alien-like succulents endemic to the area makes it a good place to visit year-round. The reserve is also home to a number of animal species, including the Namaqualand sandgrouse, the bat-eared fox and the aardwolf. There is a 17km loop on a gravel road from the gate that you can self drive, or you can explore on foot on one of the short trails.

Kamieskroon

About 70km south of Springbok, the village of **KAMIESKROON** is set among the Kamiesberg Mountains, beneath the rocky peak – or kroon – from which it takes its name. There isn't much to the village other than a pretty setting, the crisp air of the mountains and, in flower season, a sense of being at the heart of the garden of the gods.

Deeper into the mountains, at places east of Kamieskroon such as **Nourivier** and the old Moravian mission station of **Leliefontein**, the land is owned and farmed as a community project by the local Nama people. In places you'll see families living in traditional **matjieshuise** (reed huts); these settlements, many of which are still based around a mission, are connected by dirt roads, and so make good flower-viewing routes.

Namaqua National Park

22km northwest of Kamieskroon along a signposted gravel road from the N7 • Daily 8am–5pm • R60 • ☎ 027 672 1948, ⓦ sanparks.org

A place worth going to in flower season, even if you're just passing through on the highway, is the Skilpad section in the southern half of **Namaqua National Park.** The displays here, featuring great swathes of orange colour, tend to be more reliable than elsewhere, even in years with low rainfall. Butterfly fanatics and twitchers should be in for a treat, too. There's a circular five-kilometre drive around the reserve, two short walking trails and a scenic picnic site.

ACCOMMODATION

AROUND NAMAQUA NATIONAL PARK

KAMIESKROON

Kamieskroon Hotel To the right as you come off the N7 at Kamieskroon ☎ 027 672 1614, ⓦ kamieskroon hotel.com. A vibrant and creative place that runs photographic workshops during flower season, and has become the centre for a number of activities in the surrounding Kamiesberg. There are 24 rooms, a caravan and camping park, and five self-catering apartments. The restaurant offers generous farm-style meals (book dinner in advance). Camping R90, double R530, apartment R550

GARIES

If the hotel in Kamieskroon is booked up for flower season, consider staying at Garies, 45km further south along the N7.

★ **Sophia Guest House** 33 Main St ☎ 027 652 1069, ⓦ sophiaguesthouse.co.za. Well worth the detour, this whimsically renovated old hotel from the 1930s is one of the best places to stay in the area. The cosy double rooms, kitchen and salon have all been lovingly decorated in colourful florals, and there's a charming self-catering cottage out back. The friendly owners are knowledgeable about the area and can organize dinners with advance notice. Double R600, cottage R850

NAMAQUA NATIONAL PARK

Skilpad Rest Camp In the Skilpad section of the park, reservations through South African National Parks in Pretoria ☎ 012 428 9111, ⓦ sanparks.org; for camping and late bookings, contact reception directly ☎ 027 672 1948. Four three-bed chalets set in the park's rocky hills, all comfortably equipped with fireplaces, cooking equipment and enclosed verandas. You can also camp here but there is no electricity or showers and only simple toilets. Bring all supplies including firewood. Camping R95, chalet R525

Vanrhynsdorp

Travelling south from Kamieskroon, the mountains gradually give way to the bleaker landscape of the pebble-strewn **Knersvlakte** – the "plains of the gnashing teeth", referring to the sound made by wagon wheels toiling across the harsh terrain. The small agricultural town of **VANRHYNSDORP**, 196km from Kamieskroon, is the most southerly of the Namaqualand towns. Although it's officially in the Western Cape, this is the gateway to the region if you're coming from Cape Town, 307 km to the south. It also marks the crossroads between the N7 and the R27, which connects via the glorious **Bokkeveld Escarpment** with Calvinia and ultimately Upington, on the northern fringe of the Great Karoo. Set in the lee of the spectacular flat-topped Maskam Mountain, Vanrhynsdorp is pretty much deserted out of flower season.

Museums and historical sites

Vanrhynsdorp, dominated by the tall spire of its church, offers a surprising number of local museums and historical sites for a town of its size. The **Van Rhijn Museum** on Van Riebeeck Street (Mon–Fri 9am–6pm, Sat & Sun 9am–1pm; free) is diverting enough, featuring a collection of old military pieces and domestic paraphernalia from early Boer homesteaders. Also in town is the quirky **Latsky Radio Museum**, behind the church at 4 Church St (Mon–Sat 9am–noon & 2–5pm during flower season, on request the rest of the year; free; ☎027 219 1032), nurturing a collection of some two hundred valve radios dating back to the 1920s. Venture about 500m out of town along Troe Troe Street and you'll find the town's dusty little **cemetery**, which contains the touchingly derelict graves of a number of casualties of the Anglo-Boer War – some marked by nothing more than piles of stones.

Kokerboom Kwekery

74 Voortrekker St, five blocks east of the church • Mon–Fri 8am–5pm • R10 during flower season, free the rest of the year • ☎027 219 1119, ⓦ kokerboom.co.za

Worth a look in or out of the flower season, this unusual **nursery** specializes in succulents, with a fascinating display of dozens of the more unusual varieties. Around a third of the world's succulent species grow in this area, many of them endemic. There's also a small café and shop.

ARRIVAL AND INFORMATION   VANRHYNSDORP

Most buses and taxis running to and from Cape Town, Springbok or Upington stop at either the Shell or Caltex garages at the start of Van Riebeeck St after turning off the N7 highway.

By bus Intercape buses (reservations ☎021 380 4400, ⓦ intercape.co.za) run daily to Cape Town (9.20am; 6hr 15min), Upington (7am; 8hr 5min) via Springbok (3hr), and Windhoek (3.35pm; 13hr 55min).
By minibus taxi Minibus taxis to Cape Town and Springbok usually depart Vanrhynsdorp in the early

afternoon as they pass through town on the N7. Note that there are few taxis in either direction at the weekends.
Tourist information In the museum on Van Riebeeck St (Aug & Sept Mon–Fri 8am–5pm, Sat 9am–1pm; Oct–July Mon–Fri 8am–5pm; ☎027 219 1552, ⓦ namaquawestcoast.com).

ACCOMMODATION

If you're planning on staying more than one night, you're probably best off looking for farm-based accommodation in the nearby mountains, for which you'll need a vehicle.

Gifberg Holiday Farm 29km north of Vanrhynsdorp ☎027 219 1555, ⓦ gifberg.co.za. A rural retreat with self-catering chalets that sleep one to thirteen people, plus a swimming pool and an on-site coffee shop. But the real draw is the hiking in the area, which includes everything from

beginners' trails to a 21km trek to San rock art sites. R420
Namaqualand Country Lodge 22 Voortrekker St, next to the church ☎027 219 1633 or ☎082 896 6444, ⓦ namaqualodge.co.za. A family-run lodge that has been in operation for over a century, with quirky,

old-fashioned charm (think taxidermied wildlife and the country's largest collection of neckties). There's a swimming pool, and a restaurant, *Mikie's*, next door. R560

Van Rhyn Guest House Van Riebeeck St ☎ 027 219 1429, ⓦ vanrhyngh.co.za. Calm, welcoming and artsy, with nine rooms, some in converted outhouses, which have high ceilings and remain cool even during the summer heat; excellent meals can also be provided by prior arrangement. R600

Vanrhynsdorp Caravan Park 800m along Troe Troe St (which becomes Gifberg Rd) ☎ 027 219 1287, ⓦ vanrhynsdorpcaravanpark.co.za. Reasonably quiet out of season, with a cheap campsite, basic en-suite chalets (eight of them with kitchenettes) and a handful of simple double and single rooms; pay a little extra for a/c and DSTV. Camping R170, double R360, chalets R400

Vanrhynsdorp Self-Catering Resort End of Lazarus St ☎ 027 219 1810, ✉ vrdpselfsorg@nashuaisp.co.za. These comfortable, self-catering chalets are somewhat impersonal, but they are good value and some have multiple bedrooms for families or groups. R460

EATING

Aside from the options below, there are reasonable restaurants at both the Shell and Caltex garages catering mainly to passing motorists on the N7.

Mikie's Namaqualand Country Lodge, 22 Voortrekker St ☎ 027 219 1633. An unexciting place that is, nonetheless, one of the only proper restaurants in the town centre. *Mikie's* offers a fairly standard menu of steaks, burgers and other meat-based offerings from around R70. Mon–Sat 8am–10pm.

ZAR (Zuid Afrikaanse Restaurant) Vanrhynsdorp Caravan Park, 800m along Troe Troe St (which becomes Gifberg Rd) ☎ 027 219 1287. The best restaurant in town (mains R60–110), where well-prepared steaks are served with snails, mussels and other interesting combinations, all in surprisingly refined surroundings. Mon–Sat 7–10am & 6–11pm.

Nieuwoudtville

Heading east from Vanrhynsdorp on the R27 you have a very clear impression of the sudden elevation of the land from the plains up to the **Bokkeveld Escarpment**, which the road tackles by way of Van Rhyn's Pass, complete with a couple of neck-achingly tight hairpins near the top. There's an excellent viewpoint overlooking the plains, signposted soon after you reach the plateau.

Eight kilometres on from the top of Van Rhyn's Pass, just over 50km from Vanrhynsdorp, the R27 passes just to the north of the picturesque *dorp* of **NIEUWOUDTVILLE** ("Knee-voet-vil"), with an attractive collection of tin-roofed, honey-coloured sandstone buildings and the sombre ruins of early settler homesteads on the outskirts. Founded just over a century ago, it's by far the most atmospheric place to stay in the region, full of character and history. The soil here has the highest concentration of bulb species on Earth, and there are several appealing nature reserves in the vicinity. Although most of the flowering species appear in August and September, a time of spectacularly colourful display, you're likely to find something in flower here any time between March and October.

About 7km north of Nieuwoudtville on the R357 towards Loeriesfontein the Willems and Grass Rivers combine to form the Doring (thorn) River, which tumbles over 100 metres into the Maaierskloof; the flow of water during the spring months, fed by the spring rains across the Bokkeveld Escarpment, provides a fine spectacle. The waterfall is a short 100-metre walk from the parking area alongside the R357.

Hantam National Botanic Garden

Oorlogskloof Rd • During flower season (usually Aug–Oct) daily 8am–5pm • R18 • Rest of year Mon–Fri 7.30am–4.30pm • Free • ☎ 027 218 1200, ⓦ sanbi.org/gardens/hantam

One of the best places in the country for seeing wild flowers is the **Hantam National Botanic Garden**. Formerly the farm Glenlyon, it has been described by botanist and former director of Kew Gardens Sir Ghillean Prance as "a botanical treasure of international importance". The BBC Natural History Unit and Sir David

FLOWER ROUTES AROUND NIEUWOUDTVILLE

The area around Nieuwoudtville receives unusually high rainfall thanks to its location at the edge of the escarpment, and consequently boasts over three hundred different floral species; flowering starts after the first rains in April or May, and peaks in August and September. But even if you're here out of flower season, you'll still be privy to some fantastic scenery and a wealth of rare flora and fauna. The following places give a taste of what the area has to offer:

Nieuwoudtville Wildflower Reserve 3km east of Nieuwoudtville on the R27. This is the best place to see flowers, exhibiting an unparalleled variety of bulbs, notably the orange-flowered bulbinellas. There is also a short hiking trail between the rock *koppies*.

The Bokkeveld Nature Reserve 7km north of Nieuwoudtville. The main attraction of this reserve is the 30-metre waterfall which, when the Doring River is flowing between April and October, tumbles down into an impressive gorge where large raptors can sometimes be seen soaring around the tall cliffs.

Quiver Tree Forest 25km north of Nieuwoudtville, on the R357 towards Loeriesfontein. A dirt road leading towards Gannabos will take you to one of the area's botanical oddities, an extensive quiver tree forest, containing some of the tallest specimens of *Aloe dichotoma* (the kokerboom) found in South Africa. They flower in June and July.

The Matjiesfontein Flower Route On the farm of the same name, 14km south of Nieuwoudtville. This pretty and easy-to-drive route starts at the Matjiesfontein farm stall (☎ 027 218 1217), where you pay a fee of R10; it crisscrosses the surrounding fields and is only 7km, but there is a wide range of flowering bulbs to see. During the flower season, the farm stall also runs tractor and wagon tours.

The Rondekop/Naressie Route A 42km circular drive that starts and finishes in Nieuwoudtville, through an area more akin to the Karoo; hence you will find vast numbers of daisies and *vygies* along this route. The tourist office can provide a map.

Attenborough visited twice in the 1990s to film footage of the garden's extraordinary flora for the documentary series *The Private Life of Plants*. While spring is obviously the best time to visit, you'll also find a number of early-blooming flowers in winter, and autumn features brilliant displays of pink candelabra lilies and yellow crossyne.

ARRIVAL AND INFORMATION   NIEUWOUDTVILLE

By minibus taxi Public transport to Nieuwoudtville is limited to occasional minibus taxis to and from Vanrhynsdorp (45min), which drop off and pick up on Kerk St, 700m east of the tourist office.

Tourist information The Information Centre operates out of the church hall on Kerk St (mid-July to Sept Mon–Sat 9am–5pm, Sun 9am–2pm; Oct to mid-July Mon, Wed & Fri 9am–2pm; ☎ 027 218 1336, ⓦ nieuwoudtville.com). The Smidswinkel Restaurant & Information Centre, in a large sandstone building on Neethling St (☎ 027 218 1535), is another good choice for reliable advice; staff can point you to the various hiking trails in the region, and to rock-art sites.

ACCOMMODATION

Olive Caravan Park Just over 1km out of town along Kerk St; book through the Van Zijl Guesthouses (see below). A pleasant caravan park and campsite, with a large thatched braai area and six pitches with electricity and hot-water showers. R150

Papkuilsfontein Guest Farm 23km south of town off the dirt road to Clanwilliam ☎ 027 218 1246, ⓦ papkuilsfontein.com. Six lovingly restored white-washed self-catering cottages spread around the farm run by the Van Wyk family; some date back to the 1800s and are hugely atmospheric. Tasty home-cooked light lunches, cakes and coffee are available at the farm restaurant, *Die Waenhuis* (daily 10am-4pm), and dinners are by prior arrangement. Activities include hiking, birding and swimming in the farm dams. R790

Van Zijl Guesthouses 1 Neethling St ☎ 027 218 1535, ⓦ nieuwoudtville.co.za. A collection of attractive guesthouses clustered around the *Smidswinkel Restaurant*. Most of the self-catering rooms are in restored traditional sandstone buildings, complete with fireplaces and cosy old furniture. There's also a double room tucked into a snug loft above the restaurant, and another in a restored wagon shed. R740

EATING

Smidswinkel Restaurant 1 Neethling St ☎027 218 1535. For somewhere to eat, you can't do better than this excellent restaurant at the *Van Zijl Guesthouses*; the leg of lamb is famously good, especially when washed down with the local wine. For less common Afrikaner specialities like baked sheep's heads and stuffed heart, give them a day's notice. Main courses average around R100, and light meals and teas are served in the garden. Daily 7am–10pm.

Calvinia

Despite its stern name, bestowed by an early dominee, **CALVINIA**, 70km east of Nieuwoudtville, has quite an appealing setting beneath the impressive Hantam Mountains. The town acts as a service centre for the western part of the **Great Karoo**, but it isn't a place you'll want to spend a lot of time in, unless you're here for the flowers in the surrounding area (*hantam* is Khoi for "where the red bulbs grow").

INFORMATION

Tourist information 44 Church St (Mon–Fri 8am–1pm & 2–5pm, Sat 8am–noon; ☎027 341 1043); located in an old synagogue built in the 1920s, with a few farm tools and early photographs on display, they can provide details of flower routes and various hiking and 4WD trails in the Hantam district.

ACCOMMODATION AND EATING

Die Blou Nartjie 35 Water St, ☎027 341 1263, ⓦnartjie.co.za. Easily one of the most stylish places to stay in the region with eight luxurious rooms decorated in a mixture of antiques and modern bling – think silver chandeliers and velvet bedspreads – and each has a/c and DSTV. There's a small swimming pool and the excellent restaurant and bar is the focal point for the town. **R540**

Hantam Huis 42–44 Hope St ☎027 341 1606, ⓦcalvinia.co.za. An atmospheric collection of restored old homes, turned into guesthouses and filled with beautiful antique furniture. Self-catering is available, but there is also a restaurant serving traditional Afrikaner food, fresh bread, cakes and coffee. Worth a stop is the reception with its craft shop and interesting jumbled collection of collectibles on display. **R520**

The west coast and the Richtersveld

North from St Helena Bay, the hook of land 100km north of Cape Town, the long, lonely **west coast** of South Africa has two simple components: the cold, grey Atlantic Ocean, and the dominant sandveld vegetation, hardy but infertile. There isn't much more to the region: between the mouth of the Olifants River near Vanrhynsdorp and the Orange River over 400km to the north the only settlement of any size or significance is **Port Nolloth**, but there are good sealed roads connecting the N7 highway to the coast. Namaqualand's first **diamonds** were discovered in 1925, confirming that diamonds could be carried the length of the Orange, washed out into the ocean and then dispersed by currents and the processes of longshore drift. Although initial prospecting was carried out along the course of the Orange and in the coastal dunes, the diamonds lying offshore on the sea bed are now more eagerly chased, mostly by boats operating with huge underwater "vacuum cleaners" and divers working in often dangerous conditions. Whereas much of Namaqualand's coast remains off limits thanks to the presence of diamonds, the "**Diamond Coast**" from Port Nolloth to Alexander Bay, the mouth of the Orange River, is visitable. Springbok serves as a good access point.

During **flower season**, the rains fall first on the coastal areas, and you can often see displays beginning about 20km inland, making the few roads down to the coast from the N7 worthwhile detours. The tarred R355 road through the **Spektakel Pass** between Springbok and Kleinzee is one of the most spectacular drives in Namaqualand, and the **Anenous Pass** on the tarred R382 between Steinkopf and Port Nolloth is also impressive. Along this road you'll also see wandering herds of goats belonging to the pastoral **Nama** people living in the area, as well as the peaks and valleys of the |Ai-|Ais/ **Richtersveld National Park**, the protected mountain desert occupying the area immediately south of the Orange River.

Port Nolloth

PORT NOLLOTH, 136km northwest of Springbok, is an odd but delightful place. In the hazy sunshine the horizons are never quite in focus, while the heavy morning mists shroud the town in a quiet eeriness. Populated by a mix of fishermen and diamond-boat owners, Port Nolloth is also a place with a whiff of mystery and excitement, and tales are thick about "IDB" (illegal diamond buying). Attractions are limited and the Atlantic too cold for swimming, but a stroll to the **harbour** is always interesting. There are no tours on the diamond boats, but the guesthouses at McDougall's Bay, around 5km to the south, provide canoes and small boats for their guests.

ARRIVAL AND INFORMATION | PORT NOLLOTH

By minibus taxi The only public transport for Port Nolloth are the sporadic minibus taxis that run Mon–Sat between Sanddrif on the Namibian border and Springbok (enquire at the taxi rank in Springbok the day before). In Port Nolloth they stop next to the Port Nolloth Pharmacy on Main Rd (which runs parallel with Beach St). Ask the drivers about departures for the return trip.

ACCOMMODATION

Bedrock Lodge 2 Beach Rd, Port Nolloth ☎ 027 851 8865, ⓦ bedrocklodge.co.za. A stylish, laid-back old beach house with period furniture that's a great place to stay, and a good source of local information. There is also a collection of self-catering cottages of various sizes, all with sea views. **R750**

McDougall's Beach House Accommodation Voetbay St, McDougall's Bay ☎ 027 851 8064, ⓦ beachhouseportnolloth.co.za. Eleven modern self-catering houses around McDougall's Bay; fairly simple but most come with sea views and are good value for groups and families. You check in at reception (where you can also get wood for the braais) and they'll transfer you in their vehicle. **R600**

Port Indigo On Kamp St, McDougall's Bay ☎ 027 851 8012, ⓦ portindigo.co.za. One en-suite double in a B&B, plus a scattering of self-catering beachfront houses, of varying quality, with one to four bedrooms each. Can help to arrange local tours. Double **R450**, self-catering **R960**

EATING

Anita's Tavern Next to First National Bank, Coastal Rd ☎ 084 726 7090. This cosy pub is the best place in town to eat, serving good fish, mussels and calamari, plus meat and pasta dishes (mains from R70), in a rustic beachside fisherman's hut decorated with nautical bric-a-brac. Daily 10am–11pm.

Vespetti 2099 Coastal Rd ☎ 027 851 7843. This friendly set-up, with a Vespa scooter theme (the owners are fans), is well located right on the beachfront, offering an Italian-inspired menu of pizza and pasta (R45–90) and some pricier seafood dishes. Takeaways available. Tues–Sun noon–9.30pm.

Alexander Bay

The westernmost point of South Africa is **ALEXANDER BAY**, 84km north of Port Nolloth at the mouth of the Orange River, within a stone's throw of Namibia. It is named after Sir James Edward Alexander who in the 1860s began exporting copper, but it was in 1926 when the first diamonds were discovered that the little town came to life. Alluvial **diamonds** are still the town's *raison d'être*, and the largest stone ever found here, in 1944, was the Merensky Diamond, weighing in at a cool 211.5 carats. The **Alexkor** mining company controls most commercial activity in and around town and you can contact them to arrange a tour of the diamond area as well as an oyster farm and seal colony (☎ 027 877 0028, ⓦ coastofdiamonds.co.za). Tours run on Friday at 8am and you need to book at least a week in advance and supply copies of your passport (the price depends on the size of the group, generally around R175 per person).

ARRIVAL AND DEPARTURE ALEXANDER BAY

Note that there is no border crossing to Oranjemund on the Namibian coast; the border posts to Namibia are at Vioolsdrift on the N7 or the vehicle pontoon over the Orange River at Sendelingsdrift in the |Ai-|Ais/Richtersveld National Park (see below).

By minibus taxi The only public transport for Alexander Bay are the sporadic minibus taxis that run Mon–Sat between Sanddrif on the Namibian border and Springbok (enquire at the taxi rank in Springbok the day before). In Alexander Bay they stop near Pep Stores on Oranje St – ask the drivers about departures for the return trip.

|AI-|AIS/RICHTERSVELD NATIONAL PARK

Daily 7am–6pm, reception 8am–4pm • R170 • ☎ 027 831 1506, ⓦ sanparks.org

The |AI-|AIS/RICHTERSVELD NATIONAL PARK in northwestern Namaqualand – commonly known as **the Richtersveld** – covers an area roughly bounded by the Orange River to the north, the N7 to the east, the R382 to Port Nolloth to the south and the Atlantic Ocean on its western side. The starkly beautiful park was formed in 2003 by the merger of South Africa's Richtersveld National Park (by which name the new park is still often known in South Africa) and Namibia's /Ai-/Ais and Fish River Canyon Park. Tucked along either side of a loop in the Orange, the landscape is fierce and rugged; names such as Hellskloof, Skeleton Gorge, Devil's Tooth and Gorgon's Head indicate the austerity of the inhospitable brown mountainscape, tempered only by a broad range of hardy succulents, mighty rock formations, the magnificence of the light cast at dawn and dusk, and the glittering canopy of stars at night. Annual rainfall in parts of the park is under 50mm, making this the only true desert – and mountain desert at that – in South Africa. In summer the daytime heat can be unbearable – temperatures over 50°C have been recorded – while on winter nights temperatures drop below freezing.

The **best time to visit** is August and September, when the area's succulents – representing almost one-third of South Africa's species – burst into flower. There's little fauna in the park other than lizards and klipspringers, although leopards are present, if characteristically shy.

ACTIVITIES IN THE RICHTERSVELD

Between April and September it's possible to take **guided hikes** along three designated trails in the park, although note that these trails are pretty tough going and should only be attempted by experienced wilderness hikers. They are: the Vensterval Trail (four days, three nights), the Lelieshoek–Oemsberg Trail (three days, two nights) and the Kodaspiek Trail (two days, one night). Most overnights on the trails are in the Hiking Trails Base Camp in the Ganakouriep Valley within the park, which has bunks, gas stoves, fridges and hot showers. For more information and reservations contact South African National Parks in Pretoria (☎ 012 428 9111, ⓦ sanparks.org).

Several companies offer multiday **canoeing trips** on the Orange River; two-person inflatable or fibreglass canoes are used and nights are spent camping under the stars on the riverbanks. These trips are a gentle and relaxing jaunt and are not too physically challenging; children over the age of 6 can join. Expect to pay from R3000 per person for a four-day trip. A recommended canoeing company is **Bushwhacked Outdoor Adventure** (☎ 027 761 8953, ⓦ bushwhacked .co.za), based at the riverside Fiddler's Creek campsite (R75) on the Namibian border, 12km along the south bank of the river from Vioolsdrif. Also try Cape Town-based **Amanzi Trails** (☎ 021 559 1573, ⓦ amanzitrails.co.za), and **Umkulu** (☎ 021 853 7952, ⓦ orangeriverrafting.com), which have basecamps on the river where you can park and leave luggage.

ARRIVAL AND DEPARTURE | |AI-|AIS/RICHTERSVELD NATIONAL PARK

Given its remoteness this is not the place for a day visit, and there's no public transport.

By car The most direct route to the park is to drive north from Springbok on the N7 to Steinkopf (49km). From here, follow the R382 via the Annenous Pass to Port Nolloth and then Alexander Bay, from where the park is signposted. It is 93km on a gravel road from Alexander Bay to the park office at Sendelingsdrift – you will need to be at the park office before 4pm. Those coming from Namibia can take the road from the Vioolsdrift border on the N7, via Kotzehoop, Eksteenfontein and then take the Sendelingsdrift pontoon (daily 8am–4.15pm) across the Orange River, which marks the boundary between South Africa and its neighbour. Note that ordinary cars are not allowed inside the park (see below).

By tour Unless you're a skilled driver, probably the best way of seeing the |Ai-|Ais/Richtersveld National Park is as part of a tour. The most experienced operation is Richtersveld Challenge (see p.284), offering expeditions of varying lengths into the park as well as to Kgalagadi and Namibia. The Kalahari tour operators listed on p.272 can also organize tours to the park.

GETTING AROUND

By car Ordinary cars are not allowed inside the park; the only way to explore is in a 4WD or a pick-up with a high enough clearance to handle the sandy river beds and rough mountain passes between the designated campsites. Pay particular attention along the track linking the Richtersberg and De Hoop campsites, which is covered with thick sand and treacherously jagged rocks. If you are driving, it's recommended that you travel in a group of two vehicles, but note that no driving is allowed at night.

ACCOMMODATION

It's advisable to prebook accommodation; reservations should be made through South African National Parks in Pretoria (☎ 012 428 9111, ⓦ sanparks.org). For camping and late bookings, contact reception directly (☎ 027 831 1506). There is no restaurant in the park, but fuel and limited supplies (cold drinks and dried and tinned food) are available at the park headquarters at Sendelingsdrift (daily 8am–4pm), 93km from Alexander Bay. The nearest shops are at Alexander Bay, but there is far greater choice in the large supermarkets in Springbok.

Campsites Inside the park at Kokerboomkloof, Potjiespram, Richtersberg and De Hoop. There are four very basic wilderness campsites spread throughout the park. All sites have cold showers except for *Kokerboomkloof* which doesn't have showers. You'll need to bring all drinking water and jerry cans be filled at Sendelingsdrift. R195

Sendelingsdrift Rest Camp By the gate at Sendelingsdrift; ⓦ sanparks.org. Ten decent chalets sleeping between two and four people, each equipped with a/c, fridges and stoves. There are views over the Orange River from the front porches, and a swimming pool as well as a campsite. Camping R195, chalets R730

Tatasberg Wilderness Camp Inside the park at Tatasberg, on the Namibian border. Picturesque, two-person reed cabins that come with cooking facilities, set among dramatic boulders and enjoying lovely views of the surrounding mountains. Showers are provided, but bring your own drinking water. R730

The Eastern Cape

VIEW ACROSS THE KAROO

The Eastern Cape

Sandwiched between the Western Cape and KwaZulu-Natal, South Africa's two most popular coastal provinces, the Eastern Cape tends to be bypassed by visitors – and for all the wrong reasons. The relative neglect it has suffered as a tourist destination and at the hands of the government is precisely where its charm lies. You can still find traditional African villages here, and the region's 1000km of undeveloped coastline alone justifies a visit, sweeping back inland in immense undulations of vegetated dunefields. For anyone wanting to get off the beaten track, the province is, in fact, one of the most rewarding regions in South Africa.

Port Elizabeth is the province's commercial centre, principally used to start or end a trip along the Garden Route, though it's a useful springboard for launching out into the rest of South Africa – the city is the transport hub of the Eastern Cape. **Jeffrey's Bay**, 75km to the west, has a fabled reputation among surfers for its perfect waves. Around an hour's drive inland are some of the province's most significant game reserves, among them **Addo Elephant National Park**, a Big Five reserve where sightings of elephants are virtually guaranteed. Addo and the private reserves nearby are among the few game reserves in South Africa that are malaria-free throughout the year. The hinterland to the north takes in areas appropriated by English immigrants shipped out in the 1820s as ballast for a new British colony. Here, **Grahamstown** glories in its twin roles as the spiritual home of English-speaking South Africa and host to Africa's biggest arts festival.

The northwest is dominated by the sparse beauty of the **Karoo**, the thorny semi-desert stretching across much of central South Africa. The rugged **Mountain Zebra National Park**, 200km north of Port Elizabeth, is a stirring landscape of flat-topped mountains and arid plains stretching for hundreds of kilometres. A short step to the west, **Graaff-Reinet** is the quintessential eighteenth-century Cape Dutch Karoo town.

The eastern part of the province, largely the former Transkei, is by far the least developed, with rural Xhosa villages predominating. **East London**, the province's only other centre of any size, serves well as a springboard for heading into the Transkei, where the principal interest derives from political and cultural connections. **Steve Biko** was born here, and you can visit his grave in **King William's Town** to the west. Further west is **Fort Hare University**, which educated many contemporary African leaders. The only established resorts in this section are in the **Amatola Mountains**, notably

Highlights

❶ **Port Elizabeth township tour** Accessible tours to areas which were the stomping ground of a number of significant black South Africans and the site of anti-apartheid resistance. **See p.304**

❷ **Addo Elephant National Park** See pachyderms and the rest of the Big Five in the best game reserve in the malaria-free southern half of the country. **See p.307**

❸ **Grahamstown Festival** Africa's largest arts festival wakes up this pretty colonial university town. **See p.319**

❹ **The Tuishuise** The historic frontier town of Cradock offers accommodation in a street of beautifully restored and furnished Victorian houses. **See p.321**

❺ **Karoo farmstays** Experience the sharp light and panoramic landscape of the Karoo semi-desert that sweeps across South Africa's interior. **See p.327**

❻ **Bulungula Backpacker Lodge** In a remote Wild Coast village, this brilliant base offers a vivid experience of Xhosa life and culture. **See p.343**

❼ **Nelson Mandela's birthplace, Qunu** Follow in the footsteps of South Africa's greatest hero to the village where he was born and was buried in 2013, just outside Mthatha. **See p.344**

HIGHLIGHTS ARE MARKED ON THE MAP ON PP.298–299

Hogsback, where indigenous forests and mossy coolness provide relief from the dry scrublands below.

Tucked into the northeastern corner of the province, the **Eastern Cape Highlands** make a steep ascent out of the Karoo and offer trout-fishing and ancient San rock art. The focus of the area is the remote, lovely village of **Rhodes**. Further east, the **Wild Coast region** remains one of the least developed and most exciting regions in the country. The poorest part of the poorest province, the region is blessed with fabulously

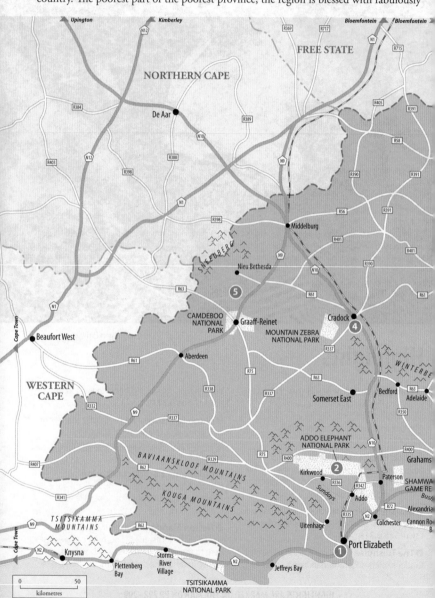

beautiful subtropical coast. Green hills roll down to the best beaches in the country, largely deserted, except for the long-horned Nguni cattle that laze on the sand. All the way to the KwaZulu-Natal border, dirt roads trundle down to the coast from the N2 to remote and indolent hillside resorts, each one dominated by a family hotel. **Port St Johns** is the biggest and best known destination, followed by Coffee Bay, both of which are blessed with tarred roads. In the rugged, goat-chewed landscape inland, Xhosa-speakers live in mud-and-tin homesteads, scraping a living herding stock and growing

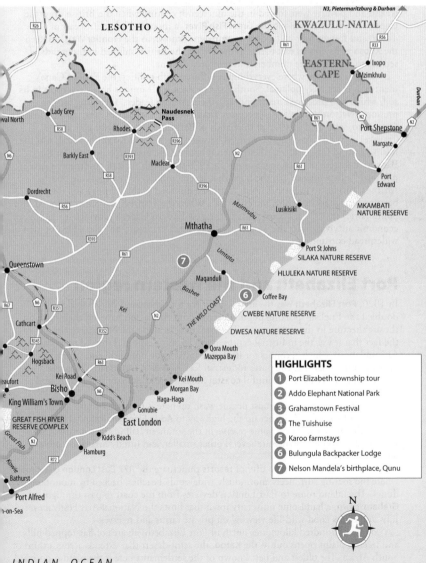

HIGHLIGHTS

1. Port Elizabeth township tour
2. Addo Elephant National Park
3. Grahamstown Festival
4. The Tuishuise
5. Karoo farmstays
6. Bulungula Backpacker Lodge
7. Nelson Mandela's birthplace, Qunu

INDIAN OCEAN

N

EASTERN CAPE

crops. Most visitors pass as quickly as possible through **Mthatha** (formerly Umtata), the ugly former capital of the Transkei – but if you're following in the footsteps of Nelson Mandela, the **Nelson Mandela Museum** in the centre of Mthatha, and **Qunu**, his birthplace and grave site, southwest of the town, are obvious ports of call.

Brief history

The Eastern Cape was carved up into black and white territories under apartheid in a more consolidated way than anywhere else in the country. The stark contrasts between wealth and poverty were forged in the nineteenth century when the British drew the Cape colonial frontier along the **Great Fish River**, a thousand kilometres east of Cape Town, and fought over half a dozen campaigns (known as the **Frontier Wars**) to keep the **Xhosa** at bay on its east bank. In the 1820s, the British shipped in thousands of settlers to bolster white numbers and reinforce the line.

Even for a country where everything is suffused with politics, the Eastern Cape's identity is excessively **political**. South Africa's black trade unions have deep roots in its soil, which also produced many anti-apartheid African leaders, including former president **Nelson Mandela**, his successor **Thabo Mbeki**, and Black Consciousness leader **Steve Biko**, who died in 1977 at the hands of Port Elizabeth security police. The Transkei or Wild Coast region, wedged between the Kei and KwaZulu-Natal, was the testing ground for grand apartheid when it became the prototype in 1963 for the Bantustan system of racial segregation. In 1976 the South African government gave it notional "independence", in the hope that several million Xhosa-speaking South Africans, surplus to industry's needs, could be dumped in the territory and thereby become foreigners in "white South Africa". When the Transkei was reincorporated into South Africa in 1994 it became part of the new Eastern Cape, a province struggling for economic survival under the weight of its apartheid-era legacy and the added burden of widespread corruption.

Port Elizabeth and the western region

In 1820, **Port Elizabeth** was the arrival point for four thousand British settlers, who doubled the English-speaking population of South Africa and have left their trace on the architecture in the town centre. The smokestacks along the N2 bear testimony to the fact that it was the industrial centre of the Eastern Cape and thrived on cheap African labour, which accounts for its deep-rooted trade unionism and strong tradition of African nationalism. The port's industrial feel, however, is mitigated by some outstanding **city beaches**, beautiful **coastal walks** a few kilometres from town, and a small **historical centre**.

However, the main reason most people wash up here is to start or finish a tour of the **Garden Route** – or head further up the highway to **Addo Elephant National Park** (see p.307), the most significant game reserve in the southern half of the country. Also within easy striking distance are several other smaller, and utterly luxurious, **private game reserves**.

East of Port Elizabeth, a handful of **resorts** punctuate the **R72 East London coast road**, where the roaring surf meets enormously wide sandy beaches, backed by mountainous dunes. The inland route to East London deviates from the coast to pass through **Grahamstown**, a handsome university town that hosts the National Arts Festival every July, and offers good wild-life viewing on private farms and reserves.

A couple of hundred kilometres north of Port Elizabeth, an area of flat-topped hills and treeless plains opens out to the **Karoo**, the semi-desert that extends across a third of South Africa. The oldest and best known of the settlements here is the picture-postcard town of **Graaff-Reinet**, a solid fixture on bus tours. Just a few kilometres away is the awesome **Valley of Desolation**, and the village of **Nieu Bethesda**, best known for its

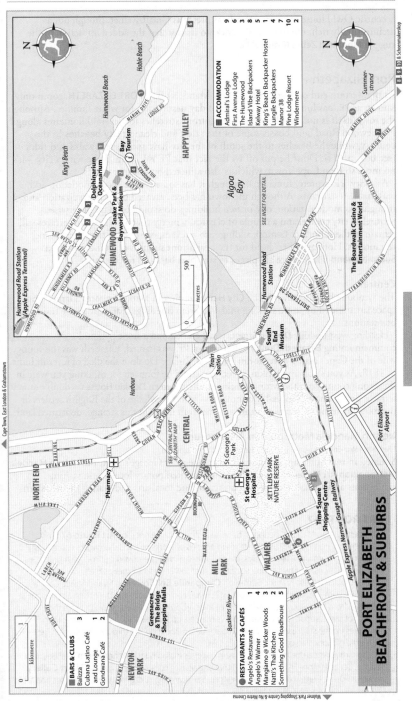

PORT ELIZABETH BEACHFRONT & SUBURBS

■ **ACCOMMODATION**

Admiral's Lodge	9
First Avenue Lodge	6
The Humewood	3
Island Vibe Backpackers	8
Kelway Hotel	5
King's Beach Backpacker Hostel	4
Lungile Backpackers	1
Manor 38	7
Pine Lodge Resort	10
Windermere	2

■ **BARS & CLUBS**

Balizza	3
Cubana Latino Café and Lounge	1
Gondwana Café	2

● **RESTAURANTS & CAFÉS**

Angelo's Restaurant	1
Angelo's Walmer	4
Mangiamo @ Wicker Woods	4
Natti's Thai Kitchen	2
Something Good Roadhouse	5

Cape Town, East London & Grahamstown

Walmer Park Shopping Centre & Nu Metro Cinema

8 9 10 & Schoenmakerskop

4

eccentric Owl House museum. Nearly as pretty as Graaff-Reinet, though not as architecturally rich, the town of **Cradock**, to its east, has the added attraction of the rugged **Mountain Zebra National Park**.

Port Elizabeth

At the western end of Algoa (aka Nelson Mandela) Bay, **PORT ELIZABETH**, commonly known as **PE**, has long been a popular holiday destination for white families. Although the town itself is no great beauty, its beachfront stretches for several kilometres along Humewood Road, and boasts some of the safest and cleanest **city beaches** in the country, while the beaches to the south of the city have some great walks and rides (see box, p.304). Don't be put off by the fact that PE is known as the windy city – it's no more so than Cape Town, which is also afflicted by summer winds.

As a city, PE is pretty functional, though it has some terrific accommodation and reasonable restaurants. Although the town has been ravaged by industrialization and thoughtless modernization, one or two buildings do stand out in an otherwise featureless **city centre**, and a couple of classically pretty rows of Victorian terraces still remain in the suburb of **Central**, sliding into a revamped street of trendy cafés and restaurants. Holidaymakers head for the beachfront suburbs of **Humewood** and **Summerstrand** where there are places to stay plus bars and restaurants.

Central

The symbolic heart of town is the **City Hall**, standing in **Market Square**, a large, empty space surrounded by some striking mid-Victorian buildings, adjacent to the train and bus stations.

Heading west up hilly **Donkin Street**, you'll come upon a stone pyramid commemorating **Elizabeth Donkin**, after whom PE was named. Elizabeth was the young wife of the Cape's acting governor in 1820, Sir Rufane Donkin; she died of fever in India in 1818. As you stroll up Donkin Street, you could be forgiven for thinking you were in the wrong country, on the wrong continent: the nineteen **Donkin Houses** – double-storey terraces that are now National Monuments – reflect the desire of the English settlers in the mid-nineteenth century to create a home from home in this strange, desiccated land.

Nelson Mandela Metropolitan Art Museum

1 Park Drive · Mon–Fri 8.30am–5pm, Sat & Sun 1–5pm · Free · ⓦ artmuseum.co.za

Situated in two buildings framing the entrance to St George's Park, the **Nelson Mandela Metropolitan Art Museum** has a collection of contemporary local work, visiting exhibitions and a small shop selling postcards and local arts and crafts. Their Eastern

---

ART ROUTE 67

Commemorating Madiba's period of 67 years fighting for democracy, **Art Route 67** is a walk round central Port Elizabeth, which takes in a series of works of art. The artworks come in all sizes ranging from small tile mosaics, to vinyl street stickers, beadworks, 30m-wall murals, metal installations, and two-tonne sculptures that tower up to six metres high.

A good place to start is at the 52m-high **Campanile Bell Tower** on Strand Street, Central (Tues–Sun 9am–12:30pm, 1–2pm; free), which you can climb to reach the observation room at the top – from here, you get a great view of the harbour and its surroundings. From the bottom of the Campanile, the route follows markers up the steps to Vuyisile Square, then continues up the staircase at St Mary's Terrace before meandering through the Donkin Reserve to reach a gigantic flag on top of the hill.

Other artworks can be found in PE's main galleries including the **Athenaeum**, at 7 Belmont Terrace, Central (Mon–Fri 8.30am–5pm) that showcases community art, and **GFI Art Gallery** at 30 Park Drive, Central (Mon–Fri 10am–4pm, Sat 10am–1pm; ⓦ gfiartgallery.com), for fine art.

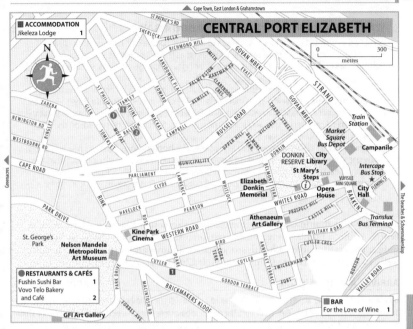

Cape art section is the area to aim for, though they have some minor European and oriental artworks which hold some interest too.

South End Museum

On the corner of Humewood Road and Walmer Boulevard • Mon–Fri 9am–4pm, Sat & Sun 10am–3pm • Free • ⓦ southendmuseum.co.za

Based in the old Seamen's Institute, the **South End Museum** recalls the bygone days of the South End, a vibrant multicultural neighbourhood which grew up because of PE's then booming harbour. As a result of the Group Areas Act it was razed street by street in the 1960s, save for a handful of churches and mosques. Today, the area is full of pricey townhouses.

The beachfront

Port Elizabeth's sandy **beaches** are its main attraction. The protection provided by Algoa Bay makes them safe for swimming (that said, it's best to do so between the lifeguard beacons), and clean enough to make **beachcombing** a pleasure.

The beachfront strip, divided from the harbour by a large wall, starts about 2km south of the city centre. The first of the beaches is beautiful, wide **King's Beach**, somewhat marred by a jumble of coal heaps and oil tanks behind it. To the southeast lies **Humewood Beach**, across the road from which is the Bayworld complex, housing the missable **Bayworld Museum** and **Snake Park** (daily 9am–4.30pm; R35; ⓦ www.bayworld.co.za). Nearby is a complex of restaurants, pubs and clubs with great views. Beyond, to the south, **Hobie Beach** and **Summerstrand** are good for walking and sunbathing.

Boardwalk Casino Complex

Beach Road, Summerstrand • Musical Fountain Show Sun–Thurs at 7pm, Fri, Sat & public holidays 8, 9 & 10pm • ⓦ www .suninternational.com/boardwalk

Summerstrand's mammouth **Boardwalk Casino Complex** is a lively place for a stroll at night, with a musical fountain show where water jets through coloured lights to create

WALKING AND RIDING ROUND SARDINIA BAY

Port Elizabeth's most beautiful coastline lies to the south of the city. From Summerstrand, Marine Drive continues 15km down the coast as far as the quiet seaside suburb of **Schoenmakerskop** (Schoenies to the locals), along an impressive coastline that alternates between rocky shores and sandy beaches. At Schoenies, you'll also find a charming beachside restaurant, the only place for refreshments in the area. From here you can walk the 8km **Sacramento Trail**, a shoreline path that leads to the huge-duned **Sardinia Bay**, the wildest and most dramatic stretch of coast in the area. To get to Sardinia Bay by road, turn right at the Schoenmakerskop intersection and follow the road until Sardinia Bay is signed, on the left. Always walk with others for safety.

The huge beach at Sardinia Bay is also a great place for **horseriding**, with treks heading along sandy paths through the coastal bush of Sardinia Bay Nature Reserve, which open out onto the dunes and beach. Heavenly Stables, 431 Sardinia Bay Rd (T 082 420 8855; R250 per hour), can accommodate beginners on quiet well-behaved horses, as well as more experienced riders.

a screen with a multimedia show. The complex also houses a large hotel, convention centre, casino, a number of reasonable restaurants, some pleasing shops, including an indigenous crafts market, a health spa, cinemas, a games arcade and ten-pin bowling, as well as a nearby golf course (Humelinks Golf Club T 041 583 2137).

ARRIVAL AND DEPARTURE — PORT ELIZABETH

4

By plane Port Elizabeth's airport is conveniently situated on the edge of Walmer suburb, 4km south from the city centre, and served by Kulula (T 0861 585 852, W kulula.com), SAA (T 041 507 1111, W flysaa.com) and Mango (T 086 100 1234, W flymango.com). There's a taxi rank outside the airport as well as the major car rental companies – arrange a car beforehand to ensure the best deal and have a car waiting for you.

Destinations Cape Town (daily; 1hr 15min); Durban (3 daily; 1hr 15min); Jo'burg (6–7 daily; 1hr 35min).

By train Port Elizabeth station (T 041 507 2662) is centrally located on the Strand, with the Shosholoza Meyl train (W www.shosholozameyl.co.za) connecting PE to Jo'burg three times a week (Mon, Wed & Sun; 20hr 35min).

By bus The Baz Bus runs in both directions along the coast and will drop off at any central location or accommodation, while Greyhound, Intercape and Translux intercity buses stop at every major town along the Garden route before pulling in at Greenacres shopping mall in Newton Park suburb, 3km from the centre; from here, you can get a taxi into town.

Destinations Cape Town (6–7 daily; 12hr); Durban (daily; 12hr 30min); Jo'burg (daily; 14hr 30min); Knysna (daily; 5hr); Mthatha (daily; 8hr 50min).

INFORMATION, TOURS AND ACTIVITIES

Tourist information The Nelson Mandela Bay Tourism office has several offices in PE, all of which can book accommodation and hand out leaflets detailing local attractions. The main office is at the corner of Mitchell Street and Walmer Boulevard, South End (Mon–Fri 8am–4.30pm; T 041 582 2575, W nmbt.co.za), but there are also branches at the airport (daily 7am–7pm; T 041 581 0456); at Shop 48 at the Boardwalk, Marine Drive, Summerstrand (daily 8am–7pm; T 041 583 2030); and in the Donkin Reserve Lighthouse Building, Belmont Terrace, Central (Mon–Fri 8am–4.30pm, Sat 8am–3pm; T 041 585 8884).

Tours The best way to see Port Elizabeth is on one of the excellent bus tours, which shed light on a city shaped by layers of political history. Calabash Tours (T 041 585 6162, W calabashtours.co.za) operates "Real City Tours" by day and *shebeen* tours by night, as well as day-trips to Addo, and most of the backpacker hostels run their own tours too, notably *Jikeleza*. The self-guided Heritage Walk (shown on a map available at the tourist office) is an excellent way to see the city centre sights, and can be combined with Art Route 67 (see box, p.302).

Boat trips Though PE is not known for whale-watching, Raggy Charters (T 073 152 2277, W raggycharters.co.za) runs recommended sea cruises (R900) from the Algoa Yatch Club in PE harbour to spot Humpback and Southern Right Whales (July–Nov) and dolphins (year-round), and to the massive penguin colony at St Croix Island.

Watersports Although the ocean around PE is not tropically clear and warm, the diving is good, especially for soft corals, and there is the chance of diving with Ragged Tooth Sharks. For dives and dive courses, as well as snorkelling, kiteboarding, stand-up paddling and kayaking, try Pro Dive, 189 Main Rd, Walmer (T 041 581 1144, W prodive.co.za).

RIGHT HOBIE BEACH, PORT ELIZABETH (P.303) >

GETTING AROUND

By car Renting a car is your best option (see p.304) for getting around PE and going to the premier destination of Addo. If you are staying in Central or the beachfront, however, it is easy enough to explore locally on foot.

Taxis PE's minibus taxis run from town to the beachfront regularly, though have been known to suffer from opportunistic muggings. There are metered taxis, which need to be booked beforehand, particularly if you are arriving in the city by bus or train: try Hurter Cabs (☎041 585 5500) or King Cab (☎041 368 5559).

ACCOMMODATION

The obvious place to stay is on the beachfront at Summerstrand or Humewood, with a wide choice of hotels, self-catering suites and B&Bs. During the December and January peak holiday period, prices are highest. Away from the beachfront, the salubrious suburb of Walmer is close to the airport and shopping hubs, with some decent B&Bs, while the suburb of Central is the oldest part of PE with Victorian houses, some good restaurants, and a short drive down the hill to the beachfront.

Admiral's Lodge 47 Admiralty Way, Summerstrand ☎041 583 1894 or 083 455 2072, ⓦadmiralslodge.co.za; map p.301. Spacious and stylish rooms at a good B&B situated at the far end of Summerstrand, roughly 7km from the centre; airport transfers are available. There's a braai area, communal lounge, pool and a trampoline for the kids. **R880**

First Avenue Lodge 3 First Ave, Summerstrand ☎041 583 5173, ⓦfirstavenuelodge.co.za; map p.301. Sixteen en-suite rooms, with their own entrances, offered on a B&B or self-catering basis (R900). It's a popular and pleasant establishment close to the beach with a lawn pool and chill-out area. **R1000**

The Humewood 33 Beach Rd, Humewood ☎041 585 8961, ⓦhumewoodhotel.co.za; map p.301. A large, old-fashioned hotel with a nostalgic hint of 1950s family seaside holidays. The rooms are large and feature wicker furniture and older-style floral prints. The service is excellent and there's a good bar and sun deck; babysitting can also be arranged. Airport transfers and laundry facilities available. **R980**

★ Island Vibe Backpackers 4 Jenvey Rd, Summerstrand ☎041 583 1256, ⓦislandvibe.co.za; map p.301. Ideal for flashpackers wanting more creature comforts without sacrificing the social backpacker atmosphere. In a beautiful setting a few minutes from the beach and restaurant strip, it has 4-bed rooms with wooden bunks, a swimming pool, jacuzzi, free wi-fi, pool and ping-pong tables. Dorm **R160**, doubles **R550**.

Jikeleza Lodge 44 Cuyler St, Central ☎041 586 3721, ⓦhighwinds.co.za; map p.303. Friendly backpacker place, recently renovated with dorms, doubles and a family room. Its adventure centre, High Winds, can sort out tours around Addo, as well as recommended combo tours to Addo and Schotia for the evening or night. Dorms **R120**, doubles **R300**

Kelway Hotel Brookes Hill Drive, Humewood ☎041 584 0638, ⓦthekelway.co.za; map p.301. Stylish hotel kitted out with timber panelling, seagrass chairs and handcrafted wooden tables. The lovely pool area with a natural rock wall, wooden decking and sun beds overlooks the sea. Standard, luxury and family rooms are available. **R1380**

King's Beach Backpacker Hostel 41 Windermere Rd, Humewood ☎041 585 8113, ⓦkingsbeachbackpackers.wozaonline.co.za; map p.301. Spotless, if slightly outdated, hostel, a block away from the beach, with camping facilities, dorms and double rooms, plus an outside bar and braai area. Although principally for self-catering, it lays on tea, coffee, bread and jams in the morning. The travel desk can book township and game park tours among others. Camping **R70**, dorm **R130**, doubles **R380**

Lungile Backpackers 12 La Roche Drive, Summerstrand ☎041 582 2042, ⓦlungilebackpackers.co.za; map p.301. Large and popular beachfront hostel with a sociable party vibe, situated in the heart of PE's beachfront nightlife strip. Perched on a hill, it has facilities for camping and a large lawn to relax on, twin rooms, a swimming pool, plus dorms inside the main house. Camping **R90**, dorm **R130**, doubles **R480**

Manor 38 38 Brighton Drive, Summerstrand ☎083 270 7771, ⓦmanorcollection.co.za; map p.301. Modern, sparklingly clean boutique hotel in an excellent location close to Summerstrand and the Boardwalk. There's a lovely pool area with sunbeds, and two communal lounge areas plus off-street parking. **R1320**

Pine Lodge Resort Off Marine Drive, Humewood ☎041 583 4004; map p.301. Right on the beach near the historic lighthouse and next to Cape Recife Nature Reserve, where you can spot owls, mongooses and antelope. The excellent-value accommodation consists of log cabins, some with full kitchens, sleeping from four up to eight people. Beside a popular bar and restaurant, the resort boasts a swimming pool, gym and games room. Four-person cabin **R875**

Windermere 35 Humewood Rd, Humewood ☎041 582 2245, ⓦthewindermere.co.za; map p.301. Stylish hotel with just nine suites, decorated in off-white to oatmeal tones contrasted with dark chocolate hues, and timber and granite surfaces. Facilities include a plunge pool, bar, laundry, secure parking, bar and discounts with Humewood Golf Course. The sea-view rooms cost no more than those without, so ask for one with a view. **R1900**

EATING, DRINKING AND NIGHTLIFE

The newly developed Richmond Hill precinct is a great area for trendy cafés and restaurants, open during the day as well as in the evening, while having a meal or drink along the beachfront is another obvious choice – wander about and see what takes your fancy. For details of occasional concerts at the PE Opera House, next to the Donkin Memorial, check out the *Daily Herald*.

RESTAURANTS

Angelo's Restaurant 45 Sixth Ave, Walmer ☎ 041 501 2899; and Shark Rock Pier, Marine Drive, Summerstrand ☎ 041 583 5862; map p.301. An institution in PE, with two branches, one at the beach, the other in Walmer. Large plates of pasta at lunchtime are popular and cheap (under R70), although be prepared to wait, as *Angelo's* is busy and known for its slow service. Daily 8am–10pm.

Fushin Sushi Bar 15 Stanley St, Richmond Hill ☎ 082 865 2707; map p.303. Sit at the long counter for the most delicious sushi in town, as well as salads and eastern-influenced tapas-style small dishes; main courses average R120. Daily noon–10pm.

Mangiamo@Wickerwoods 50 Sixth Ave, Walmer ☎ 041 581 1107 or 082 900 0777; map p.301. Many locals consider this welcoming but shabby, Italian pizzeria the best restaurant in PE and, indeed, you can't go wrong with its excellent pastas (R70), pizzas, and antipasto. Tues–Sat 6–11pm.

Natti's Thai Kitchen 5 Park Lane, Central ☎ 041 373 2763; map p.301. Unfailingly great, long-established restaurant, serving reasonably priced authentic Thai cuisine in a relaxed atmosphere, with a BYO alcohol policy; mains average R75. Mon–Sat 6.30pm till late.

★**Something Good Road House** Marine Drive, Summerstrand ☎ 041 583 6986; map p.301. Stripped-down, surfer beach bar on the seafront, where you can get pizzas, burgers, foot-long sandwiches (R60) and other classic roadhouse meals, all served out on a deck that's humming with people and has a beautiful sea view. Mon–Sun 7am–11pm.

Vovo Telo Bakery and Cafe 16 Raleigh St, Richmond Hill ☎ 041 585 5606; map p.303. This is a great place for breakfast (R60) and lunch, with Italian and French breads and pastries, real coffee and wrap-around verandah seating. Mon–Sat 7.30am–3pm.

BARS AND CLUBS

Balizza Times Square Shopping Centre, on the corner of Heugh Rd and Fifth Ave, Walmer; map p.301. With two bars, three lounges, two dancefloors and a range of cocktails and shooters, plus DJs mixing recent house anthems and oldies, you're likely to have a good night out here (beer R18). Mon–Sun 11am–2am.

Cubana Latino Café and Lounge 49 Beach Rd Humewood ☎ 041 582 5282; map p.301. A café by day and lounge by night, with an outside deck to watch the sea. There's a large cocktail menu (R50) and Cuban music and DJ's at the weekends. Note the smart casual dress code in the evening (no sneakers or shorts). Sun–Wed 8am–noon, Thurs 8am–2am, Fri & Sat 8am–4am.

For the Love Of Wine 1st Floor, 20 Stanley St, Richmond Hill ☎ 072 566 2692; map p.303. With a wrap-around balcony overlooking popular Stanley St, PE's only wine bar serves a wide selection of wines from R35 per glass. Tues–Sat 1–10pm.

Gondwana Cafe 2 Dolphin's Leap, Main Rd, Humewood; map p.301. This place is great fun; a relaxed, racially mixed restaurant by day that doubles as a club by night, plus there's jazz on Sunday afternoons (spirits from R38). Tues–Sun 9am till late.

DIRECTORY

Cinema A reasonable range of popular films is screened at the Kine Park Cinema, 3 Rink St; Nu Metro, Walmer Park Shopping Centre, Walmer; Ster Kinekor in The Bridge shopping complex; and Cinema Starz at the Boardwalk Casino Complex.
Hospitals St George's (private), 40 Park Drive, Settlers

Park (☎ 041 392 6111).
Pharmacy Mount Road Pharmacy, 559 Govan Mbeki Ave (daily til 11pm; ☎ 041 484 3838).
Post office 259 Govan Mbeki Ave (Mon–Fri 8am–5pm & Sat 8.30–1am; ☎ 041 508 4039).

Addo Elephant National Park

73km northeast of Port Elizabeth • Daily 7am–7pm • R216 • ⓦ addoelephantpark.com

A Big Five reserve, **Addo Elephant National Park** should be your first choice for an excursion from Port Elizabeth – for just one day or for several. You can also stay at one of the nearby **private reserves** – especially if you want to be pampered. On the N2 highway between PE and Grahamstown alone, there are three: **Shamwari**, **Amakhala** and **Lalibela**, while **Schotia**, 1km off the N10/N2 interchange, has exciting night drives and is the least upmarket. One big attraction of Addo and these private reserves is that, unlike the country's other major game parks, they are **malaria-free**. Beyond Addo, in the Grahamstown area, you'll also find good game watching (see box, p.320) but nowhere has as many elephants as Addo.

Addo is currently undergoing an expansion programme that will see it become one of South Africa's three largest game reserves, and the only one including coastline. **Elephants** remain the park's most obvious attraction, but with the reintroduction of a small number of **lions**, in two prides, as well as the presence of the rest of the Big Five – **buffalo**, **hippos** and **leopards** – it has become a game reserve to be reckoned with. Spotted **hyenas** have also been introduced as part of a programme to re-establish predators in the local ecosystem. Other species to look out for include cheetah, black rhino, eland, kudu, warthog, ostrich and red hartebeest.

Wildlife watching

Daytime game drives at sunrise, 9am, noon & 3pm; R280 • Sundowner game drive (including drinks & snacks) R380 • Night game drive R310 • Advance bookings essential on ☎ 042 233 8657 • ⓦ sanparks.co.za/parks/addo/tourism/activities

The Addo bush is thick, dry and prickly, making it sometimes hard to spot the 450 or so elephants and other game; when you do, though, it's often thrillingly close up. The best strategy is to ask staff at the park reception where animals have last been seen, or to head for the **water hole** in front of the restaurant and scan the bush for large grey backs quietly moving about. It's also worth taking a **guided game drive** with a knowledgeable national parks driver in an open vehicle that is higher than a normal sedan to improve viewing opportunities.

ARRIVAL AND DEPARTURE   ADDO ELEPHANT NATIONAL PARK

By car Addo's southern gate lies about 5km from *Matyholweni Camp* and is accessed off the N2 at the village of Colchester, 43km northeast of Port Elizabeth. From here, you can take a slow, scenic drive north through the park to

Main Camp, Addo's older and more established base – a journey of at least an hour along untarred, but good condition, roads. Alternatively, to reach most of the accommodation outside the park, follow the R335 along

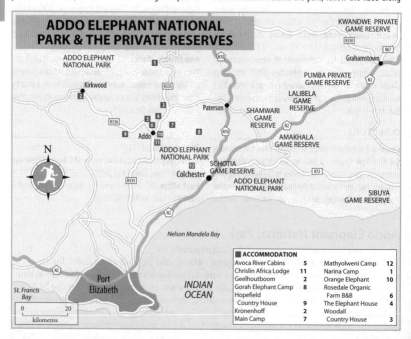

ADDO ELEPHANT NATIONAL PARK & THE PRIVATE RESERVES

■ ACCOMMODATION			
Avoca River Cabins	5	Mathyolweni Camp	12
Chrislin Africa Lodge	11	Narina Camp	1
Geelhoutboom	2	Orange Elephant	10
Gorah Elephant Camp	8	Rosedale Organic	
Hopefield		Farm B&B	6
Country House	9	The Elephant House	4
Kronenhoff	2	Woodall	
Main Camp	7	Country House	3

HORSE AND ELEPHANT RIDES IN ADDO

Two-hour **horserides** in the Nyathi area, home to the Big Five, leave at 8.30am and 2pm (R265) from stables close to Main Camp. They are only suitable for experienced riders – you need to be able to gallop in case of danger – and note that the trails may be moved due to the behaviour of some of the animals, in which case the price will be R100 less. Novices as well as experienced riders can ride in the beautiful Zuurberg section, 21km beyond *Main Camp*, where there is not much game, but ample mountain and river valley scenery to make up for it. You'll need a head for heights on the longer trails, where the calm and sure-footed horses descend the steep slopes of a ravine to cross a river at the bottom. Beginner rides leave at 9am, 11am and 2pm (1hr; R180); three-hour trails for experienced riders leave at 9am and 11am (R255); while the highly recommended full-day ride leaves at 9am (great value at R275). There is also a two-day ride that overnights at Narina bush camp on the river (R450 per day). Advance booking (☎ 042 233 8657) is required for all rides.

Elephant-back safaris are operated from a farm abutting the northern boundary of Addo (☎ 041 585 1150, ⓦ addoelephantbacksafaris.co.za; R975 per person), 90km from Port Elizabeth, off the R335. Safaris last approximately 2hr 30min and leave at 8am (includes a light breakfast), 11am (includes a light lunch) and 3pm. Transfers from Addo coast an extra R600 per person.

the park's western flank – from Port Elizabeth take the N2 east towards Grahamstown for 5km, branching off at the Addo/Motherwell/Markman signpost onto the R335 through Addo village. To get to the Zuurberg section, including *Narina Bush Camp* and the Zuurberg horse trails, turn off 1km before you reach *Main Camp*, and travel for 21km along a good gravel road. Until the park is consolidated (not imminent), you can't access the coastal section that includes the Alexandria State Forest from inside the national park.

4

INFORMATION

Main Camp The reception here has maps of the park showing picnic and braai sites. The restaurant (daily 7.30am–10pm) offers three meals a day, while the shop is well stocked with food and drink. *Main Camp* also has a bird-hide and a museum showing wildlife films more or less continuously.

ACCOMMODATION

INSIDE THE PARK

Reservations for all accommodation can be made online through SANParks (ⓦ sanparks.org/tourism/reservations) or, less than 72 hours in advance, directly with Addo (☎ 042 233 8600). Book as far ahead as possible.

Main Camp. The oldest and largest of the National Parks camps, with camping facilities, forest cabins that sleep two people and share communal kitchens, as well as more luxurious two-person chalets with their own kitchenettes. Some units sleep up to four people (but the minimum charge is for two occupants). The cheapest accommodation available is in well-designed, spacious safari tents, perfect during the summer months, with decks right next to the perimeter fence. Camping R260, safari tents R700, forest cabins R800, chalets R925

Mathyolweni Camp. National Parks accommodation in a dozen fully equipped self-catering chalets with showers, each sleeping two. Set in a secluded valley surrounded by thicket that supports a wealth of birdlife, the chalets have nice viewing decks. There is no restaurant, so bring food from PE or Colchester. R1300

Narina Camp. A small National Parks bush camp in the mountainous Zuurberg section of Addo, a remote spot, that's not in big game country. It has four safari tents that sleep four people and share washing and cooking facilities; there's no restaurant, so bring your own provisions. R1150

★ **Spekboom Tented Rest Camp**. The newest and most rustic of the National Parks accommodation has five fixed tents on decks with twin beds. Each tent is equipped with camp chairs, a table and solar light, plus communal showers and toilet within a short walking distance. There's no electricity, and you'll need to bring your own cooking equipment, sleeping gear and torches, or you can hire a box of cutlery, crockery, cooking utensils and bedding. R670

AROUND THE PARK

Private B&Bs and guesthouses are in abundance around Addo, especially among the citrus groves of the Sundays River Valley. Some offer their own day and night drives in the game reserve, or you can use them as a base, and drive yourself into the park, or drive to *Main Camp* and take an organized game drive.

Avoca River Cabins 13km northwest of Addo village on the R336 ☎ 082 677 9920, ⓦ avocarivercabins.co.za. Reasonably priced B&B and self-catering accommodation on a farm in the Sundays River Valley, ranging from budget cabins (sleeping four/five) to more comfortable thatched huts (some on the banks of the river); there is a swimming pool, pleasant walks on the farm, wi-fi (extra fee), a zip line and tree top course for kids and canoes to rent. Cabin sleeping five R600

Chrislin Africa Lodge 12km south of Addo main gate, off the R336 ☎042 233 0022 or ☎082 783 3553, ⊚chrislin.co.za. Quirky B&B with thatched huts built using traditional Xhosa construction techniques, with a lovely *lapa* (courtyard) and pool, and hearty country breakfasts, as well as dinners on request. R1100

★**The Elephant House** 5km north of Addo village on the R335 ☎042 233 2462 or ☎083 799 5671, ⊚elephanthouse.co.za. Just minutes from Addo is one of the Eastern Cape's top places to stay, a stunning thatch-roofed lodge filled with Persian rugs and antique furniture that perfectly balances luxury with a supremely relaxed atmosphere. The eight bedrooms and six garden cottages open onto a lawned courtyard. Candlelit dinners are available, as are game drives (R800/person) into Addo and the surrounding reserves. R2800

Geelhoutboom 26 Market St, Kirkwood ☎042 230 1191, ⊚geelhoutboom.co.za. A great value and homely B&B in the shade of a large yellowwood tree, with a/c rooms just a 20min drive from Addo main gate. R800

Gorah Elephant Camp 9km west along the Addo Heights Rd leading from the N10 to Addo village ☎044 501 1111, ⊚gorah.hunterhotels.com. Ultra-luxurious outfit based around a Victorian homestead decked out with mounted antelope skulls above the fireplace, evocative African landscapes, and tabletops so polished you can admire your reflection. The suites are plush, there's a beautifully landscaped swimming pool, and you can dine under the stars; meals are included in the price, as are game drives. Hefty low season discounts are available. R13,430

Hopefield Country House 20km southwest of Addo main gate ☎042 234 0333, ⊚hopefield.co.za. An atmospheric 1930s farmhouse set in beautiful English-style gardens on a citrus farm. The five bedrooms are imaginatively furnished with period pieces in a style the owners (a pair of classical musicians who occasionally give impromptu concerts for guests) describe as "farmhouse eclectic". R1200

Kronenhoff On the R336 as you enter Kirkwood ☎042 230 1448, ⊚kronenhoff.co.za. Situated in a small farming town, this is a hospitable, high-ceilinged Cape Dutch-style home, with spacious suites, polished wooden floors, large leather sofas and a sociable bar. In summer the sweet scent of orange blossom carries from the surrounding citrus groves. R1140

Orange Elephant On the R335, 8km from the National Park gate ☎042 233 0023, ⊚addobackpackers.com. Budget accommodation at a comfortable hostel, with a lively bar that is well known for its large portions of pub grub. Outings can be organized into the surrounding game reserves, such as an Addo half-day tour from R650 including refreshments, or R1000 for a full day including a braai in the park. Dorms R120, doubles R300

★**Rosedale Organic Farm B&B** On the R335, 1km north of Addo village ☎042 233 0404 or ☎083 329 8775, ⊚rosedalebnb.co.za. Very reasonably priced accommodation in eight cottages on a certified organic farm that exports citrus fruits to the EU. Hosts Keith and Nondumiso Finnemore are committed to sustainable farming and tourism – water for the cottages is solar-heated, and breakfasts are organic – and Keith offers a free one-hour walking tour of the farm. There is also a kitchen for guests who prefer to self-cater. R800

Woodall Country House About 1km west of Addo main gate ☎042 233 0128, ⊚woodall-addo.co.za. Excellent luxury guesthouse on a working citrus farm with eleven self-contained suites and rooms. There's a swimming pool, gymnasium, spa and sauna (massages are available, and there's a resident beautician). A lovely sundowner deck overlooks a small lake full of swans and other waterfowl. Renowned for its outstanding country cuisine, its restaurant offers three- to six-course dinners. R2750

The private game reserves

Although driving yourself through Addo can be extremely rewarding, nothing beats getting into the wild in an open vehicle with a trained guide – something the **private reserves** excel at. If you're strapped for cash or pushed for time, a good option is one of the day or half-day safaris that start at R980 per person offered by **Schotia** and **Amakhala**. If you want the works – game drives, outstanding food, uncompromising luxury and excellent accommodation, you'll find it at top-ranking **Shamwari**, with prices over R5000 per person a day.

ACCOMMODATION

Amakhala Game Reserve 67km north of Port Elizabeth on the N2 ☎041 581 0993, ⊚amakhala.co.za. A fantastic, family-friendly reserve stocked with the Big Five as well as cheetah, giraffe, zebra, wildebeest and

PRIVATE GAME RESERVES

antelopes. The Bushman's River meanders through the reserve allowing for canoe safaris and riverboat sundowner cruises. Safaris for day visitors include two game drives, a river cruise and lunch (R980; book ahead). The accommodation includes fabulous farmhouse lodges and a camp with beds fashioned from restored ox wagons – all with fabulous views. R5000

Lalibela Game Reserve 90km northeast of Port Elizabeth on the N2 to Grahamstown ☎ 041 581 8170, ⓦ lalibela.co.za. An excellent mid-range choice, that is home to diverse flora and fauna and the Big Five. Safaris are included in the accommodation rate, along with all meals and drinks – you can dine on terrific contemporary Eastern Cape cuisine – and they also offer an African drumming and dancing session. There are three fabulous lodges with private viewing decks, swimming pools and *bomas* to choose from. R9000

Schotia Game Reserve On the eastern flank of Addo ☎ 042 235 1436, ⓦ schotiasafaris.co.za. Schotia is the smallest and the busiest of the private reserves, on account of the excellent value it offers. Although not quite a Big Five reserve, it's really only missing the elephants, which they make up for by driving you through Addo itself. Day visitors

can be collected from Port Elizabeth or anywhere in the Addo vicinity; full-day safaris (R2000/person) involve a game drive through Addo and an evening game drive with lunch and dinner, or you can just opt for the afternoon game drive (R1000/person). An overnight stay in one of three bush lodges or eight double rooms is the cheapest of the private reserves; rates include game drives into Addo. R4000

Shamwari Game Reserve 65km north of Port Elizabeth on the N2 ☎ 041 509 3000, ⓦ shamwari.com. The largest and best known of the private reserves, Shamwari has cultivated a jetsetter fan base, hosting such celebrities as Tiger Woods and John Travolta. Voted World's Leading Eco-lodge in 2013 at the World Travel Awards, it deserves its accolades for the diverse landscapes, requisite animals and high standards of game-viewing. Accommodation is in the colonial-style, family-friendly *Long Lee Manor* or in attractive lodges and tented camps, furnished with every conceivable comfort. R9720

Jeffrey's Bay

Some 75km west of Port Elizabeth, off the N2, **JEFFREY'S BAY** (known locally as J Bay) is jammed during the holiday seasons, when thousands of visitors throng the beaches, surf shops and fast-food outlets, giving the place a tacky seaside resort feel.

Despite its unappealing suburbs and retirement homes, J Bay is said by some to be one of the world's top three **surfing** spots. If you've come to surf, head for the break at **Super Tubes**, east of the main bathing beach, which produces an impressive and consistent swirling tube of whitewater, attracting surfers from all over the world throughout the year. Riding inside the vortex of a wave is considered the ultimate experience by surf buffs, but should only be attempted if you're an expert. Other key spots are at Kitchen Windows, Magna Tubes, the Point and Albatross. Surfing gear, including wet suits, can be rented from the multitude of surfing shops along Da Gama Road, and all the international surfing clothing brands have factory shop outlets in town boasting massive reductions.

Dolphins regularly surf the waves here, and **whales** can sometimes be seen between June and October. The main **bathing areas** are Main Beach (in town) and Kabeljous-on-Sea (a few kilometres north), with seashells to be found between Main and Surfer's Point.

ARRIVAL AND INFORMATION   JEFFREY'S BAY

By Bus The Baz Bus stops at J Bay on its daily trek between Cape Town and Port Elizabeth, as do Greyhound and Intercape buses.

Tourist information In the Shell Museum Complex on the corner of Da Gama and Dromedaris roads (Mon–Fri 9am–5pm, Sat 9am–2pm; ☎ 042 293 2923, ⓦ jeffreysbaytourism.org).

ACCOMMODATION

With lots of hostels to choose from, J Bay is definitely backpacker territory, but there are also numerous good B&Bs and some self-catering places in town. It's essential to book accommodation in advance in December, January, at Easter, and during the Billabong world-championship surfing competition, usually in July, though off-season things are very quiet.

A1 Kynaston 23 & 27 Chestnut Ave ☎ 084 900 3006/8, ⓦ a1kynaston.co.za. A friendly establishment offering

B&B rooms as well as a comfortable, well-equipped, self-catering flat, in a quiet suburban area, not too far from either the beach or town centre. R850

African Perfection B&B 20 Pepper St ☎ 042 293 1401, ⓦ africanperfection.co.za. A light and airy B&B offering good-value luxury en-suite rooms with private balconies overlooking Supertubes Beach. There's also a spacious communal lounge and a fully equipped kitchen for self-caterers. R1200

African Ubuntu Backpackers 8 Cherry St, Wavecrest ☎ 042 296 0376 or 081 046 1285, ⓦ jaybay.co.za. Only 100m from the beach, with good views, a lush garden dotted with hammocks, movie nights and Friday night parties with gourmet African meals. Camping R85, dorms R110, doubles R285

Cristal Cove 49 Flame Crescent, opposite the Spar Shopping Centre on Da Gama Rd ☎ 042 293 2101, ⓦ cristalcove.co.za. Just steps away from the beach, this backpacker joint has dorms and doubles, as well as

spacious, self-contained flats that are excellent value for money. There is also a cosy pub and wi-fi. Dorm R100, double R350, flat R400

Island Vibe 10 Dageraad St ☎ 042 293 1625, ⓦ islandvibe.co.za. Backpacker lodge built on a dune, with a wooden walkway onto the beach. Offers camping, dorms and doubles, with spectacular views. There's a lounge, bar, pool table and self-catering facilities. Breakfasts are available. Camping R100, dorm R130, double R500

Super Tubes Guest House 12 Pepper St ☎ 042 293 2957, ⓦ supertubesguesthouse.co.za. A beach house whose modest en-suite rooms, with old wooden bedsteads, open onto a patio or garden, while the luxury en-suite rooms (R1780) come with a sea view, balcony and DSTV. The Super Tubes beach is practically on the doorstep. R980

EATING

The Greek Restaurant & Wine Bar Corner of Da Gama & Beverland St ☎ 083 287 6406. A Mediterranean restaurant near the beach with beautiful ocean views and Greek music, serving traditional Greek food baked in a clay oven or grilled over open coals – try the kilo of tiger prawns (R350 for two). Daily 11am–10pm, Fri & Sat 11am–11pm.

In Food Restaurant, Bakery & Deli Corner of Schelde & Jefferies St ☎ 042 293 1880. Light and airy café serving a wide range of dishes, including chicken curry (R69), plus great coffee and artisan-made breads from stoneground flour. Mon–Sat 7am–5pm.

Potters Place Coffee Shop & Restaurant 18 Oosterland St ☎ 042 293 2500. Popular quirky place offering huge breakfasts, home-baked bread, and dishes such as Cape Beef Curry (R70). Fully licensed. Daily 8am–10pm.

Walskipper Marina Martinique Seafront, Claptons Beach ☎ 042 292 0005. The town's top restaurant is incongruously housed in a weather-beaten wooden shack on the beach in Marina Martinique Harbour. Here you can tuck into lovely home-made bread, pâtés and jams while the main courses – including seafood (R125) – are cooked on an outside fire. Tues–Sat noon–8pm, Sun noon–3pm.

BEACH RIDING: J BAY TO PORT ALFRED

Long stretches of deserted, sandy beaches make this coast appealing for **horseriding**, from experienced riders who can enjoy long canters through the surf, to beginners who can walk calmly next to the breakers. Eastern Cape beaches are the best in the country for riding, while the Wild Coast beaches are even more deserted, with no vehicle access, so riding (or hiking) is the best way of exploring them.

Mkulu Kei Horse Trails ☎ 083 632 7298, ⓦ mkulukeihorsetrails.co.za. Experienced outfit that offers long and short rides on superfit trail horses along the beaches west of Port Alfred to Kenton-on-Sea, a wonderfully deserted area.

Papiesfontein Farm 65km west of Port Elizabeth, close to Jeffey's Bay ☎ 079 299 8080, ⓦ horsetrails.co.za. Here, good horses take you on a 13km route that combines bush, river and beach and is suitable for intermediate and advanced riders (R300 for 2 hours), or opt for the 15–20km full-day beach ride to Paradise Beach and back (R1300, lunch included). Papiesfontein is clearly marked on the R102 turn off, after you take the Jeffery's Bay exit from the N2.

Three Sisters Horse trails 14km east of Port Alfred, on the R72 ☎ 082 645 6345, ⓦ threesistershorsetrails.co.za. Two hour beach rides for beginners or experienced riders which take you from a farm through coastal dune bush, cantering along a beautiful deserted beach, and back past Riet River teeming with bird life (R350). They also do one- or two-night trails which combine riding with a night in a charming tree house overhanging a river on the farm and a night at a fantasy beach cabin built into a milkwood grove at Riet River; there's no electricity and one massive room for sleeping and living (R1250 per day for the ride and accommodation). Non-riding family members or friends can stay overnight for a very reasonable fee at either location.

4

Alexandria State Forest

Alexandria Hiking Trail reservation • R135 • ☎ 041 468 0916

A 50km tract of Eastern Cape beachfront, and the most deserted section of the coast, is protected by the **Alexandria State Forest**. Part of the **Woody Cape** section of the Addo Elephant National Park, it can be walked on the circular two-day **Alexandria Hiking Trail**, one of South Africa's finest coastal hikes, which winds through indigenous forest and crosses a landscape of great hulking sand dunes to the ocean.

The 35km trail starts at the Woody Cape office, 8km from the R72 (and not served by public transport), where you collect permits. If you're heading east, the signposted turn-off is on the right, just before you reach Alexandria, 86km from Port Elizabeth. If you are picnicking rather than hiking, you can visit the forest and walk the 7km Tree Dassie Trail from the Woody Cape offices.

Kenton-on-Sea

Some 115km from Port Elizabeth and 56km from Grahamstown, the resort of **KENTON-ON-SEA** lies along two river valleys, perfect for a short beach holiday. A conglomeration of holiday houses served by a few shops and places to eat, Kenton is a good choice if you want to be somewhere undemanding and very beautiful – there's little to do except enjoy the sandy beaches, rocky coves and dunes. While you can swim in the rivers, avoid getting close to the entrance to the sea, as strong **riptides** occur and drowning is a real risk.

INFORMATION

KENTON-ON-SEA   **4**

Tourist information Signposted on the main road, the tourist office (Mon–Fri 9.30am–5pm, Sat 9.30am–1pm; ☎ 046 648 2411, ⊛ kenton.co.za) is run by Erica McNulty, who also coordinates various interesting sustainable community projects run by Xhosa women.

ACCOMMODATION

Dunwerkin 5 Park Rd ☎ 046 648 1173, ⊛ dunwerkin .co.za. In a fine location, just two minutes' walk from the beach, this affordable self-catering option can accommodate either one or two families in a spanking-new four-bedroomed house. R650

★ **Oribi Haven** Kasouga Farm, 9km from Kenton, on a gravel road off the R72 (turn right at the first cattle grid) ☎ 084 477 1166, ⊛ oribihaven.co.za. Kasouga Farm sits on a hillside overlooking one of the best and least-known beaches in the country. The farm, which has been declared a Natural Heritage Site for its large population of Oribi antelope, has two well-equipped and spacious two-bedroom cottages, which can be taken on a B&B or self-catering basis. Farm game drives can be arranged, as can sundowners on the beach, and there is the use of sandboards for the dunes. R550

The Oysterbox Beach House ☎ 046 648 3466, ⊛ theoysterboxbeachhouse.co.za. Three luxury beachside properties of varying sizes, an easy walk from the sea and lagoon. They are all furnished in an appealing contemporary beach-house style, with great views and terraces. The smallest house can be rented on a self-catering basis from R1400. Double R1880

River Roost Grahamstown Rd, 1km inland from

SUNSHINE COAST CANOEING

The **Bushman's River Trail** is a two- to five-hour paddle, which heads 15km upriver through countryside lined with cycads and euphorbias. To explore the Bushman's River, you can rent **canoes** from Kenton Marina (daily 8am–4pm; ☎ 046 648 1223; R160 for 8hrs), signposted off the R72, 300m up the R343 to Grahamstown.

The **Kowie Canoe Trail**, a 21km paddle up the Kowie River from Port Alfred, is one of the few self-guided canoeing and hiking trails in South Africa. Much of its charm is the chattering birdlife, and the landscape – hills of dense, dry bush that slopes down to the river. On the trip, you stay overnight in a hut in the **Horseshoe Bend Nature Reserve**, from where you can explore the forest on foot, and climb the steep escarpment to get an impressive view over the horseshoe: book in advance with Gary McKay in Port Alfred (☎ 082 491 0590; R150 per person).

Kenton on the R343 ☎046 648 2850, ⊕riverroost
.co.za. On a hill above the Bushmans River with panoramic
views and jetty access to the river, *River Roost* provides
luxury self-catering (R2750 for a cottage) or B&B in a
French Provencal-style main house with farmhouse
kitchen, reading room and rock swimming pool. It is a few
minutes' drive from the beach. <u>**R1100**</u>

Woodlands Country House and Tea Garden 2km
from the town centre along the R343 to Grahamstown
☎046 648 2867, ⊕accommodation-kenton.co.za. A
charming, large property with acres of garden and
bush leading down to the Bushman's River, and little
cottages dotted along pathways cut through the
vegetation. <u>**R450**</u>

EATING AND DRINKING

Homewoods 1 Eastbourne Rd ☎046 648 2700. The
best-located place in Kenton, this restaurant and pub at the
mouth of the Kariega River has grand views, though the
food is run-of-the-mill burgers, fish and chips, sandwiches
and steaks (R95). Tues–Fri 11am–3pm & 6–9pm, Sat
10am–4pm & 6pm till late, Sun 9am–4pm.

Sandbar Floating Restaurant River Bend, Bushmans
River ☎046 648 2450. Moored on the lagoon, this
restaurant/pub serves light meals, seafood and grills, with
main courses around R90. Booking essential. Tues–Sun
11am till late, open Mondays in holiday season.

The Secret Garden Main Rd ☎083 650 4773. During
the day, you can get cooked breakfasts, teas and light
lunches of toasted sandwiches and salads (R35) here,
though it is in town, and not at the beach. Mon–Fri
7.30am–4pm, Sat 8am–2pm.

Stanleys Restaurant just outside Kenton on the R343
Grahamstown Road ☎082 774 9326. A casual place that
serves the best food in Kenton – succulent steaks (R95) and
fresh seafood can be eaten outside with views of
subtropical gardens and the Kariega river. Booking
required. Mon–Sat 11am till late, Sun 11.30am–3.30pm.

Port Alfred

Of all the settlements between Port Elizabeth and East London – a largely
undeveloped stretch of coast with huge dunes and exhilarating surf – only **PORT
ALFRED**, midway between the two, can make any claims to a town life outside the
holiday season, when for a few weeks the small centre is transformed into a hectic
bustle. Like many other places along the coast, it is developing apace, with housing
developments sprouting along its once lonely beaches. Besides beach walking and
swimming, it's an excellent place to do some **canoeing**, **diving**, waterskiing, abseiling,
deep-sea fishing and horseriding.

Nicknamed "Kowie" by locals, after the river, Port Alfred was named in honour of the
second son of Queen Victoria, although he never actually made it here, since he chose
to go on an elephant hunt instead. Port Alfred's attractions are firmly rooted in its
beaches and the Kowie River; the town itself has little else to offer. The landmark
Halyards Hotel and *Spur* restaurant constitute the town's ersatz caged-in waterfront; far
more authentic, however, is the river frontage on Wharf Street, next to the old bridge,
which has been revamped and the row of Victorian buildings spruced up, while the
Harbour Master and Brewery offers its own home brew.

The beaches

West Beach, where the river is sucked out to sea and the breakers pound in, makes a good
start to exploring Port Alfred. From the stone pier you can watch the surfers and see
fishing boats make dramatic entries into the river from the open ocean. Fifteen minutes'
walk west along the beach lies **Kelly's Beach**, by far the most popular stretch, where you can
swim safely in a gentle bay. **East Beach**, reached from the signposted road next to *Halyards
Hotel*, is the nicest beach for walking, with a backdrop of hilly dunes popular for
sandboarding, stretching to the horizon. For toddlers, the safest and most popular spot is
Children's Beach, a stretch of sand close to the town centre along a shallow section of river,
reached from Beach Road, a few hundred metres from the arched bridge.

ARRIVAL AND DEPARTURE   PORT ALFRED

By bus The reasonably priced SA Connection minibus
(☎043 722 0284 or 086 110 2426, ⊕saconnection.co.za)

calls in at Beavers shop at the R72 petrol station on the
west bank of town, on its way between Port Elizabeth

and East London (Mon, Wed, Fri & Sun), and between Cape Town and East London (Tues, Wed & Sat). On Tuesdays and Thursdays, the Minilux bus service (☏ 043 741 3107) connecting Port Elizabeth to East London via Grahamstown pulls into the *Halyards Hotel*, off the main

coastal road on the east side of the Kowie River. Otherwise, Wayne's Transport (☏ 046 624 2358 or ☏ 084 644 6060) offers a shuttle service from Port Elizabeth's airport, with times and drop-offs to suit passengers when you book.

INFORMATION AND ACTIVITIES

Tourist information On the riverfront at the Main Street bridge (Mon–Fri 8.30am–4.30pm, Sat 8.30am–noon; ☏ 046 624 1235, ⓦ sunshinecoasttourism.co.za).

Watersports Outdoor Focus, next to Children's Beach, Beach Road, on the West Bank (☏ 046 624 4432,

ⓦ outdoorfocus.co.za), offers courses in everything water-based, including scuba diving and skippering. They also rent out boards for sand-boarding on the massive sand dunes on East Beach, and can make bookings for horse trails and other outdoor activities.

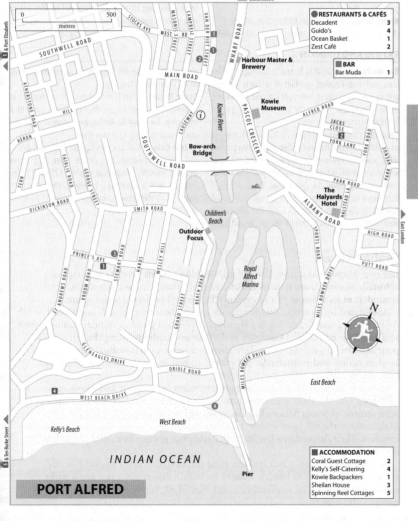

RESTAURANTS & CAFÉS
Decadent	3
Guido's	4
Ocean Basket	1
Zest Café	2

BAR
Bar Muda	1

ACCOMMODATION
Coral Guest Cottage	2
Kelly's Self-Catering	4
Kowie Backpackers	1
Sheilan House	3
Spinning Reel Cottages	5

PORT ALFRED

ACCOMMODATION

Coral Guest Cottage Jack's Close ☎046 624 2849, ⓦcoralcottages.co.za. A reasonably priced B&B on one of the East Bank hills, in a luxuriant garden, five-minutes' drive from the beach. There are comfortable rooms in a restored corrugated-iron settler cottage, though the walls are not at all soundproof, and a two-storey self-catering unit with a massive luxury room upstairs and living area downstairs. Expect to be pampered by the ebullient owner. **R650**

Kelly's West Beach Drive, opposite Kelly's Beach ☎082 657 0345, ⓦwww.kellys.co.za. As close to the main swimming beach as you could possibly be, these neat and clean self-catering apartments in a large brick house are good value. **R600**

Kowie Backpackers 13 Van Riebeeck St, off the R72, close to Beavers bus stop ☎071 266 8899, ⓦkowiebackpackers.co.za. Comfortable, clean, affordable and friendly accommodation in a modern suburban house, with a garden for camping. Convenient if you are travelling through, but a 20min walk from the beach and close to the busy R72. Camping **R80**, dorm **R140**, double **R310**

Sheilan House 27 Prince's Ave ☎046 624 4076 or ☎082 894 1851, ⓦsheilanhouse.co.za. A well-run and friendly guesthouse, with four en-suite bedrooms. Evening meals available on request, and the owners can organize a multitude of activities. **R990**

Spinning Reel Cottages, 4km from the town centre ☎046 624 4281 ⓦspinningreel.co.za. A beachside property offering fully equipped self-catering cottages, some newer and bigger, some older and smaller, but all with paths through coastal forest down to the beach. There are also B&B rooms in the main house. **R500**

EATING AND DRINKING

Bar Muda 25 Van der Riet St ☎046 624 8659. Choose from over two hundred cocktails in a lovely riverside setting, where you can sit indoors or out, and eat seafood, steaks or schnitzels (R90). Daily 10.30am–midnight, Fri & Sat open until 2am.

Decadent Postmasters Village, 20 Stewart Road ☎046 624 8282. Cheerful daytime coffee shop serving salads (R60), sweet and savoury Belgian waffles and crepes, as well as smoothies. It's quiet, green and pretty in a small complex away from the beach and town. Mon–Fri 9am–4pm, Sat 9am–2pm.

Guido's On the beach ☎046 624 5264. Port Alfred's only place right on the beach, though the pizzas and pasta dishes (R90) play second fiddle to the sundowners served on the deck. Daily 11am–9pm.

Ocean Basket In Port Frances House on Van der Riet St ☎046 624 1727. For fish and chips (R46) and sushi with a river view, the *Ocean Basket* has prompt service and the food is spot-on. Daily 11.30am–9pm.

★**Zest Cafe** 48 Van der Riet St, The Courtyard ☎046 624 5783. Port Alfred's best central coffee shop serves delicious, modern, imaginative lunches (R70) and coffee outdoors, from a kitchen in a wooden canteen that once stood at Grahamstown's railway station. Mon–Fri 8am–5pm, Sat 8am–3pm.

Grahamstown

Just over 50km inland from Port Alfred, **GRAHAMSTOWN** projects an image of a cultured, historic town, quintessentially English, Protestant and refined, with reminders of its colonial past in evidence in the well-preserved architecture.

Dominated by its cathedral, prestigious private boarding schools and one of South Africa's best universities, this is a thoroughly pleasant place to wander through, with well-maintained colonial **Georgian** and **Victorian buildings** lining the streets, and pretty suburban gardens. Every July, the town hosts an **arts festival**, the largest of its kind in Africa, and purportedly the second largest in the world after Edinburgh (see box, p.319).

As elsewhere in South Africa, there are reminders of conquest and dispossession. Climb up Gunfire Hill, where the fortress-like 1820 **Settlers Monument** celebrates the achievement of South Africa's English-speaking immigrants, and you'll see Makanaskop, the hill from which the **Xhosa** made their last stand against the British invaders. Their descendants live in desperately poor ghettos here, in a town almost devoid of industry.

Despite this, Grahamstown makes a good stopover, and is the perfect base for excursions: a number of **historic villages** are within easy reach, some **game parks** are convenient for a day or weekend visit and, best of all, kilometres of **coast** are just 45 minutes' drive away.

Brief history

Grahamstown's sedate prettiness belies its beginnings as a **military outpost** in 1811.
Colonel Graham made his – and the town's – name here, driving the Xhosa out of the
Zuurveld, an area between the Bushman's and Fish rivers. The Fish River, 60km east of
Grahamstown, marked the eastern boundary of the frontier, with Grahamstown as the
capital. The ruthless expulsion of the Xhosa sparked off a series of nineteenth-century
Frontier Wars.

The British decided to reinforce the frontier with a human barrier. With the promise
of free land, they lured the dispossessed from a depressed Britain to occupy the lands
west of the Fish River. In the migration mythology of English-speaking whites, these
much-celebrated **1820 Settlers** came to take on a larger-than-life status as ancestors to
whom many trace back their origins. However, far from discovering the hoped-for
paradise, the ill-equipped settlers found themselves in a nightmare. The plots given to
them were subject to drought, flood and disease, and the threat of Xhosa attack was
never far away.

Not surprisingly, many settlers abandoned their lands and headed to Grahamstown in
the early 1820s. This brought prosperity and growth to the town, which enjoyed a
boom in the 1840s, when it developed into the emporium of the frontier.

High Street

High Street is Grahamstown's major shopping axis, with terraces of nineteenth-century
buildings lending it a graceful air. Running from the station at its seedier east end,

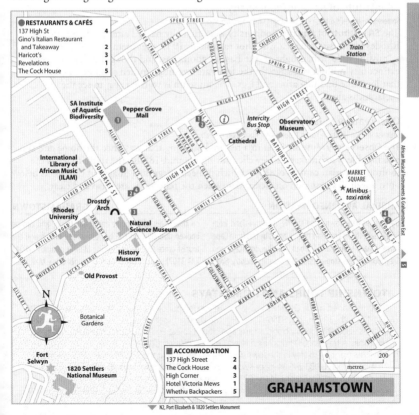

N2, Port Elizabeth & 1820 Settlers Monument

High Street continues past the cathedral at the junction of Hill Street, terminating at the 150-year-old Drostdy Arch, the whitewashed entrance gate to prestigious Rhodes University, named after Cecil John Rhodes (see box, p.263). At the centre of the street is the **Cathedral of St Michael and St George**, opened in 1830. In addition to High Street's shops, **Pepper Grove Mall**, five minutes' walk north, with entrances in African and Allen streets, is a good retail option, dominated by a large Pick n Pay supermarket.

Natural Science Museum

Somerset St • Tues–Fri 9.30am–1pm & 2–5pm, Sat 9.30am–1pm • R10

If you've time for only one museum, head for the **Natural Science Museum**, just south of the university entrance. The display of Eastern Cape fauna and flora from 250 million years ago is excellent, with intriguing plant fossils and the bones of dinosaurs that once roamed these parts. The **History Museum** next door houses a dusty collection of 1820 settler memorabilia, nineteenth-century paintings and antique firearms, as well as Xhosa beadwork and traditional dress.

ILAM

Corner of Somerset and Prince Alfred streets • Mon–Fri 8.30am–12.45pm & 2.15–4.45pm • Free • ☎ 046 603 8557, ⓦ ilam.ru.ac.za

Beyond the Drostdy Arch, tucked behind some buildings, **ILAM** is the International Library of African Music. It's an absolute treasure trove of recordings of **traditional African music** from Southern Africa, as well as Zaire, Rwanda, Uganda and Tanzania.

SA Institute of Aquatic Biodiversity

Somerset St • Mon–Fri 8.30am–1pm & 2–5pm • Free • ⓦ saiab.ac.za

The **SA Institute of Aquatic Biodiversity** was originally named after J.L.B. Smith, the Rhodes University scientist who shot to fame in 1939 after identifying the coelacanth, a "missing link" fish, caught off the East London coast and thought to have become extinct fifty million years ago. In the foyer are two huge stuffed specimens, with fins that look like budding arms and legs. The museum is worth a visit to see the coelacanths alone.

Observatory Museum

Bathurst St • Mon–Fri 9am–1pm & 2–5pm; Sat 9.30am–1pm • Donation

The Observatory Museum is set in a restored building that was once the home and shop of a notable watchmaker and jeweller during the mid-1850s. The thing to see is the rooftop Victorian **camera obscura**, which projects magnified images of the streets below onto a wall. It's best seen on a clear day, when the reflections are crisp and clear.

ARRIVAL AND INFORMATION   GRAHAMSTOWN

By bus Grahamstown is on the N2, 127km inland from Port Elizabeth, and roughly twelve hours by bus from Cape Town, Johannesburg and Durban. Translux, Intercape and Greyhound buses stop outside the *Frontier Country Hotel* on the corner of Bathurst and High streets, and can be booked directly with the bus companies or through the tourist office (see opposite). The Minilux minibus (☎ 043 741 3107) stops at the Wimpy in Pepper Grove Mall, with

---

TOWNSHIP TOURS AND HOMESTAYS

Recommended guide Otto Ntsheve will take you in your own car on a **township tour** (☎ 082 214 4242; 2hr 30min–3hr; R350). Tours visit the Umthathi self-help project, which teaches skills such as vegetable growing and an arts and crafts project Egazini Outreach Project in Joza township. A traditional Xhosa lunch is available on request (R100).

Visitors wanting to stay in the townships, especially during the Arts Festival, can book with Thabisa Xonxa (☎ 083 245 0496) or Kwam e-Makana **B&B Homestays** (☎ 046 622 3241) which will organize a stay with one of the 52 local women. Most of the homes have indoor plumbing, en-suite bathrooms, TV, lockable cupboards and off-street parking, and cost R600 per room B&B.

connections to Port Elizabeth, Port Elizabeth airport and Port Alfred (Tues, Thurs, Fri & Sun) and East London (Mon, Tues & Thurs).

Tourist information 63 High St, next to City Hall (Mon–Fri 8.30am–5pm, Sat 9am–midday; ☎046 622 3241, ⓦ grahamstown.co.za).

GETTING AROUND

By taxi Grahamstown is easily explored on foot, but if you want a taxi, use the reliable London Tours (☎046 622 7939) or JC Shuttles (☎083 590 2169).

ACCOMMODATION

The choicest places to stay in Grahamstown are in historic houses, and there's a good selection of hotels. The only time you may have difficulty finding accommodation is during the festival in July, when you'd be well advised to book as early as March – the tourist office can help with finding accommodation during this period.

The Cock House 10 Market St ☎046 636 1295, ⓦ cockhouse.co.za. Plush rooms in a handsome Victorian house with a fine restaurant, though it's not in the best location, being well away from the university and centre. It belonged once to SA writer Andre Brink who had an eye for beautiful homes. R990

★**High Corner** 122 High St ☎046 622 8284, ⓦ highcorner.co.za. A beautiful historical home in a great location across the road from the university, with six rooms furnished with Cape antiques and original art. It was formerly the home of notable South African writer and academic Guy Butler who was also an excellent carpenter, so you will find some beautiful yellowwood inside. R1040

Hotel Victoria Mews 8 New Street ☎046 622 7261 7208, ⓦ hotelvictoriamews.com. Built in 1849, this centrally located hotel has a secluded swimming pool, garden and secure off-street parking. It also boasts an Italian restaurant *Gino's* that serves pasta, steaks, salads and pizza baked in wood ovens (R89). There's also a period bar where you can enjoy occasional live music. R970

Whethu Backpackers 6 George St, on R67 to Port Alfred ☎046 636 1001 or 083 982 5966, ⓦ whethu.com. A spacious house with a garden and great views over the valley, a 20min walk from the university. Free internet, bicycles for hire, and evening meals available, often featuring local venison. Dorms sleep six or eight, and there are doubles and a family room. You can book trips here through Smileyface Tours (☎083 982 5966) to Addo Elephant National Park and the Fish River, or *shebeen* crawls and township tours. Camping R65, dorm R150, double R400

EATING, DRINKING & NIGHTLIFE

137 High St 137 High St ☎046 622 3242. A favourite meeting place for students and academics, serving good coffee, sandwiches and great cheesecake (R32). Mon–Fri 7.30am–9.30pm, Sat 8am–2pm & 5–9.30pm, Sun 8am–2pm.

The Cock House Corner of Market and George streets ☎046 636 1295. Grahamstown's best restaurant, serving country cuisine – the speciality is braised and marinated local lamb shank (R110). Sun & Mon 6.30–9pm; Tues–Sat 7.30–9.30am, 12.30–2.30pm & 6.30–9pm.

THE GRAHAMSTOWN FESTIVAL

For ten days every July, Grahamstown's population doubles, with visitors descending for the annual National Arts Festival – usually called the **Grahamstown Festival**. At this time, seemingly every home is transformed into a B&B and the streets are alive with colourful food stalls. Church halls, parks and sports fields become flea markets and several hundred shows are staged, spanning every conceivable type of performance.

This is the largest arts festival in Africa, with its own fringe festival, plus free art exhibitions at the museums and other smaller venues. The hub of the event is the 1820 Settlers Monument, which hosts drama, dance and operatic productions in its theatres, as well as art exhibitions and free early-evening concerts. While work by African performers and artists is well represented, and is perhaps the more interesting aspect of the festival, the festival-goers and performers are still predominantly white.

The **programme** – spanning jazz, classical music, drama, dance, cabaret, opera, visual arts, crafts, films and a book fair – is bulky, but essential, and it's worth planning your time carefully to avoid walking aimlessly around the potentially cold July streets, though during the festival there is a shuttle bus between venues. For more **information and bookings**, contact the Grahamstown Foundation (☎046 603 1103, ⓦ nafest.co.za).

★**Haricot's** 32 New St ☎046 622 2150. French, European and Mediterranean food in a tranquil, secluded spot, with contemporary decor and a central location – the muesli and croissant breakfasts (R60) are great. Mon–Sat 9am–9.30pm.

Revelations Coffee Shop Pepper Grove Mall, African St ☎046 636 2433. Sunny café with outdoor seating and an extensive menu including breakfast fry-ups and specials such as butternut and orange soup (R30). Mon, Tues & Thurs 7am–5pm; Wed, Fri & Sat 7.30am–9pm.

ENTERTAINMENT

Despite being the home of the country's premier arts festival (see box, p.319), and dominated by Rhodes University, Grahamstown's nightlife and entertainment scene is less exciting than you might expect. Outside the festival fortnight in July, the town's only regular evening entertainment is the **cinema** at the Pepper Grove Mall. The two main venues for **live performances** are the Monument Theatre and the

Rhodes University Theatre, where the Drama Department puts on productions from time to time. Look out for anything staged by Ubom First Physical Theatre Company, founded by a local actor with an international reputation in physical theatre. To find out what's on, check the flyposters down High Street and *Grocott's Mail*, the local rag, which comes out on Tuesday and Friday afternoons.

SHOPPING

★**African Musical Instruments** on the corner of Cloncourt and Jarvis streets ☎046 622 6252 3501, 🖰kalimba.co.za. The place in South Africa to buy an

authentic instrument, it sells reasonably priced *kalimbas*, handmade using high-quality timber, as well as many other genuine African instruments. Mon–Fri 8am–5pm.

Bathurst

A significant centre in the nineteenth century, **BATHURST**, 45km south of Grahamstown, is today little more than a picturesque straggle of smallholdings, gardens

EASTERN CAPE GAME RESERVES

The Eastern Cape is fast developing as a region for game viewing, with several fine reserves in the Grahamstown area, many of which offer day trips as well as overnight excursions.

Great Fish River Reserve Complex On the R67, 34km north of Grahamstown; office daily 8am–4.30pm; day visitors R20 ☎043 701 9600, 🖰visiteasterncape.co.za. This is an amalgamation of three separate reserves covering 430 square kilometres situated along the banks of the Fish and Kat rivers, and accessed by rough dirt roads. Although there is plenty of game, it is difficult to see, so if you want to tick off the Big Five, this reserve is not for you. In the southwestern section, closest to Grahamstown, there's accommodation in chalets for up to four people at *Mvubu*. R400

★**Kwandwe Private Game Reserve** On the R67, 41km north of Grahamstown and 160km from Port Elizabeth ☎046 603 3400, 🖰kwandwe.com. The Eastern Cape's top wildlife destination, with 30km of Fish River frontage plus the Big Five. As well as game drives, Kwandwe offers guided river walks, canoeing on the Great Fish and rhino tracking, plus cultural tours that explore the social and archeological history of the area. The accommodation ranges from a luxury lodge with nine suites and thatched roofs, wooden walkways and French windows with panoramic views, to a funky boutique-hotel-in-the-bush ingeniously designed with glass walls

that allow you to lie on your bed and feel you're totally alone in the middle of the wilderness. R10,900

Pumba Private Game Reserve 22km west of Grahamstown off the N2 ☎041 502 3050, 🖰pumbagamereserve.co.za. A good bet if you want to see lions and other game at close quarters, delivered to you, on daily game drives. You can be collected from your accommodation in Grahamstown and the early morning drive includes breakfast at the camp, while the 4pm game drive includes dinner (both R900 per person). Drives are on a ten-seater Land Rover, with no children under 8 permitted. The full overnight safari experience includes luxury accommodation, meals, drives and drinks. R10, 830

Sibuya Game Reserve Access only by boat ☎046 648 1040, 🖰sibuya.co.za. At the cheaper end of the spectrum, as it doesn't have lions, though you can still see zebra, giraffe, buffalo and rhinos on its recommended day tours where guests are collected by boat from Kenton-on-Sea for a meander up the Kariega River, with a game excursion and picnic or braai (R985, or R600 without game excursion). If you stay overnight in the luxuriously tented camps, the rate includes all meals and game activities, as well as canoeing and walking. R6450

and craft shops, anchored around the Victorian landmark of the *Pig and Whistle*, a pub. Some of the **craft shops** are good for ceramics, paintings, woollen products and creams made from beeswax and herbs produced in the village, and there's a small outdoor **Farmers' Market** on Main Road on Sundays (9am–noon), where you can buy fantastic local breads, produce and herbal ointments, and sit under the coral trees having a pancake or fry-up.

ARRIVAL AND INFORMATION
BATHURST

By bus On Tues, Thurs & Fri the Minilux bus between Grahamstown and Port Alfred stops at the *Pig and Whistle* (see below).

Tourist information The *Pig and Whistle* (see below) provides maps and directions to historical sites.

ACCOMMODATION

Kingston Farm On the R67 between Port Alfred and Grahamstown ☎ 046 625 0129 or ⊛ kingstonfarm .co.za. An Appaloosa horse stud farm offering accommodation in three comfortable self-catering apartments in a large Edwardian main house. There's also a tea garden (daily 10am–5pm) and you can book dinner in advance (R285 three courses). R1000

Pig and Whistle On the R67 as you drive into town ☎ 046 625 0673, ⊛ pigandwhistle.co.za. A colonial Victorian village inn; the old rooms upstairs, furnished with period pieces, are best, and you can sit on the veranda with a beer, while the restaurant offers traditional pub food, including breakfast, and Sunday roasts (R70). It's a good place to meet locals. R624

EATING AND DRINKING

Lara's Eatery & Deli On the Green, York Rd ☎ 071 370 1019. Rustic café in a beautiful garden serving a range of fusion and South African cuisine. The salads brimming with fresh local produce are especially popular (R68). Mon & Wed–Sat 8am–11pm, Sun 8am–3pm.

Pickwick's Pizza Corner of York & Trappes streets ☎ 046 625 0350. A cosy café-restaurant offering pasta, salads and pizza cooked in a wood oven (R60), plus coffee and cake. There's a garden for summer meals and a fireplace in winter. Tues–Sat 10am–9pm, Sun 10am–4pm.

The Eastern Cape Karoo

Between Grahamstown and the towns of Cradock and Graaff-Reinet (the Eastern Cape's two most-visited Karoo towns) is **sheep-farming country**, with the occasional *dorp* rising against the horizon, offering the experience of an archetypal one-horse outpost. The roads through this vast emptiness are quiet, passing dun-coloured sheep, angora goats and the occasional springbok grazing on brown stubble, plus groups of charcoal-and-grey ostriches in the veld.

Cradock, 240km north of Port Elizabeth, lies in the **Karoo** proper, and makes a great stopover on the Port Elizabeth to Johannesburg run, because of its excellent accommodation and its proximity to the beautiful **Mountain Zebra National Park**. Some 100km due west of Cradock, **Graaff-Reinet**, surrounded by the **Camdeboo National Park**, is one of the oldest towns in South Africa, with much of its historical centre intact. For more of a sense of the Karoo's dry timelessness, head to **Nieu Bethesda**, 50km to the north of town.

ACCOMMODATION
THE EASTERN CAPE KAROO

★**Cavers Country Guest House** Just outside Bedford, an hour north of Grahamstown ☎ 046 685 0619, ⊛ cavers.co.za. One of the best farms to stay on in the region, this is a grand 1850 refurbished

two-storey stone manor house with beautiful gardens, watered by mountain springs, on a working farm with a mountainous backdrop. The friendly owners cook delicious dinners. R1200

Cradock

The silvery windmills on the surrounding sheep farms of **CRADOCK** have become an unofficial symbol of the town; as you enter town, Xhosa hawkers sell intricately crafted wire model windmills. The town itself has some handsome colonial architecture, with

4

the main street dominated by the 1868 **Dutch Reformed Church**, based on London's St Martin-in-the-Fields. In March the annual **Karoo Food Festival** takes place here, where you can taste specialities of the region.

But poverty has overshadowed Cradock since the Frontier Wars of the nineteenth century and the subjugation of the Xhosa people. Against this history of conquest the town has provided fertile grounds for **resistance**: ANC members in the vicinity almost single-handedly kept the organization alive during the 1930s. In 1985, Cradock hit the headlines when anti-apartheid activist **Matthew Goniwe** and three colleagues were murdered. It was only in 1997, during the **Truth and Reconciliation Commission** hearings, that five Port Elizabeth security policemen were named as the perpetrators. There is a modest **memorial** to the Cradock Four in the municipal park on the banks of the Fish River, off the Middelburg Road.

Schreiner House Museum

9 Cross St • Mon–Fri 8am–12.45pm & 2–4.30pm, weekends by appointment • Donation • ☎ 048 881 5251

Schreiner House is dedicated to the writer Olive Schreiner, best known for her ground-breaking novel *The Story of an African Farm* (1883), made into a film in 2004. It was remarkable enough for a woman from the conservative backwoods of nineteenth-century Eastern Cape to write a novel, but even more amazing that she espoused such radical ideas as universal franchise for men and women irrespective of race. Schreiner died in 1921 and is buried near Cradock on the Buffelskop Peak, with her 1-day-old daughter and favourite dog. Her **burial site** has become something of a

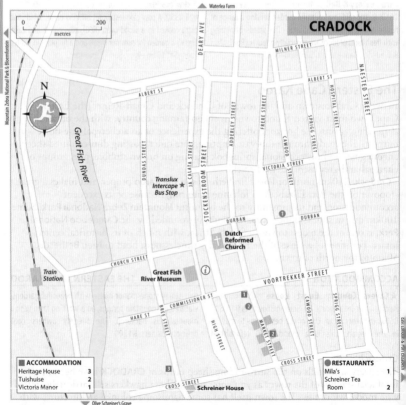

■ ACCOMMODATION	
Heritage House	3
Tuishuise	2
Victoria Manor	1

● RESTAURANTS	
Mila's	1
Schreiner Tea Room	2

place of pilgrimage, and details of how to get there are available from Schreiner House – it is a long hike up. At the house there is also an interesting exhibition on Cradock's famous literary son, Guy Butler, a writer, academic and poet.

ARRIVAL AND INFORMATION — CRADOCK

By bus Translux and Intercape buses from Port Elixabeth and Johannesburg pull in daily at Shoprite Checkers on Voortrekker St, where you can buy tickets and get information for onward travel.

By train Cradock is a daily stop on the Port Elizabeth–Johannesburg rail line; the station is on the west bank of the Great Fish River.

Information Cradock Tourist Office, JA Calata St (☎ 048 881 1137, ⓦ cradockmiddelburg.co.za) is staffed by one person who is often out, so check the website when necessary.

ACCOMMODATION

Heritage House 45 Bree St ☎ 048 881 3210, ⓦ wheretostay.co.za/heritagehouse. Set in a large tranquil garden, this Karoo-style Victorian homestead offers a welcome respite in peaceful surroundings. Each of the six double en-suite bedrooms has a private entrance from the garden. R900

★ **Tuishuise** Market St ☎ 048 881 1322, ⓦ tuishuise .co.za. Staying in this street of comfortable and stylish one- to four-bedroomed Victorian houses gives an authentic sense of colonial domestic life over a century ago. Prices are very reasonable, given that you get what amounts to a mini-museum to yourself, each house kitted out with antique furniture and crockery. R960

Victoria Manor 36 Market St ☎ 048 881 1650,

ⓦ tuishuise.co.za. Effortlessly gracious, old-fashioned hotel with excellent service, bags of character and period fittings. The rooms are en suite, dining is off silverware and the breakfasts are among the best in the country. R795

★ **Waterlea Farm** 60km north of Cradock, off the R61 ☎ 073 068 8792. Accessible via a dirt road, this self-catering cottage is on a remote Karoo farm, where magnificent Arab horses are bred for long-distance racing. Experienced riders can explore the vast plains and flat-topped mountainous landscape on a lively mount, or simply enjoy the tranquillity, farm life and hospitality of Robert and Jean Lord. You can pay extra for their wholesome farm cooking. R600

EATING

Mila's 27 Durban St ☎ 048 881 0036. A cosy, homely open-kitchen restaurant serving pizza, pasta, steaks and grills (R95). Local meat is always the thing to go for – Karoo lamb is free range and organic here. Fully licensed. Mon–Sat 4–9pm.

Schreiner Tea Room Market St ☎ 072 381 3422. The nicest place for tea, sandwiches and hot lunches of traditional *roostekoek* (bread grilled on an open fire) with various fillings, plus soups, pies and salads (R65). Summer Mon–Fri 9am–4.30pm; Winter Mon–Fri 9am–4pm, Sat 9am–1pm.

Mountain Zebra National Park

26km west of Cradock • Daily: April–Sept 7am–6pm; Oct–March 7am–5pm • Adults R144, children R72, SA citizens R36 • ☎ 048 881 2427, ⓦ sanparks.org/parks/mountain_zebra

One of the most beautiful, but least known of South Africa's parks, the **Mountain Zebra National Park** was created in 1937, when there were only five Cape **mountain zebras** left on its 65 square kilometres – and four were male. Today, the park supports several hundred in the spectacular, dry, mountainous and unpolluted Karoo landscape.

For **game viewing**, the park has a couple of good part-tar, part-gravel loop roads forming a rough figure of eight, with most game spotted on the Rooiplaat Loop where herds graze on open grassland. As well as zebra, look out for springbok, buffalo, blesbok and several large herds of wildebeest. Some big cats have been introduced, but you'll be very lucky to see them.

At the park reception, you can book morning and evening **game drives** (R160), morning **walks** (R230), **cheetah tracking** (R290), the Saltpeterkop **hike** for a magnificent view over the park (3hr; R285), and the Impofu 25km hike (3 days; R390), which takes in highlights of the park including Bakenkop, the highest peak, sleeping overnight in mountain cottages. You can also do your own **bush walk** on two trails which start from the swimming pool, and are within a fenced off area.

ARRIVAL AND SERVICES

By car To reach the park, 26km from town, head north out of Cradock on the N10 Middelburg Rd. Signposts direct you to the main gate of the reserve, from where it is approximately 12km to the accommodation, game viewing all the way. From Port Elizabeth, it is 256km on the N10.

MOUNTAIN ZEBRA NATIONAL PARK

Services A small shop at reception sells basics, souvenirs, alcohol and soft drinks, but if you're staying for a few days you should stock up in Cradock. There's a reasonable licensed à la carte restaurant (daily 7.30am–9pm), a post office, a filling station and a lovely swimming pool.

ACCOMMODATION

Park accommodation ☎ 048 881 2427, ⓦ sanparks.org /parks/mountain_zebra. Choose from either comfy two-bedroom cottages with outstanding mountain views and

their own kitchens and bathrooms, or lovely camp sites. All accommodation must be confirmed with reception by 6pm the day before you arrive. Camping R250, cottages R990

Graff-Reinet

GRAAFF-REINET is a beautiful town and one of the few places in the Eastern Cape where you'd want to wander freely day and night, taking in historical buildings and the

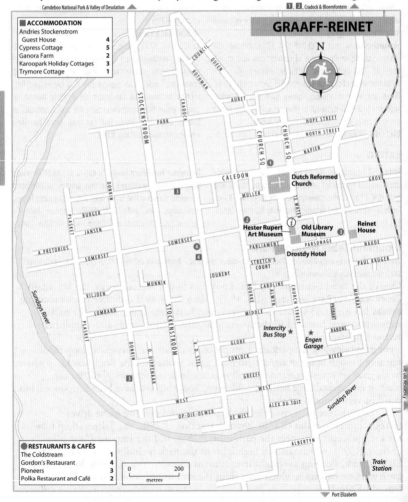

occasional museum, or having a meal and a drink. The town centres around the imposing 1886 **Dutch Reformed Church** on Church Street, the main thoroughfare, from which little roads fan out, lined with whitewashed Cape Dutch, Georgian and Victorian buildings. The dry mountains surrounding the town are part of the **Camdeboo National Park** whose main attraction is the impressive **Valley of Desolation**.

Brief history

By the late eighteenth century, Dutch burghers had extended the Cape frontier northwards into the Sneeuwberg Mountains, traditionally the stomping ground of Khoi pastoralists and San hunter-gatherers. The settlers raided Khoi cattle and attacked groups of San, killing the men and abducting women and children to use as farm and domestic labourers. Friction escalated when the Khoi and San retaliated and, in 1786, the Cape authorities sent out a *landdrost* (magistrate) to **establish Graaff-Reinet**, administer the surrounding area and pacify the frontier.

Colonial control over the district was slowly consolidated, with vast tracts turned over to grazing sheep. The **wool boom** of the 1850s brought prosperity to the town and established a pattern of farming and land ownership which continues to this day. Today, Graaff-Reinet has a large population of Afrikaans-speaking coloured people, mostly living on the south side of town, some of slave origin, others the descendants of indigenous Khoi and San.

Old Library Museum

Church St • Mon–Thurs 8am–1pm & 1.45–4.30pm, Fri 8am–1pm & 1.30–4pm, Sat & Sun 9am–1pm • R20

The only, but spectacular, attraction at the **Old Library Museum**, one block south of the Dutch Reformed church, is the compelling collection of **fossil skulls** and skeletons of reptiles that populated the prehistoric Karoo, some 230 million years ago.

Hester Rupert Art Museum

Church St • Mon–Fri 9am–12.30pm & 2–5pm, Sat & Sun 9am–noon • R20

In a restored 1821 mission church, the **Hester Rupert Art Museum** features a representative selection of work by South African artists (primarily white) active in the mid-1960s. Much of it is dreary and derivative of European art, but a few pieces stand out.

The Reinet House and the Old Residency

Reinet House Mon–Thurs 8am–4.30pm & 1.45–4.30pm, Fri 8am–1pm & 1.30–4pm, Sat & Sun 9am–1pm • R20 • The Old Residency
Mon–Thurs 8am–1pm & 1.45–4.30pm, Fri 8am–1pm & 1.30–4pm, Sat & Sun 9am–noon • R20

The graceful, whitewashed *Drostdy Hotel*, at 30 Church Street, is a historical building in its own right, as the former residence of the *landdrost*, though it is now closed, with no firm dates set for reopening. From its front steps, you can look down Parsonage Street, lined with Cape Dutch buildings, to **Reinet House**, Graaff-Reinet's finest museum. Formerly a parsonage, it was built in 1812 and is essentially a period house museum, filled with covetable furniture and intriguing household objects. Opposite Reinet House, the **Old Residency** is a well-preserved example of a early-nineteenth-century Cape Dutch H-shaped house.

ROBERT SOBUKWE AND THE AFRICANISTS

One of Graaff-Reinet's most brilliant but often-forgotten sons is **Robert Managaliso Sobukwe** (1923–1978), the charismatic founder of the Pan Africanist Congress (PAC). He is best known for launching the nationwide **anti-pass protests**, which ended in the Sharpeville massacre and his imprisonment, in solitary confinement, on Robben Island for nine years. You can visit the Sobukwe home and grave on a **township tour**, attending traditional events and music, or meeting members of Graaff-Reinet's African community; Karoo Connections (☎049 892 3978) and Camdeboo Adventures (☎049 892 2557) can both provide a reliable guide.

Camdeboo National Park

5km north of Graaff-Reinet, off the Marraysburg Rd • ☎ 049 892 3453, ⓦ sanparks.org/parks • R80 • Daily 6/7am–6/8.30pm

The low-lying **Camdeboo National Park** surrounds the town, with its entrance 5km north of the town centre. Its highlight is the strikingly deep **Valley of Desolation**, which you can gaze down into by driving the narrow tarred road from the reserve's entrance and ascending the bush-flecked mountainside; you'll pass a series of viewpoints up to the cliffs overlooking the valley. The views from the lip of the canyon, beyond the rocks and into the plains of Camdeboo, are truly thrilling, accompanied by echoing bird calls, especially when black eagles circle the dolomite towers, scanning the crevices for prey.

There are a couple of good walks: the looped **Crag Lizard Walk** (45min) along the canyon lip, well marked with a lizard emblem; and the **Eerstefontein Day Walk**, which starts and ends at Spandaukop gate, with route options of 5km, 11km and 14km.

ARRIVAL AND DEPARTURE GRAAFF-REINET

By bus Translux buses between Johannesburg and Port Elizabeth, and Intercape buses connecting Jo'burg with the Garden Route towns, pull in daily at the Engen garage on Church St. For bus tickets and timetables, check at the tourist office (see below).

INFORMATION AND TOURS

Tourist information The tourist office at 13 Church St (Mon–Fri 8am–5pm, Sat 9am–noon; ☎ 049 892 4248, ⓦ graaffreinet.co.za) provides maps and accommodation lists.

Tours Karoo Connections (☎ 049 892 3978, ⓦ karoo connections.co.za) runs recommended township tours, plus a variety of tours of the area, including of Bushman Rock Art and Gondwanaland Fossils, and to Cradock.

ACCOMMODATION

B&BS AND SELF-CATERING

Andries Stockenstrom Guest House 100 Cradock St ☎ 049 892 4575, ⓦ asghouse.co.za. This handsome listed house is one of the best upmarket stays in town, with seven comfortable rooms, done out with white percale linen on kingsize beds, and an excellent restaurant (see Gordon's Restaurant, below). **R1600**

Cypress Cottage 76 Donkin St ☎ 049 892 3965 or ☎ 083 456 1795, ⓦ cypresscottage.co.za. Two restored Karoo cottages each with three double en-suite rooms and a communal lounge and dining room. Families are welcome and the garden with swimming pool, trampoline and dolls' house is popular with kids. **R1300**

Karoopark Holiday Cottages 81 Caledon St ☎ 049 892 2557, ⓦ karoopark.co.za. A complex of self-catering cottages, set in a garden with a pool, plus dinky B&B units. It also has an in-house bar and restaurant serving traditional karoo specialities (dinner R170). Booking essential. **R650**

★**Trymore Cottage** Wellwood Farm, 31km north of town, on the road to Nieu Bethesda ☎ 049 840 0302, ⓦ wellwood.co.za. Self-catering, comfortable, four-bedroom house on a long-established, beautiful farm. Braai packs are available, as are evening dinners, with Karoo lamb or venison on the menu. The stunning private collection of Karoo reptile fossils here is open to guests. **R1300**

CAMPING

Camdeboo National Park Book in advance through Graaff Reinet Tourism ☎ 049 892 4248. There are two overnight camps in the park, both equipped with communal kitchens and showers/toilets, the Nqweba campsite (15 places) and the Lakeside Tented Camp, with four rustic furnished tents. Nqweba **R205**, Lakeside **R570**

EATING AND DRINKING

The Coldstream 3 Church Square ☎ 049 891 1181. In a handsome listed building, the former colonial Graaff-Reinet Club, with a big tree in the garden and veranda seating, this restaurant serves Karoo lamb, a considerable variety of local meats and venison, plus generous snack platters (mains around R120). Mon–Sat 9am till late.

★**Gordon's Restaurant** Andries Stockenstrom Guest House, 100 Cradock St ☎ 049 892 4575, ⓦ asghouse .co.za/veld-to-fork. Slow Karoo cooking at its finest. A 4-course set menu (R300) which changes daily using only local ingredients such as venison (hunted by Chef Gordon himself), organic karoo lamb and home-grown vegetables. Also runs 3-day cooking courses; advance booking essential. Daily 7.30–9am & 7pm til late.

Pioneers 3 Parsonage St ☎ 049 892 6059. Traditional Karoo cuisine for the adventurous – try Kudu schnitzel (R145) or Ostrich carpaccio. You can choose from four dining rooms, or sit on the stoep or in the garden. Mon 9am–9pm, Tues–Sat 9am–10pm, Sun 9am–2pm & 5–9pm.

Polka Restaurant, Café, Bakery & Deli 52 Somerset St ☎087 550 1363. A cottage restaurant on a quiet leafy side street serving well presented and delicious Karoo cuisine, such as lamb shanks (R130) and *bobotie* with unusual touches. Mon–Sat 7.30am–9pm.

Nieu Bethesda

Off the beaten track, in the mountains north of Graaff-Reinet, **NIEU BETHESDA** (ⓦnieubethesda.info) is dry and dusty, especially in midsummer when it boils with harsh, bright light. There are no streetlamps, and on winter nights temperatures plummet to zero, though the whitewashed **village** has plenty of charm, with a village shop and butcher on the main road. Once an archetypal conservative Karoo *dorp*, it has reinvented itself as a tiny artists' colony, attracting a growing number of visitors.

Bethesda Arts Centre

Muller St, opposite the police station • ☎073 028 8887, ⓦbethesdafoundation.org • **Tower Restaurant** daily 8.30am–8pm

The non-profit **Bethesda Arts Centre** has provided opportunities for craft workers, artists and performers to get trained and to sell their work; it now houses an art gallery, working studios and an open-air theatre. It's worth dropping in to check what's on, or you can enjoy a curry and rice (R80) at the quaint Tower restaurant.

Owl House

River St • Daily April–Sept 9am–5pm; Oct–March 8am–5pm • R50 • ☎049 841 1733

Most people who come to Nieu Bethesda visit the **Owl House**, once the home of Helen Martins, a reclusive artist who expressed her disturbing and fascinating inner world through her work. Every corner of the house and garden has been transformed to meet her vision. The interior walls glitter with crushed glass, owls with large eyes gaze from the tin-roofed veranda, while at the back of the house, trapped by a stone wall and high chicken wire, are hundreds of glass and cement sculptures: camels, lambs, sphinxes and human figures.

ARRIVAL AND DEPARTURE   NIEU BETHESDA

By car Nieu Bethesda is 23km off the N9 between Graaff-Reinet and Middelburg, on a dirt road, some 60km from Graaff-Reinet and 308km from Port Elizabeth. There's no ATM nor petrol in Nieu Bethesda, so fill up in Graaff-Reinet.

ACCOMMODATION

Doornberg Farm 9km north of Nieu Bethesda ☎049 841 1401, ⓦnieubethesda.co.za. For those wanting to to stay on a farm, the friendly *Doornberg Farm* serves evening meals, or you can self-cater; there's also a trampoline, pool, riding and hiking. The nicest place to stay on the farm is in *Die Vleihuisie*, a little cottage 4km away from the farmstead. B&B R600

★**Ganora Farm** Off the N9, 7km east of Nieu Bethesda ☎049 841 1302 or ☎082 698 0029, ⓦganora.co.za. A working sheep farm with B&B accommodation, plus self-catering cottages (R850). The owners arrange trips to climb Compassberg and to see Bushman rock shelters, and there's also a small fossil collection. Dinner can be ordered (R140 for a three-course meal). R960

Huis Nommer Een Murray St, book through Suzette Pienaar on ☎049 841 1700. *Huis Nommer Een* has three spacious rooms furnished in South African country style, a farm-style kitchen, and a handsome veranda. R500

Owl House Backpackers Lodge Martin St ☎049 841 1642 or 072 742 7113, ⓦowlhouse.info. Nieu Bethesda's only backpacker lodge is friendly, laidback and well organized, with dorm beds, en-suite rooms (B&B or self-catering), two self-contained cottages and a restaurant and pub opposite. They will pick you from Graaff-Reinet for R100. Camping R75, dorm R125, double R460

EATING

Auntie Evelin se Plek 4 Kloof St (just on the top of the rise on entering Pienaarsig) ☎083 873 5526. Auntie Evelin lives in Pienaarsig (the township area) where she serves traditional township food in her home. In summer meals are served on her stoep overlooking the community sports field; in winter you sit in a painted tin shack, warmed by a heater and adjacent oudoor stove. The menu varies and could include traditional *bredies*, samp-and-beans, *roosterkoek* and *lekker poeding*. (3-course meal R120). Advance booking essential; phone for opening hours.

Ibis Lounge Martin St ☎082 442 3174, ⓦtheibislounge .co.za. Lovely, comfortable place to relax and enjoy a wide range of speciality coffees. They serve breakfast, lunch and dinner and you can sit outdoors in the shade of the big stoep or inside on leather couches, warmed by fireplaces in winter. Sample the home-made pies and bread, or slow roast Karoo lamb (R80) for Sunday lunch. Daily 8am–8pm.

Two Goats Deli at The Brewery Across the dry Gats River, off New St ☎049 841 1602. A good choice for an unhurried lunch, serving its own cold beer accompanied by home-made cheese, bread, olives and salami (R65) – the only offerings on the menu. Daily 8am–5pm.

East London and the central region

Between Port Alfred and East London lies some of the Eastern Cape's least-developed **coastline**, although it has now fallen into the hands of developers as more and more people discover the beauty of the region. **East London**, the largest city in the central region of the province, though dowdy and eminently missable, has some with excellent beaches for surfing and swimming and good transport links to Johannesburg and along the coast. Inland, **Fort Hare University** near Alice has educated political leaders across the subcontinent, including Nelson Mandela, and boasts the country's finest collection of contemporary black South African art.

Sweeping up from Fort Hare's valley, the misty, wooded **Amatola Mountains** yield to the dramatic landscapes of the **Eastern Cape Drakensberg**, which offer hiking, trout fishing and remote landscapes. Before white settlers (or even the Xhosa) arrived, these towering formations were dominated by **San hunter-gatherers**, who decorated the rock faces with thousands of ritual **paintings**, many of which remain surprisingly vivid.

East London

EAST LONDON, the second-largest city in the Eastern Cape, is the obvious jumping-off point for exploring the Transkei. **Nahoon Beach** is a great **surfing spot**, and the town

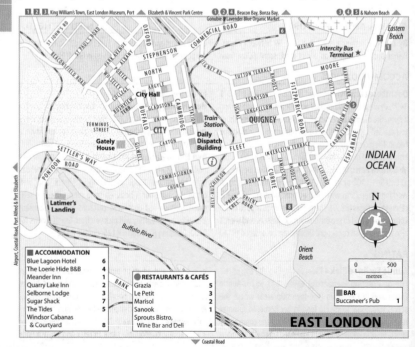

has a dedicated and lively surfing scene. It's also gradually becoming a place for black holidaymakers – a post-apartheid phenomenon. The beaches to the east of town are very beautiful, with long stretches of sand, high dunes, estuaries and luxuriant vegetation, and good swimming.

The drab city centre is dominated by **Oxford Street**, parallel to Station Street and the train station. Although a major traffic thoroughfare, it is largely deserted at night, when you shouldn't wander around alone. Apart from a couple of handsome buildings, East London's Victorian heart has progressively been demolished, though its principal landmark, the splendid terracotta and lace-white **City Hall**, opened in 1899, remains. Over the road is a rather lifeless statue of martyred Black Consciousness leader **Steve Biko** (see box 000).

Away from the holiday strip, East London is dominated by an industrial centre served by **Mdantsane**, a huge African township 20km from the city towards King William's Town.

Brief history

Before the British, and even the Xhosa, the area was home to the **Khoikhoi** people, who called it Place of the Buffaloes. The Buffalo River once teemed with game, but the animals were gradually killed off with the arrival of British hunters. East London began life as a permanent British settlement during the nineteenth-century **Frontier Wars**, when it was used as a beachhead to land military supplies needed to push back the Xhosa. Taken by its strategic possibilities as a port, the British governor Sir Harry Smith optimistically called it **London** in 1848. Later it was changed to East London, because the port was on the east side of the Buffalo River.

East London Museum

Upper Oxford St • Mon–Thurs 9.30am–4.30pm, Fri 9am–4pm • R15 • ☎ 043 743 0686

A few kilometres north of the city centre, the **East London Museum** has a stunning collection of South Nguni beadwork and contemporary wire sculpture. The museum's pride and joy, however, is its stuffed coelacanth (see p.318), caught off the coast in the 1950s.

The Esplanade

East London's **Esplanade** loops from Orient Pier in a wide and beautiful sweep of rocks, beach and sand dunes to Eastern Beach, marred only by the motley assortment of holiday apartments, hotels and restaurants lining the beachfront. It's about thirty minutes' walk from the city centre; buses here are sporadic, but it's easy enough to stroll from one end to the other.

Orient Beach

Tucked in next to Orient Pier, with dockland cranes poking their necks above the water, **Orient Beach** is a good place to swim, though it looks a bit grim and industrial, and is often crowded. There are changing rooms, and a couple of little pools for kids.

Eastern Beach

From Orient Beach, the sea-walled Esplanade continues northeast, along sand and black rocks, to **Eastern Beach**, with its high, bush-capped sand dunes. Although far more attractive, Eastern Beach has had problems with muggings, even during the day, though it remains a popular beach for surfers.

Nahoon Point Nature Reserve and Nahoon Beach

Visitor's Centre signposted off Epson Rd, Nahoon • Daily 8.30am–4pm • Free • Café Tues–Sun 9am–4pm • ☎ 083 232 5055

If you have time to visit one attraction, make it the **Nahoon Point Nature Reserve**, 5km from the centre of East London, where you can see the coastline from a good vantage point, visit the museum and have a coffee. In a building shaped like a footprint (commemorating the discovery of a young child's fossilized footprint 120,000 years old, in a nearby dune), the Coastal Education and Visitors' Centre has a worthwhile museum with displays on the town's surfing history, as well as an excellent section on the archeological finds of the area, including the famous footprint. There's also a cafe, serving light meals. From the Museum car park, you can stroll on wooden walkways along the coast, or go on longer hikes, to take in the best of the city's coastline.

Superb for swimming and surfing, **Nahoon Beach**, to the east of Nahoon Point, is a long stretch of sand, backed by dunes, with some of the best waves in the country.

Bonza Bay and Gonubie Beach

East of the Nahoon River, 10km from the centre, the coast curves into **Bonza Bay**, with kilometres of beach walks and a lazy lagoon at the mouth of the Quinera River. Further on, **Gonubie Beach**, 18km northeast of the centre, at the Gonubie River Mouth, is still close enough to be considered part of East London, with some good accommodation, a beautiful beach and walks.

ARRIVAL AND DEPARTURE   EAST LONDON

By plane East London's small airport (☎ 043 706 0306), a few kilometres west of the centre on the R72, connects the city to all major centres. The airport shuttle, the Little Red Bus (☎ 082 569 3599), meets all flights and drops off at the *Holiday Inn* near the beachfront (R100). Imonti Tours (☎ 043 741 3884 or ☎ 083 487 8975) also makes transfers from the airport to the city centre (R120).

By bus All three of the intercity buses – Translux (☎ 086 158 9282, �🌐 translux.co.za), Intercape (☎ 086 128 7287, 🌐 intercape.co.za) and Greyhound (☎ 083 915 9000, 🌐 greyhound.co.za) – offer a frequent, comprehensive and inexpensive service connecting East London to major cities. The buses drop off at the Intercity Bus Terminal at Windmill Park on Moore St. The Minilux minibus (☎ 043 741 3107), which connects Grahamstown with the airport at Port Elizabeth daily, goes on to Port Alfred on Tuesdays and Thursdays, and East London on Mon, Tues, Thurs & Fri.

By train The train station (☎ 086 000 8888) is on the eastern edge of East London's small business and shopping district. Metered taxis outside the station will get you to your accommodation.

GETTING AROUND

By car Like most South African cities, central East London is gridded; with uncongested roads and easy parking, it's far more geared to driving than walking.

By taxi Deans Taxi Service (☎ 073 194 6367 or ☎ 079 293 5132).

INFORMATION AND TOURS

Tourist information There's tourist information at the airport (Mon–Fri 8am–4.30pm; ☎ 043 736 3019) or in town at the Firestation, 2nd Floor, Fleet St (☎ 043 705 2111, 🌐 bctourism.co.za). The Eastern Cape Tourism Board office (☎ 043 701 9600, 🌐 ectourism.co.za), which provides information on the rest of the province, is quite a distance from town, at Ironwood House, Palm Square Business Park, Bonza Bay Rd, in Beacon Bay.

Tours Imonti (☎ 043 741 3884 or ☎ 083 487 8975, 🌐 imontitours.co.za) runs township and city tours (half-day from R300), as well as full-day tours to Umtata and Qunu, to see the Nelson Mandela sights (R700).

ACCOMMODATION

East London's beachfront sports graceless blocks of holiday apartments and functional hotels, redeemed only by their fabulous views of the Indian Ocean. The really cheap hotels are mostly filled with long-term residents, and are often rough drinking hangouts – best avoided. If the urban nature of the main beachfront doesn't appeal, your best bet is to head for the suburbs of Nahoon Mouth at the end of Beach Rd, Beacon Bay, Bonza Bay or Gonubie, close to the river and sea and reached via the N2 east of the city; without your own transport, you'll need to take a taxi or arrange to be picked up.

BEACHFRONT AND NORTHERN SUBURBS

Blue Lagoon Blue Bend Place, Beacon Bay ☎ 043 748 4821, 🌐 bluelagoonhotel.co.za. Very pleasant accommodation surrounded by palm trees and close to the beach. Rooms are quiet and spacious, with balconies looking onto the river. R1610

The Loerie Hide B&B 2B Sheerness Rd, off Beach Rd, Nahoon ☎ 043 735 3206, 🌐 loeriehide.co.za. Five reasonably priced en-suite rooms in the vicinity of Nahoon Beach at the bottom of a garden that gives way to indigenous bushland. R1300

Meander Inn 8 Clarendon Rd, Selborne ☎043 726 2310, ⓦmeanderinn.co.za. Ten spacious, tastefully furnished rooms with white linen and ceiling fans, five of which are in the luxurious main house, with the rest in the garden and annexe. There's a swimming pool, patio and bar, and they offer airport transfers. R1000

Quarry Lake Inn Quartzite Drive, off Pearce St, The Quarry ☎043 707 5400, ⓦquarrylakeinn.co.za. Spacious, well-appointed rooms in a lovely setting on the edge of a flooded disused quarry that has become home to abundant vegetation and birdlife. R1460

Sugar Shack Eastern Beach ☎043 722 8240, ⓦsugarshack.co.za. Basic accommodation, in brilliant location right on the beach, with terrific views. There's

transport from the hostel to the mountain resort of Hogsback (see p.332). Dorm R110, double R280

★**The Tides** 49 Harewood Drive, Nahoon ☎043 735 4454 or ☎082 828 7977, ⓔthetidesbnb@mweb.co.za. Just above Nahoon Beach, this comfortable B&B, with smart bathrooms and television, is run by friendly couple Wayne & Sue who are well informed about the area and onward travel to the Wild Coast. R825

Windsor Cabanas & Courtyard George Walker Parade ☎043 743 2225, ⓦkatleisure.co.za. A Spanish-style block near Orient Beach, offering great views. The Cabanas has comfortable one-, two- and three-bedroom self-catering apartments, while the adjacent Courtyard offers basic accommodation with standard decor. Courtyard R465, Cabanas R1155

EATING AND DRINKING

Buccaneer's Pub Eastern Beach, next to *Sugar Shack* ☎043 743 5171. A lively bar that buzzes till the early hours, with occasional live music. During the day, there are fantastic views of the rodeo riders of the surf. Good pub fare includes fish and chips and, best of all, chicken schnitzel (R79). Daily 10am–10pm.

Grazia Upper Esplanade, Beach Front Rd ☎043 722 2009 ⓦgraziafinefood.co.za. A light and airy restaurant with stunning views of the sea, serving Italian-style food (R140). The *linguini alla marinara* and layered vegetable gnocchi are recommended. Daily noon–10.30pm.

Lavender Blue Organic Market & Coffee Shop Ocean Way Drive, Beacon Bay ☎043 732 1172. The market itself sells great local produce on Saturdays, with breads, comb honey, home-made ginger beer, vegetables, bakes and preserves, and during the week you can get good coffee, salads and sit indoors or outdoors in a garden setting. Tues–Fri 8am–3.30pm, Sat 7.30am–1pm, Sun 8am–1pm.

Le Petit 54 Beach Rd Shopping Centre, Nahoon ☎043 735 3685. A highly regarded eating place serving rich Mediterranean/French-inspired food, with an emphasis

on game, seafood and veal (R142). Lunch Mon–Fri noon–2pm Dinner Mon–Sat 6–10.30pm. Sunday closed.

Marisol 3 Epson Rd, Action House, Beacon Bay ☎043 735 3236. Small, intimate restaurant serving Afro–Portuguese food. The tapas are recommended, while lunch dishes include Portuguese sardines with olive oil and salad, seafood paella (R380 for 2) and, best of all, healthy salads. Mon, Tues & Sat 6.30–10pm, Wed–Fri 11am–3pm & 6.30–10pm.

Sanook 11 Chamberlain Rd ☎043 721 3215. Cosy restaurant serving beautifully presented dishes – the thin-crust pizzas are in a wood-fired oven are recommended, as are the daily specials, such as beef fillet topped with oregano butter and marinated cherry tomatoes (R135). Mon–Sat 9am–10pm.

Sprouts Bistro, Wine Bar and Deli 11 Beach Rd, Nahoon ☎043 735 3841. Homely, popular restaurant with outdoor seating and a cool vibe. Serves breakfast, lunch and dinner, with dishes such as steaks, burgers, fish, pasta and fresh salads (R72). Mon–Sat 7.30am–10pm.

SHOPPING

For shopping and anything practical, such as banks and the post office, head to **Devereux Avenue**, 5km north of the city centre (leave the centre on Oxford St, then turn right into Devereux), in the midst of the salubrious suburbs of Vincent and Stirling. Here, you'll find the

Vincent Park Centre, a popular shopping mall with cinemas and restaurants, plus **Umzi Wethu Curio Shop**, at no. 62 (☎074 105 1935), which is the city's best curio outlet, stocking authentic Xhosa crafts, such as beautifully beaded bags.

The Amatola Mountains

Most visitors drive quickly through the scrubby, dry, impoverished area between East London and the **Amatola Mountains** proper, to reach the cool forests and holiday lands at **Hogsback**. However, it's worth deviating en route, to see the fine collection of African art at **Fort Hare University**, close to the little town of Alice, and to take in some peeling, but intact, colonial streetscapes in **King William's Town**.

STEVE BIKO AND BLACK CONSCIOUSNESS

Steve Biko's brutal interrogation and death while in police custody triggered international outrage and turned opinion further against the apartheid regime.

Steven Bantu Biko was born in 1946 in King William's Town. His political ascent was swift, due to his eloquence, charisma and focused vision. While still a medical student at Natal University during the late 1960s, he was elected president of the exclusively black **South African Students' Organization** (SASO) and started publishing articles in their journal, fiercely attacking white liberalism, which they saw as patronizing and counter-revolutionary. In an atmosphere of repression, Biko's brand of **Black Consciousness** immediately caught on. He called for blacks to take destiny into their own hands, to unify and rid themselves of the "shackles that bind them to perpetual servitude". From 1973 onwards, Biko suffered banning, detention and other harassment at the hands of the state. In 1974, he defended himself in court, presenting his case so brilliantly that his international profile soared.

Barred from leaving King William's Town, Biko continued working and writing, frequently escaping his confinement. In August 1977 he was detained and taken to Port Elizabeth where he was interrogated and tortured. A month later he died from a brain haemorrhage, after a beating by security police. No one was held accountable.

He is buried in the **Steve Biko Garden of Remembrance** in King William's Town, now part of a heritage site that includes several other Biko-related mounuments, such as his mother's Ginsberg home, Biko's office in King William's Town and the Steve Biko Bridge over the Buffalo River. You can organize a free guided tour of the memorial sights at the **Steve Biko Centre** and museum, 1 Zotshie St, King Williams Town (☎ 043 605 6700; Mon–Fri 8.30am–4.30pm & Sat 9am–1pm; R25).

Hogsback

Made sweeter by the contrast with the hot valleys below, the village of **HOGSBACK** in the Amatola Mountains, 32km north of Alice and 145km from East London, offers cool relief after hauling through prickly, overgrazed country. The name "Hogsback" applies to the area as much as to the village, and comes from the high rocky ridge (actually three peaks) resembling a bushpig's spine, which runs above the settlement.

Hogsback represents a corner of England, a fantasy fed by mists, pine plantations and exotic trees such as oak, walnut and azaleas, and snowfalls each winter. It's a great place to spend a relaxing couple of days, with plenty of walks and good air among the flowers, grasslands and forests, and there are many places to stay. The real attraction is the **Afro-montane cloud forest**, dense with yellowwood, stinkwood and Cape chestnut, singing with bird calls and waterfalls, and populated by the odd troop of **samango monkeys**, which survive on the steep slopes above the pine plantations, and the endangered Cape Parrots. Note that Hogsback can be wet and cold, even in summer, so bring a warm pullover, sturdy shoes and rain gear.

The hamlet itself is strung out along 3km of tarred road, with gravel and fairly rough lanes branching out on either side to hotels and cottages. The closest thing to a **centre** is the small conglomeration of a general store, post office and filling station. Hogsback has its own **indigenous craft** found nowhere else in the country: prepare to be pestered by hawkers selling the characteristic, and rather lovely, unfired clay horses and hogs with white markings.

The trails

Amatola Trail R150 per day per section, complete trail R750 • Book through the Department of Forestry ☎ 043 642 2571, ⒲ amatola.co.za

Hogsback is prime **rambling** country, with short, relatively easy trails indicated by hogs painted onto trees. For a rewarding taste of indigenous forest, head to the Arboretum and up the path towards **Tor Doone**, which overlooks the settlement, and is the easiest summit to climb, if steep. Alternatively, following the path to Tor Doone then turning right onto the contour path will take you on a one-hour round walk back to the Arboretum. One of the most rewarding waterfall trails is the one-hour steep downhill

FORT HARE UNIVERSITY

Despite decades of deliberate neglect, and its relegation after 1959 to a "tribal" university under apartheid, **Fort Hare**, 2km east of Alice on the R63, is assured a place in South African history. Established in 1916 as a multiracial college by missionaries, it became the first institution in South Africa to deliver tertiary education to blacks, and was attended by many prominent African leaders, including Zimbabwe's president Robert Mugabe and Tanzania's former president, Julius Nyerere. The most famous former student is Nelson Mandela (see box, p.346), making this a port of call if you're following his footsteps.

The university's **De Beers Art Gallery** (Mon–Fri 8am–4.30pm; free) is a treasury of contemporary black Southern African art, and one of the most significant and least publicized collections anywhere. The gallery also houses Fort Hare's **ethnographic collection** – a major museum of traditional crafts and artefacts, with many rare and valuable pieces. **Free tours** of the university, its art gallery and the ANC archives are run during the week (Mon–Thurs 8am–4.30pm, Fri 8am–3.30pm; ☎040 602 2050 or 2239, ⓦufh.ac.za; book in advance).

walk to the lovely **Madonna and Child Waterfall**. Walks are detailed in inexpensive **guidebooks** available at the information centre.

One of South Africa's best mountain walks, the 105km self-guided backpacking **Amatola Trail** takes in numerous waterfalls and rivers as well as grasslands, plateaus and the Hogs themselves – it's a tough hike, however, and best done in an experienced group.

ARRIVAL AND DEPARTURE   HOGSBACK

By shuttle A cheap shuttle, on demand (☎043 722 8240), connects *Sugar Shack* in East London (see p.331)

with Hogsback; *Away With The Fairies* and *Terra-Khaya* (see below) can make arrangements.

INFORMATION

Tourist information The tourist office on Main Rd (Mon–Sat 10am–4pm, Sun & Public Hols 9am–3pm; ☎045 962 1245, ⓦhogsback.com) can book accommodation, much of which is self-catering, and you

will need to stock up in a bigger centre before you come, as the pricey village shop has limited stock. Also bring cash, as the one ATM is often out of order, and although there is a petrol pump, you may be safer filling up in a bigger place.

ACCOMMODATION

Arminel Signposted along the main road ☎045 962 1005, ⓦkatleisure.co.za. The best located of the hotels, with thatched buildings and large spaces. All the rooms lead directly onto the well-kept hotel gardens, and some have their own wooden decks. B&B R1150

Away With The Fairies Hydrangea Lane; down the first turning on your right and signposted as you drive into Hogsback ☎045 962 1031, ⓦawaywiththefairies .co.za. This partying hostel, in a large converted house, has small dorms sleeping five to eight, plus twin and double rooms, some en suite and one with its own fireplace. One of the nicest features of the hostel is a platform in a tree for drinks and hanging out. It's central and ideally situated for the start of many Hogsback hikes and mountain bike trails. Camping R70, dorm R120, double R340

Back O' The Moon Holiday Cottage Trewennan Lane ☎045 962 1017, ⓦbackofthemoon.hogsback.co.za. An ideal old-world home, with obliging owners, in a beautiful six-acre garden. There are three comfortable bedrooms, a lounge with fireplace and DSTV, veranda and fully

equipped kitchen for self-catering. R650

★**The Edge** Signposted off Main Rd ☎045 962 1159, ⓦtheedge-hogsback.co.za. The best of the self-catering accommodation, with twenty comfortably and stylishly furnished cottages, and ten B&B rooms, a few kilometres from the centre of the village, along a rough road. There are superb valley and forest views, hikes, a labyrinth for contemplation, and a restaurant and bar on site. Booking is essential for the cottages. B&B R800, cottages R600.

Lowestoffe Country Lodge Off Cathcart Rd ☎045 843 1716 or ☎083 654 5935, ⓦlowestoffecountrylodge. co.za. Three fairly modern cottages on a farm where you can horseride or fish for trout. The farm is 24km out on the unpaved road to Cathcart, so its draw is the dramatic and lonely mountain scenery. There are dams and mountain pools for swimming. R800

★**Terra-Khaya** Off Plaatjieskraal Rd ☎082 897 7503, ⓦterrakhaya.co.za. Tucked into the backwoods is a wonderful and well-run backpackers on an eco-farm. While it is sociable with a lovely communal lounge

---

ON HORSEBACK AROUND HOGSBACK

Lowestoffe (☎ 045 843 1716) offers **horseriding** trails (R300) through a wide valley and up mountain slopes for beginners and experienced riders alike on a large farm, 25km outside Hogsback, where they breed appaloosas. For **forested rides** at Hogsback, contact Shane at *Terra-Khaya Backpackers* (see below), a superb horseman who rides bareback and barefooted, and will take you on one of the best rides you can do anywhere, on well-schooled horses (R250); full-day rides to the base of Hog 1 and overnight trails are recommended.

---

and kitchen area where you can get delicious meals cooked on an aga, this is a place to chill around an outdoor fire, enjoy the lovely views from the sunny verandah, or go horseriding with Shane (see box above).

There are free meals for cutting down water-guzzling alien trees. Phone for directions; it's a few, rough kilometres off Main Rd, but signposted. Camping R̲7̲0̲, dorm R̲1̲2̲0̲, double R̲2̲8̲5̲

EATING AND DRINKING

Arminel Main Rd ☎ 045 962 1005. Centrally located, this hotel has the prettiest garden setting for a terrace lunch of sandwiches, steaks or burgers (R60), or tea or drinks, and with a roaring fireplace and screen for watching sport. Daily 11am–4pm.

Butterfly Bistro Main Rd, next to the tourist office ☎ 045 962 1326. Well regarded for its wood-fired pizzas (R80), pastas and salads, with deli items for sale if you are picnicking. On Saturday mornings they host a small farmers' market under the oak tree, where you can buy breads, preserves, ready-made vegetarian meals and superb quality locally produced essential oils. Tues, Wed & Sun 9am–5pm, Thurs–Sat 9am–8pm.

King's Lodge Hotel Main Rd ☎ 045 962 1024. Well-priced pub lunches, but the hotel is principally known for its very reasonable Sunday lunch buffet as well as the Tuesday and Friday night buffet dinner special (all R80). The buffets are popular, so book in advance. Daily 8am–8pm.

Tea Thyme at The Edge Signposted off Main Rd. The best place in town for food, though it's off the main road and during the day may be best combined with a walk along the edge of the escarpment. The slow-cooked crispy duck is recommended (R125), and there are several appealing vegetarian options. Daily 8am–8pm.

The Eastern Cape Highlands

The **Eastern Cape Highlands** is the most southerly section of Southern Africa's highest and most extensive mountain chain, the Drakensberg, which that stretches east across Lesotho and up the west flank of KwaZulu-Natal into Mpumalanga. The obvious goal of this world of **San rock paintings**, sandstone **caves** and craggy sheep farms is **Rhodes**, one of the country's best-preserved and prettiest Victorian villages. Since there is no national park here, all activities are arranged through private farms.

Rhodes and around

RHODES is almost too good to be true – a remote and beautiful village girdled by mountains. Few people actually live here: like other villages in this region, Rhodes was progressively deserted as residents gravitated to the cities to make a living, leaving its Victorian tin-roofed architecture stuck in a pleasing time warp. Today, its *raison d'etre* is as a low-key holiday place for people who appreciate its isolation, wood stoves and restored cottages. Although electricity reached the village a few years ago, paraffin lamps and candles are still used. Given that Rhodes is very remote and not on the way to anywhere (on some maps it doesn't even appear), it is a place to dwell for a few days, rather than an overnight stop. While nights are cool even in summer, in winter they are freezing, and there's no central heating, so pack warm clothes.

The village itself is not much more than a few crisscrossing gravel roads lined with pine trees. At its heart is the *Rhodes Hotel* (currently closed), a general shop and a garage; there's also a post office and payphone, but no banking facilities.

Rock-art sites

Martin's Dell ☎ 045 974 9201

Rhodes is a good base for exploring millennia-old **San rock paintings**, the majority of which are on surrounding private farms which can be visited with the farmers' permission (some farms also take guests). Rhodes locals can point you to nearby farms which have their own paintings.

Close to Rhodes, **Martin's Dell** farm, 16km from the village, is worth a visit, not just for the well-preserved, photogenic paintings, but for the lovely, lonely valley you have to drive through to get there. Make an appointment with Russie or Lookie Schmidt to see them. The signposted turn-off to Martin's Dell is 8km from Rhodes on the road to Barkly East. From the turn-off it's another 8km to the site, with parking and a couple of picnic tables.

Rock art had an essentially religious purpose, usually recording experiences of trance states (see p.10 for more); shamans' visions often included powerful animals like the eland, which you can see depicted at Martin's Dell.

ARRIVAL AND INFORMATION   RHODES

By car There's no public transport in or out of the village, so you'll have to drive. Rhodes is reached from Barkly East, which itself is 130km from Aliwal North on the N6. The 60km dirt road to Rhodes from Barkly East is tortuous and rough, taking a good ninety minutes, with sheer, unfenced drops. The garage in Rhodes has a small petrol pump, though you should fill up in Barkly East to be safe.

Tourist information Dave Walker of *Walkerbouts* (see below) runs Highlands Information, 1 Vorster St (☎ 045 974 9290, ⬤ walkerbouts.co.za), which can book any activities and accommodation in the area.

ACCOMMODATION

4

Gateshead Lodges ☎ 045 974 9303, ⬤ gateshead.co.za. A range of excellent cottages and a sandstone farmhouse on huge properties in remote and rugged territory, all within a large radius of Rhodes and Barkly East – the roads are rough, however, and you'll need a vehicle with good clearance to reach some of the cottages. Basie and Carien Vosloo can also take you trout fishing or horse riding. **R500**

Rubicon Flats Old School House, signposted off Main Rd ☎ 045 974 9268, ⬤ rubiconflats.co.za. The best-value, and the warmest, place in town, this handsome old schoolhouse has been converted into self-catering rooms, each with an anthracite burner; there are also simple dorms. Good Afrikaans farm-style meals can be provided if you are staying here (3-course meal R150). **R600**

Walkerbouts Inn Signposted off the main road ☎ 045 974 9290, ⬤ walkerbouts.co.za. A relaxed house with six en-suite guest rooms. The friendly owner, Dave Walker, knows a good deal about the area and can organize almost any activity (see above). **R1270**

EATING AND DRINKING

KoesterkosKombuis Earls Farm, 1.8km from Rhodes on the Barkly East Rd, signposted Toekas ☎ 079 516 6041. Enjoy fresh local fine dining, by candlelight and looking out over panoramic mountain views – dishes include the likes of oxtail or pork belly confit (3-course dinner menu R185). Also sells farm-produced cheese and preserves. Booking essential; phone for opening times.

Walkerbouts Walkerbouts Inn, signposted off the main road ☎ 045 974 9290. The best choice in town for food, offering home-cooked meals. Breakfast (R75), pizzas for lunch and a 3-course set menu for dinner (R145). Booking essential; phone for opening times.

Naude's Nek

The most exhilarating drive out of Rhodes is on the R396 along **Naude's Nek**, the highest mountain-pass road in South Africa, connecting Rhodes with **Maclear** to the south, in a series of snaking hairpin bends and huge views. If you're chiefly looking for scenery, it's not essential to do the whole route to Maclear. Many people go from Rhodes to the top of the pass and back as a day trip, during which you can make a call from South Africa's highest phone (with a crank handle), in a corrugated-iron booth in the middle of a sheep pen at the top of the pass. Be sure to park your car facing into the wind, to ensure your car doors don't fly off, as the wind gets strong up here. There is no mobile reception, so be prepared for emergencies (food, water and sleeping bags) as few cars pass this way.

THE WILD COAST

While it's only 30km from Rhodes, the journey can take a couple of hours to the Nek because so many changing vistas en route demand stops. You'll need a car with high clearance (and a 4x4 in winter) as the road is harsh and impassable after snow.

ACCOMMODATION   NAUDE'S NEK

Tenahead Lodge 33km from Rhodes, on the R396 ☏0861 748 374 ⓦriverhotels.co.za/tenahead. Situated in a spectacular position at the top of the pass, this luxury 5-star hotel has all the amenities a resort could offer. R1880

Woodcliffe Country House, 16km before Maclear ☏045 932 1550, ⓦwoodcliffe.co.za Self-catering accommodation on a farm well below Naude's Nek in the beautiful foothills of the Drakensberg. Rooms in the farmhouse are available, or there's a three-bed cottage and flat. Meals are on request, and they also offer guided rock art and orchid trails, hiking and trout fishing in beautiful rivers. R690

The Wild Coast region

The **Wild Coast region** is aptly named: this is one of South Africa's most unspoilt areas, a vast stretch of undulating hills, lush forest and spectacular beaches skirting a section of the Indian Ocean. Its undeveloped sandy beaches stretch for hundreds of kilometres, punctuated by rivers and several wonderful, reasonably priced hotels geared to family seaside holidays. The wildness goes beyond the landscape, for this is the former **Transkei** homeland, a desperately poor region that was disenfranchised during apartheid and turned into a dumping ground for Africans too old or too young for South African industry to make use of.

The Wild Coast region's inhabitants are predominantly Xhosa, and those in rural areas live mostly in traditional rondavels dotting the landscape for as far as the eye can see. The **N2** highway runs through the middle of the region, passing through the old Transkei capital of **Mthatha** and a host of scruffy, busy little towns along the way. To the south of the highway, the **coastal region** stretches from just north of East London to the mouth of the **Mtamvuna River**. With its succession of great beaches, hidden reefs, patches of subtropical forest, rural Xhosa settlements and the attractive little towns of **Coffee Bay** and **Port St Johns** (both popular with backpackers), this region offers the most deserted and undeveloped beaches in the country.

The Wild Coast, unlike the Western Cape Garden Route, is not a stretch that you can easily tour by car. There's no coastal road, and no direct route between one seaside resort and the next. Yet in this **remoteness** lies the region's charm. Resorts are isolated down long, winding gravel roads off the N2, which sticks to the high inland plateau. Choose one or two places to stay, and stay put for a relaxing few days. Most places along this stretch of coast are known simply by the name of the hotel that nominates the settlement, though you will also see the Xhosa name of the river mouth, on which each hotel is situated, on many maps.

Cintsa

Of the smattering of resorts between East London and the Kei River, one of the best is at **CINTSA**, where endless sandy beaches back up into forested dunes, sliced through by lagoons and rivers. Cintsa is actually two places, Cintsa East and Cintsa West, divided by a river; the whole place is gorgeous. **CINTSA EAST**, 45km from East London, is an upmarket holiday village of some two hundred houses, while **CINTSA WEST** is famous for its beautiful tidal pool.

Haga-Haga

Just northeast of Cintsa, **HAGA-HAGA** is dominated by the box-like but perfectly positioned *Haga-Haga Resort* (see p.343). To reach a sandy beach from the hotel, take the 2km path to Pullens Bay, which is ideal for swimming among the breakers. A 4km walk takes you to Bead Beach, where vendors sell beads made from carnelian, and bits of pottery.

RIDING AND HIKING ALONG THE WILD COAST

Since there's no coastal road, the only way to explore stretches of the Wild Coast is **on foot** or **horseback**.

WILD COAST HIKING TRAILS

Strandloper Coastal Hiking Trail (☎ 043 841 1046, ⊛ strandlopertrails.org.za). Three-night, 58km hiking trail between Kei Mouth and Gonubie (R400 per person). Varied terrain, well-planned stages, small coastal villages and friendly pubs en route make this a popular hike, suited to family groups. Overnight accommodation is provided in comfortable twelve-bunk self-catering cabins.

Wild Coast Holiday Reservations (☎ 043 743 6181, ⊛ wildcoastholidays.co.za). Offers portered packages including transfers from East London, hotel accommodation and all meals, on three trails: the 55km Wild Coast Hotel Meander along pristine, wild coast from the Kob Inn to Morgan Bay (five nights, R6310); the 56km Wild Coast Amble starting north of Kei River and ending in Cintsa, covering terrain of moderate difficulty (four nights R6065); and the Wild

Coast Pondo Walk – five nights based at the *Mboyti River Lodge*, near Lusikisiki, including two coastal walks and two inland trails, ranging from 13km to 26km a day (R745 per day).

★ **Wild Coast Horseback Adventures** (☎ 043 831 1087, ⊛ wildcoasthorsebackadventures.com). Reputable establishment based at Sunray Farm near Kei Mouth, with fit horses and trails suitable for all levels of riding on some of the best beaches in the country – sweeping sandy bays, warm lagoons, river crossings, inland riding through traditional rural settlements, indigenous forest, rolling grasslands and green hills. Beginners start at Kei Mouth (90min; R200), intermediate/advanced ride to Morgans Bay (2hr; R350), or a full-day across the Kei River to Trennerys for a pub lunch and back (R600). They also run fantastic multi-day trips along the coast, overnighting at hotels.

4

Morgan Bay

MORGAN BAY, 90km from East London, lies magnificently in an estuary at the confluence of two rivers carving their passage through forested dunes. A hike from the *Morgan Bay Hotel*, one of the best resorts along the Wild Coast (see p.343), leads over some grassy knolls to the 50m Morbay Cliffs, an excellent vantage point for spotting dolphins and, in season, whales. The bay is pounded by massive breakers, but the estuary provides a safe and tranquil place for toddlers to paddle.

Kei Mouth and Trennery's (Qholorha Mouth)

Pontoon daily: summer 6am–6pm; winter 7am–5.30pm

From Morgan Bay, it's a short drive to the village of **KEI MOUTH**, though there's little point dallying. To get to beautiful **TRENNERY'S**, only 6km along the beach as the crow flies, but considerably longer by road, cross the Kei River on a pontoon (which you can take your car on); after disembarking, continue driving for another 17km to *Trennery's Hotel* (signposted; see p.343). From the hotel, it's a steep walk through luxuriant vegetation to the spectacular beach, where canoes and rowing boats are available.

Trevor's Trail

Daily 9am • ☎ 047 498 0006, or book through your hotel • R85

A recommended excursion from Trennery's is **Trevor's Trail**, a three-hour bush walk and boating trip to "The Gates" – the short corridor of rock face towering above the Qholorha River; it's run by local resident Trevor Wigley, who also runs a number of other trails that include a visit to a local **traditional healer**.

Wavecrest (Nxaxo Mouth)

Wavecrest, just north of Trennery's (though not drivable from there), is a tranquil location where mangrove swamps teem with wildlife. It's an ideal place for hiking, shoreline fishing and general relaxation, as well as the more strenuous **activities** – canoeing, waterskiing and deep-sea fishing. All of this can be arranged through the resort's only **accommodation**, the *Wavecrest* (see p.343).

THE GREAT CATTLE KILLING

The 1850s were a low point for the **Xhosa** nation: most of their land had been seized by the British, drought had withered their crops, and cattle-sickness had decimated their precious herds. In 1856, a young woman called **Nongqawuse**, whose uncle Mhlakaza was a prophet, claimed to have seen and heard ancestral spirits in a pool on the Gxara River. The spirits told her the Xhosa must kill all their remaining cattle and destroy their remaining crops; if they did this, new cattle and crops would arise, along with new people who would drive the whites into the sea.

As news of her **prophecy** spread, opinion was sharply divided among the Xhosa – those whose herds had been badly affected by cattle-sickness were most inclined to believe her. A turning point came when the Gcaleka paramount chief Sarili became convinced she was telling the truth and ordered his subjects to start the cull. Thousands of cattle were killed, but when the "new people" failed to materialize, the unbelievers who had not killed their herds were blamed. By February 1857, the next date for the appearance of the new people, over 200,000 cattle had been slaughtered. When the new people failed once more to materialize, it was too late for many Xhosa. By July there was **widespread starvation**; 30,000 of an estimated population of 90,000 died of hunger.

The British administration saw the famine as a perfect way to force the destitute Xhosa into working on white settlers' farms. To speed up the process, the Cape governor Sir George Grey closed down the feeding stations established by missionaries and laid the blame for the disaster on the Xhosa chiefs, imprisoning many of them on Robben Island.

Mazeppa Bay

One of two good fishing and general chill-out spots on the Wild Coast (the other being by *Kob Inn*; see below), **MAZEPPA BAY** lies northeast of *Wavecrest* – a lovely spot surrounded by dunes and coastal forest. Swimming in the bay is safe, and the surfing is good.

Kob Inn (Qora Mouth)

Just northeast of Mazeppa, **KOB INN** is situated right on the sea front at the **Qora River Mouth**. Apart from the hotel (see p.343), there is nothing else at the settlement. A small ferry traverses the river mouth and takes you to some good hiking trails along the coast, through grassland and into nearby forest patches.

Bulungula (Nqileni)

Idyllically located at the mouth of the Bulungula River, the spread-out village of **NQILENI**, focused around *Bulungula Lodge* (see p.343), gives you the opportunity to

---

SOME XHOSA TRADITIONS

The Wild Coast is largely populated by **rural Xhosa**, who practise traditions and customs that have faded in more urban areas. Many people, for example, still believe that the sea is inhabited by strange people who do not always welcome visitors, which explains the relative scarcity of the activities you would normally find thriving among seashore-dwelling people, such as fishing and diving.

Initiation for teenage boys and young men is still common, and sadly every year there are a number of deaths from infections associated with circumcision. The main circumcision period is the December holidays, when you may see white-daubed young men by the roadside, or men with ochre faces sporting English-styled tweed caps. Young men usually leave their homes to stay in "circumcision lodges", dress in distinctive white paint and costumes and learn the customs of their clan. At the circumcision ceremony the men are expected to make no sound while their foreskin is cut off (with no anaesthetic). After the ceremony, they wash off the paint and wrap themselves in new blankets, and all their former possessions are burned. There follows a feast to celebrate the beginning of manhood and the start of a year-long intermediary period during which they wear ochre-coloured clay on their faces. After this, they are considered men.

Like other African peoples, although they believe in one God, **uThixo**, or uNhkulukhulu (the great one), many Xhosa also believe that their **ancestors** play an active role in their lives. However, the ancestors' messages are often too obscure to be understood without the aid of specialists, or *amagqira*.

The Xhosa are patriarchal by tradition, with women's subordinate status symbolized by *lobola*, the **dowry** payment in cattle and cash that a prospective husband must make to her parents. If the woman is not a virgin, the man pays less. Married Xhosa women have the same right as men to smoke tobacco in **pipes**, and can sometimes still be seen doing so, the pipes' long stems designed to prevent ash falling on babies suckling at their breasts.

The Xhosa did not wear **cloth** until it was introduced by Europeans, when it was quickly adopted. Today, what is now seen as traditional Xhosa cloth is almost always worn by women, mostly in the form of long skirts, beautifully embroidered with horizontal black stripes. The breasts of unmarried women were traditionally uncovered, while those of married women were usually covered with beads or matching cloth. These days, women wear T-shirts, though almost all still cover their heads with scarves and dress modestly in rural areas. In the cities, however, young Xhosa women wear jeans and make-up. For Xhosa who had to leave the Eastern Cape, there is still a powerful connection to their place of origin. Xhosas dying in Cape Town, for example, will still be buried in the Eastern Cape with their family and ancestors. Every Friday night scores of minibuses leave Cape Town transporting mourners and corpses to Saturday **funerals** in the Eastern Cape, a journey of 12–17 hours. Funerals are the most important ritual of all for Xhosa families — and their single greatest expense.

THE EASTERN CAPE'S COASTAL NATURE RESERVES

The Eastern Cape has some undeveloped and gorgeous **coastal reserves**, Dwesa, Hluleka and Mkhambathi. All accommodation in the reserves is self-catering, and there are no shops or facilities, so you need to be fully self-sufficient and stock up before you leave the N2. The reserves are accessible in a rugged vehicle on slow, dirt roads and suitable for a stay of a few days, though they have a reputation of being poorly run. Accommodation can be booked with the Eastern Cape Parks Board (☎043 701 9600, ⓦecparks.co.za).

---

experience rural Transkei life. The river winds its way to the sea through rolling green hills dotted with rondavels, maize fields and livestock, ending at a tranquil river mouth. Here, the coastline is carpeted in dense forest stretching into kilometres of soft, white beach.

Coffee Bay and around

The densely populated, gentle hills of **COFFEE BAY**, known to the Xhosa as Tshontini after a dense wood that grows there, mark the traditional boundary between the Bomvana and Pondo clans of the Xhosa nation. Coffee Bay, with its laidback, relaxed atmosphere, draws a growing number of visitors – yet retains its feeling of idyllic obscurity.

The **landscape** consists of dramatic high cliffs dropping to sandy beaches speckled with black pebbles, which contrasts with the grasslands, forested sand dunes and lagoons further south. The **huts** around here are also very distinctive: many are thatched with a topknot made from a tyre, coloured glass or even an aloe plant – said to discourage owls, harbingers of ill-omen, from roosting on roofs. The main attraction, however, is the **coastal hikes** – the walk to Hole in the Wall is outstanding, as is the stunning two-day coastal route to Bulungula, over-nighting in *Wild Lubanzi Backpackers* (see p.343): *Coffee Shack* (see p.343) and *Bulungula Lodge* (see p.343) can both arrange guides (R150 per day) and free luggage transfer.

Village visits

An excellent community-run **village tour** can be organized through the impressive ANC Women's League veteran, Betty Madlalisa (R80, plus R100 per group to enter the kraal; ☎083 339 0454). Apart from visiting homesteads, the outing takes in the Masizame Women's Project (daily 8am–5pm), housed in a colourful building opposite the Bayview Store, 5km out of Coffee Bay on the Mthatha Road. The project is one of the very few outlets in South Africa where you can buy traditional Xhosa craftwork, including beaded bags and belts, traditional clothing, baskets, mats and blankets. With advance notice, they also offer Xhosa meals (R60) washed down with traditional beer.

Hole In The Wall

The settlement of **HOLE IN THE WALL**, 9km north west of Coffee Bay, has grown up on the shoreline near the large cliff that juts out of the sea, from which it gets its name. The cliff has a tunnel at its base through which huge waves pound during heavy seas, making a great crashing sound. As well as good fishing, safe swimming and snorkelling, there are several spectacular hikes.

ARRIVAL AND DEPARTURE   **THE WILD COAST**

TRANSPORT

By car Phone your resort in advance for up-to-date directions, as roads and conditions change, and fill up with petrol before leaving the N2. Although some of the Wild Coast roads are being surfaced as part of an upgrading programme, most remain untarred and, while generally passable in an ordinary car, it's best to carry a tool kit, a spare tyre and take the roads slowly. Watch out for livestock on all Wild Coast roads, including the N2, and avoid driving in rainy weather and at night. Do not park overnight anywhere that does not have security.

By bus The Baz Bus stops in Cintsa West and Mthatha; you can arrange to be met by hostels in Port St Johns and Coffee Bay, or in Butterworth for Mazeppa. Greyhound and other services ply the N2 between Durban and East London, stopping at Mthatha. Minibus taxis ply all routes, and you should be able to get from Mthatha quite easily to Coffee Bay or Port St Johns, both of which are along tarred and well-populated roads.

By plane If you are flying into East London and making for a specific resort, there is a useful shuttle service run by Ken Black (☎ 043 740 3060) who will quote a price when you book, depending how many people are travelling.

DIRECTIONS

Cintsa Cintsa East can be reached on a tarred road: turn off the N2 at the East Coast Resorts Rd (30km out of East London) then, after 8km, turn left at the sign to Cefane Mouth, from where the village is 7km away. Cintsa West is on the Baz Bus Route, which drops off at *Buccaneers* (see below).

Haga Haga Signposted off the N2, Haga Haga is 72km from East London, 27km of which is along a dirt road.

Wavecrest (Nxaxo Mouth) To get to *Wavecrest*, follow the 34km of tarred road to Centani from the N2 at Butterworth. At Centani, take the signposted road (to the left) to Nxaxo for 8km, then the dirt road for 24km to *Wavecrest* (on the right).

Mazeppa Bay To reach Mazeppa Bay, follow the 34km of tarred road to Centani from the N2 at Butterworth. At Centani, take the signposted road another 45km to Mazeppa.

Kob Inn (Qora Mouth) To get to *Kob Inn* from the N2, take the signposted dirt road heading east for 34km from Idutywa, passing through grassy rolling hills and Xhosa villages.

Bulungula (Nquileni) The turn-off to Bulungula is 50km along the road to Coffee Bay from the N2: you will get detailed directions when booking at *Bulungula Lodge* (see opposite), and you should aim to arrive before nightfall. The Lodge also runs a shuttle service (R90) from the Shell Ultra City in Mthatha (arrange this when booking) on Tues, Thurs, Fri & Sun. If you are coming from Coffee Bay, they will collect you from the Bulungula/Coffee Bay turn-off (called Lutubeni) so you don't need to go all the way back to Mthatha.

Lubanzi Village In the Zithulele Mission Hospital area, off the road to Coffee Bay, Lubanzi Village is two hours drive from the N2 – check directions with *Wild Lubanzi Backpackers*. There's also a Lubanzi shuttle (R15 per person) from Zithulele Hospital; book with *Lubanzi Backpackers* the day before).

Coffee Bay A tarred road leaves the N2 14km south of Mthatha's Shell Ultra City for Coffee Bay.

Hole In The Wall A 9km gravel road – a scenic drive through traditional villages and along cliffs with sea views – links Coffee Bay with Hole In The Wall.

Lambazi Bay Follow the concrete road off the R61 (1km south of Lusikisiki), and then continue for some 40km on gravel roads toward Port Grosvenor. Follow the Drifters signs to Lambazi Bay.

INFORMATION

Services Apart from Port St Johns, none of the places on the coast has a bank or ATM, so be sure to get enough money from East London or Mthatha. Petrol is available in Coffee Bay and Port St Johns.

ACCOMMODATION

The **hotels** on the Wild Coast are typically run along old-fashioned, colonial lines, with set meals, tea times and a well patronized pub. Most offer full board – aside from in Cintsa, Port St Johns and Mthatha, there are no restaurants besides those provided by the accommodation establishments. If you're travelling with children, you will find many hotels have experienced Xhosa nannies who can be employed for a day or for short stretches while you take a break. There are a number of good backpacker lodges along the coast, and plenty of campsites, but **camping** in rural areas is not advisable, even if a beach looks idyllically deserted. It's wise to **book in advance**: the well-informed Wild Coast Holiday Reservations (☎ 043 743 6181, ⊛ wildcoastholidays.co.za), based in East London, can arrange accommodation and organize **activities** in the region.

CINTSA

Buccaneer's Backpackers Cintsa West ☎ 043 734 3012, ⊛ cintsa.com. One of South Africa's most popular hostels, *Buccaneer's* has built its reputation on the excellence of its ten cottages of varying sizes, with fantastic sea and lagoon views, unspoilt beaches, and the plethora of activities they lay on. You can self-cater, or eat inexpensive breakfasts and dinners in the café and pub. It also lays on trips to a local African school and township. Dorm R145, double R330

Crawford's Lodge & Cabins Cintsa East ☎ 043 738 5000, ⊛ crawfordsbeachlodge.com. Just a few minutes' walk from the beach, *Crawford's* offers guesthouse B&B accommodation; for a room with a spectacular view, expect to pay R1800. R1400

HAGA-HAGA

Haga-Haga ☎043 841 1670 or ☎082 659 8881, ⓦhagahagahotel.co.za. This pleasant, rather old-fashioned hotel offers full board in hotel rooms, and self-catering in fourteen flatlets sleeping two or four. The en-suite rooms have balconies. A tidal swimming pool is sculpted into the rocky shoreline in front of the hotel. One of its advantages is being only 70km from East London with a mere 13km of dirt road. Flatlet R950, double R1420

MORGAN BAY

★**Morgan Bay Hotel** ☎043 841 1062, ⓦmorganbayhotel.co.za. This friendly, well-run place overlooks a gorgeous beach and is one of the best hotels along the Wild Coast, particularly for family holidays. It offers good food and fresh, airy rooms furnished with limewashed furniture; camping is also available. Rates include breakfast and dinner. It's only 76km from East London, all on tar roads. Camping R210, double R1600

TRENNERY'S (QHOLORHA MOUTH)

★**Trennery's** ☎047 498 0025/95 or ☎082 908 3134, ⓦtrennerys.co.za. This marvellous family hotel, founded in 1928, still has its heart in the 1950s or 1960s, with well-kept gardens and flowering trees, which obstruct the sea views, but offer shelter from the wind. Uniformed nannies accompany children at the pool, and in the separate children's dining room. The light, airy and spacious rooms and thatched chalets are en suite, while the English-style food is wholesome and well cooked. It is a short hop through forest to the magnificent beach, with various activities laid on. Camping R75, full board R1360

WAVECREST (NXAXO MOUTH)

★**Wavecrest** ☎047 498 0022, ⓦwavecrest.co.za. A cluster of pleasant thatched bungalows and family rooms at arguably the most beautifully positioned of the Wild Coast hotels, right on the edge of a mangrove-lined estuary. You can take a canoe and go birdwatching on the estuary, or cross it to explore the forests backing a sandy beach that stretches as far as you can see. The view from the bar and outside deck takes this all in, and when you are done gazing at the vista, you can have a massage at their modest spa. Full board R1500

MAZEPPA BAY

Mazeppa Bay ☎047 498 0033, ⓦmazeppabay .co.za. This charming hotel offers full board in comfortable cabanas or family rooms, 39 steps up from the beach. Units are thatched and surrounded by palms and tropical plants. It has the added attraction of its own island (reached along a bridge), excellent game fishing and surfing. R1540

KOB INN (QORA MOUTH)

Kob Inn ☎047 499 0011/16, ⓦkobinn.co.za. The *Kob Inn* is a favourite, with sea-facing rooms and a bar right on the rocky shore, close to the wide Mbashe River. The thatched bungalows are comfortable and spacious, and the restaurant is renowned for its seafood banquets. It has a tidal swimming pool built into the rocks. Staff can arrange a boat and fishing tackle, or equip you for canoeing, waterskiing and boardsailing. There is also a tennis court and trampoline and satellite TV. Full board R1580

BULUNGULA (NQILENI)

★**Bulungula Backpackers Lodge** ☎047 577 8900 or 083 391 5255, ⓦbulungula.com. Situated on the estuary of river and sea, *Bulungula* offers ten brightly painted rondavels (sleeping two or four) and camping with shared ablutions. It's a joint venture between the community and seasoned traveller Dave Martin. If you're looking for relaxation and an authentic cultural experience, you'll be hard pressed to find a better place to stay. Booking essential. Camping R80, rondavel R370

MBOLOMPO

Mbolompo Homestay near Zithulele Mission Hospital ☎083 275 9427 ⓦmbolompohomestay .weebly.com. Stay in a Xhosa village in an indigenous forest overlooking Mncwasa river mouth. Accommodation is in a mud thatched hut with clean linen, showers and compost toilets. Evening meals are available on request (R35). Activities available are tubing on the river, cliff jumping, fishing, birdwatching and volunteering in local activities. R180

LUBANZI VILLAGE

Wild Lubanzi Backpackers ☎078 530 8997 or 071 485 6449, ⓦwildlubanzi.co.za. Beautifully hand-crafted buildings using solar power, in a breathtaking setting of hill and sea and beach, with a friendly community vibe. Home cooked meals from the veggie garden (dinner R60). Internet available. Dorm R120, double R320

COFFEE BAY

Bomvu Paradise ☎047 575 2073 or ☎082 467 4494, ⓦbomvubackpackers.com. On the forested edge of the Bomvu river, this popular place hosts drumming sessions around an evening fire, yoga, massage and horseriding, as well as tours to the nearby village. Accommodation is in dorms and doubles, or you can camp, and there is tasty food (R60) available from the *Ubuntu Kitchen*. Camping R60, dorm R100, double R300

Coffee Shack ☎047 575 2048 or 083 656 4350, ⓦcoffeeshack.co.za. Well located on the Bomvu River, *Coffee Shack* is the liveliest of Coffee Bay's backpacker lodges, with dorm, double rooms and camping. It has a restaurant, where a two-course dinner costs just R55. Its shuttle bus plies the route between Mthatha and Coffee Bay, meeting the Baz Bus on request. Camping $\overline{R75}$, dorm $\overline{R120}$, double $\overline{R320}$

Ocean View ✆ 047 575 2005 or 2006, ⓦ oceanview .co.za. The smartest accommodation in Coffee Bay, right on the sandy bay. It's a friendly place, with bright rooms, terraced gardens, a pool area, and a trampoline and playground next to the beach. The restaurant and bar serves English-styled food. Full board. $\overline{R1588}$

White Clay ✆ 083 262 5239 or 083 979 4499 ⓔ whiteclay@vodamail.co.za. One bay west of Coffee Bay, and set on a cliff high above the water, *White Clay* has en-suite double rooms and camping facilities. No one else lives on this bay, so you have it all to yourself, and the location couldn't be better; there are gorgeous views. Whales can sometimes be seen between August and November, and dolphins all year round. They also have a fully licensed restaurant serving seafood specialities. Camping $\overline{R110}$, double $\overline{R450}$

HOLE IN THE WALL

Hole In The Wall ✆ 047 575 0009, ⓦ holeinthewall .co.za. A cluster of white thatched rondavels on a small sandy bay and surrounded by lawns, with a pool, bar and playground. The hotel has a poor reputation for food, accommodation and organization, but it is the only choice here. There are self-catering units sleeping two to eight people. $\overline{R640}$

Hole In The Wall Backpackers ✆ 047 575 0009. Owned by and run on the same site as the hotel, and guests can use the hotel facilities. There isn't the same social scene here as at the Coffee Bay hostels, but the coastline is beautiful. Dorm $\overline{R200}$, double $\overline{R250}$

LAMBAZI BAY

Drifters Lodge Lambazi Bay ✆ 011 888 1160, ⓦ drifters.co.za. On an untouched and dramatic stretch of coastline, the lodge is hidden in a grove of coastal milkwood trees, less than 100m from the beach. The en-suite rooms are in six pondo-style thatched huts with a central restaurant and bar. Full board $\overline{R1590}$

EATING

All of the resorts have their own restaurants, with meals often included in their rates. If you're self-catering, it's best to pick up supplies in a city, before heading to your accommodation. Otherwise, absolute basics can be purchased at trading stores along the main roads, but don't rely on this.

Mthatha and around

Straddling the Mthatha River and the N2 highway 235km from East London, the fractious, shambolic town of **MTHATHA** (formerly Umtata) is the erstwhile capital of the Transkei and the Wild Coast region's largest town. It's a pretty ugly place, its crowded and litter-strewn streets lined with nondescript 1970s office buildings, with the odd older architectural gem, albeit dilapidated. However, the town is useful for stocking up and drawing money, all of which can be done at the Spar Centre or Shell Ultra City on the edge of town. The only reason to venture into the town centre is to visit the **Nelson Mandela Museum**.

Nelson Mandela Museum

Corner of Owen St and Nelson Mandela Drive • 9am–4pm • Free • ✆ 047 532 5110, ⓦ mandelamuseum.org.za

The **Nelson Mandela Museum** is housed in the old **parliament**, or *bungha*, built in 1927. Refurbished in 2014, the museum's most interesting display traces the great man's life with photos and other visual material. The museum coordinates guided **trips** to **Qunu** and **Mveso** (see opposite), Mandela's birthplace, from its sister museum, the Youth and Heritage Centre in Qunu (see below).

Qunu and the Nelson Mandela Youth and Heritage Centre.

500m from N2, 30km west of Mthatha • 9am–4pm • Free • Tours by arrangement • ✆ 047 538 0217, ⓦ mandelamuseum.org.za

Some 30km from Mthatha, on the East London side, are the scattered dwellings of **Qunu**, where Mandela grew up. The N2 thunders through it, but his large and rather plain mansion, which you may photograph but not enter, is clearly visible on the roadside. Signs from the N2 direct you to the **Nelson Mandela Youth and Heritage Visitors' Centre**, where you can look around the craft centre, and arrange a free guide to accompany you in your car to visit the remains of Mandela's primary school, the rock

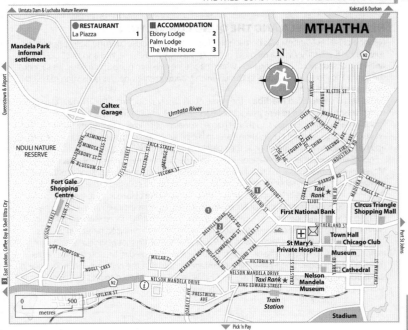

he used to slide down with friends, and the graveyard where his parents, son and daughter are buried. You can see the site of Mandela's grave in the distance from the Centre, but it is on private land is currently inaccessible. There are plans to create a pilgrimage site here, but check the current situation with the Centre before attempting to visit.

ARRIVAL AND DEPARTURE

By plane The small Mthatha airport (☎ 047 536 0115) lies 10km west of town on the Queenstown Rd, with expensive daily flights on SA Airlink (☎ 047 536 0023) to Jo'burg. There is no public transport from the airport, but you can rent a car here from Avis or Budget.

By bus Greyhound and Translux buses pull in at Shell Ultra

MTHATHA AND AROUND

City, 6km from the centre, on the N2, which is also served by the Baz Bus, and is the connecting point for backpackers to take organized shuttles to Port St Johns. There's an ATM here, and in the car park a little Eastern Cape Tourism Board caravan provides maps and basic information. Minibuses can take you into town.

INFORMATION

Tourist information The tourist office is 2.5km from town on the N2, in the Spar Shopping Centre, Savoy Building 3rd Floor, Nelson Mandela Drive (Mon–Fri 8am–4.30pm; ☎ 047 531 5290).

Self-catering supplies You can pick up groceries at the

Spar Centre (daily 7am–9pm), 2.5km from town on the N2 (next to the *Wimpy* restaurant), or Pick 'n Pay (Mon–Fri 8.30am–7pm, Sat & Sun 9am–4pm) at the Southernwood Shopping Centre on Errol Spring Avenue.

ACCOMMODATION

MTHATHA

Ebony Lodge 22 Park Rd ☎ 047 531 3933 or ☎ 083 457 7507. Close to the town centre, *Ebony* has 43 luxury en-suite rooms surrounded by lush gardens, a few swimming pools, and an à la carte restaurant open daily for breakfast, lunch (R170) & dinner. **R850**

Palm Lodge 19 Blakeway Rd ☎ 072 707 9847, ⓦ palmlodgemthatha.co.za. Near the golf course, the ten en-suite rooms here have their own entrance, plus a swimming pool, garden and braai area. Dinner available on request. **R880**

The White House 5 Mhlobo St, South Ridge Park

NELSON MANDELA AND THE QUNU CONNECTION

Nelson Rolihlahla Mandela was born in the village of **Mveso**, close to Qunu (see opposite), on July 18, 1918. His father was a member of the Xhosa royal house – he was also chief of Mveso, until he crossed swords with the local white magistrate over a minor dispute. After his sacking, the family moved to a small kraal in Qunu, which Mandela remembers as consisting of several hundred poor households.

Mandela is often called **Madiba** – the name of his family's subclan of the Thembu clan. The name Nelson was given to him by a schoolteacher, and Rolihlahla means colloquially, "troublemaker". Mandela has said that at home he was never allowed to ask any questions, but was expected to learn by observation. Later in life, he was shocked to visit the homes of whites and hear children firing questions at their parents and expecting replies.

Shortly after his father died, Mandela was summoned from Qunu to the royal palace at Mqhakeweni, where he sat in on disputes in court and learned more about Xhosa culture. At 16 he was initiated into manhood before enrolling in Clarkebury, a college for the Thembu elite, then Healdtown at Fort Beaufort, and finally the celebrated **Fort Hare** in Alice (see box, p.333), which has educated generations of African leaders. Mandela was expelled from Fort Hare after clashing with the authorities, and returned to Mqhakeweni. In 1941, faced with the prospect of an arranged marriage, he ran away to Johannesburg where he immersed himself in politics.

It was only on his release from prison in 1990 (at the age of 72) that Mandela was able to return to Qunu, visiting first the grave of his mother, who had died in his absence. He noted that the place seemed poorer than he remembered it, and that the children were now singing songs about AK47s and the armed struggle. However, he was relieved to find that none of the old spirit and warmth had left the community, and he arranged for a large home to be built there. In December 2013, he was buried in Qunu.

4

☎ 047 537 0580 or ☎ 083 458 9810, ✉ whitehouse @indepco.co.za. Twenty-five rooms, eight en suite, in two adjoining suburban houses in a quiet area just off the N2, opposite the Shell Ultra City. An evening meal can be provided if booked beforehand. **R880**

QUNU

Jonopo Cultural Village 7km north of Mandela's house ☎ 083 503 3896. Basic B&B accommodation in rondavels with a washbasin in each room and shared

outside toilet; a Xhosa dinner can be cooked if ordered in advance. The centre is open daily (8am–5pm; R5) and there are also crafts for sale and some exhibitions of rural life. Dinner, B&B **R460**

Nelson Mandela Youth and Heritage Centre Qunu (see p.344). Conference facilities that are also suitable for overnight stays comprise six simple doubles or family rooms with showers and a/c, and twelve dorms sleeping four in two double bunks. It's all self-catering and there are no restaurants in the area. Dorm **R140**, double **R300**

EATING AND DRINKING

MTHATHA

Most guesthouses have their own restaurants, so you're unlikely to need to head out for food. The town has a thriving nightlife, with bars and *shebeens*, but exploring it without a local escort isn't recommended.

La Piazza Restaurant Country Club, Delville Rd ☎ 047 531 0795. The à la carte *La Piazza Restaurant* in the Country Club is open to the public and has a thatch-covered deck overlooking the golf course (mains R120). Their steaks are recommended. Mon–Fri 11am–late, Sat 12.30–10pm

Port St Johns

The 90km drive on the R61 to **PORT ST JOHNS** from Mthatha is one of the best and scariest journeys on the Wild Coast – just don't look down the sheer drops at the cars which never made it, and make sure you tackle the drive by day. After passing tiny **Libode**, with its small hotel and restaurant, you start the dramatic descent to the coast, past craggy ravines and epic vistas of forest and rondavel-spotted grassland. The road runs alongside the Mzimvubu River for the last few kilometres, giving you a perfect view of the Gates of St John, before reaching the town square and taxi rank. The big surprise, coming from the sparse hillsides around Mthatha, is how dramatic, hilly, lush and steamy it all is.

Initially the town is quite confusing – it meanders into three distinct localities, some kilometres apart. **First Beach**, where the river meets the sea, is along the main road from the post office and offers good fishing, but is unsafe for swimming. Close to First Beach is the rather run-down town centre, where you'll find shops and minibus taxis. **Second Beach**, 5km west along a tarred road off a right turn past the post office, is a fabulous swimming beach with a lagoon, and a couple of nice places to stay nearby. The area along the river around the **Pondoland Bridge** also has some accommodation that is popular with anglers.

Port St Johns is a favoured destination for backpackers, drawn by its stunning location at the mouth of the Mzimvubu River, dominated by Mount Thesiger on the west bank and Mount Sullivan on the east. A further attraction for some visitors is the strong, good quality **cannabis** grown in the area, and the town's famously laidback atmosphere may tempt you to stay longer than you intended. Port St Johns also has good **fishing** and **swimming beaches**, a wider choice of accommodation than anywhere else on the Wild Coast, and a good tarred road all the way into town. If you are looking for a stop-off along the Wild Coast, note that Port St Johns is much better than Mthatha.

The Gates of St John
Both the mountains of the **Gates of St John** merit a stiff climb to the top, from where you get a superb view of the lush surrounding landscape. To get here by car, drive up to the aircraft landing strip at the top of Mount Thesiger. Look out for the birds of prey, making use of the updraughts.

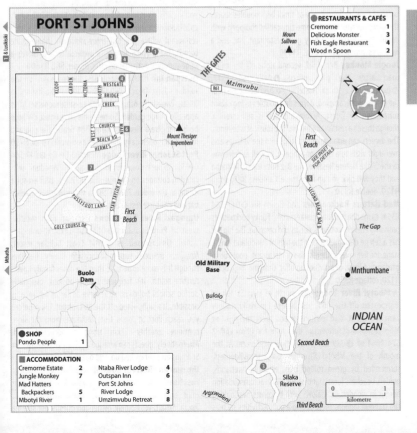

ARRIVAL AND DEPARTURE
PORT ST JOHNS

By bus and minibus taxi The Baz Bus drops off at Shell Garage, from where you can catch a shuttle bus to *Jungle Monkey* hostel (prebook on ☎ 047 564 1517); they will phone your accommodation to pick you up from there. If you're travelling from KwaZulu-Natal to Port St Johns by public transport, an alternative route is by minibus taxi via Port Edward, Bizana and Lusikisiki on the R61. This is also the route to take from Durban.

INFORMATION AND TOURS

Tourist information In an obvious building at the roundabout as you enter town (daily 8am–4.30pm; ☎ 047 564 1187), the tourist office provides maps and provide information about local Xhosa homestays.

Tours Jimmy Gila and his brother (☎ 082 507 2256, ⓦ wildcoasthikes.com) run brilliant hiking tours in the area, with overnight accommodation in huts or in xhosa villages. Guides cost R190 per day, accommodation R250 per night (including meals), and the river crossing R70.

ACCOMMODATION

Cremorne Estate 5km from the centre on the Mzimvubu River, signposted from the Pondoland Bridge ☎ 047 564 1110 or 076 430 2194, ⓦ cremorne .co.za. One of Port St Johns' few upmarket places, offering self-catering timber cottages on stilts set on tidy lawns running down to the Mzimvubu River, with views of Mount Thesiger's red-slabbed cliffs. The cottages have two en-suite bedrooms, making them very affordable for a party of three or four. A row of small B&B doubles shares the view; cheaper still are some tiny cabins equipped with double bunks. There's a very good restaurant, bar, and a relaxing swimming pool area. R1040

Jungle Monkey Berea Rd, second right off the main road after the post office ☎ 047 564 1517, ⓦ junglemonkey.co.za. Hostel in a converted house near the centre, with camping, dorms and doubles in log cabins surrounded by forest. Accommodation is self-catering, though there's a restaurant, bar and live music at weekends. The owners can arrange guided trips into the villages and overnight visits to a traditional healer, as well as drive you to the Silaka Nature Reserve. The Baz Bus stops in Mthatha and they will pick you up from there. Camping R80, dorm R120, double R350

Mad Hatters Backpackers 2nd Beach Rd ☎ 047 564 8354, ⓦ madhattersbackpackers.com. Funky backpackers providing en-suite cottages, dorms and camping. The hip bar has a serene deck overlooking the hills of Pondoland, and a stage for live music. There's also a restaurant, pool room, garden and loads of activities on offer. Camping R60, dorm R120, cottage R350

★**Mbotyi River Lodge** Just north of Port St Johns; signposted off the R61, just before Lusikisiki; follow 7km of cement road to the end, and then turn right at Mbotyi sign and follow the dust road for 19km ☎ 082 674 1064 or ☎ 039 253 7200, ⓦ mbotyi.co.za. At the mouth of the Mbotyi River in complete wilderness, surrounded by green rolling hills, estuarine wetlands, golden beaches, forests and sheer cliffs, accommodation here is in wooden bungalows with balconies overlooking the tranquil lagoon. There is also a pub. Activities such as horseriding, canoe trips, mountain bikes, fishing, trails and game viewing can be organized. They can also book pitches (R95) at a nearby campsite, run by Mbotyi Campsite Trust, a joint venture with the local community, which also has three pondo huts sleeping six (R655), electricity, water and 24hr security. Full board R1350

Ntaba River Lodge On the banks of the Mzimvubu River, signposted on the R61 from Mthatha, just before you reach Port St Johns ☎ 047 564 1707/1717, ⓦ intabariverlodge.co.za. A collection of chalets, with a restaurant where you can enjoy *idombolo* (home-made bread). The friendly service is impeccable and there's a huge variety of activities on offer. Dinner, B&B R1600

Outspan Inn In the centre, past the town hall on the road to First Beach ☎ 047 564 1057, ⓦ outspaninn .co.za. Two-storey ochre B&B with en-suite rooms set in an appealing large garden. Some rooms have unusually high beds that give a view of nearby First Beach. The pub and restaurant is open daily and there's a swimming pool. R790

Port St Johns River Lodge Mthatha Tar Rd ☎ 047 564 0005, ⓦ portstjohnsriverlodge.co.za. Wooden self-catering cottages on the riverside (R770) or B&B en-suite rooms in the lodge. There's also a swimming pool, ladies' bar and à la carte restaurant. R990

Umngazi River Bungalows Umngazi river mouth, west of Port St Johns ☎ 047 564 1115, ⓦ umngazi .co.za. Unsurpassed as a Wild Coast holiday resort, *Umngazi* delivers superb beachside family holidays though it is more expensive than the other family hotels further south. It's frequently fully booked, especially during school holidays, so reserve as far in advance as possible. It's signposted off the R61, about 10km before you reach Port St Johns from Mthatha; from the sign, continue another 11km along a potholed road. Alternatively, guests can arrange a private plane into Port St Johns and get picked up. Full board R2200

Umzimvubu Retreat Guest House Follow the road to First Beach; the entrance is clearly marked after the tar road ends ☎ 047 564 1741, ⓦ umzimvuburetreat .co.za. Smart, yet homely, owner-run guesthouse set in a vast natural garden with scenic views. All rooms are en suite, and there is self-catering available, as well as accommodation for families. Book in advance for dinner at the restaurant (R110). **R1000**

EATING AND DRINKING

If you're self-catering, you can often buy local fruit by the roadside, and sometimes fresh fish and seafood is sold by hawkers. In the centre, Boxer Supermarket has most foodstuffs you'll need.

Cremorne Mzimvubu River; follow the signs from the Pondoland Bridge ☎047 564 1110. Port St Johns' poshest eating place, serving very good fish, steaks (R85) and puddings, as well as having a pizza oven (pizzas are only served on Fri and Sat eve) and pub. Daily 7–9.30am, noon–2.30pm & 6–8.30pm.

Delicious Monster Near Second Beach ☎083 997 9856. A licensed garden restaurant, where you can get breakfast, lunch and dinner of seafood, *schwarmas* and delicious vegetarian fare, cooked with fresh herbs from the garden, as well as home-baked goodies for tea (R78). Mon–Sat 9am–3pm & 6–9pm.

Wood n Spoon Second Beach ☎083 532 8869. Fantastic little local eatery with food cooked in a campervan kitchen. There's rustic but charming outside seating where you can watch cows wandering across the beach. Breakfast, traditional African cuisine, burgers, curry and sandwiches (R79). Thurs–Tues 10.30am–9pm.

Fish Eagle Restaurant The Knoll ☎047 564 1234. Enjoy traditional South African cuisine under the fine thatched lapa or outside on a wooden deck overlooking the Umzimvubu river. Their large T-bone steaks (R80) are a good bet. Mon–Sat 8.30am–9pm.

SHOPPING

Pondo People on the east side of the Mzimvubu River across the Pondoland Bridge ☎047 564 1274. Easily the best craft shop on the Wild Coast, *Pondo People* sells beautiful beaded clothing, aiming to retain the tradition of beadwork in the Transkei. Mon–Fri 8.30am–4.30pm, Sat 8.30am–1pm.

4

KwaZulu-Natal

SHAKALAND

5

KwaZulu-Natal

KwaZulu-Natal, South Africa's most African province, has everything the continent is known for – beaches, wildlife, mountains and accessible ethnic culture. South Africans are well acquainted with KwaZulu-Natal's attractions; it's the leading province for domestic tourism, although foreign visitors haven't quite cottoned on to the incredible amount packed into this compact and beautiful region. The city of Durban is the industrial hub of the province and the country's principal harbour. British in origin, it has a heady mixture of cultural flavours deriving from its Zulu, Indian and white communities. You'll find palm trees fanning Victorian buildings, African squatters living precariously under truncated flyovers, high-rise offices towering over temples and curry houses, overdeveloped beachfronts, and everywhere an irrepressible fecundity.

To the north and south of Durban lie Africa's most developed beaches, known as the **North and South coasts**: stretching along the shore from the Eastern Cape border in the south to the Tugela River in the north, this 250km ribbon of holiday homes is South Africa's busiest and least enticing coastal strip. However, north of the Tugela River you'll find some of the most pristine shores in the country. Here, along the **Elephant Coast**, a patchwork of wetlands, freshwater lakes, wilderness and Zulu villages meets the sea at a virtually seamless stretch of sand that begins at the St Lucia Estuary and slips across the Mozambique border at Kosi Bay. Apart from **Lake St Lucia**, which is fairly developed in a low-key fashion, the Elephant Coast is one of the most isolated regions in the country, rewarding visitors with South Africa's best snorkelling and scuba diving along the coral reefs off **Sodwana Bay**.

KwaZulu-Natal's marine life is matched on land by its **game reserves**, some of which are beaten only by the Kruger National Park, and easily surpass the latter as the best place on the continent to see both black and white rhinos. Concentrated in the north, the reserves tend to be compact and feature some of the most stylish game-lodge accommodation in the country. Most famous and largest of the reserves is the **Hluhluwe-Imfolozi Park**, visited by a respectable cross section of wildlife that includes all of the Big Five.

HAWKSBILL TURTLE, SODWANA BAY

Highlights

❶ Indian curries The tangy food of KwaZulu-Natal's second-largest ethnic group can be experienced in the heart of Durban. **See p.372**

❷ Ukhahlamba Drakensberg Towering peaks and ancient San (Bushman) rock paintings in one of KwaZulu-Natal's two World Heritage Sites. **See p.388**

❸ Hluhluwe-Imfolozi Park KwaZulu-Natal's most outstanding game park, and one of the best places in the world to see both black and white rhinos. **See p.401**

❹ Lake St Lucia Highlight of the iSimangaliso Wetland Park, a World Heritage Site reserve that is home to five ecosystems, full of marine life and wildlife. **See p.404**

❺ Sodwana Bay Swim with ragged-tooth sharks, sea turtles and bright tropical fish at South Africa's premier diving and snorkelling destination. **See p.410**

❻ Eshowe's authentic Zulu culture Be a guest at a traditional Zulu wedding or coming-of-age ceremony, or inspect Zulu baskets at the Vukani Zulu Cultural Museum. **See p.419**

❼ Battlefield tours Experience the drama of the Anglo-Zulu wars with world-renowned storytellers and guides. **See p.424**

HIGHLIGHTS ARE MARKED ON THE MAP ON P.354

5

Since the nineteenth century, when missionaries were homing in on the region, the **Zulus** have captured the popular imagination of the West and remain one of the province's major draws for tourists. You'll find constant reminders of the old Zulu kingdom and its founder Shaka, including an excellent reconstruction of the beehive-hutted capital at **Ondini** and the more touristy **Shakaland** near **Eshowe**. The interior north of the Tugela River was the heartland of the Zulu kingdom and witnessed gruesome battles between Boers and Zulus, British and Zulus, and finally Boers and British. Today, the area can be explored through **Battlefield tours**, a memorable way of taking in some of South Africa's most turbulent history.

HIGHLIGHTS

1. Indian curries
2. Ukhahlamba Drakensberg
3. Hluhluwe-Imfolozi Park
4. Lake St Lucia
5. Sodwana Bay
6. Eshowe's authentic Zulu culture
7. Battlefield tours

KWAZULU-NATAL

> **KZN WILDLIFE**
>
> Most of the public game parks and wilderness areas described in this chapter fall under the auspices of **Ezemvelo KwaZulu-Natal Wildlife**, also known as Ezemvelo KZN Wildlife or KZN Wildlife (PO Box 13053, Cascades 3202; ☎033 845 1000, ⓦwww.kznwildlife.com).
> **Accommodation** in these areas is best booked in advance through them, or at Durban office on Florida Rd (☎031 322 4164; see p.369).

From the Midlands, South Africa's highest peaks sweep west into the soaring **Ukhahlamba Drakensberg** range, protected by a chain of KZN Wildlife reserves. The area's restcamps are ideal bases for walking in the mountains or heading out for ambitious hikes; with relatively little effort, you can experience crystal rivers tumbling into marbled rock pools, awe-inspiring peaks and rock faces enriched by ancient San paintings.

KwaZulu-Natal experiences considerable variations in **climate**, from the occasional heavy winter snowstorms of the Ukhahlamba Drakensberg to the mellow, sunny days and pleasant sea temperatures a couple of hundred kilometres away along the **subtropical coastline**, which offers a temperate climate year-round. This makes the region a popular winter getaway, but in midsummer the low-lying areas, including Durban, the coastal belt and the game reserves, can be uncomfortably humid.

Brief history

Despite their defeats in battles with the Boers and the British during the nineteenth century, the Zulus have remained an active force in South African politics and are particularly strong in KwaZulu-Natal. The **Inkatha Freedom Party** (IFP), formed in 1975 by former ANC Youth League member **Mangosuthu Buthelezi**, has long been associated with Zulu nationalism and draws most of its support from Zulu-speaking people. The IFP and ANC were originally allies in the fight against apartheid, but the IFP's ardent nationalism soon proved to be a major hassle for the ANC, who responded with attacks on opposing IFP members. A bitter and violent conflict between the two parties ensued during the 1980s and 1990s, which, according to some, claimed around twenty thousand lives. Although the fighting is now restricted to isolated incidents, the political rivalry continues. It is the ANC, however, which has gained the upper hand in KwaZulu-Natal and is currently in control of the provincial legislature. South Africa's president, **Jacob Zuma**, a Zulu from KwaZulu-Natal, has played an important role in trying to end the violence between the ANC and IFP. He often makes speeches in Zulu, and enjoys strong support among his people despite his controversial political career.

Durban

Until the 1970s, **DURBAN** – South Africa's third-largest city and the continent's largest port – was white South Africa's quintessential seaside playground, thanks to its tropical colours and itinerant population of surfers, hedonists and holidaying Jo'burg families. Then, in the 1980s, the collapse of apartheid saw a growing stream of Africans flood in from rural KwaZulu-Natal, and shantytowns and cardboard hovels revealed the reality of one of the most unmistakably **African conurbations** in the country. The city's second-largest group is its **Indian population**, whose mosques, bazaars and temples are juxtaposed with the Victorian buildings of the colonial centre.

Although the **beachfront** pulls thousands of Jo'burgers down to "Durbs" every year, the city's main interest lies in its gritty urbanity, a seemingly endless struggle to reconcile competing cultures. Durban also provides a logical springboard for visiting

5

the surrounding region, and is well connected to the rest of South Africa. With the opening of the King Shaka International Airport in 2010, the city now attracts a handful of international flights as well.

There's enough here to keep you busy for a few days. The pulsing warren of bazaars, alleyways and mosques that makes up the Indian area around Dr Yusuf Dadoo Street is ripe for exploration, and there are some excellent restaurants and nightlife around Durban's photogenic **harbour** area. Swanky **northern suburbs** such as the **Berea**, a desirable residential district perched on a cooler ridge, are replete with luxuriant gardens and packed with fashionable cafés, restaurants and bars.

Durban's **city centre** grew around the arrival point of the first white settlers, and the remains of the historical heart are concentrated around **Francis Farewell Square**. Durban's expansive **beachfront** on the eastern edge of the centre is lined with high-rise hotels and tacky family entertainment, and has a reputation for crime (which admittedly is improving).

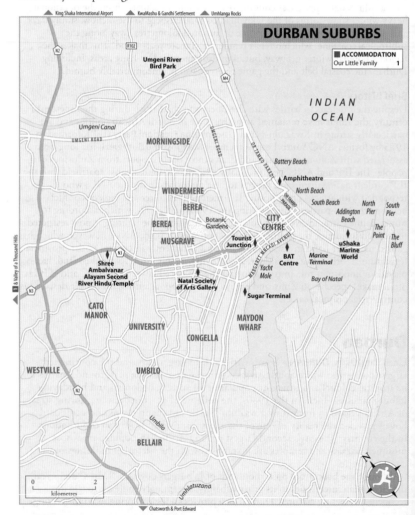

DURBAN SUBURBS

King Shaka International Airport   KwaMashu & Gandhi Settlement   Umhlanga Rocks

INDIAN OCEAN

ACCOMMODATION	
Our Little Family	1

Umgeni River Bird Park

Umgeni Canal

UMGENI ROAD

MORNINGSIDE

Battery Beach

Amphitheatre

North Beach

WINDERMERE

BEREA

South Beach   North Pier   South Pier

Addington Beach

Botanic Gardens

BEREA

CITY CENTRE

The Point

MUSGRAVE

Tourist Junction

uShaka Marine World

The Bluff

Shree Ambalvanar Alayam Second River Hindu Temple

BAT Centre

Marine Terminal

Yacht Mole

Natal Society of Arts Gallery

Bay of Natal

Sugar Terminal

CATO MANOR

MAYDON WHARF

UNIVERSITY

CONGELLA

WESTVILLE

UMBILO

Umbilo

BELLAIR

T & Valley of a Thousand Hills

Umhlatuzana

0   2
kilometres

Chatsworth & Port Edward

Much further afield lie dormitory towns for blacks who commute to work, including the apartheid **ghettos** of KwaMashu and Inanda to the northwest. **Cato Manor**, the closest township to the city, provides an easily accessible vignette of South Africa's growing urban contradictions.

Brief history

Less than two hundred years ago Durban was known to Europeans as **Port Natal**, a lagoon thick with mangroves, eyed by white adventurers who saw business opportunities in its ivory and hides. In 1824 a British party led by **Francis Farewell** persuaded the Zulu king, **Shaka**, to give them some land. Not long after, the British went on to rename the settlement **Durban** after Sir Benjamin D'Urban, governor of the Cape Colony, whose support, they believed, might not go amiss later.

Britain's tenuous toehold looked threatened in 1839, when **Boers** trundled over the Ukhahlamba Drakensberg in their ox wagons and declared their Republic of Natalia nearby. Then, the following year, a large force of now-hostile Zulus razed the settlement, forcing the British residents to take refuge at sea in the brig *Comet*. Capitalizing on the British absence, a group of Boers annexed Durban, later laying siege to a British detachment. This provided the cue for a much-celebrated piece of Victorian melodrama when teenager **Dick King** heroically rode the 1000km from Durban to Grahamstown in ten days to alert the garrison there, which promptly dispatched a rescue detachment to relieve Durban.

Industrialization and apartheid

While Cape Town was becoming a cosmopolitan centre by the 1840s, Durban's population of barely one thousand lived a basic existence in a near wilderness roamed by lions, leopards and hyenas. Things changed after Britain formally annexed the **Colony of Natal** in 1843; within ten years, a large-scale immigration of settlers from the mother country had begun. The second half of the nineteenth century was marked by the city's considerable industrial development and major influxes of other groups. Indentured **Indian labourers** arrived to work in the KwaZulu-Natal cane fields, planting the seeds for South Africa's lucrative **sugar industry** and the city's now substantial Indian community; and **Zulus** headed south after their conquest by the British, in 1879, to enter Durban's expanding economy. In 1895, the completion of the railway connecting Johannesburg and Durban accelerated the process of migrant labour. This link to South Africa's industrial heartland, and the opening of Durban's harbour mouth to large ships in 1904, ensured the city's eventual pre-eminence as South Africa's principal harbour. In 1922, in the face of growing Indian and African populations, Durban's strongly English city council introduced **legislation** controlling the sale of land in the city to non-whites, predating Afrikaner-led apartheid by 26 years.

With the strict enforcement of **apartheid** in the 1950s, Durban saw a decade of ANC-led **protests**. And when the party was banned in 1960 and formed its armed wing, the ANC made plans for a nationwide **bombing campaign** that was initiated with an explosion in Durban on December 15, 1961. Durban scored another first in 1973 when workers in the city precipitated a wildcat strike, despite a total ban on black industrial action. This heralded the rebirth of South Africa's **trade unions** and reawakened anti-apartheid activity, ushering in the final phase of the country's road to democracy.

The centre

Standing at the heart of colonial Durban, **Francis Farewell Square** is hemmed in by the centre's two main thoroughfares, Dr Pixley Kaseme (formerly West) Street and Anton Lembede (formerly Smith) Street. The square is a sultry palm-fringed garden overlooked by some fine old buildings, the focal point being the **Cenotaph**, a

5

● **RESTAURANTS & CAFÉS**
Afriportico	5
Cargo Hold	6
Little Gujarat	1
Moyo	7
Oriental	2
Roma Revolving Restaurant	4
Ulundi	3

● **SHOPS**
Adams & Co	3
Amphitheatre Fleamarket	1
BAT Centre	5
City Market	4
Victoria Street Market	2

■ **BAR & CLUB**
The Origin	1

Botanic Gardens

Airport & A3

CANONGATE ROAD

& Berea Road

Dalton Road

Sugar Terminal

Berea

M12

OSBORNE

Minibus/
Taxi Rank ★

New Durban
Train Station

Bus
Station

MASABALA YENGWA AVENUE

JEFF TAYLOR CRES.

ARCHIE GUMEDE (OLD FORT) PLACE

MITCHELL ROAD

NORTH

FIRST AVENUE

MAY

FYNN

UMGENI ROAD

NEWMARKET

ASCOT

EPSOM RD

INGCUCE (ALBERT) ROAD

CARLISLE

VICTOR LANE

ISMAIL C MEER (LORNE) STREET

MAUD LANE

CHARLOTTE MAXEKE
(BEATRICE) ROAD

FOUNTAIN LANE

M L SULTAN ROAD

CROSS

K E MASINGA (OLD FORT) ROAD

Kwa Muhle
Museum

BRAAM FISCHER (ORDINANCE) ROAD

JOHANNES NKOSI STREET

DAVID WEBSTER LEOPOLD STREET

JOSEPH NDULI (RUSSELL) STREET

BROOK

DR YUSUF DADOO STREET

DR GOONAM
(PRINCE EDWARD)
STREET

BOND

INGCUCE (ALBERT) ROAD

JOE SLOVO (FIELD) STREET

SOLDIERS WAY

Central
Park

Workshop
Mall ❷

CROSS

BERTA MKHIZE
STREET

Tourist
Junction ❶

Berea Road
Train Station

BROOK

❶

❷ Fish and
Meat Market

DENNIS HURLEY (QUEEN) STREET

Pine Arcade
Carpark P

Local Bus
Depot

JOSEPH NDULI
(RUSSELL) STREET

CATHEDRAL
ROAD

Juma Musjid

Madressa
Arcade

DR A B XUMA STREET

Emmanuel
Cathedral

MADRESSA ARCADE

RUSSELL

DAVES LANE

SAVILLE

FEEDREY
LANE
PLOWRIGHT
LANE
CRANCERY
LANE
CHANCERY
LANE

SCHOOL
LANE
GREEN
GROVE
PASS

HOOPER

MARK LANE

MERCURIES
PASSAGE

❸ @

MERCURY
LANE

DOROTHY NYEMBE (GARDINER) STREET

FRANCIS
FAREWELL
SQUARE

City
Hall

West Street
Cemetery

THEATRE LANE

DR PIXLEY KASEME (WEST) STREET

DR PIXLEY KASEME (WEST) STREET

CONVENT LANE

ANTON LEMBEDE (SMITH) STREET

DULLAR OMAR (MASONIC)
GROVE
BEACH GROVE
SALMON GROVE
TENTOR RD

JOE SLOVO (FIELD) STREET

PARRY ROAD

HERMITAGE
BEACH GROVE
DEVONSHIRE
PLACE

LESLIE

❻

❸

BEACH ROAD

WARWICK
TRIANGLE

Footbridge ❹

JULIUS NYERERE (WARWICK) AVENUE

ROAD

MARKET

DR FINCH
(BAKER) STREET

ANTON LEMBEDE (SMITH) STREET

ALEXANDRA

PARK

COLLEGE LANE

MAUD MFUSI (ST GEORGES) STREET

MCARTHUR

DIAKONIA STREET

Old House
Museum

MARGARET MNCADI AVENUE

Yacht
Mole

Albert Park

Wilson's
Wharf

DURBAN CITY CENTRE & BEACHFRONT

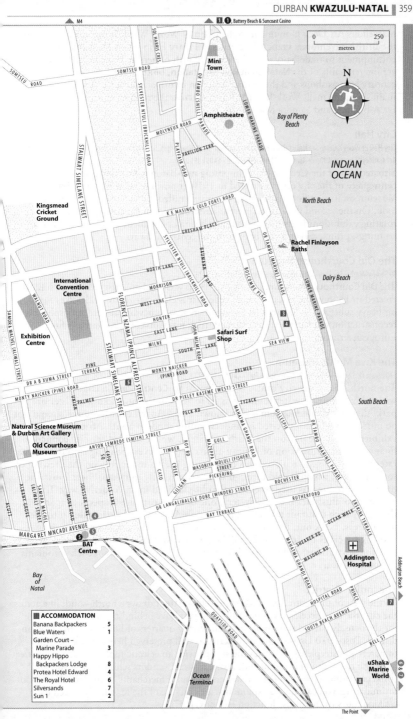

5

marvellous Art Deco monument to the fallen of World War I. It marks the site where the British adventurers Francis Farewell and Henry Fynn set up Durban's first white encampment to trade ivory with the Zulus. North of here at 160 Monty Naicker Rd are the remnants of the **Natal Great Railway Station**, built in 1894 and recycled a century later as shops and the Tourist Junction information centre. The city centre's main shopping mall, Workshop Mall, is just across the road from here on the corner of Dr A B Xuma and Samora Machel streets.

City Hall

City Hall Dr Pixley Kaseme St • **Natural Science Museum** Mon–Sat 8.30am–4pm, Sun 11am–4pm • Free • ☎ 031 311 1111 • **Durban Art Gallery** Mon–Sat 8.30am–4pm, Sun 11am–4pm • Free • ☎ 031 311 2264

Situated east of the Cenotaph, the imposing neo-Baroque **City Hall** is the monumental centrepiece of the city centre. Erected in 1910, it now houses the **Natural Science Museum** on its first floor, containing the usual stuffed animals and worth only a brief look. On the second floor is the more interesting **Durban Art Gallery**, which has rotating exhibitions in its main rooms and a small permanent collection of African paintings, prints, carvings and baskets in the central hallway.

The Old Courthouse Museum

99 Samora Machel St • Mon–Sat 8.30am–4pm • Free • ☎ 031 311 2226

The **Old Courthouse Museum**, east of City Hall, was Durban's first two-storey building, erected in 1866 in the Natal Veranda style that is characterized by wide eaves to throw off heavy subtropical downpours. Housed here in a somewhat austere atmosphere is a reconstruction of Henry Francis Fynn's wattle-and-daub cottage, Durban's first European structure.

The Kwa Muhle Museum

130 Braam Fischer Rd • Mon–Sat 8.30am–4pm • Free • ☎ 031 311 2237

The north side of the city centre is dominated by **Central Park**, a large green space with a lovely mosaic water fountain as its focus. On the northern perimeter of the park, the **Kwa Muhle Museum** – also known as the Apartheid Museum – should not be missed if you are interested in understanding modern South Africa. Permanent exhibitions include one on the Durban System, which enabled the city council to finance the administration of African affairs without ever spending a rand of white ratepayers' money. It achieved this by granting itself a monopoly on the brewing of sorghum beer, which it sold through vast, African-only municipal beer halls. The resulting revenue was used to ensure that blacks lived in an "orderly" way. The exhibit also illustrates the Pass System, one of the most hated aspects of apartheid, through which constant tabs could be kept on Africans and their influx into the urban areas. Look out, too, for photographs of life in the single-sex, artificially tribalized worker hostels, which deliberately sowed divisions among blacks by creating separations, and so played its part in many of the current social problems in South Africa.

The Indian District

To the west of the centre, where **Dr Yusuf Dadoo Street** draws a north–south line across the city, the pace accelerates perceptibly, and you leave behind the formal city centre for the densely packed warren of shops and living quarters of Durban's central **Indian district**. Post-1910 Union-style architecture is well preserved here and, along with minarets and steeples, punctuates the skyline with an eclectic roofscape. Down at street level, the rich cultural blend includes African street vendors selling herbs, fruit and trinkets outside the Indian general dealers and spice merchants. If the crowds feel too intimidating, you can always explore this area on one of the reasonably priced daily **walking tours** from Tourist Junction (see box, p.370).

Juma Musjid and the Madressa Arcade
On the corner of Dr Yusuf Dadoo and Dennis Hurley streets

The gilt-domed minarets of **Juma Musjid** were completed in 1927. It's the largest mosque in the southern hemisphere and a focal point for the area, although Durban's Indian population is predominantly Hindu. You're welcome to enter the mosque, but make sure you leave your shoes at the door. The colonnaded verandas give way to the alley of the bazaar-like **Madressa Arcade** next door, heaving with Indian traders peddling kerosene lamps, tailor-made outfits and beads. The arcade emerges with a start into Cathedral Street, dominated by the **Emmanuel Cathedral**, built in 1902 in Gothic Revival style.

Victoria Street Market
North across Dennis Hurley St

The bright-pink **Victoria Street Market** (see p.375) is popular with tourists in search of a trinket or two, while the hectic fish and meat market opposite can provide drama, particularly on Sunday mornings when the stallholders compete to sell their stocks before the afternoon close-down. Both can be explored independently, but a guided tour with a company like Markets of Warwick (see box, p.370) can be even more rewarding.

Joseph Nduli Street and the West Street Cemetery

To the west of the Victoria Street Market, African hawkers gather on **Joseph Nduli Street** (formerly Russel St), where they do a brisk trade in *umuthi* (traditional herbal medicines). West of Joseph Nduli Street and jammed between the railway tracks to the west and the N3 into town on its northern side, **West Street Cemetery** is zoned according to religion. Many of the city's colonial big names are buried here, such as Durban's first mayor, George Cato, and the Victorian documentary painter, Thomas Baines. In the Muslim section some tombstones are inscribed "*hagee*" or "*hafez*", the former indicating someone who has been to Mecca and the latter an individual who managed to memorize the entire Koran.

Warwick Triangle

In an Africanized *Bladerunner* setting west of Dr Yusuf Dadoo Street, concrete freeways run over chaotic roadways and minibus taxi ranks; here you'll find Durban's real urban heart of hawkers, shacks and *shebeens*. You'll need to be bold to explore the **Warwick Triangle**, which lies between King Dinizulu Road, Brook Street and Cannongate Road – walk with confidence, wear nothing easily snatched, and you should be fine.

The gateway to the triangle is across Brook Street – known until 1988 as Slaughterhouse Road because butchers slaughtered livestock here – through the hectic Berea station concourse full of pumping music and hawkers, and over the Market Road footbridge, where you'll come to the main **city market** (see p.375), which lies between Julius Nyerere Avenue and Market Road.

The harbour area

Margaret Mncadi Avenue (formerly Victoria Embankment), or the Esplanade, runs the length of Durban's harbour, the lifeblood of the city's economic power. Durban is one of the only cities in the world with a busy port a mere block from the city centre, but the harbour area is edged by a narrow strip of park that is too seedy to make for a very pleasant stroll. However, there are some good restaurants to be found in the area and a lively cultural scene at the BAT Centre at the eastern end, all of which are good spots from which to watch the sun glinting off the sparkling water and take in the mix of yachts and cargo ships chugging past.

The Sugar Terminal
51 Maydon Wharf Rd • Tours Mon–Thurs 8.30am, 10am, 11.30am & 2pm • R17 • Book at the SA Sugar Association Tour Centre, or at Tourist Junction • ☎ 031 365 8100

At the western edge of the harbour, where Margaret Mncadi Avenue joins Maydon

5

Wharf Road, is a photogenic complex of functional industrial architecture, most notable of which are the three dramatic sugar silos at the **Sugar Terminal**. The terminal, whose design has been patented and used internationally, has become something of a tourist attraction; a tour gives you one hour of sugary history and access to half a million tonnes of sugar.

Old House Museum

31 Diakonia St • Mon–Fri 9am–4pm • Free • ☎ 031 311 2261

Margaret Mncadi Avenue and the streets around it were the prime residential areas during the city's early development in the nineteenth century, and working your way back east from Maydon Wharf Road there's a reminder of the city's colonial heritage at the **Old House Museum**, one block north of Margaret Mncadi Avenue. Once the home of Sir John Robinson, who became Natal's first prime minister in 1893, the two rooms of this renovated settler house are crammed full of period furniture and numerous ticking clocks.

Yacht Mole and the BAT

BAT Office Mon–Fri 8am–4.30pm, Sat 9am–2pm • ☎ 031 332 0451, ⍟ batcentre.co.za

On the waterfront you'll find the **Yacht Mole**, a slender breakwater jutting into the bay and home to the Point and Royal Natal Yacht clubs. This is also the access point for the **BAT (Bartle Arts Trust) Centre**, an industrial-chic arts development and community venue boasting a concert hall, practical visual art workshops, classes and exhibition galleries (see p.373). The *Afriportico* restaurant upstairs (see p.371) provides a magnificent lookout for watching the passing harbour scene.

Ocean Terminal Building

The **Ocean Terminal Building**, which harks back to the romantic days of sea travel, is one of Durban's architectural masterpieces. Although you can't enter the building, the view from outside it at night, looking back onto the city, is spectacular. To get here, head east on Margaret Mncadi Avenue towards the Stalwart Simelane Street intersection, enter the Harbour at Port Entrance no. 3 and follow the signs.

The beachfront

Durban's **beachfront**, a high-energy holiday strip just east of the centre, is South Africa's most developed seaside; however, it's of limited appeal unless you enjoy unabashed kitsch and garish amusement parks. This 6km stretch from the Umgeni River in the north to the Point in the south was traditionally called the **Golden Mile**, though the prevalence of crime along the beachfront earned it the moniker of Mugger's Mile. However, in the build-up to the 2010 football World Cup, concerted efforts were made to clean up the beachfront: the police presence has increased significantly and CCTV cameras have been installed. These measures have improved security, although you should still exercise caution and use common sense during the day – for example, never leave valuables unattended on the beach – and avoid the beachfront altogether at night.

uShaka Marine World

Just south of Addington Beach • Wed–Fri 10am–5pm, Sat & Sun 9am–5pm • R139 to visit either Sea World or Wet 'n Wild, or R185 for both • ☎ 031 328 8000, ⍟ ushakamarineworld.co.za • uShaka Village Walk & uShaka Beach daily 9am–late

The big draw of Addington Beach – and the only really worthwhile attraction along the beachfront – is **uShaka Marine World**. This impressive water adventure wonderland is a tropical African theme park, complete with palm trees, fake rock formations and thatched *bomas*. The most appealing section is **uShaka Sea World**, designed in and around a superb mock-up of a wrecked 1920s cargo ship. The main entrance leads you down to the darkened hull with its broken wood, battered engine room, ropes and

5

sloping floors. The walls of the hull serve as windows into the "ocean" (actually a series of large tanks), where turtles, stingrays, octopus, sharks and a host of other marine life can be seen. The complex also includes a dolphin stadium and a seal pool, where daily shows (three a day) feature these creatures, as well as **uShaka Wet 'n Wild**, a series of pools and water slides, including The Drop Zone, the highest water slide in the southern hemisphere. The **uShaka Village Walk** development is home to plenty of restaurants, making it a great (and safe) night-time venue.

South Beach

Just north of uShaka Marine World lies **South Beach**, arguably South Africa's busiest beach, which heralds the start of the beachfront tourist tack. On weekends and holidays the paved promenade swarms with surfers, skateboarders and hawkers. Further along OR Tambo Parade, you'll find paddling pools, stepping stones, an aerial cableway and amusement rides.

Dairy Beach and the Rachel Finlayson Baths

OR Tambo Parade • **Rachel Finlayson Baths** Oct–April Mon–Fri 5.30am–6pm, Sat & Sun 6am–6pm; May–Sept daily 6am–5pm • R8

Dairy Beach, the next along from South Beach, is so-called because of the milking factory that once stood here. It's now regarded as one of the country's best surfing beaches, and it's home to the saltwater **Rachel Finlayson Baths**, a good spot for sheltered swimming and sunbathing.

North Beach and the Bay of Plenty

Both **North Beach** and the adjacent **Bay of Plenty**, adjoining Dairy Beach, host an international professional surfing contest held every July (see p.374). Between OR Tambo Parade and the pedestrian walkway at the Bay of Plenty is the attractively landscaped **Amphitheatre**, the venue for Sunday flea markets (see p.375).

Mini Town

141 OR Tambo Parade • Daily: Feb–June, Aug, Oct & Nov 9.30am–4.30pm; Dec, Jan, July & Sept 9.30am–5pm • R20 • ☎ 031 337 7892

Near the corner of OR Tambo Parade and KE Masinga Road, just north of North Beach, **Mini Town** is a scale replica of Durban's landmarks and great fun for kids; walkways lead you past hotels, beaches and the airport, giving you a bird's-eye view of the city.

Battery Beach and the Suncoast Casino

A kilometre north of the centre along Marine Parade, past **Battery Beach** (a good place for swimming), is the massive **Suncoast Casino**, a mock Art Deco entertainment complex with restaurants, gambling tables, eight cinemas and a pristine private beach.

The Berea

High on a north–south ridge overlooking the city centre, the **Berea** is Durban's oldest and most desirable residential district, where mansions and apartment blocks enjoy airy views of the harbour and the sea. Its palmy avenues provide an alternative to the torrid city centre and beachfront for accommodation, eating and entertainment. The term Berea actually has two meanings locally; the suburban area immediately north and west of the city centre is called the Berea, though within this is a suburb known as the Berea, as well as suburbs such as Morningside and Musgrave.

KwaZulu-Natal Society of Arts Gallery

166 Bulwer Rd • Tues–Fri 9am–5pm, Sat 9am–4pm, Sun 10am–3pm • Free • ☎ 031 277 1705, ⓦ kznsagallery.co.za

South of the N3, which passes through the Berea to the city, and east of Peter Mokaba Road, the **KwaZulu-Natal Society of Arts Gallery**, or NSA, provides a breezy venue for taking in thrice-weekly exhibitions by local artists. Designed for the local climate, the

5

DURBAN: THE BEREA

■ BARS & CLUBS

Billy The Bums	1
Dropkick Murphy's	2
Skyybar	3

■ ACCOMMODATION

Audacia Manor	2
The Benjamin	7
The Elephant House	3
Essenwood House	5
Gibela Lodge	8
Goble Palms	1
Hippo Hide Lodge and Backpackers	9
Nomad's Backpackers	10
Rosetta House	4
Tekweni Backpackers	6

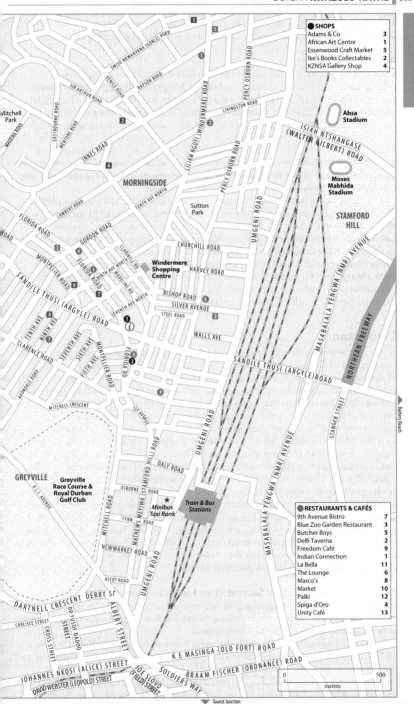

Absa Stadium

Moses Mabhida Stadium

ISIAH NTSHANGASE (WALTER GILBERT) ROAD

STAMFORD HILL

MASABALALA YENGWA (NMR) AVENUE

NORTHERN FREEWAY

Battery Beach

UMGENI ROAD

SANDILE THUSI (ARGYLE) ROAD

STANGER STREET

Mitchell Park

MADUMA ROAD
EASTBOURNE ROAD
MENTONE ROAD
SIR ARTHUR ROAD
VENICE ROAD
SMISO NEWANYANA (GOBLE) ROAD
RAPSON ROAD
LILIAN NGOYI (WINDERMERE) ROAD
PERCY OSBORN ROAD
LIVINGSTONE ROAD

INNES ROAD

MORNINGSIDE

Sutton Park

LAMBERT ROAD
TENTH AVE NORTH

FLORIDA ROAD

GORDON ROAD
CLAIRBELL RD
NINTH AVE NORTH
MADELINE RD

CHURCHILL ROAD

HARVEY ROAD

Windermere Shopping Centre

MONTPELIER ROAD
FLORIDA ROAD

SANDILE THUSI (ARGYLE) ROAD

BISHOP ROAD
SILVER AVENUE
STEEL ROAD

SEVENTH AVE NORTH

WALLS AVE

TENTH AVE
NINTH AVE
CLARENCE ROAD
SEVENTH AVE
SIXTH AVE
FIFTH AVE
MONTPELIER ROAD
FLORIDA RD

AVONDALE ROAD

MITCHELL CRESCENT

1ST AVENUE

DALY ROAD

GREYVILLE

Greyville Race Course & Royal Durban Golf Club

D.L.I. AVENUE

OSBORNE ROAD
MITCHELL ROAD
MATHEWS MEYIWA (STAMFORD HILL) ROAD
FYNN ROAD

★ Minibus Taxi Rank

Train & Bus Stations

NEWMARKET ROAD

ASCOT ROAD

UMGENI ROAD

DARTNELL CRESCENT   DERBY ST
CARLISLE STREET
CROSS STREET
DR YUSUF DADOO STREET
ALBERT STREET

JOHANNES NKOSI (ALICE) STREET
DAVID WEBSTER (LEOPOLD) STREET
JOE SLOVO (FIELD) STREET
SOLDIERS WAY
K E MASINGA (OLD FORT) ROAD
BRAAM FISCHER (ORDNANCE) ROAD

0   500
metres

5

1990s building is a mass of interlinked spaces divided by a timber screen that forms a veranda. There's a good arts and crafts shop (see p.375) and a relaxing coffee shop.

Botanic Gardens

John Zikhali Rd, enter on St Thomas Rd • Daily 7.30am–5.15pm • Free • ☎ 031 322 4021, ⓦ durbanbotanicgardens.org.za

A little way northwest of the centre and east of Musgrave, Durban's **Botanic Gardens** were established in 1849. They're famous for their cycad collection, which includes *Encephalartos woodii*, one of the rarest specimens in the world. The gardens also boast cool paths, excellent picnic spots, a lovely teahouse and a magnificent array of orchids.

Muckleneuk

220 Gladys Mazibuco Rd, corner of Steven Dlamini Rd • **Campbell Collections** Mon, Tues & Fri 9am–3pm, Sat 9am–noon • Tours by appointment R20 • ☎ 031 260 1720 • **Killie Campbell Africana Library and Museum** Mon–Fri 8.30am–4.30pm, Sat 9am–noon • Free • **Mashu Museum of Ethnology** Mon–Fri 8.30am–4.30pm, Sat 9am–noon • Free

The Cape Dutch-revival former homestead of sugar baron Sir Marshal Campbell, **Muckleneuk** houses one of the finest private collections of Africana in the country, including material relating to KwaZulu-Natal's ethnic heritage. The **Campbell Collections** comprise artworks and excellent examples of Cape Dutch furniture, while the adjacent **Killie Campbell Africana Library and Museum** is well known for its comprehensive collection of books, manuscripts and photographs. Also here is the **Mashu Museum of Ethnology**, consisting of a superb collection of Zulu crafts, including tools, weapons, beadwork and pottery. The entire complex is surrounded by a beautiful garden designed by Killie Campbell herself.

Cato Manor

A short drive west of the city centre takes you through **Cato Manor**, offering a graphic cross section of Durban's twentieth-century history, where you can see a juxtaposition of African squatter camps, Hindu temples and vegetation mingling in the heart of the city's middle-class suburbs. A large area in a valley below the Berea, Cato Manor was named after Durban's first mayor, **George Cato**, who arrived here in 1839. During the first half of the last century the district was home to much of Durban's Indian community, who built temples on its hills. They were later joined by Africans, who were forced into crowded slums because of the shortage of housing. In 1949, an incident in which an Indian trader assaulted a Zulu man flared up into Durban's worst **riot**, with thousands of Africans attacking Indian stores and houses, leaving 142 dead.

Because Cato Manor was right in the middle of white suburbs, the apartheid government began enforcing the Group Areas Act here in the 1960s, moving Africans north to KwaMashu and Indians south to Chatsworth, leaving a derelict wasteland guarded only by the handful of Hindu temples left standing. The vacuum was filled again in the late 1980s, when Africans pouring into Durban built the closely packed tin shacks that line **Vusi Mzimela Road** (formerly Bellair Rd), winding its way through Cato Manor's valley. A drive along the road is undeniably interesting, though not altogether safe – carjackers are a potential hazard.

Shree Ambalvanar Alayam Second River Hindu Temple

890 Bellair Rd • Can be visited safely on a tour (see box, p.370) • Leave the city centre on the M13, take the Felix Dlamini Rd (formerly Brickfield Rd) exit and then turn left into the M10, which becomes Vusi Mzimela Rd; the temple is on the right if you're coming from town, just before Solomon Mahlangu Drive (formerly the Edwin Swales freeway)

A National Monument, the **Shree Ambalvanar Alayam Second River Hindu Temple** is a 1947 reconstruction of the first Hindu temple in Africa, built in 1875 on the banks of the Umbilo River and subsequently destroyed by floods. The beautifully carved entrance doors are originals salvaged from the flood, while the facade is adorned with a pantheon of wonderfully garish Hindu deities. Around Easter every year the temple

5

hosts a **firewalking festival** in which unshod devotees walk across red-hot coals, emerging unscathed. Visitors are welcome to join the thousands of worshippers who come to honour the goddess Draudpadi.

Umgeni River Bird Park

490 Riverside Rd, Durban North • Daily 9am–5pm; bird shows Tues–Sun 11am & 2pm • R40 • ☎ 031 579 4600 • ⓦ umgeniriverbirdpark.co.za

The **Umgeni River Bird Park** is a tranquil place that's worth a visit for its fantastic free-flight bird shows, some of which feature critically endangered species such as the Wattled Crane. The park, which consists mostly of walk-through aviaries and open paddocks, is home to a vast collection of more than two hundred species of indigenous and exotic birds including flamingos, finches, magpies and macaws.

KwaMashu, Shembe and Inanda

Even though they're not hard to reach with your own wheels, some quintessential Durban experiences rarely make it into the pages of tourist brochures. Driving north of the city along the R102 (which becomes the M25), you can visit the place where Gandhi dreamed up passive resistance, and witness the epic religious ceremonies of the Zulu–Christian Shembe sect. A word of **warning**: driving through some of the areas covered here carries a certain risk, and you're advised to go with someone familiar with the road and local customs or on an organized tour (see box, p.370).

KwaMashu

Driving north along the M25 towards Inanda you'll pass the African township of **KwaMashu** on the left, established in the late 1950s to house residents of Cato Manor who had been forcibly resettled. It displays all the unimaginative planning typical of such low-cost housing schemes. The area is a sea of hills, vegetation and colour, which makes it tempting to romanticize the locality's poverty.

The Gandhi Settlement

Mon–Fri 8am–4pm, Sat 9am–2pm • Donation • ☎ 031 519 2555

A well-signposted turn off the M25 takes you to the **Gandhi Settlement**, also known as the Phoenix Settlement. On the eastern edge of the vast Inanda squatter camp, it's the site of a self-help scheme established by Mohandas Gandhi soon after his arrival in Durban in 1903. It was from here that Gandhi began to forge his philosophy of passive resistance; in a sad irony, violence brought it to ruin in 1985 when squatters from the adjacent camp looted and razed the settlement. With the help of the Indian Government, the settlement was rebuilt in time for its centenary celebration. A bronze bust of Gandhi now stands near the entrance to his house, **Sarvodaya** ("a place for the upliftment for all"), which is now a **museum** focusing on his time in South Africa and on Indian resistance to segregation.

Shembe

At **Ekuphakameni** ("the elated place"), west of the Gandhi Settlement along the M25, two "stars" laid in stone in the hilly landscape mark the spots where meteorites from the 1906 appearance of Halley's Comet struck the Earth. From here, you can continue to the Inanda police station at the top of the hill, then turn left to descend into the valley and cross the Umhlanga River bridge. At the next intersection, take the dirt road to the left, past the sports field, and turn left again to view the **Shembe settlement** at **Ebuhleni**. The settlement was established by the Holy Church of Nazareth as a refuge for Africans dispossessed as a result of the Land Act of 1913. According to the founding history of the Church, its prophet Isaya Shembe was "called" in 1910 to the summit of a mountain outside Durban, where he vowed before God to bring the Gospel to the Zulus. The Church's membership of tens of thousands was drawn

5

initially from rural people whose lives had been devastated by colonization and who were eager to embrace Christianity, but were unwilling to give up traditional customs. The resulting religion was a rich synthesis that rejected drinking, smoking and cults, while encouraging a work ethic centred around crafts.

Every July devotees of the Holy Church of Nazareth gather in Ebuhleni for a month of worship. On these occasions, the men and women live on different sides of the village, and the unmarried maidens live in a separate enclosure. At the entrance gates to the settlement, rows of tables display what appear to be religious knick-knacks for sale to tourists – holographic images of Isaya Shembe and key rings with religious icons embedded in perspex – but which are actually religious artefacts revered by the converted of Shembe.

Leaving Ebuhleni, ignore the dirt road turn-off and head straight on to reach the Inanda Dam. The deep gorge to your left is the **Inanda Falls**, where the Shembe have baptismal ceremonies, which visitors are welcome to attend.

ARRIVAL AND DEPARTURE   DURBAN

BY PLANE

King Shaka International Airport Durban's international airport (☎ 032 436 6585) is located 35km north of the city in the village of La Mercy. A shuttle service to the city centre runs every 45min (daily 5am–10pm; ☎ 031 465 1660; R70) and will drop you at your accommodation. A metered taxi to the city should cost no more than R450. Several car-rental companies are based here (see opposite), and there's an Absa Bank in the arrivals terminal (daily 7am–8pm) with a 24-hour ATM next to it. The following airlines are based at the airport: 1time ☎ 086 136 4728; Air Mauritius ☎ 032 436 0007; Emirates ☎ 086 160 6606; Kulula ☎ 086 158 5852; Mango ☎ 086 116 2646; and South African Airways ☎ 086 160 6606.

Destinations Bloemfontein (4 daily; 1hr 5min); Cape Town (18 daily; 2hr 15min); Dubai (2 daily; 8hr 20min); East London (3 daily; 1hr 15min); George (2 daily; 1hr 50min); Johannesburg (around 50 daily; 1hr 10min); Lanseria (5 daily; 1hr 10min); Lusaka (2 daily; 2hr 50min); Nelspruit (2 daily; 1hr 20min); Port Elizabeth (8 daily; 1hr 20min).

BY TRAIN

New Durban Station The Trans-Natal service from Johannesburg and the Trans-Oranje service from Cape Town via Free State arrive at the grim main train station off Masabalala Yengwa Avenue, just north of the main

commercial centre. The best option from here is to take a metered taxi from the rank in front of the bus station that occupies the ground level of the station complex; a ride to the beachfront or Florida Rd costs R50–60.

Destinations Cape Town (Mondays; 38hr); Johannesburg (4 weekly; 12hr 30min); Pietermaritzburg (4 weekly; 2hr 10min).

BY BUS

Intercity buses Intercape (☎ 086 128 7287), Greyhound (☎ 031 334 9702), Translux (☎ 031 361 7670) and other intercity buses arrive at and depart from the bus station attached to the New Durban station complex. The Margate Mini Coach (☎ 039 312 1406) from the South Coast pulls in here, as well as outside domestic departures at King Shaka International Airport. The Umhlanga Explorer minibus shuttle from Umhlanga Rocks (☎ 031 561 2860) drops off at a number of points in Durban, including the airport and opposite Tourist Junction (see opposite) in the city centre.

Destinations Ballito (daily; 45min); Bloemfontein (3 daily; 7hr); Cape Town (6 daily; 22hr); East London (2 daily; 9hr); Grahamstown (3 daily; 12hr); Harrismith (13 daily; 4hr 30min); Jeffrey's Bay (daily; 15hr 45min); Johannesburg (21 daily; 10hr); Knysna (3 daily; 17hr 30min); Ladysmith (3 daily; 3hr 30min); Margate (3 daily; 2hr); Melmoth (daily; 4hr); Mossel Bay (2 daily; 19hr 40min);

DURBAN'S NEW STREET NAMES

Many of Durban's main thoroughfares have been renamed to better reflect the cultural balance in the new South Africa. Well-known Durban streets, such as Point Road and West Street, now bear the names of famous and not-so-famous people who have contributed in one way or another to the democratization of South African society. However, this has been a controversial process. Some Durbanites question the merits of naming streets after foreigners such as Che Guevara and Samora Machel, and the changes have been challenged in court. Despite this, most of the proposed changes have been made and are reflected on new street signs around the city. In practice, people still commonly use the old names, and even taxi drivers might not know the new ones, so on the maps in this guide, we have given the new name followed by the old name in brackets. You can pick up a list of the affected streets, along with their new names, at Tourist Junction (see opposite).

Pietermaritzburg (18 daily; 2hr 15min); Plettenberg Bay (3 daily; 15hr 30min); Port Elizabeth (3 daily; 13hr 30min); Port Shepstone (6 daily; 1hr 30min); Pretoria (17 daily; 11hr 30min); Richards Bay (daily; 2hr 30min); Sedgefield (3 daily; 18hr); Umtata (daily; 6hr); Vryheid (daily; 6hr).

Baz Bus (☎086 122 9287, ⓦbazbus.com) stops at most of the Durban backpacker hostels. For more about Baz Bus routes, see p.49.

Destinations: Amphitheatre (4 weekly; 5hr); Chintsa (4 weekly; 10hr); Coffee Bay (4 weekly; 7hr); East London (4 weekly; 11hr); Johannesburg (4 weekly; 10hr); Kokstad (4 weekly; 4hr); Mthatha (4 weekly; 7hr); Pietermaritzburg (4 weekly; 2hr); Port Alfred (4 weekly; 11hr); Port Elizabeth (4 weekly; 15hr); Port Shepstone (4 weekly; 3hr); Pretoria (4 weekly; 11hr); Umtentweni (4 weekly; 3hr); Umzumbe (4 weekly; 2hr); Warner Beach (4 weekly; 1hr).

INFORMATION

Tourist information The most obvious port of call for information is the central Tourist Junction at Old Station Building, 160 Monty Naicker Rd (Mon–Fri 8am–5pm, Sat 9am–2pm; ☎031 366 7516, ⓦdurbanexperience.co.za), which houses the province's excellent tourist bureau Tourism KwaZulu-Natal (ⓦkzn.org.za). Durban Africa (the city's tourist bureau) is based at 90 Florida Rd (daily 8am–5pm; ☎031 322 4164), along with the KZN Wildlife and South African National Parks booking offices. There is another well-equipped tourist office at uShaka Marine World on the beachfront (daily 9am–9pm; ☎031 337 8099), and an excellent tourist information desk in the arrivals terminal at King Shaka international airport (daily 7am–9pm; ☎031 322 6046).

GETTING AROUND

By car The easiest way to explore Durban is by car. The city's freeways are well signposted and, with careful map-reading and advance planning, getting around is straightforward. There are several car rental companies in Durban, including Avis (☎032 436 7800), Budget (☎032 436 5500), Europcar (☎032 436 9500), Hertz (☎032 436 0300) and Tempest (☎032 436 9800); all are based at the airport, while Avis also has a downtown office at the *Royal Hotel* (☎031 310 9700), and Budget has an office at 50 Florence Nzama St (☎031 337 3731). The most convenient and central car parks are those at Pine Arcade, at the west end of Monty Naicker Rd, and in the Workshop Mall.

By bus Durban's most useful urban transport is the cheap and regular bus system operated by Mynah, which covers the central districts, including the city centre, the beachfront, the Berea and Florida Rd. If you want to get to the more far-flung suburbs, the Aqualine buses are quite functional, although slightly the worse for wear. For information about times and routes for all of these companies call ☎031 309 3250, or go to the bus depot on Monty Naicker Rd, which is adjacent to the Workshop Mall and is the starting point for most local bus services (you can also pick up bus schedules from the tourist office at uShaka Marine World). One useful route is Mynah's Musgrave/Mitchell Park Circle buses, which either go along Florida Rd (on the Mitchell Park Circle bus) or Musgrave Rd (on the Musgrave Rd bus). For travel within the city centre, the Durban People Mover (☎031 309 2731) operates modern buses along three routes linking the beachfront (from the Moses Mabhida Stadium to uShaka Marine World) with the centre as far west as the botanic gardens. A ride on the People Mover costs R4, while a card worth ten trips on a Mynah bus costs R24.

By minibus Minibuses cover the entire city, and run with greater frequency than the buses. You can catch a minibus in the city centre going to Florida Rd from Field St, between Anton Lembele and Dr Pixley Kaseme sts.

By taxi Reputable taxi companies in central Durban include Eagle Taxis (☎031 337 8333), Mozzies (☎086 066 9943) and Zippy (☎031 202 7067).

By bike Cycling is safe along the beachfront, but hazardous on any major road and not really recommended.

ACCOMMODATION

Durban's high-rise **accommodation** is concentrated along the beachfront and in the city centre, both convenient locations but less salubrious at night – taking taxis to your doorstep is recommended after dark. An increasingly popular alternative is the Berea residential area west and north of the centre, which boasts the best backpacker hostels in town, as well as guesthouses and B&Bs housed in beautifully renovated old homes. Durban also has a selection of **township homestays** where you can experience the warmth of urban Zulu hospitality. Durban Africa at Tourist Junction (see above) can arrange your accommodation as well as transport into the townships.

CITY CENTRE

Banana Backpackers 61 Monty Naicker Rd, 1st floor, Ambassador House ☎031 368 4062, ⓦbananaback packers.co.za; map pp.358–359. Simple dorms and doubles in an old Durban building that has seen better days, but there is a congenial courtyard with a plastic pool and it's very close to the beach, Tourist Junction and the Pine St bus terminal. Dorm R110, double R320

The Royal Hotel 267 Anton Lembede St ☎031 333 6000, ⓦtheroyal.co.za; map pp.358–359. Once

5

DURBAN TOURS AND HARBOUR RIDES

One of the safest and easiest ways to get under the skin of ethnic Durban is to take a **guided tour**. Standard three-hour tours cost around R400 per person and upwards of R1000 for a full day; we've listed a few operators below.

Isle of Capri Cruises ☎031 305 3099, ⓦisleofcapri .co.za. Harbour trips leave daily on the hour (10am–4pm) from Wilson's Wharf (R150).

Markets of Warwick ☎031 309 3880, ⓦmarketsofwarwick.co.za. A variety of fascinating walking tours that take in the multitude of markets around the Warwick Triangle, including the early morning market, the bead market, the bovine head market (where you can sample this Zulu delicacy) and many others.

Street Scene Tours ☎031 321 5079, ⓦstreetscenetours.co.za. One-day and overnight township and Durban tours with an emphasis on the

"local" experience, which can include anything from playing football with township kids to trawling through hip vintage clothing stores or trying your hand at brewing your own beer.

Tekweni Eco Tours ☎082 303 9112, ⓦtekweniecotours.co.za. Durban city tours and visits to Zulu villages in the Valley of a Thousand Hills, for a Zulu meal and beer, traditional dancing and an encounter with a traditional healer.

Walkabout Tours book at Tourist Junction. A good way to explore Durban's Indian areas is by joining one of two daily walking tours organized by the tourist office (R100 per person).

Durban's finest hotel, but now feels a little old-fashioned. Smack in the centre of town and used mainly by business visitors, it's worth considering if you can afford five-star splendour and fancy the liveried service. Discounts are often available. R1342

Sun 1 Directly opposite the bus station, near the corner of Masabalala Yengwa Ave and Jeff Taylor Crescent ☎031 301 1551, ⓦtsogosun.co.za; map pp.358–359. No-frills chain hotel that's tremendously convenient if you arrive late at night by train or bus. Rooms sleep up to three people. R460

BEACHFRONT

Blue Waters 175 OR Tambo Parade ☎031 327 7000, ⓦbluewatershotel.co.za; map pp.358–359. A delightful 1950s Durban landmark in a period building with a tiled façade, opposite Battery Beach and with great views onto the oceanfront. There's also a pleasant café on the wooden deck out front, good for watching the beach-going crowds. R1094

Garden Court – Marine Parade 167 OR Tambo Parade ☎031 337 2231, ⓦtsogosunhotels.com; map pp.358–359. All the rooms face the sea (those on the top floors are best), and the view from the thirtieth-floor swimming pool is fabulous. A cool through-breeze offers respite against the summer heat, and a back entrance across from Victoria Park provides handy access to the city centre. R1199

Happy Hippo Backpackers Lodge 222 Mahatma Gandhi Rd ☎031 368 7181, ⓦhappy-hippo.info; map pp.358–359. Extremely spacious hostel a stone's throw from uShaka Marine World and the beach, in a renovated old factory with a decidedly industrial feel. The nice rooftop bar makes it popular with a younger crowd in the mood for a party. Dorm R150, room R400

Protea Hotel Edward OR Tambo Parade, at Seaview Rd ☎031 337 3681, ⓦproteahotels.com; map pp.358–359. Crystal chandeliers, a colonial-style ambience, sea-view balconies and a ladies' bar leading onto a cool veranda make this Art Deco mansion the *grande dame* of the beachfront. R1450

Silversands 16 Erskine Terrace, near the Addington Hospital ☎031 332 1140, ⓔsilversands@worldonline .co.za; map pp.358–359. These clean, comfortable and spacious self-catering apartments sleeping four to eight people are among the best value on the beach, especially for families. R912

THE BEREA

Audacia Manor 11 Sir Arthur Rd ☎031 303 9520, ⓦafricanpridehotels.com; map pp.364–365. Luxurious guesthouse in a restored colonial mansion. The restaurant and bar on the veranda boast gorgeous sea views, and some of the rooms feature outdoor showers and jacuzzi baths. R2250

The Benjamin 141 Florida Rd ☎031 303 4233, ⓦbenjamin.co.za; map pp.364–365. A professionally run boutique hotel in an elegant old house that tends to attract corporate guests, although its location makes it perfect for tourists as well. There's a pool, free wi-fi and safe parking, and rooms are occasionally cheaper at weekends; the ones facing the courtyard tend to be quieter. R1255

★**The Elephant House** 745 Peter Mokaba Rd ☎031 208 9580 or ☎082 4522 574, ⓔelephanthouse@ mweb.co.za; map pp.364–365. If you like to feel as though you're staying in someone's home, this is one of the best B&Bs in South Africa. The home in question is the oldest in Durban, built in 1847 as a hunting lodge and oozing with character. The extremely kind and generous

5

hosts love showing travellers around. Highly recommended and excellent value for money. <u>R450/person</u>

Essenwood House 630 Steven Dlamini Rd ☎ 031 207 4547, ⓦ essenwoodhouse.co.za; map pp.364–365. This grand house with a sumptuous garden has seven large, comfortable rooms (the upstairs ones have sea views), an attractive pool and a good-natured host. <u>R1150</u>

Gibela Lodge 119 Ninth Ave, Morningside ☎ 031 303 6291, ⓦ gibelabackpackers.co.za; map pp.364–365. Quiet hostel with a restful atmosphere, tastefully decorated rooms and single-sex dorms; there's even a small pool. The owner has tremendous knowledge of Durban and the rest of the province. There's a strict no-smoking policy and no check-in after 8pm. Rates include a good breakfast. Dorm <u>R240</u>, double <u>R630</u>

Goble Palms 120 Smiso Nkwanyana Rd ☎ 031 312 2598, ⓦ goblepalms.co.za; map pp.364–365. This house, built in 1900, features a sunny patio with sea views, a pool and an intimate on-site English-style pub, as well as pretty, restful rooms. <u>R895</u>

★**Hippo Hide Lodge and Backpackers** 2 Jesmond Rd ☎ 031 207 4366 or 082 784 1816, ⓦ hippohide.co.za; map pp.364–365. A stunning, imaginative and cosy hostel in a beautiful tropical garden with a rock pool. It's clean and quiet, with a guesthouse feel, and conveniently located on the Mynah bus route to the centre (10min). One of the doubles is en suite, and there are also log cabins. Dorm <u>R140</u>, double <u>R380</u>

Nomad's Backpackers 70 Steven Dlamini Rd ☎ 031 202 9709, ⓦ nomadsbp.com; map pp.364–365. A short walk from the Musgrave Centre, this chilled-out hostel is good for nonsensical conversations at the bar or around the pool. The dorms are tidy and nicely decorated, though the lounge is a bit dark and some of the bunks are triples. Meals available on request. Dorm <u>R130</u>, double <u>R350</u>

★**Rosetta House** 126 Rosetta Rd ☎ 031 303 6180, ⓦ rosettahouse.co.za; map pp.364–365. The fact that there are just four rooms, all warmly decorated, lends an intimate feel to this cosy guesthouse. There's a lush and tranquil garden and the hosts maintain a high standard of service, serving one of the best breakfasts in town. <u>R990</u>

Tekweni Backpackers 169 Ninth Ave ☎ 031 303 1433, ⓦ tekwenibackpackers.co.za; map pp.364–365. This large hostel near Florida Rd is spread over three houses and features plenty of communal areas, a pool and bar. Braais and other social gatherings cater to a young, energetic clientele. Monthly accommodation is also available. Dorm <u>R140</u>, double <u>R470</u>

WESTVILLE

Our Little Family 35 Menston Rd ☎ 083 777 1245; map p.356. A family home in an old farmhouse stocked with historical maps and fascinating military antiques from the Boer wars, offering seven homey rooms of varying sizes. Most are self-catering and there are several braai areas, though the friendly hosts also prepare meals on request. Ten minutes from town by car. <u>R550</u>

EATING

Eating out is a favourite pastime in Durban, and although all types of cooking are found here, **Indian food** is what the city excels at – hardly surprising for a place with one of the largest Indian populations outside Asia. The Indian takeaways of the city centre are good places to try *bunny chow* – Durban's big contribution to the national fast-food scene – and the not-dissimilar *rotis* (Indian bread) stuffed with curries. **Shisanyama** outlets at the African markets and around the taxi ranks offer hunks of meat cooked over an open fire. Downtown Durban has been largely colonized by South Africa's ubiquitous chain eateries, though there are still a few good sit-down options worth trying. For a more refined dining experience, the Berea has the city's best and most diverse range of restaurants.

BEACHFRONT

Cargo Hold uShaka Marine World ☎ 031 328 8065; map pp.358–359. A rather staid international menu – half of which consists of fish dishes like prawns and kingklip (R165) – although eating in front of the giant fish tank is a thrill. Daily noon–3pm & 6pm–late.

★**Moyo** uShaka Marine World ☎ 031 332 0606; map pp.358–359. A large, breezy dining room overlooking the sea where you can order a great range of African specialities, from Moroccan *tajines* and Senegalese chicken *yassa* (R139) to Tanzanian fish curry and lamb from the Karoo. Light meals and drinks are available at the end of the pier opposite the restaurant; a good idea at sunset. Mon–Fri 11am–11pm, Sat & Sun 8am–11pm.

THE HARBOUR AREA

Afriportico BAT Arts Centre, Margaret Mncadi Ave ☎ 031 332 0451; map pp.358–359. This lively venue dishes up African fusion food like samp and beans, and ox tripe with steamed Zulu bread, as well as sandwiches for around R30. Regular jazz on Sundays and a great terrace overlooking the harbour add to the appeal. A good place to meet the locals. Daily 10am–late.

Roma Revolving Restaurant John Ross House, Margaret Mncadi Ave ☎ 031 337 6707; map pp.358–359. No visitor to Durban should miss the view from the *Roma* as it revolves above the city. The international menu includes tasty mussel starters (R47) and hit-and-miss Italian specialities like gnocchi and veal dishes, plus an excellent dessert trolley. You pay for the view as much as for

5

EATING INDIAN IN DURBAN

Inexpensive Indian **takeaways** – all open very early and usually shut by 5pm – abound in the city centre. *Little Gujarat*, 107 Dr Goonam St (Mon–Fri 8.30am–4pm, Sat 8.30am–1.30pm; ☎031 305 3148; map pp. 358–359) is noted for its vegetarian food such as potato or paneer curries (around R20 for a large), pakoras and bhajis. Otherwise, the takeaway *Oriental* at the Workshop Mall (Mon–Thurs 8am–9pm, Fri–Sun 8am–10pm; ☎031 304 5110; map pp. 358–359) serves up a hotchpotch of fare – delicious Indian-style *shawarmas*, bunny chows (R40) and curries. If you're hankering for something much slicker in the heart of town, head to *Ulundi* at *The Royal Hotel* (Mon 10am–6pm, Tues–Sat 10am–late; ☎031 333 6174; see p.369) for tasty curries and bunny chows (R40) served in a stylish and contemporary dining room.

the food; reservations required. Mon–Thurs 6–10.30pm, Fri & Sat noon–2.30pm & 6–10.30pm.

THE BEREA

★**9th Avenue Bistro** Shop 2, Avonmore Centre, Ninth Ave Morningside ☎031 312 9134; map pp.364–365. One of the most highly regarded restaurants in Durban, serving refined French-inspired dishes – for example, free-range duck in a honey-cinnamon jus (R148). Mon & Sat 6–9.30pm, Tues–Fri noon–2.30pm & 6–9.30pm.

Blue Zoo Garden Restaurant 6 Nimmo Rd, Morningside ☎031 303 2265; map pp.364–365. The varied and unusual menu features delicious lamb shank in a port wine sauce (R105), steaks, fish, and salads with mango-chilli dressing. Beautifully located in Mitchell Park and great for kids. Daily 8am–4.30pm.

Butcher Boys 170 Florida Rd ☎031 312 8248; map pp.364–365. A long-time favourite in Berea, this grill house is known for its steaks, but it also offers a wide range of other meats such as rack of lamb (R175), roasted marrow bones and cuts of game meat when available. Mon–Thurs noon–2.30pm & 6–10pm, Fri noon–3pm & 6–10.30pm, Sat 6–10.30pm, Sun noon–3pm & 6–9.30pm.

★**Delfi Taverna** 386 Lilian Ngoyi Rd, Morningside ☎031 312 7032; map pp.364–365. This cosy restaurant boasts excellent, authentic Greek dishes such as *kleffiko* (lamb shank) and *moussaka* (R80), and has a wonderfully congenial atmosphere created by friendly staff and plenty of regular customers – always a good sign. Wed–Mon noon–3pm & 6pm–late.

★**Freedom Café** 37–43 St Mary's Ave, Greyville ☎031 309 4453; map pp.364–365. An artsy café with a decidedly hipster vibe, located in and around a collection of creatively converted containers, where you can sip your milkshake out of a jam jar and nibble on home-made baked goodies. The food, which ranges from kale salad to New York-style hot dogs (R60), is wonderful, and the breakfasts are highly recommended. Sun–Thurs 7am–4pm, Fri & Sat 7am–9pm.

Indian Connection 485 Lilian Ngoyi Rd ☎031 312 1440; map pp.364–365. Set in one of the Berea's dignified old homes, this place offers North Indian specialties such as

lamb vindaloo (R95) and kormas, as well as a tasty variety of other curries. Daily 11am–3pm & 5.30–10.30pm.

La Bella Corner of Steven Dlamini and St Thomas roads ☎031 201 9176; map pp.364–365. Housed in a former power station, with outdoor seating that's good for a coffee or a stone oven-cooked pizza, with imaginative toppings such as roast lamb (R85). There's also a pub at the back. Mon–Sat 7am–midnight, Sun 7.30am–11pm.

Marco's 45 Lilian Ngoyi Rd ☎031 303 3078; map pp.364–365. This colourful and authentic little Italian restaurant prides itself on its home-made pastas, wood-fired pizzas and wonderful gnocchis (from R75), and is very popular with the locals. Its sister restaurant, *Mama Luciana's*, is in the same building with an entrance on Florida Rd. Daily noon–11pm.

Market 40 Gladys Mazibuko Rd ☎031 309 8581; map pp.364–365. With its shady courtyard sheltered from the street and sparkling with candles in the evening, this trendy bistro is the perfect spot to enjoy luxurious breakfasts, or a fresh and wholesome meal such as roasted vegetable couscous salad or a sesame lentil burger (R86). There's live music on Fridays & Sundays. Mon 7.30am–4pm, Tues–Fri 7.30am–9.30pm, Sat 8.30am–late, Sun 8am–4pm.

Palki 225 Musgrave Rd, Musgrave ☎031 201 0019; map pp.364–365. The South African representative of a chain of restaurants based in the East, this has mouthwatering, authentic dishes mainly from South India, including *pooris* and *dosas* (from R39). Vegetarians are well catered for. Daily 11am–3pm & 6–10pm.

★**Spiga d'Oro** 200 Florida Rd, Morningside ☎031 303 9511; map pp.364–365. Justifiably popular Italian restaurant serving several types of pasta dishes (around R70) and pizza, with outside tables on Florida Rd giving the place a European feel. The friendly and efficient service adds to the appeal. Sun–Wed 7am–10pm, Thurs–Sat 7am–midnight.

Unity Café Corner of Silverton and Vause roads ☎031 201 3470; map pp.364–365. A buzzing gastro-pub dishing up hearty yet sophisticated fare such as mushroom and blue cheese soup, or butternut and gorgonzola risotto (R75): also offers micro-brews on tap. Mon–Sat noon–late.

5

GAY DURBAN
Durban's **gay scene** is fairly well developed, although nothing like what you'll find in Cape Town. Among the smattering of gay or gay-friendly nightspots, *The Lounge*, 226 Mathews Meyiwa Rd, Morningside (☎031 303 9022; map pp.364–365), is one popular meeting place.

DRINKING, NIGHTLIFE AND ENTERTAINMENT
Durban has a healthy nightlife scene, with a decent number of bars, clubs and music venues. For entertainment and nightlife listings, the *Mercury* is the better of Durban's two English-language dailies. Durban Africa also publishes a monthly events brochure, available from tourist offices.

BARS AND CLUBS
Billy The Bum's 504 Lilian Ngoyi Rd, Morningside ☎031 303 1988; map pp.364–365. Acrobatic barmen juggle bottles while mixing imaginative cocktails at this popular singles' watering hole. Burgers (R60), wraps and the like are also available. Mon–Sat noon till late.

Dropkick Murphy's 219 Florida Rd ☎031 825 1858; map pp.364–365. A friendly pub perennially packed with beer-lovers attracted by the healthy range of craft brews on offer, many made in and around Durban (R45/pint). There's food as well, including Guiness and beef pie (R95), but it's the beer that's the star of the show. Mon–Thurs noon–midnight, Fri–Sun noon–2am.

The Origin 9 Clark Rd ☎031 201 9959; map pp.358–359. A long-time favourite on Durban's hard-core clubbing scene, this nightclub in an industrial area near the university attracts serious dancers with its multiple dance floors and DJs spinning mostly house music. The area can be unsafe at night, so take a taxi. Entrance R60. Sat 8pm–late, sometimes open Fri as well.

Skyybar 25 Silver Ave, Morningside ☎031 313 7424; map pp.364–365. This flashy club has a fabulous outdoor deck with views of the city, an emphasis on house music and a largely middle-class black clientele. Entrance R50. Fri & Sat 8pm–4am.

LIVE MUSIC
You'll find plenty of live indie music on offer in Durban, much of it derivative of European or North American trends. More interesting, but less accessible, are some of the Zulu forms such as *iscathamiya* and *maskanda*. On the jazz scene, the city's most indigenous offering is a spicy combination of American mixed with township jazz and Zulu forms. As for classical music, the best place to hear concerts by the **KwaZulu-Natal Philharmonic** (☎031 369 9438, ⓦkznpo.co.za) is at a sundowner concert held in the Botanic Gardens (see p.366). Check their website for the programme.

The BAT Centre Next to the harbour at 42 Maritime Place ☎031 332 0451, ⓦbatcentre.co.za. This artsy cultural centre is your best bet for live concerts. The Centre's *Afriportico* restaurant (see p.371) also has jazz sundowners on Sundays.

Moyo uShaka Marine World ☎031 332 0606. Live African music and drumming on Friday and Saturday evenings at this excellent restaurant (see p.371).

The Rainbow 23 Stanfield Lane in Pinetown, northwest of Durban ☎031 702 9161. A long-established restaurant offering monthly Sunday-lunchtime performances ranging from Afro-fusion to jazz, and more regular weekday sessions by up-and-coming bands.

THEATRE AND CINEMA
The best and most convenient cinemas are the multiscreen complexes at the Musgrave Centre, the Workshop Mall in the city centre and the Suncoast Casino on the beachfront. The only place to see art-house movies is at Gateway Mall (see p.381) in Umhlanga Rocks.

Elizabeth Sneddon Theatre University of KwaZulu-Natal, Mazisi Kunene Rd ☎031 260 2296. A modern venue for university and visiting productions.

Playhouse Drama Theatre 231 Anton Lembede St ☎031 369 9555, ⓦplayhousecompany.com. A mock-Tudor building that tends to host middle-of-the-road productions, but also sees performances by the resident progressive Playhouse Dance Company.

OUTDOOR ACTIVITIES AND SPECTATOR SPORTS
Birdwatching, a major activity in the green fringes of the city, is being aided by the Durban Metropolitan Open Space System (DMOSS), a project linking all the city parks via narrow green corridors. Promising spots include the Manor Gardens area; the Botanic Gardens; the Berea; Burman Bush, to the north of the city; Pigeon Valley, below the University of KwaZulu-Natal; the Umgeni River Mouth; Virginia Bush, on the road to Umhlanga Rocks; and the Hawaan Forest in Umhlanga, where the spotted thrush and green coucal have been seen.

Golf is a popular and rewarding activity in Durban. Enclosed within the tracks of the Greyville Race Course (see below), the Royal Durban Golf Club (☎031 309 1530, ⓦroyaldurban.co.za; R270 for eighteen holes) is notable for its unusual setting, while the Durban Country Club on Isiah Ntshangase Rd (☎031 313 1777, ⓦdcclub.co.za;

5

R425 for eighteen holes) is considered by many to be the finest course in South Africa.

Scuba diving is an obvious and pleasurable activity in KwaZulu-Natal's subtropical waters, but is somewhat limited immediately around Durban. The best diving sites are Vetches Pier at the southern tip of the beachfront, and Blood Reef at the tip of the Bluff (opposite the Point). Scuba-diving courses can be arranged through Underwater World, 251 Mahatma Gandhi Rd (☎031 332 5820, ⓦunderwaterworld.co.za); a full six-day internationally recognized NAUI or PADI course costs R3250, including use of the main gear you'll need.

Kitesurfing has started to gain a following in Durban and you can take lessons on the calm waters of La Mercy Lagoon (R900 for a half-day intro course) with Kitesports, 1 Umdloti Centre on South Beach Rd (☎031 568 2644, ⓦkitesports.co.za).

Surfing Given Durban's seafront location, watersports are extremely popular, none more so than surfing. Night surfing competitions draw enormous crowds, as does the annual Mr Price Pro (formerly the Gunston 500), which, after the Rip Curl Pro at Bells Beach, Australia, is the world's longest-running professional surfing competition and is held in Durban every July. The favourite spot for surfers is North Beach, while a good place to pick up gear is the Safari Surf Shop, 6 Milne St (☎031 337 4230, ⓦsafarisurf.com), where Spider Murphy, South Africa's top board-shaper, will custom-build a world-class board for much less than a comparable order would cost in Europe or North America. Ocean Ventures at uShaka Marine World (☎086 100 1138, ⓦoceanventures.co.za), offers surfing lessons with experienced instructors (R100/ hr, plus R100 for board rental).

Swimming Durban's largest pool is the heated King's Park Olympic Swimming Pool on Masabalala Yengwa Ave, between Sandile Thusi and Battery Beach rds in Stamford Hill (☎031 312 0404). The seawater Rachel Finlayson Baths on OR Tambo Parade are handy if you're staying near the beachfront. Entry to both is R8.

Cricket The Kingsmead Cricket Ground in the centre (☎031 335 4200) is the principal venue for local and international cricket matches and is home to the provincial cricket team, the Sunfoil Dolphins.

Horse-racing The horse-racing season runs from May to August and centres around the Greyville Race Course, Avondale Rd, Greyville (☎031 314 1500). The annual Vodacom Durban July (ⓦdurbanjuly.info), which, as the name suggests, takes place during July, is South Africa's premier horse-racing event, drawing bets from across the length and breadth of the country.

Rugby You'll have plenty of opportunity to watch rugby in season at Kings Park Stadium, Isiah Ntshangase Rd, Stamford Hill (☎031 308 8400), home to the local Sharks. The spectacular new Moses Mabhida Stadium (see below; ☎031 582 8242) is just next door.

SHOPPING

As one of South Africa's major cities, Durban is a good place to pick up general supplies and local books and records. But it's for **crafts and curios** that it scores particularly highly, with a dazzling range of handmade Zulu goods (see box opposite). The best places to browse for crafts are in the downtown markets, the weekend flea markets and the specialist shops around the city. Durban is littered with shopping malls of varying sizes, the two largest being the central Workshop Mall (see p.360) and the more upmarket Musgrave Centre in Musgrave.

BOOKS

Adams & Co Shop 223 Musgrave Centre, Musgrave ☎031 319 4450; map pp.364–365. Durban's oldest bookshop has an excellent selection of books on the history of Durban and KwaZulu-Natal. There's another branch in the city centre at 341 Dr Pixley Kaseme St (map pp.358–359). Mon–Sat 9am–6pm, Sun 9am–5pm.

★**Ike's Books & Collectables** 48a Florida Rd, Morningside ☎031 303 9214; map pp.364–365. A fascinating secondhand bookshop with an interesting range of items covering KwaZulu-Natal's history. Speciality areas include Africana and the Anglo-Boer War, travel and exploration, and South African politics. Mon–Fri 10am–5pm, Sat 9am–2pm.

EXTREME SPORTS

Durban's newest architectural landmark, the **Moses Mabhida Stadium**, may have been designed with the 2010 football World Cup in mind, but city authorities seem determined to keep it from gathering dust. These days there are a number of activities on offer at the stadium, including mounting the striking 106m central arch by **cable car** for a 360-degree view of the city (daily 9am–5pm; R55), or strapping on safety equipment and scaling the arch on foot (Sat & Sun 10am, 1pm & 4pm; R90). Adrenaline junkies can also try the **Big Rush Big Swing**, billed as the world's tallest swing, which sends you plunging off one side of the stadium to swoop across in a 220m arc (daily 9am–4pm; R695; ⓦbigrush.co.za). For more information check ⓦmmstadium.com.

ZULU CRAFTS AND CURIOS

Durban's huge range of galleries, craft shops and markets makes it one of the best places in the country to pick up **Zulu crafts**. Traditional works include functional items such as woven beer strainers and grass brooms, and basketry that can be extremely beautiful. Other traditional items are beadwork, pottery and Zulu regalia, of which *assegais* (spears), shields, leather kilts and drums are a few examples.

   The availability of cheap plastic crockery and enamelware has significantly eroded the production of traditional ceramics and woven containers for domestic use. Even so, the effects of urbanization have led to the use of new materials, or new ways of using old materials. Nowadays you'll find beautifully decorated black-and-white sandals made from recycled rubber tyres, wildly colourful baskets woven from telephone wire, and *sjamboks* (whips) decorated with bright insulation tape. On the more frivolous side, industrial materials have been married with rural life or rural materials with industrial life. Attractive tin boxes made from flattened oil cans, chickens constructed from sheet plastic, and aircraft and little 4WD vehicles carved from wood are just some of the results.

CRAFTS AND CURIOS

African Art Centre 94 Florida Rd, Morningside ☎031 312 3804, ⓦafriart.org.za; map pp.364–365. A gallery and shop where many rural artists sell their work, well worth visiting for its traditional and modern Zulu and Xhosa beadwork, beaded dolls, wire sculptures, woodcuts and tapestries. Mon–Fri 8.30am–5pm, Sat 9am–3pm.

BAT Centre Off Margaret Mncadi Ave, city centre ☎031 332 0451; map pp.358–359. A grouping of several shops selling Zulu and other African crafts, with clothing and jewellery well represented. Mon–Fri 8am–4.30pm, Sat 9am–2pm.

KZNSA Gallery Shop KZNSA Gallery, Bulwer Rd, Berea ☎031 277 1705; map pp.364–365. This menagerie of contemporary hand-crafted goods includes a wonderful selection of functional art, including pewter cutlery, etchings and paintings. Tues–Fri 9am–5pm, Sat 9am–4pm, Sun 9am–3pm.

MARKETS

Amphitheatre Fleamarket OR Tambo Parade, beachfront; map pp.358–359. Crafts and beadwork sold by both local traders and by merchants from as far afield as Zimbabwe, Malawi and Kenya. Sun 9am–5pm.

City Market Between Julius Nyerere Ave and Market Rd, Warwick Triangle; map pp.358–359. Stock up with the cheapest fruit and veg in town, from aubergines and jackfruit to betel nut for red-stained lips and a two-minute rush. Daily dawn–dusk.

Essenwood Craft Market Berea Park, Steven Dlamini Rd, Musgrave ☎031 208 1264, ⓦwww.essenwoodmarket.com; map pp.364–365. Upmarket stalls in a beautiful park setting. Sat 9am–2pm.

Victoria Street Market Corner of Dennis Hurley and Joseph Nduli streets, city centre; map pp.358–359. Traders here sell all manner of stuff, from curios and jewellery to spices with labels like "mother-in-law exterminator". Touristy, but fun nonetheless. Daily dawn–dusk.

DIRECTORY

Consulates Canada, 81 Richefond Circle, Umhlanga (☎031 536 8214); Lesotho, West Guard House, corner of Dr Pixley Kaseme and Dorothy Nyembe streets, city centre (☎031 307 2168); US, Old Mutual Centre, 31st floor, 303 Dr Pixley Kaseme St, city centre (☎031 305 7600).

Currency exchange The First National Bank bureau de change, 306 Dr Pixley Kaseme St, city centre, will cash Visa travellers' cheques without commission (Mon–Fri 9am–3.30pm, Sat 8.30am–12.30pm). American Express, Richefond Circle, Umhlanga (Mon–Fri 8.30am–4.30pm, Sat 8.30am–noon; ☎031 566 8650), replaces lost cheques and changes money.

Emergencies AA ☎083 84322.

Hospitals and medical centres The main state hospital is the Addington, Erskine Terrace, South Beach (☎031 327 2000), which offers a 24hr emergency ward. A better

alternative is Entabeni Private Hospital, 148 Mazisi Kunene Rd, Berea (☎031 204 1300), which has a casualty unit and can also treat minor conditions, but you'll have to pay a deposit on admission and settle up before leaving town. Travel Doctor, 45 Braam Fischer Rd, International Convention Centre, city centre (☎031 360 1122, ⓦdurbantraveldoctor.co.za), is a clinic offering travel information, as well as advice on malaria and the necessary jabs for visiting African countries to the north.

Internet access Copy Shop, West Tower, Dr Pixley Kaseme Rd (Mon–Fri 8am–4pm).

Pharmacies Sparkport, corner of Anton Lembede and Dr Yusuf Dadoo sts (Mon–Sat 7.30am–8.30pm, Sun 9am–7pm; ☎031 304 9767).

Post The main post office, on the corner of Dorothy Nyembe and Dr Pixley Kaseme sts, has a poste restante and enquiry desk (Mon–Fri 8am–5pm, Sat 8am–1pm).

5

The South Coast

The **South Coast**, the 160km seaboard stretching from Durban to Port Edward on the Eastern Cape border, is a ribbon of seaside suburbs linked for most of its length by the **N2** and **R102** roads, running side by side. In the winter months it's much warmer and sunnier along this stretch than on any of the beaches between here and Cape Town. Away from the sea, the land is very hilly and green, dotted with sugar-cane fields, banana plantations and palm and pecan nut trees. Note that many beaches shelve steeply into the powerful surf, so only swim where it's indicated as safe.

Margate, 133km from Durban, is the transport and holiday hub of the area, with plenty of resorts lying to the east and west of it. The highlight of the South Coast, however, lies just inland, where **Oribi Gorge Nature Reserve** has lovely forest hikes, breathtaking views and good-value accommodation.

ARRIVAL AND DEPARTURE
THE SOUTH COAST

By car Driving from Durban, head for the N2, which runs south from the city as far as Port Shepstone before heading inland to Kokstad. From Port Shepstone to Southbroom, the South Coast Toll Rd is even faster and less congested.

By bus Margate Mini Coach (5 Jenkins Drive, Margate ☎ 039 312 1406) has three to four daily bus services departing from King Shaka International Airport (domestic arrivals) and

calling at the Durban bus station (Greyhound terminal), Amanzimtoti (prebooked only), Scottburgh (prebooked only), Hibberdene, Port Shepstone (Shell Garage), Margate (Maroela Flats on Marine Parade), Sam Lameer (prebooked only) and Wild Coast Sun Casino (prebooked only). The Baz Bus between Durban and Port Elizabeth calls at Umzumbe, Umtentweni and Port Shepstone four days a week.

Aliwal Shoal

The resorts that line the first 50km of coastline south of Durban – places such as **Amanzimtoti**, 27km down – feel more like beachside suburbs than towns in their own right. For diving enthusiasts, however, the faded town of **UMKOMAAS**, 20km further down the coast from Amanzimtoti, is the perfect point to set out for **Aliwal Shoal**, a scattered reef quite close to the shore and one of Southern Africa's top **dive sites**. Rewards for experienced divers include sightings of ragged-tooth and tiger sharks, and the chance to go wreck-diving to three stunning sites. The ideal time to dive is between June and October, when visibility is at its best.

ACTIVITIES
ALIWAL SHOAL

Various dive centres organize trips to Aliwal Shoal (expect to pay around R270, plus R220 for equipment rental), as well as PADI-certified four-day Open Water diving courses

(around R3200, includes equipment); try Meridian Dive Centre (☎ 082 894 1625, ⓦ meridiandive.com) or Amatikulu Tours (☎ 039 973 2534, ⓦ amatikulu.com).

ACCOMMODATION

Agulhas House 30 Barrow St, Umkomaas ☎ 039 973 1640, ⓦ agulhashouse.com. Centrally located B&B in a renovated doctor's clinic, whose simple en-suite rooms,

with fridges and private entrances, are set around an attractive pool. They can also arrange dive packages in-house. **R980**

Oribi Gorge Nature Reserve

Daily: Oct–March 5am–7pm; April–Sept 6am–6pm • R10 • ☎ 072 042 9390

A highly scenic area traversed by the fast-flowing Umzimkulu and Umzimkulwana rivers, with cliffs rising from vast chasms and forest, the **Oribi Gorge Nature Reserve**, 21km from Port Shepstone and signposted off the N2, is the South Coast's most compelling attraction. There are numerous idyllic picnic spots on the riverbanks (though avoid swimming here, as bilharzia parasites are present in the water), and waymarked **hikes** ranging from thirty-minute to day-long excursions lead to dizzying lookout points or through the forest. A fine one-hour **walk** starts from the Umzimkulu

---

THE SARDINE RUN

Around June or July, the South Coast is witness to the extraordinary annual migration of millions of **sardines** moving northwards along the coast in massive shoals. They leave their feeding ground off the Southern Cape coast and move up the coast towards Mozambique, followed by about 23,000 dolphins, 100,000 Cape gannets and thousands of sharks and game fish, attracting fishermen from all over the province to join in the jamboree. The shoals appear as dark patches of turbulence in the water, and when they are cornered and driven ashore by game fish, hundreds of people rush into the water either to scoop them out with their hands or to net them. For updates on shoal coordinates and other information of use for sardine-spotting, call the Sardine Hotline on ☎083 913 9495 or visit ⓦshark.co.za.

---

car park, crosses the river and heads immediately up some steps into the forest. You'll only see the river when it opens out dramatically to reveal **Samango Falls** and a perfect little rock-bounded sandy beach.

   Wildlife in the reserve includes bushbuck, common reedbuck and blue and grey duiker, but not oribi, which have left for the succulent shoots of the surrounding sugar-cane plantations. More difficult to see are the shy samango monkeys hiding in the high canopy of the forest, and leopards.

INFORMATION AND ACTIVITIES

ORIBI GORGE NATURE RESERVE

Tourist information KNZ Wildlife has an office at the main gate (daily 8am–12.30pm & 2–4pm; ☎072 042 9390).

Activities There are a few adventure activities on offer in the reserve, all run by Wild 5 (☎082 566 7424, ⓦoribigorge.co.za), which operates from the *Oribi Gorge Hotel* (see below). There's an abseil (R350) with a tough half-hour walk out of the gorge afterwards; a gorge swing that requires you to leap off the top of the Lehrs Falls (R490); a gorge slide (R250), erected 160m above the gorge floor; plus rafting trips down the Umzimkulu River (R550).

ACCOMMODATION

KZN Wildlife huts ☎072 042 9390; book through KZN Wildlife ☎033 845 1000, ⓦwww.kznwildlife.com. The nicest accommodation is in the KZN Wildlife huts, which sleep two to eight people, though you can also camp. The restcamp sits at the head of the Umzimkulwana Gorge, peering into the chasm of Oribi Gorge itself. There's a swimming pool here, and all crockery, cutlery and bedding is provided. Camping R70, huts R330

Oribi Gorge Hotel Some 16km from the restcamp, off the Oribi Flats Rd ☎039 687 0253, ⓦoribigorge.co.za. This colonial-style hotel has spectacular views, including of the famous overhanging rock, and offers spacious rooms, meals to suit most budgets and a pleasant outdoor tea area. R1100

The Hibiscus Coast

The 44km of coast from Port Shepstone to Port Edward has been dubbed the **Hibiscus Coast** because of its luscious, bright gardens, luxury suburbs, beachside developments and attractive caravan parks. It's also known as the **Golf Coast**: there are nine top courses on this short stretch of coastline, and many people come specifically for its golfing opportunities. Although the whole area, centred on Margate, is built up, the Hibiscus Coast gets nicer the further south you go.

Margate and Ramsgate

Some 14km south of Port Shepstone, the brash holiday town of **MARGATE**, with its high-rise apartments, fast-food outlets and ice-cream parlours, offers little in the way of undiscovered coves or hidden beaches, but it's the liveliest town on the South Coast, with the best nightlife. Adjoining Margate to the south, **RAMSGATE** is quieter and slightly more refined – as evidenced by the Gaze Gallery (daily 8am–5pm; free; ☎039 314 4011), attached to the restaurant *Waffle House* (see p.380), just across the lagoon coming from Margate, which displays some reputable work by local artists.

5

Southbroom and Port Edward

Some 7km beyond Margate, **SOUTHBROOM** is known disparagingly as "Houghton-by-Sea" after one of Johannesburg's wealthiest suburbs, which allegedly relocates here en masse in December. The town is predominantly a sumptuous development of large holiday houses set in expansive gardens and centred on the pretty **Southbroom Golf Course** (R300 for eighteen holes; ☎039 316 6051, ⊕southbroomgolfclub.co.za). Huge dunes covered by lush vegetation sweep down to the sea, and there are good long walks along the shore. The best place for swimming is **Marina Beach**, 3km south of Southbroom Beach.

Heading on for another 10km or so brings you to **PORT EDWARD**, which marks the border with the Eastern Cape. The town has some nice sandy beaches, but its main interest lies in its proximity to the Umtamvuna Nature Reserve (see p.380).

ARRIVAL AND INFORMATION
THE HIBISCUS COAST

By bus and minibus taxi The Margate Mini Coach runs between Durban and Margate three to four times a day (1hr 30min; see p.368), and minibus taxis connect Margate to Port Shepstone, Ramsgate, Southbroom and Port Edward. The only public transport heading west from Port Edward is the minibus taxis, which form a lively rank on the R61 just outside town, collecting passengers for the Eastern Cape.

Tourist information The tourist office on the beachfront at Margate (Mon–Fri 8am–5pm, Sat 8am–1pm, Sun 9am–1pm; ☎039 312 2322, ⊕hibiscuscoast.kzn.org.za) can provide details of accommodation plus general information for the whole South Coast area.

ACCOMMODATION

UMTENTWENI

The Spot Backpackers 23 Ambleside Rd, Umtentweni, 4km north of Port Shepstone ☎039 695 1318, ⊕spotbackpackers.com. This collection of basic but comfortable dorms and cottages is right on the beach, which makes it a magnet for surfers. It's also on the Baz Bus route. Dorm R140, double R340

RAMSGATE

Beachcomber Bay 75 Marine Drive, Ramsgate ☎039 317 4473, ⊕beachcomberbay.co.za. With splendid views of the seafront and private access to the beach, this comfortable, easy-going guesthouse has six rooms, a jacuzzi and sauna and is very close to Margate's restaurants and bars. R800

BillsBest Corner of Marine Dr and Penshurst Rd, Ramsgate ☎039 314 4837, ⊕billsbest.co.za. This outfit offers a range of well-maintained and regularly serviced cabanas and self-catering units sleeping two to six people, all close to the beach and with good security. There's also B&B accommodation and the attractive *Rock Inn Lodge*, which is rented to large groups (up to 28) and idyllically located in a forest 300m from Ramsgate beach. R420

SOUTHBROOM

Southbroom Traveller's Lodge 11 Cliff Rd, Southbroom ☎039 316 8448, ⊕southbroomtravellerslodge.co.za. Budget accommodation in a quiet neighbourhood with a pool, a bright lounge area and free use of golf clubs and surfboards. Rates include breakfast. R400

★**Sunbirds** 643 Outlook Rd, Southbroom ☎039 316 8202 or 072 993 7902, ⊕sunbirds.co.za. A classy, upmarket B&B offering immaculate rooms with modern decor, flat-screen TVs, DVD players and iPod docking stations. The attentive hosts provide an imaginative, cooked-to-order breakfast and there's a lovely saltwater pool. R1200

PORT EDWARD

Ku-boboyi River Lodge Old Main Rd, Leisure Bay, Port Edward ☎072 222 7760, ⊕kuboboyi.co.za. An attractive backpacker hostel on a hilltop with sweeping views of the ocean (even the dorm has a sea view), a relaxing atmosphere and a pool, making it great value. Meals are also available. Dorm R130, double R300

EATING AND DRINKING

MARGATE

Larry's Corner of O'Connor and Panorama Parade across from the tourist office, Margate ☎039 317 2277. This quirky little diner on the beach is something of a local institution, and has been serving up reliably good seaside fare like burgers (around R55) and seafood baskets for decades. Its patio is a good place to watch the parade of holiday makers drift by. Daily 10am–late.

RAMSGATE

Flavours The Bistro Village, 1303 Marine Drive, Ramsgate ☎039 310 4437. One of the area's most highly regarded restaurants, serving good prawns, steaks and Moroccan lamb (R120). Tues–Sat noon–2pm & 6–9pm, Sun noon–2pm.

★**Pistols Saloon** Old Main Rd, Ramsgate ☎039 316 8463. A lively, slightly surreal cowboy-themed bar on the southern edge of Ramsgate (R22 for a pint of beer), where

RIGHT RAGGED-TOOTH SHARK, SODWANA BAY (P.410) >

the resident donkey is paraded in front of drinkers and there's live music (mostly from the 1960s, '70s and '80s) on Friday nights. Daily 10am–midnight.

Waffle House Marine Drive, Ramsgate ☎ 039 314 9424. The best waffles in the province, with elaborate toppings such as lemon meringue, hummus and avocado (R74) and chicken a la king. There's also a lovely wooden deck nestled in the reeds overlooking a lagoon. Daily 8am–5pm.

SOUTHBROOM

Trattoria La Terrazza Outlook Rd, Southbroom ☎ 039 316 6162. Solid Italian food such as linguine with mussels (R89) served in a lovely setting next to a lagoon where, at around sunset, thousands of swallows come home to roost. Tues–Thurs 6.30–10pm, Fri & Sat 12.30–2.30pm & 6.30–10pm, Sun 12.30–2.30pm.

Umtamvuna Nature Reserve

About 8km north of Port Edward, signposted off the R61 to Izingolweni • Daily 7am–5pm • R15 • ☎ 039 311 2383

You'll find some of the best nature walks in the whole of KwaZulu-Natal at the **Umtamvuna Nature Reserve**. Extending 19km upstream along the tropical Umtamvuna River and the forested cliffs rising above it, the reserve is well known for its spring flowers, as well as the sunbirds and sugar birds that feed on the nectar. It's home to three hundred species of birds, including a famous colony of rare **Cape vultures**, though to see where they nest you'll have to be prepared for a whole day's walk. Waymarked paths are dotted throughout the reserve.

ACCOMMODATION   **UMTAMVUNA NATURE RESERVE**

Umtamvuna River Lodge Holiday Rd, inside the reserve ☎ 039 311 3583, ⓦ boardalign.co.za. Eight rooms in tranquil, lushly forested surroundings on the banks of the river. Wakeboarding is also available, and there's a restaurant on-site. R1050

Vuna Valley Ventures 9/10 Michelle Rd, 50m from the

entrance to the reserve ☎ 083 992 6999, ⓦ vunavalleyventureskzn.co.za. This family-friendly budget guesthouse is handily located for forays into the reserve, with attractive rooms that can sleep between two and five people, plus self-catering chalets sleeping six to ten. R400

The North Coast

KwaZulu-Natal's **North Coast**, the 80km stretch along the coast north of Durban from Umhlanga Rocks to the mouth of the Tugela River, is also known as the **Dolphin Coast**. The combination of a narrow continental shelf and warm, shallow waters creates ideal conditions for attracting bottlenose dolphins, which come here to feed all year round. Though the chances of seeing a cetacean are fairly high, bear in mind that sightings are not guaranteed.

Less tacky and developed than the South Coast, the North Coast attracts an upmarket breed of holidaymaker, especially to the main resort of **Umhlanga Rocks**, which is within easy striking distance of Durban. While the Dolphin Coast is still pretty much dominated by whites, the inland towns of **Tongaat** and **KwaDukuza**, linked by the old **R102** road, have substantial Zulu and Indian populations, with Indian temples at Tongaat and the Shaka memorial at KwaDukuzu. Also on the R102 is the grave of one of the ANC's best-loved leaders, Albert Luthuli, at **Groutville**.

Umhlanga Rocks

With a permanent population of around a hundred thousand, **UMHLANGA ROCKS** is 20km from the centre of Durban and merges with the suburb of Durban North. A swish resort, the town makes a good day out from the city, with a pleasant, sandy beach dominated by a red-and-white lighthouse. The town's shopping area along Chartwell Drive has a collection of smart, well-stocked malls, while a couple of kilometres up the hill on Umhlanga Ridge, the monster **Gateway Theatre of Shopping** has four hundred shops, eighteen cinemas, a wave pool and an indoor climbing rock. To get there from Durban, follow the N2 and take the Umhlanga/Mount Edgecombe exit, then follow the signs.

KwaZulu-Natal Sharks Board

5

1a Herrwood Drive, signposted off the N2 · **Shark dissection** Tues, Wed & Thurs 9am & 2pm · R45 · ☎ 031 566 0400 · **Boat trips** daily at 6.30am; advance booking required · R300 · ☎ 082 403 9206 , ⓦ shark.co.za

A couple of kilometres north of Umhlanga's centre, the **KwaZulu-Natal Sharks Board** shows a multiscreen audiovisual about sharks and conducts a dissection of a recently caught shark, which disabuses any notions of these creatures as the hooligans of the oceans. It also plugs the board's work in maintaining the province's **shark nets**; although these nets protect swimmers all along the coast, they are controversial, as not just sharks but also endangered turtles and dolphins die in them, thus affecting the balance of the inshore ecosystem. The Sharks Board is investigating an electronic shark barrier that might improve the situation, while still ensuring safe swimming.

Sharks Board also runs **boat trips** from Wilson's Wharf in Durban, that allow you to look out for dolphins and whales and include an inspection of the shark nets.

ARRIVAL AND INFORMATION   UMHLANGA ROCKS

By shuttle and minibus taxi The Umhlanga Explorer Shuttle Service (☎ 031 561 1846) runs trips on request to the Musgrave Centre in Berea and to Durban city centre, departing from near the tourist office. Otherwise, minibus taxis make the trip to Gateway Mall from the taxi rank on Johannes Nkosi St.

Tourist information 1A Chartwell Drive (Mon–Fri 8.30am–5pm, Sat 9am–1pm; ☎ 031 561 4257, ⓦ umhlangatourism.co.za).

ACCOMMODATION

Anchor's Rest 14 Stanley Grace Crescent ☎ 031 561 7380, ⓦ anchorsrest.co.za. Centrally located and elegant Mediterranean-style guesthouse with spacious and well-decorated suites (some self-catering), as well as an expansive veranda overlooking the pool. **R980**

Beverly Hills Hotel Lighthouse Rd ☎ 031 561 2211, ⓦ southernsun.com. The oldest and most upmarket of Umhlanga's luxury beachfront hotels, occupying a prime location in the centre of town. All rooms have sea views, as does the restaurant – a good spot for a sundowner. **R4500**

Honeypot 11 Hilken Drive ☎ 031 561 3795, ⓦ honeypotguesthouse.com. An attractive B&B in a residential area, whose cosy rooms all come with private patios and their own fireplaces. There is also a self-catering flat that sleeps four, and a small pool. **R750**

★**Jessica's B&B** 35 Portland Drive ☎ 031 561 3369, ⓦ jessicaskzn.co.za. Two comfortable self-contained cottages set in a rambling tropical garden, ideal for families, plus a few double rooms in the main house. Good value, and the friendly owners will make you feel right at home. **R650**

EATING

Bar-Ba-Coa Corner of Chartwell Dr and Lighthouse Rd ☎ 031 561 4106. This Argentinean grill-house is a meat-lover's paradise, featuring chicken, fish, lamb and of course beef, flame-grilled or served in a number of other ways. There are a few vegetarian options as well, but not many. Sirloin steak goes for R115. Mon–Thurs noon–3pm & 6–10pm, Fri & Sat noon–3pm & 6–10.30pm, Sun noon–3pm & 6–9.30pm.

Ile Maurice 9 McCausland Crescent ☎ 031 561 7609. A gastronomic Franco–Mauritian restaurant run by one of Durban's renowned chefs, where rabbit cooked in red wine meets octopus curry (R155). Tues–Sun noon–3pm & 6.30–9.30pm.

Olive & Oil 19 Chartwell Centre, on the 1st floor of the building next to the tourist office ☎ 031 561 2618. Particularly good for fish and seafood, with tasty prawns from R130, though they also serve the usual Mediterranean standbys. Mon–Thurs noon–3pm & 6–10pm, Fri noon–3pm & 6–11pm, Sat noon–3pm & 6–10.30pm, Sun noon–3pm & 6–9.30pm.

Tongaat

TONGAAT lies a few kilometres inland of Umhlanga Rocks across the N2 highway, a barrier between the coastal resorts and the workings of KwaZulu-Natal's sugar industry. The town, fronted by neglected imitation Cape Dutch cottages, has long associations with South Africa's Indian community and boasts a handful of temples. The most distinguished of these, a National Monument, is the small, whitewashed **Shri Jugganath Puri Temple**, built at the turn of the last century by the Sanskrit

5

scholar Pandit Shrikishan Maharaj and dedicated to Vishnu. To get to the temple from the R102, turn west into Ganie Street, then left into Plane Street and left again into Catherine Street; the temple is at the junction of Catherine and Plane.

Ballito

There's nothing very African about **BALLITO**, a Mediterranean-style resort a further 10km up the coast from Tongaat, with a splurge of time-shares, high-rise holiday apartments and shopping malls by the sea. But it's a pleasant enough place nevertheless, with a beach offering safe swimming and full-time lifeguards.

ARRIVAL AND DEPARTURE   BALLITO

By bus and minibus taxi One of the Greyhound bus routes between Durban and Johannesburg passes through Ballito (daily; 45min to Durban, 11hr 45min to Johannesburg). Otherwise, a number of minibus taxis trundle up the coast from Durban.

ACCOMMODATION

Dolphin Holiday Resort Five minutes' walk from the beach on the corner of Compensation Beach Rd and Hillary Drive ☎ 032 946 2187, ⊚ dolphinholidayresort .co.za. A good budget option, consisting of a well-shaded campsite and a collection of self-catering cottages; minimum stay of two nights. Camping R230, cottage R630

Zimbali Lodge 1km south of Ballito ☎ 032 538 5000, ⊚ fairmont.com/zimbali-lodge. This is the swishest place to stay, with accommodation in luxury suites set in lush subtropical coastal forest in the heart of a network of wetlands. Even if you aren't staying, consider stopping here for a meal or a sundowner in the bar, raised on stilts overlooking the golf course, which rewards you with soaring views across the Indian Ocean. R1800

KwaDukuza

Head inland from Ballito and follow the R102 north for around 30km • KwaDukuza Interpretative Centre Mon–Fri 8am–4pm, Sat & Sun 9am–4pm • Free • ☎ 032 552 7210

KWADUKUZA (still widely known by its pre-1994 election name, **Stanger**) has a special place in the cosmology of Zulu nationalists. This was the site of King Shaka's last kraal (the round formation of huts where the king lived), and it was the place where he was treacherously stabbed to death in 1828 by his half-brother Dingane, who succeeded him. The warrior-king is said to have been buried upright in a grain pit, and is commemorated by a small park and memorial on King Shaka Street, right in the centre of town. Near the memorial is a rock with a groove worn into it – supposedly where Shaka sharpened his spears. At the rear of the park, the **KwaDukuza Interpretative Centre** has a small display on Shaka and a very good fifteen-minute audiovisual display. The park is also the venue of the **King Shaka Day** celebrations (see box, p.419), held every year on September 24 – which is also the Heritage Day public holiday.

Groutville

8km southwest of KwaDukuza on the R102, just across a bridge over the Mvoti River

Tiny **GROUTVILLE** is remarkable mainly for the grave of **Albert Luthuli**, one of South Africa's greatest political leaders. A teacher and chief of the Zulus in Groutville, Luthuli became President General of the ANC in 1952. Advocating a non-violent struggle against apartheid, Luthuli was awarded the Nobel Peace Prize in 1960, which at home earned him a succession of banning orders restricting him to the KwaDukuza area. He died under mysterious circumstances in 1967 in KwaDukuza, apparently knocked down by a train. He is buried next to a whitewashed, nineteenth-century corrugated-iron mission church. Luthuli's life is recounted in the moving autobiography *Let My People Go*.

The best place to stay close to KwaDukuza and Groutville is Blythdale, the closest stretch of sand to KwaDukuza, where a ban on high-rise construction has preserved the deserted appearance of its endless beach.

Mini Villas 52 Umvoti Drive ☎ 032 551 1277, ⓦ minivillas.co.za. Simply decorated but well-equipped self-catering villas sleeping four to six people, some giving out onto a garden, with a nearby path leading down to the beach. R549

Palm Dune Beach Lodge 9 Umvoti Drive ☎ 032 552 1588, ⓦ palmdune.co.za. An upmarket resort where you can opt for a classy one-, two-, or three-bedroom chalet and partake of a wide range of activities, from jetskiing to beach volleyball. R1874

Harold Johnson Nature Reserve

Signposted 24km north of KwaDukuza off the N2 – take the Zinkwazi turn-off and turn left at Darnall • Daily: April–Sept 6am–6pm; Oct–March 5am–7pm • R10 • Camping R150/2 people • ☎ 032 486 1574

Abutting the Tugela River is KZN Wildlife's **Harold Johnson Nature Reserve**. With its well-preserved coastal bush, steep cliffs and gullies, this is a fine place to come for a day's visit or to camp overnight – there are no shops or facilities, so be sure to stock up before arrival. The reserve has several hiking **trails** that take you past various historical sites, most of them connected to the Anglo-Zulu War of 1879. These include the **Ultimatum Tree**: the wild fig tree where the British issued their ultimatum to King Cetshwayo in 1878, part of which required the Zulus to demobilize their standing army.

Valley of a Thousand Hills

The evocatively named **Valley of a Thousand Hills** makes for a picturesque drive along the edge of densely folded hills where Zulu people still live in traditional homesteads, and which visitors rarely venture into. However, the area is only worth a special trip if you're not exploring the KwaZulu-Natal interior, where scenes like this occur in abundance. While the valley, 45km from Durban, is best suited to touring in your own car (take the N3 from Durban, following the Pinetown signs), there are **daily tours** from Durban offered by Tekweni Eco Tours (see box, p.370) that take in the highlights. The trip to the valley and back can be done in half a day, but there are sufficient attractions along the route to extend it to a full day's outing.

Vintage train trip

Last Sunday of the month; also check the website for occasional extra trips • Departures at 8.30am and 12.30pm, from the Kloof Station, Stockers Arms, Old Main Rd • R170 • ☎ 082 353 6003, ⓦ umgenisteamrailway.co.za

If you're in Durban, consider taking a **vintage train trip** with Umgeni Steam Railways, which boasts one of the largest collections of historic locomotives and coaches in the southern hemisphere. From Kloof, the trains chug for 45 minutes along the edge of the Valley of a Thousand Hills, terminating at Inchanga Station and its crafts market.

Phezulu Safari Park

Old Main Rd • Daily 8.30am–4.30pm • Reptile park R45 • Zulu dancing daily at 10am, 11.30am, 2pm & 3.30pm; R100 • ☎ 031 777 1000, ⓦ phezulusafaripark.co.za

Just south of the valley is **Phezulu Safari Park**, which brings you close to deadly serpents – tucked away in cramped little glass boxes – plus crocodiles and other penned animals. There's also a reconstruction of a pre-colonial Zulu village, where you can watch tourist-geared – but nonetheless spirited – displays of **Zulu dancing** set against the dramatic horizon of the valley.

5

Pietermaritzburg

Although **PIETERMARITZBURG** (often called Maritzburg), the provincial capital of KwaZulu-Natal, sells itself as the best-preserved Victorian city in South Africa, with strong British connections, little of its colonial heritage remains. It's actually a very South African city, with Zulus forming the largest community, followed by Indians, with those of British extraction a minority – albeit a high-profile one. This multiculturalism, together with a substantial student population, adds up to a fairly lively city that's also relatively safe and small enough to explore on foot, with most places of interest within easy walking distance of the centre's heart. Only 80km inland from Durban along the fast N3 freeway, Pietermaritzburg is an easy day's outing from the coastal city; it can be combined with visits to the Valley of a Thousand Hills (see p.383) along the Old Main Road (R103), or used as an overnight stop en route to the Ukhahlamba Drakensberg (see p.388) or the Battlefields in the vicinity of Ladysmith (see p.426).

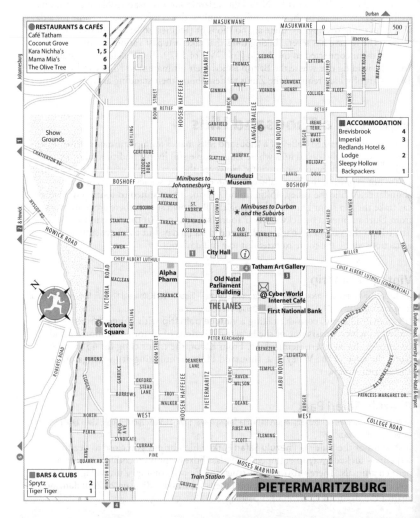

ALAN PATON

Writer, teacher and politician **Alan Paton** was born in Pietermaritzburg in 1903. His visionary first novel, *Cry, the Beloved Country*, focused international attention on the plight of black South Africans and sold millions of copies worldwide. The book was published in 1948 – the same year the National Party assumed power and began to establish apartheid – and Paton subsequently entered politics to become a founder-member of the non-racial and fiercely anti-apartheid Liberal Party. He was president of the party from 1960 until 1968, when it was forced to disband by repressive legislation forbidding multiracial political organizations.

Paton died in Durban in 1988, having published a number of works, including two biographies and his own autobiography. The following year, the **Alan Paton Centre** was established at the University of KwaZulu-Natal's archives building on Milner Rd, Scottsville (Mon–Fri 8.30am–1pm; ☏ 033 260 5926, ⊛ paton.ukzn.ac.za), where you can see a re-creation of Paton's study, as well as personal memorabilia and documents.

Brief history

Pietermaritzburg's Afrikaner origins are reflected in its name; after slaughtering three thousand Zulus at the Battle of Blood River, the Voortrekkers established the fledgling Republic of Natalia in 1839, naming their capital in honour of the Boer leaders **Piet Retief** and **Gerrit Maritz**. The republic's independence was short-lived – Britain annexed it only four years later, and by the closing decade of the nineteenth century Maritzburg was the most important centre in the colony of Natal, with a population of nearly ten thousand (more than Durban at that time). Indians arrived at the turn of the last century, mostly as indentured labourers, but also as traders. Among their number was a young, little-known lawyer called Mohandas Gandhi, who went on to change the history of India. He later traced the embryo of his devastatingly successful tactic of passive resistance to an incident in 1893, when as a non-white he was thrown out of a first-class train compartment at Pietermaritzburg station.

Tatham Art Gallery

Corner of Chief Albert Luthuli and Langalibalele sts • Tues–Sun 10am–5pm • Free • ☏ 033 392 2801, ⊛ tatham.org.za

Across from the imposing **City Hall**, a late Victorian red-brick building with an impressive 15m clock tower, you'll find the **Tatham Art Gallery**, another fine brick edifice, which was previously the Supreme Court of the Colony of Natal. This is the highlight of the city's attractions, housing one of the country's best collections of art. Pieces by black South Africans such as Zwelethu Mthethwa and Sam Nhlengethwa are exhibited alongside those by Marc Chagall, Georges Braque and Henri Matisse. A good way to enjoy the art is by attending the free **classical music concerts** that often take place at the gallery on Wednesday afternoons.

Old Natal Parliament Building, First National Bank and the Lanes

South of the Tatham on Langalibalele Street stands a series of attractive period buildings, including the typically imperial **Old Natal Parliament Building** and the **First National Bank**, which dates from 1903 and had its facade chosen from an Edwardian catalogue and shipped out from the mother country. Across from the First National Bank building is the mostly pedestrianized warren of alleyways known as **the Lanes**, which was the financial hub of Natal from 1888 to 1931 and housed four separate stock exchanges. This area is enjoyable to explore during the day, but it's a notorious stamping ground for pickpockets, so stay alert and don't come here after dark.

5

Msunduzi Museum

Langalibalele St • Mon–Fri 9am–4pm, Sat 9am–1pm • R8 • ☎ 033 394 6834, ⓦ voortrekkermuseum.co.za

The best of the town's museums is the **Msunduzi Museum**, which centres on the original Church of the Vow, built in 1838 by Boers in honour of their victory over the Zulus three years earlier at the Battle of Blood River. The church was their part of a bargain allegedly struck with God (see p.426). The museum connects with the Voortrekker roots of Pietermaritzburg and is worth a fleeting visit to gain some insight into life on a trek. The most interesting items are the home-made children's toys and beautifully embroidered *kappies* (hats) which the women used to shield themselves from the sun. Across the lovely courtyard garden is a reconstruction of the 1846 thatched house of **Andries Pretorius**, leader of the Voortrekkers at Blood River and the driving force behind the establishment of the Boer Republic of Natalia.

ARRIVAL AND INFORMATION

PIETERMARITZBURG

By bus All intercity buses pull in at the *McDonald's* on the corner of Burger and Chief Albert Luthuli streets. SA Roadlink (☎ 033 345 6890) has an office in the *McDonald's* parking lot, while Intercape's office (☎ 086 128 7287) is just across Burger St. Greyhound tickets can be bought at African Link Travel next to Intercape (☎ 033 345 3175), and Translux tickets can be bought at the train station (see below; ☎ 033 345 0165).

Destinations Bloemfontein (3 daily; 9hr 30min); Cape Town (2 daily; 21hr 45min); Durban (17 daily; 1hr 20min); Johannesburg (18 daily; 7hr); Ladysmith (3 daily; 2hr 15min); Pretoria (17 daily; 7hr 30min).

By Baz Bus The Baz Bus drops off at *Sleepy Hollow Backpackers* in Montrose (see below).

Destinations Amphitheatre (4 weekly; 3hr); Durban (4 weekly; 2hr); Johannesburg (4 weekly; 8hr); Pretoria (4 weekly; 9hr).

By plane Flights to Johannesburg (6 daily; 1hr 30min), used mainly by business travellers, depart from the city's

Oribi Airport (☎ 033 386 9577), about 6km south of the centre. The only means of getting to and from the airport and the town centre is by taxi.

By train The train station (☎ 033 897 2350) lies at the unsavoury southwest end of Langalibalele St, one of the city's main thoroughfares – it's advisable to arrange beforehand to be collected from here, particularly at night.

Destinations Durban (4 weekly at 4.58am; 2hr 20min); Johannesburg (4 weekly at 9.36pm; 10hr).

By minibus taxi Minibuses to Durban and Johannesburg leave from ranks near the Msunduzi Museum in the centre.

Tourist information Publicity House, on the corner of Langalibalele and Chief Albert Luthuli streets (Mon–Fri 8am–5pm, Sat 8am–1pm; ☎ 033 345 1348, ⓦ pmbtourism.co.za), stocks an excellent selection of books, and also has information on the Ukhahlamba Drakensberg and other nearby attractions.

GETTING AROUND

Taxi Metered taxis should be booked in advance; one of the biggest firms is Metro Taxis (☎ 033 397 1910);

alternatively, try Govender's Taxis (☎ 033 391 2902).

ACCOMMODATION

Brevisbrook 28 Waverleydale Rd, Boughton, 5km from centre ☎ 033 344 1402, ⓦ brevisbrook.co.za. All rooms in this intimate little B&B have private entrances and bathtubs, and there's a wonderful woodsy braii area and a swimming pool. Self-catering option is available, too. R850

Imperial 224 Jabu Ndlovu St, city centre ☎ 033 342 6551, ⓦ proteahotels.com/imperial. All the mod cons you'd expect, set in a lovely nineteenth-century building with a certain historical flair; Prince Louis Napoleon stayed here in 1879 before being killed in the Zulu Wars, and some of the decor is reminiscent of that era. It books up quickly, so reserve in advance. R1152

Redlands Hotel & Lodge 1 George MacFarlane Lane,

Wembley, 3km from centre ☎ 033 394 3333, ⓦ redlandshotel.co.za. This upmarket boutique hotel has luxury finishes, a swimming pool and a tennis court. Besides rooms, it offers its self-catering one- and two-bed apartments. R1420

Sleepy Hollow Backpackers 489 Town Bush Rd, Montrose ☎ 082 455 8323, ⓦ sleepyhollowbackpackers.com. Dorms at Pietermaritzburg's only backpackers are simple and small, with just three or four beds. There are bikes available for hire and regular tours of the city, including weekly pub crawls, as well as free transfers from Durban on Tuesdays and Fridays. Dorm R140, double R330

EATING, DRINKING AND NIGHTLIFE

Pietermaritzburg has a fairly good choice of **restaurants**, as well as a handful of decent **pubs** and **nightclubs**. Around Boshoff St, at the heart of the city's Indian quarter, you'll find a concentration of shops selling cheap spicy snacks like *rotis* and bunny chows, while the university quarter across the river in Scottsville can be fun for a night out.

RESTAURANTS AND CAFÉS

Café Tatham Tatham Art Gallery, Chief Albert Luthuli St ☎ 033 342 8327. A colourful little coffee shop that's the best place in town for light lunches, with sandwiches, soups and specials such as lamb tagine (R60). Tues–Sat 10am–4.30pm.

Coconut Grove 426 Langalibalele St ☎ 033 394 3337. Popular with Indian families, serving cheap curries (under R50) and an extensive range of burgers, as well as more substantial fare like seafood and roasts. Mon–Thurs 9am–7pm, Fri & Sat 9am–9pm.

★**Kara Nichha's** 470 Church St ☎ 033 345 0228. An excellent, very cheap vegetarian Indian takeaway (curries for R7.50), particularly good for filled *rotis* and Indian sweets. There's another branch at 151 Victoria Rd. Mon–Fri 7.15am–5.15pm, Sat 7.15am–3pm.

Mama Mia 101 Roberts Rd, Wembley ☎ 033 342 2778. A decent Italian restaurant offering the usual classics along with some more unusual dishes, such as roast lamb pizza with mint chutney (R88). Daily 10am–10pm.

The Olive Tree McDonald's Garden Centre, Chatterton Rd ☎ 033 394 7033. Occupying a tranquil, shaded spot overlooking the river, this pleasant café serves good breakfasts, imaginative salads and healthy lunches including sandwiches for around R35; walk through the garden centre to find it. Mon–Sat 8am–4pm, Sun 8am–3.30pm.

BARS AND CLUBS

Sprytz 40 Alan Paton Ave, Scottsville ☎ 033 342 3206. Upscale cocktail bar that draws a well-heeled, mostly black clientele. Cocktails on offer range from the classic to the more creative, and cost around R35. Tues–Thurs noon–11pm, Fri & Sat noon–2am, Sun 2pm–midnight.

Tiger Tiger Chief Albert Luthuli St ☎ 033 345 5977. Centrally located nightclub that has been a firm favourite for years, playing house music and attracting a crowd of university students and young professionals. Thursdays are student nights. Entrance R100. Thurs–Sat 8pm–late.

DIRECTORY

Emergencies AA ☎ 083 84322.
Hospital Pietermaritzburg Medi-Clinic, 90 Payn St (☎ 033 845 3700).
Internet access Cyber World Internet Café, 204 & 258

Langalibalele St (Mon–Sat 7am–6pm, Sun 10am–5pm; ☎ 072 100 8558).
Pharmacy Alpha Pharm, 62 Chief Albert Luthuli St (Mon–Fri 8am–5pm, Sat 8.30am–12.30pm; ☎ 033 342 4218).

The Midlands

For most travellers, the verdant farmland that makes up the **Midlands** is picture-postcard terrain, to be whizzed through on the two-hour journey from Durban or Pietermaritzburg to the Ukhahlamba Drakensberg. There's little reason to dally here, unless you fancy taking in the region's quaint, English-style country inns, tea shops and craft shops, several of which are on the so-called **Midlands Meander**, a route that weaves its way around the N3 on back roads between Pietermaritzburg and the **Mooi River** 60km to the northwest.

As you head north out of Pietermaritzburg on the N3 through the Midlands, you're roughly tracing the last journey of **Nelson Mandela** as a free man before his arrest in 1962. On the run from the police, Mandela had been continuing his political activities, often travelling in disguise – a practice that earned him the nickname of the "Black Pimpernel". **Howick**, 18km northwest of Pietermaritzburg, is recorded as the place where his historic detention began; the actual spot is on the R103, 2km north of a side road heading to the Tweedie junction. On this occasion, he was masquerading as the chauffeur of a white friend, when their car was stopped on the old Howick road, apparently because of a tip-off. A memorial unveiled by Mandela himself in 1996 marks the unassuming spot.

5

INFORMATION

THE MIDLANDS

A free **map** outlining the attractions on the Midlands Meander is available from most tourist offices in the vicinity, while the KZN Wildlife and the Midlands Meander Association (☎ 033 330 8195, ⓦ midlandsmeander.co.za) can provide lists of self-catering accommodation in the area and make bookings on your behalf.

ACCOMMODATION

Granny Mouse Country House Old Main Rd, Balgowan, 28km northwest of Howick on the R103 ☎ 033 234 4071, ⓦ grannymouse.co.za. Stylishly renovated and offering rooms in thatched cottages decorated with rich-textured fabrics. There's a health spa, restaurant and loads of small lounges with large comfortable chairs to relax in. R1445

Loxley House South off the Lonteni/Sani Pass Rd in the hamlet of Nottingham Rd, 30km northwest of Howick on the R103 ☎ 033 266 6362, ⓦ loxleyhouse.com. Comfortable rooms in a small B&B with its own restaurant; electric blankets on request for chilly winter nights. R1190

Rawdon's Old Main Rd, Nottingham Rd ☎ 033 266 6044, ⓦ www.rawdons.co.za. Set in a gracious thatch-roofed country estate looking onto its own trout lake, with welcoming log fires for cool misty days and airy verandas for hot summers. It also has an atmospheric pub with its own brewery on site. R1460

The Ukhahlamba Drakensberg

Hugging the border with Lesotho, South Africa's premier mountain wilderness is officially known as the **Ukhahlamba Drakensberg Park**. The tallest range in Southern Africa, the "Dragon Mountains" (or, in Zulu, the "barrier of spears") reach their highest peaks along the border with Lesotho. The range is actually an escarpment separating a high interior plateau from the coastal lowlands of KwaZulu-Natal. Although this is a continuation of the same escarpment that divides the Mpumalanga highveld from the game-rich lowveld of the Kruger National Park and continues into the northern section of the Eastern Cape, when people talk of the Berg, they invariably mean the range in KwaZulu-Natal.

For elating scenery – massive spires, rock buttresses, wide grasslands, glorious waterfalls, rivers, pools and fern-carpeted forests – the Ukhahlamba Drakensberg is unrivalled. Wild and unpopulated, it's a paradise for **hiking**. One of the richest **San rock-art** repositories in the world, the Ukhahlamba Drakensberg is also a World Heritage Site, with more than six hundred recorded sites hidden all over the mountains featuring over 22,000 individual paintings by the original inhabitants of the area; three easily accessible ones are at **Giant's Castle**, **Injisuthi** and **Kamberg.**

The park is hemmed in by rural African areas – former "homeland" territory, unsignposted and unnamed on many maps, but interesting to drive through for a slice of traditional **Zulu life** complete with beehive-shaped huts. Visitors to the Ukhahlamba Drakensberg can **stay** either in the self-catering and camping options provided by KZN Wildlife, or in hotels or backpacker hostels outside the park (the most feasible option if you don't have your own transport). As for the **weather**, summers are warm but wet; expect both dramatic thunderstorms and misty days that block out the views. Winters tend to be dry, sunny and chilly, with freezing nights and, on the high peaks, occasional snow. The best times for hiking are spring and autumn. As the weather can change rapidly at any time of year, always take sufficient clothing and food.

HANG TIGHT

The Midlands offers a couple of **adventure activities** for those itching to take to the skies. Bulwer, southwest of Pietermaritzburg, is one of the country's premier paragliding destinations, and Wild Sky Paragliding (☎ 082 395 3298, ⓦ wildsky.co.za) can provide two-day basic courses for R2500, or tandem flights for R950. Meanwhile north of Howick, at the Karkloof Nature Reserve, you can undertake a **canopy tour** with Karkloof Canopy Tours (☎ 033 330 3415, ⓦ karkloofcanopytour.co.za; R495 including lunch), where you're strapped into a harness and glide along steel cables between platforms erected high above the forest floor.

ARRIVAL AND DEPARTURE

THE UKHAHLAMBA DRAKENSBERG

By car You can reach the Southern Drakensberg using the R626 or R612/R617, both routes putting you within striking distance of Sani Pass. For the Central and Northern Drakensberg, most roads to the mountains branch off westwards from the N3 between Pietermaritzburg and the Ladysmith area, and come to a halt at various KZN Wildlife camps. With no connecting road system through the Ukhahlamba Drakensberg, it's not possible to drive from one end to the other.

By bus Public transport serving the Ukhahlamba Drakensberg is limited. Many hotels offer transfers from

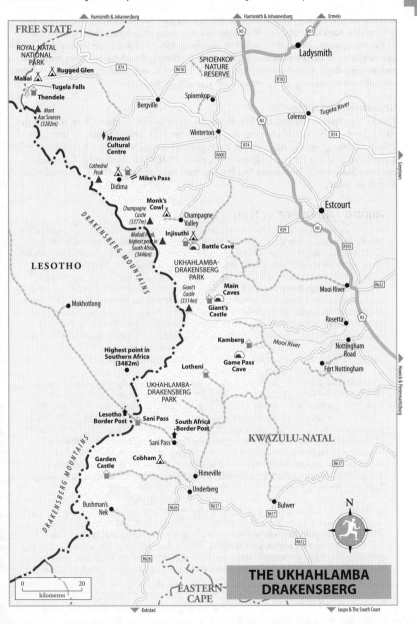

THE UKHAHLAMBA DRAKENSBERG

5

the bus terminals in Estcourt, a commercial centre 88km north of Pietermaritzburg on the N3, or Ladysmith. Underberg Express shuttle service (see p.392) runs daily between Durban and Sani Pass, while the Baz Bus Durban–Jo'burg service goes via *Amphitheatre Backpackers* (see p.398) for the Northern Drakensberg.

The Southern Drakensberg

While the southern section of the Ukhahlamba Drakensberg lacks some of the drama and varied landscape found further north, it does have an outstanding highlight: the hair-raising **Sani Pass** into Lesotho, a precipitous series of hairpins that twist to the top of the escarpment, the highest point in Southern Africa reachable on wheels. It is easily one of the most beautiful drives in the country, offering breathtaking views from the top on clear days. The area offers lots of good hiking as well, and several local operators organize pony trekking in the mountains just across the border.

Underberg and Himeville

From Pietermaritzburg and the N3, the main access to the Southern Berg is along the R617 (take the Bulwer/Underberg exit west off the N3). **UNDERBERG**, 150km west of Pietermaritzburg on the R617, is the main gateway to the Southern Drakensberg, with a good supermarket for stocking up on supplies. **HIMEVILLE**, 4km north from here, is the last village you'll find before heading up Sani Pass, and can make for a good place to stay en route.

HIKING AND OTHER ACTIVITIES

Whether you choose to take your time on easy walks or embark on a challenging three- or four-day trip into the mountains, **hiking** in the Ukhahlamba Drakensberg remains one of South Africa's top wilderness experiences. The marvel of setting out on foot in these mountains is that you're unlikely to encounter vehicles, settlements, or even other people, and the scenery is sublime.

The Ukhahlamba Drakensberg is divided into the High Berg and Little Berg, according to altitude. In the **High Berg** you're in the land of spires and great rock buttresses, where the only places to sleep are in caves or, in some areas, huts. You'll need to be totally self-sufficient and obey wilderness rules, taking a trowel and toilet paper with you and not fouling natural water with anything – which means carrying water away from the streams to wash in. Both mountaineers' huts and caves must be booked with the KZN Wildlife office you start out from, and you'll also need to write down your route details in the mountain register. Slogging up the passes to the top of the mountains requires a high degree of fitness, some hiking experience and a companion or guide who knows the terrain.

The **Little Berg**, with its gentler summits, rivers, rock paintings, valleys and forests, is equally remote and beautiful. It's also easier (and safer) to explore if you're of average fitness. If you don't want to carry a backpack and sleep in caves or huts, it's feasible to base yourself at one of the KZN Wildlife camps and set out on day hikes, of which there are endless choices. It's also possible to do a two-day walk from one of the camps, spending one night in a cave. Two excellent bases for walking are **Injisuthi** in the Giant's Castle Game Reserve (see p.394), or **Thendele** in the Royal Natal National Park (see p.398). If you want the luxury of spending the nights in a hotel, base yourself in the **Cathedral Peak** area at the *Cathedral Peak Hotel* (see p.397). With extensive grasslands, the Southern Berg is the terrain of the highly recommended **Giant's Cup Hiking Trail**, an exhilarating introduction to the mountains (see box, p.392).

KZN Wildlife offices sell books on Ukhahlamba Drakensberg walks, as well as trail maps they produce themselves (1:50,000). If you don't feel confident tackling the terrain, or are alone, note that Drakensberg Adventures, based at *Sani Lodge* (☎033 702 0330, ⬤sanilodge.co.za), offers a range of **guided hikes** across the Ukhahlamba Drakensberg and into Lesotho.

As for other activities, **angling** at Cobham Garden Castle or Giant's Castle costs R50 per day by permit only from KZN Wildlife, with a bag limit of ten trout per day. At Lotheni and Kamberg the permit costs R50 and R90 respectively, with a bag limit of ten trout. You'll need to bring all your own gear.

RIGHT TRADITIONAL HUT LOOKING TOWARD CATHEDRAL PEAK (P.396) >

5

Sani Pass

SANI PASS is the only place in the KwaZulu-Natal Ukhahlamba Drakensberg range where you can actually drive up the mountains using the only road from KwaZulu-Natal into Lesotho, connecting to the tiny highland outpost of **Mokhotlong**. It's the pass itself, zigzagging into the clouds, that draws increasing numbers into the High Berg.

Lotheni and Kamberg

Well off the beaten track, along dirt roads and seldom explored by foreign visitors, the two **KZN Wildlife camps** at Lotheni and Kamberg are worth venturing into for their isolated wilderness, good trout fishing and some exquisite San rock paintings.

In a valley in the foothills of the Berg and accessible by car either via Nottingham Road to the northeast or from Himeville to the southeast, **LOTHENI** is tranquil and beautiful, with waterfalls, grasslands and the lure of fishing in the Lotheni River, which flows through the reserve and is stocked with brown trout.

Apart from the superb fishing, the best reason to visit **KAMBERG**, 42km west of **Rosetta**, is for the rock art. At **Game Pass Cave** (one of the three caves in the Ukhahlamba Drakensberg open to the public, also known as Shelter Cave), images of stylized figures in trance states and large, polychrome eland dance across the wall. These can only be visited with a guide (arrange in advance), and the walk there and back takes around three hours, following a contoured path through the grasslands. Alternatively, you can join one of the guided tours departing daily from Kamberg restcamp at 9am (R50), which also has its own rock-art centre that's worth a vist. There are other less distinct paintings near the waterfall that you can visit at will. **Walks** from Kamberg are undemanding and very scenic, and include a 4km trail with handrails for wheelchair-users and the visually impaired.

ARRIVAL AND INFORMATION

THE SOUTHERN DRAKENSBERG

By bus For all its isolation, Sani Pass is fairly straightforward to get to. Underberg Express (☎ 079 696 7108) operates a shuttle service between Durban airport, Durban centre, Pietermaritzburg, Howick, Bulwer, Himeville and Sani Pass, which also drops off at *Sani Lodge* (see opposite). The fare from Durban's King Shaka airport to Sani Pass is R650/person and the journey takes around three and a half hours.

By car If you intend to drive up to Sani Pass, it's preferable to use a 4WD vehicle, and you'll need your passport. The South African and Lesotho border posts are both open daily from 6am to 6pm.

Tourist information The best place to get information about the region is in the centre of Underberg, at Southern Drakensberg Tourism (Mon–Fri 7.45am-4.15pm, Sat & Sun 9am–1pm; ☎ 033 701 1471, ⊚ drakensberg.org).

GIANT'S CUP HIKING TRAIL

The 60km, five-day **Giant's Cup Hiking Trail** (R80 per person per night, includes entrance fee to the reserve), part of which traverses a depression that explains the trail's name, is the only laid-out trail in the Ukhahlamba Drakensberg. It starts at the Sani Pass road, then leads through the foothills of the Southern Drakensberg and winds past eroded sandstone formations, overhangs with San paintings, grassy plains and beautiful valleys with river pools to swim in. No single day's hike is longer than 14km and, although there are some steep sections, it is not a difficult trail – you need to be fit to enjoy it, but not an athlete.

The **mountain huts** at the five overnight stops have running water, toilets, tables and benches, and bunks with mattresses. It's essential to bring a camping stove, food and a sleeping bag. The trail can be shortened by missing the first day and starting out at Pholela Hut, an old farmhouse where you spend the night, then terminating one day earlier at Swiman Hut close to the KZN Wildlife office at Garden Castle. You can also lengthen the trail by spending an extra night at Bushmen's Nek Hut, in an area with numerous caves and rock-art sites.

The trail is restricted to thirty people per day and tends to get booked out during holiday periods; **bookings** should be made through KZN Wildlife (⊚ www.kznwildlife.com), where you can also get a map and a trail booklet.

TOURS AND SERVICES

SANI PASS

Tours Roof of Africa Tours in Himeville (☎ 083 212 7856, ⓦ roofofafricatours.co.za) runs tours up the pass and into Lesotho, including a visit to a Basotho village; it also organizes trips to local cheese and wine farms, where you can view the production process, and taste the end product. In addition, it offers walking tours (3–7 hours) to visit the region's historic San rock paintings.

LOTHENI AND KAMBERG

Access and supplies The rest camps at Lotheni (☎ 033 702 0540; R25) and Kamberg (☎ 033 267 7251; R30) are open daily April–Sept 6am–6pm and Oct–March 5am–7pm. In Lotheni, there's a trading store about 10km before you reach the restcamp. At Kamberg, however, the nearest major supplies are at Rosetta, so it's best to bring all your own food and drink.

ACCOMMODATION

HIMEVILLE

Himeville Arms Arbuckle St ☎ 033 702 1305, ⓦ himevillehotel.co.za. A decent country inn that makes a good stopover before the final haul to the mountains. It organizes 4WD trips, horseriding, fishing and golf, and also has dorm accommodation for backpackers. Dorm R185, double R960

Yellowwood Cottage 8 Mackenzie St ☎ 033 702 1065, ⓔ rays@piscali.co.za. One of the nicest B&Bs in the area, with friendly hosts, and a spectacular garden boasting wonderful Berg views. There are four en-suite rooms and a fully equipped kitchenette. R580

UNDERBERG

Cedar Garden 1 Polo Way ☎ 033 701 1153 or 083 648 4111, ⓦ cedargarden.co.za. A stately old house with elegant light-filled rooms, some in the main house and others in a four-person self-catering cottage or separate self-catering house. The best rooms overlook the gardens, and there is a fireplace in the cosy lounge. R700

SANI PASS

Most accommodation is at the foot of the mountains, just before the pass hairpins its way up to the top.

Mkomazana Mountain Cottages 25km northwest of Underberg along the Sani Pass Rd ☎ 082 521 6343, ⓦ mkomazana.co.za. Self-catering in five cottages sleeping two to six people. The lodge, on the site of an old trading post, is near the start of Giant's Cup Hiking Trail. Less ambitious walks into the mountains begin right on the property, which has its own river and waterfall, and a private dam with trout. R740

★ **Sani Lodge** 19km northwest of Underberg along the Sani Pass Rd ☎ 033 702 0330, ⓦ sanilodge.co.za. There are dorms, doubles and self-catering cottages at this popular backpacker hostel, some in picturesque thatched rondavels. The view from the veranda is stunning, and delicious home-made goodies are available at the café next door. It's a good base for walking to waterfalls and rock paintings – packed lunches can be supplied – and there are also tours up Sani Pass, guided hikes and 4WD excursions on offer. Dorm R125, double R370

Sani Mountain Lodge At the top of Sani Pass, just inside Lesotho ☎ 078 634 7496, ⓦ sanimountain.co.za. The only place to stay at Sani Top in Lesotho (see p.601) which, at 2874m above sea level, makes much of its (disputed) claim to be the highest pub in Africa. The cliff-edge setting is superb, with awesome views into KwaZulu-Natal, and there's also hearty food on offer, while in the evenings you can sit on the balcony and watch the sun set over the mountaintops. Rooms are in attractive rondavels with open fireplaces, and there's camping available. Camping R95, dorm R215, double (half board) R1840

LOTHENI AND KAMBERG

Lotheni In a remote area of the park north of Sani Pass; book through KZN Wildlife ☎ 033 845 1000, ⓦ www.kznwildlife.com. A small campsite plus fourteen comfortable self-catering chalets with three to six beds, as well as bathrooms and well-equipped kitchens. Also on site is *Simes Cottage* (R1850), a stone farmhouse with a majestic outlook, its own trout lake and grounds traversed by bushbuck and eland. The cottage sleeps ten, and you have to rent the whole thing and bring all your supplies. Camping R140, chalet R440

Kamberg In the foothills of the Drakensberg, between Lotheni and Giant's Castle; book through KZN Wildlife ☎ 033 845 1000, ⓦ www.kznwildlife.com. The restcamp here consists of chalets sleeping two to six; there's a communal kitchen but no campsite. There's trout fishing to be had nearby, as well as a number of scenic walks in the area. R450

The Central Drakensberg

The **Central Drakensberg** incorporates four distinct areas, all clearly signposted from the N3. **Giant's Castle**, the site of a beautiful game reserve, is where you'll find the popular vulture hide and access to important San rock paintings. More San art is at **Injisuthi** to the north, principally a hiking destination and the place to head for if

5

you're after complete wilderness. Far more accessible and tourist-trammelled is **Champagne Valley**, which offers a healthy number of hotels with ample sporting facilities, while to the north, the hotel at **Cathedral Peak** is the best place to base yourself for some serious walking.

Giant's Castle Game Reserve

Daily: April–Sept 6am–10pm; Oct–March 5am–10pm • R30 • ☎ 036 353 3718

Giant's Castle Game Reserve was created to protect the dwindling numbers of **eland**, which lived in great numbers in the Ukhahlamba Drakensberg before the arrival of colonialists. Antelope of the montane zone are also found here – oribi, grey rhebok, mountain reedbuck and bushbuck – as well as four dozen other mammal species and around 160 bird species. The reserve is bordered to the west by three of the four highest peaks in South Africa: Mafadi (the highest at 3410m), Popple Peak (3325m) and the bulky ramparts of Giant's Castle itself (3314m). This is not a traditional game park – there are no roads inside the reserve apart from access routes, which terminate at the two main KZN Wildlife accommodation areas, **Giant's Castle** and **Injisuthi**; the only way to see the wildlife here is by hiking through the terrain.

The vulture hide

May–Sept • R645 for up to three people • Book as much as a year in advance through KZN Wildlife • ☎ 033 845 1000, ⓦ www.kznwildlife.com

One of the big attractions at the Giant's Head peak is the thrilling **vulture hide** where you may see the rare bearded vulture, or lammergeier, a giant, black and golden bird with massive wings and a diamond-shaped tail. A scavenger, the lammergeier is an evolutionary link between eagles and vultures and was thought extinct in Southern Africa until only a couple of decades ago. The bird is found only in mountainous areas such as the Himalayan foothills, and in South Africa only in the Ukhahlamba Drakensberg and Maloti mountains. In the locality you may also spot Cape vulture, black eagle, jackal buzzard and lanner falcon, attracted by the carcasses of animals put out by rangers during the winter.

Main Caves

Daily 9am–3pm • Guided walks from Giant's Castle Camp R30

Giant's Castle has one of the three major **rock-art sites** open to the public in the Ukhahlamba Drakensberg, with more than five hundred paintings at **Main Caves**, about a half-hour's easy walk up the Bushman's River Valley.

EN ROUTE TO THE BERG

The tiny hamlet of **Winterton**, some 90km north of Pietermaritzburg along the R74 as it deviates west off the N3, offers some pleasant **places to stay** if you're looking for a stopover on the way to the Central Drakensberg. One is *Lilac Lodge* at 8 Springfield Rd, the main drag as you drive into the town (☎ 036 488 1025, ⓦ lilaclodge.co.za; R300 per person), with accommodation in small cottages and its own coffee and arts and crafts shop. Another appealing choice is *Rolling M Ranch* (☎ 036 488 1751, ⓦ rollingmranch.co.za; R500), a working farm outside town on the banks of the Tugela River – to get there, head 2km north from Winterton on the R600, then turn right at the signposted Skietdrift road; the camp is around 15km down this route and has self-catering cabins and cottages as well as a bush camp. Since the farm is on the Battlefields route, there are trails from here to Spioenkop and Buller's Cross monuments.

If you fancy **whitewater rafting**, this is a good place to do it. The Tugela River east of the Drakensberg can be accessed from Winterton on trips (Dec–April) run by Four Rivers Rafting and Adventures (☎ 036 468 1693, ⓦ fourriversadventures.co.za); one-day raft forays into the river gorge cost R510/person, with multi-day trips available on request.

Injisuthi

April–Sept 6am–6pm, Oct–March 5am–7pm • R20 • Guided visits to the San paintings (R235 for up to three people; 5hr) set out from Injisuthi camp at 8.30am; book through KZN Wildlife (see box, p.355) • ☏ 036 431 9000 • To get to the camp, take the indicated turning off the R615, then follow the dirt road for 30km

In the northern section of the Giant's Castle Game Reserve, some 50km from both Winterton and Estcourt, **INJISUTHI** is a hiker's dream. You can walk straight out into the mountains, swim in the rivers or take in rock art. One of the best day walks, albeit a tough one, is up Van Heyningen's Pass to the viewpoint – the friendly staff at the main camp can direct you. There are ten different day hikes at Injisuthi, lasting from one to ten hours.

If you have even a passing interest in rock art, don't miss the paintings at **Battle Cave**, so-named because of a series of paintings that apparently depict an armed conflict between two groups of Bushmen. San art authority David Lewis-Williams has argued that these paintings are unlikely to depict a conflict over territory because there is no evidence that such conflicts took place in a society that was very loosely organized and un-territorial. Instead, he claims, the paintings are about the San spiritual experience and shamanic trance, the battles taking place in the spiritual realm where marauding

---

THE SAN AND THEIR ROCK PAINTINGS

Southern Africa's earliest inhabitants and the most direct descendants of the late Stone Age, the **San**, or Bushmen, lived in the caves and shelters of the Ukhahlamba Drakensberg for thousands of years before the arrival of the Nguni people and later the white farmers. Many liberal writers use the word "Bushmen" in a strictly non-pejorative sense to descibe these early hunter-gatherers – though the word was originally deeply insulting. Several historians and anthropologists use "San", but as this refers to a language group and not a culture, it isn't strictly accurate either. Since there is no agreed term, you'll find both words used in this book.

The San hunted and gathered on the subcontinent for a considerable period – paintings in Namibia date back 25,000 years. In the last two thousand years, the southward migration of Bantu-speaking farmers forced change on the San, but there is evidence that the two groups lived side by side. However, tensions arose when the white settlers began to annex lands for hunting and farming. As the San started to take cattle from farmers, whites felt justified in hunting them in genocidal campaigns until they were wiped off the South African map.

San artists were also **shamans**, and their paintings of hunting, dancing and animals mostly depict religious beliefs rather than realistic narratives of everyday life. It's difficult to **date** the paintings with accuracy, but the oldest are likely to be at least eight hundred years old (although Bushmen lived in the area for thousands of years before that) and the most recent are believed to have been painted towards the end of the nineteenth century. The **medicine** or **trance dance** – journeying into the spiritual world to harness healing power – was the Bushmen's most important religious ritual and is depicted in much of their art. Look out for the postures the shamans adopted during the dance, including arms outstretched behind them, bending forward, kneeling, or pointing fingers. Dots along the spine depict the sensation of energy boiling upwards, while lines on faces or coming out of the nose usually refer to trance-induced nosebleeds. Other feelings experienced in trance, such as elongation, attenuation or the sensation of flight, are expressed by feathers or streamers. The depictions of horses, cattle and white settlers mark the end of the traditional way of life for the Ukhahlamba Drakensberg Bushmen, and it is possible that the settlers were painted by shamans to try to ward off their all-too-real bullets.

You'll also see the spiral-horned **eland** depicted in every cave – not because these antelope were prolific in the Berg, but because they were considered to have more spiritual power than any other animal. Sometimes the elands are painted in layers to increase their spiritual potency. In the caves, you can see depictions of human-like figures transforming into their power animal. Besides antelope, other animals associated with trance are honeybees, felines, snakes, elephants and rhinos.

Paintings weather and fade, and many have been vandalized. People dabbing water on them to make them clearer, or touching them, has also caused them to disappear – so never be tempted. One of the best introductions to rock art is the slim **booklet** by David Lewis-Williams, *Rock Paintings of the Natal Drakensberg*, available from most decent bookshops in the area.

5

evil shamans shoot arrows of "sickness", while good shamans attempt to fight them off. There are more than 750 beautifully painted people and animals in this extensive cave, though many are faded. The paintings are fenced off, and can be visited only on a guided walk with a KZN Wildlife guide.

Champagne Castle

Champagne Castle, the second-highest peak in South Africa, provides the most popular view in the Ukhahlamba Drakensberg, with scores of resorts in the valley cashing in on the soaring backdrop. The name, so the story goes, derives from an incident in 1861, when a Major Grantham made the first recorded ascent of the peak accompanied by his batman, who inadvertently dropped the bottle of bubbly and christened the mountainside.

Champagne Valley

Monk's Cowl daily 6am–6pm • R35 • Overnight hiking R45 • ☎ 036 468 1103

Champagne Valley is an easy 32km from Winterton, and has shops, restaurants and facilities absent in other parts of the Ukhahlamba Drakensberg. This over-civilized but extremely pretty area, which lies outside the KZN Wildlife reserve, is best avoided if you want to **hike** from your doorstep – you'll have to drive west along the R600 to Monk's Cowl, from where plenty of hikes set off into the mountains.

Ardmore Ceramic Art Studio

Signposted 20km from Winterton off the R600 • Daily 8am–4.30pm • ☎ 033 940 0034, ⓦ ardmoreceramics.co.za

The **Ardmore Ceramic Art Studio** is one of the area's highlights, started in the 1980s by fine-arts graduate **Fée Halsted-Berning** with trainee **Bonnie Ntshalintshali**, a young Zulu girl suffering from polio. By 1990 they had collected a clutch of awards for their distinctive ceramic works, and the studio now has around forty people creating beautiful sculpture and crockery with wildly colourful and often impossibly irrational motifs, which have included rhinos dressed as preachers administering the sacrament to a congregation of wild animals. Bonnie died of AIDS in 1999, as have at least eight other artists at the studio, but the distinctive style she pioneered has been continued here and the works are well worth seeing and buying. There's also a less pricey local **curio shop** on the premises, selling works by other local artists.

Cathedral Peak

North of Monk's Cowl and the Champagne Valley resorts are the Mlambonja River Valley and **Cathedral Peak**, a freestanding pinnacle sticking out of the 5km-long basalt Cathedral Ridge. The peak looks nothing like a cathedral (its Zulu name, *Mponjwane*, means "the horn on a heifer's head").

Hiking trails

A number of **hiking trails** start right from the *Cathedral Peak Hotel* (see opposite), which can provide maps and books. One of the most popular day walks is to the beautiful **Rainbow Gorge**, an 11km round trip (4–5hr) that follows the Ndumeni River, with pools, rapids and falls to detain you. The hike can be wet, so wear proper walking boots. The hotel also operates nine-hour guided trips up to Cathedral Peak, which include plenty of time at the top to revel in the views. It's a very steep climb, and the final section beyond Orange Peel Gap should only be tackled by experienced climbers – you'll probably be quite satisfied to stop at this point.

Mike's Pass

Permit R30, plus R60 per vehicle

The 24hr guardhouse at the park entrance is the place to buy a permit to drive up **Mike's Pass**, a 10km twisting forestry road that takes you to a car park from where, on a clear day, you'll get outstanding views of the entire region. There's a scale model on top to help identify the peaks. An ordinary car will make the journey when the weather is dry and the road is hard, but you'll need a 4WD when it's wet.

INFORMATION AND SERVICES

Giant's Castle The reserve's only filling station is at the main entrance to Giant's Castle; you'll find the park's reception office and a shop 7km further on (daily

THE CENTRAL DRAKENSBERG

8am–4.30pm; ☎036 353 3718). The Cathedral Peak reception office is 1.5km from the park entrance (daily 7am–7pm; ☎036 488 8000).

ACCOMMODATION

GIANT'S CASTLE

Giant's Castle Camp Book through KZN Wildlife ☎033 845 1000, ⓦwww.kznwildlife.com. Comfortable self-contained two-, four- and six-bed chalets, some with wonderful picture windows looking out to the peaks, and fireplaces. For food, there's the pleasant buffet-style restaurant *Izimbali*. You can buy frozen meat for braais and some tinned food at the curio shop in the reception area, but stock up on other supplies before getting here. There are fabulous hiking trails from the camp, and the eight-person Bannerman's Hut (R44/person) is one of the Berg's best-located hiking huts. R695

White Mountain Lodge Along the road to Giant's Castle hutted camp, 34km from Estcourt and 32km from the reserve ☎036 353 3437, ⓦwhitemountain .co.za. If the KZN Wildlife accommodation is full, this is the one hotel that gives access to the reserve. They offer full board as well as self-catering cottages, and it's located in the foothills and close to Zulu villages and farmlands, so while the area is pretty, it's neither grand nor remote. Camping for two people R220, double R660

INJISUTHI

Injisuthi Camp Book through KZN Wildlife ☎033 845 1000, ⓦwww.kznwildlife.com. Accommodation here includes comfortable self-catering chalets, safari tents and campsites. However, most people come with the express purpose of taking to the hills and camping in one of the designated caves, which have absolutely no facilities and must be booked at reception. Camping R80, safari tent R300

CHAMPAGNE VALLEY

Ardmore Guest Farm Signposted off the R600, midway between Winterton and Monk's Cowl ☎036 468 1314, ⓦardmore.co.za. A thoroughly hospitable farmstay with accommodation in en-suite rondavels or cottages, some with their own fireplaces. Guests eat together from hand-crafted crockery made on the farm.

Staff can arrange horse trails into Spioenkop Game Reserve through the Battlefields. Half board R465

Champagne Castle Along the R600 ☎036 468 1063, ⓦchampagnecastle.co.za. This old-fashioned hotel, the closest accommodation to the hiking trails beginning at Monk's Cowl, has comfortable en-suite rooms and self-catering chalets sleeping six set in lovely gardens with a swimming pool. Full board R1930

Graceland Cottage Signposted off the R600 ☎036 468 1011, ⓦgracelandsa.com. A four-bedroom self-catering cottage with TV and fireplace as well as a smaller, two-bedroom cottage perched right on the edge of a mountain with spectacular views. R1600

Inkosana Lodge and Trekking Along the R600, midway between Winterton and Monk's Cowl ☎036 468 1202, ⓦinkosana.co.za. Backpacker accommodation in unpretentious, ethnic-style rooms, with beautiful indigenous gardens and a retreat-centre feel. Breakfasts and dinners are also available. Dorm R150, double R500

CATHEDRAL PEAK

★**Cathedral Peak Hotel** 44km from both Winterton and Bergville ☎036 488 1888, ⓦwww.cathedralpeak .co.za. The only hotel in the Cathedral Peak area and the closest in the Ukhahlamba Drakensberg to the mountains – also within the KZN Wildlife protected area, it's an excellent place to stay. The views are perfect and the rooms in thatched two-storey wings are comfortably furnished with pine and country-style fabrics. Half board R2480

Didima At the top of Mike's Pass; book through KZN Wildlife ☎033 845 1000, ⓦwww.kznwildlife.com. Self-catering two- to six-bed chalets with satellite TV and fireplaces, as well as campsites. You'll also find a restaurant, a bar and a shop with basic food supplies, as well as the Didima San Art Centre (R50, including park entry fee), which has displays on San rock art and shows a short film. Chalet rates include breakfast. Camping R160, chalets R900

The Northern Drakensberg

The dramatically beautiful **Northern Drakensberg** consists mainly of the **Royal Natal National Park** with a few resorts scattered around the fringes. The Tugela River and its bouldered gorge offer some of the most awe-inspiring scenery in the area, its most striking geographical feature being the **Amphitheatre**, the crescent-shaped 5km rock

5

wall over which the Tugela plunges. With a complete cross section of accommodation, the Northern Berg is a very desirable area to visit. The best place to get a real feeling of these pristine mountains and valleys is at **Thendele**, the main KZN Wildlife camp, with chalets but no camping.

Royal Natal National Park

Daily: Oct–March 5am–10pm; April–Sept 6am–10pm • R30 • ☎ 036 438 6310

The **Royal Natal National Park**, 46km west of Bergville, is famed for its views of the Amphitheatre, which probably appear on more posters and postcards than any other single feature of the Ukhahlamba Drakensberg. Almost everyone does the **Tugela Gorge walk**, a fabulous six-hour round trip from Thendele, which gives close-up views of the **Amphitheatre** and the **Tugela Falls** plummeting over the 947m rock wall.

Established in 1916, the park only earned its royal sobriquet in 1947 when the Windsors paid a visit. It sits at the northern end of the Ukhahlamba Drakensberg, tucked in between Lesotho to the west and Free State province to the north. The three defining peaks are the Sentinel (3165m), the Eastern Buttress (3048m) and the Mont Aux Sources (3282m), which is also where five rivers rise – hence its name, given by French missionaries in 1878.

ARRIVAL AND INFORMATION

By transfer Several of the resorts offer transfers from Bergville or the N3 if you book ahead, but they tend to be expensive.

By car Routes to the park are surfaced all the way. Coming from the south along the N3, take the Winterton/Berg resorts turn-off and follow the signposts through Bergville to the park entrance, 46km away.

THE NORTHERN DRAKENSBERG

Tourist information The Drakensberg Tourism Association (☎ 036 448 1557, ⓦ drakensberg.org.za) has information about the area and helps with booking accommodation, either by phone or email (there is no actual tourist office).

Supplies For supplies head to Bergville, the last place to stock up before heading into the park.

ACCOMMODATION

INSIDE THE PARK

KZN Wildlife offers some very reasonable campsites within the park, as well as some exceptional chalets. While you can book the chalets through their usual reservation system (see box, p.355), the campsites here are best booked by calling the sites themselves.

Mahai Campsite Along the river adjacent to the national park ☎ 036 438 6310. With facilities for up to four hundred campers, *Mahai* attracts hordes of South Africans over school holidays and weekends. From here you can head straight into the mountains for some of the best walks in the Berg. Minimum charge for three people. Three people R255

Rugged Glen Campsite Signposted 4km from Mahai ☎ 036 438 6310. A smaller and quieter campsite than *Mahai*, though often only open during school holidays. The views and walks here aren't as good, but there is horseback riding available (R120/hr), and the *Orion Mont-Aux-Sources Hotel* is an easy walk away – handy if you want a substantial meal. Minimum charge for two. Two people R170

★ **Thendele Hutted Camp** At the end of the road into the Royal Natal National Park ☎ 036 438 6411. This is one of the most sought-after places to stay in South Africa, with splendid views of the Amphitheatre and excellent walks right from your front door. Accommodation is in

comfortable two- and four-bed chalets, the cheapest of which have hotplates, fridges, kettles, toasters and eating utensils. If you opt for the more luxurious cottages or lodge, chefs are on hand to cook, though you need to bring the ingredients. There's a good curio and supply shop. R670

OUTSIDE THE PARK

Amphitheatre Backpackers On the R74, 21km west of Bergville ☎ 082 855 9767, ⓦ amphibackpackers .co.za. On the Baz Bus route, this place is convenient for those without their own transport who want to explore the Northern Drakensberg. Accommodation is in en-suite dorms, with private rooms also on offer. There's a bar and restaurant, and organized hiking trips, horseriding and mountain biking are available. Dorm R140, double R400

The Cavern Off the R74, about 20km from the Royal Natal National Park ☎ 036 438 6270, ⓦ cavern.co.za. This is the most tucked-away of the hotels, family-run and with an old-fashioned feel. The rooms are adequate, though suites come with fireplaces, and there's also a swimming pool, horseriding and trout fishing. Full board R1900

Hlalanathi Berg Resort About 10km from the Royal Natal National Park ☎ 036 438 6308, ⓦ hlalanathi .co.za. This family resort offers camping and self-catering thatched chalets sleeping two to six people. There's also a swimming pool and trampolines, as well as a sit-down and takeaway restaurant serving cheap burgers, sandwiches and more substantial meals. Camping R50, double R600

Mnweni Cultural Centre In the Mnweni Valley 30km west of Bergville along the Woodstock Dam/Rookdale roads ☎086 528 5841, ⓦmnweni.org. Owned by the AmaNgwane and AmaZzizi communities, accommodation in this breathtaking valley is in simple four-bed thatched rondavels with shared ablutions and kitchen facilities.

Aside from hiking in the mountains (R35 per night), there are craft stalls, horseriding and some San rock paintings, while overnight stays in traditional homesteads can also be arranged. Meals available with advance notice. Camping R50, chalets R170/person

Orion Mont-Aux-Sources Hotel About 4km from the Royal Natal National Park ☎086 148 8867, ⓦoriongroup.co.za. A smart but impersonal hotel with views of the Amphitheatre, as well as sports facilities that include tennis courts and horseriding. R1600

The Elephant Coast and Zululand game reserves

In startling contrast to the intensively developed 250km ribbon of coastline running north and south of Durban, the seaboard to the north of the Dolphin Coast drifts off into some of the wildest and most breathtaking sea frontage in South Africa – an area known as the **Elephant Coast**.

If you've travelled along the Garden Route and wondered where stereotypical Africa was, the answer is right here, in the northern reaches of the Elephant Coast – traditionally known as **Maputaland** – with its tight patchwork of wilderness and **ancestral African lands**. In this area hemmed in by Swaziland and Mozambique, **traditional life** continues: for example, there is one *nyanga* (traditional healer) for every 550 people, compared with one Western-style doctor to 18,000 people. Access can be difficult; St Lucia, Sodwana Bay and Kwa-Ngwanase can both be reached via tarred roads from the N2, but you'll still need a 4WD vehicle to visit any of the other idyllic spots along the Elephant Coast's 200km of virtually uninterrupted beachfront.

Further south, less than three hours' drive north on the N2 from Durban, is the big game country of **Hluhluwe-Imfolozi**, which rivals even the Kruger National Park for beautiful wilderness. Turn right instead of left at the Mtubatuba junction and you'll hit the southernmost extent of South Africa's most satisfyingly "tropical" coast. It's protected all the way up to Mozambique by the country's third-largest protected area, the **iSimangaliso Wetland Park** (which includes Lake St Lucia, Cape Vidal, Charter's Creek, False Bay Park, Mkhuze Game Reserve, Sodwana Bay, Lake Sibaya and Kosi Bay). This 2750-square-kilometre patchwork encompasses wetland reserve, marine sanctuaries, a UNESCO World Heritage Site and some outstanding scuba diving and fishing opportunities around **Sodwana Bay**. The coast gets remoter and more exhilarating the further north you head, with one of South Africa's best upmarket beachside stays near Mozambique at **Kosi Bay**. Note that the northern KwaZulu-Natal coastal region is **malarial**.

Mtubatuba and Hluhluwe Village

Travelling north on the N2 from Durban and the large industrial port of **Richards Bay**, you'll pass a few predominantly African villages that make adequate bases for exploring the Hluhluwe-Imfolozi Park.

Mtubatuba

Around 50km north of Richards Bay, **MTUBATUBA** (often shortened to Mtuba) is situated where the R618 intersects the N2, just twenty minutes from both the southern section of the Hluhluwe-Imfolozi Park and St Lucia. The town features lots of herbalists, traditional healers and a Zulu market, and is also a thriving centre for the local sugar-cane industry.

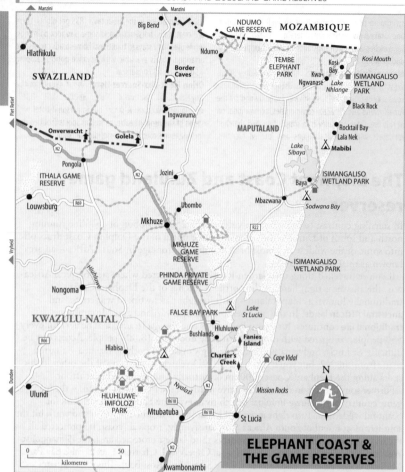

**ELEPHANT COAST &
THE GAME RESERVES**

Hluhluwe

Just off the N2, about 20km north of Mtubatuba, is the straggling village of
HLUHLUWE (pronounced "shla-shloo-wee"), which is short on charm but nonetheless
handy for accessing the northern section of the Hluhluwe-Imfolozi Park. Five
minutes' drive from Hluhluwe, **Ilala Weavers** (Mon–Fri 8am–4.30pm, Sat & Sun
8.30am–4pm; ☎087 802 1792, ⓦilala.co.za) is a hub of community projects
selling well-priced traditional **crafts** in a cheerful atmosphere: there's also a
restaurant (see opposite).

ARRIVAL AND INFORMATION — MTUBATUBA AND HLUHLUWE VILLAGE

By bus Greyhound buses from Durban (daily; 2hr
20min), Johannesburg (daily; 9hr 45min) and Pretoria
(daily; 11hr 45min) stop in Richard's Bay, from where
you can catch regular minibuses on to Hluhluwe and
Mtubatuba.

By plane There is an airport at Richard's Bay, from which

ten flights a day leave for Johannesburg (1hr 30min).
Tourist office The friendly Hluhluwe Tourist
Information office is based at the Engen filling station on
Main St (daily 8am–4.30pm; ☎035 562 0966,
ⓦvisitelephantcoast.co.za), providing details of
numerous lodges and game farms in the vicinity.

5

ACCOMMODATION

MTUBATUBA

Wendy's Country Lodge 3 Riverview Drive ☎ 035 550 0407 or 083 628 1601, ⓦ wendybnb.co.za. Eight luxurious rooms in a house with a vaguely colonial atmosphere set in tropical gardens in a suburb of Mtubatuba, plus a cottage that sleeps five. There's also a swimming pool and a restaurant on site. **R1040**

HLUHLUWE

Hluhluwe Guest House In the residential area behind the Engen garage ☎ 035 562 0838, ⓔ hluguest @iafrica.com. Comfy, en-suite B&B rooms opening onto a garden with a pool and small bar, and meals on request. There are self-catering options as well, and the guesthouse can arrange trips into Hluhluwe-Imfolozi Park. **R830**

Isinkwe Backpackers Bushcamp 20km south of Hluhluwe ☎ 083 338 3494, ⓦ isinkwe.co.za. A well-run rustic hostel offering camping, dorms and a number of small chalets, some en suite. It serves reasonably priced meals (or you can self-cater), and arranges tours to Hluhluwe-Imfolozi Park and St Lucia. Camping **R110**, dorm **R165**, double **R460**

Zulu Homestay ☎ 082 485 8498 or ☎ 082 953 5601, ⓦ mbonise.com. This homestay, organized by Mbonise Cultural Concepts and Safaris, is the most interesting accommodation option in the area. Staying with the Mdaka family, you'll also be taken to visit the Nompondo Community and a school adjacent to Hluhluwe-Imfolozi Park. You can pay extra for walking tours and the services of a Zulu guide (R120) or to witness Zulu dancing. Half board **R300/person**

EATING AND DRINKING

HLUHLUWE

The Fig Tree at *Ilala Weavers*, five minutes' drive from Hluhluwe ☎ 079 393 8773. Serves decent breakfasts and lunches, including salads and seafood dishes such as mussels (R45 for a pot), on a shaded terrace. Mon–Fri 8am–4.30pm, Sat & Sun 8.30am–4pm.

Hluhluwe-Imfolozi Park

Daily: March–Oct 6am–6pm; Nov–Feb 5am–7pm • R120 • ☎ 035 562 0848

Hluhluwe-Imfolozi is KwaZulu-Natal's most outstanding game reserve, considered by some to be even better than Kruger. While it certainly can't match Kruger's sheer scale (Hluhluwe is a twentieth of the size) or its teeming game populations, its relatively compact 960 square kilometres have a wilder feel. This has something to do with the fact that, apart from **Hilltop**, an elegant hotel-style restcamp in the northern half of the park, none of the other restcamps are fenced off, and wild animals are free to wander through. The vegetation, with subtropical forest in places, adds to the sense of adventure. The park also offers the best **trails** in the country.

The park used to be two distinct entities – hence its tongue-twisting double-barrelled name (pronounced something like "shla-shloo-wee-oom-fa-low-zee") – and the two sections retain their separate characters, reinforced by a public road slicing between them. The southern **Imfolozi section** takes its name from a corruption of *mfulawozi*, a Zulu word that refers to the fibrous bushes that grow along its rivers. The topography here is characterized by wide, deep valleys incised by the Black and White Imfolozi rivers, with altitudes varying between 60 and 650 metres. Luxuriant riverine vegetation gives way in drier areas to a variety of woodland, savannah, thickets and grassy plains. The notable feature of the northern **Hluhluwe section** is the river of the same name, a slender, slithering waterway, punctuated by elongated pools. The Hluhluwe rises in the mountains north of the park and passes along sandbanks, rock beds and steep cliffs in the game reserve before seeping away into Lake St Lucia to the east. The higher ground is covered by veld and dense thicket, while the well-watered ridges support the softer cover of ferns, lichens, mosses and orchids.

Brief history

Despite Hluhluwe-Imfolozi being the oldest proclaimed national park in Africa (it was created in 1895), its future as a game refuge has hung by a thread several times in the last two hundred years. In the nineteenth century, Imfolozi was the private hunting preserve of the **Zulu** king, Shaka. During Shaka's reign between 1818 and 1828 the area saw the most sustained campaign of hunting in Zulu history, but this was nothing compared to

5

the destruction caused by white farmers between 1929 and 1950, when a crusade of game **extermination** was launched to wipe out **nagama** disease, resulting in the slaughter of one hundred thousand head of game from sixteen species; rhinos alone were spared.

It was only in 1952, when the park was handed over to the newly formed organization now known as **KZN Wildlife**, that the slow process of resuscitating the threadbare game reserve began. The sense of pristine wilderness you now get at Hluhluwe-Imfolozi is the result of careful management, crowned by the brilliant success of re-establishing its white rhino population from twenty animals at the start of the twentieth century to 2500 today. The removal in 1994 of the **white rhino** from the World Conservation Union's endangered list was thanks mostly to conservationists in the Hluhluwe-Imfolozi Park, which has become the world's breeding bank for these animals.

ARRIVAL AND INFORMATION   HLUHLUWE-IMFOLOZI PARK

Day-trips and tours There is no public transport to Hluhluwe-Imfolozi. Without your own car, you can take a day-trip offered by any of the accommodation within an hour's drive of the park, or a tour operated by the Durban firms listed in the box on p.372.

By car Access to the park is via three gates. Just north of Mtubatuba, the R618 to Hlabisa and Nongoma reaches Nyalazi Gate after 21km, providing access to the southern

section of the park. Further north, on the N3, an unclassified but signposted and tarred road near the turning for Hluhluwe takes you via Memorial Gate into the northernmost section of the park. A third gate, Cengeni, is accessible along a 30km tarred road from Ulundi to the west.

Information Maps and information, including details of guided walks, night drives and boat trips, are available at the receptions of the *Hilltop* and *Mpila* camps.

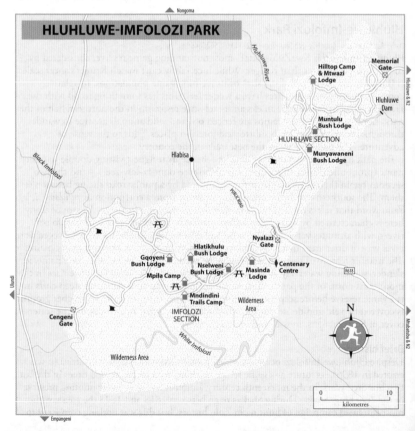

5

GAME VIEWING AND ACTIVITIES IN HLUHLUWE-IMFOLOZI

Despite its compact size, Hluhluwe-Imfolozi is home to 84 mammal species and close to 350 varieties of birds. The Big Five are all here, and it's no exaggeration to say that this is the best place in the world to see **rhinos**, both black and white. Extinct in Imfolozi until 1958, **lions** have been reintroduced, and today they number around seventy, although they're not easy to see. Other **predators** present are cheetah, spotted hyena and wild dog. **Herbivores** include blue wildebeest, buffalo, giraffe, hippo, impala, kudu, nyala and zebra. When it comes to **birds**, there are over a dozen species of **eagle**, as well as other **raptors** including hawks, goshawks and honey buzzards. Other larger birds include ground hornbills, vultures, owls and herons. **Reptile** species number in the sixties, including crocodiles and several types of venomous snake, none of which you're likely to see. Along the Hluhluwe River, keep an eye open for the harmless monitor lizards.

Where Hluhluwe-Imfolozi really scores over the Kruger is in the variety of activities on offer. Apart from **self-driving** around the park, there are also **self-guided walks** near several of the restcamps, **guided trails** in the company of an armed field ranger, guided **night drives** and a **boat trip** on the Hluhluwe Dam. South Africa's first **wilderness trail** started in Imfolozi, and the reserve remains the best place in South Africa for these (all are available from mid-March to mid-Dec). The three-night **Base Camp trail** (R3700 per person) involves day walks in the Wilderness Area, with nights spent at the Mndindini Trails camp not far from *Mpila Camp*; the three-night **Primitive trail** (R2290 per person) departs from *Mpila* and requires you to carry your own gear and sleep under the stars, wherever the ranger chooses; while the two-night **Short Wilderness trail** (R2250 per person) starts from *Mpila* at 1.30pm on Fridays and Sundays. Both the Primitive and the Short Wilderness trails can be extended by one night if you choose. On all of these trails, which must be booked through KZN Wildlife, you'll be accompanied by an armed ranger; all gear – including linen and food – is included in the price.

ACCOMMODATION

Accommodation is available in both the Imfolozi and Hluhluwe sections of the game reserve, with Imfolozi being the less developed of the two. There are no fences around the Imfolozi camps, so take care when walking around, particularly at night. Hluhluwe's *Hilltop* camp has a pleasant **restaurant**, the *Mpunyane*, and a bar lounge, the *Usavolo*. Some of the lodges include the services of a cook to prepare your meals, although you'll have to provide the ingredients. *Hilltop* and *Mpila* camps also have small stores selling very basic supplies, but it's best to stock up before you enter the park. Hluhluwe village and Mtubatuba have well-stocked **supermarkets**. In Imfolozi you'll find the **Centenary Centre** (daily 9am–4.30pm), with a small takeaway restaurant, a craft centre and *bomas* that house animals brought from other parks to be introduced here. **Bookings** are made through KZN Wildlife as usual (☎ 033 845 1000, ⊛ www.kznwildlife.com), though camping should be arranged locally.

HLUHLUWE SECTION

★ **Hilltop Camp** Probably the best publicly run safari camp in South Africa, set high on the edge of a slope with sweeping views across the park's hills and valleys. The camp has modern, comfortable and varied accommodation: budget two-bed rondavels that share communal ablutions and kitchen facilities; self-catering en-suite chalets sleeping two to four, with kitchenettes; and two-person en-suite chalets without kitchens. The camp is surrounded by an electric fence, which keeps out most animals, though nyala, zebra and other herbivores still graze around the chalets. R545

Mthwazi Lodge Near Hilltop. Four luxurious en-suite rooms in the original home of the warden, set attractively in a secluded private garden. A chef is available to prepare meals. Minimum charge for six people. R4320

Muntulu and Munyawaneni bush lodges Four bedrooms with private verandas at each of two upmarket bush lodges overlooking the Hluhluwe River. A cook is on hand to cater and a field ranger is available to take guests on walks. Minimum charge for six people. R4320

IMFOLOZI SECTION

Gqoyeni and Hlatikhulu bush lodges Both of these lodges – which have four two-bed units elevated above the Black Imfolozi River and linked to the living area by wooden walkways – need to be rented in their entirety. Their field ranger can conduct walks in the area, and there's a chef to cook meals. Gqoyeni R5400, Hlatikhulu R4800

Masinda Lodge Near Nyalazi Gate, this renovated upmarket lodge has three en-suite bedrooms decorated with Zulu art, plus the services of a cook. Minimum charge for eight people. R4000

Mpila Camp This camp in the centre of Imfolozi has excellent views of the surrounding wilderness from twelve one-roomed huts with two beds each, en-suite bathrooms and kitchenettes; two self-contained three-bedroom cottages for seven people (minimum charge for five); and

5

six self-catering chalets for five people (minimum charge for four). There's also a safari camp with twelve tents that sleep two people, and two tents that sleep four. R770 **Nselweni Bush Lodge** Located on the banks of the Black Mfolozi River, this lodge boasts wonderful views of the river and the bushveld. Its eight two-bed chalets are self-catering and share a comfortable lounge and a picturesque elevated veranda. R1130

Lake St Lucia

The most striking feature of the **isimangaliso Wetland Park** is the 360-square-kilometre **Lake St Lucia**, South Africa's largest inland body of water, formed 25,000 years ago when the oceans receded. The lake is flanked by mountainous **dunes** covered by forest and grassland, whose peaks soar to an astonishing 200m above the beach to form a slender rampart against the Indian Ocean. Aside from the lake and dune ecosystems, the reserve protects a **marine zone** of warm tropical seas, coral reefs and endless sandy beaches; the **papyrus and reed wetland** of the Mkhuze swamps, on the north of the lake; and, on the western shore, dry **savannah** and **thornveld**. Any one of these would justify conservation, but their confluence around the lake makes this a world-class wilderness. The real prize of the area is **Cape Vidal** inside the wetland park, though the limited accommodation there may necessitate your making a day-trip from St Lucia town.

St Lucia

Once a rough and remote anglers' hangout, **ST LUCIA**, which lies at the mouth of the **St Lucia Estuary** in the extreme south of the park, is in the process of reinventing itself as a well-organized eco-destination. The town's best feature is the **estuary**, the mouth of which was named Santa Lucia by Portuguese explorers when they reached it in 1576. During the second half of the eighteenth century, landlocked Boers made attempts to claim the estuary as a port, but were pipped at the post by the British, who sent HMS *Goshawk* in 1884 to annex the whole area, which then developed as a fishing resort. The estuary is hidden behind the buildings along the main drag, easy to miss if you drive quickly through.

The town of St Lucia lies 32km east of Mtubatuba, and can become pretty hectic in midsummer when **angling** fanatics descend for the school holidays. There's not much to do in St Lucia itself, but it does provide an excellent base for a number of activities (see box, p.406) and has a good choice of accommodation. Facilities in St Lucia include filling stations, a supermarket, self-service laundries, banks and ATMs.

St Lucia Crocodile Centre

Beside the park gate about 2km north of town on the road to Cape Vidal • Mon–Sat 9am–6pm, Sun 10am–5pm • Mon–Fri R40, Sat & Sun R50 • Crocodile feeding Sat 3pm & Sun 11.30am • ☎ 035 590 1386

This isn't another of the exploitative wildlife freak-shows common throughout South Africa, but a serious educative spin-off of KZN Wildlife's crocodile conservation campaign. Up until the end of the 1960s, "flat dogs" or "travelling handbags" were regarded as pests, and a hunting free-for-all saw them facing extinction in the area. Just in time, it was realized that crocs have an important role in the ecological cycle, and KZN Wildlife began a successful **breeding programme**, returning the crocs to the wild to bolster their numbers. The Crocodile Centre aims to rehabilitate the reputation of these maligned creatures, with informative displays and an astonishing cross section of species lounging around enclosed pools (only the Nile crocodile occurs in the wild in South Africa).

ARRIVAL AND INFORMATION   ST LUCIA

By taxi Taxis to Mtubatuba leave from the Dolphin Centre on the corner of McKenzie St and the R618 as you enter the village.

Tourist information The most helpful place is Advantage Tours at the Dolphin Centre on the corner of McKenzie St and the R618 as you enter the village (Mon–Fri 8am–4.30pm, Sat & Sun 8am–1pm; ☎ 035 590 1259 or 035 590 1180). The village of Khula, 7km west of St Lucia on the Mtuba Rd, has a tourist office specializing in responsible eco-tourism on the Elephant Coast (daily 7am–4.30pm; ☎ 083 447 0730).

KZN Wildlife Has an office at the south end of Pelican Rd (daily 8am–4.30pm; ☎ 035 590 1343), two blocks east of and parallel to McKenzie St.

ACCOMMODATION

Budget Backpackers 81 McKenzie St ☎ 082 627 6208, ⓦ budgetbackpackers.co.za. A spotlessly clean and well-managed hostel on the main road with a well-stocked kitchen and a comfortable lounge equipped with satellite TV. The dorms sleep five to nine, and there are a handful of doubles in cabins at the back. Dorm R150, double R380

Elephant Lake Hotel 3 Mullet St ☎ 035 590 1001, ⓦ elephantlake.co.za. St Lucia's only hotel, complete with a pool and a fantastic deck for evening drinks and views of the estuary. Rates include breakfast. R1090

iGwalagwala Guest House 91 Pelican St ☎ 035 590 1069, ⓦ igwala.co.za. The spacious en-suite rooms here are simply but elegantly decorated, and the gracious hosts make you feel right at home. Some rooms open directly onto the quiet, leafy garden and swimming pool. R860

Jo-a-Lize 116 McKenzie St ☎ 035 590 1224, ⓔ joalizelodge@futurenet.co.uk. One of the cheaper places in town, offering a variety of accommodation ranging from self-contained, self-catering flats to en-suite B&B units set around a pool. Rates include breakfast. R600

Marlin Lodge 62 Garrick Ave ☎ 035 590 1929, ⓦ marlinlodgestlucia.co.za. A friendly and convivial guesthouse whose light-filled rooms open onto a communal patio, where guests gather to braai and socialize. Some of the double rooms can be combined to accommodate families. R860

★ **St Lucia Wetlands B&B** 20 Kingfisher St ☎ 035 590 1098, ⓦ stluciawetlands.com. Six large rooms fitted out with elegant wooden furnishings, and there's a pool and a classy bar for guests. Exceptional service and the friendly atmosphere created by congenial hosts make this one of the best places to stay in St Lucia. There's even a car-washing service. R950

Sunset Lodge 154 McKenzie St ☎ 035 590 1197, ⓦ sunsetstlucia.co.za. Attractive, well-appointed self-catering log cabins sleeping two, four or five, with balconies and views of the estuary. Hippos occasionally feed on the lawn in front of the wooden pool deck. Good value, and great for families. R595

CAMPSITE

Sugarloaf Campsite On Ski-Boat Club Rd, south of town; book through KZN Wildlife ☎ 033 845 1000, ⓦ www.kznwildlife.com. A sizeable campsite on the best site in St Lucia, right on the banks of the estuary, with an on-site swimming pool and plenty of fishing and birdwatching opportunities nearby. R180/Two people

EATING AND DRINKING

Braza Georgiou Centre ☎ 035 590 1242. Portuguese specialities like *espetada* (beef skewers with peppers) and chourico (pork sausage), plus plenty of grilled meat, including a "Portuguese steak" topped with a fried egg (R89). Daily 10am–10pm.

Fisherman's 61 McKenzie St ☎ 035 590 1257. A good place for fresh seafood, this rough-and-ready local hangout is covered with fishing memorabilia. The owner himself is a fisherman, and serves up good prawns and seafood baskets (R85). At night it turns into one of the only bars in town. Daily 8am–11pm.

Ocean Basket Georgiou Centre ☎ 035 590 1241. It may be a chain, but good food and fast service make this one of the best places to eat in St Lucia. Big seafood platters and grilled fish served up in the pan (from R80) are the specialities of the house, and there's a pleasant balcony. Daily 11am–9.30pm.

Reef and Dune 51 McKenzie St ☎ 035 590 1048. A casual, family-friendly eatery decked out with picnic tables and a wrap-around deck. It serves the usual grills and seafood, along with tasty thin-crust pizzas at around R60. Daily 11.30am–9pm.

St Lucia Ski-Boat Club The end of Ski-Boat Club Rd ☎ 035 590 1376. This pub and grill has a nice patio with pleasant views of the estuary, making it a great place for sundowners. The food is mainly pub fare like burgers and fish and chips (R50). Daily noon–8.30pm.

Thyme Square Next to John Dory, McKenzie St ☎ 035 590 1692. It may be decorated like Barbie's dream house, but this civilized little café is a relaxing place to indulge in tea and crumpets with cream (R18), or a light and healthy lunch. Mon–Sat 9am–5pm, Sun 9am–4pm.

Cape Vidal

Daily: April–Oct 6am–6pm; Nov–March 5am–7pm • R35, plus R45 per vehicle • ☎ 035 590 9012

Cape Vidal, another popular fishing spot, can only be reached via a tarred road that heads north from St Lucia (the extension of McKenzie St) for 32km, navigating a narrow land bridge between the lake and the Indian Ocean. En route you'll pass through grassland and wetlands populated by small game, rhino, birdlife and the occasional leopard. There's no public transport to Cape Vidal.

There's enough stunning wilderness here to keep you chilling out for several days, even if you aren't a keen angler. The sea is only minutes from the KZN Wildlife accommodation and an offshore reef shelters the coast from the high seas, making it

5

ACTIVITIES AROUND ST LUCIA

Small as it is, St Lucia is the biggest settlement around the iSimangaliso Wetland Park, and the best place to **organize activities**. If you're using St Lucia as a base from which to visit the Hluhluwe-Imfolozi Park, informative half- and full-day game drives (from R850) are conducted by St Lucia-based Maputaland Tours, 1 Kabeljou St (☎035 590 1041 or ☎082 940 7380, ⍵maputaland.com), which also organizes other tours in and around St Lucia.

BIKING

Birders on Bikes is the best-value cycling package in town, and one of the most interesting tours available. A two- to three-hour gentle cycle leads you through the southern part of the estuary, along the beach and into the Cape Vidal reserve. Knowledgeable Zulu guides teach you about flora and fauna and the use of plants in Zulu culture and medicine. Book through Shaka Barker Tours, 43 Hornbill St (☎035 590 1162, ⍵shakabarker.co.za; R225 including bike rental).

FISHING

Deep-sea fishing trips (for novices and seasoned anglers) with a skipper, guide, experienced fisherman, bait and tackle supplied. Either tag and release your game fish or take it home to cook. Advantage Tours & Charters (☎035 590 1259) runs six-hour trips, as does the restaurant *Fisherman's* (see p.405); both cost R1000 per person. Bring your own lunch and refreshments.

HORSERIDING

Bhangazi Horse Safaris (☎083 792 7899, ⍵stlucia-adventureactivities.com) offers **rides** through bushland, forests and lakes where you can view wildlife, or along the beach (R350/hr).

KAYAKING

Kayaking in the lake system gives an unparalleled experience of the wetland. St Lucia Kayak Safaris (☎035 590 1233, ⍵kayaksafaris.co.za) runs half- and full-day outings costing R295–525, including all gear, transfers to the launch site and refreshments.

LAKE CRUISES

It's well worth going on a **lake cruise**, which gives you a good chance of seeing crocodiles and hippos, as well as pelicans, fish eagles, kingfishers and storks. Two-hour cruises are offered by most operators in town, the cheapest being KZN Wildlife (☎035 590 1340; R155), though Shaka Barker Tows (see above; R210) and Heritage Tours (☎035 590 1555, ⍵heritagetoursandsafaris .com; R195) go out in smaller boats and provide a more personalized experience.

WETLAND WILDLIFE TOURS

An outstanding range of **tours in the wetland** is led by Shaka Barker's Kian Barker, a qualified zoologist and marine biologist, including the full-day St Lucia World Heritage Tour (R625) and the interesting and unusual Night Drive (R325), which goes out in search of rhinos, hyenas, leopards and the sixteen chameleon species of the St Lucia region (a staggering fourteen of which are endemic). Also recommended is the one-night, two-day Turtle Tour (Nov–Feb; R2250) to see the annual turtle egg-laying migration at Kosi Bay (see p.413), and walks led by local guides who explain the relationship the Zulus traditionally had with the animals who share their land (R195; 3hr). Book through Shaka Barker Tours (see above).

WHALE-WATCHING

Humpback and southern right whales cruise along the wetland's shore, and in season (June–Nov) you can join a **whale-watching boat trip** to look for them. Book through Advantage Tours & Charters (see above; R950; 2hr); the trips leave from the Advantage office on McKenzie St. There's no jetty down at the beach and launching the boat into the waves is an adventure in itself – if the ocean is choppy, expect to get soaked.

safe for **swimming** and providing good opportunities for **snorkelling** – you'll see hard and soft corals, colourful fish and tiny **rock pools** full of snails, crabs, sea cucumbers, anemones and urchins – while burly anglers use the rocks for casting their lines.

Whale-watching

Cape Vidal is an excellent place for shore sightings of **humpback whales**, which, in winter, breed off Mozambique not far to the north. In October they move south, drifting on the warm Agulhas current with their calves. If you're lucky you may see these and other whales from the dunes; a **whale-watching tower**, reached through the dune forest south of the restcamp, provides an even higher viewpoint. Eighteen-metre plankton-feeding whale sharks, the largest and gentlest of the sharks, have been sighted off this coast in schools of up to seventy at a time, and manta rays and dolphins are also common.

ACCOMMODATION   CAPE VIDAL

There's a small store selling basics and a petrol pump at the beach.

Beach Log Cabins ☎035 590 9012, ⓦwww
.kznwildlife.com. A collection of five- and eight-bed
Swiss-style log cabins, all en suite and provided with linen
and cooking utensils. Minimum charge for three and four
people, respectively. Three people R1020
Bhangazi Complex ☎035 590 9012, ⓦwww
.kznwildlife.com. Cabins ranging from six beds

(minimum charge for three) to twenty in dorms let out
to groups, plus a campsite with space for fifty tents in
the dune forest near the beach, with ablution facilities.
Bookings for the campsite in particular are vital during
school holidays and over long weekends; there's a
minimum charge for four. Camping for four people
R440, three-person cabin R540

The western shore

Daily: Nov–March 5am–7pm; April–Oct 6am–6pm • R40, plus R45 per vehicle

Accessible only with your own transport or on a tour, the **western shore** of Lake St Lucia marks the old seashore, harking back aeons to a time when the ocean level was 2m higher than it is today. Decayed matter from marine animals has created a rich soil, which once supported an extensive array of animal life, and although the Big Five were shot out ages ago, **birdlife** and more than a hundred species of **butterfly** still flit about. Among the **herbivores** are suni – Africa's smallest antelope – as well as nyala and red duiker. With no dangerous predators apart from **crocodiles** (take care along the shore), the inland bushveld and woodlands are safe for walking without a guide. Only day visitors are allowed at **Charter's Creek**, at the southern end of the lake, while **Fanies Island**, 20km north of Charter's Creek, is closed completely.

False Bay Park

About 20km north of Fanies Island • Daily 6am–6pm • R25 • ☎035 562 0425

False Bay Park perches on the western shore of a small, lozenge-shaped waterway connected to Lake St Lucia by a narrow, steep-sided channel known colourfully as "Hell's Gates" (note that it's not possible to launch boats in this part of the lake because of the low water level). Two self-guided hikes, the 8km **Dugandlovu Trail** and the 10km circular **Mpophomeni Trail**, are clearly waymarked. They pass through a mixed terrain, and offer the opportunity of seeing birds and a decent variety of antelope and other small mammals such as jackals, mongooses and warthogs. The shorter 6km **Ingwe Trail** passes alongside the lake.

ARRIVAL AND ACCOMMODATION   THE WESTERN SHORE

By car You reach False Bay Park via Hluhluwe (see p.401);
continue east through the village to a T-junction at the
end of the road and follow the signposts for 15km to the
False Bay Gate.
Falaza Game Park ☎035 562 2319, ⓦfalaza.co.za.
For a touch of luxury, head for this slick tented
accommodation in a small reserve, which also boasts a
reasonably priced health spa and a pool where rhino

enjoy lounging. Activities can be arranged, such as
guided walks and boat trips or game drives into
Hluhluwe-Imfolozi Park. R1800
Sand Forest Lodge ☎082 417 6484 or 083 627 7080,
ⓦsandforest.co.za. A collection of campsites and self-
catering cottages, located on a small reserve with antelope,
zebra and wildebeest. Meals are available on request.
Camping R120, cottage R600

5

Mkhuze Game Reserve

Daily: April–Oct 6am–6pm; Nov–March 5am–7pm • R35, plus R44 per vehicle • ☏ 035 573 9004

Reached across the Lebombo Mountains, 28km east of **Mkhuze** village on the N2, **Mkhuze Game Reserve** is notable for its varied and beautiful countryside and rich birdlife, although it is also home to lions, rhinos and elephants. The reserve is a major part of the iSimangaliso Wetland Park, connected to the coastal plain by a slender corridor through which the Mkhuze River flows before emptying into Lake St Lucia. It marks the final haul of the coastal plain stretching down the east of the continent from Kenya. The landscape varies from the **Muzi Pans**, wetlands consisting of seasonal flood plains floating with waterlilies, reed beds and swamps, to savannah. Elsewhere you'll come across stands of acacias, and in the south across the Mkhuze River you can wander through the cathedral-like fig forest that echoes to the shriek of trumpeter hornbills.

ARRIVAL AND INFORMATION
MKHUZE GAME RESERVE

By car If you're driving, the easiest way to get to the reserve is to leave the N2 at Mkhuze village and follow the signs along a good dirt road to Emshopi Gate. An alternative route, which leaves the N2 further south, 35km north of Hluhluwe, involves a lot more driving on dirt and doesn't knock much off the distance. Another entry point provides quick access from Sodwana Bay via the new Ophansi Bridge that crosses the Mkhuze River on the eastern side of the reserve. From Sodwana Bay, travel south on the R22 and turn down the

D820 access road on which the bridge is built; it's about a 40min drive from Sodwana Bay to the reserve.

On a tour There's no public transport into Mkhuze, and if you don't have your own vehicle you'll need to join one of the daytime or night-time excursions into the park from Mkhuze village (see above).

Information The park reception office, 9km from the entrance gate, provides a clear map showing all routes and distances and giving general information about the park.

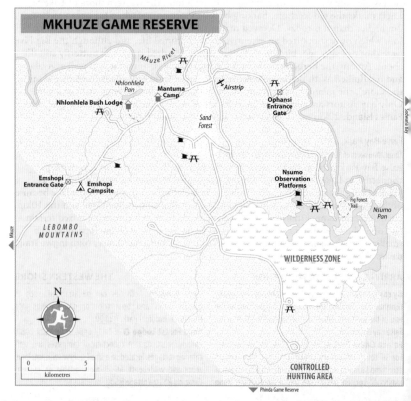

GAME VIEWING AND ACTIVITIES IN MKHUZE

Some 84km of roads traverse Mkhuze, but one of the best ways to see game is to stay put and wait for the animals to come to you. Several **hides** have been erected at artificial watering holes and on the edge of pans, which attract plenty of animals, particularly in the drier months.

Mkhuze is among the top spots for **birdwatching** in the country, with an impressive 430 species on record. Some of the prizes include Pels fishing owl and Rudd's apalis, a small, insect-eating bird with a very restricted distribution. Even if you know nothing about birds, you're likely to appreciate one of Africa's most colourful here – the lilac-breasted roller. The two hides at **Nsumo Pan**, in the southern section of the park, overlook a beautiful natural waterway, and are superbly placed for observing **waterfowl**. Between July and September, if conditions are right, you can see up to five hundred birds on the water at one time, among them flocks of pelicans and flamingos, kingfishers, fish eagles, and many other species. To arrange a specialist birding guide from the local community, contact one of the guides listed on the website of the Zululand Birding Route (w zululandbirdingroute.co.za; R300 half day, R550 full day).

The other obvious draw of Mkhuze is its black and white **rhinos**. While there are no lions, cheetah and leopard are present though rarely glimpsed – you're more likely to see jackals. You also stand a good chance of seeing several types of **antelopes**, including impala, eland and kudu. **Primates** such as baboons and vervet monkeys can generally be seen rustling around in the trees and making a nuisance of themselves on the ground, while at night you could be treated to the eerie call of the thick-tailed bushbaby from the canopy.

KZN Wildlife offers a number of activities, including recommended **night drives** from *Mantuma* (R200). During the day, you can explore Mkhuze on foot with a field ranger on two-hour **walks** (R110) that concentrate on either game or birds. Also good for birding is a guided walk (R180) along the 3km **Mkhuze Fig Forest Trail** – another highlight of the reserve. Sycamore fig forest is one of the rarest types of woodland in South Africa, and the stands of massive trees give the forest a gentle green glow. Passing monkeys and baboons pose no threat to anything but your food, but you should keep alert to the possibility of encountering black rhinos or hippos.

You can buy fuel at the entrance gate, and there's a shop selling basic supplies and books at reception, but you should stock up on provisions in Mkhuze village before heading out.

ACCOMMODATION

Ghost Mountain Inn In Mkhuze village, signposted off the N2 ☎ 035 573 1025, w ghostmountaininn.co.za. An attractive hotel, great for a drink or meal and a dunk in their pool even if you aren't staying. They organize four-hour game drives to Mkhuze (from R415 per person; minimum four people) and guided hikes up Ghost Mountain, which overlooks Mkhuze (3–4hr; R160; minimum four people). R1700

Mantuma 9km into the park in the northern section; book through KZN Wildlife ☎ 035 573 9004. A range of KZN Wildlife accommodation, the cheapest being two-bed rest huts with shared bathrooms and a kitchen. There are also larger chalets that sleep two, four or six. The most enticing units, however, are the large two- or four-person safari tents, each with its own ablutions. R410

Nhlonhlela Bush Lodge Overlooking Nhlonhlela Pan between Mantuma and Emshopi Gate; book through KZN Wildlife ☎ 035 573 9004. Four two-bed rooms run by KZN Wildlife, connected by wooden walkways to a communal kitchen and living area. There's a cook (you bring the ingredients) and a field ranger included in the price. Minimum charge for six. Six people R2350

Phinda Private Game Reserve Book through & Beyond Africa ☎ 011 809 4300, w andbeyond.com. A small private game reserve at Mkhuze's southern end, *Phinda* offers good chances of seeing lion, cheetah and both species of rhino. Accommodation is at five opulent lodges in a variety of original styles, from stilted Afro–Japanese timber houses to intimate chalets chiselled into the rock. All provide hospitality of the highest standard, and game drives and walks are accompanied by well-informed expert guides who are as good as any you'll find in South Africa. Rates include all meals and game activities. R12000

CAMPSITE

Emshopi Campsite at Emshopi Gate; book through KZN Wildlife ☎ 033 845 1000, w www.kznwildlife.com. A simple, fairly large campsite handily located at the park entrance, with hot-water showers available on site; minimum charge for three. Three people R230

Maputaland

Also known as **Maputaland**, the extreme northeast section of the Elephant Coast is the remotest tract of South Africa, mostly accessible only along dirt roads that work their tortuous way to the coast. The quickest way of reaching this area is from **Hluhluwe** village, where the tarred **R22** strikes north for some 150km, passing **Sodwana Bay** and terminating near **Kosi Bay** and the Mozambique border. Another road, 11km north of **Mkhuze** village, snakes north and then east for 133km, eventually connecting with the R22 about 40km south of Kosi Bay. This road gives access to the border village of **Ingwavuma**, home to a Zulu festival and the base for some excellent hikes, as well as the **Ndumo Game Reserve** and **Tembe Elephant Park**, both reserves reaching down from the Mozambique border.

Sodwana Bay National Park

Around 80km northeast of Hluhluwe village • Daily 24hr • R30

A tiny scoop in the Zululand Coast, **SODWANA BAY** is the only breach in an almost flawless strand extending 170km from St Lucia to Kosi Bay. It's the fortuitous convergence of the bay (which makes it easy to launch boats) with the world's southernmost coral reefs that makes Sodwana the most popular base in the country for **scuba diving** and the most popular KZN Wildlife resort. Because the continental shelf comes extremely close to shore (near-vertical drops are less than 1km away), it offers very deep waters, much loved by anglers who gather here for some of South Africa's best deep-sea **game fishing**, mostly tag and release. The abundance of game fish also makes for some of the best surf fly-fishing in the country.

When there's no one around, Sodwana Bay is paradise, with tepid waters, terrific sandy beaches, relaxed diving and snorkelling, and plenty of accommodation. Over weekends and during school holidays, however, fashion-conscious Jo'burgers tear down in their 4WDs, while thick-set anglers from Gauteng, Free State and Mpumalanga come here and drink themselves into a stupor. Thankfully, government regulations now limit the number of 4WDs using the beach as a car park. A gentler presence from mid-November to February are the leatherback and loggerhead **turtles**, who make their way onto Sodwana's beaches to reproduce, as they've been doing for the last 60,000 years.

The national park takes in the bay itself, while the desultory collection of shops and an upmarket lodge that pass for the town lie 4km to the west, back along the Mbazwana road.

The Mgobolezeni Trail

The 5km circular **Mgobolezeni trail** winds its way from just across from the park reception (see opposite) through a variety of habitats, including woodland, to the coastal lake that gives the hike its name. Arrows and signs indicate the way – but take care not to get sidetracked down one of the many game paths that crisscross it. The walk takes around three hours and there's no drinkable water along the way, so you should bring refreshment. **Crocodiles** live in the lake, as do **hippos** who leave the water to feed, usually at dusk. If you encounter a hippo on land, treat it with the utmost respect – hippos are responsible for more human deaths than any other African mammal. Avoid getting between a hippo and its line of retreat, which will generally be the most direct route to the safety of the water. If you do disturb one, find a tree to hide behind or, even better, to climb.

Apart from hippos, you may be lucky enough to see some of the other animals that inhabit the dune forest and its surrounds, among them bushbuck, duiker and Tonga squirrels. A trail **booklet** available from the park reception interprets points of interest along the way.

ARRIVAL, INFORMATION AND TOURS SODWANA BAY

By minibus taxi Minibus taxis run to Sodwana Bay from Mbazwana. If you haven't got your own vehicle, you'll have to hitchike your way around as the place is so spread out.

Tours Off-Road Adventures in the village (☎ 079 835 4132, ⓦ offroadfun.co.za) runs guided quad-bike rides (R250/hr) either within the bay area or, more ambitiously, on a

5

DIVING AND SNORKELLING IN SODWANA BAY

Unless you're a keen angler, the principal reason to come to Sodwana Bay is for the diving off the **coral reefs** that thrive here in the warm waters carried down the coast by the Agulhas current. The sea is clear, silt-free and perfect for spotting some of the 1200 varieties of **fish** that inhabit the waters off northern KwaZulu-Natal, making it second only to the Great Barrier Reef in its richness.

The closest reef to the bay, and consequently the most visited, is **Two Mile Reef**, 2km long and 900m wide, offering excellent dives. Among the others is **Five Mile Reef**, which is further north and known for its miniature staghorn corals, while beyond that, **Seven Mile Reef** is inhabited by large anemone communities and offers protection to turtles and rays, which may be found resting here.

There's excellent **snorkelling** at Jesser Point, a tiny promontory at the southern end of the bay. Just off here is **Quarter Mile Reef**, which attracts a wide variety of fish, including moray eels and rays. Low tide is the best time to venture out. You can buy competitively priced snorkels and masks (or rent them for R30 per day) from the dive shop at *Sodwana Bay Lodge*. Here you'll also find a **dive operation** offering various diving courses, diving packages and scuba equipment rental. There is also a dive operator providing similar services at *Coral Divers*.

three-hour jaunt to Lake Sibaya (R500). During December and January, when loggerhead and leatherback turtles come to nest and lay their eggs on the beach, you can join one of the guided turtle tours from Sodwana Bay. As a limited number of licences are issued each year for these, the operators change from year to year, so enquire locally.

Tourist facilities The KZN Wildlife office (Mon–Sat 8am–4pm, Sun 7am–3pm), park entry gate and a small shop with food and other camping basics, as well as an ATM, are up the hill past the town. Petrol is available at the entry gate.

GETTING AROUND

By car Your biggest challenge in Maputaland is likely to be getting around. For much of this area, a 4WD vehicle is essential and it's best to travel in two vehicles as there's nowhere to get repairs done and facilities are poor. It's also essential to carry an inflated spare tyre, jack and wheel spanner, and spare water. Watch out for unattended stray animals and school children wandering onto the roads; never resort to speeding on dirt roads to make up time, and watch out for potholes.

ACCOMMODATION

Most accommodation at Sodwana Bay lies inside the KZN Wildlife conservation area along the beach. If you're staying inside the park at the privately run *Coral Divers* or *Mseni*, you must pay a R70 daily camping fee to KZN Wildlife. *Mseni* includes the fee in its rate; to stay at *Coral Divers*, pay the fee at the KZN Wildlife office.

Coral Divers Sodwana Main Rd ☏ 035 571 0290, ⓦ coraldivers.co.za. The largest dive outfit at Sodwana Bay is a basic, rather tired divers' haunt with two-bed safari tents and two-bed cabins with or without their own bathrooms; note that at least one person in each room must be planning to dive. You can self-cater or pay for half board, and takeaways are available throughout the day. Free transport to and from the beach to coincide with dives and meal times. Self-catering R260

KZN Wildlife Accommodation At the northern end of the reserve ☏ 035 571 0051. Twenty fully equipped log cabins with either four or six beds, with minimum charges for three and four people, respectively. There are also a staggering 350 campsites here (minimum charge for four), and the seasonal population explosion allegedly makes Sodwana Bay the largest campsite in the southern hemisphere. Camping for four people R440, cabin for three people R1230

Mseni Lodge Right on the water's edge, south of the village ☏ 035 571 0284, ⓦ mseni.co.za. The only establishment with direct access to the beach, this comfortable lodge offers en-suite B&B log cabins or self-catering units sleeping two to eight people spread out amid thick coastal forest. There's a restaurant, bar, satellite TV and swimming pool. R560

Natural Moments Next to *Sodwana Bay Lodge*, Sodwana Main Rd ☏ 083 236 1756, ⓦ divesodwana .com. A friendly and somewhat bohemian backpackers offering a variety of rustic but cosy cabins, most priced as dorms and some en suite, along with a couple of family units and a big communal kitchen. During the summer there's also a good pizza joint out front, and campsites across the road. Camping R85, dorms R150, double R400

Sodwana Bay Lodge Sodwana Main Rd, in the village ☏ 035 571 6000, ⓦ sodwanabaylodge.co.za. Simple yet comfortable reed and thatched en-suite two-bed B&B chalets. A poolside bar downstairs has pool tables and a sun deck that attracts both visitors and locals. Half board R1464

5

EATING

There are several fast food kiosks at the beach. The pick of the bunch is Jabu's by the craft market, serving freshly made sandwiches and hot bunny chows.

Drunken Tree Bar Sodwana Main Rd ☎ 079 931 4737. Nightly bonfires, live music, a chess board made of bottles and a neighbourly vibe make this pub the watering hole of choice for locals and tourists alike, who come for the beer (R15), the food (R78 for steak and chips) and the late-night camaraderie. Daily except Tues noon–late.

The Lighthouse Sodwana Main Rd ☎ 083 471 0868. The classiest restaurant Sodwana has to offer, with pasta, seafood and good thin-crust pizzas (around R70) served on a pleasant patio strewn with fairy lights. Winter Thurs–Sun 8am–10pm; summer daily 8am–10pm.

Lake Sibaya

Lake Sibaya, South Africa's largest natural freshwater lake, covers 77 square kilometres and is fringed by white sandy beaches disappearing into dense forest. On a windless day, the lake, 10km due north of Sodwana Bay, appears glassy, azure and flat; the waters are so transparent that when KZN Wildlife take a hippo census they just fly over and count the dark blobs clearly visible from the air. From the margins, timid crocodiles cut the lake surface, exchanging the warmth of the sun for the safety of the water. This is not an unpopulated wilderness: the lake fringes are dotted with traditional African lands and villages. There's an exceptionally easy-going 3km **circular walk** that starts from the viewing platform behind KZN Wildlife's now closed *Baya Camp*. **Birdwatching** can be rewarding (there are two hides), with close on three hundred species present. Needless to say, with crocs and hippos lolling about, swimming in the lake is most unwise.

Mabibi

Daily 6am–6pm • R25, plus R20 per vehicle • ☎ 035 574 8998

MABIBI is probably one of the most peaceful spots to camp in South Africa, where you can pitch your tent in luxuriant subtropical forest and follow a boardwalk down the duneside to the **sea** – a walk that takes about ten minutes. Outside school holidays, there's a fair chance of having a perfect tropical beach all to yourself, and you won't get the frenetic activity of outboard motors and 4WD vehicles found further south – they're banned within the Maputaland Coastal Forest Reserve, which Mabibi falls under. The coast here offers **surf angling** and **snorkelling** matching that at Sodwana Bay, with rich tropical marine life thriving on the coral reefs offshore. A number of mammals live in the forest, but most of them – bushbabies, large-spotted genets and porcupines – only come out after dark.

ARRIVAL AND DEPARTURE   MABIBI

By car One approach to Mabibi is the tarred Kwa-Ngwanase (also called Manguzi) Rd from the N2, some 11km north of Mkhuze. At the Manzengwenya intersection, turn right and follow the (poorly marked) signboards to Mabibi. Because this final 45km from the junction is along gravel and thick sand tracks, a 4WD vehicle, or at least one with high clearance, and competent driving are essential. You can also reach Mabibi on the coastal forest link road (also called Coastal Cashews Rd) from Mbazwana; turn right at the Manzengwenya Rd and follow the signs. If you're staying at *Thonga Beach Lodge*, you'll be collected at the end of the tarred road, beyond the Manzengwenya intersection.

ACCOMMODATION

Campsite Book through Isibindi Africa ☎ 035 474 1473, ⊛ isibindi.co.za. Three remote and idyllic two-person chalets and eight camping pitches situated in subtropical forest, perched on a plateau on top of the dunes and sheltered from the wind. A boardwalk leads down to the sea. Camping R96, chalets R550

Thonga Beach Lodge ☎ 035 474 1473, ⊛ isibindi .co.za. This luxury Robinson Crusoe-style lodge offers thatched suites secluded in the coastal dune forest, along with a wellness centre, dive operation, turtle tracking tours, kayaking and sundowners at Lake Sibaya. Full board R6550

Rocktail Bay

South Africa's most sublime beachstay lies about 20km north of Mabibi along the coast at **ROCKTAIL BAY**, a stretch of sand and sea that's restricted to guests who are prepared to pay for the privilege. Few parts of the South African coastline are as unspoilt as the beaches around here. Although there's no big game to pull in the punters, there's excellent **scuba diving** offshore, and a dive centre with a qualified PADI instructor, a boat and skipper – one of the highlights is diving with pregnant ragged-tooth sharks as they migrate north up the KwaZulu-Natal coast from around late September to May. The **birdwatching** here is excellent; among a number of rare species are the green coucal, grey waxbill, Natal robin and – particularly prized – palmnut vulture.

In addition, Rocktail Bay is the best spot along the northern Elephant Coast for viewing loggerhead and leatherback **turtles**, who come here every year between October and February from as far afield as Kenya and Cape Agulhas to lay their eggs. **Surf fishing** for kingfish, barracuda, blacktail and the like is another possibility.

ACCOMMODATION ROCKTAIL BAY

Rocktail Beach Camp Book through Wilderness Safaris ☎ 011 807 1800, ⌨ wilderness-safaris.com. The comfortable *Rocktail Beach Camp* is the ideal way to get away from it all. There are seventeen luxurious yet rustic en-suite rooms a short walk from the beach, each decorated with natural materials and enjoying sweeping views of the coastal forest. There's limited solar electricity, mobile networks don't always work, and the last few kilometres are so heavy-going that you leave your vehicle at the Coastal Cashews Farm on the dirt road from Mabibi and get ferried in by 4WD (included in the rate). Rates also include excursions. Half board R2608

Kosi Bay

Kosi Mouth daily 6am–6pm • R20, plus R15 per vehicle • ☎ 035 592 0236

At the northernmost reaches of the KwaZulu-Natal coast, **KOSI BAY** is at the centre of an enthralling area of waterways fringed by forest. Despite the name, this is not a bay at all, but a system of four lakes connected by narrow reed channels, which eventually empty into the sea at Kosi Mouth.

One of the most striking images of Kosi Bay is of mazes of reed fences in the estuary and other parts of the lake system. These are **fish traps**, or kraals, built by local Tonga people, a sustainable practice that has been going on for hundreds of years. The traps are passed down from father to son, and capture only a small fraction of the fish that pass through, with trap numbers strictly controlled. To see the fish traps – and the beach – you'll need to travel to Kosi Mouth, a hard-going 20-minute drive for which you'll need 4WD. Note that a permit is required for Kosi Mouth, which you can obtain at the gate.

ACCOMMODATION KOSI BAY

In addition to KNZ's wildlife's restcamp, there are a number of locally owned and operated camps, the proprietors all enthusiastic hosts and knowledgeable guides. Directions to the camps are given when you book, and 4WD transfers from Kwa-Ngwanase (Manguzi) can be arranged for an additional charge.

★ **Kosi Forest Lodge** Inside the reserve ☎ 035 474 1473, ⌨ isibindiafrica.co.za. Arguably the most dreamy place to stay in KwaZulu-Natal, featuring eight reed-and-thatch suites in a remote landscape of palms, lakes, sand forest and bleached white beaches. There's limited electricity, and if you don't have your own 4WD you'll be collected from the Total garage in Kwa-Ngwanase and taken along sandy tracks to the lodge. Activities include game drives, guided canoeing trips, reef snorkelling and forest walks; there's a good chance you'll see hippos, crocodiles and marine turtles. The rate includes all meals and some activities. Full board R3380

KZN Wildlife Restcamp Inside the reserve on the western shore of Nhlange, the largest of the lakes ☎ 035 592 0236. Two-bed, five-bed (minimum charge for four people) and six-bed cabins, with a small campsite nearby (minimum charge for four). The price includes the park entry fee. Camping for four people R400, cabins R510 **Thobeka Backpackers** 4km north of Kwa-Ngwanase ☎ 072 446 1525, ⌨ kosi.co.za. A delightfully rustic, friendly backpackers hidden away in the forest, with bush camp-style self-catering double rooms and a cottage connected by elevated walkways. A variety of activities is

5

available, including snorkelling, tours into Mozambique, trips to a colourful border market and even courses in bush cooking. Double R300, cottage R800

Vic's Camp ✆ 082 857 3363, ✉ jenny.reservations @vodamail.co.za. A collection of campsites and basic

rondavels with a communal kitchen (bring your own provisions) and dining area. The main draw is its unique setting in the sand forest at Bhanga Nek. Camping R110, rondavels R460

Tembe Elephant Park

✆ 082 651 2868, ⓦ tembe.co.za

The easy-going and remote **Tembe Elephant Park**, on the border with Mozambique, is part-owned by the local Tembe tribe, and access is limited to those staying in the rather pricey accommodation on offer. The park is located on what was once known as the "Ivory Route" along which Zulu ivory merchants once plied their trade, and it is still home to over 220 elephants, including some of the largest in Southern Africa. The park also contains the other Big Five species, as well as game such as impala and suni antelope, and a wide variety of birds can be found flitting through its sand forests and wetlands.

ARRIVAL AND ACCOMMODATION · TEMBE ELEPHANT PARK

By car The turn-off to Tembe lies 15km or so east of Ndumo. You can reach the gate with a normal vehicle, but in the park itself 4WD is necessary – you leave your car at the gate and transfer to the park's own vehicle.

Safari tents ✆ 082 651 2868, ⓦ tembe.co.za.

Accommodation at Tembe is in luxury en-suite safari tents built on raised wooden platforms. The price includes all meals and game drives conducted by knowledgeable guides from the local community, with traditional Tembe dancers coming to perform in the evenings on request. R1900

Ndumo Game Reserve

Daily: April–Sept 6am–6pm; Oct–March 5am–7pm · R40, plus R35 per vehicle · ✆ 035 591 0058

One of the most beautiful of the KwaZulu-Natal reserves, **Ndumo** looks across the flood plain into Mozambique to the north and up to the Lebombo Mountains in the south. Its northern extent hugs the **Usutu River**, which rises in Swaziland and defines South Africa's border with Mozambique. The turn-off to the reserve is 56km north of Jozini, with the final 15km along a rough gravel track.

No great volume of animals trammel the reserve (nyala, hippo and both species of rhino are among the 62 species here), and they may be more difficult to see than elsewhere. For twitchers, however, Ndumo ranks among the country's top **bird-watching** spots. The staggering 430 different varieties recorded here include the African broadbill, Pels fishing owl and the southern banded snake eagle.

It's possible to **drive** around some areas, one of the highlights being the trip to **Redcliffs**, where there's a picnic site with a vantage point offering soaring views across the Usutu River into both Swaziland and Mozambique.

INFORMATION AND TOURS · NDUMO GAME RESERVE

KZN Wildlife operates an education centre on the reserve, 2km from the restcamp office (daily 7am–4pm; ✆ 072 804 6007). Staff can organize open-topped 4WD outings in the mornings and evenings to the lovely

Inyamiti pan, which is inhabited by hippos and crocodiles and receives visits from an array of waterfowl; guided walking trails are also available.

ACCOMMODATION

KZN Wildlife Restcamp ✆ 035 591 0058. A number of campsites and seven well-maintained, two-bed huts perched on a hill, each with a fridge and shared ablutions. A shop near the entrance gate sells basic supplies, but you're better off stocking up en route in Mkhuze village. Camping R110, huts R660

Ndumu River Lodge Just outside the park ✆ 035 592 8000, ⓦ ndumu.com. A pleasant place to stay, offering en-suite B&B rooms or self-catering chalets. There's also a restaurant and bar on site, and you can fish in the nearby river. Directions are given when you book. R1350

FROM TOP CHEETAH IN HLUHLUWE-IMFOLOZI PARK (P.401); HIPPO IN THE ST LUCIA WETLANDS (P.404) >

5

Ithala Game Reserve

Daily: March–Oct 6am–6pm; Nov–Feb 5am–7pm • R40, plus R30 per vehicle • ☎ 034 983 2540

West of Maputaland and close to the Swaziland border, the small **Ithala Game Reserve** is little known, despite being one of the country's most uncrowded and spectacularly scenic places to watch wildlife. Ithala is largely mountainous and the terrain is extremely varied, with numerous cliffs and rock faces contained within a protective basin.

Like the rest of the KwaZulu-Natal game reserves, Ithala is excellent for white **rhinos** and there's plenty of **plains game**, including zebras and giraffes. Of the **predators**, you could, if you're very lucky, encounter brown hyenas, cheetahs and leopards. If want to see the Big Five, however, Ithala is not foo you – there are no lions, though the other four make periodic appearances. The best idea is to forget the mammal checklist and take a slow drive around the mountains into the valleys and along the watercourses. One of the most rewarding **drives** is along Ngubhu Loop, with a detour to Ngubhu picnic site.

ARRIVAL, INFORMATION AND TOURS
ITHALA GAME RESERVE

By car There's no public transport to the park or near it, so driving here is your only option. The entrance gate is just off the R69.

Information The camp's reception can provide information and maps.

Tours There are some self-guided trails into the wooded mountainside above Ntshondwe Camp, which give the chance to stretch your legs if you've spent a morning driving around. Day and night drives (R190) in open vehicles can be booked through the restcamp's reception.

ACCOMMODATION

Mbizo Bush Camp ☎ 033 845 1000, ⦿ www .kznwildlife.com. For a pared-down bush experience, you can't beat this marvellous bush camp with space for just eight people, shaded by thorn trees and ilala palms, on the banks of the Mbizo River. Expect no frills here – it's cold showers in reed enclosures and cooking over wood fires, the only concession to civilization being a flushing toilet. Minimum charge for six people. <u>R2460</u>

Mhlangeni and Thalu Bush Camps ☎ 033 845 1000, ⦿ www.kznwildlife.com. A wonderful choice for something a bit wilder, these camps enjoy beautiful secluded settings and have four (minimum charge for three) or ten (minimum charge for seven) beds respectively. Both are staffed by an attendant and you can arrange a field ranger to take you on walks. Thalu (3 people) <u>R1230</u>, Mhlangeni (7 people) <u>R2870</u>

★**Ntshondwe Camp** ☎ 033 845 1000, ⦿ www .kznwildlife.com. This is one of the best game-reserve restcamps in South Africa, offering comfortable two-, four- and six-bed self-catering chalets with fully equipped kitchens, lounge areas and verandas, as well as two-bed non-self-catering units. Each chalet is surrounded by indigenous bush through which paved walkways weave their way around granite rocks and trees to the main reception area. <u>R800</u>

Ntshondwe Lodge ☎ 033 845 1000, ⦿ www .kznwildlife.com. Next to the restcamp, yet completely secluded, this luxury lodge has three beautifully decorated rooms and a small plunge pool overlooking the reserve; there's a minimum charge for five people. A cook is on hand to prepare food you bring. <u>R2750</u>

EATING

If you want to self-cater, you'll need to bring supplies – the camp shop specializes in beer and frozen meat and hasn't much by way of fresh food. Louwsburg, signed from the surfaced road along the southern section of the reserve, has a very small general store that's a little better.

Ntshondwe Camp The camp's restaurant serves a surprisingly varied range of food from *escargot* to steaks – though meat-free meals aren't always on the menu – with a dinner buffet for R165. There's also a cosy bar whose sun deck looks out over the watering hole and across the valleys. Daily 7.30–9.30am & 6.30–9pm.

Central Zululand and the Battlefields

Central Zululand – the Zulu heartland – radiates out from the unlovely modern town of **Ulundi**, some 30km west of the Hluhluwe-Imfolozi Park. At the height of its influence in the 1820s and 1830s, under King Shaka, the core of the Zulu state lay between the **Black Imfolozi River** in the north and the **Tugela River** in the south, which discharges into the Indian Ocean roughly 100km north of Durban.

Contained in a relatively small area to the west of the heartland is a series of nineteenth-century **battlefield sites**, where Zulus and Boers, then Zulus and the British, and finally Boers and Brits came to blows. Don't attempt to visit this area on your own: all you'll see is empty veld with a few memorials. It's far better to join a tour with one of the several excellent guides who make it their business to bring the region's dramatic history to life (see box, p.424).

Don't expect to see "tribal" people who conform to the Zulu myth outside theme parks like Shakaland, near Eshowe (see box, p.421). Traditional dress and the **traditional lifestyle** are largely a nineteenth-century phenomenon, deliberately smashed by the British a century ago when they imposed a poll tax that had to be paid in cash – thus ending Zulu self-sufficiency, generating urbanization and forcing the Africans into the modern industrial economy, where they were needed as workers.

You will find beautiful Zulu crafts in this part of the country, the best examples being in museums such as the little-known but outstanding **Vukani Zulu Cultural Museum** in Eshowe (see p.420). Also worth checking out is the reconstructed royal enclosure of Cetshwayo, the last king of the independent Zulu, at **Ondini**, near Ulundi.

Brief history

The truth behind the Zulus is difficult to separate from the mythology, which was fed by the Zulus themselves as well as white settlers. Accounts of the Zulu kingdom in the 1820s rely heavily on the diaries of the two adventurers, **Henry Fynn** and **Nathaniel Isaacs**, who portrayed King Shaka as a mercurial and bloodthirsty tyrant who killed his subjects willy-nilly for a bit of fun. In a letter from Isaacs to Fynn, uncovered in the 1940s, Isaacs encourages his friend to depict the Zulu kings as "bloodthirsty as you can, and describe frivolous crimes people lose their lives for. It all tends to swell up the work and make it interesting."

A current debate divides historians about the real extent of the **Zulu empire** during the nineteenth century. What we do know is that in the 1820s Shaka consolidated a state that was one of the most powerful political forces on the subcontinent, and that internal dissent to his rule culminated in his assassination by his half-brothers **Dingane and Mhlangana** in 1828.

In the 1830s, pressure from whites exacerbated internal tensions among the Zulus, which reached a climax when a relatively small party of Boers defeated Dingane's army at **Blood River**. This led to a split in the Zulu state, with one half following **King Mpande**, and collapse threatened when Mpande's sons Mbuyazi and Cetshwayo led opposing forces in a pitched battle for succession. **Cetshwayo** emerged victorious and successfully set about rebuilding the state, but too late. Seeing a powerful Zulu state as a threat to a confederated South Africa under British control, the British high commissioner, Sir Bartle Frere, delivered a Hobson's choice of an **ultimatum** on the banks of the Tugela River, demanding that Cetshwayo should dismantle his polity or face invasion.

In January 1879, the British army crossed the Tugela and suffered a humiliating disaster at **Isandlwana** – the British army's worst defeat ever at the hands of native armies – only for the tide to turn that same evening when just over a hundred British soldiers repulsed a force of between three and four thousand Zulus at **Rorke's Drift**. By the end of July, Zulu independence had been snuffed, when the British lured the reluctant (and effectively already broken) Zulus, now eager for peace, into battle at **Ulundi**. The British set alight Cetshwayo's capital at **Ondini** – a fire that blazed for four days – and the king was taken prisoner and held in the Castle in Cape Town.

5

THE ZULU HEARTLAND & THE BATTLEFIELDS

Hluhluwe

St Lucia

INDIAN OCEAN

Mkuze

N2

R618

Mtubatuba

Richards Bay

Empangeni

N2

R102

Hlabisa

R618

HLUHLUWE-IMFOLOZI PARK

White Imfolozi

Nongoma

R66

Gingindlovu

R34

Nkwalini

Melmoth

Ondini

Battle of Ulundi 1879

Ulundi

Louwsburg

R69

Black Imfolozi River

ITHALA GAME RESERVE

Shakaland

Eshowe

R66

Siege of Eshowe 1879

Battle of Gingindlovu 1879

Spirit of Emakhosini

Babanango

R68

Vryheid

R33

R34

Nqutu

Battle of Isandlwana 1879

Battle of Blood River 1838

Fugitives' Drift

Buffalo River

Tugela River

Greytown

R74

R33

Utrecht

R34

R33

Battle of Rorke's Drift 1879

Battle of Talana 1899

Helpmekaar

Moor River

R74

Dundee

R68

Glencoe

R602

Weenen

Newcastle

N11

Siege of Ladysmith 1899-1900

Estcourt

Capture of Winston Churchill 1899

Colenso

N11

N3

Chievely

R103

Ladysmith

SPIOENKOP NATURE RESERVE

Battle of Spioenkop 1900

Spioenkop

Winterton

R600

Champagne Valley

R616

Bergville

Didima

UKHAHLAMBA-DRAKENSBERG PARK

N3

R74

FREE STATE

0 — 25
kilometres

Harrismith & Johannesburg

Harrismith

Piet Retief & Ermelo

Pongola

Piet Retief

Ermelo

Eshowe

The name **ESHOWE** has an onomatopoeic Zulu derivation, evoking the sound of the wind blowing through the trees. Though visitors generally give the town a miss on the way to the more obvious drama of Ondini and the Battlefields, the place offers a gentle introduction to the Zulu heartland and deserves more than just a passing glance. Apart from its attractive setting, interlacing with the **Dlinza Forest**, the town is home to one of the world's finest collections of Zulu crafts and has a tour operator offering excellent excursions that take you out to experience some authentic Zulu culture and other aspects of life in Zululand that you would otherwise most likely miss.

Fort Nongqayi

Nongqayi Rd • R25 • ☎ 035 474 2281, ⓦ eshowemuseums.org.za

At the southwestern end of town, picturesque **Fort Nongqayi** was built in 1883 to house the barefoot Zululand Native Police Force, but has since been turned into the largest historical complex in the area. Its shady grounds are home to several worthwhile museums and replicas of historical buildings, as well as a good restaurant, and make a pleasant place to spend an afternoon. The three museums described below are all included in the Fort admission fee, while entry to the Phoenix Gallery is free.

ZULU FESTIVALS

In September and October KwaZulu-Natal is host to three significant Zulu **festivals** that until recently were only attended by the actual participants, though it's now possible to witness these with the Eshowe-based Zululand Eco-Adventures (see p.420). If you're not around in September or October, Zululand Eco-Adventures can arrange for you to attend several lower-key Zulu ceremonies that give an authentic, non-touristy insight into various aspects of Zulu life. These range from *sangoma* healing ceremonies (Wed & Sun), to Zulu weddings (Sat & Sun), coming-of-age ceremonies (Sat & Sun) and a visit to a Zulu gospel church (daily).

THE ROYAL REED DANCE

In the second week of September, the Zulu King hosts a four-day celebration at his royal residence at **Nongoma**. The event is both a rite of passage to womanhood for the young maidens of the Zulu nation, and a chance for them to show off their singing and dancing talents. The festival, known as **Umkhosi woMhlanga** in Zulu, takes its name from the riverbed reeds that play a significant role in Zulu life. Young women carry the reed sticks, which symbolize the power of nature, to the king. According to Zulu mythology, only virgins should take part, and if a woman participant is not a virgin, this will be revealed by her reed stick breaking. A second Reed Dance takes place in the last week of September at the king's other residence in Ingwavuma (see p.410).

KING SHAKA DAY

In honour of King Shaka, a celebration is held yearly on September 24 in **KwaDukuza** (see p.382), Shaka's original homestead and the place where he was murdered in 1828 by his brothers Dingane and Mhlangana. It was Shaka who brought together smaller tribes and formed them into the greatest warrior nation in Southern Africa. Today, the celebration is attended by a who's who of South African Zulu society; there are speeches by the likes of Inkatha Freedom Party leader Chief Mangosuthu Buthelezi, along with music and fantastic displays of warrior dancing, the men decked out in full ceremonial gear and armed with traditional weapons.

SHEMBE FESTIVAL

Held in mid- to late October in **Judea**, near Eshowe, the Shembe Festival is the culmination of weeks of endless rituals, dancing and prayers held throughout KwaZulu-Natal. Some thirty thousand members of the Shembe Church (see p.367) return here every year to meet their leader and celebrate their religion with prayer dances and displays of drumming.

5

Vukani Zulu Cultural Museum

Mon–Fri 8am–4pm, Sat & Sun 11am–3pm

Containing more than three thousand examples of traditional Zulu arts and crafts, the brilliant **Vukani Zulu Cultural Museum** is housed in a purpose-built structure in the grounds of Fort Nongqayi. Guided tours take you through the huge range of **baskets** (a craft at which Zulu culture excels), each made for a specific purpose, the finest of which are the ones by **Reuben Ndwandwe**, arguably the greatest Zulu basket weaver. There are also carvings, beadwork, tapestries and some outstanding ceramics, including works by **Nesta Nala**, one of the leading proponents of the form. Both Ndwandwe and Nala died about ten years ago of AIDS. The benchmark examples here allow you to form an idea of the quality of basketry and crafts you'll see for sale as you work your way around Zululand. The museum itself sells baskets and pottery by local artists, which far surpass what's on offer at the on-site crafts shop.

The museum also houses the very touching **Phoenix Gallery** (free), where drawings and paintings by the male (overwhelmingly black) inmates of Eshowe prison exhibit the stark and sometimes shocking expressions of the prisoners' alienation and anger.

Zululand Historical Museum

Mon–Fri 7.30am–4pm, Sat 9am–4pm, Sun 10am–4pm

With a collection that's eccentric and informative by turns, but never dull, the **Zululand Historical Museum** is the place to see furniture belonging to **John Dunn**, the only white man to become a Zulu chief; incidentally, he also took 49 wives, so becoming the progenitor of Eshowe's coloured community, many of whom still carry his last name. The museum also exhibits Zulu household artefacts and has displays on Zulu history.

Zululand Missionary Museum

Mon–Fri 7.30am–4pm, Sat 9am–4pm, Sun 10am–4pm

Housed in a replica of Fort Nongqayi's chapel, the **Zululand Missionary Museum** contains exhibits relating to the Norwegian missionaries who came to this part of South Africa in the nineteenth century. There's also a working **paper mill** nearby, where you can see boxes, photo frames, notepads and the like being made from sugar-cane fibre and even elephant dung.

Dlinza Forest and aerial boardwalk

Off Kangela St on the southwestern side of Eshowe (accessed from the museums complex at Fort Nongqayi) • Daily: May–Aug 7am–5pm; Sept–April 6am–5pm • R30 • ☎ 035 474 4029

A must for birdwatchers, **Dlinza Forest** is also a great place for picnics or strolling along the impressive **Dlinza Forest Aerial Boardwalk**. Wheelchair-friendly, the boardwalk spans 125m and is raised 10m into the air just beneath the forest canopy, giving visitors a chance to experience a section of the woodland normally restricted to birds. The boardwalk leads to a 20m-high stainless-steel **observation tower**, offering stunning panoramas across the treetops to the Indian Ocean shimmering in the distance. A **visitor information centre** at the foot of the boardwalk provides information about forest ecology. Among the birds you might see here are black sparrowhawks, crowned eagles and spotted ground thrushes, while eighty species of butterfly have also been recorded in the forest.

ARRIVAL AND TOURS   ESHOWE

By bus Regular minibus taxis run from Eshowe to Durban and Empangeni.

Tours Zululand Eco-Adventures, based at the *George Hotel* (☎ 035 474 2298, ⬤ zululandeco-adventures.com), runs tours that give an authentic experience of local Zulu life. It can take you to rural Zulu communities where you can attend a variety of Zulu ceremonies (see box, p.419), and see markets and *shebeens* without feeling as if you're in a theme park. The company takes an active role in the local community and will take you out to a school or an orphanage in the morning, where you'll spend an unhurried day with the kids before being picked up again in the afternoon – a rewarding experience for both you and the children, and one that involves only a negligible charge for the transport.

ACCOMMODATION

★ **Chase Guest House** About 1.5km along John Ross Highway from *KFC* on Main St ☎ 035 474 5491 or 083 265 9629, ⓦ thechase.co.za. This lovely, peaceful farm has two large en-suite rooms and endless views of the surrounding sugar-cane fields. In the grounds there are also two smart self-contained units sleeping two, with the option of B&B or self-catering. A pool, tennis court, internet access and very charming hosts add to the appeal. R700

Chennells Guesthouse 36 Pearson Ave ☎ 035 479 4919, ⓦ eshowe.com. Under the same management as the *George Hotel*, this beautiful colonial home built over a century ago boasts a large garden and very comfortable rooms, all with their own entrances. R1295

Forest View Lodge 52 Addison Rd ☎ 035 474 1282, ⓔ woodprod@iafrica.com. Pretty wood-and-brick rooms in a quiet neighbourhood, some of which come with their own balconies overlooking a flower-filled garden. There are a few family-friendly self-catering cottages as well that sleep up to four. R550

George Hotel 36 Main St ☎ 035 474 4919, ⓦ eshowe .com. Something of a focal point for the town, this busy hotel in a historic 1906 building is steeped in local history. It offers renovated en-suite rooms, many with their original wooden floors, and an on-site travel agent. R795

Thornley's 17 Mansel Terrace T035 474 4179 or 083 442 3884, ⓔ thornleys@iafrica.com. Four light and airy rooms in an old family home, run by an energetic young couple always happy to braai with guests in the garden or engage in good conversation at the little on-site bar. One of the most convivial spots in town, they have plans to expand with a lower-budget alternative next door. R700

EATING AND DRINKING

Adam's Outpost In the museum complex at Fort Nongqayi ☎ 035 474 1787. In a converted settler house, *Adams' Outpost* dishes up healthy salads, home-made bread and good curries (R70), plus a very popular Sunday lunch buffet (R130; reservations required). Mon–Fri 8am–4pm, Sun 9am–3.30pm.

George Hotel One of Eshowe's best restaurants is at the *George Hotel*, whose short but tasty selection of dishes includes German specialities like schnitzel (R70) along with the usual steak and curry. Mon–Fri 7–9am & 6–9pm, Sat & Sun 8–9.30am & 6–9pm.

Pablo Esco Bar It's only open twice a week, but if you're in town on the right night head to the bar at the *George Hotel* where you'll get to taste a beer or two brewed at the on-site Zululand Brewery (home of the famous Zulu Blond), and catch the sunset from the deck overlooking the forest. Wed & Fri 4–9.30pm.

Prawn Shak 30km east of Eshowe at Amatikulu ☎ 084 737 6493. At weekends Eshowe locals head to this rambling wooden beach house that prides itself on its heady mixture of prawns and tequila, though that's just part of the eight-course menu – expect baked camembert and "Zulu sushi" as well. The set menu is R185 per person, and there is no a-la-carte option. Payment by debit or credit card only. Sat & Sun 11.30am–5pm.

ZULU THEME PARKS

North of Eshowe, the winding R66 leaves behind the softer vistas of the Dlinza Forest, the citrus groves and green seas of cane plantations and looks across huge views of the valleys that figure in the creation mythology of the Zulu nation. In no time you're into thornveld (acacias, rocky *koppies* and aloes) and **theme park** country.

Most accessible of these "Zulu-village hotels" is **Shakaland**, 14km north of Eshowe off the R68 at Norman Hurst Farm, Nkwalini (☎ 035 460 0912, ⓦ shakaland.com). Built in 1984 as the set for the wildly romanticized TV series *Shaka Zulu*, Shakaland is a reconstruction of a nineteenth-century Zulu kraal and quite unrepresentative of how people live today. However, the theme park just about manages to remain on the acceptable side of exploiting ethnic culture, and offers the chance to sample Zulu food. **Tours** for day visitors (daily 11am & 12.30pm; R420) include an audiovisual presentation about the origin of the Zulus, a guided walk around the huts, an explanation of traditional social organization, spear-making, a beer-drinking ceremony and a buffet lunch with traditional food. The highlight, however, is probably one of the best choreographed Zulu **dancing** shows in the country, with the dramatic landscape as the backdrop – it's worth putting up with all the other stuff just to see it.

For those who want to stay the night, there is traditional-style accommodation at Shakaland in comfortable beehive huts (R2870), with untraditional luxuries such as electricity and en-suite bathrooms.

5

Ulundi

Some 90km north of Eshowe on the R66, **ULUNDI** is the former capital of the KwaZulu Bantustan and lies at the centre of the **eMakhosini Valley** (Valley of the Kings). The latter holds a semi-mythical status among Zulu nationalists as the birthplace of the Zulu state and the area where several of its founding fathers lived and are now buried. A memorial to them was erected in 2003, the Spirit of eMakhosini, on a hill 3km up the R34, beyond the junction with the R66 for Ulundi. The circular memorial is surrounded by seven large aluminium horns representing the kings that came before Shaka, while in the centre is an impressive 600-litre bronze traditional beer pot.

The **Battle of Ulundi Memorial**, just outside town on the tarred road to the Cengeni Gate of the Hluhluwe-Imfolozi Park, is the poignant spot marking the final defeat of the Zulus. An understated small stone structure with a silver dome houses a series of plaques listing all the regiments on both sides involved in the last stand of the Zulus on July 4, 1879. The rectangular park around the memorial marks the site of the hollow square formation adopted by the British infantry and supported to devastating effect by seven- and nine-pounder guns.

Ondini Historical Reserve

A few kilometres from Ulundi • Mon–Fri 8am–4pm, Sat & Sun 9am–5pm • R30 • ☎ 083 661 7942, ⓦ zulu-museum.co.za

By far the most interesting sight around here is the **Ondini Historical Reserve**, which houses the reconstruction of the royal residence of **King Cetshwayo**, a site museum and a cultural museum. After the decisive Battle of Ulundi, the royal residence at Ondini was razed to the ground and Cetshwayo was captured. Still puzzled by Britain's actions, Cetshwayo wrote to the British governor in 1881 from his exile at the Castle in Cape Town: "I have done you no wrong, therefore you must have some other object in view in invading my land." The *isigodlo*, or **royal enclosure**, has been partially reconstructed with traditional Zulu beehive huts that you can wander round, while the site museum has a model showing the full original arrangement. Among the items in the **Cultural Museum** is an impressive bead collection.

uMuzi Bushcamp ☎ 035 870 2500, ⓦ tintasafaris .co.za. Stay in a Zulu hut, ranging from beehives to rondavels or more modern concrete huts, most en suite. All the huts are located in a traditional *umuzi* (homestead) with a central fire for night-time gatherings. The camp offers tours to eMakhosini Valley, the surrounding battlefields and Hluhluwe-Imfolozi Game Park; rates include entrance to Ondini Cultural Museum. Half board **R770**

The Battlefields

Most of the major KwaZulu-Natal Battlefields lie in the northwestern corner of the province, where the Boers first came out of the mountains from the northeast into Zulu territory and inflicted a severe defeat on the Zulus at **Blood River** in 1838, 13km southeast of the tiny town of Utrecht. Some four decades later, the British spoiled for war and marched north to fight a series of battles against the Zulus, the most notable being at **Isandlwana** and **Rorke's Drift** southeast of Dundee.

Twenty years on, Britain again provoked war, this time against the **Boers** of the South African Republic and the Orange Free State to the north and west. In the early stages of the Second Anglo-Boer War (also known as the South African War) the huge, lumbering British machine proved no match for the mobile Boers. At **Ladysmith**, the British endured months of an embarrassing siege, while nearby, at **Spioenkop**, bungling British leadership snatched defeat from the jaws of victory. Although the empire successfully struck back, it took three years to subdue the South African Republic and the Orange Free State, two of the smallest states in the world, after committing half a million troops to the field in an operation that proved to be the costliest campaign since the Napoleonic Wars nearly a century earlier.

5

If you're only planning to take in one battlefield site, then Isandlwana should be the one, though you really should see Rorke's Drift as well to complete the day; both sites are eerily beautiful.

Isandlwana Battlefield

Off the R68 just over 130km northwest of Eshowe and 70km southeast of Dundee • Daily 8am–4pm • R30 • ☎ 034 271 8165

On January 22, 1879, the British suffered the most humiliating defeat in their colonial history when virtually their entire force of 1200 men at Isandlwana was obliterated by warriors armed with spears. Dominated by an eerie hill, the **Isandlwana Battlefield** remains unspoilt and unchanged apart from some small homesteads and the graves of those who fell. A small **interpretation centre** houses artefacts and mementos.

The monumental bungling and the scale of the Zulu victory over the British sent shock waves back to London. Following the British ultimatum to the Zulus, three colonial columns were sent to invade Zululand. King Cetshwayo responded by sending a force against each of these. On January 21, 1879, Zulu troops encamped 6km from Isandlwana Hill, where one of the British columns had set up camp. Unaware of the Zulus over the brow, the British commander took a large detachment to support another British force, leaving the men at Isandlwana undefended and unfortified.

Meanwhile, a British scouting party rode to the brow of a hill and was stunned to find the valley filled with some 25,000 Zulu warriors sitting in utter silence. Because of a superstition surrounding the phase of the moon, the Zulus were waiting for a more propitious moment to attack. On being discovered, they rose up and converged on the British encampment using the classic Zulu "horns of the bull" formation to outflank the unprotected British, whom they completely overran.

The British press at the time demonized the Zulus for disembowelling the dead. In fact, the practice had a religious significance for the Zulus, who believed that it released the spirit of the dead. The custom also had a less spiritual significance; a Zulu warrior was required to "wash his spear" (ie kill an enemy) before he was allowed to marry.

Rorke's Drift

15km west of Isandlwana on the D30 • Daily 8am–4pm • Field Museum and interpretation centre R30; Craft centre free • ☎ 034 642 1687

The same evening as the Isandlwana battle (see above), tattered British honour was restored when a group of British veterans successfully defended the field hospital at **Rorke's Drift**, just across the Buffalo River from the site of the earlier disaster, against four advancing Zulu regiments. Despite Cetshwayo's express orders not to attack Rorke's Drift, three to four thousand hot-headed young Zulu men were so fired up by the Isandlwana victory and so eager to "wash their spears" – they were part of a reserve force and had not yet seen action – that they launched the assault. For twelve hours spanning January 22 and 23, 1879, just over a hundred British soldiers (many of whom were ill) repulsed repeated attacks by the Zulus and so earned eleven Victoria Crosses – the largest number ever awarded in one battle.

Rorke's Drift is the most rewarding Battlefield to visit on your own, thanks to its excellent **field museum** and interpretation centre. While you're here, it's also worth taking in the **Rorke's Drift ELC Craft Centre**, known for its hand-printed fabrics and tapestries depicting rural scenes.

ACCOMMODATION AND EATING	THE BATTLEFIELDS

Accommodation around Isandlwana and Rorke's Drift is fairly spread out, most of it in small villages in the area. Many guesthouses offer meals and the owners often double as guides.

BABANANGO

Babanango Lodge Signposted 4km west of Babanango on the R68 ☎ 082 709 7951, ⊛ babanangovalley.co.za. Situated on a Natural Heritage Site deep in a beautiful valley,

where you can be taken on walks to explore the veld, rocks and river. With a degree in animal behaviour, the proprietor combines tours of Hluhluwe-Imfolozi Park and ecological topics, including birding and basic tree identification, with

5

BATTLEFIELD GUIDES

Visiting the **Battlefields** with a qualified guide will enhance the experience. The guides below specialize in different battle sites, usually those closest to their base. Most guides have negotiable fees, which vary depending on the size of the group, and some require you to have your own transport.

If you prefer to explore the battlefields on your own, the late David Rattray's excellent set of CDs *The Day of the Dead Moon*, covering Rorke's Drift and Isandlwana, makes for good company; it's available directly from *Fugitive's Drift Lodge* (see below).

RECOMMENDED GUIDES

Elisabeth Durham ☎034 212 1014, ⓦ cheznousbb.com. Informative half- and full-day tours in English and French of Rorke's Drift, Isandlwana and the route followed by the French Prince Imperial, who fell at Nqutu (R1300–1800, more if you don't have your own vehicle).

Fugitive's Drift Lodge ☎034 642 1843, ⓦ fugitives-drift-lodge.com. David Rattray, the doyen of battlefield guides, was based at this lodge (see below) near Rorke's Drift until his untimely murder during a botched robbery. The baton has now been passed to the lodge's other excellent guides, Rob Caskie, Joseph Ndima and George Irwin who, like Rattray, are great storytellers. Their half-day Isandlwana (departs at 7.30am) and Rorke's Drift (departs at 3pm in winter and 3.15pm in summer) tours cost R770–995 per person for both battlefields, depending on the season.

Ron Gold, KwaZulu-Natal Tours ☎033 263 1908 or 083 556 4068, ⓦ kwazulu-natal-tours.com. Gold specializes in the battles of Spioenkop, Willow Grange and Colenso, and the site of Churchill's arrest, offering both half- and full-day tours (R1800–2500).

Evan Jones ☎034 212 4040 or ☎082 807 8598, ⓦ battleguide.co.za. Extensive full-day tours of all the Battlefields (from R1400) by a guide with a vast repository of knowledge, who breathes life into the battles.

Pat Rundgren ☎034 212 4560 or 082 690 7812, ✉ gunners@trustnet.co.za. A large, burly man of Scandinavian/Irish descent, Pat, a military specialist, provides an alternative perspective on the battles around the Dundee area. Tours cost R400 per person per day, including transport.

Foy Vermaak ☎034 642 1925, ⓦ www.penny .co.za. Based close to Isandlwana and Rorke's Drift, in which he specializes; he also covers Helpmekaar and Fugitive's Drift. Tour rates are R1000 per day for up to six people, using your own vehicle.

Zulu historical sites and the Anglo-Zulu Battlefields. Accommodation is in pleasant en-suite rooms at the main lodge, or in a self-catering cottage nearby (R350/person). Lodge room (half board) <u>R2900</u>

HELPMEKAAR

Penny Farthing Along the R33 south of Rorke's Drift and 30km south of Dundee ☎034 642 1925, ⓦwww .pennyf.co.za. Near the minuscule settlement of Helpmekaar, *Penny Farthing* is an historic pioneer farm still furnished with original objects and generations of hunting trophies, set in an area of big open grasslands and hills, crisscrossed with hiking trails. The host Foy Vermaak is a Battlefields guide (see box above) who enjoys fireside chats on the subject, and has a personal collection of memorabilia. <u>R1120</u>

NEAR RORKE'S DRIFT

Fugitives' Drift Lodge 9km north of Rorke's Drift along the D31 dirt road ☎034 642 1843, ⓦfugitives -drift-lodge.com. The ultimate Battlefields place to stay, this luxury lodge, located on a huge game farm, overlooks the drift where the few British survivors of Isandlwana fled across the Buffalo River. The colonial-style rooms are in individual cottages that open onto lawns and gardens, and there is also an annexe that sleeps four. Guests eat together in a central dining room among the world's largest Zulu battlefield memorabilia collection. Rates include full board. Double <u>R7000</u>, annexe <u>R7200</u>

Dundee

Some 32km west of the Rorke's Drift turn-off, along the R68, **DUNDEE** has little to offer except shops, supermarkets and pharmacies, but does serve as a good base for exploring the surrounding areas. For those with some time to kill in town, Dundee Tourism's brochure includes an historical walking tour of the buildings dating back to Dundee's early days as a coal-fuelled boom town.

5

The Talana Museum and Kwakunje Cultural Village

2km outside Dundee on the R33 to Vryheid • **Museum** Mon–Fri 8am–4.30pm, Sat & Sun 9am–4.30pm • R25 • ☎ 034 212 2654 •
Cultural Village Mon–Fri 8am–4.30pm, Sat & Sun 9am–4.30pm • R8 • ☎ 072 796 0844 • ⓦ talana.co.za

Under shady blue gums, the excellent **Talana Museum** museum consists of ten historic whitewashed buildings from the time of the 1899 Battle of Talana Hill, the first engagement of the Anglo-Boer War. The most interesting of these is **Talana House**, which gives information about northern KwaZulu-Natal conflicts including the Anglo-Zulu, Zulu-Boer and Anglo-Boer wars. The displays include weapons and uniforms, but most evocative are the photographs that really personalize the wars and reveal fascinating details such as the POW camps Boers were exiled to in far-flung parts of the British Empire, including St Helena and the Far East. Often-neglected aspects of the Anglo-Boer War, including the roles of Africans and Indians, also get some coverage. In a photograph of Indian stretcher-bearers you may be able to spot the youthful Mohandas Gandhi, who carried wounded British soldiers off the Spioenkop and Colenso Battlefields. The museum curator can arrange guided tours of the museum and surrounding Battlefields.

On the same site, Kwakunje Cultural Village (*kwakunje* means "it was like this") is a model village in which guides demonstrate and explain Zulu traditions and the way they've changed over the years. Zulu meals and dancing can also be arranged, if you call in advance.

ARRIVAL AND INFORMATION   DUNDEE

By minibus taxi The only public transport to Dundee is by minibus taxi, many of which, when coming from the east, require you to change in Vryheid. There are also direct routes to Ladysmith.

Tourist information Dundee Tourism, just off Victoria St in Civic Gardens (Mon–Fri 9am–5pm; ☎ 034 212 2121, ⓦ tourdundee.co.za), can recommend local tour guides, and provide information about the various re-enactments staged from time to time to coincide with the anniversaries of famous battles.

ACCOMMODATION

Battlefields Backpackers International 90 Victoria St ☎ 034 212 4040, ⓦ bbibackpackers.co.za. A small family-run hostel offering somewhat cramped but friendly backpackers accommodation in two doubles and two bunk rooms, with dogs to play with and a free drink on arrival. Excellent battlefield tours are also conducted by owner Evan Jones (see box, opposite). R340

Chez Nous 39 Tatham St ☎ 034 212 1014, ⓦ cheznousbb.co.za. You can stay on a B&B or self-catering basis at *Chez Nous*, run by gregarious French hostess Elisabeth Durham, who cooks delicious three-course dinners on request, and also leads tours of the Battlefields (see box opposite). Accommodation is in spacious doubles or cottages sleeping up to six. R660

Lennox Cottage 3km east of town on the R68 ☎ 034 218 2201, ⓦ lennox.co.za. Advance booking is essential at the unpretentious and comfortable *Lennox Cottage*, on an organic farm run by former rugby Springbok Dirk Froneman and his wife, Salome, who cooks good dinners. R1340

EATING

Royal Country Inn 61 Victoria St ☎ 034 212 2147, ⓦ royalcountryinn.com. A short and simple menu of well-prepared Old World dishes such as oxtail soup (R90), steaks and apple tart, served in the subdued colonial elegance of Dundee's historic hotel, built in 1886. Daily 6am–8pm.

Ncome Blood River

The **battle of Blood River** takes its name from reports that the Ncome River turned red with blood when, on December 16, 1838, Andries Pretorius' band of 470 Voortrekkers barricaded themselves behind their wagons and defeated an army of 10,000 to 15,000 Zulu soldiers commanded by King Dingane. The resulting Zulu casualties numbered in the thousands, according to official counts, while the Voortrekkers suffered nothing more than injuries. Although the event has become a defining moment for Afrikaner nationalists, some historians argue that the number of Zulu dead was most likely inflated by the victors. Today the battlefield is the site of an impressive Boer monument, plus a museum that presents a more balanced perspective on events.

5

Blood River Battlefield

48km from Dundee on the way to Vryheid, off the R33 • Daily 8am–4.30pm • R25 • ☎ 034 632 1695

You can't fail to be amazed by the monument at the **Blood River Battlefield**. Of all the Afrikaner quasi-religious shrines across the country, this definitely takes the biscuit, comprising a replica laager of 64 life-size bronze wagons on the site of the battle. During the apartheid years, the date of the battle, December 16, was celebrated by Afrikaners as the **Day of the Vow**, a public holiday honouring a supposed covenant made by the Boers with God himself that if he granted them victory, they would hold the day sacred. Afrikaners still visit the monument on this day, but under the new government the public holiday has been recycled as the **Day of Reconciliation**, with Blood River also referred to by its Zulu name, Ncome.

Ncome Monument and Museum Complex

On the eastern side of Ncome Blood River • Daily 8am–4.30pm • Free • ☎ 034 271 8121, ⓦ www.ncomemuseum.org.za

The **Ncome Monument and Museum Complex**, across the river from the Blood River Monument, does a good job presenting the Zulu side of the conflict, with its horn-shaped design inspired by the Zulu martial formation. Exhibits include a display about battle strategy, and a reed garden relating the importance of river reeds in Zulu life. The video shown here gives a good sense of the battle as it unfolded, making Blood River one of the easier sites to take in without the help of a guide. Together with the Boer monument, the museum illustrates the difficulties inherent in South African historical memory.

Ladysmith

LADYSMITH, 61km south of Dundee on the N11, owes its modest fame to one of the worst sieges in British military history nearly a century ago – the best reason to linger is to learn about the Anglo-Boer War at the Ladysmith Siege Museum – and more recently to **Ladysmith Black Mambazo**, the local vocal group that helped Paul Simon revive a flagging career in the mid-1980s.

It's easy enough to walk around Ladysmith's small centre; **Murchison Street** is the main artery running through town, where you'll find banks, the post office and shops.

Ladysmith Siege Museum

Corner of Queen and Murchison streets • Mon–Fri 9am–4pm, Sat 9am–1pm • R11 • ☎ 036 637 2992

The **Ladysmith Siege Museum** is the obvious starting point for any tour of the Anglo-Boer Battlefields. The siege began on November 2, 1899, and lasted 118 days, with twelve thousand British troops suffering the indignity of being pinned down by undisciplined farmers. This compelling little museum tells the story of the war through text and photographs, conveying the appalling conditions during the siege as well as key points in a war that helped shape twentieth-century South Africa, paving the way for its unification. The museum is also a good place to browse books about the war, written from both the British and Boer points of view.

ARRIVAL, INFORMATION AND TOURS

LADYSMITH

By bus Greyhound Johannesburg–Durban buses pull in at the Caltex Service Station on Murchison St.
By train The train station (☎ 036 271 2020) is 500m east of the town hall on Lyell St, though night-time arrival and departure times make the train an unrealistic option.

Tourist information At the Siege Museum (Mon–Fri 9am–4pm, Sat 9am–1pm; ☎ 036 637 2992).
Tours Local guide Liz Spiret (☎ 036 637 7702 or 072 262 9669, ⓔ lizs@telkomsa.net) charges R950 for a battlefields tour for up to four people (you'll need your own transport).

ACCOMMODATION

Budleigh House 12 Berea Rd ☎ 036 635 7700 or 084 512 2756, ⓔ slabb12@telkomsa.net. Rooms at this elegant guesthouse are pleasantly decorated, featuring wooden floors and a subtle African feel. There's also a pool and sunny patio on which to enjoy the lovely garden. R750
Bullers Rest Lodge 59/61 Cove Crescent ☎ 036 637

6154, ⓦbullersrestlodge.co.za. A smart thatched establishment with cosy, country-style furnishings, a large wooden deck overlooking town, and a small swimming pool. The on-site pub is filled with original battlefield artefacts. Packed lunches provided on request, and dinners available Mon–Fri. **R830**

Hunters' Lodge 6 Hunter St ⓣ036 637 2359, ⓦhunterslodgekzn.co.za. This lovely old home is located in a peaceful neighbourhood and has fifteen en-suite

rooms surrounding a well-manicured garden. Dinners are available on request Mon–Thurs. **R1000**

Royal Hotel 140 Murchison St ⓣ036 637 2176, ⓦroyalhotel.co.za. In the heart of town, this is the hotel that harboured the upper classes during the siege – and was regularly shelled by the Boers. Now a mid-range establishment catering mainly to travelling reps, it's full during the week, which makes booking essential at any time of year. It can be noisy due to traffic. **R1195**

EATING

Royal Hotel 140 Murchison St ⓣ036 637 2176. The restaurant at the *Royal Hotel* was patronized in former times by the more privileged of the besieged, including Frank Rhodes (brother of the more famous Cecil). It is

still the best place to eat in town, though the food – mostly pub fare and steaks (around R85) – is not particularly sophisticated. Mon–Sat 6.30am–9pm, Sun 7am–10pm.

Spioenkop

35km west of Ladysmith • **Spioenkop Battlefield** daily 9am–5pm • R30 • ⓣ036 637 2992 • **Spioenkop Nature Reserve** daily: April–Sept 6am–6pm; Oct–March 5am–7pm • R20 • ⓣ036 488 1578

Spioenkop Battlefield is set in the Spioenkop Nature Reserve, though its access point is off the road to Bergville. The bloodiest of all the Anglo-Boer War battles, Spioenkop took more British lives than any other and taught the British command that wars fought by means of set-piece battles were no longer viable. After this, the guerrilla-style tactics of modern warfare were increasingly adopted.

Some 1700 British troops took the hill under cover of a mist without firing a shot, but were able to dig only shallow trenches because the surface was so hard. When the mist lifted they discovered that they had misjudged the crest of the hill, but their real failure was one of flawed command and desperately poor intelligence. Had the British reconnoitred properly, they might have discovered that they were facing a motley collection of fewer than five hundred Boers with only seven pieces of artillery, and they could have called in their sixteen hundred reserves to relieve them. Despite holding lower ground, the Boers were able to keep the British, crammed eight men per metre into their trenches, pinned down for an entire sweltering midsummer day. Around six hundred British troops perished and were buried where they fell on the so-called "acre of massacre".

Meanwhile the Boers, who were aware of the British reinforcements at the base of the hill, had gradually been drifting off, and, by the end of the day, unbeknownst to the British, there were only 350 Boers left. In the evening the British withdrew, leaving the hill to the enemy.

Today you can stand at the summit of the rocky hill and look out over the desolate battlefield, where small plaques mark out the positions of the two sides. A mass grave marks the final resting place of hundreds of fallen British troops.

ACCOMMODATION   SPIOENKOP

KZN Wildlife Ipika Bush Camp On the slopes of Spioenkop Mountain ⓣ036 488 1578. This simple bush camp consists of just one four-bed safari tent plus camping pitches. There's a minimum charge for three people for the safari tent and two for the campsites. Camping (two people) **R140**, safari tent (three people) **R630**

Three Tree Hill Lodge Adjoining the reserve ⓣ036 448 1171, ⓦthreetreehill.co.za. Tours of the battlefield and outdoor activities, including wildlife-spotting, can be arranged at this colonially stylish lodge. Each room has its own veranda overlooking the valley, and there is both a spacious two-bedroom suite and a separate cottage for families. Full board **R4230**

Free State

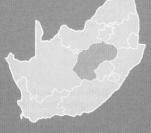

AARDVARK, NEAR CLARENS

6

Free State

The Maloti Route, one of South Africa's most scenic drives, skirts the mountainous eastern flank of the Free State, the traditional heartland of conservative Afrikanerdom, which lies landlocked at the centre of the country. If you're driving from Johannesburg to Eastern or Western Cape, the Eastern Highlands, which sweep up to the subcontinent's highest peaks in the Lesotho Drakensberg, are worth the detour. Bloemfontein, the capital, is only worth visiting if you are passing through, but once there you'll find very good guesthouses, restaurants and museums. Closer to Johannesburg, the riverside town of Parys is a pleasant rural escape that long ago was ground zero for a massive meteorite impact.

The highlight of the Eastern Highlands is the **Golden Gate National Park**, designated as such for the beauty of the Maloti Mountains, with their stripy red sandstone outcrops. Southeast of Golden Gate you can drive to the Sentinel car park – access point for hikes up to the highest plateaus of the Drakensberg – via the interesting **Basotho Cultural Village**. West of Golden Gate is **Clarens**, by far the nicest of the string of towns along the Lesotho border. In the rest of the province, flat farmlands roll away into kilometres of bright-yellow sunflowers and mauve- and pink-petalled cosmos, with maize and wheat fields glowing under immense blue skies.

Brief history

Intriguing though it sounds, the name "Free State" applies to former redneck country. For nearly 150 years, the only free people in the Free State were its white settlers, who in 1854 were granted independence from Britain in a territory between the Orange and Vaal rivers, where they created a Boer Republic called the **Orange Free State** (the "Orange" part of the name came from the royal Dutch House of Orange). The system of government in the republic, inspired by the US Constitution, was highly democratic – if you were white and male. Women couldn't vote, while Africans had no rights at all, and were even forbidden from owning land. In 1912 the ANC was formed in the Bloemfontein township of Batho, while the Nationalist Party was founded two years later in Bloemfontein itself. In 1914, the Orange Free State became a bastion of apartheid, being the only province to ban anyone of Asian descent from remaining within its borders for longer than 24 hours. Africans fared little better; in 1970, under the grand apartheid scheme, a tiny barren enclave wedged between Lesotho, KwaZulu-Natal and the Free State became QwaQwa, a "homeland" for Southern Sotho people – a result of forced clearances from white-designated areas. The Bantustans have since been reincorporated into South Africa and, after an ANC landslide in Free State province in the 1994 elections, the "Orange" part of the name, with its Dutch Calvinist associations, was dropped.

GOLDEN GATE HIGHLANDS NATIONAL PARK

Highlights

❶ Maloti Route A scenic drive skirting the Lesotho border, past massive rock formations, cherry orchards and sandstone farming towns, including the delightfully artsy town of Clarens. **See p.436**

❷ Drakensberg Escarpment Catch some of South Africa's most spectacular mountain views by climbing to the highest point on the escarpment via a chain ladder. **See p.436**

❸ Basotho vernacular architecture See the decorative adobe huts typical of the Eastern Free State and Lesotho at the Basotho Cultural Village, and spend the night in a comfortable rondavel. **See p.437**

❹ Golden Gate Highlands National Park Hike or drive through this stunning reserve, dominated by the beautiful Maloti Mountains with their stripy red sandstone outcrops. **See p.437**

❺ Parys Tour the remnants of the massive impact dome made by a meteorite two billion years ago, or simply relax in the town centre, shop for antiques, eat *vetkoek* and paddle down the Vaal River. **See p.442**

HIGHLIGHTS ARE MARKED ON THE MAP ON P.432

6

Bloemfontein

BLOEMFONTEIN, part of Mangaung municipality, is located at the crossroads of South Africa, which means that many travellers break their journey across the country here. Despite its reputation as the hick capital of South Africa, Bloem (or "flower", as it is lovingly called) is actually quite agreeable, and there's enough diversion for a day or two. The city's surprisingly fine **Oliewenhuis Art Museum** is set in beautiful gardens, while the unmistakably provincial **President Brand Street** is lined with handsome, sandstone public buildings paying a pick 'n' mix homage to Mediterranean, British, Renaissance and Classical influences. Bloem is also the seat of the provincial parliament and South Africa's Court of Appeal.

As an overnight stop, the city offers good accommodation at reasonable prices, upmarket shopping centres and a couple of nightlife opportunities. In common with other South African cities, the white population has deserted the city centre. Instead, the suburbs just northwest of the city centre have become the place to shop and hang out. The **Loch Logan Waterfront Mall** beside the stadium and Westdene's four-storey Mimosa Mall in nearby Kellner Street provide coffee shops, chain restaurants, banks, bookshops and more.

If you're around in August, visit the Castle Granaat Rock Festival at the Oliewenhuis Art Museum, which sees popular South African bands perform in a very family-friendly atmosphere. In October, try to catch the ten-day Manguang African Cultural

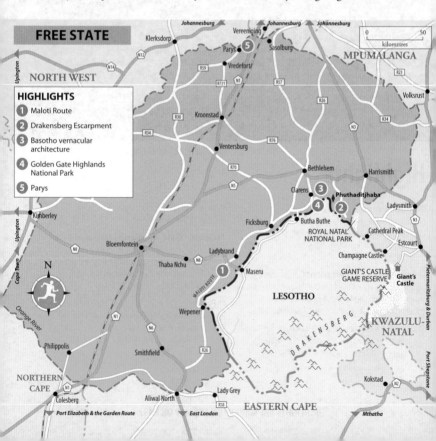

FREE STATE

HIGHLIGHTS
1. Maloti Route
2. Drakensberg Escarpment
3. Basotho vernacular architecture
4. Golden Gate Highlands National Park
5. Parys

Festival (🌐macufe.co.za), which fills the city with storytelling, poetry, art, music and dance, and attracts people from all over the country.

President Brand Street

For a rewarding stroll in the centre, head down **President Brand Street**, starting at the City Hall at the north end on the corner of Charles Street. Built in 1934, the building was designed in the "new tradition style" by Gordon Leith, a former employee of Sir Herbert Baker, and features large animal skulls above the windows.

South of the City Hall stands the Roman-style Appeal Court of South Africa, built in 1929. Staring at it from across the road is the imposing sandstone and red-brick Fourth Raadsaal from 1890, the last parliament building of the independent Orange Free State republic (it's now the provincial legislature). Further south on the corner of Selborne Avenue is the Supreme Court, completed in 1906. The Old Presidency, diagonally opposite, was built on the site of the home of **Major Henry Warden**, the founder of Bloemfontein. It was built in 1861 in "Scottish baronial style" as the official seat of the head of the republic.

National Museum

36 Aliwal St • Mon–Fri 8am–5pm, Sat 10am–5pm, Sun noon–5pm • R5 • ☎ 051 447 9609, 🌐 nasmus.co.za

To the east of President Brand Street is the **National Museum**, well worth a visit for its good dinosaur fossil collection, the 260,000-year-old Florisbad human skull and an impressive reconstruction of a turn-of-the-twentieth-century Bloemfontein street. There's also an interesting exhibit on the township of Batho, birthplace of the ANC, which includes a replica of a typical Batho house and interviews with township residents.

First Raadsaal

95 St George's St • Mon–Fri 10am–1pm, Sat & Sun 2–5pm • Free • ☎ 051 447 9609, 🌐 nasmus.co.za

Bloemfontein's oldest building, the **First Raadsaal** is a small thatched pioneer cottage that was built by Warden (see above) as the town's first school, but used later as an assembly hall for the first parliament. Inside, and in a grander adjacent building, is a dry exhibition on the history of the establishment of Free State.

The small **King's Park** gardens are wedged between Loch Logan and the zoo, and are a lovely spot for a picnic or an afternoon stroll, especially when the roses are in bloom in summer; Bloemfontein is sometimes known as the "city of roses", and over four thousand of the colourful bushes have been planted in the park.

Bloemfontein Zoo

Daily: Oct–March 8am–6pm; April–Sept 8am–5pm • R45

Occupying the western half of King's Park, **Bloemfontein Zoo** is a reasonable place to see the Big Five, hippos, tigers and antelope. It's well known for the breeding programme it had for the liger, a cross between a lion and a tiger, although the last liger died in the 1990s.

The waterfront and stadium

Built on the opposite site of Loch Logan lake to the zoo, the **Loch Logan Waterfront Mall** boasts shops, cafés, several chain restaurants and a cinema. Connected to the mall is the **Vodacom Stadium**, used mainly for rugby.

Freshford House Museum

31 Kellner St • Mon–Fri 10am–1pm, Sat & Sun 2–5pm • R10 • 🌐 nasmus.co.za

To the north of the city centre, just across Nelson Mandela Drive, the **Freshford House Museum** is a beautifully maintained Edwardian house from 1897, which was designed and inhabited by architect John Edwin Harrisson. The interior has been refurbished impeccably in Victorian and Edwardian style, giving great insight into the daily life of that era.

National Women's Monument and War Museum

Monument Rd • Mon–Fri 8am–4.30pm, Sat 10am–5pm, Sun 11am–5pm • R10 • ☎ 051 447 3447, ⊛ anglo-boer.co.za

Just over 2km south of the centre, in an industrial part of town, a sandstone needle pointing skywards marks the **National Women's Monument and War Museum**. This stands as a memorial to the 26,370 Afrikaner women and children who died in British concentration camps during the second Anglo-Boer War. The suffering depicted in the museum isn't an exaggeration, but it is a little heavy-handed. Two cursory panels on concentration camps for Africans are a post-apartheid afterthought that at least provide a partial record of the more than 14,000 black South Africans who died incarcerated.

Oliewenhuis Art Museum

16 Harry Smith St, 2km north of the centre off Aliwal St • Mon–Fri 8am–5pm, Sat & Sun 9am–4pm • Free • ☎ 051 447 9609, ⊛ nasmus.co.za

The best of Bloemfontein's museums, the **Oliewenhuis Art Museum**'s collection – which includes a surprisingly good range of South African sculpture and painting – is housed in the former residency of South African presidents, a beautifully light, neo-Cape Dutch manor set in large, attractive gardens, surrounded by wild bush traversed by short walking

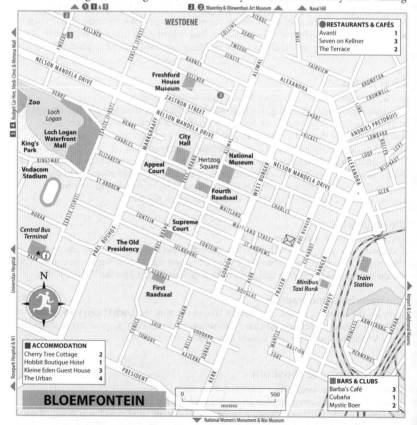

BLOEMFONTEIN

RESTAURANTS & CAFÉS
Avanti	1
Seven on Kellner	3
The Terrace	2

ACCOMMODATION
Cherry Tree Cottage	2
Hobbit Boutique Hotel	1
Kleine Eden Guest House	3
The Urban	4

BARS & CLUBS
Barba's Café	3
Cubaña	1
Mystic Boer	2

TOLKIEN IN BLOEMFONTEIN

Bloemfontein's biggest surprise is that it's the birthplace of **John Ronald Reuel Tolkien**, author of *The Lord of the Rings* and *The Hobbit*, a fact the city seems curiously reluctant to publicize. Tolkien's father, Arthur, left his native Birmingham to work in the colonies, eventually becoming manager of the Bank of Africa in Bloemfontein. Tolkien was born in 1892, in a house standing on the corner of West Burger and Maitland streets, a couple of blocks east of President Brand Street. When Arthur Tolkien died three years after Tolkien's birth, his wife returned to England with her two infant sons; their house was later torn down to make way for a furniture shop.

trails. Even if you're not interested in the gallery, it's still worth having tea at *The Terrace*, the café on the lawn (see p.436) – its trees and fountain make it the most harmonious location in town, and there's art here too, most notably the quirky African Carousel.

ARRIVAL AND DEPARTURE

BLOEMFONTEIN

By bus Translux, Intercape, SA Roadlink and Greyhound buses pull in at the central bus terminal in the tourist complex on Park Rd, 500m south of Loch Logan mall.

Destinations: Cape Town (9 daily; 12hr); Durban (4 daily; 9hr); East London (4 daily; 8hr 30min); Johannesburg (21 daily; 6hr); Mossel Bay (2 daily; 9hr 30min); Pietermaritzburg (3 daily; 8hr); Port Elizabeth (6 daily; 9hr); Pretoria (21 daily; 7hr); Upington (daily; 7hr 30min).

By plane The small airport (T 051 407 2240) is located 10km east of town on the N8; there are pricey SAA flights between here and the major cities, and budget flights to Cape Town by Mango. There are no regular shuttle buses from the airport into town, so your only choice is to hail or phone for a taxi, or rent a car. The following rental agencies are based at the airport: Avis T 051 433 2331; Europcar T 051 433 3511; and Hertz T 051 433 2627. Budget's office is on Nelson Mandela street (T 051 447 9947).

Destinations: Cape Town (4–5 daily; 2hrs); Durban (2 daily; 1hr); Johannesburg (11 daily ; 1hr).

By train Trains operate from Bloemfontein Station (T 051 408 4843) on Harvey Rd, at the east end of Maitland St.

Destinations: Johannesburg (Wed, Fri & Sun; 7hr); Port Elizabeth (Wed, Fri, Sun; 13hr).

INFORMATION

Tourist information Inside the tourist complex and bus terminal on Park Rd (Mon–Fri 7.45am–4.15pm, Sat 8am–noon; T 051 405 8489).

GETTING AROUND

By taxi The minibus taxi rank lies one block west of the train station on Hanger St. The area around the station and the minibus taxi rank is regarded by some residents as the dodgiest in the city centre, but there have been few actual incidents; stay alert, and avoid the area at night. Fortunately, metered taxis usually gather outside the train and bus stations; alternatively, you can phone for one (Bloem Taxis T 051 433 3776; GG Taxis T 051 522 6969).

ACCOMMODATION

The more central suburbs of Westdene and Waverley, both just north of the centre, are the best areas to stay in. If you are driving through and need a bed for the night, do ring guesthouses in advance, rather than just turning up.

Cherry Tree Cottage 12A Peter Crescent, Waverley T 051 436 4334 or T 072 291 0336, E cherrytree@imaginet.za. A peaceful, a/c B&B set in a beautifully landscaped garden and bordering a reserve with resident giraffe. The four bedrooms each have their own separate entrances, and the price includes a cooked breakfast. **R850**

★ **Hobbit Boutique Hotel** 19 President Steyn Ave, Westdene T 051 447 0663, W hobbit.co.za. Inspired by Tolkien's *The Hobbit*, this is the best place to stay in Bloemfontein; a luxurious establishment filled with beautiful and comfortable antique furniture, with teddy bears tucked into every bed under handmade quilts. Excellent three-course dinners are available for small groups (phone by lunchtime). Book well in advance. **R950**

Kleine Eden Guest House 2 Moffett St, Fichardt Park T 051 525 2633, W kleine-eden.co.za. Well-maintained guesthouse with B&B, self-catering and family units. Rooms all have their own entrance and private garden. Breakfast extra. **R630**

The Urban 101 Parfitt St, Park West T 051 444 3142, W urbanhotel.co.za. A slick and surprisingly affordable designer hotel decorated in white, black and red. Rooms are small, functional and stylish, though slightly impersonal. **R840**

EATING AND DRINKING

While Bloemfontein is no culinary capital and there are few regional specialities to sample, you can still have a good and inexpensive meal here. Westdene's Second Avenue has a handful of restaurants and is safe to stroll about at night.

Avanti 53 Second Ave, Westdene ☎051 447 4198. Bloemfontein's best Italian restaurant features mostly well-done classics, alongside a few more adventurous offerings like lamb ravioli (R90) and "Italian spring rolls". There is a delicious array of focaccia as well. Booking recommended. Mon–Thurs 11.30am–10pm, Fri & Sat 11.30am–10.30pm, Sun 11.30am–3pm.

Barba's Café 16 Second Ave, Westdene ☎051 430 2542. Serves excellent Greek food like *pita souvlakia* (R50), but is mainly known for its Saturday-night bashes which go on into the small hours. Wed–Sun 3pm–4am.

Cubaña Corner of Second Ave and President Reitz St, Westdene ☎051 447 1920. A bustling Latino restaurant and bar serving large portions of decent food such as quesadillas (R45) and meat platters. Later on in the evenings, cocktails (around R35) are served and DJs play Latino music. Wednesday is a rowdy student night. Mon–

Wed 8am–midnight, Thurs–Sat 8am–2am.

Mystic Boer 84 Kellner St, Westdene ☎051 430 2206. A great place to down a few tequilas, with pizzas available for around R80, and different music styles and special offers throughout the week. There's live music on Sundays. The best place in town for a night out. Mon–Sun 2pm–2am, Sun 5pm–midnight.

Seven on Kellner 7 Kellner St, Westdene ☎051 447 7928. Upmarket dining in a fine old house, with a short but inventive menu that includes grilled meat and fish as well as imaginative wood-fired pizzas for around R90. Mon–Fri noon–2pm & 6.30pm–late, Sat 6.30pm–late.

The Terrace 16 Harry Smith St ☎051 448 6834. A pleasant location in the formal gardens of the Oliewenhuis Art Museum, leading onto a nature reserve, make this Bloemfontein's nicest place for afternoon tea and cake (R25 per slice). Tues–Fri 9am–5pm, Sat & Sun 10am–5pm.

DIRECTORY

Emergencies ☎082 911.
Hospitals The main state hospital is Universitas (☎051 405 3911), offering a free 24hr emergency ward, but you may wait hours and the level of care is variable. The private hospitals are a better choice: Medi-Clinic, Kellner St (☎051 404 6666); Rosepark Hospital, Fichmed Centre, Gustav Crescent (☎051 505 5111).

Pharmacies Dis-Chem, Loch Logan Waterfront mall, First Ave (☎051 411 6140; Mon–Fri 9am–6pm, Sat 8am–5pm, Sun 9am–2pm).
Post office Corner of Oos Burger and Maitland sts (Mon, Tues, Thurs & Fri 8am–4.30pm, Wed 8.30am–4.30pm, Sat 8am–noon).

The Maloti Route

Hugging the Lesotho border for 280km from Phuthaditjhaba (Witsieshoek) in the north to Wepener in the south, the tarred **Maloti Route** offers one of South Africa's most scenic drives, taking you past massive rock formations streaked with red and ochre, cherry orchards and sandstone farming towns. Wedged into a corner between Lesotho and northern KwaZulu-Natal, **Phuthaditjhaba** is the gateway to the Sentinel, from where it's easy to hike the Drakensberg Escarpment. Not far to the west is the highlight of the region, **Golden Gate Highlands National Park**, encompassing wide-open mountain country. The park is an easy three- to four-hour drive from Johannesburg, which means you could easily use it as a first- or last-night stop if you're arriving or leaving from Johannesburg and don't want to spend the night in the city. Nearby, the **Basotho Cultural Village** is worth visiting to gain some insight into Basotho traditions.

HIKING THE DRAKENSBERG AMPHITHEATRE

The easiest hiking access onto the high **Drakensberg Escarpment** and some of South Africa's most dramatic mountain scenery can be found just southeast of the Golden Gate park. A five-hour return hike leads past two metal ladders to the top of the chunky **Sentinel Peak**, with fantastic views of the Drakensberg amphitheatre and the Tugela waterfall, at 948m the second highest in the world. The starting point is at the Sentinel car park, near the *Witsieshoek Mountain Lodge*, south of Phuthaditjhaba; this can only be reached with private transport.

HIKING UP THE DRAKENSBERG ESCARPMENT

South Africa's most spectacular mountain views are from the **Drakensberg Escarpment**, the broad area right at the top of the major peaks, and from the top of the **Amphitheatre**, the grand sweep of mountains dominating the Royal Natal National Park. Both of these require a high level of fitness to reach if approached from KwaZulu-Natal (see box, p.390) but can be achieved relatively easily via the Free State from the Sentinel car park. A tough ten-hour climb from the Mahai campsite in the Royal Natal National Park (see p.398) or a 2.5-hour walk from the Sentinel car park brings you to the foot of a 30m-high chain ladder leading up an almost vertical face; from the top, you can make the final short onslaught to the highest peak on the escarpment (3278m). Don't be lulled by your apparently easy conquest: it's the Berg's prerogative to have the last word. Always tackle the ladder with enough food, water, clothes and a tent in which to sit out violent storms, and set out early so you have the whole day for the excursion.

For those bitten by the mountain bug, some serious hikes are available, including a two-week trek along the escarpment plateau to Sani Pass in the southern Drakensberg. You can also take in the most dramatic parts of the Berg on a five-day, 62km escarpment traverse, sleeping in caves, from the Sentinel car park to Cathedral Peak in the Natal Drakensberg Park, roughly 40km to the southwest. For any hikes of this nature you'll need a map and the excellent *Best Walks of the Drakensberg* by David Bristow (see p.663), available in most bookshops.

The closest village to the Golden Gate Park is **Clarens**, a centre for arts and crafts and the most attractive of all the villages along the route.

Basotho Cultural Village

20km east of Golden Gate National Park and signposted from the main road • Mon–Fri 9am–4.30pm, Sat & Sun 9am–5pm • R70 • ☎ 058 721 0300, ⓦ sanparks.org

The **Basotho Cultural Village** is a great place to learn about the traditional lives of the Basotho people, who have lived in the vicinity and just across the border in Lesotho for centuries. The main display in the reconstructed village is a courtyard of beautiful Basotho huts, from organic circular sixteenth-century constructions to square huts with tin roofs, bright interior decor and European blankets and utensils. Visitors are taken on a tour run by actors in traditional dress, meeting the chief, sampling traditional beer, hearing musicians play and seeing a traditional healer; you also learn about the curious spiral aloe, plants unique to the Drakensberg.

The views across the surrounding **QwaQwa Nature Park** are awesome, and there's an endless choice of walks and pony rides. The curio shop sells some quality local crafts (look out for raffia mats and baskets and the conical hats unique to this area), and the open-air tea garden serves teas and traditional food.

You can stay the night here in some traditional Basotho rondavel huts with views over the plain (see p.438).

Golden Gate Highlands National Park

300km northeast of Bloemfontein on the R712 • R144/day for hiking, driving through is free • ☎ 058 255 1000, ⓦ sanparks.org

The **Golden Gate Highlands National Park** was designated for its outstanding beauty rather than its wildlife. Although eland, zebra, mountain reedbuck and black wildebeest roam the hillsides, the real attraction here is the unfettered space, eroded sandstone bastions and seamless blue skies. These rocks, grassy plateaus and incised valleys belong to the Drakensberg range (see p.388), characterized here by spectacular yellow and red cliffs and overhangs.

A number of hour-long rambles into the sandstone ravines start from a direction board near the footbridge at the *Glen Reenen Rest Camp*. There aren't many medium-length hikes

6

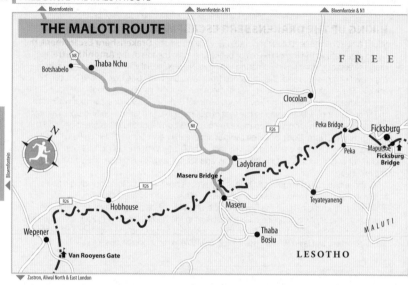

in the park, the only exception being a sometimes steep and physically challenging half-day walk up Wodehouse Kop, which offers great views. The most strenuous hike, available for groups only, is the demanding two-day circular Rhebok Trail, which reaches the highest and lowest points of the park; hikers need to book the basic overnight accommodation through South African National Parks (see p.64). In the summer you can swim in a natural waterfall pool close to the *Glen Reenen* campsite; other activities at Golden Gate include horseriding, fossil tours, scenic drives and hiking trails, all arranged via the *Glen Reenen* reception. For those quickly driving through, two asphalted loops signposted off the main road take in fields populated by zebra and antelope, a carcass-strewn vulture feeding spot, and stunning views of the highest peaks of the Drakensberg.

ARRIVAL AND DEPARTURE
THE MALOTI ROUTE

BASOTHO CULTURAL VILLAGE
Occasional **minibus taxis** run along the R712 between Clarens and Phuthaditjhaba via the Golden Gate Park, dropping visitors off at the access road to the Basotho Cultural Village, from where it's a 2km walk.

GOLDEN GATE HIGHLANDS NATIONAL PARK
Golden Gate is almost equidistant from Bloemfontein and Johannesburg (320km to the north on good, tarred roads), and is easily reached from either city. There are no entry gates to the park, which is open 24 hours.

ACCOMMODATION

BASOTHO CULTURAL VILLAGE
Basotho Cultural Village Rest Camp ☎ 012 428 9111, ⓦ sanparks.org. The cosy self-catering rondavels in the beautifully situated museum village are meant to resemble those of an eighteenth-century Basotho settlement, and offer magnificent views over the plains. **R700**

THE ESCARPMENT
Witsieshoek Mountain Lodge End of the R57 Rd ☎ 058 713 6361 or ☎ 073 228 7391, ⓦ witsieshoek .co.za. Currently being upgraded after years of neglect, the lodge is spectacularly set at 2283m above sea level, making

it the highest lodge in the country. It has functional rooms in chalets and bungalows, some with excellent views of the mountains – those that have already been renovated are slightly more expensive – and there is also a restaurant and pub. **R880**

GOLDEN GATE HIGHLANDS NATIONAL PARK
The *Golden Gate Hotel* has a restaurant and the rest camp has a basic shop, but otherwise all accommodation is self-catering – and the nearest alternative for food is Clarens, 20km away, which is also the place to head if all

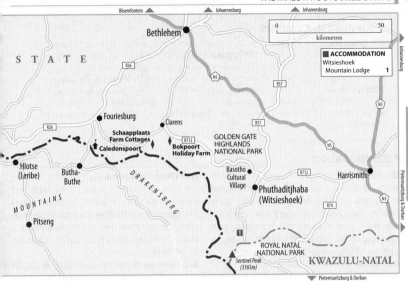

accommodation is full at the park (see below).

Glen Reenen Rest Camp ☎012 428 9111 or ☎058 255 1000 on the day, ⓦsanparks.org. In the centre of the park, but unfortunately right beside a road that has truck traffic all night. Camping, rondavels and basic four-bed cottages are available. As well as the provisions store, there's also a swimming pool, picnic sites and a filling station. Camping R180/for 2 people, rondavel R740, cottage R1100

Golden Gate Hotel ☎012 428 9111 or ☎058 255 1000

on the day, ⓦsanparks.org. This is the smartest place to stay in the park, with well-equipped self-catering chalets and comfortable B&B rooms, most with fantastic views. Breakfast and dinner are available on request. Room R1035, chalet R990

Highlands Mountain Retreat ☎012 428 9111 or ☎058 255 1000 on the day, ⓦsanparks.org. Away from the crowds, and beautifully located in the foothills off the Oribi Loop Rd, the *Highlands Mountain Retreat* offers luxury family log cabins sleeping two to four people. R1200

Clarens

Some 20km west of Golden Gate Highlands National Park lies the tree-fringed village of **CLARENS**, the most appealing of the settlements along the Maloti Route. Founded in 1912, Clarens is especially remarkable for its dressed stone architecture, which glows under the sandstone massif of the Rooiberge (Red Mountains) and the Malotis to the southeast. The best time to see the village is spring, when the fruit trees blossom, or autumn, when the poplar leaves are turning. But at any time of year Clarens' relaxed air makes it a rare phenomenon in the Free State – a *dorp* you'd actually want to explore, or sip a sidewalk lager and simply hang out in. The scenery is a magnet for artists and photographers all year round, but especially during autumn when the leaves are ablaze in russet gold.

Clarens is an arts and crafts centre, with a number of studios and shops peppering the streets. If you arrive around lunchtime on a weekend there's a chance you'll catch some local live music at one of the streetside cafés around President Square, effectively the town centre in the middle of Main Street.

INFORMATION   **CLARENS**

Tourist information There is no official tourist information office, but Clarens Destinations on Swart St by the main highway is a useful accommodation booking and information service (Mon–Fri 9am–5pm, Sat 9am–1pm;

☎058 256 1189, ⓦgoclarens.co.za). Mountain Odyssey on Main St (Mon–Fri 9am–5pm, Sat 9am–2pm, Sun 9am–noon; ☎058 256 1480) also books accommodation, and can help organize activities in the area.

6

SHOPPING IN CLARENS

The **galleries** in the village centre are great for gifts and souvenirs. Just west of the square, the excellent bookshop **Bibliophile** (313 Church St; Mon–Sat 9am–5pm, Sun 9am–3pm; ☎ 058 256 1692) is a good place to stock up on photo books, fiction, Lesotho maps and literature. The most charming shop is the **Di Mezza & De Jager Trading Store** (Sias Oosthuizen Street; Mon–Sat 8.30am–1pm & 2–5pm; ☎ 058 256 1313), signposted as "The Blanket Shop". This genuine old-style general dealer is run by Gertie and Minnie, who can advise on quality woollen Basotho blankets (R250–1300) in various sizes and patterns.

ACCOMMODATION

Clarens Inn 93 Van Reenen St ☎ 076 369 9283 or ☎ 082 377 3621, ☯ clarensinn.com. The cheapest place to stay, with the choice between a functional dorm, camping, dome-shaped huts, a very basic honeymoon suite and a range of equally basic self-catering units sleeping up to eight people (from R200/person). Camping R100, dorm R150, suite R500

Cottage Pie 89 Malherbe St ☎ 058 256 1214 or ☎ 082 853 5947, ☯ cottagepiebb.co.za. One of the town's best B&Bs with a lovely setting in a lush garden along a stream. There's a garden chalet and two rooms inside the thatched main house, with excellent breakfasts (R85 extra) served on the patio. R530

Lake Clarens Guesthouse 1 Lake Clarens Drive ☎ 058 256 1446, ☯ lakeclarensgh.co.za. Pretty rooms in a characterful old sandstone building overlooking a pond filled with geese, with breakfast served on a pleasant rose-covered terrace out front. There are a few cheaper rooms in an annex at the back, and a self-catering flat as well (R350/person). R800

Red Mountain House President Square ☎ 058 256 1456, ☯ redmountainhouse.co.za. Centrally situated B&B that has rooms on the upper floor opening onto balconies with views onto the square and the mountains. Rooms have fireplaces and are luxuriously furnished with Persian rugs and Victorian antiques. R1160

EATING AND DRINKING

On weekends, when the crowds arrive in town, most restaurants are packed and service is slow – it's best to book in advance or to arrive early if you're hungry.

278 on Main 278 Main St ☎ 082 556 5208, ☯ 278onmain.co.za. A good variety of sweet and hearty breakfasts (around R50), pasta, meat dishes, pancakes and desserts in a artsy interior, at the very end of the row of restaurants in the village. Tues–Sat 7.30am–9pm, Sun 7.30am–1pm.

Clarens Brewery President Square, next to Red Mountain House ☎ 058 256 1193. Seven delicious beers (R25/pint) and a collection of ciders are proudly brewed on site at this friendly biergarten, which also serves a few German-inspired dishes like bratwurst (R35). The perfect place for a drink in the sun. Mon–Thurs 10am–6pm, Fri & Sat 10am–7pm, Sun 10am–5pm.

Clementines Church St ☎ 082 453 7060. Booking is essential at Clarens' best restaurant, housed in an atmospheric old tin bus maintenance shed. Try the steaks, a slow-food oxtail stew, or grilled local rainbow trout (R95), washed down with beer from the Clarens Brewery. There's plenty of space in the garden for romping kids. Tues–Thurs 11am–2.30pm & 5.30–8pm, Fri 11am–2.30pm & 5.30–9pm, Sat & Sun 10.30am–2.30pm & 5.30–9pm.

The Highlander President Square ☎ 058 256 1912. A cosy restaurant with a fire in winter and a terrace for when the weather is fine; it's especially recommended for its home-made pies, pizza, breakfasts and cheesecake (R45). Daily 7.30am–10pm.

Ficksburg

FICKSBURG, 82km southwest of Clarens, is the centre of South Africa's cherry and asparagus farming. The town's sandstone architecture gives it a pleasant ambience, and it's a good place to make a stop halfway down the Maloti Route. An annual Cherry Festival in the third week of November is the highlight of Ficksburg's calendar; it features a marathon, floats, stalls, a "cherry queen" competition and a popular beer festival.

ARRIVAL AND DEPARTURE   FICKSBURG

By minibus taxi Minibus taxis from the Maputsoe border crossing on the eastern edge of town link Ficksburg to

Bloemfontein (3hr 30min), Johannesburg (10hr) and other towns.

ACCOMMODATION

Bella Rosa 21 Bloem St ☎051 933 2623. A hugely popular and well-priced pair of Victorian sandstone houses

set in a lovely garden, with nicely furnished en-suite rooms. Breakfast is included in the rate. R580

Ladybrand

LADYBRAND lies on the main route into Lesotho, just over 50km southwest of Ficksburg. It's one of the few small towns in the Free State that is booming, owing to its proximity to Lesotho's capital, 12km away. Many people working on projects in Lesotho stay in Ladybrand rather than in Maseru because of its calm and family-friendly village atmosphere.

The area is certainly fine **horseriding** country, and *Bokpoort and Schaapplaats* (see box, below) offer superlative guided riding in isolated mountains.

ARRIVAL AND DEPARTURE   LADYBRAND

By bus and minibus taxi Minibus taxis run regularly between Ladybrand and the Maseru bridge border crossing

16km away, as well as connecting to Johannesburg and Bloemfontein.

ACCOMMODATION

Cranberry Cottage 37 Beeton St ☎051 923 1500 or ☎082 921 1575, ⓦcranberry.co.za. One of the best and most popular options in town, offering 43 comfortable country-style rooms (some with kitchens) set in a rambling garden. There's a gym and spa here, and the owners have reams of information on day-trips and rock-art sites. R960

Living Life Station House 1 Princess St ☎082 854 8550, ⓦlivinglifesa.co.za. Run by a charity that provides employment to women, these four stylish rooms near the old train station are airy and spacious, beautifully done up with whitewashed wood and crisp linens. All come with bathtubs and private porches, and there's also a spa on site. R570

FARMSTAYS AND HORSERIDING AROUND CLARENS

Horseriding is big along the Eastern Highlands. A couple of farms near Clarens – both excellent family destinations – provide outstanding riding onto the Drakensberg Escarpment, from where you can gaze across into Lesotho and view Southern Africa's highest peaks.

The friendly and very Afrikaans *Bokpoort Holiday Farm* (☎083 744 4245, ⓦbokpoort.co.za) has a range of accommodation, from en-suite chalets with fireplaces and kitchenettes (R500), to dorm beds (R150) in an old sandstone barn. If you're camping (R75), there's a good communal cooking and dining area. Reasonably priced meals, including dinner, can be ordered from the farmhouse kitchen, while a small shop sells basics.

Bokpoort's big draw is the memorable **Western-style riding** in deep, comfortable cowboy saddles on sure-footed horses. Short rides from the farmhouse (R350 for 2hr) take in San rock paintings and swimmable river pools, with the chance of seeing eland, zebra and springbok on the adjoining game farm. Two-day riding trails into the mountains on the Lesotho border cost R1600 per person all-inclusive, or R1200 if you self-cater; a 4WD vehicle brings the food and bedding (you sleep on mattresses in a remote mountain hut), and you ride about six hours a day.

High-quality horses and riding are also available at *Schaapplaats Farm Cottages & Ashgar Equestrian Centre* (☎058 256 1176 or ☎083 630 3713, ⓦashgarhorses.co.za), in the mountains 6km south of Clarens off the R711. An establishment with a more English flavour, this turn-of-the-twentieth-century farm has four self-catering sandstone cottages sleeping two to four people (R250/person). From here you can go on terrific **mountain hikes**, visit Boer War graves and San rock paintings and, of course, go ride horses (R300 per person for 2hr). There's also a chance to brush up your equestrian skills, as the owner is a qualified riding teacher. Moreover, there is some game on the farm (zebra, wildebeest, antelope etc), which adds zest to any ride.

6

EATING

Cranberry's Restaurant 37 Beeton St ☎051 923 1500. *Cranberry Cottage's* popular restaurant serves excellent international meals, including an assortment of seafood, pastas and grills like lamb chops (R110). In summer, guests are seated out on the candle-lit terrace by the pond. Daily 7am–9.30pm.

★**Station Café** 1 Princess St, ☎051 924 2834 or 082 854 8550. Ladybrand's former train station is now an attractive restaurant run by the charity Living Life, with wonderful organic South African dishes like focaccia pizza (R60) and delicious salads. The ingredients are sourced from the region, and some from the café's own garden. Tues–Sat 8am–4.30pm.

Parys and the Vredefort Dome

The small town of **PARYS**, just off the N1 highway 300km northeast of Bloemfontein and 100km from Johannesburg, makes a good stopover on the long trek across the country, or an interesting day-trip from Jo'burg. The town, with its galleries, antique shops, adventure sports and the meandering Vaal River, is pleasant enough, but its main claim to fame is harder to spot as it's situated near **Vredefort**, the epicentre of a massive meteorite impact some two billion years ago. What remains of the huge 300km-wide crater is now South Africa's most abstract World Heritage Site (it can only properly be seen from space), but by joining a tour (see box below) it is possible to get a good idea of what happened and to view what's left of the impact dome, the mass of molten rock that was thrust upwards after the meteorite struck.

Early November is a good time to visit Parys, when outdoor enthusiasts descend on the town for dragon-boat racing and live music during the annual Dome Adventure Festival (🖥domefest.co.za).

INFORMATION   PARYS

Tourist information 30 Water St (Mon–Fri 8am–5pm, Sat & Sun 9am–1pm; ☎056 811 4000, 🖥parys.info).

ACCOMMODATION

Art Lovers Guesthouse 89 Breë St ☎056 817 6515, 🖥artloversguesthouse.co.za. Six spacious and artistically furnished suites with antique furniture, chandeliers and Persian carpets, plus nice personal touches like a glass of sherry to welcome guests. No children under 12. R1100

THE VREDEFORT DOME

Some two billion years ago, an **asteroid** the size of Cape Town's Table Mountain slammed into Earth at a speed of 30,000 kilometres per hour, forming a 300km-wide crater. The impact at **Vredefort**, 10km south of Parys, vaporized the asteroid and part of the Earth's crust, melting, pulverizing and shattering rocks for kilometres around. It also forced rocks beneath the impact area briefly down before these rebounded, raising and upending rock layers to form a dome structure. Even though the Earth's surface has eroded about 10km since the impact, the weathered **concentric rings** of this dome can still be seen, forming the hills around Parys. The rim of the crater, originally up to 150km away, has not survived the elements, though it's thanks to the downward sagging of the gold-bearing layers around the dome, caused by the impact, that the richest source of gold in the world was preserved from erosion before the first gold diggers discovered these layers in Johannesburg, in 1886.

The dome area is best experienced on a **tour**, which takes in the view of the dome remnants and tracks down strange melt rock formations. *Otters' Haunt Lodge*, 2km from Parys (Kopjeskraal Rd; ☎056 818184 or ☎084 245 2490, 🖥otters.co.za), organizes dome walks (half day; R335/ person) and guided drives in your own car (full day; R565/person). For both, there is a minimum charge for three people. Six kilometres from Parys, the *Kopjeskraal Country Lodge* (☎083 406 0841, 🖥kopjeskraal.co.za/tours.htm) also offers dome walks (2hr; R100) and two-and-a-half-hour 4WD drive tours (R150/person for groups of three or more, or R200/person for two people).

Secret Place 21A Venus Rd ☎081 414 6822, ⓦsecretplace.co.za. An elegant guesthouse infused with the flavour of France – it even boasts its own formal garden – with beautiful rooms decorated in a romantic, antique style. Each room is different: one has an outdoor shower, while another overlooks a herb garden. <u>R800</u>

EATING AND DRINKING

O's Restaurant 1 De Villiers St ☎056 811 3683. Homey Boer comfort food like *bobotie* (R80) alongside more sophisticated Continental fare like escargots and smoked chicken pasta, all served in a pretty and peaceful riverside garden. Bookings recommended. Wed–Sat 11am–10pm, Sun 11am–3pm.

Vetkoek Paleis & Kerrie Huis 62 Breë St ☎056 817 6833. Snack on Afrikaner *vetkoek*, deep-fried pastries with various fillings, at this local institution whose name means "fat cake palace and curry house". A *vetkoek* filled with beef curry will run you R49. Normal breakfasts and pancakes are also served. Mon–Thurs 8.30am–3pm, Fri 8.30am–5pm, Sat 8am–2pm, Sun 8.30am–2pm.

6

Gauteng

JOHANNESBURG AT DUSK

Gauteng

Gauteng is South Africa's smallest region, comprising less than two percent of its landmass, yet contributing around forty percent of the GDP. Home to over twelve million people, Gauteng is almost entirely urban; while the province encompasses a section of the Magaliesberg Mountains to the east and the gold-rich Witwatersrand to the south and west, the area is dominated by the huge conurbation incorporating Johannesburg, Pretoria and a host of industrial towns and townships that surround them. Although lacking the spectacular natural attractions of the Cape Province or Mpumalanga, Gauteng has a subtle physical power. Startling outcrops of rock known as *koppies*, with intriguing and often lucrative geology, are found in the sprawling suburbs and grassy plains of deep-red earth that fringe the cities.

The older parts of Johannesburg and Pretoria are gloriously green in summer: both are among the most tree-rich cities on Earth, and Johannesburg, home to ten million of them, is proudly described by locals as the world's largest man-made forest. The ubiquitous jacaranda trees blossom in October, turning the suburbs purple.

Gauteng is dominated by **Johannesburg**, whose origins lie in the exploitation of **gold** (Gauteng means "Place of Gold" in Sotho). Although it has grown rapidly since the discovery of gold in 1886 to become the richest metropolis in Africa, it is a hectic city, home to extreme contrasts of wealth and poverty. The city has a reputation among both visitors and South Africans as a place to avoid, but those who acquire a taste for Jo'burg – something you can do in just a few days – are seduced by its energy and vibrancy, unmatched by any other city in South Africa. A highly cosmopolitan city, and the most Africanized in the country, Jo'burg boasts South Africa's most famous townships, its most active and diverse cultural life, some of its best restaurants and the most progressive nightlife.

Some 50km north lies dignified **Pretoria**, the country's administrative capital. Historically an Afrikaner stronghold, today it's a cosmopolitan mix of civil servants, diplomats and students from South Africa and around the world. Smaller and more relaxed than Johannesburg, Pretoria is an intriguing destination in its own right, with a range of interesting museums and historic buildings. The Gautrain rapid rail connection between Jo'burg and Pretoria was nothing less than a transport revolution when it opened in 2010, finally offering locals and travellers a safe and affordable alternative to the tedious traffic jams on the N1.

Less than an hour from the centre of Jo'burg, the section of the **Magaliesberg Mountains** that extends into Gauteng is a magnet for Johannesburgers desperate to escape the city's hectic tempo. Although the hills can hardly be described as remote and untamed, you'll find ample opportunities for nature trailing and hiking. As in much of Gauteng, however, the important part lies underground, with a series of caves and

TOWNSHIP HOUSE IN SOWETO

Highlights

❶ Downtown Johannesburg Experience a truly pan-African urban buzz at the heart of the continent's richest city. **See p.451**

❷ Melville Hang out with Jo'burg's students and hipsters in one of the city's few places where bars, cafés and decent restaurants line the street. **See p.463**

❸ The Apartheid Museum, Jo'burg A powerful, inspiring journey through the South African struggle for freedom. **See p.466**

❹ Soweto tours Sample the vibrancy of South Africa's most historically significant township. **See p.467**

❺ Live music Make the effort and you'll find that Jo'burg has the best scene in the country. **See p.479**

❻ The big match Whether it's Chiefs v Pirates or Springboks v All Blacks, sport in Jo'burg is always big news. **See p.481**

❼ Cradle of Humankind A series of caves on the fringe of Johannesburg provides vital fossil evidence of human ancestry. **See p.484**

❽ Voortrekker Monument and The Freedom Park, Pretoria These two monuments are dramatic tributes to the old and new South Africa. **See p.492**

HIGHLIGHTS ARE MARKED ON THE MAP ON P.448

archeological sites making up the **Cradle of Humankind** World Heritage Site. Most famous of these sites are the **Sterkfontein Caves**, where some of the world's most important discoveries of pre-human primate fossils have been made.

Johannesburg

Back in October 1886, when gold was discovered, what is now **JOHANNESBURG** was an expanse of sleepy, treeless veld. Now the economic engine of Africa, it's the sprawling,

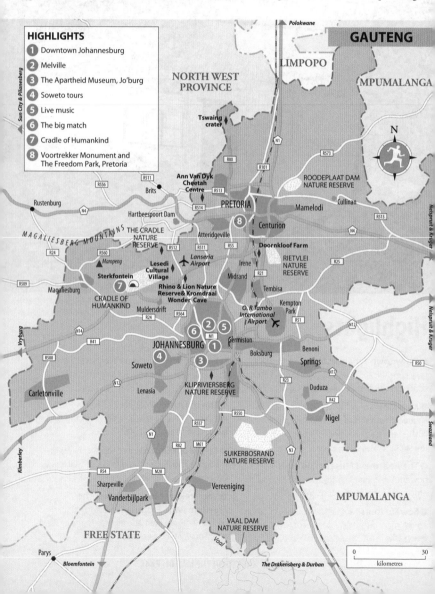

HIGHLIGHTS

1. Downtown Johannesburg
2. Melville
3. The Apartheid Museum, Jo'burg
4. Soweto tours
5. Live music
6. The big match
7. Cradle of Humankind
8. Voortrekker Monument and The Freedom Park, Pretoria

GAUTENG

LIMPOPO

NORTH WEST PROVINCE

MPUMALANGA

N

Polokwane

Tswaing crater

Sun City & Pilanesberg

Rustenburg

Brits

Hartbeespoort Dam

Ann Van Dyk Cheetah Centre

PRETORIA

Mameledi

Cullinan

ROODEPLAAT DAM NATURE RESERVE

MAGALIESBERG MOUNTAINS

THE CRADLE NATURE RESERVE

Centurion

Atteridgeville

Lanseria Airport

Irene

Doornkloof Farm

RIETVLEI NATURE RESERVE

Maropeng

Lesedi Cultural Village

Midrand

Magaliesburg

Sterkfontein

Rhino & Lion Nature Reserve & Kromdraai Wonder Cave

Tembisa

CRADLE OF HUMANKIND

Muldersdrift

Kempton Park

O. R. Tambo International Airport

JOHANNESBURG

Germiston

Benoni

Soweto

Boksburg

Springs

Carletonville

Lenasia

KLIPRIVIERSBERG NATURE RESERVE

Duduza

Nigel

Sharpeville

Vanderbijlpark

SUIKERBOSRAND NATURE RESERVE

MPUMALANGA

FREE STATE

Parys

Bloemfontein

VAAL DAM NATURE RESERVE

Vaal

Vereeniging

The Drakensberg & Durban

Nelspruit & Kruger

Swaziland

Vryburg

Kimberley

0   30
kilometres

infuriating, invigorating home to six million people, but never the country's seat of government or national political power.

During the apartheid era, Jo'burg was the city in which black resistance and urban culture were most strident – Nelson Mandela and Walter Sisulu formed the country's first black law firm here in 1952 – while the democratic era has seen the city become the vanguard of the gradual deracialization of South African society. The country's burgeoning **black elite** and **middle class** are concentrated here, and the city is a giant soup of ethnicities: Zulu and Sotho-speaking blacks, Afrikaners and English-speaking whites predominate, but Jozi culture is also enriched by immigrants from across Africa, as well as sizeable Indian, coloured, Chinese, Greek, Jewish, Portuguese and Lebanese communities. Jo'burg is an unpretentious, loud, ballsy city; outsiders are quickly accepted, and a pervasive social warmth keeps many of its more relaxed citizens from leaving.

Even so, there are still astonishing extremes of wealth and poverty here: mansions in verdant **suburbs** are protected by high walls and electrified fences, only a kilometre or two from sprawling **shantytowns** such as the inner-city flatlands of Hillbrow and Yeoville, where hundreds of thousands of immigrants, mostly from Zimbabwe, have formed a teeming ghetto economy, since the formal job market cannot absorb most of them.

The bewildering size of Jo'burg can be daunting, and some visitors venture out only to the bland, safe, covered shopping malls and restaurants of the northern suburbs while making hasty plans to move on. However, once you've found a convenient way of getting around, either by car, on the new **Gautrain** trains and buses, or in the company of a tour guide, the history, diversity and crackling energy of the city can quickly become compelling.

The **central business district**, which in the 1990s was all but abandoned by big business fleeing crime and grime, is undergoing a slow rebirth, with crime rates dropping and investors moving in. New City Improvement Districts have been implemented to oversee the cleaning, sprucing up and guarding of the central areas, most effectively so far in Braamfontein; security guards and cameras can now be seen on many street corners and, as a result, it's now relatively safe to walk around the CBD during the day.

Shopping is Jo'burg's biggest addiction, and the city offers an abundance of superb contemporary African art, fashion and design. And then there are the **townships**, most easily explored on a tour but, in some cases, possible to get to under your own steam.

Jo'burg is also a great place to watch **sport**, with soccer, rugby and cricket teams commanding feverish support. The 2010 Football World Cup was headquartered in the city; the one-hundred-thousand-seat FNB Stadium (formerly Soccer City) is a proud reminder of the event, and is regularly used for games, concerts and other gatherings.

Brief history

Johannesburg dates back to 1886, when Australian prospector **George Harrison** found the main Witwatersrand gold-bearing reef. Almost immediately, this quiet area of the Transvaal became swamped with diggers from near and far, and a tented city sprang up around the site. The Pretoria authorities were forced to proclaim a township nearby: they chose a useless triangle of land called the Randjeslaagte, which had been left unclaimed by local farmers. **Johan Rissik**, the surveyor, called it Johannesburg, either after himself or Christiaan Johannes Joubert, the chief of mining, or the president of the South African Republic (ZAR), Paul Johannes Kruger.

Mining magnates such as Cecil Rhodes and Barney Barnato possessed the capital necessary to exploit the world's richest gold reef, and their **Chamber of Mines** (a self-regulatory body for mine owners, founded in 1889) attempted to bring some order to the digging frenzy, with common policies on recruitment, wages and working conditions. In 1893, due partly to pressure from white workers, and with the approval of the ZAR government, the chamber introduced the **colour bar**, which excluded black workers from all but manual labour.

By 1895, Johannesburg's population had soared to over one hundred thousand, many of whom were not Boers and had no interest in the ZAR's independence. Kruger and the burghers regarded these *uitlanders* (foreigners) as a potential threat to their political supremacy, and denied them the vote despite the income they generated for the state's coffers. Legislation was also passed to control the influx of blacks to Johannesburg, and Indians were forcibly moved out of the city into a western location. Before long, large shantytowns filled with blacks and Indians were springing up on the outskirts of Johannesburg.

The Anglo-Boer War

In 1900, during the Anglo-Boer War, Johannesburg fell to the British, who had been attempting to annex the gold-rich area for some time. At the same time, more black townships were established, including **Sophiatown** (1903) in an area previously used for dumping sewage, and **Alexandra** (1905). Bubonic plague erupted on the northern fringes of the city in 1904, providing justification for the authorities to burn several Indian and African locations, including **Newtown**, just west of the centre.

Meanwhile, white mine workers were becoming unionized, and outbreaks of fighting over pay and working hours were a frequent occurrence. Their poorly paid black counterparts were also mobilizing; their main grievance was the ruling that skilled jobs were the preserve of white workers. Resentments came to a head in the **Rand Revolt** of 1922, after the Chamber of Mines, anxious to cut costs, decided to allow blacks into the skilled jobs previously held only by whites. White workers were furious: street battles broke out and lasted for four days. Government troops were called in to restore order and over two hundred men were killed. Alarmed at the scale of white discontent, Prime Minister Jan Smuts ruled that the colour bar be maintained, and throughout the 1920s the government passed laws restricting the movement of blacks.

Populating Soweto

During the 1930s, the township of **Orlando** became established southwest of the city, with accommodation for eighty thousand blacks; this was the nucleus around which **Soweto** evolved. By 1945, four hundred thousand blacks were living in and around Johannesburg – an increase of one hundred percent in a decade. In August 1946, seventy thousand African Mineworkers Union members went on strike over working conditions. The government sent police in, and twelve miners were killed and over a thousand injured.

Forced removals of black residents from Johannesburg's inner suburbs, particularly from Sophiatown, began in 1955. Thousands were dumped far from the city centre, in the new township of Meadowlands, next to Orlando, and Sophiatown was crassly renamed Triomf (triumph). The **ANC** (see p.643) established itself as the most important black protest organization during this period, proclaiming the **Freedom Charter** in Kliptown, Soweto, that year.

During the 1950s, a vigorous black urban culture began to emerge in the townships, and the new *marabi* jazz and its offspring, the jubilant *kwela* pennywhistle style, were played in illegal drinking houses called *shebeens*. This was also the era of *Drum Magazine*, which celebrated a glamorous, sophisticated township zeitgeist, and introduced a host of talented journalists, such as Can Temba and Casey "Kid" Motsisi, to the city and the world. Mbaqanga music emerged later, with its heavy basslines and sensuous melodies capturing the bittersweet essence of life in the townships.

Resistance and democracy

The formation in 1972 of the **Black Consciousness Movement** (BCM) rekindled political activism, particularly among Soweto students. On June 16, 1976, student riots erupted in

SAFETY IN JOHANNESBURG

With Johannesburg's extremes of poverty and wealth, its brash, get-ahead culture and the presence of illegal firearms, it's hardly surprising that the city can be a dangerous place. Despite its unenviable reputation, it's important to retain a sense of proportion about potential risks and not to let paranoia ruin your stay. Most crime happens in the outlying townships, and the vast majority of Jo'burgers are exceedingly friendly; as in all major cities, taking simple precautions (see p.72 and below) is likely to see you through safely.

If you're wandering around **on foot**, the most likely risk of crime is from mugging. Although significant effort has gone into making the riskiest central areas safer – such as the installation of security cameras – you should remain alert when exploring the central business district (CBD), Braamfontein and Newtown, do your touring in daylight, use busy streets and never be complacent.

Joubert Park, Hillbrow and Berea should only be entered with a local guide; Yeoville and Observatory are safer and generally fine if you're confident or have someone to show you around. You're very unlikely to be mugged on the streets of Melville, Parktown, Rosebank or Sandton. If you want to walk around one of the riskier areas, study maps beforehand (not on street corners), don't walk around with luggage and avoid groups of young men. If you're carrying valuables, make a portion of them easily available, so that muggers are likely be quickly satisfied. Never resist muggers. You're unlikely to be mugged on **public transport** but, as always, stay alert, especially at busy spots such as Park Station and taxi ranks, and be extra vigilant when getting off minibus taxis. Waiting for buses in the northern suburbs is generally safe.

If you're **driving** around, there is a small risk of "smash and grab" theft or carjacking; keep all bags and valuables locked in the trunk, lock the car doors and keep windows up when driving after dark and in central areas. Always seek out secure – preferably guarded – parking; in Jo'burg this is in ample supply. Although urban legend suggests you can cruise through red traffic lights at night, this is dangerous and illegal; stop, keep a good distance from the car in front of you and be aware of anyone approaching the car.

Don't expect too much from the **police**, who normally have priorities other than keeping an eye out for tourists. In the city centre and Rosebank, **private guards**, identifiable by their yellow armbands and stationed on street corners, provide an effective anti-crime presence on the street.

the township, and the unrest spread nationwide (see box, p.470). The youth's war against the State escalated in the 1980s, resulting in regular "**states of emergency**", during which the armed forces had permission to do anything they liked to contain revolt. Towards the end of the decade, the government relaxed "petty" apartheid, turning a blind eye to the growth of "grey" areas like Hillbrow – white suburbs where blacks were moving in.

The three years after Nelson Mandela's release in 1990 saw widespread political violence in Gauteng right up until the day before the elections. However, as elsewhere in South Africa, the election on April 27, 1994, went off peacefully. The ANC won comfortably in Gauteng then, and retained their hold in 1999 and 2004. They also carried the province in 2009, despite a growing feeling that the ANC have not totally lived up to their promises. Black South Africans have indeed made steady inroads into positions of influence in business and politics, but, as an increasing number of township dwellers move to the suburbs, Johannesburg's infrastructure has struggled to cope: low-income housing is not being built fast enough, energy supply is wobbling as demand surges, and traffic is often hellish, though the new Gautrain rail network has improved the situation along the north–south routes, while the efficient Rea Vaya bus network is also steadily expanding its routes northwards.

The central business district (CBD)

Johannesburg's **CBD**, the grid of streets and tightly packed skyscrapers just to the south of the Witwatersrand Ridge, is the most recognizable part of the city. For a century after the first mining camp was built, on what is now Commissioner Street, the CBD

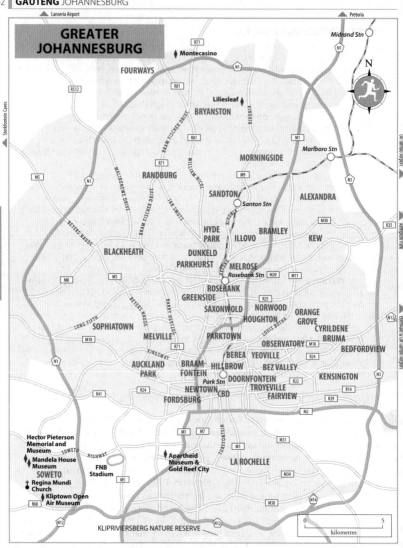

was the core of Jo'burg's buzzing commercial and financial life. Then there was the mass exodus during the crime-ridden 1980s and 1990s, and when the Jo'burg Stock Exchange moved out in 1999 in favour of Sandton, the city centre was all but written off. Today, however, Central Jo'burg is back on the map, with several regeneration projects having a profound effect on how the locals experience their city. A visit to the CBD offers the chance to see buildings and institutions with a fascinating history and get a taste of the bustle, sounds and thrills of a genuinely African city.

The Carlton Centre and around

Commissioner St • Centre and viewpoint daily 9am–7pm • R10; ticket office on the lower ground floor • Parking free for tower ticket holders • ☎ 011 308 2876

A good place to start exploring the CBD, the **Carlton Centre** complex has a lively shopping mall on the lower and underground floors and a convenient car park across Main Street. Its main attraction, however, is the **Top of Africa viewpoint** on the fiftieth floor of the Carlton Tower, Africa's tallest building (222m), which offers breathtaking views of the centre of Johannesburg, and shows how the mines, mine dumps and city concrete exist cheek by jowl. The adjacent *Carlton Hotel* was once the best hotel on the continent, but now stands empty after being closed in 1997.

Main Street

Main Street, partially pedestrianized for six blocks west of the regenerated Gandhi Square near the Carlton Centre, is home to the offices of various mining companies and makes a great introduction to Jo'burg's mining history. Industrial relics such as trains, wooden stampmills and a headgear lift tower have been placed along the road; walk right to the western end to see the fabulous 1940s Art Deco **AngloGold Ashanti head office** buildings, fronted by a fountain with a beautiful statue of a herd of springboks jumping over a pond.

7

   North of the courthouse, on the corner of Fox and Gerard Sekoto streets, the recently renovated **Chancellor House** is where Nelson Mandela and Oliver Tambo started their law firm in the 1950s. The ground floor windows have a small exhibition about the history of the building, while the impressive statue outside, based on the famous photo by *Drum* magazine's Bob Gosani, shows a young Mandela shadowboxing.

Gauteng Legislature and around

Corner of Rissik and Market streets

The impressive **Gauteng Legislature** was built in 1915 as the City Hall and is fronted by huge palm trees. Beside it stands the city's daintiest little skyscraper, the ten-storey **Barbican**, built in 1931, which was saved from neglect and destruction when it was renovated in 2010. Directly opposite the Legislature, the former **Rissik Street Post Office** was not as lucky, and its burnt-out shell stands testimony to the indifference of the current city management to its heritage; squatters accidentally set it on fire in 2009 and little has happened since. When this building was completed in 1897 it was the tallest in the city. Neo-Baroque in style, its fourth floor and clock tower were later additions, timed to coincide with the accession of the British king, Edward VII, in 1902.

GANDHI IN JOHANNESBURG

It was the ten years that **Mohandas Gandhi** spent in Johannesburg between 1903 and 1913 that first tested the philosophies for which he is famous. As an advocate, he frequently appeared in the Transvaal Law Courts (now demolished), which stood in what has since been renamed Gandhi Square in downtown Jo'burg. Defending mainly South African Indians accused of breaking the restrictive and racist registration laws, Gandhi began to see practical applications for his concept of **Satyagraha**, soul force, or passive resistance, as a means of defying immoral state oppression.

   Gandhi himself was twice imprisoned, along with other passive resisters, in the fort in Braamfontein, on what is now Constitution Hill. On one of these occasions he was taken from his cell to the office of General Jan Smuts to negotiate the prisoners' release, but finding himself at liberty had to borrow the railway fare home from the general's secretary.

   Gandhi's ideas found resonance in the non-violent ideals of those who established the **African National Congress** in 1912. Forty years later, only a few years after Gandhi's successful use of Satyagraha to end the British Raj in India, the start of the ANC's Defiance Campaign against the pass laws in 1952 owed much to his principles. MuseuMAfricA (see p.457) contains displays on Gandhi's time in Johannesburg, and he is commemorated with a statue on Gandhi Square.

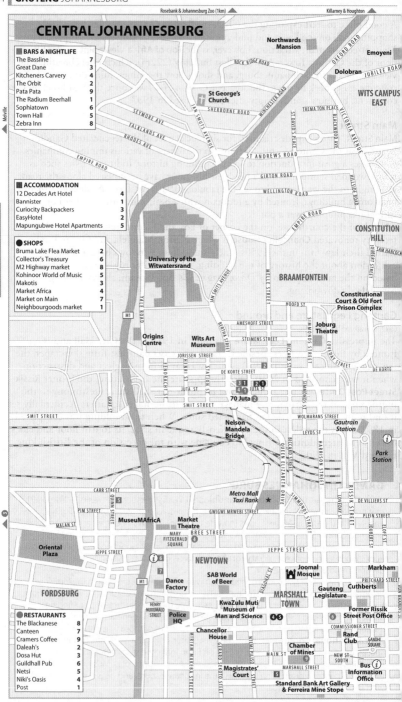

CENTRAL JOHANNESBURG

BARS & NIGHTLIFE

The Bassline	7
Great Dane	3
Kitcheners Carvery	4
The Orbit	2
Pata Pata	9
The Radium Beerhall	1
Sophiatown	6
Town Hall	5
Zebra Inn	8

ACCOMMODATION

12 Decades Art Hotel	4
Bannister	1
Curiocity Backpackers	3
EasyHotel	2
Mapungubwe Hotel Apartments	5

SHOPS

Bruma Lake Flea Market	2
Collector's Treasury	6
M2 Highway market	8
Kohinoor World of Music	5
Makotis	3
Market Africa	4
Market on Main	7
Neighbourgoods market	1

RESTAURANTS

The Blackanese	8
Canteen	7
Cramers Coffee	9
Daleah's	2
Dosa Hut	3
Guildhall Pub	6
Netsi	5
Niki's Oasis	4
Post	1

Rosebank & Johannesburg Zoo (1km)

Killarney & Houghton

Northwards Mansion

Emoyeni

Dolobran

WITS CAMPUS EAST

St George's Church

WINCHESTER ROAD

ROCK RIDGE ROAD

OXFORD ROAD

JUBILEE ROAD

SHERBORNE ROAD

SEYMORE AVE

FALKLANDS AVE

RHODES AVE

EMPIRE ROAD

ST ANDREWS ROAD

GIRTON ROAD

WELLINGTON ROAD

EMPIRE ROAD

CONSTITUTION HILL

University of the Witwatersrand

BRAAMFONTEIN

Constitutional Court & Old Fort Prison Complex

HOOFD ST

Origins Centre

Wits Art Museum

Joburg Theatre

AMESHOFF STREET

STEIMENS STREET

JORISSEN STREET

DE KORTE STREET

DE KORTE

JUTA ST

70 Juta

SMIT STREET

SMIT STREET

WOLMARANS STREET

Nelson Mandela Bridge

Gautrain Station

LEYDS ST

Park Station

CARR STREET

PIM STREET

Metro Mall Taxi Rank ★

DE VILLIERS ST

PLEIN STREET

MALAN ST

GWIGWI MRWEBI STREET

MuseuMAfricA

Market Theatre

BREE STREET

Oriental Plaza

JEPPE STREET

JEPPE STREET

MARY FITZGERALD SQUARE

NEWTOWN

Markham

FORDSBURG

Dance Factory

SAB World of Beer

Joomal Mosque

Cuthberts

MARSHALL TOWN

Gauteng Legislature

Police HQ

KwaZulu Muti Museum of Man and Science

Former Rissik Street Post Office

COMMISSIONER STREET

Chancellor House

Rand Club

GANDHI SQUARE

Chamber of Mines

MAIN ST

Bus Information Office

Magistrates' Court

MARSHALL STREET

Standard Bank Art Gallery & Ferreira Mine Stope

Killarney, Houghton & Norwood

0 — 500 metres

PARKTOWN

The Wilds

N

7

Linder Auditorium

Hazeldene Hall

The View

BEREA

YEOVILLE

Norwood & Orange Grove

Observatory & Cyrildene

HILLBROW

HIGHLANDS

Ponte City Tower

Windybrow Theatre

Johannesburg Stadium

JOUBERT PARK

DOORNFONTEIN

Johannesburg Art Gallery

NEW DOORNFONTEIN

Ellis Park Stadium

Park Central Taxi Terminus

St Mary's Cathedral

High Court

MOAD Museum of African Design

Carlton Centre & Top of Africa

Main Street Life

Arts on Main

Bioscope cinema

MABONENG

& Bezuidenhout Valley (1.5km)

Kensington

Rand Club

33 Loveday St • Visits by prior arrangement only, book at least a week in advance • Free if followed by lunch at the club • ☎ 011 870 4268, ✉ catering@randclub.co.za

The grandiose **Rand Club** is where mining magnates, nicknamed Randlords, have come to dine and unwind for over 125 years. Although the club was founded in 1887, the current building was completed in 1904 and is the fourth to occupy the site, as each successive clubhouse was replaced to reflect the members' growing wealth. The impressive hall with its stained-glass dome is surrounded by various dining rooms, a library and the *Main Bar*, home to the longest bar in Africa, which snakes around the room. Non-members can join tours of the building, lunch, dine or drink at the club (all with prior booking). Visitors must observe the dress code: a shirt and smart trousers and shoes for the men, smart casual for the women.

Standard Bank Art Gallery

Frederick St • Mon–Fri 8am–4.30pm, Sat 9am–1pm • Free • ☎ 011 631 1889, 🌐 standardbankarts.co.za

At the superb **Standard Bank Art Gallery**, changing exhibitions consistently show off some of the best contemporary African art in South Africa. The gallery is especially good at uncovering new talent; keep an eye out for the annual exhibition by the Standard Bank Young Artist Award winner.

Ferreira Mine Stope

5 Simmonds St • Daily 8.30am–5pm • Free

In the Standard Bank's head office, opposite their Art Gallery, it's possible to take a lift from the main concourse down to the **Ferreira Mine Stope**, an old mine access tunnel discovered when the building was being constructed in 1986. The plain rock face you see still bears pick-axe scars, and there's a simple but fascinating display putting the history of Johannesburg in context; look out for the old sepia photographs of the mine and early Jo'burg.

Diagonal Street

Diagonal Street, at the western end of Pritchard Street, lies at the heart of one of the most fascinating areas of the CBD. In the shadow of various concrete and glass behemoths, including the former Johannesburg Stock Exchange, is a street of old two-storey buildings, some of which date back to the 1890s; the lines of washing on the upstairs balconies show that they are still residential. The streets are home to a number of traders and shops peddling traditional medicines (*umuthi*), Sotho blankets and paraffin stoves alongside mobile phones. Though it might not feel so at first, the area is fairly safe, and with businessmen mingling with hawkers it has a very urban-African buzz. At the southern end of the street there are two lovely statues of ANC heroes Walter and Albertina Sisulu.

KwaZulu Muti Museum of Man and Science

14 Diagonal St • Mon–Fri 7.30am–5pm, Sat 7.30am–1pm • Free • ☎ 011 836 4470

The rather spooky **KwaZulu Muti Museum of Man and Science** is in fact a shop selling all kinds of traditional medicines, often manufactured from the dried animal skins hanging from the ceiling. You might also find yourself brushing against dangling ostrich feet or a pair of monkey skulls.

Newtown

On the western edge of the CBD between Diagonal Street and the M1 motorway flyover, **Newtown** is an area of redevelopment where some of Johannesburg's cultural hot spots can be found. The striking Nelson Mandela Bridge provides a swift link to the district from Braamfontein and the northern suburbs, while the large newly-opened Newtown Junction shopping mall beside the bridge is expected to breathe new life into the area. Newtown is a safe place to visit, both by day for strolling along the signposted heritage trail (see ⓦnewtown.co.za/heritage), and at night, when the handful of music and theatre venues are in full swing.

MuseuMAfricA

Mary Fitzgerald Square • Tues–Sun 9am–5pm • Free • ☎ 011 833 5624

At the heart of Newtown is the excellent **MuseuMAfricA**. The sheer size of the museum building – formerly the city's fruit and vegetable market – can make it seem a bit sparse and empty, but in fact the permanent exhibitions and numerous temporary displays are well worth seeing. Most successful is Sounds of the City, which features imaginative re-creations of shacks and *shebeens* in Sophiatown, home to famous musicians such as Hugh Masekela and Miriam Makeba, and which describes the different musical styles that were forged in this township during the 1950s. In a side room, look out for Tried for Treason, an exhibition dedicated to the Treason Trial (1956–61), when 156 people, including Nelson Mandela and many well-known ANC activists of all races, were accused of plotting against the state.

Market Theatre and The Bassline

Theatre Mary Fitzgerald Square, entrance at the eastern end of MuseuMAfricA

The famous **Market Theatre** (see p.480) has been a reliable source of stimulating and often ground-breaking dramatic output over the last thirty years or so. Outside, there's a handful of shops and places to eat and drink. The cultural theme continues south of Jeppe Street, with Jo'burg's best live music venue, **The Bassline** (see p.479), and a dance rehearsal and performing space called the Dance Factory, which is used for the annual Arts Alive Festival (see box, p.480).

South African Breweries (SAB) World of Beer

On the corner of President and Gerard sts • Tues–Sat 11am–3pm • R75 • ☎ 011 836 4900, ⓦ worldofbeer.co.za

The ninety-minute tour of the **South African Breweries (SAB) World of Beer** takes you through six thousand years of brewing history, which begs the question why SAB's ubiquitous end product, the anaemic, fizzy Castle lager, is so disappointing. Still, the reconstructed gold-rush pubs and 1960s *shebeen* are fun, along with the greenhouse where sample crops of barley and hops grow; use your two free beers to wash down a pub lunch on the balcony of the *Tap Room* bar and watch the city rush by.

Police Headquarters, Oriental Plaza and Mint Road

Main Reef Rd

At the infamous Johannesburg **police headquarters**, anti-apartheid activists were detained and tortured, and some fell to their deaths having "jumped" from the tenth floor. After this, it's a pleasant relief to find the remains of the old Indian neighbourhood of **Fordsburg** just further west, where Jeppe Street passes under the M1 flyover. This busy commercial street ends up at the **Oriental Plaza**, a hugely popular, Indian-owned shopping complex, selling everything from fabrics to spices and where haggling is *de rigueur*. Just beyond the Plaza, **Mint Road** is the scene of a fascinating Asian market (Thurs–Sat evening from 5pm) with dozens of stalls and good food. Most of Newtown's once-thriving Indian community, however, was forcibly removed in 1904 to make way for whites.

Johannesburg Art Gallery

Joubert Park • Tues–Sun 10am–5pm • Free • ☎ 011 725 3130, ⓦ joburg.org.za

On the eastern side of Park Station, **Joubert Park**, named after General Piet Joubert (who lost the South African Republic general election to Paul Kruger in 1893), is the only inner-city green space but largely regarded as a no-go area.

The one sight you can visit here is the **Johannesburg Art Gallery**, housed in an elegant, predominantly nineteenth-century building accessed via King George Street (with safe parking). This is one of the most progressive galleries in the country and regular exhibits include vast wooden sculptures by the visionary Venda artist Jackson Hlungwani that tower up to the ceilings. Elsewhere, there's a very South African mixture of African artworks and artefacts from the ceremonial to the purely decorative, and a range of European paintings, including some minor Dutch Masters. The special exhibitions are usually excellent, too.

The Maboneng Precinct

Between Main and Fox Streets, bordered by Berea and Auret Streets • ⓦ mabonengprecinct.com • Best reached from the M2 highway via Joe Slovo Drive (M31); take the R24 Market St exit and follow signs to the right

Around Main Street, east of the city centre, several city blocks have been transformed into a hive of cultural activity, and are perhaps the best place to get a taste of the potential of the city centre, and of how Jo'burg is changing for the better. It all started with **Arts on Main**, a former warehouse complex that now houses art workshops and galleries, the LoveJozi clothing shop, an arts bookshop, a restaurant and a rooftop bar, where you can do salsa dancing on Sundays. It positively buzzes with people during the excellent **Market on Main** every Sunday, when clothing, accessories and healthy food are for sale. Just 200m down the road, **Main Street Life** is a 1970s industrial building that has been converted into a complex with an exhibition space, apartments, the *12 Decades Art Hotel* (see p.474), the Bioscope art-house cinema (see p.480), the *Pata Pata* bar (see p.478) and a rooftop bar with great CBD views. Several other adjacent buildings have also been renovated to house a dozen boutiques and small restaurants that attract a hip crowd on Sundays. Two blocks north, at 281 Commissioner St, the **Museum of African Design**, or MOAD (Tues–Sun 10am–5pm; R30; ☏ 084 951 2060, ⓦ moadjhb.com), hosts worthwhile changing exhibitions and events in a large hall. The area is safe to visit, even at night, with plenty of security guards around.

The central suburbs

Grouped around the CBD are various suburbs which, given Johannesburg's itinerant population and fast-changing demography, seem to be in a state of constant change. Some, particularly Hillbrow, Berea and Yeoville, were once the "grey areas" of Johannesburg, where apartheid first started to break down in the 1980s. The police turned a blind eye as large numbers of blacks started moving from the townships into these previously all-white areas. Today, most whites have left these neighbourhoods – though they still reside in leafy, residential Observatory, just east of Yeoville – while migrants from all over Africa have flooded in. The hectic street life of Yeoville, Berea and Hillbrow can be very exciting, but you should not venture into these areas at night and should consider going with a street-smart guide during the day.

Braamfontein

It's not just for the transport facilities at Park Station that you might have cause to visit **Braamfontein** (ⓦ braamfontein.org.za), which starts at the main train station and extends north as far as Empire Road. Helped by its small size and clear physical boundaries, Johannesburg's prime student district has been regenerated after successful city improvement projects, increased policing and security, numerous new artworks and dozens of office-space-to-budget-accommodation conversions. It's a fun place to start exploring the new Johannesburg, especially on Saturday when the food market is on, and the developments in Braamfontein seem to fit comfortably in the urban fabric, with plenty of local students livening up the scene.

70 Juta and around

Corner of Juta and De Beer streets • ⓦ playbraamfontein.co.za/70-juta-street

A small development with a handful of fashion boutiques, shops, galleries and café, **70 Juta** is where the regeneration of Braamfontein took off. Across the street, the historical *Milner Park Hotel*, dating from 1906, is now home to fashionable bars and creative companies, while a dozen other boutiques, cafés and restaurants have since opened up along nearby De Beer and Melle streets. The best time to visit is on Saturdays between 9am and 3pm, when the car park at 73 Juta Street is home to the bustling **Neighbourgoods market** (see p.482).

Constitution Hill and Old Fort prison complex

Joubert St • Tours of the prisons every hour Mon–Fri 9am–5pm, Sat & Sun 10am–5pm • Tours take 1–2hr • R30–70 • ☎ 011 381 3100, ⓦ www.constitutionhill.org.za

Since 2003, **Constitution Hill** has been the home of the Constitutional Court, South Africa's highest court. Its hearings are fascinating for those interested in law or political science: the Court must tread a difficult path between the constitution's array of popular rights and the frustrating realities of a state that is struggling to guarantee them. The Court was built using the bricks of a demolished men's prison and is decorated with over two hundred mostly excellent modern and contemporary South African paintings and sculptures, worth seeing in themselves.

The adjacent **Old Fort prison complex** was built by Paul Kruger during the second Anglo-Boer War to protect the Afrikaners against the English and to keep an eye on the gold mine in the village below. The fort was subsequently converted to a prison and used to incarcerate and torture black men during apartheid for breaking racist laws or fighting for their repeal. You can visit the spine-chilling **Number Four prison building**, where Gandhi and Pan-Africanist Congress leader Robert Sobukwe were both held, and the cell where Mandela was kept briefly after his arrest in 1962.

The **Women's Jail**, built in 1910, is a grand Edwardian building that held black and white women prisoners in separate sections. The notorious serial poisoner Daisy de Melker was kept here when she was on death row, but major political leaders such as Winnie Madikizela-Mandela, Albertina Sisulu, Helen Joseph and Ruth First also became familiar with its cells. From the 1950s onward, most of the prison's inmates were pass-law offenders, until the systematic restriction of the movement of black people was repealed in 1986. Rich in symbolism, the Court and the prison complex provide a subtle but arresting testimony to the country's ongoing transformation, eloquently expressing the pride South Africans have in their new constitution and the democratic principles enshrined therein.

Origins Centre

Yale Rd • Daily 10am–5pm • R75 • ☎ 011 717 1365, ⓦ origins.org.za

On the campus of the University of the Witwatersrand, also known as "Wits", the **Origins Centre** uses a combination of films and exhibits to explain the African origins of humanity – where you can see a 75,000-year-old engraved ochre rock that's considered the world's first artwork – before moving on to its main focus: the beliefs, traditions and rock art of the San people (see box, p.395). This is the museum's main strength, and the displays give a useful overview for those intending to explore the San rock-art sites in KwaZulu-Natal.

Wits Art Museum

Corner of Jorissen St and Jan Smuts Ave • Wed–Sun 10am–4pm • Free • ☎ 011 717 1363, ⓦ wits.ac.za/wam

The new **Wits Art Museum** presents the university's rich art collection, built up over seventy years, in exhibitions that change every month or so. It's especially worth checking out the West and Central African art, though the modern photography and other genres are equally fascinating. There's a very good café on site, too.

Hillbrow

Smit Street marks the boundary of Joubert Park with infamous and densely populated **Hillbrow**, dominated by high-rise apartment buildings all crammed with people. Hillbrow has always attracted Jo'burg's new immigrants. Immediately after World War II, the typical immigrant was English, Italian or East European Jewish. These days, Africans from all over the continent are arriving in numbers, giving Hillbrow a uniquely pan-African atmosphere, with music from Lagos to Kinshasa to Harare pumping from the bars, clubs and markets that line the main thoroughfares. Along the many side streets, the scene is distinctly seedy, with drug pushers loitering outside lurid strip joints. The suburb is widely regarded as a no-go area for tourists, but the excellent **walking tours** by local NGO Dlala Nje, that leave from R180, Shop 1, Ponte City, Saratoga Avenue (☎072 397 2269, ⌨dlalanje.org), are a safe and fun way to visit Hillbrow and neighbouring Yeoville, while contributing to Dlala Nje's community centre and social projects. The walks visit the huge Ponte City residential tower, renovated parks and apartment buildings, as well as some fascinating hijacked high-rise buildings, while the evening tours take in Yeoville's food and nightlife scene.

The northern suburbs

Safe, prosperous and packed with shops and restaurants, the **northern suburbs** seem a world apart from the CBD and its surrounds. The name is actually a catch-all term for the seemingly endless urban sprawl running over 30km from Parktown, beyond the N1 ring road and into an area known as **Midrand**, which is itself creeping toward the southern edge of Pretoria. With the notable exception of Alexandra, this is a moneyed area, where plush shopping malls are often the only communal meeting points, and the majority of homes use high walls, iron gates and electric fences to advertise how security-conscious a life the owners lead. Despite the often numbing sheen of affluence, however, interesting pockets do exist, such as the centres of the suburbs of Melville,

---

SIR HERBERT BAKER

South Africa's most famous architect, **Sir Herbert Baker**, was born in Kent, England, in 1862. Apprenticed to his architect uncle in London at the age of 17, Baker attended classes at the Royal Academy and Architectural Association. By the time he left for the Cape in 1892, Baker was already a convert to the new so-called **Free Style**, which advocated an often bizarre, but roughly historical, eclecticism. The young architect's favourite influences, which would crop up again and again in his work, were Renaissance Italian and medieval Kentish.

Once in the Cape, Baker met **Cecil Rhodes**, which established him as a major architectural player. The second Anglo-Boer War began in 1899 and Rhodes, assuming eventual British victory, sent Baker off to study the Classical architecture of Italy and Greece, hoping that he would return to create a British imperial architecture in South Africa. Baker returned to South Africa deeply influenced by what he had seen, and was summoned by **Lord Alfred Milner**, the administrator of the defeated Transvaal, to fulfil Rhodes' hopes.

Baker began with the homes of the so-called "kindergarten", the young Oxford- and Cambridge-educated men whom Milner had imported to govern the defeated territory. The result was the **Parktown mansions**, opulent houses lining the roads of Johannesburg's wealthiest suburb. Baker trained local craftsmen and used local materials for these mansions, pioneering the use of local *koppie* stone.

Baker's major public commissions were **St George's Cathedral** in Cape Town, the **South African Institute for Medical Research** in Johannesburg, and the sober **Union Buildings** in Pretoria, which express the British imperial dream – obsessed with Classical precedent, and in a location chosen because of its similarity to the site of the Acropolis in Athens.

Baker left South Africa in 1913 to design the Secretariat in New Delhi, India, returning to England on its completion, where he worked on South Africa House in Trafalgar Square, London. He was knighted in 1923; he died in 1946, and is buried in Westminster Abbey.

● RESTAURANTS				
Assaggi	2	Red Chamber	1	
Craft	5	Tashas	11	
Doppio Zero	6	Vovo Telo	7	
DW Eleven 13	3	Wolfpack	8	
Flames	12	Wolves	4	
Moyo	13	Zoo Lake Bowling Club	14	
Nice on Fourth	9			
Odd Cafe	10			

■ BARS & NIGHTLIFE			
Katzy's	2	Goodman Art Gallery	9
Southern Sun	1	Kim Sacks Art Gallery	10
Hyde Park Bar		Melrose Arch	3
		Sandton City Shopping Centre	2
● SHOPS		The Mall of Rosebank	5
Bryanston Organic Market	1	Rosebank Art & Craft Market	7
Everard Read Gallery	4	Rosebank Sunday Market	8
Exclusive Books	2, 6		

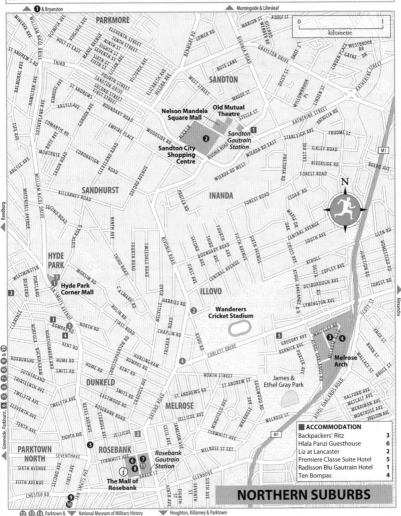

■ ACCOMMODATION	
Backpackers' Ritz	3
Hlala Panzi Guesthouse	6
Liz at Lancaster	2
Premiere Classe Suite Hotel	5
Radisson Blu Gautrain Hotel	1
Ten Bompas	4

Rosebank and Parkhurst. Most of the suburbs are close to major arterial roads and best explored by car, though the Gautrain, its bus routes and the Rea Vaya buses also offer easy access to some areas.

Parktown

The first elite residential area in Johannesburg, **Parktown** has retained its upmarket status despite its proximity to Hillbrow, which lies just southeast on the other side of

7

PARKTOWN'S RANDLORD MANSIONS

Parktown's main attraction lies in its distinctive architecture, largely the legacy of Sir Herbert Baker (see box, p.460). Baker's influence is still evident today in the opulent **mansions** of the Randlords, the rich mine owners, lining the streets. The Johannesburg Heritage Trust (see p.473) runs regular tours, usually on Saturday afternoons, to some of the notable buildings in Parktown as well as to other districts in Johannesburg; and the Heritage Weekend (second weekend in September), also organized by the Trust, features more tours and special events around the Parktown mansions and city centre.

High walls make viewing the buildings tricky on an independent visit, though most now have blue plaques with information outside. A good place to start is the area around Ridge Road, just north of the Randjeslaagte beacon, which marks the northern point of old Johannesburg. The *Sunnyside Park Hotel* here is a massive complex that Lord Alfred Milner used as his governor's residence from 1900. The best of the houses nearby are **Hazeldene Hall**, built in 1902 and featuring cast-iron verandas imported from Glasgow, and **The View**, built in 1897, with carved wooden verandas and an elegant red-brick exterior. To the north of Ridge Road, York Road curves to the left into Jubilee Road, with several palaces on its northern side; the neo-Queen Anne-style **Emoyeni**, at no. 15, built in 1905, is especially striking. At the corner of Jubilee Road and Victoria Avenue stands **Dolobran**, a weird and impressive house, also built in 1905, with a perfect veranda, wonderful red-brick chimneys, red Marseilles roof tiles and hallucinatory stained glass.

Crossing the busy M1 onto Rock Ridge Road, you'll reach the **Northwards Mansion**, built by Sir Herbert Baker in 1904 and home of the Parktown Trust. Unfortunately, there's no access along the road to Baker's own residence at no. 5. On the parallel Sherborne Road, you can see Baker's attractive St George's Church and its rectory, which mix Kentish and Italian features and were built in local rock.

Empire Road. The first people to settle in Parktown were Sir Lionel Philips, president of the Chamber of Mines, and his wife Lady Florence. In 1892, seeking a residence that looked onto the Magaliesberg rather than the mine dumps, they had a house built on what was then the Braamfontein farm. The rest of the farm was planted with eucalyptus trees and became known as the Sachsenwald Forest, some of which was given over to the Johannesburg Zoo a few years later. The remaining land was cleared in 1925 to make way for more residential developments.

Johannesburg Zoo

Roughly 2km north of Parktown, off Jan Smuts Ave • Daily 8.30am–5.30pm • R65 • ☎ 011 646 2000, ⓦ jhbzoo.org.za
Johannesburg Zoo is home to about two thousand species, including polar bears, gorillas, rhinos, white lions and red pandas. The zoo is slowly being spruced up, and it remains immensely popular, especially on warm weekends. The café beside the chimp enclosure is an excellent spot for lunch.

Zoo Lake

Opposite the zoo, on the west side of Jan Smuts Ave • At weekends the Gautrain bus from Rosebank runs here every 30 minutes (9am–6.30pm), via Jo'burg Zoo and the National Museum of Military History.
The park at **Zoo Lake** is a popular and safe walking and picnic spot that occasionally hosts outdoor performances, including an all-day music event every September during the Arts Alive festival. You can rent a rowing boat and pootle around the lake, or sample African cuisine at the lakeside restaurant, which has outdoor and indoor tables and plenty of peaceful, shady nooks.

National Museum of Military History

Erlswold Way 22 • Daily 9am–4.30pm • R30 • ☎ 010 001 3515, ⓦ ditsong.org.za/militaryhistory.htm
The **National Museum of Military History**, next to the zoo, has a fascinating collection of intimidating tanks, guns and uniforms, and a display on Umkhonto we Sizwe (MK),

the armed wing of the ANC – although the other liberation armies are conspicuous by their absence. The display focuses on the MK's commander, Joe Modise, who became Minister of Defence in the ANC government.

Melville

Together with Parkhurst, **Melville** is one of the more relaxed of the northern suburbs. When so many shops and restaurants in Jo'burg are tucked away in soulless malls, it's refreshing to find streets that are pleasant to walk and full of cafés, second-hand bookshops and quirky antique dealers as well as a main drag (Seventh Street) lined with restaurants, bars and clubs for every taste.

Melville Koppies

North of Melville • Melville Koppies Central tours every Sun; check website for hours • R50 • ☎ 011 482 4797, ⊛ mk.org.za

The **Koppies** is a pleasant 3km-long hilltop park that is split into three distinct sections that contain hundreds of species of indigenous flora and fauna. Melville Koppies Central is a nature reserve that can only be visited on tours (starting on Judith Road opposite Marks Park; 3hr) and which is lovingly maintained by volunteers who weed out tons of invasive non-African plants every year. Tours take in the archeological remains of both Stone Age and Iron Age settlements near the top of the hill. Flanking the reserve on either side, Melville Koppies East and West are public parks that are open daily from dawn until dusk; the main appeal of Melville Koppies East, reached

7

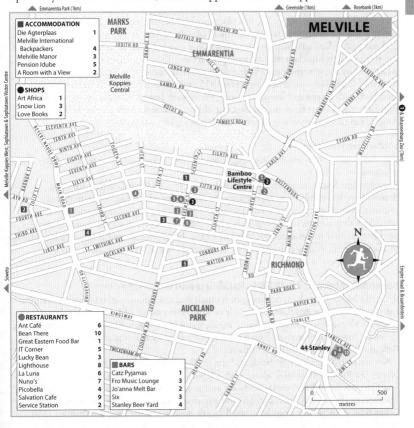

from Zambesi Road (a short walk from the restaurants in the Bamboo Centre), is the hilltop, which offers fantastic views over central Jo'burg and the leafy suburbs. Melville Koppies West has a number of good walking trails – to get there, follow Ayr Road (off Melville's Main Road), which becomes Korea and then Arundel Road, and then turn right into the Third Avenue dead-end.

Emmarentia Park and Dam
Beyers Naude Drive • Daily 8am–5pm • Free • ☎ 011 782 7064

Emmarentia Park, a large spread of green parkland running north and west of the city for several kilometres, contains the beautiful **Johannesburg Botanic Garden** in its northeast corner. Situated beside Emmarentia Dam, a popular lake for paddling and rowing, the garden is noted for its wide-open spaces and routes for joggers, cyclists and walkers, which are safe during daylight hours when others are around. Apart from the fields, the botanical gardens have some attractive formal herb and rose gardens that are perfect for picnics. The main field is regularly used for concerts and festivals.

Sophiatown

West of Melville, the suburb of **Sophiatown** is unremarkable architecturally but significant in the history of apartheid – it was here that **Archbishop Trevor Huddleston**, the English cleric who established the Anti-Apartheid Movement, worked in the 1950s. When he died in 1998, his ashes were brought from London to be scattered in Sophiatown. For many years, Sophiatown was one of the few places within the city where blacks owned property, and as a result it became a creative whirlpool of culture, jazz, literature, cinema, journalism and political radicalism; Miriam Makeba had her musical roots here, and Huddleston gave the young Hugh Masekela his first trumpet. In the 1950s, the suburb was designated a white area by the government, which sent in the bulldozers, scattering some sixty-five thousand inhabitants to Soweto between 1955 and 1960, regardless of their claim to the land and, with a degree of irony, renaming the suburb **Triomf**. Nothing of the original suburb remains apart from two houses, the old orphanage and the Christ the King Anglican church, from where Trevor Huddleston conducted his ministry.

Sophiatown Visitor Centre
Corner of Toby St and Edward Rd • Mon–Thurs 10am–2pm, Sat 9am–1pm • Free; musuem tour R35; suburb tours R120 • ☎ 011 673 1271, ⓦ sophiatown.net

The excellent **Sophiatown Visitor Centre**, located in a 1930s house that survived destruction, has exhibitions on the suburb, its culture, the music styles that were popular, "tsotsi" gang culture, and the area's destruction. The enthusiastic staff can provide walking tours of Sophiatown when called in advance, or you can join the weekly tour that leaves every Saturday at 11am. Jazz concerts are held on the last Friday of every month. A new cultural centre is currently being built next door and is expected to open in 2015.

Rosebank, Melrose, Hyde Park, Parkhurst and Greenside
Recently boosted by the renovation of its mall and the opening of a Gautrain station, the small suburb of **Rosebank**, a couple of kilometres north of Jo'burg Zoo, boasts one of the city's most appealing shopping malls, the African Craft Market and a series of art galleries. Just to the north of Rosebank, the two swanky suburbs of **Melrose** and **Hyde Park** also have malls as their main focus.

Not far to the west of Rosebank and the gracious but sleepy old suburb of Parktown North lies **Parkhurst**, which, along with Melville, is one of the few northern suburbs to boast decent street life – particularly on and around Fourth Avenue, which is full of upmarket cafés, restaurants, antique and interior design shops. West of Parkhurst is **Greenside**, another hip neighbourhood worth heading to for food and drinks.

Sandton

Some 20km north of the CBD, **Sandton** is the archetypal northern suburb. It is outrageously rich, with plush shopping centres and endless rows of lavish villas. In the 1980s and 1990s, it became the retreat of choice for banks and large corporations fleeing the CBD. A stroll through the connected Sandton City and Nelson Mandela Square shopping centres, complete with a pseudo-Italian piazza crammed with restaurants and cafés, may make you shudder at the ostentation, but with cash to burn you'll have some fun.

At one end of **Nelson Mandela Square** is a large bronze statue of the man himself: sadly, it's a mediocre work, achieving neither a compelling likeness nor any originality of approach.

Liliesleaf

7 George Ave, Rivonia • Mon–Fri 8.30am–5pm, Sat & Sun 9am–4pm • R60; tours R110 • ☏ 011 803 7882, ⊛ liliesleaf.co.za

Once a remote farmhouse but now swallowed up by Jo'burg's suburban sprawl, the **Liliesleaf** heritage site just north of Sandton is where the underground resistance movement had their headquarters and safe house until the police raid of July 11, 1963, when several important ANC and MK leaders were arrested. Mandela, who also spent time in hiding here as a caretaker, was serving five years in prison at the time but was sent to trial anyway together with his comrades. The Rivonia Trial ended in life sentences on Robben Island for Mandela, Walter Sisulu, Ahmed Kathrada, Govan Mbeki and others, and sparked global interest in the ANC's struggle. The old farm and adjacent new buildings now house informative interactive displays about the house, key figures of the resistance, Mandela's stay, the arrests and the trial. There's an overland safari truck on display, used by the ANC to smuggle weapons into South Africa right beneath the seats of unsuspecting tourists. The site has a good café called *Cedric*, after the farm's code name.

Alexandra

Jeff Mulaudzi's Alexandra Tours runs excellent 2–3hr bike tours • R300–400 • ☏ 071 279 3654, ⊛ alexandratours.co.za • Soweto-based Imbizo Tours runs tours that combine the main points of interest in Soweto and Alexandra • R550–980 • ☏ 011 838 2667, ⊛ imbizotours.co.za

The contrast between desperately poor **Alexandra**, just east of the M1, and the surrounding suburbs could hardly be greater. When it was founded, this black township was one of the few places where blacks could own property. The sense of ownership and independence helped Alex, as it's commonly known, to avoid the forced removals of former governments. Despite the simple grid design its map suggests, the township is actually a bewildering maze with overcrowded housing and a woeful lack of basic services such as sewerage and water. Half a million people live here in an area of less than eight square kilometres, with immigrants from places such as Mozambique, Malawi and Zimbabwe putting additional pressure on the township's inadequate infrastructure. In 2008, a series of riots was sparked when immigrants were attacked in Alexandra: the riots killed two people and injured forty more, and triggered further **xenophobic violence** elsewhere in the country.

"Exhilarating and precarious" was how Nelson Mandela described Alex when he lived here in the early 1940s after running away from the Eastern Cape to find work in Jo'burg as an articled law clerk. In those days, the township was well known for its gangsters as well as its developing political militancy, which saw **bus boycotts** preventing bus companies from raising their fares, one of the first examples of mass action by blacks achieving political results. Alexandra has long been an ANC stronghold, and paid dearly for it until the collapse of apartheid, with ongoing warfare between Inkatha vigilantes and the ANC in the 1980s leading to one section of Alex being dubbed "Beirut".

While the old spirit of Alex lives on in the bustling streets on the western side of the polluted Jukskei River, the eastern bank is lined with new houses, some built by government funding and others by middle-class blacks looking to improve their quality of life but wanting to remain in the township. Not far from here a patch of land has been turned into a **cricket oval**; it's surreal to watch this most colonial of games being played against a backdrop of densely packed township shacks, with the skyscrapers of opulent Sandton peeking over the horizon beyond. While less popular than those of Soweto, tours of Alexandra are safe, authentic and very enjoyable, enabling visitors to learn about township life, just minutes from the malls of Sandton.

The eastern and southern suburbs

Among the oldest of the city's suburbs, and for years home to Johannesburg's Jewish and Portuguese communities, the eastern suburb of **Bezuidenhout Valley** (better known as Bez Valley) has changed dramatically in recent years, with whites moving out of much of the old housing to make way for township and immigrant blacks. **Cyrildene**, to the northeast of Bez Valley, has become the city's new Chinatown, with a fascinating collection of Chinese supermarkets, businesses and authentic restaurants along Derrick Avenue.

Most visitors to this area, however, come to **Bruma Lake**, an artificial stretch of water that is disappointing save for its popular and lively flea market (see p.481). Nearby is one of Jo'burg's more accessible green spaces, **Gillooly's Farm**, a park set around a dam. The park is overlooked by a dramatic *koppie* that can be climbed in twenty minutes.

The suburbs immediately **south of the city centre** were traditionally the preserve of the white working class. After the repeal of the Group Areas Act in 1990, blacks started moving in; unusually in contemporary South Africa, many are wealthier than the original residents.

Gold Reef City

Northern Parkway, corner of Data Crescent, Ormonde (8km south of the city centre along the M1) • Wed–Sun 9.30am–5pm • 2hr mine tours at 9am, 10am, 11am, 2pm & 3pm • R165 • ☎ 011 248 6800, ⓦ goldreefcity.co.za

Gold Reef City is where old Johannesburg meets Disneyland: a large, gaudy, tacky entertainment complex built around the old no. 14 shaft of the Crown Mines. Essentially a theme park, it has some points of interest, notably the old gold mine itself, into which you can descend 200m and get an inkling of what it's like to work underground. Look out, too, for the excellent tribal dancing that takes place three times a day.

You can wander round the streets filled with period houses, shops and museums, though most are generally disappointing, with the exception of those dedicated to early Johannesburg, such as Ohlthaver and Nourse House. Otherwise, the most enjoyable thing to do in Gold Reef City is to go on one of the thrill rides (all included in the entrance ticket), such as the Raging Rapids water ride and the terrifying Anaconda roller coaster. Various restaurants serve decent if pricey food, but the main focus of this section of Gold Reef City is the vast casino.

The Apartheid Museum

Northern Parkway, corner of Gold Reef Road, Ormonde (Gold Reef City complex, 8km south of the city centre along the M1) • Daily 9am–5pm • R70 • ⓦ apartheidmuseum.org

The excellent **Apartheid Museum**, featuring separate entrances for "whites" and "non-whites" (your race is randomly assigned), is a world-class museum, delivering a sophisticated visual history that is distressing, inspiring and illuminating. The museum offers a nuanced insight into the deep social damage wrought by apartheid – and by colonial policies that long preceded it – and helps to explain the persistence of poverty and racial tension in the new South Africa. On the other hand, the museum's visual account of the jubilant advent of democracy serves to remind us how miraculous the transition was.

Allow at least two hours for the museum, three to four hours if you'd like to see all the exhibits in detail; there's a good lunch café and a bookshop on site too. Also allow time to view the exhibition of photographs by Peter Magubane of the 1976 Soweto uprising, and don't miss the exhilarating short documentary on the State of Emergency during the mid-1980s, when a wave of mass demonstrations and riots, though violently suppressed, shook the resolve of the regime.

Klipriviersberg Nature Reserve

15km south of the centre on Ormonde Drive, Mondeor • Dawn–dusk • Free • ⓦ klipriviersberg.org.za

Few Jo'burgers know about this undeveloped, unspoilt parkland, just beyond the N12 in the suburb of Mondeor. Beyond the riverside picnic spot, there are easy valley trails on which you can spot zebras, wildebeest, hartebeest and other wildlife, as well as strenuous uphill hikes rewarded by wonderful views of the city to the north.

Soweto

South Africa's most famous township, **Soweto** (short for South West Townships), is a place of surreal contrasts. The area was home to two Nobel Peace Prize winners, yet suffers one of the highest rates of murder and rape in the world; it is the richest township in South Africa, home to a growing number of millionaires, but has some of the most desperate poverty; it is the most political township, yet has the most nihilistic youth.

Southwest of the city centre, Soweto is huge, stretching as far as the eye can see, with a population estimated at between three and four million. Like any city of that size, it is divided into a number of different suburbs, with middle- and upper-class neighbourhoods among them. At first sight, it appears an endless jumble of houses and shacks, overshadowed by palls of smoke, though parts of it have a villagey feel. Apart from the Hector Pieterson Memorial and Museum, most of Soweto's **tourist highlights** are physically unimpressive, their fame stemming from historical associations. That history, however, is enthralling, not least because here it is told with a perspective and context rarely found in the rest of South Africa. For visitors it provides an insight not just into a place much mentioned in 1980s news bulletins for funerals and fighting, but into a way of life most Westerners rarely encounter.

A visit to Soweto with one of the many **tours** (see box, p.486) is the single most popular attraction in Johannesburg. Where once these had a whiff of daring and originality, a well-trodden tourist trail has developed, and unless you're content to follow the herds of minibuses and coaches around the conventional sights, visiting the same shantytowns and *shebeens*, it's well worth using an operator who mixes the highlights with lesser-known sights. Most outfits are keen for you to "meet the people", though conversations can tend to be strained and lead to your leaving a "donation" or buying local craftwork. While this gets a few tourist dollars directly into the townships, it often leaves visitors feeling pressurized and vulnerable.

At one time, taking yourself to Soweto would have meant a display of bravado bordering on foolhardiness, but it's now possible to visit the main sights **independently**. In Soweto, residents will stop to greet you or to chat, regardless of your colour. There are surprisingly few criminal incidents affecting tourists, though as ever it pays to remain vigilant; exploring less-visited areas by yourself, or going after dark, isn't recommended. If you want to drive to Soweto, you'll need good navigational skills – the lack of obvious landmarks amid kilometre upon kilometre of boxy little houses can be highly confusing. The Rea Vaya bus route from the city centre that passes near Vilakazi Street offers a good alternative to taking a minibus taxi to Soweto, which are more confusing than dangerous, as it isn't always easy to ascertain which part of the township they are heading for. Forming a cross with two fingers is the recognized minibus signal indicating that you want to go to "crossroads", which will bring you to the centre of Soweto. From here you can pick up another taxi to whichever sight you want to visit, though even in a taxi you may be let out on one of the main roads and have to walk a little way to reach your target.

VISITING SOWETO

The most convenient way to visit Soweto is with a **tour operator**. CitySightseeing Jo'burg's hop-on hop-off bus tour (see p.473) offers daily two-hour tours around Soweto, departing from their Gold Reef City stop. For a more personal experience try Imbizo Tours (☎011 838 2667, ⓦimbizotours.co.za), run by the irrepressible Mandy Mankazana. She runs three-hour, half-day and night tours, some including the Apartheid Museum and Alexandra township; particularly recommended are her evening *shebeen* crawls lasting up to five hours.

Smaller outfits offer imaginative **alternative tours** such as jazz outings, walks around Orlando West and Diepkloof, visits to Sowetan artists or local churches, language immersion tours and homestays with locals: try Phaphama (☎011 982 2088, ⓦphaphama.org) or Past Experiences (☎011 678 3905, ⓦpastexperiences.co.za). Another highly recommended way to experience the township is on bicycle and tuk-tuk tours offered by Soweto Bicycle Tours (☎011 936 3444, ⓦsowetobicycletours.com). Alternatively, you can visit independently using the safe Rea Vaya BRT bus system; for further **information**, head to the Soweto Tourism Information Centre on Walter Sisulu Square in Kliptown (Mon–Fri 8am–5pm; ☎011 342 4316, ⓦjoburgtourism.com).

Orlando West and Dube

Set in the northern part of Soweto, **Orlando West** and **Dube** qualify as two of its more affluent suburbs, with a number of sights and the greatest concentration of places to eat and drink. **Orlando East**, across Klipspruit Valley from Orlando West, was the first part of Soweto to be established in 1932, and the area is fairly easily accessible by car off the Soweto Highway (M70).

Hector Pieterson Memorial and Museum

8287 Khumalo St, Orlando West • Mon–Sat 10am–5pm, Sun 10am–4.30pm • R30 • ☎011 536 0611 • Using the Rea Vaya BRT bus from Jo'burg CBD, get off at Boomtown stop, and then walk or take the F4 feeder bus to Vilakazi St

The **Hector Pieterson Memorial and Museum**, opened in 2002, was named after the first student to be killed in the Soweto uprising (see box, p.470). Dedicated to all the students who died, the museum focuses specifically on the events surrounding and leading up to the 1976 Soweto uprising. The startling brutality used in the repression of student activists is depicted in video and pictures, including images from well-known black photographers such as Peter Magubane and Sam Nzima.

The Mandela House Museum

Vilakazi St • Daily 9am–4.45pm • R60 • ☎011 936 7754, ⓦmandelahouse.com • Take the Rea Vaya BRT bus T1 from Jo'burg CBD to Boomtown; here, change to the F4 to Vilakazi St, or cross the bridge and walk a few minutes up the road

Vilakazi Street was once home to Nelson Mandela and Desmond Tutu. **Mandela's bungalow** is where he lived with Winnie in the late 1950s and early 1960s, before his imprisonment on Robben Island, and where Winnie lived until exiled to the Free State (from which she returned to an imposing brick house with high walls and security cameras, just down the road). On his release, Nelson insisted on returning to his old home, but its small size and lack of security proved too much of a strain, and he moved out of Soweto. The old bungalow displays some fascinatingly mundane memorabilia, including some original furnishings, a collection of Winnie and Nelson's photographs and audiovisual displays describing living conditions in Soweto at the time Mandela lived there.

Regina Mundi Church

Near the junction of Klipspruit Valley (M10) and Potchefstroom (M68) roads • Daily 9am–5pm, outside church services • R20 • ☎011 986 2546, ⓦreginamundichurch.co.za • Lakeview is the closest Rea Vaya BRT bus stop

The **Regina Mundi Church** is Soweto's largest Catholic church and was the focus of numerous gatherings in the struggle years. Again, its impact owes more to historical

aura than aesthetic appeal, although with so few large buildings in the township it has a certain presence. The caretaker shows visitors around; look out for the bullet holes left in the ceiling by the South African police, and the (black) Madonna and Child painting near the altar.

Kliptown Open Air Museum

Walter Sisulu Square • Mon–Sat 10am–5pm, Sun 10am–4.30pm • Free • The Rea Vaya BRT feeder bus F5 travels from Lakeview to Klipspruitvalley Rd for Sisulu Square

The **Walter Sisulu Square of Dedication** is the site where the ANC's Freedom Charter was proclaimed to thousands in 1955. The square is also home to the **Kliptown Open Air Museum**, on its western side, which explains the history behind the Freedom Charter through photographs, documents and news clippings, and is worth a look once you've finished with the Hector Pieterson and Mandela House museums.

FNB Stadium

Nasrec, Soweto • Tours by appointment only • R80 • ☏ 011 247 5300, ⓦ stadiummanagement.co.za

Halfway between the CBD and Soweto in Nasrec and known as Soccer City during the 2010 Football World Cup, the **FNB Stadium** is Africa's largest stadium. A beautiful structure, it was designed by South African architects and built on top of an older football stadium that was used for Mandela's first speech after his release from prison in

7

THE SOWETO UPRISING OF 1976

The **student uprising** that began in Soweto in June 1976 was sparked off by a government ruling that **Afrikaans** should be used on an equal basis with English in black secondary schools. While this was feasible in some rural areas, it was impossible in the townships, where neither pupils nor teachers knew the language.

On June 16, student delegates from every Soweto school launched a mass protest march through the township and a rally at the Orlando football stadium. Incredibly, details of the plan were kept secret from the omnipresent *impimpis* (informers). Soon after the march started, however, the police attacked, throwing tear gas and then firing. The crowd panicked, and demonstrators started throwing stones at the police. The police fired again. Out of this bedlam came the famous photograph of the first student to die, Hector Pieterson, bleeding at the mouth, being carried by a friend, while his sister Antoinette (who now works in the Hector Pieterson Memorial and Museum; see p.468) looks on in anguished horror.

The police retreated to Orlando East, and students rushed to collect the injured and dead, erect barricades, and destroy everything they could belonging to the municipal authority, including beer halls. The attacks heightened the antagonism between the youth and older people who thought that class boycotts were irresponsible, given the students' already dismal employment prospects. Students accused their elders of apathy, which they attributed in part to drunkenness. In a society that has traditionally regarded respect for the old as sacrosanct, this was a historic departure.

In the days following June 16, all Soweto schools were closed indefinitely, thousands of police were stationed throughout the township, and police brutality continued unabated. In the face of worldwide condemnation, the government ascribed the violence to Communist agitation, citing as evidence the clenched-fist salutes of the students, though this was really an indication of their support for South Africa's **Black Consciousness Movement**, founded by Steve Biko (see box, p.332). Meanwhile, rebellion spread to other townships, particularly in Cape Town. In Soweto, schools did not reopen until 1978, by which time many students had abandoned any hope of formal education. Some had left the country to join the military wings of the ANC and PAC, while others stayed at home, forming "street committees" to politicize and police the communities. Others drifted into unemployment.

Now the armed struggle is over, the problems that face the former students of 1976 are manifold. As their parents warned, their lack of qualifications counts against them in the job market, even if June 16 is now a national holiday, during which they are praised for their role in the struggle. The street committees have dissolved, but the guns remain.

1990. With earth colours on the exterior that blend in nicely with the adjacent mine dumps, the interior is larger than you'd expect, with 94,000 orange seats spread across three tiers. Unlike some other World Cup venues in South Africa, this stadium is no white elephant and regularly fills to capacity for matches, concerts and rallies. If you can't make it to a game, the sixty- to ninety-minute tours of the stadium are very worthwhile, taking in the players' rooms and VIP areas.

ARRIVAL AND DEPARTURE   JOHANNESBURG

BY PLANE

OR Tambo International Airport (☎086 727 7888, ⓦairports.co.za), named after the ANC's greatest leader in exile, lies 20km east of the city centre. On the ground floor of the international arrivals hall there's a tourist information desk (daily 5.30am–10pm; ☎011 390 3614) and 24-hour facilities for changing money; ATMs, a post office and an internet café can be found on the first floor.

ONWARD TRANSPORT

Gautrain The fastest and easiest way to get to the city – especially during the dreaded morning and afternoon rush hours – is on the Gautrain rail link (daily 5.30am–8.30pm; see p.473), which takes fifteen minutes to reach Sandton station (R135, plus R13 card), where you can change for trains south to Rosebank and Park stations and north to Pretoria, or use the Gautrain feeder buses to Sandton's hotels.

Buses The Airport Shuttle (☎0861 397 488, ⓦairportshuttle.co.za; R300–580) offers a round-the-clock pick-up and drop-off service from the airport; book a day in advance. Alternatively, the Magic Bus service offers door-to-door transfers to the main suburbs (R465–775); book ahead or buy tickets at the company's office (☎011 548 0822, ⓦmagicbus.co.za) on the ground floor of the domestic car park building.

Courtesy buses The more expensive hotels often provide courtesy buses, while most backpacker hostels and some smaller guesthouses or B&Bs offer free pick-ups (best booked when making your reservation) and sometimes free drop-offs back to the airport.

Taxis Taking a metered taxi from the airport is convenient and safe, though you should make certain the driver knows where you're going before you set off, and get a quote beforehand. The official ORTIA Taxi Association (☎0861 243 243, ⓦjiata.co.za/ortiata) has a stand next to the tourist office in the arrivals hall where you can book rides. You should pay around R400 to get to central Jo'burg, Rosebank or Sandton, and no more than R550 to reach a far northern or western suburb.

Car rental Standard car rental deals are available from the main companies such as Avis (☎011 921 6262), Budget (☎086 101 6622), EuropCar (☎011 390 3909) and Tempest (☎0861 836 737), which all have offices at both airports and in several city locations. It's often much cheaper to rent one of these company's cars using a broker website like ⓦcarhire.co.za, or try Apex Rent-a-Wreck, 13 Siemert Rd, CBD (☎011 402 5150,

ⓦrentawreck.co.za), or Comet, which meets customers at the airport (☎011 974 9618, ⓦcometcar.co.za). Beware of police checkpoints at the airport; heed all stop signs and speed limits or you risk getting fined.

Airline information All of the following airlines have ticket offices at OR Tambo International Airport: Air France/KLM ☎011 390 8560; British Airways ☎011 441 8600; Lufthansa ☎0861 842 538; South African Airways ☎011 978 2888; and SA Airlink ☎011 451 7300. Qantas, 195 Jan Smuts Ave, Parktown North (☎011 441 8550), Virgin Atlantic, 50 Sixth Rd, Hyde Park (☎011 340 3500), have offices in the city.

Destinations Bloemfontein (5–12 daily; 1hr); Cape Town (70 daily; 2hr); Durban (50 daily; 1hr); East London (9 daily; 1hr 25min); Hoedspruit (2 daily; 1hr); Kimberley (3–7 daily; 1hr 30min); Nelspruit (5–6 daily; 1hr 50min); Port Elizabeth (15 daily; 1hr 40min).

LANSERIA AIRPORT

Jo'burg's secondary Lanseria Airport (☎011 367 0300, ⓦlanseria.co.za) is 30km northwest of the city centre and used by an increasing number of budget airlines. Taxis don't tend to wait at this airport and there's no public transport, so either organize a transfer with your accommodation or call a taxi (see p.473).

BY CAR

Toll roads The much-hated electronic road toll system on the N1, N3, N12 and R21 highways around Jo'burg and up to Pretoria charges all vehicles about R0.50 per kilometre. Rental cars are fitted with devices to register the toll payments, others must register beforehand at ⓦwww.nra.co.za.

Rush hour When driving to Pretoria, avoid the afternoon rush hour northwards (3.30–5pm), when travel time can double to 2hr; this is also when a quick 45min drive to OR Tambo airport can turn into a two-hour ordeal.

BY BUS AND MINIBUS

Baz Bus (☎0861 229 287, ⓦbazbus.com) operates 22-seater bus services from Johannesburg to Cape Town via the Drakensberg, Durban and the Garden Route (4–5 weekly), stopping at hostels en route.

Greyhound, Intercape and Translux These intercity buses arrive at Park Station in the centre of town. Once notoriously unsafe, Park Station has been significantly improved and the main concourse is big, open and secure, with information desks for all the bus companies. That said, it's not a good idea to walk around the surrounding area with a lot of luggage, so you're best off taking the Gautrain or a taxi to your final destination, or arranging a pick-up with your accommodation. Park Station has a number of car rental offices conveniently located on the upper concourse, usually listed under "Braamfontein" on their websites.

Destinations: Beitbridge (3 daily; 7hr); Bloemfontein (16 daily; 5hr); Cape Town (6 daily; 19hr 30min); Durban (16 daily; 8–11hr); East London (12 daily; 12hr 45min); Kimberley (5 daily; 6hr 30min); King William's Town (3 daily; 12hr 15min); Knysna (daily; 17hr); Kuruman (daily; 7hr); Ladysmith (2 daily; 5hr 45min); Mossel Bay (2 daily; 17hr); Nelspruit (6 daily; 5hr); Newcastle (daily; 5hr); Oudtshoorn (2 daily; 14hr 30min); Pietermaritzburg (16 daily; 7hr); Plettenberg Bay (daily; 17hr 30min); Port Elizabeth (4 daily; 13hr 15min); Pretoria (over 30 daily; 1hr); Umtata (daily; 11hr 30min).

BY TRAIN

Intercity and Gautrain Trains pull in at Park Station in the centre of town (see p.471). The Airport Shuttle (see p.471) can provide a pick-up and drop-off service from Sandton Gautrain station.

Destinations Cape Town (Tues, Wed, Fri & Sun; 26hr); Durban (Mon, Wed, Fri & Sun; 14hr); East London, via Bloemfontein (Wed, Fri & Sun; 20hr); Kimberley (daily; 8hr 15min); Komatipoort (for the border crossing into Mozambique; Wed, Fri; 13h), Messina (for the Beitbridge border crossing into Zimbabwe; Fri; 16h), Port Elizabeth, via Bloemfontein (Wed, Fri & Sun; 20hr); Pretoria (30 daily; 45min).

GETTING AROUND

Johannesburg's **public transport** system is improving fast, with the Gautrain rail and bus network and the Rea Vaya rapid bus (BRT) system being very well received by city residents. Rea Vaya is steadily expanding northwards from its trunk routes to and from Soweto. However, driving still remains very much the order of the day in Jo'burg, though the CBD and some suburbs, notably Melville, are easily explored on foot. **Private taxis**, which should be booked in advance by telephone (see opposite), are an expensive option, as a simple journey to the CBD from the northern suburbs will cost at least R200.

BY CAR

Getting around The best way to explore Johannesburg is still by car. Although road signs can be poor and the local drivers pushy, familiarity with a few key roads, a GPS device or some careful map reading before you set out makes driving around relatively straightforward. In the city centre, the grid system does make navigation reasonably logical, though it's beset by one-way streets, and gridlock traffic in rush hour.

Routes The M1 connects the centre to the northern suburbs, crossing above Newtown on a flyover, through Braamfontein and Parktown, and heading into Houghton and Sandton, eventually turning into the N1 for Pretoria. South of the centre, the M1 is one of the best routes to Soweto. The next artery west of the M1, also useful for heading north, is Oxford Rd, which starts off in Parktown, and becomes Rivonia Rd once it enters Sandton. West again is Jan Smuts Avenue, which passes through Rosebank and Dunkeld before hitting Hyde Park.

Parking If you're travelling into the city centre by car, guarded parking can be found underneath Gandhi Square, in the Carlton Centre car park on Main St (connected to the Centre via an underground passage; free parking if you have the ticket stamped at the Top of Africa office) or at the new Newtown Junction mall.

BY BUS

Metrobus Most of Jo'burg's municipal Metrobus routes start and end at the main terminus in Gandhi Square, off Eloff St in the city centre. There's a bus information office in the Gandhi Mall on the southern side of Gandhi Square (Mon–Fri 6am–6pm, Sat 8am–2pm; ☎ 011 833 5918, ⓦ mbus.co.za), where you can pick up timetables. Buses only run between the suburbs and the centre, so are useless for getting from one suburb to another, unless they both lie on the same route to town. Most buses stop by 6.30pm, though a small number keep going until 9.30pm. At weekends very few routes have services and there are waits of at least an hour between buses. Fares (R9–25, depending on distance) should be paid to the driver; ensure you get a ticket as you may need to show it to a ticket inspector. Useful routes include the #67 to Melville and the #05CD to Rosebank and Sandton.

BRT The Rea Vaya Bus Rapid Transit (BRT) system (ⓦ reavaya.org.za) is a fast and safe way to get from the CBD and Melville to Soweto as it uses dedicated roads and lanes; the high-floor buses stop at specially designed raised bus stops, which are clean, enclosed and well guarded. The network is steadily expanding into the northern suburbs; the latest line to open runs from Park Station to Soweto via Milpark (for 44 Stanley Avenue) and Empire Road (passing near Melville). The T1 trunk line from Ellis Park in the CBD to Thokoza Park in Soweto has several feeder (F) bus routes, and links up with the C3 inner-city circular route. Handy for tourists, the C3 links the Johannesburg Art Gallery with the Old Fort on Constitution Hill, the Origins Centre in Braamfontein, Park Station, Rissik St, Newtown and the Carlton Centre, where you can transfer to the T1 to Soweto. You'll need a rechargeable smartcard, sold at the Park Station and Carlton Centre bus stops, to use the system;

rides cost R12–25. Buses on the trunk routes run every 10–20 minutes on weekdays from about 6am to 7pm, and every 20–30min at weekends between 7am and 6pm; the inner-city circular route has buses every 15–20min on weekdays from 6am to 8.30pm, and every 15–30min at weekends between 7am and 5.30pm. The Rea Vaya website has handy maps showing the main city sights in relation to the bus stops.

Gautrain feeder buses The gold Gautrain feeder buses (Ⓦ gautrain.co.za) serve all Gautrain stations except for the airport station (Mon–Fri; R20, R6 if combined with a train journey); you'll need a preloaded Gautrain Gold Card to travel on them. Useful routes include: from Park Station to Parktown, from Rosebank Station to Hyde Park Corner mall and Melrose Arch mall, and from Sandton Station to the Montecasino complex in Fourways. The only line to run at weekends (9am–6.30pm, every 30 minutes) is from Rosebank Station via Jo'burg Zoo and the National Museum of Military History to Zoo Lake park. Route information can be found at stations, bus stops and online; call Ⓣ 010 223 1098 for the exact arrival time of the next bus.

BY MINIBUS TAXI
Minibus taxis transport the vast majority of commuters, and cover the widest area. They can be picked up at taxi ranks or hailed mid-route by raising your forefinger if you're heading into town, pointing downwards if you are going uptown or pointing towards yourself if you want Park Central Taxi Terminus, where most of the city's minibus taxis terminate. This is a hectic place and can be a little intimidating: be vigilant and discreet with your valuables.

Minibuses for Melville leave from rank #1, for Sandton from rank #2 and for Orlando West in Soweto from rank #9. Fares start at R8 for short rides.

BY TRAIN
Gautrain The rapid rail network (Ⓣ 011 4288 7242, Ⓦ gautrain.co.za) connects Johannesburg's Park Station to Pretoria via Rosebank and Sandton, with an airport line branching off at Sandton. Security is very tight with guards at stations and on every train car. The system uses Gold Cards (R13) that can be purchased and charged with money at stations and used to pay for train travel, as well as on the feeder buses and for parking. Trains run daily from 5.30am to 8pm at intervals of 15 to 30 minutes. The fare from Park Station to Rosebank is R25, to Sandton R27.

Metrorail The city's other suburban train system, Metrorail, has a poor security reputation, very limited services and is best avoided.

BY TAXI
Reliable taxi companies include Maxi Taxis (Ⓣ 011 648 1258) and Rose Taxi (Ⓣ 011 403 0000), usually charging fixed rates of around R12 a kilometre, with a minimum of R50. Taxis often also wait outside the large hotels and the main Gautrain stations.

BY TUKTUK
Sheshatuks (Ⓣ 0861 743 742, Ⓦ sheshatuks.co.za) in Sandton (at the Gautrain station) and Rosebank and E-tuktuk (Ⓣ 072 316 8099, Ⓦ e-tuktuk.co.za) in Melville scoot passengers around in small tuk-tuks; from R25 for 3km.

INFORMATION AND TOURS

Tourist information Gauteng Tourism's main office is in Newtown at 1 Central Place, Henry Nxumalo St (Mon–Fri 8am–5pm; Ⓣ 011 214 0700, Ⓦ gauteng.net). More useful is the Jo'burg city tourism office at Park Station (Mon–Fri 9am–5pm, Sat 9am-2pm; Ⓣ 011 333 1486). The excellent city guide Johannesburg In Your Pocket (R30, Ⓦ johannesburg.inyourpocket.com) is the best source of information for concerts, shows, exhibitions, sports and other events; it's available online, and at bookshops and accommodation across town.

Tours Gerald Garner (Ⓣ 082 894 5216, Ⓦ joburgplaces .com) and Chris Green (Ⓣ 082 491 9370, Ⓦ cashanafrica .com) are excellent local guides that can take you on tailor-made tours around the city centre, into the suburbs and beyond. Mainstreetwalks (Ⓣ 072 880 9583, Ⓦ mainstreetwalks.co.za), based in the *Curiocity Backpackers* hostel, has several interesting three-hour inner city walking tours (Tues–Sat at 10am). The Past Experiences travel agency (Ⓣ 011 478 3647, Ⓦ pastexperiences.co.za) offers tailor-made tours of Johannesburg and the archeological sites west of town,

and also runs regular weekend group tours based around themes such as street art, shopping and graffiti; these often use public transport, allowing for interaction with all kinds of Jo'burgers. The Johannesburg Heritage Trust (Ⓣ 011 482 3349, Ⓦ www.joburgheritage.co.za) conducts historical walking and bus tours for an older crowd (from R110) most Saturday afternoons to destinations in the city centre and the suburbs.

Bus tour The red open-topped city tour buses run by CitySightseeing Jo'burg (Ⓣ 0861 733 287, Ⓦ citysightseeing .co.za) are popular and safe, with daily departures every 40 minutes (every 30 minutes at weekends), between 9am and around 3.30pm, from the Gautrain Park Station, running via the CBD to the Apartheid Museum, Gold Reef City, Newtown, Braamfontein and Constitution Hill, then back to Park Station. Riding the full circle takes about 2 hours, but you can hop off and on again at any of the twelve stops. At the Gold Reef City stop, you can join an additional 2-hour tour through the main sights in Soweto. Tickets purchased online cost R130 (R350 including Soweto); from the driver (credit cards only) it's R30–70 more.

7

ACCOMMODATION

There's plenty of accommodation in Jo'burg's northern suburbs and in the city centre, both good options if you are relying on public transport. Melville is relatively close to the CBD and offers a characterful community with cafés, restaurants and bars within safe walking distance of a great number of guesthouses. Rosebank is well located at the heart of the northern suburbs, and has a decent selection of places to eat out and shop. Sandton has a wealth of pricey chain hotels aimed at business executives. It is also possible to stay in a guesthouse in the townships, though the most rewarding option is to stay with locals, something best arranged through an experienced tour operator (see box, p.468).

CBD & CENTRAL SUBURBS

12 Decades Art Hotel 286 Fox St, Maboneng, CBD ☏ 010 007 0102, ⊚ urbanhiphotels.com/12-decades; map pp.454–455. Each room at this self-catering hotel on the top floor of the Main St Life building has been designed by a local artist to reflect a specific decade in the life of Jo'burg. Mining, theatre, apartheid (with race laws printed in the toilet bowl) and the Ponte building are just a few of the themes. **R900**

Bannister 9 De Beer St, Braamfontein ☏ 011 403 6888, ⊚ bannisterhotel.co.za; map pp.454–455. A classy new luxury budget hotel with small but fresh en-suite rooms and some dorm beds. It's in the heart of "Braamies", at crawling distance from the nightlife and Saturday market. Dorms **R150**, doubles **R495**

★ **Curiocity Backpackers** 302 Fox St, Maboneng, CBD ☏ 011 592 0515, ⊚ curiocitybackpackers.com; map pp.454–455. A basic but friendly hostel with spacious dorm and double rooms, set above a lively bar full of locals (which closes at 11pm) in the upcoming Maboneng Precinct. Plenty of activities are organized, from city walks and bike rides to pub crawls, bar concerts and volunteering. There's a free city centre shuttle service and a tiny swimming pool. Dorm **R160**, doubles **R360**

EasyHotel 90 De Korte St, Braamfontein ☏ 011 242 8600, ⊚ easyhotel.com; map pp.454–455. Part of the great orange chain, *EasyHotel* is simply an affordable and central option situated on a lively small square with several good eateries nearby. **R565**

Mapungubwe Hotel Apartments 54 Marshall St, Marshalltown, CBD ☏ 011 429 2600, ⊚ mapungubwe hotel.co.za; map pp.454–455. Set in a former bank building, the first luxury hotel to open in the city centre for decades has an impressive foyer, stylishly furnished rooms and apartments, and a bar in the old underground bank vaults. Free CBD shuttle service. **R1145**

NORTHERN SUBURBS

Backpackers' Ritz 1a North Rd (off Jan Smuts Ave), Dunkeld West ☏ 011 325 7125, ⊚ backpackers-ritz .com; map p.461. A well-known, busy lodge in a large suburban house halfway between Rosebank and Sandton, with a pool, gardens and travel centre. Dorm **R150**, double **R450**

Hlala Panzi Guesthouse 41 Fifth St, Parkhurst ☏ 011 788 7988, ⊚ hlalapanzi.co.za; map p.461.

Convenient for the boutiques and restaurants along Parkhurst's 4th Avenue, this charming and tiny guesthouse has five lovely en-suite rooms, most overlooking the garden and pool. **R600**

Liz at Lancaster 79 Lancaster Ave, Craighall Park ☏ 011 442 8083, ⊚ lizatlancaster.co.za; map p.461. A classy and very highly regarded guesthouse halfway between the restaurants and boutiques of Parkhurst's 4th Avenue, and the upmarket Hyde Park Corner mall. Decorated with local art, the large rooms overlook a garden with a pool. **R900**

Premiere Classe Suite Hotel 62 Corlett Drive, Melrose North ☏ 011 788 1967, ⊚ premiereclasse.co.za; map p.461. A calm, quiet and friendly hotel with comfortable suites with fully equipped kitchens. It's close to the Melrose Arch complex and the Wanderers cricket stadium. Long-term rates available. **R850**

Radisson Blu Gautrain Hotel Rivonia Road, corner West Street, Sandton ☏ 011 286 1000, ⊚ radissonblu .com; map p.461. There's no need to stay out at the airport with this excellent upmarket chain hotel positioned right next to the Sandton Gautrain station. Good for business visitors and shoppers, it has a free shuttle to the nearby Nelson Mandela Square mall. **R2590**

★ **Ten Bompas** 10 Bompas Rd, Dunkeld West ☏ 011 341 0282, ⊚ tenbompas.com; map p.461. One of Jo'burg's most stylish small hotels, with each of its quiet and intimate suites (all with fireplaces and separate living areas) decorated by a different interior designer. Rates include laundry. **R3500**

MELVILLE

★ **Die Agterplaas** 66 Sixth Ave, Melville ☏ 011 726 8452, ⊚ agterplaas.co.za; map p.463. Just a minute's walk from Melville's restaurants and cafés, this neat, tasteful guesthouse has balconied rooms with views over the Melville *koppies*, and more accommodation in a house across the road. There's a wonderful lounge, where the famed breakfasts prepared by chef Badia are served; non-guests are welcome as well (until 10am, 11am at weekends). **R840**

Melville International Backpackers 37 First Ave, Melville ☏ 011 482 5797, ⊚ melvillebackpackers.co.za; map p.463. A small, relaxed hostel between Melville's Main and 7th streets, with wooden floors, ornate pressed metal ceilings and a pool. Dorm **R150**, double **R450**

★**Melville Manor** 80 Second Ave, Melville ☎011 726 8765, ⓦmelvillemanor.co.za; map p.463. In an elegantly restored Victorian house, this welcoming, well-run guesthouse with a pool and a great communal kitchen and dining area is less than a minute's walk from the Melville restaurant strip. R730

Pension Idube 11 Walton Ave, Auckland Park ☎011 482 9512, ⓦpensionidube.co.za; map p.463. A great budget guesthouse with tastefully decorated doubles, a communal kitchen and lounge, a pool and a friendly, easy-going atmosphere, just a few blocks from Melville's cafés and nightlife. R550

A Room with a View 1 Tolip St, Melville ☎011 482 5435, ⓦaroomwithaview.co.za; map p.463. A grand and charmingly surreal two-storey Italian-style villa, laid out and decorated in exuberant style, with twelve rooms, an indoor pool, efficient service and plenty of light provided by balconies and skylights. R1070

EASTERN SUBURBS

Airport en Route 97 Boden Rd, Benoni Small Farms, Benoni ☎011 963 3389, ⓦsa-venues.com/visit /airportenroute. A tidy, congenial budget lodge located 15 minutes from the airport (pickups from R80) in the famously sleepy suburb where film star Charlize Theron grew up. Accommodation is in cosy, three-bed log cabins, some of which are en suite, and two rooms sleeping up to four people (R550); camping is also available. Camping R80, cabin R300

The Aviator Kempton Rd, on the corner of Bosch Av, Kempton Park ☎011 921 8300, ⓦtheaviator.co.za. Just 3km from the airport, this hotel has everything you need for a stopover: modern rooms, a pool with deckchairs, a decent restaurant, and free transfers to and from the airport and Rhodesfield Gautrain station. R710

City Lodge OR Tambo airport ☎011 552 7600, ⓦclhg.com. Conveniently plonked right on top of the airport parking garage, this is the best value hotel within walking distance of the gates. Rooms are well sized, very quiet and overlook the Gautrain station. R1540

French Guest House 16 Meintjies St, Rhodesfield, Kempton Park ☎011 394 5245, ⓦjoburg-french guesthouse.com. A simple French-owned guesthouse 1km from the airport but away from the noise, offering a pool, free airport shuttle and French meals. A stone's throw from the Rhodesfield Gautrain station, for cheap and fast transport into the city. R700

★**Purple Palms** 71 Geranium St, Birch Acres, Kempton Park ☎011 391 8851, ⓦpurple-palms.co.za. Cheerful, organized and clean self-catering set-up close to the airport with a small pool, garden, free internet and book exchanges, plus a "day stay" option for short airport stopovers. There's a supermarket within easy walking distance. More luxurious than your average hostel. Dorm R130, double R180

SOWETO

Lebo's Soweto Backpackers 10823a Pooe St, Orlando West ☎011 936 3444, ⓦsowetobackpackers.com. One of the country's few black-owned backpacker hostels, with dorms, singles, doubles, camping and a great vibe when guests gather at the beach bar or around the fireplace. Walking, cycling and tuk tuk tours, and volunteer opportunities in Soweto are also available. Camping R105, dorm R160, double R390

Lolo's Guest House 1320 Diepkloof Extension, Diepkloof ☎011 985 9183, ⓔlolosbb@mweb.co.za. A smart and modern guesthouse run by former teacher Mrs Lolo Mabitsela in the historic Diepkloof district. There's a small garden, guarded parking and a conference room; tailor-made tours, including Soweto bar crawls, can be arranged. R700

EATING

Johannesburg has a huge range of places to eat out, with authentic French, Italian, Chinese, Greek and Portuguese restaurants, plus increasing numbers of African restaurants – not just township South African but also Congolese, Moroccan, Ethiopian and Cape Malay. Prices are higher than elsewhere in the country outside Cape Town and the Winelands, and you can blow out in spectacular style, but an average meal out is still good value. The bulk of Jo'burg's restaurants are in the **northern suburbs**; the key places to try are Fourth Avenue in Parkhurst (west of Parktown North), Seventh Street in Melville, the junction of Greenway and Gleneagles in Greenside and at the Melrose Arch complex in Melrose. In the city centre dozens of small new restaurants are opening up around De Beer Street in Braamfontein and Fox Street in the Maboneng Precinct. Jo'burg's **shopping malls** are well stocked with takeaways and chain restaurants, though some top-notch venues do exist in malls.

CBD & CENTRAL SUBURBS

The Blackanese 20 Kruger St, Maboneng ☎011 024 9455, ⓦtheblackanese.co.za; map pp.454–455. Exciting African–Asian cuisine, where sushi and curries meet African flavours and ingredients. Come on Tuesday for the R110 all-you-can-eat sessions, or on Sunday for the prawn braai. Tues–Sun 11am–9pm.

★**Canteen** 264 Fox St, Maboneng ☎011 334 5947, ⓔcanteen.245@iafrica.com; map pp.454–455. The restaurant in the Arts on Main courtyard has seating below the olive trees, and a varied international menu including some great burgers (R80). Book ahead for Sundays when the market is on. Tues & Wed 9am–4pm, Thurs–Sun 9am–1am.

7

7

Cramers Coffee Main St, Marshalltown ☎ 011 833 2699, ⓦ cramerscoffee.com; map pp.454–455. A good place for a break on a tour of the sights along Main Street; excellent coffee, cinnamon buns and other snacks. Free wi-fi, too. Mon–Fri 6am–5.30pm, Sat 7am–1.30pm.

Daleah's 6 De Beer St, Braamfontein ☎ 011 403 0243; map pp.454–455. A pleasant high-ceilinged cafe inside a bright green building, with breakfast (full, R65), chicken prego (R65), asparagus salad (R55) and glorious cake. Tues–Fri 8.30am–5.30pm, Sat 9am–5.30pm.

★ **Dosa Hut** 48 Central Rd, Fordsburg ☎ 011 492 1456; map pp.454–455. One of several authentic options in the lively Indian district, one block south of the weekend market, this South Indian restaurant serves masala dosa platters (R26), mutton *uttappam* (R40) and spicy fish curry. Daily 10am–9.30pm.

Guildhall Pub Market St, corner of Harrison St ☎ 011 833 1770; map pp.454–455. A wonderful, traditional pub founded in 1888 just after gold was discovered, making it Jo'burg's oldest watering hole. It still looks the part, though nowadays tasty Portuguese food (steak R89) is served along with the beer. Have lunch on the first-floor balcony for rare CBD street views. Mon–Wed 11am–8pm, Thurs–Fri 11am–2am, Sat 11am–7pm.

Netsi 220 Jeppe St, Shop 123, CBD ☎ 083 345 6789; map pp.454–455. The converted Medical Arts building is now "Litte Addis", home to dozens of fascinating Ethiopian shops, hairdressers and eateries. It may look a bit dodgy from the outside, but just walk up to the second floor and ask for Netsi, housed in a wood-panelled office. Here, the delicious vegetarian platter for two (spongy injera bread heaped up with veggie snacks, eaten with your right hand) costs just R30. There's good coffee too. Mon–Fri 6am–5pm, Sat & Sun 6.30am–3pm.

Niki's Oasis 138 Bree St, Newtown ☎ 011 492 1134; map pp.454–455. Local staples such as oxtail, tripe, *potjiekos* (stew) and *pap* (mostly around R80), and regular live jazz. Situated opposite the Market Theatre. Mon–Sat 11.30am–midnight.

Post 70 Juta St, Braamfontein ☎ 072 248 2078; map pp.454–455. A hip little café serving healthy sandwiches (pork belly, R35), cheesecake in a jar (R25), coffee and home-made lemonade. There are large windows, and a stack of LPs to select the background music from. Mon–Fri 6.30am–4pm, Sat 8.30am–2pm.

ROSEBANK, MELROSE, HYDE PARK AND SANDTON

Assaggi 30 Rudd Rd, Post Office Centre, Illovo ☎ 011 268 1370, ⓦ assaggi.co.za; map p.461. Despite the setting in an ugly mall, this is one of Jo'burg's best Italian restaurants, with a new menu every month reflecting the seasonal dishes (main courses around R100). Mon 6.30–9pm, Tues–Sat 12.30–2pm & 6.30–9pm.

DW Eleven 13 Jan Smuts Ave, on the corner of Bompas Rd, Dunkeld West ☎ 011 341 0663, ⓦ dw11-13.co.za; map p.461. Gourmet dining in an old shopping mall. The glamourous dining room is a great place to sample experimental, classic cuisine like spiced springbok loin (R190) or hammed duck (R175) plus top-of-the-range wines. Their *Grazing Room* next door serves upmarket tapas. Tues–Sat noon–2.30pm & 6.30–10pm, Sun noon–3.30pm.

★ **Flames** 67 Jan Smuts Ave, Westcliff ☎ 011 481 6000, ⓦ westcliff.co.za; map p.461. The terrace restaurant at the deluxe *Westcliff* hotel is perched on a steep hill, overlooking Jo'burg zoo and the lush green expanse of the northern suburbs. Come here for high tea, sundowner cocktails or a fantastic meal, and you'll remember the view and the sounds of the elephants and lions below. Daily 10am–11pm.

Moyo Melrose Arch, Melrose ☎ 011 684 1477, ⓦ www.moyo.co.za; map p.461. In the upmarket Melrose Arch complex, this sleek but slightly touristy venue occupying five floors offers a good variety of African dishes, from ostrich with Ethiopian spices (R189) to veggie options such as Cape lentil curry (R79), accompanied by dance and music performances. There's another branch at Zoo Lake. Book ahead. Daily 11am–11pm.

Red Chamber Jan Smuts Avenue, corner of Sixth Rd, Hyde Park Corner Mall, Sandton ☎ 011 325 6048, ⓦ redchamber.co.za; map p.461. The usual Chinese dishes plus more original creations, such as sizzling ostrich with spring onion (R117), and a good Peking duck (R179), served in much plusher surroundings than you tend to get in Chinatown. Daily noon–10.30pm.

Tashas Oxford Rd, The Zone, Mall of Rosebank ☎ 011 447 7972, ⓦ tashascafe.com; map p.461. A well-designed chain restaurant with a varied bistro menu covering everything from breakfasts and sandwiches to steaks and Turkish flat bread wraps; R60–100. Book ahead to be certain of a table. Mon–Sat 7.30am–7pm, Sun 7.30am–4pm.

Wolves 3 Corlett Drive, Melrose ☎ 011 447 2360, ⓦ wolves.co.za; map p.461. A fantastic little café, halfway between Rosebank and Sandton, serving killer red velvet cake, healthy breakfasts and sandwiches. Drop by on Thursday evenings for the Howl night, with live folk music by South African bands. Mon–Wed 7.30am–7pm, Thurs & Fri 7am–11.30pm, Sat & Sun 9am–3.30pm.

Zoo Lake Bowling Club Prince of Wales Drive, Zoo Lake Park, Parkwood ☎ 011 646 1131; map p.461. The quaint old clubhouse of the local lawn bowling club has become something of a hipster hangout, and the terrace overlooking the greens is a wonderful spot for a cheap beer. There's pub food too – burgers for R50 and Portuguese steak fillet for R85. Guarded parking available. Daily 10am–11pm.

GREENSIDE AND PARKHURST

★**Craft** 33 Fourth Ave, corner of 13th Av, Parktown ☎ 011 788 7111, ⓦ craftrestaurant.co.za; map p.461. An informal pizzeria and grill restaurant for beer lovers, with tables spilling out onto the pavements for optimal craft beer swilling and people-watching. The oven churns out magnificent pizza, priced from R90, pies, meat dishes and other wood-fired delicacies. Daily 7am–11pm.

Doppio Zero Corner of Barry Herzog and Gleneagles Rd, Greenside ☎ 011 646 8740; map p.461. Unpretentious and hugely popular Italian place with an eclectic menu. Breakfast (from R35) is a big draw, and the omelettes are exceptional. Most pizzas and pasta dishes are R60–90. Mon & Sun 7am–9pm, Tues–Sat 7am–10.30pm.

Nice on Fourth Corner of 14th St and Fourth Ave, Parkhurst ☎ 011 788 6286, ⓦ niceon4th.co.za; map p.461. One of the best breakfast spots around, it's also good any time of the day for sandwiches, salads or cake. Tues–Sun 7.30am–4pm.

Odd Café 116 Greenway, Greenside ☎ 011 486 3631, ⓦ oddcafe.co.za; map p.461. Slightly odd indeed, this small place rustles up delicious "comfort food with a twist", such as spinakopita spinach pie and Mediterranean sandwiches (R40–70), for eating inside or on the pavement terrace. Look out for the wacky graffitied building. Mon 7am–5pm, Tues–Sat 7am–11pm, Sun 8am–5pm.

Vovo Telo Cobbles Centre, Fourth Ave, Parkhurst ☎ 011 447 5939, ⓦ vovotelo.com; map p.461. A calm and classy bakery café serving tasty home-baked products and light meals, such as chicken breast in lemon yoghurt (R70). Also at the 44 Stanley complex and other outlets. Mon–Sat 7am–9pm, Sun 7am–8.30pm.

Wolfpack 21 Fourth Ave, Parkhurst ☎ 011 447 7705; map p.461. A crowded and noisy little burger joint in Parkhurst's nightlife zone, where the beef patties come with excellent sides and salads. Booking required, except at weekends when you'll probably have to wait for a table. Tues–Sat noon–midnight, Sun noon–8pm.

MELVILLE

Ant Café 11 Seventh St ☎ 076 476 5671; map p.463. A classic Melville hangout, *Ant* has delicious crisp thin-crust pizzas (bacon avocado feta or chicken liver pizza for R75), friendly service, a few comfy chairs on the pavement, and after all these years still only accepts cash. Food is served till late here. Daily 8am–11pm.

Bean There 44 Stanley Rd, Milpark ☎ 087 310 3100, ⓦ beanthere.co.za; map p.463. A bean roastery and café inside a bright old warehouse, with a tiny garden terrace. The coffee and freshly roasted beans are also available to take away. Mon–Fri 7.30am–4pm, Sat 9am–3pm, Sun 9am–noon.

★**Great Eastern Food Bar** 53 Rustenburg Rd, Bamboo Lifestyle Centre ☎ 011 482 2910; map p.463. Introducing adventurous Asian cooking and flavours that are new to South Africa, the self-taught chef here makes a selection of ramen noodle dishes (R110), seasonal dumplings, bento-style lunch boxes (R100–120) and rice cakes (R35). There's a Korean braai party every weekend too. Mon 6–11pm, Tues–Sun noon–11pm.

IT Corner Seventh St, corner of Second Ave ☎ 011 482 6090, ⓦ theitcorner.co.za; map p.463. A boutique internet café with free wi-fi, laptop rental (R20/hr) and excellent food and drinks; stuffed croissants for breakfast (R45), *kefta* beef burgers (R39), carrot cake, crêpes and Moroccan mint tea. Mon–Fri 7.30am–7.30pm, Sat & Sun 8.30am–7.30pm.

La Luna 9a Seventh St ☎ 011 482 7451, ⓦ laluna -melville.co.za; map p.463. The swankiest spot on the strip offers quality dining in a refined setting. Enjoy dishes like pumpkin ravioli (R85) or salmon fillet (R170). Tues–Sat 11.30am–10pm, Mon 5.30–10pm.

Lighthouse 10 Seventh St ☎ 061 729 2216; map p.463. The only two-storey place in Melville has live music on Thurs & Fri, occasional poetry slams, nice views from the balcony, and a menu of strictly organic meals with farm-sourced ingredients. Try the grilled haloumi and spinach sandwich (R40) or the salad buffet (R35). Daily 10.30–2.30am.

Lucky Bean 16 Seventh St ☎ 011 482 5572, ⓦ luckybeantree.co.za; map p.463. A trendy place at the calm bottom end of the street, with comfy sofas and an imaginative menu that includes ostrich burger (R85) and wild mushroom risotto and springbok pie (mains R90). Tues–Fri 11am–10pm, Sat & Sun 10am–11pm.

Nuno's 5 Seventh St ☎ 011 482 6990; map p.463. This popular Portuguese restaurant has a prawn platter for two (R231), *trinchado* rump cubes in spicy sauce (R89) and *espetada* skewers as well as more generic pastas and salads. The outside tables are great for people-watching and there's a relaxed bohemian atmosphere, which continues after dark in the attached Mozambican-themed bar, *Xai Xai*. Daily 8am–midnight.

Picobella 66 Fourth Ave ☎ 011 482 4309; map p.463. This converted villa with a lovely porch is the best Italian place for miles; pizzas are served in a flash, with toppings such as spicy chicken strips, mushrooms and avocado (R60). Daily 8am–10pm.

★**Salvation Cafe** 44 Stanley Rd, Milpark, between Braamfontein and Melville ☎ 011 482 7795, ⓦ salvationcafe.co.za; map p.463. A delightful eatery at 44 Stanley, a former industrial complex that now hosts various boutiques, restaurants and bars. There's an excellent chicken caesar salad (R82), the house breakfast will fill you up for R72, and you should always leave space for a New York cheese cake (R39) before you leave. Tues–Sun 8am–4pm.

7

7

★**Service Station** 53 Rustenburg Rd, Bamboo Lifestyle Centre ☎011 726 1701; map p.463. A superbly stylish daytime café-deli in a converted garage, with appetizing and healthy breakfasts and lunches (like zesty lemon chicken sandwich, R65), a pay-by-weight buffet of quiche and salads (from 12.30pm; R120/kg), and home-made ice cream. Walk it all off afterwards by hiking up to the nearby Melville Koppies viewpoint. Mon–Fri 7.30am–5pm, Sat 8am–5pm, Sun 8.30am–3.30pm.

SOWETO

Soweto tours (see box, p.468) usually stop off for a meal in a local restaurant, bar or *shebeen*, and so long as you're not part of a huge group of tourists, it's not a bad way to meet some locals. If you're heading to Soweto under your own steam or with a local contact, any of the places below are worth checking out and will give you a warm welcome. Commonly, some kind of meat and *pap* is the main dish on offer, often alongside local favourites such as tripe or ox shin.

Chaf-Pozi Corner of Chris Hani Drive and Nicholas St, Diepkloof ☎011 463 8895, ⓦchafpozi.co.za. *Shebeen* chic at the foot of Soweto's iconic Orlando cooling towers; there's both traditional *pap en vleis* (cornmeal and meat)

dishes (from R30) and sirloin steak available here – choose your meat of choice at the butchery and it gets grilled on the spot. Daily 10am–10pm.

The Rock 1987 Vundla Drive, Rockville ☎011 986 8182. A massively popular upmarket venue for eating, drinking and dancing, with DJs or live jazz on offer most nights. The roof deck is a wonderful spot to unwind, get an overview of Soweto, and enjoy a sundowner. Mon–Fri 6pm–4am, Sat & Sun noon–2am.

Sakhumzi 6980 Vilakazi St, Orlando West, opposite the Mandela House Museum ☎011 536 1379, ⓦsakhumzi .co.za. Once a small *shebeen*, the restaurant has completely taken over this residential home now, and is a great place to try typical "Kasi" Sowetan food (buffet R120). The lively streetside terrace is the best place in the area to enjoy drinks and watch the "Black Diamonds" park their oversized cars. Daily 11am–11pm.

Wandie's Place 618 Makhalemele St, Dube ☎011 982 2796, ⓦwandies.co.za. Situated 2km west of Vilakazi St, this was once Soweto's archetypal tourist-friendly *shebeen*, and is now the area's smartest eating spot, though it retains its popularity with locals. A buffet of local African food costs R120. Daily 10am–11pm.

BARS AND CLUBS

Jo'burg has the country's most racially mixed nightlife, with a modest nightlife strip along **Melville's Seventh Street**, which is great fun for drinking. In the city centre, weekend nights are hopping in Braamfontein and Maboneng. In many parts of the city, particularly the **northern suburbs**, old-school pubs and bars have been replaced by café/bar/restaurants, commonly located in shopping centres. Irish theme pubs and sports bars are often packed and jovial, if not exactly cutting-edge. You can visit some **Soweto** *shebeens* during the day (see above); at night it's wise to visit the townships in the company of a guide.

CBD & CENTRAL SUBURBS

Great Dane 5 De Beer St ☎011 403 1136 map pp.454–455. A popular, grungy bar with a remarkable floor, consisting of R8000 worth of 5ct coins. There's no reason to sit – DJs get the crowd jumping around after 9pm, and "gourmet hot dogs" and boerewors snacks are for sale (R35–45). Thurs–Sat noon–2am.

★**Kitcheners Carvery** 5 De Beer St, corner of Juta St ☎011 043 0166; map pp.454–455. The well-preserved pub in the century-old former *Milner Hotel* has regular punters propping up the bar during the week, with hip youngsters taking over on Wed–Sat nights, when DJs and bands perform; funk and soul during the week, house and electro at weekends. Daily 10am till late.

Pata Pata 286 Fox St, Maboneng ☎073 036 9031; map pp.454–455. Named after a song by famous local singer Miriam Makeba, this large ground-floor bar has a mix of secondhand furniture to lounge on, a menu of African meals and a small stage for live jazz music on Fri & Sat. Daily 7am–2am.

Sophiatown 1 Central Place, off Mary Fitzgerald Square, Newtown ☎011 836 5999,

ⓦsophiatownbarlounge.co.za; map pp.454–455. This township retro bar is popular with chic black Jo'burgers, and is often heaving at weekends. There's jazz on Wednesday, live music on Saturday and sports on the large screens plus old- and nu-school Afrojazz and Afropop most other days. There's another branch on Seventh St in Melville. Mon–Wed 10.30am–9pm, Thurs–Sat 10.30–2am, Sun 11.30am–8pm.

Zebra Inn 252 Albertina Sisulu Rd, corner of Kruger St, Maboneng ☎082 494 7763; map pp.454–455. No need to head out to Kruger for your alcohol-soaked safari experience; take snapshots of the hundred trophy game heads crammed on the walls of this unmissable bar. It's also a great escape from the hipsters draped around all the other bars in the area. Ring the bell and head upstairs. Daily from noon till late.

NORTHERN SUBURBS

Southern Sun Hyde Park Bar First Rd, Hyde Park ☎011 341 8080; map p.461. A hotel bar with a difference – this designer bar is perched on top of the Hyde Park Corner mall with excellent sunset views, and is crammed with trendy people downing drinks on weekend nights. Daily 6pm–2am.

MELVILLE

Catz Pyjamas 12 Main Rd, Melville ☎ 011 726 8596, ⓦ catzpyjamas.co.za; map p.463. A large first-floor bar and food stop; it's nothing special during daylight hours, but gets interesting when it fills up in the wee hours with party-minded patrons from nearby clubs. Daily 24 hours.

Fro Music Lounge 2 Seventh St, Melville ☎ 078 856 8782; map p.463. A hopping little bar with regular concerts by local bands. Tues–Sun noon–midnight.

Jo'anna Melt Bar 7 Seventh St ☎ 072 733 5966. An attractive and busy open-fronted bar, with plenty of exposed brickwork, inventively decorated with the pressed iron panels traditionally used for ceilings. Jo'Anna specializes in melted cheese with various toppings; cheddar with sweet mustard for example, for R49. There's craft beer, too. Mon–Thurs noon–12.30am, Fri & Sat noon–2am.

Six 6 Seventh St, Melville; map p.463. One of the more popular bars along Melville's nightlife strip, attracting a funky leftie and/or gay cocktail-drinking crowd. Expect people dancing in any available space as the night proceeds. Daily noon–2am.

★Stanley Beer Yard 44 Stanley Rd, Milpark ☎ 011 482 482 5791, ⓦ stanleybar.co.za; map p.463. A wonderful hangout for beer lovers. Looking like a cross between a barn and a garage, the *Beer Yard* sells a dozen good craft beers, and puts on live country and folk music in the Beergarden on Saturday afternoon. Mon–Sat noon–11pm, Sun 11am–6pm.

LIVE MUSIC

Johannesburg dominates the South African music scene, offering a much wider spectrum of sounds than Cape Town or Durban. Friday and Saturday nights are the busiest times for gigs. Jo'burg is always discovering superb new **jazz** talent, but established artists to look out for include the gifted vocalist Simphiwe Dana, singer-songwriter Vusi Mahlasela, Afro-fusion merchants Freshlyground and trumpeters Marcus Wyatt and Hugh Masakela. Newtown and a couple of venues in the northern suburbs are your best bets for live jazz. **Indie** acts worth catching live include Desmond and the Tutus, Kid of Doom, Us Kids Know, João Orrechia, Black Hotels and BLK JKS. Kwaito, the hugely popular **township-house** genre, is rarely performed live except at major concerts. You might hear some from **hip-hop** artists such as the excellent Hip-Hop Pantsula (HHP), Teargas, Skwatta Kamp or Pitch Black Afro. As for classical music, the Johannesburg Philharmonic Orchestra performs regularly at Linder Auditorium in the Wits University campus (entrance on St Andrews Rd) in Parktown (☎ 011 789 2733, ⓦ jpo.co.za). A useful **online gig guide** is provided by ⓦ jhblive.co.za, and tickets are usually available via ⓦ computicket.com.

CBD

★The Bassline 10 Henry Nxumalo St, Newtown ☎ 011 838 9142, ⓦ bassline.co.za; map pp.454–455. The city's leading live venue by some distance; the hottest local artists across the genres play here, and world-class acts from west and central Africa also stop by. Thursday is reggae night. Guarded parking to the rear, entered below the flyover. Open for events only.

★The Orbit 81 De Korte St, Braamfontein ☎ 011 339 6645, ⓦ theorbit.co.za; map pp.454–455. A huge jazz club with a stylish restaurant space and terrace on the ground floor, and a concert room upstairs. There's free live music at lunchtime, and paid concerts (admission R40–150) every night; see website for the programme. The menu includes sirloin beef for R110 and a mushroom risotto for R75. Tues–Sun 11.30–2am.

Town Hall 66 Carr St, Newtown ☎ 082 332 5772; map pp. 454–455. A trendy nightspot in the warehouse district west of the M1 flyover. Regular DJ and live music performances, sometimes spilling over into *The Woods* bar next door. Thurs–Sat 9pm–3am.

NORTHERN AND EASTERN SUBURBS

Katzy's 282 Louis Botha Ave, The Firs Mall, Rosebank ☎ 011 880 3945, ⓦ katzys.co.za; map p.461. A stylish and upmarket jazz bar in the mall attached to the *Hyatt* hotel. There's live music daily, as well as occasional comedy nights. Book ahead if you'd like to sit, and dress up a little. Mon–Sat noon–midnight.

The Radium Beerhall 282 Louis Botha Ave, Orange Grove ☎ 011 728 3866, ⓦ theradium.co.za; map pp.454–455. A charmingly shabby Victorian pub – probably the second oldest in town – with live music several nights a week, and Portuguese food on the menu. On the first Sun of every month, don't miss the entertaining eighteen-piece Phat Brass band playing jazz and swing. Daily 10am till late.

ENTERTAINMENT

Johannesburg has the best **entertainment** in South Africa, and draws top international performers. The Johannesburg city guide In Your Pocket (ⓦ johannesburg.inyourpocket.com) has a handy online events guide that's updated weekly and geared towards foreign visitors. On Fridays, the *Mail & Guardian* carries cinema listings and articles on the main events, while the *Daily Star* lists mainstream cinema and theatre. Otherwise, listen to local radio stations and check roadside posters and leaflets. **Tickets** for most events can be booked through Computicket (☎ 083 915 8000, ⓦ computicket.com).

7

7

JOHANNESBURG ARTS FESTIVALS

Arts Alive Festival ⓦ artsalive.co.za. The city's major festival for the performing arts takes place over three weeks every September at various venues, mainly in Newtown, but also in some townships. Live music dominates, but dance, cabaret and theatre are also well represented. "Jazz on the Lake", on Zoo Lake, is a mainstay of the festival, and always features major South African artists in front of big crowds.

FNB Dance Umbrella Wits Theatre, Braamfontein ⓦ danceforumsouthafrica.co.za. Over ten days in February/March, Africa's largest festival of dance and choreography hosts international companies but also acts as the major national platform for work by South African talent.

Jo'burg City Fest Venues across central Johannesburg ⓦ joburgcityfest.co.za. Exhibitions, concerts, dance, fashion, city tours and culinary events over four days in early October, in dozens of venues.

Joy of Jazz Festival Newtown ⓦ joyofjazz.co.za. A weekend festival in late August/early September that draws the cream of South African jazz, including the likes of Pops Mohamed and Hugh Masekela, along with international guest stars.

THEATRE, OPERA AND DANCE

Barnyard Theatre Cresta Shopping Centre, Beyers Naude Drive, Cresta ☎ 011 478 5300, ⓦ barnyardtheatre .co.za. The most central of a popular chain of theatres staging musical tribute shows, theatre and cabaret. On the lower ground floor of Cresta Shopping Centre, ten minutes' drive north of Melville.

The Dance Factory 10 Henry Nxumalo St, Newtown ☎ 011 833 1347. An interesting but irregular programme of dance by both professionals and township kids in a purpose-built dance studio.

Joburg Theatre Loveday St, Braamfontein ☎ 011 877 6800, ⓦ joburgtheatre.com. Top venue offering a good mix of mainstream and more adventurous theatre, ballet and opera productions at an impressive four-stage venue, buried inside a huge brutalist block of concrete. There's underground parking, entered from Simmonds St.

Market Theatre 56 Margaret Mcingana St, corner of Bree St, Newtown ☎ 011 832 1641, ⓦ markettheatre .co.za. The venue for some of Johannesburg's finest stage productions and top-grade visiting music acts; also celebrated for its innovative community theatre, and the odd costly epic.

Montecasino Theatre Montecasino, corner of William Nicol Dr and Witkoppen Rd, Fourways ☎ 011 511 1988, ⓦ montecasino.co.za. Two stages for comedies, musicals and touring shows, and the huge 1800-seat Teatro at Montecasino which stages musicals.

Old Mutual Theatre on the Square Nelson Mandela Square, Sandton ☎ 011 883 8606, ⓦ theatreonthe square.co.za. Lightweight drama, some political theatre and a handful of mainstream music or cultural acts. There are regular free lunchtime concerts on weekdays too.

CINEMAS

Bioscope 286 Fox St, Maboneng ⓦ thebioscope.co.za. An excellent art-house movie cinema in the Main St Life complex where anything goes: environmental documentaries, Japanese splatter films, foreign film festivals, gay flicks and Asian movie nights that include food. Don't miss the regular screenings of the hilarious local cult documentary *Unhinged – Surviving Joburg*. Tickets cost R30–60.

Ster-Kinekor ⓦ sterkinekor.com. Cinema complexes in the Rosebank, Sandton and other malls. Their separate Cinema Nouveau brand, with a branch in Rosebank Mall, has art-house films and regular festivals themed by country, which are sometimes free to visit. Otherwise tickets cost R30–60.

SHOPPING

Johannesburg is the best place in South Africa to buy arts and crafts, with excellent flea markets and galleries offering a plethora of goods, some very high quality. The city is also home to over twenty major malls (typically open daily 8am–6pm), most of which are depressingly anonymous, though the handful listed below are so plush that they merit visiting in their own right. The craft, music and book shops, galleries and markets below follow regular shop opening hours unless mentioned otherwise.

MALLS

Hyde Park Corner Jan Smuts Ave, Hyde Park ⓦ hydeparkshopping.co.za; map p.461. A trendy and upmarket mall, awash and haute couture outlets. The excellent chain Exclusive Books has a large branch here, and the restaurants are much better than in other malls.

The Mall of Rosebank Corner of Baker St and Cradock Ave, Rosebank ⓦ themallofrosebank.co.za; map p.461. One of the city's least soulless malls, with exclusive boutiques, craft shops, the Sunday crafts market and plenty of outdoor cafés and restaurants in the pedestrian streets of the adjoining The Zone centre. Famed for its

African crafts market, every Sunday on the top parking deck. Right next to the Rosebank Gautrain station.

Melrose Arch Athol Oaklands Drive, Melrose North ⓦmelrosearch.co.za; map p.461. A beautifully designed city quarter, surrounded by tight security, with European-style streets, plazas, restaurants, bars, hotels and an upmarket mall, all built on top of a huge parking garage.

Sandton City Shopping Centre Corner of Sandton Drive and Rivonia Rd, Sandton ⓦsandtoncity.com; map p.461. Linked to the opulent Nelson Mandela Square shopping centre, this enormous complex has a mind-boggling abundance of shops (including some good bookshops), plus cinemas and African art galleries.

CRAFT SHOPS, MARKETS AND PRIVATE ART GALLERIES

44 Stanley 44 Stanley Avenue, Milpark ⓦ44stanley.co.za; map p.463. A deeply hip design and art complex between Braamfontein and Melville, with cafés, restaurants and galleries, and shops selling antiques, furniture and gifts.

Art Africa 62 Tyrone Ave, Parkview ☎011 486 2052, ⓔartafrica@tiscali.co.za; map p.463. Just west of the zoo, this shop has a very good selection of innovative and more familiar crafts from South Africa and the region, many ingeniously created out of recycled material.

Bamboo Lifestyle Centre 53 Rustenburg Rd ⓦbamboo-online.co.za; map p.463. A small converted filling station now holds a few excellent restaurants, a bookshop and shops selling Jo'burg-themed fashion. Every Saturday morning there's a small farmers' market on the roof, which is open until they sell out around noon.

Bruma Lake Flea Market Bruma Lake, east of the centre; map pp.454–455. A huge, permanent and very popular market of mostly African crafts and souvenirs, mainly mainstream and fairly inexpensive. At weekends, the crowds are entertained with music.

Bryanston Organic Market Culross Rd, off Main Rd,

Bryanston ☎011 706 3671, ⓦbryanstonorganicmarket.co.za; map p.461. Right-on collection of stalls selling lovely organic food, unusual home crafts and handmade clothes. Thurs & Sat 9am–3pm.

Everard Read Gallery 6 Jellicoe Ave, Rosebank ☎011 788 4805, ⓦeverard-read.co.za; map p.461. A renowned gallery worth visiting for exhibitions of fine contemporary artists. The landmark cylindrical Circa exhibition building offers great views over the leafy suburbs.

Goodman Art Gallery 163 Jan Smuts Ave, Rosebank ☎011 788 1113, ⓦgoodman-gallery.com; map p.461. The city's leading contemporary gallery, regularly hosting shows by globally renowned South African artists such as William Kentridge, David Goldblatt and Moshekwa Langa.

Kim Sacks Art Gallery 153 Jan Smuts Ave, Rosebank ☎011 447 5804, ⓦkimsacksgallery.blogspot.com; map p.461. A trove of magnificent crafts and traditional art from across Africa. The prices can be hefty, but the quality is consistently exceptional.

M2 Highway market CBD; map pp.454–455. An informal market stretching underneath this major artery, a few blocks south of Anderson St. Most stalls specialize in *umuthi* folk medicine, but there are plenty of local crafts as well.

Makotis 112 President St, CBD ☎011 337 1435, ⓦmakotis.co.za; map pp.454–455. Traditional African shweshwe designs sold by the metre at very affordable prices, or as finished dresses and other clothing. Also sells colourful woolen Basotho blankets.

Market Africa Newtown; map pp.454–455. A flea market held next to the Market Theatre every Saturday; rifle through colourful blankets from Mali, Congolese masks and statues, local beadwork animals and objects, and more. Sat 9am–4pm.

Market on Main 264 Fox St, Maboneng ☎011 334 5947; map pp.454–455. Food, design and entertainment at the Arts on Main complex. All shops and restaurants in

7

SPECTATOR SPORT IN JO'BURG

The biggest sport in Johannesburg is **football**, and there's a passionate rivalry between Jo'burg's two main teams, the **Kaizer Chiefs** and **Orlando Pirates** – for decades local derbies have pulled mammoth crowds of seventy thousand. It's worth trying to go to a home game of either team, especially one against Pretoria giants Mamelodi Sundowns. Tickets are cheap, the football can be exciting and the atmosphere exhilarating. Crowd violence is very rare, and there is secure parking.

Ellis Park stadium in central Jo'burg is a South African **rugby** shrine. As well as hosting international fixtures it's also home ground to the provincial **Gauteng Lions** team. The best way to get there is on the park-and-ride system that operates for big games, with buses shuttling in from car parks outside the centre.

The major **cricket** games, including five-day test matches, are played at the Wanderers Stadium, off Corlett Drive, Illovo, though if you check the programme for visiting international teams you may find fixtures scheduled to be played in Soweto or Alexandra.

the Maboneng district are open on Sunday as well, making it the best time to visit. Sun 10am–3pm.

Neighbourgoods Market De Korte St, Braamfontein ⓦneighbourgoodsmarket.co.za; map pp.454–455. A bustling market selling mainly food, plus some art and design, in an old parking garage. This is where the young and beautiful get their Balkan Burger fix. As the afternoon progresses, everyone somehow ends up on the terrace by the bar. Sat 9am–3pm.

Rosebank Art & Craft Market The Mall of Rosebank, 50 Bath Ave, Rosebank; map p.461. Not to be confused with the Sunday market, this permanent and entertaining two-storey market has an impressive array of cottage-industry crafts and clothes. Daily 9am–6pm.

Rosebank Sunday Market Corner of Baker St and Cradock Ave, Rosebank ⓦfinderskeepersmarket.co.za; map p.461. An excellent market with handmade African arts, souvenirs, fashion, jewellery, household items and more; held on the spacious top floor of the mall parking garage. There's also food and live music. Sun 9am–4pm.

Snow Lion 12b Seventh St, Melville ⓣ011 482 2795, ⓦwww.snowlion.co.za; map p.463. Creative South African-themed T-shirts for children and adults (showing Mandela's smiling face or well-known South African brands), plus New Age artefacts. Daily 10am–9pm.

BOOKS & MUSIC

The Musica and Look & Listen chains, found in most malls, sell soul and rock import CDs, with small selections of local music. In the CBD there are dozens of small shops selling CDs of African sounds.

Collector's Treasury CTP House, 244 Commissioner St, CBD ⓣ011 482 6516; map pp.454–455. For decades, the Treasury has been a book-lover's dream come true, with some two million second-hand books (including lots of Africana) stacked on shelves and left in random piles over several floors.

Exclusive Books ⓦexclus1ves.co.za; map p.461. South Africa's biggest and best bookshop chain, with all the latest titles. There are branches in many malls, but the best shops are in Hyde Park Mall (ⓣ011 325 4298), Mandela Square, Sandton (ⓣ011 748 5416) and The Mall of Rosebank (ⓣ011 447 3028).

Kohinoor World of Music 163 Albertina Sisulu Rd, CBD ⓣ011 834 1361; map pp.454–455. Excellent vinyl selection, as well as a range of tapes and CDs. The focus is on jazz, but you'll find all manner of South African styles here, ranging from gospel to maskanda and mbaqanga.

Love Books 53 Rustenburg Rd, Bamboo Lifestyle Centre ⓣ011 726 7408, ⓦlovebooks.co.za; map p.463. A delightful small bookstore selling African literature, imported novels, Jo'burg books and with comfortable seats. Next to the Service Station café.

DIRECTORY

Banks and exchange There are ATMs everywhere, but beware scammers: only use a safe indoor ATM and refuse any kind of help from strangers while using it. The main shopping malls have banks and exchange offices where you can change money.

Hospitals and ambulance services In any medical emergency, call the private Netcare 911 ambulance service on ⓣ082 911 (ⓦnetcare.co.za). Patients are taken to a Netcare private hospital, which will be expensive but more dependable than a public hospital. State-run hospitals with 24hr casualty departments include Johannesburg General Hospital, Parktown (ⓣ011 488 3334/5), and Helen Joseph Hospital, Auckland Park (ⓣ011 489 1011). Private hospitals include Milpark Hospital, Guild St, Parktown (ⓣ011 480 5600), and Morningside Medi-Clinic, off Rivonia Rd in Morningside (ⓣ011 282 5000). Private hospitals are always the best option, but without proof of medical insurance, a hefty payment will be needed on admission.

Post offices Most major suburbs have a centrally located post office, often inside shopping centres or malls. There's a landside post office at OR Tambo airport for last-minute mailings (sending a package up to 30kg to Europe by surface mail costs around R270, but can take three months to arrive). The main poste restante post office is on Jeppe St in the CBD.

Swimming & gyms Public swimming pools around Johannesburg are not always in great repair, one exception being the superb, outdoor, heated Olympic-sized Ellis Park pool (Mon–Fri 7am–7pm, Sat–Sun 8am–5pm; ⓣ011 402 5565). As for gyms, try the chain of Virgin Active gyms around the city (ⓣ086 020 0911, ⓦvirginactive.co.za); some hotels will give you a voucher for a visit to the gym, or you can pay a single-visit fee of R140.

Around Johannesburg

Johannesburgers wanting to get away from it all tend to head northwest towards the ancient **Magaliesberg Mountains**, stretching from Pretoria in the east to Rustenberg in the west. Formed over two billion years ago, the mountain range has steadily eroded over the millenia, so you won't see a horizon of impressive peaks: much of the area is

7

MRS PLES AND FRIENDS

Embedded in the dolomitic rock within a dozen caves in the area now called the Cradle of Humankind are the fossilized remains of **hominids** that lived in South Africa up to 3.5 million years ago. Samples of fossilized pollen, plant material and animal bones also found in the caves indicate that the area was once a **tropical rainforest** inhabited by giant monkeys, long-legged hunting hyenas and sabre-toothed cats.

Quite when hominids arrived on the scene isn't certain, but scientists now believe that the human lineage split from apes in Africa around five to six million years ago. The oldest identified group of hominids is *Australopithecus*, a bipedal, small-brained form of man. The first *Australopithecus* discovery in South Africa was in 1924, when Professor Raymond Dart discovered the **Taung child** in what is now North West Province. In 1936, australopithecine fossils were first found in the Sterkfontein Caves, and in 1947 Dr Robert Broom excavated a nearly complete skull which he first called *Plesianthropus transvaalensis* ("near-man" of the Transvaal), later confirmed as a 2.6-million-year-old *Australopithecus africanus*. Identified as a female, she was nicknamed "**Mrs Ples**", and for many years she was the closest thing the world had to "**the missing link**".

A number of even older fossils have since been discovered at Sterkfontein and nearby caves, along with evidence of several other genera and species, including *Australopithecus robustus*, dating from between one and two million years ago, and *Homo ergaster*, possibly the immediate predecessor of *Homo sapiens*, who used stone tools and fire.

If you want to learn more and visit some of the caves and dig sites not open to the general public, try one of the excellent **tours** offered by Palaeo Tours (☎082 804 2899, ⓦpalaeotours .com) or Past Experiences (☎011 678 3905, ⓦpastexperiences.co.za).

farmland running across rolling countryside, with some ridges, cliffs, *kloofs* (gorges) and refreshingly wide vistas. A series of caves on the southeastern (Johannesburg) side holds some of the world's most important information about human evolution stretching back some 3.5 million years. These caves, including the renowned Sterkfontein Caves, are now protected as part of the **Cradle of Humankind**, one of South Africa's first World Heritage Sites.

The Cradle of Humankind

Covering some 47,000 hectares, the **Cradle of Humankind** is the name given to the area in which a series of dolomitic caves has in the last fifty years or so produced nearly two-fifths of the world's hominid fossil discoveries. Given its accessibility and the richness of the finds, it has now arguably overtaken Tanzania's Olduvai Gorge as Africa's most important paleontological site.

Sterkfontein Caves

Daily 9am–5pm, tours every half hour until 4pm • R150, or R215 including Maropeng museum; 10 percent cheaper online • ☎011 577 9000, ⓦmaropeng.co.za

The best-known of the Cradle of Humankind sites are the **Sterkfontein Caves**, believed to have been inhabited by pre-human primates who lived here up to 3.5 million years ago. They first came to European attention in 1896, when an Italian lime prospector, Gulgimo Martinaglia, stumbled upon them. Martinaglia was only interested in the bat droppings, and promptly stripped them out, thus destroying the caves' dolomite formation. Archeologist Dr Robert Broom excavated the caves between 1936 and 1951; in 1947, he found the skull of a female hominid (nicknamed "Mrs Ples") that was over 2.5 million years old. In 1995, another archeologist, Ronald Clarke, found "Little Foot", the bones of a 3-million-year-old walking hominid, with big toes that functioned like our thumbs do today. In 1998 an *Australopithecus* skeleton discovered here was the oldest complete specimen known, reckoned to be 3.3 million years old. There's a small museum that you can browse before being taken on a tour through the cave.

Kromdraai Wonder Cave

Mon–Fri 8am–5pm, Sat & Sun 8am–6pm • Tours depart on the hour • R90, R210 including the Rhino & Lion Nature Reserve • ☎ 011 957 0006, ⓦ gauteng.net/attractions/entry/wonder_cave • The best access is through the Rhino and Lion Nature Reserve – the alternative route is on a longer, rough dirt road.

The only other cave with public access is the **Kromdraai Wonder Cave**, located within the Rhino and Lion Nature Reserve (see below) to the northeast of Sterkfontein. Also mined for lime in the 1890s, this cave hasn't revealed any paleontological finds, and the main focus of attention is the extraordinary stalactites, stalagmites and rimstone pools to be found in a huge underground chamber. Once you've descended into the cave by a lift, carefully placed lighting and marked trails make the experience theatrical and unashamedly commercial.

The Rhino and Lion Nature Reserve

Daily 8am–4pm • R140, R210 including the Kromdraai Wonder Cave • ☎ 011 957 0349, ⓦ rhinolion.co.za

The fourteen-square-kilometre **Rhino and Lion Nature Reserve** is really more a safari park than anything resembling a wilderness game reserve as found in other parts of South Africa, but it is Gauteng's best site for seeing large mammals. The main section of the reserve has white rhino, wildebeest, hartebeest and zebra roaming free, while the Lion and Predator Camp has several large enclosures containing lions, cheetahs and wild dogs. Elsewhere, there's a vulture hide, a series of hippo pools (located opposite the main gate) and a breeding centre. At the animal crèche, you can pet lion cubs – though you should realize that these animals usually end up on hunting game farms. Visits can also be organized to the nearby **Old Kromdraai Gold Mine**, the second-oldest mine on the Witwatersrand, where you can follow the original mining tunnel 150m into the hillside.

Maropeng Museum

Down the R400 turn-off from the R563, northwest of the Sterkfontein Caves • Daily 9am–5pm • R145, R215 with Sterkfontein Caves; 10 percent cheaper online • ☎ 014 577 9000, ⓦ maropeng.co.za

Housed in a striking building, the Tumulus, half clad in grassy earth to simulate a burial mound, **Maropeng** ("returning to the place of our ancestors" in SeTswana) is an impressive museum dedicated to human origins and evolution. Visitors can take a short underground boat ride into the mists of time, and then browse through some child-friendly interactive displays and other exhibits explaining the history of human development. A room full of original hominid, plant and animal fossils, loaned from various institutions across South Africa, provides a fitting finale.

ARRIVAL AND DEPARTURE   THE CRADLE OF HUMANKIND

By car The Cradle of Humankind can only be reliably reached by car: head west out of Johannesburg on the R47 (Hendrik Potgieter Rd) or M5 (Beyers Naude Drive), then follow the N14 to the R563 junction. A few kilometres northwest along the R563 is a right turn to the Sterkfontein Caves turn-off.

ACCOMMODATION

Forum Homini Kromdraai Rd ☎ 011 668 7000, ⓦ forumhomini.com. Set in a private game farm that's home to antelopes and hippos, this award-winning hotel has beautiful "cave chic" rooms overlooking a lake. The fantastic gourmet restaurant *Roots*, which serves set lunches and dinners, is worth the trip alone; plan to spend several hours eating here. Rates include meals. R3500

Maropeng Hotel Off the R400 ☎ 014 577 9100, ⓦ maropeng.co.za. The chic hotel next to the Maropeng Museum is not cheap, but each of its classy earth-toned rooms has a patio commanding a dramatic Magaliesberg view. R2182

Pretoria

Gauteng's two major cities are just 50km apart, but could hardly be more different. With its graceful government buildings, wide avenues of purple flowering jacarandas, and stolid Boer farming origins, **PRETORIA** – or **TSHWANE** as the metropolitan area is now officially known – was for a long time a staid, sleepy city. However, since the arrival of democracy, the country's capital has become increasingly cosmopolitan, with a substantial diplomatic community living in Arcadia and Hatfield, east of the city centre, and middle-class blacks swelling the ranks of civil servants. Nowadays, most Pretorians are not Afrikaners, but Pedi and Tswana; and thousands of black students studying at the city's several universities have further diluted Pretoria's traditional Afrikaans roots. Connected to the Gautrain system, Pretoria is easily reached from Johannesburg and the airport, and the **nightlife** here is energetic and fun.

Pretoria's city centre is a compact grid of wide, busy streets, comparatively safe to explore on foot. Its central hub is **Church Square**, where you can see some fascinating architecture; and there are other historic buildings and museums close by. To the north lie the vast **National Zoological Gardens**, while the Arcadia district is the site of the city's famous **Union Buildings** and the **Mandela monument**. On the southern fringes of the city is the remarkable **Voortrekker Monument**, and **Freedom Park**, a memorial that attempts to come to terms with South Africa's past conflicts. While Central Pretoria is fairly safe to walk around, you should be careful when wandering north of Church Square around busy Johannes Ramokhoase and Struben streets, and also be vigilant in the Sunnyside district, east of the CBD.

Brief history

Unlike Johannesburg, Pretoria developed at a leisurely pace from its humble origins as a **Boer farming community** on the fertile land around the Apies River. When the city was founded in 1855 by **Marthinus Pretorius**, who named it after his father, Andries Pretorius, it was intended to be the capital around which the new South African Republic (ZAR) would prosper. Embodying the Afrikaners' conviction that the land they took was God-given, Pretoria's first building was a church. The town was then laid out with streets wide enough for teams of oxen brought in by farmers to make U-turns.

In 1860, the city was proclaimed the capital of the ZAR, the result of tireless efforts by Stephanus Schoeman to unite the squabbling statelets of the Transvaal. From this base, the settlers continued their campaigns against local African peoples, bringing thousands into service, particularly on farms. Infighting also continued among the settlers, and violent skirmishes between faction leaders were common. These leaders bought most of the best land, resulting in the dispossession of many white trekkers, and also in the massacre of most of the animals of the region, particularly its elephants.

The Boer Wars

The British annexed Pretoria in 1877, and investment followed in their wake. Although the town prospered and grew, farmer **Paul Kruger**, who was determined not to be subjugated by the British again, mobilized commandos of Afrikaner farmers to drive them out, resulting in the first Anglo-Boer War (1877–81). After defeat at Majuba on the Natal border, the colonial government abandoned the war and ceded **independence** in 1884. Paul Kruger became ZAR president until 1903. However, his mission to keep the ZAR Boer was confounded by the discovery of **gold** in the Witwatersrand, which precipitated an unstoppable flood of foreigners. Kruger's policy of taxing the newcomers, while retaining the Boer monopoly on political power, worked for a while. Most of the elegant buildings of Church Square were built with mining revenues, while the Raadsaal (parliament) remained firmly in Boer hands. ZAR independence ended with the second Anglo-Boer War (1899–1902), but, despite the brutality of the conflict, Pretoria remained unscathed. With the creation of the **Union of South Africa** in 1910, the city became the administrative capital of the entire country.

In 1928, the government laid the foundations of Pretoria's industry by establishing the **Iron and Steel Industrial Corporation** (Iscor), which rapidly generated a whole series of related and service industries. These, together with the civil service, ensured white

Pretoria's quiet, insular prosperity. Meanwhile, increasing landlessness among blacks drove many of them into the city's burgeoning **townships**. Marabastad and Atteridgeville are the oldest, and Mamelodi is the biggest and poorest.

After the introduction of apartheid by the National Party in 1948, Pretoria acquired a hated reputation among the black population. Its supreme court and central prison were notorious as the source of the laws that made their lives a nightmare.

Democracy

Mandela's **inauguration** at the Union Buildings in 1994 was the symbolic new beginning for Pretoria's political redemption. Through the 1990s, the stages of South Africa's revolution could be seen as clearly here as anywhere else: the gradual replacement of the diehards from institutions like the army and civil service, new faces in almost all the old government offices, the return of foreign diplomats and the influx of students.

Pretoria's metropolitan area was renamed **Tshwane** in 2005 by the city council, after a Tswana-Ndebele chief who ruled in the area before Boer settlers arrived, and dozens of city-centre streets have been recently re-named after resistance heroes. The central business district remains Pretoria, but the compromise is awkward, with most media, and indeed most citizens, still calling the whole city Pretoria. Many Afrikaners resent what they see as a spiteful and costly attempt to erase the city's historic origins from public memory, while many black Pretorians don't see why a post-apartheid, mainly black city should still bear a name deeply associated with racial oppression. It seems likely that the city will lug two names around for years to come.

7

Church Square

The heart of Pretoria is **Church Square**, surrounded by dramatic and important buildings. It was here that Boer farmers outspanned their oxen when they came into town for the quarterly *Nagmaal* (Holy Communion) of the Dutch Reformed Church, turning the square temporarily into a campsite.

Indeed, nearly every important white meeting, protest or takeover the city has known happened in Church Square; the ZAR Vierkleur ("four colours") flag was lowered here in 1877 to make way for the Union Jack, only to rise again in 1881, after the British eviction from the republic; the British flag flew again in 1900 but was lowered for the last time in 1910; Paul Kruger was proclaimed head of state here four times, and thirty thousand people crammed into the square in 1904 for his memorial service. Such historical resonances are viewed differently by Pretoria's black community, and the square's central **statue of Paul Kruger** is for many an unwanted relic of a dismal past.

Raadsaal and the Old Nederlandsche Bank Building

On the southwest corner of Church Square, the old **Raadsaal** (parliament) was built in neo-Renaissance style in 1891, and still exudes the bourgeois respectability yearned for by the parliamentarians of the ZAR. Ask the security guard for a peek inside, and to look at the room where Paul Kruger spent most of his time during the final stages of the Anglo-Boer War.

Next to the Raadsaal is the **Old Nederlandsche Bank Building**, home of the tourist office (see p.494). Incredibly, it took a gathering of ten thousand people in 1975 and five years of deliberation to reverse a decision to demolish this building and the Raadsaal.

Palace of Justice

In the northwest corner of Church Square, the grandiose **Palace of Justice** was started in 1897 and, half completed, used as a hospital for British troops during the second Anglo-Boer War. Home to the Transvaal Supreme Court for many years after its completion in 1902, it was the location of the Rivonia Trial in 1963–64, which saw

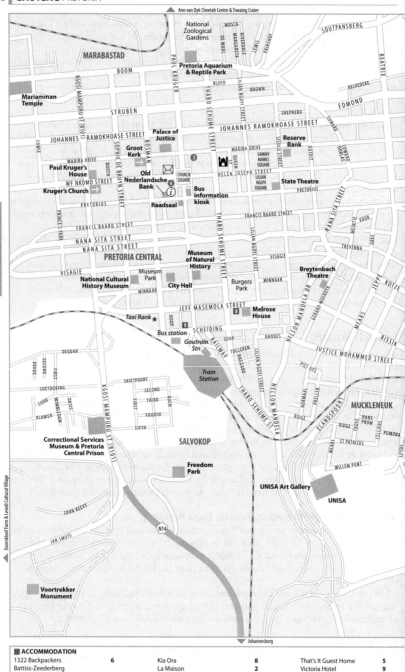

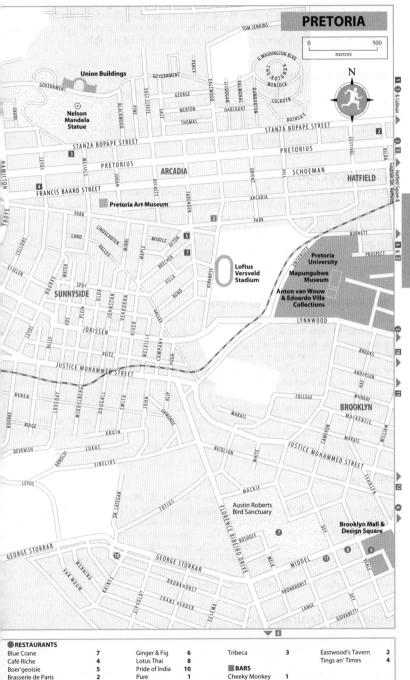

PRETORIA

0   500
metres

N

7

Union Buildings

Nelson Mandela Statue

ARCADIA

HATFIELD

Pretoria Art Museum

Loftus Versveld Stadium

Pretoria University

Mapungubwe Museum

Anton van Wouw & Edoardo Villa Collections

SUNNYSIDE

BROOKLYN

JUSTICE MOHAMMED STREET

Austin Roberts Bird Sanctuary

Brooklyn Mall & Design Square

GEORGE STORRAR

● RESTAURANTS					
Blue Crane	7	Ginger & Fig	6	Tribeca	3
Café Riche	4	Lotus Thai	8		
Boer'geoisie	5	Pride of India	10	■ BARS	
Brasserie de Paris	2	Pure	1	Cheeky Monkey	1
Crawdaddy's	11	Tashas	9	Drop Zone	3

Eastwood's Tavern   2
Tings an' Times   4

Nelson Mandela and other leaders of the ANC sentenced to life imprisonment. Restoration work has revealed and repaired the splendid facade and balconies, although the new court is an ugly box sitting squatly in a street behind the Palace.

Queen Street Mosque

A small passageway off Queen Street brings you to the unexpected site of a bright white **mosque**, oriented at an angle to the city grid so as to face Mecca. Pretoria's Muslims, who reportedly got on well with Kruger, acquired the site in 1896, and the current building was constructed in 1927 by Cape artisans. The mosque is now hemmed in by ugly tower blocks, but is somehow all the more indomitable for that.

Lilian Ngoyi Square

Lilian Ngoyi Square is named after the anti-apartheid activist who was one of the leaders of the 1956 Women's March that started on this spot. Until 2006 this was called Strijdom Square, and was the site of a vast and horrific bust of the man himself. Prime minister from 1954 to 1958, **Johannes Strijdom** began the wave of apartheid legislation that peaked under his successor, Hendrik Verwoerd, and was a firm believer in "white supremacy". Dramatically, on May 31, 2001, forty years to the day after the statue was completed, a structural fault caused it to collapse.

Paul Kruger's House and around

60 WK Nkomo St (formerly Church St) • Mon–Fri 8.30am–4.30pm, Sat & Sun 9am–4.30pm • R35 • ☎ 012 000 0010, ⊛ ditsong.org.za

Paul Kruger's House was built in 1884 by the English-speaking Charles Clark, described by Kruger as one of his "tame Englishmen", who mixed his cement with milk instead of water. Inside, the **museum** is rather dull, though you may find some interest in Kruger's effects, such as his large collection of spittoons. The *stoep* (veranda) is the most famous feature of the house, for here the old president would sit and chat to any white person who chose to join him. At the back is Kruger's private railway coach, built in 1898, which he used during the second Anglo-Boer War.

Opposite is a characteristically grim Reformed church known as **Kruger's Church**. The **Groot Kerk** (Great Church), on the corner of Madiba Drive and Bosman streets, is more impressive; its strikingly ornate tower is one of the finest in the country.

Melrose House

275 Jeff Masemole St (formerly Jacob Maré St) • Tues–Sun 10am–5pm • R20 • ☎ 012 322 2805, ⊛ melrosehouse.co.za

Opposite the restful **Burgers Park** (named after ineffective ZAR president Thomas Burgers, who was in office between 1873 and 1877), with its manucured lawns, you'll find **Melrose House**, an over-decorated Victorian domicile with a wonderful conservatory and interesting exhibitions. The house was built in 1886 for local businessman George Heys, who made his money running mailcoach services. Lord Kitchener used the house during the second Anglo-Boer War, and the treaty of Vereeniging that ended hostilities was signed inside.

Museum of Natural History

432 Paul Kruger St • Daily 8am–4pm • R30 • ☎ 012 322 7632, ⊛ ditsong.org.za

The grand **Museum of Natural History** is Pretoria's oldest museum and home to plenty of stuffed animals, bird exhibits, models of dinosaurs and casts of fossil remains. The originals can be viewed by appointment only. This is a good place to come to put the discoveries of the nearby Cradle of Humankind (see p.484) into context: alongside a bronze bust of Robert Broom staring into the three-million-year-old eye sockets of Mrs Ples is an assortment of fossilized discoveries and reconstructions of early hominid life.

City Hall
Paul Kruger St

Forming an architectural ensemble with the Museum of Natural History directly opposite, the **City Hall** was built in 1935 in a mix of Greek and Roman architectural styles. The park in front of the building has a series of fountains and well-tended flowerbeds and statues of the city's founding fathers Andries and Marthinus Pretorius and – added in 2006 – founding grandfather Chief Tshwane.

National Cultural History Museum
149 Visagie St • Daily 8am–4pm • R35 • ☎ 012 324 6082, ⓦ ditsong.org.za

The permanent exhibitions at the **National Cultural History Museum**, west of the City Hall, are eclectic to the point of being a bit unconnected: they include displays of San rock art, and a room showing work by J.H. Pierneef (1886–1957), one of the country's most famous artists, who is known for his dramatically stylized bushveld landscapes.

National Zoological Gardens
232 Boom St • Daily 8.30am–5.30pm • R55; cableway R10 • **Night tour** Wed, Fri & Sat 6.30pm; R100 • **Camping tour** Fri & Sat 5pm; R150 • ☎ 012 328 3265, ⓦ nzg.ac.za

Pretoria's spacious and recommended **zoo** houses rare species of antelope, a white rhinoceros, and a wide selection of South American as well as African animals. Next door, the **Pretoria Aquarium and Reptile Park** (included in the price) is less impressive, but nonetheless houses plenty of beasts, some weird and highly venomous. A cable-car ride takes you right over the zoo, across the Apies River and to the top of the ridge for fine views of the city. It's well worth trying to book one of the **night tours**, when you'll see some of the zoo's nocturnal creatures, like bats, owls and lions, at their most active; it's also possible to spend the night in the zoo on a camping tour.

Mariamman Temple
Seventh St, Marabastad • Daily 9am–5pm • ☎ 012 358 1430

The scruffy streets of Marabastad, the city's first "non-white" area, lie to the west of the zoo and, while fascinating, can feel quite intimidating if visiting alone. Don't miss the intricately decorated Hindu **Mariamman Temple** from 1930, next to the market, which was built in Tamil style with a colourful Gorpuram tower, and is dedicated to the consort of the god Shiva, who protects against infectious diseases.

The Correctional Services Museum
Kgosi Mampuru St (formerly Potgieter St) • Tues–Fri 9am–3pm • Free • ☎ 012 314 1766, ⓦ dcs.gov.za

The chilling **Correctional Services Museum** at Pretoria Central Prison, along the R101 towards Johannesburg, is well worth a visit. You'll see the notorious prison, where many famous political prisoners were held (and executed), on your right. Be prepared to walk past depressed-looking visiting relatives on your way in. Inside the museum you can see artwork made by prisoners, including a life-size statue of an inmate crawling towards an expressionless prison warder, who has his arms outstretched, ready to correct him. There are also exhibits of knives concealed in Bibles and shoes, files in cakes and so forth. Most alarming are the group photos of various forbidding-looking prison warders through the ages, which seem a strange sort of propaganda for the prison service. For a first-hand account of the conditions inside, Charles Herman Bosman's Cold Stone Jug is a fascinating collection of short stories about his four-year stay in this prison in the 1920s.

The Freedom Park

Salvokop Hill • Guided tours daily at 9am, noon & 3pm • R45 • ☎ 012 336 4000, ⓦ freedompark.co.za

Freedom Park, which sits atop Salvokop Hill, is punctuated by a sculpture of ascending "reeds" that are dramatically illuminated at night. Started in 2000 in response to the Truth and Reconciliation Commission's (see box, p.650) call for new symbols to resolve past conflicts, and still partly under construction, the park is a courageous and successful attempt to create a memorial that speaks to all sections of post-apartheid society in South Africa. Visits are by guided tour only and take you past the **Wall of Names**, inscribed with the names of 75,000 victims of various South African conflicts, an eternal flame to the unknown soldier, and boulders representing important moments in the history of the country's nine provinces – Gauteng's rock symbolizes the peaceful marches in Soweto, Sharpville, Mamelodi and other townships that were met by police violence. Tours also take in the new **//hapo Museum**, named after the Khoi word for dream, which tells about local creation legends and the country's history from an African perspective.

The Voortrekker Monument

Eeufees Rd • Daily: May–Aug 8am–5pm, Sept–April 8am–6pm • R55 • ☎ 012 326 6770, ⓦ vtm.org.za

A symbol of Afrikaner domination in the old South Africa, the **Voortrekker Monument and Museum** is a striking, austere block of granite, built in 1940 to commemorate the Boer victory over the Zulu army at Blood River on December 16, 1838 (see p.425). The monument is enclosed by reliefs of ox wagons, with a large statue of a woman standing outside, shaking her fist at imaginary oppressors. Inside, a series of moving reliefs depicts scenes from the Great Trek, and you can climb to the top of the tower for a peek down into the hall, or for dramatic views of the surrounding nature reserve. This has various hiking and mountain-bike trails, leading to lookout points over Pretoria.

The Union Buildings

In the Arcadia district, Pretoria's **Union Buildings**, the headquarters of the South African government, perch majestically on the main hill. Designed by Herbert Baker in 1910 to symbolize the union of Briton and Boer, the lashings of colonnades and lavish amphitheatre seem to glorify British imperial self-confidence. Nelson Mandela had an office here after his release from prison, and the buildings were the site of his inauguration as president in 1994. This was perhaps the first time their imperialist symbols were transformed, not least by the African praise-singers who delivered their odes from the amphitheatre, proclaiming Mandela as the latest in a long line of African heroes from Shaka to Hintsa, and beyond. The buildings are not open to the public, but you can walk around the terrace and the attractive gardens below to enjoy great views over the city. Just below the main terrace stands the nine-metre high, wide-armed **Nelson Mandela statue**, unveiled the day after Mandela's burial in December 2013. The sculptors had added a small rabbit inside the sculpture's ear, referring to the time pressure they were under ("*haas*" in Afrikaans means haste as well as hare) but, although Mandela would probably have appreciated the joke, the humourless new guardians of the ANC had it removed because "Nelson Mandela never had a rabbit in his ear".

Pretoria Art Museum

Corner of Francis Baard and Wessels streets • Tues–Sun 10am–5pm • R20 • ☎ 012 344 1807, ⓦ pretoriaartmuseum.co.za

South of the Union Buildings, the **Pretoria Art Museum** is housed in a modernist pavilion overlooking a park. Inside is a modestly sized but excellent selection of South African and early Dutch-inspired art, modern photography, some works of "resistance art" by the likes of William Kentridge and a number of black artists, including Ephraim Ngatane and Gerard Sekoto.

Sunnyside and Pretoria University

Southeast of the centre, desegregated **Sunnyside** is the central suburb with the strongest African feel, with a lively street life, distinctive old houses and a multitude of cafés – though it's best not to walk around alone here. Robert Sobukwe Street is the busiest thoroughfare, brimming with bars and street hawkers. East of Sunnyside, the huge **Loftus Versveld Stadium** is home to Pretoria's hugely popular sporting giants – the Bulls rugby team and the Mamelodi Sundowns football team – while further east still is the vast **Pretoria University**, with two worthwhile museums.

7

Mapungubwe Museum

Lynnwood Rd, Old Arts Building, Pretoria University campus • Tues–Fri 10am–4pm • Free • ☎ 012 420 5450, ⓦ www.up.ac.za

The small **Mapungubwe Museum** is dedicated to the remarkable archeological finds at Mapungubwe (see p.572), a hilltop fort near the Limpopo River that was the ancient capital of a major southern African kingdom. Among the artefacts on display are a rhinoceros made from thin gold foil, figurines, jewellery and decorated pots, all at least seven hundred years old.

Anton van Wouw and Edoardo Villa Collections

Lynnwood Rd, Old Merensky Library, Pretoria University campus • Tues–Fri 10am–4pm • Free • ☎ 012 420 5450, ⓦ www.up.ac.za

The acclaimed Dutch-born sculptor **Anton van Wouw** was responsible for most of the brooding effigies of Afrikaner public figures from the 1890s to the 1930s that are scattered around the country, including the Kruger statue in Pretoria's Church Square and the Voortrekker Monument. The university's collection, in an elegant 1930s library building, includes two striking pieces, one of a mine worker, the other an accused man standing in the dock. Look out, too, for *The Guitar Player*, a feisty-looking woman strumming away with a trace of a smile on her face. Also on display here are dozens of impressive modern steel sculptures, spanning more than sixty years, by Italian artist **Edoardo Villa**, who was a prisoner of war in South Africa in 1947.

UNISA Art Gallery

Preller St, Kgorong Building, UNISA University campus • Tues–Fri 10am–4pm • Free • ☎ 012 441 5681, ⓦ unisa.ac.za/gallery

Travelling south of the centre on Elandspoort Road, you can't miss the enormous and head-shakingly ugly **UNISA**, South Africa's largest university, with more than two hundred thousand students – though most of them study by correspondence. The university's very good **art gallery**, inside the entrance building, hosts some of Pretoria's most innovative exhibitions of visual and conceptual art, as well as a permanent collection exhibiting young South African talent of all backgrounds.

ARRIVAL AND INFORMATION   **PRETORIA**

By plane Johannesburg's OR Tambo International Airport (see p.471) is 55km to the southeast of Pretoria. The Gautrain (see p.473) connects the airport to Pretoria and Hatfield stations, with a change in Sandton or Marlboro, daily between 5.30am and 8.30pm; tickets from the airport to Pretoria or Hatfield stations are R155. The Airport Shuttle (☎ 086 1748 8853, ⓦ airportshuttle.co.za) also goes to Pretoria from OR Tambo and Lanseria airports for around R500, though it's often cheaper to ask your accommodation to arrange collection from the airport.

7

By train The Gautrain runs every twelve to twenty minutes (5.30am–8.30pm) from Johannesburg to Pretoria station, situated just south of the city centre and Hatfield station. A ticket from Pretoria station to Sandton costs R57, to Rosebank R61 and to Park Station R64.

By bus Intercity buses stop beside the main train station, while minibus taxis from Jo'burg and other destinations arrive nearby at the corner of Jeff Masemola and Bosman streets. Destinations Bloemfontein (10 daily; 7hr); Cape Town (6 daily; 20hr); Durban (18 daily; 9hr); Johannesburg (over 30 daily; 1hr); Kimberley (4 daily; 7hr); Nelspruit (6 daily; 6hr).

Information The tourist office is in the Old Nederlandsche Bank building on Church Square (Mon–Fri 7.30am–4pm; ☎ 012 358 1430).

GETTING AROUND

By bus Gautrain bus lines (see above) loop from Pretoria station through the city centre, while the suburbs, malls and embassies in Arcadia, Brooklyn and Menlyn are served by Gautrain buses from Hatfield station. (You can also take the Gautrain between Hatfield and Pretoria station for R25.) Municipal bus services to other suburbs start along Madiba Drive between Bosman and Thabo Sehume streets. The driver sells tickets (R10) and has timetables available, otherwise visit the information kiosk in Church Square (☎ 012 358 0839).

By taxi Recommended local taxi firms are Rixi Taxi (☎ 086 100 7494, ⊛ rixitaxi.co.za) and Dial-a-Dove Taxi (☎ 012 323 2040).

ACCOMMODATION

Besides the many chain hotels, Pretoria has numerous guesthouses dotted around Brooklyn and Hatfield, offering good nightlife and easy access to Loftus Versveld Stadium and the Gautrain station; Pretoria's Bed & Breakfast Association has a central booking site at ⊛ bbapt.co.za. As with Jo'burg, it's worth booking your first night before you arrive.

1322 Backpackers 1322 Arcadia St, Hatfield ☎ 012 362 3905, ⊛ 1322backpackers.com. A popular hostel near the embassies and Hatfield's nightlife, with a kitchen, pool and travel desk. Just a short walk east of the Gautrain station. Dorm R150, double R350

Battiss-Zeederberg Guesthouse Fook Island, 92 Twentieth St, Menlo Park ☎ 012 460 7318. Comfortable B&B accommodation in the original home of eccentric Walter Battiss, one of South Africa's greatest twentieth-century artists, with brightly painted floors, unusual decorations and a distinctly Greek feel. R800

★ **Brooks Cottage** 283 Brooks St, Brooklyn ☎ 012 362 3150, ⊛ brookscottage.co.za. An elegant Cape Dutch-style home – a national monument – with smart rooms, satellite TV and breakfast served on the porch overlooking the pool. R900

Hotel 224 Corner of Francis Baard and Leyds streets ☎ 012 440 5281, ⊛ hotel224.com. A characterful and excellent budget hotel, with modern single and double rooms, plus a restaurant and bar attached and safe parking. R750

Kia Ora 257 Jeff Masemola St ☎ 012 322 4803. In a prime location opposite Burgers Park, this basic but friendly hostel is ideal for sightseeing. The dorms and private rooms are clean and comfortable, and there's a congenial bar next door. Dorm R150, double R330

La Maison 235 Hilda St, Hatfield ☎ 012 430 4341, ⊛ lamaison.co.za. A very pleasant guesthouse in a mock castle dating from 1922, with lovely gardens, six Victorian-styled rooms full of antiques, and an outstanding Portuguese restaurant. R1000

Osborne House 82 Anderson St, Brooklyn ☎ 012 362 2334, ⊛ osborneguesthouse.com. A wonderfully elegant guesthouse in a restored Edwardian manor house with lovely furniture, big windows, wooden floors and a secluded pool with a deck, perfect for breakfasts in the sun. R1100

Pretoria Backpackers 425 Farenden St, Clydesdale ☎ 012 343 9754, ⊛ pretoriabackpackers.net. A relatively upmarket backpacker place near the Loftus Versveld Stadium, with doubles as well as smallish dorms, spread over two lovely old houses with original features, a relaxing garden *stoep* and a pool. There's also a useful travel centre. Dorm R150, double R400

Sheraton Pretoria 643 Stanza Bopape St, Arcadia ☎ 012 429 9999, ⊛ sheraton.com/pretoria. This good-value five-star hotel boasts all the usual *Sheraton* touches, but most importantly has the best views in town of the Union Buildings. If you can't afford a room with a view, head to the terrace beside *Tiffens Bar & Lounge* for high tea. R1045

That's It Guest Home 5 Brecher St, Clydesdale ☎ 012 344 3404, ⊛ thatsit.co.za. Near Loftus Versveld Stadium is this neat, reasonably priced B&B in a family home with four rooms, a relaxing garden and pool. R900

Victoria Hotel Corner of Scheiding and Paul Kruger streets ☎ 012 323 6054, ✉ hvic@absamail.co.za. The interior of this 1894 building opposite the train station has seen better days, but there's a friendly atmosphere and you can rent rooms for the day, which is handy if you're waiting for bus connections. R650

★ **Whistletree Lodge** 1267 Whistletree Drive, Queenswood ☎ 012 333 9915, ⊛ whistletreelodge.com. Roughly 7km northeast of the centre, this small boutique hotel is adorned with beautiful antiques, eclectic artwork and stylish furniture, giving the place a refined and luxurious atmosphere. Facilities include a pool, sauna and tennis courts; all rooms have private balconies, and the service is impeccable. R800

EATING

★**Blue Crane** 156 Melk St, New Muckleneuk ☎012 460 7615, ⓦbluecranerestaurant.co.za. A fairly smart restaurant in a unique location, overlooking the lake and Austin Roberts Bird Sanctuary. The large menu includes lamb shank and ostrich kebabs (mains R90–120). Mon 7.30am–3pm, Tues–Fri 7.30am–11pm, Sat 9am–11pm, Sun 9am–4pm.

Boer'geoisie Greenlyn Village, Thirteenth St, Menlo Park ☎012 460 0264, ⓦbistrotboergeoisie.co.za. Traditional Afrikaner *boerekos* (farmers' food) jazzed up with bistro-cuisine flourishes. The *potjies* (stews) are the house speciality; options include lamb with Karoo dumplings (R124). Mains around R120. Mon–Fri noon–3pm & 6–10pm, Sat 6–10pm, Sun noon–3pm.

Brasserie de Paris 381 Aries St, Waterkloof Ridge ☎012 460 3583. This reproduction of a classic Parisian café has a French-inspired menu, including dishes such as scallop vol-au-vent and steak tartare. Most mains R100–170. Mon–Fri noon–2.30pm & 7–9pm, Sat 7–9.30pm.

Café Riche 2 Church Square, CBD ☎012 328 3173. Opened in 1905, this classic café overlooking the square is a must for a quick coffee or simple pub meal. It still has its original fittings, continental atmosphere and hosts quirky events, including late-night philosophical discussions (last Fri of the month). Daily 6am–6pm.

Crawdaddy's Corner of Middel and Dey streets, Piazza mall, Brooklyn ☎012 460 0889, ⓦcrawdaddys.co.za. A popular Cajun-themed restaurant, serving chowder and surf-and-turf-style dishes such as prawns and calamari with a meat accompaniment (mains R60–100). Sun–Wed 11am–10pm, Thurs–Sat 11am–11.30pm.

★**Ginger & Fig** Jan Shoba St, corner Lynnwood Rd, Brooklyn ☎012 362 5926, ⓦgingerandfig.co.za. Delicious modern cooking in a shopfront "artisan eatery"

run by ambitious young cooks. Everything here is home made, free range, organic and tasty – try the beetroot veggie burger (R65), a pear and blue cheese salad (R60) or some sweet-potato crisps. Mon 7.30am–5.30pm, Tues–Fri 6am–9pm, Sat 7am–3pm.

Lotus Thai 281 Middel St, Brooklyn ☎012 346 5406. An elegant, authentic Thai restaurant in the heart of Brooklyn, with stylish, contemporary decor and efficient staff. Plenty of curry and stir-fry dishes (R60–120), as well as sushi. Daily noon–10pm.

Pride of India Groenkloof Plaza, George Storrar Drive, Groenkloof ☎012 346 3684, ⓦprideofindiarestaurant .com. Filled with exquisite, imported Indian artefacts and oozing class and confidence, this is the place in town for beautifully prepared North Indian and Goan curries (mostly around R75). Mon–Sat 11.30am–midnight, Sat 4pm–midnight, Sun 11.30am–4pm.

Pure 137 Thomson St, corner Gordon Rd, Hatfield ☎012 342 1443, ⓦpurecafe.co.za. A lovely café near the highway to Polokwane serving breakfast and lunch, cakes and coffee. Try the chai-mango smoothies for R29, a spring meadow salad for R58, or the stuffed aubergine for R69. Mon–Fri 7am–4pm, Sat 8am–3pm.

Tashas Design Square mall, corner of Bronkhorst and Veal streets, Brooklyn ☎012 460 2951, ⓦtashas.co.za. An immensely popular chain bistro with a beautiful, simple design and an extensive menu offering breakfasts, good freshly squeezed juices (rare in South Africa), sandwiches, pasta and cakes; mains cost R60–100. Book ahead or expect to queue. Mon 6.30am–9pm, Tues–Sat 6.30am–10pm, Sun 7.30am–9pm.

★**Tribeca** 220 Madiba Dr, CBD ☎012 321 8876, ⓦtribeca.co.za. Excellent coffee, breakfast, cake and light meals, just northeast of Church Square. Their outlet at Design Square mall in Brooklyn mall is a popular gay meeting place. Mon–Fri 7am–5pm.

BARS AND CLUBS

Most of the city's action is in Hatfield and, to a lesser extent, Brooklyn. **Hatfield**, where the students hang out, is Pretoria's liveliest area, with Hatfield Square being the hub of activity and the trendiest hangouts and nightlife spreading along Burnett Street, where you'll find a plethora of studenty cafés, bars and restaurants. Southeast of the university, the wealthy suburb of **Brooklyn** attracts an older, more upmarket crowd.

Cheeky Monkey Burnett St, Hatfield Square ⓦcheekymonkeybar.co.za. The best of the dozen bars on lively Hatfield Square, *Cheeky Monkey* is often crammed with students downing beer, cocktails or snacks from the in-house restaurant/pizzeria. Daily noon till late.

Drop Zone Burnett St, Hatfield Square ☎012 362 6528, ⓦclubdropzone.co.za. A student nightclub with plenty of daily drinks specials, live acts, foam parties and

loud music that rarely deviates from the mainstream. No under 21s. Daily 8pm till late.

Eastwood's Tavern 391 Eastwood St, Arcadia ☎012 344 0243, ⓦeastwoods.co.za. An often raucous pub-restaurant near Loftus Versveld Stadium popular with meat- and beer-loving sports fans. Select a raw piece of steak (R70) and chuck it on the braai yourself. Mon–Sat 8am–2am, Sun 8am–10pm.

★**Tings an' Times** Corner of Garsfontein and January

Masilela roads, Waterglen Centre, Waterkloof Glen ☎012 993 0233, ⓦtings.co.za. Reggae predominates at this eclectic bar, which is also the best place in town to catch live bands; drop by on Sundays for their free unplugged sessions. There's food too, such as pita bread with falafel (R50) or beef cumin (R68) and other snacks. Daily noon–1.30am.

ENTERTAINMENT

Pretoria lacks the dynamism and breadth of Johannesburg's arts and music scene, but there's still a fair amount going on. The *Pretoria News* is good for listings for theatre and cinema, while the *Mail & Guardian* covers the visual arts, theatre and major musical events. Computicket (ⓦcomputicket.com) is the big central ticket outlet for most arts and sports events.

Breytenbach Theatre 137 Gerard Moerdyk St, Sunnyside ☎012 440 4834. The "Breytie" is a venue for lively student theatre, though it's said to be haunted since the time it was a hospital.
State Theatre 320 Pretorius St ☎012 392 4000, ⓦstatetheatre.co.za. The city's main venue for dance, theatre, opera and classical concerts. Under the leadership of Hugh Masekela and then Aubrey Sekhabi, it also puts on an interesting programme of jazz and black theatre.

DIRECTORY

Banks Most banks are around Church Square and east along Church St.
Bookshops Exclusive Books has a branch at Brooklyn Mall, Bronkhorst St, Brooklyn (☎012 346 5864, ⓦexclus1ves .co.za). Protea Book House, 1067 Burnett St, Hatfield (☎012 362 5683, ⓦproteaboekhuis.com), offers a wide range of new and secondhand books.
Embassies and consulates Australia, 292 Orient St, Arcadia (☎012 423 6000); Canada, 1103 Arcadia St, Hatfield (☎012 422 3000); Ireland, 570 Fehrsen St, Brooklyn (☎012 452 1000); Lesotho, 391 Anderson St, Menlo Park (☎012 460 7648); Malawi, 770 Government Ave, Arcadia (☎012 342 0146); Mozambique, 529 Edmond St, Arcadia (☎012 401 0300); Namibia, 197 Blackwood St, Arcadia (☎012 481 9100); Swaziland, 715 Government Ave, Arcadia (☎012 344 1910); UK, 255 Hill St, Arcadia (☎012 421 7500); US, 877 Pretorius St, Arcadia (☎011 431 4000); Zambia, 570 Ziervogel Ave, Arcadia (☎012 326 1854); Zimbabwe, 798 Merton Av, Arcadia (☎012 342 5125).
Emergencies Private ambulance (Netcare) ☎082 911; ambulance & fire ☎10177; police ☎10111.
Flea market Hatfield Flea Market, 1122 Burnett St (every Sun), is Pretoria's best flea market, with crafts, bric-a-brac and lively banter.
Hospitals Those with 24hr casualty services include Steve Biko Academic Hospital, Voortrekker Rd (☎012 354 1590), and Wilgers Hospital, Denneboom Rd (☎012 807 8100).
Pharmacies In virtually every shopping mall; there are also 24hr pharmacies at Wilgers Hospital (see above) and the Muelmed Medi-Clinic, 577 Pretorius St (☎012 440 1457).
Post office Church St (Mon, Tues, Thurs & Fri 8am–4.30pm, Wed 8.30am–4.30pm, Sat 8am–noon).

Around Pretoria

The most absorbing sight in the vicinity of Pretoria is **Doornkloof Farm**, the former home of Prime Minister Jan Smuts. Further out, to the east of Pretoria, the mining town of **Cullinan** harks back to the pioneering days of diamond prospecting, while north of the city the **Tswaing meteorite crater** is a great place for a short hike. To the west, **Lesedi Cultural Village** has become a victim of its own popularity, while those interested in wildlife conservation should not miss the **De Wildt Cheetah and Wildlife Trust**.

Doornkloof Farm

Jan Smuts Ave, off Nellmapius Ave, Irene, signposted 20km south of Pretoria along the R21 • Mon–Fri 8am–4pm, Sat & Sun 8.30am–4.30pm • R15 • ☎012 667 1176, ⓦsmutshouse.co.za

Doornkloof Farm was the home of **Jan Smuts** for much of his life, including during his periods as prime minister of South Africa. His simple wood-and-corrugated-iron house is now a museum, which sheds light on one of South Africa's most enigmatic politicians. The massive library here reflects Smuts' intellectual range, while numerous mementos confirm his internationalism. Other displays focus on Smuts' role as one of the most successful commanders of Boer forces during the Anglo-Boer Wars. The surrounding farm is part of the museum, and features the pleasant 2.5-kilometre **Oubaas Trail**, leading from the house to the top of a nearby *koppie*, a walk the nature-loving Smuts took every day. Scattered near the house are various pieces of military hardware such as cannon and armoured vehicles – a little incongruously, given the declarations of peace and tranquillity posted along the trail and elsewhere.

Cullinan's Premier Mine

50km east of Pretoria • **Surface tours** Mon–Fri 10.30am & 2pm, Sat & Sun 10.30am & 12.15pm • 2hr • R115 • **Underground tours** Mon & Fri 10.30am, Tues–Thurs 9.30am, Sat 7.30am • 8hr • R500 • Booking required • ☎ 012 734 0081, ⓦ diamondtourscullinan.co.za • **Diamond Express train** R200 • ☎ 012 767 7913, ⓦ friendsoftherail.com

The quaint town of **Cullinan** is home to the **Premier Mine**, still worked today, where the world's largest diamond, the 3106-carat **Star of Africa**, was discovered in 1905. Mine enthusiasts can take a surface tour of the mine, or dress in protective clothing and see operations from close up, 760m underground. The best way to visit is on the **Diamond Express** steam-train day-trip organized about once a month by Friends of the Rail, departing from Pretoria's Hermanstad depot at 8am and returning at 5.30pm, leaving enough time in Cullinan to wander the streets and have a relaxed lunch.

Tswaing Crater

Onderstepoort Rd, Soshanguve, off the M35 • Daily 7.30am–4pm • R25 • ☎ 076 9455 911, ⓦ ditsong.org.za/tswaing.htm

Tswaing Crater is one of the youngest and best-preserved meteorite craters in the world, a 1.4km-wide and 200m-deep depression created around 220,000 years ago. Tswaing means "place of salt" in Tswana, and the rich deposits of salt and soda around the edge of the shallow crater lake have attracted people since ancient times; artefacts up to 150,000 years old have been discovered here. Register at the visitors' centre on the main road before driving to the car park, from where a pleasant 7km trail crosses the veld to the crater, down to the lake and back; alternatively, park closer to the rim from where it's a short stroll to the crater.

Lesedi Cultural Village

Southwest of Pretoria, off the R512, north of Lanseria Airport • Tours daily at 11.30am & 4.30pm • R260 tour only, R400 for the tour plus a meal and dance performance • Accommodation R800 • ☎ 087 940 9993, ⓦ lesedi.com

Lesedi Cultural Village crams five cultural villages into one bewildering experience, with the Zulu, Pedi, Xhosa, Ndebele and Basotho all represented. Tourists are escorted round the fairly authentic kraals, entertained by a lively display of colourful costumes, singing and dancing, then fed heartily with a traditional African feast in the vividly decorated restaurant. You can also stay the night in one of the village huts, or in a grass hut with a Lesedi family.

Ann van Dyk Cheetah Centre

West of Pretoria, just off the R513 towards Brits • **Cheetah run and tour** Tues, Thurs, Sat & Sun 8am • R400 • **Tours** Mon, Wed, Fri 8.30am; Tues, Thurs, Sat & Sun 1.30pm • R300 • Book in advance • ☎ 012 504 9906, ⓦ dewildt.co.za

The **Ann van Dyk Cheetah Centre** is a world-renowned conservation project. The centre's mission is to protect the cheetah by developing predator management policies with farmers, breeding cubs in captivity (over 750 have been raised to date) and then generally transporting them to game reserves. Other endangered animals bred and/or cared for at the centre include African wild dogs, vultures and brown hyenas. Visitors can get up close to the centre's senior cheetahs, who are relaxed in human company, and there's a tour of the centre and enclosures housing the other animals. Photographing cheetahs on the run is a big draw, and there's also a cheetah adoption programme.

North West Province

WILDEBEEST IN MADIKWE GAME RESERVE

North West Province

South Africa's North West Province is one of the country's least-understood regions – renowned, among tourists at least, for the opulent Sun City resort and the Big Five Pilanesberg National Park, but not much else. Few people venture beyond these attractions to explore this area in greater depth; consequently, it can be curiously rewarding to do so. The old-fashioned hospitality of the myriad little *dorps* scattered throughout the region, and the tranquillity of the endless stretches of grassland and fields of *mielies* (sweetcorn) make a refreshing change after hectic Johannesburg and Pretoria.

North West Province extends west from Gauteng to the Botswana border and the Kalahari Desert. Along the province's eastern flank, essentially separating it from Gauteng, loom the **Magaliesberg mountains**, one hundred times older than the Himalayas and dotted with **holiday** resorts for nature-starved Jo'burgers. The **N4** from Pretoria cuts through the mountains to the main town of the northeastern part of the province, **Rustenburg**, gateway to the windswept **Kgaswane Mountain Reserve**, where you can hike high enough to gaze down onto the shimmering plains beneath. **Groot Marico**, further west along the N4, is a friendly *dorp* with powerful home-brews and laidback people to share them with. Further to the west lies the provincial capital of **Mafikeng** – famed for its siege during the second Anglo-Boer War – while near the Botswana border **Madikwe Game Reserve** is one of South Africa's undiscovered wildlife gems, a massive Big Five park which sees remarkably few visitors and boasts some superb game lodges.

Brief history

San hunter-gatherers were the province's first inhabitants; they were displaced 500–1000 years ago by cattle-herding Iron Age peoples from the north, who pitched their first settlements on low ground near watercourses. These settlements developed into stone-walled towns on hilltops; and by 1820 the largest, Karechuenya (near Madikwe), was estimated to have more inhabitants than Cape Town. By the nineteenth century, the dominance of the Rolong, Taung, Tlhaping and Tlokwa clans was established. European observers classified them all as **Tswana**, but it's unclear whether these people regarded themselves as very different from people further east classified as "Sotho".

The outbreak of intense **inter-clan violence** in the early 1800s was due to displacements caused by the expansion of white trekboers, and the growing availability of firearms. Victory went to those who made alliances with the new arrivals, whether **Griqua** from the Northern Cape or **Afrikaners** from further south. However, the clans' victories were short lived and their Griqua and Afrikaner allies soon evicted them from their land and forced them into service. Various mini-states were formed until, in 1860, they were all amalgamated to form the **South African Republic** (ZAR), with Pretoria as its capital.

The first Anglo-Boer War (1877–81) left most of the province unaffected. Of far greater impact was the **second Anglo-Boer War** (1899–1902). As well as the celebrated

Visiting North West Province p.503   The siege of Mafikeng p.515
Mampoer p.512

Highlights

❶ Kgaswane Mountain Reserve High above Rustenburg, in the Magaliesberg mountains, varied trails allow you to hike through savannah, rolling hills and rocky kloofs, and past sparkling streams. **See p.506**

❷ Sun City Las Vegas meets the bushveld at this unique fantasyland of hotels, slot machines, stage shows, elephant safaris, lush golf courses and a fun-filled water park. **See p.506**

❸ Pilanesberg Park The most accessible Big Five park from Johannesburg and Pretoria, with beautiful landscapes in a former volcano crater, and terrific game viewing. **See p.508**

❹ Groot Marico One of the most characterful of South Africa's tiny dorps, or small farming towns, famed for its warm welcome, literary connections and the potency of the local fruit spirit, *mampoer*. **See p.511**

❺ Madikwe Game Reserve An often-overlooked Big Five reserve in the corner of the province; prepare to be pampered in some of South Africa's classiest wildlife lodges. **See p.512**

HIGHLIGHTS ARE MARKED ON THE MAP ON P.502

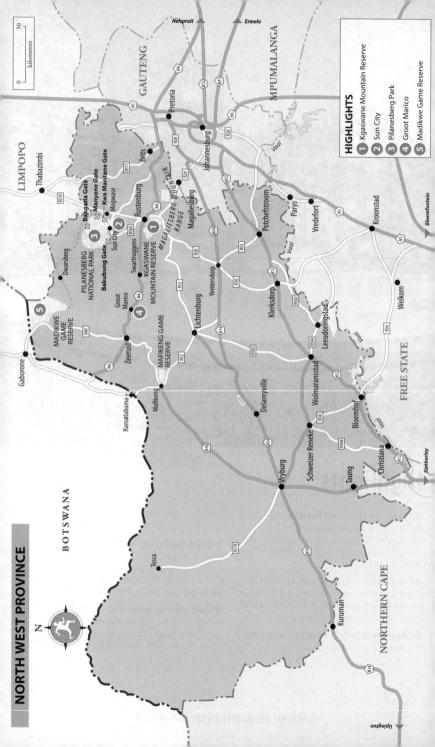

NORTH WEST PROVINCE

HIGHLIGHTS

1. Kgaswane Mountain Reserve
2. Sun City
3. Pilanesberg Park
4. Groot Marico
5. Madikwe Game Reserve

BOTSWANA

LIMPOPO

GAUTENG

MPUMALANGA

FREE STATE

NORTHERN CAPE

Nelspruit

Ermelo

Pretoria

Johannesburg

Thabazimbi

Dwarsberg

Bakgatla Gate

Manyane Gate

Kwa Maritane Gate

Mogwase

Brits

Rustenburg

PILANESBERG NATIONAL PARK

Bakubung Gate

Sun City

Swartruggens

Groot Marico

KGASWANE MOUNTAIN RESERVE

MADIKWE GAME RESERVE

MAGALIESBERG MOUNTAIN RANGE

Magaliesburg

Potchefstroom

Parys

Vredefort

Kroonstad

Welkom

Ventersdorp

Klerksdorp

Leeudoringstad

MAFIKENG GAME RESERVE

Zeerust

Lichtenburg

Mafikeng

Ramatlabama

Gaborone

Delareyville

Wolmaransstad

Bloemhof

Schweizer Reneke

Christiana

Taung

Vryburg

Tosca

Kuruman

Bloemfontein

Kimberley

Upington

Vaal

Vaal

Vaal

N1

N4

N12

N17

N3

N14

R510

R511

R565

R24

R28

R26

R30

R53

R52

R49

R502

R505

R504

R34

R506

R378

N

0   50
kilometres

siege of Mafikeng, where British and Tswana forces held out for 217 days against Afrikaner troops, there were protracted skirmishes up and down the Vaal River. After the British victory, both Afrikaner and Tswana had their lands torched and many were thrown into concentration camps.

The Union Treaty of 1910 left the province, as the western part of the Transvaal, firmly in Afrikaner hands. Its smaller *dorps* soon became synonymous with rural racism, epitomized in the 1980s by the fascistic AWB led by **Eugene Terreblanche**, whose power base was here. In addition, the province played a relatively minor role in the national struggle against apartheid due to the absence of a significant black working class after the migration of many Tswana men to work in the gold mines of the Witwatersrand.

In 1977, the **Bophuthatswana Bantustan** homeland – or "Bop" – was created around Mmabatho in the western part of the province out of the old "native reserves", the poor-quality land into which Tswana had been forced. Far from being a long-awaited "independent" homeland for the blacks in this area, Bop proved to be a confusing amalgamation of enclaves, ruled by the corrupt **Lucas Mangope**, who grew rich on the revenues from **Sol Kerzner**'s casinos in Sun City and Mmabatho and the discovery of platinum. Bophuthatswana's short life came to an end in March 1994, a month before South Africa's elections, when its army mutinied. Mangope called in hundreds of armed AWB neo-fascists to help quell the uprising, but the AWB – and Mangope – were ingloriously defeated.

The mining industry continues to dominate the province's economics, but in recent years there have been frequent and violent miners' strikes, most infamously in 2012 at the Lonmin mine in the Marikana area near Rustenburg. Forty-four people were killed there, thirty-four of them by the South African Police, in the **Marikana massacre**, the worst case of state violence against civilians since the Sharpeville shootings in 1960.

8

Bojanala Region

Bordering Gauteng, **Bojanala Region** lies in North West Province's northeastern bushveld and is a popular weekend destination for Jo'burgers. One of the more distinctive parts of this largely empty and flat province is the **Magaliesberg mountain range**, which gets its name from the Tswana chief **Mogale** of the Kwena clan. Kwena people lived here from the seventeenth century until 1825, when most of them were forced out by the Ndebele chief **Mzilikazi**. Afrikaner farmers continued the process of eviction, and today the dispossession and expulsion of the Kwena in the Magaliesberg is complete.

Great chunks of the Magaliesberg have been fenced off and turned into time-shares or resorts, but there are oases of unspoilt nature, in particular **Kgaswane Mountain Reserve**, accessed from the region's main town, **Rustenburg**; preserved in something like its previous natural state, it is well stocked with wildlife. Further north, occupying an ancient volcanic crater, is the outstanding **Pilanesberg National Park** – the "Big Five" mainstay of Gauteng-based safari operators. If you're in the mood for a fun-in-the-sun water park and some surreal tourist opulence, **Sun City** is worth checking out, if only as a stopover on your way to Pilanesberg.

VISITING NORTH WEST PROVINCE

Relentless sun alleviated only by torrential rain makes **summer** in North West Province something of an endurance test: aim to come here in **spring** or **autumn**. For the more adventurous, **camping** in the quiet and timeless veld is especially rewarding in this part of South Africa. **Tourist information** for the province is provided by the North West Parks & Tourism Board (☎ 0861 111 866, ⓦ tourismnorthwest.co.za); its website has information and links to all of the region's parks. **Malaria** is absent throughout the province.

Rustenburg

Some 120km northwest of Johannesburg lies the dreary platinum-mining town of **RUSTENBURG**, the oldest town in the former Western Transvaal. With its grid of prefabricated chain stores and shopping malls, the place is eminently missable. Still, you may end up having to stay if you're visiting the glorious Kgaswane Mountain Reserve, 7km south of town.

Rustenburg's historic centre is limited to two blocks of Burger Street, from Nelson Mandela Drive to Oliver Tambo Drive. Here you'll find two churches: the old **Anglican church**, dating from 1871, and the 1850 **Dutch Reformed church**. Facing the latter is the graceful 1935 town hall and a **statue of Paul Kruger** by French sculptor Jean Georges Achard, showing the president in his last days in exile in France, sitting grumpily in an armchair. After a quick tour round these few low-key sites, head to the gleaming 160-shop **Waterfall Mall** (Mon–Fri 9am–6pm, Sat 9am–5pm, Sun 9am–1pm; ⓦ waterfallmall.co.za), 5km east of town (follow Nelson Mandela Drive), for the province's best shopping.

ARRIVAL AND DEPARTURE

By bus and minibus taxi None of the major bus companies has scheduled stops in Rustenburg. Long-distance minibus taxis and the daily Bojanala bus (☎ 014 565 6550, ⓦ bojanalabus.co.za) from Mafikeng (3hr, not via Groot Marico) arrive at the terminal at the western end of Nelson Mandela Drive by Beneden St. Long-distance minibus taxis depart regularly, covering most of the province, including Groot Marico (1hr 30min; take the Zeerust taxi) and Mafikeng (3hr 30min), and also go to Lesotho (daily; 9hr). Bays are clearly marked with destinations, and tickets are available on the buses; it's best to check your options the day before you travel. When leaving the bus terminal, avoid its dodgy northern section.

By car Car rental is available from Avis at 56a Von Wielligh St (☎ 014 592 9902, ⓦ avis.co.za).

INFORMATION

Tourist information The excellent tourist information office has friendly staff and maps and brochures for attractions and hotels across the province; it's 2km from the centre at the eastern entrance of town, in a small compound on Kloof Rd, between Nelson Mandela Drive and Fatima Bhayat St (Mon–Fri 8am–4.30pm, Sat 8am–noon; ☎ 014 597 0904, ✉ tidcrust@mweb.co.za).

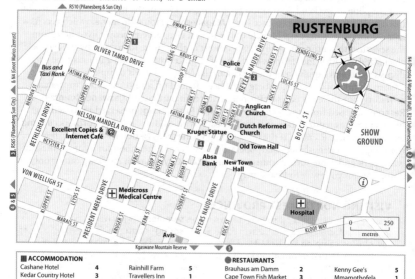

■ ACCOMMODATION			
Cashane Hotel	4	Rainhill Farm	5
Kedar Country Hotel	3	Travellers Inn	1
Palm Lodge	2		

● RESTAURANTS			
Brauhaus am Damm	2	Kenny Gee's	5
Cape Town Fish Market	3	Mmamothofela	1
Hartley's	4		

ACCOMMODATION

You'll get the most out of the area by staying out of town. You can camp at Kgaswane Mountain Reserve (see p.506), and there are dozens of rural (and sometimes quite flashy) B&Bs and resorts in the surrounding countryside – you'll find a selection online at ⊚ rustenburgaccommodation.co.za . There's safe parking at all the following recommendations.

Cashane Hotel 66 Steen St ☎014 592 8541, ⊕ cashanehotel@telkomsa.net. A well-kept hotel on six floors, with comfortable, well-equipped rooms and views over town. Built in 1968, it was Rustenburg's first multistorey building, and has a good bar with pub food. R500

Kedar Country Hotel 20km northwest of town in Boshoek, 500m off the R565 to Sun City ☎014 573 3218, ⊕ kedar.co.za. Set amid plentiful game and birdlife, this lovingly restored farmhouse once belonged to President Kruger, who's honoured by a small museum. The luxurious Afrikaner-style decor makes for a refreshingly tranquil rural getaway, and there's also a swimming pool, plus two suites with private plunge pools. Doubles R1130, suites R8525

Palm Lodge 99 Beyers Naude Drive ☎014 597 2520, ⊕ palmrtb.co.za. A large thatch-roofed complex appearing swankier than it is, with dozens of small, dark rooms, one-bedroom self-catering units, a swimming pool, two bars and a restaurant. R500

Rainhill Farm 4km southwest of town; follow Bethlehem Drive, turn right on Brink St, left on Watsonia Rd, right at the end ☎014 592 8911, ⊕ rainhill.co.za. Four charming rooms in 1940s chalets decked out with antiques, perfect for families or honeymooners. Catch a minibus taxi to Rustenburg Kloof. R560

★ **Travellers Inn** 99 Leyds St ☎014 592 7658, ⊕ travellersinn.co.za. Offering good modern rooms, with a large poolside dorm for backpackers. There's a lovely rustic bar and superb food, all a short walk from the town centre and bus stop. Gay and lesbian couples welcome. Breakfast R90 extra. Dorm R200, double R500

EATING, DRINKING AND NIGHTLIFE

Rustenburg is dominated by fast-food joints: Nelson Mandela Drive and Fatima Bhayat St have plenty, while there are more appealing restaurants at some of the hotels and in the Waterfall Mall. There are some good spots for traditional African food, including the food stands in and around the bus terminal (although exercise caution in all of these areas day and night).

★ **Brauhaus am Damm** R24, 18km from Rustenburg ☎087 802 5519, ⊕ brauhaus.co.za. Set up by descendants of German immigrants from nearby Kroondal, this brewery restaurant can be found beside Olifantsnek lake, along the main route to Jo'burg – it's especially popular at weekends. Six types of tasty German beer are brewed here (half a litre costs R32), and you can also buy it bottled to take away. The beer is served with tasty food, such as a meat and cheese platter (R80), or fried noodles, known as *spaetzle* (R35). Call ahead for the one-hour brewery tours (R50 including tasting and a glass). Tues–Sat 11am–11pm, Sun 10am–4pm.

Cape Town Fish Market Waterfall Mall, 1 Augrabies Ave ☎014 537 3663, ⊕ ctfm.co.za. This quality chain restaurant is one of the best food options in the mall, with good fresh fish dishes, sushi and bento boxes. Daily 11am–11pm.

Hartley's *Rainhill Farm* (see above) ☎014 594 1992. Tranquil, country-style pub and family restaurant. The pub area is called *The Milk Shed*, while *The Pack House* is the more formal, non-smoking restaurant. The food at both (R55–90) ranges from ribs and steaks to prawns and seafood platters – don't miss the farm's famous orange marmalade. Daily noon–10pm.

Kenny Gee's 67 Brink St, corner of Kock St ☎014 592 8079, ⊕ kennygees@telkomsa.net. The best central-ish option, this non-chain restaurant serves good breakfasts (from R37), a feta chicken avocado grill (R76) and banana cinnamon pancakes (R29). There's modest partying too, with live music on Wednesday and Fridays. Mon–Fri 6.45am–8pm, Sat 8am–2pm.

Mmamothofela Boom St, Bafokeng Plaza, ☎014 592 9527. The best traditional African fast food option in town, though you can also get an English breakfast for R30. Lunch includes stew, steak and chicken served with *pap*, *samp* and beans, rice and vegetables (all around R45) – the R600 beef & chicken kebab platter will feed a family. Mon–Sat 6.30am–4pm.

DIRECTORY

Banks Absa at Waterfall Mall has an exchange office.
Emergencies Private ambulance (Netcare) ☎014 568 4338 or ☎082 911; ambulance ☎014 556 2073; fire ☎014 590 3334; police ☎014 590 4111.
Health Doctors and dentists are available at Medicross

Medical Centre, on the corner of President Mbeki Drive and Von Wielligh St ☎014 523 5100.
Internet Excellent Copies & Internet Café, Nelson Mandela Drive, on the corner of President Mbeki Drive.

8

Kgaswane Mountain Reserve

7km south of Rustenburg • Daily: April–Aug 6am–6pm; Sept–March 5.30am–7.30pm • R30, plus R10 per vehicle • ☏ 014 533 2050,
Ⓦ tourismnorthwest.co.za/kgaswane

Kgaswane Mountain Reserve spans a spectacular forty-square-kilometre portion of the Magaliesberg and is dotted with rock formations, created by millennia of erosion, areas of dry veld and streams coursing through the valleys. The reserve's unique **flora** includes aloes indigenous to the Magaliesberg and the discreet *frithiapulchra*, a succulent with only its leaf tips exposed, flowering between November and March. The many crags are perfect for predatory **birds**; keep a lookout for the rare black eagle, Martial eagle and Cape vulture, as well as parrots and paradise flycatchers. Kgaswane is also home to eight hundred **antelopes**, representing most of South Africa's species, and also zebras. Predators are few in number and limited to caracal, aardwolf, black-backed jackals and the elusive leopard.

The reserve can be explored on foot or by bicycle (bring your own). There are two short trails for day hikes: the 5km **Peglarae Trail** follows a relatively easy path through rocky terrain and takes in most of the reserve's best features and views, while the shorter and flatter **Vleiramble Trail** (2km) leads to a viewing hut on the *vlei* (grassy valley) that is popular with birders. Longer walks follow the **Rustenburg Hiking Trail** (19.5km or 23.5km) and last two days and two nights.

ARRIVAL AND INFORMATION   KGASWANE MOUNTAIN RESERVE

By car You'll need your own vehicle to reach the reserve: take the R24 from central Rustenburg towards Johannesburg and turn right at the traffic lights just after the Waterfall Mall (or just before the mall when coming from Jo'burg), and follow the road up the hill, turning left onto the signposted road to the reserve gate. Or follow Beyers Naude St southwest across the highway and keep following Helen Joseph St. From here, the road winds dramatically up to the visitor centre in a broad valley near the mountaintop.

Information The Visitor Centre is in the middle of the park (can be closed in winter; check at the entrance gate), stocking useful maps and information on hikes and trails.

ACCOMMODATION

Campsite ☏ 014 5332050, Ⓦ tourismnorthwest .co.za/kgaswane. The visitor centre has sheltered camping, a cottage sleeping 5, and braai facilities that are open year-round; there's no shop so bring all supplies you need. In winter, count on very cold nights. Camping R80, cottage R500

Sun City

Day visitors R60 • ☏ 011 780 7810, Ⓦ suncity.co.za

A surreal pocket of high-rise hotels and tinkling gaming machines in the endless bushveld, **SUN CITY** consists of four hotel resorts tightly packed together with golf courses, a water park and various other attractions. When entrepreneur Sol Kerzner began building the vast complex in the 1970s, the area was part of the Bophuthatswana Bantustan and therefore one of the few places in the country where you could **gamble** legally. Thousands visited from "across the border" to sample Kerzner's blend of gaming, topless shows and over-the-top hotels. However, now that gambling is legal in South Africa, Sun City has altered its focus, promoting itself these days as a **family destination** – indeed, if you have kids to entertain, this is an excellent place to bring them. The resort also makes a good base for exploring Pilanesberg National Park.

Cabanas and Waterworld

Daily 10am–5pm

Animal World, at the *Cabanas* hotel, is the area that young kids will enjoy most: it has a small zoo, horseriding, a crèche, an aviary with summer flying displays by hawks, falcons and owls, and a crocodile sanctuary, where you can feed the hungry denizens at 4.30pm. Behind it is **Waterworld**, a large artificial lake used for a range of watersports, from parasailing to waterskiing.

Entertainment Centre

Daily 10am–2am

The **Entertainment Centre** next to the towering triangle of *Cascades* hotel is the focal point of Sun City, with rows of bleeping slot machines and arcade games, a cinema, upmarket shops, and a concert hall hosting various musical acts and other events. Next to the Entertainment Centre you'll find an aviary, tennis courts, health spa and the renowned Gary Player Country Club golf course (green fee R790–890; book well in advance as a waiting list of several months is not uncommon).

Lost City and Valley of Waves

Valley of Waves daily: early May & mid-June to Aug 10am–5pm (closed mid-May to mid-June); Sept–April 9am–6pm • R120–150, free if you're staying at one of the hotels • **Palace Tour** 11.30am–4pm 8 daily departing from the Welcome Centre • R60

The **Lost City** is the resort's showpiece, separated from the rest of the complex by the vibrating Bridge of Time. Inside is the **Valley of Waves**, a gigantic water park designed to look like a beach, complete with sand, palm trees, three water slides and a machine producing 2m-high breakers suitable for surfing. Deeper into the acres of specially planted rainforest above the Valley, you'll find waterfalls, trickling streams and a network of explorable paths, all interspersed with "remains" of the Lost City. Overlooking the whole scene is the staggering *Palace of the Lost City* (see below); you can pop in for a drink if you're not staying, or join a *Palace* tour for a more thorough look.

ARRIVAL AND DEPARTURE   SUN CITY

8

By car Driving from Pretoria or Jo'burg, follow the N4 past the Brits turn-off, and turn right onto the R556, from where it's roughly 70km. There's parking near the Welcome Centre, though when it's busy day visitors use the vast car park by the main gate and hop on a monorail train to the Welcome Centre.

By minibus taxi Regular minibus taxis from Rustenburg to Mogwase pass the Sun City entrance, and daily shuttle

buses operated by Ingelosi Tours (R400 one way; ☎ 012 546 3827, ⓦ ingelositours.co.za) drive from OR Tambo International Airport, Sandton and Pretoria.

On a day-trip A large number of operators in Pretoria and Jo'burg (see p.477) offer day tours here; expect to pay at least R400–500, plus R200–350 if combined with a short safari at Pilanesberg.

INFORMATION AND TOURS

Tourist information Sun City's Welcome Centre (Mon–Thurs & Sun 8am–7pm, Fri & Sat 8am–10pm; ☎ 014 557 1544) can provide maps, leaflets and details of special offers. There's also an information desk for the North West Parks & Tourism Board (Mon–Fri 8am–5pm, Sat 9am–4pm, Sun 9am–2pm; ☎ 014 552 2116).

Tours Gametrackers (☎ 014 552 5020, ⓦ gametrac.co.za)

has a desk at the Welcome Centre where you can book game drives, balloon flights and other outdoor activities at the small Letsatsing Game Reserve, a twenty-minute drive from the Welcome Centre. Here, you can do quad biking (R475–745), clay pigeon shooting (R445–735), archery (R270), drumming and dancing lessons (R195). The desk will also arrange all transport out to the reserve.

ACCOMMODATION

Sun City's hotels are all located within a short distance of each other in the centre of the valley. Rooms can be booked through Sun City Reservations (☎ 011 780 7810, ⓦ suninternational.co.za), but will be considerably cheaper if arranged through a tour company as part of a package, or over the internet. All hotels are enormous – *Cascades*, the smallest, has a mere 243 rooms.

Cabanas ☎ 011 780 7810, ⓦ suninternational.co.za. The cheapest accommodation in Sun City, and close to most of the kids' activities, this is the obvious base for families. The rooms are small and somewhat dated, but the atmosphere is relaxed and there's a good indoor pool and reasonably priced restaurants. R2046

Cascades ☎ 011 7807810, ⓦ suninternational.co.za. After the *Palace*, this is the resort's most comfortable place

to stay, though the rooms and service are bland. Next door to the Entertainment Centre, it's a stylish pyramid-shaped high-rise with tropical decor, a mini rainforest and aviary, and outside lifts offering splendid views. The inviting pool and bar are for residents only. R2819

★Palace of the Lost City ☎ 011 780 7810, ⓦ suninternational.co.za. Like something out of an *Indiana Jones* film, the enormous *Palace* is a fantastically opulent and imaginative hotel, designed as a soaring African jungle palace with towers, domes, extravagant carvings and sculptures. Rooms are large and beautifully furnished, and although a stay here is bank-breakingly expensive (you'll find better value elsewhere), the experience is unforgettable. R4172

Sun City Hotel ☎ 011 780 7810, ⓦ suninternational .co.za. The resort's original hotel houses the main casino, so is a good choice if gambling is your main reason for visiting Sun City. The large, balconied rooms have great views and there are four decent restaurants. R3103

EATING, DRINKING AND NIGHTLIFE

The Entertainment Centre has lots of moderately priced restaurants, snack bars, cafés, a casino and a cinema. There's **drinking** and **dancing** at the *Traders* bar and nightclub (admission free) on the upper level of the Entertainment Centre, which is where you'll also find an alcohol-free nightclub for teenagers.

Crystal Court *Palace of the Lost City*. The classically furnished *Crystal Court* hosts two recommended dining experiences: a sumptuous breakfast buffet and afternoon high tea; otherwise there's a buffet on weekdays and à la carte dining on weekends.

Santorini *Cascades Hotel*. This chain restaurant, situated beside the lovely pool at *Cascades*, is known for its affordable, tasty Mediterranean food (R90–200) including Greek *kleftiko*, pitta dishes and pizza.

Pilanesberg Game Reserve

Daily: March, April, Sept & Oct 6am–6.30pm; May–Aug 6.30am–6pm; Nov–Feb 5.30am–7pm • R65, plus R20 per car • ☎ 014 555 1600, ⓦ parksnorthwest.co.za/pilanesberg

Adjacent to Sun City and home to a huge variety of animals, the **PILANESBERG GAME RESERVE** is North West Province's biggest tourist draw. The artificially created reserve was, until 1979, occupied by farmers and the **Tswana** people, who were unceremoniously evicted when **Operation Genesis** saw over six thousand animals shipped in from all over the country to fill the park. Just two to three hours' drive from Pretoria and Jo'burg, Pilanesberg is definitely the place to come to see some game if you're based in Gauteng and have only limited time in South Africa. Like any other game parks, you'll get the most from your visit if you stay in or near the reserve so that you're in the best position to head out at prime game-viewing time: at dawn, before the day visitors arrive.

Don't let the crowds or the managed nature of the place put you off: the park offers game-viewing thrills aplenty, with a good chance of seeing all the **Big Five**, along with hippo, brown hyena, giraffe and zebra. The majority of antelope species are here, too, and there's a vast array of birdlife – over 365 species recorded so far. At night, some fantastic creatures emerge, including civet, porcupine and caracal, though you'll be lucky to spot them. The areas known for popular animals can become congested during the day; the traffic disappears after dark, when only tour buses on night-game drives are allowed in, making this one of the optimum times to visit the park (although be sure to bring warm clothes on winter nights).

Covering some 650 square kilometres, and with 200km of good-quality tar and gravel roads, you'll need at least a full day to do Pilanesberg justice. The reserve is easily explored by car, especially with the official map (for sale at the gates and camp shops). The park's many beautiful hills – the result of an unusual volcanic eruption that occurred 1300 million years ago – are in some ways Pilanesberg's finest feature, though they are often ignored by visitors more interested in scouring their slopes for wildlife. Pilanesberg's natural focus, for visitors and wildlife alike, is the alkaline **Lake Mankwe** ("place of the leopard"), whose goings-on are best observed from several walk-in hides. The various picnic spots and hides dotted around are ideal for breaking the drive – the hides in particular aren't used by many visitors and as a result can be cool, peaceful places to appreciate the natural surroundings. If you're self-driving, don't hesitate to ask the safari jeep drivers for sighting tips; they are all in radio contact with each other and know exactly what's going on.

ARRIVAL AND DEPARTURE

By car There are four entrance gates to the reserve; the most commonly used are Manyane, on the eastern side of the reserve near Mogwase, and Bakubung in the south, just to the west of Sun City off the R565.

By minibus taxi Frequent minibus taxis run the 54km from Rustenburg to Manyane Gate (ask for Mogwase).

On a tour Prices for day-trips from Gauteng average R700–1000 per person on a scheduled tour; private tours start at around R1600 for the day. Rates for overnight trips vary according to where you stay, but expect to pay upwards of R3500. Ulysses Tours & Safaris

PILANESBERG GAME RESERVE

(☎012 653 0018, ⌨ulysses.co.za) is a well-regarded and professionally run upmarket outfit based in Pretoria, which offers day-trips to Pilanesberg every Saturday or otherwise on demand, from R1050, and two-day trips from R4450. While all activities can be booked on arrival, it's best to reserve them in advance either directly or through your lodge to avoid missing out. The special activities organized by Mankwe Gametrackers (see below) can usually be incorporated into trips run by other operators, particularly if you have the flexibility of a private tour.

INFORMATION AND ACTIVITIES

Information At both gates you'll find useful notice boards giving details of wildlife sightings, as well as the excellent official map and park guidebook explaining the various habitats, enabling you to plan your journey around what you most want to see. The Pilanesberg Centre in the middle of the park contains a café, gift shop and open-air restaurant with good pizza and a wonderful terrace overlooking a watering hole usually teeming with less timid wildlife.

Mankwe Gametrackers ☎014 552 5020, ⌨mankwegametrackers.co.za. Sun City's activity operator offers spectacular balloon flights over the park (R3995), day and night game drives (from R475), game walks (R550) and outdoor activities including quad biking (from R465), clay target shooting (from R410), archery (R270), paintball (from R290) and drumming lessons (R180). Pick-ups from some of the resorts and lodges around the park are possible.

ACCOMMODATION

Pilanesberg's accommodation ranges from upmarket lodges where game drives are included in the price, to large, resort-style complexes on the fringes of the park, and cheaper, more basic camps just outside the park gates. Camping is possible at Golden Leopard's *Bakgatla* and *Manyane* resorts. The more luxury lodges usually include all meals, game drives and walks in their rates, or can organize them for you; some may insist on two-night stays at weekends. *Bakubung* and *Kwa Maritane* have shuttle buses every other hour to and from Sun City.

Bakgatla Resort Near Bakgatla Gate at the foot of Garamoga Hills ☎014 555 1045, ⌨goldenleopardresorts.co.za. A large collection of reasonable chalets, safari tents with attached bathrooms and shady verandas, plus a big campsite. There's a decent restaurant and a large pool, too. Camping R180, safari tent R1815

Bakubung Bush Lodge On the southern edge of the park, just west of Sun City ☎014 552 6000, ⌨legacyhotels.co.za. The highlight at this large, modern lodge is the hippo pool, a stone's throw from the restaurant from where you can watch the hippos bathing. The hotel rooms and chalets are pleasant if bland. R4180

Ivory Tree Lodge Near Bakgatla Gate ☎014 556 8100, ⌨ivorytreegamelodge.com. Luxurious lodge with stylish rooms (with en-suite toilets and showers outside), a health spa, conference centre and a rather hotel-like feel. R5136

Kwa Maritane Bush Lodge Near Kwa Maritane Gate ☎014 5525100, ⌨legacyhotels.co.za. A beautiful, upmarket resort in the park's southeast corner near

Pilanesberg Airport. Recently refurbished, it has decent rooms, a good restaurant and a pool with views over to the reserve. R4180

Manyane Resort Just outside Manyane Gate ☎014 555 1000, ⌨goldenleopardresorts.co.za. Low cost and convenience compensate for the distinctly un-bushlike atmosphere of the park's main camp. Stay in thatched chalets with a/c, safari tents or bring a tent or caravan; there's also a bar and restaurant, pool, mini-golf and walking trails. Camping R180, safari tent R1095, chalet R1585

Tshukudu Bush Lodge 8km from Bakubung Gate within the park ☎014 552 6255, ⌨legacyhotels.co.za. Watch big game at the water hole from your veranda at Pilanesberg's most upmarket and exclusive lodge, attractively located on a hilltop with sweeping views. The six picturesque thatched cottages offer luxury accommodation with sunken baths and roaring log fires; there's also a swimming pool. No children under 12. Rates include full board and game drives. R8620

The Central Region

Thanks to its scrawny and desolate dryness, North West Province's Central Region feels especially remote, and there are not all that many towns worth visiting. **Mmabatho**, once the capital of Bophuthatswana and now incorporated into neighbouring **Mafikeng**, the provincial capital, forces reluctant bureaucratic pilgrimages on people from all over the province. The region's appeal lies elsewhere, in the brooding plains and lush river valleys of **Marico** and the rarely visited game reserves, including **Madikwe** on the Botswana border. And then there are the people themselves: local Tswana and Afrikaners are both short on English but long on hospitality, at least to visitors, a trait best experienced at the village of **Groot Marico**, famed nationwide for its *mampoer* peach brandy and quintessentially laidback spirit.

Groot Marico

GROOT MARICO, a tiny, dusty and characterful *dorp* resting contentedly by the banks of the Marico River, just south of the N4 and 90km west of Rustenburg, gained fame through **Herman Charles Bosman**'s short stories based on his time as a teacher here. In mid-October, Groot Marico hosts the literary **Bosman Weekend**, drawing fans of one of South Africa's best-loved authors from far and wide – those unfamiliar with his work should start by reading the hilarious "*In the Withaak's shade*", about an encounter with a leopard.

Although prone to stultifying heat in summer (the best months to visit are March to May and September to November), the hills of the Marico district around the town are good for hiking, and when it all gets too much the river provides cool relief. The water of the **Marico Oog** ("Marico Eye"), a deep spring 20km south of town, is particularly clear and refreshing: festooned with water lilies and surrounded by beautiful dolomitic rocks, it makes a tranquil place for a picnic, and can be paradise for birdwatchers, with over four hundred species recorded here. It's also a favoured spot for scuba divers; contact the town's information centre for more details.

Herman Charles Bosman Living Museum

Kerk St • Daily 8am–6pm • R10 • ☎ 014 503 0085 , ⟨W⟩ marico.co.za • Rondavels and camping from R60

The tourist information centre arranges short tours of the modest **Herman Charles Bosman Living Museum**, a community project with reconstructed mud dwellings, that were common in the area a hundred years ago. There's also a re-creation of the school where Bosman taught, and two charming BaTswana homestead rondavels, where you can stay overnight; book ahead via the information centre to stay in the rondavels or to camp.

ARRIVAL AND INFORMATION   GROOT MARICO

By bus and minibus taxi The Intercape bus from Johannesburg/Pretoria (daily 3–4hr) to Gaborone in Botswana (3hr) drops passengers off at the petrol station at the Groot Marico turn-off along the N4, a shady twenty-minute walk north of the village centre. Minibus taxis travelling along the N4 from Pretoria or Rustenburg to Zeerust or Botswana also stop here.

Information South Africa's most welcoming tourist information centre is on Paul Kruger St (daily sunrise to sunset; ☎ 014 503 0085 or ☎ 083 2722 958, ⟨W⟩ marico.co.za),

in an enclosure built by Italian POWs in World War II. It's run by a knowledgeable couple who provide a welter of information on the town and its activities, can arrange visits to the nearby Bosman Living Museum, and organize half- and full-day dorp tours which take in a *mampoer* distillery (see box, p.512). Email in advance, and they'll suggest and book suitable accommodation. The room beside the front porch houses an art and crafts shop, selling Tswana cultural artefacts, locally made Afrikaner crafts such as wooden pipes, whips and clocks, and books by Herman Charles Bosman.

ACCOMMODATION AND EATING

The local guesthouses are your best bet for **a meal**, though it's a good idea to book ahead for the day of arrival. The *Groot Marico Bushveld Hotel* on Paul Kruger Street has the pick of the town's **bars**, where white locals, inspired by beer, brandy and their own good humour, have been known to dance traditional Afrikaans two-steps.

8

> ## MAMPOER
>
> According to legend, a Pedi chief by the name of Mampuru introduced the art of distilling peach brandy to the Boers. Named **mampoer** in his honour, the fearsomely strong spirit has inspired locals and visitors alike ever since. In the old days the alcohol content was measured by throwing a chunk of lard into a sample: if it floated halfway, the *mampoer* was perfect. Today, you just hold a match over it – the higher and cleaner the blue flame, the better the brew. Any fruit can be used to make *mampoer*, but peach was the most traditional: until 1878, much of North West Province's farmland grew peach trees solely devoted to this purpose, though disease put an end to that and now most *mampoer* is made with citrus and wildfruit. Things also changed with the ZAR government's distilling tax, and the new licensing system introduced in 1894, when thousands of *mampoer* stills were destroyed. A few, however, escaped detection. A local story recounts that one farmer cleaned out his entire drainage system, but made no attempt to conceal his fifteen barrels of *mampoer*. The inspectors found the barrels, split them open and poured the entire contents down the drain. Meanwhile, the canny farmer had his family stationed in the field where the pipe ended up with every container the household possessed, and managed to recover fourteen of the fifteen barrels.
>
> To **sample** and buy *mampoer*, join a *mampoer* tour organized by Groot Marico's information centre (half day R200, including a farm lunch), or head to Maruthwane Farm (see below) where you can also see demonstrations of how the stuff is made.

Angela's Guest House Fakkel St, between the village and the N4 highway ☏ 014 503 0082, ✉ angela_s @telkomsa.net. *Angela's* has four comfortable en-suite rooms and a self-catering chalet set in a lovely garden and orchard; it can also organize massage and beauty treatments as well as meals. R600

Djembe 3km south of the village ☏ 079 955 8119, ✉ jolenemuir@ymail.com. Groot Marico's backpacker option has comfortable double rooms and a pleasant dorm room. There are shared kitchen facilities for self-caters, or you can book meals. Pickups from the N4 and bike rental are possible. The place comes alive in the evening when travellers gather around the fireplace and the drums come out. Dorm R50, doubles R160

Marico Moon Café and Witchazel's Tea Garden Paul Kruger St, near the information centre ☏ 014 503 0926 or ☏ 072 617 7019. A lovely little lunch café, serving traditional dishes such as shepherd's pie, and fruit salad with Jerepigo wine cream. The tea garden (and nursery) serves light meals, salads, home-made bread rollls and soup, and will prepare picnic baskets. Café Fri–Sun 9am–3pm; open for dinner on request; Tea Garden Tues–Sun 9am–3pm.

Marunthwane Farm 12km west of Groot Marico on the N4 ☏ 083 239 6662. An active game farm with antelope, wild boar and kudu in the bush, and one-hour *mampoer* tasting tours (R30; R60 with lunch). Two chalets overlooking the lawn and three rooms in the farmhouse offer comfortable lodging. R300

River Still Guest Farm 6km south of the village ☏ 083 272 2958, 🌐 riverstill.co.za. Four charming self-catering cottages sleeping 2–8 people, down by the river in a secluded and heavily forested valley, just perfect for birders. Swimming in the river is possible, and there are also canoes for rent and drumming sessions on weekends. R550

Madikwe Game Reserve

Gate fee R55; day visitor R160, including game drive and lunch • ☏ 018 350 9931, 🌐 parksnorthwest.co.za/madikwe

Tucked up in the very north of the province near the Botswana border lies the 765-square-kilometre, malaria-free **MADIKWE GAME RESERVE**, one of South Africa's largest wildlife areas. The reserve was established in 1991 from reclaimed farmland, thanks to **Operation Phoenix**, which saw the reintroduction of over eight thousand animals. Today, Madikwe's largely low-lying plains of woodland and grassland are amply stocked with the Big Five, plus dozens of other mammals, including cheetah, wild dogs, spotted hyena and most of Southern Africa's plains antelopes. Twitchers won't be disappointed, with some 350 bird species recorded so far; the Marico River, on the eastern border, and the *koppies* scattered all around, are particularly rewarding birding areas.

Madikwe remains one of the least known of South Africa's large wildlife areas, even though there are more than twenty **lodges** here. Access is reserved to guests of its lodges and **day visitors**, who must book a package through one of the lodges that includes a **game drive** and lunch; independent day visits are not allowed.

ARRIVAL AND DEPARTURE — MADIKWE GAME RESERVE

By car Road access to Madikwe is normally through Tau Gate, 12km off the R49, although the reserve can also be approached from the east via Molatedi Gate. Whichever approach you take, you'll need to inform your lodge prior to arrival. The park is 360km from Johannesburg.

By plane It's possible to fly to the small airport inside the reserve on the two to three daily flights from Johannesburg which take 45 minutes (around R2500 plus R150 landing fee); book through the lodges or directly with Madikwe Air (T 011 805 4888, W madikwecharters.com) or Federal Air (T 011 395 9000, W fedair.com), which can also arrange private charters. The lodges take care of transport to and from the airport.

ACCOMMODATION

Accommodation rates at all lodges include full board, day and night game drives, and guided bush walks. There is no budget accommodation or camping.

Jaci's Safari Lodge & Tree Lodges T 083 700 2071, W madikwe.com. Two exceptional lodges whose sense of style, comfort and laidback luxury are hard to beat. The *Safari Lodge* overlooks a water hole on the Marico River and has a natural rock swimming pool nearby, while the *Tree Lodges'* rooms are built around trees several metres off the ground. Children welcome. R5950

Madikwe Hills T 018 3509200; reservations T 011 781 5431, W madikwehills.com. Another gem, this one built around a *koppie* close to the riverbank. Rooms are modern and have views over the veld. There are even better views from the sundowner terrace and its small swimming pool, plus there's a gym, spa, childcare facilities and the food is excellent. R10600

Mateya Safari Lodge T 014 778 9200, W mateyasafari.com. Experience the ultimate in bush chic at these five luxurious suites, each boasting its own swimming pool, as well as both indoor and outdoor showers. There's a spa and the lodge's excellent food is best sampled on the terrace overlooking the veld. No children under 16. R14000

★**Mosetlha Bush Camp & Eco Lodge** T 011 444 9345, W thebushcamp.com. Slightly cheaper than Madikwe's other accommodation and offering the most intense wilderness experience. Located in the reserve's centre, there's no perimeter fence here and accommodation is in very simple open-sided log cabins, with no electricity – the hot outdoor showers are delivered by an ingenious donkey boiler and bucket system. What it lacks in luxury it makes up for in atmosphere and expertise, with the emphasis placed on game walks as much as drives. R4190

8

Mafikeng

Mafikeng, 25km south of the Ramatlabama border post with Botswana, 100km from Groot Marico, and also known as Mahikeng, is a shopping and transport hub for the wide area of farmland that surrounds it. The government offices at the former Bophuthatswana capital of **Mmabatho**, now a suburb to the north of town, offer a unique portrait of the vision of apartheid and its deep contradictions. However, Mafikeng remains most famous for Baden-Powell and the Boer siege of 1899–1900 (see box, p.515).

Mafikeng Museum

Martin St • Mon–Fri 8am–4.30pm • Donation • T 018 388 9000

The town's main attraction is the recently renovated **Mafikeng Museum**, housed in the impressive former town hall, which was built in 1902, two years after the siege ended (see box p.515). There's a restored steam locomotive outside, in use from 1901 until 1971 when it pulled the Kimberley–Bulawayo Express. Inside, you'll find San hunting weapons and poisons, and a life-size re-creation of a traditional Tswana hut, complete with its trademark enclosed porch. The siege of Mafikeng is given a room of its own, filled with classic British imperial memorabilia, from weaponry to a wonderful collection of photos. Keep an eye out too for the fascinating exhibit on Mafikeng and the railways, which provides

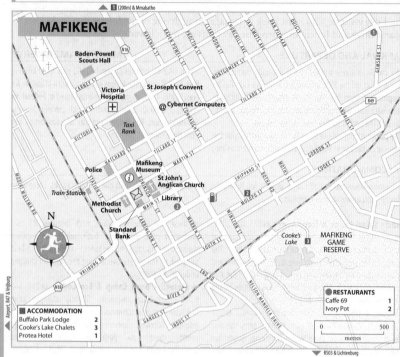

evidence of the connection between their spread from Cape Town and Rhodes' mission to colonize Africa.

Mafikeng Game Reserve

On the eastern edge of town • Daily: May–Aug 7.30am–6pm; Sept–April 7.30am–7pm • R35, plus R5 per car • ☎ 018 397 1675, ⊕ parksnorthwest.co.za/mafikeng_reserve • There are two entrances to the reserve, one 10km east of Mafikeng along the R49 towards Zeerust, the other 2km from the town centre, southeast along the R503.

The 48-square-kilometre **Mafikeng Game Reserve** is worth a quick drive around for its acacia-strewn bushveld landscape and herbivorous plains game, including white rhino and buffalo. Cooke's Lake, in the reserve's western corner next to town, is a good spot for waxbill, colourful finches, waterfowl and mongooses (and the snakes they prey on).

ARRIVAL   MAFIKENG

By bus and minibus taxi None of the major intercity bus companies serves Mafikeng, but Atamelang (☎ 018 381 2680) runs a daily service to and from Johannesburg (3hr), while Bojanala Bus (☎ 014 565 6550) crawls once a day to and from Rustenburg (3hr). There are minibus taxis to most destinations within the province, as well as two to three daily services to Kimberley (5hr). The hassle-free bus and minibus taxi terminal can be found between Victoria and Hatchard Streets on the northern side of town.

ACCOMMODATION, EATING AND DRINKING

Mafikeng is no culinary paradise, and your best option for good food is to eat at one of the hotels or fast-food joints scattered across town. Walking around at night is not recommended and, as Mafikeng lacks a telephone taxi service, unless you have wheels or can find a local to accompany you, nightlife is limited to within a block or two of your hotel.

THE SIEGE OF MAFIKENG

Mafikeng was besieged within three days of the start of the **second Anglo-Boer War** (1899–1902) by generals Snyman and Cronje. **Colonel Robert Baden-Powell** (founder of the Boy Scouts) had the task of defending the town. This he did for 217 days, from October 16, 1899, until May 17, 1900, when relief arrived from Rhodesia and from the south. In the process, Baden-Powell became a British household name and hero, and the exuberant scenes of jubilation in London that greeted news of the relief gave rise to a new word in the English language: **maffick**, which meant to celebrate unduly.

Strategically, Mafikeng was irrelevant to the war; Baden-Powell's real achievement was to distract the six thousand Afrikaners besieging the town from fighting elsewhere. He relied heavily on the **Barolong** people for defence, labour and reconnaissance, but failed to record this either in his dispatches to London or in his memoirs, despite the fact that four hundred Barolong lost their lives during the siege – twice as many as British. Some of the British casualties of the siege are marked by white iron crosses in the town's **cemetery** on Carrington Street, next to the railway sidings. Until the 1980s this was a whites-only cemetery, and today it still commemorates only the Europeans who died during the siege. The Barolong also received far fewer rations, and over one thousand subsequently died of starvation; they received none of the £29,000 raised in Britain for the rehabilitation of Mafikeng. To add insult to injury, not one Barolong was decorated for bravery, in contrast to the plentiful medals dished out to the British regiments, and none of the promises Baden-Powell made about land grants to them was ever kept. An important legacy of the involvement of the black population was the diary of the siege kept by **Sol Plaatje**, one of the first black writers to make an impact on English literature, who was later to become a founder member of the South African Native Congress, forerunner to the ANC.

8

Buffalo Park Lodge 59 Molopo St, at the corner of Botha Rd 📞018 381 2159, 🌐buffalolodge.co.za. A family-run place with small, cool and well-kept twin bedrooms with TVs, a good pub-restaurant, and a small swimming pool. Restaurant Mon–Sat 9.30am–9.30pm, Sun 9.30am–6pm. R730

Caffe 69 Corner of Tillard and Gemsbok streets 📞018 381 0700, 🌐caffe69.co.za. This slightly rundown restaurant and bar is the town's main independent restaurant and drinking hole, with reliably good South African and international dishes (steak R85; chicken schnitzel R65), and several beers on tap. There's a DJ, music and dancing at weekends. Mon–Wed 10am–midnight, Thurs–Sat 10am–4am.

Cooke's Lake Chalets Cooke's Lake, access on Nelson Mandela Drive 📞018 386 6380, 🌐goldenleopardresorts.co.za. Near the city centre and overlooking the pretty lake with plenty of birdlife, these beautiful two-storey wood-and-thatch chalets are the most attractive places to stay in Mafikeng. The reception building has a large, average restaurant overlooking the lake too. R800

Ivory Pot 11 Shippard St 📞082 577 8267. Cheap and authentic African meals consisting of meat with *ting* (sour sorghum porridge), *samp* (corn kernels), *pap* or rice, serv ed in a cheerful orange room. Meals cost R32; add a beer for R14 or a home-made ginger soda for R7. Mon–Fri 8am–5pm, Sat 8am-4pm.

Protea Hotel 80 Nelson Mandela Drive 📞018 381 0400, 🌐proteahotels.com. Just north of the centre, Mafikeng's best hotel has comfortable rooms, a good pool, and cheerful staff. Their Mafika restaurant is very good – try the sirloin steak for R120. Restaurant daily noon–10pm. R940

DIRECTORY

Hospital The best hospital in town is the Victoria Private Hospital, in the city centre at Victoria St (📞018 381 2043); it also has on-site walk-in doctors' clinics and a pharmacy, **Internet access** Cybernet Computers, Nelson Mandela Drive, opposite Game Shopping Centre.

Police Corner of Tillard and Carrington streets 📞086 001 0111.
Post The post office is on Carrington St.

Mpumalanga

LEOPARD, SABI SANDS RESERVE

9

Mpumalanga

Mpumalanga, "the land of the rising sun" to its Siswati- and Zulu-speaking
residents, extends east from Gauteng to Mozambique and Swaziland. The
province is synonymous with the Kruger National Park, the real draw of
South Africa's east flank, and one of Africa's best game parks. Kruger
occupies most of Mpumalanga and Limpopo's borders with Mozambique, and covers
over 20,000 square kilometres – an area the size of Israel or El Salvador.
Unashamedly populist, Kruger is the easiest African game park to drive
around on your own, with many well-run restcamps for accommodation. On
its western border lie a number of private reserves and game farms, called
the Greater Kruger, offering the chance – at a price – to escape the Kruger
crush, with well-informed rangers conducting safaris in open vehicles.

Apart from the irresistible magnet of big-game country, Mpumalanga also has some
spectacular scenery in the mountainous area known as the **Escarpment**, usually
passed through en route to Kruger. The most famous viewpoints – **God's Window**,
Bourke's Luck Potholes and **Three Rondavels** – are along the lip of the Escarpment,
the best of which is the Potholes. Descending the Escarpment on one of four
mountain passes takes you into the tropical-fruit-growing and bushveld country of
the **lowveld**, with impressive views back towards the towering massif of the
Escarpment. Nearest to the Blydepoort Dam at the base of the Escarpment is the
service centre of **Hoedspruit** (actually in Limpopo Province, but covered here
because of its proximity to Kruger) with its own airport, a jumping-off point for
safaris in the central and northern section of the park, as well as a number of private
game reserves. Note that **malaria** (see p.70) is a potential hazard in the lowveld and
Kruger, particularly in summer.

There is great pressure on the land that lies between the mountains and Kruger: you'll
see stretches of commercial tropical fruit farms, and very populous areas that were
allocated for Sotho, Shangaan and Tsonga speakers during Apartheid, where thousands
of very poor people live harsh rural lives. Between here and the park itself lies a thick
buffer of private game farms and wildlife reserves. Many of these reserves have taken
down the fences that separate them from Kruger and animals roam freely between the
park and the reserves; it is here, in Greater Kruger, that you will find a plethora of safari
lodges and camps, both ultra-luxurious and more reasonably priced ones.

Highlights

❶ Horseriding Head off on horseback to spot wild horses near Nelspruit, or on a big game safari in the Karongwe. **See p.530**

❷ Drive the R40 This road, which takes you along Kruger's western flank, is the best way to experience how rural Shangaan and Tsonga people really live. **See p.534**

❸ Aerial cable trail Glide in a harness through the air, over tree tops and the river, on a 1.2km trail near Hazyview. **See p.534**

❹ Brushing an elephant Enjoy a close encounter grooming an elephant or walking hand-in-trunk, at the Hazyview Elephant

Sanctuary. **See p.535**

❺ African meals at the Shangana Cultural Village Sample crocodile and unusual vegetables, cooked over open fires, and watch stirring traditional dances. **See p.536**

❻ Walking safaris in Kruger It's worth leaving behind the security of a vehicle for the thrill of potential close encounters with animals. **See p.539**

❼ Leopard-spotting The luxury camps in the Sabi Sands Game Reserve offer excellent opportunities to observe leopards. **See p.549**

HIGHLIGHTS ARE MARKED ON THE MAP ON P.521

9

VISITING KRUGER NATIONAL PARK

Kruger National Park, stretching for 414km along the border with Mozambique, remains South Africa's biggest wildlife draw. The park is administered by the government-run South African National Parks (SANParks; **w** sanparks.org), while on its western flank, thousands of square kilometres of land is divided into privately administered farms and reserves, known as Greater Kruger. As far as animals are concerned, however, the private and public areas are joined in an enormous, seamless whole. How you experience the park – or Greater Kruger – depends to a large extent on what you can afford; at the top end, expect exclusivity and a greater sense of the wilderness, while those on a tight budget may want to consider either a self-drive visit or an organized tour.

Whatever you choose, and whatever your budget, don't get too obsessed with seeing the **Big Five** – wildlife-viewing always involves an element of luck, which is what makes it so addictive, and the very experience of being in Kruger is undeniably exciting in itself.

GETTING TO THE PARK

Johannesburg boasts to the best transport connections to Kruger, with regular flights and buses, as well as organized tours, on offer; if you're planning on self-driving, it makes the best major entry point. Visiting from **Cape Town**, your best option is to fly the two-thousand-odd kilometres to get here – though prices are high as only one airline (SA Airlink; **w** flyairlink.com) offers (daily) flights. Nelspruit, the modern capital of Mpumalanga, boasts the best transport connections in the region, and makes a good jumping-off point for the park; flights arrive into Kruger Mpumalanga International, 20km north of the town. The other airports serving the park are at Hoedspruit, Phalaborwa and Skukuza.

BUDGET AND MID-RANGE OPTIONS

Kruger is designed for **self-driving** and **self-catering**; if you're travelling with young children, on a budget, or want to manage your time in the park yourself, this is likely to be the best way of seeing the park's animals. There are restaurants and shops at each of the camps, and the roads are a mix of tarred and dirt, making it possible to explore a fair amount of Kruger in a normal car, though you may not see a great deal being so low down. The park's popularity does mean that you are likely to share major animal sightings with several other motorists, some of whom may behave badly – hogging the sightings, or making noises to frighten the animals. A number of game drives are run by the park, operating out of each camp, which offer a greater chance of spotting the more elusive animals. On the plus side, it is very exciting when you are able to find animals yourself, and are able to watch them at your leisure. It's also possible to explore Kruger on a walking safari (see box, p.543).

Accommodation in the park can be over-subscribed; if you can't get a place you may want to consider staying in nearby Hazyview or close to an entry gate, where there are well-priced accommodation options, and then either driving into Kruger yourself each day, or taking one of their organized game-drives. Another option is to stay in a backpackers' lodge in Nelspruit, Hazyview or Phalaborwa, all of which offer their own trips into the park; alternatively you can take a three to four day trip with a tour operators from Johannesburg (see box, p.542).

LUXURY OPTIONS

With more to spend, choosing a private reserve in Greater Kruger is the obvious choice (and it's worth noting that some are more reasonably-priced than others). The three major private reserves are **Sabi Sands** (to the south; see p.549), and **Timbavati** and **Manyeleti**, both of which adjoin the central section of the national park (see p.549). With no tarred roads, and no self-driving, the private reserves offer a much greater sense of the wilderness, and you can be assured that you won't be sharing your sightings with a bunch of other cars. Accommodation is often in very romantic rooms or luxury "tents", overlooking the savannah or a river, and you'll be taken out on game drives in comfortable, open-topped 4WDs, with plenty of information and photo opportunities provided. Several of the luxury camps also cater for children, offering special kids' safaris and activities.

The Escarpment

Four hours' drive east of Johannesburg International Airport is one of the city's favoured mountain retreats: the waving grasslands and luxury guesthouses of the Mpumalanga Drakensberg, generally known as the **Escarpment**. While most travellers visit the region purely because of its proximity to Kruger National Park, it provides some of the most dramatic views in the country, which can be enjoyed with little effort, even if you are simply passing through en route to the park. This tour of these highlands, known as the **Panorama Route**, can also be taken as an organized day-trip by numerous tour operators in Nelspruit (see p.528). The main draw of the Escarpment is

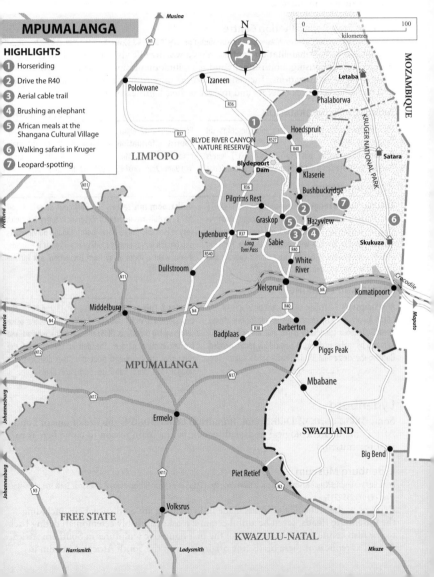

MPUMALANGA

HIGHLIGHTS

1. Horseriding
2. Drive the R40
3. Aerial cable trail
4. Brushing an elephant
5. African meals at the Shangana Cultural Village
6. Walking safaris in Kruger
7. Leopard-spotting

9

the **Blyde River Canyon**, whose dizzying views into one of the world's great gorges appear in countless South African tourist brochures, though it is often overshadowed by the allure of the game on the plains below.

Dullstroom

Unless your passion is fly-fishing, chances are you'll find the crossroads settlement of **DULLSTROOM**, some 209km east of Johannesburg, as unexciting as its name suggests, though it can be a useful place to stop on your way to Kruger National Park. The town is often proclaimed as "a drinking town with a fishing problem" – unsurprisingly, you'll find a thriving pub life here.

Birds of Prey Rehabilitation Centre

1km outside Dullstroom on the R540 • Daily 9am–4pm • R50 • Demonstrations daily 10.30am & 2.30pm • ☎ 076 557 7069, ⊛ birdsofprey.co.za

The **Birds of Prey Rehabilitation Centre** makes a worthwhile visit and is exclusively devoted to the housing, nourishment and rehabilitation of raptors, with very good daily flying demonstrations. The centre offers the opportunity to see magnificent eagles and other birds of prey close up and marvel at their lightness and agility.

ARRIVAL AND INFORMATION   DULLSTROOM

By car Dullstroom is 260km from Johannesburg's OR Tambo airport (3hr).

By bus City to City bus (☎ 015 781 1037) leaves Johannesburg Station daily at 8am, arriving at Tonteldoos Restaurant at 12.30pm.

Tourist information Auldstone House, on the main road, Naledi Drive (Mon–Fri 9am–5pm, Sat 9am–4.30pm, Sun 9am–2pm; ☎ 013 254 0254, ⊛ dullstroom.biz).

ACCOMMODATION

Critchley Hackle Lodge Teding van Berkhout St ☎ 013 254 0149, ⊛ urbanhiphotels.com. A gracious, country-style hotel, offering stone and brick cottages, each with a fireplace, and a veranda with outdoor seating. Facilities include a restaurant, a bar for after-dinner cognac, and there's also a patio for tea and scones. R2270

Dullstroom Inn Teding van Berkhout St ☎ 013 254 0071, ⊛ dullstroom.net. A Victorian country inn, with very reasonably priced floral rooms, though no views. Its pub (which serves hearty food) gets packed at weekends; if you want a room away from the action, ask for the annexe. R785

EATING AND DRINKING

Mrs Simpson's 94 Teding van Berkhout St ☎ 013 254 0088. An always busy country restaurant for fine dining. Their Dullstroom trout with garlic and almonds (R115), followed by malva pudding, is particularly recommended. Booking ahead essential. Mon & Thurs–Sat 11.30am–3pm & 7–10pm, Sun 11.30am–3pm.

Pickles & Things 86 Naledi Drive ☎ 013 254 0115. The best place in town for (fair-trade) coffee, this popular place serves up big breakfasts (R65) and home-made bread, and has an inviting garden. The deli at the front of the restaurant stocks smoked trout and other delicacies like nougat. Mon, Wed–Sun 7am–5pm, Tues 7am–3pm.

Lydenburg

Some 58km north of Dullstroom, humdrum **LYDENBURG** is the site of one of South Africa's major archeological finds; subsequently, the main reason to come here is to visit the museum.

Lydenburg Museum

In the Gustav Klingbiel Nature Reserve, 3km out of town along the R37 to Sabie • Mon–Fri 9am–noon & 2–4.15pm, Sat & Sun 10am–4pm • Free • ☎ 013 235 2213

Replicas of the archeological finds made in Lydenburg are on display here, including the **Lydenburg Heads**, seven beautiful ceramic masks (probably ceremonial) dating back to the fifth century, which are some of the first figurative sculptures in Southern Africa. As well as replicas of these heads (the originals are in the South African Museum in

---

ADVENTURE ACTIVITIES IN SABIE

With its forest, massive gorge and mountains, the Escarpment offers good opportunities for adventure activities. Among the operators running a range of these is Sabie Xtreme Adventures, based at *Sabie Backpackers Lodge* (see below). The activities on offer include **rockclimbing**, **caving by candlelight** in the Lone Creek Caves, **waterfall abseiling** at the Sabie Falls, **whitewater tubing** and **canyoning**.

Induna Adventures is recommended (Sabie Rd; Mon–Sun 8am–5pm; ☎013 737 8308/1, ⓦindunaadventures.com) for **river rafting** on the Sabie River; its half-day trip (R400) takes three hours, on Grade 2 and 3 rapids. It also specializes in mountain biking, taking you through forests and pine and eucalyptus plantations, crossing the Mac Mac and Sabie rivers several times (R400 for 90mins).

Cape Town; see p.96), there are excellent displays on human activity in the vicinity over the past million years or so.

Sabie and around

Lying on the R37 beyond Long Tom Pass, **SABIE** (pronounced "Saabie", like the car) is the centre of Mpumalanga's agroforestry industry. The extensive pine plantations that cover the surrounding hills look monotonous compared to the rich, jungly variety of the remaining pockets of indigenous woodland. It is a missable town, worthwhile as a stop only for the activities on offer in the surrounding area – Sabie is one of the best places in the country for mountain biking, valued for the intensity of the climbs and technical complexity of the trails.

Numerous **waterfalls** drop down the slopes outside Sabie. Just 7km from town, down the Old Lydenburg Road, you can visit three of the most impressive: **Bridal Veil**, **Horseshoe** and, appropriately at the end of the road, **Lone Creek Falls**. The loveliest of the three, Lone Creek is reached down a paved path that crosses a river and works its way back to the car park.

Mac Mac Falls

Falls 13km north of the town along the Graskop Rd • R10 • **Pools** 11km north of town • R10

The most visited of the falls around Sabie are the spectacular 65m **Mac Mac Falls**, named after the many people of Scottish descent who died looking for gold in the area and whose names appear on dozens of tombstones in the vicinity. While you can't swim in the inviting waterfall pool at the base of the falls, there is a river pool at the **Mac Mac Pools**, 2km before you reach the falls themselves, where there's also a picnic and braai area, and the 3km **Secretary Bird walking trail**.

ARRIVAL AND INFORMATION   SABIE AND AROUND

Sabie is 60km from Nelspruit on a windy road, often slowed down by logging trucks.

By bus Public transport to Sabie is limited to minibus taxis plying the routes from neighbouring towns.

Tourist information There are two information offices in the village, the best of which is on Market Square (Mon–Fri 9am–5pm, Sat 9am–1pm; ☎013 767 1833, ⓦsabie .co.za).

ACCOMMODATION

Hillwatering Country House 50 Marula St ☎013 764 1421, ⓦhillwatering.co.za. Renovated 1950s home with four large bedrooms, each with its own veranda, overlooking the Bridal Veil Falls. The reception is warm and breakfast excellent. R880

Merry Pebbles Holiday Resort 2km west from the centre on the Old Lydenburg Rd ☎013 764 2266,

ⓦmerrypebbles.com. Go for the newer units at this resort, which offers camping as well as self-catering and en-suite chalets. The facilities include a lovely, big heated pool and a children's playground. Camping R190, chalet R1000

Sabie Backpackers Lodge 185 Main Rd ☎013 764 2118, ⓦsabiextreme.co.za. A well-run, fun hostel, with camping, dorms and doubles, featuring sturdy beds and

9

warm bedding. There's also accommodation for two in a tree house. Xtreme Adventures, based here, organizes a host of adventure activities (see box, p.523), and the lodge

has good weekend packages available, with wall-to-wall adventure activities. Camping R70, dorm R120, double R260

EATING AND DRINKING

The Wild Fig Tree On the corner of Main and Louis Trichardt sts ☎013 764 2239. South African dishes and venison including ostrich, kudu (R90) and crocodile are the speciality at this pleasant restaurant, the best in town, with a wide deck to make the most of the weather. Daily 8.30am–8.30pm.

Woodsman Restaurant On the corner of Main and Mac Mac rds ☎013 764 2204. A licensed restaurant with a beer garden, serving Greek Cypriot food, including vegetarian *meze* (R60) plus local specialities such as ostrich and trout. Also good for coffee and snacks on the terrace, or by the cosy fire in winter. Daily 7.30am–9pm.

Pilgrim's Rest

Hiding in a valley 35km north of Sabie, **PILGRIM'S REST**, an almost too-perfectly restored gold-mining town, is an irresistible port of call for tour buses. With a collection of red-roofed, corrugated-iron buildings, including the characterful *Royal Hotel* brimming with Victoriana, the place is undeniably photogenic. But you can't help feeling there's little substance behind the romanticized gold-rush image, especially when the village nods off after 5pm once the day-trippers have been spirited away. If you do want to visit a real gold mine, you're best off heading to Barberton (see p.533).

Pilgrim's Rest stretches along its one main road and is divided into Uptown and Downtown. Commercialized **Uptown** has the greatest concentration of shops and restaurants and draws the bulk of tourists; **downtown**, just 1km to the west, has a more down-to-earth atmosphere. Apart from souvenir hunting and lingering in the cafés and tea shops, the main activity in Pilgrim's Rest is visiting its handful of **museums**, and the place to absorb the history best is at the old cemetery, where the losses tell their own story.

Brief history

Pilgrim's Rest owes its origins to South Africa's first **gold rush**, which predates the uncovering of the great Gauteng seams. In 1873, Alex "Wheelbarrow" Patterson discovered gold here, though his attempts to keep his discovery secret were a total failure, and by the end of the year Patterson had been joined by 1500 diggers frantically working four thousand claims. Many diggers arrived malnourished, suffering from dysentery and malaria after punishing journeys. Those who survived could expect drab lives in tents or, if they struck lucky, more permanent wattle-and-daub huts. Mining slowed right down a hundred years later, and Pilgrim's Rest was declared a historic monument in the 1980s.

Diggings Site Museum

Graskop Rd · Guided tours only, daily at 10am, 11am, noon, 2pm & 3pm · R20, buy tickets from the tourist office (see opposite)

To get an authentic impression of the gold-mining days, head for the open-air **Diggings Site Museum** on the eastern edge of town, where you can see demonstrations of alluvial gold-panning and get a guided tour around the bleak diggers' huts and the remnants of workings and machinery from the early mining days.

Alanglade House Museum

Main St · Guided tours only, daily 11am & 2pm · R20, buy tickets from the tourist office (see opposite)

If you want to see how mine owners and managers lived, visit **Alanglade**, the reconstructed home of the former general manager of the mine, just west of the Downtown area. The house has a wonderful collection of early twentieth-century British fashion and decorative arts and reveals a sheltered way of life far removed from either Africa or mining.

ARRIVAL AND INFORMATION
PILGRIM'S REST

By car Pilgrim's Rest is 41km from Sabie and is easily accessed by car on the exceptionally winding R532, or on the R535 from Graskop, 17km away.
By minibus taxis There are no scheduled buses; minibus taxis run here from Sabie and Graskop.

Tourist information Signposted on the main road in Uptown, close to the *Royal Hotel* (daily 9am–12.45pm, 1.45–4pm; ☎013 768 1060, ⓦpilgrims-rest.co.za); tickets for local museums can be bought here.

ACCOMMODATION

Pilgrim's Rest has a few restaurants and teashops that provide for the daily influx of visitors, all situated along the main road and, apart from the hotel, open only during daytime. Catering for the tourist trade, the food is nothing to write home about.

Royal Hotel Main St, Uptown ☎013 768 1100, ⓦroyal-hotel.co.za. Atmospheric hotel that dates back to the gold-rush days and brims with Victoriana, with

guests mostly accommodated in restored houses on the main road. A visit to the pub is essential. R900

EATING AND DRINKING

Peach Tree Creek Restaurant Royal Hotel, Main St, Uptown ☎013 768 1100. The nicest place in town, where you can take in the historical atmosphere while having a steak and salad (R120) or an English breakfast. A visit to the colonial-styled pub *Church Bar* is mandatory

at any time of day. Daily 8am–9pm.
Stable Café Main St, Uptown ☎013 768 1061. Enjoy a beer or glass of wine with traditional South African food like *bobotie* and rice (R55) or fried doughnut balls (*vetkoek*) with various fillings. Tues–Sat 10am–4pm.

Graskop

Some 17km east of Pilgrim's Rest, **GRASKOP** owes its place on the tourist map to *Harrie's Pancake Shop*, which serves much-imitated but rarely rivalled crêpes, and attracts all the tour buses doing the Escarpment viewpoints. The town itself is very ordinary, with timber trucks rumbling heavily through, but its location close to the **Blyde River Canyon** is the major consolation.

Africa Silks Weavery and Showroom

Showroom Louis Trichardt Ave • Daily 8am–5pm • **Farm** 23km from Graskop, on the R533 • Mon–Sat 8am–5pm, Sun 8am–noon – Guided tours daily 9.30am, 10.30am, noon, 2pm & 3pm • ☎013 767 1665, ⓦafricasilks.com

The **Africa Silks Weavery and Showroom** is a notable village industry, and sells a range of products made by local African women from the silk of mopane silkworms. The silk-filled duvets, cushion covers and scarves are particularly fabulous. It's also possible to visit the farm where the silk is produced.

Big Swing

☎013 737 8191 or ☎082 412 7295 • R320

Graskop's **Big Swing** is the best of all the big swings on the Escarpment – a 68m free fall done in under three seconds, on one of the world's highest cable gorge swings. After the drop, you "fly free" across the gorge on a 135m highwire "*foefie* slide*", 130m above ground, to glimpse the Graskop Falls. It's also possible to swing tandem (R580). Book in advance – they will either pick you up or direct you to the gorge.

INFORMATION
GRASKOP

Tourist information Big 5 Country Tourism, Louis Trichardt St (Mon–Sat 8am–5pm, Sun 10am–1pm; ☎013 767 573, ⓦtours-tickets.co.za), can book accommodation, safaris into Kruger Park, adventure activities and transfers.

They also have the clearest map of the region and decent activity booklets, and you can purchase tickets online for almost everything worth doing around Kruger and the Escarpment.

9

ACCOMMODATION

★**Graskop Hotel** On the corner of High and Louis Trichardt sts ☎013 767 1244, ⓦgraskophotel.co.za. One of the nicest places to stay on the Escarpment, with a personal and relaxed atmosphere. Though unprepossessing from the outside, it actually has a very stylish interior of retro furniture, African baskets, fabrics and sculptures. The rooms, some of which are in garden wings, are airy and decorated with considerable flair, and there is an on-site gallery with contemporary artwork. R860

Sheris Lodge & Backpackers 66 Oorwinning St ☎072 623 5583, ⓦsherislodge.co.za. A clean and friendly backpackers', situated near the centre of town. Dorms and self-catering doubles are on offer, all in rondavels, and there's a kitchen, and a dining and entertainment area that boasts a pool table. Dorm 150, double R540

EATING

Canimambo On the corner of Hoof and Louis Trichardt sts ☎013 767 1868. Excellent Portuguese and Mozambican cuisine, with an cheerful, informal atmosphere, and a fire in winter. There is spicy bean stew for vegetarians, while a carnivorous speciality is rump steak done with butter, garlic and whiskey (R100), though the Mozambican peri-peri chicken never fails to please. Daily 9am–9pm.

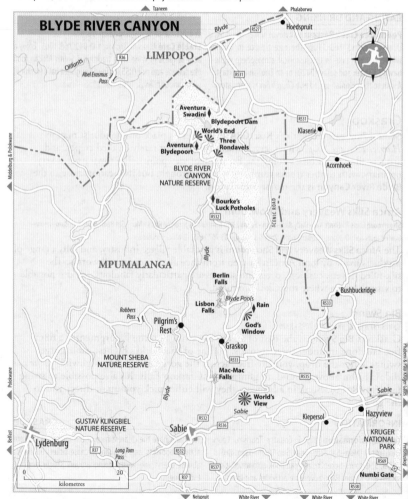

Harrie's Pancake House Louis Trichardt St ☎ 013 767 1273. The legendary and well-signposted *Harrie's* serves the best sweet and savoury pancakes in town, with local specialities such as trout pancake (R88). There is a nice outdoor terrace, as well as an inside dining room with a roaring log fire in winter. Daily 8.30am–5pm.

9

Blyde River Canyon

There are few places in South Africa where you can enjoy such easily accessible and dramatic scenery as that of the colossal **Blyde River Canyon**, weathered out of strata of red rock and dropping sharply away from the Escarpment into the lowveld. The **Blyde River Canyon Nature Reserve** stretches from a narrow tail near Graskop in the south, and broadens into a great amphitheatre partially flooded by the **Blydepoort Dam** about 60km to the north.

The drive along the canyon lip

Viewpoints R25

The views of the canyon are wonderful from both above and below, but the nicest way to take in the vistas is on an easy half-day's drive along the canyon lip. Some 3km north of Graskop, the R534 makes a 15km loop past a series of superb **viewpoints**. The road winds through pine plantations until it comes to the turn-off to the **Pinnacle**, a gigantic quartzite column topped with trees, rising out of a ferny gorge. After another 4km the road reaches the sheer drop and lowveld views of **God's Window**, one of the most famous of the viewpoints; it's also one of the most developed, with toilets and curio stalls. The looping road returns to rejoin the R532, which continues north for 28km beyond the turn-off to reach **Bourke's Luck Potholes** at the confluence of the Treur and Blyde rivers – a collection of strange, smoothly scooped formations carved into the rocks by water-driven pebbles. If you only have time for one spot, this is the best choice, with an easy but rewarding 45-minute walk, though there are no facilities.

Another fine viewpoint lies 14km beyond, at the **Three Rondavels**. The name describes only one small feature of this cinemascope vista: three cylinders in the shape of huts with the meandering Blyde River twisting its way hundreds of metres below. No photograph does justice to the sheer enormity of the view, punctuated by one series of cliffs after another buttressing into the valley.

Three Rondavels to Blydepoort Dam

The 90km **drive** from the Three Rondavels viewpoint to the base of the canyon provides spectacular views of the Escarpment cliffs rising out of the lowveld and is easily incorporated into your itinerary if you're heading to or from Kruger. The drive winds west to join with the R36 and heads north to begin its descent through the Abel Erasmus Pass and then the J.G. Strijdom Tunnel through the mountain, with the wide lowveld plains opening out on the other side. The road takes a wide arching trajectory to circumnavigate the canyon.

Blydepoort Dam and boat trips

26km from Hoedspruit; follow signs on the R531 for Forever Swadini Resort – the jetty is 5km beyond the resort• **Boat trips** daily 11am & 3pm • R120 plus R20 per car • Booking in advance essential •☎ 015 795 5961, ✉ bookings@blydecanyon.co.za

At the heart of the Blyde River Canyon is the man-made **Blydepoort Dam**, most notable for the staggering views it gives of the canyon, looking up from the water. Here you can take recommended ninety-minute boat trips – probably the best way to experience the impressive canyon – to take in spectacular mountain ravines and the Three Rondavels from below, as well as a number of impressive waterfalls. You'll also see the formations created by calcium deposits from the natural springs, and you may catch sight of hippos or crocs in the dam.

9

The lowveld

South Africa's **lowveld**, wedged between the Mpumalanga section of the Drakensberg and Mozambique, is part of a vast subtropical region of savanna that stretches north through Zimbabwe and Zambia as far as Central Africa. Closely associated at the turn of the last century with fortune-seekers, hunters, gold-diggers and adventurers, these days the South African lowveld's claim to fame is its proximity to the Kruger National Park and the adjacent private game reserves. The towns here all act as gateways to the park.

Largest of the lowveld towns, and the capital of Mpumalanga, is **Nelspruit**, accessible by air and bus (including buses from Maputo in Mozambique). East of Nelspruit, the N4 runs close to the southern border of the Kruger, providing easy access to its Malelane and Crocodile Bridge gates; the latter is just 12km north of **Komatipoort**, a humid frontier town on the border with **Mozambique**. From Nelspruit, you can also head 32km south to **Barberton**, with strong mining connections, or continue another 41km to **Swaziland**.

The R40 north of the provincial capital passes through **White River**, **Hazyview**, **Hoedspruit** and **Phalaborwa**, a series of small towns that act as bases for exploring Kruger. Each town is well supplied with accommodation, and has a Kruger entrance gate nearby; tours are available from some. The closest to Nelspruit and an entry point into the Park, Hazyview is now leader of the pack. Hoedspruit and Phalaborwa actually fall within Limpopo Province, but for the sake of continuity have been included in this chapter.

Nelspruit

Prosperous **NELSPRUIT** (nel-sprait), 358km east of Johannesburg on the N4, grew in the 1890s as a base for traders, farmers and prospectors, but there is little evidence left of these origins. Most of the old buildings have been ripped out and replaced by shopping malls and freeways, and the town has a bustling and prosperous feel. It's a

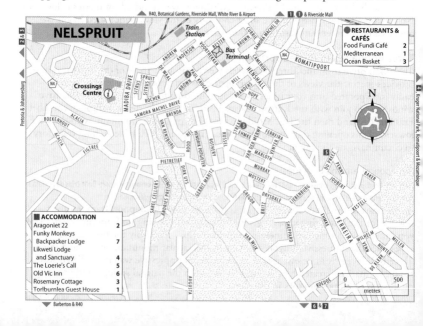

NELSPRUIT

Train Station

Bus Terminal

RESTAURANTS & CAFÉS
Food Fundi Café 2
Mediterranean 1
Ocean Basket 3

N

ACCOMMODATION
Aragoniet 22 — 2
Funky Monkeys
 Backpacker Lodge — 7
Likweti Lodge
 and Sanctuary — 4
The Loerie's Call — 5
Old Vic Inn — 6
Rosemary Cottage — 3
Torlburnlea Guest House — 1

0 — 500
metres

major commercial centre, not only for the lowveld but also for shoppers from Swaziland and Mozambique. The municipality is called Mbombela, and you are may see that name on some road signs, rather than Nelspruit.

The town also has the best **transport connections** in the province, including air links with Johannesburg, Cape Town and Durban, as well as to Maputo. Nelspruit also has an excellent hospital and all the facilities and shops you might need.

Lowveld National Botanical Garden

Signposted off the R40 to White River · Daily 8am–5pm · R15

Nelspruit's major attraction is the **Lowveld National Botanical Garden**. Set on the banks of the Crocodile River, the garden comes a close second to Cape Town's Kirstenbosch Gardens (see p.106). Natural waterfalls and walks through rainforest make a pleasant break from the midday heat, with **trees** grouped according to habitat and helpfully identified with labels. The garden specializes in **cycads** from around the world, and there's also a grove of baobabs from South Africa and other African countries. A useful brochure sold at the entrance gate has a map showing the highlights of the garden and the paths through it, and you'll find a tea room open for refreshments, as well as a restaurant with good views.

Chimpanzee Eden

10km out of Nelspruit on the R40 to Barberton · Daily 10am, noon & 2pm · R160 · ☎ 079 7771514, ⓦ janegoodall.co.za

The Jane Goodall-sponsored **Chimpanzee Eden** is dedicated to the rescue and rehabilitation of chimpanzees. Here, on the obligatory tours, you can see the primates, who have been rescued from terrible conditions in places like Angola and Somalia, re-learning to climb trees, foraging for food in the leaves, carefully grooming each other and establishing troop relationships, though you don't get to touch or interact with them in any way at all.

ARRIVAL AND DEPARTURE   NELSPRUIT

By plane Flights, run by SA Airlink (ⓦ flyairlink.com), arrive at the tiny, thatched Kruger Mpumalanga International Airport (KMIA; ☎ 013 753 7500), 20km north of town off the R40 to White River. Unfortunately, flights to Nelspruit are among the most expensive in the country, and it may work out cheaper to fly into Johannesburg and continue here by car. All the major car rental companies, including Avis (☎ 013 741 1087), have rental desks at the airport. If you're not hiring a car, your best option for onward travel is a private shuttle: Summit Tours and Safaris (☎ 013 794 4300 or ☎ 084 991 6783,

ⓦ summittoursandsafaris.com) meets flights on request and provides reliable transfers into Nelspruit (or into Kruger and the private reserves, to Hazyview, and onwards from Nelspruit to Mozambique). Otherwise, try Jackson Mahlati (☎ 083 414 0801, ⓔ jacksontransfers@gmail.com), which offers the cheapest shuttle into town (R400).

Destinations: Cape Town (daily; 3hr); Durban (2 daily; 1hr); Johannesburg (5 daily; 1hr).

By bus From Johannesburg, the City Bug (☎ 0861 33 44 33, ⓦ citybug.co.za) is the best option, with six departures daily 8am–6pm (4hr), leaving from OR Tambo Airport and

HEADING INTO MOZAMBIQUE

Maputo is only 200km from Nelspruit, an easy journey by car on the N4, though there are two toll gates to pass through (R60). The Cheetah Express (☎ 013 755 1988; R260) is a **shuttle service** between the two cities – it leaves Nelspruit at 4.15pm daily; the journey takes three hours. Tickets can be purchased from the tourist office at the Crossings Centre (see p.530) and **visas** (R750) must be purchased beforehand at the Mozambique Consulate (Ferriera Street, opposite Absa Square; ☎ 013 753 2089). You'll need a whole day for this – arrive at the Embassy first thing to hand in your forms, and collect your visa in the early afternoon. Visas can be issued at the border itself, but this can be unpredictable, so it's best to arrange your visa beforehand.

To find out how best to explore the Mozambican side of Kruger Park, east of Phalaborwa Gate, speak to the well-informed company Great Limpopo Wilderness Camps & Trails (☎ 021 701 7860, ⓦ dolimpopo.com).

9

HORSERIDING NEAR NELSPRUIT

One of the best things to do around Nelspruit is horseriding, where you stand a good chance of seeing **wild horses** – or you can ride among plains game on a wildlife conservancy.

Kaapsehoop Horse Trails Kaapsehoop, 35km west of Nelspruit, off the N4 ☎082 774 5826, ⓦ horsebacktrails.co.za. Wild horses roam around Kaapsehoop, a mountainous, forested area close to Nelspruit; Kaapsehoop Horse Trails offer one-hour rides for beginners (R230), and two-hour (R420) and full day (R780) rides for competent riders. There is very nice, reasonably priced self-catering accommodation (R500) on offer at the riding centre,

with friendly staff and a relaxed vibe.

Kwa Madwala Reserve 80km east of Nelspruit, off the N4 ☎082 779 2153, ⓦ kwamadwala.net. Horserides are offers on this massive game conservancy, where you can ride amongst plains game (no predators or elephants); one-hour rides for beginners (R300), and a choice of two-hour (R550) and half-day (R800) rides for more experienced riders.

arriving in Nelspruit at the BP garage in the Sonpark Centre, Piet Retief St, just south of the city centre. You'll need to arrange a taxi beforehand (it's too far to walk into

town) – Edgars Taxi Service (☎072 147 1677) is recommended – or to get someone from your accommodation to meet you.

INFORMATION

Tourist information Lowveld Tourism (Mon–Fri 7am–6pm, Sat 8am–1.30pm; ☎013 755 1988/1989, ⓦ krugerlowveld.com), at the Crossings Centre, corner of the N4 and General Dan Pienaar St, is the town's main tourist office. It provides maps and basic information,

and arranges accommodation, including bookings for Kruger's restcamps, as well as day-trips with various tour operators. Lowveld Tourism also has a kiosk at the upmarket Riverside Mall, just north of the city centre on the R40.

ACCOMMODATION

Nelspruit's accommodation is largely geared towards business travellers, and none is close to restaurants. Most places have swimming pools, outdoor eating areas and tropical gardens. There are also some excellent options a few kilometres out, on farms, and a game lodge virtually at the airport.

Aragoniet 22 Aragoniet St ☎083 631 2136, ⓦ aragonietlodge.co.za. Spotless and cheap self-catering in four rooms, in a convenient location, with a garden and pool, attractive mainly for the price. They can also arrange to have you collected from the bus or airport. R600

Funky Monkeys Backpacker Lodge 102 Van Wijk St ☎013 744 1310, ⓦ funkymonkeys.co.za. Popular hostel with a licensed bar, pool table, shady veranda, swimming pool and broadband internet. It offers one- to three-day tours into Kruger and can arrange pick-ups from the town centre or airport. Dorm R140, double R390

Likweti Lodge and Sanctuary On the R358 between Nelspruit and White River, 5km from KMI airport ☎082 939 0629, ⓦ likweti.co.za. Planes are not allowed to fly over Likweti's 1400 acres of rocky outcrops and open plains, which are home to rhino, buffalo, zebra and giraffe. Two types of accommodation are available: the lodge, set on a ridge, faces the sunrise, with supremely comfortable rooms and excellent food; or you can self-cater in a two-storey chalet that sleeps four. Chalet R770, lodge R2420

The Loerie's Call 2 Du Preez St ☎013 744 1251 or ☎083 283 6190, ⓦ loeriescall.co.za. A modern place, with a pool and sub-tropical gardens, offering upmarket en-suite rooms with private verandas, as well as an appealing lounge and terrace. It's often fully booked, so reserve well ahead. There is also a restaurant on site. R1200

Old Vic Inn 12 Impala St, 3km from town ☎013 744 0993 or ☎082 340 1508, ⓦ krugerandmore.co.za. Six clean, comfortable doubles, some en suite, and a dorm in a quiet backpacker hostel, with a pool, garden and walks in the adjoining nature reserve. There are also three self-catering units suitable for families. The owners can arrange transport from the centre of town and from the airport, and can organize tours, including to Mozambique and Kruger. Their in-house tour company is the only backpackers' tour company that will get you a bed right in Kruger Park; the tours are normally run by the owner himself. Dorm R145, double R400, en suite R600

Rosemary Cottage 16km west of Nelspruit, off the N4 ☎084 205 9522, ⓦ alkmaarrosemarycottage.co.za. A charming two-bedroom self-catering cottage with a veranda and a veg and herb garden, on a working orange

9

and macadamia nut farm, a 20min drive from Nelspruit. If you opt for B&B, you'll be treated to home-baked bread and preserves. R700

★ **Torlburnlea Guest House** Mataffin Macadamia Village, 5km east of town ☎072 884 8872, ⓦtorburnlea.co.za. Pick of the Nelspruit guesthouses, *Torburnlea* is the beautifully renovated 1920s family home of friendly and informed hosts Andrew and Kim Hall, with a gracious colonial-style veranda looking from a hill onto lychee and macadamia nut orchards and sugarcane fields. The rooms are spacious and elegant, with luxurious fittings and linen, and you'll get fresh fruit juice and tropical fruit from the farm for breakfast. R1700

EATING AND DRINKING

Food Fundii Cafe Absa Square, Paul Kruger St ☎013 755 4969. A daytime spot in the centre of town with pavement seating under a tree, serving really good coffee, open sandwiches, wraps, cakes and salads. Their rooibos-smoked chicken sandwich with cashew nuts is very tasty (R58), and you can get interesting combos such as biltong and cheddar sarnies with jalpeno. Mon–Fri 7am–4pm, Sat 8am–1pm.

Mediterranean Ilanga Mall, N4 ☎013 757 0170; Riverside Mall, White River Rd (R40) ☎013 757 0170. A popular seafood and sushi choice, where you can try Greek-style Mozambican prawns (R75), or a whole fish baked, steamed or fried (R99). The menu is extensive – ask to see the display of fresh fish from the kitchen. Mon–Thurs & Sun 11.30am–9pm, Fri & Sat 11.30am–10pm.

Ocean Basket 17 Ferreira St ☎013 752 7193. A reasonably priced chain fish restaurant in a central and pleasant location, with the benefit of outdoor seating on balmy evenings. If hake and chips (R45), prawns, sole or kingklip don't cut it, steaks are always available. Mon–Sat 11am–9.30pm, Sun 11am–9pm.

DIRECTORY

Embassies Mozambique, Bell St (☎013 752 7396).
Emergencies Ambulance ☎013 741 1620.
Hospital Nelspruit Private Hospital, 10 Rothery St (☎013 759 0500).
Internet access There are internet cafés in the shopping malls.
Pharmacy Chemist Mopani, Crossings Centre (Mon–Fri 8am–6pm, Sat 8am–3pm; ☎013 755 5500, out of hours ☎082 761 1603); Ilanga Centre (Mon–Fri 9am–6pm, Sat 9am–4pm, Sun 9am–1pm; ☎013 742 2225).
Post office Voortrekker St (Mon–Fri 8.30am–4pm, Sat 8.30–11am); each shopping mall has a Postnet, which is easier to use than the post office.
Shopping There are three major malls in Nelspruit: Riverside Mall, towards White River heading north on the R40; the more central Crossings Centre; and Ilanga Mall, to the west towards Johannesburg, off the N4.

Kruger's southern fringe

The N4 east of Nelspruit roughly follows the progress of the **Crocodile River**, which traces the southern boundary of Kruger National Park. For 58km to the tiny farming settlement of **Malelane**, the road travels within view of the Crocodile's riverine forest, passing lush, subtropical farmlands and the Dalí-esque formations of granite *koppies*. Some 4km further on, the road turns off to Kruger's **Malelane Gate**, the most convenient entry point for *Berg-en-Dal* restcamp (see p.545). The only blight on the journey is the smoke stacks from the Malelane sugar-cane mill.

BARBERTON MINING TOURS AND TRAILS

Barberton offers the opportunity to experience an excellent tour down a fascinating historical gold mine. **Galaxy Gold Mines** offers daily tours at 8am, 11am and 2pm at the historical Pioneer Mine, 15km out of town (book through Barberton Odyssey ☎079 180 1488; 2hr 30min; R220), for which you will be provided with gum boots, a hard hat and a headlamp, and shown how to pan for gold.

The area around Barberton is a **UNESCO geological heritage sight** as the surrounding Mahonjwa mountains have a global reputation for being the best preserved ancient rocks on earth – 3.5 billion years old – with fossils recording the earliest life forms on the planet. Odyssey (☎079 180 1488) offers a three-hour guided motor geo-trail (R700) along the beautiful old Bulembu Road with several stops of geological interest along the way.

ACCOMMODATION

KRUGER'S SOUTHERN FRINGE

Buhala Game Lodge 12km east of Malelane Gate ☎ 082 940 8630, ⓦ buhala.co.za. A fabulous guesthouse on a mango, sugar-cane and papaya farm, on the banks of the Crocodile River, with views from a wooden deck across the slow water into Kruger, plus a swimming pool, and ten a/c elegant doubles. Day drives with a ranger into Kruger be arranged from here for R990 per person, as well as three-hour walks there for R550. Golfers stay here too, for the nearby Leopard Creek course. **R2885**

Kwa Madwala Game Reserve Signposted off the N4, between Malelane and Crocodile Bridge gates ☎ 082 779 2153, ⓦ kwamadwala.net. A game lodge experience at B&B prices, set in a beautiful area of bushveld, dotted with granite hills and roamed by four of the Big Five. Accommodation at their main lodge, *Manyatta*, consists of chalets built into granite outcrops, and there's a nice pool and good views, though with farmland and a sugar-processing mill not too far away, it doesn't have a totally wild feeling. Rates include dinner, bed and breakfast; game drives and horseriding are extra. **R3200**

Barberton

BARBERTON, 36km south of Nelspruit, began its urban existence after **gold** was discovered in 1883. An influx of shopkeepers, hoteliers, barmen, prostitutes, even ministers of religion, soon joined the diggers in the growing frontier town, which consisted of tents, tin, thatch and mud, with nearly every second building functioning as a boozing joint. During the fabulous boom of the 1880s the mines slipped out of the grasp of the small-time prospectors and came under the control of the large corporations that still own them today. There are seven working **mines** around Barberton, each with its own recreational area for miners only, which means you won't find miners packing out public bars as in the wild days of old, and the whole place feels rather run down these days.

This is the best place in the country, however, to take an **underground gold-mining tour**, in a working mine, or learn to do gold panning. This attraction aside, there's no real reason to detour to Barberton as it is sadly devoid of the charms it once had.

Barberton Museum

36 Pilgrim St • Mon–Fri 9am–4pm, Sat & Sun 9am–1pm & 2–4pm • Free

You can explore the mining history of the town at the **Barberton Museum**; housed in a well-designed, modern building, the museum has good displays on the gold-rush era. The museum can also provide a map of the town's **Heritage Walk**, on which green and white signposts direct you to some historical houses and monuments, including the worthwhile Belhaven House and Stopforth House.

ARRIVAL AND INFORMATION

BARBERTON

By minibus taxi There is no scheduled public transport to Barberton, though from Nelspruit you can take a minibus taxi (36km).

Tourist information Crown St (Mon–Fri 7.30am–4.30pm, Sat 8am–1pm; ☎ 013 712 2880, ⓦ barberton.co.za).

Activities and tours Barberton Odyssey (☎ 079 180 1488) offers a guided historical walk of Barberton (R55), as well as mining and geological tours.

ACCOMMODATION

Aloe Ridge Guest Farm 10km north of Barberton on the R38 ☎ 082 456 3442, ⓦ aloeridgeguestfarm.com.

Peaceful and reasonably priced accommodation on an organic farm, with excellent birding opportunities. The

---

HEADING INTO SWAZILAND

The closest route **into Swaziland** is through the border crossing at Bulembu (daily 8am–4pm), but the road is poor and should be avoided in the summer unless you're in a 4WD vehicle, though an ordinary car can make it in the winter (dry season). The quickest and best route is through Jeppe's Reef/Matsamo (daily 7am–8pm). This road gives you views of the impressive Maguga Dam just south of Piggs Peak in Swaziland.

9

three rooms in the main house are all furnished with wooden furniture, with cotton bedding, and do not have television. R550

Mazwita Bush Camp 17km towards Nelspruit on the

R40 ☎082 604 1190, ⓦmazwita.com. A small game farm with thatched rondavels, wooden walkways and lovely hilly surrounds where you can walk, cycle or drive to view plains game in the bush without predator dangers. R1100

EATING AND DRINKING

Co-Co Pan Resttaurant and Pub Crown St ☎013 712 2653. The most central spot to eat is the cheap and friendly no-frills *Co-Co Pan*, which serves straightforward hamburgers (R40), steaks and omelettes, but is probably a better choice for a beer (R18). Daily 8am–9pm.

Victorian Tea Garden Next to the tourist office on Crown St ☎013 712 4985. The pleasant *Victorian Tea Garden*, with a white gazebo straight out of a London park, serves cheap toasted sandwiches (R25) outdoors, as well as tea and desserts. Mon–Fri 8am–5pm, Sat 8am–2pm.

Kruger's western flank – the R40

The **R40** heads north from Nelspruit along the western border of Kruger National Park, passing through some prosperous tropical-fruit-growing farmlands around Hazyview, but for the most part through densely populated and very poor African areas, the biggest conglomeration of which is called Bushbuck Ridge. It is a fascinating drive, however, to see a slice of busy, rural South African life, where tiny brick houses and shacks exist alongside more prosperous dwellings. It contrasts starkly to wild, protected Kruger, a reserve that the majority of people in this area have never had the means to enter.

The R40 yields access to the private game reserves – **Sabi Sands**, **Manyeleti** and **Timbavati** – as well as the Kruger Park gates of Numbi, Phabeni, Paul Kruger and Orpen Though marked prominently on maps, **Klaserie**, which lies on the border of Mpumalanga and Limpopo Province, is little more than an easily missed petrol station and shop, surrounded by a number of private game farms.

Continuing northwards into Limpopo, you reach **Hoedspruit**, a shopping and service centre that is good for access to several large private game reserves and to Orpen Gate (69km away). Further north is the mining town of **Phalaborwa**, a convenient 2km from Phalaborwa Gate into central Kruger and the rewarding camps of Letaba and Olifants.

Hazyview

HAZYVIEW, 43km north of Nelspruit, is a service centre for Southern Kruger, with **Phabeni Gate** situated a mere 10km from town. It's the last town to stock up in before reaching the major Paul Kruger Gate into Skukuza, Kruger's "capital", as well as the entrance to the Sabi Sands Reserve. It is a centre too for surrounding farms, with large shopping centres and busy roadside market stalls selling fruit and goods to the surrounding, densely populated African areas. The town is one of the best bases for visitors who want to stay outside the park and take part in some adventure **activities** and **tours**, as well as view game. Hazyview is spread out, but **Perry's Bridge**, on the corner of the R536 and R40, is a central stop-off with a small complex of luxury shops, craft outlets and restaurants.

The Skyway Trails

Perry's Bridge Trading Post · R480 · ☎082 825 0209 or ☎013 737 6747, ⓦskywaytrails.com

The **aerial cable way**, Skyway Trails, offers three-hour jaunts above the trees, on which

---

DRIVING THE R40

If you're driving the **R40**, take great care as the road has many potholes that can easily damage a wheel, as well as wandering goats and cattle, unaware pedestrians and a hair-raising combination of minibus taxis tearing along and heavy trucks travelling between Phalaborwa Mine and Mozambique. Given the potential hazards, don't travel along this route in the dark, and allow for a slow journey – it's a very busy road, with only a single lane in each direction.

you glide from platform to platform over the valley, securely clipped to a stout cable. Helmets and harnesses are provided and the guides are capable and fun. No skills are needed, other than a degree of calmness and a head for heights, and children aged 6–10 can ride with a guide. You meet at *Gecko Lodge*, 3km along on the R536 from Hazyview, where you are kitted up and given a short lesson before being transported to the hilltop where the trail begins. Book in advance.

The Elephant Sanctuary

5km from Hazyview on the R536 road to Sabie • Brush Down R545 • Trunk in Hand R545 • Elephant ride R750 • ☎ 079 624 9436, ⓦ elephantsanctuary.co.za. Book elephant activities ahead on the website.

The **Elephant Sanctuary** offers the opportunity to touch and feed the two orphaned elephants rescued from a culling programme. A variety of programmes offer close encounters with the elephants – the "Brush Down", where you groom the animals and feel the texture of their skin and ears, combined with "Trunk in Hand", where you walk alongside them, lightly holding their trunks, is recommended. Rides are also available.

ARRIVAL AND DEPARTURE   HAZYVIEW

By car The shortest and quickest route here from Johannesburg, 421km away, is via the N4 and Nelspruit (53km south).

By minibus taxi The only form of public transport serving Hazyview is minibus taxis.

INFORMATION

Tourist information Big 5 Country Tourism, Perry's Bridge, R40 (Mon–Sat 8am–5pm, Sun 10am–1pm; ☎ 013 737 8191, ⓦ tours-tickets.co.za) is the best information office in Mpumalanga, and able to book accommodation, safaris into Kruger Park, adventure activities and transfers (it also has a branch in Graskop; see p.525). It publishes the clearest map of the region and has its own activity booklets; it also cover the Escarpment. You can purchase tickets online for almost everything worth doing around Kruger and the Escarpment, from gold-panning in Barberton to ballooning, horseriding or visiting animal rehab centres. Staff also offer game drives and walks in the Sabi Sands private reserve, as well as in Kruger.

ACCOMMODATION

Guesthouses here are set mostly in farmland strung along the roads radiating out to the neighbouring towns of Sabie (the R536), Graskop (the R535) and White River (the R538), as well as to Kruger's Paul Kruger Gate (the R40).

Bohms Zeederberg Country House 17km from Hazyview, on the R536 ☎ 013 737 8101, ⓦ bohms .co.za. Well-run chalets with an old-fashioned feel, set in subtropical gardens around a swimming pool, with magnificent views and walking trails to the river below. Wheelchair-friendly. R1760

Gecko Backpackers 3km from Hazyview on the R536 ☎ 082 342 6598, ⓦ backpackers-gecko.co.za. Situated next to *Gecko Lodge* (see below), with a swimming pool, camping, dorms and doubles, plus a funky bar and home-cooked meals. Transfers to and from Nelspruit, and trips of varying length into Kruger Park and the Escarpment are also available. Camping R80, dorm R120, double R350

Gecko Lodge 3km from Hazyview on the R536 ☎ 013 590 1020 or ☎ 082 556 6458, ⓦ geckolodge.co.za. Probably the nicest setting in Hazyview, with lush riverine vegetation and a stream running through the grounds. Rooms are decent and well priced, and there is an on-site pub as well as a restaurant. The lodge is also the starting point for the aerial cable trails. R990

Idle and Wild 6km from Hazyview, on the R536 ☎ 013 737 8173 or ☎ 082 381 7408, ⓦ idleandwild.co.za. This mango farm in a lush valley on the banks of the Sabie River offers two thatched rondavels, a cottage (sleeping up to four) and two honeymoon suites (with their own spa bath) in the lush garden, as well as two en-suite bedrooms in the main house. All have kitchenettes, and there's a jacuzzi, sauna and swimming pool. Quad biking and river rafting on site. Rondavel R520, cottage R1050, double R1010

Nkambeni Safari Camp Numbi Gate, 25km south of Hazyview ☎ 013 590 1011 or ☎ 021 910 1780, ⓦ nkambeni.com. Very large, popular safari camp just inside the Kruger park boundaries, offering a no-frills game viewing experience at reasonable prices. Accommodation is in pleasant safari tents with indoor and outdoor showers, though situated rather too close together. Massive buffet meals are served in an open-air thatched dining room overlooking the bush and swimming pool. Day and sunset safaris are available, though you can also use it as a base for self-driving in

9

Kruger. Rates include half board. R1560
Numbi Main Rd ☎013 737 7301, ⓦhotelnumbi.co.za.
An old-fashioned, comfortable place, right in the centre,
offering camping, garden suites and hotel rooms. The
grounds are shady and the hotel's restaurant serves
excellent steaks. Camping R110, double R1130
Rissington Inn 2km south of town, just off the R40

☎013 737 7700 or ☎082 327 6842, ⓦrissington.co.za.
A relaxed, well-run and informal place with fourteen rooms
set in the gardens of a large thatched homestead. Best are
the garden suites which have roofless outside showers, so
you can still feel as if you are in a bush-lodge. There's also a
swimming pool, a bar and good restaurant, so you don't
have to go out to eat. It is, however, on the busy R40. R950

EATING AND DRINKING

Kuka Perry's Bridge Centre ☎013 737 6957.
Sophisticated Afro-chic restaurant and cocktail bar with
colourful, modern decor and both indoor and outdoor
seating. As well as game such as kudu (R145) and meat
dishes, there are good salads. Daily 7am–10pm.
Shangana Cultural Village 4km out of town on the
R535 to Graskop ☎013 737 5804/5, ⓦshangana.co.za.
Delicious African dinners (from R423; booking essential)
cooked in massive pots over an open fire. The menu might
include crocodile in spicy peanut sauce and beef and
honey-glazed sweet potato, and vegetarians are well
catered for. You eat in huts and are served very graciously
by women from the household. The meals are the climax of
a tour of the village and an energetic show of dancing, all of

which is included in the price; a minimum of fifteen people
is required to run. Daily 5pm.
Summerfields River Café 4.5km out of town on the
R536 Sabie Rd ☎013 737 6500, ⓦsummerfields.co.za.
Beauty, harmony and healthy living are offered at this spa
and restaurant on a rose farm. Breakfast and light lunches
are served outdoors on a wooden deck next to the Sabie
River, with vegetables and salads grown on the property,
while dinners at their indoor venue, the *Kitchen*, feature the
likes of lamb loin or organic vegetable risotto (R100), with
tasty starters of smoked goats cheese, white bean puree
and onion flowers (R75), and desserts such as macadamia
nut parfait. Mon & Sun 8am–11am & noon–3pm, Tues–
Sat 8–11am, noon–3pm & 6.30–9pm.

Orpen Gate

After Hazyview, the R40 passes through Bushbuck Ridge – although any bushbucks
that might once have wandered here have long since been eaten and displaced by
cattle and goats. People live crammed at a density six times greater than the
provincial average, a left-over from Apartheid land divisions. Forty-five kilometres
east from here lies **Orpen Gate** into Kruger, the road heading east to Satara into the
centre of the Park. Orpen is also the access point for the Manyeleti and Timbavati
private game reserves.

ACCOMMODATION   ORPEN GATE

★**Timbavati Safari Lodge** Orpen Gate Rd, 20km
from Open Gate ☎015 793 0415 or ☎082 362 2922,
ⓦtimbavatisafarilodge.com. The pick of the places to
stay in the vicinity with space for couples or large groups
in thatched Ndebele-styled huts, plus a pool, bar and
pleasant outdoor dining with wholesome, hearty
dinners under the stars. It has an established feel with
well-tended grounds full of trees and tropical
vegetation, and a lawn kept cropped by resident
warthogs. Guided walks on the property itself offer the

chance of sighting giraffe, zebra, wildebeest and buck,
and adventure activities and worthwhile visits to the
tribal villages across the road can be arranged (real
village life, rather than a village created for tourists).
They have traversing rights into Manyeleti for their own
game drives, which is rich in game with very few
vehicles about to share the sightings, and thus superior
in many ways to going into Kruger itself. Its value for
money makes it a popular base for self-drive into Kruger;
prices include half board. R1500

Hoedspruit

Lurking in the undulating lowveld, 153km north of Nelspruit, with the hazy blue
mountains of the Escarpment visible on the distant horizon, is the small but busy
service centre of **HOEDSPRUIT** ("hood-sprait"). The town lies at the heart of a
concentration of **private game reserves** and lodges, and is a good base for specialist
activities, such as horseriding, rafting on the Blyde River, visiting animal rehabilitation
centres and lazy hot-air ballooning over the bush. Hoedspruit is a significant arrival
point for air travellers heading to Kruger and the nearby private reserves, which include
Timbavati, Manyeleti and Balule.

ACTIVITIES IN AND AROUND HOEDSPRUIT

Hot-air ballooning is a fabulous way to appreciate the surrounding landscape, and recommended flights are offered by Sun Catchers, based near Hoedspruit (☎ 087 806 2079 or ☎ 082 572 2223, ⓦ suncatchers.co.za; R3249). Conditions have to be perfect, and flights are generally very early in the morning when the weather is at its most stable. They leave from different locations depending on the weather – you'll be advised in good time where to meet your flight, and set your alarm clock!

   Horseriding is on offer in Hoedspruit itself, at the Hoedspruit Wildlife Estate, where both beginners and experienced riders can view the reserve's game – zebra, giraffe and antelope, among others. Book through African Dream Horse Safaris (☎ 084 582 5442, ⓦ africandreamhorsesafari.co.za; from R270).

   For experienced riders, Wait a Little Safaris (☎ 083 273 9788, ⓦ waitalittle.co.za) offers the unforgettable experience of horseriding through big game country. Running from their base in the Karongwe Nature Reserve, 70km north of Hoedspruit, their **Big Five horseriding safaris** range from six to ten days, on highly disciplined horses, with first-class accommodation and food; the trails also venture into Makali Reserve, dependent on date and package. Prices start at R30,000 per person.

Moholoholo Wildlife Rehabilitation Centre

17km from Hoedspruit, on the R531 between the R40 and R527, about 3km from the tarred turn-off to the Blydepoort Dam • **Tours** Mon–Sat 9.30am & 3pm, and during school holidays Sun at 3pm • R120 • Booking essential • ☎ 015 795 5236, ⓦ moholoholo.co.za

At the **Moholoholo Wildlife Rehabilitation Centre**, ex-ranger Brian Jones has embarked on an individual crusade to rescue and rehabilitate injured and abandoned animals, notably raptors, but also lions, leopards and others. Tours are informative and you get to see a lot of endangered animals close up. The centre is part of a wider reserve and both night drives and early-morning walks are offered, and there is also accommodation (see below).

Monsoon Gallery

Along the R527, near its junction with the R36 • Daily 8.30am–4.30pm • Free • ☎ 015 795 5114, ⓦ bluecottages.co.za

The **Monsoon Gallery**, 29km north west of Hoedspruit, makes a good place to pause on your journey. Its great African arts and crafts shop has an absorbing selection of authentic artefacts, including ironwork and woodcarving from Zimbabwe, superb tapestries from the Karosswerkers factory near Tzaneen, Venda pots and jewellery, plus silk items, and African music CDs and books.

ARRIVAL, DEPARTURE AND TOURS   HOEDSPRUIT

By plane Hoedspruit airport, Eastgate, 14km south of town, is served by two daily flights from Johannesburg and three weekly flights from Cape Town; both routes are run by SA Airlink (ⓦ flyairlink.com) and ticket prices are very high. Car hire is available at the airport through Avis (☎ 015 793 2014, ⓦ avis.co.za). For transfers to game lodges from the airport, contact Eastgate Safaris (☎ 015 793 3678 or ☎ 082 774 9544, ⓦ eastgatesafaris .co.za), though most lodges send their own vehicles to meet guests.

By shuttle Ashton's Tours and Safaris (☎ 021 683 0234, ⓦ ashtonstours.com) runs a daily shuttle (R720) from Johannesburg OR Tambo Airport (6.30am) to Hoedspruit, and will pick up within a 5km radius of OR Tambo. It drops off in town, at the airport, or at your safari lodge; the journey takes just under six hours.

Tours Eastgate Safaris (☎ 015 793 3678 or ☎ 082 774 9544, ⓦ eastgatesafaris.co.za) offers a number of tours in the area, including a full-day game drive in Kruger National Park (R1290).

ACCOMMODATION

★**Blue Cottages Country House** 27km from Hoedspruit on the R527 ☎ 015 795 5750 or ☎ 082 853 7741, ⓦ bluecottages.co.za. Comfortable suites in a farmhouse filled with African artefacts and fabrics, set in an enticingly cool and colourful tropical garden; more modest, but also lovely, are the garden cottages. You can have dinner served in the garden or on the veranda, if you book in advance. R720

Moholoholo Forest Camp 26km from Hoedspruit, on the R531 ☎ 013 795 5236, ⓦ moholoholo.co.za. In the

9

ACTIVITIES AROUND PHALABORWA

Keen **golfers** shouldn't miss the chance of a round at the signposted Hans Merensky Country Club, Copper Road (☎015 781 3931, ⓦhansmerenskygolf.co.za), where it's not unusual to see giraffes and elephants sauntering across the fairways, built over a vast area of indigenous bush (18 holes; R350).

You can whet your appetite before heading into Kruger Park with a **sundowner boat trip** with Jumbo River Safaris (booking essential; ☎082 070 1477 or ☎083 580 5703; R130), which sets out at 3.30pm down the Olifants River, frequently encountering game – including elephants – and guaranteeing sightings of crocs and hippos. Kruger Park's own activities, run from **Phalaborwa Gate** (☎013 735 3548), are definitely worth doing and must be booked in advance; they include half-, full-day and night drives (from R350), and bush walks (from R450).

foothills of the Drakensberg Escarpment, this is an unshowy safari camp with plenty of game, including rhino, on the property. The price includes meals, a night drive, morning walk and a tour to the nearby rehabilitation centre. R3210
Trackers 25km from Hoedspruit, on the R531 ☎082 494 4266, ⓦtrackers.co.za. A variety of accommodation – camping, and self-catering or B&B chalets – on a farm with indigenous bushveld vegetation, where you may see zebra and antelope. Bring your own drinks, as you can't buy any here. A botanist living on the farm runs recommended guided walks through the bush. Camping R100, chalet R500

Phalaborwa

PHALABORWA ("pal-a-bore-wa"), 74km north of Hoedspruit, gives access to the central and northern part of Kruger Park. The name Phalaborwa means "better than the south", a cheeky sobriquet coined as the town developed on the back of its extensive mineral wealth. During the 1960s, the borders of the park near Phalaborwa suddenly developed a kink, and large copper deposits were found, miraculously, just outside the protected national park area. Mining actually began at Phalaborwa some time after 200 AD, and the **Masorini Heritage Site**, close to Phalaborwa Gate, is a reconstruction of an iron-smelting village.

ARRIVAL AND DEPARTURE   PHALABORWA

By plane SA Airlink (☎015 781 5823, ⓦflyairlink.com) flights arrive daily from Johannesburg (1hr) at Phalaborwa Airport, a 5min drive from Kruger's Phalaborwa Gate, off President Steyn St, and virtually in the town itself. Unfortunately, this is one of the most expensive flights in the country. There are a number of car rental firms represented at the airport, including Avis (☎015 781 3169)

and Budget (☎015 781 5404); alternatively, arrange for your accommodation to pick you up.
By bus City to City (☎0861 589 282, ⓦcitytocity.co.za) runs daily from Johannesburg (7am; 8hr 30min), via Lydenburg. The better, more comfortable option is the daily Translux service (☎0861 589 282, ⓦtranslux.co.za); 9.30am; 7hr), via Polokwane.

INFORMATION

Tourist information Sureturnkey Travel, 73a Sealene St (Mon–Fri 8.30am–5pm, Sat 9–11am; ☎015 781 1037,

ⓦphalaborwa.co.za), makes bookings for Kruger, accommodation and car rental.

ACCOMMODATION

Daan & Zena's 15 Birkenhead St ☎015 781 6049, ⓦdaanzena.co.za. Brightly painted and friendly B&B (self-catering available) offering en-suite rooms located in three neighbouring houses, with a/c and TV in each room, and three swimming pools to choose from. R400
Elephant Walk 30 Anna Scheepers St ☎015 781 5860 or ☎082 495 0575, ⓦaccommodation-phalaborwa .com. A small and friendly hostel and B&B, in a pleasant suburban home with a large garden, 2km from the Kruger gate, with camping facilities and budget tours into the

park, plus a booking service for Phalaborwa/Kruger activities. Besides dorms and twins, they have four en-suite garden rooms, and a swimming pool in the garden. Camping R100, dorm R120, double R570
Kaia Tani Guest House 29 Boekenhout St ☎015 781 1358, ⓦkaitani.com. Almost at the gate into Kruger, this upmarket and comfortable guesthouse is run by an energetic and flambouyant Italian, Daniela, who can meet you at the airport. There is a pool, tropical garden and you can arrange meals here, too. R1500

EATING AND DRINKING

★**The Hat & Creek** 2 Hendrik van Eck St ☎015 781 2517. The top place to eat in town, right at the gate into Kruger Park, offering steak and chips, or lighter café options like cappuccinos and red velvet cake (R55). There is outdoor seating on the terrace and a fire for winter nights, plus free wi-fi. Mon–Sat 9am–10pm, Sun 9am–8pm.

Villa Luso 6 Grosvenor Crescent ☎015 781 5670. Mozambican food, including recommended seafood platters and sole, and tender T-bone steaks (R100), is served at this relaxed and comfortable place with checked tableclothes and nice outdoor seating under thatch. Mon–Sat 7am till late.

Kruger National Park

KRUGER NATIONAL PARK is arguably the emblem of South African tourism, the place that delivers best what most visitors to Africa want to see – scores of elephants, lions and a cast of thousands of other game roaming the savanna. A narrow strip of land hugging the Mozambique border, Kruger stretches across Limpopo Province and Mpumalanga, an astonishing 414km drive from Pafuri Gate in the north to Malelane Gate in the south, all of it along tar, with many well-kept gravel roads looping off to provide routes for game drives.

Visiting Kruger (see box, p.520) invariably means choosing between self-driving (staying either in the park itself, or in one of the nearby towns), an organised safari tour, or staying on an exclusive reserve. How you experience the park will largely depend on your budget – but regardless of whether you are roughing it on a backpacker tour, or in your own luxury riverside suite, your experience of Kruger, and its animals, will be memorable.

Brief history

It's highly questionable whether Kruger National Park can be considered ˙a pristine wilderness", as it's frequently called, given that people have been living in or around it for thousands of years. **San hunter-gatherers** have left their mark in the form of paintings and engravings at 150 sites so far discovered, and there is evidence of farming cultures at many places in the park.

Around 1000–1300 AD, centrally organized states were building stone palaces and engaging in **trade** that brought Chinese porcelain, jewellery and cloth into the area, but it was the arrival of white **fortune-seekers** in the second half of the nineteenth century that made the greatest impact on the region. African farmers were kicked off their traditional lands in the early twentieth century to create the

---

KRUGER PARK BUSH WALKS AND GAME DRIVES

Whether you're staying in Kruger or not, you can still join one of the early morning, mid-morning, sunset or night **game drives** organized by the park (R450–500). Not only are these drives one of the cheapest ways of accessing the park, but the viewing is good because of the height of the open vehicles. The drives leave from every camp in the park (book at reception or, even better, when you make your reservation) and, for those staying outside the park, from these entrance gates: Crocodile Bridge (☎013 735 6012), Malelane (☎013 735 6152), Numbi (☎013 735 5133), Paul Kruger (☎013 735 5107), Phabeni (☎013 735 5890) and Phalaborwa (☎013 735 3547/3548).

For those staying inside the park, three-hour **game walks** (R490) are conducted every morning at dawn from each camp. Groups are restricted to eight people, so it's worth booking beforehand. "**Park and braais**", departing from some entry gates, combine a short drive with a barbecue (R450); it's likely to be the only meal for which you'll ever have to sign an indemnity form. Kruger also runs several three-night **wilderness trails** (see box, p.543) in different parts of the park, led by armed rangers – a fabulous way of getting in touch with the wilderness, but one you'll have to book months in advance.

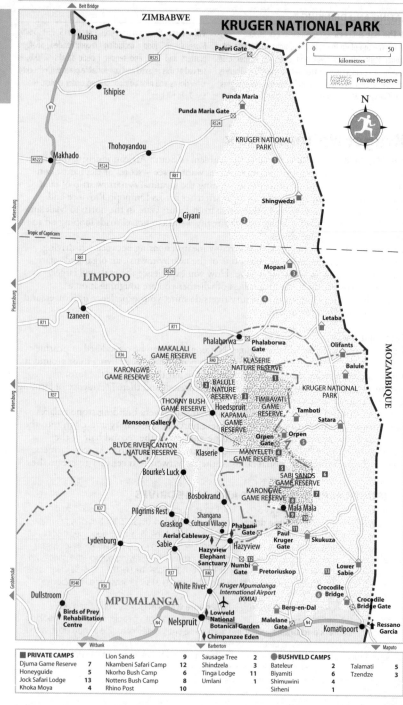

KRUGER NATIONAL PARK

PRIVATE CAMPS		Lion Sands	9	Sausage Tree	2	● BUSHVELD CAMPS	
Djuma Game Reserve	7	Nkambeni Safari Camp	12	Shindzela	3	Bateleur	2
Honeyguide	5	Nkorho Bush Camp	6	Tinga Lodge	11	Biyamiti	6
Jock Safari Lodge	13	Nottens Bush Camp	8	Umlani	1	Shimuwini	4
Khoka Moya	4	Rhino Post	10			Sirheni	1

Talamati	5
Tzendze	3

park, and hunters and poachers made their livelihoods here decimating game populations.

Paul Kruger, former president of the South African Republic, is usually credited with having the foresight to set aside land for wildlife conservation. Kruger figures as a shrewd, larger-than-life character in Afrikaner history, and it was **James Stevenson-Hamilton**, the first warden of the national park, who cunningly put forward Kruger's name in order to soften up Afrikaner opposition to the park's creation. In fact, Stevenson-Hamilton knew that Kruger was no conservationist and was actually an inveterate hunter; Kruger "never in his life thought of animals except as biltong", he wrote in a private letter, and it was his tenacity that saved the animals that hadn't been shot out, rather than Kruger's.

The park was extended into Mozambique with the establishment of the Great Limpopo Transfrontier Park in 2000, and two border posts linking Kruger to Mozambique have been created, one right at the north of the park at Pafuri near *Punda Maria Camp*, the other at Giriyondo, between *Letaba* and *Mopani* camps.

ESSENTIALS
KRUGER NATIONAL PARK

Opening hours Daily: April, Aug & Sept 6am–6pm; May–July 6am–5.30pm; Oct & March 5.30am–6pm; Nov–Feb 5.30am–6.30pm
Entry Fee R248 per day (SA residents R62).

Internet Available at Berg-en-Dal and Skukuza.
Petrol stations At all main rest camps (petrol and diesel); all are cash only.

ARRIVAL AND DEPARTURE

Johannesburg is the city with the best connections to Kruger, by both land and air. An easy option if you are flying in or out of Johannesburg is to see the park as part of a tour that starts and ends in the city (see box, p.542). Alternatively, rent a car at the airport for the easy five-hour drive to the park; the airport is on the N4 motorway to Kruger.

By plane The four local airports servicing Kruger are Skukuza Nelspruit, (see p.528; for the southern section see p.545), Hoedspruit (see p.536; for the central and northern sections) and Phalaborwa (see p.538; for the northern section); car rental is available at each airport, or you will be picked up by your safari lodge. Unfortunately, flights to airports near Kruger are pricey, and all are run by SA Airlink (w flyairlink.com).
By bus There are regular buses servicing Nelspruit, Hoedspruit and Phalaborwa from Johannesburg; from these towns, you can book on one of the many Kruger tours on offer at the backpacker lodges: the *Old Vic Inn* and *Funky Monkeys* in Nelspruit and *Elephant Walk* in Phalaborwa can arrange tours.

KRUGER FLORA AND FAUNA

Among the nearly 150 species of **mammals** seen in the park are cheetah, leopard, lion, spotted hyena, wild dog, black and white rhino, blue wildebeest, buffalo, Burchell's zebra, bushbuck, eland, elephant, giraffe, hippo, impala, kudu, mountain reedbuck, nyala, oribi, reedbuck, roan antelope, sable antelope, tsessebe, warthog and waterbuck. Rhino poaching remains an ongoing problem; despite many campaigns and plans of action, nothing seems to staunch the steady flow towards decimation, with at least two rhinos killed here every day.

The staggering 507 **bird species** include raptors, hefty-beaked hornbills, ostriches and countless colourful specimens. The **birders' "Big Six"** are the saddle-billed stork, kori bustard, martial eagle, lappet-faced vulture, Pel's fishing owl and ground hornbill. SanParks has a good birding page overviewing the different areas and species with details of bird hides (w sanparks .org/groups/birders).

Keep your eyes open and you'll also see a variety of **reptiles**, **amphibians** and **insects** – most rewardingly in the grounds of the restcamps themselves: there's always something to see up the trees, in the bushes or even inside your rondavel. If you spot a miniature ET-like reptile crawling upside down on the ceiling, don't be tempted to kill it; it's an insect-eating gecko and is doing you a good turn. If, however, you have a horror of insects or frogs, stay away from Kruger in the rainy season (Nov–March).

Common among the three-hundred-plus **tree** species are the baobab, cluster fig, knobthorn, Natal mahogany, monkey orange, raisin bush, tamboti, coral tree, fever tree, jackalberry, leadwood, marula, mopane, lala palm and sausage tree.

9

KRUGER TOUR OPERATORS

There are many **tours** to Kruger, several of which depart from Johannesburg. Prices given below are per person unless otherwise noted, and most include park entry fees, meals and transport to and from Johannesburg. Backpacker hostels in Nelspruit, Hazyview and Phalaborwa also run tours to Kruger at reasonable prices. In addition, in the Nelspruit and Hazyview area are some excellent tour guides who will take you into the Park, or organize trips in Mpumalanga. When choosing a tour from Johannesburg, a minimum of three nights (ideally four) is advisable to allow for the long journey time (six to seven hours to get from Jo'burg into the park), more opportunities to view game, and more drives.

★**Nguni Africa** ☎082 221 4177, ⊛nguniafrica .co.za. Extremely knowledgeable and personable guide Andrew Hall, based in Nelspruit, can put together a package for you to see Kruger, and beyond if necessary. He has a great passion for the Lowveld, where his family were pioneers, and runs trips into the park in a Land Rover, where you'll be assured of spotting plenty of game, even on a day trip (from R6800 including meals and fees); the exclusivity of the experience, rather than being in a vehicle with several strangers, is a real bonus. He also offers airport or lodge transfers.
Outlook Small Group Explorations ☎011 894 5406 or ☎079 473 2443, ⊛outlook.co.za. A number of options departing from Jo'burg, where they have a nice guesthouse

not far from the airport that's ideal for before and after your safari. Options include camping in Kruger (R7650) or a combo of Kruger and Sabi Sands (two nights camping in Kruger and one night in a Sabi Sands Lodge; R12,500).
Viva Safaris ☎071 842 5547, ⊛vivasafaris.com. Departing from Jo'burg, and geared towards a price-conscious market, Viva's trips offer all you might want from a Kruger experience (and include a stop at Blyde River Canyon, too). Of the different packages they offer, the most attractive is two nights in *Tremisana Bush Lodge* in Balule, where there is plenty of game , and one or two nights at *Marc's Camp*, which gives you a more rustic, closer to nature bush experience, though there are fewer animals (3 nights R7595).

DRIVING IN KRUGER

When driving, only approved roads should be used; don't drive on unmarked roads and never drive off-road. In heavy rainfall some roads become unusable; check ⊛sanparks.org/parks/kruger for the latest information. Do buy a Kruger map showing all the marked roads. Roads have numbers rather than names; some are tarred, some are dirt. Speed limits are 50km/hr on tar, 40km/hr on untarred roads and 20km/hr in restcamps; speed traps operate in some parts of the park. Never leave your car (it's illegal and dangerous), except at designated sites. If you're trying to get from one part of the park to another, note that although it's far more fun driving inside, the **speed limit** makes it a slow journey – the rule of thumb is to estimate that you will be driving at 25km/h between camps – and you're bound to make frequent stops to watch animals. Bicycles and motorbikes are not allowed.

CHOOSING YOUR ROUTE

The public section of Kruger can be divided roughly into three sections, each with a distinct character and terrain. If your time is limited, it's best to choose just one or two areas to explore, but if you're staying for five days or more, consider driving the length of the park slowly, savouring the changes in landscape along the way. The southern, central and northern sections are sometimes referred to as "the circus", "the zoo" and "the wilderness" – sobriquets that carry more than a germ of truth. Each camp is like a small village in a vast area, with *Skukuza* in the south the largest.
Southern Kruger The south has the greatest

concentration of game, attracts the highest number of visitors, and is the most easily accessible part of the park if you're coming from Johannesburg.
Central Kruger The central areas offer excellent game viewing, as well as two of the most attractive camps in the park at *Olifants* and *Letaba*.
Northern Kruger The north has fewer animals, being drier and flatter than the other areas, but offers an increased sense of wilderness, reaching its zenith at the marvellously old-fashioned *Punda Maria* camp and the lovely Pafuri river area. It is best for a second visit to Kruger, or one which also incorporates time in the south.

WHEN TO VISIT

Kruger is rewarding at any time of the year, though each season has its advantages and drawbacks. If you don't like the heat, avoid **high summer** (Dec–Feb), when temperatures are in the mid- to high thirties, with short thunder showers; a lot of the accommodation in air-conditioned, however. At this time of the year, everything becomes green, the grass is high, animals are born and birds and insects are prolific. There's little rain during the **cooler winter** months of April to August; the vegetation withers over this period, making it easier to spot game. Although daytime temperatures rise to the mid-twenties (days are invariably bright and sunny throughout winter), the nights and early mornings can be very cold, especially in June and July, when you'll definitely need a very warm jacket and woolly hat. **September and October** are the peak months for wildlife viewing.

ACCOMMODATION

At most of the fourteen main **restcamps** inside Kruger, the sounds of the African night tend to get drowned out by air conditioning and the merriment of braais and beer. Nearly all camps have swimming pools, electricity, petrol stations, shops (though they don't stock much in the way of fruit or vegetables), restaurants and laundrettes. The restcamps are pleasant, but hardly wild, with walks around the edges, labelled trees to help you identify what you see on drives, and plenty of birds and smaller creatures around the camps themselves. You'll find thatched rondavels, each with an outdoor eating area, facing communally towards each other rather than out towards the views. The best rondavels are on the camp perimeters or directly facing onto rivers.

Just about all restcamps have a **campsite** (with shared kitchen and washing facilities), which provides the park's cheapest accommodation, but the stands are generally very close together, and you may not get shade. Sites for caravans and camper vans are available wherever there's camping and often have a power point. Most camps have furnished permanent safari tents and huts in configurations usually sleeping two to four people. These are fully equipped, with shared communal kitchens and ablutions. Bungalows and cottages sleep up to six people and come in several variations, with fully equipped kitchens and bathrooms.

WALKING TRAILS

Undertaken with the guidance of an experienced ranger, Kruger Park's three-night **wilderness trails** pass through landscapes of notable beauty with diverse plant and animal life. However, they don't bring you nearer to game than driving; they're really about getting closer to the vegetation and smaller creatures, though you have a good chance of encountering big game. Groups are limited to eight people staying in the same camp, comprising four rustic, two-bed huts, served by reed-walled showers and flush toilets; simple meals are provided. You walk for five hours in the morning, return to the camp for lunch and a siesta, and go walking again for an hour or two in the evening, returning to sit around a campfire. The trails are heavily subscribed; you can **book** up to eleven months in advance through SANParks (see p.64). The cost is around R4000 per person, including accommodation and meals.

In addition, there are three **backpacking trails** where you carry your own stuff on a guided, three-night walk: the Olifants River Trail, following the course of the Olifants River; the Lonely Bull Trail, which leaves from *Mopani*; and the Mphongolo Trail leaving from *Shingwedzi*. These trails offer one of the ultimate adventure wildlife experiences in Africa, where you are unpampered and self-sufficient, sleeping out in the wild every night with no facilities.

More expensive, and a lot easier to get a booking on, are the fabulous two- or three-night walking safaris in a magnificently wild concession near Skukuza, run by Rhino Post Walking Safaris (3 nights R12,000; W isibindiafrica.co.za), which uses Plains Camp as its base (see p.551), with the option of a sleep-out in a treehouse, where you spend the night cosily bedded on an elevated platform, able to see the stars and hear the sometimes chilling sounds of the night. Of the same calibre, offering a luxury walking and camping experience, deep in the Kruger Park, is Jock's Safaris (see p.551); the two-night Explorer experience costs R6000 per person and runs every weekend.

In addition, there are a number of cheaper walking trails within Greater Kruger, accessed from Hoedspruit and with organized departures from Johannesburg. Transfrontiers (T 015 793 0719, W transfrontiers.com) offers four-night walking safaris for R7500, using a camp in Balule, where the Big Five roam; accommodation is in safari tents or chalets. Another recommended operator is Africa on Foot (T 021 421 8433, W africaonfoot.com), which runs a combination of walking and driving trails in the Klaserie area, adjoining the Timbavati Reserve (three nights from R6600 per person). This area is wild and lovely, and their safari camp very pleasant; you walk for two to four hours in the morning, and enjoy game drives in the afternoons and evenings – the combination of safaris should allow you to see more game.

9

For a more rustic experience, head out to one of the handful of **bushveld camps** away from day-to-day trivialities and the tourist pack. The bushveld camps have accommodation of the same standard as the main restcamps, but accommodate fewer people, and are far smaller. They dispense with shops and restaurants, but are within reasonable reach of the restcamps.

Kruger's restcamps and bushveld camps are administered by SANParks (☎ 012 428 9111 or 082 233 9111, ⊕ sanparks .org/tourism/reservations) – **bookings** can only be made in advance online or by telephone, or at various satellite offices (see website). Advance bookings are a necessity – book as early as possible, especially for over school holidays and weekends, and don't turn up without a booking and expect to find accommodation. Even with advance booking, anticipate that you will most likely have to take any camp that is available, as demand far outstrips supply. Booking opens eleven months in advance.

SOUTHERN KRUGER RESTCAMPS

The so-called circus is the busiest section of the Kruger, with its hub at *Skukuza*, the biggest of all the Kruger camps, and *Lower Sabie*, one of the most popular. Apart from containing some of the best places for seeing large quantities of game, southern Kruger is also easily reached

GAME VIEWING AND PICNIC SITES IN SOUTHERN KRUGER

GAME VIEWING

Berg-en-Dal The focus of the camp is the Rhino Trail along the perimeter fence (with Braille facilities), meandering under riverine trees along the Matjulu dam, where there are resident crocodiles and nesting fish eagles. Game includes white rhino, leopards and lions, and plenty of kudu. Some say this is the best camp from which to set out on a guided morning walk because of the likelihood of encountering white rhino, and the pretty scenery.

Crocodile Bridge Try the tarred H4 north and dirt S25 east for elephant, rhino and buffalo. For cheetah, among the best places are the open plains along the S28 Nhola Road. If you're pushing north to *Lower Sabie*, it's worth taking the drive slowly, as this area, dotted with knobthorn and marula trees, is known for its herbivores, which include giraffe, wildebeest, zebra and buffalo, as well as ostrich, warthog and the magnificent black sable antelope. You should also keep your eyes peeled for predators such as lion, cheetah, hyena and jackal.

Lake Panic Only a twenty-minute drive (7km) from *Skukuza* (see opposite), Lake Panic has one of the best bird hides in the park, where you'll see herons, kingfishers, ducks, geese, dikkop and African jacanas, as well as hippos and crocodiles.

Lower Sabie The must-drive roads here include the H10 for lion and cheetah, the S130 for white rhino and the H4-1 for leopard. Sunset Dam, just outside *Lower Sabie*, is a favourite sunset spot, where you can get really close to the water, and is worthwhile at any time of day.

Pretoriuskop A decent focus for a day drive is Transport Dam, on the H1-1, a good place to see buffalo and elephant, and there's invariably other game to be found.

Skukuza Most people drive along the Sabie River to *Lower Sabie*, on the H4, one of the best places to see game. The tangled riverine forest, flanked by acacia bush and mixed savanna, is the most fertile and varied in the park. Another great drive is northeast on the H1–2 to Tshokwane picnic site, stopping at Elephant, Jones, Leeupan and Siloweni water holes. The area around *Skukuza* is also one of the best places to see endangered African wild dogs; worth trying is the S114 between Skukuza and Berg-en-Dal, the S1 between Phabeni Gate and Skukuza, and the H11 between Paul Kruger Gate and Skukuza.

PICNIC SITES

One of the park's nicest picnic sites is at **Afsaal**, between *Berg-en-Dal* and *Skukuza* on the H3, a good focus for a day drive. Once here, look out for the African scops-owl which sleeps in a tamboti tree nearly every day – the tree is marked so that you can try to spot the camouflaged bird. There's a shop on site.

Another top picnic spot is **Mlondozi**, north of *Lower Sabie* on the S29, which overlooks a dam from a thatched *lapa*, with some tables and chairs under trees. **Tshokwane** Picnic Site, 40km north of *Lower Sabie* on the H10, is much busier, but you can buy meals here.

from Johannesburg along the N4. At peak times of year, the area buzzes with vehicles jostling to get up close anywhere that big cats are sighted – events which always seem to induce bad human behaviour. As with all restcamps in Kruger, book in advance with SANParks (☎012 428 9111, ⓦsanparks.org/parks/kruger/).

Berg-en-Dal In the southwest corner of the park, 12km northwest of Malelane Gate ☎013 735 6106. Attractively set among *koppies* in a shallow grassy basin, *Berg-en-Dal* overlooks the Matjulu stream and dam, and has modern, fully equipped bungalows sleeping three people, or family cottages sleeping six, all landscaped among indigenous bushveld vegetation and widely spaced to provide privacy. Facilities include a beautifully positioned swimming pool, a shop with a good range of food, restaurants, a petrol station and a laundry. The area is known for rhinos. Camping R250, bungalow R1060, cottage R1980

Crocodile Bridge 12km north of Komatiport on N4 ☎013 735 6012. The least impressive of Kruger's restcamps – its position at the very southern edge of the park, overlooking sugar-cane farms, does nothing to enhance your bush experience. However, old hands say this is a tremendously underrated camp as there is a high density of general game, and you have an excellent chance of seeing the Big Five. Moreover it is quiet and has a lovely campsite with plenty of big trees for shade. Accommodation includes camping, two-bed permanent tents and en-suite bungalows sleeping two to three, with cooking facilities. Amenities are limited to a laundry and filling station, and a shop selling basic supplies. Camping R250, tent R540, bungalow R1160

★**Lower Sabie** 35km north of Crocodile Bridge ☎013 735 6056/6057. Usually fully booked, *Lower Sabie* occupies game-rich country, with an outlook over the Sabie River, which places it among the top three restcamps in the Kruger for animal-spotting. One of its biggest attractions is the large wooden viewing deck

outside the restaurant (open to day visitors) where you can have a snack while often watching elephants crossing the river in front of you. Accommodation includes camping, safari tents, bungalows and guest cottages, some with river views. There's a *Mugg & Bean* restaurant, a shop, a swimming pool, a filling station and a laundry. Camping R250, rondavel R510, bungalow R1060, cottage R1980

Pretoriuskop 9km east of Numbi Gate ☎013 735 5128/5132. The area surrounding Pretoriuskop is good for predators, however, given the dense bush, game viewing can be disappointing, and you may only see larger species such as kudus and giraffes. Accommodation here consists of en-suite cottages and guesthouses, bungalows and cheaper huts, and camping with shared ablution and cooking facilities. The camp has a Wimpy restaurant, a snack bar, a shop, a laundry, a semi-natural rock swimming pool – one of the most beautiful in Kruger, with a surrounding garden and picnic area – and a petrol station. Around the perimeter fence at night, you're almost certain to see patrolling hyenas, waiting for scraps from braais. One feature of the camp is the tame impala that wander freely around. Camping R250, hut R510, bungalow R985, cottage R1980

Skukuza 12km east of Paul Kruger Gate ☎013 735 4265/4196. Kruger's largest restcamp accommodates over a thousand people and lies at the centre of the best game-viewing area in the park. Its position is a mixed blessing; although you get large amounts of game, hordes of humans aren't far behind, and cars speeding at animal sightings can chase away the very animals they are trying to see. Accommodation is in a range of en-suite guesthouses, cottages and bungalows, or more cheaply in huts, safari tents and campsites, with shared ablutions and kitchens. *Skukuza* is the hub of Kruger; with its own airport (SA Airlink, private airlines and charters) and car-rental agency, and its sprawling collection of rondavels and staff village, it resembles a small town and all the cars can be

9

irksome. There are two swimming pools, and a deli café with internet facilities, plus a post office, a bank, a petrol station and garage, a *Cattle Baron & Bistro* steakhouse and a really good library (Mon–Fri 8.30am–4pm & 7–9pm, Sat 8.30am–12.45pm, 1.45–4pm & 7–9pm, Sun 8.30am–12.45pm & 1.45–4pm) with a collection of natural history books and exhibits. Golf at *Skukuza* is also a draw, where you'll have to sign an indemnity form in case of bumping into wildlife on the course. There is a special area designated for day visitors, with its own swimming pool and picnic area. Camping R250, tent R510, bungalow R1040, cottage R2000

CENTRAL KRUGER RESTCAMPS

Game viewing can be extremely good in the "zoo", the rough triangle between *Orpen*, *Satara* and *Letaba*, which is reckoned to be one of the global hot spots for lions. At *Olifants* you'll find the Kruger's most dramatically located camp, with fantastic views into a river gorge, while *Satara* is one of the most popular – its placement is ideal for making sorties into fertile wildlife country. It is estimated that there are about sixty lion prides in this central area, but, even so, you may not be lucky enough to see one. As with all restcamps in Kruger, book in advance with SANParks (☎012 428 9111, ⊚sanparks .org/parks/kruger).

Balule On the southern bank of the Olifants River, 41km north of Satara and 87km from Phalaborwa Gate ☎013 735 6606. A very basic satellite to *Olifants* (11km to the north), *Balule* is one of the few restcamps where two can stay for R500 without resorting to camping. The restcamp has two sections, one consisting of six rustic three-bed rondavels and another of fifteen camping and caravan sites. Each section has its own communal ablution and cooking facilities. You can forget about a/c; the only electricity is in the fence to keep out lions, and paraffin lamps are provided for lighting. Guests have to bring their own crockery, cutlery and utensils, and must report to *Satara* or *Olifants* at least half an hour before the gates close. Camping R250, rondavel R380

Letaba 52km east of Phalaborwa Gate ☎013 735 6636. *Letaba* is set in *mopane* shrubland along the Letaba River. Old and quite large, the camp is beautifully located on an oxbow curve, and though very few of the rondavels afford a view, the restaurant does have great vistas; you can spend a day just watching herds of buffalo mooching around, elephants drifting past and a host of other plains game. There is a full range of accommodation and the camp offers the usual shopping and laundry facilities, a *Mugg & Bean* restaurant, a swimming pool, a vehicle-repair workshop, and an interesting museum, Elephant Hall, with exhibits on the life of elephants, including a display on the Magnificent Seven, bulls with inordinately large tusks that once roamed the area, with six pairs of their tusks on display. Camping R250, tent R510, rondavel R630, bungalow R1040, cottage R2000

Olifants 80km east of Phalaborwa Gate ☎013 735 6606/6607. With a terrific setting on cliffs overlooking the braided Olifants River, *Olifants* is reckoned by many to be the best restcamp in Kruger. It's possible to spend hours sitting on the benches on the covered look-out terrace, gazing into the valley whose airspace is crisscrossed by Bateleur eagles and yellow-billed kites cruising the thermals, while the rushing of the water below creates a hypnotic rhythm. Of the thatched, en-suite rondavels, numbers 1–24 boast superb views overlooking the valley; it's worth booking well in advance to get one of these. You can eat at the *Mugg & Bean* restaurant, and there's a shop and a laundry. This is also promising country for spotting elephant, giraffe, lion, hyena and cheetah, and you should look out for the tiny klipspringer, a pretty antelope that inhabits rocky terrain, which it nimbly negotiates by boulder-hopping. R965

Orpen and **Maroela** Right by Orpen Gate, 45km east of Klaserie ☎013 735 6355. Recommended mainly if you're arriving late and don't have time to get further into the park before the camp gates close. However, *Orpen* is very good for game viewing, because the substantial Timbavati Private Game Reserve lies to the west, so you're

---

GAME VIEWING AND PICNIC SITES IN CENTRAL KRUGER

N'wanetsi River Road One of the best-known drives in the park is along the S100, with a stop at N'wanetsi Picnic Site, and beautiful scenery of riverine trees and open acacia savanna. It passes through a variety of terrain, which besides being scenic, means it attracts large herds of buffalo, giraffe, zebra, wildebeest, kudu and waterbuck and, in their wake, big cats. The S100 is one of the best roads to try to find lions.

Satara Rewarding drives are the Timbavati River Road (S39) and the drive east of *Satara* along the S100, which snakes along the N'wanetsi River towards the Lebombo Mountains, marking the border with Mozambique.

Tshokwane picnic site About halfway along the tarred road between *Satara* and *Skukuza*, the area around this picnic site can be good for lions, hence the number of motorists usually present.

GAME-VIEWING TIPS

- The best times of day for game viewing are when it's cooler, during the early morning and late afternoon. Set out as soon as the camp gates open in the morning and go out again as the temperature starts dropping in the afternoon. Take a siesta during the midday heat, just as the animals do, when they head for deep shade where you're less likely to see them.
- It's worth investing in a detailed **map of Kruger** (available at virtually every restcamp) in order to choose a route that includes rivers or pans where you can stop and enjoy the scenery and birdlife while you wait for game to come down to drink, especially in the late afternoon.
- **Driving really slowly** pays off, particularly if you stop often, in which case switch off your engine, open your window and use your senses. Stopping where other cars have already stopped or slowed down is probably the best strategy you could choose.
- Don't embark on overambitious drives from your restcamp. Plan carefully.
- **Binoculars** are a must for scanning the horizon.
- Take **food and drink** with you, and remember you can only use toilets and get out at the **picnic sites**, where there's always boiling water available, braai places powered with gas, and, at some sites, food or snacks for sale.

already well into the wilderness once you get here. There's a waterhole right in front of the camp, and animals come and go all the time. The camp is small, peaceful and shaded by beautiful trees; facilities include a petrol station, a shop and a swimming pool overlooking a waterhole, and accommodation is in bungalows and en-suite guest cottages, with communal kitchens. If you want to camp, you'll need to go to the small *Maroela* satellite camping area, overlooking the Timbavati River, approximately 4km from *Orpen*. You must report to *Orpen* reception to check in before going to the campsite, which has electricity. Camping R250, bungalow R1080, cottage R2000

★**Satara** 46km due east of Orpen Gate ☎013 735 6306/6307. *Satara* ranks second only to *Skukuza* (92km to the south) in size and the excellence of its game viewing. Set in the middle of flat grasslands, the camp commands no great views, but is preferable to *Skukuza* because it avoids the feeling of suburban boxes on top of each other. Very busy in season, accommodation ranges from camping, through bungalows and cottages arranged around lawned areas shaded by large trees, to secluded guesthouses; besides a shop, petrol station, laundry and an AA vehicle repair workshop, there's also a swimming pool, pizzeria and café. *Satara* itself is usually good for sighting grazers such as buffalo, wildebeest, zebra, kudu, impala and elephant; the night drives are particularly recommended. Camping R220, bungalow R1040, cottage R2025

Tamboti Turn left 2km after Orpen and continue for 1km ☎013 735 6355. Not far from Orpen Gate, *Tamboti* is Kruger's only tented camp. You sleep in tents in a tranquil position on the banks of the frequently dry Timbavati River, set among apple leaf trees, sycamore figs and jackalberries. From the tents, elephants can often be seen just beyond the electrified fence, digging in the river bed for moisture, hence the camp's popularity. Each walk-in tent has its own

deck overlooking the river, but best of all are numbers 21 and 22, which enjoy the deep shade of large riverine trees, something you'll appreciate in the midsummer heat. The tents have fridges and electric lighting, while all kitchen, washing and toilet facilities are in two shared central blocks (bring your own cooking and eating utensils). R535

NORTHERN KRUGER RESTCAMPS

You won't find edge-to-edge game in the northern section, the least visited of Kruger's regions, but you do get a much stronger feeling here of being in the wilds, particularly after you've crossed the Tropic of Capricorn north of *Mopani* camp and hit *Punda Maria* camp, which still has the flavour of an old-time outpost in the bush. As with all restcamps in Kruger, book in advance with SANParks (☎012 428 9111, ⓦ sanparks.org/parks/kruger).

Mopani 42km north of Letaba ☎013 735 6535/6536. *Mopani* overlooks the Pioneer Dam, one of the few water sources in the vicinity, which attracts animals to drink and provides an outstanding lookout for a variety of wildlife, including elephant, buffalo and antelope. This is a sprawling place in the middle of monotonous *mopane* scrub, with en-suite accommodation built of rough-hewn stone and thatch, and a restaurant and a bar with a good view across to the dam. Other facilities include a shop, a laundry and a petrol station; the swimming pool, one of the best in the park, provides cool relief after a long drive. Bungalow R1020, cottage R1160

★**Punda Maria** 71km beyond Shingwedzi ☎013 735 6873. Kruger's northernmost camp is a relaxed, tropical outpost near the Zimbabwe border. It is the least-visited camp and is unpretentious and peaceful. There's less of a concentration of game up here, but this isn't to say you won't see wildlife (the Big Five all breeze through from time to time). The real rewards of *Punda* are in its landscapes and stunningly varied vegetation, with a

9

GAME VIEWING AND PICNIC SITES IN NORTHERN KRUGER

Red Rocks Loop The S52 southwest of Shingwedzi is a favoured road for elephant sightings; if you drive it in the early morning, look out for leopards.

★**Pafuri picnic site** 46km north of *Punda*. This picnic site should on no account be missed, as it's here that you'll experience the true richness of northern Kruger, and it is rated as the top birding spot in the park. The site is a large area under the shade of massive thorn trees, leadwoods and jackalberry trees on the banks of the Luvuvhu River and is the ultimate place for lunch. An interpretation board gives a fascinating account of human history in the area. There are braai facilities, a constantly boiling kettle to make your own tea, and the attendant can sell you ice-cold canned drinks.

---

remarkable nine biomes all converging here, which also makes it a paradise for birdwatchers, notably along the Pafuri River. The landscape around *Punda* has many craggy sandstone cliffs, the hilltops crowned with giant baobabs, some as old as 4000 years. Accommodation is camping, in safari tents with communal cooking and ablution areas or en-suite fully equipped bungalows. The camp has a restaurant, a small shop, a petrol station, a swimming pool and a bird hide. Camping R220, bungalow R880, tent R975, cottage R2000

Shingwedzi 63km north of Mopani ☎013 735 6806/6807. A fairly large camp featuring a campsite, square, brick huts and a few older, colonial-style whitewashed, thatched bungalows, as well as a cottage and a guesthouse, sited in extensive grounds shaded by *pals* and *mopane* trees. From the terrace you get a long view down across the usually dry Shingwedzi River. Look out for the weavers' nests with their long, tube-like entrances hanging from the eaves outside reception. Camping R220, hut R490, bungalow R895, cottage R1385

BUSHVELD CAMPS

If you want to stay at a bushveld camp, book as early as possible, as demand for the bush experience they offer is pretty high. Note that the camps are out of bounds to anyone not booked in to stay. Most offer walks, night drives and hides. As with all camps in Kruger, book in advance with SANParks (☎012 428 9111, ⌨sanparks .org/parks/kruger).

★**Bateleur** About 40km southwest of Shingwedzi restcamp ☎013 735 6843. Well off the beaten track, in the remote northern section of the park on the banks of the frequently dry Mashokwe stream. The camp has a timber viewing-deck, excellently placed for views of game coming to drink at a seasonally full water hole. The nearby Silver Fish and Rooibosrand dams also attract game as well as birdlife in prodigious quantities. There are three six-bed cottages and four four-bed cottages; each has its own kitchenette and fridge, with electricity provided by solar panels. R1675

★**Biyamiti** 41km northeast of the Malelane Gate

and 26km west of Crocodile Bridge Gate ☎013 735 6171. *Biyamiti* lies on the banks of the Mbiyamiti River; its proximity is one of the main advantages of this very southerly camp, and the surrounding terrain attracts large numbers of game including lion, elephant and rhinos. There are ten two-bed guest cottages and five one-bed cottages, all with fully equipped kitchens. R975

Shimuwini About 50km from the Phalaborwa Gate on the Mooiplaas Rd ☎013 735 6683. *Shimuwini* lies on the upper reaches of the Shimuwini Dam, which is filled by the Letaba River. Situated in *mopane* and bushwillow country, with sycamore figs along the banks of the river, this peaceful camp is not known for its game but is a perennial favourite among birdwatchers. It's an excellent place for spotting riverine bird species, including fish eagles. Accommodation is in fourteen two-bedroom cottages (nine of which are especially nice) and one three-bedroom cottage. R1425

Sirheni Roughly 54km south of Punda Maria ☎013 735 6860. *Sirheni* is on the bank of Sirheni Dam. It's a fine spot for birdwatching, beautifully tucked into riverine forest, with some game also passing through the area. The big pull, however, is its remote bushveld atmosphere in an area that sees few visitors. There are five four-bedroom cottages and ten smaller cottages, all en suite and equipped with kitchens. The camp's two bird hides are a great pull. R1420

Talamati About 31km south of Orpen Gate ☎013 735 6343. Lying on the banks of the usually dry Nwaswitsontso stream, the mixed bushwillow woodland setting of *Talamati* attracts giraffe, kudu, wildebeest, zebra and predators like lion, hyena and jackal, as well as rhino and sable. Two hides within the perimeter of the camp overlook a water hole, where game viewing can be excellent. The camp has ten comfortable two-bedroom and four smaller one-bedroom cottages arranged in an L-shape along the river in a forest of leadwoods and russet bushwillows. R1550

Tzendze Rustic Camp 7km south of Mopani ☎013 735 6535/6536. The back-to-basics *Tzendze Rustic Camp* caters for those who wish to escape the typical Kruger camp vibe.

There is no electricity here – the lighting in the ablutions is from a solar battery system and hot water in the outdoor showers is from gas geysers. There are thirty camping sites (sites 14, 15 and 16 are best), but as each is surrounded by trees and scrub the atmosphere is wild and rustic. The nearest shop is at *Mopani*. **R230**

Private reserves – Greater Kruger

Kruger's western flank is comprised of private reserves, whose boundaries with Kruger are unfenced – the whole zone is often referred to as **Greater Kruger**. Within each reserve are a number of gorgeous safari lodges, each on a large tract of land. Some establishments have three different lodges on their properties, each one different in character, and with some price variations.

It's in these private reserves that you'll find utterly luxurious and romantic accommodation, fabulous food and classic safaris on Land Rovers, where you'll see plenty of big game, smaller animals and birds. All lodges follow the same basic formula: full board, with dawn and late-afternoon game drives conducted by a ranger, assisted by a tracker, in open vehicles. Afternoon outings usually turn into night drives following sundowners in the bush. In winter months you'll be given blankets on the vehicle and even hot water bottles in some places, to cope with the cold. Dinners are inevitably lamplit, around a fire, in the open. Several offer bushwalks, usually after breakfast, and most overlook water holes, rivers or plains, so that you can look out for animals during the time you're in camp, when you're not lazing around the pool, making use of the spa or gym facilities or perusing their collection of animal books on gigantic sofas.

The **Sabi Sands reserve** (ⓦsabi.krugerpark.co.za) is one of the best places in the world for seeing leopards and lions. **Sabi Sands South** is the most exclusive of all the game-viewing areas in South Africa, not only because of the superb game, but also because of its proximity to Nelspruit, and by car it's a two- to three-hour easy run to the lodges from KMIA airport. **Sabi Sands North** is cheaper, and the game is good, but access is more difficult. From the R40 you turn east at Acornhoek, travelling along dirt roads through traditional African villages for a couple of hours to reach the lodges. **Manyeleti**, north of Sabi Sands, is easily accessed from Orpen Gate; **Timbavati**, accessed off the R40 Hoedspruit/Eastgate turnoff, is easy to reach, with less travelling on dirt roads than to reach Sabi Sands North.

Even easier to reach, but as a result closer to roads and the sounds of civilization, are the private reserves abutting the R40, and accessible from Hoedspruit – Kapama, Thorneybush, Balule and Karongwe.

ACCOMMODATION   PRIVATE RESERVES

Prices are undeniably very steep in the private reserves – you're paying for the African wilderness experience, and for rangers who are dedicated to showing you as much as possible. Prices quoted below include all meals and all game activities. You need to book ahead, and get driving instructions to your camp, as no pop-ins are allowed.

MANYELETI

Honeyguide 4km from Orpen Gate ☏015 793 1729, ⓦhoneyguidecamp.com. One of the more reasonably priced camps, and the only one to offer tented accommodation at each of its two locations, *Khoka Moya*, which takes children and is contemporary in design, and *Mantobeni*, which has more of a traditional safari camp feel. With a lack of tended gardens, the camps maximize the bush feel, and although they don't have views of a river or a water hole, they make up for it with attentive staff and superb rangers and trackers. Each tent is enormous and has its own bathroom with double showers and basins. The best thing about *Honeyguide* is that there is an imaginative children's programme, and great tolerance of children of all ages. Rangers will take your kids off your hands and make casts of animal tracks in the bush, teach them about wildlife and in the evenings sit them on cushions around the campfire. Meals are plated, and all beverages, including wine, are included in the price. **R7560**

TIMBAVATI

Shindzela 33km inside the reserve, accessed from Timbavati Gate ☏087 943 6442 or ☏082 307 9493,

9

WILDLIFE IN THE PRIVATE RESERVES

If it's **leopards** you're after, Sabi Sands is best, especially in the south, where they have become quite blasé about people and vehicles. Timbavati is much quieter and wilder than Sabi Sands, and is known for its large herds of **buffalo**, with plenty of lions and elephants, though it's not good for viewing leopards and cheetah. Timbavati's name is associated with the extraordinary phenomenon of **white lions**, and while you may see some prides carrying the recessive gene which makes them look a little paler, the last sighting of an adult white lion was in 1993 – though a dozen cubs have been born since, but with the high mortality rate, it is not known whether two which were doing well in 2010 have survived. Manyeleti has a good spread of all game, with some stirring landscapes of open grasslands and rocky outcrops, where it borders Kruger. During the apartheid days, Manyeleti was the only part of Kruger that black people were allowed in, and consequently is far less developed than the other reserves, with little accommodation, which works to its advantage in that there are fewer vehicles about.

ⓦ shindzela.co.za. *Shindzela's* draw is its small size, affordability and walking opportunities. It is a twelve-bed unfenced, no-frills tented lodge, with early morning walks of two to four hours, or game drives if you prefer. They also offer transfers from Johannesburg. R3500

★ **Umlani** Close to Orpen Gate, accessed from Orpen Rd ☎ 021 785 5547, ⓦ umlani.com. Eight reed-walled huts overlooking the dry Nhlaralumi River, each with an attached open-topped bush shower, heated by a wood boiler (there's no electricity). *Umlani* (meaning "place of rest") isn't fenced off, the emphasis being very much on a bush experience, and windows are covered with flimsy blinds so that you get to hear all the sounds of the night. The decor is simple, as is the food, though it's delicious and you don't end up overstuffed. Altogether, *Umlani* delivers a much more satisfying experience of the wilds than many other places, and offers very good value. Check out their specials for some great deals. R6000

SABI SANDS NORTH

Djuma Game Reserve ☎ 013 735 5555 or ☎ 083 574 1660, ⓦ djuma.com. The best of *Djuma's* camps is *Vuyatela*, combining a hip, contemporary African feel with township art and funky fittings, plus good wildlife spotting. Each five-star suite has its own plunge pool and mini-bar. Moreover, there is a library, gym and wellness centre for massages and beauty treatments. *Djuma* is one of the more socially minded establishments, with traditional village trips organized during the day between game drives, and they support preschools in Dixi village. R10500

Nkorho Bush Camp ☎ 013 735 5367, ⓦ nkorho.com. A small, family-operated outfit in thinly wooded grassland, *Nkorho* scores on affordability. There are six simple chalets with showers, catering to a maximum of sixteen guests. The communal areas comprise an open-air lounge, a bar with a pool table and an African fantasy of a *boma* – constructed from gnarled tree trunks – where evening

meals are served around an open fire. The swimming pool overlooks a productive water hole. R6130

SABI SANDS SOUTH

Lion Sands ☎ 013 735 5000, ⓦ lionsands.com. One of the top game lodges in Sabi Sands, with accommodation in suites, with bathrooms that couldn't be more romantic, overlooking the Sabi River. *River Lodge's* eighteen suites come with their own butler, combined with terrific game viewing. The food is top-notch, and the two swimming pools, heated in winter, are placed right next to the river so you can hang out and watch the hippos. Close to River Lodge, and actually in the Kruger itself, is *Tinga Lodge*, with gorgeous riverside suites, each with a deck and heated plunge pool overlooking the water. *River Lodge* R14,600; *Tinga* R18,000

★ **Nottens Bush Camp** ☎ 013 735 5105, ⓦ nottens .com. Four decades old and still resisting the temptation to expand, this family-run outfit feels as if you are staying on a sociable friend's farm. Meals are served around a fire, or on a massive deck that acts as a viewing platform. The camp houses just eighteen (children over 8 welcome) in large tin-roofed chalets, facing the plain and lit by paraffin oil lamps. The lack of electricity in the bedrooms is meant to bring guests into better contact with the bush. It offers very good value for a five-star game-viewing experience, and has a swimming pool where you can actually swim laps, next to the massage room. R7750

BALULE

★ **Sausage Tree** Balule Nature Reserve, off the R40, 22km north of Hoedspruit ☎ 083 349 6007, ⓦ sausagetree.co.za. The pick of the crop of safari camps in Balule Reserve . Balule is well stocked with all the big game, and has the lovely Oliphants River defining its northern border, though you are aware of the R40 not far away. *Sausage Tree* represents great value for money; the game drives are excellent, the rooms are comfortable with every detail thought through, and meals are served on the deck which is set high up with long views across the bushveld. It is also a small camp with very personalized attention, so that you begin to feel like one of the family, sitting around the roaring campfire. <u>R3600</u>

PRIVATE CAMPS CLOSE TO SKUKUZA

★**Jock Safari Lodge** Kruger National Park, 38km from Skukuza ☎041 509 3000, ⍵jocksafarilodge .com. Fabulous location in a game hotspot deep in the southern Kruger, at the confluence of two seasonal rivers. Majestic riverine trees shade the twelve thatched luxury suites: choose a north-facing room if you can, where you can doze on the sunny daybed on your private deck above the river bank. The lodge also has a spa and small gym, and a library with internet. Jock also offers a two night package of walking with a ranger and staying over at a rustic camp. Watch for specials which can be a third cheaper. <u>R12,000</u>

★**Rhino Post Walking Safaris and Plains Camp** ☎035 474 1473 or ☎035 474 1490, ⍵isibindiafrica .co.za. Two safari camps on this magnificent, wild concession near *Skukuza*, offering different experiences. *Rhino Post Lodge* has eight suites built out of stone, wood and thatch, above a sandy river bed, while *Plains Camp* has four super-comfy safari tents, overlooking a plain that is rarely absent of game. *Plains Camp*, simply furnished in a pioneer style, is marvellously peaceful with a maximum of eight guests, has been built with no trees cut down or concrete used, and is solar powered. For an ultimate wilderness experience, walk with a superbly informed armed guide to the tree-house overnight camp, which has basic beds under mosquito nets set on high wooden platforms, where you hear all the African night sounds. <u>R8450</u>

Limpopo

BAOBAB TREES

10

Limpopo

Limpopo Province is considered by many to be South Africa's no-man's-land: a hot, thornbush-covered area caught between the dynamic heartland of Gauteng to the south and, to the north, the Limpopo River, which acts as South Africa's border with Zimbabwe and Botswana. The real highlights of Limpopo are often overshadowed by the busy N1 highway, South Africa's umbilical cord to the rest of the continent, which dissects the province. But this is where you'll find vast open spaces with wildlife galore and breathtaking mountainous landscapes covered in mist, all accessible at lower prices than elsewhere in the country. Culturally, Limpopo also stands out: seven of South Africa's eleven official languages are spoken here, and you stand a good chance of meeting people from the majority of the country's ethnic groupings while travelling around the province. The region is also well endowed with a remarkable and ever-increasing number of wildlife and nature reserves, housing the country's highest population of rhinos and a multitude of elegant species of antelope, and ensuring that there is brilliant game viewing to be had.

The eastern side of the province is lowveld, dominated by the 70km-wide strip of Kruger National Park abutting the Mozambique border. This part of Limpopo is covered, along with Kruger itself, in the preceding chapter. The principal attractions of the rest of the province lie in its three wild and distinctive **mountain escarpments**. The best known of these is the **Drakensberg** Escarpment, making the descent from highveld to lowveld through lush forests in the Letaba to the west of Kruger.

Polokwane, the provincial capital, lies west of the Drakensberg along the N1, while further to the west lies the sedate **Waterberg** massif, a region dedicated to wildlife conservation and offering malaria-free Big Five game viewing. In the north, parallel to the Limpopo River and bisected by the N1, are the subtropical **Soutpansberg Mountains**, and the intriguing and still very independently minded **Venda** region, a homeland during the apartheid era, to the east. North of the Soutpansberg are wide plains dominated by surreal baobab trees, much in evidence along the N1 as it leads to the only border post between South Africa and Zimbabwe, at Beitbridge. Hugging the border to the west, stifling hot Mapungubwe National Park provides a fascinating insight into what is now recognized as Africa's earliest kingdom.

Brief history

The first black Africans arrived in South Africa across the Limpopo River some time before 300 AD. The various movements and migrations, and of course trading, ensured a fluidity in the people who established themselves here, and the historical and cultural

VHAVENDA HUT WITH SOLAR PANEL

Highlights

❶ Exploring the Letaba Experience this otherworldly area of lush forests, subtropical tea plantations and upmarket country-house guesthouses, and the quirky, time-warped town of Haenertsburg in its midst. **See p.561**

❷ Horseriding in the Waterberg This mountain range offers some of South Africa's finest wilderness riding and horseback safaris, with outrides among zebra and giraffe, and the occasional rhino tagging along. **See p.564**

❸ Soutpansberg Mountains Spend the night in the mountains watching the magical display

of stars above and let the soothing sound of the gushing waterfall gently lull you to sleep. **See p.568**

❹ Venda crafts Explore the remote, simple villages of the mystical Venda region and discover its skilful and distinctive art, pottery and woodcarvings. **See p.569**

❺ Mapungubwe archeology Climb the Hill of Jackals and see the remains of Africa's earliest kingdom, then continue to the fantastic nearby San cave paintings. **See p.572**

HIGHLIGHTS ARE MARKED ON THE MAP ON PP.556–557

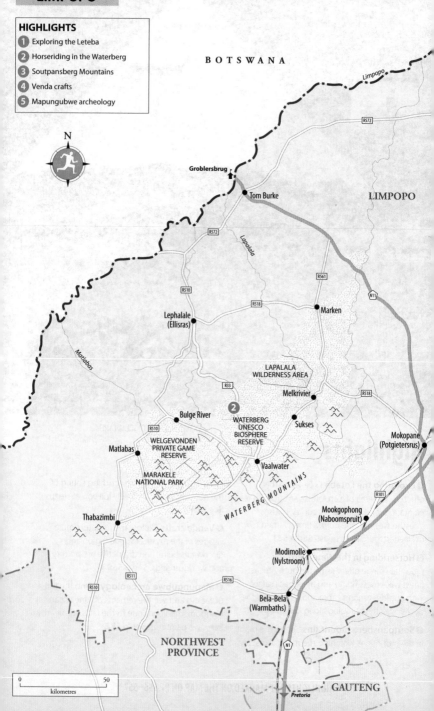

LIMPOPO

HIGHLIGHTS

1 Exploring the Leteba
2 Horseriding in the Waterberg
3 Soutpansberg Mountains
4 Venda crafts
5 Mapungubwe archeology

N

BOTSWANA

Limpopo

R572

LIMPOPO

Groblersbrug

Tom Burke

R572

Lapalala

R510

R518

R561

Lephalale
(Ellisras)

Marken

N11

Matlabos

LAPALALA
WILDERNESS AREA

R33

Melkrivier

R518

2

Bulge River

WATERBERG
UNESCO
BIOSPHERE
RESERVE

Sukses

Mokopane
(Potgietersrus)

R510

WELGEVONDEN
PRIVATE GAME
RESERVE

Matlabas

Vaalwater

MARAKELE
NATIONAL PARK

WATERBERG MOUNTAINS

Mookgophong
(Naboomspruit)

R101

Thabazimbi

Modimolle
(Nylstroom)

R510

R511

R516

Bela-Bela
(Warmbaths)

N1

**NORTHWEST
PROVINCE**

GAUTENG

0   50
kilometres

Pretoria

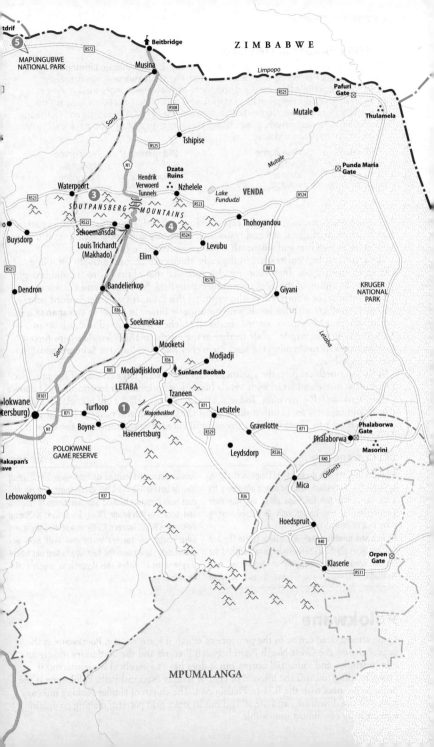

tdrif

5 MAPUNGUBWE NATIONAL PARK

R572

✈ **Beitbridge**

ZIMBABWE

Musina

Limpopo

R525

Pafuri Gate ⊠

R508

Sand

Mutale

Thulamela

R525

● **Tshipise**

N1

Mutale

Dzata Ruins

Hendrik Verwoerd Tunnels

Waterpoort

3

● **Nzhelele**

VENDA

Lake Fundudzi

R523

R524

S O U T P A N S B E R G   M O U N T A I N S

⊠ **Punda Maria Gate**

R523

R522

4

● **Thohoyandou**

Buysdorp

Schoemansdal

R524

Louis Trichardt (Makhado)

● **Levubu**

R21

Elim

R81

● **Dendron**

Bandelierkop

R578

KRUGER NATIONAL PARK

● **Giyani**

o

R36

Soekmekaar

Sand

● **Mooketsi**

● **Modjadji**

R36

Letaba

R81

Modjadjiskloof

🍃 **Sunland Baobab**

LETABA

Tzaneen

olokwane tersburg)

R101

Turfloop

1

Magoebaskloof

R71

Letsitele

R71

N1

Boyne

Haenertsburg

● **Gravelotte**

R71

Phalaborwa

⊠ **Phalaborwa Gate**

R329

akapan's ave

POLOKWANE GAME RESERVE

● **Leydsdorp**

● **Masorini**

R526

R40

Lebowakgomo

R37

Olifants

R36

● **Mica**

Hoedspruit

R40

Klaserie

⊠ **Orpen Gate**

R531

MPUMALANGA

10

NAME CHANGES IN LIMPOPO

What was once known as South Africa's Northern Province was renamed **Limpopo** in 2002, and the capital, Pietersburg, was subsequently renamed **Polokwane**. A number of other towns with "colonial" names have also undergone official name changes, though some of these changes have been taken to court for various political and procedural reasons – the name change of Louis Trichardt to Makhado was reversed in 2007. Road signs and local usage yet have to catch up with officialdom, and examples of changes that you'll come across while travelling in the province include:

Old name	New name	Old name	New name
Ellisras	Lephalale	Nylstroom	Modimolle
Messina	Musina	Potgietersrus	Mokopane
Naboomspruit	Mookgophong	Warmbaths	Bela-Bela

ties to the north are, as you might expect, stronger in this region than in other parts of South Africa. Traditional arts and crafts such as **pottery** and **woodcarving** are still an important part of life; and **witchcraft** is still encountered in many places.

The arrival of the **Voortrekkers** in the early nineteenth century brought profound changes to the region. Their route roughly followed that of the N1 today, and brought about the founding of the towns now called Bela-Bela, Modimolle and Polokwane, among others. The Voortrekkers who ventured this far north were determined people, and their conflicts with the locals were notoriously bitter. In 1850, at **Makapan's Cave** off the N1 near Mokopane, several thousand Ndebele were starved to death by an avenging Boer commando, while further to the north, in 1867, Venda troops forced the Voortrekkers to abandon the settlement they had established at **Schoemansdal** in the Soutpansberg.

In the twentieth century, the apartheid years saw several large chunks of the province hived off as homeland areas, with Venda becoming notionally independent and Lebowa and Gazankulu self-governing. Today the contrasts between the old homelands and the white farming areas are manifest throughout the province, and poverty, HIV and corruption are rife. However, the province still voted overwhelmingly in favour of the ANC in 2014.

GETTING AROUND   LIMPOPO

By car Cutting through the middle of Limpopo, the N1 is, by South African standards, fast and easy, if often busy. It's a toll road, with five toll stops along the way from Johannesburg to the border with Zimbabwe costing between R30–40 each time.

By bus and minibus taxi SA Roadlink, City to City and Translux buses ply the N1 between Johannesburg and the Musina border post, stopping at Polokwane and Makhado. Translux also runs buses between

Johannesburg and Tzaneen via Polokwane. The Tzaneng Shuttle bus (☏ 073 110 4180, ⊛ tzanengshuttle.zxq.net) runs from Pretoria's Hatfield Gautrain station to Tzaneen and back via Polokwane (Wed, Fri & Sun; 4h30min; Polokwane R250, Tzaneen R300). In addition, these other routes are covered by minibus taxis from any moderately sized town; the best way to find out where they're going and when they depart is to enquire at the taxi rank.

Polokwane

Lying almost dead centre in the province of which it is the capital, **Polokwane** is the largest city on the Great North Road between Pretoria and the border. It's mostly an administrative and industrial centre, but it does have an excellent museum, and if you're heading towards the lowveld or central Kruger National Park, Polokwane is the point to connect with the R71 to Phalaborwa. The clutch of similar-looking one-way streets in the downtown area are all laid out in strict grid pattern, making navigation, especially by car, almost impossible.

MALARIA IN LIMPOPO

Parts of Limpopo are **malarial**; you will need to take prophylactics, and exercise caution against mosquitoes if you are travelling in the lowveld, including Kruger National Park, or north of the Soutpansberg Mountains. The Waterberg area was not affected at the time of writing, though it's worth double-checking the current situation with your accommodation or safari provider before you go.

Civic Square

At the heart of Polokwane's busy, compact CBD is the **Civic Square**, a park area bounded on two sides by Landros Mare and Thabo Mbeki streets. Streets on either side are abuzz with the bustle from street traders competing with stores and selling anything from top designer gear to Chinese enamelware.

Bakone Malapa Museum

9km southeast of town on the R37 • Mon–Fri 8.30am–4.30pm, Sat 9.30am–3.30pm • R10 • ☎ 015 290 2540

Polokwane's one sight really worth seeing is the open-air **Bakone Malapa Museum**. A simple but genuine project, it succeeds in conveying some of the old way of life of the local Bakone people – a grouping within the Northern Sotho – where many flashier examples have fallen short. A village of huts has been built in the traditional style, and ten people live permanently on site, working on crafts such as pottery and leatherworking through the day. One of them also acts as a guide, and will explain the different activities you see, as well as the architecture, history and legends of the site.

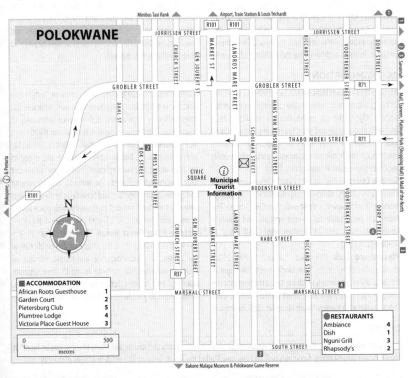

Polokwane Game Reserve

Silicon Road, along the R37 near the stadium, 3km south of town • Daily 7am–4.30pm • R19, car R29 • ☎ 015 290 2331

If you're not heading to Kruger, the 3200-hectare municipal **Polokwane Game Reserve** is a good place to spot white rhino, eland, sable antelope and some fifty other species of game, plus two hundred bird species. The well-kept trails through fertile grassland are suitable for regular cars, and there are hiking trails of 5–21km, too.

ARRIVAL AND DEPARTURE

By plane SA Airlink (☎ 015 288 0166, ⓦ flyairlink.com) flies from Johannesburg (Mon–Thurs & Sat 1–2 daily, Fri & Sun 3 daily; 1hr) to Polkwane's Gateway Airport, on the N1, 5km north of the city (☎ 015 288 1622, ⓦ gaal.co.za): the airport is also served by the odd international connection from neighbouring countries. All the city's car-rental firms have offices at the airport, including Avis (☎ 015 288 0171), Budget (☎ 015 288 0169) and Europcar (☎ 015 288 0097), while taxis line up outside (City Taxi ☎ 015 288 0142).

By bus All intercity buses from Johannesburg to Polokwane (7 daily; 4–6hr) pass through the centre of town: Translux and City-to-City stop at the train station, Greyhound stops on Thabo Mbeki St near Civic Square and at the Mall of the North and Savannah Mall. The Tzaneng Shuttle bus (see p.588) stops at the Savannah Mall.

By train The train station is on the northern edge of the city centre, just off the R521 (an extension of Market St). A twice-weekly train leaves Johannesburg every Wednesday and Friday at 7pm, arriving in Polokwane at 3.50am, then continuing to Louis Trichardt (arrival 8am) and Musina, near the Zimbabwe border (arrival 11.15am). The return trains leaves Musina every Sunday and Thursday at 3.25pm, arriving at Louis Trichardt at 6.15pm, Polokwane at 10.35pm, and Johannesburg at 5.44am the following day. Tickets from Johannesburg to Polokwane are R100 for an ecomony seat, R180 for a sleeper berth.

INFORMATION

Tourist information There are two tourist information offices in Polokwane. One is the municipal tourist information service (Mon–Fri 7.30am–5pm, Sat 9am–1pm; ☎ 015 290 2010) at the Civic Square, which can help with information about the city's accommodation, attractions and transport. The other is Limpopo Tourism and Parks, on the outskirts of town on the western side of the N1 when coming from Johannesburg (Mon–Fri 8am–4.30pm; ☎ 015 293 3600, ⓦ golimpopo.com), which runs a provincial service and stocks an array of brochures and maps. There is also a helpful budget travellers' tourist agent, SA Tours and Bookings (☎ 082 375 3870, ⓔ satours@mweb.co.za), at *Plumtree Lodge* (see below).

ACCOMMODATION

African Roots Guesthouse 58a Devenish St ☎ 015 297 0113, ⓦ africanroots.info. On the corner of Oost St at the eastern edge of the city centre, this is a relaxed, tasteful spot with immaculate and stylish rooms given character by local and foreign works of art selected by the designer proprietors. The breakfast restaurant also serves evening meals on request. Wi-fi throughout. R780

Garden Court On the corner of Thabo Mbeki and Bok St ☎ 015 291 2030, ⓦ www.tsogosunhotels.com. Large modern hotel complex, a short walk from Civic Square. The rooms are predictable but decent enough, and there's a good restaurant and an outdoor pool. Half price at weekends. R1200

Pietersburg Club 119 South St ☎ 015 291 2900, ⓦ pietersburgclub.co.za. Four blocks from Civic Square, this traditional gentlemen's club has taken the leap into the twenty-first century and now offers comfortable en-suite rooms, some with garden-facing verandas ideal for sipping sundowners. The club also has an excellent restaurant and a bizarre remnant from days gone by, a men-only bar. The "members only" sign at the club entrance refers only to residents of Polokwane. Free wi-fi throughout. R800

★ **Plumtree Lodge** 138 Marshall St ☎ 015 295 6153, ⓦ plumtree.co.za. Not far from the centre, this is one of the city's oldest and most efficiently run lodges, with smart rooms set in high-ceilinged villas around a large compound and garden, a poolside bar, and breakfasts to die for. This is probably the friendliest and most comfortable place to stay in town. Cheaper rates (R715) over the weekend. R915

Victoria Place Guest House 32 Burger St ☎ 015 295 7599, ⓦ victoriaplace.co.za. Situated a short walk east of the centre, this Victorian-style guesthouse consists of fourteen individualistic en-suite rooms in three separate buildings and a self-catering section across the street. Known especially for its hearty breakfasts. R935

EATING

True to its functional role, Polokwane has no shortage of chain restaurants and takeaways. Many of these can be found at the city's two largest malls: Savannah Mall and the new Mall of the North, both on the western fringes of the city.

Ambiance 34 Rabe St ☎015 291 4012, ⓦambiancerestaurant.co.za. Classy, contemporary restaurant serving tasty light meals, including wraps (R65–85) and quiche (R49), as well as hearty dinners like biltong and avocado steak (R111), plus delicious cakes and teatime treats. There's also outdoor seating below the jacaranda trees in the pretty garden. Mon–Fri 8am–10pm, Sat 9am–2pm.

★ **Dish** 96 Burger St, on the corner of Rissik St ☎079 553 3790. A delightful café, restaurant and bar in an old house with a large garden. *Dish* serves cakes, sandwiches (try a biltong cheese sandwich, R55) and hot meals such as stuffed trout (R105) and traditional oxtail (R115). Mon 9am–5pm, Tues–Fri 9am–midnight, Sat & Sun 9am–3pm.

Nguni Grill De Wet Drive ☎082 314 8788. On the corner of Morris St, this is a proper steak house serving weird things like "puff adder" sausages (sausages made of minced kidney and liver), grilled tortoise (actually lamb's liver) and lots of other unusual but tasty meat dishes. Tues–Sat 11am–11pm, Sun 11am–4pm.

Rhapsody's 1 Pamelo Street, Platinum Park shopping centre ☎015 297 1296, ⓦrhapsodys.co.za. Part of a pan-African chain of fine dining restaurants, *Rhapsody's* specializes in beautiful slow-cooked lamb shank and other grilled mains of around R160. This is also a great place for breakfast, with about ten different options such as poached eggs served with spinach and hollandaise sauce, and a full-on traditional English fry-up. Mon–Thurs 7am–10.30pm, Fri 7am–11pm, Sat 8am–11pm, Sun 9am–3pm.

10

Letaba

East of Polokwane, the **Letaba** is a forested, lush, mountainous area, contrasting very sharply with the hot lowveld and bushveld abutting it east towards Kruger and west towards Polokwane. It marks the first dramatic rise of the Drakensberg Escarpment as it begins its sweep south through Mpumalanga. The forest begins around the mountain village of **Haenertsburg** and follows two very scenic parallel valleys to Limpopo's second-largest but missable town, **Tzaneen**. The valleys are filled with lakes surrounded by dark pine forests, sparkling rivers, misty peaks and, towards Tzaneen, subtropical

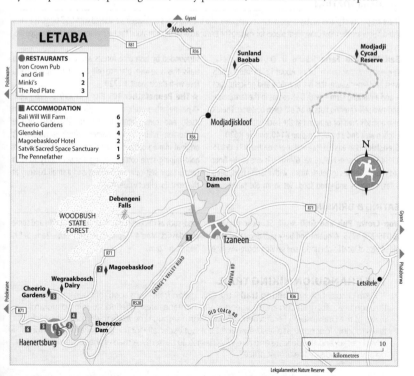

LETABA

● **RESTAURANTS**
Iron Crown Pub and Grill	1
Minki's	2
The Red Plate	3

■ **ACCOMMODATION**
Bali Will Will Farm	6
Cheerio Gardens	3
Glenshiel	4
Magoebaskloof Hotel	2
Satvik Sacred Space Sanctuary	1
The Pennefather	5

crops such as macadamia nuts and avocados. With some very comfortable and beautifully located guesthouses, farm-stalls and tea rooms, hiking trails and trout fishing, the Letaba is in many ways an attractive, less-well-known alternative to Mpumalanga's crowded highlands, although it is gradually making solid inroads onto the tourist route.

Haenertsburg

Mellow **Haenertsburg** lies 60km from Polokwane, high on a hillside tucked away behind the R71 as the road winds down into the thickly wooded Magoebaskloof Valleys. Once an old gold-rush village, Haenertsburg has wonderful views over the area known as the Land of the Silver Mist; that is, when it's not covered in a light carpet of mist that gives it its nickname. With few fences or gates to protect private property, the town has an unusual and unmistakable time-warped feel to it – as if existing within an isolated bubble. This is apparently due to the town's many eccentric residents, some of whom are said to use otherworldly powers to protect the town. There's not much more to Haenertsburg than its **main street**, Rissik Street, which is lined with various quaint olde-worlde shops, including a secondhand bookshop, art gallery and antique and curio shops.

ARRIVAL AND INFORMATION   HAENERTSBURG

By bus Three times weekly, the Tzaneng Shuttle bus between Tzaneen and Pretoria (see p.558) stops along the R71 in Haenertsburg, five minutes' walk from the village centre. Regular minibus taxis from Polokwane and Tzaneen also pass by.

Information The town's informal tourism office (daily 9am–7pm; ⓦ magoebaskloftourism.co.za) is inside the bookshop at *The Pennefather* hotel on Rissik St, and hands out the useful free Mountain Getaways map and guide.

ACCOMMODATION

There are plenty of places to stay in the Haenertsburg area, and the two roads to Tzaneen are littered with B&B signs. The ones listed below are the most convenient places for visiting the town; accommodation along the two routes is covered on opposite.

Bali Will Will Farm D3 Rd D ⓣ 015 276 2212, ⓔ glmccomb@absamail.co.za. About 1.5km into the hills west of Haenertsburg, this is a beautiful and peaceful spot – and a working farm – with B&B rooms in the farmhouse and two self-catering flats in an old farm building. There's also a shady area for camping at the back with showers, a kitchen area and a braai. Camping R140, double R620

Glenshiel 2km east of Haenertsburg on the R71 ⓣ 015 276 4335, ⓦ glenshiel.co.za. *Glenshiel* is one of the finer old country lodges in South Africa, with roaring fires, deep sofas, antiques and good food. Set in an old farmhouse surrounded by lush pine forests and a number of hiking trails, this is an ideal place to chill out for a couple of days. Free wi-fi throughout. R1720

★**The Pennefather** 105 Rissik St ⓣ 015 276 4885, ⓔ pennefather@telkomsa.net. The only option in town itself, and conveniently located for the start of the Changuion hiking trail. Named after Haenertsburg's original mining company, *The Pennefather* consists of six gold-mining-style cottages lining a small courtyard with comfortable self-catering facilities and a small balcony at the front. Excellent value. R660

EATING & DRINKING

Iron Crown Pub and Grill Rissik St, near the R71 ⓣ 015 276 4755. A quaint and busy pub decorated with old photos of local lumberjacks, and serving above-average

food, such as chicken curry (R65), prawns (R120) and some pub classics. Mon 4–10pm, Tues–Fri 10am–2am, Sat & Sun 9am–2am.

THE CHANGUION HIKING TRAIL

A 10km circular historical **hiking trail** – the Changuion Trail – runs south of Haenertsburg through beautiful grassland and indigenous afromontane forest, offering stunning panoramic views of the Drakensberg Escarpment. It's well worth setting time aside to do the trail, which takes roughly four hours at a leisurely pace. Look out especially for the blue swallow, Methuens Dwarf gecko, and the delicate and rare Wolkberg Zulu butterfly. A map of the route is painted on a wall outside by the tourist office.

Minki's Rissik St, corner of Rush St ☎ 015 276 4781. A bright and modern coffee shop and lunchroom overlooking the main crossing in town: it also sells art and craft supplies. There's excellent coffee and freshly baked goods such as Belgian waffles, as well as light meals like the prego steak roll (R65) and oven-baked trout (R79). Mon– Sat 9am–4.30pm, Sun 9am–3pm.

★**The Red Plate** Rissik St 161 ☎ 083 305 2851, ⓦ redplate.co.za. With a shady terrace overlooking downtown Haenertsburg, *The Red Plate* serves excellent food throughout the day including freshly caught trout (R75), an array of tasty salads, the usual burgers and steaks, and a good malva pudding with custard (R26). Mon noon– 8pm, Tues & Sun 9am–3.30pm, Wed–Sat 9am–8pm.

10

Along the two valley roads to Tzaneen

Just east of Haenertsburg is a turning off the main R71 for the R528 which offers an alternative route to Tzaneen via **Georges Valley Road**. There is, in fact, little to choose between the two options in terms of both distance and stunning scenery. Along the Georges Valley Road lies a memorial to **John Buchan**, author of *The Thirty-Nine Steps*. Further along, the tranquil **Tzaneen Dam** is an atmospheric spot for swimming and picnicking.

Taking the R71, the Magoebaskloof Valley Road, will lead you through the dramatic **Magoebaskloof Valley**, named after the rogue chief Makgoba, who in 1895 had his head chopped off by native warriors serving under the Boer leader Abel Erasmus. The grand *Magoebaskloof Hotel* (see below) here is a good place from which to start exploring: there's a number of hiking trails (ranging from easy to steep), including an attractive 1.5km waterfall walk and a 5km trail through the neighbouring Lesodi forest, home to monkeys and the beautiful Knysna Turaco bird.

After the turn-off to the Debengeni Falls, the valley becomes broader, the rolling hillsides covered with huge stands of citrus, avocado, kiwi and banana trees, as well as by the rich green texture of tea bushes.

Cheerio Gardens

4km out of Haenertsburg, off the Georges Valley Rd • Free • Tearooms Wed–Sat 9am–5pm, Sun 9am–4pm • ☎ 083 355 0835, ⓦ cheeriogardens.co.za

The tranquil **Cheerio Gardens** stem from the post Boer war era when the new government began to establish forestry in the area. The garden was part of the forestry commissioner's estate and today makes a peaceful place for a wander among the mass of pretty cherry trees, while the tearooms – set next to a small pond – are a good place to stop for delicious home-made cakes and scones. The gardens hold an annual Cherry Blossom Festival at the end of September when the plants are at their most colourful. You can also do a spot of trout fishing in one of the many ponds, and there are also some self-catering cottages here (see below).

Wegraakbosch Dairy

4km out of Haenertsburg, off the Georges Valley Rd • Daily 7am–5pm • Tours at 10am, booking recommended • R60 • ☎ 071 687 5218

Along the same dirt road as Cheerio Gardens, the tiny **Wegraakbosch Dairy** is another wonderful piece of backwoods life. At the dairy, organic cheese is handmade in traditional style over an open fire in a huge copper cauldron with milk from the farm's Brown Swiss cattle. It's a very idyllic setting with geese and duck wandering freely among the rustic-looking farm buildings. The one-hour tours give you an opportunity to see the cheese being made, amazingly without any electrical or mechanical devices, and afterwards you get a chance to sample the freshly made cheese – some decidedly better than others. You can also buy the cheese at weekends from the farm stall opposite the petrol station in Haenertsburg.

ACCOMMODATION	ALONG THE TWO VALLEY ROADS TO TZANEEN

Cheerio Gardens 4km out of Haenertsburg, off the Georges Valley Rd ☎ 083 355 0835, ⓦ cheerio.co.za. A range of eight different self-catering cottages strategically placed around the Cheerio Gardens, with lots of privacy and beautiful mountain views, some even with private gardens. The comfortable cottages are all former homes of the

Thompson family and have loads of character and atmosphere. R425

Magoebaskloof Hotel Magoebaskloof Valley Rd ☏ 015 276 5400, ⓦ magoebaskloof.co.za. This grand hotel boasts the most spectacular view in the area from its restaurant deck, and from all the room balconies. The 68 rooms are large and comfortable. There's a pool, DSTV, a choice of two bars and a restaurant. Mountain bikes can be rented for R50 per day, hiking and biking maps are available, and picnic baskets and braaipacks can be ordered too. R1600

Satvik Sacred Space Sanctuary Georges Valley Rd, 4km from Tzaneen ☏ 071 6124 851 or ☏ 084 556 2414, ⓦ satvik.co.za. Down a steep dirt track, this is an unusual and appealing backpacker lodge, housed in old workers' shacks, with a range of basic rooms, some self-contained, others sharing a shower block. There's a picturesque waterside bar and braai area, and various walking trails on the vast property, including one leading through indigenous forest. Dorm R120, double R320

Modjadji Cycad Reserve

Daily 7.30am–6pm · R10, car R20 · Guided tours R125 per person · Traditional self-catering rondavels R920 · ☏ 015 781 0690 · ⓦ africanivoryroute.co.za

The area around the village of **Modjadjiskloof**, 40km northeast of Tzaneen on the R36, is the home of the famous **Rain Queen**, the hereditary female monarch of the Modjadji people, who, according to legend, has the power to make rain – a useful talent in these often parched northern areas – and who provides royal protection of the regal cycad. Currently, there is no queen in post, so to speak, but her royal kraal is up the mist-covered mountainside. At the top of the mountain is the **Modjadji Cycad Reserve**, where a special form of ancient cycad flourishes – the unique Modjadji cycad. The 1300-acre reserve contains some of the world's oldest and largest cycads and incorporates some fine views (often obscured by mist) and various steep but pleasant trails. Near the car park at the top, there's a picnic area and a souvenir shop, and you can also rent traditional self-catering rondavels (see above), along the access road, at the bottom of the mountain and in the reserve.

Sunland Baobab

4km off the Modjadji road, near the R36 · Daily 7am–5pm · R20 · ☏ 083 453 2228, ⓦ bigbaobab.co.za

Surrounded by avocado plantations, the massive 1000-year old **Sunland Farm Baobab Tree** is the biggest in the world, with a vast 33-metre circumference. The tree is hollow and can be entered; it used to house a pub inside with enough seating for a small group. Sunland Farm, where it is located, also organizes activities, such as quad-biking and hiking, and rents out several basic chalets (R600).

Waterberg

Rising out of the plains to the west of the Great North Road, the **Waterberg** was until recently one of the least known of South Africa's significant massifs. However, it has been "discovered" by Johannesburgers, and is now a hugely popular weekend destination. Once an area of lakes and swamps – hence its name – the elevated plateau can often seem as dry as its surrounding northern bushveld, yet it harbours a diversity of vegetation and topography that for years supported extensive farming and cattle-ranching. In recent times, the majority of the old ranches have been converted into private reserves catering either for the hugely lucrative hunting market, or less profitable game viewing, with white rhino often the star attraction, along with giraffe, large antelope and leopard. Today the entire area, some 14,500 square kilometres of both private and publicly owned land, is encompassed by one of the country's foremost conservation projects – the **Waterberg Savanna Biosphere Reserve** (ⓦ waterbergbiosphere.org), designated a biosphere reserve by UNESCO in 2001. It was founded by a close-knit association of landowners who wished to combine wildlife conservation with the benefits of tourism. They have set up an extensive management plan for the area, developing various remarkable tourism initiatives, such as the useful GPS signboarding that helps navigation in the area.

As a game-viewing destination, the Waterberg makes a decent alternative to the lowveld areas around Kruger National Park, with the important advantage that malaria isn't present. It has impressive credentials as a vast area of true wilderness, and it is certainly a lot less commercialized than Kruger. **Vaalwater** – the only settlement of any size – is located at the heart of the biosphere reserve. West of Vaalwater, and also included within the biosphere reserve, are two large game reserves that are home to the Big Five: **Marakele National Park** and the privately owned **Welgevonden** reserve. North of Vaalwater is the highly regarded **Lapalala Wilderness Area**, where the biosphere reserve was originally instigated.

10

The only reserve you can visit for a game-viewing day-trip under your own steam is Marakele National Park; Lapalala Wilderness Area can be visited with a guide from *Waterberg Cottages* (see p.567). Otherwise, to gain access to the reserves, large or small, you'll almost always be expected to book into accommodation on the reserve itself; as most accommodation in the Waterberg is on reserves, this is generally hard to avoid.

Vaalwater

The small farming town of **VAALWATER** offers the visitor little more than a couple of useful places to stay and eat, and an orientation point on the R33, which connects the N1 at Modimolle with Lephalale. Vaalwater marks the junction between the R33 and the tarred road to Melkrivier and Marken. The **Zeederberg Homestead**, 1.5km northwest of the main crossing along the R33, beside the Spar supermarket, was the town's first settlement and home to the legendary Zeederberg stagecoaches that used to crisscross Limpopo and Zimbabwe to service settler outposts. Today, the complex offers good self-catering accommodation, a restaurant, and an excellent crafts shop (see p.567).

Lapalala Wilderness Area

55km north of Vaalwater; turn left down a dirt road at the Melkrivier junction on the R518 Marken Rd · Guided day safari R600, including lunch · ⓦ lapalala.com

Providing sanctuary for endangered and rare animals, the 244-square-kilometre **Lapalala Wilderness Area** has developed into one of the foremost conservation projects

---

COMMUNITY PROJECTS IN THE WATERBERG

There are a number of community projects throughout the Waterberg that provide employment to the many farm labourers who lost their jobs when tobacco farming stopped being lucrative, and support the area's high percentage of HIV/AIDS sufferers by giving them employment when they are well enough to work. The useful **Waterberg Meander brochure** (see p.566) gives a detailed breakdown of community projects that are worth visiting, generally catering for the tourist trade. You can watch wonderful crafts being made, go on guided tours into traditional homesteads, or on mountain trails past Stone Age settlements and San rock art.

The best of the bunch near Vaalwater is the innovative **Beadle Crafts Workshop** (Mon–Fri 7.30am–5pm, Sat & Sun 7.30am–1pm; ☎083 258 4850, ⓦ beadle.co.za), where you can see the colourful and intricate beadwork on leather items such as belts (R800), bracelets and sandals (R500–600) being made by trainees. Next to the workshop is a tearoom and a shop where you can buy the goods; all products can be ordered online too. The workshop is a short drive northeast of Vaalwater near Horizon Horseback Adventure & Safaris (see p.567); head along the R518 to Melkriver for 24km, then turn right onto the gravel road to Sterkstroom and continue for another 4km.

in the country. It was the first private game reserve in South Africa to obtain the highly endangered black rhino and it is now equally well known for its Wilderness School, which introduces some three thousand children a year from all over Africa to the principles and practices of conservation during week-long courses. To visit Lapalala on a **day safari**, book through *Waterberg Cottages* (see opposite).

Marakele National Park

100km west of Vaalwater • Daily 7am–4pm • R152 • Sunrise/sunset drive R200 • ☎ 014 777 6928, ⓦ sanparks.org/parks/marakele

In the mountains to the northeast of the mining and hunting town of **Thabazimbi** lies the 670-square-kilometre **Marakele National Park**, reached via a 12km tarred road from Thabazimbi. At its core is the **Kransberg**, a striking assortment of odd-shaped peaks, plateaus and cliffs. The fauna includes tsessebe, roan and sable antelope, red hartebeest and eight hundred breeding pairs of the endangered Cape vulture. Larger game such as elephant, rhino and lion have also been introduced, many from Kruger National Park.

While the park has a great deal of potential, **day visitors** are restricted to a small area, which includes Kransberg, with its inspiring views. The roads here don't require a 4WD, but for off-road exploration, you can join one of the excellent two- to three-hour organized sunrise and sunset drives, which meet at the main gate.

Welgevonden Private Game Reserve

25km west of Vaalwater on the tarred road towards Thabazimbi, abutting Marakele • ⓦ welgevonden.org

Privately owned by an association of landowners, the 380-square-kilometre **Welgevonden Private Game Reserve** is managed as one large conservation area, which strictly regulates the number of lodges that can be built and visitor numbers in the park. This results in some fantastic undisturbed and relatively easy-to-view wildlife throughout the entire area, including the Big Five, a host of antelope and a plethora of colourful birds. All eight commercial lodges in Welgevonden – the rest are private – have their own unique features, such as bush spas, romantic fireplaces, outdoor showers, and granite swimming pools, and are comfortably kitted out with plush sofas and soft beds. With well-qualified and experienced game guides at hand at all times, there's no question that this is an expensive place, with all-inclusive rates hovering around R3000 per person per day.

ARRIVAL AND INFORMATION

WATERBERG

By minibus taxi The only public transport to Vaalwater is by minibus taxi.

Tourist information The new Waterberg Biosphere Reserve information office, at 2 Sanddrif Rd, opposite the FNB bank (Mon–Fri 9am–5pm, Sat 9am–1pm; ☎ 083 947 2333), has information on attractions and activities in the region, a small crafts shop, and hands out the useful *Waterberg Meander* brochure, which is based around a

series sightseeing routes demarcated by GPS reference points and signboarded throughout the Waterberg area. It's an excellent tool if you get lost – which is not that uncommon. You can also get the brochure at most lodges or download it on ⓦ waterbergmeander.co.za. There's internet access at R1 per minute at the Sign Centre shop (Mon–Fri 8am–5pm, Sat 8am–1pm), next to *La Fleur* (see opposite).

ACCOMMODATION

MARAKELE NATIONAL PARK

Bontle Camping Site 2km from the main gate ⓦ sanparks.org/parks/marakele. Run by South African National Parks, this is a shaded campsite with fully kitted kitchen and ablution blocks, the obligatory braai area, and the option of a power point. R205

Tlopi Tented Camp 17km from the main entrance ⓦ sanparks.org/parks/marakele. A romantic self-catering tented camp on the banks of the Matlabas River, with luxuriously equipped tents sleeping two hovering on stilts over the water's edge. R1065

WELGEVONDEN PRIVATE GAME RESERVE

Shibula Lodge ☎082 7885100, ⓦshibulalodge.co.za. A good, friendly option, right in the middle of the reserve. The lodge overlooks a busy watering hole visited by birds, antelope and the occasional elephant, with a large family of boisterous and entertaining baboons inhabiting the neighbouring cliffside. You need to book in advance and will be picked up at the main gate. Prices include game drives (and drink and snacks on the game drives) plus all meals. R4400

VAALWATER AND AROUND

Ant's Nest and Ant's Hill Off the dirt road to Dorset from Vaalwater ☎081 572 2624, ⓦwaterberg.net. Two super-luxurious lodges, offering all-inclusive pampering in the wild including horseriding, game drives, mountain biking and guided game walks, before ending each day with a sundowner at one of the 50-square-kilometre reserve's beautiful viewpoints. Successful breeders of sable antelope and passionate about conservation, the owners are happy to share their vast knowledge and experience. Rates are all-inclusive. R6500

★**Horizon Horseback Adventures & Safari** 5km off the Vaalwater–Melkrivier Rd ☎014 755 4003, ⓦridinginafrica.com. A well-established and highly professional outfit with 80 horses and 13,000 hectares of beautiful bushland inhabited by hippos, giraffe, zebra and antelope. There's lovely lakeside accommodation in individual chalets, and also a magical lantern-lit bushcamp with a pool and great views. Riders can tackle activities such as cattle-mustering, polocrosse and a cross-country course. Suitable for riders of all levels; last-minute discounted rates available. Rates are all-inclusive. R5460

Lindani Lindani Reserve ☎083 631 5579, ⓦlindani .co.za. On a 31-square-kilometre reserve halfway between Vaalwater and Marken, *Lindani* comprises eight secluded and attractive thatched self-catering lodges sleeping between four and eighteen people. What makes *Lindani* unique is the many hiking and mountain-biking trails crisscrossing the reserve, which guests are free to use unsupervised, making this an ideal spot to explore the bush at your own pace. With tranquil picnic spots along rivers and the potential for encountering giraffe and various antelope, it's not surprising this is one of the most popular game lodges in the Waterberg. Minimum stay two nights. R670

Waterberg Cottages Triple B Ranch ☎014 755 4425, ⓦwaterbergcottages.co.za. Pleasant self-catering accommodation in five old farmhouse buildings on the working Triple B Ranch. The ranch is famous for its hardy Bonsmara cattle, which you can learn more about on their farm tours. The unpolluted wide-open skies above also make this an ideal spot for stargazing, hence the offer of brilliant two-hour star tours. R520

Zeederberg Cottages Right behind the shops and petrol station in Vaalwater ☎082 332 7088, ⓦzeederbergs.co.za. The best choice in Vaalwater town, set around a large, relaxing garden with a pool. The cluster of comfortable self-catering cottages includes a Zulu-style rondavel, and budget rooms. Guests have access to the kitchen and living room in the main house, and there's free wi-fi at the reception. Camping R90, budget room R280, double R600

EATING

The only places to eat or go out in Waterberg are in Vaalwater itself, so you'll need to be self-catering or staying at one of the all-inclusive game lodges when away from the town. Vaalwater also houses the Waterberg's only two supermarkets and the area's only banks.

★**Bush Stop Café** Zeederberg Complex ☎083 326 5098. With a fabulous and slightly quirky breakfast and lunch menu, *Bush Stop* dishes up the town's best French toast (served with banana and bacon) and pancakes, and a whole host of weird and wonderful salads, such as a delightful butternut squash salad (R52) – when in season. It uses only fresh produce and cooks everything from scratch, so it would be a shame to miss this place when travelling through Vaalwater. Mon–Fri 7.30am–5pm, Sat 8am–1.30pm.

La Fleur 361 Voortrekker St, near the main crossing on the R33 ☎014 755 3975. A popular place for home-made ice cream, pizza, coffee and cake, plus also a good option for salads and steak. This is where all the lodge employees hang out on their days off. Mon–Fri 7.30am–6pm, Sat 7.30am–1pm.

Sport on Main Near the main crossing on the R33, opposite *La Fleur* ☎014 755 3567. This hugely popular pub is the place to watch sports on TV. It also serves pizza, hearty steaks and a 200g Big Burger (R67), and sometimes stays open into the wee hours. Mon–Sat 7.30am–9.30pm, Sun 9am–3pm.

SHOPPING

★**Black Mamba Crafts Gallery** In the Zeederburg Complex ☎014 755 3518, ⓔtheblackmamba@absa .co.za. This excellent gallery sells beautiful crafts from throughout southern Africa, as well as books and nature guides. Mon–Fri 8.30am–5pm, Sat 8.30am–1.30pm, Sun 9.30am–1pm.

10

10

The far north

The northernmost part of Limpopo Province is a hot, green, undeveloped rural region that has much in common with Zimbabwe. Its essential geographical features are the **Limpopo River**, the border between South Africa and Zimbabwe (and, further west, Botswana), and the alluring **Soutpansberg mountain range**, aligned east–west just to the north of the area's main town, Louis Trichardt (often signposted as Makhado), an unremarkable settlement and not worth a stopover.

Perhaps the most distinctive area is the **Venda** region, formerly an "independent" homeland under apartheid. Although economically impoverished, it remains rich in tradition, art and legend. East of the Venda lands is the northern tip of **Kruger National Park**, a less-visited but intriguing part of the park (see p.539); there are two entry gates to the park here, at **Punda Maria** and **Pafuri**.

Both the Limpopo River and the Soutpansberg range lie in the path of the N1 highway, which crosses into Zimbabwe at **Beitbridge**. About 70km west of here, the **Mapungubwe National Park** encompasses a UNESCO World Heritage Iron-Age site which for archeology buffs is probably the area's most enticing attraction.

The Soutpansberg

The **Soutpansberg**, an impressive range of hills, particularly when approached from the south, attracts sufficient rainfall to create a subtropical climate, and spectacularly lush farms along the southern slopes produce a range of exotic crops such as avocados and macadamia nuts. In other parts, the rocky *kloofs* and green hillsides offer unspoilt mountain retreats, shaded by up to 580 different species of tree, and the home of monkeys, small antelopes, warthogs and some raptors. The uniqueness of the area led to it being designated a UNESCO Biosphere Reserve in 2009, along with the Waterberg Savanna Biosphere Reserve (see p.564).

The N1 highway bisects the range, passing through missable Louis Trichardt, situated in the southern shadow of the mountains, then climbing over a low pass and descending through a pair of tunnels on the northern side. Once over the escarpment, the highway runs north across mostly empty baobab plains to **Musina** and the **Limpopo River**.

ACCOMMODATION   THE SOUTPANSBERG

139 on Munnik Guest House 139 Munnik St, Louis Trichardt ☎083 407 0124, ⍟139onmunnik.co.za. A comfortable, upmarket guesthouse on a quiet street in the northern part of town, with cosy rooms and a pool in a shady garden. An excellent dinner is available on request, and during the day the on-site coffee shop serves lunch. R880

Bergpan Eco Resort On the north side of the mountains and east of Waterpoort along the R523 ☎015 593 0127, ✉bergpan@mweb.co.za. Twelve basic self-catering chalets sleeping two plus self-catering cottages in a well-run resort. You can take tours of the saltpans that gave the mountains their name and experience salt-making, along with hiking. R400

★**Leshiba Wilderness** 36km west of Louis Trichardt along the R522 ☎011 726 6347, ⍟leshiba.co.za. Located in a spectacular valley atop the mountain range, *Leshiba* is a truly unique experience, well worth the long uphill drive (safest in a 4WD, or book a R190 transfer). The internationally acclaimed artist Noria Mabasa has used the ruins of old rondavels to create a replica Venda village, alive with plump sculpted figures that guests can admire when lounging by the pool or enjoying the quirky accommodation – each one different with absolutely no straight lines. Rates include all meals. R3200

★**Madi a Thava Mountain Resort** 10km west of Louis Trichardt on the R522 ☎015 516 0220, ⍟madiathavha.com. A beautiful fair-trade lodge on the southern slopes of the Soutpansberg, where lovely villas and guest rooms are furnished and decorated with local crafts. There's a guest lounge, swimming pool, and guided day-trips and birding walks. It even has an onsite art gallery, Dancing Fish, which promotes Venda crafts and artists. Camping R90, rooms R1180

Venda

To the east and north of Louis Trichardt lies the intriguing land of the **VhaVenda** people, a culturally and linguistically distinct African grouping known for their mystical legends, political independence and arts and crafts. **Venda** was demarcated as a homeland under the apartheid system in the 1950s, and became one of three notionally independent homelands in South Africa in the late 1970s. Of all the homelands, Venda was one of the least compromised, keeping both its geographic and cultural integrity, and largely being left to mind its own business during the dark years of apartheid. Nowadays, its boundaries have regained their former fuzziness within Limpopo, but the region has retained its strong, independent identity.

Aside from a sprinkling of accommodation in Thohoyandou (see below), you'll find almost no tourist-oriented infrastructure whatsoever in Venda, but travelling here can be wonderfully rewarding.

10

The R523 west from Thohoyandou

Some 70km east of Louis Trichardt on the R524, **Thohoyandou** is a chaotic place with nothing much to see – if you're heading on to Kruger, you'll be thankful that the road bypasses the centre of town. However, if you head west of Thohoyandou, through a valley traced by the R523 road along the northern side of the Soutpansberg, you'll find the lush forests, waterfalls and mountains that give Venda its mystical atmosphere – this is the most appealing core of VhaVenda history and legend.

Driving from Thohoyandou, climb out of town to the north and then west, leaving the suburbs to get among the elevated green scenery which lies enticingly ahead. You'll pass the **Vondo Dam**, created in the early 1990s and surrounded by pine forests, then climb over the **Thate Vondo Pass**. Over the summit, a small shack marks the entrance to a network of forest roads that take you into the area containing the most important lake in Venda, **Lake Fundudzi**, and the **Sacred Forest**, an area of dense indigenous forest which contains the burial ground of Venda chiefs. In the past you could only look at both from afar, as getting closer was a matter of deep sensitivity and you had to gain permission from the VhaVenda chief. Today, access is unrestricted but there isn't a readily available map showing you the network of roads around the forest, and

---

VHAVENDA HISTORY AND CULTURE

The people who today call themselves **VhaVenda** are descended from a number of ancient groupings who migrated from the Great Lakes area in east-central Africa in the eleventh and twelfth centuries. Their identity gelled when a group under Chief Dimbanyika arrived at Dzata in the northern Soutpansberg, where a walled fort was later built. From here, they consolidated their power in the region, fending off attack from a number of different African groupings (including the Voortrekkers, whom they drove from their settlement at Schoemansdal in 1867). Although the VhaVenda suffered a reverse at the hands of the Boers in 1898, the onset of the Anglo-Boer War prevented that victory being consolidated.

The **culture** of the VhaVenda is a fascinating one, steeped in mysticism and vivid legend. One pervading theme is water – always an important concern in hot, seasonal climates, but a resource in which Venda is unusually abundant. Lakes, rivers, waterfalls and lush forests all form sacred sites, while legends abound of *zwidutwane*, or water sprites, and snakes who live at the bottom of dark pools or lakes.

Many VhaVenda **ceremonies** and **rituals** still hold great importance, with the most famous being the python, or *domba*, dance performed by young female initiates. Naked but for jewellery and a small piece of cloth around their waists, the teenage girls form a long chain, swaying and shuffling as the "snake" winds around a fire to the sound of a beating drum – another sacred object in Venda – often for hours on end. Your chances of seeing it performed are limited. The genuine thing is most common during spring; Heritage Day around the end of August or the beginning of September is a good time for celebrations.

some of the roads require 4WD; you may be better off joining a **tour** from *Khoroni Hotel* (see below) or hooking up with a local guide. Beyond the crest of the Thate Vondo Pass, the R523 follows the **Nzhelele River** down a valley of scattered but mostly unbroken settlement.

INFORMATION AND ACCOMMODATION

VENDA

Information The best place to get information about the area is from one of the established accommodation options such as *Shiluvari Lakeside Lodge* (see below) or *Khoroni Hotel*, both of which have lists of tour guides offering trips in the area.

Bougainvilla Lodge Mphephu Drive Unit C 36–37, Thohoyandou ☎ 015 962 3411, ⊛ bourgainvillalodge .com. A simple place, covered in colourful bougainvillea, offering motel-like rooms – some with a/c – and the option of evening meals if ordered in advance. R595

Khoroni Hotel Mphephu St, Thohoyandou; from Louis Trichardt turn left off the R524 at the petrol station, and right at the third traffic lights ☎ 015 962 4600, ⊛ www.khoroni.co.za. Set in the heart of downtown Thohoyandou, surrounded by trees, but not far beyond the road and tatty shopping mall. The hotel makes a living through its casino but also has a pool, and decent rooms. It has an impressive record of supporting Venda arts and crafts, with useful maps and tours available. R1300

Elim and around

Southeast of Louis Trichardt along the R578 lie some areas that used to form part of the self-governing Tsonga homeland of **Gazankulu**. They feature the vibrant roadside action typical of such rural areas – most notably at **ELIM**, a cluster of stalls, minibuses and hoardings on the site of a long-established Swiss mission hospital.

Continuing on the R578 from Elim crossroads, towards the town of **Giyani**, you'll come upon a series of rural arts and crafts workshops (see box below). The traditions and skills in arts and crafts are not dissimilar to what you find in Venda, and most of the workshops and small factories have simple, rural roots, making the trip to see them a worthwhile adventure. *Shiluvari Lakeside Lodge* (see below) can help with guides to arts and crafts workshops in the area, and sells products from many of them in its exquisite and well-stocked crafts boutique.

ACCOMMODATION

ELIM AND AROUND

★**Shiluvari Lakeside Lodge** A short way from Elim; turn left at the hospital junction towards Thohoyandou, and follow the signs down a gravel road to the left ☎ 015 556 3406, ⊛ shiluvari.com. The peaceful *Shiluvari Lakeside Lodge* has lawns running down to the edge of Albasini Dam lake and great views over the water to the

Soutpansberg. There are large rooms in the cottages with gardens, and lakeside rondavels, all decorated with local art. The owners have strong links with the local community and have helped set up the art route that has made visiting this area so popular (see box below). A tasty three-course dinner can be preordered for R160. R1050

TSONGA AND VENDA ARTS AND CRAFTS

The **Venda** and **Tsonga** regions have a strong reputation for **arts and crafts**. The best known of these are clay pots distinctively marked with angular designs in graphite silver and ochre. Also growing in status are woodcarvings, ranging from abstract to practical – the best of these can be imaginative and bold, though many are unfinished and overpriced. You'll also come across tapestries, fabrics, basketwork and painting. Finding your way to these **craft villages** can be quite an adventure, as they are widely scattered and the roads are poor, so the Ribolla Tourism Association, behind the Swiss mission hospital in Elim (Mon–Fri 8.30am–4.30pm; ☎ 015 556 4262 or ☎ 072 235 4543, ❸ ribollata@mweb.co.za), has set up a demarcated **art route** in the area, and hands out free maps of the route. It also has knowledgeable guides to take you around. Alternatively, try the **shops** selling craft products at the *Shiluvari Lakeside Lodge* (see above) and at *Madi a Thava* (see p.568), or check out the fine local crafts at the Thohoyandou Arts and Crafts Centre, on the R524 on the outskirts of Thohoyandou.

Mapungubwe National Park

Around 60km west of Musina along the R572 road to Pontdrift • Daily April–Oct 6.30am–6pm; Sept–March 6am–6.30pm • R152 • Sunset and night drives R235 • ☎ 015 534 7923, ⓦ sanparks.org/parks/mapungubwe

The **Mapungubwe National Park** is a UNESCO World Heritage Site, primarily due to its famous Iron Age site known as the Hill of Jackals, thought to be the site of the first kingdom in Africa. The park is situated at the confluence of the Limpopo and Shashi rivers, where South Africa, Zimbabwe and Botswana meet, and is well worth a detour if you have even the faintest interest in archeology. The park is divided into an eastern and a western side connected only by the main road, with a large plot of private land in between. The main entrance is on the eastern side nearest Musina, which is also where you'll find the Hill of the Jackals and most of the accommodation.

The park offers excellent game viewing with a scenic backdrop of unusual sandstone formations, mopane woodland, riverine forest, and a landscape scattered with otherworldly baobab trees housing wildlife such as elephant, giraffe, white rhino, plus various different antelope, including eland and gemsbok. You can explore the park either in your own car or on three-hour guided drives. If you're lucky, you may spot predators such as lion, leopard and hyenas, and there are over four hundred bird species including kori bustard, tropical boubou and the magnificent pel's fishing owl.

The long-term goal is eventually to develop the park into a tri-border park incorporating Mashatu Reserve in Botswana and the Tuli Circle in Zimbabwe.

Hill of the Jackals

Heritage site tour at 7am & 10am from the main gate • R200 plus park fee • Book at the main gate or on ☎ 015 534 7923

The **Hill of the Jackals** – one hour's drive from the main entrance – held a spiritual and mythological importance to local Modimo people long before it was "discovered" in 1932, when a local farmer climbed the dome-shaped granite hill and found various remains, including a tiny one-horned rhinoceros and a bowl, both made out of gold. It is thought that the years 1000–1300 AD were the heyday of a civilization centred at Mapungubwe. Prior to this, the Khoi and San people both left their footprints in the area with numerous sites of important rock art. Most impressive of these is found on land outside the national park (but still within the UNESCO World Heritage Site) at *Kaoxa Bush Camp* (see below).

The amazing domed and vaulted **Mapungubwe Interpretation Centre** near the park's main entrance houses an informative exhibition, and has won awards for its architecture. However, owing to conservation and security worries only a few of the original gold items found at the site are on display here – you can see a replica of the golden rhino, as the original one is in Pretoria's Mapungubwe Museum (see p.493).

To view the Hill of the Jackals, you need to join a two-hour **Heritage Site Tour**. A knowledgeable guide will talk you through the finds from an archeological dig in front of the hill, before climbing the steps up the hill to where the king and his extended family lived.

Kaoxa Bush Camp

Nestled in between the eastern and western section of Mapungubwe National Park is the privately owned Kaoxa wilderness area housing **Kaoxa Bush Camp**, a beautiful rustic camp set upon a hillside overlooking the confluence of the Limpopo and Shashi rivers across to Zimbabwe and Botswana. Stretching down to these two rivers, the camp is frequently visited by wild animals from Zimbabwe and Botswana, and signs at the camp make it clear that elephants have right of way. In contrast to the national park, visitors are free to move around independently (after signing lengthy indemnity forms) – on foot or by car. But bearing in mind the many hungry animals you may encounter, it's a good idea to seek advice before setting off. The only area that you're not allowed to explore by yourself is the amazing rock-art site with unique locust images, which one of the camp staff will take you to.

MAPUNGUBWE AND OTHER ARCHEOLOGICAL SITES

As one of the early melting pots of southern Africa, Limpopo has a number of important **archeological sites** where excavations have helped piece together a picture of the different people who inhabited the land for thousands of years. Some of the most interesting sites are at places where iron was smelted, as the development from what was essentially a Stone Age culture to an Iron Age culture, with its associated improvement in tools for cultivation and war, was a vital part of the migration of African tribes into South Africa around 1500 years ago. The presence of slag and other wastes provides the strongest clues – the iron itself seldom survives the processes of erosion. Some of the most revealing excavations have taken place at **Thulamela**, inside Kruger National Park not far from the Punda Maria Gate, **Bakone Malapa** cultural village outside Polokwane (see p.559), **Makapan's Cave** near Mokopane (see p.558), **Masorini**, also in the Kruger park, not far from Phalaborwa (see p.538), and the single most important site in Limpopo Province, **Mapungubwe** (Hill of the Jackals), west of Musina (see opposite).

10

ARRIVAL AND DEPARTURE
MAPUNGUBWE NATIONAL PARK

By public transport The only public transport to the park is by non-timetabled minibus taxis from Musina; however in practice this is only really useful if you are joining the Heritage Site Tour, then moving on.

ACCOMMODATION

Kaoxa Bush Camp 📞072 536 6297, 🌐kaoxacamp .com. Accommodation at the camp comprises three rustic stone cabins with breathtaking views from large terraces, which compensate for the fact that there's electricity but no a/c (and it gets very hot here). There are also three comfortable furnished safari tents with equally wonderful views. All the accommodation is self-catering, with shared kitchen and dining facilities. **R700**

SAN Parks Accommodation 🌐sanparks.org. There are a number of different accommodation options within the park: spacious cottages (with a natural rock pool) at the beautiful *Leokwe Camp*, the luxurious *Tshugulu Lodge*, forest tents and a fully equipped campsite. There are no other facilities, however, so if you're camping, you'll need to be fully self-sufficient. Camping **R205**, Leokwe cottages **R1010**

Lesotho

THE MALOTI MOUNTAINS

Lesotho

Entirely surrounded by South Africa, the aptly named "mountain kingdom" of
Lesotho (pronounced "Lee-su-tu") is proudly independent and very different
in character from its dominant neighbour. Whereas the Rainbow Nation next
door is, in many respects, distinctly European, laidback Lesotho prides itself
on its staunchly African heritage. Few people in the highlands of this
fabulously beautiful and rugged land speak English or Afrikaans, though
language isn't a barrier when the country's inhabitants – the BASOTHO
– count among the most hospitable people in Southern Africa. Another
refreshing physical (and psychological) contrast is the almost total absence
of fences, which means you can hike into the upland regions at will.

11

Travelling almost anywhere in Lesotho is an adventure: there are no highways or slick
intercity buses here (nor too many timetables), though the tarred **road network** is good,
covered by rickety minibuses held together in some cases by little more than prayers.
For many Basotho, **ponies** are the preferred method of transport, particularly in the
highlands. You can do the same from pony-trekking lodges all over the country.

Lesotho is the only country in the world to lie entirely above an altitude of 1000m,
earning its nickname of "the kingdom in the sky". Even the sandstone **Lesotho
lowlands** – which form a crescent along the country's western rim – would be
highlands anywhere else. It's here that you'll find all the nation's major towns, including
the busily practical capital of **Maseru**, with its very African mix of new glass buildings,
honking taxis and dusty streets, which began life as tax-collection centres for the British
administration. Lowland attractions include the weavers of **Teya-Teyaneng**,
extraordinary caves near **Mateka**, rock paintings at **Liphofung**, and the mountain
fortress at **Thaba Bosiu**, established by Lesotho's founder, King Moshoeshoe I.

At around 1400m above sea level, sandstone gives way to basalt, which forms the
bulk of the ruggedly beautiful **Lesotho highlands**. Once up the steep, twisting roads
that lead into the mountains you can visit the engineering masterpieces of the **Katse**
and **Mohale dams**, ski in the Maloti Mountains, fish from rivers everywhere and,
above all, wander through the countryside, dividing your time between remote
villages of simple stone-and-thatch huts and the peaceful solitude of the mountains.
Three protected areas in particular are worth the effort of getting to: **Ts'ehlanyane
National Park** and **Bokong Nature Reserve**, both in the Front Range of the Maloti
Mountains and easily accessed by saloon car, and the exceedingly remote
Sehlabathebe National Park in the east of the country, offering gloriously rugged
hiking terrain.

PONY TREAKKING NEAR MALEALEA

Highlights

❶ Pony trekking The ideal way to see Lesotho, following paths from village to village through spectacular mountain scenery and past towering waterfalls; you can also walk alongside while the pony takes your luggage. **See p.586**

❷ Thaba Bosiu The hilltop fortress from which Lesotho's greatest king, Moshoeshoe I, defended his kingdom against attackers offers fabulous views. **See p.589**

❸ Maletsunyane Falls A dramatic 200m waterfall plunging into a vast gorge deep in the remote highland region, reached on foot or by pony. **See p.593**

❻ Highlands Water Project Go on a tour inside Africa's secod-highest dam at Katse, visit the power plant at 'Muela and learn about Lesotho's ambitious water project. **See p.597 & p.599**

❹ "Roof of Africa" route The winding road from Butha-Buthe to the Sani Pass travels through dramatic mountain passes and valleys, and passes Africa's best ski resort. **See p.601**

❺ Sehlabathebe National Park A lonely mountain reserve with superb hiking. **See p.608**

HIGHLIGHTS ARE MARKED ON THE MAP ON P.578

Lesotho's **winter** runs from May to July, when it often snows in the highlands and sometimes in the lowlands too. Although the days are usually clear and warm, it gets extremely cold at night and ice can make driving hazardous in the highlands, while snowfall blocks even tarred highways for days at a time. **Spring** (Aug–Oct), when the snow melts, is a beautiful time, with new plants sprouting up everywhere. November to January is **summer**, when Lesotho gets most of its rain, often torrential, turning dirt roads into mudslides. Still, when it isn't raining the weather is usually sunny and the landscape is coloured in vivid shades of green. **Autumn** (Feb–April) is one of the best times to visit, as it doesn't usually rain too much and temperatures are moderate. Whatever the time of year, Lesotho can be very cold at night, particularly in the highlands, and prone to rapid weather changes, for which it's always wise to be prepared.

Brief history

Lesotho exists because of the determined efforts of one man, **Moshoeshoe I** (1786–1870), to secure land for his people in the face of intense social upheaval and the insatiable land-hunger of others. Before the arrival of Moshoeshoe's ancestors, around 900 AD, the San inhabited Lesotho unchallenged. Today the San are gone,

HIGHLIGHTS
1. Pony trekking
2. Thaba Bosiu
3. Maletsunyane Falls
4. Highlands Water Project
5. "Roof of Africa" route
6. Sehlabathebe National Park

BORDER POST OPENING TIMES

Monontsa Pass	8am–4pm	Makhaleng Bridge	8am–4pm
Caledonspoort	6am–10pm	Tele Bridge	6am–10pm
Ficksburg Bridge	Open 24hr	Ongeluk's Nek	8am–4pm
Peka Bridge	8am–4pm	Qacha's Nek	6am–10pm
Maseru Bridge	Open 24hr	Ramatseliso's Gate	8am–6pm
Van Rooyen's Gate	6am–10pm	Nkonkoana Gate	8am–4pm
Sephapho's Gate	8am–4pm	Sani Pass	8am–4pm

exterminated in 1873 by the last of many British campaigns against them. However, they left their mark in the country's rock paintings and elements of their tongue in the Sesotho language (including impossible buzzes and clicks), while traces of their vaguely oriental features and paler skin can still be discerned in some Basotho faces.

The Basotho first settled the fertile plains that today form the Lesotho lowlands and South Africa's Free State, before going on to colonize the mountains. They farmed these plains relatively peacefully for centuries, but by Moshoeshoe's time, tribes from elsewhere had forced thousands of Basotho off their land.

Moshoeshoe became chief in 1820 and established himself on top of a mountain near **Butha-Buthe**, where he became patron to many refugees in search of safety. However, after a particularly vicious attack on Butha-Buthe in 1824, Moshoeshoe decided it was no longer safe and trekked south with his followers in search of a better mountain. He found one at **Thaba Bosiu**, which, though subsequently attacked repeatedly, was never taken. Moshoeshoe earned an almost mythical reputation for wisdom and generosity among ordinary Basotho that survives to this day.

The Europeans in Lesotho

The kingdom was encroached upon by land-hungry Europeans from the 1840s onwards, and the **Orange Free State** government invaded in 1858, their soldiers destroying Morija and then launching a failed attack on Thaba Bosiu. They nonetheless captured plenty of farmland, whose acquisition was sanctioned by a British treaty in 1860. In 1865, the Orange Free State government cited Basotho cattle theft as the pretext for a new conflict, though few could deny Moshoeshoe's bitter assertion that "my great sin is that I possess a good and fertile country". The ensuing **Seqiti War** resulted in the destruction of Basotho crops, forcing Moshoeshoe into a humiliating treaty in 1866 that signed over most of his remaining good land. The war resumed in 1867, and was halted only by the British taking over what was left of the kingdom as the protectorate of **Basotholand** in 1868. The Treaty of Aliwal North in 1869 restored Moshoeshoe's land east of the Caledon but left the rest with the Free State, where it has remained to this day – a loss that still stings.

Moshoeshoe died in 1870 and the British handed Basotholand to the Cape administration a year later, which began taxing its new subjects, establishing a series of hut tax-collection points that have since grown into Lesotho's modest collection of small towns. Discontent turned to open rebellion in 1879, when the Cape government decided to confiscate all Basotho firearms. The result was the **Gun War**, one of few colonial-era conflicts in which the locals came out on top; the prize for the victorious Basotho was the resumption of direct rule from Britain in 1884.

Independence

Along with Bechuanaland and Swaziland, Basotholand rejected incorporation into the union of South Africa in 1910, with **King Letsie II** instead helping found the South African Native National Congress (later the ANC) in 1912. During the following years, the monarchy and chiefs' position declined, partly because British reforms forced their uneasy conversion into a junior arm of the colonial civil service, but also because social changes at work in the region, like migration, urbanization and rising education levels, proved too much for them to adapt to. In 1960, when **Moshoeshoe II** was crowned king, independence politics were in full swing, spearheaded by Pan-Africanist Ntsa Mokhele's Basotho Congress Party (BCP), and rivalled by the more conservative Basotho National Party (BNP). After narrowly winning the 1965 elections, the BNP led newly named Lesotho into **independence** on October 4, 1966. However, after losing the 1970 election, prime minister Leabua Jonathan annulled the result, declared a **state of emergency**, and carried on ruling until he was toppled in 1986 by a **military coup** led by Major General Metsing Lekhanya. Lekhanya ordered the **expulsion of the ANC** from Lesotho and signed an agreement that year with apartheid South Africa for

LESOTHO TRAVEL BASICS

BOOKS AND MAPS

The Morija Museum (see p.602) and some lodges sell books on Lesotho; a number of these also stock a very good 1:250,000 **topographical map** of Lesotho that marks most trails; it's also available from the Department of Lands, Surveys and Physical Planning on Lerotholi Road, near the corner of Constitution Road, in Maseru (☎ 2232 2376). This is also the only place where you can buy the really detailed 1:50,000 maps, essential for serious hiking.

MONEY

Lesotho's currency is the **loti**, plural **maluti** (M), divided into 100 lisenti; the loti is tied to the South African rand (R1=M1). You can also use South African rand throughout Lesotho, but you cannot use or exchange maluti anywhere outside Lesotho (apart from in some border towns such as Ladybrand), so make sure you use them up or exchange them before leaving.

FOOD

The Basotho staple **food** is *papa,* maize meal which is boiled and stirred until it resembles stiff, white mashed potato. An alternative is *nyekoe,* brown beans mixed with sorghum and wheat. Both are fairly bland but filling and usually served with some kind of *nama* (meat) and *moroho* (leafy vegetable – usually spinach or cabbage). On the street, you'll find *dipapata,* delicious steamed bread, and a fried snack called *makoenya* or fat cakes.

PHONE NUMBERS

Lesotho's **country code** is ☎ 266, unless you're calling from South Africa, in which case it's ☎ 09266. There are no **area codes**. To call collect, dial the international operator on ☎ 109.

PUBLIC HOLIDAYS

January 1 New Year's Day	**May 1** Workers' Day
March 11 Moshoeshoe Day	**May 25** Heroes' Day
Good Friday	**July 17** King's Birthday
Easter Monday	**Ascension Day** (Thursday)

the **Lesotho Highlands Water Project** (see box, p.597) – Africa's biggest engineering project to date, aiming to divert much of Lesotho's ample water resources to the thirsty South African province of Gauteng.

In 1990, Lekhanya sent Moshoeshoe II into exile and installed Moshoeshoe's son on the throne as **Letsie III**, but a year later Lekhanya was himself ousted by Major General Phisona, who then gave way to a **democratically elected government** led by Mokhele's BCP in 1993. Letsie stood down in favour of his father in 1995, but Moshoeshoe II died in a car crash the next year, and Letsie regained the throne.

In 1997, the BCP split with Mokhele and most of his cabinet, breaking away to form the Lesotho Congress for Democracy (LCD). The following year Mokhele's health deteriorated and he was forced to step down just before the **1998 elections**, which his successor Pakalitha Mosisili won by a landslide. Opposition parties cried foul amid widespread allegations of **vote-rigging**, and in July and August, crowds gathered outside the Royal Palace in Maseru demanding that the results be overturned – these protests subsequently developed into a **mutiny** by Lesotho Defence Force soldiers. In September, under the flag of a Southern African Development Community (SADC) peacekeeping force, **South African troops** crossed the border, and fierce fighting took place around military bases and at the strategically vital Katse Dam. Meanwhile, thousands of demonstrators protested at what they regarded as South Africa's heavy-handed intervention, and a large number of shops and offices across the country were looted and burned. After the 1998 riots, Lesotho's electoral system was changed to combine majority voting and proportional representation: eighty parliamentary seats to

October 4 Independence Day
December 25 Christmas Day

December 26 Boxing Day

RED TAPE AND VISAS

Visas are not required for most citizens of Western Europe and the US. If you've travelled through a **yellow fever zone**, you'll need an International Certificate of Vaccination against yellow fever. The standard entry permit is for 14 or 28 days; should you need an extension, visit the Department of Immigration on Assisi Road in Maseru (☎ 2232 3771).

ROAD TAX

A "road fund" **fee** of M30 is payable when entering Lesotho by car.

TOUR OPERATORS

Lesotho's tourist infrastructure remains sketchy in some areas, and arranging activities such as pony trekking and visits to the natural parks can be time-consuming, especially without your own transport. If you're short on time, consider an **organized tour**. *Malealea Lodge* (see p.605) in the southwest offers some innovative pony trekking and 4WD combinations, while the *Trading Post Guest House* in Roma (see p.592) is probably the best source of information on 4WD trails. Coming from South Africa, Thaba Tours (☎ 0027 33 701 2888, ⓦ thabatours.co.za) in Underberg specializes in overland trips in Lesotho via Sani Pass, pony trekking, biking and hiking.

WEBSITES

ⓦ **www.gov.ls** The Lesotho government's portal with national news and links to its ministries.
ⓦ **publiceye.co.ls** An independent local website with news, politics, business and events.
ⓦ **seelesotho.com** A wealth of information about the history, culture, flora and fauna of Lesotho, plus tips on where to visit and how to get there.
ⓦ **sesotho.web.za** The first stop if you are interested in learning Sesotho, with guidance in greetings and basic phrases in addition to references for Sesotho publications. There's an online dictionary too.
ⓦ **visitlesotho.travel** Lesotho's official tourism website has maps, accommodation and restaurant listings, driving route tips and contact details.

11

be elected by the first-past-the-post system, forty through proportional representation. Despite some scandals and unrest, subsequent elections passed off with little incident.

Current challenges

Aside from politics, there are some promising economic opportunities for Lesotho. **Mining** brings in significant revenue: since reopening in 2004, the diamond mine at Letseng has discovered three of the world's largest diamonds, and has the potential to provide up to twenty percent of Lesotho's GDP. The government continues to attract funding from international donors to battle poverty. And the royalties from the **Lesotho Highlands Water Project** are guaranteed for the foreseeable future.

However, a number of gargantuan challenges remain unanswered. **Poverty** remains entrenched, particularly in the rural areas of the country where the majority rely on small-scale agriculture. It was these areas that were pushed to the brink of emergency in 2007 when Lesotho suffered its worst **drought** in thirty years, resulting in a government appeal for food aid from the international community. **Environmental degradation** remains an issue too, ever visible in the numerous dongas across the country. And economically, Lesotho is still recovering from the massive losses in its textile exports after increased Chinese competition, and suffers very high levels of **unemployment**. Most devastating of all is the scourge of **HIV/AIDS**; with 23 percent of the population HIV positive, and twenty-five thousand new cases reported in 2013 alone, the prevalence of the pandemic in Lesotho is the highest in the world after Swaziland, and life expectancy for the nation has plummeted to 35 years.

SOME SIMPLE SESOTHO

The Basotho language is **Sesotho**. It can be tricky to speak, as spellings rarely correspond with pronunciation, a legacy of the bizarre nineteenth-century transcription by French missionaries, in which locals take a perverse pride. For more information about Sesotho and tips on learning the language, see ⓦ sesotho.web.za.

BASICS

Yes	*E* ("aye")
No	*E-e* ("ai-ai" as in the ai of hair)
Thank you	*Kea leboha* ("Kiya lee-bowa")
Today	*Kajeno* ("Ka-jen-noo")
Tomorrow	*Hosane* ("Ho-san-nee")
Yesterday	*Moobane* ("Mow-ban-nee")
Where is …?	*E kae …?* ("O kai …")
Where can we stay?	*Nka lula hokae?* ("N-ka dula o kai")
Where are you going?	*U ea kae?* ("Oo ya kai")
Where are you from?	*U tsoa kae?* ("Oo tswa kai")
How much?	*Ke bokae?* ("Ke bo-kai")
I speak Sesotho a little	*Ke bua Sesotho ha nyane* ("Ke boo-a Sesotho han-yaney")

GREETINGS AND RESPONSES

Hello (informal)	*Khotso* ("Khot-so" – literally "peace")
Hello (to one)	*Lumela* ("Do-mela")
…father (used to address any man)	*Ntate* ("N-dar-tay")
…mother (used to address any woman)	*Me* ("Mmeh")
…brother (used to address any boy)	*Abuti* ("A-boo-ti")
…sister (used to address any girl)	*Ausi* ("A-woo-si")
Hello (to many)	*Lumelang* ("Do-melang")
How are you?(formal)	*U phela jooang* ("O pela jwan")
I'm fine (formal)	Ke phela hantle ("Ke pela hank-le") with a clicked *k*
Goodbye (said by person leaving)	*Sala hantle* ("Sala hank-le" – literally "go well")
Goodbye (said by people remaining)	*Tsamaea hantle* ("Ts-my-ya hank-le" – literally "stay well")

Corruption, incompetence and political infighting has seriously hindered progress in all these fields, and the future prospects of the mountain kingdom rest on whether it can overcome these challenges.

ARRIVAL AND DEPARTURE

By plane Flights to Lesotho only run from Johannesburg. South African Airlink operates three flights a day (1hr) to Moshoeshoe I International Airport, 18km southeast of the city, from Monday to Friday and two on the weekends. Taxis and shuttle buses (M50) connect the airport with Maseru.

By bus There are limited bus services from South African cities to Lesotho's main overland border at Maseru Bridge (2km from Maseru city centre).

By minibus taxi There are frequent minibus taxis throughout the day from Johannesburg, Bloemfontein and Durban, and less frequently from a host of smaller towns in the Free State and North West Province to various border crossings in Lesotho's western lowlands – particularly Maseru Bridge, Ficksburg Bridge (near Maputsoe) and

Caledonspoort (near Butha-Buthe). All these places have plentiful onward transport connections within Lesotho, with shared taxis shuttling between the border and the nearest towns. It's also possible to enter Lesotho from the south via the spectacular Sani Pass by taking a 4WD car or hired transport from Underberg in KwaZulu-Natal (see p.390).

By car Travelling to Lesotho by car, you have a choice of fourteen border crossings. Easiest to reach are the western lowlands crossings, including Caledonspoort (the closest to Johannesburg, an easy 350km, 4–5 hour drive), Ficksburg Bridge and Maseru Bridge. The main crossings get very busy with returning migrants around weekends, and it may make sense to take a detour via a smaller crossing. For border opening times, see the map on p.578. If you've rented a car in South Africa, you'll need the agency to provide paperwork for crossing the border

(usually costs R500 extra) – also check whether the insurance covers you for Lesotho, especially for gravel roads and in winter.

GETTING AROUND

By car Lesotho has a good tarred road network, though you can't avoid dirt (and often boulder-strewn) roads when heading to more out-of-the-way places. However, keep your eyes on the road as even the best stretches of have deep potholes that can wreck a wheel, or worse. The main route from Maseru north is good tar until Oxbow, after which there's potholes all the way to the border at Sani Pass. The beautiful road from Leribe to Katse Dam is tarred, as is the road from Maseru to Thaba-Tseka; as the gravel road between Thaba-Tseka and Katse can be handled by saloon cars this makes a big two- or three-day loop from Maseru via Thaba-Tseka and Katse to Leribe possible. The southern route from Maseru is tarred as far as Mphaki, but is passable in an ordinary saloon up to Qacha's Nek. Fuel costs roughly the same as in South Africa; unleaded is readily available in Maseru, but can be scarce elsewhere. When approaching a police roadblock, be sure to wait at the stop sign until you are waved through. The speed limit is 80km/h, and 50km/h in urban areas. Hitching is much safer than in South Africa and is a good way to get around.

By minibus taxi Inexpensive minibus taxis are often the main form of transport, and run on major routes, at least until early afternoon.

By bus Slower but safer than minibus taxis, and very inexpensive. While there are lots of buses in Lesotho, only one company – the Lesotho Freight and Bus Services Corporation – keeps to a timetable. Other buses simply leave when they're full, and operate just like minibus taxis.

Maseru and the central districts

A convenient entry point from South Africa, and the country's most sophisticated urban centre by far, **Maseru** is a handy first stop for exploring Lesotho, and is the place to fill up on supplies, use an ATM and organize onward transport. Apart from a few elegant colonial sandstone buildings, there's not a great deal to see here. However, if you're in town for a few days there are plenty of excursions into the surrounding countryside, including to **Thaba Bosiu**, the so-called "Mountain of the Night" where the founder of the nation, Moshoeshoe I, ruled for almost fifty years.

Further afield, **Roma** is the country's academic centre, surrounded by beautiful sandstone hills and with a historic Catholic mission. South of Roma, a road ascends into the **central highlands** – one of the most striking drives in the country. At the end of the road, the village of **Semonkong** has a superb lodge, a spectacular waterfall nearby and a wide variety of outdoor activities on offer. Continuing along the A3 east of Roma, a wonderful tarred road heads up into Lesotho's **Central Range**, with particularly spectacular driving between the impressive Mohale Dam and **Thaba-Tseka**.

Maseru

Sprawling **MASERU**, the nation's capital and only big town, spreads east from the Caledon River, which marks the border with South Africa. Maseru was established by the British in 1869 as the administrative centre for newly annexed Basotholand, but Britain put as little effort into developing the town as it did the rest of the country, no doubt expecting it to become just a minor South African town when Basotholand was incorporated into South Africa.

Surrounded by sprawling shantytown suburbs, the city has grown swiftly over recent years, poverty in Lesotho's rural areas having driven people to the capital in search of a better life. Few have found it yet, and the city has a high unemployment rate. Yet Maseru's compact centre has all the marks of an upwardly mobile African city, with slick fashions and mobile phones much in evidence.

Maseru's older buildings, as well as some stylish new ones, are built from well-crafted local **sandstone** – from which the city gets its name – though a number of ugly concrete

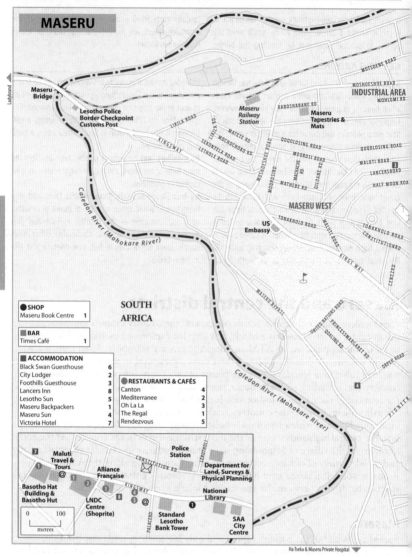

MASERU

11

Ladybrand

Maseru Bridge

Lesotho Police Border Checkpoint Customs Post

Maseru Railway Station

Maseru Tapestries & Mats

INDUSTRIAL AREA

MOTSOENE ROAD
MOSHOESHOE ROAD
MOHLOMI RD

RABOSHABANE RD

LIKILA ROAD
MATETE RD
DR J M MOCHOCHOKO RD
SEKONYELA ROAD
LETHOLE ROAD
MOCHOCHOKO RD
MATHEBE RD
MACHACHE RD
GILDANE RD
QOOQOLOSING ROAD
MOOROSI RD
QOOQOLOSING ROAD
MALUTI ROAD
LANCERS ROAD
HALF MOON ROA

KINGSWAY

MOSHOESHOE ROAD
MOOROSI ROAD

MASERU WEST

US Embassy

TONAKHOLO ROAD
TONAKHOLO ROAD
CONSTITUTION RD

MALUTI ROAD
KINGS WAY
CENEXZO

MASERU BYPASS

SOUTH AFRICA

Caledon River (Mohokare River)

UNITED NATIONS ROAD
PRINCESS MARGARET RD
QOALING RD
OPPEN ROAD

● **SHOP**
Maseru Book Centre   1

■ **BAR**
Times Café   1

■ **ACCOMMODATION**
Black Swan Guesthouse	6
City Lodger	2
Foothills Guesthouse	3
Lancers Inn	8
Lesotho Sun	5
Maseru Backpackers	1
Maseru Sun	4
Victoria Hotel	7

● **RESTAURANTS & CAFÉS**
Canton	4
Mediterranee	2
Oh La La	3
The Regal	1
Rendezvous	5

Caledon River (Mohokare River)

PIONEER

Police Station

Maluti Travel & Tours

Alliance Française

CONSTITUTION RD

LEROTHOLI RD

Department for Land, Surveys & Physical Planning

Basotho Hat Building & Basotho Hut

LNDC Centre (Shoprite)

KINGSWAY
PALIKELI RD

National Library

Standard Lesotho Bank Tower

SAA City Centre

0   100
metres

Ha Tseka & Maseru Private Hospital ▼

box buildings diminish the effect and, unfortunately, dominate the skyline. Most of the city's daytime action happens on or around **Kingsway**, the road that runs through town, becoming increasingly downmarket and lively as it heads east towards the cathedral. Compared with most towns and cities in South Africa, Maseru is relatively safe, and as long as you take the **safety precautions** you would in any other African city, you can walk around here comfortably by day. It's not advised to walk around at night, however.

Maseru's landmarks

The town's most famous landmarks used to be the trio of neo-traditional thatched buildings at the west end of Kingsway: unfortunately the **Basotho Shield** building which

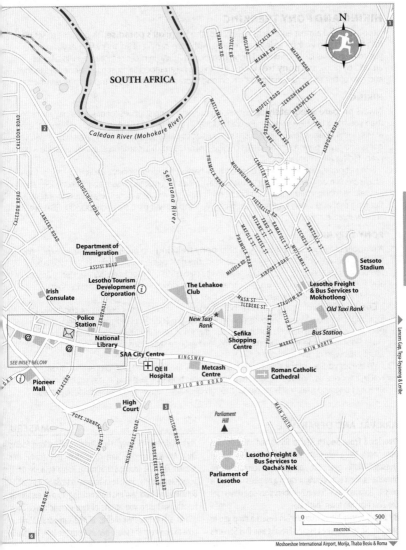

11

SOUTH AFRICA

Caledon River (Mohokare River)

Seputana River

Department of
Immigration

ASSIST ROAD

Lesotho Tourism
Development (i)
Corporation

Irish
Consulate

Police
Station

National
Library

SAA City Centre

KINGSWAY

SEE INSET BELOW

(i)
Pioneer
Mall

QE II
Hospital

Metcash
Centre

MPILO BO ROAD

High
Court

Parliament
Hill ▲

The Lehakoe
Club

*New Taxi
Rank*

Sefika
Shopping
Centre

Setsoto
Stadium

Lesotho Freight
& Bus Services to
Mokhotlong

Old Taxi Rank

Bus Station

MAIN NORTH

Roman Catholic
Cathedral

MAIN SOUTH

Lesotho Freight &
Bus Services to
Qacha's Nek

Parliament of
Lesotho

Lancers Gap, Teya-Teyaneng & Leribe

0   500
metres

Moshoeshoe International Airport, Morija, Thaba Bosiu & Roma ▼

housed the tourist office burnt down in 2011; what remains is the **Basotho Hut**, home to the *Regal* restaurant, and the appropriately shaped **Mokorotlo (Basotho Hat) Building**, housing the well-stocked Lesotho Cooperative Handicrafts shop (see box, p.587). The main part of town lies east of here along Kingsway, though there's not much to see other than a handful of colonial-era buildings: the **Alliance Française** in the former library at the corner with Pioneer Road, the former **Anglican church** next to it, and the 1891 **Resident Commissioner's House** (now a government department), on the left beyond the towering **Post Office** building – evidence of Maseru's intention to create a thoroughly modern capital. Kingsway comes to an end at the traffic circle by the impressively large sandstone **Roman Catholic Cathedral**, where it splits into Main North Road and Main South Road.

11

HIKING AND PONY TREKKING

Hospitable and almost entirely fenceless, Lesotho is a **hiker's paradise**. It's possible to set off into the hills and walk for as long as you like, with no prospect of an angry farmer yelling at you to get off his land – quite a change from South Africa. In more remote areas, locals get around by pony, and **pony trekking** – which can be arranged at most tourist-oriented lodges and two of the three national parks – is an undoubted highlight of any trip to the country.

HIKING

Always **prepare adequately** before setting out, and bring supplies for at least a day more than you think the hike will take. Be warned that in the highest reaches of the highlands there are very few villages; lovely as this is, it's also risky, so make sure someone knows where you've gone, and don't hike in remote areas on your own. Lesotho's weather is notoriously fickle – be prepared for all eventualities.

Bring enough cash (you can't count on rural banks changing money), a torch, plenty of food (there aren't many shops in remote rural areas), a water container, water-purifying tablets, an all-weather cooker with fuel (don't count on finding firewood), a genuinely waterproof tent, a sleeping mat and a very warm sleeping bag. A compass and map (see box, pp.580–581) are also invaluable.

PONY TREKKING

A number of lodges and other places offer **pony trekking** (no previous equestrian experience needed) though only a few are well organized, the best being the *Malealea Lodge* (see p.605), *Semonkong Lodge* (see p.593) and *Maliba Lodge* (see p.599). Semonkong, Mokhotlong, Bokong and Ts'ehlanyane are all high up; the others are lower down, with less variable weather conditions, though the terrain is harder on the ponies.

Costs vary according to group size, but tend to average M250 per person for short two to four hour trips; for overnights, count on an extra M100–200 per person, which can include a pack horse as well as accommodation. A full-day's ride typically involves six or seven hours (10–15km) in the saddle, so overnight trips can be quite strenuous. Children under 12 are not usually allowed on overnighters.

Wherever you go, make sure you bring a wide-brimmed sunhat, sun protection cream, waterproof gear, swimwear in summer, and a water bottle (and, if you're staying overnight, a sleeping bag and mat, torch and food, though cooking utensils and fuel should be provided).

ARRIVAL AND DEPARTURE

MASERU

Overland from South Africa Buses and minibus taxis from South Africa terminate at the Maseru Bridge border crossing. Walk over the bridge and complete the formalities, then either walk or catch a minibus taxi or a "4 plus 1" (saloon taxi – four passengers plus one driver) for the 2km ride into town (both M5).

By bus Intercity buses from within Lesotho drop you in Stadium Road near the Lesotho Freight and Bus Services station, ten minutes' walk east of the city centre, or M5–6 by minibus or local taxi. Walking by day with luggage is safe, if a somewhat amusing sight for locals. Most buses leave from the chaotic bus station between Market St and Pitso Ground, northeast of the cathedral roundabout. Early morning long-distance buses to Mokhotlong and Qacha's Nek are operated by Lesotho Freight and Bus Services (☎ 2240 0583); for Mokhotlong they depart from Stadium Road next to Maseru Mart; to Qacha's Nek they depart from Main Road South, 500m south of the cathedral.

Destinations Bokong (daily; 7hr 30min); Leribe (8 daily; 2hr); Mafeteng (5 daily; 1hr 30min); Mokhotlong (daily; 7hr); Morija (hourly; 50min); Qacha's Nek (daily; 9hr 30min); Quthing (daily; 3hr 30min); Roma (4 daily; 1hr); Semonkong (daily; 5hr); Teya-Teyaneng (8 daily; 45min).

By minibus taxi Minibus taxis arriving from elsewhere in Lesotho will drop you at one of two chaotic ranks, both within a few hundred metres of the cathedral. Minibus taxis to and from the south depart from the New Taxi Rank (also known as Sefika Taxi Rank), next to the Sefika Shopping Centre on Moshoeshoe Rd. Minibus taxis to and from the east and north use the Old Taxi Rank, 200m east of the bus station. Regular minibus taxis link both taxi ranks to the city centre.

By plane Moshoeshoe I International Airport (☎ 2235 0777), 18km southeast of town off Main South Rd (the A2 towards Mafeteng), is served by daily flights from Johannesburg (4 daily; 1hr) by South African Airlink (☎ 2235 0418, ⊛ saairlink.co.za). South African Airlink operates a shuttle bus to and from Maseru (M50), which can pick you up or drop you at a hotel; call ahead to book the ride back to the airport. Private taxis (see below) and the private Airport Shuttle Service (☎5885 5527, ✉airportshuttle@ymail.com) charge around M100. Alternatively, wait for an infrequent

minibus taxi at the airport gate. Avis (☎2235 0328, ⓦavis.com), Budget (☎2231 6344, ⓦbudget.com) and Europcar (☎2235 0299, ⓦeuropcar.com) have offices at the airport.

GETTING AROUND

The city centre is compact and easy to get around on foot during the day; at night it's recommended to take a taxi. There are lots of **minibus taxis** running up and down Kingsway and into the suburbs, from just before dawn to around 8pm. At night, **private taxis** are the only option; operators include Luxury Telephone Taxis (☎2232 6211), Moonlite Taxis (☎2231 2695) and Perfect Taxis (☎2232 5222).

INFORMATION

Tourist information Lesotho Tourism Development Corporation headquarters, Linare Rd, corner Parliament Rd (Mon–Fri 9am–5pm; ☎2231 2238,

ⓦvisitlesotho.travel); also in the Pioneer Mall, Pioneer Rd (Mon–Fri 9am–5pm, Sat 9am–1pm).

ACCOMMODATION

Maseru is the only place in the country where there's much choice of accommodation, offering everything from camping to luxury suites in plush hotels. The central options, on or near Kingsway, are the most practical if you don't have your own transport.

Black Swan Guesthouse 28 Manong Rd, Hillsview ☎2231 7700, ⓦblackswan.co.ls. Located in a quiet area of town, this hotel has sixteen clean and attractive rooms and a small indoor pool set around a tidy compound with a duck pond. M850

City Lodger 221 Moshoeshoe Rd, Maseru West ☎2232 4215, ⓦcitylodger.co.za. A boutique guesthouse north of the centre near the industrial area; the elegant rooms with sandstone brick walls are nicely decorated with sleek bathrooms. M680

Foothills Guesthouse 121 Maluti Rd, Maseru West ☎5870 6566, ⓦmelvin@xsinet.co.za. This colonial-style sandstone house offers simple, homely accommodation in a quiet area of town; in addition to the six comfortable and spotless rooms, there are a couple of self-catering chalets. M480

Lancers Inn Kingsway, corner of Pioneer Rd ☎2231 2114, ⓦlancersinn.co.ls. Maseru's most central, characterful and pleasant place to stay, set in an attractive complex around a sandstone building. There are

well-priced and comfortable rondavels and chalets with en-suite bathrooms, a pool and a good beer garden and restaurant, all set in pretty gardens. M845

Lesotho Sun Hilton Rd ☎2224 3000, ⓦsuninternational.com. Maseru's largest and smartest accommodation option, this resort has comfortable (if smallish) rooms with TVs and good views over town, plus loads of sports facilities, a health spa, casino, cinema and several good restaurants. M1935

Maseru Backpackers Airport Rd ☎2232 5166, ⓦlesothodurhamlink.org. The best camping option in Maseru, with clean shower blocks and a well-equipped kitchen, plus very comfortable four-bed rondavels and decent backpacker accommodation in small dormitories. The site, signposted as "Lesotho Durham Link" just beyond the old airport, overlooks the Maqalika Dam, and they can arrange a number of outdoor activities. Camping M50, dorm M140, rondavel M500

Maseru Sun 12 Orpen Rd, ☎2231 2434, ⓦsuninternational.com. The second of the town's *Sun*

HANDICRAFTS IN MASERU

Woollen bags, carpets, tapestries and traditional Basotho hats are the most sought-after crafts in Lesotho. The Basotho Hat Building in the city centre is home to the impressive **Lesotho Cooperative Handicrafts shop** (Mon–Fri 8am–5pm, Sat 8am–4.30am; ☎2232 2523, ✉lch@basothohat.co.ls; accepts credit cards). You'll find a few more crafts, mostly woven Basotho hats (*mokorotlo*), sold on the pavements around this end of town. Good handicraft outlets on the outskirts of town include **Maseru Tapestries & Mats** (☎2231 1733, ✉maserutapestry@yahoo.com), signposted on Raboshabane Road, in the industrial area, which has handwoven tapestries and carpets; and the similar **Seithati Weavers**, 8km out along the Mafeteng road (☎2231 3975, ⓦvillageweavers.co.ls).

hotels, with decent rooms in soothing, well-tended garden surroundings, which are popular with locals in the evenings. There is also a good restaurant and a large, attractive swimming pool. M1415

Victoria Hotel Kingsway ☎ 2231 3687. This plain concrete hotel towering over Kingsway, opposite the Basotho Hat Building, offers comfortable if unremarkable rooms, a good pool, a restaurant and a club. M690

EATING AND DRINKING

As you'd expect, Maseru has the best selection of restaurants in Lesotho. Several pricey, upmarket places can be found in the Lesotho and Maseru *Sun* hotels.

Canton Moposo House, Kingsway ☎ 2231 2003. Despite the tacky interior, this is an excellent Chinese restaurant, spread across two floors. Try Lesotho-style stew for M25, or Chinese dumplings (M12), fried beef (M48) or duck (M80). Mon–Thurs & Sun 9.30am–9.30pm, Fri & Sat 9.30am–11pm.

Mediterranee Pioneer Rd, LNDC Shopping Centre ☎ 2832 9638. Opposite *Lancer's Inn*, this unpretentious pizzeria and coffee shop is popular for its excellent-value pizza, pasta and burgers, and the DJs playing jazz on Sunday evenings. Offerings include a biltong pizza (M50) and a Hawaii pizza (M53). Mon–Thurs 7.30am–10pm, Fri & Sat 7.30am–midnight, Sun 8am–10pm.

Oh La La Kingsway, corner of Pioneer Rd. With terrace seating in the small park next to the Alliance Française, this rondavel houses the best café in town, with fresh sandwiches (M27), croissants, crepes (ham & mozzarella M26), pastries and pies, plus good coffee and fresh juice. Mon–Fri 7.30am–10pm, Sat 7.30am–4pm.

The Regal Kingsway ☎ 2231 3930. The best non-hotel dining experience in the country. The Regal has a stylish dining room and balcony on the first floor of the thatched Basotho Hut building, and serves very good Indian food; lamb korma (M95), butter chicken (M85), vegetarian *paneer tikka* (M70) and seafood from M70. Mon–Sat 11.30am–2.30pm & 6–9.30pm.

Rendezvous Lancers Inn, Kingsway ☎ 2231 2114. Maseru's classiest restaurant (King Letsie is known to dine here regularly), with an African- and French-themed menu and a candlelit atmosphere. There's a spicy peri-peri chicken burger for M45, Thai curry for M45, and delicious local mountain trout for M86. The outdoor seating is popular at lunchtime. Daily noon–2pm, 5.30–9.30pm.

Times Café First floor of LNDC Centre, Kingsway ☎ 2231 5303. Trendy bar that serves a selection of European food like sandwiches (M25), schnitzel (M60), steak (from M80) and trout (M140), in addition to coffees and cakes. If you can stand the constant blaring of taxi horns, eat alfresco on the balcony. Daily 4pm–4am.

DIRECTORY

Banks and currency exchange The main branches and ATMs of Standard Lesotho Bank, Nedbank and First National Bank are on Kingsway. The best place for foreign exchange is the Standard Bank on the ground floor of the Standard Lesotho Bank Tower, on Kingsway.

Books Maseru Book Centre on Kingsway, just east of the Lesotho Bank, has a number of historical and cultural works published by Morija Museum; the craft shop in the Basotho Hat Building also has a small selection.

Embassies and consulates Canada, Quadrant Sales Building, Orpen Rd (☎ 2231 5365, ⊛ canadainternational .gc.ca); Ireland, Tona-kholo Rd (☎ 2231 4068, ⊛ embassyofireland.org.ls); South Africa, corner Kingsway and Old School Rd (☎ 2231 5758, ⊛ dfa.gov .za); USA, 254 Kingsway (☎ 2231 2666, ⊛ maseru .usembassy.gov).

Gym The Lehakoe Club, on the corner of Parliament and Moshoeshoe rds (☎ 2223 2300), offers everything from exercise classes, indoor and outdoor pools, to squash, tennis and a well-equipped gym, all open to non-members.

Hospitals Queen Elizabeth II Hospital, Kingsway (☎ 2231 2501); Maseru Private Hospital, Thetsane Rd (☎ 2231 3260).

Internet access Newland Internet Cafe, on Kingsway opposite the Post Office (Mon–Fri 8.30am–5.30pm, Sat 8.30am–3.30pm, Sun 9am–2pm); Leo Internet Cafe, on Kingsway, 200m to the west (Mon–Fri 8am–5pm).

Pharmacy MHS Pharmacy, LNDC Centre, Kingsway (☎ 2232 5189).

Police Constitution Rd (☎ 5888 1024).

Post office Kingsway (Mon–Fri 8am–4.30pm, Sat 8am–noon).

Supermarkets A large, well-stocked Pick 'n Pay supermarket can be found in the Pioneer Mall on Pioneer Rd (Mon–Sat 8am–8pm, Sun 8am–5pm).

Travel agents Flight ticketing and Intercape bus tickets are available through SAA City Centre Maseru Travel, next to the Maseru Book Centre, Kingsway (☎ 2231 4536, ⊜ mampek.maserutravel@galileosa.co.za), and Maluti Travel & Tours, next to First National Bank on Kingsway (☎ 2232 7172, ⊜ valentinem.maluti@galileo.co.za). Intercape bus tickets are sold at the Shoprite supermarket in the LNDC Centre.

Around Maseru

Although you're unlikely to spend much time in Lesotho in Maseru itself, there are a number of rewarding places to visit within easy reach of the capital. A little oddly in a country dominated by towering mountains, it is two of the smaller hills, **Thaba Bosiu**, Moshoeshoe I's impregnable hilltop fortress, and nearby **Qiloane**, model for the Basotho hat (*mokorotlo*), which are the most famous, both ranking among the most important historical sites in the country. South of Maseru, the **Qeme Plateau** offers views over the city and surrounding countryside.

Thaba Bosiu

About 20km east of Maseru • ☎ 2835 7207 • M40

Thaba Bosiu is Lesotho's most important historical sight, a steep mountain with a large flat top that was the capital of the kingdom in the days of Moshoeshoe I. It is a place of great significance to the people of Lesotho, and the burial ground of the country's kings, and well worth a visit.

Moshoeshoe I trekked with his followers from Butha-Buthe to Thaba Bosiu in July 1824 in a bid to settle somewhere far from the warrior clans then terrorizing the flat plains to the north and west, and somewhere that would be extremely hard for anyone to capture. Thaba Bosiu, with its crown of near-vertical cliffs, good grazing and seven or eight freshwater springs on top, fitted the bill perfectly, and despite numerous attacks, the mountain was never taken. The name means "Mountain of the Night", perhaps because, as legend has it, Moshoeshoe first arrived there in the evening, and immediate protective measures took all night to install. A more compelling reason, and

11

TAKING THABA BOSIU

In 1828, the Ngwane were the first to attack Thaba Bosiu, but were decisively beaten, after which they never troubled Moshoeshoe again. **Mzilikhazi**, King of the Ndebele, who later conquered much of modern-day Zimbabwe, tried to take the mountain in 1831, but his men were defeated by a mass of great boulders flung down from the top by the Basotho; Moshoeshoe is reputed to have sent the Ndebele a large number of fat oxen after their defeat, an unprecedented move for a victorious chief – as if to say that he understood that their attack had been inspired by hunger and that he wanted to help them out.

There followed a twenty-year period of relative calm, during which time Moshoeshoe would receive visitors wearing a beautifully tailored dark-blue military uniform, complete with cloak, and offer them tea from a prized china tea service. He allowed the French missionary **Eugene Casalis** to establish a mission at the bottom of the mountain in 1837, and employed him as his secretary and interpreter. In 1852 a British punitive force led by the Cape governor **Sir George Cathcart** didn't even make it as far as the mountain, instead being attacked a short distance away by Moshoeshoe's well-armed troops, who forced their hasty withdrawal. **Afrikaner forces** fighting for the Orange Free State (OFS) made a brief attempt on Thaba Bosiu in 1858, but came back in 1865 in a more determined manner, armed with heavy artillery, and began steadily shelling the mountain, launching two simultaneous assaults a few days later. Eight men made it to the top, but were seriously wounded as soon as they did so, and speedily retreated back down. A week later, more Afrikaner troops and the OFS president turned up, and another assault was launched. **General Wepener** led his men right to the top of the Khubelu Pass, but he was shot at the top and mortally wounded. The Basotho then mounted a counterattack, and the Afrikaners withdrew. They continued the siege for a month, though, during which time most of the livestock on Thaba Bosiu died of hunger and the Basotho became so short of bullets that they melted down the shells being fired at them to make home-made ones.

Although they won this battle, the Basotho lost the war, and Moshoeshoe signed a humiliating treaty in 1866 that surrendered most of Lesotho's farmland to the OFS. Four years later the old king died and was buried on the top of Thaba Bosiu, and two years after that Lesotho was annexed to the Cape Colony.

the one most Basotho prefer, is that the mountain, which does not look particularly high or impressive by day, seems to grow inexorably as night falls, becoming huge and unconquerable.

Visiting Thaba Bosiu

An official guide from the visitor centre will walk you up the steep **Khubelu Pass** (or "Red Pass"), a cleft in the cliffs marked by two flagpoles, where the Afrikaner General Louw Wepener was killed trying to storm the mountain in 1865 (see box, p.589), and on to the remains of Moshoeshoe's **European house**, built for him by a deserter from the 72nd Seaforth Highlanders, David F. Webber. From here, it's a short walk to the remains of Moshoeshoe's royal court and then to the **royal graveyard**, where the tombs of Moshoeshoe I and most of his successors are marked with simple stone cairns. On the eastern edge of the plateau you get a great view of **Qiloane**, a strange cone-shaped mountain with a large nodule on the top, which was apparently the inspiration for the national headdress, the distinctive Basotho hat.

11

ARRIVAL AND DEPARTURE

THABA BOSIU

By car To get to Thaba Bosiu by car, take Main South Road from Maseru, turning left 4km beyond the cathedral at the Engen petrol station. Follow this road for 10km and turn left at the T-junction for another 3km. Alternatively, follow Main South Road further towards Roma and follow signs to Thaba Bosiu.

By minibus taxi During the day, frequent minibus taxis run here from Maseru's New Taxi Rank.

INFORMATION

Tourist information At the foot of the mountain (☎2235 7207, ✉m.mokuku@ltdc.org.ls). Contact them a day in advance and they can arrange ponies for a pleasant guided two-hour trip around the main sights on the mountain (M200). There's also another two-hour route taking in some rock paintings and cave dwellings. Outside opening hours you're officially not allowed up the mountain, but there's nothing to stop you.

ACCOMMODATION

Mmelesi Lodge ☎5886 1116, ⊕mmelesilodge.co.ls. A pleasant lodge, next to the mountain and within walking distance of the visitor centre. It has a braai area, and comfortable en-suite rondavels at the back. The pleasant *Mokhoro* restaurant serves moderately priced dishes such as burgers (from M25) and sole fillet (M75). <u>M640</u>

Roma and around

About 30km from Maseru along a good tar road, the mission town of **ROMA** has a beautiful location amid sandstone foothills and is home to the **National University of Lesotho**, which began life in 1945 as Pius XII College, run by the Roman Catholic Church. Between 1964 and 1971 it was the university of all three of the former British southern African protectorates, now Lesotho, Botswana and Swaziland.

A kilometre or so further up the road is **Roma Mission**, most of which was built by French missionaries after 1862. Though grander than its counterpart in Morija (see p.602), the mission is a little run-down, and there's not much reason to linger.

The road to Semonkong

The road from Roma to Semonkong is one of the most spectacular in Lesotho, with superb views as you climb into the highlands. At **Moitsupeli**, 18.5km beyond Roma, look ahead towards the twin summits of the appropriately named **Thabana-li-Mele** (Breast Mountains). After the next village of Ha Dinzulu, the road continues to climb, peaking at 2000m at Nkesi's Pass and then dropping down to the village of **RAMABANTA**.

FROM TOP MALETSUNYANE FALLS (P.593); BASOTHO MAN >

ARRIVAL AND DEPARTURE

ROMA AND AROUND

By bus and minibus taxi Several buses and dozens of minibus taxis travel daily between Maseru and Roma, making this one of the busiest public transport routes in the country. Minibus taxis to Roma depart from the New Taxi Rank in Maseru and take 30–45min.

Destinations Maseru (5 daily; 1hr); Semonkong (4 daily; 4hr).

ACCOMMODATION

ROMA

Trading Post Guest House Signposted off the main road 2km before the centre of Roma ☎ 2234 0202, after 5.30pm ☎ 2234 0267, ⊛ tradingpost.co.za. The best accommodation in Roma, built in 1903 as a trading store by John Thomas Thorn, and lived in by his family ever since. This ivy-festooned guesthouse offers luxury rondavels, en-suite doubles and backpacker twin rooms with shared bathrooms in the original sandstone house; plus a self-catering cottage and camping. Decent meals are available by prior arrangement, there's a small swimming pool, and the family can help arrange activities including pony-trekking in the surrounding hills and walks to nearby dinosaur footprints. Camping M85, dorm M175, cottage M500, double M520

RAMABANTA

Ramabanta Trading Post Lodge ☎ 2234 0202, after 5.30pm ☎ 2234 0267, ⊛ tradingpost.co.za. Sister establishment to the *Trading Post Guest House* (see above), boasting seven lovely en-suite rooms in converted stables, three luxury rondavels sleeping four, backpacker accommodation in three-bed dorms and a campsite. Meals are available and, like the guesthouse in Roma, hikes and pony rides can be arranged, as can 4WD adventures (in your own car) with overnights in villages. Camping M85, dorm M150, double M650

Semonkong and around

Crossing the Makhaleng River and the 3000m-high Thaba Putsoa mountain range from Maseru gets you to the curiously straggly town of **SEMONKONG**. The region was inhabited by the San until 1873, when – after a series of **genocidal campaigns** against them by the British – the last of Lesotho's San were finally exterminated by an expedition led by a certain Colonel Bowker. The town itself began life in the 1880s following the Gun War as a refuge for displaced Basotho from the lowlands. The town offers a few basic stores, plenty of **bars**, and even a post office and bank, though you can't rely on either. If you're here in winter, try to catch the local **horse races** on the last Saturday of every month.

Ketane Falls

From the lodge in Semonkong (see opposite), it's a day's hike or pony trek west (see box below) into the pretty Thaba Putsoa mountains to the pristine 120m **Ketane Falls**.

ACTIVITIES AROUND SEMONKONG

Working in conjunction with the local community, *Semonkong Lodge* offers a bewildering choice of **outdoor activities**, ranging from short walks through town and along the river in search of bald ibis, to abseiling and adventurous pony treks lasting several days and overnighting in basic huts. Advance bookings are required for overnight rides. Semonkong boasts the longest commercially run **abseil** in the world, a 204m descent down the Maletsunyane Falls (M825). It's an electrifying thirty-minute descent, just metres away from the crashing water. You'll be given training on a small cliff near the lodge before taking the challenge the next day, and receive photos of the experience afterwards.

There is also a variety of **pony treks**, from short jaunts visiting nearby sights to overnight expeditions. Per-person costs work out cheaper in larger groups; the maximum is fifteen people; couples pay M275 per person for a full day's ride. Overnight trips, including the guide and pack horse, are around M900 per person for one night and M1400 per person for two nights. For overnight hikes, pack horses are optional but recommended. For day-trips on foot, a guide costs M15 per hour.

The falls are inaccessible by any other means of transport, and the pony trek is considered one of the best in the country. The falls can also be visited on a popular multi-day pony trek from *Malealea Lodge* (see p.605).

Maletsunyane Falls

The dramatic **Maletsunyane Falls** (or Le Bihan Falls, after a French missionary) are a pretty one-hour walk downriver from Semonkong. The dramatic falls, the highest single drop in Southern Africa, plunge nearly 200m down a sheer and scary cliff into a swimmable pool, whose mist gives the falls their name: "Smoking Water". There's a steep path down to the bottom, where you can swim or camp. The pool usually freezes by June, but the waterfall keeps going all winter, spraying the surrounding rocks with ice, and forming an impressive ice cage over the pool.

ARRIVAL AND DEPARTURE SEMONKONG AND AROUND

By car The 130km drive from Maseru to Semonkong takes about three hours by car. This road, and the new one from Semonkong to Qacha's Nek, have recently been asphalted and are now fantastic routes for drivers.

By bus From Maseru, a Lesotho Freight and Bus Services bus leaves daily around 9–10am, returning from Semonkong around 6–7am; the ride takes around five hours and terminates in the village centre, a few minutes' walk from the lodge.

ACCOMMODATION

Semonkong Lodge 1km south of the village centre beside the Maletsunyane River ☎ 2700 6037, ⓦ placeofsmoke.co.ls. One of the best lodges in Lesotho, this laidback and well-run place offers en-suite doubles and a dormitory in cosy thatch-and-stone buildings, complete with electricity and hot showers, and with fireplaces in some rooms. There's also a campsite, a kitchen for self-caterers, a great bar with pool table, balcony and a decent selection of music, and delicious meals (including vegetarian). But the main reason for staying here is for the immense selection of outdoor activities on offer (see box opposite). Camping M80, dorm M145, double M660

Ha Baroana

About 45km east of Maseru, a few kilometres north of Nazareth village • Daily 8am–5pm • M10

Ha Baroana has what were once some of the finest rock paintings in the country. They are still interesting, with discernible figures of animals, dancers and hunters, but they have been damaged by guides who throw water at them to make them more visible for tourists. The easiest way to get to the paintings is along a difficult dirt road, signposted off the main road. After 3.5km you'll reach the village of Ha Khotso; take the second turning on your right and then continue straight on for another 3km to Ha Baroana. The attractive **visitors' centre provides** a (compulsory) guide to accompany you on the fifteen-minute walk down into the gorge.

Thaba-Tseka

The road from Mohale Dam (see box, p.594) to **THABA-TSEKA** is a dramatic one, peaking in the heart of the Central Range at the 2860m **Mokhoabong Pass**, before descending to the town, which is over 2200m above sea level – although once here there's very little in this 1980s purpose-built administrative centre to detain you. The magnificent route from Mohale Dam has recently been asphalted, and it's now easy to drive from Maseru via Katse and Thaba-Tseka to Leribe, or vice versa, in two to three days

ARRIVAL AND DEPARTURE THABA-TSEKA

By bus Lesotho Freight and Bus Services operates three buses daily between Maseru and Thaba-Tseka, leaving from both directions in the early morning.

By car With your own vehicle you could tackle the spectacular road to Mokhotlong and the Sani Pass, but it's not one you should attempt in anything other than a 4WD. The fairly flat gravel road to Katse is suitable for ordinary saloon cars.

MOHALE DAM

About 80km east of Maseru and signposted off the A3, Mohale Dam was completed in 2004 as Phase 1b of the Lesotho Highlands Water Project (see box, p.597). Unlike the astonishing engineering grace of Katse Dam (see p.597), Mohale is little more than an enormous pile of concrete-faced rubble, the highest of its kind in Africa, whose 145m-high barrier holds back almost a billion cubic metres of water. Connected to the Katse Dam by a 32km-long tunnel, its main purpose is to feed more water north towards South Africa. A **visitor centre** (Mon–Fri 8am–5pm, Sat & Sun 10am–4pm; ☎ 2293 6217, ✉ lerotm@lhda.org.ls), with a stunning location overlooking the lake, runs daily **tours** (M10) of the site at 9am and 2pm on weekdays, and either 9am or noon on weekends. There are cruises (M300–500 for two people) on the lake, taking in Thaba-Chitja Island and the dam wall. The visitor centre is difficult to reach without your own transport but is well signposted: follow the signs 6km beyond Mohale Camp on the A3.

ACCOMMODATION

11

Buffalo's Hotel At the western side of Thaba-Tseka, ☎ 2290 0415, ✉ senatentabe@leo.co.ls. A neat compound of twelve comfortable rooms set back from the main road, with a decent restaurant. M450

Mohale Lodge Near Mohale Dam, Likalaneng ☎ 2293 6134, 🌐 mohalelodge.co.za. A modern hotel with bland if comfortable rooms, and some self-catering cottages. There's a good restaurant too. Near the impressive Mohale Dam, which is visible in the distance. M1100

Mohale oa Masite 10km east of Thaba-Tseka along the main road ☎ 2290 0980. A pleasant hotel with en-suite rooms and rondavels, a restaurant and a bar. Popular with the 4WD crowd crossing Lesotho. M450

The northern districts

The route north from Maseru right the way round to the **Sani Pass** takes in the best of Lesotho's lowlands and highlands. The road is tarred all the way to Mokhotlong, and although it's breaking up in places, is fine for 2WD vehicles except in winter. The stretch from Mokhotlong to Sani Pass, and the dramatic winding road down the mighty Drakensberg into South Africa, is gravel, for which 4WD is strongly advised, even if it remains just about passable in a saloon car in good weather.

Teya-Teyaneng

TEYA-TEYANENG (usually abbreviated to "T.Y.") means "place of shifting sands", after the way the nearby river changes its course from time to time. T.Y. is the **crafts capital** of Lesotho, specializing in all manner of weavings (see box opposite), from jerseys to elaborately designed wall hangings.

Ha Kome Cave Village

About 2km from the village of Mateka • Daily 8am–5pm • M43 • ☎ 5775 7437

Kome Cave Village is an increasingly popular tourist destination, and well worth the short detour from the northern main road. Seven quaint and inhabited mud dwellings sit under a huge rock overhang, looking more like igloos or West African mud architecture than anything usually found in Southern Africa.

At the modern **visitor and crafts centre**, visible on approach from the main road, an obligatory guide accompanies you on the ten-minute walk down to the site, where the ladies living in the huts will happily show you their dwellings and pose for photos.

Leribe (Hlotse)

Some 15km east of Maputsoe, a messy border town opposite Ficksburg in South Africa

THE WEAVING INDUSTRY IN TEYA-TEYANENG

There are four weaving outlets in Teya-Teyaneng (all open Mon–Fri 8am– 5pm, Sat 9am–5pm & Sun 10am–5pm). The most central is **Setsoto Design** (☎ 5808 6312, ⊛ setsotodesign.com), 300m from the *Blue Mountain Inn* (see p.596), where you can see tapestries being made. A good selection of woven products, crafts and elusive Lesotho postcards is sold in the adjacent shop: expect to pay around M120 for a bag and M1500 for a large tapestry. Credit cards and online orders are accepted. Three kilometres south of town, on the left as you come in from Maseru, look for signs to the small showroom of **Hatooa Mose Mosali** (☎ 2250 0772), which translates as "women must stand up and work hard". There's a fairly limited range in stock but its catalogue displays some very special wall hangings, which you need to order as they take a week or two to make. A short distance further on, signposted to the right of the main road, the pleasant Anglican St Agnes Mission is home to **Helang Basali Handicrafts** (☎ 2250 1546), whose showroom has a limited selection of woven crafts. For the best choice of products, head to **Elelloang Basali Weavers** (☎ 5851 0992, ⊛ africancrafts.com/artist/elelloang), about 5km north of town on the road to Leribe (the last building in town, constructed from recycled cans), where you'll find an extensive range of wall hangings, floor rugs, table mats and bags (from M130).

11

that's only good for its transport connections, **LERIBE** is a dilapidated but still pleasant little town, officially called **Hlotse** but more commonly known by the name of the surrounding district. It was founded in 1876 by an Anglican missionary, Reverend John Widdicombe, and suffered repeated sieges during the Gun War. With some effort, it's possible to view excellent **dinosaur footprints** at the turn-of-the-twentieth-century **Tsikoane Mission,** just over 7km south of town. To get there, turn off the main road at the white Tsikoane school sign and ask directions to the mission, where you can tip a local to guide you up the steep slope to the rock overhang above the church. Here you'll find a large chunk of rock that fell from the overhang, which has dozens of clear three-toed Lesothosaurus footprints of varying sizes; the negative prints can be seen on the overhang ceiling.

Leribe Craft Centre

Mon–Fri 8am–4.30pm, Sat & Sun 9.30am–1pm; outside official opening hours ask around and someone will open up • ☎ 2240 0323

The **Leribe Craft Centre**, at the major intersection on the main road, sells wonderful mohair scarves and shawls (M150–450), blankets and tablemats made by people with disabilities, plus maps, postcards and a few books about Lesotho and its history.

ARRIVAL AND DEPARTURE

THE NORTHERN DISTRICTS

TEYA-TEYANENG

By car The scenic A1 Main North Road takes you through sandstone mountain-studded lowlands.

By bus and minibus taxi The bus and taxi rank is 100m east of the main highway on the road to Mapoteng. There's plenty of transport to and from Maseru (40min) and further north to Leribe (45min) and Butha-Buthe (1hr), and you rarely have to wait long.

KOME CAVE VILLAGE

By pubic transport Getting to the caves is easiest via Teya-Teyaneng, where you can pick up fairly regular minibus taxis to Mateka, 19km to the southeast; from here it's an easy 30min walk down the hill to the visitor centre and Kome.

By car The caves are signposted along the road from Teya-Teyaneng to Mateka; turn right onto the gravel track

behind the football field in Mateka to find the road going downhill to the visitor centre. For a scenic option from Maseru, turn right onto the B31 after 4km, signposted to Sefikeng and Kome Cave Village; this road climbs up a steep series of hairpins to Lancer's Gap, an extraordinary ridge with a great gap in the middle through which the road passes, so named because a Lancers regiment was allegedly ambushed and defeated in it during the Gun War. From Thaba Bosiu (30km away), there's also a decent, direct gravel road; however, the steep 30m stretch of road between Sefikeng and Mateka could be problematic for saloon cars in bad weather, when you should only approach from Teya-Teyaneng.

LERIBE

By car The highway from Maseru passes to the south of town, and between the two petrol stations you'll find the

11

CULTURE AS FASHION: THE BLANKET AND THE HAT

In a region of Africa where **traditional dress** has all but died out, Lesotho stands out as the exception. The **mokorotlo** (Basotho traditional hat) is not widely worn these days, admittedly, though you'll still regularly see its distinctive cone and bobble in Lesotho. Apparently modelled on the shape of Qiloane Mountain near Thaba Bosiu, and made of woven straw, the *mokorotlo* has become the standard Basotho souvenir, sold in every craft shop, usually for M50 or less.

More prevalent than the *mokorotlo* is the Basotho **blanket**, made from high-quality woven wool and worn all over the country in all seasons. European traders started bringing these from England to Lesotho in the 1860s, though nowadays they are made in South Africa.

The symbols woven into the blankets were originally English design, but acquired significance for the Basotho over time; maize cobs were associated with fertility, for example. Young brides are supposed to wear a blanket around their hips until their first child is conceived, and boys wear different blankets before and after circumcision. The ubiquitous Fraser's Stores, which you find all over the country, first established themselves by selling blankets, and still stock them today; otherwise, the Di Mezza & De Jager Trading Store, just across the border in Clarens (see p.439), is a great place to see a collection of historical blankets, as well as modern ones. Good ones (made of pure wool) cost M400–600, a fortune by local standards.

Although they have always been foreign imports, and are the commodities on which many European trader fortunes have been built, the blankets remain quintessentially Basotho, and a source of national pride.

main intersection. The road on the left if coming from Maseru leads up the hill to the town centre.

By bus and minibus taxi The taxi rank is reached along the road branching off at the *Mountain View Hotel*.

There's plenty of transport, though if you're heading south it may be quickest to grab a seat on one of the frequent minibuses west to Maputsoe (10min) and change there.

ACCOMMODATION AND EATING

TEYA-TEYANENG

Blue Mountain Inn A couple of hundred metres past the post office and its transmitter ☎ 2250 0362, ⓦ bmilesotho.com. A spacious and well-run hotel with dozens of small and old-fashioned but comfortable chalets, plus a block with smarter, better-value rooms. It also has a restaurant, serving tasty meals (M40–80), plus a pizzeria, three bars, a pool and a large lawn with shaded tables. **M700**

Ka Pitseng Guest House Signposted below the main road as you approach the town from Maseru ☎ 2250 1638, ⓦ molengoane-kapitseng.co.ls. A more modest option than *Blue Mountain Inn*, with clean rooms and a decent restaurant that serves a Basotho lunch buffet (R50) on Wednesdays. **M680**

LERIBE

Bird Haven Jlisimeng II, three streets east of the main

crossing ☎ 5954 3030, ⓦ birdhavenleribe.com. A good central option with five charming rondavel chalets with kitchenettes and private bathrooms in a suburban garden, plus two rooms in the main house. **M600**

Mountain View Hotel Just up the road from the main intersection ☎ 2240 0559, ⓦ skymountainhotels.com. A range of rooms in the main buildings and in chalets and rondavels scattered around the pleasant gardens. The restaurant serves tasty meat and fish dishes, and light snacks. There's also a lively bar, which is especially busy at weekends. **M750**

Naleli Guest House 2km from the centre along the old road north to Butha-Buthe ☎ 2240 0409, ⓦ naleliguesthouse.co.ls. The best accommodation and food in town, with a set of nicely furnished rooms that overlook a well-tended garden and terrace. The restaurant serves hake and chips (M60), steak (M70) and Basotho cuisine on Thursdays. **M685**

The road to Katse Dam

To the east of Leribe rises the impressive Front Range of the Maloti Mountains. The region is at the heart of Phase 1a of the ambitious **Lesotho Highlands Water Project** (see box opposite), whose centrepiece is the massive dam and reservoir at **Katse**. The 100km A8 highway built for the dam from Leribe is a remarkable journey almost worth making for the drive alone, rising steeply up from the lowlands and over the

3090m **Mefika Lisiu Pass**, before reaching the Bokong Nature Reserve and dropping down to Katse Dam.

Bokong Nature Reserve

Just off the A8 • Daily 8am–4.30pm • ☎ 2246 0723, ⓦ lhda.org.ls • M30 • Guides M30/day • Horses M150/half day, M210/day

Established as part of the Highlands Water Project (see box below), and a paradise for high-altitude hikers, the highlight of the breathtaking **Bokong Nature Reserve** is the dramatic **Lepaqoa Waterfall**, which freezes in winter to form a column of ice.

The reserve's **entrance** is next to the **visitor centre**, along the highway 3km beyond the pass. Perched dramatically on the edge of a 100m cliff overlooking the Lepaqoa valley, the visitor centre offers a 45-minute walk along a poorly marked footpath to the top of the Lepaqoa Waterfall, as well as guides and horses for hire. Call to enquire about the two to three day pony-riding or hiking trips across the plateau, 32km north to Ts'ehlanyane National Park.

The Katse Dam

11

Visitor centre Mon–Fri 8am–noon & 1–4pm, Sat & Sun 8am–noon • **Dam wall tours** Mon–Fri 9am & 2pm, Sat & Sun 9am & 11am • M10 • **Botanical gardens** Mon–Fri 7am–5pm, Sat & Sun 9am–2pm • M5 • ☎ 2291 0377, ⓦ lhda.org.ls

Katse village, a former engineers' village overlooking the lake, is drab and boring, with uniform box-like houses. But the massive **dam** below (see box below), which holds back nearly two billion cubic metres of water, really is impressive, even if you aren't usually interested in engineering. To find out more, head for the **visitor centre**, with its bright blue roof, just before the village and dam. The hour-long **tours** take in the tunnels running from inside the dam into the mountainside, as well as the road on top, from where you can look straight down the wall.

During initial excavations it was discovered that the bedrock was seismically unstable, so a moveable joint was incorporated into the dam's base, allowing it to flex. Even so, the rapid filling of the reservoir caused a series of minor **earth tremors**. This was all to be expected, said the engineers, but not by the inhabitants of Ha Mapaleng, where a tremor ripped a 30cm-wide, 1.5km-long gash through the village. The local prophetess explained that a huge **underground snake** had been disturbed by the dam's construction and that the entire village would be gobbled up. No one hung around to find out, and the village was eventually relocated 1km away.

THE LESOTHO HIGHLANDS WATER PROJECT

Lesotho's abundance of water but shortage of cash and Gauteng's monetary wealth and water poverty are the facts behind the stunningly ambitious **Lesotho Highlands Water Project** – Africa's largest engineering venture to date. The essence of the project is to dam Lesotho's major south-flowing rivers, then divert the water north through gravity tunnels (the longest in the world) via a hydroelectric power station at 'Muela to the Ash River, north of Clarens in South Africa, from where the water flows into the Vaal and to Gauteng. For this, South Africa pays Lesotho royalties of around R24 million a month.

The treaty formalizing the project was signed in 1986, although without much popular consultation or assessment of the environmental impact. Various compensation arrangements have been put in place for villagers affected by flooding, though not unexpectedly there are grumbles that these promises have not been met.

The project's first phase, which concluded in 2004, saw the construction of the 185m-high Katse Dam, an underground hydroelectric plant at 'Muela, tunnels to the Ash River, and all the road infrastructure. Facilities were developed at Liphofung Cave, Katse and the nature reserves as part of this phase, the idea being that local communities would benefit from tourism revenues. It also saw the construction of Mohale Dam on the Senqunyane River, linked to Katse reservoir by tunnel. In 2014, the second phase of the project kicked off with the construction of the 2,2 billion litre Polihali dam in Mokhotlong district, which will transfer water through another tunnel to Katse reservoir; completion of this new dam is expected in 2020.

Situated in the village and overlooking the dam lake, the **botanical gardens** are beautiful to visit, with several "Afro-alpine" ecosystems represented on the sloping terrain, attracting colourful birds. It's something of a refugee camp for thousands of critically endangered spiral aloes rescued from the construction sites and thieves, and a programme to plant seedlings of spiral aloes and montane bamboo is under way.

ARRIVAL AND DEPARTURE

BOKONG NATURE RESERVE

By minibus taxi The reserve can be reached from Leribe on minibus taxis that run roughly every two hours to Katse; ask to be dropped off at the visitor centre, 100m off the main road. If the minibuses returning from Katse to Leribe are full, try a minibus going 15km east to nearby Ha Lejone and pick up transport there.

THE ROAD TO KATSE DAM

KATSE

By bus and minibus taxi Public transport arrives at and departs from the taxi rank at the entrance to Katse village. There are daily buses to Maseru, leaving around 6am (6hr), and minibus taxis every two hours or so to Leribe (3hr). There are several buses and minibus taxis every day to and from Thaba-Tseka, two to three hours south along a good gravel road.

ACCOMMODATION

PITSENG

★**Aloes Guest House** Follow the signs from the A8 ☎ 2700 5626, ✉ aloesguesthouse@gmail.com. Dreary Pitseng, on the A8, is notable only for this stylish guesthouse, which offers thatched bungalows set around a grassy compound with a small pool, self-catering facilities and food served on request. Camping and dorm beds are also available. Quadbikes, pony trekking and guided hikes can be arranged. Camping M80, dorm M200, double M600

BOKONG NATURE RESERVE

Reserve accommodation Contact the LHDA Nature Reserves Booking Office in Butha-Buthe ☎ 2246 0723 or ☎ 2291 3206, ✉ nature@lhda.org.ls. Camping is possible throughout the reserve, and there are also two stone-and-thatch rondavels close to the falls (each with

four single beds) with a shared kitchen and bathroom. They have gas and bedding, but you need to bring your own food. Five large chalets are under construction next to the visitor centre, where a basic restaurant serves meals (M25) on request. Advance booking for the restaurant, accommodation and ponies is recommended. Camping M50, rondavels & chalets M400

KATSE

Orion Katse Lodge Katse village ☎ 2291 0202, ⊛ katselodge.co.za. The lodge has drab rooms with fine views of the lake and its impressive birdlife, and a good restaurant serving a decent selection of meals. There are also a number of cheaper dorm rooms and flats in the compound. The hotel can arrange boat cruises (M600–1000), biking, pony trekking and hiking. Dorm M200, flats M660, lodge M1100

Butha-Buthe

BUTHA-BUTHE (meaning "Lie Down") has a frontier feel – noisy, dirty and dusty – and offers little reason to stay, although it makes a good base for visiting nearby attractions. The town was founded in 1884 because the local chief refused to go to Leribe to pay taxes, necessitating a new tax centre nearer his residence. Butha-Buthe attracted traders from the outset, and is one of few towns in Lesotho with a sizeable Muslim Indian community.

Butha-Buthe Mountain, just east of town, is where Moshoeshoe I had his first stronghold before retreating to Thaba Bosiu in 1824. It's a stiff but not particularly difficult climb and the summit provides tremendous views. You can cut the hiking distance by catching a minibus taxi as far as Ha Mopeli.

ARRIVAL AND DEPARTURE

BUTHA-BUTHE

By minibus taxi There are frequent buses and minibus taxis from the main crossroads in town to Maseru (2hr)

and Katse (3hr), and two to three a day to Mokhotlong (7hr).

ACCOMMODATION

Crocodile Inn Hotel Hospital Rd ☎ 2246 0223, ✉ crocodileinn@yahoo.com. The only central place to stay,

the basic *Crocodile Inn*, next to the hospital, has shabby en-suite rooms and better rooms in rondavels. There are two bars, which attract dedicated drinkers until well into the morning, and an inexpensive restaurant. M600

Likileng Lodge 1km out of town, on the left-hand side of the road if heading towards Oxbow ☎ 2246 0686, ✉ likilenglodge@tsebo.co.ls. The best accommodation in town, set in a large compound and offering clean and functional en-suite rooms, plus a bar and a restaurant serving tasty meals. M530

Ts'ehlanyane National Park

Daily 8am–5pm • M30, plus M10 per vehicle and M10 if staying overnight • Horses are available for hire by prior arrangement M180/3hr, M210/half day, M410/day • ☎ 2246 0723 or 2291 3206 • ✉ nature@lhda.org.ls

An asphalt road starting 9km southeast of Butha-Buthe leads 32km southeast into the western scarp of the Front Range, following a very picturesque valley. Covering 56 square kilometres of extremely rugged hiking terrain at the confluence of the Ts'ehlanyane and Holomo rivers, **Ts'ehlanyane National Park** is intended to protect several areas of ecological importance, particularly the indigenous **Leucosidea sericea woodland** known locally as *Ouhout* or *Che-che* – one of Lesotho's very few forested areas. Equally rare are stands of montane bamboo. **Mammals** present include mainly duikers, baboons and serval cats, and the fenced-in mountain opposite the Maliba Lodge is home to a herd of huge eland antelope. There's also the endangered *Metisella syrinx* butterfly, bearded vultures (*lammergeiers*) and ground woodpeckers. The **best time to visit** is in spring, when the small yellow flowers along the riverbanks that give their unpronounceable name to the reserve are in flower. The highlight for serious hikers and pony trekkers is a spectacular 35km trail linking the park with Bokong Nature Reserve to the south (see p.597), with swimming possible in streams along the way.

ARRIVAL AND DEPARTURE   **TS'EHLANYANE NATIONAL PARK**

By minibus taxi There are regular minibus taxis from Butha-Buthe to the national park, stopping at the park gates.

ACCOMMODATION

★ **Maliba Lodge** ☎ 0027 31 702 8791, ⊛ maliba-lodge .com. Inside the national park, this de luxe private lodge has Lesotho's best accommodation in six beautiful thatched "Mountain Lodge" suites, each with underfloor heating, fireplaces, and a private balcony with views of the protected forest and mountains. There are also riverside rooms in several sleek lodges sleeping up to eight, and smaller huts. The lodge arranges pony trekking tours in the national park (M280/person for up to 3hr, M350 for up to 5hr, M410/day)

and village visits (M80), and there are maps for hiking and 4WD trips. Massage and other treatments are available in the spa. Rates for huts and suites include meals; the lodges are self-catering. Riverside lodge chalet M1650, huts M2100, suites M3360

National Park Accommodation ☎ 2246 0723 or 2291 3206. There's accommodation in a guesthouse near the park's reception, which sleeps six people, or in three-bed dormitories. Dorm M150, guesthouse M450

'Muela

Power plant Tours daily 9am & 2pm • M30 • **Visitor centre** ☎ 2224 8000

Heading northeast from Butha-Buthe, the A1 road begins to climb into the Maloti Mountains. After 22km, you reach the small settlement of Khukhune where a road on the right leads up to **'MUELA**, an integral part of the Lesotho Highlands Water Project (see box, p.597). Here the water flowing down the delivery tunnel from Katse Reservoir to South Africa powers an underground hydroelectric station that supplies all of Lesotho with electricity. The real attraction lies underground, and **tours** of the power plant (run by the visitor centre) take you past the three large turbines that power much of Lesotho.

Liphofung Cave Cultural Historical Site

3km off the main road north, 7km beyond the 'Muela turn-off • Daily 8am–5pm • M30 • Pony trekking M100 per half day

The **Liphofung Cave Cultural Historical Site** is actually a large sandstone overhang boasting an impressive series of San **rock paintings**, from whose images it gets its name, "Place of the Eland". The site is well worth a visit and is also significant for the Basotho in its role as a hideout for the young Moshoeshoe I. Guided tours of the site start from the visitor centre, where you can also see three traditional Basotho huts. Ponies can be hired from the visitor centre for guided treks, where cultural performances can also be arranged.

ACCOMMODATION   **LIPHOFUNG CAVE CULTURAL HISTORICAL SITE**

Liphofung Visitor Centre ☎ 2246 0723. At the site's visitor centre are a couple of delightful self-catering rondavels that each sleep four people. Camping M40, rondavels M250

Mamohase Rural Stay B&B Signposted off the main road just south of Liphofung, then 2km down a tough dirt track ☎ 5805 8438 or 5804 5597, ⓦ mamohaseruralstay.com. A homely set-up, offering local meals in the family dining room and a few beds in thatched rondavels next door, with bucket showers and an outdoor toilet. M500

Oxbow

The A1 into the highlands is one of the most dramatic roads in Lesotho, passing through some particularly striking sandstone cliffs before twisting tortuously up a chain of heart-stopping hairpins into the basalt. Some 20km beyond Liphofung, past **Moteng Pass** (2820m), Oxbow is a string of unremarkable buildings in a narrow valley. In winter, the place is packed out with South Africans looking at snow. Between June and August, **skiing** is the main draw 16km up the road from Oxbow, where AfriSki (June–Aug daily 9am–4pm; ski pass M400/day, equipment rental M340/day) has a fun 2km intermediate ski slope complete with a modern ski lift and snow-making equipment.

ACCOMMODATION   **OXBOW**

AfriSki Mahlasela Basin ☎ 5954 4734, ⓦ afriski.net. About 10km up the road from Oxbow, at 3220m, this fledgling resort overlooking the ski slope is popular with South Africans in winter. Accommodation at the resort must be booked via the central reservation office; the 250 beds on offer range from basic backpacker dorms to very comfortable en-suite rooms. Dorm M100, double M1200

New Oxbow Lodge Oxbow ☎ 0027 51 933 2247 (South Africa), ⓦ oxbow.co.za. This lodge has seen better days but still has perfectly comfortable, warm rooms, a well-stocked bar, and a restaurant serving reasonably priced meals. There's good trout fishing on the Malibamatso River, and wonderful hiking in any direction. M1050

The Roof of Africa route

The scenic road from Oxbow to Mokhotlong is often called "the Roof of Africa route", peaking at **Tlaeeng Pass** (3251m) and passing the ugly **Letseng diamond mine** en route. The road is fully tarred, although the extremes of temperature and heavy mining trucks here have caused damage, and there are numerous potholes.

Mokhotlong

Perched on the banks of the scraggly Mokhotlong River, the wind-blown town of **MOKHOTLONG** ("Place of the Bald Ibis") was once known as the "Loneliest Place in Africa", and it's easy to see why, since it still gets cut off from the rest of civilization for days or weeks at a time in winter. Mokhotlong began life as a remote police outpost in 1905, and gradually evolved into a trading centre for the region's highlanders, but remained isolated from the rest of Lesotho for years, with radio contact only established in 1947. An airstrip was constructed in 1948 and a rudimentary road link built in the 1950s, but Mokhotlong continued to get the bulk of its supplies by pony from Natal, via Sani, for a long time afterwards. Even today it feels remote, with locals usually riding into town for a shop and a drink on ponies, resplendent in their gumboots and blankets. However, it's the only town of any size in eastern Lesotho and a good place to stock up with supplies if you are using the Sani Top border post.

ARRIVAL AND INFORMATION | **MOKHOTLONG**

By bus and minibus taxi Getting to Mokhotlong's main crossroad is easiest on the daily 7am Lesotho Freight and Bus Services bus from Maseru (9hr), which makes the return journey at 8am. There are also several minibus taxis a day from Butha-Buthe (6hr), and up to three to Sani Top (1hr 30min); the early morning bus from Mokhotlong to

Sani Top usually continues down the pass to Underberg, returning in the afternoon; additionally, *Sani Mountain Lodge* (see p.393) has a shuttle service between their lodge and the South African border post at the bottom of the pass road.

Bank There's a Standard Lesotho Bank ATM in town.

ACCOMMODATION

Farmers' Training Centre 2km north of town, signposted as "FTC" ☎ 2292 0235. Basic and cheap dorm accommodation with clean rooms but grubby shared bathrooms. The highlight is the pleasant location on the edge of town. No food available. M70

Molumong Guest House 20km southwest of town along the road to Thaba-Tseka, ☎ 0027 83 254 3323 (South Africa), ⊛ molumong.wordpress.com. The remotest of Lesotho's lodges is a rustic but characterful 1920s place with fantastic mountain views. The main house is self-catering, with very cosy doubles and a great lounge to relax in. There's also a bunkhouse and a campsite. Only basic supplies are available in the village so come well stocked. The lodge also offers inexpensive pony trekking, and is a good base for hiking. It can be reached on the

hourly minibuses from Mokhotlong to Ha Janteau. Camping M80, double M340

Senqu Hotel On the edge of town as you enter on the A1 ☎ 2292 0330. Some of the rooms are very nice (request one with a balcony and a good view), while the older rooms are clean but looking a bit shabby. The restaurant is the best place to eat in town, and there's a bar too. M500

St James Lodge 4km along the road from Mokhotlong to Tsaba-Tseka ☎ 071 6726801, ⊛ tjameslodge.co.za. In the grounds of the St James Mission, this self-catering lodge offers pleasant en-suite rooms, cheaper rondavels with separate bathrooms, and camping. Pony trekking, cultural visits to the village and a church tour are all available. Camping M70, rondavel M300, double M400

11

Sani and around

The gravel road to **SANI** branches off the main road to Mokhotlong 5km before town, and twists its way in spectacular fashion for nearly 60km along the Sehonkong River, peaking at **Kotisephola Pass** (3240m) before dropping to 2895m at **Sani Top**, a few kilometres from the South African border.

At Sani Top there are plenty of rewarding hikes, including a stiff 12km climb up **Thabana Ntlenyana**, at 3482m the highest point in Southern Africa and walkable in a day if you start early. Also tough but stunningly beautiful is the 40km **Top-of-the-Berg** hike to Sehlabathebe National Park, which takes about four days.

The descent from Sani, down the dramatic, hairpin-bend-filled **Sani Pass** into South Africa (see p.392), is only allowed with a 4WD car. In winter, the pass is frequently blocked by snow or ice. Talk of tarring the road has horrified off-road enthusiasts across the subcontinent. **Accommodation** is available just across the border at *Sani Mountain Lodge* (see p.393).

ARRIVAL AND INFORMATION | **SANI AND AROUND**

By bus and minibus Getting to Sani is only possible in good weather; if it's been snowing, you can forget it. Some five buses go from *Sani Mountain Lodge* to Mokhotlong every day (1hr 30min). On the South African side, 4WD vehicles run up to *Sani Mountain Lodge* daily at

11.30am and 3.30pm, going back down at 10.30am and 2.30pm (R250).

Crossing the border The border, between *Sani Mountain Lodge* and Sani Pass, is open daily from 8am to 4pm; the Lesotho side stays open till 5pm to let vehicles through.

The southern districts

The country's **southern districts** can't match the mountains of north and central Lesotho for sheer scale, but they do hold some dramatic countryside that is relatively easy to visit – especially on horseback from the excellent tourist lodges at **Malealea** and **Semonkong**. The nineteenth-century mission town of **Morija** is perhaps the most historic in the country. Morija also has dinosaur footprints in the vicinity, as does **Mohale's Hoek** and, more accessibly, **Quthing**, further south. Moving on northeast past the town of **Qacha's Nek**, the isolated delights of **Sehlabathebe National Park** are so remote as to make visits here a true adventure.

Morija

Set at the foot of the Makhoarane Plateau, 44km from Maseru, the pleasant little town of **MORIJA** houses the country's main museum and Lesotho's oldest building, church and printing press. The town was established in 1833 at Moshoeshoe I's behest as the country's first Christian mission, and granted to three missionaries of the Paris Evangelical Missionary Society. The bucolic setting, attractive accommodation and easy access make it a good base for exploring western Lesotho.

Lesotho Evangelical Church
In the middle of the village

The large, red-brick **Lesotho Evangelical Church**, with its impressive teak-beamed roof, is usually open on Sundays. Begun in 1847, this is the third church built on the site, using the labour of Pedi economic migrants on their way to Cape Colony, though its tall steeple was only built in 1905. Interestingly, the pillars inside were made from old ships' masts, transported here by ox-cart from Port Elizabeth.

Maeder House Gallery
Next to the Evangelical Church • Tues–Sun 10am–4pm • ☎ 5946 7681, ✉ prorke@gmail.com

Most of Morija was razed to the ground by Afrikaner troops in 1858, and almost the only building left standing was the historical **Maeder House**, built in 1843 and the oldest building in the country. It's now used as a gallery selling striking modern paintings, mosaics and wonderful pottery by Patrick Rorke and crafts by other local artists. There's an **art centre** for local children and visiting artists, and any donations of art books or supplies are very welcome. An adjacent building houses the historic **printing works**, which have produced Basotho literature since the 1860s as well as the country's oldest newspaper, *Leselinyana la Lesotho* (Little Light of Lesotho), which has been in almost continual publication since 1863.

Morija Museum
Just uphill from the Evangelical Church • Tues–Sat 11am–4pm, Sun 1–4pm • M20 • ☎ 2236 0308, ⊛ morija.co.ls

The bright-yellow **Morija Museum** is an excellent reason for coming to town. The exhibits, displayed in a large room and an adjoining hallway, are a stimulating combination of geological and fossil finds, meteorite fragments, ethnographic material and historic items connected with Moshoeshoe (see p.578) and his contemporaries. The museum also sells a range of books including the recommended *Guide to Morija* (M20), and can organize tours of the village and surroundings, taking in the church and Maeder House Gallery. The museum **archive** is the best collection of books on Lesotho anywhere. Curator Stephen Gill is the main authority on Lesotho's history and culture.

In the last week of September and the first week of October the museum organizes the **Morija Arts and Cultural Festival** (⊛ morija.co.ls), the largest and most significant event of its kind in the country, where traditional music, jazz, dancing, horse races and crafts mix with theatre, cinema, sport and children's events.

RIGHT SANI PASS (P.601) >

11

ARRIVAL AND INFORMATION

By bus and minibus taxi Getting to Morija is easy, with buses and minibus taxis running throughout the day from Maseru (45min–1hr). There's no bus or taxi rank; transport finishing in Morija drops you outside the post office close to the museum, while buses running from Maseru to Mafeteng and Mohale's Hoek drop off and pick up on the highway 1km west of the centre.

Tourist information Morija Museum (see p.602) also doubles up as the town's tourist information.

Activities Pony treks can be arranged through *Morija Guest Houses* (see below) or the museum, and range from one-hour jaunts (from M100) to day-trips (from M385). The best of various **walking** trails from Morija leads to an impressive sets of avian dinosaur footprints on one side of a large rock halfway up the Makhoarane Plateau, 45 minutes beyond the guesthouse. Guides are available for these walks; there are no fixed prices.

ACCOMMODATION

Lindy's B&B ☏ 6285 5309, ⓦ lindysbnb.co.ls. Two nicely furnished cottages sleeping up to four; one historical and one new, up on the hill above the museum (follow the white stones). Lunch and dinner can be ordered in advance. M600
★**Morija Guest Houses** ☏ 2236 0306, ⓦ morijaguesthouses.com. One of Lesotho's most attractive lodgings, set in a dramatic spot right at the top of town (follow the white stones from the museum). The

beautiful thatched house contains several comfortable rooms, plus a fully equipped kitchen, lounge, and veranda with fantastic views over the surrounding area. Just below the guesthouse stand several attractive self-catering Basotho cottages. Mountain bikes are for rent at M65/hr. Meals can be provided by prior arrangement. Arrive by public transport and pay M160 for the best available bed, in any room. M620

EATING AND DRINKING

Morija Museum Tea Shop The museum's tea shop, in a traditional rondavel in the lovely gardens behind the main building, offers cold drinks and simple Basotho meals; enjoy them sitting on the terrace with valley views. Mon–Sat 9am–4.30pm, Sun 2–4.30pm.

Snack bar Opposite the post office. You can get drinks and excellent cheap Basotho meals for a very modest M20 in the snack bar attached to the grocer's, a few minutes' walk downhill from the museum. Daily 8am–7pm.

Malealea

The bustling minibus taxi stop at **Motsekuoa**, 10km south of Morija, marks the turning for the village of **MALEALEA**, one of the best-known places in Lesotho thanks to the hugely popular *Malealea Lodge & Pony Trek Centre* (see opposite). Now a spacious forested compound, set in a spectacular spot in the foothills of the Thaba Putsoa range, the lodge was originally a small trading store established by the British adventurer Mervyn Bosworth-Smith in 1905. It was Bosworth-Smith who wrote the words on the brass plaque at the top of the magnificent Gate of Paradise Pass, 6km before the lodge: "Wayfarer, pause and look upon a gateway of Paradise".

ACTIVITIES AROUND MALEALEA

Malealea Lodge (see opposite) runs a series of **guided pony treks**, from short jaunts to as many days as your bottom and wallet can stand, with nights in basic huts equipped with gas cookers, kitchen utensils and floor mattresses. Trips can be arranged at short notice. **Costs** vary according to where you go and group size, but count on around M475 for a full day and night, plus M100 for village accommodation, or M10 per hour of hiking. Riders cannot weigh more than 90kg, you must have medical insurance, and luggage is limited to 12.5kg including food. A good alternative to the pony trekking (which can be quite hard on the body if you're not used to it) is simply to **walk** and use a pony as a pack animal. The pony can carry four people's packs, provided they're not excessively heavy.

Short trips include **village walks** and a consultation with a traditional healer (*sangoma*). Longer day-trips, either afoot or in the saddle, go to Botsoela Waterfall (a beautiful four-hour trip that's recommended for saddle-sore, novice riders; from M240), Pitseng Canyon and its rock pool, San rock paintings, and the Gates of Paradise Pass along Matelile Ridge.

ARRIVAL AND DEPARTURE

MALEALEA

By public transport A daily minibus taxi leaves from Maseru's New Taxi Rank at around 11am direct to the gates of *Malealea Lodge* (85km, 2hr).

By taxi Take one of the hourly taxis from Maseru to Mafeteng and change at Motsekuoa (1hr), where you'll find onward taxis to Malealea (5 daily; 1hr).

ACCOMMODATION

★**Malealea Lodge & Pony Trek Centre** ☎0027 82 552 4215, ⓦmalealea.com. Simple but comfortable accommodation in huts, chalets and rondavels spread out in a pretty forested compound. The lodge is always a lively place; next to the dining room (set meals served at set times) is a great little bar and most evenings guests congregate around an open fire outside. Every afternoon a local choir and band perform for guests, the latter bashing out tunes on home-made instruments. The local community benefits greatly from the lodge through employment and special projects funded by the Malealea Development Trust, and visitors can experience heart-warming hospitality when venturing out. Meals are optional: breakfast M80, lunch M100, dinner M135. Camping M100, huts M350, farmhouse rooms M580, rondavels M700

11

Mafeteng and around

The bustling town of **MAFETENG**, 18km from Van Rooyenshek **border post**, will be the first place you come to in Lesotho if crossing from Wepener in the Free State. It means "the place of Lefeta's people", after the son of a French missionary Emile Rolland, who was the district's first magistrate and was nicknamed Lefeta, or "he who passes", by locals, who regarded him as virtually Basotho except for the fact that he skipped (or "passed by") initiation. Much of the town suffered in the 1998 riots, but the centre has now recovered. The only building of any interest is the **District Administrator's office** on the main street, worth a quick look for the carved animal heads studding its front wall.

Thabana Morena Plateau

About 20km east of Mafeteng is the impressive **Thabana Morena Plateau**, which makes a good excursion, though you'll need your own transport. Rising above the village of the same name, it rewards those who make the steep hour-long climb with good views of the Free State plains to the west and the Thaba Putsoa range to the east.

ARRIVAL AND DEPARTURE

MAFETENG AND AROUND

By bus As befits a border town, Mafeteng has a very busy bus station at the main crossroads in the centre of town where you can easily find transport north to Morija (30min) and Maseru (1hr), and southeast to Mohale's Hoek (45min), Quthing (1hr30min) and beyond (five buses and numerous minibus taxis daily each way).

ACCOMMODATION AND EATING

Golden Hotel To the right of the highway from Maseru, just before you enter Mafeteng proper ☎2270 0566. The anonymous-looking *Golden Hotel* offers functional en-suite rooms and a dining room serving pizzas and meat dishes. M390

Mafeteng Hotel & Restaurant On the south side of town down the small street near the telecommunications tower ☎2270 0236. Looks like a 1960s airport control tower, but offers pleasant and spacious en-suite rooms, all with satellite TV, plus some cottages in a secluded garden and a good swimming pool. It's a good idea to ask in advance if the loud disco will be active when you plan to sleep here. Its restaurant may be the best place to eat in town, with a range of moderately priced meat dishes. M400

Mohale's Hoek

MOHALE'S HOEK, a short distance from the little-used Makhaleng Bridge borderpost, is a rather bedraggled little town, but it has a decent hotel and some interesting sites in the surrounding hills, including some well-preserved **dinosaur footprints**. Mohale was Moshoeshoe's younger brother, appointed to look after the area by the king as part of his bid to wrest control of the district from chief

11

DONGAS AND SOIL EROSION IN LESOTHO

One thing you'll quickly notice about Lesotho is that the entire country is virtually **treeless**. Indeed, the country – once the grain basket of the region – is in deep ecological trouble, and acres of irreplaceable topsoil, loosened by decades of over-farming, are washed away down its rivers each year.

The problems began with the expropriation of the best land by the OFS in the 1860s, which forced the Basotho to start farming hilly areas that had previously only been used for winter grazing. This process continues to this day, and you will even see crops being grown at over 2000m in districts like Semonkong and Mokhotlong. Mountains are no substitute for fertile plains, however, and Lesotho has been a net importer of food since the 1920s.

The ecological effect of the unrelenting cultivation of the Lesotho mountains has been devastating. The soil fertility has plummeted and, more seriously, huge quantities of topsoil are simply washed away in each summer's rains. In many places so much topsoil has gone that great ravines called **dongas** have opened up. Though they often look green enough, the remaining soil tends to lie close to the surface rock, making it useless for serious cultivation.

Efforts to slow this process have been under way for some time, most noticeably through the terracing of hillside fields. For one of the best examples of how simply dongas can be reclaimed, ask to be shown the way to the Musi family donga in the village beside *Malealea Lodge* (see p.605) – reclamation of the donga began two decades ago by Fanuel Musi, and is now carried on by his grandson and wife; donations are appreciated.

Moorosi. There are still quite a few of Moorosi's Baphuthi clan here, though, whose language is in some ways closer to Xhosa than Basotho. There's nothing to see or do here apart from the excellent drive, walk or pony trek into the little-visited **Mokhele Mountain Range** (see below).

Mokhele Mountain Range

Ten kilometres east of Mohale's Hoek, the beautiful and little-visited **Mokhele Mountain Range** is perfect for a drive, walk or pony trek (ask about treks at *Mount Maluti Hotel*; see below). To get here, travel a few kilometres south on the main road to the little village of Mesitsaneng; turn left at the signpost for the primary school and head 11km east along a rough dirt track to the historic French **Maphutseng Mission**, in whose roof locals once hid from attacking Boers. When the road bends sharply to the left, branch right down a smaller track and you'll see a plateau a short walk away, where you'll find some **dinosaur footprints** and the remnants of an inscription recording their discovery in 1959.

ARRIVAL AND DEPARTURE   MOHALE'S HOEK

By bus and minibus taxi Buses arrive at the busy station in the centre of Mohale's Hoek, while minibus taxis congregate on the main street near the Engen petrol station – between them and the buses (6 daily in both directions) you should be able to find transport heading both north to Maseru (2hr) and south to Quthing (45min) throughout the day.

ACCOMMODATION AND EATING

Mount Maluti Hotel ✆ 2278 5224, ⊛ hmmlesotho .com. Comfortable rooms with TVs, plus a bar, tennis court and swimming pool. The hotel restaurant is the best place to eat in southern Lesotho and offers decent cuisine including superb pizzas (M45–95) fresh from the oven. M680

Quthing and around

QUTHING, also known as **Moyeni** ("Place of the Wind"), is a curious split-level town established by the British after the Gun War in 1884. The town itself is messy, though it has an attractive setting beside a river gorge, with views of the surrounding hills improving as you climb to the upper part of town.

Dinosaur footprints

Daily 8am–4pm • M10

The most accessible **dinosaur footprints** in Lesotho are very near the lower section of Quthing. On the road to Mount Moorosi, about 400m from the junction to Quthing town centre, look out for the shed-like building with the thatched **visitor centre** beside it on the left of the road. The shed protects a variety of clearly discernible footprints, and there's also a limited range of handicrafts for sale.

Masitise Cave House

A few kilometres west of Quthing • Mon–Fri 8.30am–5pm, Sat & Sun 8.30am–2pm • M10 • ☎ 5875 8187, Ⓦ masitisecavehouse .blogspot.com

The **Masitise Cave House** is well worth a visit. This extraordinary house was built into the side of a rock overhang in 1866 by the Swiss missionary D.F. Ellenberger – whose *History of the Basuto: Ancient & Modern*, published in 1912, was the first study of its kind. The house has been converted into a museum and contains interesting displays about the history of the Quthing area, the Ellenbergers' fascinating home, and an explanation about the dinosaur footprints in the roof of one of the rooms in the house. To find it, turn right off the main road from Mafeting at the "Masitise Primary" sign and follow the rutted road past the church; the curator, Aaron Ntsonyana, will guide you around. Homestay accommodation can be arranged by Rev. Ramonotsi (☎ 2700 5760).

ARRIVAL AND DEPARTURE

QUTHING AND AROUND

By bus and minibus taxi Five daily buses and numerous minibus taxis run north from the bus stop at the main crossroads to Maseru (2hr30min), and much more infrequent services head northeast towards Qacha's Nek (including a 10am Lesotho Freight and Bus Services bus from Maseru every other day of the week; 5hr). You'll also find minibus taxis heading for the nearby Tele Bridge border post (daily 6am–10pm) where you can pick up transport to Sterkspruit in the Eastern Cape.

ACCOMMODATION

Fuleng Guest House In town, near the first hairpin bend to upper Quthing ☎ 2275 0260. Excellent-value rooms in simple rondavels (although check as they vary in standard), or more luxurious and stylish rooms with TVs. Rondavels M360, rooms M450

Mountain Side Hotel About 100m down the dirt track just beyond Fuleng ☎ 2275 0257. The intimate *Mountain Side Hotel* has mostly adequate rooms. There's a cosy private bar, a friendly public one and a decent restaurant with a tasty fixed menu. M750

Mount Moorosi and around

Just over 40km beyond Quthing, the small town of **MOUNT MOOROSI** was named after a chief who moved to the region in the 1850s. He was an ally of the San and had several San wives, but made an enemy of the British in the 1870s. British troops attacked his stronghold in 1879, but he held out for eight months until soldiers used scaling ladders on the steep cliffs and finally captured him, after which they cut off and publicly displayed his severed head. **Thaba Moorosi**, where the main battle took place, is 1km or so further along the main road on the right. The site is marked by some stone slabs in which British soldiers sent to catch the chief engraved their names. It's quite a tricky climb, though, so be sure to let someone in Mount Moorosi know where you are going.

Shortly after rounding Thaba Moorosi, the main road leaves the Senqu River and heads swiftly into the highlands through the impressive **Quthing Gorge**, peaking after about 10km at the **Lebelonyane Pass** (2456m), with superb views. A far less used route into the highlands than the northern road to Mokhotlong, the mountain road to Sehlabathebe is ruggedly beautiful, and according to some the most rewarding drive in the country.

Qacha's Nek

Some 34km east of Mphaki at **Sekake**, the recently asphalted road rejoins the southern banks of the Senqu. It's a beautiful, undulating drive, though once you reach the approach to **QACHA'S NEK** you'll see the depressingly familiar soil erosion and dongas (see box, p.606). Named after chief Moorosi's son Ncatya, Qacha's Nek was an area famed for its banditry when the British founded the town in 1888 in an attempt to forestall the kind of trouble they'd experienced with chief Moorosi. Many of the "bandits" were in fact desperate San, hounded from their homes and having no means of survival; this left the British unmoved, and they hunted them to extermination throughout the 1860s and 1870s. Moorosi's Baphuthi people had started moving there in the 1850s, rapidly wiping out all the game, and turning the land over to grazing and cultivation instead. The area has unusually high rainfall, and the weather conditions favour conifers, including a few massive Canadian redwoods, giving Qacha's Nek an atmosphere completely different from most of virtually treeless Lesotho.

There's little to see in town, except the elegant **St Joseph's Church** at its eastern end, but the entire surrounding mountainous countryside is great for **hiking**.

ARRIVAL AND DEPARTURE — QACHA'S NEK

By bus and minibus taxi Qacha's Nek is an important border town and there's usually plenty of public transport heading southwest towards Quthing from the petrol station in the centre of town. There's a daily bus to and from Maseru; it leaves from both Maseru and Qacha's Nek at 6.30am, and takes up to ten hours. You can hear minibus taxis a mile off, thanks to the cowbells tied to their front. On the other side of the border you'll find transport (roughly hourly) heading for the Eastern Cape town of Matatiele, from where it's easy to find buses and minibus taxis on to Kokstad and beyond.

ACCOMMODATION

Anna's B&B Just past the Central Hotel, near the Farmers' Training Centre ⓣ2295 0374, ⓔannasb&b@leo.co.ls. This friendly B&B also offers a restaurant and choice of accommodation, either older rooms with shared bath or newer en-suite ones. **M380**

Letloepe Lodge Coming from the border post, turn right at the roundaboat ⓣ2295 0383, ⓦmaleaatours.com. The town's best accommodation, in an attractive and well-signposted setting at the bottom of the Letloepe cliff on the edge of town, just a few minutes' drive from the border. The lodge offers decent en-suite rondavels with TVs, some with their own kitchenettes, and there is a restaurant with set meals. They also have cheaper backpacker accommodation in twin or triple rooms with shared bathrooms (M125). **M420**

Nthatuoa Hotel The first building on the left as you enter Qacha's Nek on the main road from Quthing ⓣ2295 0260. A variety of rooms, each more luxurious than the last; all are en suite, and you're also welcome to pitch a tent (M50). All tariffs include a substantial breakfast. Their pub and restaurant also serves lunch and dinner. **M350**

Sehlabathebe National Park

Free

The oldest nature reserve in the country, and on UNESCO's World Heritage list since 2013 as part of the Maloti-Drakensberg Park, **Sehlabathebe National Park** is remote and almost inaccessible, but predictably peaceful and stunningly beautiful. Set on the border with South Africa in the southern reaches of the Drakensberg at an average altitude of 2400m, the park is best known for its prolific birdlife, excellent trout fishing, waterfalls, rock paintings and seemingly endless open spaces just perfect for hiking. There are also a few game animals: baboons, rhebok, eland and the secretive oribi antelope, mongoose, otters, wild cats and jackals. In good weather you probably won't be in any hurry to leave, but at any time of year mist and rain can emerge out of nowhere, even on the finest of days, so come prepared.

ARRIVAL AND DEPARTURE

SEHLABATHEBE NATIONAL PARK

By bus or car To get to the park from the Lesotho side of the border you'll need either a 4WD or to catch the daily Lesotho Freight and Bus Services bus from Qacha's Nek to Sehlabathebe village, just outside the park (departs at noon, returns at 5.30am), which can tackle the road and takes four to five hours.

On foot The only other way into the park from the Lesotho side is to hike 40km along the Top-of-the-Berg route from Sani Top. From South Africa, it's a day's walk to the park through the southern section of South Africa's Ukhahlamba Drakensberg Park along a dramatic path starting at Bushman's Nek, 38km from Underberg in KwaZulu-Natal.

INFORMATION

Sehlabathebe Ranger Station Information about the park and hikes. If you want to do some serious hiking, go to the Department of Lands, Surveys and Physical Planning in Maseru (see box, pp.580–581), where you should be able to pick up some detailed maps of the area.

ACCOMMODATION

Camping is permitted anywhere in the park, provided you get a permit from the lodge. Wherever you're staying, you'll need to be self-sufficient in food and bring spare fuel too. The only accommodation inside the park, *Jonathan's Lodge*, has closed down to be replaced by the new 72-bed dorm-only *Sehlabathebe Lodge* (☏ 5802 8729, ✉ kretha2010@yahoo.com), though at time of writing the opening date was unknown.

Sehlabathebe Ranger Station Sehlabathebe village ☏ 2295 0551 or ☏ 5807 1433, ✉ semakhetha@gmail .com. There are basic dormitory rooms with about thirty beds in total and decent facilities at this elegant bungalow guesthouse, situated near the entrance gate of the national park. There's a restaurant too; breakfast M40, lunch and dinner M70. **M70**

11

Swaziland

UMHLANGA REED DANCE

Swaziland

A tiny landlocked kingdom, Swaziland lies in the spanner-like grip of South Africa, which surrounds it on three sides, with Mozambique providing its eastern border along the Lubombo Mountains. Although South Africa's influence predominates, Swaziland was a British protectorate from 1903 until its full independence in 1968, and today the country offers an intriguing mix of colonial heritage and home-grown confidence, giving the place a friendlier, more relaxed and often safer feeling than its larger neighbour. Though Swaziland still feels a lot more commercialized than, say, Lesotho, its outstanding scenery, along with its commitment to wildlife conservation, makes it well worth a visit. With a car and a bit of time, you can explore some of the less trampled reserves, make overnight stops in unspoilt, out-of-the-way settlements and, if you time your visit well, take in something of Swaziland's well-preserved cultural traditions.

12

Swaziland is also something of a draw for **backpackers**, with an inexpensive network of minibus Kombi taxis covering all corners of the country, and some good backpacker lodges to boot. There are also plenty of adventure activities on offer – from mountain biking and horseriding to whitewater rafting and tree-top canopy gliding. Swaziland has six **national parks** exemplifying the country's geographical diversity, all offering good-value accommodation. While not as efficiently run as South African national parks, the Swazi reserves are less officious, and many people warm to their easy-going nature.

Laidback **Mbabane**, the country's tiny capital city, makes a useful base from which to explore the attractive central **eZulwini Valley**, home to the royal palace and the **Mlilwane Wildlife Sanctuary**. With your own transport, or a bit of determination and public transport, you can venture further afield, heading into the highveld of the northwest and up to the fantastically beautiful **Malolotja Nature Reserve**, with its fabulous hiking country, soaring valleys and cliffs.

Summers are hot, particularly in the eastern lowveld. **Winter** is usually sunny, but nights can be very chilly in the western highveld around the Malolotja Nature Reserve. In summer, rainfall is usually limited to short, drenching storms that play havoc with the smaller untarred roads. Note that Swaziland's eastern lowveld, including Hlane Royal National Park, is **malarial** during the summer months (Nov–May). For details on necessary precautions, see p.70.

Brief history

The history of Swaziland dates back to the **Dlamini** clan and their king, **Ngwane**, who crossed the Lubombo Mountains from present-day Mozambique in around 1750. Pushed into southeast Swaziland by the Ndwandwe people of Zululand, the clan eventually settled

Highlights

❶ **Royal festivals** The spectacular ceremonies of Ncwala and Umhlanga are colourful affirmations of Swazi national identity. **See p.625**

❷ **Malandela's Homestead** A collection of buildings bursting with creativity and enterprise, including the funky performance space and live music venue House on Fire, and Gone Rural, one of the best of Swaziland's many attractive arts and crafts outlets. **See p.626**

❸ **Myxo's cultural tours, KaPhunga** Get a true taste of life in rural Swaziland – this enterprising project allows you to live as part of a village for a few days. **See p.628**

❹ **Mkhaya Game Reserve** Swaziland's best wildlife experience, where you can walk with rhino before sleeping in luxurious open-sided cottages in the bush. **See p.630**

❺ **Whitewater rafting on the Great Usutu** As action-packed as anything south of the Zambezi – you can paddle a two-man inflatable croc raft down Swaziland's largest river. **See p.631**

❻ **Malolotja** A wild, rugged and breathtakingly beautiful reserve attracting hundreds of different bird species, with a network of trails perfect for hiking. **See p.634**

HIGHLIGHTS ARE MARKED ON THE MAP ON P.614

at Mhlosheni and then Zombodze in the southwest, where Ngwane reigned precariously, under constant threat of Ndwandwe attack. His grandson, **Sobhuza I**, was forced to flee north from the Ndwandwe, but they in turn were defeated by the Zulu king Shaka in 1819. Sobhuza then established a new capital suitably far from Shaka in the eZulwini Valley, and made peace with the Ndwandwe by marrying the king's daughter.

Sobhuza's power grew as he brought more and more clans under his wing. His alliance with the newly arrived Afrikaners in the 1830s, forged out of mutual fear of

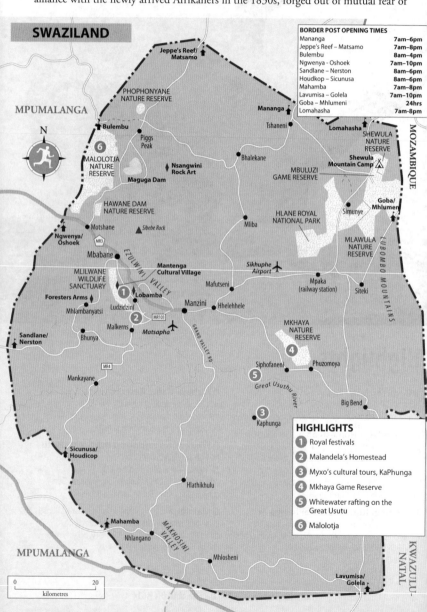

SWAZILAND

BORDER POST OPENING TIMES

Mananga	7am–6pm
Jeppe's Reef – Matsamo	7am–8pm
Bulembu	8am–4pm
Ngwenya - Oshoek	7am–10pm
Sandlane - Nerston	8am–6pm
Houdkop – Sicunusa	8am–6pm
Mahamba	7am–8pm
Lavumisa – Golela	7am–10pm
Goba – Mhlumeni	24hrs
Lomahasha	7am–8pm

HIGHLIGHTS

1. Royal festivals
2. Malandela's Homestead
3. Myxo's cultural tours, KaPhunga
4. Mkhaya Game Reserve
5. Whitewater rafting on the Great Usutu
6. Malolotja

SWAZILAND 615

CHOOSING THE KING

Swazi monarchs are always men of the **Dlamini** family, and over the course of their reign they marry a number of women carefully selected from different clans to cement national unity. In theory, the king marries women from increasingly important families as he goes along, which means that the son of the last wife is always a strong contender for the succession. In practice, however, other wives with older sons are also in with a chance, resulting in unrest and power-struggles every time the king dies. After his death, the royal council, or *liqoqo*, selects the new **Queen Mother**, who rules as regent until her son is old enough to take charge. She usually has to work hard to ensure her position against ambitious uncles. The main advantage of this awkward process is that by the time the new king is old enough to rule, he and his mother have generally garnered enough support for him to do so effectively.

the Zulu, was continued by his son **Mswati II** (after whom the Swazi people are named), who stretched his kingdom north to the Sabi River and sent raiding parties as far as the Limpopo River and east to the Indian Ocean.

Europeans arrived in greater numbers throughout the 1880s, after the discovery of gold in neighbouring Transvaal and at Piggs Peak and Forbes Reef in Swaziland. Mswati's son, **Mbandzeni**, granted large chunks of his territory in concessions to the new arrivals, emboldening Britain to ignore his claims to most of the rest; by the time Swaziland became a protectorate of South Africa in 1894, there was precious little land left. After their victory in the Second Anglo-Boer War, Britain assumed control of the territory and retained it until 1968.

After World War II the British invested in their protectorate, establishing enormous **sugar plantations** in the northeast and an **iron-ore mine** at Ngwenya in the highveld (today, the country's major export is sugar). Meanwhile **Sobhuza II**, who had become king of the Swazis in 1921, concentrated on buying back his kingdom, and had acquired about half of it by the time independence came in 1968. The Swazi aristocracy managed the transition to independence skilfully, with its Imbokodvo party winning every parliamentary seat in the first elections. In 1973 a radical pan-Africanist party won three seats, prompting Sobhuza to **ban political parties** and declare a state of emergency, which technically has been in place ever since.

After Sobhuza's death in 1982 a period of intrigue ensued, with the Queen Mother Dzeliwe assuming the regency until deposed by Prince Bhekimpi, who ruled until 1985, purging all the opposition he could. The current king, **Mswati III**, the son of one of Sobhuza's seventy wives, was recalled from an English public school to become king in 1986, and parliamentary elections were held in 1987. New opposition began to emerge, most notably the **People's United Democratic Movement** (PUDEMO), which has strong support among Swazi workers.

12

SISWATI PHRASES

BASICS

Yes	*Yebo* (also a casual greeting)
No	*Cha*
Thank you	*Ngiyabonga*
It's nice/tasty	*Kumnandzi*
Today	*Lamuhla*
Tomorrow	*Kusasa*
Yesterday	*Itolo*

GREETINGS AND RESPONSES

Hello (to one)	*Sawubona*
Hello (to many)	*Sanibona*
How are you?	*Kunjani?*
I'm fine	*Ngikhona*
Goodbye (said by person leaving)	*Sala kahle*
Goodbye (said by person remaining)	*Hamba kahle*

TRAVEL

Where is... ?	*Iphi l... ?*
Where can we stay?	*Singahlala kuphi?*
Where are you going?	*U ya phi?*
How much?	*Malini?*

SWAZILAND TRAVEL BASICS

MONEY

Currency is the **lilangeni** – plural **emalangeni** (E) – which is tied to the South African rand (1 rand = 1 lilangeni). The rand is legal tender in Swaziland, so you won't have to change any money, but note that emalangeni are not convertible outside Swaziland.

PHONES AND PHONE NUMBERS

The **country code** for Swaziland is 🕿 268, followed by the destination number (there are no area codes). The code for phoning out from Swaziland is 🕿 00, followed by the country and area codes and finally the destination number. To arrange a **collect call**, dial 🕿 94.

Swaziland has only one mobile phone network – MTN – which generally works well throughout the country.

PUBLIC HOLIDAYS

January 1	**July 22** (King Sobhuza II's birthday)
Good Friday	**August/September** (Umhlanga Dance Day)
Easter Monday	
April 19 (King Mswati III's birthday)	**September 6** (Independence Day)
April 25 (National Flag Day)	**December/January** (Ncwala Day)
May 1 (Workers' Day)	**December 25** (Christmas Day)
Ascension Day	**December 26** (Boxing Day)

RED TAPE AND VISAS

Nationals of most Commonwealth countries (excluding Bangladesh, India, Pakistan and Sri Lanka), the US, Canada, South Africa, Australia and all EU countries do not require a **visa** if staying sixty days or less. Other nationals must obtain visas before arrival. For details of Swaziland's embassies see p.620.

TOUR OPERATORS

The country's biggest **tour operator** is Swazi Trails (🕿 24162180, 🌐 swazitrails.co.sz), next to the Mantenga Craft Centre (see p.623), offering tours to the royal village and game parks along with whitewater rafting, quad biking, caving and other activities. There are also a handful of smaller local operations, including Taman Tours (🕿 4163370, 🌐 tamantours.com), which runs tours to different parts of Swaziland, and All Out Africa (🕿 24162260, 🌐 alloutafrica.com), which organizes a selection of adventure tours such as river tubing on the Ngwempisi River, and also helps find volunteering opportunities within the country. The tourist office in Mbabane (see p.619) keeps information on other tour guides.

WEBSITES

🌐 **biggameparks.org** Provides information on three of the country's most visited reserves, the Hlane, Mlilwane and Mkhaya parks, with practical information about activities, and an accommodation booking site.

🌐 **swazi.travel** Hosted by Swazi Trails, with an efficient online accommodation booking service, reams of information about shopping and restaurants, and details of tours and activities around Swaziland.

🌐 **welcometoswaziland.com** Swaziland's official tourism website is packed with useful information, including hotel listings.

But in general Swazis are proud of their distinctive kingdom, and as a result calls for change are tempered by an unwillingness to show disloyalty to the king or to expose Swaziland to what many see as the predatory ambitions of South Africa.

Thus the maintenance of tradition and appeals to broad nationalism have been key components of Swazi royalty's strategy to retain power. Although Mswati III is sometimes said to favour reform, the authorities have worked hard to keep dissent bottled up through sporadic police repression; opposition leaders have been prevented from speaking freely in the media, and poor turnouts marked the "elections" of 1993, 1998, 2003, 2008 and 2013. In 2011, demonstrations triggered by the "Arab Spring", calling for **multi-party** democracy and condemning the government's mismanagement of funds, were stopped in their tracks with the arrest of demonstration organizers. Currently Swaziland is the only country in Southern Africa not practising multiparty democracy, though it seems only a matter of time before it is coerced by the other regional powers into doing so.

ARRIVAL AND DEPARTURE

BORDER CROSSINGS

Crossing the border is usually very straightforward: you simply have to show your passport and pay E50 in road tax per car. There are eleven border posts serving traffic from South Africa, and two crossings into Mozambique. We've listed the most convenient ones below:

Ngwenya/Oshoek (7am–10pm) is the most popular, closest to Johannesburg and the easiest route to Mbabane. Can be very busy during holidays and weekends.

Sandlane/Nerston (8am–6pm) is a good alternative 35km further south, roughly 70km from Johannesburg.

Sicunusa/Houdkop (8am–6pm) is just off the N2 from Piet Retief in the southwest, which leads to the wonderfully scenic and fast MR4.

Bulembu (8am–4pm), via Piggs Peak in the north, is perhaps the most spectacular crossing in the country, but the bad road makes it a hard journey in an ordinary car.

Jeppe's Reef/Matsamo (7am–8pm) in the north, handy if you're coming in from Kruger Park and Nelspruit.

Lavumisa/Golela (7am–10pm) in the southeast, close to the KwaZulu-Natal coast, is the second-busiest crossing.

Mahamba (7am–10pm) in the south, runs lots of traffic from N2/Piet Retief and beyond.

Goba/Mhlumeni (24hr) is a busy crossing into Mozambique and the main route for traffic from the southern half of South Africa, so expect lots of lorries.

Lomahasha (7am–8pm) is the second crossing into Mozambique, passing through Hlane Royal National Park and the scenic Lebombo mountains.

BY PLANE

Swaziland has one international airport, Matsapha (often referred to as "Manzini"), between Mbabane and Manzini. Airlink Swaziland (☎ 25186155, ⊕ flyswaziland.com), a partner of SAA, through whom it can be contacted in South Africa, flies four times daily to and from Johannesburg (1hr). An airport tax fee of E100 is payable when flying out of Matsapha Airport. A new international airport – Sikhuphe – has recently been completed about 50km from Mbabane on the road to Hlane, but it currently stands empty.

BY BUS

At the time of writing, the only timetabled bus company connecting South Africa and Swaziland is TransMagnifique (☎ 24049977, ⊕ goswaziland.co.sz), which runs two daily buses between Mbabane and Johannesburg (4hr; E500), stopping at Witbank, Eastgate, Johannesburg Airport and Sandton. It also runs a Saturday bus to Nelspruit (E350) and Kruger National Park (E450). Book in advance online. Swaziland Cultural Tours (☎ 76426780, ⊕ swaziculturaltours.com) run buses on request to Nelspruit (E1200), Maputo (E1200) and St Lucia (E950), which include lunch and visits to markets and natural reserves en route. A cheaper option is to catch Kombi minibuses (see below), which ply the main routes into Swaziland from Johannesburg and Nelspruit, and depart when they are full.

12

GETTING AROUND

By car Driving is the best way to see Swaziland; distances are small, all the main tourist sites are near tarred roads, and the major gravel roads are in decent condition. Most dirt roads are passable with an ordinary vehicle in dry months. Driving standards, however, leave a lot to be desired – two of the last four ministers of transport died in road accidents. Also, the general speed limit of 80km/h outside towns is universally ignored and very rarely enforced. For Swazi car rental, see p.619.

By Kombi minibus Swaziland is crisscrossed by a network of Kombi minibus routes that covers almost every corner of the country. The Kombis leave when full from bus stations in the main towns, and ply the main routes linking the towns, calling at set stops along the way. Kombi travel is cheap – a ticket from Mbabane to *Lidwala Backpacker Lodge* in the eZulwini Valley costs E7. Ask at the local bus station about the best route to get to your destination. The stations are organized by destination, so all Kombis to, say, Manzini will leave from one corner of the station, and to Big Bend from another. Although buses tend to get quite packed, they are an efficient way of getting around, and a great way of meeting people.

Mbabane

Tucked into the jumble of granite peaks and valleys that makes up the Dlangeni hills, Swaziland's administrative capital, **MBABANE** (pronounced "M-buh-ban"), is small, relaxed and unpretentious, with a population of only about 61,000. The city roughly marks the point where the mountainous Southern African highveld descends briefly into middleveld, before bottoming out further east as dry lowveld.

There's not much to do in Mbabane, but most visitors find it more agreeable than hectic Manzini, especially if you need to stock up on supplies or plan your trip ahead. This is a good base from which to start exploring Swaziland, especially if you're without your own transport: the Mlilwane Wildlife Sanctuary (see p.624) lies not far south, and the royal village of Lobamba (see p.624) makes an easy day-trip – useful if you're here when the *Umhlanga* or *Ncwala* ceremonies take place and everything nearer the village is fully booked.

Mbabane's hilly **centre** is a low-key jumble of office blocks, markets, malls and shacks that you can very easily explore on foot – which is just as well, as driving here can be stressful without a sound grasp of the street layout and confusing one-way system.

Gwamile Street is the closest the city has to a main street; running south into the central business district (CBD), it's lined in parts by colonial administrative buildings which are attractive to look at, but can only be entered on official

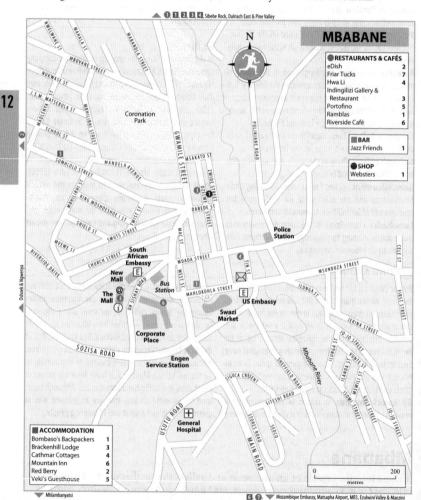

MBABANE

● **RESTAURANTS & CAFÉS**
eDish	2
Friar Tucks	7
Hwa Li	4
Indingilizi Gallery & Restaurant	3
Portofino	5
Ramblas	1
Riverside Café	6

■ **BAR**
| Jazz Friends | 1 |

● **SHOP**
| Websters | 1 |

■ **ACCOMMODATION**
Bombaso's Backpackers	1
Brackenhill Lodge	3
Cathmar Cottages	4
Mountain Inn	6
Red Berry	2
Veki's Guesthouse	5

SIBEBE ROCK TRAILS

About 10km north of Mbabane along the Pine Valley road is Swaziland's most famous geological feature, a huge granite dome called **Sibebe Rock**. Situated among the Mubuluzi Mountains, the area boasts springs you can swim in and a network of trails leading to various breathtaking viewpoints. Rising 300m above the Mubuluzi River Valley, the vast slabs of granite are very steep and dangerous in places, but among the scattered boulders at the summit are Bushman paintings indicating that the rock was inhabited by humans thousands of years ago. While the hard, coarse surface of the granite offers more grip than other types of rock, it can be very dangerous, so a guide is essential for any ascent. Local resident Anna McGinn, who lives at the base of the rock, can organize tours and guides (half day E160 per person, full day E240 per person; reduced prices for groups larger than two; ☎ 78207700, ✉annamcgin@gmail.com). For an adrenaline-fuelled ascent up the front face of the rock dome, Swazi Trails (see p.623) offers a challenge it describes as "the steepest walk in the world". It also organizes **caving trips** in the same mountain range, which involves a lot of squeezing through narow spaces and navigation by little more than a head torch and the encouraging words of your guide – it's a memorable adventure for those who don't mind enclosed spaces and a few bumps and scratches.

business. At the end of Gwamile Street, on the banks of the Mbabane River, lies the daily **Swazi Market** where fresh fruit and vegetable stalls make for a colourful scene.

The main focus of the city centre, however, is the sprawl of shopping malls down the hill from Gwamile Street. Most of Mbabane's main shops, banks and services are located in either **Corporate Place** or the more upmarket **Mall** and **New Mall**.

Note that Central Mbabane empties at night, and **muggings** are a risk for those wandering the streets alone. If you're going out after dark, arrange for a taxi to pick you up.

ARRIVAL AND DEPARTURE

By plane Matsapha Airport (☎25184390), 25km southeast of Mbabane, just west of Manzini, is Swaziland's only international airport. There's no public transport from here into Mbabane, so if you haven't arranged a pick-up with your hotel, you'll need to take a taxi (around E150) or rent a car; Avis (☎25186222) and Europcar (☎25184393) are located at the airport. There's another Europcar agent at the Engen service station at the junction of Gwamile Street

MBABANE

and Main Road (☎24040459), though Affordable Car Hire (☎4049136) in Corporate Place is cheaper.

By Kombi Kombi buses and minibuses from South Africa stop at the main bus station on Dr Sishay Road beside Corporate Place. From here you can catch minibus Kombis to Manzini and Piggs Peak, and local buses within the Mbabane area. Kombis plying the Mbabane–Manzini route leave from the western side of the bus station.

INFORMATION

Tourist office The Mall (Mon–Fri 8am–5pm, Sat 9am–5pm; ☎24042531). Has a good supply of maps,

brochures and a list of recommended tour guides. They can also help with hotel bookings (free).

GETTING AROUND

By Kombi Kombi minibuses leave from the bus station near Corporate Place.

By taxi Private taxis congregate near the bus station in the centre.

ACCOMMODATION

Mbabane's accommodation is somewhat limited, with no worthwhile options in the town centre. The rest are a short minibus journey or taxi ride away. If you have your own transport, most establishments in the eZulwini Valley (see p.621) are close enough to make for viable alternatives.

Bombaso's Backpackers Lukhalo Rd, 3km north of the centre, off Pine Valley Rd ☎24045465, ⟨⟩bombasos .co.za. Funky, young backpackers' place with four- and eight-bed dorms, and three smart doubles sharing facilities.

You can pitch a tent in the large garden, which has a pool and great views of Sibebe Rock. There's also a self-catering kitchen, chill-out lounge, various games rooms and a bar. Camping E80, dorm E145, double E290

Brackenhill Lodge Mountain Drive, off Fonteyn Rd ☎ 24042887, ⊛ brackenhillswazi.com. Luxurious B&B on a quiet hillside 4.5km north of the city centre. The comfortable rooms are often full so it's a good idea to book in advance. Facilities include a swimming pool, lovely hiking trails, a gym and a steam room; dinner is also available when ordered in advance. E870

Cathmar Cottages 3km north of Mbabane on Pine Valley Rd ☎ 24043387 or ☎ 24041165, ✉ shieldguest @yahoo.com. A laidback place offering a range of fully equipped self-catering rooms and cottages in a lovely location north of town with views of Sibebe Rock. Facilities include TV and fridge in the cottages, and a swimming pool; breakfast is E75. E360

Mountain Inn 4km southeast of Mbabane off MR3 ☎ 24042781, ⊛ mountaininn.sz. A large, efficient,

family-run hotel with 52 spacious rooms and good facilities, including a lovely pool and the *Friar Tuck* restaurant, located on an airy mountainside plot with wonderful views down the eZulwini Valley. E1160

Red Berry Mseni Drive, 3km north of Mbabane, off Pine Valley Rd ☎ 24045217, ⊛ redberrybb.co.sz. A smart, modern place with wonderful views of the Pine Valley, encompassing six tidy and fully equipped rooms, and a lovely terrace where breakfast is served. Self-catering facilities are also available. E780

Veki's Guesthouse 233 Somhlolo Rd ☎ 24048485 or ☎ 76036396, ✉ veni@mweb.co.sz. Three simple but comfortable rooms in a residential area not far from the city centre, set in a house with a communal lounge and self-catering kitchen. Meals are available on request, and breakfast is extra (E40). R400

EATING AND DRINKING

Nightlife in Mbabane is limited during the week and only slightly more lively at weekends. For the best nightlife, however, most locals head out to the eZulwini Valley, especially to *Malandela's* (see p.626), where local and international bands often headline at the House on Fire. Women travellers on their own are likely to encounter some unwanted attention in bars and clubs, but the pestering probably won't be aggressive or persistent.

RESTAURANTS

★**eDish** Somhlolo Rd ☎ 24045504. An unexpectedly funky café with comfy couches and a wooden deck on which to enjoy the delicious gourmet sandwiches – try the oxtail or blue arugula (E50). Freshly baked pastries and good coffee make this a great place for breakfast as well, and there's free wi-fi. Mon–Sat 8am–5pm.

Friar Tucks Mountain Inn, 4km southeast of the city centre ☎ 24042781. Elaborate buffet lunches (E155) during the week, as well as international à la carte meals (such as well-prepared baby chicken and Swazi goat casserole; E97) the rest of the time, in an intimate vaulted cellar or outdoors overlooking the pool. Good selection of wine, too. Daily 12.30–2pm & 7–9.30pm.

Hwa Li Dhlanubeka House, Mdada St ☎ 24045986. A reliable Chinese restaurant serving good-value chow mein (E48), spring rolls, stir fries and the like. Mon–Sat noon–3pm & 6–10pm.

Indingilizi Gallery & Restaurant 112 Dzeliwe St ☎ 24046213. A very pleasant place to come for lunch, situated in the gallery's back garden, serving light, wholesome dishes such as omelettes, salads and burgers with tasty fillings like garlic and blue cheese (E59). Mon–Fri 8am–5pm, Sat 8.30am–1pm.

Portofino The Mall ☎ 76846136. Downstairs in The Mall,

along the central walkway, this is the place to go for Italian ice cream (E12/scoop), beautiful cake, good coffee, and well-prepared breakfasts and lunches, all at reasonable prices. Mon–Fri 7.45am–5.30pm, Sat 7.45am–5pm, Sun 8.15am–2.30pm.

Ramblas Mantsholo St ☎ 24044147. A favourite among locals, this tastefully decorated restaurant is perched on breezy hill near the golf course. It serves good breakfasts, pizzas and grilled meats like rump steak and pork ribs (E105), and there's a jungle gym to keep kids occupied. Mon–Fri 8am–late, Sat 8.30am–late.

Riverside Café Corporate Place ☎ 24049547. On the first floor of Corporate Place Mall, overlooking the river and the busy bus station, this café serves excellent-value breakfasts, light lunches and salads as well as more substantial meals such as "chicken liver for chilli addicts" (E40) and peri-peri baby chicken. Mon–Fri 8am–5pm, Sat 8am–3pm.

BAR

Jazz Friends Gwamile St ☎ 24048684. Exactly what it says on the tin: a popular, smoky bar frequented by jazz fiends and friends, with music (live or recorded) on most nights and cold beer on tap (E13/pint). Mon–Fri 11am–late, Sat 1pm–late, Sun 2pm–late.

DIRECTORY

Banks Most banks are found in Corporate Place. Branches include First National, Nedbank and Standard. Hours are generally Mon–Fri 8.30am–3.30pm & Sat 8.30–11am.

Bookshops Websters at 120 Dzeliwe St (Mon–Fri

7.45am–5pm, Sat 7.45am–1pm; ☎ 24042560).

Embassies Mozambique, Princess Drive (☎ 24043700); South Africa, New Mall (☎ 24044651); US, 7th Floor Central Bank building, Mahlokohla St (☎ 24046441). Note that the

UK's representation in Swaziland is a Pretoria-based consul; for details, see ⓦ fco.gov.uk.
Emergencies Fire ☎ 933; Police ☎ 999.
Hospitals Mbabane Clinic Service (private), St Michael St (☎ 24042423); Government Hospital (public), Usutu Rd (☎ 24046954).
Internet access Real Image in The Mall (Mon–Fri

8am–6pm, Sat 9am–3pm; ☎ 24091060).
Pharmacy Green Cross in The Mall (Mon–Fri 9am–6pm, Sat 9am–2pm, Sun 10am–2pm; ☎ 24048450).
Post office The main post office is on Mahlokohla St (Mon–Fri 8am–4pm, Sat 8–11am), and there's a smaller one in the Swazi Plaza.

The eZulwini Valley

After passing through Mbabane from the Ngwenya border, the smooth, four-lane **MR3** winds down the steep sides of **Malagwane Hill** in a series of sweeping curves made hazardous by crawling lorries and reckless minibus taxis. The road then heads off southeast along the eZulwini Valley, but unless you're bound directly for Manzini and beyond, take the turning to the right not long after the foot of the hill onto the older and quieter **MR103** – also known as the eZulwini Valley Road – which links most of the main sights of the **eZulwini Valley** (Place of Heaven). In the 1960s a succession of casinos, strip joints, hotels and caravan parks sprang up here, catering mainly for South African tourists. When gambling became legal in South Africa in the mid-1990s, however, the number of pleasure-seekers dropped; the tourist industry had to start looking beyond the noise of the slot machines and karaoke to the valley's cultural and natural assets, and places such as the **Mantenga Cultural Village** were developed while the royal residences of **Lobamba** and **Ludzidzini**, as well as **Mlilwane Wildlife Sanctuary**, became more recognized as attractive to visitors. The latter, in particular, is one of Swaziland's main attractions, with its range of accommodation and numerous activities, including hiking trails and game viewing from a mountain bike.

12

The Mantenga Valley

The first five kilometres or so of the **eZulwini Valley Road** take you past a strip of glossy, anonymous-looking and hugely overpriced casino hotels. Turning south along Mantenga Drive (signposted to *Mantenga Lodge*) will take you to the much more interesting **Mantenga Valley**, which follows the course of the Lusushwana (or Little Usutu) River. Most prominent in the valley is the twin-peaked **Lugogo Mountain**, also known as "Sheba's Breasts", which featured in H. Rider Haggard's famous adventure novel *King Solomon's Mines*. Further along, on the western horizon, Execution Rock is a stark reminder of the days when murderers and thieves were punished by being forced to jump off the rock to certain death below. Just beyond the turning to the Mantenga Valley is the **Gables Shopping Centre**, which boasts ATMs, banks and a large supermarket.

FINE DINING AT FORESTERS ARMS

Just before the small town of Mhlambanyatsi, on the back road to the Sandlane border post – and 27km from Mbabane – the **Foresters Arms hotel and restaurant** (☎ 24674377, ⓦ forestersarms.co.za; E830) is well worth a detour. The hotel is set in a picturesque clearing in the woodland, which can be explored by foot, or on horseback or mountain bike, both of which are available at the hotel, and the rooms are cosy with fireplaces and wonderful mountain views. But the main reason to stop here is for the outstanding meals, predominantly made with home-grown and locally sourced produce such as hearty farm-style chicken and corn soup, unusual but mouth-watering tropical salmon, and delicious lamb confit with bean cassoulet. On Sundays, people from all over the country pour in to feast on the hotel's superb buffet lunch (E160) – you'll need to book ahead to be sure of a table.

12

▲ **①** & Mbabane

EZULWINI VALLEY

■ ACCOMMODATION
Legends Backpacker Lodge	3
Lidwala Backpacker Lodge	2
Malandela's B&B	9
Mantenga Lodge	4
Mlilwane Main Rest Camp	7
Nyanza Cottage	10
Reilly's Rock Hilltop Lodge	5
Sondzela Backpacker Lodge	8
Sundowners Backpackers	6
Timbali Lodge	1

● RESTAURANTS & CAFÉS
Bakers Corner	4
Boma	3
Calabash	2
Edlandleni	1
Hippo Haunt	5
Malandela's Farmhouse Restaurant	7
Sondzela	6

■ BAR
Malandela's Pub	1

MR103

MR3

MANTENGA VALLEY

MR103

Lusushwana River

MR3

Mantenga Cultural Village

① ② Swazi Trails

③

Somhlolo Stadium

Parliament

National Museum

Lusushwana River

MLILWANE WILDLIFE SANCTUARY

LUDZIDZINI

MR103

MR1

⑤ & Manzini

④

④ ⑥

⑥ ⑦

Malandela's Homestead

MR27

②①
⑨

House on Fire

MR103

Manzini

N

MALKERNS VALLEY

MR27

Nyanza Farm

⑩

MR4

③

0   1
kilometre

● SHOPS
Gables Shopping Centre	2
Mantenga Craft Centre	1
Swazi Candles Craft Centre	3

Mantenga Craft Centre

Mantenga Drive, less than 1km from the northern turn-off from the eZulwini Valley Rd • Daily 8am–5pm

The **Mantenga Craft Centre** consists of an attractive purpose-built village of craft shops, specializing in more exclusive and individual crafts than found in many other parts of Swaziland, including African Fantasy artwork, silver-smithing, and beautiful and quirky carving and sculptures, all sold at fair prices.

INFORMATION

Tourist information Across from the Craft Centre behind *Legends Backpacker Lodge*, the main booking office for Swazi Trails also doubles as the country's best tourist office (daily 8am–5pm; ☎ 24162180 or ☎ 76020261 after hours, Ⓦ swazitrails.co.sz), which can help you with accommodation booking and trip planning. As the country's leading tour operator, Swazi Trails organizes a wide range of cultural and adventure trips including a half-day arts and crafts trail, whitewater rafting (see box, p.631) and adventure caving.

THE MANTENGA VALLEY

ACCOMMODATION

Legends Backpacker Lodge Across from Mantenga Craft Centre ☎ 24161870, Ⓦ legends.co.sz. Rather run-down but friendly, with dorms sleeping twelve, ten doubles, a yard for camping, internet access and a communal kitchen. It's a great place to base yourself if you're on a tight budget and want easy access to all that the valley has to offer. Camping E60, dorm E150, double E400

★ **Lidwala Backpacker Lodge** On the Ezulwini Rd just before the Mantenga Valley turn-off ☎ 76905865, Ⓦ lidwala.co.sz. A brilliant backpackers' place on a hillside above the All Out Africa responsible travel company office (see box, p.616). It's made up of comfortable four- and six-bed dorms, a few en-suite doubles and a grassy bit for camping, and there's also a fully equipped kitchen, a packed library and computers with internet access. Camping E114, dorm E155, double E406

Mantenga Lodge From the Mantenga Craft Centre, continue along a dirt road for about 200m (follow the signs) ☎ 24161049, Ⓦ mantengalodge.com. Nestled between Sheba's Breasts, this is a stunningly located, family-run mid-priced lodge with 38 en-suite rooms, some in cosy chalets on the valley-side, as well as a pool, terrace bar and top-notch restaurant with especially good views of Execution Rock. E710

Timbali Lodge On the eZulwini Valley Rd, 1km after the turn-off from the MR3 ☎ 24161156, Ⓦ timbalilodge .co.sz. A former caravan park that has been transformed into a stylish guest lodge with shaded double chalets, self-catering cottages sleeping five, and a large shady area for camping (though the showers for campers are cold). Camping E80, double E670, cottage E850

EATING

Bakers Corner Corner Plaza ☎ 24162930. A café serving healthy and wholesome dishes like quinoa salad (E55), salmon and gnocchi, and "breakfast in a glass": a delicious smoothie filled with fruits, yogurt, coconut and honey. The freshly baked pastries are also good, and there are plenty of good vegetarian options. Mon–Fri 7am–6pm, Sat 7am–4.30pm, Sun 8am–3.30pm.

Boma Timbali Lodge (see above). Under an enormous thatched roof *Boma* specializes in pizza (around E70) from their pizza oven, alongside the usual selection of carvery dishes and fish. Daily 11am–10.30pm.

Calabash Next door to Timbali Lodge ☎ 24161187. One of Swaziland's best and most upscale restaurants, serving an excellent range of fresh seafood and specializing in German, Swiss and French dishes such as beef tartare and proper Wiener schnitzel for E125. Fine dining at its best. Daily 12.30–2.30pm & 6–10.30pm.

★ **Edlandleni** Near Mvubu Falls, signposted off the MR3 2km west of the Mantenga turnoff ☎ 76184103. A lovely café set beside a babbling brook, run by a Swazi woman determined to revive the lost cuisine of her country. The traditional Swazi dishes are delicious, and include *umbidvo wetintsanga* (pumpkin shoot and groundnuts in mealie porridge), warthog (E95), melon pie and traditional yaswara tea. Daily 11am–3pm & 6–10pm.

Mantenga Cultural Village

Daily 8am–5pm • E100 • ☎ 24161151, Ⓦ sntc.org.sz

Mantenga Drive ends at the grand entrance to the tiny **Mantenga Nature Reserve**, only really worth visiting for its cultural village. This open-air living museum replicates a nineteenth-century Swazi homestead with sixteen beehive huts, all built in traditional style using wooden frames joined by leather strips, reed thatch, cow dung and termite-hill earth. Cattle and goats wander about, and there are often demonstrations of traditional activities and crafts. Twice daily (11.15am & 3.15pm) an enchanting thirty-minute traditional music and dance performance takes place in a small open-air arena, telling a story of Swazi soldiers in the Anglo-Boer War, and the love and witchcraft they encounter when they return home.

Although the cultural village is the main attraction of the nature reserve, it's worth finding time to follow the short trail to the scenic 95m **Mantenga Falls** with its pretty **picnic** and **swimming spots**; it's a signposted fifteen-minute walk from the café.

Lobamba

Some 20km south of Mbabane, at the heart of the eZulwini Valley, the small royal village of **LOBAMBA** was originally built in 1830 for King Sobhuza I, and became the royal kraal (residence) of Sobhuza II. The **Houses of Parliament** are situated here, and must be one of the few in the world to have cattle grazing undisturbed in surrounding fields.

National Museum

Next door to the Parliament building • Mon–Fri 8am–4.30pm, Sat & Sun 10am–4pm • E80 • T24161516

A paved road to the north of the MR103 leads to the **National Museum**, which provides a helpful potted history of the country through displays of cultural artefacts, a mishmash of old photographs of Manzini and Mbabane when they were one-horse towns, and sweaty British administrators in full colonial regalia. The only really interesting item in the natural history wing is a replica of a sixteenth-century head of Krishna that was discovered nearby. It was all that was found of what was a full-bodied statuette, and the find has been interpreted as an indication of the high level of trade with the East at the time. Outside the museum stands a life-size re-creation of a traditional Swazi homestead. Remarkably, given their size, these huts are actually portable.

Somhlolo stadium

In front of the Parliament and Museum

Lobamba's **Somhlolo stadium** is the country's venue for major events and football matches, which are usually highly entertaining. For a few emalangeni on a Sunday afternoon you can treat yourself to genial games of occasional great skill, with a good-humoured and vociferous crowd. Consult the local *Times of Swaziland* for details, or ask locally.

Ludzidzini

On the other side of the MR103 from Lobamba, the village of **LUDZIDZINI** is the kraal of the present king, Mswati III, and the Queen Mother. Ludzidzini cannot be visited or even photographed at all except during *Ncwala* (around New Year) and *Umhlanga* (end Aug/early Sept), when permission must be obtained (see box, opposite).

Mlilwane Wildlife Sanctuary

Daily 24hr • E40 • W biggameparks.org

For many visitors to Swaziland the highlight of the eZulwini Valley is **Mlilwane Wildlife Sanctuary**, with its relaxed atmosphere and attractive, game-filled plains. The name Mlilwane refers to the "little fire" that sometimes appears when lightning strikes the granite mountains. As well as offering good game viewing and activities, Mlilwane is an easy alternative to staying in Mbabane or on the eZulwini strip. Given its popularity, it's wise to book ahead if you intend to stay overnight.

The reserve holds a special place in the history of wildlife conservation in Swaziland; it was here that Ted Reilly (see box, p.626) first realized his dream of a sanctuary for Swaziland's fast-disappearing **wildlife**. Mlilwane's animals are mainly herbivorous, and include zebra, bountiful numbers of antelope and the sanctuary's emblem, the warthog.

NCWALA AND UMHLANGA

The most sacred of Swaziland's ceremonies, **Ncwala** celebrates kingship, national unity and the first fruits of the new year. Its timing coincides with the new moon in November, when a group of selected men travel to the ancestral home of the Swazi people on the shores of the Indian Ocean to collect foam from the waves. While they are there, the *Ncwala* ceremony begins in Lobamba, with songs and rituals performed until the afternoon of the full moon in December/early January, when the six days of the full *Ncwala* begin. Young Swazi men gather branches of the *lusekwane* tree, from which they build a bower for the king. Warriors gather and sing songs that can only be sung at this time, while the king dances with them. On the sixth day, objects representing the previous year are burnt on a massive bonfire, and prayers are offered to Swazi ancestors. The ceremony ends amid raucous singing, dancing and feasting. Visitors are allowed to attend most of *Ncwala*, but photography is prohibited during certain times (a free permit is also required; contact the Ministry of Information, PO Box 642, Mbabane; ☎ 24054000, ⓦ gov.sz), so be sure to ask first to avoid having your camera smashed.

The **Umhlanga** is a **fertility** or reed **dance** that gets its name from the large reeds brought to the residence of the Queen Mother by young women to repair her kraal, usually in late August or early September. The sixth and seventh days are the most spectacular, when you can watch up to 25,000 young women, dressed in elaborate and carefully coded costumes, sing and dance before the king and Queen Mother at Lobamba, giving the king an opportunity to pick a **new wife**. The former king, Sobhuza II, invariably plucked a new mate from the bevy of young beauties and racked up a total of seventy wives during his lifetime. His successor, Mswati III, now in his 40s, has proved a little more restrained with only thirteen wives so far.

There's also the occasional crocodile and hippopotamus, which means you still need to be cautious if viewing the game on foot, bike or horseback.

12

ARRIVAL AND DEPARTURE

By car To get to Mlilwane take the turning from the eZulwini Valley Rd, signposted about 1km beyond the turn-off to Ludzidzini. From here it's 3.5km along a dirt road to the entrance gate, where you pay your entrance fee – if arriving after 6pm entry fees are paid at the main restcamp the following morning. Note that you'll need to show both

MLILWANE WILDLIFE SANCTUARY

your entry and accommodation receipts in order to leave the sanctuary again, or they may charge you twice.
By shuttle bus There is a daily shuttle bus that runs between *Sondzela* and Malandela's Homestead, leaving Sondzela at 8am (see p.626) and Malandela's about half an hour later.

INFORMATION AND ACTIVITIES

Maps The park office, easy to spot in the middle of the main restcamp, sells maps of cycling and hiking routes in the sanctuary for E25.
Guided trails Guided walks and game drives are available through the park office at the main restcamp. There are also guided mountain-bike tours and horseback trails, both fairly relaxed ways of taking in the park's attractions. For those with a little more horseback experience, various overnight trails involve camping in caves and rustic trail camps in the more remote parts of the reserve. For details, contact Big Game Parks central reservations (see below).

Self-guided trails Over 40km of road enables you to drive through the park to view game. There are also a number of good cycling routes running throughout the park; the main rest camp rents out mountain bikes for E130/hour. The best of the self-guided walking trails is the Macobane Hill Trail, a gentle, four-hour hike through the mountains. The more adventurous can climb to the top of Nyonyane, the "Execution Rock", which rises so prominently in the north of the reserve. Whichever route you choose to take, it's important you tell a ranger of your plans before heading out; they keep track of who's out on their own and come out to find you if you're not back by dusk.

ACCOMMODATION

The reserve offers a wide variety of accommodation, which should be booked through Swaziland Big Game Parks Central Reservations (☎ 25283944, ⓦ biggameparks.org), though *Sondzela* (see p.626) can also be booked directly.

Main Rest Camp About 3.5km from the gate ☎ 25283992. A wide variety of accommodation (all basic but clean and tidy), including a campsite, traditional beehive huts and two- and four-person huts, plus a swimming pool. Self-

TED REILLY AND THE SWAZI NATURE CONSERVATION STORY

Swaziland owes the creation and survival of three of its major wildlife sanctuaries – Mlilwane, Mkhaya and Hlane – to **Ted Reilly**, who was born in Mlilwane in 1938, the son of a British Anglo-Boer War soldier who had stayed on. As Reilly was growing up, Swazi wildlife and its natural habitats were coming under serious threat from poachers and commercial farmers. In 1959 Reilly lobbied the colonial government to set aside land for parks, but was defeated by farmers who wanted the land for commercial agriculture. Undeterred, he turned his Mlilwane estate into a park anyway, and set about cultivating a relationship with **King Sobhuza II**. After Swazi independence Sobhuza became much more powerful, and Reilly's relationship with him lent weight to his nature conservation efforts.

Despite rickety finances, the **Mlilwane Wildlife Sanctuary** opened in 1961, and the restocking and reintroduction of species has continued ever since. Meanwhile, Sobhuza asked Reilly to help stamp out poaching at Hlane. Reilly's tough approach resulted in shootouts with the poachers, earning him the praise of some, but the enmity of many.

Reilly's dependence on royal connections has also generated controversy, and some critics also assert that Reilly subordinates wildlife management principles to the needs of the tourist industry. Reilly's answer to his critics is simply to point to the three game parks his company runs. It's a powerful argument – without Reilly, the parks would not exist. Ted Reilly still lives at Mlilwane and remains active in Swazi conservation.

catering and B&B options available. Camping E90, huts E690
Reilly's Rock Hilltop Lodge On a hilltop about 30min drive from Main Rest Camp. A lovely colonial home full of antiques and hardwood furniture, situated on a hilltop surrounded by woodland and prolific birdlife. With only six rooms, it's more upmarket than a guesthouse but more rustic than a game lodge, and guests can enjoy fantastic views over the Mdzimba Mountains, and wander round the gardens that surround the house. Rates include half board. E1780
Sondzela Backpacker Lodge A 15min walk from Main Rest Camp ☎ 25283992. A friendly place firmly established on the backpacking circuit, with dorms, doubles, and comfortable adobe rondavels sleeping two overlooking the valley, all with communal ablution facilities. Campings also an option (tents only) and there's a lush garden, bar and large swimming pool. Camping E80, dorm E105, double E300

EATING

You can only buy basic supplies at the Main Rest Camp, so if you've opted for self-catering accommodation it's best to stock up at the Gables Shopping Centre (see p.621) beforehand.

Hippo Haunt At the Main Rest Camp. The only restaurant at Mlilwane serves up some good à la carte steaks, curries and pan-fried fish (E55), and buffet dinners on busy nights (E145). There's also a well-stocked bar. The restaurant overlooks an artificially created pond, which is home to hippos, crocs and a huge variety of birds, and is a superb place to while away a few hours. Daily 6.30am–10pm.

Sondzela Backpacker Lodge A 15min walk from Main Rest Camp ☎ 25283992. Inexpensive breakfasts (E40) and dinners (E60) are available at *Sondzela*, served in front of the campfire. There's only one dish on offer – such as stewed impala prepared in cast iron pots over an open fire – in addition to a vegetarian option. Dinner must be ordered in advance. Dinner daily 6pm.

Malandela's Homestead

1km southeast of the Mahlanya junction, off the MR103 • **Homestead** Daily 11am–3pm & 6pm–late • ☎ 25283115, ⓦ malandelas.com • **Gone Rural** Mon–Sat 8am–5pm, Sun 9am–5pm • ☎ 25504936, ⓦ goneruralswazi.com • **House on Fire** Tickets E50–80, gigs from 8pm • ☎ 25282110, ⓦ house-on-fire.com • **Bush Fire music festival** Day ticket E150–250, whole festival E600 • ☎ 25282040, ⓦ bush-fire.com

The scenic Malkerns Valley, lined with pineapple and sugar-cane fields, is home to **Malandela's Homestead**. Initially just a collection of rustic farm buildings, it has now developed into a lively family-run arts and crafts venue that attracts locals and visitors alike to its top-of-the-range gigs, performances and exhibitions, while its pub and restaurant always seem to be filled to capacity. One of the highlights of the homestead is Gone Rural, one of the most successful and creative **local handicrafts**

projects in Swaziland; the colourful and well-designed woven mats and baskets on sale here are made by a huge network of women working from villages all over the country. Next to Gone Rural, the funky music venue **House on Fire** doubles as an art gallery and amphitheatre-like performance space, and is worth checking out for contemporary African crafts and exuberant design. With live gigs most weekends – mostly up-and-coming local talent, with the occasional big international act – this is the hottest music venue in Swaziland at the moment. Over the last three days of May, House on Fire is also the venue for the hugely successful **Bush Fire music festival**, with acts like Hugh Masekela, Johnny Clegg and Ladysmith Black Mambazo headlining in the past, and camping on fields next to the homestead. Tickets can be bought via the website.

INFORMATION   MALANDELA'S HOMESTEAD

Tourist information All Out Africa is next door to Gone Rural (Mon–Sat 8am–5pm, Sun 9am–5pm; ☎ 25283423, ⊛ alloutafrica.com); along with organizing tours, it has a good array of tourist information leaflets, a few online computers, and wi-fi.

ACCOMMODATION

Malandela's B&B ☎ 25283448, ⊛ malandelas.com. Delightful Afro-chic double rooms built in natural and recycled materials, with lavish breakfasts served on a terrace facing sugar-cane fields, a pool and a tranquil garden. It tends to be full when there's a concert happening at House on Fire (see above), in which case advance booking is essential. **E630**

EATING AND DRINKING

Malandela's Farmhouse Restaurant ☎ 25283115. Situated under a large thatched roof and offering a European-style menu with good-value à la carte meals, including stews, game and fresh fish dishes, plus a fabulous range of salads like pawpaw, bacon and feta (E55). The restaurant's outdoor dining area provides excellent views of the adjoining sugar-cane fields and distant mountains. Daily 9.30–11am, noon–3pm & 6–9.30pm.

Malandela's Pub Adjoining the restaurant, this cosy and homey pub has Guinness on tap (E33/pint) and is a popular spot for locals to watch rugby and football on cable TV. Daily 9am–10pm.

Along the MR4

The idyllic **Nyanza Farm** (☎ 76085779 or ☎ 76214181, ⊛ nyanza.co.sz), situated on the MR4 a few kilometres from the MR103 junction, offers cross-country and mountain horse rides lasting from half an hour to a whole day (E190/hr). It's an appealingly cluttered working farm roamed by friendly dogs, cats, geese, turkeys, peacocks, horses and Jersey cows. A little further along the MR4 is the **Swazi Candles Craft Centre** (daily 8am–5pm; ☎ 25283219, ⊛ swazicandles.com), which in addition to a dedicated store producing and selling a bewildering array of brightly patterned wax candles also encompasses a number of local crafts outlets, including the colourful Baobab Batiks (☎ 25283242, ⊛ baobab-batik.com), the mohair weavers of Rosecraft (☎ 25282039) and Kwazi Swazi (☎ 25283110), selling books, art and a good selection of music.

ACCOMMODATION   ALONG THE MR4

★ **Nyanza Cottage** Nyanza Farm ☎ 76085779 or ☎ 76214181, ⊛ nyanza.co.sz. Simple yet delightful self-catering accommodation in two spacious, rustic cottages sleeping five at the bottom of a farm track, plus a double room and bunk beds suitable for groups. A great place for animal lovers and kids who want the hands-on experience of a real family farm. Double **E420**, cottage **E650**

Sundowners Backpackers At the MR103 junction to the Malkerns Valley, 9km west of Manzini, behind Sundowners Lodge ☎ 76878941, ⊛ swazisundowners .com. A laidback backpackers with tidy dorms, four decent doubles and some grassy areas outside for camping (tents can be rented for an additional E10). There's also a pool with a pleasant bar, which tends to bring guests together for long conversation over beers. Trips to various attractions and activities such as quad biking can be organized. Camping **E70**, dorm **E120**, doubles **E250**

12

KAPHUNGA VILLAGE CULTURAL TOURS

An ambitious community tourism project in **KaPhunga** village, about 55km into the mountains southeast of Manzini, provides an excellent off-the-beaten-track opportunity to see the real rural Swaziland. The village is the second-highest settlement in the country and spreads over the top of a mountain rise with absolutely breathtaking views of the valley below – sugar-cane fields galore and the Lebombo Mountains in the distance. Here a young Swazi, Myxo, has built a mini homestead with authentic huts, separate from the main village so that a certain amount of privacy is allowed both visitors and villagers. You're encouraged to stay at least one night and sleep in the traditional Swazi way, on a mattress on the hut floor. Facilities are fairly basic, but the gorgeous and authentically rustic setting makes this more than adequate. During the day visitors can join in whatever is going on in the village, such as building projects, farming work, brewing beer or helping at the local primary school. Two-day trips (one night) to KaPhunga, including full board, transport from Manzini and contributions to the village, cost E1386 per person. Extra nights can be arranged. Day-trips including transport and meals cost E1210 per person. To book, contact Myxo on ☎ 25058363 or ☎ 76044102, ⊕ swaziculturaltours.com.

Manzini

MANZINI is Swaziland's largest city and its commercial hub. Almost all of the country's industrial and commercial sector is based in or around here, and the city is dominated by office blocks and malls obscuring its few attractive edifices. With a rising crime rate and an atmosphere far less relaxed than Mbabane, Manzini would be an eminently missable place were it not for its outstanding **market** (Mon–Sat) on the corner of Mhlakuvane and Mancishane streets, which is best on Thursday morning when traders from neighbouring countries come to town. Much of Manzini's market is devoted to fruit and vegetables, household goods and traditional medicines, while an upper section that spills onto the steps below sells **crafts** and **fabrics**. The crafts selection is bigger, more varied and much better value than any other market in Swaziland, while the fabrics – from Zimbabwe, Congo and Mozambique – are hard to find elsewhere in the country.

ARRIVAL AND DEPARTURE

MANZINI

By bus Buses from all over the country and South Africa pull in at Manzini's busy main bus and taxi rank at the end of Louw St, just north of Ngwane St.

By plane Matsapha airport (☎ 25184390) lies 8km west of the city centre; a taxi into central Manzini costs E50.

ACCOMMODATION

The George Hotel Northern end of Ngwane St ☎ 25052260, ⊕ tgh.sz. A comfortable business-class hotel offering luxurious, spacious en-suite doubles with plush soft carpets; facilities include a pool, three restaurants, a bar, and a beauty salon and spa. E940
Matsapha Inn 6km outside town on the MR103,

shortly after the Matsapha airport turn-off ☎ 25187482 or ☎ 5186888. A good, quiet motel-like option outside the centre, with smart en-suite doubles lining a long corridor, and a bar-restaurant; rates include breakfast. Convenient for the airport. E567

EATING AND DRINKING

Egg Yolk The George Hotel, northern end of Ngwane St. The town's best coffee and also a fine place to eat, selling food prepared at the hotel's posher restaurant, at half the price. Try the Ungcwembe Special – grilled meat served with *pap* and lettuce garnish in a wooden bowl for sharing (E150 for two). Daily 8am–10pm.

Tandoori Express In the bus station ☎ 25058936. Some of Manzini's best food is to be had at this innocuous takeaway in the bus station, which does at least offer plastic chairs on which to enjoy its delicious kormas, biryanis, curries and tandoori chicken (E50). Daily 7.30am–7.30pm.

FROM TOP BEEHIVE HUTS; MALOLOTJA NATURE RESERVE (P.634) >

The south

Approaching Swaziland from one of its border crossings in the south is an excellent idea if you're travelling from northern KwaZulu-Natal through to the Kruger National Park or Mpumulanga. The scenery, particularly along the drive between **Mahamba** and Manzini through the **Grand Valley**, is really superb, and the road passes near most of the historical sites of the Swazi royal house. The south is also home to the **Mkhaya Nature Reserve**, Swaziland's most upmarket reserve and a sanctuary for the rare black rhino.

Mkhaya Game Reserve

35km east of Manzini · Pick up at 10am and 4pm · ☎ 25283944, ⓦ biggameparks.org

Mkhaya Game Reserve is situated along a turn-off from the wonderfully named village of **Phuzumoya** ("drink the wind") in classic lowveld scrubland, filled with acacia and thorn trees. A sanctuary for the rare **black rhino**, Mkhaya also accommodates **white rhino**, **elephant** and numerous antelopes such as nyala, sable and eland. In addition, Mkhaya operates as a refuge where endangered species such **roan antelope** and **tsessebe** are bred. Rubbing shoulders with them, in the reserve section closest to the road, are herds of **Nguni cattle**.

INFORMATION   MKHAYA GAME RESERVE

Essentials You'll need to book your visit to Mkhaya through Swazi Big Game Parks Central Reservations (☎ 25283944, ⓦ biggameparks.org). Day visits cost E650, including lunch. Day visits and overnight stays at Mkhaya must be booked in advance (see above), and you can't tour Mkhaya in your own vehicle, but must arrange to be met at the gate (10am or 4pm) from where you'll drive in convoy to the reserve's ranger base and the starting point of the first game drives – Kombi buses from Manzini to Big Bend stop at the gate; ask for the Phuzamoya shop drop.

Game Dives Day visitors are taken on a game drive from the ranger base, and you'll have a high chance of encountering much of the big game. A generous lunch at the main camp is included in the price. For overnighters, morning and evening game drives are included in the accommodation price. Unlike game reserves in South Africa, Mkhaya's experienced Swazi rangers have few qualms about stopping in the middle of a game drive and inviting visitors to get out of the vehicle and walk quite close to white rhino. If you're staying overnight, early-morning game walks can also be organized.

ACCCOMMODATION

Stone Camp ☎ 25283944, ⓦ biggameparks.org. The reserve's only camp makes up for the lack of elevation in the reserve with an atmospheric bush setting beside the dry Ngwenyane river bed. Accommodation is offered in seductively luxurious open-plan and open-sided thatched stone huts with en-suite toilets and showers, which give you a wonderful sense of sleeping right in the bush. Beautifully prepared three-course meals are served around a large campfire in the main part of the camp, under the shade of a massive sausage tree (its seed pods look like sausages), and staff have been known to treat guests to traditional dancing. E3050

The northeast

Northeast Swaziland is dominated by sugar plantations stretching into the distance, shimmering from the constant water spray, wreaking havoc with the water table – and leaving many locals without (hence the need for the new Maguga Dam; see p.634) – but earning the country valuable foreign exchange. Three large tracts of bush – **Hlane**, **Mlawula** and **Mbuluzi** – have been preserved as wildlife and nature reserves, and these are the main attractions for visitors to this region, together with the smaller **Shewula Nature Reserve**. They all form part of the **Lubombo Conservancy**, a grouping of protected land in the **Lubombo Mountains** that runs along Swaziland's eastern border and provides fantastic views of both Swaziland and the western fringes of Mozambique.

The most direct and obvious route to the reserves from Mbabane and Manzini is to follow the signposted and tarred road towards Siteki for 100km and 65km

WHITEWATER RAFTING

One of the most exhilarating things you can do in southern Swaziland is to **whitewater raft** on the beautiful Great Usutu River, located in the east of the country near the Mkhaya Nature Reserve. One of the best whitewater rivers in southern Africa, it's also one of the few where you can take a trip in a two-man "croc" raft. The route runs for 15km in summer (a bit less in winter), and crosses over rapids classed in grades two to four. The scenery en route is stunning, but hard to appreciate once you hit the rapids, which leave you paddling like crazy and doing your best not to fall in the water. Trips include pick-ups from various points in the eZulwini Valley and en route to the river as well as a picnic lunch; they cost E950 for a half day and E1200 for a full day. Contact Swazi Trails (☎ 24162180, ⊛ swazitrails.co.sz) for bookings and further information.

respectively. Turning north roughly 10km before Siteki leads to the reserves listed below.

Mbuluzi Game Reserve

Daily 6am–6pm • E35 • ☎ 2383 8861, ⊛ www.mbuluzigamereserve.co.sz

Privately owned and little known, **Mbuluzi** is about 1km off the Manzini–Lomahasha road, and straddles the road to Mlawula Nature Reserve. Set in classic lowveld bush, it encompasses two perennial rivers, riverine forest and some rocky precipices, but dominant in Mbuluzi are the thorn trees. The park has recently been restocked with game, including hippo and giraffe, which you can view in your own vehicle or on a bike. The absence of predators in Mbuluzi also means that you can walk along a network of clearly demarcated **trails**.

ARRIVAL AND DEPARTURE   MBULUZI GAME RESERVE

By Kombi Minibus Kombis from Manzini and Simunye to the Lomahasha border stop at the Maphiveni junction, from where it's a 15min hike to the gate.

ACCOMMODATION

Campsite ⊛ www.mbuluzigamereserve.co.sz. The well-equipped campsite is situated in the northern section of the reserve, close to the Mbuluzi River. Facilities include a shower block (with hot water) and the obligatory braai area. Book in advance. **E100**

Lodges ⊛ www.mbuluzigamereserve.co.sz. Mbuluzi's more upmarket accommodation consists of six privately owned self-catering lodges located – with lots of space between them – in the southern section of the reserve, south of the road to Mlawula. The immensely luxurious lodges are only available when not being used by their owners, and feature creature comforts such as swimming pools, DSTV and a/c. Three of the lodges sleep eight, one sleeps six and one five, and a studio cottage sleeps two. Book in advance. **E800**

Mlawula Nature Reserve

Daily 6am–6pm • E30 • ☎ 23838885, ⊛ sntc.org.sz

The largest single protected area in the Lubombo Mountains is the 165-square-kilometre **Mlawula Nature Reserve** south of the Mbuluzi River, where you can spend some time exploring a network of self-guided hiking **trails**. As well as climbing into the mountains and onto the plateau at the top of the Lubombo range where unique species of ironwood trees and cycads grow, the trails wend their way around the river heading for caves, a waterfall and a hyena pool, and hikes vary in length from two to eight hours. The bush throughout the reserve is quite dense, however, which prevents you from seeing much game. Guides are available to lead you on the hiking trails.

The Mlawula stream and more substantial Mbuluzi River both flow through some spectacular valleys in this reserve, and Stone Age tools over one million years old have been found along their beds. **Antelope**, **zebra** and **wildebeest** congregate near the water, but so do **crocodiles**, so resist the temptation to swim.

12

12

SHEWULA MOUNTAIN CAMP

Although isolated and time-consuming to reach, **Shewula Mountain Camp** (booking essential ☏ 76051160, ⊛ shewulacamp.org; E440) is well worth the effort with its spectacular setting at one end of the Lubombo plateau. To get here, take a bumpy dirt road eastwards into the mountains for 16km, from a turn-off 10km north of the Mubuluzi junction on the Manzini–Lomahasha road. Here, the local Shewula community manages a well-run camp with stupendous views west across northeast Swaziland and even, on a clear day, to the skyscrapers of Maputo to the east. It also offers an interesting insight into rural life in Swaziland. Accommodation is in seven rondavels (which sleep up to five people), with bunks or doubles, some with communal ablution facilities, but there's no electricity and cooking in a large kitchen/dining area is done on gas. **Activities** include guided hiking through Shewula Nature Reserve to the Mubuluzi River (E50/person) or a two-hour visit to the nearby village where there's a school for AIDS orphans and a local crafts centre (E40/person). If you don't want to self-cater, meals can be arranged in advance.

ARRIVAL AND INFORMATION

By car To get here by car, turn east off the Manzini–Lomahasha Rd at the Maphiveni junction and continue past the Mbuluzi Reserve for a few kilometres until you see a sign pointing to the Mlawula Reserve on your right. There's also a second gate on the eastern side of the reserve, not far from the Mhlumeni/Goba border crossing from Mozambique, on the main road to Siteki.
By Kombi Minibus Kombis from Manzini and Simunye to

MLAWULA NATURE RESERVE

the Lomahasha border stop at the Maphiveni junction, from where it's a 4km hike to the main Mlawula Nature Reserve gate. Kombis linking the Mhlumeni/Goba border crossing to Siteki stop outside the gate.
Information You can pick up various leaflets at the park gate but no supplies, so stock up beforehand at the nearby supermarket in Simunye.

ACCOMMODATION

Magadzavane Chalets ☏ 23838885, ⊛ sntc.org.sz. A cluster of twenty modern en-suite thatched rondavels near the gate by the Mozambican border, each with a spacious veranda at the front offering fabulous views of the valley. They have electricity so are fully kitted with stove, fridge and TV, and the site also encompasses a pool and

restaurant. Book in advance. E800
Siphiso Campsite ☏ 23838885, ⊛ sntc.org.sz. A shaded site next to the Siphiso River, with a toilet and shower block and braai stands. There's also an area for caravans, and two thatched shelters that are handy should the weather turn nasty. Book in advance. E70

Hlane Royal National Park

Daily 6am–6pm • E40 • ⊛ biggameparks.org

Some 67km northeast of Manzini, **Hlane Royal National Park** is the largest of Swaziland's parks. Formerly a private royal hunting ground, the main attraction here is the presence of big game, including **elephant**, **rhino**, **lion** and **leopard**. Hlane has a large population of easy-to-spot elephants and rhino in the northern area of the park, which you can also visit in your own vehicle, and rhino-sighting is virtually guaranteed. Other animals in this section include giraffe, zebra and waterbuck.

Various **southern enclosures** contain lion and leopard, along with some more elephant and rhino. Although the enclosures guarantee lion sightings, the animals are well habituated to vehicles and look completely uninterested. Hlane is also home to the largest population of nesting vultures in Africa.

ARRIVAL AND INFORMATION

By car The entrance to Hlane is roughly 7km south of Simunye, off the Manzini–Lomahasha Rd.
By Kombi Kombis running between Manzini and Simunye stop 300m from the park gate.
Guided tours Birding tours on foot (E170 for 2hr 30min) are available any time during the day from the

HLANE ROYAL NATIONAL PARK

reception at Main Camp. You can join a guided tour in one of the park's Land Rovers (E280 for 2hr 30min), with sunrise (5.30am) and sunset (4.30pm) tours also available (E310 for 2hr 30min); the sunrise and sunset tours are the most magical, with most sightings; bookings at Main Camp reception.

ACCOMMODATION

Bhubesi Camp 14km from Main Camp along a dirt track ☎ 25283944, ⓦ biggameparks.org. These four-person self-catering stone cottages overlook a dry river and feel much more remote than the main campsite, though they do have electricity. **E720**

Ndlovu Main Camp ☎ 25283944, ⓦ biggameparks .org. Situated near the gate, with large self-catering thatched cottages that sleep up to eight people and en-suite rondavels sleeping two. There's no electricity (paraffin lamps and gas cooker are provided), but the basic but adequate accommodation provides a relaxed setting, allowing you to focus on the surrounding wildlife. **E730**

Ndlovu Camping Area Main Camp ☎ 25283944, ⓦ biggameparks.org. Open camping ground with plenty of soft grass and trees using a communal kitchen and ablution block (with hot water) and plenty of firewood available in the braai area. **E90**

EATING

Ndlovu Restaurant Main Camp. A large thatched restaurant and lounge area, with a wide deck overlooking a nearby watering hole that attracts rhino, elephant and giraffe. There's a reliable à la carte menu offering the usual gamut of chicken and burgers, as well as a buffet at dinner time (E145). Unless there's a large group staying, the wide deck is fairly relaxed, with plenty of trees and shady spots to sit. Daily 7am–8pm.

The northwest

The highveld of the **northwest** is unquestionably the most beautiful region of Swaziland, with rolling hills perfect for hiking, countless sparkling streams, a sprinkling of waterfalls and some wonderful accommodation.

Most visitors to the northwest are en route to or from Kruger National Park (see p.539), but beautiful **Phophonyane Nature Reserve** is only 64km north of Mbabane and well worth a visit, too. The most spectacular – and rugged – entrance into the country is via the Bulembu road from Barberton in Mpumalanga.

Phophonyane Nature Reserve

40km south of the Matsamo border • Daily 8am–4.30pm • E30 • ☎ 24313429, ⓦ phophonyane.co.sz

The relaxing, private **Phophonyane Nature Reserve** is situated five slow kilometres away from the MR1, making it best reached with your own transport (public transport drops off on the main road, from where it's a hike to get here). The five-square-kilometre reserve's carefully laid-out **trails** ensure there's plenty to see, including the Phophonyane Waterfall on its northwestern side. The vegetation is subtropical and attracts hundreds of colourful **bird species**, while animals include mongooses, bushbabies, otters and numerous snakes, though all are hard to spot. The **lodge** in the reserve is one of the most beautiful places to stay in Swaziland (see below); if you can't afford to stay, it's still worth stopping here for a short hike and a meal in the thatched restaurant.

ACCOMMODATION · PHOPHONYANE NATURE RESERVE

êPhophonyane Nature Reserve ☎ 24313429, ⓦ phophonyane.co.sz. Five secluded two-person safari tents next to the Phophonyane River, with private bathroom facilities in separate huts a few steps up from the tents. There are also family cottages sleeping up to five, with private kitchens and gardens, and two gorgeously romantic beehive huts. The reserve has two pools; one with salt water next to the restaurant, the other blended cleverly into the rocks beside the tumbling river and with a stunning location, looking out onto endless mountains and surrounded by luxuriant vegetation. **E1310**

Nsangwini Rock Art

Komati Valley • E25 • From the Mbabane–Matsamo Rd follow the Muguga Dam Loop Rd eastwards, following signs down a dirt road turn-off to the east; the hike begins after 7km

A thirty-minute hike down a mountainside trail in the Komati Valley will lead you to a wide expanse of rock art, found in a rock shelter dramatically perched over the Komati River Valley, with breathtaking views of the mountain. The rock art is estimated to be around 4000 years old, and is absolutely mind-boggling; you'll find that the longer you look at the rocks, the more you see, including human figures in a trance-like dance holding spears, and the sacred preying mantis. To visit the site you need to hire a guide from the Nsangwini community, who are well informed. You can find one waiting in a shelter at the start at the hiking trail, or you can book a guided walk though *Maguga Lodge* (see below).

Maguga Dam

On the Maguga Dam Loop Rd, eastwards off the Mbabane–Matsamo Rd · Information Centre daily 8am–5pm · Free · ☎ 24371056

The hydroelectric **Maguga Dam** sits snugly in a lowveld dip surrounded on all four sides by the often mist-covered mountains. The dam, primarily constructed to provide water for the vast sugar-cane plantations downstream, was completed in 2002 and filled in 2006. You can ponder the vastness of the construction in the on-site café, while the **information centre**, on a ledge overlooking the dam, shows a short video on the dam's history.

Many people come to Maguga Dam to fish for bass, but the area also makes for some good hiking. The surrounding countryside is spectacular, and there are trails leading to the "the Gap" on the Nkomati River, a point at which the river flows through naturally occuring holes and fantastic formations in the rock. Contact *Maguga Lodge* (see below) to arrange a local guide.

12

ACCOMMODATON
MAGUGA DAM

Maguga Lodge Next to the Maguga Dam on the Maguga Dam loop road ☎ 24373975, ⊚ magugalodge .com. This scenically located lodge has 33 comfortable en-suite rondavels and a fully equiped campsite. It offers relaxing boat trips on the dam (E120/person), giving you an opportunity to see the dam's rich birdlife, as well as visits to a local homestead and fishing expeditions. There's also an outstanding restaurant that overlooks the dam from a large thatched balcony. Camping **E105**, rondavel **E880**

Malolotja Nature Reserve

Daily 6am–6pm · E30 · ☎ 24443241, ⊚ sntc.org.sz

Swaziland's least touristy park, the easy-going **Malolotja Nature Reserve** offers awesome scenery and some of the finest hiking in Southern Africa. This is a place to come for rugged, wild nature and tranquillity, rather than for game spotting. The mountains here, among the oldest in the world (3.6 billion years old), are covered in grassland and graced by myriad streams and waterfalls, including the 95m-high **Malolotja Falls**.

Nearly three hundred species of **birds** are found in Malolotja, with an impressive colony of the rare bald ibis just by the waterfalls. You'll have to look harder for **game**, although wildebeest, blesbok and zebra are often visible, and there are leopards lurking somewhere in the gaping tracts of mountain and valley. Malolotja's small network of roads passes some fine viewpoints and picnic sites, but to really savour this park's rugged wilderness and see its waterfalls you'll need to hike. A variety of **trails** is laid out in the reserve, from easy half-day excursions to seven-day marathons, with basic campsites available en route (see opposite). **Forbes Reef Gold Mine**, a few kilometres south of the reserve's main entrance on the main tarred road, can be visited alone, but take care on the slippery banks; you can find it using the map you get on arrival at the main entrance.

ARRIVAL AND INFORMATION
MALOLOTJA NATURE RESERVE

By Kombi Minibus Kombis between Mbabane and Piggs Peak stop at the main gate, which is clearly signposted on the Mbabane–Matsamo Rd. **Information and supplies** Brochures and maps are available from the reserve's reception building, 500m from the main entrance gate. The reception also houses a nice

UP IN THE TREES

An alternative way of experiencing the reserve is through **Canopy Tours** (☏ 76606755, ⓦ malolotjacanopytour.com; E495 for two and a half hours), which involves gliding on wires between elevated forest platforms while securely kitted out with lots of tackle. You can't really see much wildlife while whooshing along, but there's a good adrenalin kick when stepping off the first platform. Tours include a light lunch. Booking is essential; tours start from the reserve's reception building.

restaurant (daily 8am–4pm; ☏ 76606755) and there's a curio shop that sells basic provisions, but it's wiser to stock up in Piggs Peak or Mbabane.

Climate If you're on a long hike during the summer, be prepared for hot days; however, temperatures drop dramatically in winter, when the nights can be freezing.

ACCOMMODATION

Campsites ☏ 24443241, ⓦ sntc.org.sz. For those attempting longer hikes there are 21 scenic overnight camps scattered around the reserve, all with natural water sources but few other facilities (except braai areas); you'll need to bring all your own equipment. Camps 11 and 12 are near Malolotja Falls. Book in advance. E50
Main Restcamp ☏ 24443241, ⓦ sntc.org.sz. Fifteen

tent sites with hot water in a communal ablutions block, and braai areas, as well as thirteen comfortable log cabins, each sleeping up to five people and kitted out with their own fireplaces. Both are a short walk from the main reception so you can eat at the restaurant there if you don't fancy cooking. Book in advance. Camping E70, cabin E250 per person

Hawane Dam Nature Reserve

12km south of Malolotja Nature Reserve main gate on the Mbabane road, on the eastern side of the road • Daily 6am–6pm • E30 •
☏ 76606755, ⓦ sntc.org.sz

12

Though technically part of the Malolotja Nature Reserve, **Hawane Dam Nature Reserve** is not directly connected. This is a small area around the northern end of the Hawane Dam, designed to protect part of the Black Mbuluzi River wetlands. Hawane's main attraction is its wealth of **birdlife**, and there's an excellent trail for birdwatching.

ACCOMMODATION
HAWANE DAM NATURE RESERVE

Hawane Resort Signposted on the Mbabane Rd down a 1km track, on the opposite side of the main road to the dam ☏ 24441744, ⓦ www.hawane.co.sz. Funky accommodation in quirky triangular adobe chalets or thatched rondavels sleeping two, and comfortable

twin-bed backpacker accommodation in a nearby converted barn. With large stables housing well-trained horses, this is the place to head if you fancy exploring the attractive surrounding countryside on horseback (E135/hr). Dorms E120, chalet E966

EATING

êTaste of Africa Hawane Resort ☏ 24441744. An outstanding restaurant in a large thatched circular structure, which serves delicious food best defined as

African fusion. Try the seafood-packed Mozambican north-coast soup (E60), coconut crepes (E60), or the delectable honey and cashew-nut ice cream (E43). Daily 6am–9pm.

Ngwenya Glass factory

On the MR3, west of Motshane • Mon–Fri 6.50am–4.30pm, Sat & Sun 8am–4pm • ☏ 24424053, ⓦ ngwenyaglass.co.sz

The Mbabane–Matsamo road meets the fast MR3 between the Ngwenya/Oshoek border post and Mbabane at the small settlement of **Motshane**. A kilometre west of Motshane, along the MR3 towards the border, follow the signs to where one of Swaziland's best-known exports, **Ngwenya glass**, is made. Their products, which range from attractive wine glasses to endless trinkets in the shape of rotund animals, are made from recycled glass and produced by highly skilled workers; it's well worth stopping here just to see them blowing and crafting the glass from the viewing balcony above the roaring furnaces. The adjoining gift shop and **café** are usually swamped by coach-loads of tourists.

NELSON MANDELA DEPICTED IN STAINED GLASS, SOWETO

Contexts

History

Recent fossil finds show that *Homo sapiens* existed along Africa's southern coast over fifty thousand years ago. The descendants of these nomadic Stone-Age people – ochre-skinned San hunter-gatherers and Khoikhoi herders (see below) – still inhabited the Western Cape when Europeans arrived in the fifteenth century. By the time of the Dutch settlement at the Cape in the mid-seventeenth century, much of the eastern half of the country was occupied by people who had begun crossing the Limpopo around the time of Christ's birth.

The stage was now set for the complex drama of South Africa's modern history, which in crude terms was a battle for the control of scarce resources between the various indigenous people, African states and the European colonizers. The twentieth century saw the temporary victory of colonialism, the unification of South Africa and the attempts by whites to keep at bay black demands for civil rights, culminating in the implementation of South Africa's most notorious social invention – **apartheid**. Ultimately, it was multiracialism that was victorious and, despite numerous problems, South Africa's lively 2014 elections were proof that democracy was still alive after twenty years.

The first South Africans

Rock art provides evidence of human culture in the subcontinent dating back nearly 30,000 years and represents Southern Africa's oldest and most enduring artistic tradition. The artists were hunter-gatherers, sometimes called Bushmen, but more commonly **San**. The most direct descendants of the late Stone Age, San people have survived in tiny pockets, mostly in Namibia and Botswana, making theirs the longest-spanning culture in the subcontinent. At one time they probably spread throughout sub-Saharan Africa, having pretty well perfected their **nomadic lifestyle**, which involved an enviable twenty-hour working week spent by the men hunting and the women gathering. This left considerable time for artistic and religious pursuits. People lived in small, loosely connected bands comprising family units and were free to leave and join up with other groups. The concept of private property had little meaning because everything required for survival could be obtained from the environment.

About two thousand years ago, this changed when some groups in northern Botswana laid their hands on fat-tailed sheep and cattle from Northern Africa, thus transforming themselves into herding communities. The introduction of livestock revolutionized social organization, creating the idea of ownership and accumulation. Social divisions developed, and political units became larger and centred around a chief, who had important powers, such as the allocation of pasturage.

These were the first South Africans encountered by Portuguese mariners, who landed along the Cape coast in the fifteenth century. Known as **Khoikhoi** (meaning "men of men"), they were not ethnically distinct from the San, as many anthropologists once believed, but simply represented a distinct social organization. According to current thinking it was possible for Khoi who lost their livestock to revert to being San, and for San to lay their hands on animals to become Khoi, giving rise to the collective term "Khoisan".

30,000 BC	500 BC	500 AD	1488
Hunter-gatherers occupy Cape Peninsula	Khoikhoi sheep herders drift southwards into South Africa, eventually reaching southern coast	Tall Bantu-speaking farmers cross Limpopo River and begin dispersing down South Africa's east coast	Bartholomeu Dias becomes first European to set foot on South African soil at Mossel Bay

Farms and crafts

Around two thousand years ago, tall, dark-skinned people who practised mixed farming – raising both crops and livestock – crossed the Limpopo River into what is today South Africa. These **Bantu-speaking** farmers were the ancestors of South Africa's majority African population, who gradually drifted south, to occupy the entire eastern half of the subcontinent as far as the Eastern Cape, where they were first encountered by Europeans in the sixteenth century.

Apart from having highly developed farming know-how and a far more sedentary life than the Khoisan, the early Bantu speakers were skilled craft workers and knew about mining and smelting metals, including gold, copper and iron, which became an important factor in the extensive network of trade that developed.

The Cape goes Dutch

In the fifteenth century, Portuguese mariners led by **Bartholomeu Dias** became the first Europeans to set foot in South Africa, but it was another 170 years before any European settlement was established here. In 1652, a group of white employees of the **Dutch East India Company**, which was trading between the Netherlands and the East Indies, pulled into Table Bay to set up a refreshment station to resupply company ships.

Despite the view of station commander Jan van Riebeeck that the indigenous Khoi were savages "living without conscience", from the start, the Dutch were dependent on them to provide livestock, which were traded for trinkets. As the settlement developed, Van Riebeeck needed more labour to keep the show going. Much to his annoyance, the bosses back in Holland had forbidden him from enslaving the locals, and refused his request for slaves from elsewhere in the company's empire.

This kicked off the process of colonization of the lands around the fort, when a number of Dutch men were released in 1657 from their contracts to farm as free burghers on land granted by the company. The idea was that they would sell their produce to the company at a fixed price, thereby overcoming the labour shortage. The move sparked the first of a series of Khoikhoi–Dutch wars. Although the first campaign ended in stalemate, the Khoikhoi were ultimately no match for the Dutch, who had the advantage of superior mobility and firepower in horses and guns.

Meanwhile, in 1658, Van Riebeeck established slavery at the Cape via the back door, when he purloined a shipload of slaves from West Africa. The Dutch East India Company itself became the biggest slave owner at the Cape and continued importing slaves, mostly from the East Indies, at such a pace that by 1711 there were more slaves than burghers in the colony. With the help of this ready workforce, the embryonic Cape Colony expanded outwards displacing the Peninsula Khoikhoi, who by 1713 had lost everything. Most of their livestock (nearly fifty thousand head) and most of their land west of the Hottentots Holland Mountains (90km southeast of present-day Cape Town) had been swallowed by the Dutch East India Company. Dispossession and diseases like smallpox, previously unknown in South Africa, decimated their numbers and shattered their social system. By the middle of the eighteenth century, those who remained had been reduced to a condition of miserable servitude to the colonists.

1652	**1657**	**1658**	**1679**
Dutch East India Company establishes supply station at Cape for trade ships sailing to Indies	Company releases indentured labourers to farm as free settlers	First slaves introduced at Cape and within fifty years slaves outnumber settlers	Castle of Good Hope completed

THE TREKBOERS

Like the Khoikhoi, impoverished whites living at the fringes of colonial society had limited options. Many just packed up their wagons and rolled out into the interior, where they lived by the gun, either hunting game or taking cattle from the Khoi by force. Beyond the control of the Dutch East India Company, these nomadic trekboers began to assume a pastoral niche previously occupied by the Khoi. By the turn of the nineteenth century, trekboers had penetrated well into the Eastern Cape, pushing back the Khoi and San in the process.

As their lives became disrupted and living by **traditional** means became impossible, the Khoisan began to prey on the cattle and sheep of the trekboers. The trekboers responded by hunting the San as vermin, killing the men and often taking women and children as slaves. After the British occupation of the Cape in 1795, the trekboer migration from the Cape accelerated.

Rise of the Zulus

While in the west of the country trekboers were migrating from the Cape Colony, in the east equally significant movements were under way. Throughout the seventeenth and eighteenth centuries, descendants of the first Bantu-speakers to penetrate into South Africa had been swelling their numbers and had expanded right across the eastern half of the country.

Nowhere was this more marked than in **KwaZulu-Natal**, where, prompted by pressures on grazing land, chiefdoms survived by subduing and absorbing their neighbours. By the early nineteenth century, two chiefdoms, the Ndwandwe and the Mthethwa, dominated eastern South Africa around the Tugela River. During the late 1810s a major confrontation between them ended in the defeat of the Mthethwa. Out of their ruins emerged the **Zulus**, who were to become one of the most powerful polities in Southern Africa. Around 1816, **Shaka** assumed the chieftaincy of the Zulus, whose fighting tactics he quickly transformed.

By 1820, the Zulus had become the dominant regional power and by the middle of the century had established a centralized military state with a forty-thousand-strong standing army. One of the strengths of the system lay in its ability to absorb the survivors of conflict, who became members of the expanding Zulu state. Throughout the 1820s, Shaka sent his armies to invade neighbouring territory. But in 1828 he was stabbed to death by two of his half-brothers, one of whom, Dingane, succeeded him. Dingane continued with his brother's ruthless but devastatingly successful policies and tactics.

The rise of the Zulu state reverberated across Southern Africa and led to the creation of a series of **centralized Nguni states** as well as paving the way for **Boer** expansion into the interior. In a movement of forced migrations known as the **mfecane**, huge areas of the country were laid waste and people across eastern South Africa were driven off their lands. They attempted to survive either in small groups or by banding together to form larger political organizations.

To the north of the Zulu kingdom another Nguni group with strong cultural and linguistic affinities with the Zulus came together under **Sobhuza I** and his son Mswati II, after whom their new state **Swaziland** took its name. In North West Province, a few hundred Zulus under **Mzilikazi** were displaced by Shaka and relocated to

1713	1795	1816–1828	1820s
Khoikhoi dispossessed of livestock by settlers and reduced to servitude	Company goes bust and English becomes official language when British take over	Shaka assumes chieftainship of Zulus and forges militarized regional power in southeast	As defence against Shaka, Nguni states form in Swaziland, Lesotho and Matabeleland

Matabeleland, now southwestern Zimbabwe, where they re-established themselves as the **Matabele** kingdom. In the Drakensberg, on the west flank of KwaZulu-Natal, **Moshoeshoe I** used diplomacy and cunning to establish the territory that became the modern state of **Lesotho**.

The Great Trek

Back in the Cape, many Afrikaners were becoming fed up with British rule. Their principal grievance was the way in which the colonial authorities were tampering with labour relations and destroying what they saw as a divine distinction between blacks and whites. In 1828 a proclamation gave Khoi residents and free blacks equality with whites before the law. The **abolition of slavery** in 1834 was the last straw.

Fifteen thousand Afrikaners (one out of ten living in the colony) left the Cape to escape the meddlesome British. When they arrived in the eastern half of the country, they were delighted to find vast tracts of apparently unoccupied land. In fact, they were merely stumbling into the eye of the **mfecane** storm – areas that had been temporarily cleared either by war parties or by fearful refugees hiding out to escape detection. As they fanned out further they encountered the Nguni states and a series of battles followed. By the middle of the nineteenth century, descendants of the Dutch had consolidated control and established the two Boer states of the **South African Republic** (now Mpumalanga, North West and Limpopo provinces) and the **Orange Free State** (now Free State). Britain recognized the independence of both of these states in the 1850s.

The Anglo-Boer War

Despite the benefits it brought, the discovery of gold (see box below) was also one of the principal causes of the **Anglo-Boer War**. Gold-mining had shifted the economic centre of South Africa from the British-controlled Cape to the South African Republic, while at the same time Britain's European rival, Germany, was beginning to make political and economic inroads in the Boer republics. Britain feared losing its strategic Cape naval base, but perhaps even more important were questions of international

> ### GOLD AND DIAMONDS
>
> In the 1850s Britain wasn't too concerned about the interior of South Africa. Its strategic position aside, South Africa was a chaotic backwater at the butt-end of the empire. Things changed in the 1860s, with the discovery of **diamonds** (the world's largest deposit) around modern-day Kimberley, and even more significantly in the 1880s, with the discovery of **gold** on the Witwatersrand (now Gauteng). Together, these finds were the catalyst that transformed South Africa from a down-at-heel rural society into an urbanized industrial one. In the process great fortunes were made by capitalists like Cecil Rhodes, traditional African society was crushed and the independence of the Boer republics ended.
>
> Although the **Gauteng goldfields** were exceptionally well endowed, they were also particularly difficult to mine, requiring the sinking of deep shafts. Exploiting the mines required costly equipment and cheap labour. Capital quickly flowed in from Western investors eager for profit.

1820s	**1834**	**1843**
British settlers arrive at Port Elizabeth as bulwark against Xhosa on eastern frontier	Abolition of slavery leads many Boers to leave Cape and establish two republics	British annex Natal, settlers arrive and indentured Indian labourers brought to work cane fields

finance and the substantial British investment in the mines. London was at the heart of world trade and was eager to see a flourishing gold-mining industry in South Africa, but the Boers seemed rather sluggish about modernizing their infrastructure to assist the exploitation of the mines.

In any case, a number of Britons had for some time seen the unification of South Africa as the key to securing British interests in the subcontinent. To this end, under a wafer-thin pretext, Britain had declared war and subdued the last of the independent African kingdoms by means of the **Zulu War of 1879**. This secured KwaZulu-Natal, bringing all the coastal territories of South Africa under British control. To control the entire subcontinent south of the Limpopo, Britain needed to bring the two Boer republics under the Union flag.

During the closing years of the nineteenth century, Britain demanded that the South African Republic grant voting rights to British miners living there – a demand that, if met, would have meant the end of Boer political control over their own state, since they were outnumbered by the foreigners. The Boers turned down the request and war broke out in October 1899. The British command believed they were looking at a walkover: in the words of **Lord Kitchener**, a "teatime war" that would get the troops home by Christmas.

In fact, the campaign turned into Britain's most expensive since the Napoleonic Wars. During the early stages, the Boers took the imperial power by surprise and penetrated into British-controlled KwaZulu-Natal and the Northern Cape, inflicting a series of humiliating defeats. By June, a reinforced British army was pushing the Boers back, but the Boers fought on for another two years. Lord Kitchener responded with a **scorched-earth policy** that left the countryside a wasteland and thousands of women and children homeless. To house them, the British invented the **concentration camps**, in which 26,370 Boer women and children died. For some Afrikaners, this episode remains a major source of bitterness against the British even today. Less widely publicized were the **African concentration camps** which took 14,000 lives. By 1902, the Boers were demoralized, and in May the Afrikaner republics surrendered their independence in exchange for British promises of reconstruction. By the end of the so-called teatime war, Britain had committed nearly half a million men to the field and lost 22,000 of them. Of the 88,000 Boers who fought, 7000 died in combat. With the two Boer republics and the two British colonies under imperial control, the way was clear for the federation of the **Union of South Africa** in 1910.

Migrant labour and the Bambatha Rebellion

Between the conclusion of the Anglo-Boer War and the unification of South Africa, the mines suffered a **shortage of unskilled labour**. Most Africans still lived by agriculture. To counter this, the government took measures to compel them to supply their labour to the mines. One method was the imposition of **taxes** that had to be paid in coin, thus forcing Africans from subsistence farming and into the cash economy. Responding to one such tax, in 1906 a group of Zulus refused to pay. The authorities declared martial law and dealt mercilessly with the protesters, burning their homes and seizing their possessions. This provoked a full-blown rebellion led by Chief Bambatha, which was

1860s	**1879**	**1886**
Discovery of world's biggest diamond deposit at Kimberley	Britain declares war on Zulus, suffers humiliating defeat at Isandlwana, but eventually wins	Discovery of gold around Johannesburg

ruthlessly put down, at a cost of four thousand rebel lives. Armed resistance by Africans was thus ended for over half a century. After the defeat of the **Bambatha Rebellion**, the number of African men from Zululand working in the Gauteng mines shot up by sixty percent. By 1909, eighty percent of adult males in the territory were away from home, working as migrant labourers. **Migrant labour**, with its shattering effects on family life, became one of the foundations of South Africa's economic and social system, and a basic cornerstone of apartheid.

Kick-starting Afrikanerdom

In a parallel development, large numbers of **Afrikaners** were forced to leave rural areas in the early part of the twentieth century. This was partly a result of the war, but also of overcrowding, drought and pestilence. Many Afrikaners joined the ranks of a swelling poor **white working class** whose members often felt despised by the English-speaking capitalists who commanded the economy, and threatened by lower-paid Africans competing for their jobs.

In 1918 a group of Afrikaners formed the **Broederbond** ("the brotherhood"), a secret society to promote the interest of Afrikaners. It aimed to uplift impoverished members of the **volk** ("people") and to develop a sense of pride in their language, religion and culture (see box below). The Broederbond would come to dominate every aspect of the way the country was run for half a century.

During the 1930s, a number of young Afrikaner intellectuals travelled to Europe, where they were inspired by fascism. It was around this time that Afrikaner intellectuals began using the term **apartheid** (pronounced "apart-hate"). Among those kicking their heels in Germany in the 1930s were **Nico Diederichs**, who became a minister of finance

---

NEW WORD ORDER

In the late nineteenth century, Afrikaans-speaking whites, fighting for an identity, sought to create a "racially pure" culture by driving a wedge between themselves and coloured Afrikaans-speakers. They reinvented **Afrikaans** as a "white man's language", eradicating the supposed stigma of its coloured ties by substituting Dutch words for those with Asian or African roots. In 1925, the dialect of Afrikaans spoken by upper-crust whites became an official language alongside English, and the dialects spoken by coloureds were treated as inferior deviations from correct usage.

For Afrikaner nationalists this wasn't enough, and after the introduction of apartheid in 1948, they attempted to codify perceived racial differences. Under the **Population Registration Act**, all South Africans were classified as white, coloured or African. These classifications became fundamental to what kind of life you could expect. There are numerous cases of families in which one sibling was classified coloured with limited rights and another white with the right to live in comfortable white areas, enjoy superior job opportunities, and be able to send their children to better schools and universities.

With the demise of apartheid, the make-up of residential areas is slowly (very slowly) shifting – and so is the thinking on ethnic terminology. Some people now reject the term "coloured" because of its apartheid associations, and refuse any racial definitions; others, proudly embrace the term, as a means of acknowledging their distinct culture, with its slave, East Indies and Khoikhoi roots.

1899–1901	**1910**	**1912**
Britain defeats Afrikaners in Anglo-Boer War to gain total hegemony over South Africa	Boer republics and British colonies merge into Union of South Africa	ANC forms to fight for universal suffrage

under the Afrikaner Nationalist Party; **Hendrik Frensch Verwoerd**, apartheid's leading theorist and prime minister from 1958 to 1966; and **Piet Meyer**, controller of the state broadcasting service, who named his son Izan ("Nazi" spelled backwards – he later claimed this was sheer coincidence).

In 1939, the Broederbond introduced a scheme that, in the space of a decade, launched ten thousand Afrikaner businesses, some of which are still among the leading players in South Africa's economy.

Africans' claims

Despite having relied on African cooperation for their victory in the Anglo-Boer War and having hinted at enhanced rights for blacks after the war, the British excluded blacks from the cosy federal deal between themselves and the Afrikaners. It wasn't long, in fact, before the white Union government began eroding African rights. In response, a group of middle-class mission-educated Africans formed the **South African Native National Congress** (later to become the ANC) in 1912 to campaign for universal suffrage. In 1914, the leaders went to London to protest against the 1913 **Natives' Land Act**, which confined the black majority to less than ten percent of the land. The trip failed and the Land Act became the foundation for apartheid some 35 years later.

Through the early half of the twentieth century, the ANC remained conservative, unwilling to engage in active protest. In response, a number of alternative mass organizations arose, among them the **Industrial and Commercial Union**, an African trade union founded in 1919, which at its peak in 1928 had gathered an impressive 150,000 members. But in the 1930s it ran out of steam. The first political movement in the country not organized along ethnic lines was the South African Communist Party, founded in 1921 with a multiracial executive. While it never gained widespread membership itself, it became an important force inside the ANC.

Throughout the 1930s, the ANC plodded on with speeches, petitions and pleas, which proved completely fruitless.

Young Turks and striking miners

In 1944, a hotheaded young student named **Nelson Mandela** with friends **Oliver Tambo**, **Walter Sisulu** and **Anton Lembede** formed the **ANC Youth League**. The League's founding manifesto criticized the ANC leadership for being "gentlemen with clean hands". The 1945 annual conference of the ANC adopted a document called "**Africans' Claims in South Africa**", which reflected an emerging politicization. The document demanded **universal franchise** and an end to the **colour bar**, which reserved most skilled jobs for whites.

In 1946 the African Mineworkers' Union launched one of the biggest strikes in the country's history in protest against falling living standards. Virtually the entire Gauteng gold-mining region came to a standstill as one hundred thousand workers downed tools. Prime Minister Jan Smuts sent in police who forced the workers back down the shafts at gunpoint.

The following year Nelson Mandela took his first step into public life when he was elected general secretary of the ANC.

1913	1918	1920s	1930s
Land Act gives whites (20 percent of population) 92 percent of the land	Afrikaner secret society, Broederbond, forms and Nelson Mandela born	Agatha Christie surfs at Muizenberg, Cape Town	Orlando, the nucleus of Soweto, begins evolving

Winds of change

For years, the white government had been hinting at easing up on segregation, and even Smuts himself, no soft liberal, had reckoned that it would have to end at some point. The relentless influx of Africans into the urban areas was breaking the stereotype of them as rural tribespeople. The government appointed the **Fagan Commission** to look into the question of the **pass laws**, which controlled the movement of Africans and sought to keep them out of the white cities unless they had a job.

When the Fagan Commission reported its findings in 1948, it concluded that "the trend to urbanization is irreversible and the pass laws should be eased". While some blacks may have felt heartened by this whiff of reform, this was the last thing many whites wanted to hear. Afrikaner farmers were alarmed by the idea of a labour shortage caused by Africans leaving the rural areas for better prospects in the cities, while white workers feared the prospect of losing jobs to lower-paid African workers.

The National Party comes to power

Against this background of black aspiration and white fears, the Smuts government called a **general election**. The opposition **National Party**, which promoted Afrikaner nationalism, campaigned on a *swart gevaar* or "black peril" ticket, playing on white insecurity and fear. With an eye on the vote of Afrikaner workers and farmers, they promised to reverse the tide of Africans into the cities and to send them all back to the reserves. For white business they made the conflicting promise to bring black workers into the cities as a cheap and plentiful supply of labour.

On Friday May 28, 1948, South Africa awoke to a National Party victory at the polls. Party leader **D.F. Malan** told a group of ecstatic supporters: "For the first time, South Africa is our own. May God grant that it always remains our own. It is to us that millions of barbarous blacks look for guidance, justice and the Christian way of life."

Meanwhile, the **ANC** was driven by its own power struggle. Fed up with the ineffectiveness of the old guard, the Youth League staged a coup, voted in its own leadership with Nelson Mandela on the executive and adopted the League's radical Programme of Action, with an arsenal of tactics that Mandela explained would include "the new weapons of boycott, strike, civil disobedience and non-cooperation".

The 1950s: peaceful protest

During the 1950s, the National Party began putting in place a barrage of laws that would eventually constitute the structure of apartheid. Some early onslaughts on black civil rights included the **Bantu Authorities Act**, which set up puppet authorities to govern Africans in the reserves; the **Population Registration Act**, which classified every South African at birth as "white, native or coloured" (see box, p.642); the **Group Areas Act**, which divided South Africa into ethnically distinct areas; and the **Suppression of Communism Act**, which made any anti-apartheid opposition (Communist or not) a criminal offence.

The ANC responded in 1952 with the **Defiance Campaign**, aimed at achieving full civil rights for blacks. During the campaign, eight thousand volunteers deliberately broke the apartheid laws and were jailed. The campaign rolled on through 1952 until the police provoked violence in October by firing on a prayer meeting in East London.

1939	**1948**	**1949**
World War splits Afrikaners, with future prime minister John Vorster among those supporting Germany	National Party wins election and goes full throttle on segregation	Government bans inter-racial marriage and sex, followed by slew of other discriminatory laws

THE FREEDOM CHARTER

- The people shall govern.
- All national groups shall have equal rights.
- The people shall share the nation's wealth.
- The land shall be shared by those who work it.
- All shall be equal before the law.
- All shall enjoy equal human rights.
- There shall be work and security for all.
- The doors of learning and culture shall be opened.
- There shall be houses, security and comfort.
- There shall be peace and friendship.

A riot followed in which two white people were killed, thus appearing to discredit claims that the campaign was non-violent. The government used this pretext to swoop on the homes of the ANC leadership, resulting in the detention and then **banning** of over one hundred ANC organizers. Bannings restricted a person's movement and political activities: a banned person was prohibited from seeing more than one person at a time or talking to any other banned person; prohibited from entering certain buildings; kept under surveillance; required to report regularly to the police; and could not be quoted or published.

The most far-reaching event of the decade was the **Congress of the People**, held near Johannesburg in 1955. At a mass meeting of three thousand delegates, four organizations, representing Africans, coloureds, whites and Indians, formed a strategic partnership called the Congress Alliance. ANC leader **Chief Albert Luthuli** explained that "for the first time in the history of our multiracial nation its people will meet as equals, irrespective of race, colour and creed, to formulate a freedom charter for all the people of our country". Adopted at the Congress of the People, the Freedom Charter (see box above) became the principal document defining ANC policy.

The government rounded up 156 opposition leaders and charged them with treason. Evidence at the Treason Trial was based on the Freedom Charter, described as a "blueprint for violent Communist revolution". Although all the defendants were acquitted, the four-year trial disrupted the ANC and splits began to emerge. In 1958 a group of Africanists led by the charismatic **Robert Mangaliso Sobukwe** (see box, p.325) broke away from the ANC to form the **Pan Africanist Congress (PAC)**, arguing that cooperation with white activists was not in the interests of black liberation.

Sharpeville

On March 21, 1960, Sobukwe and thousands of followers presented themselves without passes to police stations across Gauteng and the Western Cape. At **Sharpeville** police station, south of Johannesburg, the police opened fire, killing 69 and injuring nearly 200. Most were shot in the back.

Demonstrations swept the country on March 27. The next day Africans staged a total stay-away from work and thousands joined a public pass-burning demonstration. The day after that, the government declared a **state of emergency**, rounded up 22,000

1952	1955	1958
Mandela leads Defiance Campaign against apartheid legislation	Mass non-racial meeting drafts the Freedom Charter, which becomes policy of ANC	New prime minister Verwoerd creates ten ethnic "homelands", the cornerstone of Grand Apartheid

people and banned the ANC and PAC. White South Africa panicked as the value of the rand slipped and shares slid. Some feared an imminent and bloody revolution.

Later that month, Prime Minister Hendrik Verwoerd was shot in the head by a half-crazed white farmer. Many hoped that if he died, apartheid would be ditched. But Dr Verwoerd survived, his appetite for apartheid stronger than ever. More than anyone, Verwoerd made apartheid his own and formulated the system of **Bantustans** – notionally independent statelets in which Africans were to exercise their political rights away from the white areas. The aim was to dismantle the black majority into several separate "tribal" minorities, none of which on its own could outnumber whites.

In 1961 Nelson Mandela called for a national convention "to determine a non-racial democratic constitution". Instead, Verwoerd appointed one-time neo-Nazi John Vorster as justice minister. A trained lawyer, Vorster eagerly set about passing repressive legislation that circumvented the rule of law.

Nelson Mandela saw the writing on the wall. "The time comes in the life of any nation when there remain only two choices: submit or fight. That time has now come to South Africa. We shall not submit," he told the BBC, before going underground as commander in chief of **Umkhonto we Sizwe** (Spear of the Nation, aka MK), the newly formed armed wing of the ANC. The organization was dedicated to economic and symbolic acts of sabotage and was under strict orders not to kill or injure people. In August 1962 Mandela was captured, tried and with nine other ANC leaders he was handed a **life sentence**.

Apartheid: everything going white

With the leadership of the liberation movement behind bars, the 1960s was the decade in which everything seemed to be going the white government's way. Resistance was stifled, the state grew more powerful, and for white South Africans, businessmen and foreign investors life seemed perfect. For black South Africans, poverty deepened – a state of affairs enforced by apartheid legislation and repressive measures that included bannings, detentions without trial, house arrests and murders of political prisoners.

The ANC was impotent, and resistance by its armed wing MK was virtually nonexistent. But as South Africa swung into the 1970s, the uneasy peace began to fray, prompted at first by deteriorating black living standards, which reawakened industrial action. Trade unions came to fill the vacuum left by the ANC.

The **Soweto uprising** of June 16, 1976, signalled the transfer of protest from the workplace to the townships, as black youths took to the streets in protest against the imposition of Afrikaans as a medium of instruction in their schools. The protest spread across the country and by the following February, 575 people (nearly a quarter of them children) had been killed in the rolling series of revolts that followed.

The government relied increasingly on armed police to impose order. Even this was unable to stop the mushrooming of new liberation organizations, many of them part of the broadly based **Black Consciousness Movement**. As the unrest rumbled on into 1977, the government responded by banning all the new black organizations and detaining their leadership. In September 1977, **Steve Biko** (one of the detained) became the 46th political prisoner to be killed in jail.

1960	1961	1962
Sixty-nine Africans shot dead at anti-pass law protest; government bans anti-apartheid opposition	South Africa leaves Commonwealth and becomes republic; ANC launches armed struggle	ANC leadership jailed for treason on Robben Island

The banned organizations were rapidly replaced by new movements and the government never again successfully put the lid on opposition. By the late 1970s business was complaining that apartheid wasn't working any more, and even the government was having its doubts. The growth of the black population was outstripping that of whites; from a peak of 21 percent of the population in 1910, whites now made up only 16 percent. This proportion was set to fall to 10 percent by the end of the century. The sums just didn't add up.

Total Strategy

It was becoming clear that the deployment of the police couldn't solve South Africa's problems, and in 1978 defence minister **Pieter Willem (P.W.) Botha** became prime minister in a palace coup. Botha adopted a two-handed strategy, of reform accompanied by unprecedented repression. He devised his so-called **Total Strategy**, which aimed to draw every facet of white society into the fight against the opponents of apartheid. This included military training programmes in white schools, propaganda campaigns, the extension of conscription, and political reforms aimed at co-opting Indians and coloureds.

Despite this, the 1980s saw the growing use of sabotage against the apartheid state. Botha began contemplating reform and moved Nelson Mandela and other ANC leaders from **Robben Island** to Pollsmoor Prison in mainland Cape Town. But he also poured ever-increasing numbers of troops into African townships to stop unrest, while intimidating neighbouring countries. Between 1981 and 1983, the army launched operations into every one of the country's black-ruled neighbours, Angola, Mozambique, Botswana, Zimbabwe, Swaziland and Lesotho.

In 1983 Botha came up with another scheme to shore up apartheid: the so-called New Constitution in which coloureds and Indians would be granted the vote for their own racially segregated – and powerless – chambers. For Africans, apartheid was to continue as usual.

Around the same time, 15,000 **anti-apartheid** delegates met at Mitchell's Plain in Cape Town to form the **United Democratic Front** (UDF), a multiracial umbrella for 575 opposition organizations. The UDF became a proxy for the ANC as two years of strikes, protest and boycotts followed.

Towards the end of the decade, the world watched as apartheid troops and police were regularly shown on TV beating up and shooting unarmed Africans. The Commonwealth condemned the apartheid government, the United States and Australia severed air links and the US Congress passed legislation promoting disinvestment. An increasingly desperate Botha offered to release Mandela "if he renounces violence".

Mandela replied: "I am surprised by the conditions the government wants to impose. I am not a violent man. It was only when all other forms of resistance were no longer open to us that we turned to armed struggle. Let Botha … renounce violence."

As events unfolded, a subtle shift became palpable: Botha was the prisoner and Mandela held the keys. While black resistance wasn't abating, Botha was now also facing a white right-wing backlash. The ultra-right Conservative Party was winning electoral support and the neo-Nazi Afrikaner Weerstand Beweging (Afrikaner Resistance Movement, aka AWB) was darkly muttering about civil war.

1966–1970s	**1970**	**1976**
About 3.5 million Africans and coloureds forcibly removed from "white" areas	Africans stripped of SA citizenship and assigned to impoverished ethnic "homelands"	Police shoot dead over 600 during countrywide protests, which start in Soweto schools

Crisis

In 1986, Botha declared yet another **state of emergency** accompanied by assassinations, mass arrests, detentions, treason trials and torture. Alarmed by the violence engulfing the country, a group of South African businessmen, mostly Afrikaners, flew to Senegal in 1987 to meet an ANC delegation headed by **Thabo Mbeki**. A joint statement pressed for unequivocal support for a negotiated settlement.

In July 1988 Mandela was rushed to Tygerberg Hospital in Cape Town, suffering from tuberculosis. Although he was better by October, the government announced that he wouldn't be returning to Pollsmoor **Prison**. Instead he was moved to a prison warder's cottage at **Victor Verster** (now Groot Drakenstein) Prison just outside Paarl. Outside the prison walls, Botha's policies had collapsed and the army top brass were telling him that there could be no decisive military victory over the anti-apartheid opposition – and that South Africa's undeclared war in Angola was bleeding the treasury dry.

At the beginning of 1989, Mandela wrote to Botha from Victor Verster calling for negotiations. The intransigent Botha found himself with little room to manoeuvre. When he suffered a stroke, his party colleagues moved swiftly to oust him and replaced him with **Frederik Willem (F.W.) De Klerk**.

De Klerk made it clear that he was opposed to majority rule. But he inherited a massive pile of problems that could no longer be ignored: the economy was in trouble and the cost of maintaining apartheid prohibitive; the illegal influx of Africans from the country to the city had become unstoppable; blacks hadn't been taken in by Botha's constitutional reforms, and even South Africa's friends were losing patience. In September 1989, US President George Bush (the elder) told De Klerk that if there wasn't progress on releasing Mandela within six months, he would extend US sanctions.

De Klerk gambled on his ability to outmanoeuvre the opposition. In February 1990, he announced the unbanning of the ANC, the PAC, the Communist Party and 33 other organizations, as well as the **release of Mandela**. On Sunday February 11, at around 4pm, Mandela stepped out of Victor Verster Prison and was driven to City Hall in Cape Town, from where he spoke publicly for the first time in three decades. That May, Mandela and De Klerk signed an agreement in which the government undertook to repeal repressive laws and release political prisoners, while the ANC agreed to suspend the armed struggle. As events moved towards full-blown negotiations it became clear that De Klerk still clung to race-based notions for a settlement: "Majority rule is not suitable for South Africa," he said, "because it will lead to the domination of minorities."

Negotiations

The **negotiating** process, from 1990 to 1994, was fragile, and at many points a descent into chaos looked likely. Obstacles included violence linked to a sinister element in the apartheid security forces who were working behind the scenes to destabilize the ANC; **threats of civil war** from heavily armed right-wingers; and a low-key war of attrition in KwaZulu-Natal between Zulu nationalists of the **Inkatha Freedom Party** and ANC supporters, which had already claimed three thousand lives between 1987 and 1990.

1978	1980s	1983	1989
Hawkish former defence minister P.W. Botha becomes president	Botha floods townships with troops and sends army into neighbouring countries	Government cracks down further on opposition after formation of ANC-proxy, United Democratic Front	Botha rebuffs Mandela's appeal from prison for negotiations "to avert civil war"

In April 1993 it looked as if it would all fall apart with the **assassination** of Chris Hani, the most popular ANC leader after Mandela. Hani's slaying by a right-wing gunman touched deep fears among all South Africans. A descent into civil war loomed, and for three consecutive nights the nation watched as Mandela appeared on prime-time television appealing for calm. This marked the decisive turning point as it became obvious that only the ANC president could stave off chaos, while De Klerk kept his head down. Pushing his strategic advantage, Mandela called for the immediate setting of an election date. Shortly afterwards the date for elections was set for April 27, 1994.

The 1994 election

The election passed peacefully. At the age of 76, Nelson Mandela, along with millions of his fellow citizens, voted for the first time in his life in a national election. On May 2, De Klerk conceded defeat after an ANC landslide, in which they took 62.7 percent of the vote. Of the remaining significant parties, the National Party fared best with 20.4 percent, followed by the Inkatha Freedom Party with 10.5 percent. The ANC was dominant in all of the provinces apart from **Western Cape** and **KwaZulu-Natal**. One of the disappointments for the ANC was its inability to appeal broadly to non-Africans.

For the ANC, the real struggle was only beginning. It inherited a country of 38 million people. Of these it was estimated that six million were unemployed, nine million were destitute, ten million had no access to running water, and twenty million had no electricity. Among adult blacks, sixty percent were illiterate and fewer than fifty percent of black children under 14 went to school. Infant mortality ran at eighty deaths per thousand among Africans, compared with just seven among whites.

The Mandela era

Few people in recorded history have been the subject of such high expectations; still fewer have matched them; Mandela has exceeded them. We knew of his fortitude before he left jail; we have since experienced his extraordinary reserves of goodwill, his sense of fun and the depth of his maturity. As others' prisoner, he very nearly decided the date of his own release; as president, he has wisely chosen the moment of his going. Any other nation would consider itself privileged to have his equal as its leader. His last full year in power provides us with an occasion again to consider his achievement in bringing and holding our fractious land together.

Mail & Guardian, December 24, 1998

South Africa's first five years of democracy are inextricably linked to the towering figure of **Nelson Mandela**. On the one hand, he had to temper the impatience of a black majority that, having finally achieved civil rights, found it hard to understand why economic advancement wasn't following quickly. And on the other, he had to mollify the many fearful whites. The achievements of the government, however, were more uneven than those of its leader.

The overriding theme of the Mandela presidency was that of **reconciliation**. Perhaps the highlight of this policy was in May and June 1995, when the rugby union World Cup was staged in South Africa. **The Springboks**, for many years international pariahs due to their whites-only membership, won, watched by Mandela, sporting Springbok colours – events portrayed in Clint Eastwood's 2009 film *Invictus* (based on a book by John Carlin).

1989	1990	1994	1999
Botha suffers stroke and is replaced by F.W. De Klerk, who unbans ANC	Mandela walks to freedom	Mandela votes in election for first time and becomes president when ANC wins	Thabo Mbeki succeeds Mandela

THE TRUTH AND RECONCILIATION COMMISSION

As you type, you don't know you are crying until you feel and see the tears on your hands.

Chief typist of the transcripts of the TRC hearings
as told to Archbishop Tutu

By the time South Africa achieved **democracy** in 1994, it was internationally accepted that apartheid was, in the words of a UN resolution, "a crime against humanity", and that atrocities had been committed in its name. But no one could have imagined how systematic and horrific these atrocities had been. This emerged at the hearings of the **Truth and Reconciliation Commission** (TRC), set up to investigate gross abuses of human rights under apartheid. Under the chairmanship of Nobel Peace laureate, Archbishop Desmond Tutu, the commission examined acts committed between March 1960, the date of the Sharpeville massacre, and May 10, 1994, the day of Mandela's inauguration as president.

Evidence was heard from victims and perpetrators under a provision that amnesty would be given in exchange for "full disclosure of all the relevant facts". Unsurprisingly, the commission found that "the South African government was the primary perpetrator of gross human rights abuses in South Africa". It confirmed that from the 1970s to the 1990s the state had been involved in criminal activities including "extra-judicial killings of political opponents". Among the violations it listed were torture, abduction, sexual abuse, incursions across South Africa's borders to kill opponents in exile, and the deployment of hit squads. It also found that the ANC (and a number of other organizations, including the PAC and Inkatha) was guilty of human-rights violations.

There was considerable criticism of the TRC from all quarters. Many felt that justice would have been better served by a Nuremberg-style trial of those guilty of gross violations, but Tutu argued that this would have been impossible in South Africa, given that neither side had won a military victory.

The most significant sideshow of the period was the **Truth and Reconciliation Commission**, set up to examine gross human rights abuses in South Africa between 1960 and 1993 (see box above).

The **New Constitution**, approved in May 1996, ensured that South Africa would remain a parliamentary democracy with an executive president. One of the most progressive constitutions in the world, it incorporated an extensive bill of rights.

Despite the victory of liberal democratic principles, South Africa still displayed a singular lack of the trappings associated with civil society. Crime, sensationalized daily in the media, continued to dog the country. In the closing stages of the ANC's first five years, the police were reporting an average of 52 murders a day, a rape every half hour (including a frightening rise in child rape), and one car theft every nine minutes.

Mr Delivery doesn't

In 1999 **Thabo Mbeki** succeeded Mandela as president of South Africa. A hopeful media dubbed Mbeki "Mr Delivery", believing that this clever, well-educated technocrat would confront poverty and build schools, hospitals and houses – and at the same time create badly needed jobs. Mbeki's business-friendly policies produced healthy **economic growth**, expanded the black middle class and created a small coterie

2003	2007	2009	2010
J.M. Coetzee wins Nobel Prize for Literature	Mbeki replaced as president by Jacob Zuma, at the time facing bribery and racketeering charges	Charges against Zuma dropped on eve of general election; ANC wins by landslide	SA stages successful football World Cup and unleashes vuvuzela on unsuspecting planet

of mega-rich black entrepreneurs. But it did little for the poor fifty percent of the population, and the gulf of inequality became wider than ever.

The poor also bore the brunt of Mbeki's misguided policies on **AIDS**. Holding the view that there was no link between HIV and AIDS, he blocked the provision of **anti-retrovirals** in state hospitals, which contributed to over five million deaths from AIDS-related illnesses and left a million children orphaned.

And like the virus, **corruption** seemed to be infecting society, the most far-reaching example being the arms deal, in which the ANC government bought military equipment that South Africa's own defence force deemed unsuitable and too expensive. Newspapers alleged that the defence minister at the time was bribed and that a massive donation was paid to the ANC.

While money was squandered on arms, a raft of **social problems** festered. At the beginning of 2007, eight years after Mbeki assumed power, eight million people were living in shacks, millions had no water-borne sewerage and unemployment was running at forty percent. Disquiet at the slow pace of change was growing, and **protests** erupted on the streets of the townships. In 2005 alone, there were six thousand protests, and at the end of 2007 Mbeki was unseated by his party.

His replacement was the controversial former deputy president, **Jacob Zuma**, who was facing charges of bribery, fraud, racketeering, money laundering and tax evasion. A supreme populist, he portrayed himself as the people's president fighting off a conspiracy by an Mbeki-led elite. Miraculously, just two weeks before the April 2009 elections, top-secret recordings surfaced, purporting to prove that former president Mbeki had interfered in the Zuma case and charges against Zuma were dropped.

As expected, the Zuma-led ANC **won by a landslide**, while the Democratic Alliance (DA), the official opposition, increased its proportion of the vote. Support for the two main parties split down broadly racial lines, with the ANC getting most of its support from Africans and the DA from whites and coloureds. Given the ANC's overwhelming dominance of South African politics, it perhaps comes as no surprise that South Africa's most significant post-Mandela politics has taken place away from parliament – inside the ANC itself or on the streets.

After the vuvuzelas

For a brief period during 2010, South Africans united in a fever of vuvuzela-blowing euphoria, during the highly successful staging of the **Fifa World Cup**. But there was a return to politics as usual once the visitors had left and the country had returned to work – or not, as in the case of a million public sector workers who staged a three-week strike in August over pay increases and housing allowances. Trade union leader **Zwelinzima Vavi** attacked the ANC for leading South Africa on the path to becoming "a predator state" in which an "elite of political hyenas increasingly controls the state as a vehicle for accumulation".

Vavi's views represented the feelings of millions of South Africa's poor and dispossessed, who, nearly two decades after winning democracy, were still waiting for its economic fruits to be delivered. During Zuma's first two years of tenure, frustration with the ruling party accelerated. There were twice as many service-delivery protests in just 2009 and 2010 than there had been in the previous five Mbeki years.

2011	2012	2013
South Africa joins BRIC (Brazil, Russia, India and China), club of the most important developing nations.	Forty-four striking miners are shot in the back by police in the Marikana Massacre	South Africa and the world mourn the passing of Nelson Mandela – and of an era

By 2011, forty percent of South Africa's municipalities had been hit by popular street protests and there were attacks on Zuma from inside his own party. ANC Youth League leader **Julius Malema**, who had helped replace Mbeki with Zuma, now viciously attacked the president as being "worse than Mbeki", leading to Malema's expulsion from the ANC and his formation of a new populist party the **Economic Freedom Fighters** (EFF).

Meanwhile dissatisfaction festered in the platinum mines, with workers staging a **wildcat strike** at the Marikana mine in 2012. In an echo of the 1960 Sharpeville massacre (see p.645), one of apartheid's darkest hours, police fired on and killed 44 strikers at Marikana and wounded many more. Most of those killed in the **Marikana Massacre** were shot in the back – just as they had been at Sharpeville – delivering massive political capital to Julius Malema, who made a point of appearing at Marikana and proffering his support to the miners following the bloodshed. Malema traded on his purported working-class credentials all the way to the 2014 general election.

While mineworkers were dying in the cause of decent living conditions and millions of citizens were struggling to make ends meet, President Zuma was using taxpayers' money – over R200m of it – to refurbish his private residence at **Nkandla** in rural KwaZulu-Natal. With **Nelson Mandela's death** on 5 December 2013, the nation – and the world – mourned, not just because it had lost one of the country's greatest statesmen, but also because his passing symbolized the passing of an idealistic era that had promised a new dawn for South Africa. When President Zuma took the podium during the ten-day state memorial service, he was booed by sections of the crowd, in reaction to the dark clouds of corruption hanging over him.

These clouds proved to have a silver lining, however, when South Africa's political system demonstrated an encouraging robustness. The **Nkandla scandal** was widely reported by the independent media, and, perhaps more importantly, it was referred to the office of the Public Protector, a constitutional watchdog that protects citizens against abuses of state power. Despite official attempts to derail her investigations, the fiercely courageous Public Protector, **Thuli Madonsela** delivered a measured report in 2014, in which she found, among other things, serious flaws in the tendering process for the upgrade of Zuma's home and numerous violations of the government's ethics code. She ordered Zuma to pay back millions of rands.

Strangely, the Nkandla scandal did little to dent the ANC's performance in the **2014 general election**. Despite losing some support, much of it to Julius Malema's EFF which won 25 seats, the ANC still managed to win the poll by a very healthy 62 percent majority. Jacob Zuma's own future, however, is looking less secure. Many in the party believe that the ANC needs to be more responsive to the country's workers and the disenchanted dispossessed, and a number of commentators think that Zuma is becoming a liability to his party. It's looking increasingly likely that he may quietly – or, if needs be, not so quietly – be shown the door before the next election.

2014	**2014**	**2014**
Public Protector orders President Zuma to repay some of the R200m of taxpayers' money spent on upgrading his private residence	ANC wins general election by landslide	Nobel Prize-winning author Nadine Gordimer dies, aged 90

Music

Music from South Africa has a deserved following. The country has some of Africa's most diverse recorded music and its music industry is among the continent's most developed. It doesn't take much effort for an interested listener to encounter anything from indigenous African sounds that have remained largely unchanged for the last two hundred years, to the latest Afropop as well as a variety of white pop styles that would not be out of place anywhere in the Western world.

Gospel

Choral harmony and melody are perhaps black South Africa's greatest musical gifts to the world, and nowhere are they better manifested than in its **churches**. In the mainstream Catholic, Anglican and Methodist denominations a tradition of choral singing has evolved that has taken the style of European classical composers and loosened it up, added rhythm and, as always, some great dance routines.

In the Pentecostal churches, the music is more American-influenced, yet the harmonies and melodies remain uniquely South African and intensely moving. Pentecostal gospel music is the main recorded style; look out for groups like **Lord Comforters**, **Joyous Celebration**, **Pure Magic**, **Lusanda Spiritual Group** and the powerful **Rebecca Malope** (see box below).

Kwaito and hip-hop

South Africa's definitive youth sound, **kwaito**, has been around for about two decades. DJs importing dance music in the early 1990s, so the story goes, found white clubs unresponsive to Chicago house. DJs found that black clubbers preferred the records slowed down from 45 to 33rpm.

In an accurate reflection of the depressed and nihilistic mood of township youth culture, *kwaito*'s vibe tends to be downbeat, and the music frequently carries a strong association with gangsterism and explicit sexuality.

Some artists worth looking out for include **Tokollo** (ex-TKZee), **Mzekezeke**, **Kabelo**, the hard-rock-influenced **Mandoza**, and the matchstick-chewing, gangster-styled **Zola**. **Kalawa Jazmee**, a record label run by Oscar Mdlongwa, aka **DJ Oskido**, has been responsible for several successful *kwaito* groups including **Trompies**, **Bongo Maffin** and the self-consciously retro **Mafikizolo**.

REBECCA MALOPE

Diminutive **Rebecca Malope** is South Africa's biggest-selling music star, enjoying years at the top of the **gospel scene**, with only stadia able to hold her fans, every album going gold or platinum, popular magazines full of her photos, views and story, and everyone knowing the lyrics of her songs. Well, nearly everyone that is, for Rebecca Malope is virtually unknown outside Africa.

The daughter of a Sotho father and Swazi mother, Rebecca was born in Nelspruit, Mpumalanga, in 1969, and soon began singing in the local Assemblies of God church, where her grandfather was a pastor. Her initial recordings were mostly forgettable bubblegum pop. She was spotted in Jo'burg by **Sizwe Zako**, who became her lynchpin keyboard player. Under his tutelage and, so she says, because of letters from fans pleading that she sing God's songs, Rebecca returned to gospel in 1990, where she has been amply rewarded.

Rebecca's musical formula, engineered by Zako, who also produces, rarely varies. The songs are anthems characterized by swirling keyboards and excellent backing singers, and are delivered in her tremendous, soaring and sometimes husky voice, accompanied by dramatic gestures.

BRENDA FASSIE

Kwaito killed the careers of many of the 1980s pop stars, but the late **Brenda Fassie** managed not only to survive the new music, but to thrive on it. Brenda was South Africa's true pop queen and the one local artist whose music is still pretty much guaranteed to get things going on the dancefloor, wherever you are in the country.

Brenda began her career in the early 1980s as the lead singer for **Brenda and the Big Dudes**, enjoying a string of bubblegum hits, including the classic "Weekend Special", which for years was a South African disco anthem. Her sound mixed *kwaito*, *mbaqanga*, gospel and her own extraordinary persona, earning massive and deserved success.

During the 1990s, while some contemporaries produced comfortable material aimed more at middle-class and middle-aged audiences, Brenda made a point of hanging out with the youth in Soweto and in Hillbrow, Johannesburg's fastest-paced inner-city patch. The result was a lesbian affair that thrilled the tabloids, a bad crack habit, a tendency to lose the plot completely on stage – and the best music she had ever produced.

Tragically, her many demons eventually caught up with her, and after falling into a two-week-long coma, which even saw President Thabo Mbeki coming to her hospital bedside, she died in 2004. Her funeral was a massive media event that witnessed an outpouring of grief exceeding that attending the deaths of most "struggle" veterans.

Local hip-hop artists are more likely than their *kwaito* counterparts to use English, and tend to come from middle-class backgrounds instead of the townships – as a result of which they can afford to spend more on production. Among the notable hip-hopsters are **Skwatta Kamp**, **Optical Illusion**, **Cashless Society**, **Zubz**, **Lions of Zion** (who, as their name suggests, blend hip-hop and reggae), comedian and rapper **Ifani**, and **Pro** who is rated for the creativity of his lyrics.

House, rap and reggae

DJ-mixed South African **house** attracts practitioners and fans from all parts of the country's racial and cultural divisions, but it is black DJs such as **DJ Fresh**, **DJ Ready D**, **Glen Lewis**, **DJ Mbuso**, **Thibo Tazz**, **DJ Fosta** and **Oskido** who for years have been garnering attention from the local media. The recordings they mix with are almost exclusively from either the UK or France, while **Pex Africa** is renowned for his use of traditional African sounds.

South African **rap** has enjoyed sustained popularity since the early 1990s, but has remained almost completely ghettoized within the coloured community of the Western Cape. Heavily influenced by African American rappers, the performers often exude a palpable sense of being "Americans trapped in Africa". Pioneers of the style were the heavily politicized **Prophets of Da City**, several members of which made names for themselves as solo artists after the group's break-up, most notably **Rahim**, **Junior Solela** and **Ishmael**. Other performers who have since come up are **Brasse Van Die Kaap** (who rap in Afrikaans), **Reddy D** and **Godessa**, while Cape Town-based record and production company, African Dope, has enjoyed success with **Teba**, **Funny Carp** and crossover jazz–Latin–hip-hop–funksters **Moodphase5ive**, among others.

What is unusual as regards the place of **Lucky Dube** (who died tragically in 2007 in a hijacking) in the local **reggae** scene is the total lack of successful emulators. An energetic, disciplined and talented live performer, Dube could also deliver a falsetto like Smokey Robinson's, which added a distinct twist to his otherwise familiar roots reggae sound.

Neo-traditional music

As with *kwaito*, the instrumentation in **neo-traditional music** is really just a backdrop to the lyrics and the dance routines. One of its major stars is the Shangaan singer **Thomas Chauke**, perhaps the single bestselling artist in any neo-traditional genre.

Hailing from Limpopo Province, he makes heavy use of a drum machine and an electronic keyboard and often picks out some intricate lead-guitar work to complement his vocals.

In Sotho neo-traditional music, the bass lines are good, the shouting is first class and the accordions can take on an almost Cajun tinge. **Tau Oa Matshela** and **Tau Oa Linare** are some of the groups to look out for.

Zulu neo-trad is pervasive, both in its a cappella form, known as *iscathamiya*, and as a vocal/guitar-based style called *maskanda*. For particularly fine examples of the art, look out for **Phuzekhemisi**, **Shiyani Ncgobo** and the late, great **Mfaz'Omnyama**. Another star of the neo-traditional scene is the queen of Ndebele music, **Nothembi Mkhwebane**. As well as being a talented and veteran performer, Nothembi, who sings and plays electric guitar, is also known for her sensational outfits, decorated with typically intricate Ndebele bead and metalwork.

Jazz

Jazz has been widely popular in South Africa for decades, and you can almost always find performances in Johannesburg, Pretoria or Cape Town on virtually any weekend, and sometimes midweek too. It was **South African jazz** that was the music most associated with the struggle against apartheid, especially after the music's main exponents went into self-imposed exile in the 1960s.

Jazz's roots in the country are much older than this, harking back to the emergence of *marabi* music in Johannesburg's African slums some time after World War I. During World War II, American swing became popular and fused with *marabi* into a new style usually referred to as African jazz. This remained predominant throughout the 1940s and 1950s, and produced the first South African musical exiles in vocalists **Miriam Makeba** and the **Manhattan Brothers**.

The next development was a move in the direction of the American avant-garde, the two early, prime exponents of this in South Africa being the **Jazz Epistles** and the **Blue Notes**. Legislation prohibiting mixed-race public performances caused most of the Epistles to individually leave South Africa in the early 1960s, while the Blue Notes departed en masse in 1964. Some exiled South African jazzers detached themselves from their roots, while others such as **Hugh Masekela** reinterpreted their township

LADYSMITH BLACK MAMBAZO AND THE ISCATHAMIYA SOUND

The best known of South Africa's many neo-traditional musical genres is Zulu *iscathamiya* (or *mbube*), the distinctive male a cappella choral style made internationally famous by **Ladysmith Black Mambazo**. The style originated among Zulu rural migrants in urban hostels following World War I, and by 1939 the first commercial hit, "Mbube" by Solomon Linda and His Original Evening Birds, had been recorded, eventually selling over 100,000 copies. The song was later reworked as "The Lion Sleeps Tonight", which became a number one hit in both the US and UK.

In 1973, after recording for the SABC for several years, Ladysmith Black Mambazo made their first commercial release, *Amabutho*, for the Gallo label. It quickly sold over 25,000 copies (gold-disc status in South Africa), and since that time the group has recorded over fifty others, most of which have also gone gold. Following their collaboration with him on *Graceland*, Paul Simon produced their *Shaka* Zulu album, which sold 100,000 copies around the world and took *iscathamiya* to the international stage. In 1997, Ladysmith Black Mambazo extended its Afropop credentials with *Heavenly*, an album that featured collaborations with, among other international artists, Dolly Parton. Following the exposure of their song "Inkanyezi Nezazi" in a British TV advertisement for Heinz baked beans, the group went on to sell over a million units in the UK, an all-time record for a South African act. In 2013 they won their fourth Grammy Award, this time in the best world music category, for their album *Live: Singing for Peace Around the World*.

influences. Back home, old-style African jazz as performed by the **Elite Swingsters** and **Ntemi Piliso's Alexandra All Stars** remained popular.

In the 1970s and 1980s, various South African strains were fused with funk, soul and rock influences to produce a more accessible, populist brand of jazz, from bands such as **Sakile**, **The Drive** and the **Jazz Ministers**. Following the end of apartheid, the surviving exiles began to trickle back and a new, younger generation of jazz musicians yet again married old local traditions with contemporary international trends.

Post-apartheid, a large group of new jazz names emerged that includes vocalists (**Gloria Bosman**, **Judith Sephuma**, **Sibongile Kumalo**), saxophonists (**McCoy Mrubata**, **Zim Ngqawana**), keyboard players (**Paul Hamner**, **Themba Mkhize**), guitarists (**Jimmy Dludlu**, **Selaelo Selota**) and the odd trumpeter (**Prince Lengoasa**, **Marcus Wyatt**). Although many of the stars of this new generation emulate the smooth style of the Earl Klugh school, there are others whose tastes are considerably more muscular. Three artists that have come to the fore over the last decade or so are the talented Eastern Cape singer **Simphiwe Dana**, who fuses jazz, soul and traditional music, pianist **Bokani Dyer**, and vocalist **Tutu Puoane**.

Afropop

Afropop is a catch-all category, yet it's arguably where many contemporary South African artists sit most comfortably. Afropop is characterized by a knack for combining local African styles with Western popular influences, the ability to attract a multiracial audience, and the eschewing of computer-generated backing in favour of actual instruments.

Afropop goes back to Miriam Makeba's first American recordings in the early 1960s. More contemporary examples would include Paul Simon's 1987 *Graceland*, a collaboration with Ladysmith Black Mambazo and other local African artists; and the music of **Juluka** and **Savuka**, two bands led in the 1980s and 1990s by Johnny Clegg, whose melding of mainstream pop harmonies with Zulu dance routines and a touch of *mbaqanga* gained great popularity both in South Africa and in France. The music of bubblegum-pop queen **Yvonne Chaka Chaka** from the 1980s and 1990s could also be deemed Afropop. Artists who have subsequently adopted similar formulas include **Jabu Khanyile**, **Vusi Mahlasela**, **Ringo** and **Busi Mhlongo**.

The most successful proponents of the style are Cape Town-based **Freshlyground**, who, because of their broad appeal and engaging sound, were chosen to accompany Shakira in jamming to a billion viewers at the opening and closing ceremonies of the **2010 Fifa World Cup**. The group are still going strong, with plenty of live performances – their bedrock – and an album *The Legend* released in 2013.

White pop and rock

English-speaking South Africans have successfully replicated virtually every popular Western musical style going, and some have found fame in the outside world. Among the first and most famous of these are the alternative rockers the **Springbok Nude Girls**, who performed as the opening act for U2 during their 2011 tour of South Africa. Many local artists, such as **Manfred Mann** in the 1960s and more recently **Dave Matthews**, **Seether**, **Just Jinger** and **Wonderboom**, are known internationally, but there are many other gifted performers who have remained in South Africa. These include **Goldfish**, the **Parlotones**, string-maestro **Steve Newman** and **Tananas**, a string trio Newman plays with for a couple of months each year. A new Cape Town talent worth catching is folk singer **Jeremy Loops**, who reached number in the South African iTunes chart in 2014 with his artistry on loop pedal, guitar, harmonica and beatbox.

Like South African jazz, **Afrikaans music** is another world unto itself, with a multitude of sub-categories and a long list of heroes and heroines. From the late 1920s until the 1960s American country was its greatest outside influence, but by the early 1970s it looked to the

ENTER DIE ANTWOORD

Die Antwoord (meaning "the answer") was an overnight sensation – an unknown crew from Cape Town that stormed the internet. Rapping in lowlife Cape Flats slang known as *zef*, they represented the voice of the Mother City's mean streets. That was the story, at least.

Their success was real enough: in February 2010, internet traffic to their website (Ⓦ dieantwoord.com), which was streaming their debut album *o*, was so heavy (fifteen million hits) that it crashed. Their signature foul-mouthed lyrics aside, there's nothing crude about their artistry. If you aren't convinced, note the tight machine-gun vocals (likened by *Rolling Stone* to "Eminem's 'Lose Yourself' on mescaline"), the slick art direction, the careful choreography and the cool Keith Haring-esque graphics on their video *Enter the Ninja*. The second and third albums, *Ten$Ion* and *Donker Mag* were released on their own label, Zef Recordz, which they founded in 2011.

Far from being the band that came in from the Flats, Die Antwoord (frontman Ninja, helium-voiced Yo-landi Vi$$er and DJ Hi-Tek) is the latest surreal vehicle for Waddy Tudor Jones (Ninja), whose previous excursions included hip-hop rig Max Normal and the Constructus Corporation. Jones's history of taking on personas has led detractors to grumble that Die Antwoord "aren't real", while fans declare him a creative genius. Does it matter? The fact is, Die Antwoord deliver an unmistakably Cape Town sound that cooks.

lighter end of foreign pop and in particular Eurodisco. A long line of bouncy Afrikaans pop stars ensued, while a more sober side was represented by the light operatic style of Gé Korsten, probably the single most popular Afrikaans artist of the period.

Following the end of apartheid, a general concern about the future of the Afrikaans language and culture spurred a revival of interest in Afrikaans music. There is undoubtedly more stylistic variety now than ever before: witness the house/disco of **Juanita**, the heavy rock of **Karen Zoid** and **Jackhammer**, the modernized *boeremusiek* of the **Klipwerf Orkes**, and the Neil Diamond-esque songs of **Steve Hofmeyer** (the bestselling Afrikaans music artist). More recent sounds are the punk-rock riffs of **Fokofpolisiekar** and the studied banality of rapper **Jack Parow**.

New wave dance and electronica

Like Afropop, **new wave dance and electronica** is a catch-all phrase, in this case to describe a menagerie of sounds unleashed on South Africa's dancefloors over the past decade, and which began making their mark after 2010 in clubs in the US, Britain and the rest of Europe. Local musicians such as **Spoek Mathambo**, **DJ Mujava**, **Culoe De Song**, **Markus Wormstorm** and **Sibot** have been pumping out their blend of local sounds at the world's nightspots – and getting signed up by international labels.

Although global in flavour, the sounds are still distinctly South African, incorporating afro-beat, *kwaito*, *mbaqanga* and anything else that's to hand. Most successful at riding the new wave so far are foul-mouthed zef-rappers **Die Antwoord** (see box above).

Discography

In the reviews below, items marked with an asterisk are international releases. Other items are South African releases, issued either by local labels or by the South African operations of international labels.

CROSS-GENRE COMPILATIONS

Various Artists *The Rough Guide to the Music of South Africa* (World Music Network*). Excellent cross section of sounds combining big names with some interesting less-known musicians.

Various Artists *Mzansi Music: Young Urban South Africa* (Trikont*). Fifteen-track collection that captures the city beat of Mzansi's (South Africa's) youth.

Various Artists *Putumayo Presents: South Africa* (Trikont*). An interesting cross section that unlike the other two compilations doesn't restrict itself to black music.

MBAQANGA

Mahlathini and the Mahotella Queens *The Best of Mahlathini and the Mahotella Queens* (Gallo). Perfect introduction to the sound of this most stomping of *mbaqanga* outfits.

Soul Brothers *Igobondela*, *The Best of The Soul Brothers* and *The Early Years* (Gallo). If *The Best of* whets your appetite, investigate *The Early Years*, a series comprising the classic first twelve albums, recorded in the 1970s and early 1980s, while *Thul' Ubheke* (2010) showcases them relaxed and at the top of their game.

Various Artists *From Marabi to Disco* (Gallo). A mini-encyclopedia of the development of township musical style from the late 1930s to the early 1980s.

Various Artists *The Indestructible Beat of Soweto Volumes 1–6* (Earthworks*). Superb compilation, mainly featuring 1980s *mbaqanga*.

GOSPEL

Imvuselelo Yase Natali *Izigi* (BMG). One of the most extraordinary gospel acts in South Africa, fronted by the charismatic – and at times plain bizarre – Reverend Makitaza.

IPCC *Ummeli Wethu* (Gallo). An excellent offering from one of South Africa's most popular gospel choirs.

Lusanda Spiritual Group *Abanye Bayawela* (Gallo). The biggest-selling album from a gospel music sensation.

Pure Magic *Greatest Hits* (EMI). Simply wonderful melodic gospel-pop, featuring the silky lead vocals of Vuyo Mokoena.

Rebecca Malope *Shwele Baba* (CCP). One of Rebecca's finest albums, with the title track a strong contender for her best-ever song.

Solly Moholo *Abanye Bayawela Motlhang ke Kolobetswa "Die poppe sal dans"* (CCP). A beautiful release from the country's finest Sotho gospel artist.

Various *Joyous Celebration* (Sony, SA). Umpteen albums and still proliferating (they'd hit volume 18 by 2014) of classic gospel.

Various Artists *Choirs of South Africa* (Roi Music). Stirring gospel anthems delivered by mass choirs with exuberance and power.

Various Artists *Rough Guide to South African Gospel* (Rough Guides*). A comprehensive survey of South African gospel going back to the 1950s.

KWAITO AND HIP-HOP

Bongo Maffin *Bongolution* (Sony Music). A fine release from a popular group which combines Jamaican-style ragga lyrics with *kwaito* beats.

Brenda Fassie *African Princess of Pop* and *Memeza* (CCP). The former is a posthumous survey covering the entire career of South Africa's very own Madonna; the latter, featuring the massive hit "Vul'Ndlela", was Brenda's most commercially successful effort.

H20 *Amanzi'mtoti* (Outrageous Records). Debut album that launched hip-hop duo Siphiwe Norten and Menzi Dludla into Africa.

Kabelo *And the Beat Goes On* (Universal). A monster hit from one of the biggest *kwaito* stars.

Mafikizolo *Sibongile* (Sony Music). Solid melodies, well sung and harmonized (the trio's female vocalist, Sibongile Nkosi, is outstanding).

Makhendlas *Jammer* (CCP). Features two massive hits, "Emenwe" and "Ayeye Aho", from the brother of *kwaito* pioneer Arthur. Makhendlas tragically shot himself after killing a troublesome fan after a gig in 1998.

Malaika *Malaika* (Sony Music). Hugely successful, this is very much in the style pioneered by Mafikizolo but features even more contemporary African-American influences.

Mandoza *Nakalakala* (CCP). Not only was this album massively popular with African urban youth, the title track has been one of very few *kwaito* recordings to truly cross over into the white pop arena.

M'Du *No Pas No Special* (Sony Music). A popular though somewhat downbeat album from one of *kwaito*'s most enduring stars.

Skwatta Kamp *Khut En Joyn* (Nkuli). A fairly relentless first offering from the *enfants terribles* of the local hip-hop scene.

TKZee *Halloween* (BMG). Complete with trademark catchy anthems and R&B-based sounds, this is a solid early (1998) offering from these popular *kwaito* artists.

Trompies *Boostin' Kabelz* (Sony Music). Kicking sounds from one of the coolest *kwaito* acts on the circuit.

Various Artists *Cape of Good Dope Volumes 1 & 2* (African Dope Records). Eclectic mix showcasing the label's artists, including Lions of Zion, Godessa, Moodphase5ive and Max Normal (an earlier incarnation of Die Antwoord's Ninja).

Various Artists *Yizo Yizo Volumes 1–3* (CCP). The soundtrack to South Africa's hippest TV drama, with cuts from virtually every major *kwaito* artist.

Zola *Mdlwembe* (EMI). The first solo album of "Mr Ghetto Fabulous", full of menacing rhythms.

RAP AND REGGAE

Lucky Dube *Prisoner* (Gallo). Dube's reggae album *Prisoner* was at one time South Africa's second bestselling album ever, full of stirring Peter Tosh-style roots tunes.

Prophets of Da City *Ghetto Code* (Universal). South Africa's rap supremos' finest release, full of tough but articulate rhymes and some seriously funky backing tracks, all in true Cape Flats style.

NEO-TRADITIONAL

Amampondo *Drums for Tomorrow* (Melt 2000). South Africa's most famous marimba band deliver a fine and well-produced set here, full of their distinctive Xhosa melodies and powerful polyrhythms.

Ladysmith Black Mambazo *Favourites* (Gallo). A fine greatest hits selection from the group's first decade in the 1970s and early 1980s. *Congratulations South Africa: The Ultimate Collection* (Wrasse*). This double CD is a mixed bag of Afropop and 1990s *iscathamiya*, including "Inkanyezi Nezazi", which gained the group plenty of new fans after being used in a Heinz baked-beans advert.

Mfaz'Omnyama *Ngisebenzile Mama* (Gallo). The title means "I have been working, Mum", and is amply justified by this superb set, featuring some of the best *maskanda* ever recorded.

Nothembi Mkhwebane *Akanamandl' Usathana* (Gallo). Beautiful guitar-driven sounds from the Ndebele music queen, with a cover showing Nothembi in one of her impressive traditional outfits.

Phuzekhemisi *Ngo 49* (Gallo). Every album recorded by this reigning *maskanda* champion features stunning guitar work, great vocals and murderous bass lines.

Ringo *Sondelani* (CCP). A superb modern reworking of traditional Xhosa sounds by this bald Capetonian heart-throb, including the hit track "Sondela", which has become one of South Africa's most popular love songs.

Shiyani Ncgobo *Introducing* (Sheer Sound). Fine *maskanda* album aimed at a foreign audience, and thus with far more variety than a domestic offering would feature.

Women of Mambazo *Mamizolo* (Gallo). Beautiful *iscathamiya* melodies and harmonizations, not rendered by the usual male line-up but by a female group led by Nellie Shabalala, the late wife of Ladysmith Black Mambazo leader Joseph Shabalala.

JAZZ

Abdullah Ibrahim *African Marketplace* (Discovery/WEA). Ibrahim's best album – a wistful, nostalgic, other-worldly journey.

Gloria Bosman *Tranquillity* (Sheer/Limelight*). A young and compelling jazz vocalist, Bosman juggles African and American styles with consummate ease.

Hugh Masekela *Still Grazing* (Universal) and *Black to the Future* (Sony Music). *Still Grazing* is the best available compilation of Masekela's work in the 1960s and 1970s. In the late 1990s Masekela scored a deserved hit with *Black to the Future*.

Jimmy Dludlu *Essence of Rhythm* (Universal). Dludlu is the essence of smooth jazz, and is arguably the single most popular representative of what is in turn the most commercially successful jazz style in South Africa today.

Manhattan Brothers *The Very Best of The Manhattan Brothers* (Sterns*). Classic recordings cut between 1948 and 1959 by this seminal vocal quartet, who crossed African-American secular harmonies with indigenous influences.

Miriam Makeba and the Skylarks *Miriam Makeba and the Skylarks* (Teal) and *Welela* (Universal*). *Welela*, from 1989, is probably the finest album by Makeba, who died in 2008 – great songs, wonderfully performed.

Moses Taiwa Molelekwa *Genes and Spirits* (Melt 2000).

Fascinating jazz/drum 'n' bass fusion by a talented young pianist, who died tragically in 2001.

Paul Hanmer *Trains to Taung* (Sheer Sound). Constructed around Hanmer's dreamy, acoustic piano-based compositions, this album is now considered a classic.

Robbie Jansen *Nomad Jez* (EMI). Great, if slightly flawed, album from veteran saxophonist Jansen, playing with other luminaries of the local jazz scene.

Sakile *Sakile* (Sony Music). A prime example of the jazz fusion popular in the 1980s, Sakile spawned two major figures in saxophonist Khaya Mahlangu and bass player Sipho Gumede.

Sibongile Khumalo *Ancient Evenings* (Sony Music). Classically trained opera singer, Khumalo takes on jazz and a variety of traditional melodies on this wonderful album.

Various Artists *African Connection Parts I–IV* (Sheer Sound). This series of double-CD compilations from the country's premier independent label provides an accessible survey of South African jazz up to 2004.

Winston Mankunku *Crossroads* (Nkomo/Sheer). Sinuous, upbeat township jazz from the veteran Cape Town saxman.

Zim Ngqawana *Vadzimu* (Sheer Sound). Ngqawana is one of the most revered figures in local jazz, despite being the antithesis of the smooth style that currently dominates.

POLITICAL

Mzwakhe Mbuli *Resistance is Defence* (Earthworks*). Great sample of the militant lyricism of the people's poet, including a moving ode to Mandela's release.

Various Artists *South African Freedom Songs* (Making Music Productions). Superb double-CD set documenting the "struggle music" that helped power anti-apartheid resistance.

AFROPOP

Bayete *Umkhaya-Lo* (Polygram). A seminal fusion of South African sounds with laidback soul and funk, spiced with beautifully soothing vocals.

Busi Mhlongo *Urbanzulu* (Melt 2000). An immaculately and expensively produced Zulu *maskanda*-pop classic from this powerful jazz vocalist.

Freshlyground *Ma'Cheri* (Freeground Records/Sony BMG). Voted Album of the Year at the 2008 SA Music Awards, *Ma'Cheri* showcases the most enduring of South Africa's Afro-popsters.

Johnny Clegg *Best of Juluka/Savuka* (Universal). Born in England, the prolific Clegg mixes white pop harmonies and township rhythms, gaining him a multiracial following in South Africa.

Ladysmith Black Mambazo *Heavenly* (Gallo/Spectrum*). An inspired foray into Afropop, featuring solo versions of various pop classics as well as vocal collaborations with Dolly Parton and Lou Rawls.

Vusi Mahlasela *Silang Mabele* (BMG). Lush harmonies and melodies from this sweet-voiced township balladeer.

Yvonne Chaka Chaka *Bombani* (Teal) and *The Best of Yvonne Chaka Chaka* (Teal, SA). *Bombani* bombed, yet is Yvonne's most intricate and interesting release, mixing a range of traditional styles and featuring wonderful melodies. *The Best of* is pretty much all the 1980s disco-style Yvonne you need.

WHITE POP AND ROCK

Jeremy Loops *Trading Change* (Sheer Sound). Debut folk album, which shot to number one on the South Africa iTunes chart in 2014, trouncing international divas Toni Braxton and Shakira.

Just Jinger *All Comes Around* (BMG). Unexpectedly racking up sales of over 50,000 copies, this classic 1997 release demonstrated that local English rock was far from dead.

Mango Groove *The Best of Mango Groove* (Gallo). Mango Groove's mixture of white pop leavened with a touch of pennywhistle/township jive was briefly – from the late 1980s up to the dawn of democracy – the most commercially successful sound in South African music.

Springbok Nude Girls *Apes with Shade* (Sony Music). First album following their disbanding in 2007 and subsequent re-forming in 2011 from one of South Africa's most popular white rock bands.

Various Artists *The Best of SA Pop Vols 1–3* (Gallo). Three double CDs covering all the biggest radio hits of the local English pop scene from the 1960s through to the early 1980s.

AFRIKAANS

Anton Goosen *Bushrock* (Gallo). Goosen is one of South Africa's finest songwriters and performers. His style might best be described as Afrikaans folk rock. *Bushrock* is his one English-language album.

Fokofpolisiekar *Swanesang* (Rhythm Records/The Orchard). One of South Africa's most successful live bands has helped redefine Afrikaner identity for the post-apartheid generation with its punk-rock-influenced sound, while outraging the conservative establishment, starting with their name which translates as "fuck off police car".

Johannes Kerkorrel *Ge-Trans-To-Meer* (Gallo-Tusk). The late Kerkorrel was the leading light of the Afrikaans alternative scene of the 1990s, his brand of angst-laden pop also popular in Holland and Belgium.

Steve Hofmeyr *Toeka* (EMI). A smooth pop vocalist, Hofmeyr is the most commercially successful artist in Afrikaans music.

NEW WAVE DANCE AND ELECTRONICA

BLK JKS *Mystery* (Secretly Canadian*). Picked out by *Rolling Stone* magazine in 2009 as "artists to watch", the band (pronounced: "black jacks") went on to perform at the 2010 football World Cup kick-off. *Mystery* features their dizzying excursions across a succession of genres, from indie rock to psychedelia, tinged with traditional South African sounds.

Culoe De Song *We Baba* (Innervisions/!K7 Records*). Described as Deep House for grown-ups, the intoxicating title track of De Song's two-track EP takes its time to reach a lush climax, gradually piling on textures that include an electro beat, looped chanting and animal-like calls.

Die Antwoord *O* (Rhythm Records*). Signature album of the zef rave rap style that brought the trio to the world's attention, featuring their addictive – and plain weird – anthem track *Enter the Ninja*.

Felix Laband *Dark Days Exit* (Compost Records/GoodToGo*). Spacey folk-rock-tinged electronic tone poems spliced with old TV soundtracks as well as jazz and classical samples to generate chilled, minimalist mindscapes that justify repeated listening.

Goldfish *Perceptions of Pacha* (Pacha Recordings/Finetunes*). Cape Town-based jazz-boogie duo, who weave acoustic sounds into their predominantly electronica-based grooves to crank out one addictively upbeat track after another.

Spoek Mathambo *Mshini Wam* (BBE/!K7 Records*). Fascinating debut solo album from self-styled Afro-futurist, Mathambo, this multi-layered affair features a killer *kwaito* cover version of the Joy Division classic "She's Lost Control".

Various *Zoo City: The Soundtrack* (African Dope). Album issued to accompany the award-winning novel of the same name by Lauren Beukes (see p.663) showcases a number of the contemporary proponents of South African electronica in its attempt to evoke the gritty atmosphere of Joburg's Hillbrow.

With contributions by Rob Allingham

Books

For a country with a proportionately small reading and book-buying public, South Africa generates a substantial amount of literature, particularly on subjects the literate feel guilty about – namely, politics and history. Titles marked ★ are particularly recommended.

HISTORY, SOCIETY AND ANTHROPOLOGY

Ian Berry *Living Apart.* Superbly evocative and moving photographs spanning the 1950s to 1990s, which chart a compelling vision of the politics of the nation, but at the level of the individual.

Richard Calland *Anatomy of South Africa: Who Holds the Power?* An incisive dissection of politics and power in South Africa during the first decade of the twenty-first century, from one of the country's most respected commentators. In 2013, Calland wrote a sequel, *The Zuma Years*.

John Carlin *Playing the Enemy: Nelson Mandela and the Game that made a Nation.* Gripping account of Nelson Mandela's use of the 1995 rugby World Cup to unite a fractious nation in danger of collapsing into civil war. Also published as *Invictus*, the title of the Clint Eastwood film, which starred Matt Damon and Morgan Freeman.

Paul Faber *Group Portrait South Africa: Nine Family Histories.* Fascinating account revealing the complexities of South Africa past and present, through the histories of nine South African families of different races, backgrounds and aspirations. Includes photos and illustrations.

Andrew Feinstein *After the Party: Corruption, the ANC and South Africa's Uncertain Future.* A personal account of how South Africa's government has lost its way, by a former ANC member of parliament.

★ **Douglas Foster** *After Mandela: The Struggle for Freedom in Post-Apartheid South Africa.* Former editor of Mother Jones, Foster brings together political analysis and street level accounts based on interviews recorded over six years to create one of the past decade's most interesting and penetrating accounts of a country poised between liberation and decline.

Hermann Giliomee and Bernard Mbenga *A New History of South Africa.* A comprehensive, reliable and entertaining illustrated account of South Africa's history.

★ **Peter Harris** *In a Different Time: The Inside Story of the Delmas Four.* Brilliantly told true historical drama about four young South Africans sent on a mission by the ANC-in-exile, which ultimately led to Death Row. As their defence lawyer, Harris had unique and sympathetic insight into their personalities and motivations. Also published as *A Just Defiance: The Bombmakers, the Insurgents and a Legendary Treason Trial.*

★ **Antjie Krog** *Country of My Skull.* A deeply personal and gripping account of the hearings of the Truth and Reconciliation Commission. Krog, an Afrikaner former-SABC radio journalist and poet, reveals the complexity of horrors committed by apartheid.

★ **J.D. Lewis-Williams** *Discovering Southern African Rock Art* and *Images of Power: Understanding Bushman Rock Art.* Concise books written by an expert in the field, full of drawings and photos.

Hein Marais *Pushed to the Limit.* An assessment of why the privileged classes remain just that with a handful of conglomerates dominating the South African economy and how this relates to Jacob Zuma's rise to power.

★ **Noel Mostert** *Frontiers: The Epic of South Africa's Creation and the Tragedy of the Xhosa People.* An academically solid, brilliantly written history of the Xhosa of the Eastern Cape, and their tragic fate in the frontier wars against the British.

★ **Thomas Pakenham** *The Boer War.* The definitive liberal history of the Anglo-Boer War that reads grippingly like a novel.

Charlene Smith *Robben Island.* Comprehensive and well-written account of Robben Island from prehistoric times to the present, including coverage of its most notorious period – as a prison for opponents of apartheid.

Allister Sparks *First Drafts: South African History in the Making.* A marvellous cross section of incisive writings about South African politics and history during the first decade of the twenty-first century written as he saw it at the time without the benefit of hindsight, by one of the country's most eminent journalists.

Desmond Tutu *No Future Without Forgiveness.* The Truth and Reconciliation Commission as described by its chairman. There are better accounts of the hearings, but the book offers essential insight into one of South Africa's most unlikely heroes.

Frank Welsh *A History of South Africa.* Solid scholarship and a strong sense of overall narrative mark this publication as a much-needed addition to South African historiography.

Francis Wilson *Dinosaurs, Diamonds & Democracy: A Short, Short History of South Africa.* Brilliant and sweeping account that packs two billion years into 128 pages, making it the perfect bluffer's guide to South Africa's history.

★ **Nigel Worden, Elizabeth van Heyningen and Vivian Bickford-Smith** *Cape Town: The Making of a City.* The definitive and highly readable illustrated account of the social and political development of South Africa's first city from 1620 to 1899. A companion volume covers the twentieth century.

AUTOBIOGRAPHY AND BIOGRAPHY

J.M. Coetzee *Boyhood: Scenes from Provincial Life* and *Youth*. Two riveting and disquieting accounts of growing up in a provincial town, and the author subsequently finding his way in the world, both in South Africa and London. Coetzee won the 2003 Nobel prize for literature.

★**Mark Gevisser** *Portraits of Power: Profiles of a Changing South Africa*. Although now well over a decade old, this collection of forty mini-biographies cutting through a cross section of South African society still offers acute insights into a number of the country's significant players.

★**Sindiwe Magoma** *To My Children's Children*. A fascinating autobiography – initially started so that her family would never forget their roots – that traces Magoma's life from the rural Transkei to the hard townships of Cape Town, and from political innocence to wisdom born of bitter experience.

★**Nelson Mandela** *Long Walk to Freedom*. The superb bestselling autobiography of the former South African president. Mandela's generosity of spirit and tremendous understanding of the delicate balance between principle and tactics come through very strongly, and the book is wonderfully evocative of his early years and intensely moving about his long years in prison.

★**Benjamin Pogrund** *How Can Man Die Better? The Life of Robert Sobukwe*. The story of one of the most important anti-apartheid liberation heroes. The late leader of the Pan Africanist Congress and a contemporary of Nelson Mandela, Sobukwe was so feared by the white government that they passed a special law – The Sobukwe Clause – to keep him in solitary confinement on Robben Island after he'd served his sentence.

Anthony Sampson *Mandela, The Authorised Biography*. Released to coincide with Mandela's retirement from the presidency in 1999, Sampson's authoritative volume competes favourably with *Long Walk to Freedom*, offering a broader perspective and sharper analysis than the autobiography.

Chris van Wyk *Shirley, Goodness and Mercy: A Childhood Memoir*. A memoir of growing up in a working-class coloured family in Johannesburg during the apartheid era, with humorous and poignant touches.

THE ARTS

Marion Arnold *Women and Art in South Africa*. Comprehensive, pioneering study of women artists from the early twentieth century to the present.

David Coplan *In Township Tonight: South Africa's Black City Music and Theatre*. Classic, updated in 2008, that traces local music from its indigenous roots through slave orchestras and looks at its humanizing influence in the harsh environment of the townships.

Thorsten Deckler, Anne Graupner, Henning Rasmuss *Contemporary South African Architecture in a Landscape of Transition*. Lavishly illustrated coverage of fifty outstanding architectural projects completed since 1994, all of which, the authors say, display a sense of South African identity.

S. Francis and Rico *Madam and Eve*. Various volumes of witty cartoons conveying the daily struggle between an African domestic worker and her white madam in the northern suburbs of Johannesburg, these cartoons say more about post-apartheid society than countless academic tomes.

Steve Gordon *Beyond the Blues: Township Jazz of the Sixties and Seventies*. Portraits, in words and pictures, of the country's jazz greats such as Kippie Moeketsi, Basil Coetzee and Abdullah Ibrahim (Dollar Brand).

★**Andy Mason** *What's so Funny?: Under the Skin of South African Cartooning*. Insightful, fascinating and thoroughly collectable wade through the history of South African visual satire from the colonial period, through the apartheid years to the present.

Ralf-Peter Seippel *South African Photography: 1950–2010*. South Africa's history has provided a rich vein of material for photographers and this volume covers the work of some of the country's most celebrated lensmen, whose work is divided into three periods: apartheid, struggle and freedom.

Paul Weinberg *Then & Now*. Collection by eight photographers, tracing the changes in their subjects and approaches as South Africa moved from apartheid into the present democratic era.

Sue Williamson *South African Art Now*. A survey of South African art from the "Resistance Art" of the 1960s to the present, covering movements, genres and leading artists such as Marlene Dumas and William Kentridge, by one of the country's most influential commentators and an accomplished artist in her own right.

★**Zapiro** A series of annual cartoon collections by South Africa's leading, and always excellent, political cartoonist. In a country where satire is in notoriously short supply, Zapiro consistently reveals what needs to be exposed (ⓦzapiro.com).

TRAVEL WRITING

Richard Dobson *Karoo Moons: A Photographic Journey*. If you need encouragement to explore the desert interior of South Africa, these enticing images should do the trick.

★**Sihle Khumalo** *Dark Continent, My Black Arse*. Insightful and witty account by a black South African who quit his well-paid job to realize a dream of travelling from the Cape to Cairo by public transport.

Julia Martin *A Millimetre of Dust: Visiting Ancestral Sites*.

Sensitively crafted narrative that begins on the Cape Peninsula and takes the author, her husband and two children on a journey to important archeological sites in the Northern Cape, raising ethical, ecological and philosophical questions along the way.

Dervla Murphy *South from the Limpopo: Travels Through South Africa*. A fascinating and intrepid journey

– by bicycle – through the new South Africa. The author isn't afraid to explore the complexities and paradoxes of this country.

Paul Theroux *Dark Star Safari*. Theroux's powerful account of his overland trip from Cairo to Cape Town, with a couple of chapters on South Africa, including an account of meeting writer Nadine Gordimer (see, p.665).

SPECIALIST GUIDES

G.M. Branch *Two Oceans*. Don't be put off by the coffee-table format; this is a comprehensive guide to Southern Africa's marine life.

David Bristow *Best Hikes in Southern Africa* and *Best Walks of the Drakensberg*. The South Africa book is a well-written and reliable guide that does your homework for you, selecting the best trails from a confusingly extensive lot. The Drakensberg paperback is indispensable for anyone exploring the massif, with detailed route instructions and informative background about natural history.

Hugh Chittenden (ed) *Robert's Bird Guide*. The definitive, and very weighty, reference work on the subcontinent's entire avifauna population: if it's not in Robert's, it doesn't exist.

Richard D. Estes *Safari Companion: A Guide to Watching African Mammals*. A vital handbook on how to understand African wildlife, with interesting and readable information on the behaviour and social structures of the major species. Highly recommended for anyone wanting to go beyond the checklists.

★**Mike Lundy** *Best Walks in the Cape Peninsula*. Handy, solidly researched guide to some of the peninsula's many walks, and small enough to fit comfortably in a backpack.

L. McMahon and M. Fraser *A Fynbos Year*. Exquisitely illustrated and well-written book about South Africa's unique floral kingdom.

Willie and Sandra Olivier *Hiking Trails of Southern Africa*. Guide to major hikes, from strolls to expeditions lasting several days, throughout South Africa with information and where to get permits.

Colin Paterson-Jones *Best Walks of the Garden Route*. Handy for accessing some of South Africa's premier coastline and forests, away from the ribbon of development along the Garden Route.

Steve Pike *Surfing in South Africa: Swells, Spots and Surf African Culture*. Classic guide to everything you need to know about riding the waves along the country's 3000km coastline, written by veteran journalist, surfing aficionado and founder of the definitive surfing website wavescape.co.za.

Ian Sinclair, Phil Hockey and Warwick Tarboton *Sasol Birds of Southern Africa*. Comprehensive volume full of photos geared to the field, with useful pointers to aid quick identification.

Chris and Tilde Stuart *Field Guide to the Mammals of Southern Africa*. One of the best books on this subject, providing excellent background and clear illustrations to help you recognize species.

★**Philip van Zyl** (ed) *John Platter South African Wines*. One of the bestselling titles in South Africa – an annually updated pocket book that rates virtually every wine produced in the country.

FICTION

Tatamkhulu Afrika *The Innocents*. Set in the struggle years, this novel examines the moral and ethical issues of the time from a Muslim perspective.

Mark Behr *The Smell of Apples*. Powerful first novel set in the 1970s recounts the gradual falling of the scales from the eyes of an eleven-year-old Afrikaner boy, whose father is a major-general in the apartheid army.

Lauren Beukes *Zoo City*. Winner in 2011 of the Arthur C. Clarke award for science fiction, this amazing novel is set in an alternative Johannesburg where convicts are sentenced to be "animalled" – to have an animal familiar attached to them. A soundtrack album featuring a compilation of South African electronica tracks intended to evoke the atmosphere of the book has been issued to accompany the book (see, p.660). TV rights have been acquired by Leonardo DiCaprio's Appian Way to Beukes' latest novel *The Shining Girls*.

★**Herman Charles Bosman** *Unto Dust*. A superb collection of short stories from South Africa's master of the

genre, all set in the tiny Afrikaner farming district of Groot Marico in the 1930s. The tales share a narrator who, with delicious irony, reveals the passions and foibles of his community.

André Brink *A Chain of Voices*. This hugely evocative tale of eighteenth-century Cape life explores the impact of slavery on one farming family.

★**Michael Chapman** *Omnibus of a Century of South African Short Stories*. The most comprehensive ever collection of South African tale-telling, starting with San oral stories and working up to twenty-first-century writing, including work by Olive Schreiner, Alan Paton, Es'kia Mphahlele and Ivan Vladislavic.

★**J.M. Coetzee** *Age of Iron* and *Disgrace*. In a *Mail & Guardian* poll of writers, *Age of Iron* emerged as the finest South African novel of the 1990s. The book depicts a white female classics professor dying from cancer during the political craziness of the 1980s. She is joined by a tramp who

CRIME FICTION

South African **crime fiction** was a rarity prior to 1994, but the post-apartheid era has seen the genre blossoming, with a number of local crime writers, among them Margie Orford, Roger Smith and Deon Meyer, making a splash internationally. So marked is the emergence of the home-grown crime novel that it has spawned a flurry of academic studies pondering its nature and asking why it is happening precisely now. The notion that it is somehow a response to South Africa's sky-high crime rates doesn't wash, given that Scandanavia and Japan – countries with low crime rates – have both also experienced a recent boom in crime fiction.

One possible explanation for the genre's post-apartheid explosion is that previously, when the police were regarded as instruments of a repressive state, a storyline with a sympathetic protagonist who was also a cop would have been difficult to navigate. Another suggestion is that the crime thriller offers an opportunity to examine South African society – a niche previously occupied by the political "resistance novel". As one commentator remarks, South African crime fiction is often a "whydunnit?" rather than a "whodunit?" Others speculate that in the crime novel resolution and catharsis is possible – symbolically, at least, making up for the failures of the Truth and Reconciliation Commission (see box, p.650) to deliver justice, and for the inadequacies of the country's overburdened judicial system. Whatever the reason, the popularity of the form suggests that, for readers and writers, crime does pay.

TEN KILLER SOUTH AFRICAN CRIME WRITERS

Joanne Hichens *Divine Justice*. Cape Town, dark humour and extreme characters – among them a fanatical preacher with a penchant for amputees – provide the backdrop for private eye Rae Valentine's search for missing jewels, as the body count grows.

Angela Makhowa *Red Ink*. Journalist-turned-investigator Lucy Khambule is asked to write the biography of a serial killer in a world of Jo'burg bling where the murders mount, and nothing is what it seems.

James McClure *The Song Dog*. One of a series of novels that pair up white detective Tromp Kramer and his black sidekick Mickey Zondi, by one of the rare apartheid-era crime writers, who is now regarded as the father of the genre in South Africa.

Deon Meyer *Thirteen Hours*. This offering from South Africa's hottest crime writer is, as usual, a riveting read, but may be uncomfortably close to the bone for some – one thread follows Detective Benny Griessel's quest to find and save the life of an American backpacker on the run from Cape Town gangsters after her travelling companion has been murdered.

Mike Nicol *Payback*. Hard-boiled thriller, one of several by established novelist Nicol (who has been compared to Elmore Leonard and Cormac McCarthy),

follows a pair of gun-runners drawn back from retirement into Cape Town's dark underworld.

Sifiso Nzobi *Young Blood*. Exploration of the attractions of crime – cars, money, women – for a young man finding his identity in Umlazi township in KwaZulu-Natal, and his struggle to break free from its tentacles.

Margie Orford *Water Music*. One of the Clare Hart novels by internationally acclaimed writer Orford, this engrossing read, set in picturesque Hout Bay, delves into the dark depths of child abuse.

Michele Rowe *What Hidden Lies*. Expertly crafted police procedural, in which Detective Persy Jonas winkles dark secrets from the inhabitants of several close-knit Cape Peninsula communities, after a floating body is discovered.

Roger Smith *Mixed Blood*. Relentless noir thriller set on the Cape Flats, and written with a brutal eloquence that requires a strong stomach as it traverses the ugly landscape of a violence-ruled gangland. *Mixed Blood* and another Smith novel *Wake Up Dead* have been optioned for Hollywood productions.

Diale Tlholwe *Counting the Coffins*. South Africa's first magical realist murder novel has Detective Thabang Maje navigating corruption and crime on the mean streets of Jo'burg.

sets up home in her garden, and thus evolves a curious and fascinating relationship. But even better is *Disgrace*, a disturbing story of a university professor's fall from grace, set in the Eastern Cape. No writer better portrays the ever-present undercurrents of violence and unease in South Africa.

Achmat Dangor *Bitter Fruit* and *The Z Town Trilogy*. From one of the best Cape Town writers, *Bitter Fruit* is the story of the son of two anti-apartheid activists, and of an act of violence and injustice threading two generations, which is

resurrected by the Truth and Reconciliation Commission. The book portrays a brittle family, a dysfunctional society, and how we fail to address the past's deepest wounds. *The Z Town Trilogy* takes place in a town much like Cape Town, during one of apartheid South Africa's many states of emergency, which is burrowing in intricate ways into the psyches of his characters.

Tracey Farren *Whiplash*. Powerful, acclaimed, and by turns relentless and funny, debut novel written in the voice of a Cape Town prostitute coming to terms with her past and present on her own personal walk to freedom.

Damon Galgut *In a Strange Room*. The writer, some say, best placed to fill J.M. Coetzee's literary shoes, Damon Galgut has scooped several literary awards: *In a Strange Room* was shortlisted for the 2010 Man Booker Prize for fiction. Unusually for Galgut, it's set outside South Africa and describes in interchanging first and third person the global travels and relationships of a protagonist named, like the author, Damon. Quirky, beautifully written and highly readable.

Nadine Gordimer *July's People*. This controversial work by Nobel Literature Prize winner Gordimer was first banned by the apartheid regime for being subversive and later temporarily removed from schools by the ANC-governed Gauteng education department for being "deeply racist, superior and patronizing". Published in the 1980s when revolution in South Africa looked increasingly possible, it tells the story of a liberal white family rescued by its gardener July from a political deluge, and taken to his home village for safety.

Lily Herne *Deadlands*. South Africa's street-smart answer to *Twilight* follows the adventures and romance of 17-year-old Lele as she navigates the shattered, dystopian and zombie-infested suburbs of a post-apocalyptic Cape Town.

Dan Jacobson *The Trap* and *A Dance in the Sun*. Taut novellas written in the 1950s and published in one volume, skilfully portraying the developing tensions and nuances of the white-versus-black lives of the era.

Pamela Jooste *Dance with a Poor Man's Daughter*. The fragile world of a young coloured girl during the early apartheid years is sensitively imagined in this hugely successful first novel.

Fred Khumalo *Seven Steps to Heaven*. Ostensibly a coming-of-age story of two friends and their encounters with sex, *shebeens*, violence and revenge, journalist Khumalo's novel vividly evokes the flavour of South African township life.

★ **Alex La Guma** *A Walk in the Night and Other Stories*. An evocative collection of short stories by this talented political activist/author, set in District Six, the ethnically mixed quarter of Cape Town razed by the apartheid government.

Anne Landsman *The Devil's Chimney*. A stylish and entertaining piece of magical realism set in the Karoo town of Oudtshoorn in the days of the ostrich-feather boom.

Songeziwe Mahlangu *Penumbra*. Semi-autobiographical debut novel that etches a unique vision of Cape Town through the eyes of a young man employed by a large insurance company. Torn by turns between mindless web-surfing, drug-induced mania and charismatic Christianity, Manga charts his course through the southern suburbs of the Mother City.

Zakes Mda *Ways of Dying*, *His Madonna of Excelsior* and *The Heart of Redness*. The first is a brilliant tale of a professional mourner, full of sly insights into the culture of black South Africa; *Madonna* focuses on a family at the heart of the scandalous case in the Free State in which nineteen people from the small town of Excelsior were charged with sex across the races; while *Heart*, which won the *Sunday Times* Fiction Prize, weaves the historical story of the Eastern Cape cattle killings with a contemporary narrative.

Niq Mhlongo *Dog Eat Dog*. One of the irreverent exponents of post-apartheid literature, Mhlongo has been described as "the voice of the *kwaito* [hip-hop] generation". This novel looks at the life of a student who spends his time bunking classes, picking up girls and playing the system.

Phaswane Mpe *Welcome to Our Hillbrow*. A young black man from the rural areas hits the fleshpots of present-day Hillbrow, where xenophobia, violence and AIDS (from which the author subsequently died) reign.

★ **Es'kia Mphahlele** *Down Second Avenue*. A classic autobiographical novel set in the 1940s in the impoverished township of Alexandra, where Mphahlele grew up as part of a large extended family battling daily to survive.

★ **Alan Paton** *Cry, The Beloved Country*. Classic 1948 novel encapsulating the deep injustices of the country, by one of South Africa's great liberals. With tremendous lyricism, the book describes the journey of a black pastor from rural Natal to Johannesburg to rescue his missing son from the city's clutches.

Kathy Perkins *Black South African Women – An Anthology of Plays*. Ground-breaking collection of ten plays by a wide range of known and unknown playwrights such as Gcina Mhlope, Sindiwe Magona, Muthal Naidoo and Lueen Conning.

Sol Plaatje *Mhudi*. The first English novel by a black South African writer, *Mhudi* is set in the 1830s, at a time when the Afrikaner Great Trek had just begun. It's the epic tale of a young rural woman who saves her future husband from the raids of the Ndebele, who were then a powerful state in the Marico region.

Linda Rode and Jakes Gerwel *Crossing Over*. Collection of 26 stories by new and emerging South African writers on the experiences of adolescence and early adulthood in a period of political transition.

★ **Olive Schreiner** *Story of an African Farm*. The first-ever South African novel, written in 1883. Though subject to the ideologies of the era, the book nonetheless explores with a genuinely open vision the tale of two female cousins living on a remote Karoo farm.

★ **Ivan Vladislavic** *The Restless Supermarket*, *The Exploded View* and *Portrait with Keys: Joburg and What-What*. *The Restless Supermarket* is a dark and intricate urban satire from South Africa's most exciting contemporary writer, about Johannesburg's notorious Hillbrow district during the last days of apartheid. *The Exploded View* is a collection of four interlinked pieces, a great follow-up from a writer who's unrivalled at evoking the contradictions and fascinations of Jo'burg, while *Portrait* is not so much a novel as an account, in a series of numbered texts, of the city that inspires Vladislavic's imagination.

Language

South Africa has eleven official languages, all of which have equal status under the law. In practice, however, **English** is the lingua franca that dominates politics, commerce and the media. If you're staying in the main cities and national parks you'll rarely, if ever, need to use any other language. **Afrikaans**, although a language you seldom need to speak, nevertheless remains very much in evidence and you will certainly encounter it on official forms and countless signs, particularly on the road; for this reason we give a comprehensive list of written Afrikaans terms you could come across (see opposite).

Unless you're planning on staying a very long time, there's little point trying to get to grips with the whole gamut of **indigenous African languages**, of which there are nine official ones and several unofficial ones. Having said that, it's always useful to know a few phrases of the local indigenous language, especially greetings – the use of which will always be appreciated even if you aren't able to carry your foray through to a proper conversation (see box, pp.668–669).

The nine official African languages are split into four groups: **Nguni**, which consists of Zulu, Xhosa, siSwati and Ndebele; **Sotho**, which comprises Northern Sotho, Southern Sotho (or Sesotho) and Tswana; **Venda** and **Tsonga**. Most black people speak languages in the first two groups. In common with all indigenous Southern African languages, these operate under very different principles from European languages in that their sentences are dominated by the noun, with which the other words, such as verbs and adjectives, must agree in person, gender, number or case. Known as concordal agreement, this is achieved by supplementing word stems – the basic element of each word – with prefixes or suffixes to change meaning.

The Nguni group, and Southern Sotho, both contain a few **clicks** adopted from San languages, which are difficult for speakers of European languages. In practice, most English-speaking South Africans sidestep the issue altogether and pronounce African names in ways that are often only approximations.

English

South African English is a mixed bag, one language with many variants. Forty percent of whites are mother-tongue English-speakers, many of whom believe that they are (or at least should be) speaking standard British English. In fact, South African English has its own distinct character, and is as different from the Queen's English as is Australian. Its most notable characteristic is its huge and rich vocabulary, with unique words and usages, some drawn from Afrikaans and the indigenous African languages. The hefty *Oxford Dictionary of South African English* makes an interesting browse.

As a language used widely by non-native speakers, there is great **variation in pronunciation** and usage – largely a result of mother-tongue interference from other languages. Take, for example, the sentence "The bad bird sat on the bed", which speakers of some African languages (which don't distinguish between some of the vowel sounds of English) might pronounce as "The bed bed set on the bed". While some English-speaking whites feel that their language is being mangled and misused, linguists argue that it is simply being transformed.

Afrikaans

Broadly speaking, **Afrikaans** is a dialect of Dutch, which became modified on the Cape frontier through its encounter with French, German and English settlers, and is peppered with words and phrases from indigenous tongues as well as African and Asian languages used by slaves. Some historians argue, very plausibly, that Afrikaans was first written in Arabic script in the early nineteenth century by Cape Muslims.

Despite this heritage, the language was used by Afrikaners from the late nineteenth century onwards as a key element in the construction of their racially exclusive ethnic identity. The attempt, in 1976, by the apartheid government to make Afrikaans the medium of instruction in black schools, which led to the Soweto uprising, confirmed the hated status of the language for many urban Africans, which persists to this day.

Contrary to popular belief outside South Africa, the majority of Afrikaans-speakers are not white but coloured, and the language, far from dying out, is in fact understood by more South Africans than any other language. It's the predominant tongue in the Western and Northern Cape provinces, and in the Free State it is the language of the media.

Afrikaans signs

Bed en Ontbyt	Bed and breakfast	**Perron**	Platform (train station)
Dankie	Thank you	**Plaas**	Farm
Derde	Third	**Poskantoor**	Post office
Doeane	Customs	**Regs**	Right
Drankwinkel	Liquor shop	**Ry**	Go
Droe vrugte	Dry fruit	**Sentrum**	Centre
Eerste	First	**Singel**	Crescent
Geen ingang	No entry	**Slaghuis**	Butcher
Gevaar	Danger	**Stad**	City
Grens	Border	**Stadig**	Slow
Hoof	Main	**Stad sentrum**	City/town centre
Hoog	High	**Stasie**	Station
Ingang	Entry	**Straat**	Street
Inligting	Information	**Strand**	Beach
Kantoor	Office	**Swembad**	Swimming pool
Kerk	Church	**Toegang**	Admission
Kort	Short	**Tweede**	Second
Links	Left	**Verbode**	Prohibited
Lughawe	Airport	**Verkeer**	Traffic
Mans	Men	**Versigtig**	Carefully
Mark	Market	**Vierde**	Fourth
Ompad	Detour	**Vrouens**	Women
Pad	Road	**Vrugte**	Fruit
Padwerke voor	Roadworks ahead	**Vyfde**	Fifth
Pastorie	Parsonage		

The Nguni group

Zulu (or isiZulu), the most widely spoken black African language in South Africa, is understood by around twelve million people. It's the mother tongue of residents of the southeastern parts of the country, including the whole of KwaZulu-Natal, the eastern Free State, southern Mpumalanga and Gauteng – as well as South Africa's president, Jacob Zuma. Some linguists believe that Zulu's broad reach could make it an alternative to English as a South African lingua franca. Don't confuse Zulu with **Fanakalo**, which is a pidgin Zulu mixed with other languages. Still sometimes spoken in the mines, it is not popular with most Zulu-speakers, though many white South Africans tend to believe it is.

For all practical purposes, **siSwati**, the language spoken in Swaziland, is almost identical to Zulu, but for historical reasons has developed its own identity. The same applies to **Ndebele**, which shares around 95 percent in common with Zulu. It broke off from Zulu (around the same time as siSwati) when a group of Zulu-speakers fled north to escape the expansionism of the Zulu chief Shaka. Ndebele is now spoken in pockets of Gauteng and North West provinces as well as throughout southern Zimbabwe.

Xhosa (itself an example of a word beginning with a click sound) is Nelson Mandela's mother tongue, which he shares with seven million other South Africans, predominantly in the Eastern Cape. The language is also spoken by Africans in the Western Cape, most of whom are concentrated in Cape Town.

The Sotho group

Northern Sotho dialects, which are numerous and diverse, are spoken by around 2.5 million people in a huge arc of South Africa that takes in the country around the Kruger National Park, around to the Botswana border and south from there to Pretoria. **Southern Sotho**, one of the first African languages to be written, is spoken in the Free State, parts of Gauteng, as well as Lesotho and the areas of the Eastern Cape bordering it.

Tswana, also characterized by a great diversity of dialects, is geographically the most widespread language in Southern Africa, and is the principal language of Botswana. In South Africa its dialects are dispersed through the Northern Cape, the Free State and North West provinces.

As with the Nguni languages, the distinctions between the languages in the Sotho group owe more to history, politics and geography than to pure linguistic factors; speakers of some Northern Sotho dialects can understand some dialects of Tswana more readily than they can other Northern Sotho dialects.

Pronouncing place names

The largest number of unfamiliar **place names** that visitors are likely to encounter in South Africa are of Afrikaans origin, followed by names with origins in the Nguni group of languages. Afrikaans and English names are found across the country, while African names tend to be more localized, according to the predominant language in that area. Nguni group pronunciations generally apply in the Eastern Cape, KwaZulu-Natal, parts of Mpumalanga and Swaziland, while Sotho group names will be found in North West Province, Limpopo, the Northern Cape, Free State and parts of Gauteng. Sometimes you'll encounter names with Khoisan derivations, such as "Tsitsikamma" (in which the ts is pronounced as in "tsunami"). The pronunciation tips below are intended as a guide and are neither comprehensive nor definitive.

Afrikaans

In common with other Germanic languages, Afrikaans has a number of consonants that are **guttural**. Apart from these, most consonant sounds will be unproblematic

BASIC GREETINGS AND FAREWELLS

ENGLISH	AFRIKAANS	NORTHERN SOTHO	SESOTHO
Yes	Ja	Ee	E!
No	Nee	Aowa	Tjhe
Please	Asseblief	Hle.../...hle	(Ka kopo) hle
Thank you	Dankie	Ke a leboga	Ke a leboha
Excuse me	Verskoon my	Tshwarelo	Ntshwarele
Good morning	Goiemore	Thobela/dumela	Dumela (ng)
Good afternoon	Goeiemiddag	Thobela/dumela	Dumela (ng)
Good evening	Goeinaand	Thobela/dumela	Fonaneng
Goodbye	Totsiens	Sala gabotse/sepele gabotse	Sala(ng) hantle
See you later	Sien jou later	Re tla bonana	Re tla bonana
Until we meet again	Totsiens	Go fihla re kopana gape	Ho fihlela re bona
How do you do?	Aangename kennis?	Ke leboga go le tseba?	Ke thabela ho o ts
How are you?	Hoe gaan dit?	Le kae?	O/le sa phela?

for English-speakers. However, Afrikaans has numerous vowels and diphthongs, which have rough English equivalents but which are frequently spelled in an unfamiliar way – take, for example, the variation in the pronunciation of the letter "e" in the list below.

VOWELS AND DIPHTHONGS

a as in Kakam*a*s	**u** as in p*u*p	**eu** as in K*eu*rboomstrand	**u** as in c*u*re
aa as in Br*aa*mfontein	**a** as in c*a*r	**i** as in Cal*i*tzdorp	**e** as in ang*e*l
ae as in H*ae*nertsburg	**a** as in c*a*r but slightly lengthened	**ie** as in D*ie*pwalle	**i** as in p*i*ck
		o as in B*o*ntebok	**o** as in c*o*rk, but clipped
aai as in Smitswinkelb*aai*	**y** as in dr*y*	**oe** as in Bl*oe*mfontein	**oo** as in b*oo*k
au as in *Au*grabies	**o** as in bl*o*w	**oo** as in Kl*oo*f	**oo** as in b*oo*r
ar as in G*ar*ies	**u** as in b*u*rrow	**ou** as in *Ou*drif	**o** as in wr*o*te
e as in B*o*ntebok	**er** as in rubb*er*, but clipped	**u** as in W*u*ppertaal	**i** as in p*i*ck
		ui as in Nelspr*ui*t	**a** as in g*a*te
e as in Cl*a*rens	**e** as in ang*e*l	**uu** as in S*uu*rbraak	**o** as in wr*o*te
ee as in R*ie*beeck	**ee** as in b*ee*r	**y** as in Vanrhynsdorp	**ai** as in p*ai*n
ei as in Bloemfont*ei*n	**ai** as in p*ai*n		

CONSONANTS

d as in Suikerbosran*d*	**t** as in run*t*	**tj** as in Mat*j*iesfontein	**k** as in *k*ey
g as in Ma*g*ersfontein	guttural **ch** as in the Scottish lo*ch*	**v** as in Nysl*v*lei	**f** as in *f*ig
		w as in *W*aterkant	**v** as in *v*ase

Nguni group

The clicks in Nguni languages are the most unfamiliar and difficult sounds for English-speakers to pronounce. The three basic clicks – which, as it happens, occur in the names of three places featured in the Wild Coast of the Eastern Cape (see p.336) – are: the **dental click** (transliterated using "c", as in the Cwebe Nature Reserve), made by pulling the tongue away from the front teeth as one would when expressing disapproval in "tsk tsk"; the **palatal click** (transliterated "q", as in Qholorha Mouth), made by pulling the tongue away from the palate as you would when trying to replicate the sound of a bubbly cork being popped; and the **lateral click** (transliterated "x", as in Nxaxo Mouth), made by pulling away the tongue from the side teeth. To complicate matters, each click can be pronounced in one of three ways (aspirated, nasalized or delayed) and may change when spoken in combination with other consonants.

TSWANA	XHOSA	ZULU
Ee	Ewe	Yebo
Nnyaa	Hayi	Cha
Tsweetswee	Nceda	Uxolo
Ke a leboga	Enkosi	Ngiyabonga
Intshwarele	Uxolo	Uxolo
Dumela	Molo/bhota	Sawubona
Dumela	Molo/bhoto	Sawubona
Dumela	Molo/bhota	Sawubona
Sala sentle	Nisale kakuhle	Sala kahle
Ke tla go bona	Sobe sibonane	Sizobanana
Go fitlhelela re bonana gape	De sibonane kwakhona	Size sibonane
O tsogile jang?	Kunjani?	Ninjani?
O tsogile jang?	Kunjani?	Ninjani?

VOWELS

a as in Kw*a*Zulu	a as in f*a*ther	**o** as in Umkom*aa*s	a as in t*a*ll
e as in Cw*e*be	e as in b*e*nd	**u** as in Hl*u*hl*u*we	u as in p*u*t
i as in Kwambonamb*i*	ee as in fl*ee*		

CONSONANTS

dl as in *Dl*inza	aspirated ll as in the Welsh *Ll*ewellyn	**ph** as in M*ph*ephu	p as in *p*ass followed by a rapid rush of air
g as in Ha*g*a-Ha*g*a	hard g as in hu*g*	**r** as in Q*h*olo*rh*a	guttural ch as in the Scottish lo*ch*
hl as in *Hl*uhluwe	aspirated ll as in the Welsh llewellyn (though often pronounced like the shl in *shl*emiel by English-speakers)	**ty** as in Idu*ty*wa	approximately the initial sound in *tu*be

Sotho group

VOWELS

a as in Th*a*ba	a as in f*a*ther	**o** as in Mantseb*o*	o as in b*o*re, but curtailed
e as in M*o*tsekuoa	e as in h*e*	**u** as in B*u*tha	u as in f*u*ll

CONSONANTS

j as in Ha-Le*j*one	y as in *y*es	**ph** as in Ma*ph*utseng	p as in *p*ool
hl as in *Hl*otse	aspirated ll as in the Welsh *Ll*ewellyn (often pronounced like the shl in *shl*emiel by English-speakers)	**th** as in *Th*aba	t as in *t*ar

Glossary

Words whose spelling makes it hard to guess how to render them have their approximate pronunciation given in italics. Where *gh* occurs in the pronunciation, it denotes the **ch** sound in the Scottish word "loch". Sometimes we've used the letter "r" in the pronunciation even though the word in question doesn't contain this letter; for example, we've given the pronunciation of "Egoli" as "air-gaw-lee". In these instances the syllable containing the "r" is meant to represent a familiar word or sound from English; the "r" itself shouldn't be pronounced.

African In the context of South Africa, an indigenous South African

Aloe Family of spiky indigenous succulents, often with dramatic orange flowers

Apartheid (apart-hate) Term used from the 1940s for the National Party's official policy of "racial separation"

Assegai (assa-guy) Short stabbing spear introduced by Shaka to the Zulu armies

Baai (buy) Afrikaans word meaning "bay"; also a common suffix in place names, eg Stilbaai

Bakkie (bucky) Light truck or van

Bantu (bun-two) Unscientific apartheid term for indigenous black people; in linguistics, a group of indigenous Southern African languages

Bantustan Term used under apartheid for the territories for Africans

Bergie A vagrant living on the slopes of Table Mountain in Cape Town

Black Imprecise term that sometimes refers collectively to Africans, Indians and coloureds, but more usually is used to mean Africans

Boer (boor) Literally "farmer", but also refers to early Dutch colonists at the Cape and Afrikaners

Boland (boor-lunt) Southern part of the Western Cape

Boma An enclosure or palisade

Boy Offensive term used to refer to an adult African man who is a servant

Bundu (approximately boon-doo, but with the vowels shortened) Wilderness or back country

Burgher Literally a citizen, but more specifically members of the Dutch community at the Cape in the seventeenth and eighteenth centuries

Bushman Southern Africa's earliest, but now almost extinct, inhabitants who lived by hunting and gathering

Bushveld Country composed largely of thorny bush

Cape Dutch Nineteenth-century, whitewashed, gabled style of architecture

Ciskei (sis-kye) Eastern Cape region west of the Kei River, declared a "self-governing territory" for Xhosa-speakers in 1972, and now reincorporated into South Africa

Cocopan Small tip truck on rails used to transport gold ore

Coloured Mulattos or people of mixed race

Commandos Burgher military units during the Frontier and Boer wars

Dagga (dugh-a) Marijuana

Dagha (dah-ga) Mud used in indigenous construction

Dassie (dussy) Hyrax

Disa (die-za) One of twenty species of beautiful indigenous orchids, most famous of which is the red disa or "Pride of Table Mountain"

Dominee (dour-min-ee) Reverend (abbreviated to DS)

Donga Dry, eroded ditch

Dorp Country town or village (from Afrikaans)

Drift Fording point in a river (from Afrikaans)

Drostdy (dross-tea) Historically, the building of the *landdrost* or magistrate

Egoli (air-gaw-lee) Zulu name for Johannesburg (literally "city of gold")

Fanakalo or **fanagalo** (fun-a-galaw) Pidgin mixture of English, Zulu and Afrikaans used to facilitate communication between white foremen and African workers

Fundi Expert

Fynbos (fayn-boss) Term for vast range of fine-leafed species that predominate in the southern part of the Western Cape (see box, p.106)

Girl Offensive term used to refer to an African woman who is a servant

Gogga (gho-gha) Creepy-crawly or insect

Griqua Person of mixed white, Bushman and Hottentot descent

Group Areas Act Now-defunct law passed in 1950 that provided for the establishment of separate areas for each "racial group"

Highveld High-lying areas of Gauteng and Mpumalanga

Homeland See Bantustan

Hottentot Now unfashionable term for indigenous Khoisan herders encountered by the first settlers at the Cape

Impi Zulu regiment

Indaba Zulu term meaning a group discussion and now used in South African English for any meeting or conference

Inkatha (in-ka-ta) Fiercely nationalist Zulu political party, formed in 1928 as a cultural organization

Jislaaik! (yis-like) Exclamation equivalent to "Geez!" or "Crikey!"

Joeys Affectionate abbreviation for Johannesburg

Jol Party, celebration

Jozi Affectionate abbreviation for Johannesburg

Kaffir Highly objectionable term of abuse for Africans

Karoo Arid plateau that occupies a large proportion of the South African interior

Khoikhoi (ghoy-ghoy) Self-styled name of South Africa's original herding inhabitants

Kloof (klo-ef; rhymes with "boor") Ravine or gorge

Knobkerrie (the "k" is silent) Wooden club

Kokerboom (both the first and last syllable rhyme with "boor") Quiver tree – a type of aloe found in the Northern Cape

Kopje Dutch spelling of *koppie*

Koppie Hillock

Kraal Enclosure of huts for farm animals or collection of traditional huts occupied by an extended family

Kramat (crum-mutt) Shrine of a Muslim holy man

Krans (crunce) Sheer cliff face

Laager (lager) A circular encampment of ox wagons, used as fortification by *voortrekkers*

Lapa Courtyard of group of Ndebele houses; also used to describe an enclosed area at safari camps, where braais are held

Lebowa (lab-o-a) Now-defunct homeland for North Sotho-speakers

Lekker Nice

Lobola (la-ball-a) Bride price, paid by an African man to his wife's parents

Location Old-fashioned term for segregated African area on the outskirts of a town or farm

Lowveld Low-lying subtropical region of Mpumalanga and Limpopo provinces

Malay Misnomer for Cape Muslims of Asian descent

Matjieshuis (mikeys-hace) Reed hut

Mbaqanga (m-ba-kung-a) A genre of music that originated in Soweto in the 1960s

Mbira (m-beer-a) African thumb piano, often made with a gourd

MK Umkhonto we Sizwe (Spear of the Nation) The armed wing of the ANC, now incorporated into the national army

Mlungu (m-loon-goo) African term for a white person, equivalent to *honkie*

Moffie (mawf-ee) Gay person

Nek Saddle between two mountains

Nguni (n-goo-nee) Group of southeastern Bantu-speaking people comprising Zulu, Xhosa and Swazi

Nkosi Sikelel 'i Afrika "God Bless Africa", anthem of the ANC and now of South Africa

Nyanga (nyun-ga) Traditional healer

Outspan A place set aside for animals to rest; can also mean to unharness oxen from a wagon

Pass Document that Africans used to have to carry at all times, which essentially rendered them aliens in their own country

Pastorie (puss-tour-ee) Parsonage

Platteland (plutta-lunt) Country districts

Poort Narrow pass through mountains along river course

Pronk (prawnk) Characteristic jump of springbok or impala

Protea National flower of South Africa

Qwaqwa Now-defunct homeland for South Sotho-speakers

Raadsaal (the "d" is pronounced "t") Council or parliament building

Restcamp Accommodation in national parks

Robot Traffic light

Rondavel (ron-daa-vil, with the stress on the middle syllable) Circular building based on traditional African huts

SABC South African Broadcasting Authority

Sangoma (sun-gom-a) Traditional spirit medium and healer

Shebeen (sha-bean) Unlicensed tavern

Shell Ultra City Clean, bright stops along major national roads, with a filling station, restaurant, shop and sometimes a hotel

Sjambok (sham-bok) Rawhide whip

Southeaster Prevailing wind in the Western Cape

Spaza shops (spa-za) Small stall or kiosk

Strandloper Name given by the Dutch to the indigenous people of the Cape; literally beachcomber

Stoep Veranda

Tackie Sneakers or plimsolls

Township Areas set aside under apartheid for Africans

Transkei (trans-kye) Now-defunct homeland for Xhosa-speakers

Trekboer (trek-boor) Nomadic Afrikaner farmers, usually in the eighteenth and nineteenth centuries

Umuthi (oo-moo-tee) Traditional herbal medicine

Velskoen (fel-scoon) Rough suede shoes

Vlei (flay) Swamp

VOC Verenigde Oostindische Compagnie, the Dutch East India Company

Voortrekker (the first syllable rhymes with "boor") Dutch burghers who migrated inland in their ox wagons in the nineteenth century to escape British colonialism

ZAR Zuid Afrikaansche Republiek; an independent Boer republic that included present-day Gauteng, Mpumalanga and Limpopo provinces and which was Britain's main opponent in the Anglo-Boer War

Food and drink

Amarula Liqueur made from the berries of the marula tree

Begrafnisrys (ba-ghruff-niss-race) Literally "funeral rice"; traditional Cape Muslim dish of yellow rice cooked with raisins

Biltong Sun-dried salted strip of meat, chewed as a snack

Blatjang (blutt-young) Cape Muslim chutney that has become a standard condiment on South African dinner tables

Bobotie (ba-boor-tea) Traditional Cape curried mince topped with a savoury custard and often cooked with apricots and almonds

Boerekos (boor-a-coss) Farm food, usually consisting of loads of meat and vegetables cooked using butter and sugar

Boerewors (boor-a-vorce) Spicy lengths of sausage that are *de rigueur* at braais

Bokkoms Dried fish, much like salt fish

Braai or **braaivleis** (bry-flace) Barbecue

Bredie Cape vegetable and meat stew

Bunny chow Originally a curried takeaway served in a scooped-out half loaf of bread, but now often wrapped in a roti

Cane or cane spirit A potent vodka-like spirit distilled from sugar cane and generally mixed with a soft drink such as Coke

Cap Classique Sparkling wine fermented in the bottle in exactly the same way as Champagne; also called Méthode Cap Classic

Cape gooseberry Fruit of the physalis; a sweet yellow berry

Cape salmon or **geelbek** (ghear-l-beck) Delicious firm-fleshed sea fish (unrelated to northern-hemisphere salmon)

Cape Velvet A sweet liqueur-and-cream dessert beverage that resembles Irish Cream liqueur

Denningvleis (den-ning-flace) Spicy traditional Cape lamb stew

Frikkadel Fried onion and meatballs

Hanepoort (harner-poort) Delicious sweet dessert grape

Kabeljou (cobble-yo) Common South African marine fish, also called kob

Kerrievis (kerry-fiss) See Pickled fish

Kingklip Highly prized deepwater fish caught along the Atlantic and Indian ocean coasts

Koeksister (cook-sister) Deep-fried plaited doughnut, dripping with syrup

Maas or **amasi** or **amaas** Traditional African beverage consisting of naturally soured milk, available as a packaged dairy product in supermarkets

Maaskaas Cottage cheese made from *maas*

Mageu or **mahewu** or **maheu** (ma-gh-weh) Traditional African beer made from maize meal and water, now packaged and commercially available

Malva Very rich and very sweet traditional baked Cape dessert

Mampoer (mum-poor) Moonshine; home-distilled spirit made from soft fruit, commonly peaches

Melktert (melk-tairt) Traditional Cape custard pie

Mielie Maize

Mielie pap (mealy pup) Maize porridge, varying from a thin mixture to a stiff one that can resemble polenta

Mopani worm (ma-parny) Black spotted caterpillar that is a delicacy among Africans in some parts of the country

Mqomboti (m-qom-booty) Traditional African beer made from fermented sorghum

Musselcracker Large-headed fish with powerful jaws and firm, white flesh

Naartjie (nar-chee) Tangerine or mandarin

Pap (pup) Porridge

Peri-peri Delicious hottish spice of Portuguese origin commonly used with grilled chicken

Perlemoen (pear-la-moon) Abalone

Pickled fish Traditional Cape dish of fish preserved with onions, vinegar and curry; available tinned in supermarkets

Pinotage A uniquely South African cultivar hybridized from Pinot Noir and Hermitage grapes and from which a wine of the same name is made

Potjiekos or potjie (poy-key-kos) Food cooked slowly over embers in a three-legged cast-iron pot

Putu (poo-too) Traditional African *mielie pap* (see above) prepared until it forms dry crumbs

Roti A chapati; called rooti in the Western Cape

Rusks Tasty biscuits made from sweetened bread that has been slow-cooked

Salmon trout Freshwater fish that is often smoked to create a cheaper and pretty good imitation of smoked salmon

Salomie Cape version of a *roti*; unleavened bread

Sambals (sam-bills) Accompaniments, such as chopped bananas, green peppers, desiccated coconut and chutney, served with Cape curries

Samp Traditional African dish of broken maize kernels, frequently cooked with beans

Skokiaan (skok-ee-yan) Potent home-brew

Smoorsnoek (smore-snook) Smoked *snoek*

Snoek (snook) Large fish that features in many traditional Cape recipes

Sosatie (so-sah-ti) Spicy skewered mince

Spanspek (spon-speck) A sweet melon

Steenbras (ste-en-bruss) A delicious white-fleshed fish

Van der Hum South African *naartjie*-flavoured liqueur

Vetkoek (fet-cook) Deep-fried doughnut-like cake

Waterblommetjiebredie (vata-blom-a-key-bree-dee) Cape meat stew made with waterlily rhizomes

Witblits (vit-blitz) Moonshine

Yellowtail Delicious darkish-fleshed marine fish

Small print and index

A ROUGH GUIDE TO ROUGH GUIDES

Published in 1982, the first Rough Guide – to Greece – was a student scheme that became a publishing phenomenon. Mark Ellingham, a recent graduate in English from Bristol University, had been travelling in Greece the previous summer and couldn't find the right guidebook. With a small group of friends he wrote his own guide, combining a highly contemporary, journalistic style with a thoroughly practical approach to travellers' needs.

The immediate success of the book spawned a series that rapidly covered dozens of destinations. And, in addition to impecunious backpackers, Rough Guides soon acquired a much broader readership that relished the guides' wit and inquisitiveness as much as their enthusiastic, critical approach and value-for-money ethos.

These days, Rough Guides include recommendations from budget to luxury and cover more than 120 destinations around the globe, as well as producing an ever-growing range of ebooks.

Visit **roughguides.com** to find all our latest books, read articles, get inspired and share travel tips with the Rough Guides community.

ABOUT THE AUTHORS

Hilary Heuler originally hails from California but has spent the past decade writing from Europe, Asia and Africa, where she has lived in a hut in Guinea, travelled up the Niger River to Timbuktu and hitchhiked from Ethiopia to Cape Town. She now works as a journalist in Nairobi, Kenya.

Jeroen van Marle grew up in England, studied Human Geography in the Netherlands, learnt Romanian and moved to Eastern Europe, where he hitchhiked from St Petersburg to Bulgaria and founded a city guide company in Bucharest. He has moved 25 times and lived in nine countries; for now he's based in Berlin. He has most recently worked on Rough Guides to Bali and Lombok, South Africa and Germany.

Barbara McCrea was born in Zimbabwe and taught African literature at the University of Natal. She lived in London for fifteen years, working on Rough Guides to Zimbabwe, South Africa and Cape Town before returning to South Africa. She now lives close to the beach in Cape Town, where she swims, rides horses and climbs mountains.

Tony Pinchuck launched his travels as a schoolboy hitching around South Africa in the 1970s and his explorations of the subcontinent have continued ever since. Now resident in Cape Town, he is production editor on the investigative magazine noseweek.

Lizzie Williams has been working and travelling in Africa for more than 20 years; first as a tour guide on overland trucks across the continent and now as a guidebook author. She's authored more than forty titles on African countries for various publishers and regularly contributes to magazines and websites on all aspects of African travel. When not on the road, Lizzie lives in beautiful Cape Town.

Rough Guide credits

Editor: Mandy Tomlin, Emma Gibbs
Layout: Ankur Guha
Cartography: Ashutosh Bharti
Picture editor: Michalle Bhatia
Proofreader: Susannah Wight
Managing editor: Keith Drew
Assistant editor: Prema Dutta
Production: Emma Sparks

Cover design: Nicole Newman and Roger Mapp
Photographer: Alex Robinson
Editorial assistant: Rebecca Hallett
Senior pre-press designer: Dan May
Programme manager: Helen Blount
Publisher: Joanna Kirby
Publishing director: Georgina Dee

Publishing information

This eighth edition published February 2015 by
Rough Guides Ltd,
80 Strand, London WC2R 0RL
11, Community Centre, Panchsheel Park,
New Delhi 110017, India
Distributed by Penguin Random House
Penguin Books Ltd,
80 Strand, London WC2R 0RL
Penguin Group (USA)
345 Hudson Street, NY 10014, USA
Penguin Group (Australia)
250 Camberwell Road, Camberwell,
Victoria 3124, Australia
Penguin Group (NZ)
67 Apollo Drive, Mairangi Bay, Auckland 1310,
New Zealand
Penguin Group (South Africa)
Block D, Rosebank Office Park, 181 Jan Smuts Avenue,
Parktown North, Gauteng, South Africa 2193
Rough Guides is represented in Canada by Tourmaline
Editions Inc. 662 King Street West, Suite 304, Toronto,
Ontario M5V 1M7
Printed in Singapore by Toppan Security Printing Pte. Ltd.

MIX
Paper from
responsible sources
FSC™ C018179
www.fsc.org

Acknowledgements

Hilary Heuler: My travels have been filled with people
who have helped me out along the way, making my
research both easier and infinitely more fun. They include
the hospitable Evan and Moira Jones in Dundee; the good
people at Igwalagwala Guesthouse and St Lucia Wetlands
Guesthouse in St Lucia; Kian Barker and his amazing
chameleons; Simon and Wendy in Eshowe; Anna McGinn
in Swaziland; and, as ever, Elaine and Brian Agar at the
inimitable Elephant House in Durban.

Jeroen van Marle: Many thanks to Mandy, Emma and
Keith at Rough Guides. Special thanks in Johannesburg
to Santie Wolvaardt and Jannie du Toit at Die Agterplaas,
Nicholas Wolpe at Lilliesleaf and Heather Mason. In
Limpopo, thanks to Laura and the team at Horizon
Horseback and Betty Hlungwani at Shiluvari; in North West
Province, thanks to Santa and Egbert van Bart and Jacques
du Plessis; in Lesotho, thanks to Di, Michael and Debbie at
Malealea. And thanks to Soulafa for the safari of a lifetime.

Barbara McCrea: Thanks to Rosie Downey for her
hard work and upbeat contributions to nightlife and
other essential aspects in urban Cape Town, plus help
with Garden Route factual research, and to Carolyn
Howell for help with fact-checking in the Eastern Cape
and Mpumalanga. Thanks to the people who gave

us accommodation and other help during research
trips, notably Andrew Hall in Nelspruit; Rob McCrea at
Timbavati; Wait a Little Horse Safaris at Kruger and Wild
Coast Horse Trails near Kei Mouth for the rides of our
lives; Joe Simpson in Franschhoek; Janet Cherry in Port
Elizabeth; Joek and Jeanette for a lovely drives up the
N2 and R62; Steve and Colleen Kirk-Cohen on wine and
food related topics; and a number of B&B owners in the
Winelands, along the Garden Route, Route R62 and
the Whale Coast who helped with information and
comfortable beds. Thanks, of course, to editors Emma
Gibbs and Mandy Tomlin for holding it all together and
their incredible levels of accuracy; to Tony for competent
steering and meticulous maps; to Gabriel for being a good
teenage critic and putting up with Rough Guides for his
entire life; and to everyone else in the network of support
whom I haven't mentioned by name.

Tony Pinchuck: I would like to thank my co-author
Barbara McCrea for carrying much of the burden of
researching and updating our section of this edition; and
our editor Mandy Tomlin for her patience, skilful pruning
and for holding everything together. Thanks also to editor
Emma Gibbs; co-authors Jeroen, Lizzie and Hilary; the
cartography department and all the unsung participants
in the production of this book.

Help us update

We've gone to a lot of effort to ensure that the eighth edition of **The Rough Guide to South Africa** is accurate and up-to-date. However, things change – places get "discovered", opening hours are notoriously fickle, restaurants and rooms raise prices or lower standards. If you feel we've got it wrong or left something out, we'd like to know, and if you can remember the address, the price, the hours, the phone number, so much the better.

Please send your comments with the subject line "**Rough Guide South Africa Update**" to ✉ mail @uk.roughguides.com. We'll credit all contributions and send a copy of the next edition (or any other Rough Guide if you prefer) for the very best emails.

Find more travel information, connect with fellow travellers and plan your trip on ✇ roughguides.com.

Photo credits

All photos © Rough Guides except the following:
(Key: t-top; c-centre; b-bottom; l-left; r-right)

p.1 Kim Walker/Robert Harding Picture Library
p.2 Peter Adams/AWL Images
p.4 Michaeljung/Dreamstime.com (t)
p.5 Hoberman Collection/Corbis
p.9 Malcolm Schuyl/FLPA (t); Yadid Levy/Robert Harding Picture Library (b)
p.10 B. Bahr/Getty Images
p.11 Prisma Bildagentur/Alamy
p.12 Piccaya/Dreamstime.com
p.13 Sean Tilden/Alamy (t); Gideon Mendel/Corbis (c); Ian Trower/SuperStock (b)
p.14 SuperStock (t); Alamy (c); Steve Toon/Robert Harding Picture Library (b)
p.15 Keren Su/Corbis (t); Clive Sawyer/Corbis (b)
p.16 Niels van Gijn/Corbis (t); SuperStock (c); Michaeljung/Dreamstime.com (b)
p.17 Africa Media/Alamy (tl); Robert Harding/Alamy (tr); Tim Jackson/Getty Images (bl)
p.18 SuperStock (t); Birdiegal717/Dreamstime.com (cl); Photolibrary (cr); Frans Lanting/Corbis (b)
p.19 AfriPics/Alamy (t); Hoberman Collection/Corbis (b)
p.20 Atlantide Phototravel (t); Heintz Jean/Corbis (c); Bulungula Lodge (b)
p.21 Bradleyvdw/Dreamstime.com (t); Bobby Haas/Getty Images (c); Frans Lemmens/Alamy (b)
p.22 AfriPics/Alamy (tl); Denny Allen/Getty Images (tr)
p.25 Konrad Wothe/FLPA (tl); Chris and Tilde Stuart/FLPA (tr); Heinrich van den Berg/Getty Images (c); Christian Heinrich/FLPA (bl); Sami Sarkis/Getty Images (br)
p.27 Michael Krabs/FLPA (tl); Nigel Dennis/SuperStock (tr); Blickwinkel/Alamy (c); Jurgen & Christine Sohns/FLPA (br); Pete Oxford/FLPA (bl)
p.29 SuperStock (tl); Dirscherl Reinhard/SuperStock (tr); Shem Compion/Getty Images (cl); Tier Images (cr); Wendy Dennis/FLPA (b)
p.31 Michael Krabs/FLPA (t); Nigel Dennis/Getty Images (cl); Philip Perry/FLPA (cr); Getty Images (b)
p.33 Malcolm Schuyl/FLPA (t); Heinrich van den Berg/Getty Images (c); Richard Du Toit/FLPA (b)
p.35 Winfried Wisniewski/FLPA (t); Chris and Tilde Stuart/FLPA (cl); Jurgen & Christine Sohns/FLPA (cr); Nigel Dennis/SuperStock (bl); Getty Images (br)
p.37 Nigel Dennis/Getty Images (tl); James Hager/Getty Images (tr); Tier Images/Getty Images (cl); Steve Toon/Corbis (cr); Sean Tilden/Alamy (bl); Prisma Bildagentur/Alamy (br)
p.39 Martin Harvey/Corbis (t); Stu Porter/Dreamstime.com (b)
p.41 Vatikaki/Dreamstime.com (t); Friedrichsmeier/Alamy (b)
p.43 ImageBroker/FLPA (t); Christian Heinrich/FLPA (c); Fabio Chironi/Getty Images (cl); SuperStock (cr); Richard Du Toit/FLPA (b)
p.45 Steve Toon/Getty Images (tl); Tilde Stuart/FLPA (tr, c); FLPA (b)
p.46 Marco Calore/Corbis
p.82 Maisant Ludovic/SuperStock
p.131 Neilbrad/Dreamstime.com (b)

p.151 Michelle Smit/Alba Lounge (tl); Ariadne Van Zandbergen/Alamy (tr); Quay 4 (bl); Hoberman Collection/Getty Images (br)
p.162 Ariadne Van Zandbergen/Alamy
p.165 Mssulaiman/Alamy
p.181 Kim Walker/Robert Harding Picture Library
p.213 Peter Chadwick/Getty Images (tl); Nigel Dennis/Getty Images (tr); Peter Chadwick/Getty Images (br)
p.243 /Getty Images Paul Thompson/Getty Images
p.257 Herman du Plessis/Getty Images (b)
p.262 Rob Cousins/SuperStock
p.265 Eric Nathan/Getty Images
p.287 Vittorio Ricci/Flickr RF/Getty Images
p.299 Frans Lanting/Corbis (t); Eric Nathan/Getty Images (b)
p.302 LOOK Die Bildagentur der Fotografen/Alamy
p.305 AfriPics/Alamy (t)
p.313 Roger de la Harpe/Getty Images
p.329 Steve Toon/Getty Images (t); Robert Harding/Alamy (b).
p.345 Africa Media Online/Alamy (t)
p.363 Peter Pinnock/Getty Images
p.364 Michele Burgess/Alamy
p.387 Getty Images
p.401 Ian Trower/AWL Images
p.427 Herbert Kratky/SuperStock (t); Frans Lemmens/Alamy (b)
p.440 Nigel Dennis/SuperStock
p.443 Micheal Krabs/SuperStock
p.456 Allan Baxter/Getty Images
p.459 SuperStock
p.479 Giovanni Mereghetti/SuperStock
p.495 Gallo Images/Getty Images (t); Africa Media Online/Alamy (b).
p.510 Heeb Christian/SuperStock
p.513 Eric Nathan/Getty Images
p.521 Graham De Lacy/Corbis (t); Peter Groenendijk/SuperStock (b)
p.528 Image Source/Corbis
p.531 AfriPics/Alamy
p.541 Gideon Mendel/Corbis (tl); Warren Little/Getty Images (tr); Walter Bibikow/SuperStock (b)
p.564 AfriPics/Alamy
p.567 AfriPics/Alamy
p.581 Piotr Naskrecki/Getty Images (tl); AfriPics/Alamy (tr); John Warburton-Lee/Alamy (b)
p.586–587 Hannest/Dreamstime.com
p.589 Gary Cook/Alamy
p.603 Joe Alblas/Getty Images (t); SuperStock (br)
p.615 Getty Images (bl)
p.622 Getty Images
p.625 SuperStock
p.645 Ariadne Van Zandbergen/Getty Images (t)
p.648 Ian Trower/AWL Images (b)

Front cover and spine: John Snelling/Getty Images
Back cover: Chmura Frank/Robert Harding Picture Library (t); Martin Harvey/Corbis (bl); Aurora Photos/AWL Images (br)

Index

Maps are marked in **grey**

K

L

M

Map symbols

The symbols below are used on maps throughout the book

✈	Airport	☪	Mosque	⛰	Mountain range	----	Unpaved road
★	Transport stop	✡	Synagogue	▲	Mountain peak	-----	Pedestrian road
P	Parking	⚱	Garden	◠	Cave	⊔⊔⊔	Steps
⊠	Gate	⛺	Mountain refuge/lodge	♨	Hot spring	═══	Railway
♦	Place of interest	⚔	Battle site	⚲	Waterfall	────	Wall
⊠	Post office	∴	Ruins	⌇	Lighthouse	▦	Building
@	Internet access	⬛	Hide	⚘	Vineyards	▭	Market
✚	Hospital	♜	Castle	──	Ferry	⇨	Church
ⓘ	Information centre	⛳	Golf course	●-●-●	Cable car	◯	Stadium
E	Embassy	🏛	Monument	──	Tram line	▱	Park
⚠	Campsite	♨	Swimming pool	----	Footpath	▭	Christian cemetery
⛽	Fuel/gas station	⊼	Picnic site	──	Road	▱	Beach
↟	Border crossing post	�	Viewpoint	▨▨▨	Motorway		

Listings key

■	Accommodation
●	Restaurant/café
■	Bar/club
●	Shop